The Middle Ages · SIMPSON

The Sixteenth Century · GREENBLATT / LOGAN

The Early Seventeenth Century
MAUS

The Restoration and the Eighteenth Century
NOGGLE

The Romantic Period · LYNCH

The Victorian Age · ROBSON

The Twentieth and Twenty-First Centuries
RAMAZANI

THE NORTON ANTHOLOGY OF

ENGLISH

LITERATURE

TENTH EDITION

VOLUME C

THE RESTORATION
AND
THE EIGHTEENTH CENTURY

THE NORTON ANTHOLOGY OF

ENGLISH

LITERATURE

TENTH EDITION

Stephen Greenblatt, *General Editor*

COGAN UNIVERSITY PROFESSOR OF THE HUMANITIES
HARVARD UNIVERSITY

VOLUME C

THE RESTORATION AND
THE EIGHTEENTH CENTURY

James Noggle

W · W · NORTON & COMPANY
NEW YORK · LONDON

W. W. Norton & Company has been independent since its founding in 1923, when William Warder Norton and Mary D. Herter Norton first published lectures delivered at the People's Institute, the adult education division of New York City's Cooper Union. The firm soon expanded its program beyond the Institute, publishing books by celebrated academics from America and abroad. By midcentury, the two major pillars of Norton's publishing program—trade books and college texts—were firmly established. In the 1950s, the Norton family transferred control of the company to its employees, and today—with a staff of four hundred and a comparable number of trade, college, and professional titles published each year—W. W. Norton & Company stands as the largest and oldest publishing house owned wholly by its employees.

Editors: Julia Reidhead and Marian Johnson
Assistant Editor, Print: Rachel Taylor
Manuscript Editors: Michael Fleming, Katharine Ings, Candace Levy
Media Editor: Carly Fraser Doria
Assistant Editor, Media: Ava Bramson
Marketing Manager, Literature: Kimberly Bowers
Managing Editor, College Digital Media: Kim Yi
Production Manager: Sean Mintus
Text design: Jo Anne Metsch
Art director: Rubina Yeh
Photo Editor: Nelson Colon
Permissions Manager: Megan Jackson Schindel
Permissions Clearing: Nancy J. Rodwan
Cartographer: Adrian Kitzinger
Composition: Westchester Book Company
Manufacturing: LSC Crawfordsville

Since this page cannot legibly accommodate all the copyright notices, the Permissions Acknowledgments constitute an extension of the copyright page.

ISBN: 978-0-393-60304-0

W. W. Norton & Company, Inc., 500 Fifth Avenue, New York, NY 10110
wwnorton.com

W. W. Norton & Company Ltd., 15 Carlisle Street, London W1D 3BS

3 4 5 6 7 8 9 0

Contents*

The Restoration and
the Eighteenth Century (1660–1785)

* Additional readings are available on the NAEL Archive (digital.wwnorton.com/englishlit10abc).

Preface to the Tenth Edition

For centuries the study of literature has occupied a central place in the Humanities curriculum. The power of great literature to reach across time and space, its exploration of the expressive potential of language, and its ability to capture the whole range of experiences from the most exalted to the everyday have made it an essential part of education. But there are significant challenges to any attempt to derive the full measure of enlightenment and pleasure from this precious resource. In a world in which distraction reigns, savoring works of literature requires quiet focus. In a society in which new media clamor for attention, attending to words on the page can prove difficult. And in a period obsessed with the present at its most instantaneous, it takes a certain effort to look at anything penned earlier than late last night.

The Norton Anthology of English Literature is designed to meet these challenges. It is deeply rewarding to enter the sensibility of a different place, to hear a new voice, to be touched by an unfamiliar era. It is critically important to escape the narrow boundaries of our immediate preoccupations and to respond with empathy to lives other than our own. It is moving, even astonishing, to feel that someone you never met is speaking directly to you. But for any of this to happen requires help. The overarching goal of the Norton Anthology—as it has been for over fifty-five years and ten editions—is to help instructors energize their classrooms, engage their students, and bring literature to life.* At a time when the Humanities are under great pressure, we are committed to facilitating the special joy that comes with encountering significant works of art.

The works anthologized in these six volumes generally form the core of courses designed to introduce students to English literature. The selections reach back to the earliest moments of literary creativity in English, when the language itself was still molten, and extend to some of the most recent experiments, when, once again, English seems remarkably fluid and open. That openness—a recurrent characteristic of a language that has never been officially regulated and that has constantly renewed itself—helps to account for the sense of freshness that characterizes the works brought together here.

One of the joys of literature in English is its spectacular abundance. Even within the geographical confines of England, Scotland, Wales, and Ireland, where the majority of texts in this collection originated, one can find more than enough distinguished and exciting works to fill the pages of this

---

* For more on the help we offer and how to access it, see "Additional Resources for Instructors and Students," p. xxii.

anthology many times over. But English literature is not confined to the British Isles; it is a global phenomenon. This border-crossing is not a consequence of modernity alone. It is fitting that among the first works here is *Beowulf*, a powerful epic written in the Germanic language known as Old English about a singularly restless Scandinavian hero. *Beowulf*'s remarkable translator in *The Norton Anthology of English Literature*, Seamus Heaney, was one of the great contemporary masters of English literature—he was awarded the Nobel Prize for Literature in 1995—but it would be potentially misleading to call him an "English poet" for he was born in Northern Ireland and was not in fact English. It would be still more misleading to call him a "British poet," as if the British Empire were the most salient fact about the language he spoke and wrote in or the culture by which he was shaped. What matters is that the language in which Heaney wrote is English, and this fact links him powerfully with the authors assembled in these volumes, a linguistic community that stubbornly refuses to fit comfortably within any firm geographical or ethnic or national boundaries. So too, to glance at other authors and writings in the anthology, in the twelfth century, the noblewoman Marie de France wrote her short stories in an Anglo-Norman dialect at home on both sides of the channel; in the sixteenth century William Tyndale, in exile in the Low Countries and inspired by German religious reformers, translated the New Testament from Greek and thereby changed the course of the English language; in the seventeenth century Aphra Behn touched readers with a story that moves from Africa, where its hero is born, to South America, where Behn herself may have witnessed some of the tragic events she describes; and early in the twentieth century Joseph Conrad, born in Ukraine of Polish parents, wrote in eloquent English a celebrated novella whose ironic vision of European empire gave way by the century's end to the voices of those over whom the empire, now in ruins, had once hoped to rule: the Caribbean-born Claude McKay, Louise Bennett, Derek Walcott, Kamau Brathwaite, V. S. Naipaul, and Grace Nichols; the African-born Chinua Achebe, J. M. Coetzee, Ngũgĩ Wa Thiong'o, and Chimamanda Ngozi Adichie; and the Indian-born A. K. Ramanujan and Salman Rushdie.

A vital literary culture is always on the move. This principle was the watchword of M. H. Abrams, the distinguished literary critic who first conceived *The Norton Anthology of English Literature*, brought together the original team of editors, and, with characteristic insight, diplomacy, and humor, oversaw seven editions. Abrams wisely understood that new scholarly discoveries and the shifting interests of readers constantly alter the landscape of literary history. To stay vital, the anthology, therefore, would need to undergo a process of periodic revision, guided by advice from teachers, as well as students, who view the anthology with a loyal but critical eye. As with past editions, we have benefited from detailed information on the works actually assigned and suggestions for improvements from 273 reviewers. Their participation has been crucial as the editors grapple with the task of strengthening the selection of more traditional texts while adding texts that reflect the expansion of the field of English studies.

With each edition, *The Norton Anthology of English Literature* has offered a broadened canon without sacrificing major writers and a selection of complete longer texts in which readers can immerse themselves. Perhaps the most emblematic of these great texts are the epics *Beowulf* and *Paradise*

Lost. Among the many other complete longer works in the Tenth Edition are *Sir Gawain and the Green Knight* (in Simon Armitage's spectacular translation), Sir Thomas More's *Utopia*, Sir Philip Sidney's *Defense of Poesy*, William Shakespeare's *Twelfth Night* and *Othello*, Samuel Johnson's *Rasselas*, Aphra Behn's *Oroonoko*, Jonathan Swift's *Gulliver's Travels*, Laurence Sterne's *A Sentimental Journey through France and Italy*, Charles Dickens's *A Christmas Carol*, Robert Louis Stevenson's *The Strange Case of Dr. Jekyll and Mr. Hyde*, Rudyard Kipling's *The Man Who Would Be King*, Joseph Conrad's *Heart of Darkness*, Virginia Woolf's *Mrs. Dalloway*, James Joyce's *Portrait of the Artist as a Young Man*, Samuel Beckett's *Waiting for Godot*, Harold Pinter's *The Dumb Waiter*, and Tom Stoppard's *Arcadia*. To augment the number of complete longer works instructors can assign, and—a special concern—better to represent the achievements of novelists, the publisher is making available the full list of Norton Critical Editions, more than 240 titles, including such frequently assigned novels as Jane Austen's *Pride and Prejudice*, Mary Shelley's *Frankenstein*, Charles Dickens's *Hard Times*, and Chinua Achebe's *Things Fall Apart*. A Norton Critical Edition may be included with either package (volumes A, B, C and volumes D, E, F) or any individual volume at a discounted price (contact your Norton representative for details).

We have in this edition continued to expand the selection of writing by women in several historical periods. The sustained work of scholars in recent years has recovered dozens of significant authors who had been marginalized or neglected by a male-dominated literary tradition and has deepened our understanding of those women writers who had managed, against considerable odds, to claim a place in that tradition. The First Edition of the Norton Anthology included 6 women writers; this Tenth Edition includes 84, of whom 12 are newly added and 10 are reselected or expanded. Poets and dramatists whose names were scarcely mentioned even in the specialized literary histories of earlier generations—Aemilia Lanyer, Lady Mary Wroth, Margaret Cavendish, Mary Leapor, Anna Letitia Barbauld, Charlotte Smith, Letitia Elizabeth Landon, Mary Elizabeth Coleridge, Mina Loy, and many others—now appear in the company of their male contemporaries. There are in addition four complete long prose works by women—Aphra Behn's *Oroonoko*, Eliza Haywood's *Fantomina*, Jane Austen's *Love and Friendship*, and Virginia Woolf's *Mrs. Dalloway*—along with selections from such celebrated fiction writers as Maria Edgeworth, Jean Rhys, Katherine Mansfield, Doris Lessing, Margaret Atwood, Kiran Desai, Zadie Smith, and new authors Hilary Mantel and Chimamanda Ngozi Adichie.

Building on an innovation introduced in the First Edition, the editors have expanded the array of topical clusters that gather together short texts illuminating the cultural, historical, intellectual, and literary concerns of each of the periods. We have designed these clusters with three aims: to make them lively and accessible, to ensure that they can be taught effectively in a class meeting or two, and to make clear their relevance to the surrounding works of literature. Hence, for example, in the Sixteenth Century, a new cluster, "The Wider World," showcases the English fascination with narratives of adventure, exploration, trade, and reconnaissance. New in the Eighteenth Century, "Print Culture and the Rise of the Novel" offers statements on the emergence of what would become English literature's most popular form as well as excerpts from *Robinson Crusoe* and *Evelina*. And in the Romantic

Period, a new cluster on "The Romantic Imagination and the 'Oriental Nations'" joins contemporary discussion of the literature of those nations with selections from William Beckford's *Vathek* and Byron's *The Giaour*, among other texts. Across the volumes the clusters provide an exciting way to broaden the field of the literary and to set masterpieces in a wider cultural, social, and historical framework

Now, as in the past, cultures define themselves by the songs they sing and the stories they tell. But the central importance of visual media in contemporary culture has heightened our awareness of the ways in which songs and stories have always been closely linked to the images that societies have fashioned and viewed. The Tenth Edition of *The Norton Anthology of English Literature* features fifty-six pages of color plates (in seven color inserts) and more than 120 black-and-white illustrations throughout the volumes, including six new maps. In selecting visual material—from the Sutton Hoo treasure of the seventh century to Yinka Shonibare's *Nelson's Ship in a Bottle* in the twenty-first century—the editors sought to provide images that conjure up, whether directly or indirectly, the individual writers in each section; that relate specifically to individual works in the anthology; and that shape and illuminate the culture of a particular literary period. We have tried to choose visually striking images that will interest students and provoke discussion, and our captions draw attention to important details and cross-reference related texts in the anthology.

Period-by-Period Revisions

The Middle Ages. Edited by James Simpson, this period, huge in its scope and immensely varied in its voices, continues to offer exciting surprises. The heart of the Anglo-Saxon portion is the great epic *Beowulf*, in the acclaimed translation by Seamus Heaney. Now accompanied by a map of England at the time, the Anglo-Saxon texts include the haunting poems "Wulf and Eadwacer" and "The Ruin" as well as an intriguing collection of Anglo-Saxon riddles. These new works join verse translations of the *Dream of the Rood*, the *Wanderer*, and *The Wife's Lament*. An Irish Literature selection features a tale from *The Tain* and a group of ninth-century lyrics. The Anglo-Norman section—a key bridge between the Anglo-Saxon period and the time of Chaucer—offers a new pairing of texts about the tragic story of Tristan and Ysolt; an illuminating cluster on the Romance, with three stories by Marie de France (in award-winning translations); and *Sir Orfeo*, a comic version of the Orpheus and Eurydice story. The Middle English section centers, as always, on Chaucer, with a generous selection of tales and poems glossed and annotated so as to heighten their accessibility. Simon Armitage's brilliant verse translation of *Sir Gawain and the Green Knight* appears once again, and we offer newly modernized versions both of Thomas Hoccleve's *My Complaint*, a startlingly personal account of the speaker's attempt to reenter society after a period of mental instability, and of the playfully ironic and spiritually moving *Second Shepherds' Play*. "Talking Animals," a delightful new cluster, presents texts by Marie de France, Chaucer, and Robert Henryson that show how medieval writers used animals in stories that reveal much about humankind.

The Sixteenth Century, edited by Stephen Greenblatt and George Logan, features eight extraordinary longer texts in their entirety: More's *Utopia* (with two letters from More to Peter Giles); Book 1 of Spenser's *Faerie Queene* and, new to this edition, the posthumously published *Mutabilitie Cantos,* which arguably offer some of Spenser's finest poetry; Marlowe's *Hero and Leander* and *Doctor Faustus,* Sidney's *Defense of Poesy;* and Shakespeare's *Twelfth Night* and *Othello,* which has been added to the Tenth Edition by instructor request. Two exciting new topical clusters join the section. "An Elizabethan Miscellany" is a full, richly teachable grouping of sixteenth-century poems in English, by writers from George Gascoigne to Michael Drayton to Thomas Campion, among others, and provides access the period's explosion of lyric genius. "The Wider World" showcases the English Renaissance fascination with narratives of adventure, exploration, trade, and reconnaissance. Ranging from Africa to the Muslim East to the New World, the texts are compelling reading in our contemporary global context and offer particularly suggestive insights into the world of Shakespeare's *Othello.*

The Early Seventeenth Century. At the heart of this period, edited by Katharine Eisaman Maus, is John Milton's *Paradise Lost,* presented in its entirety. New to the Tenth Edition are the Arguments to each book, which are especially helpful for students first reading this magnificent, compelling epic. Along with Milton's "Lycidas" and *Samson Agonistes,* which is new to this edition, other complete longer works include John Donne's *Satire 3* and *The Anatomy of the World: The First Anniversary;* Aemilia Lanyer's country-house poem "The Description of Cookham"; Ben Jonson's *Volpone* and the moving Cary-Morison ode; and John Webster's tragedy *The Duchess of Malfi.* Generous selections from Donne, Mary Wroth, George Herbert, Katherine Philips, Andrew Marvell, and others, as well as the clusters "Inquiry and Experience," "Gender Relations," and "Crisis of Authority," together make for an exciting and thorough representation of the period.

The Restoration and the Eighteenth Century. The impressive array of complete longer texts in this period, edited by James Noggle, includes Dryden's *Absalom and Achitophel* and *MacFlecknoe;* Aphra Behn's *Oroonoko* (now with its dedicatory epistle); Congreve's comedy *The Way of the World;* Swift's *Gulliver's Travels* (newly complete, with illustrations from the first edition); Pope's *Essay on Criticism, The Rape of the Lock,* and *Epistle to Dr. Arbuthnot;* Gay's *Beggar's Opera;* Eliza Haywood's novella of sexual role-playing, *Fantomina;* Hogarth's graphic satire "Marriage A-la-Mode"; Johnson's *Vanity of Human Wishes* and *Rasselas;* Laurence Sterne's *A Sentimental Journey through France and Italy* (new to this edition); Gray's "Elegy Written in a Country Churchyard"; and Goldsmith's "The Deserted Village." An exciting new topical cluster, "Print Culture and the Rise of the Novel," with selections by Daniel Defoe, Henry Fielding, Samuel Richardson, Frances Burney, Clara Reeve, and others, enables readers to explore the origins of English literature's most popular form.

The Romantic Period. Edited by Deidre Shauna Lynch, this period again offers many remarkable additions. Chief among them are two topical clusters: "Romantic Literature and Wartime," which, through texts by Godwin, Wordsworth, Coleridge, Barbauld, Byron, De Quincey, and others, explores the varied ways in which war's violence came home to English literature; and "The Romantic Imagination and the 'Oriental Nations,'" which shows how English writers of the late eighteenth and early nineteenth centuries looked eastward for new, often contradictory themes of cultural identity and difference and for "exotic" subjects that were novel and enticing to the English audience. Also new to this period are poems by Barbauld, Robinson, Charlotte Smith, Wordsworth, Shelley, Hemans, and Landon. We are excited to include an excerpt from *The History of Mary Prince, a West Indian Slave*—the first slave narrative by a woman. John Clare, the increasingly appreciated "natural poet," receives four new texts.

The Victorian Age, edited by Catherine Robson, offers an impressive array of complete longer works. New to the prose selections is Charles Dickens's *A Christmas Carol,* complete with its original illustrations. Dickens's celebrated tale, which entertains at the same time that it deals brilliantly with matters social, economic, and spiritual, joins Robert Louis Stevenson's *The Strange Case of Dr. Jekyll and Mr. Hyde,* Arthur Conan Doyle's *The Speckled Band,* Elizabeth Gaskell's *The Old Nurse's Story,* and Rudyard Kipling's *The Man Who Would Be King.* Authors with significant longer poems include Elizabeth Barrett Browning, Alfred, Lord Tennyson, Robert Browning, Dante Gabriel Rossetti, Christina Rossetti, Algernon Charles Swinburne, and Gerard Manley Hopkins. Plays include Oscar Wilde's *The Importance of Being Earnest* and George Bernard Shaw's controversial drama on prostitution, *Mrs Warren's Profession.* And, continuing the tradition of enabling readers to grapple with the period's most resonant and often fiercely contentious issues, the Tenth Edition offers an exciting new cluster, "Beacons of the Future? Education in Victorian Britain," which brings together powerful reflections by John Stuart Mill and others, government reports on the nature of education, and illuminating excerpts from *Hard Times, Alice's Adventures in Wonderland, Tom Brown's School Days,* and *Jude the Obscure.*

The Twentieth and Twenty-First Centuries. The editor, Jahan Ramazani, continues his careful revision of this, the most rapidly changing period in the anthology. Once again its core is three modernist masterpieces: Virginia Woolf's *Mrs. Dalloway,* James Joyce's *Portrait of the Artist as a Young Man,* and Samuel Beckett's *Waiting for Godot,* all complete. These works are surrounded by a dazzling array of other fiction and drama. New to the Tenth Edition are the recent recipient of the Nobel Prize for Literature, Kazuo Ishiguro, along with Hilary Mantel, Caryl Phillips, and Chimamanda Ngozi Adichie. Their works join Joseph Conrad's *Heart of Darkness,* Harold Pinter's *The Dumb Waiter,* Tom Stoppard's *Arcadia,* and stories by D. H. Lawrence, Katherine Mansfield, Jean Rhys, Doris Lessing, Nadine Gordimer, Kiran Desai, and Zadie Smith. A generous representation of poetry centers on substantial selections from Thomas Hardy, William Butler Yeats, and T. S. Eliot, and extends out to a wide range of other poets, from A. E. Housman, Wilfred Owen, and W. H. Auden to Philip Larkin, Derek Walcott, and Seamus

Heaney. Two new poets, frequently requested by our readers, join the anthology: Anne Carson and Simon Armitage; and there are new poems by Yeats, Heaney, Geoffrey Hill, and Carol Ann Duffy. Visual aids have proved very helpful in teaching this period, and new ones include facsimile manuscript pages of poems by Isaac Rosenberg and Wilfred Owen, plus five new maps, which illustrate, among other things, the dramatic changes in the British Empire from 1891 to the late twentieth century, the movement of peoples to and from England during this time, and the journeys around London of the central characters in Woolf's *Mrs. Dalloway*. Linton Kwesi Johnson, Bernardine Evaristo, Patience Agbabi, and Dajlit Nagra join Claude McKay, Louise Bennett, Kamau Brathwaite, Ngũgĩ Wa Thiong'o, M. NourbeSe Philip, Salman Rushdie, and Grace Nichols in the much-praised cluster "Nation, Race, and Language"—together they bear witness to the global diffusion of English, the urgency of issues of nation and identity, and the rich complexity of literary history.

Editorial Procedures and Format

The Tenth Edition adheres to the principles that have always characterized *The Norton Anthology of English Literature*. Period introductions, headnotes, and annotations are designed to enhance students' reading and, without imposing an interpretation, to give students the information they need to understand each text. The aim of these editorial materials is to make the anthology self-sufficient, so that it can be read anywhere—in a coffeeshop, on a bus, under a tree.

The *Norton Anthology of English Literature* prides itself on both the scholarly accuracy and the readability of its texts. To ease students' encounter with some works, we have normalized spelling and capitalization in texts up to and including the Romantic period—for the most part they now follow the conventions of modern English. We leave unaltered, however, texts in which such modernizing would change semantic or metrical qualities. From the Victorian period onward, we have used the original spelling and punctuation. We continue other editorial procedures that have proved useful in the past. After each work, we cite the date of first publication on the right; in some instances, this date is followed by the date of a revised edition for which the author was responsible. Dates of composition, when they differ from those of publication and when they are known, are provided on the left. We use square brackets to indicate titles supplied by the editors for the convenience of readers. Whenever a portion of a text is omitted, we indicate that omission with three asterisks. If the omitted portion is important for following the plot or argument, we provide a brief summary within the text or in a footnote. Finally, we have reconsidered annotations throughout and increased the number of marginal glosses for archaic, dialect, or unfamiliar words.

The Tenth Edition includes the useful "Literary Terminology" appendix, a quick-reference alphabetical glossary with examples from works in the anthology. We have also updated the General Bibliography that appears in the print volumes, as well as the period and author bibliographies, which appear online, where they can be easily searched and updated.

Additional Resources for Instructors and Students

The idea that a vital literary culture is always on the move applies not only to the print anthology but also to the resources that accompany it. For the Tenth Edition, we have added exciting new resources and improved and updated existing resources to make them more useful and easy to find.

We are pleased to launch the new NAEL Archive site, found at digital .wwnorton.com/englishlit10abc (for volumes A, B, C) and digital.wwnorton .com/englishlit10def (for volumes D, E, F). This searchable and sortable site contains thousands of resources for students and instructors in one centralized place at no additional cost. Following are some highlights:

- A series of twenty brand-new video modules designed to enhance classroom presentation of the literary works. These videos, conceived of and narrated by the anthology editors, bring various texts from the anthology to life by providing a closer look at a rarely seen manuscript, visiting a place of literary significance, or offering a conversation with a living writer.
- Over 1,000 additional readings from the Middle Ages to the turn of the twentieth century, edited, glossed, and annotated to the scholarly standards and with the sensitivity to classroom use for which the Norton Anthology is renowned. Teachers who wish to add to the selections in the print anthology will find numerous exciting works, including Wycherley's *The Country Wife*, Joanna Baillie's "A Mother to Her Waking Infant," and Edward Lear's "The Jumblies." In addition, there are many fascinating topical clusters—"The First Crusade: Sanctifying War," "Genius," and "The Satanic and Byronic Hero," to name only a few—all designed to draw readers into larger cultural contexts and to expose them to a wide spectrum of voices.
- Hundreds of images—maps, author portraits, literary places, and manuscripts—available for student browsing or instructor download for in-class presentation.
- Several hours of audio recordings.
- Annotated bibliographies for all periods and authors in the anthology.

The NAEL Archive also provides a wealth of teaching resources that are unlocked on instructor log-in:

- "Quick read" summaries, teaching notes, and discussion questions for every work in the anthology, from the much-praised *Teaching with* The Norton Anthology of English Literature: *A Guide for Instructors* by Naomi Howell (University of Exeter), Philip Schwyzer (University of Exeter), Judyta Frodyma (University of Northern British Columbia), and Sondra Archimedes (University of California–Santa Cruz).
- Downloadable PowerPoints featuring images and audio for in-class presentation

In addition to the wealth of resources in the NAEL Archive, Norton offers a downloadable coursepack that allows instructors to easily add high-quality Norton digital media to online, hybrid, or lecture courses—all at no cost.

Norton Coursepacks work within existing learning management systems; there's no new system to learn, and access is free and easy. Content is customizable and includes over seventy-four reading-comprehension quizzes, short-answer questions with suggested answers, links to the video modules, and more.

The editors are deeply grateful to the hundreds of teachers worldwide who have helped us to improve *The Norton Anthology of English Literature*. A list of the instructors who replied to a detailed questionnaire follows, under Acknowledgments. The editors would like to express appreciation for their assistance to Jessica Berman (University of Maryland Baltimore County), Lara Bovilsky (University of Oregon), Gordon Braden (University of Virginia), Bruce Bradley (Clongowes Wood College), Dympna Callaghan (Syracuse University), Ariel Churchill (Harvard University), Joseph Connors (Harvard University), Taylor Cowdery (University of North Carolina at Chapel Hill), Maria Devlin (Harvard University), Lars Engel (University of Tulsa), James Engell (Harvard University), Aubrey Everett (Harvard University), Anne Fernald (Fordham University), Kevis Goodman (University of California, Berkeley), Alexander Gourlay (Rhode Island School of Design), John Hale (University of Otago), Stephen Hequembourg (University of Virginia), Seth Herbst (United States Military Academy, West Point), Rhema Hokama (Singapore University of Technology and Design), Jean Howard (Columbia University), Robert Irvine (University of Edinburgh), Thomas Keirstead (University of Toronto), Margaret Kelleher (University College Dublin), Cara Lewis (Indiana University Northwest), Mario Menendez (Harvard University), Tara Menon (New York University), John Miller (University of Virginia), Peter Miller (University of Virginia), A. J. Odasso (Wellesley College), Declan O'Keeffe (Clongowes Wood College), Juan Christian Pellicer (University of Oslo), Robert Pinsky (Boston University), Will Porter (Harvard University), Mark Rankin (James Madison University), Josephine Reece (Harvard University), Jessica Rosenberg (University of Miami), Suparna Roychoudhury (Mount Holyoke College), Peter Sacks (Harvard University), Ray Siemens (University of Victoria), Kim Simpson (University of Southampton), Bailey Sincox (Harvard University), Ramie Targoff (Brandeis University), Misha Teramura (Reed College), Gordon Teskey (Harvard University), Katie Trumpener (Yale University), Paul Westover (Brigham Young University), Katy Woodring (Harvard University), and Faye Zhang (Harvard University).

We also thank the many people at Norton, an employee-owned publishing house with a commitment to excellence, who contributed to the Tenth Edition. In planning this edition, Julia Reidhead served, as she has done in the past, as our wise and effective collaborator. In addition, we are now working with Marian Johnson, literature editor and managing editor for college books, a splendid new collaborator who has helped us bring the Tenth Edition to fruition. With admirable equanimity and skill, Carly Frasier Doria, electronic media editor and course guide editor, fashioned the new video modules and brought together the dazzling array of web resources and other pedagogical aids. We also have debts of gratitude to Katharine Ings, Candace Levy, and Michael Fleming, manuscript editors; Sean Mintus, senior production manager; Kimberly Bowers, marketing manager for literature; Megan Jackson Schindel and Nancy Rodwan, permissions; Jo Anne Metsch, designer; Nelson

Colon, photo editor; and Rachel Taylor and Ava Bramson, assistant editor and assistant media editor, respectively. All these friends provided the editors with indispensable help in meeting the challenge of representing the unparalleled range and variety of English literature.

STEPHEN GREENBLATT

Acknowledgments

The editors would like to express appreciation and thanks to the hundreds of teachers who provided reviews:

Michel Aaij (Auburn University at Montgomery), Jerry J. Alexander (Presbyterian College), Sarah Alexander (The University of Vermont), Marshall N. Armintor (University of North Texas), Marilyn Judith Atlas (Ohio University), Alison Baker (California State Polytechnic University, Pomona), Reid Barbour (University of North Carolina, Chapel Hill), Jessica Barnes-Pietruszynski (West Virginia State University), Jessica Barr (Eureka College), Chris Barrett (Louisiana State University), Craig Barrette (Brescia University), Carol Beran (St. Mary's College), Peter Berek (Amherst College), David Bergman (Towson University), Scott Black (University of Utah), William R. "Beau" Black III (Weatherford College), Justin Blessinger (Dakota State University), William E. Bolton (La Salle University), Wyatt Bonikowski (Suffolk University), Rebecca Bossie (University of Texas at El Paso), Bruce Brandt (South Dakota State University), Heather Braun (University of Akron), Mark Brown (University of Jamestown), Logan D. Browning (Rice University), Monica Brzezinski Potkay (College of William and Mary), Rebecca Bushnell (University of Pennsylvania), Claire Busse (La Salle University), Thomas Butler (Eastern Kentucky University), Jim Casey (Arcadia University), Susan P. Cerasano (Colgate University), Maria Chappell (University of Georgia), Brinda Charry (Keene State College), Susannah Chewning (Union County College), Lin Chih-hsin (National Chengchi University), Kathryn Chittick (Trent University), Rita Colanzi (Immaculata University), Nora Corrigan (Mississippi University for Women), David Cowart (University of South Carolina), Catherine Craft-Fairchild (University of St. Thomas), Susan Crisafulli (Franklin College), Jenny Crisp (Dalton State College), Ashley Cross (Manhattan College), James P. Crowley (Bridgewater State University), Susie Crowson (Del Mar College), Rebecca Crump (Louisiana State University), Cyrus Mulready (SUNY New Paltz), Lisa Darien (Hartwick College), Sean Dempsey (University of Arkansas), Anthony Ding (Grossmont Community College), Lorraine Eadie (Hillsdale College), Schuyler Eastin (San Diego Christian College), Gary Eddy (Winona State University), J. Craig Eller (Louisburg College), Robert Ellison (Marshall University), Nikolai Endres (Western Kentucky University), Robert Epstein (Fairfield University), Richard Erable (Franklin College), Simon C. Estok (Sungkyunkwan University), Michael Faitell (Mohawk Valley Community College), Jonathan Farina (Seton Hall University), Tyler Farrell (Marquette University), Jennifer

Feather (The University of North Carolina Greensboro), Annette Federico (James Madison University), Kerstin Feindert (Cosumnes River College), Maryanne Felter (Cayuga Community College), Benjamin Fischer (Northwest Nazarene University), Matthew Fisher (University of California, Los Angeles), Chris Fletcher (North Central University), Michael J. Flynn (The University of North Dakota), James E. Foley (Worcester State University), Walter C. Foreman (University of Kentucky), Ann Frank Wake (Elmhurst College), Michael D. Friedman (University of Scranton), Lee Garver (Butler University), Paul L. Gaston (Kent State University), Sara E. Gerend (Aurora University), Avilah Getzler (Grand View University), Edward Gieskes (University of South Carolina), Elaine Glanz (Immaculata University), Adam Golaski (Brown University), Rachel Goldberg (Northeastern CPS), Augusta Gooch (University of Alabama–Huntsville), Nathan Gorelick (Utah Valley University), Robert Gorsch (Saint Mary's College of California), Carey Goyette (Clinton Community College), Richard J. Grande (Pennsylvania State University–Abington), David A. Grant (Columbus State Community College), Sian Griffiths (Weber State University), Ann H. Guess (Alvin Community College), Audley Hall (North West Arkansas Community College), Jenni Halpin (Savannah State University), Brian Harries (Concordia University Wisconsin), Samantha Harvey (Boise State University), Raychel Haugrud Reiff (University of Wisconsin–Superior), Erica Haugtvedt (The Ohio State University), Mary Hayes (University of Mississippi), Joshua R. Held (Indiana University, Bloomington), Roze Hentschell (Colorado State University), Erich Hertz (Siena College), Natalie Hewitt (Hope International University), Lisa Hinrichsen (University of Arkansas), Lorretta Holloway (Framingham State University), Catherine Howard (University of Houston), Chia-Yin Huang (Chinese Culture University), Sister Marie Hubert Kealy (Immaculata University), Elizabeth Hutcheon (Huntingdon College), Peter Hyland (Huron University College, Western University), Eileen Jankowski (Chapman University), Alan Johnson (Idaho State University), Brian Jukes (Yuba College), Kari Kalve (Earlham College), Parmita Kapadia (Northern Kentucky University), Deborah Kennedy (Saint Mary's University), Mark Kipperman (Northern Illinois University), Cindy Klestinec (Miami University–Ohio), Neal W. Kramer (Brigham Young University), Kathryn Laity (College of Saint Rose), Jameela Lares (University of Southern Mississippi), Caroline Levine (University of Wisconsin–Madison), Melinda Linscott (Idaho State University), Janet Madden (El Camino College), Gerald Margolis (Temple University), Elizabeth Mazzola (The City College of New York), Keely McCarthy (Chestnut Hill College), Cathryn McCarthy Donahue (College of Mount Saint Vincent), Mary H. McMurran (University of Western Ontario), Josephine A. McQuail (Tennessee Technological University), Brett Mertins (Metropolitan Community College), Christian Michener (Saint Mary's University), Brook Miller (University of Minnesota, Morris), Kristine Miller (Utah State University), Jacqueline T. Miller (Rutgers University), Richard J. Moll (University of Western Ontario), Lorne Mook (Taylor University), Rod Moore (Los Angeles Valley College), Rory Moore (University of California, Riverside), Grant Moss (Utah Valley University), Nicholas D. Nace (Hampden-Sydney College), Jonathan Naito (St. Olaf College), Mary Nelson (Dallas Baptist University), Mary Anne Nunn (Central Connecticut State University), John O'Brien (University of Virginia), Onno Oerlemans (Hamilton College),

Michael Oishi (Leeward Community College), Sylvia Pamboukian (Robert Morris University), Adam Parkes (University of Georgia), Michelle Parkinson (University of Wisconsin–River Falls), Geoffrey Payne (Macquarie University), Anna Peak (Temple University), Dan Pearce (Brigham Young University–Idaho), Christopher Penna (University of Delaware), Zina Petersen (Brigham Young University), Kaara L. Peterson (Miami University of Ohio), Keith Peterson (Brigham Young University–Hawaii), Professor Maggie Piccolo (Rowan University), Ann Pleiss Morris (Ripon College), Michael Pogach (Northampton Community College), Matthew Potolsky (The University of Utah), Miguel Powers (Fullerton College), Gregory Priebe (Harford Community College), Jonathan Purkiss (Pulaski Technical College), Kevin A. Quarmby (Oxford College of Emory University), Mark Rankin (James Madison University), Tawnya Ravy (The George Washington University), Joan Ray (University of Colorado, Colorado Springs), Helaine Razovsky (Northwestern State University of Louisiana), Vince Redder (Dakota Wesleyan University), Elizabeth Rich (Saginaw Valley State University), Patricia Rigg (Acadia University), Albert J. Rivero (Marquette University), Phillip Ronald Stormer (Culver-Stockton College), Kenneth Rooney (University College Cork, Ireland), David Ruiter (University of Texas at El Paso), Kathryn Rummell (California Polytechnic State University), Richard Ruppel (Chapman University), Jonathan Sachs (Concordia University), David A. Salomon (Russell Sage College), Abigail Scherer (Nicholls State University), Roger Schmidt (Idaho State University), William Sheldon (Hutchinson Community College), Christian Sheridan (Bridgewater College), Nicole Sidhu (East Carolina University), Lisa Siefker Bailey (Indiana University–Purdue University Columbus), Samuel Smith (Messiah College), Cindy Soldan (Lakehead University), Diana Solomon (Simon Fraser University), Vivasvan Soni (Northwestern University), Timothy Spurgin (Lawrence University), Felicia Jean Steele (The College of New Jersey), Carole Lynn Stewart (Brock University), Judy Suh (Duquesne University), Dean Swinford (Fayetteville State University), Allison Symonds (Cecil College), Brenda Tuberville (Rogers State University), Verne Underwood (Rogue Community College), Janine Utell (Widener University), Paul Varner (Abilene Christian University), Deborah Vause (York College of Pennsylvania), Nicholas Wallerstein (Black Hills State University), Rod Waterman (Central Connecticut State University), Eleanor Welsh (Chesapeake College), Paul Westover (Brigham Young University), Christopher Wheatley (The Catholic University of America), Miranda Wilcox (Brigham Young University), Brett D. Wilson (College of William & Mary), Lorraine Wood (Brigham Young University), Nicholas A. Wright (Marist College), Michael Wutz (Weber State University).

THE NORTON ANTHOLOGY OF

ENGLISH

LITERATURE

TENTH EDITION

VOLUME C

THE RESTORATION
AND
THE EIGHTEENTH CENTURY

The Restoration and the Eighteenth Century 1660–1785

The Restoration and the eighteenth century brought vast changes to the island of Great Britain, which became a single nation after 1707, when the Act of Union joined Scotland to England and Wales. After the prolonged civil and religious strife of the seventeenth century, Britain attained political stability and unprecedented commercial vigor. The countryside kept its seemingly timeless agricultural rhythms, even as the nation's great families consolidated their control over the land and those who worked it. Change came most dramatically to cities, which absorbed much of a national population that nearly doubled in the period, to ten million. Britons came together in civil society—the public but nongovernmental institutions and practices that became newly powerful in the period. The theaters (reopened at the Restoration),

A Philosopher Giving That Lecture on the Orrery, in Which a Lamp Is Put in Place of the Sun (detail), 1766, Joseph Wright. For more information about this painting, see the color insert in this volume.

coffeehouses, concert halls, pleasure gardens, lending libraries, picture exhibitions, and shopping districts gave life in London and elsewhere a feeling of bustle and friction. Reflecting and stimulating this activity, an expanding assortment of printed works vied to interest literate women and men, whose numbers grew to include most of the middle classes and many among the poor. Civil society also linked people to an increasingly global economy, as they shopped for diverse goods from around the world. The rich and even the moderately well off could profit or go broke from investments in joint-stock companies, which controlled much of Britain's international trade, including its lucrative traffic in slaves. At home, new systems of canals and turnpikes stimulated domestic trade, industry, and travel, bringing distant parts of the country closer together. The cohesion of the nation also depended on ideas of social order—some old and clear, many subtle and new. An ethos of politeness came to prevail, a standard of social behavior to which more and more could aspire yet that served to distinguish the privileged sharply from the rude and vulgar. This and other ideas, of order and hierarchy, of liberty and rights, of sentiment and sympathy, helped determine the ways in which an expanding diversity of people could seek to participate in Britain's thriving cultural life.

RELIGION AND POLITICS

The Restoration of 1660—the return of Charles Stuart (son of the beheaded King Charles I) and, with him, the monarchy to England—brought hope to a divided nation, exhausted by years of civil war and political turmoil. Almost all of Charles's subjects welcomed him home. After the abdication of Richard Cromwell in 1659 the country had seemed at the brink of chaos, and Britons were eager to believe that their king would bring order and law and a spirit of mildness back into the national life. But no political settlement could be stable until the religious issues had been resolved. The restoration of the monarchy meant that the established church would also be restored, and though Charles was willing to pardon or ignore many former enemies (such as Milton), the bishops and Anglican clergy were less tolerant of dissent. When Parliament reimposed the Book of Common Prayer in 1662 and then in 1664 barred Nonconformists from religious meetings outside the established church, thousands of clergymen resigned their livings, and the jails were filled with preachers like John Bunyan who refused to be silenced. In 1673 the Test Act required all holders of civil and military offices to take the sacrament in an Anglican church and to deny belief in transubstantiation. Thus Protestant Dissenters and Roman Catholics were largely excluded from public life; for instance, Alexander Pope, a Catholic, could not attend a university, own land, or vote. The scorn of Anglicans for Nonconformist zeal or "enthusiasm" (a belief in private revelation) bursts out in Samuel Butler's popular *Hudibras* (1663), a caricature of Presbyterians and Independents. And English Catholics were widely regarded as potential traitors and (wrongly) thought to have set the Great Fire that destroyed much of London in 1666.

Yet the triumph of the established church did not resolve the constitutional issues that had divided Charles I and Parliament. Charles II had promised to govern through Parliament but slyly tried to consolidate royal power. Steering away from crises, he hid his Catholic sympathies and avoided a test of strength with Parliament—except on one occasion. In 1678 the report of the Popish Plot, in which Catholics would rise and murder their Protestant foes, terrified London; and though the charge turned out to be a fraud, the House of Commons exploited the fear by trying to force Charles to exclude his Catholic brother, James, duke of York, from succession to the throne. The turmoil of this period is captured brilliantly by Dryden's *Absalom and Achitophel* (1681). Finally, Charles defeated the Exclusion Bill by dissolving Parliament. But the crisis resulted in a basic division of the country between two new political parties: the Tories, who supported the king, and the Whigs, the king's opponents.

Neither party could live with James II. After he came to the throne in 1685, he claimed the right to make his own laws, suspended the Test Act, and began to fill the army and government with fellow Catholics. The birth of James's son in 1688 brought matters to a head, confronting the nation with the prospect of a Catholic dynasty. Secret negotiations paved the way for the Dutchman William of Orange, a champion of Protestantism and the husband of James's Protestant daughter Mary. William landed with a small army in southwestern England and marched toward London. As he advanced the king's allies melted away, and James fled to a permanent exile in France. But the house of Stuart would be heard from again. For more than half a century some loyal Jacobites (from the Latin *Jacobus*, "James"), especially in Scotland, supported James, his son ("the Old Pretender"), and his grandson ("the Young Pretender" or "Bonnie Prince Charlie") as the legitimate rulers of Britain. Moreover, a good many writers, from Aphra Behn and Dryden (and arguably Pope and Johnson) to Robert Burns, privately sympathized with Jacobitism. But after the failure of one last rising in 1745, the cause would dwindle gradually into a wistful sentiment. In retrospect, the coming of William and Mary in 1688—the Glorious, or Bloodless, Revolution—came to be seen as the beginning of a stabilized, unified Great Britain.

A number of innovations made this stability possible. In 1689 a Bill of Rights revoked James's actions; the bill limited the powers of the Crown, reaffirmed the supremacy of Parliament, and guaranteed some individual rights. The same year the Toleration Act relaxed the strain of religious conflict by granting a limited freedom of worship to Dissenters (although not to Catholics or Jews) so long as they swore allegiance to the Crown. This proved to be a workable compromise. The passage of the Act of Settlement in 1701 seemed finally to resolve the difficult problem of succession that had bedeviled the monarchy. Sophia, the electress of Hanover, and her descendants were put in line for the throne. As the granddaughter of James I, she was the closest Protestant relative of Princess Anne, James II's younger daughter (whose sole surviving child died in that year). The principles established in these years endured unaltered in essentials until the Reform Bill of 1832.

But the political rancor that often animates contests for power did not vanish, and during Anne's reign (1702–14), new tensions embittered the nation. In the War of the Spanish Succession (1702–13), England and its allies defeated France and Spain. As these commercial rivals were weakened and war profits flowed in, the Whig lords and London merchants supporting the war grew rich. The spoils included new colonies and the *asiento*, a contract to supply slaves to the Spanish Empire. The hero of the war, Captain-General John Churchill, duke of Marlborough, won the famous victory of Blenheim; was showered with honors and wealth; and, with his duchess, dominated the queen until 1710. But the Whigs and Marlborough pushed their luck too hard. When the Whigs tried to reward the Dissenters for their loyalty by removing the Test, Anne fought back to defend the established church. She dismissed her Whig ministers and the Marlboroughs and called in Robert Harley and the brilliant young Henry St. John to form a Tory ministry. These ministers employed prominent writers like Defoe and Swift and commissioned Matthew Prior to negotiate the Peace of Utrecht (1713). But to Swift's despair—he later burlesqued events at court in *Gulliver's Travels*—a bitter rivalry broke out between Harley (now earl of Oxford) and St. John (now Viscount Bolingbroke). Though Bolingbroke succeeded in ousting Oxford, the death of Anne in 1714 reversed his fortunes. The Whigs returned to power, and George I (Sophia's son) became the first Hanoverian king (he would reign until 1727). Harley was imprisoned in the Tower of London until 1717; and Bolingbroke, charged with being a Jacobite traitor, fled to France. Government was now securely in the hands of the Whigs.

The political principles of the Whig and Tory parties, which bring so much fire to eighteenth-century public debate, evolved through the period to address changing circumstances. Now we tend to think of Tories as conservative and Whigs as liberal. (Members of today's Conservative Party in the United Kingdom are sometimes called Tories.) During the Exclusion Crisis of the 1680s the Whigs asserted the liberties of the English subject against the royal prerogatives of Charles II, whom Tories such as Dryden supported. After both parties survived the 1688 Glorious Revolution, the Tories guarded the preeminence of the established church (sometimes styling themselves the Church Party), while Whigs tended to support toleration of Dissenters. Economically, too, Tories defined themselves as traditionalists, affirming landownership as the proper basis of wealth, power, and privilege (though most thought trade honorable), whereas the Whigs came to be seen as supporting a new "moneyed interest" (as Swift called it): managers of the Bank of England (founded 1694), contrivers of the system of public credit, and investors in the stock market. But conservatism and liberalism did not exist as ideological labels in the period, and the vicissitudes of party dispute offer many surprises. When Bolingbroke returned to England in 1724 after being pardoned, he led a Tory opposition that decried the "ministerial tyranny" of the Whig government. This opposition patriotically hailed liberty in a manner recalling the Whig rhetoric of earlier decades, appealed to both landed gentry and urban merchants, and anticipated the antigovernment radicalism of the end of the eighteenth century. Conversely, the Whigs sought to secure a centralized fiscal and military state machine and a web of financial interdependence controlled by the wealthiest aristocrats.

The great architect of this Whig policy was Robert Walpole, who came to power as a result of the "South Sea bubble" (1720), a stock market crash. His ability to restore confidence and keep the country running smoothly, as well as to juggle money, would mark his long ascendancy. Coming to be known as Britain's first "prime" minister, he consolidated his power during the reign of George II (1727–60). More involved in British affairs than his essentially German father, George II came to appreciate the efficient administration of the patronage system under Walpole, who installed dependents in government offices and controlled the House of Commons by financially rewarding its members. Many great writers found these methods offensive and embraced Bolingbroke's new Tory rhetoric extolling the Englishman's fierce independence from the corrupting power of centralized government and concentrations of wealth. Gay's *Beggar's Opera* (1728) and Fielding's *Jonathan Wild* (1743) draw parallels between great criminals and great politicians, and Pope's *Dunciad* uses Walpole as an emblem of the venal commercialization of the whole social fabric. This distaste, however, did not prevent Pope himself from marketing his poems as cleverly as he wrote them.

Walpole fell in 1742 because he was unwilling to go to war against the French and Spanish, a war he thought would cost too much but that many perceived would enhance Britain's wealth still further. The next major English statesman, William Pitt the Elder, appealed to a spirit of patriotism and called for the expansion of British power and commerce overseas. The defeat of the French in the Seven Years' War (1756–63), especially in North America, was largely his doing. The long reign of George III (1760–1820) was dominated by two great concerns: the emergence of Britain as a colonial power and the cry for a new social order based on liberty and radical reform. In 1763 the Peace of Paris consolidated British rule over Canada and India, and not even the later loss of the American colonies could stem the rise of the empire. Great Britain was no longer an isolated island but a nation with interests and responsibilities around the world.

At home, however, there was discontent. The wealth brought to England by industrialism and foreign trade had not spread to the great mass of the poor. For much of the century, few had questioned the idea that those at the top of the social hierarchy rightfully held power. Rich families' alliances and rivalries, national and local, dominated politics; while male property owners could vote in Parliamentary elections, they and others of the middle classes and the poor had mostly followed the powerful people who could best help them thrive or at least survive. But toward the end of the century it seemed to many that the bonds of custom that once held people together had finally broken, and now money alone was respected. Protestants turned against Catholics; in 1780 the Gordon Riots put London temporarily under mob rule. The king was popular with his subjects and tried to take government into his own hands, rising above partisanship, but his efforts often backfired—as when the American colonists took him for a tyrant. From 1788 to the end of his life, moreover, an inherited disease (porphyria) periodically unhinged his mind, as in a memorable scene described by Frances Burney. Meanwhile, reformers such as John Wilkes, Richard Price, and Catharine Macaulay called for a new political republic. Fear of their radicalism would contribute to the British reaction against the French Revolution. In the last decades of the century British authors would be torn between two opposing attitudes: loyalty to the old traditions of subordination, mutual obligations, and local self-sufficiency, and yearning for a new dispensation founded on principles of liberty, the rule of reason, and human rights.

THE CONTEXT OF IDEAS

Much of the most powerful writing after 1660 exposed divisions in the nation's thinking inherited from the tumult of earlier decades. As the possibility of a Christian Commonwealth receded, the great republican John Milton published *Paradise Lost* (final version, 1674), and John Bunyan's immensely popular masterwork *Pilgrim's Progress* (1679) expressed the conscience of a Nonconformist. Conversely, an aristocratic culture, led by Charles II himself, aggressively celebrated pleasure and the right of the elite to behave as they wished. Members of the court scandalized respectable London citizens and considered their wives and daughters fair game. The court's hero, the earl of Rochester, became a celebrity for enacting the creed of a libertine and rake. The delights of the court also took more refined forms. French and Italian musicians, as well as painters from the Low Countries, migrated to England, and playhouses—closed by the Puritans since 1642—sprang back to life. In 1660 Charles authorized two new companies of actors, the King's Players and the Duke's; their repertory included witty, bawdy comedies written and acted by women as well as men. But as stark as the contrasts were during the Restoration between libertine and religious intellectuals, royalists and republicans, High Churchmen and Nonconformists, the court and the rest of the country, a spirit of compromise was brewing.

Perhaps the most widely shared intellectual impulse of the age was a distrust of dogmatism. Nearly everybody blamed it for the civil strife through which the nation had recently passed. Opinions varied widely about which dogmatism was most dangerous—Puritan enthusiasm, papal infallibility, the divine right of kings, medieval scholastic or modern Cartesian philosophy—but these were denounced in remarkably similar terms. As far apart intellectually and temperamentally as Rochester and Milton were, both portray overconfidence in human reasoning as the supreme disaster. It is the theme of Butler's *Hudibras* and much of the work of Dryden. Many philosophers, scientists, and divines began to embrace a mitigated skepticism, which argued that human beings could readily achieve a sufficient degree of necessary knowledge (sometimes called "moral certainty") but also contended that the pursuit of absolute certainty was vain, mad, and socially calamitous. If, as the commentator Martin Clifford put it in *A Treatise of Humane Reason* (1675), "in this vast latitude of probabilities," a person thinks "there is none can lead one to salvation, but the path wherein he treads himself, we may see the evident and necessary consequence of eternal troubles and confusions." Such writers insist that a distrust of human capacities is fully compatible with religious faith: for them the inability of reason and sensory evidence to settle important questions reveals our need to accept Christian mysteries as our intellectual foundation. Dryden's poem *Religio Laici* (1682) explains: "So pale grows reason in religion's sight; / So dies, and so dissolves in supernatural light."

Far from inhibiting fresh thinking, however, the distrust of old dogmas inspired new theories, projects, and explorations. In *Leviathan* (1651), Thomas Hobbes jettisoned the notion of a divine basis for kingly authority, proposing instead a naturalistic argument for royal absolutism begun from the claim that mere "matter in motion" composes the universe: if not checked by an absolute sovereign, humankind's "perpetual and restless desire

Frontispiece to Thomas Sprat's *History of the Royal Society*;
Wenceslaus Hollar, engraving, London, 1667. A bust of King
Charles II, called the "author and patron of the Royal Society"
(Latin), is being crowned by Fame. To the left is the Royal Society's
president, Lord Bruckner; to the right, Francis Bacon, pointing to
mathematical and military technology. On the left side are shelves
full of books, and in the background, more scientific instruments,
including Robert Boyle's air pump (center left).

of power after power" could lead to civic collapse. Other materialist philosophies derived from ancient Epicurean thought, which was Christianized by
the French philosopher Pierre Gassendi (1592–1655). The Epicurean doctrine that the universe consists only of minuscule atoms and void unnerved
some thinkers—Swift roundly mocks it in *A Tale of a Tub*—but it also energized efforts to examine the world with deliberate, acute attention. This
new scientific impulse advanced Francis Bacon's program of methodical
experimentation and inductive reasoning formulated earlier in the century.

Charles II gave official approval to the scientific revolution by charter-
ing the Royal Society of London for the Improving of Natural Knowledge in
1662. But observations of nature advanced both formally and informally in an
eclectic range of areas: the specialized, professional "scientist" we know today
did not yet exist. And new features of the world were disclosed to everyone
who had the chance to look. Two wonderful inventions, the microscope and

telescope, had begun to reveal that nature is more extravagant—teeming with tiny creatures and boundless galaxies—than anyone had ever imagined. One book that stayed popular for more than a century, Fontenelle's *Conversations on the Plurality of Worlds* (1686; translated from French by Behn and later by Burney), suggested that an infinite number of alternate worlds and living creatures might exist, not only in outer space but under our feet, invisibly small. Travels to unfamiliar regions of the globe also enlarged understandings of what nature could do: Behn's classifying and collecting of South American flora and fauna in *Oroonoko* show how the appetite for wondrous facts kept pace with the economic motives of world exploration and colonization. Encounters with hitherto little known societies in the Far East, Africa, and the Americas enlarged Europeans' understanding of human norms as well. In *Gulliver's Travels*, Swift shows the comical, painful ways in which the discovery of new cultures forces one average Briton to reexamine his own.

Scientific discovery and exploration also affected religious attitudes. Alongside "natural history" (the collection and description of facts of nature) and "natural philosophy" (the study of the causes of what happens in nature), thinkers of the period placed "natural religion" (the study of nature as a book written by God). Newly discovered natural laws, such as Newton's laws of optics and celestial mechanics, seemed evidence of a universal order in creation, which implied God's hand in the design of the universe, as a watch implies a watchmaker. Expanded knowledge of peoples around the world who had never heard of Christianity led theologians to formulate supposedly universal religious tenets available to all rational beings. Some intellectuals embraced Deism, the doctrine that religion need not depend on mystery or biblical truths and could rely on reason alone, which recognized the goodness and wisdom of natural law and its creator. Natural religion could not, however, discern an active God who punished vice and rewarded virtue in this life; evidently the First Cause had withdrawn from the universe He set in motion. Many orthodox Christians shuddered at the vision of a vast, impersonal machine of nature. Instead they rested their faith on the revelation of Scripture, the scheme of salvation in which Christ died to redeem our sins. Other Christians, such as Pope in *An Essay on Man* and Thomson in *The Seasons*, espoused arguments for natural religion that they felt did not conflict with or diminish orthodox belief.

Some people began to argue that the achievements of modern inquiry had eclipsed those of the ancients (and the fathers of the church), who had not known about the solar system, the New World, microscopic organisms, or the circulation of the blood. The school curriculum still began with years of Latin and Greek, inculcating a long-established humanistic tradition cherished by many authors, including Swift and Pope. A battle of the books erupted in the late seventeenth century between champions of ancient and of modern learning. Swift crusaded fiercely in this battle: *Gulliver's Travels* denounces the pointlessness and arrogance he saw in experiments of the Royal Society, while "A Modest Proposal" depicts a peculiar new cruelty and indifference to moral purpose made possible by statistics and economics (two fields pioneered by Royal Society member Sir William Petty). But as sharp as such disagreements were, accommodation was also possible. Even as works such as Newton's *Principia* (1687) and *Opticks* (1704) revolutionized previously held views of the world, Newton himself maintained a seemly diffidence, comparing himself to "a boy playing on the sea-shore" "whilst the great ocean of truth lay all undiscovered before me." He and other modest modern inquirers such as Locke won the admiration of Pope and many ardent defenders of the past.

The widespread devotion to the direct observation of experience established empiricism as the dominant intellectual attitude of the age, which would become Britain's great legacy to world philosophy. Locke and his heirs George Berkeley and David Hume pursue the experiential approach in widely divergent directions. But even when they reach conclusions shocking to common sense, they tend to reassert the security of our prior knowledge. Berkeley insists we know the world only through our senses and thus cannot prove that any material thing exists, but he uses that argument to demonstrate the necessity of faith, because reality amounts to no more than a perception in the mind of God. Hume's famous argument about causation—that "causes and effects are discoverable, not by reason but by experience"—grounds our sense of the world not on rational reflection but on spontaneous, unreflective beliefs and feelings. Perhaps Locke best expresses the temper of his times in the *Essay Concerning Human Understanding* (1690):

> If by this inquiry into the nature of the understanding, I can discover the powers thereof; how far they reach; to what things they are in any degree proportionate; and where they fail us, I suppose it may be of use, to prevail with the busy mind of man to be more cautious in meddling with things exceeding its comprehension; to stop when it is at the utmost extent of its tether; and to sit down in a quiet ignorance of those things which, upon examination, are found to be beyond the reach of our capacities. . . . Our business here is not to know all things, but those which concern our conduct.

Such a position is Swift's, when he inveighs against metaphysics, abstract logical deductions, and theoretical science. It is similar to Pope's warning against human presumption in *An Essay on Man*. It prompts Johnson to talk of "the business of living" and to restrain the flights of unbridled imagination. And it helps account for the Anglican clergy's dislike of emotion and "enthusiasm" in religion and for their emphasis on good works, rather than faith, as the way to salvation. Locke's attitudes pervaded eighteenth-century British thought on politics, education, and morals as well as on philosophy; Johnson's great *Dictionary* (1755) uses more than fifteen hundred illustrations from his writings.

Yet one momentous new idea at the turn of the eighteenth century was set against Lockean thinking. The groundbreaking intellectual Mary Astell, in *A Serious Proposal to the Ladies* (1694) and *Some Reflections upon Marriage* (1700, 1706), initiated a powerful strain of modern feminism, arguing for the establishment of women's educational institutions and decrying the tyranny that husbands legally exercised over their wives. She nonetheless mocked the calls for political rights and liberty by Locke and other Whig theorists, rights that pointedly did not extend to women. Instead, she and other early feminists, including Sarah Fyge Egerton and Mary, Lady Chudleigh, embraced the Tory principle of obedience to royal and church authority. Women's advocates had to fight "tyrant Custom" (in Egerton's words), rooted in ancient traditions of domestic power and enshrined in the Bible and mythic human prehistory. This struggle seemed distinct from public political denunciations of the tyranny of some relatively recent Charles or James. Astell feared the doctrines of male revolutionaries could produce civil chaos and so jeopardize the best that women could hope for in her day: the freedom to become fully educated, practice their religion, and marry (or not) according to their own enlightened judgment.

Other thinkers, male and female, began to advocate improving women's education as part of a wider commitment to enhancing and extending sociability. Richard Steele's periodical *The Tatler* satirized Astell as "Madonella" because she seemed to recommend women to a nunlike, "recluse life." In *The Spectator* (1711–12; 1714), conversely, Steele and Joseph Addison encouraged women to learn to participate in an increasingly sociable, intellectually sophisticated, urbane world, where all sorts of people could mingle, as in the streets, parks, and pleasure grounds of a thriving city like London. Such periodicals sought to teach as large a readership as possible to think and behave politely. On a more aristocratic plane, the *Characteristics of Men, Manners, Opinions, and Times* (1711) by the third earl of Shaftesbury similarly asserted the naturally social meaning of human character and meditated on the affections, the witty intercourse, and the standards of politeness that bind people together. Such ideas led to the popularity around midcentury of a new word, *sentimental*, which locates the bases of social conduct in instinctual feeling rather than divinely sanctioned moral codes. Religion itself, according to Laurence Sterne, might be a "Great Sensorium," a sort of central nervous system that connects the feelings of all living creatures in one great benevolent soul. And people began to feel exquisite pleasure in the exercise of charity. The cult of sensibility fostered a philanthropy that led to social reforms seldom envisioned in earlier times—to the improvement of jails, the relief of imprisoned debtors, the establishment of foundling hospitals and of homes for penitent prostitutes, and ultimately the abolition of the slave trade. And it also loosed a ready flow of sympathetic responses to the joys and sorrows of fellow human beings.

As they cultivated fine feelings, Britons also pursued their fascination with the material world. Scientific discoveries increasingly found practical applications in industry, the arts, and even entertainment. By the late 1740s, as knowledge of electricity advanced, public experiments offered fashionable British crowds the opportunity to electrocute themselves. Amateurs everywhere amused themselves with air pumps and chemical explosions. Birmingham became famous as a center where science and manufacturing were combining to change the world: in the early 1760s Matthew Boulton (1728–1809) established the most impressive factory of the age just outside town, producing vast quantities of pins, buckles, and buttons; in subsequent decades, his applications and manufacture of the new steam engine invented by Scotsman James Watt (1736–1819) helped build an industry to drive all others. Practical chemistry also led to industrial improvements: domestic porcelain production became established in the 1750s; and from the 1760s Josiah Wedgwood (1730–1795) developed glazing, manufacturing, and marketing techniques that enabled British ceramics to compete with China for fashionable taste. (In 1765 he named his creamware "Queen's ware" to remind customers of its place on Queen Charlotte's table.) Wedgwood and others

Robert Dighton, **Mr. Deputy Dumpling and Family Enjoying a
Summer Afternoon**, 1781. A family of the middling sort, the father
self-important, the mother beaming, visit Bagnigge Wells, one of
many resorts in London catering to specific classes.

answered an ever-increasing demand in Britain for beautiful objects. Artist
William Hogarth satirized this appetite of the upper and middle classes for
the accumulation of finery: a chaotic collection of china figurines crowds the
mantel in Plate 2 of *Marriage A-la-Mode* (1743–45). Yet the images that made
Hogarth famous would soon decorate English ceramic teapots and plates and
be turned into porcelain figurines themselves.

New forms of religious devotion sprang up amid Britain's spectacular
material success. The evangelical revival known as Methodism began in the
1730s, led by three Oxford graduates: John Wesley (1703–1791), his brother
Charles (1707–1788), and George Whitefield (1714–1770). The Methodists
took their gospel to the common people, warning that all were sinners and
damned, unless they accepted "amazing grace," salvation through faith.
Often denied the privilege of preaching in village churches, evangelicals
preached to thousands in barns or the open fields. The emotionalism of such
revival meetings repelled the somnolent Anglican Church and the upper

classes, who feared that the fury and zeal of the Puritan sects were returning. Methodism was sometimes related to madness; convinced that he was damned forever, the poet William Cowper broke down and became a recluse. But the religious awakening persisted and affected many clergymen and laymen within the Establishment, who reanimated the church and promoted unworldliness and piety. Nor did the insistence of Methodists on faith over works as the way to salvation prevent them or their Anglican allies from fighting for social reforms. The campaign to abolish slavery and the slave trade was driven largely by a passion to save souls.

Sentimentalism, evangelicalism, and the pursuits of wealth and luxury in different ways all placed a new importance on individuals—the gratification of their tastes and ambitions or their yearning for personal encounters with each other or a personal God. Diary keeping, elaborate letter writing, and the novel also testified to the growing importance of the private, individual life. Few histories of kings or nations could rival Richardson's novel *Clarissa* in length, popularity, or documentary detail: it was subtitled "The History of a Young Lady." The older hierarchical system had tended to subordinate individuals to their social rank or station. In the eighteenth century that fixed system began to break down, and people's sense of themselves began to change. By the end of the century many issues of politics and the law revolve around rights, not traditions. The modern individual had been invented; no product of the age is more enduring.

CONDITIONS OF LITERARY PRODUCTION

Publishing boomed as never before in eighteenth-century Britain, as the number of titles appearing annually and the periodicals published in London and the provincial towns dramatically increased. This expansion in part resulted from a loosening of legal restraints on printing. Through much of the previous three centuries, the government had licensed the texts deemed suitable for publication and refused to license those it wanted suppressed (a practice called "prior restraint"). After the Restoration, the new Printing Act (1662) tightened licensing controls, though unlike his Stuart predecessors Charles II now shared this power with Parliament. But in 1695, during the reign of William III, the last in a series of printing acts was not renewed. Debate in Parliament on the matter was more practical than idealistic: it was argued that licensing fettered the printing trades and was ineffective at preventing obnoxious publications anyway, which could be better constrained after publication by enforcing laws against seditious libel, obscenity, and treason. As the two-party system consolidated, both Whigs and Tories seemed to realize that prepublication censorship could bite them when their own side happened to be out of power. Various governments attempted to revive licensing during political crises throughout the eighteenth century, but it was gone for good.

This did not end the legal liabilities, and the prosecutions, of authors. Daniel Defoe, for instance, was convicted of seditious libel and faced the pillory and jail for his satirical pamphlet "The Shortest Way with the Dissenters" (1702), which imitated High Church zeal so extravagantly that it provoked both the Tories and the Dissenters he had set about to defend. And licensing of the stage returned: irritated especially by Henry Fielding's anti-government play *The Historical Register for the Year 1736*, Robert Walpole pushed the Stage Licensing Act through Parliament in 1737, which authorized the Lord Chamberlain to license all plays and reduced the number of London theaters to two (Drury Lane and Covent Garden), closing Fielding's New Theatre in the Haymarket and driving him to a new career as a novelist. But despite such constraints, Hume could begin his essay "Of the Liberty of the Press" (1741) by citing "the extreme liberty we enjoy in this country of communicating whatever we please to the public" as an internationally recognized commonplace. This freedom allowed eighteenth-century Britain to build an exemplary version of what historians have called "the public sphere": a cultural arena, free of direct government control, consisting of not just published comment on matters of national interest but also the public venues—coffeehouses, clubs, taverns—where readers circulated, discussed, and conceived responses to it. The first regular daily London newspaper, the *Daily Courant*, appeared in 1702; in 1731, the first magazine, the *Gentleman's Magazine*. The latter was followed both by imitations and by successful literary journals like the *Monthly Review* (1749) and the *Critical Review* (1756). Each audience attracted some periodical tailored to it, as with the *Female Tatler* (1709) and Eliza Haywood's *Female Spectator* (1744–46).

After 1695, the legal status of printed matter became ambiguous, and in 1710 Parliament enacted the Statute of Anne—"An Act for the Encouragement of Learning by Vesting the Copies of Printed Books in the Authors or Purchasers of Such Copies"—the first copyright law in British history not tied to government approval of works' contents. Typically, these copyrights were held by booksellers, who operated much as publishers do today (in the eighteenth century, *publisher* referred to one who distributed books). A bookseller paid an author for a work's copyright and, after registering the work with the Stationers' Company for a fee, had exclusive right for fourteen years to publish it; if alive when this term expired, he owned it another fourteen years. Payments to authors for copyright varied. Pope got £15 for the 1714 version of *The Rape of the Lock*, while Samuel Johnson's *Rasselas* earned him £100. The Statute of Anne spurred the book trade by enhancing booksellers' control over works and hence their chance to profit by them. But the government soon introduced a new constraint. In 1712, the first Stamp Act put a tax on all newspapers, advertisements, paper, and pamphlets (effectively any work under a hundred pages or so): all printed matter had to carry the stamp indicating the taxes had been paid. Happily for Anne and her ministry, the act both raised government revenue and drove a number of the more irresponsible, ephemeral newspapers out of business, though the *Spectator* simply doubled its price and thrived. Stamp Acts were in effect throughout the century, and duties tended to increase when the government needed to raise money and rein in the press, as during the Seven Years' War in 1757.

But such constraints were not heavy enough to hold back the publishing market, which began to sustain the first true professional class of authors in British literary history. The lower echelon of the profession was called "Grub Street," which was, as Johnson's *Dictionary* explains, "originally the name of a street in Moorfields in London, much inhabited by writers of small histories, dictionaries, and temporary poems." The market increasingly motivated the literary elite too, and Johnson himself came to remark that "no man but a blockhead ever wrote, except for money." As a young writer, he sold articles to the *Gentleman's Magazine*, and many other men and women struggled to survive doing piecework for periodicals. The enhanced opportunity to sell their works on the open market meant that fewer authors needed to look to aristocratic patrons for support. But a new practice, publication by subscription, blended elements of patronage and literary capitalism and created the century's most spectacular authorial fortunes. Wealthy readers could subscribe to a work in progress, usually by agreeing to pay the author half in advance and half upon receipt of the book. Subscribers were rewarded with an edition more sumptuous than the common run and the appearance of their names in a list in the book's front pages. Major works by famous authors, such as Dryden's translation of Virgil (1697) and the 1718 edition of Prior's poems, generated the most subscription sales; the grandest success was Pope's translation of Homer's *Iliad* (1715–20), which gained him about £5000; his *Odyssey* (1725–26) raised nearly that much. But smaller projects deemed to need special encouragement also sold by subscription, including nearly all books of poetry by women, such as Mary Leapor's poems (1751).

Not all entered the literary market with equal advantages; and social class played a role, though hardly a simple one, in preparing authors for success. The better educated were better placed to be taken seriously: many eminent male writers, including Dryden, Locke, Addison, Swift, Hume, Johnson, Burke—the list could go on and on—had at least some university education, either at Oxford or Cambridge or at Scottish or Irish universities, where attendance by members of the laboring classes was virtually nil. Also universities were officially closed to non-Anglicans. Some important writers attended the Dissenting academies that sprang up to fulfill Nonconformists' educational aspirations: Defoe went to an excellent one at Newington Green. A few celebrated authors such as Rochester and Henry Fielding had aristocratic backgrounds, but many came from the "middle class," though those in this category show how heterogeneous it was. Pope, a Catholic, obtained his education privately, and his father was a linen wholesaler, but he eventually became intimate with earls and viscounts, whereas Richardson, who had a family background in trade and (as he said) "only common school-learning," was a successful printer before he became a novelist. Both were middle class in a sense and made their own fortunes in eighteenth-century print culture, yet they inhabited vastly different social worlds.

Despite the general exclusion of the poor from education and other means of social advancement, some self-educated writers of the laboring classes fought their way into print. A few became celebrities, aided by the increasing popularity of the idea, famously expressed by Gray in his "Elegy Written in a Country Churchyard," that there must be unknown geniuses among the poor. Stephen Duck, an agricultural worker from Wiltshire, published his popular *Poems on Several Subjects* in 1730, which included "The Thresher's Labor" (he became known as the Thresher Poet). Queen Caroline herself retained him to be keeper of her library in Richmond. Several authors of the "common sort" followed in Duck's wake, including Mary Collier, whose poem "The Woman's Labor: An Epistle to Mr. Duck" (1739) defended country women against charges of idleness. Apart from such visible successes, eighteenth-century print culture afforded work for many from lower socioeconomic levels, if not as authors, then as hawkers of newspapers on city streets and singers of political ballads (who were often illiterate and female), bookbinders, papermakers, and printing-press workers. The vigor of the literary market demanded the labor of all classes.

As all women were barred from universities and faced innumerable other disadvantages and varieties of repression, the story of virtually every woman author in the period is one of self-education, courage, and extraordinary initiative. Yet women did publish widely for the first time in the period, and the examples that can be assembled are as diverse as they are impressive. During the Restoration and early eighteenth century, a few aristocratic women poets were hailed as marvelous exceptions and given fanciful names: the poems of Katherine Philips (1631–1664), "the matchless Orinda," were published posthumously in 1667; and others, including Anne Finch, Anne Killigrew, and later, Lady Mary Wortley Montagu, printed poems or circulated them in manuscript among fashionable circles. A more broadly public sort of female authorship was more ambivalently received. Though Aphra Behn built a successful career in the theater and in print, her sexually frank works were sometimes denounced as unbecoming a woman. Many women writers of popular literature after her in the early eighteenth century assumed "scandalous" public roles. Delarivier Manley published transparent fictionalizations of the doings of the Whig nobility, including *The New Atalantis* (1709), while Eliza Haywood produced stories about seduction and sex (though her late works, including *The History of Miss Betsy Thoughtless*, 1751, courted a rising taste for morality). Male defenders of high culture found it easy to denounce these women and their works as affronts simultaneously to sexual decency and to good literary taste: Pope's *Dunciad* (1728) awards Haywood as the prize in a pissing contest between scurrilous male booksellers.

Many women writers after midcentury were determined to be perceived as more moral than their predecessors. Around 1750, intellectual women established clubs of their own under the leadership of Elizabeth Vesey and Elizabeth Montagu, cousin to Lady Mary. Proclaiming a high religious and intellectual standard, these women came to be called "bluestockings" (after the inelegant worsted hose of an early member). Eminent men joined the bluestockings for literary conversation, including Samuel Johnson, Samuel Richardson, Horace Walpole (novelist, celebrated letter writer, and son of the prime minister), and David Garrick, preeminent actor of his day. The literary accomplishments of bluestockings ranged widely: in 1758 Elizabeth Carter published her translation of the Greek philosopher Epictetus, while Hannah More won fame as a poet, abolitionist, and educational theorist. Some of the most considerable literary achievements of women after midcentury came in the novel, a form increasingly associated with women readers (though men read them too), often exploring the moral difficulties of young women approaching marriage. The satirical novel *The Female Quixote* (1752) by Charlotte Lennox describes one such heroine deluded by the extravagant romances she reads, while Frances Burney's *Evelina* (1778) unfolds the sexual and other dangers besetting its naive but good-hearted heroine.

Readers' abilities and inclinations to consume literature helped determine the volume and variety of published works. While historians disagree about how exactly the literacy rate changed in Britain through the early modern period, there is widespread consensus that by 1800 between 60

Richard Samuel, *Portraits in the Characters of the Muses in the Temple of Apollo* (*The Nine Living Muses of Great Britain*), 1778. A mythological depiction of some "bluestockings," women who made outstanding contributions to British literature and culture after the mid-18th century. *Standing, left to right*: Elizabeth Carter, Anna Barbauld, Elizabeth Sheridan, Hannah More, and Charlotte Lennox; *seated, left to right*: Angelica Kauffmann, Catharine Macaulay, Elizabeth Montagu, and Elizabeth Griffith.

and 70 percent of adult men could read, in contrast to 25 percent in 1600. Because historians use the ability to sign one's name as an indicator of literacy, the evidence is even sketchier for women, who were less often parties to legal contracts: perhaps a third of women could read by the mid-eighteenth century. Reading was commoner among the relatively well off than among the very poor, and among the latter, more prevalent in urban centers than the countryside. Most decisively, cultural commentators throughout the century portrayed literacy as a good in itself: everyone in a Protestant country such as Britain, most thought, would benefit from direct access to the Bible and devotional works, and increasingly employers found literacy among servants and other laborers useful, especially those working in cities. Moral commentators did their best to steer inexperienced readers away from the frivolous and idle realm of popular imaginative literature, though literacy could not but give its new possessors freedom to explore their own tastes and inclinations.

Cost placed another limit on readership: few of the laboring classes would have disposable income to buy a cheap edition of Milton (around two shillings at midcentury) or even a copy of the *Gentleman's Magazine* (six pence), let alone the spare time or sense of entitlement to peruse such things. Nonetheless, reading material was widely shared (Addison optimistically calculated "twenty readers to every paper" of the *Spectator*), and occasionally servants were given access to the libraries of their employers or the rich family of the neighborhood. In the 1740s, circulating libraries began to emerge in cities and towns throughout Britain. Though the yearly fee they usually charged put them beyond the reach of the poor, these libraries gave the middle classes access to a wider array of books than they could afford to assemble on their own. Records of such libraries indicate that travels, histories, letters, and novels were most popular, though patrons borrowed many specialized, technical works as well. One fascinating index of change in the character of the reading public was the very look of words on the page. In the past, printers had rather capriciously capitalized many nouns—words as common as *Wood* or *Happiness*—and frequently italicized various words for emphasis. But around the middle of the eighteenth century, new conventions arose: initial capitals were reserved for proper names, and the use of italics was reduced. Such changes indicate that the reading public was becoming sophisticated enough not to require such overt pointing to the meanings of what they read. The modern, eighteenth-century reader had come to expect that all English writing, no matter how old or new, on any topic, in any genre, would be printed in the same consistent, uncluttered style. No innovation of the eighteenth-century culture of reading more immediately demonstrates its linkage to our own.

LITERARY PRINCIPLES

The literature appearing between 1660 and 1785 divides conveniently into three shorter periods of about forty years each. The first, extending to the death of Dryden in 1700, is characterized by an effort to bring a new refinement to English literature according to sound critical principles of what is fitting and right; the second, ending with the deaths of Pope in 1744 and Swift in 1745, extends that effort to a wider circle of readers, with special satirical attention to what is unfitting and wrong; the third, concluding with the death of Johnson in 1784 and the publication of Cowper's *The Task* in 1785, confronts the old principles with revolutionary ideas that would come to the fore in the Romantic movement of the late eighteenth and early nineteenth centuries.

A sudden change of taste seemed to occur around 1660. The change had been long prepared, however, by a trend in European culture, especially in seventeenth-century France: the desire for an elegant simplicity. Reacting against the difficulty and occasional extravagance of late Renaissance literature, writers and critics called for a new restraint, clarity, regularity, and good sense. Donne's "metaphysics" and Milton's bold storming of heaven, for instance, seemed overdone to some Restoration readers. Hence Dryden and Andrew Marvell both were tempted to revise *Paradise Lost*, smoothing away its sublime but arduous idiosyncrasies. As daring and imaginative as Dryden's verse is, he tempers even its highly dramatic moments with an ease and sense of control definitive of the taste of his times.

This movement produced in France an impressive body of classical literature that distinguished the age of Louis XIV. In England it produced a literature often termed "Augustan," after the writers who flourished during the reign of Augustus Caesar, the first Roman emperor. Rome's Augustan Age reestablished stability after the civil war that followed the assassination of Julius Caesar. Its chief poets, Virgil, Horace, and Ovid, addressed their polished works to a sophisticated aristocracy among whom they looked for patrons. Dryden's generation took advantage of the analogy between post–civil war England and Augustan Rome. Later generations would be suspicious of that analogy; after 1700 most writers stressed that Augustus had been a tyrant who thought himself greater than the law. But in 1660 there was hope that Charles would be a better Augustus, bringing England the civilized virtues of an Augustan age without its vices.

Charles and his followers brought back from exile an admiration of French literature as well as French fashions, and the theoretical "correctness" of such writers as Pierre Corneille, René Rapin, and Nicolas Boileau came into vogue. England also had a native tradition of classicism, derived from Ben Jonson and his followers, whose couplets embodied a refinement Dryden eagerly inherited and helped codify. The effort to formulate rules of good writing appealed to many critics of the age. Even Shakespeare had sometimes been careless; and although writers could not expect to surpass his genius, they might hope to avoid his faults. But "neoclassical" English literature aimed to be not only classical but *new*. Rochester and Dryden drew on literary traditions of variety, humor, and freewheeling fancy represented by Chaucer, Spenser, Shakespeare, Jonson, and Milton to infuse fresh life into Greek or Latin or French classical models.

Above all, the new simplicity of style aimed to give pleasure to readers—to express passions that everyone could recognize in language that everyone could understand. According to Dryden, Donne's amorous verse misguidedly "perplexes the minds of the fair sex with nice speculations of philosophy, when he should engage their hearts, and entertain them with the softnesses of love." Dryden's poems would not make that mistake; like subsequent English critics, he values poetry according to its power to move an audience. Thus Timotheus, in Dryden's "Alexander's Feast," is not only a musician but an archetypal poet who can make Alexander tearful or loving or angry at will. Readers, in turn, were supposed to cooperate with authors through the exercise of their own imaginations, creating pictures in the mind. When Timotheus describes vengeful ghosts holding torches, Alexander hallucinates in response and seizes a torch "with zeal to destroy." Much eighteenth-century poetry demands to be visualized. A phrase from Horace's *Art of Poetry, ut pictura poesis* (as in painting, so in poetry), was interpreted to mean that poetry ought to be a visual as well as verbal art. Pope's "Eloisa to Abelard," for instance, begins by picturing two rival female personifications: "heavenly-pensive contemplation" and "ever-musing melancholy" (in the older typographical style, the nouns would be capitalized). Readers were expected to *see* these figures: Contemplation, in the habit of a nun, whose eyes roll upward toward heaven; and the black goddess Melancholy, in wings and drapery, who broods upon the darkness. These two competing visions fight for Eloisa's soul throughout the poem, which we see entirely through her perspective. Eighteenth-century readers knew how to translate words into pictures, and modern readers can share their pleasure by learning to see poetic images in the mind's eye.

What poets most tried to see and represent was *Nature*—a word of many meanings. The Augustans focused especially on one: Nature as the universal and permanent elements in human experience. External nature, the landscape, attracted attention throughout the eighteenth century as a source of pleasure and an object of inquiry. But as Finch muses on the landscape, in "A Nocturnal Reverie," it is her own soul she discovers. Pope's injunction to the critic, "First follow Nature," has primarily *human* nature in view. Nature consists of the enduring, general truths that have been, are, and will be true for everyone in all times, everywhere. Hence the business of the poet, according to Johnson's *Rasselas*, is "to examine, not the individual, but the species; to remark general properties and large appearances . . . to exhibit in his portraits of nature such prominent and striking features as recall the original to every mind." Yet if human nature was held to be uniform, human beings were known to be infinitely varied. Pope praises Shakespeare's characters as "Nature herself," but continues that "every single character in Shakespeare is as much an individual as those in life itself; it is . . . impossible to find any two alike." The general need not exclude the particular. In *The Vanity of Human Wishes*, Johnson describes the sorrows of an old woman: "Now kindred Merit fills the sable Bier, / Now lacerated Friendship claims a tear." Here "kindred Merit" refers particularly to a worthy relative who has died, and "lacerated Friendship" refers to a friend who has been wasted by violence or disease. Yet Merit and Friendship are also personifications, and the lines imply that the woman may be mourning the passing of goodness like her own or a broken friendship; values and sympathies can die as well as people. This play on words is not a pun. Rather, it indicates a state of mind in which life assumes the form of a perpetual allegory and some abiding truth shines through each circumstance as it passes. The particular is already the general, in good eighteenth-century verse.

To study Nature was also to study the ancients. Nature and Homer, according to Pope, were the same; and both Pope and his readers applied Horace's satires on Rome to their own world, because Horace had expressed the perennial forms of life. Moreover, modern writers could learn from the ancients how to practice their craft. If a poem is an object to be made, the *poet* (a word derived from the Greek for "maker") must make the object to proper specifications. Thus poets were taught to plan their works in one of the classical "kinds" or genres—epic, tragedy, comedy, pastoral, satire, or ode—to choose a language appropriate to that genre, and to select the right style and tone and rhetorical figures. The rules of art, as Pope had said, "are Nature methodized." At the same time, however, writers needed *wit*: quickness of mind, inventiveness, a knack for conceiving images and metaphors and for perceiving resemblances between things apparently unlike. Shakespeare had surpassed the ancients themselves in wit, and no one could deny that Pope was witty. Hence a major project of the age was to combine good method with wit, or judgment with fancy. Nature intended them to be one, and the role of judgment was not to suppress passion, energy, and originality but to make them more effective through discipline: "The winged courser, like a generous horse, / Shows most true mettle when you check his course."

The test of a poet's true mettle is language. When Wordsworth, in the preface to *Lyrical Ballads* (1800), declared that he wrote "in a selection of the language really used by men," he went on to attack eighteenth-century poets for their use of an artificial and stock "poetic diction." Many poets did employ a special language. It is characterized by personification, representing a thing or abstraction in human form, as when an "Ace of Hearts steps forth" or "Melancholy frowns"; by periphrasis (a roundabout way of avoiding homely words: "finny tribes" for *fish*, or "household feathery people" for *chickens*); by stock phrases such as "shining sword," "verdant mead," "bounding main," and "checkered shade"; by words used in their original Latin sense, such as "genial," "gelid," and "horrid"; and by English sentences forced into Latin syntax ("Here rests his head upon the lap of Earth / A youth to Fortune and to Fame unknown," where *youth* is the subject of the verb *rests*). This language originated in the attempt of Renaissance poets to rival the elegant diction of Virgil and other Roman writers, and Milton depended on it to help him obtain "answerable style" for the lofty theme of *Paradise Lost*. When used mechanically it could become a mannerism. But Thomas Gray contrives subtle, expressive effects from artificial diction and syntax, as in the ironic inflation of "Ode on the Death of a Favorite Cat" or a famous stanza from "Elegy Written in a Country Churchyard":

> The boast of heraldry, the pomp of power,
> And all that beauty, all that wealth e'er gave,
> Awaits alike the inevitable hour.
> The paths of glory lead but to the grave.

It is easy to misread the first sentence. What is the subject of *awaits*? The answer must be *hour* (the only available singular noun), which lurks at the end of the sentence, ready to spring a trap not only on the reader but on all those aristocratic, powerful, beautiful, wealthy people who forget that their hour will come. Moreover, the intricacy of that sentence sets off the simplicity of the next, which says the same thing with deadly directness. The artful mix in the "Elegy" of a special poetic language—a language that nobody speaks—with sentiments that everybody feels helps account for the poem's enduring popularity.

Versification also tests a poet's skill. The heroic couplet was brought to such perfection by Pope, Johnson thought, that "to attempt any further improvement of versification will be dangerous." Pope's couplets, in rhymed iambic pentameter, typically present a complete statement, closed by a punctuation mark. Within the binary system of these two lines, a world of distinctions can be compressed. The second line of the couplet might closely parallel the first in structure and meaning, for instance, or the two lines might antithetically play against each other. Similarly, because a slight pause called a "caesura" often divides the typical pentameter line ("Know then thyself, presume not God to scan"), one part of the line can be made parallel with or antithetical to the other or even to one part of the following line. An often quoted and parodied passage of Sir John Denham's "Cooper's Hill" (1642) illustrates these effects. The poem addresses the Thames and builds up a witty comparison between the flow of a river and the flow of verse (italics are added to highlight the terms compared):

"Here rests his head . . ." Through a crumbling Gothic arch
appears a youth reading on a tombstone the epitaph that concludes
Thomas Gray's "Elegy Written in a Country Churchyard." Illustration, *Designs by Mr. R. Bentley for Six Poems by Mr. T. Gray* (1753).

	O could I flow like thee,	and make thy stream
Parallelism:	*My great example,*	as it is *my theme!*
Double balance:	Though *deep,* yet *clear,*	though *gentle,* yet not *dull,*
Double balance:	*Strong* without *rage,*	without *o'erflowing, full.*

Once Dryden and Pope had bound such passages more tightly together with
alliteration and assonance, the typical metrical-rhetorical wit of the new
age had been perfected. For most of the eighteenth century its only metrical rival was blank verse: iambic pentameter that does not rhyme and is
not closed in couplets. Milton's blank verse in *Paradise Lost* provided one
model, and the dramatic blank verse of Shakespeare and Dryden provided
another. This more expansive form appealed to poets who cared less for wit
than for stories and thoughts with plenty of room to develop. Blank verse
was favored as the best medium for descriptive and meditative poems, from
Thomson's *Seasons* (1726–30) to Cowper's *The Task* (1785), and the tradition continued in Wordsworth's "Tintern Abbey" and *Prelude*.

   Yet not all poets chose to compete with Pope's wit or Milton's heroic stri-
ing. Ordinary people also wrote and read verse, and many of them neither

knew nor regarded the classics. Only a minority of men, and very few women, had the chance to study Latin and Greek, but that did not keep a good many from playing with verse as a pastime or writing about their own lives. Hence the eighteenth century is the first age to reflect the modern tension between "high" and "low" art. While the heroic couplet was being perfected, doggerel also thrived, and Milton's blank verse was sometimes reduced to describing a drunk or an oyster. Burlesque and broad humor characterize the common run of eighteenth-century verse. As the audience for poetry became more diversified, so did the subject matter. No readership was too small to address; Isaac Watts, and later Anna Laetitia Barbauld and William Blake, wrote songs for children. The rise of unconventional forms and topics of verse subverted an older poetic ideal: the Olympian art that only a handful of the elect could possibly master. The eighteenth century brought poetry down to earth. In the future, art that claimed to be high would have to find ways to distinguish itself from the low.

RESTORATION LITERATURE, 1660-1700

Dryden brought England a *modern* literature between 1660 and 1700. He combined a cosmopolitan outlook on the latest European trends with some of the richness and variety he admired in Chaucer and Shakespeare. In most of the important contemporary forms—occasional verse, comedy, tragedy, heroic play, ode, satire, translation, and critical essay—both his example and his precepts influenced others. As a critic, he spread the word that English literature, particularly his own, could vie with the best of the past. As a translator, he made such classics as Ovid and Virgil available to a wide public; for the first time, a large number of women and men without a formal education could feel included in the literary world.

Restoration prose clearly indicated the desire to reach a new audience. The styles of Donne's sermons, Milton's pamphlets, or Browne's treatises now seemed too elaborate and rhetorical for simple communication. By contrast, Pepys and Behn head straight to the point, informally and unself-consciously. The Royal Society asked its members to employ a plain, utilitarian prose style that spelled out scientific truths; rhetorical flourishes and striking metaphors might be acceptable in poetry, which engaged the emotions, but they had no place in rational discourse. In polite literature, exemplified by Cowley, Dryden, and Sir William Temple, the ideal of good prose came to be a style with the ease and poise of well-bred urbane conversation. This is a social prose for a sociable age. Later, it became the mainstay of essayists like Addison and Steele, of eighteenth-century novelists, and of the host of brilliant eighteenth-century letter writers, including Montagu, Horace Walpole, Gray, Cowper, and Burney, who still give readers the sense of being their intimate friends.

Yet despite its broad appeal to the public, Restoration literature kept its ties to an aristocratic heroic ideal. The "fierce wars and faithful loves" of epic poems were expected to offer patterns of virtue for noble emulation. These ideals lived on in popular French prose romances and in Behn's *Oroonoko*. But the ideal was most fully expressed in heroic plays like those written by Dryden, which push to extremes the conflict between love and honor in the hearts of impossibly valiant heroes and impossibly high-minded and attractive heroines. Dryden's best serious drama, however, was his blank verse tragedy *All for Love* (produced 1677), based on the story of Antony and Cleopatra. Instead of Shakespeare's worldwide panorama, his rapid shifts of scene and complex characters, this version follows the unities of time, place, and action, compressing the plot to the tragic last hours of the lovers. Two other tragic playwrights were celebrated in the Restoration and for a long time to come: Nathaniel Lee (ca. 1649–1692), known for violent plots and wild ranting, and the passionately sensitive Thomas Otway (1652–1685).

But comedy was the real distinction of Restoration drama. The best plays of Sir George Etherege (*The Man of Mode,* 1676), William Wycherley (*The Country Wife,* 1675), Aphra Behn (*The Rover,* 1677), William Congreve (*Love for Love,* 1695; *The Way of the World,* 1700), and later George Farquhar (*The Beaux' Stratagem,* 1707) can still hold the stage today. These "comedies of manners" pick social behavior apart, exposing the nasty struggles for power among the upper classes, who use wit and manners as weapons. Human nature in these plays often conforms to the worst fears of Hobbes; sensual, false-hearted, selfish characters prey on each other. The male hero lives for pleasure and for the money and women that he can conquer. The object of his game of sexual intrigue is a beautiful, witty, pleasure-loving, and emancipated lady, every bit his equal in the strategies of love. What makes the favored couple stand out is the true wit and well-bred grace with which they step through the minefield of the plot. But during the 1690s "Societies for the Reformation of Manners" began to attack the blasphemy and obscenity they detected in such plays, and they sometimes brought offenders to trial. When Dryden died in 1700, a more respectable society was coming into being.

EIGHTEENTH-CENTURY LITERATURE, 1700–1745

Early in the eighteenth century a new and brilliant group of writers emerged: Swift, with *A Tale of a Tub* (1704–10); Addison, with *The Campaign* (1705), a poetic celebration of the battle of Blenheim; Prior, with *Poems on Several Occasions* (1707); Steele, with the *Tatler* (1709); and the youthful Pope, in the same year, with his *Pastorals.* These writers consolidate and popularize the social graces of the previous age. Determined to preserve good sense and civilized values, they turn their wit against fanaticism and innovation. Hence this is a great age of satire. Deeply conservative but also playful, their finest works often cast a strange light on modern times by viewing them through the screen of classical myths and classical forms. Thus Pope exposes the frivolity of fashionable London, in *The Rape of the Lock,* through the incongruity of verse that casts the idle rich as epic heroes. Similarly, Swift uses epic similes to mock the moderns in *The Battle of the Books,* and John Gay's *Trivia, or the Art of Walking the Streets of London* (1716) uses mock georgics to order his tour of the city. Such incongruities are not entirely negative. They also provide a fresh perspective on things that had once seemed too low for poetry to notice—for instance, in *The Rape of the Lock,* a girl putting on her makeup. In this way a parallel with classical literature can show not only how far the modern world has fallen but also how fascinating and magical it is when seen with "quick, poetic eyes."

The Augustans' effort to popularize and enforce high literary and social values was set against the new mass and multiplicity of writings that responded more spontaneously to the expanding commercial possibilities of print. The array of popular prose genres—news, thinly disguised political allegories, biographies of notorious criminals, travelogues, gossip, romantic tales—often blended facts and patently fictional elements, cemented by a rich lode of exaggeration, misrepresentations, and outright lies. Out of this matrix the modern novel would come to be born. The great master of such works was Daniel Defoe, producing first-person accounts such as *Robinson Crusoe* (1719), the famous castaway, and *Moll Flanders* (1722), mistress of lowlife crime. Claims that such works present (as the "editor" of *Crusoe* says) "a just history of fact," believed or not, sharpened the public's avidity for them. Defoe shows his readers a world plausibly like the one they know, where ordinary people negotiate familiar, entangled problems of financial, emotional, and spiritual existence. Jane Barker, Mary Davys, and many others brought women's work and daily lives as well as love affairs to fiction. Such stories were not only amusing but also served as models of conduct; they influenced the stories that real people told about themselves.

The theater also began to change its themes and effects to appeal to a wider audience. The clergyman Jeremy Collier had vehemently taken Dryden, Wycherley, and Congreve to task in *A Short View of the Immorality and Profaneness of the English Stage* (1698), which spoke for the moral outrage of the pious middle classes. The wits retreated. The comedy of manners was replaced by a new kind, later called "sentimental" not only because goodness triumphs over vice but also because it deals in high moral sentiments rather than witty dialogue and because the embarrassments of its heroines and heroes move the audience not to laughter but to tears. Virtue refuses to bow to aristocratic codes. In one crucial scene of Steele's influential play *The Conscious Lovers* (1722) the hero would rather accept dishonor than fight a duel with a friend. Piety and middle-class values typify tragedies such as George Lillo's *London Merchant* (1731). One luxury invented in eighteenth-century Europe was the delicious pleasure of weeping, and comedies as well as tragedies brought that pleasure to playgoers through many decades. Some plays resisted the tide. Gay's cynical *Beggar's Opera* (1728) was a tremendous success, and later in the century the comedies of Goldsmith and Sheridan proved that sentiment is not necessarily an enemy to wit and laughter. Yet larger and larger audiences responded more to spectacles and special effects than to sophisticated writing. Although the *stage* prospered during the eighteenth century, and the star system produced idolized actors and actresses (such as David Garrick and Sarah Siddons), the authors of *drama* tended to fade to the background.

Despite the sociable impulses of much the period's writing, readers also craved less crowded, more meditative works. Since the seventeenth century, no poems had been more popular than those about the pleasures of retirement, which invited the reader to dream about a safe retreat in the country or to meditate, like Finch, on scenery and the soul. But after 1726, when Thomson published *Winter*, the first of his cycle on the seasons, the poetry of natural description came into its own. A taste for gentle, picturesque beauty found expression not only in verse but in the elaborate, cultivated art of landscape gardening, and finally in the cherished English art of landscape painting in watercolor or oils (often illustrating Thomson's *Seasons*). Many readers also learned to enjoy a thrilling pleasure or fear in the presence of the sublime in nature: rushing waters, wild prospects, and mountains shrouded in mist. Whether enthusiasts went to the landscape in search of God or merely of heightened sensations, they came back feeling that they had been touched by something beyond the life they knew, by something that could hardly be expressed. Tourists as well as poets roamed the countryside, frequently quoting verse as they gazed at some evocative scene. A partiality for the sublime passed from Thomson to Collins to inspire the poetry of the Romantic age to come.

THE EMERGENCE OF NEW LITERARY THEMES AND MODES, 1740–85

When Matthew Arnold called the eighteenth century an "age of prose," he meant to belittle its poetry, but he also stated a significant fact: great prose does dominate the age. Until the 1740s, poetry tended to set the standards of literature. But the growth of new kinds of prose took the initiative away from verse. Novelists became better known than poets. Intellectual prose also flourished, with the achievements of Johnson in the essay and literary criticism, of Boswell in biography, of Hume in philosophy, of Burke in politics, of Edward Gibbon in history, of Sir Joshua Reynolds in aesthetics, of Gilbert White in natural history, and of Adam Smith in economics. Each of these authors is a master stylist, whose effort to express himself clearly and fully demands an art as carefully wrought as poetry. Other writers of prose were more informal. The memoirs of such women as Laetitia Pilkington, Charlotte Charke, Hester Thrale Piozzi, and Frances Burney bring each reader into their private lives and also remind us that the new print culture created celebrities, who wrote not only about themselves but about other celebrities they knew. The interest of readers in Samuel Johnson helped sell his own books as well as a host of books that quoted his sayings. But the prose of the age also had to do justice to difficult and complicated ideas. An unprecedented effort to formulate the first principles of philosophy, history, psychology, and art required a new style of persuasion.

Johnson helped codify that language, not only with his writings but with the first great English *Dictionary* (1755). This work established him as a national man of letters; eventually the period would be known as "the Age of Johnson." But his dominance was based on an ideal of service to others. The *Dictionary* illustrates its definitions with more than 114,000 quotations from the best English writers, thus building a bridge from past to present usage; and Johnson's essays, poems, and criticism also reflect his desire to preserve the lessons of the past. Yet he looks to the future as well, trying both to reach and to mold a nation of readers. If Johnson speaks for his age, one reason is his faith in common sense and the common reader. "By the common sense of readers uncorrupted with literary prejudices," he wrote in the last of his *Lives of the Poets* (1781), "must be finally decided all claim to poetical honors." A similar respect for the good judgment of ordinary people, and for standards of taste and behavior that anyone can share, marks many writers of the age. Both Burke, the great conservative statesman and author, and Thomas Paine, his radical adversary, proclaim themselves apostles of common sense.

No prose form better united availability to the common reader and seriousness of artistic purpose than the novel in the hands of two of its early masters, Samuel Richardson and Henry Fielding. Like many writers of fiction earlier in the century, Richardson initially did not set out to entertain the public with an avowedly invented tale: he conceived *Pamela, or Virtue Rewarded* (1740) while compiling a little book of model letters. The letters grew into a story about a captivating young servant who resists her master's base designs on her virtue until he gives up and marries her. The combination of a high moral tone with sexual titillation and a minute analysis of the heroine's emotions and state of mind proved irresistible to readers, in Britain and in Europe at large. Richardson topped *Pamela*'s success with *Clarissa* (1747–48), another epistolary novel, which explored the conflict between the libertine Lovelace, an attractive and diabolical aristocrat, and the angelic Clarissa, a middle-class paragon who struggles to stay pure. The sympathy that readers felt for Clarissa was magnified by a host of sentimental novels, including Frances Sheridan's *Memoirs of Miss Sidney Bidulph* (1761), Rousseau's *Julie, or The New Heloise* (1761), and Henry Mackenzie's *The Man of Feeling* (1771).

Henry Fielding made his entrance into the novel by turning *Pamela* farcically upside down, as the hero of *Joseph Andrews* (1742), Pamela's brother, defends his chastity from the lewd advances of Lady Booby. Fielding's true model, however, is Cervantes's great *Don Quixote* (1605–15), from which he took an ironic, antiromantic style; a plot of wandering around the countryside; and an idealistic central character (Parson Adams) who keeps mistaking appearances for reality. The ambition of writing what Fielding called "a comic epic-poem in prose" went still further in *The History of Tom Jones, a Foundling* (1749). Crowded with incidents and comments on the state of England, the novel contrasts a good-natured, generous, wayward hero (who needs to learn prudence) with cold-hearted people who use moral codes and the law for their own selfish interests. This emphasis on instinctive virtue and vice, instead of Richardson's devotion to good principles, put off respectable readers like Johnson and Burney. But Coleridge thought that *Tom Jones* (along with *Oedipus Rex* and Jonson's *Alchemist*) was one of "the three most perfect plots ever planned."

An age of great prose can burden its poets. To Gray, Collins, Mark Akenside, and the brothers Joseph and Thomas Warton, it seemed that the spirit of poetry might be dying, driven out by the spirit of prose, by uninspiring truth, by the end of superstitions that had once peopled the land with poetic fairies and demons. In an age barren of magic, they ask, where has poetry gone? That question haunts many poems, suffusing them with melancholy. Poets who muse in silence are never far from thoughts of death, and a morbid fascination with suicide and the grave preoccupies many at midcentury. Such an attitude has little in common with that of poets like Dryden and Pope, social beings who live in a crowded world and seldom confess their private feelings in public. Pope's *Essay on Man* had taken a sunny view of providence; Edward Young's *The Complaint: or Night Thoughts on Life, Death, and Immortality* (1742–46), an immensely long poem in blank verse, is darkened by Christian fear of the life to come.

Often the melancholy poet withdraws into himself and yearns to be living in some other time and place. In his "Ode to Fancy" (1746), Joseph Warton associated "fancy" with visions in the wilderness and spontaneous passions; the true poet was no longer defined as a craftsman or maker but as a seer or nature's priest. "The public has seen all that art can do," William Shenstone wrote in 1761, welcoming James Macpherson's *Ossian*, "and they want the more striking efforts of wild, original, enthusiastic genius." Macpherson filled the bill. His primitive, sentimental epics, supposedly translated from an ancient Gaelic warrior-bard, won the hearts of readers around the world; Napoleon and Thomas Jefferson, for instance, both thought that Ossian was greater than Homer. Poets began to cultivate archaic language and antique forms. Inspired by Thomas Percy's edition of *Reliques of Ancient English Poetry* (1765), Thomas Chatterton passed off his own ballads as medieval; he died at seventeen, soon after his forgeries were exposed, but the Romantics later idolized his precocious genius.

The most remarkable consequence of the medieval revival, however, was the invention of the Gothic novel. Horace Walpole set *The Castle of Otranto* (1765), a dreamlike tale of terror, in a simulacrum of Strawberry Hill, his own tiny, pseudo-medieval castle, which helped revive a taste for Gothic architecture. Walpole created a mode of fiction that retains its popularity to the present day. In a typical Gothic romance, amid the glooms and secret passages of some remote castle, the laws of nightmare replace the laws of probability. Forbidden themes—incest, murder, necrophilia, atheism, and the torments of sexual desire—are allowed free play. Most such romances, like William Beckford's *Vathek* (1786) and Matthew Lewis's *The Monk* (1796), revel in sensationalism and the grotesque. The Gothic vogue suggested that classical canons of taste—simplicity and harmonious balance—might count for less than the pleasures of fancy—intricate puzzles and a willful excess. But Gothicism also resulted in works, like Ann Radcliffe's, that temper romance with reality as well as in serious novels of social purpose, like William Godwin's *Caleb Williams* (1794) and Mary Wollstonecraft's *Maria, or The Wrongs of Woman* (1798); and Mary Shelley, the daughter of Wollstonecraft and

Bertie Greatheed, *Diego and Jaquez Frightened by the Giant Foot*, 1791. A scene from Horace Walpole's Gothic novel *The Castle of Otranto* (1764), showing servants terrified by the supernatural appearance of an oversize stone foot in the castle.

Godwin, eventually composed a romantic nightmare, *Frankenstein* (1818), that continues to haunt our dreams.

The century abounded in other remarkable experiments in fiction, anticipating many of the forms that novelists still use today. Tobias Smollett's picaresque *Roderick Random* (1748) and *Humphry Clinker* (1771) delight in coarse practical jokes, the freaks and strong odors of life. But the most *novel* novelist of the age was Laurence Sterne, a humorous, sentimental clergyman who loves to play tricks on his readers. *The Life and Opinions of Tristram Shandy* (1760–67) abandons clock time for psychological time, whimsically follows chance associations, interrupts its own stories, violates the conventions of print by putting chapters 18 and 19 after chapter 25, sneaks in double entendres, and seems ready to go on forever. Sterne's second masterpiece, *A Sentimental Journey through France and Italy* (1768), gives us a narrator, Yorick, who cultivates his feelings so self-consciously and renders them in such convincing detail that we are unsure whether to laugh at or weep along with him. Such uncertainty helps us recognize that our sympathies are as volatile and ambiguous as those of Sterne's characters. As unique as Sterne's fictional world is, his interest in private life matched the concerns of the novel toward the end of the century: depictions of characters' intimate feelings dominated the tradition of domestic fiction that included Burney, Radcliffe, and, later, Maria Edgeworth, culminating in the masterworks of Jane Austen. A more "masculine" orientation emerged at the beginning of the next century, as Walter Scott's works, with their broad historical scope and outdoor scenes of men at work and war, appealed to a large readership. Yet the copious, acute, often ironic attention to details of private life by Richardson, Sterne, and Austen continued to influence the novel profoundly through its subsequent history.

CONTINUITY AND REVOLUTION

The history of eighteenth-century literature was first composed by the Romantics, who wrote it to serve their own interests. Prizing originality, they naturally preferred to stress how different they were from writers of the previous age. Later historians have tended to follow their lead, competing to prove that everything changed in 1776, or 1789, or 1798. This revolutionary view of history accounts for what happened to the word *revolution*. The older meaning referred to a movement around a point, a recurrence or cycle, as in the revolutions of the planets; the newer meaning signified a violent break with the past, an overthrow of the existing order, as in the Big Bang or the French Revolution. Romantic rhetoric made heavy use of such dramatic upheavals. Yet every history devoted to truth must take account of both sorts of revolution, of continuities as well as changes. The ideals that many Romantics made their own—the passion for liberty and equality, the founding of justice on individual rights, the distrust of institutions, the love of nature, the reverence for imagination, and even the embrace of change— grew from seeds that had been planted long before. Nor did Augustan literature abruptly vanish on that day in 1798 when Wordsworth and Coleridge anonymously published a small and unsuccessful volume of poems called

Lyrical Ballads. Even when they rebel against the work of Pope and Johnson and Gray, Romantic writers incorporate much of their language and values.

What Restoration and eighteenth-century literature passed on to the future, in fact, was chiefly a set of unresolved problems. The age of Enlightenment was also, in England, an age that insisted on holding fast to older beliefs and customs; the age of population explosion was also an age of individualism; the age that developed the slave trade was also the age that gave rise to the abolitionist movement; the age that codified rigid standards of conduct for women was also an age when many women took the chance to read and write and think for themselves; the age of reason was also the age when sensibility flourished; the last classical age was also the first modern age. These contradictions are far from abstract; writers were forced to choose their own directions. When young James Boswell looked for a mentor whose biography he might write, he considered not only Samuel Johnson but also David Hume, whose skeptical views of morality, truth, and religion were everything Johnson abhorred. The two writers seem to inhabit different worlds, yet Boswell traveled freely between them. That was exciting and also instructive. "Without Contraries is no progression," according to one citizen of Johnson's London, William Blake, who also thought that "Opposition is true Friendship." Good conversation was a lively eighteenth-century art, and sharp disagreements did not keep people from talking. The conversations the period started have not ended yet.

The Restoration and
the Eighteenth Century

TEXTS	CONTEXTS
1660 Samuel Pepys begins his diary	**1660** Charles II restored to the throne. Reopening of the theaters
1662 Samuel Butler, *Hudibras*, part 1	**1662** Act of Uniformity requires all clergy to obey the Church of England. Chartering of the Royal Society
	1664–66 Great Plague of London
	1666 Fire destroys the City of London
1667 John Milton, *Paradise Lost*	
1668 John Dryden, *Essay of Dramatic Poesy*	**1668** Dryden becomes poet laureate
	1673 Test Act requires all officeholders to swear allegiance to Anglicanism
1678 John Bunyan, *Pilgrim's Progress*, part 1	**1678** The "Popish Plot" inflames anti-Catholic feeling
1681 Dryden, *Absalom and Achitophel*	**1681** Charles II dissolves Parliament
	1685 Death of Charles II. James II, his Catholic brother, takes the throne
1687 Sir Isaac Newton, *Principia Mathematica*	
1688 Aphra Behn, *Oroonoko*	**1688–89** The Glorious Revolution. James II exiled and succeeded by his Protestant daughter, Mary, and her husband, William of Orange
1690 John Locke, *An Essay Concerning Human Understanding*	
1700 William Congreve, *The Way of the World*. Mary Astell, *Some Reflections upon Marriage*	
	1702 War of the Spanish Succession begins. Death of William III. Succession of Anne (Protestant daughter of James II)
1704 Jonathan Swift, *A Tale of a Tub*. Newton, *Opticks*	
	1707 Act of Union with Scotland
	1710 Tories take power
1711 Alexander Pope, *An Essay on Criticism*. Joseph Addison and Sir Richard Steele, *Spectator* (1711–12, 1714)	
	1713 Treaty of Utrecht ends War of the Spanish Succession
	1714 Death of Queen Anne. George I (great-grandson of James I) becomes the first Hanoverian king. Tory government replaced by Whigs
1716 Lady Mary Wortley Montagu writes her letters from Turkey (1716–18)	
1717 Pope, *The Rape of the Lock* (final version)	

TEXTS	CONTEXTS
1719 Daniel Defoe, *Robinson Crusoe*	
	1720 South Sea Bubble collapses
	1721 Robert Walpole comes to power
1726 Swift, *Gulliver's Travels*	
	1727 George I dies. George II succeeds
1728 John Gay, *The Beggar's Opera*	
1733 Pope, *An Essay on Man*	
	1737 Licensing Act censors the stage
1740 Samuel Richardson, *Pamela*	
1742 Henry Fielding, *Joseph Andrews*	1742 Walpole resigns
1743 Pope, *The Dunciad* (final version). William Hogarth, *Marriage A-la-Mode*	
1746 William Collins's *Odes*	1746 Charles Edward Stuart's defeat at Culloden ends the last Jacobite rebellion
1747 Richardson, *Clarissa*	
1749 Fielding, *Tom Jones*	
1751 Thomas Gray, "Elegy Written in a Country Churchyard"	1751 Robert Clive seizes Arcot, the prelude to English control of India
1755 Samuel Johnson, *Dictionary*	
	1756 Beginning of Seven Years' War
1759 Johnson, *Rasselas*. Voltaire, *Candide*	1759 James Wolfe's capture of Quebec ensures British control of Canada
1760 Laurence Sterne, *Tristram Shandy* (1760–67)	1760 George III succeeds to the throne
1765 Johnson's edition of Shakespeare	
1768 Sterne, *A Sentimental Journey through France and Italy*	1768 Captain James Cook voyages to Australia and New Zealand
1770 Oliver Goldsmith, "The Deserted Village"	
	1775 American Revolution (1775–83). James Watt produces steam engines
1776 Adam Smith, *The Wealth of Nations*	
1778 Frances Burney, *Evelina*	
1779 Johnson, *Lives of the Poets* (1779–81)	
	1780 Gordon Riots in London
1783 George Crabbe, *The Village*	1783 William Pitt becomes prime minister
1785 William Cowper, *The Task*	

JOHN DRYDEN
1631–1700

Although John Dryden's parents seem to have sided with Parliament against the king, there is no evidence that the poet grew up in a strict Puritan family. His father, a country gentleman of moderate fortune, gave his son a gentleman's education at Westminster School, under the renowned Dr. Richard Busby, who used the rod as a pedagogical aid in imparting a sound knowledge of the learned languages and literatures to his charges (among others John Locke and Matthew Prior). From Westminster, Dryden went to Trinity College, Cambridge, where he took his A.B. in 1654. His first important poem, "Heroic Stanzas" (1659), was written to commemorate the death of Cromwell. The next year, however, in "Astraea Redux," Dryden joined his countrymen in celebrating the return of Charles II to his throne. During the rest of his life Dryden was to remain entirely loyal to Charles and to his successor, James II.

Dryden is the commanding literary figure of the last four decades of the seventeenth century. Every important aspect of the life of his times—political, religious, philosophical, artistic—finds expression somewhere in his writings. Dryden is the least personal of poets. He is not at all the solitary, subjective poet listening to the murmur of his own voice and preoccupied with his own feelings but rather a citizen of the world commenting publicly on matters of public concern.

From the beginning to the end of his literary career, Dryden's nondramatic poems are most typically occasional poems, which commemorate particular events of a public character—a coronation, a military victory, a death, or a political crisis. Such poems are social and often ceremonial, written not for the self but for the nation. Dryden's principal achievements in this form are the two poems on the king's return and his coronation; *Annus Mirabilis* (1667), which celebrates the English naval victory over the Dutch and the fortitude of the people of London and the king during the Great Fire, both events of that "wonderful year," 1666; the political poems; the lines on the death of Oldham (1684); and odes such as "Alexander's Feast."

Between 1664 and 1681, however, Dryden was mainly a playwright. The newly chartered theaters needed a modern repertory, and he set out to supply the need. Dryden wrote his plays, as he frankly confessed, to please his audiences, which were not heterogeneous like Shakespeare's but were largely drawn from the court and from people of fashion. In the style of the time, he produced rhymed heroic plays, in which incredibly noble heroes and heroines face incredibly difficult choices between love and honor; comedies, in which male and female rakes engage in intrigue and bright repartee; and later, libretti for the newly introduced dramatic form, the opera. His one great tragedy, *All for Love* (1677), in blank verse, adapts Shakespeare's *Antony and Cleopatra* to the unities of time, place, and action. As his *Essay of Dramatic Poesy* (1668) shows, Dryden had studied the works of the great playwrights of Greece and Rome, of the English Renaissance, and of contemporary France, seeking sound theoretical principles on which to construct the new drama that the age demanded. Indeed, his fine critical intelligence always supported his creative powers, and, because he took literature seriously and enjoyed discussing it, he became, almost casually, what Samuel Johnson called him: "the father of English criticism." His abilities as both poet and dramatist brought him to the attention of the king, who in 1668 made him poet laureate. Two years later the post of historiographer royal was added to the laureateship at a combined stipend of £200, enough money to live comfortably on.

Between 1678 and 1681, when he was nearing fifty, Dryden discovered his great gift for writing formal verse satire. A quarrel with the playwright Thomas Shadwell prompted the mock-heroic episode "Mac Flecknoe," probably written in 1678 or 1679 but not published until 1682. Out of the stresses occasioned by the Popish Plot (1678) and its political aftermath came his major political satires, *Absalom and Achitophel* (1681), and "The Medal" (1682), his final attack on the villain of *Absalom and Achitophel,* the earl of Shaftesbury. Twenty years' experience as poet and playwright had prepared him technically for the triumph of *Absalom and Achitophel.* He had mastered the heroic couplet, having fashioned it into an instrument suitable in his hands for every sort of discourse from the thrust and parry of quick logical argument, to lyric feeling, rapid narrative, or forensic declamation. Thanks to this long discipline, he was able in one stride to rival the masters of verse satire: Horace, Juvenal, Persius, in ancient Rome, and Boileau, his French contemporary.

The consideration of religious and political questions that the events of 1678–81 forced on Dryden brought a new seriousness to his mind and works. In 1682 he published *Religio Laici,* a poem in which he examined the grounds of his religious faith and defended the middle way of the Anglican Church against the rationalism of Deism on the one hand and the authoritarianism of Rome on the other. But he had moved closer to Rome than he perhaps realized when he wrote the poem. Charles II died in 1685 and was succeeded by his Catholic brother, James II. Within a year Dryden and his two sons converted to Catholicism. Though his enemies accused him of opportunism, he proved his sincerity by his steadfast loyalty to the Roman Church after James abdicated and the Protestant William and Mary came in; as a result he was to lose his offices and their much-needed stipends. From his new position as a Roman Catholic, Dryden wrote in 1687 *The Hind and the Panther,* in which a milk-white Hind (the Roman Church) and a spotted Panther (the Anglican Church) eloquently debate theology. The Hind has the better of the argument, but Dryden already knew that James's policies were failing, and with them the Catholic cause in England.

Dryden was now nearing sixty, with a family to support on a much-diminished income. To earn a living, he resumed writing plays and turned to translations. In 1693 appeared his versions of Juvenal and Persius, with a long dedicatory epistle on satire; and in 1697, his greatest achievement in this mode, the works of Virgil. At the very end, two months before his death, came the *Fables Ancient and Modern,* prefaced by one of the finest of his critical essays and made up of translations from Ovid, Boccaccio, and Chaucer.

Dryden's foremost achievement was to bring the pleasures of literature to the ever-increasing reading public of Britain. As a critic and translator, he made many classics available to men and women who lacked a classical education. His canons of taste and theoretical principles would set the standard for the next generation. As a writer of prose, he helped establish a popular new style, shaped to the cadences of good conversation. Johnson praised its apparent artlessness: "every word seems to drop by chance, though it falls into its proper place. Nothing is cold or languid; the whole is airy, animated, and vigorous . . . though all is easy, nothing is feeble; though all seems careless, there is nothing harsh." Although Dryden's plays went out of fashion, his poems did not. His satire inspired the most brilliant verse satirist of the next century, Alexander Pope, and the energy and variety of his metrics launched the long-standing vogue of heroic couplets. Augustan style is at its best in his poems: lively, dignified, precise, and always musical—a flexible instrument of public speech. "By him we were taught *sapere et fari,* to think naturally and express forcibly," Johnson concluded. "What was said of Rome, adorned by Augustus, may be applied by an easy metaphor to English poetry embellished by Dryden, *lateritiam invenit, marmoream reliquit,* he found it brick, and he left it marble."

From Annus Mirabilis[1]

* * *

[LONDON REBORN]

845   Yet London, empress of the northern clime,
      By an high fate thou greatly didst expire;
    Great as the world's, which at the death of time
      Must fall, and rise a nobler frame by fire.[2]

    As when some dire usurper Heaven provides,
850   To scourge his country with a lawless sway:[3]
    His birth, perhaps, some petty village hides,
      And sets his cradle out of fortune's way:

    Till fully ripe his swelling fate breaks out,
      And hurries him to mighty mischiefs on:
855   His Prince, surprised at first, no ill could doubt,°   *fear*
      And wants the power to meet it when 'tis known:

    Such was the rise of this prodigious fire,
      Which in mean buildings first obscurely bred,
    From thence did soon to open streets aspire,
860   And straight to palaces and temples spread.

* * *

    Me-thinks already, from this chymic° flame,   *alchemic, transmuting*
1170   I see a city of more precious mold:
    Rich as the town which gives the Indies name,°   *Mexico*
      With silver paved, and all divine with gold.

    Already, laboring with a mighty fate,
      She shakes the rubbish from her mounting brow,
1175   And seems to have renewed her charter's date,
      Which Heaven will to the death of time allow.

    More great than human, now, and more August,[4]
      New deified she from her fires does rise:

1. The year 1666 was a "year of wonders" (*annus mirabilis*; Latin): war, plague, and the Great Fire of London. According to the enemies of Charles II, God was visiting His wrath on the English people to signify that the reign of an unholy king would soon come to an end. Dryden's long "historical poem" *Annus Mirabilis*, written the same year, interprets the wonders differently: as trials sent by God to punish rebellious spirits and to bind the king and his people together. "Never had prince or people more mutual reason to love each other," Dryden wrote, "if suffering for each other can endear affection." Charles had endured rejection and exile, England had been torn by civil wars. Dryden views these sufferings as a covenant, a pledge of better times to come. Out of Charles's troubles, he predicts in heroic stanzas modeled on Virgil, the king shall arise like a new Augustus, the ruler of a great empire, and out of fire, London shall arise like the phoenix, ready to take its place as trade center for the world, in the glory of a new Augustan age.
2. Dryden's footnote cites Ovid, *Metamorphoses* 1, which foretells that the world will be purged by fire. The fire of London, which utterly consumed the central city, burned for four days, September 2–6. By September 10, Christopher Wren had already submitted a plan, much of it later adopted, for rebuilding the city on a grander scale. For a dramatic contemporary depiction of the event, see *The Great Fire of London, 1666,* in the color insert in this volume.
3. Probably a reference to Oliver Cromwell.
4. Augusta, the old name of London [Dryden's note].

Her widening streets on new foundations trust,
1180   And, opening, into larger parts she flies.

Before, she like some shepherdess did show,
    Who sat to bathe her by a river's side:
Not answering to her fame, but rude and low,
    Nor taught the beauteous arts of modern pride.

1185 Now, like a Maiden Queen, she will behold,
    From her high turrets, hourly suitors come:
The East with incense, and the West with gold,
    Will stand, like suppliants, to receive her doom.°   *judgment, decree*

The silver Thames, her own domestic flood,
1190   Shall bear her vessels like a sweeping train;
And often wind (as of his mistress proud)
    With longing eyes to meet her face again.

The wealthy Tagus,[5] and the wealthier Rhine,
    The glory of their towns no more shall boast;
1195 And Seine, that would with Belgian rivers join,[6]
    Shall find her luster stained, and traffic lost.

The venturous merchant, who designed° more far,   *intended to go*
    And touches on our hospitable shore,
Charmed with the splendor of this northern star,
1200   Shall here unlade him, and depart no more.

Our powerful navy shall no longer meet,
    The wealth of France or Holland to invade;
The beauty of this Town, without a fleet,
    From all the world shall vindicate° her trade.   *defend, protect*

1205 And while this famed emporium we prepare,
    The British ocean shall such triumphs boast,
That those who now disdain our trade to share,
    Shall rob like pirates on our wealthy coast.

Already we have conquered half the war,
1210   And the less dangerous part is left behind:
Our trouble now is but to make them dare,
    And not so great to vanquish as to find.

Thus to the eastern wealth through storms we go,
    But now, the Cape once doubled,° fear no more;   *sailed around*
1215 A constant trade-wind will securely blow,
    And gently lay us on the spicy shore.

1666   1667

5. The river Tagus flows into the Atlantic at Lisbon.
6. France and Holland (which then included Belgium) had made an alliance for trade, as well as war, against England.

Song from *Marriage à la Mode*

1

Why should a foolish marriage vow,
    Which long ago was made,
Oblige us to each other now,
    When passion is decayed?
5   We loved, and we loved, as long as we could,
        Till our love was loved out in us both;
But our marriage is dead when the pleasure is fled:
    'Twas pleasure first made it an oath.

2

If I have pleasures for a friend,
10   And farther love in store,
What wrong has he whose joys did end,
    And who could give no more?
'Tis a madness that he should be jealous of me,
    Or that I should bar him of another:
15   For all we can gain is to give ourselves pain,
    When neither can hinder the other.

ca. 1672   1673

Absalom and Achitophel   In 1678 a dangerous crisis, both religious and political, threatened to undo the Restoration settlement and to precipitate England once again into civil war. The Popish Plot and its aftermath not only whipped up extreme anti-Catholic passions, but led between 1679 and 1681 to a bitter political struggle between Charles II (whose adherents came to be called Tories) and the earl of Shaftesbury (whose followers were termed Whigs). The issues were nothing less than the prerogatives of the crown and the possible exclusion of the king's Catholic brother, James, duke of York, from his position as heir-presumptive to the throne. Charles's cool courage and brilliant, if unscrupulous, political genius saved the throne for his brother and gave at least temporary peace to his people.

    Charles was a Catholic at heart—he received the last rites of that church on his deathbed—and was eager to do what he could do discreetly for the relief of his Catholic subjects, who suffered severe civil and religious disabilities imposed by their numerically superior Protestant compatriots. James openly professed the Catholic religion, an awkward fact politically, for he was next in line of succession because Charles had no legitimate children. The household of the duke, as well as that of Charles's neglected queen, Catherine of Braganza, inevitably became the center of Catholic life and intrigue at court and consequently of Protestant prejudice and suspicion.

    No one understood, however, that the situation was explosive until 1678, when Titus Oates (a renegade Catholic convert of infamous character) offered sworn testimony of the existence of a Jesuit plot to assassinate the king, burn London, massacre Protestants, and reestablish the Roman Church.

    The country might have kept its head and come to realize (what no historian has doubted) that Oates and his confederates were perjured rascals, as Charles himself quickly perceived. But panic was created by the discovery of the body of a prominent London justice of the peace, Sir Edmund Berry Godfrey, who a few days before had received for safekeeping a copy of Oates's testimony. The murder, immediately ascribed to the Catholics, has never been solved. Fear and indignation reached a hysterical pitch when the seizure of the papers of the duke of York's secretary revealed that he had been in correspondence with the confessor of Louis XIV regarding the reestablishment of the Roman Church in England. Before the terror subsided many innocent men were executed on the increasingly bold and always false evidence of Oates and his accomplices.

The earl of Shaftesbury, the duke of Buckingham, and others quickly took advantage of the situation. With the support of the Commons and the City of London, they moved to exclude the duke of York from the succession. Between 1679 and 1681 Charles and Shaftesbury were engaged in a mighty struggle. The Whigs found a candidate of their own in the king's favorite illegitimate son, the handsome and engaging duke of Monmouth, whom they advanced as a proper successor to his father. They urged Charles to legitimize him, and when he refused, they whispered that there was proof that the king had secretly married Monmouth's mother. The young man allowed himself to be used against his father. He was sent on a triumphant progress, through western England, where he was enthusiastically received. Twice an Exclusion Bill nearly passed both houses. But by early 1681 Charles had secured his own position by secretly accepting from Louis XIV a three-year subsidy that made him independent of Parliament, which had tried to force his hand by refusing to vote him funds. He summoned Parliament to meet at Oxford in the spring of 1681, and a few moments after the Commons had passed the Exclusion Bill, in a bold stroke he abruptly dissolved Parliament, which never met again during his reign. Already, as Charles was aware, a reaction had set in against the violence of the Whigs. In midsummer, when he felt it safe to move against his enemies, Shaftesbury was sent to the Tower of London, charged with high treason. In November, the grand jury, packed with Whigs, threw out the indictment, and the earl was free, but his power was broken, and he lived only two more years.

Shortly before the grand jury acted, Dryden published anonymously the first part of *Absalom and Achitophel,* apparently hoping to influence their verdict. The issues in question were grave; the chief actors, the most important men in the realm. Dryden, therefore, could not use burlesque and caricature as had Butler, or the mock heroic as he himself had done in "Mac Flecknoe." Only a heroic style and manner were appropriate to his weighty material, and the poem is most original in its blending of the heroic and the satiric. Dryden's task called for all his tact and literary skill; he had to mention, but to gloss over, the king's faults: his indolence and love of pleasure; his neglect of his wife, and his devotion to his mistresses—conduct that had left him with many children, but no heir except his Catholic brother. He had to deal gently with Monmouth, whom Charles still loved. And he had to present, or appear to present, the king's case objectively.

The remarkable parallels between the rebellion of Absalom against his father, King David (2 Samuel 13–18), had already been noticed in sermons, satires, and pamphlets. Dryden took the hint and gave contemporary events a due distance and additional dignity by approaching them indirectly through their biblical analogues. The poem is famous for its brilliant portraits of the king's enemies and friends, but equally admirable are the temptation scene (which, like other passages, is indebted to *Paradise Lost*) and the exceptionally astute analysis of the Popish Plot itself.

A second part of *Absalom and Achitophel* appeared in 1682. Most of it is the work of Nahum Tate, but lines 310–509, which include the devastating portraits of Doeg and Og (two Whig poets, Elkanah Settle and Thomas Shadwell), are certainly by Dryden.

Absalom and Achitophel: A Poem

In pious times, ere priestcraft[1] did begin,
Before polygamy was made a sin;
When man on many multiplied his kind,
Ere one to one was cursedly confined;
5   When nature prompted and no law denied
Promiscuous use of concubine and bride;
Then Israel's monarch after Heaven's own heart,[2]
His vigorous warmth did variously impart
To wives and slaves; and, wide as his command,
10   Scattered his Maker's image through the land.
Michal,[3] of royal blood, the crown did wear,
A soil ungrateful to the tiller's care:
Not so the rest; for several mothers bore
To godlike David several sons before.
15   But since like slaves his bed they did ascend,
No true succession could their seed attend.
Of all this numerous progeny was none
So beautiful, so brave, as Absalom:[4]
Whether, inspired by some diviner lust,
20   His father got him with a greater gust,°   *relish, pleasure*
Or that his conscious destiny made way,
By manly beauty, to imperial sway.
Early in foreign fields he won renown,
With kings and states allied to Israel's crown:[5]
25   In peace the thoughts of war he could remove,
And seemed as he were only born for love.
Whate'er he did, was done with so much ease,
In him alone 'twas natural to please;
His motions all accompanied with grace;
30   And paradise was opened in his face.
With secret joy indulgent David viewed
His youthful image in his son renewed:
To all his wishes nothing he denied;
And made the charming Annabel[6] his bride.
35   What faults he had (for who from faults is free?)
His father could not, or he would not see.
Some warm excesses which the law forbore,
Were cònstrued youth that purged by boiling o'er:
And Amnon's murther,[7] by a specious name,
40   Was called a just revenge for injured fame.
Thus praised and loved the noble youth remained,

1. "Religious frauds; management of wicked priests to gain power" (Johnson's *Dictionary*).
2. David ("a man after [God's] own heart," according to 1 Samuel 13.14) represents Charles II.
3. One of David's wives, who represents the childless queen, Catherine of Braganza.
4. James Scott, duke of Monmouth (1649–1685).
5. Monmouth had won repute as a soldier fighting for France against Holland and for Holland against France.
6. Anne Scott, duchess of Buccleuch (pronounced *Bue-cloo*), a beauty and a great heiress.
7. Absalom killed his half-brother Amnon, who had raped Absalom's sister Tamar (2 Samuel 13.28–29). The parallel with Monmouth is vague. He is known to have committed acts of violence in his youth, but certainly not fratricide.

While David, undisturbed, in Sion° reigned.   *London*
But life can never be sincerely° blest;   *wholly*
Heaven punishes the bad, and proves° the best.   *tests*
45 The Jews,° a headstrong, moody, murmuring race, *English*
As ever tried the extent and stretch of grace;
God's pampered people, whom, debauched with ease,
No king could govern, nor no God could please
(Gods they had tried of every shape and size
50 That god-smiths could produce, or priests devise);[8]
These Adam-wits, too fortunately free,
Began to dream they wanted liberty;[9]
And when no rule, no precedent was found,
Of men by laws less circumscribed and bound,
55 They led their wild desires to woods and caves,
And thought that all but savages were slaves.
They who, when Saul[1] was dead, without a blow,
Made foolish Ishbosheth[2] the crown forgo;
Who banished David did from Hebron[3] bring,
60 And with a general shout proclaimed him king:
Those very Jews, who, at their very best,
Their humor° more than loyalty expressed,   *caprice*
Now wondered why so long they had obeyed
An idol monarch, which their hands had made;
65 Thought they might ruin him they could create,
Or melt him to that golden calf,[4] a state.°   *republic*
But these were random bolts;° no formed design   *shots*
Nor interest made the factious crowd to join:
The sober part of Israel, free from stain,
70 Well knew the value of a peaceful reign;
And, looking backward with a wise affright,
Saw seams of wounds, dishonest° to the sight: *disgraceful*
In contemplation of whose ugly scars
They cursed the memory of civil wars.
75 The moderate sort of men, thus qualified,°   *assuaged*
Inclined the balance to the better side;
And David's mildness managed it so well,
The bad found no occasion to rebel.
But when to sin our biased[5] nature leans,
80 The careful Devil is still at hand with means;
And providently pimps for ill desires:
The Good Old Cause[6] revived, a plot requires.
Plots, true or false, are necessary things,
To raise up commonwealths and ruin kings.
85   The inhabitants of old Jerusalem

---

8. Dryden recalls the political and religious controversies that, since the Reformation, had divided England and finally caused civil wars.
9. Adam rebelled because he felt he lacked ("wanted") liberty because he was forbidden to eat the fruit of one tree.
1. Oliver Cromwell.
2. Saul's son. He stands for Richard Cromwell, who succeeded his father as lord protector.
3. Where David reigned over Judah after the death of Saul and before he became king of Israel (2 Samuel 1–5). Charles had been crowned in Scotland in 1651.
4. The image worshiped by the children of Israel during the period that Moses spent on Mount Sinai, receiving the law from God.
5. Inclined (cf. "Mac Flecknoe," line 189 and p. 68, n. 8).
6. The Commonwealth. Dryden stigmatizes the Whigs by associating them with subversion.

Were Jebusites;[7] the town so called from them;
And theirs the native right.
But when the chosen people° grew more strong,   *Protestants*
The rightful cause at length became the wrong;
90 And every loss the men of Jebus bore,
They still were thought God's enemies the more.
Thus worn and weakened, well or ill content,
Submit they must to David's government:
Impoverished and deprived of all command,
95 Their taxes doubled as they lost their land;
And, what was harder yet to flesh and blood,
Their gods disgraced, and burnt like common wood.[8]
This set the heathen priesthood° in a flame;   *Roman Catholic clergy*
For priests of all religions are the same:
100 Of whatsoe'er descent their godhead be,
Stock, stone, or other homely pedigree,
In his defense his servants are as bold,
As if he had been born of beaten gold.
The Jewish rabbins,° though their enemies,   *Anglican clergy*
105 In this conclude them honest men and wise:
For 'twas their duty, all the learned think,
To espouse his cause, by whom they eat and drink.
From hence began that Plot, the nation's curse,
Bad in itself, but represented worse;
110 Raised in extremes, and in extremes decried;
With oaths affirmed, with dying vows denied;
Not weighed or winnowed by the multitude;
But swallowed in the mass, unchewed and crude.
Some truth there was, but dashed° and brewed with lies,   *adulterated*
115 To please the fools, and puzzle all the wise.
Succeeding times did equal folly call,
Believing nothing, or believing all.
The Egyptian[9] rites the Jebusites embraced,
Where gods were recommended by their taste.[1]
120 Such savory deities must needs be good,
As served at once for worship and for food.
By force they could not introduce these gods,
For ten to one in former days was odds;
So fraud was used (the sacrificer's trade):
125 Fools are more hard to conquer than persuade.
Their busy teachers mingled with the Jews,
And raked for converts even the court and stews:°   *brothels*
Which Hebrew priests the more unkindly took,
Because the fleece accompanies the flock.[2]
130 Some thought they God's anointed° meant to slay   *the king*
By guns, invented since full many a day:

7. Roman Catholics. The original name of Jerusalem (here, London) was Jebus.
8. Such oppressive laws against Roman Catholics date from the time of Elizabeth I.
9. French, therefore Catholic.
1. Here Dryden sneers at the doctrine of transubstantiation.
2. Dryden charges that the Anglican clergy ("Hebrew priests") resented proselytizing by Catholics chiefly because they stood to lose their tithes ("fleece").

Our author swears it not; but who can know
How far the Devil and Jebusites may go?
This Plot, which failed for want of common sense,
135 Had yet a deep and dangerous consequence:
For, as when raging fevers boil the blood,
The standing lake soon floats into a flood,
And every hostile humor,[3] which before
Slept quiet in its channels, bubbles o'er;
140 So several factions from this first ferment
Work up to foam, and threat the government.
Some by their friends, more by themselves thought wise,
Opposed the power to which they could not rise.
Some had in courts been great, and thrown from thence,
145 Like fiends were hardened in impenitence;
Some, by their monarch's fatal mercy, grown
From pardoned rebels kinsmen to the throne,
Were raised in power and public office high;
Strong bands, if bands ungrateful men could tie.
150   Of these the false Achitophel[4] was first;
A name to all succeeding ages cursed:
For close designs, and crooked counsels fit;
Sagacious, bold, and turbulent of wit;°   *unruly intellect*
Restless, unfixed in principles and place;
155 In power unpleased, impatient of disgrace:
A fiery soul, which, working out its way, ⎫
Fretted the pygmy body to decay,   ⎬
And o'er-informed the tenement of clay.[5] ⎭
A daring pilot in extremity;
160 Pleased with the danger, when the waves went high,
He sought the storms; but, for a calm unfit,
Would steer too nigh the sands, to boast his wit.
Great wits° are sure to madness near allied,[6]   *men of genius*
And thin partitions do their bounds divide;
165 Else why should he, with wealth and honor blest,
Refuse his age the needful hours of rest?
Punish a body which he could not please;
Bankrupt of life, yet prodigal of ease?
And all to leave what with his toil he won,
170 To that unfeathered two-legged thing,[7] a son;
Got, while his soul did huddled° notions try;   *confused, hurried*
And born a shapeless lump, like anarchy.
In friendship false, implacable in hate,
Resolved to ruin or to rule the state.

---

3. Bodily fluid. Such fluids were thought to determine health and temperament.
4. Anthony Ashley Cooper, first earl of Shaftesbury (1621–1683). He had served in the parliamentary army and been a member of Cromwell's council of state. He later helped bring back Charles and, in 1670, was made a member of the notorious Cabal Ministry, which formed an alliance with Louis XIV in which England betrayed her ally, Holland, and joined France in war against that country. In 1672 he became lord chancellor, but with the dissolution of the cabal in 1673, he was removed from office. Lines 146–49 apply perfectly to him.
5. The soul is thought of as the animating principle, the force that puts the body in motion. Shaftesbury's body seemed too small to house his fiery, energetic soul.
6. That genius and madness are akin is a very old idea.
7. Cf. Plato's definition of a human: "a featherless biped."

175 To compass this the triple bond[8] he broke, ⎫
     The pillars of the public safety shook,   ⎬
     And fitted Israel for a foreign yoke;   ⎭
     Then seized with fear, yet still affecting fame,
     Usurped a patriot's all-atoning name.
180 So easy still it proves in factious times,
     With public zeal to cancel private crimes.
     How safe is treason, and how sacred ill,
     Where none can sin against the people's will!
     Where crowds can wink, and no offense be known,
185 Since in another's guilt they find their own!
     Yet fame deserved, no enemy can grudge;
     The statesman we abhor, but praise the judge.
     In Israel's courts ne'er sat an Abbethdin[9]
     With more discerning eyes, or hands more clean;
190 Unbribed, unsought, the wretched to redress;
     Swift of dispatch, and easy of access.
     Oh, had he been content to serve the crown,
     With virtues only proper to the gown°   *judge's robe*
     Or had the rankness of the soil been freed
195 From cockle,° that oppressed the noble seed;   *weeds*
     David for him his tuneful harp had strung,
     And Heaven had wanted one immortal song.[1]
     But wild Ambition loves to slide, not stand,
     And Fortune's ice prefers to Virtue's land.
200 Achitophel, grown weary to possess
     A lawful fame, and lazy happiness,
     Disdained the golden fruit to gather free,
     And lent the crowd his arm to shake the tree.
     Now, manifest of° crimes contrived long since,   *detected in*
205 He stood at bold defiance with his prince;
     Held up the buckler of the people's cause
     Against the crown, and skulked behind the laws.
     The wished occasion of the Plot he takes;
     Some circumstances finds, but more he makes.
210 By buzzing emissaries fills the ears
     Of listening crowds with jealousies° and fears   *suspicions*
     Of arbitrary counsels brought to light,
     And proves the king himself a Jebusite.
     Weak arguments! which yet he knew full well
215 Were strong with people easy to rebel.
     For, governed by the moon, the giddy Jews
     Tread the same track when she the prime renews;
     And once in twenty years, their scribes record,[2]

8. The triple alliance of England, Sweden, and Holland against France, 1668. Shaftesbury helped bring about the war against Holland in 1672.
9. The chief of the seventy elders who composed the Jewish supreme court. The allusion is to Shaftesbury's serving as lord chancellor from 1672 to 1673.
1. I.e., David would have had occasion to write one fewer song of praise to heaven. The refer-

ence may be to 2 Samuel 22 or to Psalms 4.
2. The moon "renews her prime" when its several phases recur on the same day of the solar calendar (i.e., complete a cycle) as happens approximately every twenty years. The crisis between Charles I and Parliament began to grow acute about 1640; Charles II returned in 1660; it is now 1680 and a full cycle has been completed.

By natural instinct they change their lord.
220 Achitophel still wants a chief, and none
Was found so fit as warlike Absalom:
Not that he wished his greatness to create
(For politicians neither love nor hate),
But, for he knew his title not allowed,
225 Would keep him still depending on the crowd,
That° kingly power, thus ebbing out, might be   *so that*
Drawn to the dregs of a democracy.[3]
Him he attempts with studied arts to please,
And sheds his venom in such words as these:
230   "Auspicious prince, at whose nativity
Some royal planet[4] ruled the southern sky;
Thy longing country's darling and desire;
Their cloudy pillar and their guardian fire:
Their second Moses, whose extended wand
235 Divides the seas, and shows the promised land;[5]
Whose dawning day in every distant age
Has exercised the sacred prophet's rage:
The people's prayer, the glad diviners' theme,
The young men's vision, and the old men's dream![6]
240 Thee, savior, thee, the nation's vows[7] confess,
And, never satisfied with seeing, bless:
Swift unbespoken° pomps thy steps proclaim,   *spontaneous*
And stammering babes are taught to lisp thy name.
How long wilt thou the general joy detain,
245 Starve and defraud the people of thy reign?
Content ingloriously to pass thy days
Like one of Virtue's fools that feeds on praise;
Till thy fresh glories, which now shine so bright,
Grow stale and tarnish with our daily sight.
250 Believe me, royal youth, thy fruit must be
Or gathered ripe, or rot upon the tree.
Heaven has to all allotted, soon or late,
Some lucky revolution of their fate;
Whose motions if we watch and guide with skill
255 (For human good depends on human will),
Our Fortune rolls as from a smooth descent,
And from the first impression takes the bent;
But, if unseized, she glides away like wind,
And leaves repenting Folly far behind.
260 Now, now she meets you with a glorious prize,
And spreads her locks before her as she flies.[8]
Had thus old David, from whose loins you spring,

3. I.e., mob rule. To Dryden, *democracy* meant "popular government."
4. A planet whose influence destines him to kingship.
5. After their exodus from Egypt under the leadership of Moses, whose "extended wand" separated the waters of the Red Sea so that they crossed over on dry land, the Israelites were led in their forty-year wandering in the wilderness by a pillar of cloud by day and a pillar of fire by night (Exodus 13–14).
6. Cf. Joel 2.28.
7. Solemn promises of fidelity.
8. Achitophel gives to Fortune the traditional attributes of the allegorical personification of Opportunity: bald except for a forelock, she can be seized only as she approaches.

Not dared, when Fortune called him, to be king,
At Gath[9] an exile he might still remain,
265   And heaven's anointing[1] oil had been in vain.
Let his successful youth your hopes engage;
But shun the example of declining age;
Behold him setting in his western skies,
The shadows lengthening as the vapors rise.
270   He is not now, as when on Jordan's sand[2]   ⎫
The joyful people thronged to see him land,   ⎬
Covering the beach, and blackening all the strand;   ⎭
But, like the Prince of Angels, from his height
Comes tumbling downward with diminished light;[3]
275   Betrayed by one poor plot to public scorn
(Our only blessing since his cursed return),
Those heaps of people which one sheaf did bind,
Blown off and scattered by a puff of wind.
What strength can he to your designs oppose,
280   Naked of friends, and round beset with foes?
If Pharaoh's[4] doubtful succor he should use,
A foreign aid would more incense the Jews:
Proud Egypt would dissembled friendship bring;
Foment the war, but not support the king:
285   Nor would the royal party e'er unite
With Pharaoh's arms to assist the Jebusite;
Or if they should, their interest soon would break,
And with such odious aid make David weak.
All sorts of men by my successful arts,
290   Abhorring kings, estrange their altered hearts
From David's rule: and 'tis the general cry,
'Religion, commonwealth, and liberty.'[5]
If you, as champion of the public good,
Add to their arms a chief of royal blood,
295   What may not Israel hope, and what applause
Might such a general gain by such a cause?
Not barren praise alone, that gaudy flower
Fair only to the sight, but solid power;
And nobler is a limited command,
300   Given by the love of all your native land,
Than a successive title,[6] long and dark,
Drawn from the moldy rolls of Noah's ark."
      What cannot praise effect in mighty minds,
When flattery soothes, and when ambition blinds!
305   Desire of power, on earth a vicious weed,
Yet, sprung from high, is of celestial seed:
In God 'tis glory; and when men aspire,

9. Brussels, where Charles spent his last years in exile. David took refuge from Saul in Gath (1 Samuel 27.4).
1. After God rejected Saul, he sent Samuel to anoint the boy David, as a token that he should finally come to the throne (1 Samuel 16.1–13).
2. The seashore at Dover, where Charles landed (May 25, 1660).

3. Cf. the fall of Satan in *Paradise Lost* 1.50–124, which dims the brightness of the archangel. The choice of the undignified word *tumbling* is deliberate.
4. Pharaoh is Louis XIV of France.
5. Cf. line 82 and p. 41, n. 6.
6. A title to the crown based on succession.

'Tis but a spark too much of heavenly fire.
The ambitious youth, too covetous of fame,
310   Too full of angels' metal[7] in his frame,
Unwarily was led from virtue's ways,
Made drunk with honor, and debauched with praise.
Half loath, and half consenting to the ill
(For loyal blood within him struggled still),
315   He thus replied: "And what pretense have I
To take up arms for public liberty?
My father governs with unquestioned right;
The faith's defender, and mankind's delight,
Good, gracious, just, observant of the laws:
320   And heaven by wonders has espoused his cause.
Whom has he wronged in all his peaceful reign?
Who sues for justice to his throne in vain?
What millions has he pardoned of his foes,
Whom just revenge did to his wrath expose?
325   Mild, easy, humble, studious of our good,
Inclined to mercy, and averse from blood;
If mildness ill with stubborn Israel suit,
His crime is God's beloved attribute.
What could he gain, his people to betray,
330   Or change his right for arbitrary sway?
Let haughty Pharaoh curse, with such a reign
His fruitful Nile, and yoke a servile train.
If David's rule Jerusalem displease,
The Dog Star[8] heats their brains to this disease.
335   Why then should I, encouraging the bad,
Turn rebel and run popularly mad?
Were he a tyrant, who, by lawless might
Oppressed the Jews, and raised the Jebusite,
Well might I mourn; but nature's holy bands
340   Would curb my spirits and restrain my hands:
The people might assert° their liberty,   *claim*
But what was right in them were crime in me.
His favor leaves me nothing to require;
Prevents my wishes, and outruns desire.
345   What more can I expect while David lives?
All but his kingly diadem he gives:
And that"—But there he paused; then sighing, said—
"Is justly destined for a worthier head.
For when my father from his toils shall rest
350   And late augment the number of the blest,
His lawful issue shall the throne ascend,
Or the collateral line,[9] where that shall end.
His brother, though oppressed with vulgar spite,[1]

---

7. An alternative spelling of *mettle* (i.e., spirit). But a pun on *metal* is intended, as is obvious from the pun *angel* (a purely intellectual being and a coin). Ambition caused the revolt of the angels in heaven.
8. Sirius, which in midsummer rises and sets with the sun and is thus associated with the maddening heat of the "dog days."
9. In the event of Charles's dying without legitimate issue, the throne would constitutionally pass to his brother, James, or his descendants, the "collateral line."
1. Anger of the common people.

Yet dauntless, and secure of native right,
355 Of every royal virtue stands possessed;
Still dear to all the bravest and the best.
His courage foes, his friends his truth proclaim;
His loyalty the king, the world his fame.
His mercy even the offending crowd will find,
360 For sure he comes of a forgiving kind.[2]
Why should I then repine at heaven's decree,
Which gives me no pretense to royalty?
Yet O that fate, propitiously inclined,
Had raised my birth, or had debased my mind;
365 To my large soul not all her treasure lent,
And then betrayed it to a mean descent!
I find, I find my mounting spirits bold,
And David's part disdains my mother's mold.
Why am I scanted by a niggard birth?[3]
370 My soul disclaims the kindred of her earth;
And, made for empire, whispers me within,
'Desire of greatness is a godlike sin.'"
    Him staggering so when hell's dire agent found,
While fainting Virtue scarce maintained her ground,
375 He pours fresh forces in, and thus replies:
    "The eternal god, supremely good and wise,
Imparts not these prodigious gifts in vain:
What wonders are reserved to bless your reign!
Against your will, your arguments have shown,
380 Such virtue's only given to guide a throne.
Not that your father's mildness I contemn,
But manly force becomes the diadem.
'Tis true he grants the people all they crave;
And more, perhaps, than subjects ought to have:
385 For lavish grants suppose a monarch tame,
And more his goodness than his wit° proclaim.   *intelligence*
But when should people strive their bonds to break,
If not when kings are negligent or weak?
Let him give on till he can give no more,
390 The thrifty Sanhedrin[4] shall keep him poor;
And every shekel which he can receive,
Shall cost a limb of his prerogative.[5]
To ply him with new plots shall be my care;
Or plunge him deep in some expensive war;
395 Which when his treasure can no more supply,
He must, with the remains of kingship, buy.
His faithful friends our jealousies and fears
Call Jebusites, and Pharaoh's pensioners;
Whom when our fury from his aid has torn,
400 He shall be naked left to public scorn.

2. Race, in the sense of family.
3. Why does my mean birth impose such limits on me?
4. The highest judicial counsel of the Jews, here, Parliament.
5. The Whigs hoped to limit the special privileges of the Crown (the royal "prerogative") by refusing to vote money to Charles. He circumvented them by living on French subsidies and refusing to summon Parliament.

The next successor, whom I fear and hate,
My arts have made obnoxious to the state;
Turned all his virtues to his overthrow,
And gained our elders[6] to pronounce a foe.
405 His right, for sums of necessary gold,
Shall first be pawned, and afterward be sold;
Till time shall ever-wanting David draw,
To pass your doubtful title into law:
If not, the people have a right supreme
410 To make their kings; for kings are made for them.
All empire is no more than power in trust,
Which, when resumed,° can be no longer just.   *taken back*
Succession, for the general good designed,
In its own wrong a nation cannot bind;
415 If altering that the people can relieve,
Better one suffer than a nation grieve.
The Jews well know their power: ere Saul they chose,[7]
God was their king, and God they durst depose.
Urge now your piety,[8] your filial name,
420 A father's right and fear of future fame;
The public good, that universal call,
To which even heaven submitted, answers all.
Nor let his love enchant your generous mind;
'Tis Nature's trick to propagate her kind.
425 Our fond begetters, who would never die,
Love but themselves in their posterity.
Or let his kindness by the effects be tried,
Or let him lay his vain pretense aside.
God said he loved your father; could he bring
430 A better proof than to anoint him king?
It surely showed he loved the shepherd well,
Who gave so fair a flock as Israel.
Would David have you thought his darling son?
What means he then, to alienate[9] the crown?
435 The name of godly he may blush to bear:
'Tis after God's own heart[1] to cheat his heir.
He to his brother gives supreme command;
To you a legacy of barren land,[2]
Perhaps the old harp, on which he thrums his lays,
440 Or some dull Hebrew ballad in your praise.
Then the next heir, a prince severe and wise,
Already looks on you with jealous eyes;
Sees through the thin disguises of your arts,
And marks your progress in the people's hearts.
445 Though now his mighty soul its grief contains,

6. The chief magistrates and rulers of the Jews. Shaftesbury had won over ("gained") country gentlemen and nobles to his hostile view of James.
7. Before Saul, the first king of Israel, came to the throne, the Jews were governed by judges. Similarly Oliver Cromwell as lord protector took over the reins of government, after he had dissolved the Rump Parliament in 1653.
8. Dutifulness to a parent.
9. In law, to convey the title to property to another person.
1. An irony (cf. line 7 and n. 2).
2. James was given the title of generalissimo in 1678. In 1679 Monmouth was banished and withdrew to Holland.

He meditates revenge who least complains;
And, like a lion, slumbering in the way,
Or sleep dissembling, while he waits his prey,
His fearless foes within his distance draws,
450 Constrains his roaring, and contracts his paws;
Till at the last, his time for fury found,
He shoots with sudden vengeance from the ground;
The prostrate vulgar° passes o'er and spares,   *common people*
But with a lordly rage his hunters tears.
455 Your case no tame expedients will afford:
Resolve on death, or conquest by the sword,
Which for no less a stake than life you draw;
And self-defense is nature's eldest law.
Leave the warm people no considering time;
460 For then rebellion may be thought a crime.
Prevail yourself of what occasion gives,
But try your title while your father lives;
And that your arms may have a fair pretense,°   *pretext*
Proclaim you take them in the king's defense;
465 Whose sacred life each minute would expose
To plots, from seeming friends, and secret foes.
And who can sound the depth of David's soul?
Perhaps his fear his kindness may control.
He fears his brother, though he loves his son,
470 For plighted vows too late to be undone.
If so, by force he wishes to be gained,
Like women's lechery, to seem constrained.°   *forced*
Doubt not; but when he most affects the frown,
Commit a pleasing rape upon the crown.
475 Secure his person to secure your cause:
They who possess the prince, possess the laws."
    He said, and this advice above the rest
With Absalom's mild nature suited best:
Unblamed of life (ambition set aside),
480 Not stained with cruelty, nor puffed with pride,
How happy had he been, if destiny
Had higher placed his birth, or not so high!
His kingly virtues might have claimed a throne,
And blest all other countries but his own.
485 But charming greatness since so few refuse,
'Tis juster to lament him than accuse.
Strong were his hopes a rival to remove,
With blandishments to gain the public love;
To head the faction while their zeal was hot,
490 And popularly prosecute the Plot.
To further this, Achitophel unites
The malcontents of all the Israelites;
Whose differing parties he could wisely join,
For several ends, to serve the same design:
495 The best (and of the princes some were such),
Who thought the power of monarchy too much;
Mistaken men, and patriots in their hearts;

Not wicked, but seduced by impious arts.
By these the springs of property were bent,
500 And wound so high, they cracked the government.
The next for interest sought to embroil the state,
To sell their duty at a dearer rate;
And make their Jewish markets of the throne,
Pretending public good, to serve their own.
505 Others thought kings an useless heavy load,
Who cost too much, and did too little good.
These were for laying honest David by,
On principles of pure good husbandry.°   economy
With them joined all the haranguers of the throng,
510 That thought to get preferment by the tongue.
Who follow next, a double danger bring,
Not only hating David, but the king:
The Solymaean rout,[3] well-versed of old
In godly faction, and in treason bold;
515 Cowering and quaking at a conqueror's sword,
But lofty to a lawful prince restored;
Saw with disdain an ethnic[4] plot begun,
And scorned by Jebusites to be outdone.
Hot Levites[5] headed these; who, pulled before
520 From the ark, which in the Judges' days they bore,
Resumed their cant, and with a zealous cry
Pursued their old beloved theocracy:
Where Sanhedrin and priest enslaved the nation,
And justified their spoils by inspiration:
525 For who so fit for reign as Aaron's race,[6]
If once dominion they could found in grace?
These led the pack; though not of surest scent,
Yet deepest-mouthed[7] against the government.
A numerous host of dreaming saints[8] succeed,
530 Of the true old enthusiastic breed:
'Gainst form and order they their power employ,
Nothing to build, and all things to destroy.
But far more numerous was the herd of such,
Who think too little, and who talk too much.
535 These out of mere instinct, they knew not why,
Adored their fathers' God and property;
And, by the same blind benefit of fate,
The Devil and the Jebusite did hate:
Born to be saved, even in their own despite,

3. London rabble. Solyma was a name for Jerusalem.
4. Gentile; here, Roman Catholic.
5. I.e., Presbyterian clergymen. The tribe of Levi, assigned to duties in the tabernacle, carried the Ark of the Covenant during the forty-year sojourn in the wilderness (Numbers 4). Under the Commonwealth ("in the Judges' days") Presbyterianism became the state religion, and its clergy, therefore, "bore the ark." The Act of Uniformity (1662) forced the Presbyterian clergy out of their livings: in short, before the Popish Plot, they had been

"pulled from the ark." They are represented here as joining the Whigs in the hope of restoring the commonwealth, "their old beloved theocracy."
6. Priests had to be descendants of Aaron (Exodus 28.1, Numbers 18.7).
7. Loudest. The phrase is applied to hunting dogs. "Pack" and "scent" sustain the image.
8. Term used by certain Dissenters for those elected to salvation. The extreme fanaticism of the "saints" and their claims to inspiration are characterized as a form of religious madness ("enthusiastic," line 530).

540   Because they could not help believing right.
       Such were the tools; but a whole Hydra more
       Remains, of sprouting heads too long to score.°   *count*
       Some of their chiefs were princes of the land:
       In the first rank of these did Zimri[9] stand;
545   A man so various, that he seemed to be
       Not one, but all mankind's epitome:
       Stiff in opinions, always in the wrong;
       Was everything by starts, and nothing long;
       But, in the course of one revolving moon,
550   Was chymist,° fiddler, statesman, and buffoon: *chemist*
       Then all for women, painting, rhyming, drinking,
       Besides ten thousand freaks that died in thinking.
       Blest madman, who could every hour employ,
       With something new to wish, or to enjoy!
555   Railing° and praising were his usual themes;   *reviling, abusing*
       And both (to show his judgment) in extremes:
       So over-violent, or over-civil,
       That every man, with him, was God or Devil.
       In squandering wealth was his peculiar art:
560   Nothing went unrewarded but desert.
       Beggared by fools, whom still° he found° too late,   *constantly / found out*
       He had his jest, and they had his estate.
       He laughed himself from court; then sought relief
       By forming parties, but could ne'er be chief;
565   For, spite of him, the weight of business fell
       On Absalom and wise Achitophel:
       Thus, wicked but in will, of means bereft,
       He left not faction, but of that was left.
          Titles and names 'twere tedious to rehearse
570   Of lords, below the dignity of verse.
       Wits, warriors, Commonwealth's men, were the best;
       Kind husbands, and mere nobles, all the rest.
       And therefore, in the name of dullness, be
       The well-hung Balaam and cold Caleb,[1] free;
575   And canting Nadab[2] let oblivion damn,
       Who made new porridge for the paschal lamb.[3]
       Let friendship's holy band some names assure;
       Some their own worth, and some let scorn secure.
       Nor shall the rascal rabble here have place,

---

9. George Villiers, second duke of Buckingham (1628–1687), wealthy, brilliant, dissolute, and unstable. He had been an influential member of the cabal, but after 1673 had joined Shaftesbury in opposition to the court party. This is the least political of the satirical portraits in the poem. Buckingham had been the chief author of *The Rehearsal* (1671), the play that satirized heroic tragedy and ridiculed Dryden in the character of Mr. Bayes. Politics gave Dryden an opportunity to retaliate. He comments on this portrait in his "A Discourse Concerning the Original and Progress of Satire." Dryden had two biblical Zimris in mind: the Zimri destroyed for his lustfulness and blasphemy (Numbers 25) and the conspirator and regicide of 1 Kings 16.8–20 and 2 Kings 9.31.

1. See Numbers 13–14. "Well-hung": fluent of speech or sexually potent or both. For Balaam, see Numbers 22–24. "Cold": contrasts with the second meaning of *well-hung*.

2. See Leviticus 10.1–2. "Canting": points to a Nonconformist, as does "new porridge"; for Dissenters referred to the Book of Common Prayer contemptuously as "porridge," a hodgepodge, unsubstantial stuff.

3. The lamb slain during Passover; here, Christ. The identities of Balaam, Caleb, and Nadab have not been certainly established, although various Whig nobles have been suggested.

580 Whom kings no titles gave, and God no grace:
Not bull-faced Jonas,[4] who could statutes draw
To mean rebellion, and make treason law.
But he, though bad, is followed by a worse,
The wretch who heaven's anointed dared to curse:
585 Shimei,[5] whose youth did early promise bring
Of zeal to God and hatred to his king,
Did wisely from expensive sins refrain,
And never broke the Sabbath, but for gain;
Nor ever was he known an oath to vent,
590 Or curse, unless against the government.
Thus heaping wealth, by the most ready way
Among the Jews, which was to cheat and pray,
The city, to reward his pious hate
Against his master, chose him magistrate.
595 His hand a vare° of justice did uphold;   *staff*
His neck was loaded with a chain of gold.
During his office, treason was no crime;
The sons of Belial[6] had a glorious time;
For Shimei, though not prodigal of pelf,°   *free with money*
600 Yet loved his wicked neighbor as himself.
When two or three were gathered to declaim ⎫
Against the monarch of Jerusalem,   ⎬
Shimei was always in the midst of them;   ⎭
And if they cursed the king when he was by,
605 Would rather curse than break good company.
If any durst his factious friends accuse,
He packed a jury of dissenting Jews;
Whose fellow-feeling in the godly cause
Would free the suffering saint from human laws.
610 For laws are only made to punish those
Who serve the king, and to protect his foes.
If any leisure time he had from power
(Because 'tis sin to misemploy an hour),
His business was, by writing, to persuade
615 That kings were useless, and a clog to trade;
And, that his noble style he might refine,
No Rechabite[7] more shunned the fumes of wine.
Chaste were his cellars, and his shrieval board[8]
The grossness of a city feast abhorred:
620 His cooks, with long disuse, their trade forgot;
Cool was his kitchen, though his brains were hot,
Such frugal virtue malice may accuse,
But sure 'twas necessary to the Jews:

---

4. Sir William Jones, attorney general, had been largely responsible for the passage of the first Exclusion Bill by the House of Commons. He prosecuted the accused in the Popish Plot.
5. He cursed and stoned David when he fled into the wilderness during Absalom's revolt (2 Samuel 16.5–14). His name is used here for one of the two sheriffs of London: Slingsby Bethel, a Whig, former republican, and virulent enemy of Charles. He packed juries with Whigs and so secured the acquittal of enemies of the court, among them Shaftesbury himself.
6. Sons of wickedness (cf. Milton, *Paradise Lost* 1.490–505). Dryden probably intended a pun on Balliol, the Oxford college in which leading Whigs stayed during the brief and fateful meeting of Parliament at Oxford in 1681.
7. An austere Jewish sect that drank no wine (Jeremiah 35.2–19).
8. Sheriff's dinner table.

　　　　For towns once burnt[9] such magistrates require
625　　As dare not tempt God's providence by fire.
　　　　With spiritual food he fed his servants well,
　　　　But free from flesh that made the Jews rebel;
　　　　And Moses' laws he held in more account,
　　　　For forty days of fasting in the mount.[1]
630　　To speak the rest, who better are forgot,
　　　　Would tire a well-breathed witness of the Plot.
　　　　Yet, Corah,[2] thou shalt from oblivion pass:
　　　　Erect thyself, thou monumental brass,
　　　　High as the serpent of thy metal made,[3]
635　　While nations stand secure beneath thy shade.
　　　　What though his birth were base, yet comets rise
　　　　From earthy vapors, ere they shine in skies.
　　　　Prodigious actions may as well be done
　　　　By weaver's issue,[4] as by prince's son.
640　　This arch-attestor for the public good
　　　　By that one deed ennobles all his blood.
　　　　Who ever asked the witnesses' high race
　　　　Whose oath with martyrdom did Stephen[5] grace?
　　　　Ours was a Levite, and as times went then,
645　　His tribe were God Almighty's gentlemen.
　　　　Sunk were his eyes, his voice was harsh and loud,
　　　　Sure signs he neither choleric° was nor proud:　　　　　　　　prone to anger
　　　　His long chin proved his wit; his saintlike grace
　　　　A church vermilion, and a Moses' face.[6]
650　　His memory, miraculously great,
　　　　Could plots, exceeding man's belief, repeat;
　　　　Which therefore cannot be accounted lies,
　　　　For human wit could never such devise.
　　　　Some future truths are mingled in his book;
655　　But where the witness failed, the prophet spoke:
　　　　Some things like visionary flights appear;
　　　　The spirit caught him up, the Lord knows where,
　　　　And gave him his rabbinical degree,
　　　　Unknown to foreign university.[7]
660　　His judgment yet his memory did excel;
　　　　Which pieced his wondrous evidence so well,
　　　　And suited to the temper of the times,
　　　　Then groaning under Jebusitic crimes.
　　　　Let Israel's foes suspect his heavenly call,
665　　And rashly judge his writ apocryphal;[8]

9. London burned in 1666.
1. Mount Sinai, where, during a fast of forty days, Moses received the law (Exodus 34.28).
2. Or Korah, a rebellious Levite, swallowed up by the earth because of his crimes (Numbers 16). Corah is Titus Oates, the self-appointed, perjured, and "well-breathed" (long-winded) witness of the plot.
3. Moses erected a brazen serpent to heal the Jews bitten by fiery serpents (Numbers 21.4–9). Brass also means impudence or shamelessness.
4. Oates's father, a clergyman, belonged to an obscure family of ribbon weavers.
5. The first Christian martyr, accused by false witnesses (Acts 6–7).
6. Moses's face shone when he came down from Mount Sinai with the tables of the law (Exodus 34.29–30). Oates's face suggests high living, not spiritual illumination.
7. Oates falsely claimed to be a doctor of divinity in the University of Salamanca.
8. Not inspired and hence excluded from Holy Writ.

Our laws for such affronts have forfeits made:
He takes his life, who takes away his trade.
Were I myself in witness Corah's place,
The wretch who did me such a dire disgrace
670 Should whet my memory, though once forgot,
To make him an appendix of my plot.
His zeal to heaven made him his prince despise,
And load his person with indignities;
But zeal peculiar privilege affords,
675 Indulging latitude to deeds and words;
And Corah might for Agag's[9] murder call,
In terms as coarse as Samuel used to Saul.[1]
What others in his evidence did join
(The best that could be had for love or coin),
680 In Corah's own predicament will fall;
For *witness* is a common name to all.
    Surrounded thus with friends of every sort,
Deluded Absalom forsakes the court:
Impatient of high hopes, urged with renown,
685 And fired with near possession of a crown.
The admiring crowd are dazzled with surprise,
And on his goodly person feed their eyes:
His joy concealed, he sets himself to show,
On each side bowing popularly[2] low;
690 His looks, his gestures, and his words he frames,
And with familiar ease repeats their names.
Thus formed by nature, furnished out with arts,
He glides unfelt into their secret hearts.
Then, with a kind compassionating look,
695 And sighs, bespeaking pity ere he spoke,
Few words he said; but easy those and fit,
More slow than Hybla-drops,[3] and far more sweet.
    "I mourn, my countrymen, your lost estate;
Though far unable to prevent your fate:
700 Behold a banished man, for your dear cause
Exposed a prey to arbitrary laws!
Yet oh! that I alone could be undone,
Cut off from empire, and no more a son!
Now all your liberties a spoil are made;
705 Egypt° and Tyrus° intercept your trade,   *France / Holland*
And Jebusites your sacred rites invade.
My father, whom with reverence yet I name,
Charmed into ease, is careless of his fame;
And, bribed with petty sums of foreign gold,
710 Is grown in Bathsheba's[4] embraces old;

9. Agag is probably one of the five Catholic peers executed for the Popish Plot in 1680, most likely Lord Stafford, against whom Oates fabricated testimony. He is almost certainly not, as is usually suggested, Sir Edmund Berry Godfrey (see headnote, p. 38).
1. See 1 Samuel 15, where "Agag's murder" also occurs.

2. "So as to please the crowd" (Johnson's *Dictionary*).
3. The famous honey of Hybla in Sicily.
4. The woman with whom David committed adultery (2 Samuel 11). Here, Charles II's French mistress, Louise de Keroualle, duchess of Portsmouth.

Exalts his enemies, his friends destroys;
And all his power against himself employs.
He gives, and let him give, my right away;
But why should he his own, and yours betray?
715　He only, he can make the nation bleed,
And he alone from my revenge is freed.
Take then my tears (with that he wiped his eyes),
'Tis all the aid my present power supplies:
No court-informer can these arms accuse,
720　These arms may sons against their fathers use:
And 'tis my wish, the next successor's reign
May make no other Israelite complain."
　　Youth, beauty, graceful action seldom fail;
But common interest always will prevail;
725　And pity never ceases to be shown
To him who makes the people's wrongs his own.
The crowd (that still believe their kings oppress)
With lifted hands their young Messiah bless:
Who now begins his progress to ordain
730　With chariots, horsemen, and a numerous train;
From east to west his glories he displays,[5]
And, like the sun, the promised land surveys.
Fame runs before him as the morning star,
And shouts of joy salute him from afar:
735　Each house receives him as a guardian god,
And consecrates the place of his abode:
But hospitable treats did most commend
Wise Issachar,[6] his wealthy western friend.
This moving court, that caught the people's eyes,
740　And seemed but pomp, did other ends disguise:
Achitophel had formed it, with intent
To sound the depths, and fathom, where it went,
The people's hearts; distinguish friends from foes,
And try their strength, before they came to blows.
745　Yet all was colored with a smooth pretense
Of specious love, and duty to their prince.
Religion, and redress of grievances,
Two names that always cheat and always please,
Are often urged; and good King David's life
750　Endangered by a brother and a wife.[7]
Thus, in a pageant show, a plot is made,
And peace itself is war in masquerade.
O foolish Israel! never warned by ill,
Still the same bait, and circumvented still!
755　Did ever men forsake their present ease,
In midst of health imagine a disease;
Take pains contingent mischiefs to foresee,

5. In 1680 Monmouth made a progress through the west of England, seeking popular support for his cause.
6. Thomas Thynne of Longleat. He entertained Monmouth on his journey in the west. *Wise* is, of course, ironic.
7. Titus Oates had sworn that both James, duke of York, and the queen were involved in a similar plot to poison Charles II.

Make heirs for monarchs, and for God decree?
What shall we think! Can people give away
760   Both for themselves and sons, their native sway?
Then they are left defenseless to the sword
Of each unbounded, arbitrary lord:
And laws are vain, by which we right enjoy,
If kings unquestioned can those laws destroy.
765   Yet if the crowd be judge of fit and just,
And kings are only officers in trust,
Then this resuming covenant was declared
When kings were made, or is forever barred.
If those who gave the scepter could not tie
770   By their own deed their own posterity,
How then could Adam bind his future race?
How could his forfeit on mankind take place?
Or how could heavenly justice damn us all,
Who ne'er consented to our father's fall?
775   Then kings are slaves to those whom they command,
And tenants to their people's pleasure stand.
Add, that the power for property allowed
Is mischievously seated in the crowd;
For who can be secure of private right,
780   If sovereign sway may be dissolved by might?
Nor is the people's judgment always true:
The most may err as grossly as the few;
And faultless kings run down, by common cry,
For vice, oppression, and for tyranny.
785   What standard is there in a fickle rout,
Which, flowing to the mark,° runs faster out?   *highwater mark*
Nor only crowds, but Sanhedrins may be
Infected with this public lunacy,[8]
And share the madness of rebellious times,
790   To murder monarchs for imagined crimes.[9]
If they may give and take whene'er they please,
Not kings alone (the Godhead's images),
But government itself at length must fall
To nature's state, where all have right to all.
795   Yet, grant our lords the people kings can make,
What prudent men a settled throne would shake?
For whatsoe'er their sufferings were before,
That change they covet makes them suffer more.
All other errors but disturb a state,
800   But innovation is the blow of fate.
If ancient fabrics nod, and threat to fall,
To patch the flaws, and buttress up the wall,
Thus far 'tis duty; but here fix the mark;
For all beyond it is to touch our ark.[1]
805   To change foundations, cast the frame anew,

8. The fickle crowd flows and ebbs like the tide, which is pulled back and forth by the moon (hence "lunacy," after the Latin *luna*, or "moon").
9. An allusion to the execution of Charles I.

1. Uzzah was struck dead because he sacrilegiously touched the Ark of the Covenant (2 Samuel 6.6–7).

Is work for rebels, who base ends pursue,
At once divine and human laws control,
And mend the parts by ruin of the whole.
The tampering world is subject to this curse,
810   To physic their disease into a worse.
    Now what relief can righteous David bring?
How fatal 'tis to be too good a king!
Friends he has few, so high the madness grows:
Who dare be such, must be the people's foes:
815   Yet some there were, even in the worst of days;
Some let me name, and naming is to praise.
    In this short file Barzillai[2] first appears;
Barzillai, crowned with honor and with years:
Long since, the rising rebels he withstood
820   In regions waste, beyond the Jordan's flood:
Unfortunately brave to buoy the State;
But sinking underneath his master's fate:
In exile with his godlike prince he mourned;
For him he suffered, and with him returned.
825   The court he practiced, not the courtier's art:
Large was his wealth, but larger was his heart:
Which well the noblest objects knew to choose,
The fighting warrior, and recording Muse.
His bed could once a fruitful issue boast;
830   Now more than half a father's name is lost.
His eldest hope,[3] with every grace adorned,
By me (so Heaven will have it) always mourned,
And always honored, snatched in manhood's prime
By unequal fates, and Providence's crime:
835   Yet not before the goal of honor won,
All parts fulfilled of subject and of son;
Swift was the race, but short the time to run.
O narrow circle, but of power divine,
Scanted in space, but perfect in thy line!
840   By sea, by land, thy matchless worth was known,
Arms thy delight, and war was all thy own:
Thy force, infused, the fainting Tyrians° propped;   *the Dutch*
And haughty Pharaoh found his fortune stopped.
Oh ancient honor! Oh unconquered hand,
845   Whom foes unpunished never could withstand!
But Israel was unworthy of thy name:
Short is the date of all immoderate fame.
It looks as Heaven our ruin had designed,
And durst not trust thy fortune and thy mind.
850   Now, free from earth, thy disencumbered soul
Mounts up, and leaves behind the clouds and starry pole:
From thence thy kindred legions mayst thou bring,

2. James Butler, duke of Ormond (1610–1688), who was famous for his loyalty to the Stuart cause. He fought for Charles I in Ireland, and when that cause was hopeless, he joined Charles II in his exile abroad. He spent a large fortune on behalf of the king and continued to serve him loyally after the Restoration. Six of his ten children were dead (see line 830). Cf. 2 Samuel 19.31–39.
3. Ormond's son Thomas, earl of Ossory (1634–1680), a famous soldier and, like his father, devoted to Charles II.

To aid the guardian angel of thy king.
Here stop my Muse, here cease thy painful flight;
855 No pinions can pursue immortal height:
Tell good Barzillai thou canst sing no more,
And tell thy soul she should have fled before:
Or fled she with his life, and left this verse
To hang on her departed patron's hearse?
860 Now take thy steepy flight from heaven, and see
If thou canst find on earth another *he*:
Another *he* would be too hard to find;
See then whom thou canst see not far behind.
Zadoc[4] the priest, whom, shunning power and place,
865 His lowly mind advanced to David's grace:
With him the Sagan[5] of Jerusalem,
Of hospitable soul, and noble stem;
Him of the western dome,[6] whose weighty sense
Flows in fit words and heavenly eloquence.
870 The prophets' sons,[7] by such example led,
To learning and to loyalty were bred:
For colleges on bounteous kinds depend,
And never rebel was to arts a friend.
To these succeed the pillars of the laws,
875 Who best could plead, and best can judge a cause.
Next them a train of loyal peers ascend;
Sharp-judging Adriel,[8] the Muses' friend,
Himself a Muse—in Sanhedrin's debate
True to his prince, but not a slave of state:
880 Whom David's love with honors did adorn,
That from his disobedient son were torn.
Jotham[9] of piercing wit, and pregnant thought,
Indued by nature, and by learning taught
To move assemblies, who but only tried
885 The worse a while, then chose the better side;
Nor chose alone, but turned the balance too;
So much the weight of one brave man can do.
Hushar,[1] the friend of David in distress,
In public storms, of manly steadfastness:
890 By foreign treaties he informed his youth,
And joined experience to his native truth.
His frugal care supplied the wanting throne,
Frugal for that, but bounteous of his own:
'Tis easy conduct when exchequers flow,
895 But hard the task to manage well the low;
For sovereign power is too depressed or high,
When kings are forced to sell, or crowds to buy.
Indulge one labor more, my weary Muse,
For Amiel:[2] who can Amiel's praise refuse?

---

4. William Sancroft, archbishop of Canterbury.
5. Henry Compton, bishop of London.
6. John Dolben, dean of Westminster.
7. The boys of Westminster School, which Dryden had attended.

8. John Sheffield, earl of Mulgrave.
9. George Savile, marquis of Halifax.
1. Laurence Hyde, earl of Rochester.
2. Edward Seymour, speaker of the House of Commons.

900 Of ancient race by birth, but nobler yet
In his own worth, and without title great:
The Sanhedrin long time as chief he ruled,
Their reason guided, and their passion cooled:
So dexterous was he in the crown's defense,
905 So formed to speak a loyal nation's sense,
That, as their band was Israel's tribes in small,
So fit was he to represent them all.
Now rasher charioteers the seat ascend,
Whose loose careers his steady skill commend:°   *set off to advantage*
910 They like the unequal ruler of the day,
Misguide the seasons, and mistake the way;
While he withdrawn at their mad labor smiles,
And safe enjoys the sabbath of his toils.
    These were the chief, a small but faithful band ⎫
915 Of worthies, in the breach who dared to stand, ⎬
And tempt the united fury of the land. ⎭
With grief they viewed such powerful engines bent,
To batter down the lawful government:
A numerous faction, with pretended frights,
920 In Sanhedrins to plume° the regal rights;   *pluck, plunder*
The true successor from the court removed:[3]
The Plot, by hireling witnesses, improved.
These ills they saw, and, as their duty bound,
They showed the king the danger of the wound:
925 That no concessions from the throne would please,
But lenitives° fomented the disease;   *pain relievers*
That Absalom, ambitious of the crown,
Was made the lure to draw the people down;
That false Achitophel's pernicious hate
930 Had turned the Plot to ruin Church and State:
The council violent, the rabble worse;
That Shimei taught Jerusalem to curse.
    With all these loads of injuries oppressed,
And long revolving, in his careful breast,
935 The event of things, at last, his patience tired,
Thus from his royal throne, by Heaven inspired,
The godlike David spoke: with awful fear
His train their Maker in their master hear.
    "Thus long have I, by native mercy swayed,
940 My wrongs dissembled, my revenge delayed:
So willing to forgive the offending age,
So much the father did the king assuage.
But now so far my clemency they slight,
The offenders question my forgiving right.
945 That one was made for many, they contend;
But 'tis to rule; for that's a monarch's end.
They call my tenderness of blood, my fear;
Though manly tempers can the longest bear.
Yet, since they will divert my native course,

---

3. The duke of York had been banished from England.

950   'Tis time to show I am not good by force.
       Those heaped affronts that haughty subjects bring,
       Are burdens for a camel, not a king:
       Kings are the public pillars of the State,
       Born to sustain and prop the nation's weight:
955   If my young Samson will pretend a call
       To shake the column, let him share the fall:[4]
       But, oh, that yet he would repent and live!
       How easy 'tis for parents to forgive!
       With how few tears a pardon might be won
960   From nature, pleading for a darling son!
       Poor pitied youth, by my paternal care
       Raised up to all the height his frame could bear:
       Had God ordained his fate for empire born,
       He would have given his soul another turn:
965   Gulled° with a patriot's name, whose modern sense   *deceived*
       Is one that would by law supplant his prince:
       The people's brave,° the politician's tool;   *bully*
       Never was patriot yet, but was a fool.
       Whence comes it that religion and the laws
970   Should more be Absalom's than David's cause?
       His old instructor,[5] ere he lost his place,
       Was never thought indued with so much grace.
       Good heavens, how faction can a patriot paint!
       My rebel ever proves my people's saint:
975   Would *they* impose an heir upon the throne?
       Let Sanhedrins be taught to give their own.°   *what's theirs to give*
       A king's at least a part of government,
       And mine as requisite as their consent;
       Without my leave a future king to choose,
980   Infers a right the present to depose:
       True, they petition me to approve their choice;
       But Esau's hands suit ill with Jacob's voice.[6]
       My pious subjects for my safety pray,
       Which to secure, they take my power away.
985   From plots and treasons Heaven preserve my years,
       But save me most from my petitioners.
       Unsatiate as the barren womb or grave;
       God cannot grant so much as they can crave.
       What then is left but with a jealous eye
990   To guard the small remains of royalty?
       The law shall still direct my peaceful sway,
       And the same law teach rebels to obey:
       Votes shall no more established power control—
       Such votes as make a part exceed the whole:
995   No groundless clamors shall my friends remove,
       Nor crowds have power to punish ere they prove:
       For gods and godlike kings, their care express,
       Still to defend their servants in distress.

4. Judges 16.   6. Genesis 27.22.
5. The earl of Shaftesbury.

O that my power to saving were confined: ⎫
1000 Why am I forced, like Heaven, against my mind, ⎬
To make examples of another kind? ⎭
Must I at length the sword of justice draw?
O curst effects of necessary law!
How ill my fear they by my mercy scan!°   *judge*
1005 Beware the fury of a patient man.
Law they require, let Law then show her face;
They could not be content to look on Grace,
Her hinder parts, but with a daring eye
To tempt the terror of her front and die.[7]
1010 By their own arts, 'tis righteously decreed,
Those dire artificers of death shall bleed.
Against themselves their witnesses will swear,
Till viper-like their mother Plot they tear:
And suck for nutriment that bloody gore,
1015 Which was their principle of life before.
Their Belial with their Belzebub[8] will fight;
Thus on my foes, my foes shall do me right:
Nor doubt the event; for factious crowds engage,
In their first onset, all their brutal rage.
1020 Then let 'em take an unresisted course,
Retire and traverse,° and delude their force: *thwart*
But when they stand all breathless, urge the fight,
And rise upon 'em with redoubled might:
For lawful power is still superior found,
1025 When long driven back, at length it stands the ground."
    He said. The Almighty, nodding, gave consent;
And peals of thunder shook the firmament.
Henceforth a series of new time began,
The mighty years in long procession ran:
1030 Once more the godlike David was restored,
And willing nations knew their lawful lord.

                                                   1681

Mac Flecknoe   The target of this superb satire, which is cast in the form of a mock-heroic episode, is Thomas Shadwell (1640–1692), the playwright, with whom Dryden had been on good terms for a number of years, certainly as late as March 1678. Shadwell considered himself the successor of Ben Jonson and the champion of the type of comedy that Jonson had written, the "comedy of humors," in which each character is presented under the domination of a single psychological trait or eccentricity, his humor. His plays are not without merit, but they are often clumsy and prolix and certainly much inferior to Jonson's. For many years he had conducted a public argument with Dryden on the merits of Jonson's comedies, which he thought Dryden undervalued. Exactly what moved Dryden to attack him is a matter of conjecture: he may simply have grown progressively bored and irritated by Shadwell and his tedious argument. The poem seems to have been written in late 1678 or 1679

---

7. Moses was not allowed to see the countenance of Jehovah (Exodus 33.20–23).

8. A god of the Philistines. "Belial": the incarnation of all evil.

and to have circulated only in manuscript until it was printed in 1682 in a pirated edition by an obscure publisher. By that time, the two playwrights were alienated by politics as well as by literary quarrels. Shadwell was a violent Whig and the reputed author of a sharp attack on Dryden as the Tory author of *Absalom and Achitophel* and "The Medal." It was probably for this reason that the printer added the subtitle referring to Shadwell's Whiggism in the phrase "true-blue-Protestant poet." Political passions were running high, and sales would be helped if the poem seemed to refer to the events of the day.

Whereas Butler had debased and degraded his victims by using burlesque, caricature, and the grotesque, Dryden exposed Shadwell to ridicule by using the devices of mock epic, which treats the low, mean, or absurd in the grand language, lofty style, and solemn tone of epic poetry. The obvious disparity between subject and style makes the satiric point. In 1678, a prolific, untalented writer, Richard Flecknoe, died. Dryden conceived the idea of presenting Shadwell (the self-proclaimed heir of Ben Jonson, the laureate) as the son and successor of Flecknoe (an irony also because Flecknoe was a Catholic priest)—hence *Mac* (son of) *Flecknoe*—from whom he inherits the throne of dullness. Flecknoe in the triple role of king, priest, and poet hails his successor, pronounces a panegyric on his perfect fitness for the throne, anoints and crowns him, foretells his glorious reign, and as he sinks (leaden dullness cannot soar), leaves his mantle to fall symbolically on Shadwell's shoulders. The poem abounds in literary allusions—to Roman legend and history and to the *Aeneid*, to Cowley's fragmentary epic *The Davideis*, to *Paradise Lost*, and to Shadwell's own plays. Biblical allusions add an unexpected dimension of incongruous dignity to the low scene. The coronation takes place in the City, to the plaudits of the citizens, who are fit to admire only what is dull. In 217 lines, Dryden created an image of Shadwell that has fixed his reputation to this day.

Mac Flecknoe

Or a Satire upon the True-Blue-Protestant Poet, T. S.

All human things are subject to decay,
And when fate summons, monarchs must obey.
This Flecknoe found, who, like Augustus,[1] young
Was called to empire, and had governed long;
5　In prose and verse, was owned, without dispute,
Through all the realms of Nonsense, absolute.
This aged prince, now flourishing in peace,
And blest with issue of a large increase,
Worn out with business, did at length debate
10　To settle the succession of the state;
And, pondering which of all his sons was fit
To reign, and wage immortal war with wit,
Cried: "'Tis resolved; for nature pleads that he
Should only rule, who most resembles me.
15　Sh——[2] alone my perfect image bears,
Mature in dullness from his tender years:
Sh—— alone, of all my sons, is he

---

1. In 31 B.C.E. Octavian became the first Roman emperor, at the age of thirty-two. He assumed the title Augustus in 27 B.C.E.
2. Thomas Shadwell. The initial and second letter of the name followed by a dash give the appearance, but only the appearance, of protecting Dryden's victim by concealing his name. A common device in the satire of the period.

Who stands confirmed in full stupidity.
The rest to some faint meaning make pretense,
20   But Sh—— never deviates into sense.
Some beams of wit on other souls may fall,
Strike through, and make a lucid interval;
But Sh——'s genuine night admits no ray,
His rising fogs prevail upon the day.
25   Besides, his goodly fabric[3] fills the eye,
And seems designed for thoughtless majesty:
Thoughtless as monarch oaks that shade the plain,
And, spread in solemn state, supinely reign.
Heywood and Shirley were but types of thee,[4]
30   Thou last great prophet of tautology.[5]
Even I, a dunce of more renown than they,
Was sent before but to prepare thy way;
And, coarsely clad in Norwich drugget,° came   *coarse woolen cloth*
To teach the nations in thy greater name.[6]
35   My warbling lute, the lute I whilom° strung,   *formerly*
When to King John of Portugal[7] I sung,
Was but the prelude to that glorious day,
When thou on silver Thames didst cut thy way,
With well-timed oars before the royal barge,
40   Swelled with the pride of thy celestial charge;
And big with hymn, commander of a host,
The like was ne'er in Epsom blankets tossed.[8]
Methinks I see the new Arion[9] sail,
The lute still trembling underneath thy nail.
45   At thy well-sharpened thumb from shore to shore
The treble squeaks for fear, the basses roar;
Echoes from Pissing Alley[1] Sh—— call,
And Sh—— they resound from Aston Hall.
About thy boat the little fishes throng,
50   As at the morning toast° that floats along.   *sewage*
Sometimes, as prince of thy harmonious band,
Thou wield'st thy papers in thy threshing hand,
St. André's[2] feet ne'er kept more equal time,
Not ev'n the feet of thy own *Psyche's* rhyme;
55   Though they in number as in sense excel:

---

3. His body. Shadwell was a corpulent man.
4. Thomas Heywood (ca. 1570–1641) and James Shirley (1596–1666), playwrights popular before the closing of the theaters in 1642 but now out of fashion. They are introduced here as "types" (i.e., prefigurings) of Shadwell, in the sense that Solomon was regarded as an Old Testament prefiguring of Christ, the "last [final] great prophet."
5. Unnecessary repetition of meaning in different words.
6. The parallel between Flecknoe, as forerunner of Shadwell, and John the Baptist, as forerunner of Jesus, is made plain in lines 32–34 by the use of details and even words taken from Matthew 3.3–4 and John 1.23.

7. Flecknoe boasted of the patronage of the Portuguese king.
8. A reference to Shadwell's comedy *Epsom Wells* and to the farcical scene in his *Virtuoso*, in which Sir Samuel Hearty is tossed in a blanket.
9. A legendary Greek poet. Returning home by sea, he was robbed and thrown overboard by the sailors, but was saved by a dolphin that had been charmed by his music.
1. Actual London street name, changed to Little Friday Street in 1848.
2. A French dancer who designed the choreography of Shadwell's opera *Psyche* (1675). Dryden's sneer at the mechanical metrics of the songs in *Psyche* is justified.

So just, so like tautology, they fell,
That, pale with envy, Singleton[3] forswore
The lute and sword, which he in triumph bore, ⎤
And vowed he ne'er would act Villerius[4] more." ⎦

60 Here stopped the good old sire, and wept for joy
In silent raptures of the hopeful boy.
All arguments, but most his plays, persuade,
That for anointed dullness[5] he was made.
    Close to the walls which fair Augusta° bind   *London*
65 (The fair Augusta much to fears inclined),[6]
An ancient fabric,° raised to inform the sight,   *building*
There stood of yore, and Barbican it hight:°   *was called*
A watchtower once; but now, so fate ordains,
Of all the pile an empty name remains.
70 From its old ruins brothel houses rise,
Scenes of lewd loves, and of polluted joys,
Where their vast courts the mother-strumpets keep,
And, undisturbed by watch, in silence sleep.
Near these a Nursery[7] erects its head,
75 Where queens are formed, and future heroes bred;
Where unfledged actors learn to laugh and cry, ⎤
Where infant punks° their tender voices try,   ⎬   *prostitutes*
And little Maximins[8] the gods defy.   ⎦
Great Fletcher[9] never treads in buskins here,
80 Nor greater Jonson dares in socks[1] appear;
But gentle Simkin[2] just reception finds
Amidst this monument of vanished minds:
Pure clinches° the suburbian Muse affords,   *puns*
And Panton[3] waging harmless war with words.
85 Here Flecknoe, as a place to fame well known,
Ambitiously design'd his Sh——'s throne;
For ancient Dekker[4] prophesied long since, ⎤
That in this pile would reign a mighty prince, ⎬
Born for a scourge of wit, and flail of sense; ⎦
90 To whom true dullness should some *Psyches* owe,
But worlds of *Misers* from his pen should flow;
Humorists and *Hypocrites*[5] it should produce,
Whole Raymond families, and tribes of Bruce.[6]
    Now Empress Fame had published the renown
95 Of Sh——'s coronation through the town.
Roused by report of Fame, the nations meet,

3. John Singleton (d. 1686), a musician at the
Theatre Royal.
4. A character in Sir William Davenant's *Siege
of Rhodes* (1656), the first English opera.
5. The anticipated phrase is "anointed *majesty*."
English kings are anointed with oil at their
coronations.
6. This line alludes to the fears excited by the
Popish Plot (cf. *Absalom and Achitophel*, p. 38).
7. The name of a training school for young actors.
8. Maximin is the cruel emperor, in Dryden's
Tyrannic Love (1669), notorious for his bombast.
9. John Fletcher (1579–1625), the playwright

and collaborator with Francis Beaumont (ca.
1584–1616).
1. "Buskins" and "socks" were the symbols of
tragedy and comedy, respectively.
2. A popular character in low farces.
3. Said to have been a celebrated punster.
4. Thomas Dekker (ca. 1572–1632), the playwright, whom Jonson had satirized in *The
Poetaster*.
5. Three of Shadwell's plays; *The Hypocrite*, a
failure, was not published.
6. Raymond and Bruce are characters in *The
Humorists* and *The Virtuoso*, respectively.

From near Bunhill, and distant Watling Street.[7]
No Persian carpets spread the imperial way,
But scattered limbs of mangled poets lay;
100   From dusty shops neglected authors come,
Martyrs of pies, and relics of the bum.[8]
Much Heywood, Shirley, Ogilby[9] there lay,
But loads of Sh—— almost choked the way.
Bilked stationers for yeomen stood prepared,
105   And Herringman was captain of the guard.[1]
The hoary prince in majesty appeared,
High on a throne of his own labors reared.
At his right hand our young Ascanius sate,
Rome's other hope, and pillar of the state.
110   His brows thick fogs, instead of glories, grace,
And lambent dullness played around his face.[2]
As Hannibal did to the altars come,
Sworn by his sire a mortal foe to Rome,[3]
So Sh—— swore, nor should his vow be vain,
115   That he till death true dullness would maintain;
And, in his father's right, and realm's defense,
Ne'er to have peace with wit, nor truce with sense.
The king himself the sacred unction[4] made,
As king by office, and as priest by trade.
120   In his siníster° hand, instead of ball,   *left*
He placed a mighty mug of potent ale;
Love's Kingdom to his right he did convey,
At once his scepter, and his rule of sway;
Whose righteous lore the prince had practiced young,
125   And from whose loins recorded *Psyche* sprung.
His temples, last, with poppies were o'erspread,
That nodding seemed to consecrate his head.[5]
Just at that point of time, if fame not lie,
On his left hand twelve reverend owls did fly.[6]
130   So Romulus, 'tis sung, by Tiber's brook,
Presage of sway from twice six vultures took.
The admiring throng loud acclamations make,
And omens of his future empire take.
The sire then shook the honors[7] of his head,

7. Because Bunhill is about a quarter mile and Watling Street little more than a half mile from the site of the Nursery, where the coronation is held, Shadwell's fame is narrowly circumscribed. Moreover, his subjects live in the heart of the City, regarded by men of wit and fashion as the abode of bad taste and middle-class vulgarity.
8. Unsold books were used to line pie plates and as toilet paper.
9. John Ogilby, a translator of Homer and Virgil, ridiculed by both Dryden and Pope as a bad poet.
1. "Bilked stationers": cheated publishers, acting as "yeomen" of the guard, led by Henry Herringman, who until 1679 was the publisher of both Shadwell and Dryden.
2. Ascanius, or Iulus, was the son of Aeneas. Virgil referred to him as *"spes altera Romae"* ("Rome's other hope," *Aeneid* 12.168). As Troy fell, he was marked as favored by the gods when a flickering

("lambent") flame played round his head (*Aeneid* 2.680–84).
3. Hannibal, who almost conquered Rome in 216 B.C.E., during the second Punic War, took this oath at the age of nine (Livy 21.1).
4. The sacramental oil, used in the coronation.
5. During the coronation a British monarch holds two symbols of the throne: a globe ("ball") representing the world in the left hand and a scepter in the right. Shadwell's symbols of monarchy are a mug of ale, Flecknoe's dreary play *Love's Kingdom*, and a crown of poppies, which suggest heaviness, dullness, and drowsiness. The poppies also refer obliquely to Shadwell's addiction to opium.
6. Birds of night. Appropriate substitutes for the twelve vultures whose flight confirmed to Romulus the destined site of Rome, of which he was founder and king.
7. Ornaments, hence locks.

135 And from his brows damps of oblivion shed
   Full on the filial dullness: long he stood,
   Repelling from his breast the raging god; }
   At length burst out in this prophetic mood:
      "Heavens bless my son, from Ireland let him reign
140 To far Barbadoes on the western main;[8]
   Of his dominion may no end be known,
   And greater than his father's be his throne;
   Beyond *Love's Kingdom* let him stretch his pen!"
   He paused, and all the people cried, "Amen."
145 Then thus continued he: "My son, advance
   Still in new impudence, new ignorance.
   Success let others teach, learn thou from me
   Pangs without birth, and fruitless industry.
   Let *Virtuosos* in five years be writ;
150 Yet not one thought accuse thy toil of wit.
   Let gentle George[9] in triumph tread the stage,
   Make Dorimant betray, and Loveit rage;
   Let Cully, Cockwood, Fopling, charm the pit,
   And in their folly show the writer's wit.
155 Yet still thy fools shall stand in thy defense,
   And justify their author's want of sense.
   Let 'em be all by thy own model made
   Of dullness, and desire no foreign aid;
   That they to future ages may be known,
160 Not copies drawn, but issue of thy own.
   Nay, let thy men of wit too be the same,
   All full of thee, and differing but in name.
   But let no alien S—dl—y[1] interpose,
   To lard with wit[2] thy hungry *Epsom* prose.
165 And when false flowers of rhetoric thou wouldst cull,
   Trust nature, do not labor to be dull;
   But write thy best, and top; and, in each line,
   Sir Formal's[3] oratory will be thine:
   Sir Formal, though unsought, attends thy quill,
170 And does thy northern dedications[4] fill.
   Nor let false friends seduce thy mind to fame,
   By arrogating Jonson's hostile name.
   Let father Flecknoe fire thy mind with praise,
   And uncle Ogilby thy envy raise.
175 Thou art my blood, where Jonson has no part:
   What share have we in nature, or in art?
   Where did his wit on learning fix a brand,
   And rail at arts he did not understand?
   Where made he love in Prince Nicander's vein,[5]

8. Shadwell's empire is vast but empty.
9. Sir George Etherege (ca. 1635–1691), a writer of brilliant comedies. In the next couplet Dryden names characters from his plays.
1. Sir Charles Sedley (1638–1701), wit, rake, poet, and playwright. Dryden hints that he contributed more than the prologue to Shadwell's *Epsom Wells*.

2. This phrase recalls a sentence in Burton's *Anatomy of Melancholy*: "They lard their lean books with the fat of others' works."
3. Sir Formal Trifle, the ridiculous and vapid orator in *The Virtuoso*.
4. Shadwell frequently dedicated his works to the duke of Newcastle and members of his family.
5. In *Psyche*.

180 Or swept the dust in *Psyche's* humble strain?
Where sold he bargains, 'whip-stitch,[6] kiss my arse,'
Promised a play and dwindled to a farce?[7]
When did his Muse from Fletcher scenes purloin,
As thou whole Eth'rege dost transfuse to thine?
185 But so transfused, as oil on water's flow,
His always floats above, thine sinks below.
This is thy province, this thy wondrous way,
New humors to invent for each new play:
This is that boasted bias[8] of thy mind,
190 By which one way, to dullness, 'tis inclined;
Which makes thy writings lean on one side still,
And, in all changes, that way bends thy will.
Nor let thy mountain-belly make pretense
Of likeness; thine's a tympany[9] of sense.
195 A tun° of man in thy large bulk is writ,   large cask
But sure thou'rt but a kilderkin° of wit.   small cask
Like mine, thy gentle numbers feebly creep;
Thy tragic Muse gives smiles, thy comic sleep.
With whate'er gall thou sett'st thyself to write,
200 Thy inoffensive satires never bite.
In thy felonious heart though venom lies,
It does but touch thy Irish pen,[1] and dies.
Thy genius calls thee not to purchase fame
In keen iambics,° but mild anagram.   sharp satire
205 Leave writing plays, and choose for thy command
Some peaceful province in acrostic[2] land.
There thou may'st wings display and altars raise,[3]
And torture one poor word ten thousand ways.
Or, if thou wouldst thy different talent suit,
210 Set thy own songs, and sing them to thy lute."
    He said: but his last words were scarcely heard ⎤
For Bruce and Longville had a trap prepared,   ⎬
And down they sent the yet declaiming bard.[4] ⎦
Sinking he left his drugget robe behind,
215 Borne upwards by a subterranean wind.
The mantle fell to the young prophet's part,[5]
With double portion of his father's art.

ca. 1679   1682

6. A nonsense word frequently used by Sir Samuel Hearty in *The Virtuoso*. "Sold...bargains": answered an innocent question with a coarse or indecent phrase, as in this line.
7. Low comedy that depends largely on situation rather than wit, consistently condemned by Dryden and other serious playwrights.
8. In bowling, the spin given to the ball that causes it to swerve. Dryden closely parodies a passage in Shadwell's epilogue to *The Humorists*.
9. A swelling in some part of the body caused by wind.
1. Dryden accuses Flecknoe and his "son" of being Irish. Ireland suggested only poverty, superstition, and barbarity to 17th-century Londoners.
2. A poem in which the first letter of each line,

read downward, makes up the name of the person or thing that is the subject of the poem. "Anagram": the transposition of letters in a word so as to make a new one.
3. "Wings" and "altars" refer to poems in the shape of these objects as in George Herbert's "Easter Wings" and "The Altar." Dryden is citing instances of triviality and overingenuity in literature.
4. In *The Virtuoso*, Bruce and Longville play this trick on Sir Formal Trifle while he makes a speech.
5. When the prophet Elijah was carried to heaven in a chariot of fire borne on a whirlwind, his mantle fell on his successor, the younger prophet Elisha (2 Kings 2.8–14). Flecknoe, prophet of dullness, naturally cannot ascend, but must sink.

To the Memory of Mr. Oldham[1]

Farewell, too little, and too lately known,
Whom I began to think and call my own:
For sure our souls were near allied, and thine
Cast in the same poetic mold with mine.
5   One common note on either lyre did strike,
And knaves and fools[2] we both abhorred alike.
To the same goal did both our studies drive;
The last set out the soonest did arrive.
Thus Nisus fell upon the slippery place,
10 While his young friend[3] performed and won the race.
O early ripe! to thy abundant store
What could advancing age have added more?
It might (what nature never gives the young)
Have taught the numbers° of thy native tongue.   *metrics, verse*
15 But satire needs not those, and wit will shine
Through the harsh cadence of a rugged line.[4]
A noble error, and but seldom made,
When poets are by too much force betrayed.
Thy generous fruits, though gathered ere their prime,   ⎫
20 Still showed a quickness;[5] and maturing time   ⎬
But mellows what we write to the dull sweets of rhyme.   ⎭
Once more, hail and farewell;[6] farewell, thou young,
But ah too short, Marcellus[7] of our tongue;
Thy brows with ivy, and with laurels bound;[8]
25 But fate and gloomy night encompass thee around.

1684

A Song for St. Cecilia's Day[1]

1

From harmony, from heavenly harmony
This universal frame began:

1. John Oldham (1653–1683), the young poet whose *Satires upon the Jesuits* (1681), which Dryden admired, were written in 1679, before Dryden's major satires appeared (see line 8). This elegy was published in Oldham's *Remains in Verse and Prose* (1684).
2. Objects of satire.
3. Nisus, on the point of winning a footrace, slipped in a pool of blood. His "young friend" was Euryalus (Virgil's *Aeneid* 5.315–39).
4. Dryden repeats the Renaissance idea that the satirist should avoid smoothness and affect rough meters ("harsh cadence").
5. Sharpness of flavor.
6. Dryden echoes the famous words that conclude Catullus's elegy to his brother: "*Atque in perpetuum, frater, ave atque vale*" (And forever, brother, hail and farewell!).
7. The nephew of Augustus, adopted by him as his successor. After winning military fame as a youth, he died at the age of twenty. Virgil celebrated him in the *Aeneid* 6.854–86. The last line of Dryden's poem is a reminiscence of *Aeneid* 6.866.
8. The poet's wreath (cf. Milton's *Lycidas*, lines 1–2).
1. St. Cecilia, a Roman lady, was an early Christian martyr. She has long been regarded as the patroness of music and the supposed inventor of the organ. Celebrations of her festival day (November 22) in England were usually devoted to music and the praise of music, and from about 1683 to 1703 the Musical Society in London annually commemorated it with a religious service and a public concert. This concert always included an ode written and set to music for the occasion, of which the two by Dryden ("A Song for St. Cecilia's

When Nature underneath a heap
        Of jarring atoms lay,
5   And could not heave her head,
The tuneful voice was heard from high:
        "Arise, ye more than dead."
Then cold, and hot, and moist, and dry,[2]
        In order to their stations leap,
10   And Music's power obey.
From harmony, from heavenly harmony
        This universal frame began:
        From harmony to harmony
Through all the compass of the notes it ran,
15   The diapason[3] closing full in man.

2

What passion cannot Music raise and quell![4]
        When Jubal struck the corded shell,[5]
        His listening brethren stood around,
        And, wondering, on their faces fell
20   To worship that celestial sound.
Less than a god they thought there could not dwell
        Within the hollow of that shell
        That spoke so sweetly and so well.
What passion cannot Music raise and quell!

3

25   The trumpet's loud clangor
        Excites us to arms,
With shrill notes of anger,
        And mortal alarms.
The double double double beat
30   Of the thundering drum
Cries: "Hark! the foes come;
Charge, charge, 'tis too late to retreat."

Day," 1687, and "Alexander's Feast," 1697) are the most distinguished. G. B. Draghi, an Italian brought to England by Charles II, set this ode to music; but Handel's fine score, composed in 1739, has completely obscured the original setting. This is an irregular ode in the manner of Cowley. In stanzas 3–6, Dryden boldly attempted to suggest in the sounds of his words the characteristic tones of the instruments mentioned.
2. "Nature": created nature, ordered by the Divine Wisdom out of chaos, which Dryden, adopting the physics of the Greek philosopher Epicurus, describes as composed of the warring and discordant ("jarring") atoms of the four elements: earth, fire, water, and air ("cold," "hot," "moist," and "dry").
3. The entire compass of tones in the scale.

Dryden is thinking of the Chain of Being, the ordered creation from inanimate nature up to humans, God's latest and final work. The just gradations of notes in a scale are analogous to the equally just gradations in the ascending scale of created beings. Both are the result of harmony.
4. The power of music to describe, evoke, or subdue emotion ("passion") is a frequent theme in 17th-century literature. In stanzas 2–6, the poet considers music as awakening religious awe, warlike courage, sorrow for unrequited love, jealousy and fury, and the impulse to worship God.
5. According to Genesis 4.21, Jubal was the inventor of the lyre and the pipe. Dryden imagines Jubal's lyre to have been made of a tortoiseshell ("corded shell").

4

The soft complaining flute
In dying notes discovers
35   The woes of hopeless lovers,
Whose dirge is whispered by the warbling lute.

5

Sharp violins[6] proclaim
Their jealous pangs, and desperation,
Fury, frantic indignation,
40   Depth of pains, and height of passion,
For the fair, disdainful dame.

6

But O! what art can teach,
What human voice can reach,
The sacred organ's praise?
45   Notes inspiring holy love,
Notes that wing their heavenly ways
To mend the choirs above.

7

Orpheus[7] could lead the savage race;
And trees unrooted left their place,
50   Sequacious of° the lyre;   *following*
But bright Cecilia raised the wonder higher:
When to her organ vocal breath was given,
An angel heard, and straight appeared,[8]
Mistaking earth for heaven.

GRAND CHORUS

55   *As from the power of sacred lays*
      The spheres began to move,
And sung the great Creator's praise[9]
      To all the blest above;
So, when the last and dreadful hour
60   *This crumbling pageant*[1] *shall devour,*
The trumpet shall be heard on high, ⎤
The dead shall live, the living die, ⎬
And Music shall untune the sky.[2] ⎦

1687

6. A reference to the bright tone of the modern violin, introduced into England at the Restoration. The tone of the old-fashioned viol is much duller.
7. Legendary poet, son of one of the Muses, who played so wonderfully on the lyre that wild beasts ("the savage race") grew tame and followed him, as did even rocks and trees.
8. According to the legend, it was Cecilia's piety, not her music, that brought an angel to visit her.
9. As it was harmony that ordered the universe, so it was angelic song ("sacred lays") that put the celestial bodies ("spheres") in motion. The harmonious chord that results from the traditional "music of the spheres" is a hymn of "praise" sung by created nature to its "Creator."
1. The universe, the stage on which the drama of human salvation has been acted out.
2. The "last trump" of 1 Corinthians 15.52, which will announce the Resurrection and the Last Judgment.

Epigram on Milton[1]

Three poets,[2] in three distant ages born,
Greece, Italy, and England did adorn.
The first in loftiness of thought surpassed,
The next in majesty, in both the last:
5 The force of Nature could no farther go;
To make a third, she joined the former two.

1688

Alexander's Feast[1]

Or the Power of Music; An Ode in Honor of St. Cecilia's Day

I

'Twas at the royal feast, for Persia won
    By Philip's[2] warlike son:
  Aloft in awful state
  The godlike hero sate
5   On his imperial throne;
  His valiant peers were placed around;
Their brows with roses and with myrtles[3] bound:
  (So should desert in arms be crowned).
The lovely Thaïs, by his side,
10 Sate like a blooming Eastern bride
In flower of youth and beauty's pride.
    Happy, happy, happy pair!
    None but the brave,
    None but the brave,
15   None but the brave deserves the fair.

CHORUS

Happy, happy, happy pair!
None but the brave,
None but the brave,
None but the brave deserves the fair.

1. Engraved beneath the portrait of Milton in Jacob Tonson's edition of *Paradise Lost* (1688).
2. I.e., Homer, Virgil, and Milton.
1. After his defeat of the Persian emperor Darius III and the fall of the Persian capital Persepolis (331 B.C.E.), Alexander the Great held a feast for his officers. Thaïs his Athenian mistress, persuaded him to set fire to the palace in revenge for the burning of Athens by the Persians under Xerxes in 480 B.C.E. According to Plutarch, Alexander was moved by love and wine, not by music, but Dryden, perhaps altering an old tradition that Alexander's musician Timotheus once by his flute-playing caused the hero to start up and arm himself, attributes the burning of Persepolis to the power of music. The original music was by Jeremiah Clarke, but Handel's score of 1736 is better known.
2. King Philip II of Macedonia, father of Alexander the Great.
3. Emblems of love. The Greeks and Romans wore wreaths of flowers at banquets.

2

20 Timotheus, placed on high
        Amid the tuneful choir,
            With flying fingers touched the lyre:
    The trembling notes ascend the sky,
            And heavenly joys inspire.
25 The song began from Jove,
    Who left his blissful seats above
    (Such is the power of mighty love).
    A dragon's fiery form belied the god:[4]
    Sublime on radiant spires[5] he rode,
30   When he to fair Olympia pressed;
            And while he sought her snowy breast:
    Then, round her slender waist he curled,
    And stamped an image of himself, a sovereign of the world.
    The listening crowd admire° the lofty sound: *wonder at*
35 "A present deity," they shout around;
    "A present deity," the vaulted roofs rebound.
        With ravished ears
        The monarch hears,
        Assumes the god,
40   Affects to nod,
    And seems to shake the spheres.[6]

CHORUS

With ravished ears
The monarch hears,
Assumes the god,
45 *Affects to nod,*
    And seems to shake the spheres.

3

    The praise of Bacchus° then the sweet musician sung,   *god of wine*
        Of Bacchus ever fair and ever young:
            The jolly god in triumph comes;
50   Sound the trumpets; beat the drums;
                Flushed with a purple grace
                He shows his honest face:
    Now give the hautboys° breath; he comes, he comes!   *oboes*
            Bacchus, ever fair and young
55   Drinking joys did first ordain;
        Bacchus' blessings are a treasure,
        Drinking is a soldier's pleasure;
            Rich the treasure,

---

4. An oracle had declared that Alexander was the son of Zeus ("Jove") by Philip's wife Olympias (not, as Dryden calls her in line 30, "Olympia"), thus conferring on him that semidivinity often claimed by heroes. Zeus habitually conducted his amours with mortals in the guise of an animal, in this case a dragon.

5. High on shining coils ("radiant spires"). "Spires" for the coils of a serpent is derived from the Latin word *spira*, which Virgil use in this sense, *Aeneid* 2.217 (cf. *Paradise Lost* 9.502).
6. According to Virgil (*Aeneid* 10.115) the nod of Jove causes earthquakes.

Sweet the pleasure,
60 Sweet is pleasure after pain.

CHORUS

Bacchus' blessings are a treasure,
Drinking is the soldier's pleasure;
 Rich the treasure,
 Sweet the pleasure,
65 *Sweet is pleasure after pain.*

4

Soothed with the sound, the king grew vain;
 Fought all his battles o'er again,
And thrice he routed all his foes, and thrice he slew the slain.
The master saw the madness rise,
70 His glowing cheeks, his ardent eyes;
And, while he° heaven and earth defied,   *Alexander*
Changed his° hand, and checked his° pride. *Timotheus's / Alexander's*
 He chose a mournful Muse,
  Soft pity to infuse:
75 He sung Darius great and good,
  By too severe a fate
Fallen, fallen, fallen, fallen,
  Fallen from his high estate,
   And weltering in his blood;
80 Deserted at his utmost need
By those his former bounty fed;
On the bare earth exposed he lies,
With not a friend to close his eyes.[7]
With downcast looks the joyless victor sate,
85 Revolving° in his altered soul   *pondering*
  The various turns of chance below;
And, now and then, a sigh he stole,
And tears began to flow.

CHORUS

Revolving in his altered soul
90 *The various turns of chance below;*
 And, now and then, a sigh he stole,
 And tears began to flow.

5

The mighty master smiled to see
That love was in the next degree;
95 'Twas but[8] a kindred sound to move,
For pity melts the mind to love.
 Softly sweet, in Lydian[9] measures,

---

7. After his final defeat by Alexander, Darius was assassinated by his own followers.
8. I.e., it was necessary only.

9. In Greek music the Lydian mode expressed the plaintive and the sad.

Soon he soothed his soul to pleasures.
"War," he sung, "is toil and trouble;
100 Honor, but an empty bubble.
   Never ending, still beginning,
Fighting still, and still destroying:
   If the world be worth thy winning,
Think, O think it worth enjoying.
105   Lovely Thaïs sits beside thee,
   Take the good the gods provide thee."
The many° rend the skies with loud applause;   *crowd, retinue*
So Love was crowned, but Music won the cause.
   The prince, unable to conceal his pain,
110   Gazed on the fair
       Who caused his care,
   And sighed and looked, sighed and looked,
Sighed and looked, and sighed again:
At length, with love and wine at once oppressed,
115 The vanquished victor sunk upon her breast.

CHORUS

The prince, unable to conceal his pain,
    Gazed on the fair
    Who caused his care,
  And sighed and looked, sighed and looked,
120 *Sighed and looked, and sighed again:*
    At length, with love and wine at once oppressed,
    The vanquished victor sunk upon her breast.

6

Now strike the golden lyre again:
A louder yet, and yet a louder strain.
125 Break his bands of sleep asunder,
And rouse him, like a rattling peal of thunder.
    Hark, hark, the horrid° sound   *rough*
      Has raised up his head:
      As waked from the dead,
130   And amazed, he stares around,
"Revenge, revenge!" Timotheus cries,
    "See the Furies[1] arise!
   See the snakes that they rear,
   How they hiss in their hair,
135   And the sparkles that flash from their eyes!
    Behold a ghastly band,
    Each a torch in his hand!
Those are Grecian ghosts, that in battle were slain,
    And unburied remain[2]
140   Inglorious on the plain:
    Give the vengeance due

1. The Erinyes of the Greeks, avengers of crimes against the natural and the social orders. They are described as women with snakes in their hair and wrapped around their waists and arms.
2. According to Greek beliefs, the shades of the dead could not rest until their bodies were buried.

To the valiant crew.
Behold how they toss their torches on high,
How they point to the Persian abodes,
145 And glittering temples of their hostile gods!"
The princes applaud, with a furious joy;
And the king seized a flambeau° with zeal to destroy;   *torch*
Thaïs led the way,
To light him to his prey,
150 And, like another Helen, fired another Troy.[3]

CHORUS

And the king seized a flambeau with zeal to destroy;
Thaïs led the way,
To light him to his prey,
And, like another Helen, fired another Troy.

7

155 Thus long ago,
Ere heaving bellows learned to blow,
While organs yet were mute;
Timotheus, to his breathing flute,
And sounding lyre,
160 Could swell the soul to rage, or kindle soft desire.
At last, divine Cecilia came,
Inventress of the vocal frame;°   *organ*
The sweet enthusiast,[4] from her sacred store,
Enlarged the former narrow bounds,
165 And added length to solemn sounds,
With nature's mother wit, and arts unknown before.
Let old Timotheus yield the prize,
Or both divide the crown:
He raised a mortal to the skies;
170 She drew an angel down.

GRAND CHORUS

At last, divine Cecilia came,
Inventress of the vocal frame;
The sweet enthusiast, from her sacred store,
Enlarged the former narrow bounds,
175 *And added length to solemn sounds,*
With nature's mother wit, and arts unknown before.
Let old Timotheus yield the prize,
Or both divide the crown:
He raised a mortal to the skies;
180 *She drew an angel down.*

1697

3. Helen's elopement to Troy with Paris brought on the Trojan War and the ultimate destruction of the city by the Greeks.
4. Usually at this time a disparaging word, frequently, though not always, applied to a religious zealot or fanatic. Here it is used approvingly and in its literal sense, "possessed by a god," an allusion to Cecilia's angelic companion referred to in line 170 (but see "Song for St. Cecilia's Day," line 53 and p. 71, n. 8).

CRITICISM

Dryden's impulse to write criticism came from his practical urge to explain and justify his own writings; his attraction to clear, ordered theoretical principles; and his growing sense of himself as a leader of English literary taste and judgment. The Elizabethans, largely impelled by the example of Italian humanists, had produced an interesting but unsystematic body of critical writings. Dryden could look back to such pioneer works as George Puttenham's *Art of English Poesy* (1589), Sir Philip Sidney's *Defense of Poesy* (1595), Samuel Daniel's *Defense of Rhyme* (ca. 1603), and Ben Jonson's *Timber, or Discoveries* (1641). These and later writings Dryden knew, as he knew the ancients and the important contemporary French critics, notably Pierre Corneille, René Rapin, and Nicolas Boileau. Taken as a whole, his critical prefaces and dedications, which appeared between 1664 and 1700, are the work of a man of independent mind who has made his own synthesis of critical canons from wide reading, a great deal of thinking, and the constant practice of the art of writing. As a critic he is no one's disciple, and he has the saving grace of being always willing to change his mind.

All but a very few of Dryden's critical works (most notably *An Essay of Dramatic Poesy*) grew out of the works to which they served as prefaces: comedies, heroic plays, tragedies, translations, and poems of various sorts. Each work posed problems that Dryden was eager to discuss with his readers, and the topics that he treated proved to be important in the development of the new literature of which he was the principal advocate. He dealt with the processes of literary creation, the poet's relation to tradition, the forms of modern drama, the craft of poetry, and above all the genius of earlier poets: Shakespeare, Jonson, Chaucer, Juvenal, Horace, Homer, and Virgil. For nearly forty years this voice was heard in the land; and when it was finally silenced, a set of critical standards had come into existence and a new age had been given its direction.

From An Essay of Dramatic Poesy[1]

[TWO SORTS OF BAD POETRY]

* * * "I have a mortal apprehension of two poets,[2] whom this victory, with the help of both her wings, will never be able to escape." " 'Tis easy to guess

1. With the reopening of the theaters in 1660, older plays were revived, but despite their power and charm, they seemed old-fashioned. Although new playwrights, ambitious to create a modern English drama, soon appeared, they were uncertain of their direction. What, if anything, useful could they learn from the dramatic practice of the ancients? Should they ignore the English dramatists of the late 16th and early 17th centuries? Should they make their example the vigorous contemporary drama of France? Dryden addresses himself to these and other problems in this essay, his first extended piece of criticism. Its purpose, he tells us, was "chiefly to vindicate the honor of our English writers from the censure of those who unjustly prefer the French before them." Its method is skeptical: Dryden presents several points of view, but imposes none. The form is a dialogue among friends, like the *Tusculan Disputations* or the *Brutus* of Cicero. Crites praises the drama of the ancients; Eugenius protests against their authority and argues for the idea of progress in the arts; Lisideius urges the

excellence of French plays; and Neander, speaking in the climactic position, defends the native tradition and the greatness of Shakespeare, Fletcher, and Jonson. The dialogue takes place on June 3, 1665, in a boat on the Thames. The four friends are rowed downstream to listen to the cannonading of the English and Dutch fleets, engaged in battle off the Suffolk coast. As the gunfire recedes they are assured of victory and order their boatman to return to London, and naturally enough they fall to discussing the number of bad poems that the victory will evoke.

2. Crites here is probably referring to Robert Wilde and possibly to Richard Flecknoe, whom Dryden later ridiculed in "Mac Flecknoe." Their actual identity is unimportant, for they merely represent two extremes in poetry, both deplorable: the fantastic and extravagant manner of decadent metaphysical wit and its opposite, the flat and the dull. The new poetry was to seek a mean between these extremes (cf. Pope, *An Essay on Criticism* 2.239–42 and 289–300, pp. 495 and 496–97).

whom you intend," said Lisideius; "and without naming them, I ask you if one of them does not perpetually pay us with clenches[3] upon words, and a certain clownish kind of raillery?[4] if now and then he does not offer at a catachresis or Clevelandism, wresting and torturing a word into another meaning: in fine, if he be not one of those whom the French would call *un mauvais buffon*;[5] one who is so much a well-willer to the satire, that he spares no man; and though he cannot strike a blow to hurt any, yet ought to be punished for the malice of the action, as our witches are justly hanged, because they think themselves so, and suffer deservedly for believing they did mischief, because they meant it." "You have described him," said Crites, "so exactly that I am afraid to come after you with my other extremity of poetry. He is one of those who, having had some advantage of education and converse, knows better than the other what a poet should be, but puts it into practice more unluckily than any man; his style and matter are everywhere alike: he is the most calm, peaceable writer you ever read: he never disquiets your passions with the least concernment, but still leaves you in as even a temper as he found you; he is a very Leveller[6] in poetry: he creeps along with ten little words in every line, and helps out his numbers with *for to*, and *unto*, and all the pretty expletives[7] he can find, till he drags them to the end of another line; while the sense is left tired halfway behind it: he doubly starves all his verses, first for want of thought, and then of expression; his poetry neither has wit in it, nor seems to have it; like him in Martial:

Pauper videri Cinna vult, et est pauper.[8]

"He affects plainness, to cover his want of imagination: when he writes the serious way, the highest flight of his fancy is some miserable antithesis, or seeming contradiction; and in the comic he is still reaching at some thin conceit, the ghost of a jest, and that too flies before him, never to be caught; these swallows which we see before us on the Thames are the just resemblance of his wit: you may observe how near the water they stoop, how many proffers they make to dip, and yet how seldom they touch it; and when they do, it is but the surface: they skim over it but to catch a gnat, and then mount into the air and leave it."

[THE WIT OF THE ANCIENTS: THE UNIVERSAL][9]

* * * "A thing well said will be wit in all languages; and though it may lose something in the translation, yet to him who reads it in the original, 'tis still the same: he has an idea of its excellency, though it cannot pass from his mind into any other expression or words than those in which he finds it. When Phaedria, in the *Eunuch*,[1] had a command from his mistress to be

---

3. Puns.
4. Boorish banter.
5. A malicious jester (French). "Catachresis": the use of a word in a sense remote from its normal meaning. A legitimate figure of speech used by all poets, it had been abused by John Cleveland (1613–1658), who was at first admired for his ingenuity, but whose reputation declined rapidly after the Restoration. A Clevelandism: "The marigold, whose courtier's face / *Echoes* the sun."
6. The Levellers were radical egalitarians and

republicans, a powerful political force in the Puritan army about 1648. They were suppressed by Cromwell. "Passions": emotions. "Still": always.
7. Words used merely to fill out a line of verse (cf. Pope, *An Essay on Criticism* 2.346–47, p. 498).
8. Cinna wishes to seem poor, and he is poor (Latin; *Epigrams* 8.19).
9. Eugenius is in the midst of remarks about the limitations of the ancients.
1. A comedy by the Roman poet Terence (ca. 185–159 B.C.E.).

absent two days, and, encouraging himself to go through with it, said, 'Tandem ego non ilia caream, si sit opus, vel totum triduum?'[2]—Parmeno, to mock the softness of his master, lifting up his hands and eyes, cries out, as it were in admiration, 'Hui! universum triduum!'[3] the elegancy of which universum, though it cannot be rendered in our language, yet leaves an impression on our souls: but this happens seldom in him; in Plautus[4] oftener, who is infinitely too bold in his metaphors and coining words, out of which many times his wit is nothing; which questionless was one reason why Horace falls upon him so severely in those verses:

> Sed proavi nostri Plautinos et numeros et
> Laudavere sales, nimium patienter utrumque,
> Ne dicam stolide.[5]

For Horace himself was cautious to obtrude a new word on his readers, and makes custom and common use the best measure of receiving it into our writings:

> Multa renascentur quae nunc cecidere, cadentque
> Quae nunc sunt in honore vocabula, si volet usus,
> Quem penes arbitrium est, et jus, et norma loquendi.[6]

"The not observing this rule is that which the world has blamed in our satirist, Cleveland: to express a thing hard and unnaturally is his new way of elocution. 'Tis true no poet but may sometimes use a catachresis: Virgil does it—

> Mistaque ridenti colocasia fundet acantho[7]—

in his eclogue of Pollio; and in his seventh Aeneid:

> mirantur et undae,
> Miratur nemus insuetum fulgentia longe
> Scuta virum fluvio pictasque innare carinas.[8]

And Ovid once so modestly that he asks leave to do it:

> quem, si verbo audacia detur,
> Haud metuam summi dixisse Palatia caeli.[9]

calling the court of Jupiter by the name of Augustus his palace; though in another place he is more bold, where he says, 'et longas visent Capitolia pompas.'[1] But to do this always, and never be able to write a line without it,

2. Shall I not then do without her, if need be, for three whole days? (Latin).
3. The wit of Parmeno's exclamation, "Oh, three entire days," depends on universum, which suggests that a lover may regard three days as an eternity. "Admiration": wonder.
4. Titus Maccus Plautus, (ca. 254–184 B.C.E.), Roman comic poet.
5. But our ancestors too tolerantly (I do not say foolishly) praised both the verse and the wit of Plautus (Latin; Art of Poetry, lines 270–72). Dryden misquotes slightly.
6. Many words that have perished will be born again, and those shall perish that are now esteemed, if usage wills it, in whose power are the judgment, the law, and the pattern of speech

(Latin; Art of Poetry, lines 70–72).
7. [The earth] shall give forth the Egyptian bean, mingled with the smiling acanthus (Latin; Eclogues 4.20). "Smiling acanthus" is a catachresis.
8. Actually Aeneid 8.91–93. Dryden's paraphrase makes the point clearly: "The woods and waters wonder at the gleam / Of shields and painted ships that stem the stream" (Latin; Aeneid. 8.125–26). "Wonder" is a catachresis.
9. [This is the place] which, if boldness of expression be permitted, I shall not hesitate to call the Palace of high heaven (Latin; Metamorphoses 1.175–76).
1. And the Capitol shall see the long processions (Latin; Metamorphoses 1.561).

though it may be admired by some few pedants, will not pass upon those who know that wit is best conveyed to us in the most easy language; and is most to be admired when a great thought comes dressed in words so commonly received that it is understood by the meanest apprehensions, as the best meat is the most easily digested: but we cannot read a verse of Cleveland's without making a face at it, as if every word were a pill to swallow: he gives us many times a hard nut to break our teeth, without a kernel for our pains. So that there is this difference betwixt his satires and Doctor Donne's; that the one gives us deep thoughts in common language, though rough cadence; the other gives us common thoughts in abstruse words: 'tis true in some places his wit is independent of his words, as in that of the *Rebel Scot:*

> Had Cain been Scot, God would have changed his doom;
> Not forced him wander, but confined him home.[2]

"*Si sic omnia dixisset!*[3] This is wit in all languages: it is like mercury, never to be lost or killed: and so that other—

> For beauty, like white powder, makes no noise,
> And yet the silent hypocrite destroys.[4]

You see that the last line is highly metaphorical, but it is so soft and gentle that it does not shock us as we read it."

[SHAKESPEARE AND BEN JONSON COMPARED][5]

"To begin, then, with Shakespeare. He was the man who of all modern, and perhaps ancient poets, had the largest and most comprehensive soul. All the images of Nature were still present to him, and he drew them, not laboriously, but luckily; when he describes anything, you more than see it, you feel it too. Those who accuse him to have wanted learning, give him the greater commendation: he was naturally learned; he needed not the spectacles of books to read Nature; he looked inwards, and found her there. I cannot say he is everywhere alike; were he so, I should do him injury to compare him with the greatest of mankind. He is many times flat, insipid; his comic wit degenerating into clenches, his serious swelling into bombast. But he is always great when some great occasion is presented to him; no man can say he ever had a fit subject for his wit and did not then raise himself as high above the rest of poets,

Quantum lenta solent inter viburna cupressi.[6]

The consideration of this made Mr. Hales[7] of Eton say that there was no subject of which any poet ever writ, but he would produce it much better treated of in Shakespeare; and however others are now generally preferred before him, yet the age wherein he lived, which had contemporaries with him Fletcher and Jonson, never equaled them to him in their esteem: and in

2. Lines 63–64.
3. Had he said everything thus! (Latin; Juvenal's *Satires* 10.123–24).
4. From *Rupertismus*, lines 39–40. Mercury is said to be "killed" if its fluidity is destroyed.
5. Neander's contrast of Shakespeare and Jonson introduces an extended commentary on the

latter's play *Epicoene; or the Silent Woman.*
6. As do cypresses among the bending shrubs (Latin; Virgil's *Eclogues* 1.25).
7. The learned John Hales (1584–1656), provost of Eton. He is reputed to have said this to Jonson himself.

the last king's court, when Ben's reputation was at highest, Sir John Suck-ling,[8] and with him the greater part of the courtiers, set our Shakespeare far above him. . . .

"As for Jonson, to whose character I am now arrived, if we look upon him while he was himself (for his last plays were but his dotages), I think him the most learned and judicious writer which any theater ever had. He was a most severe judge of himself, as well as others. One cannot say he wanted wit, but rather that he was frugal of it. In his works you find little to retrench[9] or alter. Wit, and language, and humor also in some measure, we had before him; but something of art[1] was wanting to the drama till he came. He managed his strength to more advantage than any who preceded him. You seldom find him making love in any of his scenes or endeavoring to move the passions; his genius was too sullen and saturnine[2] to do it gracefully, especially when he knew he came after those who had performed both to such an height. Humor was his proper sphere: and in that he delighted most to represent mechanic people.[3] He was deeply conversant in the ancients, both Greek and Latin, and he borrowed boldly from them: there is scarce a poet or historian among the Roman authors of those times whom he has not translated in *Sejanus* and *Catiline*.[4] But he has done his robberies so openly, that one may see he fears not to be taxed by any law. He invades authors like a monarch; and what would be theft in other poets is only victory in him. With the spoils of these writers he so represents old Rome to us, in its rites, ceremonies, and customs, that if one of their poets had written either of his tragedies, we had seen less of it than in him. If there was any fault in his language, 'twas that he weaved it too closely and laboriously, in his serious plays:[5] perhaps, too, he did a little too much Romanize our tongue, leaving the words which he translated almost as much Latin as he found them: wherein, though he learnedly fol-lowed the idiom of their language, he did not enough comply with the idiom of ours. If I would compare him with Shakespeare, I must acknowledge him the more correct poet, but Shakespeare the greater wit.[6] Shakespeare was the Homer, or father of our dramatic poets; Jonson was the Virgil, the pattern of elaborate writing; I admire him, but I love Shakespeare. To conclude of him; as he has given us the most correct plays, so in the precepts which he has laid down in his *Discoveries*, we have as many and profitable rules for perfecting the stage, as any wherewith the French can furnish us."

1668

---

8. Courtier, poet, playwright, much admired in Dryden's time for his wit and the easy naturalness of his style. "King's court": that of Charles I.
9. Delete.
1. Craftsmanship.
2. Heavy.
3. I.e., artisans. In Jonson's comedies the charac-ters are seen under the domination of some psy-chological trait, ruling passion, or affectation—i.e.,
some "humor"—that makes them unique and ridiculous.
4. Jonson's two Roman plays, dated 1605 and 1611, respectively.
5. This is the reading of the first edition. Curiously enough, in the second edition Dryden altered the phrase to "in his comedies especially."
6. Genius.

From The Author's Apology for Heroic Poetry and Heroic License[1]

["BOLDNESS" OF FIGURES AND TROPES DEFENDED: THE APPEAL TO "NATURE"]

* * * They, who would combat general authority with particular opinion, must first establish themselves a reputation of understanding better than other men. Are all the flights of heroic poetry to be concluded bombast, unnatural, and mere madness, because they are not affected with their excellencies? It is just as reasonable as to conclude there is no day, because a blind man cannot distinguish of light and colors. Ought they not rather, in modesty, to doubt of their own judgments, when they think this or that expression in Homer, Virgil, Tasso, or Milton's *Paradise* to be too far strained, than positively to conclude that 'tis all fustian and mere nonsense? 'Tis true there are limits to be set betwixt the boldness and rashness of a poet; but he must understand those limits who pretends to judge as well as he who undertakes to write: and he who has no liking to the whole ought, in reason, to be excluded from censuring of the parts. He must be a lawyer before he mounts the tribunal; and the judicature of one court, too, does not qualify a man to preside in another. He may be an excellent pleader in the Chancery, who is not fit to rule the Common Pleas.[2] But I will presume for once to tell them that the boldest strokes of poetry, when they are managed artfully, are those which most delight the reader.

Virgil and Horace, the severest writers of the severest age, have made frequent use of the hardest metaphors and of the strongest hyperboles; and in this case the best authority is the best argument, for generally to have pleased, and through all ages, must bear the force of universal tradition. And if you would appeal from thence to right reason, you will gain no more by it in effect than, first, to set up your reason against those authors, and, secondly, against all those who have admired them. You must prove why that ought not to have pleased which has pleased the most learned and the most judicious; and, to be thought knowing, you must first put the fool upon all mankind. If you can enter more deeply than they have done into the causes and resorts[3] of that which moves pleasure in a reader, the field is open, you may be heard: but those springs of human nature are not so easily discovered by every superficial judge: it requires philosophy, as well as poetry, to sound the depth of all the passions, what they are in themselves, and how they are to be provoked; and in this science the best poets have excelled. * * * From hence have sprung the tropes and figures,[4] for which they wanted a name who first practiced them and succeeded in them. Thus I grant you

---

1. This essay was prefixed to Dryden's *State of Innocence*, the libretto for an opera (never produced), based on *Paradise Lost*. Dryden had been ridiculed for the extravagant and bold imagery and rhetorical figures that are typical of the style of his rhymed heroic plays. This preface is a defense not only of his own predilection for what Samuel Johnson described as "wild and daring sallies of sentiment, in the irregular and eccentric violence of wit" but also of the theory that heroic and idealized materials should be treated in lofty

and boldly metaphorical style; hence his definition of wit as propriety.
2. Court in which civil actions could be brought by one subject against another. "Chancery": a high court presided over by the lord chancellor.
3. Mechanical springs that set something in motion.
4. I.e., such figures of speech as metaphors and similes. "Tropes": the uses of words in a figurative sense.

that the knowledge of Nature was the original rule, and that all poets ought to study her, as well as Aristotle and Horace, her interpreters.[5] But then this also undeniably follows, that those things which delight all ages must have been an imitation of Nature—which is all I contend. Therefore is rhetoric made an art; therefore the names of so many tropes and figures were invented, because it was observed they had such and such effect upon the audience. Therefore catachreses and hyperboles[6] have found their place amongst them; not that they were to be avoided, but to be used judiciously and placed in poetry as heightenings and shadows are in painting, to make the figure bolder, and cause it to stand off to sight. * * *

[WIT AS "PROPRIETY"]

* * * [Wit] is a propriety of thoughts and words; or, in other terms, thought and words elegantly adapted to the subject. If our critics will join issue on this definition, that we may *convenire in aliquo tertio;*[7] if they will take it as a granted principle, it will be easy to put an end to this dispute. No man will disagree from another's judgment concerning the dignity of style in heroic poetry; but all reasonable men will conclude it necessary that sublime subjects ought to be adorned with the sublimest, and, consequently, often with the most figurative expressions. * * *

1677

From A Discourse Concerning the Original and Progress of Satire[1]

[THE ART OF SATIRE]

* * * How easy is it to call rogue and villain, and that wittily! But how hard to make a man appear a fool, a blockhead, or a knave without using any of those opprobrious terms! To spare the grossness of the names, and to do the thing yet more severely, is to draw a full face, and to make the nose and cheeks stand out, and yet not to employ any depth of shadowing.[2] This is the mystery of that noble trade, which yet no master can teach to his apprentice; he may give the rules, but the scholar is never the nearer in his practice. Neither is it true that this fineness of raillery[3] is offensive. A witty man is tickled while he is hurt in this manner, and a fool feels it not. The occasion

---

5. In the words of the French critic René Rapin, the rules (largely derived from Aristotle's *Poetics* and Horace's *Art of Poetry*) were made to "reduce Nature to method" (cf. Pope, *An Essay on Criticism* 1.88–89, p. 492).
6. Deliberate overstatement or exaggeration. "Catachresis": the use of a word in a sense remote from its normal meaning.
7. To find some means of agreement, in a third term, between the two opposites [Latin].
1. This passage is an excerpt from the long and rambling preface that served as the dedication of a translation of the satires of the Roman satirists Juvenal and Persius to Charles Sackville, sixth earl of Dorset. The translations were made by

Dryden and other writers, among them William Congreve. Dryden traces the origin and development of verse satire in Rome and in a very fine passage contrasts Horace and Juvenal as satiric poets. It is plain that he prefers the "tragic" satire of Juvenal to the urbane and laughing satire of Horace. But in the passage printed here, he praises his own satiric character of Zimri (the duke of Buckingham) in *Absalom and Achitophel* for the very reason that it is modeled on Horatian "raillery," not Juvenalian invective.
2. Early English miniaturists prided themselves on the art of giving roundness to the full face without painting in shadows.
3. Satirical mirth, good-natured satire.

of an offense may possibly be given, but he cannot take it. If it be granted that in effect this way does more mischief; that a man is secretly wounded, and though he be not sensible himself, yet the malicious world will find it out for him; yet there is still a vast difference betwixt the slovenly butchering of a man, and the fineness of a stroke that separates the head from the body, and leaves it standing in its place. A man may be capable, as Jack Ketch's[4] wife said of his servant, of a plain piece of work, a bare hanging; but to make a malefactor die sweetly was only belonging to her husband. I wish I could apply it to myself, if the reader would be kind enough to think it belongs to me. The character of Zimri in my *Absalom*[5] is, in my opinion, worth the whole poem: it is not bloody, but it is ridiculous enough; and he, for whom it was intended, was too witty to resent it as an injury. If I had railed,[6] I might have suffered for it justly; but I managed my own work more happily, perhaps more dexterously. I avoided the mention of great crimes, and applied myself to the representing of blindsides, and little extravagancies; to which, the wittier a man is, he is generally the more obnoxious.[7] It succeeded as I wished; the jest went round, and he was laughed at in his turn who began the frolic. * * *

1693

From The Preface to *Fables Ancient and Modern*[1]

[IN PRAISE OF CHAUCER]

In the first place, as he is the father of English poetry, I hold him in the same degree of veneration as the Grecians held Homer, or the Romans Virgil. He is a perpetual fountain of good sense; learned in all sciences;[2] and, therefore, speaks properly on all subjects. As he knew what to say, so he knows also when to leave off; a continence which is practiced by few writers, and scarcely by any of the ancients, excepting Virgil and Horace. * * *

Chaucer followed Nature everywhere, but was never so bold to go beyond her; and there is a great difference of being *poeta* and *nimis poeta*,[3] if we may believe Catullus, as much as betwixt a modest behavior and affectation. The verse of Chaucer, I confess, is not harmonious to us; but 'tis like the eloquence of one whom Tacitus commends, it was *auribus istius temporis accommodata:*[4] they who lived with him, and some time after him, thought it musical; and it continues so, even in our judgment, if compared with the

---

4. A notorious public executioner of Dryden's time (d. 1686). His name later became a generic term for all members of his profession.
5. *Absalom and Achitophel*, lines 544–68 (p. 52).
6. Reviled, abused. Observe that the verb differed in meaning from its noun, defined above.
7. Liable.
1. Dryden's final work, published in the year of his death, was a collection of translations from Homer, Ovid, Boccaccio, and Chaucer, and one or two other pieces. The Preface is Dryden's ripest and finest critical essay. He is not concerned here with critical theory or with a formalistic approach

to literature but is simply a man, grown old in the reading and writing of poetry, who is eager to talk informally with his readers about some of his favorite authors. His praise of Chaucer (unusually sympathetic and perceptive for 1700) is animated by that love of great literature that is manifest in everything that Dryden wrote.
2. Branches of learning.
3. A poet (*"poeta"*) and too much of a poet (*"nimis poeta"*). The phrase is not from Catullus but from Martial (*Epigrams* 3.44).
4. Suitable to the ears of that time (Latin). Tacitus (ca. 55–ca. 117 C.E.), Roman historian and writer on oratory.

numbers of Lydgate and Gower,[5] his contemporaries; there is the rude sweetness of a Scotch tune in it, which is natural and pleasing, though not perfect. 'Tis true I cannot go so far as he who published the last edition of him;[6] for he would make us believe the fault is in our ears, and that there were really ten syllables in a verse where we find but nine; but this opinion is not worth confuting; 'tis so gross and obvious an error that common sense (which is a rule in everything but matters of faith and revelation) must convince the reader that equality of numbers in every verse which we call heroic[7] was either not known, or not always practiced in Chaucer's age. It were an easy matter to produce some thousands of his verses which are lame for want of half a foot, and sometimes a whole one, and which no pronunciation can make otherwise. We can only say that he lived in the infancy of our poetry, and that nothing is brought to perfection at the first. * * *

He must have been a man of a most wonderful comprehensive nature, because, as it has been truly observed of him, he has taken into the compass of his *Canterbury Tales* the various manners and humors (as we now call them) of the whole English nation in his age. Not a single character has escaped him. All his pilgrims are severally distinguished from each other; and not only in their inclinations but in their very physiognomies and persons. Baptista Porta[8] could not have described their natures better than by the marks which the poet gives them. The matter and manner of their tales, and of their telling, are so suited to their different educations, humors, and callings that each of them would be improper in any other mouth. Even the grave and serious characters are distinguished by their several sorts of gravity: their discourses are such as belong to their age, their calling, and their breeding; such as are becoming of them, and of them only. Some of his persons are vicious, and some virtuous; some are unlearned, or (as Chaucer calls them) lewd, and some are learned. Even the ribaldry of the low characters is different: the Reeve, the Miller, and the Cook are several[9] men, and distinguished from each other as much as the mincing Lady Prioress and the broad-speaking, gap-toothed Wife of Bath. But enough of this; there is such a variety of game springing up before me that I am distracted in my choice, and know not which to follow. 'Tis sufficient to say, according to the proverb, that here is God's plenty. * * *

1700

---

5. John Gower (d. 1408), poet and friend of Chaucer. "Numbers": versification. John Lydgate (ca. 1370–ca. 1449) wrote poetry that shows the influence of Chaucer.
6. Thomas Speght's Chaucer, which Dryden used, was first published in 1598; the second edition, published in 1602, was reprinted in 1687.
7. The pentameter line. In Dryden's time few readers knew how to pronounce Middle English, especially the syllabic *e*. Moreover, Chaucer's works were known only in corrupt printed texts. As a consequence Chaucer's verse seemed rough and irregular.
8. Giambattista della Porta (ca. 1535–1615), author of a Latin treatise on physiognomy.
9. Different.

SAMUEL PEPYS
1633–1703

S amuel Pepys (pronounced "Peeps") was the son of a London tailor. With the help of a scholarship he took a degree at Cambridge; with the help of a cousin he found a place in the Navy Office. Eventually, through hard work and an eye for detail, he rose to secretary of the Admiralty. His defense of the Navy Office and himself before Parliament in 1668 won him a reputation as a good administrator, and his career continued to prosper until it was broken, first by false accusations of treason in 1679 and finally by the fall of James II in 1688. But Pepys was more than a bureaucrat. A Londoner to his core, he was interested in all the activities of the city: the theater, music, the social whirl, business, religion, literary life, and the scientific experiments of the Royal Society (which he served as president from 1684 to 1686). He also found plenty of chances to indulge his two obsessions: chasing after women and making money.

Pepys kept his diary from 1660 to 1669 (when his eyesight began to fail). Writing in shorthand and sometimes in code, he was utterly frank in recording the events of his day, both public and private, the major affairs of state or his quarrels with his wife. Altogether he wrote about 1.3 million words. When the diary was first deciphered and published in the nineteenth century, it made him newly famous. As a document of social history it is unsurpassed for its rich detail, honesty, and immediacy. But more than that, it gives us a sense of somebody else's world: what it was like to live in the Restoration, and what it was like to see through the eyes of Pepys.

From The Diary

[THE GREAT FIRE]

September 2, 1666

Lords day. Some of our maids sitting up late last night to get things ready against our feast today, Jane called us up, about 3 in the morning, to tell us of a great fire they saw in the City.[1] So I rose, and slipped on my nightgown and went to her window, and thought it to be on the back side of Mark Lane[2] at the furthest; but being unused to such fires as followed, I thought it far enough off, and so went to bed again and to sleep. About 7 rose again to dress myself, and there looked out at the window and saw the fire not so much as it was, and further off. So to my closet[3] to set things to rights after yesterday's cleaning. By and by Jane comes and tells me that she hears that above 300 houses have been burned down tonight by the fire we saw, and that it was now burning down all Fish Street by London Bridge. So I made myself ready presently,[4] and walked to the Tower and there got up upon one of the high places,

---

1. The fire of London, which was to destroy four-fifths of the central city, had begun an hour earlier. For another description see Dryden's *Annus Mirabilis* (p. 36).

2. Near Pepys's own house in Seething Lane.
3. A small private room or study.
4. Immediately.

Sir J. Robinson's little son going up with me; and there I did see the houses at that end of the bridge all on fire, and an infinite great fire on this and the other side the end of the bridge—which, among other people, did trouble me for poor little Michell and our Sarah[5] on the Bridge. So down, with my heart full of trouble, to the Lieutenant of the Tower, who tells me that it begun this morning in the King's baker's house in Pudding Lane, and that it hath burned down St. Magnus' Church and most part of Fish Street already. So I down to the waterside and there got a boat and through bridge, and there saw a lamentable fire. Poor Michell's house, as far as the Old Swan,[6] already burned that way and the fire running further, that in a very little time it got as far as the Steelyard while I was there. Everybody endeavoring to remove their goods, and flinging into the river or bringing them into lighters[7] that lay off. Poor people staying in their houses as long as till the very fire touched them, and then running into boats or clambering from one pair of stair by the waterside to another. And among other things, the poor pigeons I perceive were loath to leave their houses, but hovered about the windows and balconies till they were some of them burned, their wings, and fell down.

Having stayed, and in an hour's time seen the fire rage every way, and nobody to my sight endeavoring to quench it, but to remove their goods and leave all to the fire; and having seen it get as far as the Steelyard, and the wind mighty high and driving it into the city, and everything, after so long a drought, proving combustible, even the very stones of churches, and among other things, the poor steeple by which pretty Mrs.   [8] lives, and whereof my old school-fellow Elborough is parson, taken fire in the very top and there burned till it fell down—I to Whitehall[9] with a gentleman with me who desired to go off from the Tower to see the fire in my boat—to Whitehall, and there up to the King's closet in the chapel, where people came about me and I did give them an account dismayed them all; and word was carried in to the King, so I was called for and did tell the King and Duke of York what I saw, and that unless his Majesty did command houses to be pulled down, nothing could stop the fire. They seemed much troubled, and the King commanded me to go to my Lord Mayor from him and command him to spare no houses but to pull down before the fire every way. The Duke of York bid me tell him that if he would have any more soldiers, he shall; and so did my Lord Arlington afterward, as a great secret. Here meeting with Captain Cocke, I in his coach, which he lent me, and Creed with me, to Paul's;[1] and there walked along Watling Street as well as I could, every creature coming away loaden with goods to save—and here and there sick people carried away in beds. Extraordinary good goods carried in carts and on backs. At last met my Lord Mayor in Canning Street, like a man spent, with a hankercher[2] about his neck. To the King's message, he cried like a fainting woman, "Lord, what can I do? I am spent. People will not obey me. I have been pulling down houses. But the fire overtakes us faster than we can do it." That he needed no more soldiers; and that for himself, he must go and refresh himself, having been up

5. William Michell and his wife, Betty, one of Pepys's old flames, lived near London Bridge. Sarah had been a maid of the Pepyses'.
6. A tavern in Thames Street, near the source of the fire.
7. Barges.

8. Mrs. Horsely, a beauty admired and pursued by Pepys.
9. Palace in central London.
1. St. Paul's Cathedral, later ravaged by the fire.
2. Handkerchief.

all night. So he left me, and I him, and walked home—seeing people all almost distracted and no manner of means used to quench the fire. The houses too, so very thick thereabouts, and full of matter for burning, as pitch and tar, in Thames Street—and warehouses of oil and wines and brandy and other things. Here I saw Mr. Isaak Houblon, that handsome man—prettily dressed and dirty at his door at Dowgate, receiving some of his brothers' things whose houses were on fire; and as he says, have been removed twice already, and he doubts[3] (as it soon proved) that they must be in a little time removed from his house also—which was a sad consideration. And to see the churches all filling with goods, by people who themselves should have been quietly there at this time.

By this time it was about 12 o'clock, and so home and there find my guests, which was Mr. Wood and his wife, Barbary Shelden, and also Mr. Moone— she mighty fine, and her husband, for aught I see, a likely[4] man. But Mr. Moone's design and mine, which was to look over my closet and please him with the sight thereof, which he hath long desired, was wholly disappointed, for we were in great trouble and disturbance at this fire, not knowing what to think of it. However, we had an extraordinary good dinner, and as merry as at this time we could be.

While at dinner, Mrs. Batelier came to enquire after Mr. Woolfe and Stanes (who it seems are related to them), whose houses in Fish Street are all burned, and they in a sad condition. She would not stay in the fright.

As soon as dined, I and Moone away and walked through the City, the streets full of nothing but people and horses and carts loaden with goods, ready to run over one another, and removing goods from one burned house to another—they now removing out of Canning Street (which received goods in the morning) into Lumbard Street and further; and among others, I now saw my little goldsmith Stokes receiving some friend's goods, whose house itself was burned the day after. We parted at Paul's, he home and I to Paul's Wharf, where I had appointed a boat to attend me; and took in Mr. Carcasse and his brother, whom I met in the street, and carried them below and above bridge, to and again, to see the fire, which was now got further, both below and above, and no likelihood of stopping it. Met with the King and Duke of York in their barge, and with them to Queenhithe and there called Sir Rd. Browne[5] to them. Their order was only to pull down houses apace, and so below bridge at the waterside; but little was or could be done, the fire coming upon them so fast. Good hopes there was of stopping it at the Three Cranes above, and at Buttolph's Wharf below bridge, if care be used; but the wind carries it into the City, so as we know not by the water- side what it doth there. River full of lighters and boats taking in goods, and good goods swimming in the water; and only, I observed that hardly one lighter or boat in three that had the goods of a house in, but there was a pair of virginals[6] in it. Having seen as much as I could now, I away to Whitehall by appointment, and there walked to St. James's Park, and there met my wife and Creed and Wood and his wife and walked to my boat, and there upon the water again, and to the fire up and down, it still increasing and the wind

---

3. Fears.
4. Promising.
5. Sir Richard Browne was a former lord mayor.

Queenhithe is a harbor in Thames Street.
6. Table-size harpsichord, popular at the time.

great. So near the fire as we could for smoke; and all over the Thames, with one's face in the wind you were almost burned with a shower of firedrops— this is very true—so as houses were burned by these drops and flakes of fire, three or four, nay five or six houses, one from another. When we could endure no more upon the water, we to a little alehouse on the Bankside over against the Three Cranes, and there stayed till it was dark almost and saw the fire grow; and as it grew darker, appeared more and more, and in corners and upon steeples and between churches and houses, as far as we could see up the hill of the City, in a most horrid malicious bloody flame, not like the fine flame of an ordinary fire. Barbary[7] and her husband away before us. We stayed till, it being darkish, we saw the fire as only one entire arch of fire from this to the other side the bridge, and in a bow up the hill, for an arch of above a mile long. It made me weep to see it. The churches, houses, and all on fire and flaming at once, and a horrid noise the flames made, and the cracking of houses at their ruin. So home with a sad heart, and there find everybody discoursing and lamenting the fire; and poor Tom Hater came with some few of his goods saved out of his house, which is burned upon Fish Street hill. I invited him to lie at my house, and did receive his goods: but was deceived in his lying there,[8] the noise coming every moment of the growth of the fire, so as we were forced to begin to pack up our own goods and prepare for their removal. And did by moonshine (it being brave,[9] dry, and moonshine and warm weather) carry much of my goods into the garden, and Mr. Hater and I did remove my money and iron chests into my cellar—as thinking that the safest place. And got my bags of gold into my office ready to carry away, and my chief papers of accounts also there, and my tallies[1] into a box by themselves. So great was our fear, as Sir W. Batten had carts come out of the country to fetch away his goods this night. We did put Mr. Hater, poor man, to bed a little; but he got but very little rest, so much noise being in my house, taking down of goods.

September 5, 1666

I lay down in the office again upon W. Hewer's[2] quilt, being mighty weary and sore in my feet with going till I was hardly able to stand. About 2 in the morning my wife calls me up and tells of new cries of "Fire!"—it being come to Barking Church, which is the bottom of our lane. I up; and finding it so, resolved presently to take her away; and did, and took my gold (which was about £2350), W. Hewer, and Jane down by Poundy's boat to Woolwich.[3] But Lord, what a sad sight it was by moonlight to see the whole City almost on fire—that you might see it plain at Woolwich, as if you were by it. There when I came, I find the gates shut, but no guard kept at all; which troubled me, because of discourses now begun that there is plot in it and that the French had done it.[4] I got the gates open, and to Mr. Shelden's,[5] where I

---

7. The actress Elizabeth Knepp, another of Pepys's mistresses. He calls her "Barbary" because she had enchanted him by singing *Barbary Allen*.
8. I.e., mistaken in asking him to stay.
9. Fine.
1. Receipts notched on sticks.
2. William Hewer, Pepys's chief clerk. Pepys had packed or sent away all his own goods.

3. Suburb on the east side of London.
4. There were rumors that the French had set the fire and were invading the city. "Gates": at the dockyard.
5. William Shelden, a Woolwich official at whose home Mrs. Pepys had stayed the year before, during the plague.

locked up my gold and charged my wife and W. Hewer never to leave the room without one of them in it night nor day. So back again, by the way seeing my goods well in the lighters at Deptford and watched well by people. Home, and whereas I expected to have seen our house on fire, it being now about 7 o'clock, it was not. But to the fire, and there find greater hopes than I expected; for my confidence of finding our office on fire was such, that I durst not ask anybody how it was with us, till I came and saw it not burned. But going to the fire, I find, by the blowing up of houses and the great help given by the workmen out of the King's yards, sent up by Sir W. Penn, there is a good stop given to it, as well at Mark Lane end as ours—it having only burned the dial[6] of Barking Church, and part of the porch, and was there quenched. I up to the top of Barking steeple, and there saw the saddest sight of desolation that I ever saw. Everywhere great fires. Oil cellars and brimstone and other things burning. I became afeared to stay there long; and therefore down again as fast as I could, the fire being spread as far as I could see it, and to Sir W. Penn's and there eat a piece of cold meat, having eaten nothing since Sunday but the remains of Sunday's dinner.

Here I met with Mr. Young and Whistler; and having removed all my things, and received good hopes that the fire at our end is stopped, they and I walked into the town and find Fanchurch Street, Gracious Street, and Lumbard Street all in dust. The Exchange a sad sight, nothing standing there of all the statues or pillars but Sir Tho. Gresham's picture in the corner.[7] Walked into Moore-fields (our feet ready to burn, walking through the town among the hot coals) and find that full of people, and poor wretches carrying their goods there, and everybody keeping his goods together by themselves (and a great blessing it is to them that it is fair weather for them to keep abroad[8] night and day); drank there, and paid twopence for a plain penny loaf.

Thence homeward, having passed through Cheapside and Newgate Market, all burned—and seen Anthony Joyce's house in fire. And took up (which I keep by me) a piece of glass of Mercer's Chapel in the street, where much more was, so melted and buckled with the heat of the fire, like parchment. I also did see a poor cat taken out of a hole in the chimney joining to the wall of the Exchange, with the hair all burned off the body and yet alive. So home at night, and find there good hopes of saving our office—but great endeavors of watching all night and having men ready; and so we lodged them in the office and had drink and bread and cheese for them. And I lay down and slept a good night about midnight—though when I rose, I hear that there had been a great alarm of French and Dutch being risen—which proved nothing. But it is a strange thing to see how long this time did look since Sunday, having been always full of variety of actions, and little sleep, that it looked like a week or more. And I had forgot almost the day of the week.[9]

---

6. Clock. "Yards": i.e., dockyards.
7. Sir Thomas Gresham had founded the Royal Exchange, a center for shopping and trading, in 1568. It was rebuilt in 1669.
8. Out of doors.
9. A day later the fire was under control. Pepys's own house was spared.

[THE DEB WILLET AFFAIR]

October 25, 1668

Lords day. Up, and discoursing with my wife about our house and many new things we are doing of; and so to church I, and there find Jack Fen come, and his wife, a pretty black[1] woman; I never saw her before, nor took notice of her now. So home and to dinner; and after dinner, all the afternoon got my wife and boy[2] to read to me. And at night W. Batelier comes and sups with us; and after supper, to have my head combed by Deb,[3] which occasioned the greatest sorrow to me that ever I knew in this world; for my wife, coming up suddenly, did find me embracing the girl con my hand sub su coats; and indeed, I was with my main in her cunny.[4] I was at a wonderful loss upon it, and the girl also; and I endeavored to put it off, but my wife was struck mute and grew angry, and as her voice came to her, grew quite out of order; and I do say little, but to bed; and my wife said little also, but could not sleep all night; but about 2 in the morning waked me and cried, and fell to tell me as a great secret that she was a Roman Catholic and had received the Holy Sacrament;[5] which troubled me but I took no notice of it, but she went on from one thing to another, till at last it appeared plainly her trouble was at what she saw; but yet I did not know how much she saw and therefore said nothing to her. But after her much crying and reproaching me with inconstancy and preferring a sorry girl before her, I did give her no provocations but did promise all fair usage to her, and love, and foreswore any hurt that I did with her—till at last she seemed to be at ease again; and so toward morning, a little sleep; [*Oct. 26*] and so I, with some little repose and rest, rose, and up and by water to Whitehall, but with my mind mightily troubled for the poor girl, whom I fear I have undone by this, my wife telling me that she would turn her out of door. However, I was obliged to attend the Duke of York, thinking to have had a meeting of Tanger[6] today, but had not; but he did take me and Mr. Wren into his closet, and there did press me to prepare what I had to say upon the answers of my fellow-officers to his great letter; which I promised to do against[7] his coming to town again the next week; and so to other discourse, finding plainly that he is in trouble and apprehensions of the reformers, and would be found to do what he can towards reforming himself. And so thence to my Lord Sandwich; where after long stay, he being in talk with others privately, I to him; and there he taking physic and keeping his chamber, I had an hour's talk with him about the ill posture of things at this time, while the King gives countenance to Sir Ch. Sidly and Lord Buckhurst,[8] telling him their late story of running up and down the streets a little while since all night, and their being beaten and clapped up all night by the constable, who is since chid and imprisoned for his pains.

---

1. Dark-haired.
2. Servant. Pepys had no children.
3. Deborah Willett, Mrs. Pepys's maid.
4. With his hand under her skirts and in her vulva.
5. When unhappy with her husband, Elizabeth Pepys sometimes threatened to convert to the Church of Rome. She never did.
6. Committee supervising the British naval base at Tangier, later evacuated under Pepys's supervision.
7. Before. Pepys had drafted a letter for the duke of York (later James II), high admiral of the navy, defending him from charges of mismanagement.
8. Sir Charles Sedley and Lord Buckhurst were riotous rakes and well-known writers; they are often identified with Lisideius and Eugenius in Dryden's *Essay of Dramatic Poesy.*

He tells me that he thinks his matters do stand well with the King—and hopes to have dispatch to his mind;[9] but I doubt it, and do see that he doth fear it too. He told me my Lady Carteret's trouble about my writing of that letter of the Duke of York's lately to the office; which I did not own, but declared to be of no injury to G. Carteret[1] and that I would write a letter to him to satisfy him therein. But this I am in pain how to do without doing myself wrong, and the end I had, of preparing a justification to myself here-after, when the faults of the Navy come to be found out. However, I will do it in the best manner I can.

Thence by coach home and to dinner, finding my wife mightily discon-tented and the girl sad, and no words from my wife to her. So after dinner, they out[2] with me about two or three things; and so home again, I all the evening busy and my wife full of trouble in her looks; and anon to bed—where about midnight, she wakes me and there falls foul on me again, affirming that she saw me hug and kiss the girl; the latter I denied, and truly; the other I confessed and no more. And upon her pressing me, did offer to give her under my hand that I would never see Mrs. Pierce more, nor Knepp, but did promise her particular demonstrations of my true love to her, owning some indiscretion in what I did, but that there was no harm in it. She at last on these promises was quiet, and very kind we were, and so to sleep; [Oct. 27] and in the morning up, but with my mind troubled for the poor girl, with whom I could not get opportunity to speak; but to the office, my mind mighty full of sorrow for her, where all the morning, and to dinner with my people and to the office all the afternoon; and so at night home and there busy to get some things ready against tomorrow's meeting of Tanger; and that being done and my clerks gone, my wife did towards bedtime begin to be in a mighty rage from some new matter that she had got in her head, and did most part of the night in bed rant at me in most high terms, of threats of publishing[3] my shame; and when I offered to rise, would have rose too, and caused a candle to be lit, to burn by her all night in the chimney while she ranted; while I, that knew myself to have given some grounds for it, did make it my business to appease her all I could possibly, and by good words and fair promises did make her very quiet; and so rested all night and rose with perfect good peace, being heartily afflicted for this folly of mine that did occasion it; but was forced to be silent about the girl, which I have no mind to part with, but much less that the poor girl should be undone by my folly. [Oct. 28] So up, with mighty kindness from my wife and a thorough peace; and being up, did by a note advise the girl what I had done and owned, which note I was in pain for till she told me that she had burned it. This evening, Mr. Spong came and sat late with me, and first told me of the instrument called Parrallogram,[4] which I must have one of, showing me his practice thereon by a map of England.

9. A message to his liking.
1. Sir George Carteret, former treasurer of the navy (which Pepys had plans to reform), was later censured for having kept poor accounts.
2. Went out.
3. Making public.
4. The pantograph, a mechanism for copying maps or plans.

November 14, 1668

Up, and had a mighty mind to have seen or given a note to Deb or to have given her a little money; to which purpose I wrapped up 40s in a paper, thinking to give her; but my wife rose presently, and would not let me be out of her sight; and went down before me into the kitchen, and came up and told me that she was in the kitchen, and therefore would have me go round the other way; which she repeating, and I vexed at it, answered her a little angrily; upon which she instantly flew out into a rage, calling me dog and rogue, and that I had a rotten heart; all which, knowing that I deserved it, I bore with; and word being brought presently up that she was gone away by coach with her things, my wife was friends; and so all quiet, and I to the office with my heart sad, and find that I cannot forget the girl, and vexed I know not where to look for her—and more troubled to see how my wife is by this means likely for ever to have her hand over me, that I shall for ever be a slave to her; that is to say, only in matters of pleasure, but in other things she will make her business, I know, to please me and to keep me right to her—which I will labor to be indeed, for she deserves it of me, though it will be I fear a little time before I shall be able to wear Deb out of my mind. At the office all the morning, and merry at noon at dinner; and after dinner to the office, where all the afternoon and doing much business late; my mind being free of all troubles, I thank God, but[5] only for my thoughts of this girl, which hang after her. And so at night home to supper, and there did sleep with great content with my wife. I must here remember that I have lain with my moher[6] as a husband more times since this falling-out then in I believe twelve months before—and with more pleasure to her then I think in all the time of our marriage before.

November 18, 1668

Lay long in bed, talking with my wife, she being unwilling to have me go abroad, being and declaring herself jealous of my going out, for fear of my going to Deb; which I do deny—for which God forgive me, for I was no sooner out about noon but I did go by coach directly to Somerset House and there inquired among the porters there for Dr. Allbun;[7] and the first I spoke with told me he knew him, and that he was newly gone into Lincoln's Inn fields, but whither he could not tell me, but that one of his fellows, not then in the way, did carry a chest of drawers thither with him, and that when he comes he would ask him. This put me in some hopes; and I to Whitehall and thence to Mr. Povy's, but he at dinner; and therefore I away and walked up and down the Strand between the two turnstiles,[8] hoping to see her out of a window; and then employed a porter, one Osbeston, to find out this doctor's lodgings thereabouts; who by appointment comes to me to Hercules' Pillars, where I dined alone, but tells me that he cannot find out any such but will inquire further. Thence back to Whitehall to the treasury a while, and thence to the Strand; and towards night did meet with the porter that carried the chest of drawers with this doctor, but he would not tell me where he

---

5. Except.
6. Woman or wife (*mujer* in Spanish).
7. Pepys's wife had told him that Deb was stay-

ing with a man named Allbon.
8. To keep traffic, except for pedestrians, out of the street.

lived, being his good master he told me; but if I would have a message to him, he would deliver it. At last, I told him my business was not with him, but a little gentlewoman, one Mrs. Willet, that is with him; and sent him to see how she did, from her friend in London, and no other token. He goes while I walk in Somerset House walk there in the court; at last he comes back and tells me she is well, and that I may see her if I will—but no more. So I could not be commanded by my reason, but I must go this very night; and so by coach, it being now dark, I to her, close by my tailor's; and there she came into the coach to me, and yo did besar her and tocar her thing, but ella was against it and labored with much earnestness, such as I believed to be real; and yet at last yo did make her tener mi cosa in her mano, while mi mano was sobra her pectus, and so did hazer[9] with grand delight. I did nevertheless give her the best counsel I could, to have a care of her honor and to fear God and suffer no man para haver to do con her—as yo have done— which she promised. Yo did give her 20s and directions para laisser sealed in paper at any time the name of the place of her being, at Herringman's my bookseller in the Change[1]—by which I might go para her. And so bid her good-night, with much content to my mind and resolution to look after her no more till I heard from her. And so home, and there told my wife a fair tale, God knows, how I spent the whole day; with which the poor wretch was satisfied, or at least seemed so; and so to supper and to bed, she having been mighty busy all day in getting of her house in order against tomorrow, to hang up our new hangings and furnishing our best chamber.

November 19, 1668

Up, and at the office all the morning, with my heart full of joy to think in what a safe condition all my matters now stand between my wife and Deb and me; and at noon, running upstairs to see the upholsters, who are at work upon hanging my best room and setting up my new bed, I find my wife sitting sad in the dining-room; which inquiring into the reason of, she begun to call me all the false, rotten-hearted rogues in the world, letting me understand that I was with Deb yesterday; which, thinking impossible for her ever to understand, I did a while deny; but at last did, for the ease of my mind and hers, and for ever to discharge my heart of this wicked business, I did confess all; and above-stairs in our bed-chamber there, I did endure the sorrow of her threats and vows and curses all the afternoon. And which was worst, she swore by all that was good that she would slit the nose of this girl, and be gone herself this very night from me; and did there demand 3 or 400*l* of me to buy my peace, that she might be gone without making any noise, or else protested that she would make all the world know of it. So, with most perfect confusion of face and heart, and sorrow and shame, in the greatest agony in the world, I did pass this afternoon, fearing that it will never have an end; but at last I did call for W. Hewer, who I was forced to make privy now to all; and the poor fellow did cry like a child and obtained what I could not, that she would be pacified, upon condition that I would give it under my hand never to see or speak with Deb while I live, as I did before of Pierce

9. Carry on. "Besar": kiss. "Tocar": touch. "Ella": she. "Tener mi cosa in her mano": take my thing in her hand. "Mi mano was sobra her pectus": my hand was on her breast.
1. I.e., the Royal Exchange, a center for shopping, business, and trade. "Para laisser": to leave.

and Knepp; and which I did also, God knows, promise for Deb too, but I have the confidence to deny it, to the perjuring of myself. So before it was late, there was, beyond my hopes as well as desert, a tolerable peace; and so to supper, and pretty kind words, and to bed, and there yo did hazer con ella to her content; and so with some rest spent the night in bed, being most absolutely resolved, if ever I can master this bout, never to give her occasion while I live of more trouble of this or any other kind, there being no curse in the world so great as this of the difference between myself and her; and therefore I do by the grace of God promise never to offend her more, and did this night begin to pray to God upon my knees alone in my chamber; which God knows I cannot yet do heartily, but I hope God will give me the grace more and more every day to fear Him, and to be true to my poor wife. This night the upholsters did finish the hanging of my best chamber, but my sorrow and trouble is so great about this business, that put me out of all joy in looking upon it or minding how it was.[2]

2. Despite his promises, Pepys continued to hanker for Deb, and they had a few brief encounters. Mrs. Pepys accused him of talking to Deb in his dreams, and she once threatened him with red-hot tongs. But so far as is known the affair was never consummated.

JOHN BUNYAN
1628–1688

John Bunyan is one of the most remarkable figures in seventeenth-century literature. The son of a poor Bedfordshire tinker (a maker and mender of metal pots), he received only meager schooling and then learned his father's craft. Nothing in the circumstances of his early life could have suggested that he would become a writer known the world over.

Grace Abounding to the Chief of Sinners (1666), his spiritual autobiography, records his transformation from a self-doubting sinner into an eloquent and fearless Baptist preacher. Preachers, both male and female, often even less educated than Bunyan, were common phenomena among the sects during the Commonwealth. They wished no ordination but the "call," and they could dispense with learning because they abounded in inspiration, inner light, and the gifts conferred by the Holy Spirit. In November 1660, the Anglican Church began to persecute and silence the dissenting sects. Jails filled with unlicensed Nonconformist preachers, and Bunyan was one of the prisoners. Refusing to keep silent, he chose imprisonment and so for twelve years remained in Bedford jail, preaching to his fellow prisoners and writing religious books. Upon his release, he was called to the pastorate of a Nonconformist group in Bedford. It was during a second imprisonment, in 1675, when the Test Act was once again rigorously enforced against Nonconformists, that he wrote his greatest work, *The Pilgrim's Progress from This World to That Which Is to Come* (1678), revised and augmented in the third edition (1679). Bunyan was a prolific writer: part 2 of *The Pilgrim's Progress*, dealing with the journey of Christian's wife and children, appeared in 1684; *The Life and Death of Mr. Badman*, in 1680; *The Holy War*, in 1682. And these major works form only a small part of all his writings.

The Pilgrim's Progress is the most popular allegory in English. Its basic metaphor—life is a journey—is simple and familiar; the objects that the pilgrim Christian meets are homely and commonplace: a quagmire, the highway, the bypaths and shortcuts through pleasant meadows, the inn, the steep hill, the town fair on market day, and the river that must be forded. As in the equally homely parables of Jesus, however, these simple things are charged with spiritual significance. Moreover, this is a tale of adventure. If the road that Christian travels is the King's Highway, it is also a perilous path along which we encounter giants, wild beasts, hobgoblins, and the terrible Apollyon, "the angel of the bottomless pit," whom Christian must fight. Bunyan keeps the tale firmly based on human experience, and his style, modeled on the prose of the English Bible, together with his concrete language and carefully observed details, enables even the simplest reader to share the experiences of the characters. What could be better than the following sentence? "Some cry out against sin even as the mother cries out against her child in her lap, when she calleth it slut and naughty girl, and then falls to hugging and kissing it." The Pilgrim's Progress is no longer a household book, but it survives in the phrases it gave to our language: "the slough of despond," "the house beautiful," "Mr. Worldly-Wiseman," and "Vanity Fair." And it lives again for anyone who reads beyond the first page.

From The Pilgrim's Progress

From This World to That Which Is to Come: Delivered under the Similitude of a Dream

[CHRISTIAN SETS OUT FOR THE CELESTIAL CITY]

As I walked through the wilderness of this world, I lighted on a certain place where was a den, and I laid me down in that place to sleep; and, as I slept, I dreamed a dream. I dreamed, and behold I saw a man clothed with rags, standing in a certain place, with his face from his own house, a book in his hand, and a great burden upon his back (Isaiah lxiv.6; Luke xiv.33; Psalms xxxviii.4; Habakkuk ii.2; Acts xvi.31). I looked and saw him open the book and read therein; and, as he read, he wept, and trembled; and not being able longer to contain, he brake out with a lamentable cry, saying, "What shall I do?" (Acts ii.37).

In this plight, therefore, he went home and refrained himself as long as he could, that his wife and children should not perceive his distress; but he could not be silent long, because that his trouble increased. Wherefore at length he brake his mind to his wife and children; and thus he began to talk to them. O my dear wife, said he, and you the children of my bowels, I your dear friend am in myself undone by reason of a burden that lieth hard upon me; moreover, I am for certain informed that this our city will be burned with fire from heaven, in which fearful overthrow both myself, with thee, my wife, and you, my sweet babes, shall miserably come to ruin, except (the which yet I see not) some way of escape can be found, whereby we may be delivered. At this his relations were sore amazed; not for that they believed that what he had said to them was true, but because they thought that some frenzy distemper[1] had got into his head; therefore, it drawing towards night, and they

---

1. A malady causing madness. The use of *frenzy* as an adjective was not uncommon in the 17th century.

hoping that sleep might settle his brains, with all haste they got him to bed; but the night was as troublesome to him as the day; wherefore, instead of sleeping, he spent it in sighs and tears. So when the morning was come, they would know how he did. He told them, Worse and worse; he also set to talking to them again, but they began to be hardened. They also thought to drive away his distemper by harsh and surly carriages[2] to him: sometimes they would deride, sometimes they would chide, and sometimes they would quite neglect him. Wherefore he began to retire himself to his chamber, to pray for and pity them, and also to condole his own misery; he would also walk solitarily in the fields, sometimes reading, and sometimes praying; and thus for some days he spent his time.

Now I saw, upon a time, when he was walking in the fields, that he was (as he was wont) reading in this book, and greatly distressed in his mind; and as he read, he burst out, as he had done before, crying, "What shall I do to be saved?"

I saw also that he looked this way and that way, as if he would run; yet he stood still, because (as I perceived) he could not tell which way to go. I looked then, and saw a man named Evangelist[3] coming to him, who asked, Wherefore dost thou cry? (Job xxxiii.23). He answered, Sir, I perceive by the book in my hand that I am condemned to die, and after that to come to judgment (Hebrews ix.27), and I find that I am not willing to do the first (Job xvi.21), nor able to do the second (Ezekiel xxii.14). . . .

Then said Evangelist, Why not willing to die, since this life is attended with so many evils? The man answered, Because I fear that this burden that is upon my back will sink me lower than the grave, and I shall fall into Tophet[4] (Isaiah xxx.33). And, sir, if I be not fit to go to prison, I am not fit to go to judgment, and from thence to execution; and the thoughts of these things make me cry.[5]

Then said Evangelist, If this be thy condition, why standest thou still? He answered, Because I know not whither to go. Then he gave him a parchment roll, and there was written within, "Fly from the wrath to come" (Matthew iii.7).

The man therefore read it, and looking upon Evangelist very carefully,[6] said, Whither must I fly? Then said Evangelist, pointing with his finger over a very wide field, Do you see yonder wicketgate?[7] (Matthew vii. 13, 14.) The man said, No. Then said the other, Do you see yonder shining light? (Psalms cxix.105; II Peter i.19.) He said, I think I do. Then said Evangelist, Keep that light in your eye, and go up directly thereto; so shalt thou see the gate; at which when thou knockest it shall be told thee what thou shalt do.

So I saw in my dream that the man began to run. Now, he had not run far from his own door, but his wife and children perceiving it, began to cry after him to return; but the man put his fingers in his ears, and ran on, crying, Life! life! eternal life! (Luke xiv.26.) So he looked not behind him, but fled towards the middle of the plain (Genesis xix.17).

---

2. Behavior.
3. A preacher of the Gospel; literally, a bearer of good news.
4. The place near Jerusalem where bodies and filth were burned; hence, by association, a name for hell.
5. Cry out.
6. Sorrowfully.
7. A small gate in or beside a larger gate.

The neighbors also came out to see him run (Jeremiah xx.10); and as he ran some mocked, others threatened, and some cried after him to return; and, among those that did so, there were two that resolved to fetch him back by force. The name of the one was Obstinate, and the name of the other Pliable. Now by this time the man was got a good distance from them; but, however, they were resolved to pursue him, which they did, and in a little time they overtook him. Then said the man, Neighbors, wherefore are ye come? They said, To persuade you to go back with us. But he said, That can by no means be; you dwell, said he, in the City of Destruction (the place also where I was born) I see it to be so; and, dying there, sooner or later, you will sink lower than the grave, into a place that burns with fire and brimstone; be content, good neighbors, and go along with me.

OBST. What! said Obstinate, and leave our friends and our comforts behind us?

CHR. Yes, said Christian (for that was his name), because that ALL which you shall forsake is not worthy to be compared with a little of that which I am seeking to enjoy (II Corinthians v.17); and, if you will go along with me, and hold it, you shall fare as I myself; for there, where I go, is enough and to spare (Luke xv.17). Come away, and prove my words.

OBST. What are the things you seek, since you leave all the world to find them?

CHR. I seek an inheritance incorruptible, undefiled, and that fadeth not away (I Peter i.4), and it is laid up in heaven, and safe there (Hebrews xi.16), to be bestowed, at the time appointed, on them that diligently seek it. Read it so, if you will, in my book.

OBST. Tush! said Obstinate, away with your book; will you go back with us or no?

CHR. No, not I, said the other, because I have laid my hand to the plow (Luke ix.62).

OBST. Come, then, neighbor Pliable, let us turn again, and go home without him; there is a company of these crazed-headed coxcombs, that, when they take a fancy[8] by the end, are wiser in their own eyes than seven men that can render a reason (Proverbs xxvi.16).

PLI. Then said Pliable, Don't revile; if what the good Christian says is true, the things he looks after are better than ours; my heart inclines to go with my neighbor.

OBST. What! more fools still? Be ruled by me, go back; who knows whither such a brain-sick fellow will lead you? Go back, go back, and be wise.

CHR. Nay, but do thou come with thy neighbor, Pliable; there are such things to be had which I spoke of, and many more glories besides. If you believe not me, read here in this book; and for the truth of what is expressed therein, behold, all is confirmed by the blood of Him that made it (Hebrews ix.17–22; xiii.20).

PLI. Well, neighbor Obstinate, said Pliable, I begin to come to a point,[9] I intend to go along with this good man, and to cast in my lot with him: but, my good companion, do you know the way to this desired place?

8. Delusion. "Coxcombs": fools. 9. Decision.

CHR. I am directed by a man, whose name is Evangelist, to speed me to a little gate that is before us, where we shall receive instructions about the way.

PLI. Come, then, good neighbor, let us be going. Then they went both together. * * *

[THE SLOUGH OF DESPOND]

Now I saw in my dream, that just as they had ended this talk they drew near to a very miry slough,[1] that was in the midst of the plain; and they, being heedless, did both fall suddenly into the bog. The name of the slough was Despond. Here, therefore, they wallowed for a time, being grievously bedaubed with dirt; and Christian, because of the burden that was on his back, began to sink in the mire.

PLI. Then said Pliable, Ah, neighbor Christian, where are you now?

CHR. Truly, said Christian, I do not know.

PLI. At that Pliable began to be offended, and angrily said to his fellow, Is this the happiness you have told me all this while of? If we have such ill speed at our first setting out, what may we expect 'twixt this and our journey's end? May I get out again with my life, you shall possess the brave[2] country alone for me. And, with that, he gave a desperate struggle or two, and got out of the mire on that side of the slough which was next[3] to his own house: so away he went, and Christian saw him no more.

Wherefore Christian was left to tumble in the Slough of Despond alone: but still he endeavored to struggle to that side of the slough that was further from his own house, and next to the wicket-gate; the which he did, but could not get out, because of the burden that was upon his back: but I beheld in my dream, that a man came to him, whose name was Help, and asked him what he did there?

CHR. Sir, said Christian, I was bid go this way by a man called Evangelist, who directed me also to yonder gate, that I might escape the wrath to come; and as I was going thither I fell in here.

HELP. But why did not you look for the steps?

CHR. Fear followed me so hard that I fled the next way, and fell in.

HELP. Then said he, Give me thy hand; so he gave him his hand, and he drew him out, and set him upon sound ground, and bid him go on his way.

Then I stepped to him that plucked him out, and said, Sir, wherefore, since over this place is the way from the City of Destruction to yonder gate, is it that this plat[4] is not mended, that poor travelers might go thither with more security? And he said unto me, This miry slough is such a place as cannot be mended; it is the descent whither the scum and filth that attends conviction for sin doth continually run, and therefore it was called the Slough of Despond; for still, as the sinner is awakened about his lost condition, there ariseth in his soul many fears, and doubts, and discouraging apprehensions, which all of them get together, and settle in his place. And this is the reason of the badness of this ground. * * *

---

1. Swamp (pronounced to rhyme with *now*).
2. Fine.
3. Nearest.
4. A plot of ground.

[VANITY FAIR]⁵

Then I saw in my dream, that when they were got out of the wilderness, they presently saw a town before them, and the name of that town is Vanity; and at the town there is a fair kept, called Vanity Fair; it is kept all the year long; it beareth the name of Vanity Fair because the town where it is kept is lighter than vanity; and also because all that is there sold, or that cometh thither, is vanity. As is the saying of the wise, "All that cometh is vanity" (Ecclesiastes i.2, 14; ii.11, 17; xi.8; Isaiah xl.17).

This fair is no new-erected business, but a thing of ancient standing; I will show you the original of it.

Almost five thousand years agone, there were pilgrims walking to the Celestial City, as these two honest persons are; and Beelzebub, Apollyon, and Legion,⁶ with their companions, perceiving by the path that the pilgrims made, that their way to the city lay through this town of Vanity, they contrived here to set up a fair; a fair wherein should be sold all sorts of vanity, and that it should last all the year long. Therefore at this fair are all such merchandise sold, as houses, lands, trades, places, honors, preferments,⁷ titles, countries, kingdoms, lusts, pleasures, and delights of all sorts, as whores, bawds, wives, husbands, children, masters, servants, lives, blood, bodies, souls, silver, gold, pearls, precious stones, and what not.

And, moreover, at this fair there is at all times to be seen jugglings, cheats, games, plays, fools, apes, knaves, and rogues, and that of every kind.

Here are to be seen, too, and that for nothing, thefts, murders, adulteries, false swearers, and that of a blood-red color.

And as in other fairs of less moment, there are the several rows and streets, under their proper names, where such and such wares are vended; so here likewise you have the proper places, rows, streets (viz., countries and kingdoms), where the wares of this fair are soonest to be found. Here is the Britain Row, the French Row, the Italian Row, the Spanish Row, the German Row, where several sorts of vanities are to be sold. But, as in other fairs, some one commodity is as the chief of all the fair, so the ware of Rome and her merchandise⁸ is greatly promoted in this fair; only our English nation, with some others, have taken a dislike thereat.

Now, as I said, the way to the Celestial City lies just through this town where this lusty⁹ fair is kept; and he that will go to the City, and yet not go through this town, must needs "go out of the world" (I Corinthians v.10). The Prince of princes himself, when here, went through this town to his

---

5. In this, perhaps the best-known episode in the book, Bunyan characteristically turns one of the most familiar institutions in contemporary England—annual fairs—into an allegory of universal spiritual significance. Christian and his companion Faithful pass through the town of Vanity at the season of the local fair. *Vanity* means "emptiness" or "worthlessness," and hence the fair is an allegory of worldliness and the corruption of the religious life through the attractions of the world. From earliest times numerous fairs were held for stated periods throughout Britain; to them the most important merchants from all over Europe brought their wares. The serious business

of buying and selling was accompanied by all sorts of diversions—eating, drinking, and other fleshly pleasures, as well as spectacles of strange animals, acrobats, and other wonders.

6. The "unclean spirit" sent by Jesus into the Gadarene swine (Mark 5.9). Beelzebub, prince of the devils (Matthew 12.24). Apollyon, the destroyer, "the Angel of the bottomless pit" (Revelation 9.11).

7. Appointments and promotions to political or ecclesiastical positions.

8. The practices and the temporal power of the Roman Catholic Church.

9. Cheerful, lustful.

own country, and that upon a fair-day too,[1] yea, and as I think, it was Beel-zebub, the chief lord of this fair, that invited him to buy of his vanities; yea, would have made him lord of the fair, would he but have done him reverence as he went through the town. (Matthew iv.8; Luke iv.5–7.) Yea, because he was such a person of honor, Beelzebub had him from street to street, and showed him all the kingdoms of the world in a little time, that he might, if possible, allure the Blessed One to cheapen[2] and buy some of his vanities; but he had no mind to the merchandise, and therefore left the town, without laying out so much as one farthing upon these vanities. This fair, therefore, is an ancient thing, of long standing, and a very great fair.

Now these pilgrims, as I said, must needs go through this fair. Well, so they did; but, behold, even as they entered into the fair, all the people in the fair were moved, and the town itself as it were in a hubbub about them; and that for several reasons: for

First, The pilgrims were clothed with such kind of raiment as was diverse from the raiment of any that traded in that fair. The people, therefore, of the fair, made a great gazing upon them: some said they were fools, some they were bedlams, and some they are outlandish[3] men. (I Corinthians ii.7, 8.)

Secondly, And as they wondered at their apparel, so they did likewise at their speech; for few could understand what they said; they naturally spoke the language of Canaan, but they that kept the fair were the men of this world; so that, from one end of the fair to the other, they seemed barbarians[4] each to the other.

Thirdly, But that which did not a little amuse the merchandisers was that these pilgrims set very light by all their wares; they cared not so much as to look upon them; and if they called upon them to buy, they would put their fingers in their ears, and cry, "Turn away mine eyes from beholding vanity," and look upwards, signifying that their trade and traffic was in heaven. (Psalms cxix.37; Philippians iii.19, 20.)

One chanced mockingly, beholding the carriages of the men, to say unto them, What will ye buy? But they, looking-gravely upon him, said, "We buy the truth" (Proverbs xxiii.23). At that there was an occasion taken to despise the men the more; some mocking, some taunting, some speaking reproachfully, and some calling upon others to smite them. At last things came to an hubbub and great stir in the fair, insomuch that all order was confounded. Now was word presently brought to the great one of the fair, who quickly came down, and deputed some of his most trusty friends to take these men into examination, about whom the fair was almost overturned. So the men were brought to examination; and they that sat upon them[5] asked them whence they came, whither they went, and what they did there, in such an unusual garb? The men told them that they were pilgrims and strangers in the world, and that they were going to their own country, which was the Heavenly Jerusalem (Hebrews xi.13–16); and that they had given no occasion to the men of the town, nor yet to the merchandisers, thus to abuse them,

1. The temptation of Jesus in the wilderness (Matthew 4.1–11).
2. Ask the price of.
3. Foreign. "Bedlams": lunatics from Bethlehem Hospital, the insane asylum in London.
4. The Greeks and Romans so designated all those who spoke a foreign tongue. "Canaan": the

Promised Land, ultimately conquered by the Children of Israel (Joshua 4) and settled by them; hence the pilgrims speak the language of the Bible and of the true religion. Dissenters were notorious for their habitual use of biblical language.
5. Interrogated and tried them.

and to let[6] them in their journey, except it was for that, when one asked them what they would buy, they said they would buy the truth. But they that were appointed to examine them did not believe them to be any other than bedlams and mad, or else such as came to put all things into a confusion in the fair. Therefore they took them and beat them, and besmeared them with dirt, and then put them into the cage, that they might be made a spectacle to all the men of the fair. * * *

[THE RIVER OF DEATH AND THE CELESTIAL CITY]

So I saw that when they[7] awoke, they addressed themselves to go up to the City; but, as I said, the reflection of the sun upon the City (for the City was pure gold, Revelation xxi.18) was so extremely glorious, that they could not, as yet, with open face behold it, but through an instrument made for that purpose. (II Corinthians iii.18.) So I saw that as I went on, there met them two men, in raiment that shone like gold; also their faces shone as the light.

These men asked the pilgrims whence they came; and they told them. They also asked them where they had lodged, what difficulties and dangers, what comforts and pleasures they had met in the way; and they told them. Then said the men that met them, You have but two difficulties more to meet with, and then you are in the City.

Christian then and his companion asked the men to go along with them; so they told them they would. But, said they, you must obtain it by your own faith. So I saw in my dream that they went on together till they came in sight of the gate.

Now I further saw that betwixt them and the gate was a river, but there was no bridge to go over; the river was very deep. At the sight, therefore, of this river, the pilgrims were much stunned;[8] but the men that went with them said, You must go through, or you cannot come at the gate.

The pilgrims then began to inquire if there was no other way to the gate; to which they answered, Yes; but there hath not any, save two, to wit, Enoch and Elijah,[9] been permitted to tread that path, since the foundation of the world, nor shall, until the last trumpet shall sound. (I Corinthians xv.51, 52.) The pilgrims then, especially Christian, began to despond in his mind, and looked this way and that, but no way could be found by them by which they might escape the river. Then they asked the men if the waters were all of a depth. They said no; yet they could not help them in that case; for, said they, you shall find it deeper or shallower, as you believe in the King of the place.

They then addressed themselves to the water; and entering, Christian began to sink, and crying out to his good friend Hopeful, he said, I sink in deep waters; the billows go over my head, all his waves go over me! Selah.[1]

Then said the other, Be of good cheer, my brother, I feel the bottom, and it is good. Then said Christian, Ah, my friend, the sorrows of death have compassed me about; I shall not see the land that flows with milk and honey. And with that a great darkness and horror fell upon Christian, so that he

6. Hinder.
7. Christian and his companion, Hopeful. Ignorance, who appears tragically in the final paragraph, had tried to accompany the two pilgrims but had dropped behind because of his hobbling gait.
8. Amazed.
9. Both were "translated" alive to heaven (Genesis 5.24, Hebrews 11.5, 2 Kings 2.11–12).
1. A word of uncertain meaning that occurs frequently at the end of a verse in the Psalms. Bunyan may have supposed it to signify the end.

could not see before him. Also here he in great measure lost his senses, so that he could neither remember nor orderly talk of any of those sweet refreshments that he had met with in the way of his pilgrimage. But all the words that he spake still tended to discover[2] that he had horror of mind, and heart-fears that he should die in that river, and never obtain entrance in at the gate. Here also, as they that stood by perceived, he was much in the troublesome thoughts of the sins that he had committed, both since and before he began to be a pilgrim. 'Twas also observed that he was troubled with apparitions of hobgoblins and evil spirits; for ever and anon he would intimate so much by words. Hopeful, therefore, here had much ado to keep his brother's head above water; yea, sometimes he would be quite gone down, and then, ere a while, he would rise up again half dead. Hopeful also would endeavor to comfort him, saying, Brother, I see the gate and men standing by to receive us; but Christian would answer, 'Tis you, 'tis you they wait for; you have been Hopeful ever since I knew you. And so have you, said he to Christian. Ah, brother, said he, surely if I was right he would now arise to help me; but for my sins he hath brought me into the snare, and hath left me. Then said Hopeful, My brother, you have quite forgot the text, where it is said of the wicked, "There are no bands in their death, but their strength is firm. They are not in trouble as other men, neither are they plagued like other men" (Psalms lxxiii.4, 5). These troubles and distresses that you go through in these waters are no sign that God hath forsaken you, but are sent to try you, whether you will call to mind that which heretofore you have received of his goodness, and live upon him in your distresses.

Then I saw in my dream that Christian was as in a muse[3] a while, to whom also Hopeful added this word, Be of good cheer. Jesus Christ maketh thee whole. And with that Christian brake out with a loud voice, Oh, I see him again! and he tells me, "When thou passest through the waters, I will be with thee; and through the rivers, they shall not overflow thee" (Isaiah xliii.2). Then they both took courage, and the Enemy was after that as still as a stone, until they were gone over. Christian therefore presently found ground to stand upon, and so it followed that the rest of the river was but shallow. Thus they got over. Now, upon the bank of the river on the other side, they saw the two Shining Men again, who there waited for them. Wherefore, being come out of the river, they saluted[4] them saying, We are ministering spirits, sent forth to minister for those that shall be heirs of salvation. Thus they went along towards the gate. * * *

Now when they were come up to the gate, there was written over it in letters of gold, "Blessed are they that do his commandments, that they may have right to the tree of life, and may enter in through the gates into the city" (Revelation xxii.14).

Then I saw in my dream, that the Shining Men bid them call at the gate; the which, when they did, some from above looked over the gate, to wit, Enoch, Moses, and Elijah, etc., to whom it was said, These pilgrims are come from the City of Destruction, for the love that they bear to the King of this place; and then the pilgrims gave in unto them each man his certificate, which they had received in the beginning; those, therefore, were carried in

---

2. Reveal.
3. A deep meditation.
4. Greeted.

to the King, who, when he had read them, said, Where are the men? To whom it was answered, They are standing without the gate. The King then commanded to open the gate, "That the righteous nation," said he, "which keepeth the truth, may enter in" (Isaiah xxvi.2).

Now I saw in my dream that these two men went in at the gate; and lo, as they entered, they were transfigured, and they had raiment put on that shone like gold. There was also that met them with harps and crowns, and gave them to them: the harps to praise withal, and the crowns in token of honor. Then I heard in my dream that all the bells in the city rang again for joy, and that it was said unto them, "ENTER YE INTO THE JOY OF OUR LORD" (Matthew xxv.21). I also heard the men themselves, that they sang with a loud voice, saying, "BLESSING AND HONOR, GLORY AND POWER, BE TO HIM THAT SITTETH UPON THE THRONE, AND TO THE LAMB FOREVER AND EVER" (Revelation v.13).

Now just as the gates were opened to let in the men, I looked in after them, and, behold, the City shone like the sun; the streets also were paved with gold, and in them walked many men, with crowns on their heads, palms in their hands, and golden harps to sing praises withal.

There were also of them that had wings, and they answered one another without intermission, saying, "Holy, holy, holy is the Lord" (Revelation iv.8). And after that they shut up the gates, which when I had seen I wished myself among them.

Now while I was gazing upon all these things, I turned my head to look back, and saw Ignorance come up to the riverside; but he soon got over, and that without half that difficulty which the other two men met with. For it happened that there was then in that place one Vain-hope, a ferryman, that with his boat helped him over; so he, as the other, I saw, did ascend the hill to come up to the gate, only he came alone; neither did any man meet him with the least encouragement. When he was come up to the gate, he looked up to the writing that was above, and then began to knock, supposing that entrance should have been quickly administered to him; but he was asked by the men that looked over the top of the gate, Whence came you? and what would you have? He answered, I have eat and drank in the presence of the King, and he has taught in our streets. Then they asked him for his certificate, that they might go in and show it to the King; so he fumbled in his bosom for one, and found none. Then said they, Have you none? But the man answered never a word. So they told the King, but he would not come down to see him, but commanded the two Shining Ones that conducted Christian and Hopeful to the City, to go out and take Ignorance, and bind him hand and foot, and have him away. Then they took him up, and carried him through the air, to the door that I saw in the side of the hill, and put him in there. Then I saw that there was a way to hell, even from the gates of heaven, as well as from the City of Destruction. So I awoke, and behold it was a dream.

1678

JOHN LOCKE
1632–1704

John Locke's *Essay Concerning Human Understanding* (1690) is "a history-book," according to Laurence Sterne, "of what passes in a man's own mind." Like Montaigne's essays, it aims to explore the human mind in general by closely watching one particular mind. When Locke analyzed his ideas, the ways they were acquired and put together, he found they were clear when they were based on direct experience and adequate when they were clear. Usually, it appeared, problems occurred when basic ideas were blurred or confused or did not refer to anything determinate. Thus a critical analysis of the ideas in an individual mind could lead straight to a rule about adequate ideas in general and the sort of subject where adequate ideas were possible. On the basis of such a limitation, individuals might reach rational agreement with one another and so set up an area of natural law, within which a common rule of understanding was available.

Locke's new "way of ideas" strikes a humble, antidogmatic note, but readers quickly perceived its far-reaching implications. By basing knowledge on the ideas immediately "before the mind," Locke comports with and helps codify the movement of his times away from the authority of traditions of medieval, scholastic philosophy. His approach also alarmed some divines who argued that the foundation of human life—the mysteries of faith—could never be reduced to clear, distinct ideas. Locke indirectly accepts the Christian scriptures in the *Essay* in the midst of his famous critique of "enthusiasm," the belief in private revelation, but his main impulse is to restrain rather than to encourage religious speculations. (His fullest theological work, *The Reasonableness of Christianity,* 1695, argues that scriptural revelation is necessary for right-thinking people but not incompatible with ordinary reasonable beliefs gathered from personal experience and history.) The *Essay* also contains an unsettling discussion of personal identity (in the chapter "Of Identity and Diversity" added to the second edition in 1694). Locke argues that a person's sense of selfhood derives not from the "identity of soul" but rather from "consciousness of present and past actions": I am myself now because I remember my past, not because a unique substance ("me") underlies everything I experience. This account drew critical responses from numerous distinguished thinkers throughout the eighteenth century, notably Bishop Joseph Butler (1692–1752).

Locke spent his life in thought. His background and connections were all with the Puritan movement, but he was disillusioned early with the enthusiastic moods and persecutions to which he found the Puritans prone. Having a small but steady private income, he became a student, chiefly at Oxford, learning enough medicine to act as a physician, holding an occasional appointive office, but never allowing any of these activities to limit his controlling passion: the urge to think. After 1667, he was personal physician and tutor in the household of a violent, crafty politician, the first earl of Shaftesbury (Dryden's "Achitophel"). But Locke himself was always a grave, dispassionate man. On one occasion, Shaftesbury's political enemies at Oxford had Locke watched for several years on end, during which he was not heard to say one word either critical of the government or favorable to it. When times are turbulent, so much discretion is suspicious in itself, and Locke found it convenient to go abroad for several years during the 1680s. He lived quietly in Holland and pursued his thoughts. The Glorious Revolution of 1688–89 and the accession of William III brought him back to England and made possible the publication of the *Essay,* on which he had been working for many years. Its publication foreshadowed the coming age, not only in the positive ideas that the book advanced but in the quiet way it set aside as insoluble a range of problems about absolute authority and absolute assurance that had torn society apart earlier in the seventeenth century.

From An Essay Concerning Human Understanding

From *The Epistle to the Reader*

Reader,

I here put into thy hands what has been the diversion of some of my idle and heavy hours; if it has the good luck to prove so of any of thine, and thou hast but half so much pleasure in reading as I had in writing it, thou wilt as little think thy money, as I do my pains, ill-bestowed. Mistake not this for a commendation of my work; nor conclude, because I was pleased with the doing of it, that therefore I am fondly taken with it now it is done. He that hawks at larks and sparrows, has no less sport, though a much less considerable quarry, than he that flies at nobler game: and he is little acquainted with the subject of this treatise, the Understanding, who does not know, that as it is the most elevated faculty of the soul, so it is employed with a greater and more constant delight than any of the other. Its searches after truth are a sort of hawking and hunting, wherein the very pursuit makes a great part of the pleasure. Every step the mind takes in its progress towards knowledge makes some discovery, which is not only new, but the best, too, for the time at least.

For the understanding, like the eye, judging of objects only by its own sight, cannot but be pleased with what it discovers, having less regret for what has escaped it, because it is unknown. Thus he who has raised himself above the alms-basket, and, not content to live lazily on scraps of begged opinions, sets his own thoughts on work to find and follow truth, will (whatever he lights on) not miss the hunter's satisfaction; every moment of his pursuit will reward his pains with some delight, and he will have reason to think his time not ill-spent, even when he cannot much boast of any great acquisition.

This, reader, is the entertainment of those who let loose their own thoughts, and follow them in writing; which thou oughtest not to envy them, since they afford thee an opportunity of the like diversion, if thou wilt make use of thy own thoughts in reading. It is to them, if they are thy own, that I refer myself; but if they are taken upon trust from others, it is no great matter what they are, they not following truth, but some meaner consideration; and it is not worthwhile to be concerned what he says or thinks, who says or thinks only as he is directed by another. If thou judgest for thyself, I know thou wilt judge candidly; and then I shall not be harmed or offended, whatever be thy censure. For, though it be certain that there is nothing in this treatise of the truth whereof I am not fully persuaded, yet I consider myself as liable to mistakes as I can think thee; and know that this book must stand or fall with thee, not by any opinion I have of it, but thy own. If thou findest little in it new or instructive to thee, thou art not to blame me for it. It was not meant for those that had already mastered this subject, and made a thorough acquaintance with their own understandings, but for my own information, and the satisfaction of a few friends, who acknowledged themselves not to have sufficiently considered it. Were it fit to trouble thee with the history of this Essay, I should tell thee, that five or six friends, meeting at my chamber, and discoursing on a subject very remote from this, found themselves quickly at a stand by the difficulties that rose on every side. After we had awhile puzzled ourselves, without coming any nearer a resolution of those doubts which perplexed us, it came into my thoughts, that we took a wrong course; and that, before we set ourselves upon inquiries of that nature, it was necessary to examine our own abilities, and see what objects our understandings were or were not fitted to deal with. This I proposed to the company, who all readily assented; and thereupon it was agreed, that this should be our first inquiry. Some hasty and undigested thoughts, on a subject I had never before considered, which I set down against[1] our next meeting, gave the first entrance into this discourse, which, having been thus begun by chance, was continued by entreaty; written by incoherent parcels; and, after long intervals of neglect, resumed again, as my humor or occasions permitted; and at last, in a retirement, where an attendance on my health gave me leisure, it was brought into that order thou now seest it.

This discontinued way of writing may have occasioned, besides others, two contrary faults; viz., that too little and too much may be said in it. If thou findest anything wanting, I shall be glad that what I have writ gives thee any desire that I should have gone farther: if it seems too much to thee, thou must blame the subject; for when I first put pen to paper, I thought all I should have to say on this matter would have been contained in one sheet of paper; but the farther I went, the larger prospect I had: new discoveries led me still on, and so it grew insensibly to the bulk it now appears in. I will not deny but possibly it might be reduced to a narrower compass than it is; and that some parts of it might be contracted; the way it has been writ in, by catches,[2] and many long intervals of interruption, being apt to cause some repetitions. But, to confess the truth, I am now too lazy or too busy to make it shorter.

* * * I pretend not to publish this Essay for the information of men of large thoughts and quick apprehensions; to such masters of knowledge, I profess myself a scholar, and therefore warn them beforehand not to expect anything here but what, being spun out of my own coarse thoughts, is fitted to men of my own size, to whom, perhaps, it will not be unacceptable that I have taken some pains to make plain and familiar to their thoughts some truths, which established prejudice or the abstractness of the ideas themselves might render difficult.

* * *

The commonwealth of learning is not at this time without masterbuilders, whose mighty designs in advancing, the sciences will leave lasting monuments to the admiration of posterity: but everyone must not hope to be a Boyle or a Sydenham; and in an age that produces such masters as the great Huygenius, and the incomparable Mr. Newton,[3] with some other of

1. Before.
2. Fragments.
3. Sir Isaac Newton. Robert Boyle, the great Anglo-Irish chemist and physicist. Thomas Sydenham, a physician and authority on the treatment of fevers. Christiaan Huygens, Dutch mathematician and astronomer.

that strain, it is ambition enough to be employed as an under-laborer in clearing the ground a little, and removing some of the rubbish that lies in the way to knowledge; which certainly had been very much more advanced in the world, if the endeavors of ingenious and industrious men had not been much cumbered with the learned but frivolous use of uncouth, affected, or unintelligible terms introduced into the sciences, and there made an art of to that degree that philosophy, which is nothing but the true knowledge of things, was thought unfit or uncapable to be brought into well-bred company and polite conversation.[4] Vague and insignificant forms of speech, and abuse of language, have so long passed for mysteries of science; and hard or misapplied words, with little or no meaning, have, by prescription, such a right to be mistaken for deep learning and height of speculation; that it will not be easy to persuade either those who speak or those who hear them, that they are but the covers of ignorance, and hindrance of true knowledge. * * *

The booksellers, preparing for the fourth edition of my Essay, gave me notice of it, that I might, if I had leisure, make any additions or alterations I should think fit. Whereupon I thought it convenient to advertise the reader, that besides several corrections I had made here and there, there was one alteration which it was necessary to mention, because it ran through the whole book, and is of consequence to be rightly understood. What I thereupon said, was this:—

"Clear and distinct ideas" are terms which, though familiar and frequent in men's mouths, I have reason to think everyone who uses does not perfectly understand. And possibly it is but here and there one who gives himself the trouble to consider them so far as to know what he himself or others precisely mean by them. I have therefore, in most places, chose to put "determinate" or "determined,"[5] instead of "clear" and "distinct," as more likely to direct men's thoughts to my meaning in this matter. By those denominations, I mean some object in the mind, and consequently determined, i.e., such as it is there seen and perceived to be. This, I think, may fitly be called a "determinate" or "determined" idea, when such as it is at any time objectively in the mind, and so determined there, it is annexed, and without variation determined, to a name or articulate sound which is to be steadily the sign of that very same object of the mind, or determinate idea.

To explain this a little more particularly: By "determinate," when applied to a simple idea, I mean that simple appearance which the mind has in its view, or perceives in itself, when that idea is said to be in it. By "determined," when applied to a complex idea, I mean such an one as consists of a determinate number of certain simple or less complex ideas, joined in such a proportion and situation as the mind has before its view, and sees in itself, when that idea is present in it, or should be present in it, when a man gives a name to it. I say "should be"; because it is not everyone, nor perhaps anyone, who is so careful of his language as to use no word till he views in his mind the precise determined idea which he resolves to make it the sign of. The want

4. Locke was tutor to Anthony Ashley Cooper, third earl of Shaftesbury, whose philosophical writings make of genteel social conversation and civilized good humor something like guides to ultimate truth.
5. Definite, limited, fixed in value.

of this is the cause of no small obscurity and confusion in men's thoughts and discourses.

I know there are not words enough in any language to answer all the variety of ideas that enter into men's discourses and reasonings. But this hinders not but that when anyone uses any term, he may have in his mind a determined idea which he makes it the sign of, and to which he should keep it steadily annexed during that present discourse. Where he does not or cannot do this, he in vain pretends to clear or distinct ideas: it is plain his are not so; and therefore there can be expected nothing but obscurity and confusion, where such terms are made use of which have not such a precise determination.

Upon this ground I have thought "determined ideas" a way of speaking less liable to mistake than "clear and distinct"; and where men have got such determined ideas of all that they reason, inquire, or argue about, they will find a great part of their doubts and disputes at an end; the greatest part of the questions and controversies that perplex mankind depending on the doubtful and uncertain use of words, or (which is the same) indetermined ideas, which they are made to stand for. I have made choice of these terms to signify, 1. Some immediate object of the mind, which it perceives and has before it, distinct from the sound it uses as a sign of it. 2. That this idea, thus determined, i.e., which the mind has in itself, and knows and sees there, be determined without any change to that name, and that name determined to that precise idea. If men had such determined ideas in their inquiries and discourses, they would both discern how far their own inquiries and discourses went, and avoid the greatest part of the disputes and wranglings they have with others.

*   *   *

1690, 1700

SIR ISAAC NEWTON
1642–1727

Isaac Newton was the posthumous son of a Lincolnshire farmer. As a boy, he invented machines; as an undergraduate, he made major discoveries in optics and mathematics; and in 1667—at twenty-five—he was elected a fellow of Trinity College, Cambridge. Two years later his teacher, Isaac Barrow, resigned the Lucasian Chair of Mathematics in his favor. By then, in secret, Newton had already begun to rethink the universe. His mind worked incessantly, at the highest level of insight, both theoretical and experimental. He designed the first reflecting telescope and explained why the sky looks blue; contemporaneously with Leibniz, he invented calculus; he revolutionized the study of mechanics and physics with three basic laws of motion; and as everyone knows, he discovered the universal law of gravity. Although Newton's *Principia* (*Mathematical Principles of Natural Philosophy*, 1687) made possible the modern understanding of the cosmos, his *Opticks* (1704) had a still greater impact on his contemporaries, not only for its discoveries about light and color but also for its formulation of a proper scientific method.

Newton reported most of his scientific findings in Latin, the language of international scholarship; but when he chose, he could express himself in crisp and vigorous English. His early experiments on light and color were described in a letter to Henry Oldenburg, secretary of the Royal Society, and quickly published in the society's journal. By analyzing the spectrum, Newton had discovered something amazing, the "oddest if not the most considerable detection, which hath hitherto been made in the operations of nature": light is not homogeneous, as everyone thought, but a compound of heterogeneous rays, and white is not the absence of color but a composite of all sorts of colors. Newton assumes that a clear account of his experiments and reasoning will compel assent; when, at the end of his summary, he drops a very heavy word, he clinches the point like a carpenter nailing a box shut. But other scientists resisted the theory. In years to come, Newton would be more wary; eventually he would leave the university to become master of the mint in London and to devote himself to religious studies. Yet all the while his fame would continue to grow. "There could be only one Newton," Napoleon was told a century later: "there was only one world to discover."

From A Letter of Mr. Isaac Newton, Professor of the Mathematics in the University of Cambridge, Containing His New Theory about Light and Colors

Sent by the Author to the Publisher from Cambridge, Febr. 6, 1672, in order to Be Communicated to the Royal Society

Sir,

To perform my late promise to you, I shall without further ceremony acquaint you that in the beginning of the year 1666 (at which time I applied myself to the grinding of optic glasses of other figures than spherical) I procured me a triangular glass prism to try therewith the celebrated phenomena of colors. And in order thereto having darkened my chamber and made a small hole in my window-shuts to let in a convenient quantity of the sun's light, I placed my prism at his entrance that it might be thereby refracted[1] to the opposite wall. It was at first a very pleasing divertissement to view the vivid and intense colors produced thereby; but after a while, applying myself to consider them more circumspectly, I became surprised to see them in an *oblong* form, which according to the received laws of refraction I expected should have been *circular*.

They were terminated at the sides with straight lines, but at the ends the decay of light was so gradual that it was difficult to determine justly what was their figure; yet they seemed *semicircular*.

Comparing the length of this colored spectrum with its breadth, I found it about five times greater, a disproportion so extravagant that it excited me to a more than ordinary curiosity of examining from whence it might proceed. I could scarce think that the various thickness of the glass or the termina-

---

1. I.e., that the light's direction might be diverted from a straight path.

tion with shadow or darkness could have any influence on light to produce such an effect; yet I thought it not amiss first to examine those circumstances, and so tried what would happen by transmitting light through parts of the glass of divers thicknesses, or through holes in the window of divers bignesses, or by setting the prism without, so that the light might pass through it and be refracted before it was terminated by the hole. But I found none of those circumstances material. The fashion of the colors was in all these cases the same.

Then I suspected whether by any unevenness in the glass or other contingent irregularity these colors might be thus dilated. And to try this, I took another prism like the former and so placed it that the light, passing through them both, might be refracted contrary ways, and so by the latter returned into that course from which the former had diverted it. For by this means I thought the regular effects of the first prism would be destroyed by the second prism, but the irregular ones more augmented by the multiplicity of refractions. The event was that the light, which by the first prism was diffused into an oblong form, was by the second reduced into an orbicular one with as much regularity as when it did not at all pass through them. So that, whatever was the cause of that length, 'twas not any contingent irregularity.[2]

* * *

The gradual removal of these suspicions at length led me to the *experimentum crucis*,[3] which was this: I took two boards, and placed one of them close behind the prism at the window, so that the light might pass through a small hole made in it for the purpose and fall on the other board, which I placed at about 12 foot distance, having first made a small hole in it also, for some of that incident[4] light to pass through. Then I placed another prism behind this second board so that the light, trajected through both the boards, might pass through that also, and be again refracted before it arrived at the wall. This done, I took the first prism in my hand, and turned it to and fro slowly about its axis, so much as to make the several parts of the image, cast on the second board, successively pass through the hole in it, that I might observe to what places on the wall the second prism would refract them. And I saw by the variation of those places that the light, tending to that end of the image towards which the refraction of the first prism was made, did in the second prism suffer a refraction considerably greater than the light tending to the other end. And so the true cause of the length of that image was detected to be no other than that light consists of *rays differently refrangible*, which, without any respect to a difference in their incidence, were, according to their degrees of refrangibility, transmitted towards divers parts of the wall.[5]

* * *

2. Newton goes on to describe several experiments and calculations by which he disposed of alternative theories—that rays coming from different parts of the sun caused the diffusion of light into an oblong or that the rays of light traveled in curved paths after leaving the prism.
3. Crucial experiment (Latin); turning point.
4. From the Latin *incidere*, to fall into or onto. Newton uses it in reference to light striking an obstacle.

5. This insight enables Newton to design a greatly improved telescope, which uses reflections to correct the distortions caused by the scattering of refracted rays. He adds in passing that his experiments were interrupted for two years by the plague; but at last he returns to some further and even more important characteristics of light. "Refrangible": susceptible to being refracted.

I shall now proceed to acquaint you with another more notable difformity[6] in its rays, wherein the *origin of colors* is infolded. A naturalist[7] would scarce expect to see the science of those become mathematical, and yet I dare affirm that there is as much certainty in it as in any other part of optics. For what I shall tell concerning them is not an hypothesis but most rigid consequence, not conjectured by barely inferring 'tis thus because not otherwise or because it satisfied all phenomena (the philosophers' universal topic) but evinced by the mediation of experiments concluding directly and without any suspicion of doubt. * * *

The doctrine you will find comprehended and illustrated in the following propositions.

1. As the rays of light differ in degrees of refrangibility, so they also differ in their disposition to exhibit this or that particular color. Colors are not *qualifications of light*, derived from refractions or reflections of natural bodies (as 'tis generally believed), but *original and connate properties* which in divers rays are divers. Some rays are disposed to exhibit a red color and no other; some a yellow and no other, some a green and no other, and so of the rest. Nor are there only rays proper and particular to the more eminent colors, but even to all their intermediate gradations.

2. To the same degree of refrangibility ever belongs the same color, and to the same color ever belongs the same degree of refrangibility. The least refrangible rays are all disposed to exhibit a red color, and contrarily those rays which are disposed to exhibit a red color are all the least refrangible. So the most refrangible rays are all disposed to exhibit a deep violet color, and contrarily those which are apt to exhibit such a violet color are all the most refrangible. And so to all the intermediate colors in a continued series belong intermediate degrees of refrangibility. And this analogy 'twixt colors and refrangibility is very precise and strict; the rays always either exactly agreeing in both or proportionally disagreeing in both.

3. The species of color and degree of refrangibility proper to any particular sort of rays is not mutable by refraction, nor by reflection from natural bodies, nor by any other cause that I could yet observe. When any one sort of rays hath been well parted from those of other kinds, it hath afterwards obstinately retained its color, notwithstanding my utmost endeavors to change it. I have refracted it with prisms and reflected it with bodies which in daylight were of other colors; I have intercepted it with the colored film of air interceding two compressed plates of glass; transmitted it through colored mediums and through mediums irradiated with other sorts of rays, and diversely terminated it; and yet could never produce any new color out of it. It would by contracting or dilating become more brisk or faint and by the loss of many rays in some cases very obscure and dark; but I could never see it changed *in specie*.[8]

4. Yet seeming transmutations of colors may be made, where there is any mixture of divers sorts of rays. For in such mixtures, the component colors appear not, but by their mutual allaying each other constitute a middling color. And therefore, if by refraction or any other of the aforesaid causes the difform rays latent in such a mixture be separated, there shall emerge colors

6. Diversity of forms.
7. A student of physics or "natural philosophy."
8. In kind.

different from the color of the composition. Which colors are not new generated, but only made apparent by being parted; for if they be again entirely mixed and blended together, they will again compose that color which they did before separation. And for the same reason, transmutations made by the convening of divers colors are not real; for when the difform rays are again severed, they will exhibit the very same colors which they did before they entered the composition—as you see blue and yellow powders when finely mixed appear to the naked eye green, and yet the colors of the component corpuscles are not thereby transmuted, but only blended. For, when viewed with a good microscope, they still appear blue and yellow interspersedly.

5. There are therefore two sorts of colors: the one original and simple, the other compounded of these. The original or primary colors are red, yellow, green, blue, and a violet-purple, together with orange, indigo, and an indefinite variety of intermediate graduations.

6. The same colors *in specie* with these primary ones may be also produced by composition. For a mixture of yellow and blue makes green; of red and yellow makes orange; of orange and yellowish green makes yellow. And in general, if any two colors be mixed which, in the series of those generated by the prism, are not too far distant one from another, they by their mutual alloy compound that color which in the said series appeareth in the mid-way between them. But those which are situated at too great a distance, do not so. Orange and indigo produce not the intermediate green, nor scarlet and green the intermediate yellow.

7. But the most surprising and wonderful composition was that of *whiteness*. There is no one sort of rays which alone can exhibit this. 'Tis ever compounded, and to its composition are requisite all the aforesaid primary colors, mixed in a due proportion. I have often with admiration beheld that all the colors of the prism, being made to converge, and thereby to be again mixed as they were in the light before it was incident upon the prism, reproduced light entirely and perfectly white, and not at all sensibly differing from a direct light of the sun, unless when the glasses I used were not sufficiently clear; for then they would a little incline it to *their* color.

8. Hence therefore it comes to pass that *whiteness* is the usual color of light, for light is a confused aggregate of rays endued with all sorts of colors, as they are promiscuously darted from the various parts of luminous bodies. And of such a confused aggregate, as I said, is generated whiteness, if there be a due proportion of the ingredients; but if any one predominate, the light must incline to that color, as it happens in the blue flame of brimstone, the yellow flame of a candle, and the various colors of the fixed stars.

9. These things considered, the manner how colors are produced by the prism is evident. For of the rays constituting the incident light, since those which differ in color proportionally differ in refrangibility, they by their unequal refractions must be severed and dispersed into an oblong form in an orderly succession from the least refracted scarlet to the most refracted violet. And for the same reason it is that objects, when looked upon through a prism, appear colored. For the difform rays, by their unequal refractions, are made to diverge towards several parts of the retina, and there express the images of things colored, as in the former case they did the sun's image upon a wall. And by this inequality of refractions they become not only colored, but also very confused and indistinct.

10. Why the colors of the rainbow appear in falling drops of rain is also from hence evident. For those drops which refract the rays disposed to appear purple in greatest quantity to the spectator's eye, refract the rays of other sorts so much less as to make them pass beside it;[9] and such are the drops on the inside of the primary bow and on the outside of the secondary or exterior one. So those drops which refract in greatest plenty the rays apt to appear red toward the spectator's eye, refract those of other sorts so much more as to make them pass beside it; and such are the drops on the exterior part of the primary and interior part of the secondary bow.

* * *

13. I might add more instances of this nature, but I shall conclude with this general one, that the colors of all natural bodies have no other origin than this, that they are variously qualified to reflect one sort of light in greater plenty than another. And this I have experimented in a dark room by illuminating those bodies with uncompounded light of divers colors. For by that means any body may be made to appear of any color. They have there no appropriate color, but ever appear of the color of the light cast upon them, but yet with this difference, that they are most brisk and vivid in the light of their own daylight color. *Minium* appeareth there of any color indifferently with which 'tis illustrated, but yet most luminous in red, and so *Bise*[1] appeareth indifferently of any color with which 'tis illustrated, but yet most luminous in blue. And therefore *minium* reflecteth rays of any color, but most copiously those endued with red; and consequently when illustrated with daylight, that is, with all sorts of rays promiscuously blended, those qualified with red shall abound most in the reflected light, and by their prevalence cause it to appear of that color. And for the same reason *bise*, reflecting blue most copiously, shall appear blue by the excess of those rays in its reflected light; and the like of other bodies. And that this is the entire and adequate cause of their colors is manifest, because they have no power to change or alter the colors of any sort of rays incident apart, but put on all colors indifferently with which they are enlightened.

These things being so, it can no longer be disputed whether there be colors in the dark, nor whether they be the qualities of the objects we see, no, nor perhaps whether light be a body. For since colors are the qualities of light, having its rays for their entire and immediate subject,[2] how can we think those rays qualities also, unless one quality may be the subject of and sustain another—which in effect is to call it substance. We should not know bodies for substances were it not for their sensible qualities, and the principal of those being now found due to something else, we have as good reason to believe that to be a substance also.[3]

Besides, who ever thought any quality to be a heterogeneous aggregate, such as light is discovered to be? But to determine more absolutely what light is, after what manner refracted, and by what modes or actions it pro-

---

9. I.e., disappear alongside it.
1. Azurite blue. "Minium": red lead. "Illustrated": illuminated.
2. That of which a thing consists.
3. I.e., the only way we know bodies are substances is that our senses perceive their qualities.

The chief of these qualities, color, is now known to be a quality of light, not body; our conclusion can perfectly well be that light is a form of substance, as well as body, and that we know it to be so through its quality, color.

duceth in our minds the phantasms of colors, is not so easy. And I shall not mingle conjectures with certainties.

＊　＊　＊

1672

SAMUEL BUTLER
1612–1680

Samuel Butler passed his middle years during the fury of the civil wars and under the Commonwealth, sardonically observing the behavior and lovingly memorizing the faults of the Puritan rulers. He despised them and found relief for his feelings by satirizing them, though, naturally enough, he could not publish while they were in power. He served as clerk to several Puritan justices of the peace in the west of England, one of whom, according to tradition, was the original of Sir Hudibras (the *s* is pronounced). *Hudibras,* part 1, was published late in 1662 (the edition bears the date 1663) and pleased the triumphant Royalists. King Charles II admired and often quoted the poem and rewarded its author with a gift of £300; it was, after all, a relief to laugh at what he had earlier hated and feared. The first part, attacking Presbyterians and Independents, proved more vigorous and effective than parts 2 and 3, which followed in 1664 and 1678, respectively. After his initial success, Butler was neglected by the people he had pleased. He died in poverty, and not until 1721 was a monument to his memory erected in Westminster Abbey.

Hudibras is a travesty, or burlesque: it takes a serious subject and debases it by using a low style or distorts it by grotesque exaggeration. Butler carried this mode even into his verse, for he reduced the iambic tetrameter line (used subtly and seriously by such seventeenth-century poets as John Donne, John Milton, and Andrew Marvell) to something approaching doggerel, and his boldly comic rhymes add to the effect of broad comedy that he sought to create. Burlesque was a popular form of satire during the seventeenth century, especially after the French poet Paul Scarron published his *Virgile Travesti* (1648), which retells the *Aeneid* in slang. Butler's use of burlesque expresses his contempt for the Puritans and their commonwealth; the history of England from 1642 to 1660 is made to appear mere sound and fury.

Butler took his hero's name from Spenser's *Faerie Queene* 2.2, where Sir Huddibras appears briefly as a rash adventurer and lover. The questing knight of chivalric romance is degraded into the meddling, hypocritical busybody Hudibras, who goes out, like an officer in Cromwell's army, "a-coloneling" against the popular sport of bear baiting. The knight and his squire, Ralph, suggest Don Quixote and Sancho Panza, but the temper of Butler's mind is as remote from Cervantes's warm humanity as it is from Spenser's ardent idealism. Butler had no illusions; he was skeptical in philosophy and conservative in politics, distrusting theoretical reasoning and the new science, disdainful of claims of inspiration and illumination, contemptuous of Catholicism and dubious of bishops, Anglican no less than Roman. It is difficult to think of anything that he approved unless it was peace, common sense, and the wisdom that emerges from the experience of humankind through the ages.

William Hogarth, *Hudibras, the Manner How He Sallied Forth*; engraving, 1726. Hudibras riding out to go a-coloneling, with his squire Ralph. From *Hudibras*, by Samuel Butler (1793).

From Hudibras

From *Part 1, Canto 1*

THE ARGUMENT

Sir Hudibras, his passing worth,
The manner how he sallied forth,
His arms and equipage are shown,
His horse's virtues and his own:
The adventure of the Bear and Fiddle
Is sung, but breaks off in the middle.

When civil fury[1] first grew high,
And men fell out, they knew not why;
When hard words, jealousies, and fears
Set folks together by the ears
5   And made them fight, like mad or drunk,
For Dame Religion as for punk,°   prostitute
Whose honesty they all durst swear for,
Though not a man of them knew wherefore;
When gospel-trumpeter,[2] surrounded
10 With long-eared rout,[3] to battle sounded,
And pulpit, drum ecclesiastic,[4]

1. The civil wars between Royalists and Parliamentarians (1642–49).
2. A Presbyterian minister vehemently preaching rebellion.
3. A mob of Puritans or Roundheads, so called because they wore their hair short instead of in

flowing curls and thus exposed their ears, which to many satirists suggested the long ears of the ass.
4. The Presbyterian clergy were said to have preached the country into the civil wars. Hence, in pounding their pulpits with their fists, they are said to beat their ecclesiastical drums.

Was beat with fist instead of a stick;
Then did Sir Knight abandon dwelling,
And out he rode a-coloneling.[5]
15   A wight° he was whose very sight would   *creature*
Entitle him Mirror of Knighthood;
That never bent his stubborn knee
To anything but chivalry,
Nor put up blow but that which laid
20   Right worshipful on shoulder blade;[6]
Chief of domestic knights and errant,[7]
Either for chartel[8] or for warrant;
Great on the bench, great in the saddle,[9]
That could as well bind o'er as swaddle.[1]
25   Mighty he was at both of these,
And styled of war as well as peace.
(So some rats of amphibious nature
Are either for the land or water.)
But here our authors make a doubt
30   Whether he were more wise or stout.
Some hold the one and some the other;
But howsoe'er they make a pother,
The difference was so small his brain
Outweighed his rage but half a grain;
35   Which made some take him for a tool
That knaves do work with, called a fool,
And offer to lay wagers that,
As Montaigne, playing with his cat,
Complains she thought him but an ass,[2]
40   Much more she would Sir Hudibras
(For that's the name our valiant knight
To all his challenges did write).
But they're mistaken very much,
'Tis plain enough he was no such.
45   We grant, although he had much wit,
He was very shy of using it;
As being loath to wear it out,
And therefore bore it not about,
Unless on holidays, or so,
50   As men their best apparel do.
Beside, 'tis known he could speak Greek
As naturally as pigs squeak;
That Latin was no more difficile
Than to a blackbird 'tis to whistle.

5. Here pronounced *có-lo-nel-ing.*
6. When a man is knighted he kneels and is tapped on the shoulder by his overlord's sword.
7. Spelled and pronounced *arrant.*
8. A written challenge to combat, such as a knight-errant sends.
9. Hudibras, as justice of the peace ("domestic knight"), could also issue a "warrant" (a writ authorizing an arrest, a seizure, or a search). Hence he is satirically called "great on the [jus-

tice's] bench" as well as in the saddle.
1. Both justice of the peace and soldier, he is equally able to "bind over" a malefactor to be tried at the next sessions or, in his role of colonel, to beat ("swaddle") him.
2. In his "Apology for Raymond Sebond," Michel de Montaigne (1533–1592), French skeptic and essayist, wondered whether he played with his cat or his cat played with him.

55 Being rich in both, he never scanted
His bounty unto such as wanted,
But much of either would afford
To many that had not one word.
For Hebrew roots, although they're found
60 To flourish most in barren ground,[3]
He had such plenty as sufficed
To make some think him circumcised;
And truly so perhaps he was,
'Tis many a pious Christian's case.
65   He was in logic a great critic,
Profoundly skilled in analytic.
He could distinguish and divide
A hair 'twixt south and southwest side;
On either which he would dispute,
70 Confute, change hands, and still confute.
He'd undertake to prove, by force
Of argument, a man's no horse;
He'd prove a buzzard is no fowl,
And that a lord may be an owl,
75 A calf an alderman, a goose a justice,
And rooks committee-men and trustees.[4]
He'd run in debt by disputation,
And pay with ratiocination.
All this by syllogism true,
80 In mood and figure,[5] he would do.
    For rhetoric, he could not ope
His mouth but out there flew a trope°   *figure of speech*
And when he happened to break off
In the middle of his speech, or cough,[6]
85 He had hard words ready to show why,
And tell what rules he did it by.
Else, when with greatest art he spoke,
You'd think he talked like other folk;
For all a rhetorician's rules
90 Teach nothing but to name his tools.
His ordinary rate of speech
In loftiness of sound was rich,
A Babylonish dialect,[7]
Which learned pedants much affect.[8]
95 It was a parti-colored dress
Of patched and piebald languages;
'Twas English cut on Greek and Latin,

---

3. Hebrew, the language of Adam, was thought of as the primitive language, the one that people in a state of nature would naturally speak.
4. Committees were set up in the counties by Parliament and given authority to imprison Royalists and to sequestrate their estates. "Rooks": a kind of blackbird; here, cheats (slang).
5. The "figure" of a syllogism is "the proper dispo-sition of the middle term with the parts of the question." "Mood": the form of an argument.
6. Some pulpit orators regarded hemming and coughing as ornaments of speech.
7. Alludes to the confusion of languages with which God afflicts the builders of the Tower of Babel (Genesis 11.4–9).
8. Pedants affected the use of foreign words.

Like fustian heretofore on satin.[9]
It had an odd promiscuous tone,
100 As if he had talked three parts in one;
Which made some think, when he did gabble,
They had heard three laborers of Babel,
Or Cerberus himself pronounce
A leash of languages at once.[1]
105 This he as volubly would vent
As if his stock would ne'er be spent;
And truly, to support that charge,
He had supplies as vast and large.
For he could coin or counterfeit
110 New words with little or no wit;[2]
Words so debased and hard no stone
Was hard enough to touch them on.[3]
And when with hasty noise he spoke 'em,
The ignorant for current took 'em;
115 That had the orator, who once
Did fill his mouth with pebble-stones
When he harangued,[4] but known his phrase,
He would have used no other ways.
      In mathematics he was greater
120 Than Tycho Brahe, or Erra Pater:[5]
For he, by geometric scale,
Could take the size of pots of ale;
Resolve by sines and tangents straight,
If bread or butter wanted weight;
125 And wisely tell what hour o' the day
The clock does strike, by algebra.
      Beside, he was a shrewd philosopher,
And had read every text and gloss over;
Whate'er the crabbed'st author hath,
130 He understood by implicit faith;
Whatever skeptic could inquire for,
For every *why* he had a *wherefore*;
Knew more than forty of them do,
As far as words and terms could go.
135 All which he understood by rote
And, as occasion served, would quote,
No matter whether right or wrong;
They might be either said or sung.
His notions fitted things so well
140 That which was which he could not tell,
But oftentimes mistook the one

9. Clothes made of coarse cloth ("fustian") were slashed to display the richer satin lining. "Fustian" also means pompous, banal speech.
1. The sporting term "leash" denotes a group of three dogs, hawks, deer, etc., hence, three in general. Cerberus was the three-headed dog that guarded the entrance to Hades.
2. The Presbyterians and other sects invented a special religious vocabulary, much ridiculed by Anglicans: *out-goings, workings-out, gospel-walking-times*, etc.
3. Touchstones were used to test gold and silver for purity.
4. Demosthenes cured a stutter by speaking with pebbles in his mouth.
5. Butler's contemptuous name for the popular astrologer William Lilly (1602–1681). Brahe (1546–1601), a Danish astronomer.

For the other, as great clerks° have done.⁶   *scholars*
He could reduce all things to acts,
And knew their natures by abstracts;
145 Where entity and quiddity,
The ghosts of defunct bodies,⁷ fly;
Where truth in person does appear,
Like words congealed in northern air.⁸
He knew what's what, and that's as high
150 As metaphysic wit can fly.
    In school-divinity° as able   *scholastic theology*
As he that hight Irrefragable;⁹
Profound in all the nominal
And real ways beyond them all;¹
155 And with as delicate a hand
Could twist as tough a rope of sand;
And weave fine cobwebs, fit for skull
That's empty when the moon is full;²
Such as take lodgings in a head
160 That's to be let unfurnishèd
He could raise scruples dark and nice,³
And after solve 'em in a trice;
As if divinity had catched
The itch on purpose to be scratched,
165 Or, like a mountebank,⁴ did wound
And stab herself with doubts profound,
Only to show with how small pain
The sores of faith are cured again;
Although by woeful proof we find
170 They always leave a scar behind.
He knew the seat of paradise,⁵
Could tell in what degree it lies;
And, as he was disposed, could prove it
Below the moon, or else above it;
175 What Adam dreamt of when his bride
Came from her closet in his side;
Whether the devil tempted her
By a High Dutch interpreter;
If either of them had a navel;
180 Who first made music malleable;⁶

---

6. Elsewhere Butler wrote, "Notions are but pictures of things in the imagination of man, and if they agree with their originals in nature, they are true, and if not, false."
7. In the hairsplitting logic of medieval Scholastic philosophy, a distinction was drawn between the "entity," or *being,* and the "quiddity," or *essence,* of bodies. Butler calls entity and quiddity "ghosts" because they were held to be independent realities and so to survive the bodies in which they lodge.
8. The notion, as old as the Greek wit Lucian, that in arctic regions words freeze as they are uttered and become audible only when they thaw.
9. A reference to Alexander of Hales (d. 1245), called irrefragable because his system seemed incontrovertible.
1. These lines refer to the debate, continuous

throughout the Middle Ages, about whether the objects of our concepts exist in nature or are mere intellectual abstractions. The "nominalists" denied their objective reality, the "realists" affirmed it.
2. The frenzies of the insane were supposed to wax and wane with the moon (hence "lunatic").
3. Obscure ("dark") and subtle ("nice") intellectual perplexities ("scruples").
4. A seller of quack medicines.
5. The problem of the precise location of the Garden of Eden and the similar problems listed in the ensuing dozen lines had all been the subject of controversy among theologians.
6. Capable of being fashioned into form. Pythagoras is said to have organized sounds into the musical scale.

Whether the serpent at the fall
Had cloven feet or none at all:
All this without a gloss or comment
He could unriddle in a moment,
185　In proper terms, such as men smatter
When they throw out and miss the matter.
　　For his religion, it was fit
To match his learning and his wit:
'Twas Presbyterian true blue,[7]
190　For he was of that stubborn crew
Of errant saints[8] whom all men grant
To be the true church militant,
Such as do build their faith upon
The holy text of pike and gun;
195　Decide all controversies by
Infallible artillery,
And prove their doctrine orthodox
By apostolic blows and knocks;
Call fire, and sword, and desolation
200　A godly, thorough reformation,
Which always must be carried on
And still be doing, never done;
As if religion were intended
For nothing else but to be mended.
205　A sect whose chief devotion lies
In odd, perverse antipathies;[9]
In falling out with that or this,
And finding somewhat still amiss;
More peevish, cross, and splènetic
210　Than dog distract or monkey sick;
That with more care keep holiday
The wrong, than others the right way;
Compound for° sins they are inclined to　　　　*excuse*
By damning those they have no mind to;
215　Still so perverse and opposite
As if they worshiped God for spite.
The selfsame thing they will abhor
One way and long another for.
Free-will they one way disavow,[1]
220　Another, nothing else allow:
All piety consists therein
In them, in other men all sin.
Rather than fail, they will defy
That which they love most tenderly;

---

7. Supporters of Scotland's (Presbyterian) National Covenant adopted blue as their color, in contrast to the Royalist red. Blue is the color of constancy; hence, "true blue," staunch, unwavering.
8. A pun: *arrant,* meaning "unmitigated," and *errant,* meaning "wandering," were both pronounced *arrant.* The Puritans frequently called themselves "saints."

9. The hostility of the sects to everything Anglican or Roman Catholic laid them open to the charge of opposing innocent practices out of mere perverse antipathy. Some extreme Presbyterians fasted at Christmas, instead of following the old custom of feasting and rejoicing (cf. lines 211–12).
1. By the doctrine of predestination.

225 Quarrel with minced pies and disparage
Their best and dearest friend, plum-porridge;
Fat pig and goose itself oppose,
And blaspheme custard through the nose.[2]

1663

2. A reference to the nasal whine of the pious sectarians.

JOHN WILMOT, SECOND EARL OF ROCHESTER
1647–1680

John Wilmot, second earl of Rochester, was the precocious son of one of Charles II's most loyal followers in exile. He won the king's favor at the Restoration and, in 1664, after education at Oxford and on the Continent, took a place at court, at the age of seventeen. There he soon distinguished himself as "the man who has the most wit and the least honor in England." For one escapade, the abduction of Elizabeth Malet, an heiress, he was imprisoned in the Tower of London. But he regained his position by courageous service in the naval war against the Dutch, and in 1667 he married Malet. The rest of his career was no less stormy. His satiric wit, directed not only at ordinary mortals but at Dryden and Charles II himself, embroiled him in constant quarrels and exiles; his practical jokes, his affairs, and his dissipation were legendary. He circulated his works, always intellectually daring and often obscene, to a limited court readership in manuscripts executed by professional scribes—a common way of handling writing deemed too ideologically or morally scandalous for print. An early printed collection of his poems did appear in 1680, though the title page read "Antwerp," probably to hide its London origin. The air of scandal and disguise surrounding his writing only intensified his notoriety as the exemplar of the dissolute, libertine ways of court culture. He told his biographer, Gilbert Burnet, that "for five years together he was continually drunk." Just before his death, however, he was converted to Christian repentance, and for posterity, Rochester became a favorite moral topic: the libertine who had seen the error of his ways.

Wit, in the Restoration, meant not only a clever turn of phrase but mental capacity and intellectual power. Rochester was famous for both kinds of wit. His fierce intelligence, impatient of sham and convention, helped design a way of life based on style, cleverness, and self-interest—a way of life observable in Restoration plays (Dorimant, in Etherege's The Man of Mode, strongly resembles Rochester). Stylistically, Rochester infuses forms such as the heroic couplet with a volatility that contrasts with the pointed and balanced manner of its other masters. From the very first line of "A Satire against Reason and Mankind"—"Were I (who to my cost already am"—he plunges the reader into a couplet mode energized by speculation, self-interruption, and enjambment; and he frequently employs extravagant effects (such as the alliterations "love's lesser lightning" and "balmy brinks of bliss" in "The Imperfect Enjoyment") to flaunt his delight in dramatizing situations, sensations, and himself. "The Disabled Debauchee," composed in "heroic stanzas" like those of Dryden's *Annus Mirabilis,* subverts the very notion of heroism by turning conventions upside down. Philosophically, Rochester is daring and destabilizing. In "A Satire," he rejects high-flown, theoretical reason and consigns its "misguided follower" to an abyss of doubt. The poem's speaker himself happily embraces the "right reason" of instinct, celebrating the life of a "natural man." The poem thus accords with Hobbes's doctrine that all laws, even our notions of good and evil, are artificial social checks on natural human desires. Yet it remains unclear, in Rochester's world of intellectual risk and conflict, whether he thinks humanity's paradoxical predicament can ever finally be escaped. Often called a skeptic himself, he seems to hint that the doubt raised by reason's collapse may surge to engulf him too.

The Disabled Debauchee

As some brave admiral, in former war
    Deprived of force, but pressed with courage still,
Two rival fleets appearing from afar,
    Crawls to the top of an adjacent hill;

5 From whence, with thoughts full of concern, he views
    The wise and daring conduct of the fight,
And each bold action to his mind renews
    His present glory and his past delight;

From his fierce eyes flashes of fire he throws,
10   As from black clouds when lightning breaks away;
Transported, thinks himself amidst his foes,
    And absent, yet enjoys the bloody day;

So, when my days of impotence approach,
    And I'm by pox° and wine's unlucky chance   *syphilis*
15 Forced from the pleasing billows of debauch
    On the dull shore of lazy temperance,

My pains at least some respite shall afford
    While I behold the battles you maintain
When fleets of glasses sail about the board,°   *table*
20   From whose broadsides[1] volleys of wit shall rain.

Nor shall the sight of honorable scars,
    Which my too forward valor did procure,
Frighten new-listed° soldiers from the wars: *newly enlisted*
    Past joys have more than paid what I endure.

25 Should any youth (worth being drunk) prove nice,° *coy, fastidious*
    And from his fair inviter meanly shrink,
'Twill please the ghost of my departed vice
    If, at my counsel, he repent and drink.

1. The sides of the table; artillery on a ship; sheets on which satirical verses were printed.

Or should some cold-complexioned sot forbid,
30   With his dull morals, our bold night-alarms,
I'll fire his blood by telling what I did
    When I was strong and able to bear arms.

I'll tell of whores attacked, their lords at home;
    Bawds' quarters beaten up, and fortress won;
35 Windows demolished, watches° overcome;   *watchmen*
    And handsome ills by my contrivance done.

Nor shall our love-fits, Chloris, be forgot,
    When each the well-looked linkboy[2] strove t' enjoy,
And the best kiss was the deciding lot
40   Whether the boy used[3] you, or I the boy.

With tales like these I will such thoughts inspire
    As to important mischief shall incline:
I'll make him long some ancient church to fire,
    And fear no lewdness he's called to by wine.

45 Thus, statesmanlike, I'll saucily impose,
    And safe from action, valiantly advise;
Sheltered in impotence, urge you to blows,
    And being good for nothing else, be wise.

                                    1680

The Imperfect Enjoyment[1]

Naked she lay, clasped in my longing arms,
I filled with love, and she all over charms;
Both equally inspired with eager fire,
Melting through kindness, flaming in desire.
5 With arms, legs, lips close clinging to embrace,
She clips° me to her breast, and sucks me to her face.   *hugs*
Her nimble tongue, Love's lesser lightning, played
Within my mouth, and to my thoughts conveyed
Swift orders that I should prepare to throw
10 The all-dissolving thunderbolt below.
My fluttering soul, sprung[2] with the pointed kiss,
Hangs hovering o'er her balmy brinks of bliss.
But whilst her busy hand would guide that part
Which should convey my soul up to her heart,
15 In liquid raptures I dissolve all o'er,
Melt into sperm, and spend at every pore.

2. Good-looking boy employed to light the way with a link or torch.
3. The meaning of "used," which appears in the first printed version and many manuscript versions, includes but extends beyond that of "fucked," another prevalent alternative and one preferred by most modern editors.

1. The genre of poems about the downfall of male "pride"—not only a swelled head but an erection—derives from Ovid's *Amores* 3.7. For a woman's treatment of this situation, see Aphra Behn's "The Disappointment" (p. 136).
2. Startled from cover, like a game bird.

A touch from any part of her had done 't:
Her hand, her foot, her very look's a cunt.
   Smiling, she chides in a kind murmuring noise,
20 And from her body wipes the clammy joys,
When, with a thousand kisses wandering o'er
My panting bosom, "Is there then no more?"
She cries. "All this to love and rapture's due;
Must we not pay a debt to pleasure too?"
25   But I, the most forlorn, lost man alive,
To show my wished obedience vainly strive:
I sigh, alas! and kiss, but cannot swive.°   screw
Eager desires confound my first intent, ⎫
Succeeding shame does more success prevent, ⎬
30 And rage at last confirms me impotent. ⎭
Ev'n her fair hand, which might bid heat return
To frozen age, and make cold hermits burn,
Applied to my dead cinder, warms no more
Than fire to ashes could past flames restore.
35 Trembling, confused, despairing, limber, dry,
A wishing, weak, unmoving lump I lie.
This dart of love, whose piercing point, oft tried,
With virgin blood ten thousand maids have dyed;
Which nature still directed with such art
40 That it through every cunt reached every heart—
Stiffly resolved, 'twould carelessly invade ⎫
Woman or man, nor aught° its fury stayed: ⎬   anything
Where'er it pierced, a cunt it found or made— ⎭
Now languid lies in this unhappy hour,
45 Shrunk up and sapless like a withered flower.
   Thou treacherous, base deserter of my flame,
False to my passion, fatal to my fame,
Through what mistaken magic dost thou prove
So true to lewdness, so untrue to love?
50 What oyster-cinder-beggar-common whore
Didst thou e'er fail in all thy life before?
When vice, disease, and scandal lead the way,
With what officious haste dost thou obey!
Like a rude, roaring hector° in the streets   bully
55 Who scuffles, cuffs, and justles all he meets,
But if his King or country claim his aid,
The rakehell villain shrinks and hides his head;
Ev'n so thy brutal valor is displayed,
Breaks every stew,³ does each small whore invade,
60 But when great Love the onset does command,
Base recreant to thy prince, thou dar'st not stand.
Worst part of me, and henceforth hated most,
Through all the town a common fucking post,
On whom each whore relieves her tingling cunt
65 As hogs on gates do rub themselves and grunt,
Mayst thou to ravenous chancres be a prey,

---

3. Breaks into every brothel.

Or in consuming weepings[4] waste away;
May strangury and stone[5] thy days attend;
May'st thou ne'er piss, who didst refuse to spend
70   When all my joys did on false thee depend.
    And may ten thousand abler pricks agree
    To do the wronged Corinna right for thee.

          1680

Upon Nothing

Nothing, thou elder brother even to shade,
Thou hadst a being ere the world was made
And (well fixed) art alone of ending not afraid.

Ere time and place were, time and place were not,
5 When primitive Nothing Something straight begot,
Then all proceeded from the great united *What*.

Something, the general attribute of all,
Severed from thee, its sole original,
Into thy boundless self must undistinguished fall.

10 Yet Something did thy mighty power command
And from thy fruitful emptiness's hand
Snatched men, beasts, birds, fire, water, air, and land.

Matter, the wick'dst offspring of thy race,
By form assisted, flew from thy embrace,
15 And rebel light obscured thy reverend dusky face.

With form and matter, time and place did join,
Body thy foe, with these did leagues combine[1]
To spoil thy peaceful realm and ruin all thy line.

But turncoat time assists the foe in vain
20 And bribed by thee destroys their short-lived reign
And to thy hungry womb drives back thy slaves again.

Though mysteries are barred from laic eyes[2]
And the divine alone with warrant pries
Into thy bosom where thy truth in private lies,

25 Yet this of thee the wise may truly say:
Thou from the virtuous, nothing tak'st away,[3]
And to be part of thee, the wicked wisely pray.

---

4. "Chancres" and "weepings" are signs of venereal disease.
5. "Strangury" and "stone" cause slow and painful urination.
1. Form, matter, time, and place combined in
alliances against Nothing.
2. I.e., the eyes of the laity, who are uninitiated
in Nothing's mysteries.
3. You, Nothing, do not take anything away from
the virtuous.

Great negative, how vainly would the wise
Enquire, define, distinguish, teach, devise,
30   Didst thou not stand to point° their blind philosophies.   *expose*

Is or Is Not, the two great ends of fate,
And true or false, the subject of debate
That perfect or destroy the vast designs of state,

When they have racked the politician's breast,
35   Within thy bosom most securely rest
And when reduced to thee are least unsafe and best.

But Nothing, why does Something still permit
That sacred monarchs should at council sit
With persons highly thought, at best, for nothing fit;

40   Whilst weighty Something modestly abstains
From princes' coffers[4] and from statesmen's brains
And Nothing there like stately Something reigns?

Nothing, who dwellst with fools in grave disguise,
For whom they reverend shapes and forms devise,
45   Lawn-sleeves and furs and gowns,[5] when they like thee look wise;

French truth, Dutch prowess, British policy,
Hibernian° learning, Scotch civility,   *Irish*
Spaniards' dispatch, Danes' wit[6] are mainly seen in thee;

The great man's gratitude to his best friend,
50   Kings' promises, whores' vows, towards thee they bend,
Flow swiftly into thee and in thee ever end.

1679

A Satire against Reason and Mankind

"He had a strange vivacity of thought, and vigor of expression," said Bishop Gilbert Burnet of his friend and contemporary, Rochester: "his wit had a subtility and sublimity both, that were scarce imitable." Rochester displays these characteristics nowhere more vividly than in his most famous poem, "A Satire against Reason and Mankind." Many of the thoughts in the poem were familiar by Rochester's time. The idea that animals are better equipped to lead successful lives than human beings, for instance, had been a commonplace among moralists for centuries: Michel de Montaigne (1533–1592) makes much of it in his best-known, most comprehensively skeptical essay, "An Apology for Raymond Sebond." Other elements of the skeptical tradition, particularly a comic appreciation of the weakness of reason, receive ample play in the "Satire." The poem in general loosely follows *Satire VIII* by the influential French neoclassical poet and critic, Nicolas Boileau (1636–1711). But everywhere Rochester's energetic intellectual distinctiveness bursts through. Perhaps most unnervingly, he both claims to

4. Charles II's coffers were notably empty, and he was forced to declare bankruptcy in 1672.
5. Worn by judges. "Lawn": a fine linen or cotton fabric, worn by bishops.

6. All proverbial deficiencies of the various nationalities mentioned, many of them exposed during the Anglo-Dutch war (1672–74).

restrict his thinking to immediate, instinctual reason and gestures toward the "limits of the boundless universe" and "mysterious truths, which no man can conceive." Framed as it is by paradoxes and mysteries, his commonsensical instinct has seemed less stable to many readers than Rochester himself would have us believe. Still, these and other extravagant conflicts surely suit Rochester's fundamental aim: to throw as dramatic a light as he can on himself and his thinking.

A Satire against Reason and Mankind

Were I (who to my cost already am
One of those strange prodigious creatures, man)
A spirit free to choose, for my own share,
What case of flesh and blood I pleased to wear,
5   I'd be a dog, a monkey, or a bear;
Or anything but that vain animal
Who is so proud of being rational.
The senses are too gross, and he'll contrive
A sixth[1] to contradict the other five:
10   And before certain instinct will prefer
Reason, which fifty times for one does err.
Reason, an ignis fatuus[2] of the mind,
Which leaving light of nature, sense, behind,
Pathless and dangerous wandering ways it takes,
15   Through Error's fenny bogs and thorny brakes:°   *thickets*
Whilst the misguided follower climbs with pain
Mountains of whimsies heaped in his own brain;
Stumbling from thought to thought, falls headlong down
Into doubt's boundless sea, where like° to drown,   *likely*
20   Books bear him up awhile, and make him try
To swim with bladders[3] of philosophy;
In hopes still to o'ertake th'escaping light,
The vapor dances in his dazzled sight,
Till spent, it leaves him to eternal night.
25   Then old age and experience, hand in hand,
Lead him to death, and make him understand,
After a search so painful and so long,
That all his life he has been in the wrong.
Huddled in dirt the reasoning engine° lies,   *brain*
30   Who was so proud, so witty and so wise.
Pride drew him in (as cheats their bubbles° catch)   *dupes*
And made him venture to be made a wretch.
His wisdom did his happiness destroy,
Aiming to know that world he should enjoy;
35   And wit was his vain frivolous pretence
Of pleasing others at his own expense:
For wits are treated just like common whores,
First they're enjoyed and then kicked out of doors.

---

1. Here, reason.
2. Foolish fire (Latin). Sometimes called the will-o'-the-wisp, a light appearing in marshy lands that proverbially misleads travelers.
3. Inflated animal bladders used for buoyancy in the water.

Jacob Huysmans, *Lord Rochester with a Monkey and a Book*,
1665–70. Rochester bestowing a laurel wreath, symbol of poetic
excellence, on a monkey, who holds a page torn from a book.

The pleasure past, a threatening doubt remains,
40   That frights th'enjoyer with succeeding pains:[4]
Women and men of wit are dangerous tools,
And ever fatal to admiring fools.
Pleasure allures, and when the fops escape, ⎫
'Tis not that they're beloved, but fortunate; ⎬
45   And therefore what they fear, at heart they hate.[5] ⎭
     But now methinks some formal band and beard[6]
Takes me to task. Come on, Sir, I'm prepared:
"Then by your favor any thing that's writ
Against this gibing,° jingling knack called wit,   *jeering*
50   Likes° me abundantly, but you take care   *pleases*
Upon this point not to be too severe.
Perhaps my Muse were fitter for this part, ⎫
For I profess I can be very smart ⎬
On wit, which I abhor with all my heart. ⎭

4. The doubt that wits leave behind resembles
venereal disease left by "common whores."
5. Though allured by wits, fops also fear and
hate them.
6. Clergyman, wearing a clerical collar.

55 I long to lash it in some sharp essay, }
     But your grand indiscretion bids me stay,
     And turns my tide of ink another way.
     What rage ferments in your degenerate mind,
     To make you rail at reason and mankind?
60 Blest glorious man! to whom alone kind heaven
     An everlasting soul has freely given;
     Whom his creator took such care to make,
     That from himself he did the image take,
     And this fair frame° in shining reason dressed,   *physical body*
65 To dignify his nature above beast.
     Reason, by whose aspiring influence
     We take a flight beyond material sense;
     Dive into mysteries, then soaring pierce
     The flaming limits of the universe;
70 Search heaven and hell, find out what's acted there,
     And give the world true grounds of hope and fear."[7]
          Hold, mighty man, I cry, all this we know,
     From the pathetic pen of Ingelo,[8]
     From Patrick's *Pilgrim,* Sibbs'[9] soliloquies;
75 And 'tis this very reason I despise;
     This supernatural gift, that makes a mite
     Think he's the image of the infinite,
     Comparing his short life, void of all rest,
     To the eternal and the ever blest;
80 This busy puzzling stirrer-up of doubt,
     That frames deep mysteries, then finds them out;
     Filling with frantic crowds of thinking fools
     Those reverend Bedlams,° colleges and schools;   *madhouses*
     Borne on whose wings each heavy sot can pierce
85 The limits of the boundless universe;
     So charming ointments make an old witch fly,
     And bear a crippled carcass through the sky.
     'Tis this exalted power whose business lies
     In nonsense and impossibilities.
90 This made a whimsical philosopher
     Before the spacious world his tub prefer.[1]
     And we have modern cloistered coxcombs, who
     Retire to think, 'cause they have naught to do:
     But thoughts are given for action's government,
95 Where action ceases, thought's impertinent.
     Our sphere of action is life's happiness,
     And he who thinks beyond, thinks like an ass.
     Thus, whilst against false reasoning I inveigh,
     I own° right reason, which I would obey: *avow*
100 That reason which distinguishes by sense,

7. Teach the world about salvation and damnation.
8. Nathaniel Ingelo (d. 1683), author of the long religious allegory *Bentivolio and Urania* (1660).
9. Richard Sibbes, Puritan preacher who published volumes of sermons, though none called "soliloquies." Simon Patrick (1626–1707), author of the devotional work *The Parable of the Pilgrim* (1665).
1. Diogenes the Cynic (5th century B.C.E.), who lived in a tub to exemplify the virtues of asceticism.

And gives us rules of good and ill from thence;
That bounds desires with a reforming will,
To keep them more in vigor, not to kill.
Your reason hinders, mine helps to enjoy,
105 Renewing appetites yours would destroy.
My reason is my friend, yours is a cheat,
Hunger calls out, my reason bids me eat;
Perversely, yours your appetites does mock:
They ask for food, that answers, "what's a clock?"°   *what time is it?*
110 This plain distinction, Sir, your doubt secures,°   *resolves*
'Tis not true reason I despise, but yours.
      Thus I think reason righted, but for man,
I'll ne'er recant, defend him if you can.
For all his pride and his philosophy,
115 'Tis evident beasts are, in their degree,
As wise at least, and better far than he.
Those creatures are the wisest who attain
By surest means, the ends at which they aim.
If therefore Jowler[2] finds and kills his hares
120 Better than Meres[3] supplies committee chairs,
Though one's a statesman, th'other but a hound,
Jowler in justice would be wiser found.
You see how far man's wisdom here extends;
Look next if human nature makes amends;
125 Whose principles most generous are and just,
And to whose morals you would sooner trust.
Be judge yourself, I'll bring it to the test,
Which is the basest creature, man or beast.
Birds feed on birds, beasts on each other prey,
130 But savage man alone does man betray;
Pressed by necessity they kill for food,
Man undoes man to do himself no good.
With teeth and claws by nature armed, they hunt
Nature's allowance to supply their want.
135 But man with smiles, embraces, friendship, praise,
Inhumanly his fellow's life betrays;
With voluntary° pains works his distress,   *deliberate*
Not through necessity, but wantonness.
For hunger or for love they fight and tear,
140 Whilst wretched man is still° in arms for fear;   *always*
For fear he arms, and is of arms afraid,
By fear to fear successively betrayed.
Base fear! The source whence his best passion came,
His boasted honor, and his dear bought fame;
145 That lust of power to which he's such a slave,
And for the which alone he dares be brave,
To which his various projects are designed,
Which makes him generous, affable, and kind;
For which he takes such pains to be thought wise

2. A common name for hunting dogs.
3. Sir Thomas Meres (1635–1715), a busy parliamentarian of the day.

150   And screws his actions in a forced disguise;
      Leading a tedious life in misery
      Under laborious mean hypocrisy.
      Look to the bottom of his vast design,
      Wherein man's wisdom, power, and glory join;
155   The good he acts, the ill he does endure,
      'Tis all from fear to make himself secure.
      Merely for safety after fame we thirst,
      For all men would be cowards if they durst.
      And honesty's against all common sense;
160   Men must be knaves, 'tis in their own defense.
      Mankind's dishonest, if you think it fair
      Amongst known cheats to play upon the square,°   *honestly*
      You'll be undone—
      Nor can weak truth your reputation save;
165   The knaves will all agree to call you knave.
      Wronged shall he live, insulted o'er, oppressed,
      Who dares be less a villain than the rest.
            Thus Sir, you see what human nature craves:
      Most men are cowards, all men should be knaves.
170   The difference lies, as far as I can see,
      Not in the thing itself, but the degree,
      And all the subject matter of debate
      Is only who's a knave of the first rate.

                        Addition[4]

      All this with indignation have I hurled
175   At the pretending° part of the proud world,   *affected*
      Who swollen with selfish vanity, devise ⎫
      False freedoms, holy cheats, and formal lies, ⎬
      Over their fellow slaves to tyrannize.   ⎭
            But if in court so just a man there be
180   (In court a just man yet unknown to me),
      Who does his needful flattery direct,
      Not to oppress and ruin, but protect
      (Since flattery, which way so ever laid,
      Is still a tax on that unhappy trade);[5]
185   If so upright a statesman you can find,
      Whose passions bend to his unbiased mind;
      Who does his arts and policies apply
      To raise his country, not his family,
      Nor while his pride owned avarice withstands,
190   Receives close bribes from friends' corrupted hands[6]—
            Is there a churchman who on God relies,
      Whose life his faith and doctrine justifies?
      Not one blown up with vain prelatic[7] pride,
      Who for reproof of sins does man deride;

4. The second part was also circulated as a separate poem.
5. Even good men must pay the tax of flattery if they "trade" at the royal court at Whitehall.
6. Nor while he proudly rejects open greed, still arranges that his friends collect secret bribes for him.
7. Of prelates, high church officials.

195 Whose envious heart makes preaching a pretense, ⎫
    With his obstreperous saucy eloquence,   ⎬
    To chide at kings, and rail at men of sense; ⎭
    Who from his pulpit vents more peevish lies,
    More bitter railings, scandals, calumnies,
200 Than at a gossiping are thrown about
    When the good wives get drunk and then fall out;
    None of that sensual tribe, whose talents lie
    In avarice, pride, sloth and gluttony,
    Who hunt good livings,[8] but abhor good lives, ⎫
205 Whose lust exalted to that height arrives,   ⎬
    They act adultery with their own wives;[9]   ⎭
    And ere a score of years completed be, ⎫
    Can from the lofty pulpit proudly see   ⎬
    Half a large parish their own progeny. ⎭
210 Nor doating° bishop who would be adored   *senile*
    For domineering at the council board,[1]
    A greater fop in business at fourscore,
    Fonder of serious toys,° affected more   *trifles*
    Than the gay glittering fool at twenty proves,
215 With all his noise, his tawdry clothes and loves;
       But a meek humble man of honest sense,
    Who, preaching peace, does practice continence;
    Whose pious life's a proof he does believe
    Mysterious truths, which no man can conceive;
220 If upon earth there dwell such God-like men,
    I'll here recant my paradox[2] to them;
    Adore those shrines of virtue, homage pay,
    And with the rabble world, their laws obey.
       If such there be, yet grant me this at least,
225 Man differs more from man, than man from beast.

1679

8. Ecclesiastical appointments.
9. Married women of their parishes. Rochester
also suggests that these clergymen act out their
adulterous lusts with their own spouses.

1. In the Privy Council, a meeting of advisers to
the monarch.
2. That beasts are superior to humans.

APHRA BEHN
1640?–1689

"A woman wit has often graced the stage," Dryden wrote in 1681. Soon after actresses first appeared in English public theaters, there was an even more striking debut by a woman writer who boldly signed her plays and talked back to her critics. In a dozen years, Aphra Behn turned out at least that many plays, discovering fresh dramatic possibilities in casts that included women with warm bodies and clever heads. She also drew attention as a warm and witty poet of love. When writing for the stage became less profitable, she turned to the emerging field of prose fiction, composing a pioneering epistolary novel, *Love Letters between a Nobleman and His Sister,* and diverse short tales—not to mention a raft of translations from the French, pindarics to her beloved Stuart rulers, compilations, prologues, complimentary verses, all the piecework and puffery that were the stock in trade of the Restoration town wit. She worked in haste and with flair for nearly two decades and more than held her own as a professional writer. In the end, no author of her time—except Dryden himself—proved more versatile, more alive to new currents of thought, or more inventive in recasting fashionable forms.

Much of Behn's life remains a mystery. Although her books have been accompanied—and often all but buried—by volumes of rumor, hard facts are elusive. She was almost certainly from East Kent; she may well have been named Johnson. But she herself seems to have left no record of her date and place of birth, her family name and upbringing, or the identity of the shadowy Mr. Behn whom she reportedly married. Her many references to nuns and convents, as well as praise for prominent Catholic lords (*Oroonoko* is dedicated to one), have prompted speculation that she may have been raised as a Catholic and educated in a convent abroad. Without doubt, she drew on a range of worldly experience that would be closed to women in the more genteel ages to come. The circumstantial detail of *Oroonoko* supports her claim that she was in the new sugar colony of Surinam early in 1664. Perhaps she exaggerated her social position to enhance her tale, but many particulars—from dialect words and the location of plantations to methods of selling and torturing slaves—can be authenticated. During the trade war that broke out in 1665—which left her "vast and charming world" a Dutch prize—Behn traveled to the Low Countries on a spying mission for King Charles II. The king could be lax about payment, however, and Behn had to petition desperately to escape debtor's prison. In 1670 she brought out her first plays, "forced to write for bread," she confessed, "and not ashamed to own it."

In London, Behn flourished in the cosmopolitan world of the playhouse and the court. Dryden and other wits encouraged her; she mixed with actresses and managers and playwrights and exchanged verses with a lively literary set that she called her "cabal." Surviving letters record a passionate, troubled attachment to a lawyer named John Hoyle, a bisexual with libertine views. She kept up with the most advanced thinking and joined public debates with pointed satire against the Whigs. But the festivity of the Restoration world was fading out in bitter party acrimony. In 1682 Behn was placed under arrest for "abusive reflections" on the king's illegitimate son, the Whig duke of Monmouth (Dryden's Absalom). Her Royalist opinions and the immodesty of her public role made her a target; gleeful lampoons declared that she was aging and ill and once again poor. She responded by bringing out her works at a still faster rate, composing *Oroonoko,* her dedication claims, "in a few hours . . . for I never rested my pen a moment for thought." In some last works she recorded her hope that her writings would live: "I value fame as much as if I had been born a hero." When she died she was buried in Westminster Abbey.

"All women together ought to let flowers fall upon the grave of Aphra Behn," Virginia Woolf wrote, "for it was she who earned them the right to speak their minds." Behn herself spoke her mind. She scorned hypocrisy and calculation in her society and commented freely on religion, science, and philosophy. Moreover, she spoke as a woman. Denied the classical education of most male authors, she dismissed "musty rules" and lessons and relished the immediate human appeal of popular forms. Her first play, *The Forced Marriage,* exposes the bondage of matches arranged for money and status, and many later works invoke the powerful natural force of love, whose energy breaks through conventions. In a range of genres, from simple pastoral songs to complex plots of intrigue, she candidly explores the sexual feelings of women, their schooling in disguise, their need to "love upon the honest square" (for this her work was later denounced as coarse and impure). *Oroonoko* represents another departure for Behn and prose fiction. It achieves something new both in its narrative form and in extending some of her favorite themes to an original subject: the destiny of a black male hero on a world historical stage.

Oroonoko cannot be classified as fact or fiction, realism or romance. In the still unshaped field of prose narrative—where a "history" could mean any story, true or false—Behn combined the attractions of three older forms. First, she presents the work as a memoir, a personal account of what she has heard and seen. According to a friend, Behn had told this tale over and over; perhaps that explains the conversational ease with which she turns back and forth, interpreting faraway scenes for her readers at home. Second, *Oroonoko* is a travel narrative in three parts. It turns west to a new world often extolled as a paradise, then east to Africa and the amorous intrigues of a corrupt old-world court (popular reading fare), then finally west again with its hero across the infamous "Middle Passage"—over which millions of slaves would be transported during the next century—to the conflicts of a raw colonial world. Exotic scenes fascinate Behn, but she wants even more to talk to people and learn about their ways of life. As in imaginary voyages, from Sir Thomas More's *Utopia* to *Gulliver's Travels* and *Rasselas,* encounters with foreign cultures sharply challenge Europeans to reexamine themselves. Behn's primitive Indians and noble Africans live by a code of virtue, by principles of fidelity and honor, that "civilized" Christians often ignore or betray. Oroonoko embodies this code. Above all, the book is his biography. Courageous, high-minded, and great hearted, he rivals the heroes of classical epics and Plutarch's *Lives* and is equally worthy of fame. Nor does he lack gentler virtues. Like the heroes of seventeenth-century heroic dramas and romances, he shines in the company of women and proves his nobility by his passionate and constant love for Imoinda, his ideal counterpart. Yet finally a contradiction dooms Oroonoko: he is at once prince and chattel, a "royal slave."

Behn handles her forms dynamically, drawing out their inner discords and tensions. In the biography, Oroonoko's deepest values are turned against him. His trust in friendship and scrupulous truth to his word expose him to the treachery of Europeans who calculate human worth on a yardstick of profit. A hero cannot survive in such a world. His self-respect demands action, even when he can find no clear path through the tangle of assurances and lies. Moreover, the colony too seems tangled in contradictions. Behn's travel narrative reveals a broken paradise where, in the absence of secure authority, the settlers descend into a series of unstable alliances, improvised power relations, and escalating suspicions. Here every term—friend and foe, tenderness and brutality, savagery and civilization—can suddenly turn into its opposite. And the author also seems caught between worlds. The cultivated Englishwoman who narrates and acts in this memoir thinks highly of her hero's code of honor and shares his contempt for the riffraff who plague him. Yet her own role is ambiguous: she lacks the power to save Oroonoko and might even be viewed as implicated in his downfall. Only as a writer can she take control, preserving the hero in her work.

The story of Oroonoko did not end with Behn. Compassion for the royal slave and outrage at his fate were enlisted in the long battle against the slave trade. Reprinted, translated, serialized, dramatized, and much imitated, *Oroonoko* helped teach a mass audience to feel for all victims of the brutal commerce in human beings. A hundred years later, the popular writer Hannah More testified to the widening influence of the story: "No individual griefs my bosom melt, / For millions feel what Oroonoko felt." Women especially identified with the experience of personal injustice and everyday indignity—the pain of being treated as something less than fully human. Perhaps it is appropriate that the writer who made the suffering of the royal slave famous had known the pride and lowliness of being "a female pen."

The Disappointment[1]

One day the amorous Lysander,
By an impatient passion swayed,
Surprised fair Cloris, that loved maid,
Who could defend herself no longer.
5   All things did with his love conspire;
The gilded planet of the day,°   *the sun*
In his gay chariot drawn by fire,
Was now descending to the sea,
And left no light to guide the world
10   But what from Cloris' brighter eyes was hurled.

In a lone thicket made for love,
Silent as yielding maid's consent,
She with a charming languishment,
Permits his force, yet gently strove;
15   Her hands his bosom softly meet,
But not to put him back designed,
Rather to draw 'em on inclined:
Whilst he lay trembling at her feet,
Resistance 'tis in vain to show:
20   She wants° the power to say—*Ah! what d'ye do?*   *lacks*

Her bright eyes sweet and yet severe,
Where love and shame confusedly strive,
Fresh vigor to Lysander give;
And breathing faintly in his ear,
25   She cried—*Cease, cease—your vain desire,*
Or I'll call out—what would you do?
My dearer honor even to you
I cannot, must not give—Retire,
Or take this life, whose chiefest part
30   *I gave you with the conquest of my heart.*

But he as much unused to fear,
As he was capable of love,
The blessed minutes to improve
Kisses her mouth, her neck, her hair;
35   Each touch her new desire alarms;
His burning, trembling hand he pressed
Upon her swelling snowy breast,
While she lay panting in his arms.
All her unguarded beauties lie
40   The spoils and trophies of the enemy.

---

1. This variation on the "imperfect enjoyment" genre compares with Rochester's (p. 124); it first appeared in a collection of his poems. But Behn gives the theme of impotence her own twist. Freely translating a French poem, Cantenac's "The Lost Chance Recovered," she cuts the conclusion, in which the French lover regained his potency, and she highlights the woman's feelings as well as the man's.

And now without respect or fear
He seeks the object of his vows
(His love no modesty allows)
By swift degrees advancing—where
45   His daring hand that altar seized,
Where gods of love do sacrifice:
That awful throne, that paradise
Where rage is calmed, and anger pleased;
That fountain where delight still flows,
50   And gives the universal world repose.

Her balmy lips encountering his,
Their bodies, as their souls, are joined;
Where both in transports unconfined
Extend themselves upon the moss.
55   Cloris half dead and breathless lay;
Her soft eyes cast a humid light
Such as divides the day and night;
Or falling stars, whose fires decay:
And now no signs of life she shows,
60   But what in short-breathed sighs returns and goes.

He saw how at her length she lay;
He saw her rising bosom bare;
Her loose thin robes, through which appear
A shape designed for love and play;
65   Abandoned by her pride and shame
She does her softest joys dispense,
Offering her virgin innocence
A victim to love's sacred flame;
While the o'er-ravished shepherd lies
70   Unable to perform the sacrifice.

Ready to taste a thousand joys,
The too transported hapless swain
Found the vast pleasure turned to pain;
Pleasure which too much love destroys:
75   The willing garments by he laid,[2]
And heaven all opened to his view.
Mad to possess, himself he threw
On the defenseless lovely maid.
But oh what envying god conspires
80   To snatch his power, yet leave him the desire!

Nature's support (without whose aid
She can no human being give)
Itself now wants the art[3] to live;
Faintness its slackened nerves invade:
85   In vain th'enraged youth essayed
To call its fleeting vigor back;

---

2. He took off her compliant clothes.   3. Lacks the capacity.

No motion 'twill from motion take;
Excess of love his love betrayed:
In vain he toils, in vain commands:
90 The insensible[4] fell weeping in his hand.

In this so amorous cruel strife,
Where love and fate were too severe,
The poor Lysander in despair
Renounced his reason with his life:
95 Now all the brisk and active fire
That should the nobler part inflame
Served to increase his rage and shame,
And left no spark for new desire:
Not all her naked charms could move
100 Or calm that rage that had debauched his love.

Cloris returning from the trance
Which love and soft desire had bred,
Her timorous hand she gently laid
(Or guided by design or chance)
105 Upon that fabulous Priapus,[5]
That potent god, as poets feign:
But never did young shepherdess,
Gathering the fern upon the plain,
More nimbly draw her fingers back,
110 Finding beneath the verdant leaves a snake,

Than Cloris her fair hand withdrew,
Finding that god of her desires
Disarmed of all his awful fires,
And cold as flowers bathed in the morning dew.
115 Who can the nymph's confusion guess?
The blood forsook the hinder place,
And strewed with blushes all her face,
Which both disdain and shame expressed:
And from Lysander's arms she fled,
120 Leaving him fainting on the gloomy bed.

Like lightning through the grove she hies,
Or Daphne from the Delphic god;[6]
No print upon the grassy road
She leaves, to instruct pursuing eyes.
125 The wind that wantoned in her hair
And with her ruffled garments played,
Discovered in the flying maid
All that the gods e'er made, if fair.
So Venus, when her love[7] was slain,
130 With fear and haste flew o'er the fatal plain.

---

4. Devoid of feeling and too small to be noticed.
5. Phallus. The ancient god Priapus is always pictured with an outstanding erection.

6. Apollo, from whom the Greek nymph Daphne fled until she turned into a laurel tree.
7. Adonis, who was killed by a boar.

The nymph's resentments none but I
Can well imagine or condole:
But none can guess Lysander's soul,
But those who swayed his destiny.
135 His silent griefs swell up to storms,
And not one god his fury spares;
He cursed his birth, his fate, his stars;
But more the shepherdess's charms,
Whose soft bewitching influence
140 Had damned him to the hell of impotence.[8]

1680

Oroonoko; or, The Royal Slave[1]

Epistle Dedicatory

To the Right Honorable the Lord Maitland[2]

My Lord,

Since the world is grown so nice[3] and critical upon dedications, and will needs be judging the book by the wit of the patron; we ought, with a great deal of circumspection, to choose a person against whom there can be no exception; and whose wit, and worth, truly merits all that one is capable of saying upon that occasion.

The most part of dedications are charged with flattery; and if the world knows a man has some vices, they will not allow one to speak of his virtues. This, my lord, is for want of thinking rightly; if men would consider with reason, they would have another sort of opinion and esteem of dedications; and would believe almost every great man has enough to make him worthy of all that can be said of him there. My lord, a picture-drawer, when he intends to make a good picture, essays[4] the face many ways, and in many lights, before he begins; that he may choose from the several turns of it which is most agreeable and gives it the best grace; and if there be a scar, an ungrateful mole, or any little defect, they leave it out; and yet make the picture extremely like. But he who has the good fortune to draw a face that is exactly charming in all its parts and features, what colors or agreements[5] can be added to make it finer? All that he can give is but its due, and glories in a piece whose original alone gives it its perfection. An ill hand may diminish, but a good hand cannot augment its beauty. A poet is a painter in his way; he draws to the life, but in another kind; we draw the nobler part, the soul and mind; the pictures of the pen shall outlast those of the pencil,[6] and even worlds themselves. 'Tis

8. Blaming the woman for an imperfect enjoyment is typical of the genre.
1. The text, prepared by Joanna Lipking, is based on the 1688 edition, the sole edition published during Behn's lifetime. The critical edition of G. C. Duchovnay (diss., Indiana, 1971), which collates the four 17th-century editions, has been consulted.

2. Richard Maitland (1653–1695), fourth earl of Lauderdale, Scottish nobleman loyal to James II, who would soon join his king in France after the revolution of 1688 deposed him.
3. Fussy, overparticular.
4. Tries to depict.
5. Attractive features.
6. Fine-tipped brush for delicate painting.

a short chronicle of those lives that possibly would be forgotten by other historians, or lie neglected there, however deserving an immortal fame; for men of eminent parts[7] are as exemplary as even monarchs themselves; and virtue is a noble lesson to be learned, and 'tis by comparison we can judge and chose. 'Tis by such illustrious presidents[8] as your lordship the world can be bettered and refined; when a great part of the lazy nobility shall, with shame, behold the admirable accomplishments of a man so great, and so young.

Your lordship has read innumerable volumes of men and books; not vainly for the gust of[9] novelty, but knowledge, excellent knowledge. Like the industrious bee, from every flower you return laden with the precious dew, which you are sure to turn to the public good. You hoard no one perfection, but lay it all out in the glorious service of your religion and country; to both which you are a useful and necessary honor. They both want[1] such supporters; and 'tis only men of so elevated parts, and fine knowledge, such noble principles of loyalty and religion this nation sighs for. Where shall we find a man so young, like St. Augustine,[2] in the midst of all his youth and gaiety, teaching the world divine precepts, true notions of faith, and excellent morality, and at the same time be also a perfect pattern of all that accomplish a great man? You have, my lord, all that refined wit that charms, and the affability that obliges; a generosity that gives a luster to your nobility; that hospitality and greatness of mind that engages the world; and that admirable conduct that so well instructs it. Our nation ought to regret and bemoan their misfortunes, for not being able to claim the honor of the birth of a man who is so fit to serve his majesty and his kingdoms, in all great and public affairs; and to the glory of your nation be it spoken, it produces more considerable men, for all fine sense, wit, wisdom, breeding and generosity (for the generality of the nobility) than all other nations can boast; and the fruitfulness of your virtues sufficiently make amends for the barrenness of your soil: which however cannot be incommode[3] to your lordship; since your quality and the veneration that the commonalty naturally pay their lords creates a flowing plenty there—that makes you happy. And to complete your happiness, my lord, heaven has blest you with a lady to whom it has given all the graces, beauties, and virtues of her sex; all the youth, sweetness of nature, of a most illustrious family; and who is a most rare example to all wives of quality, for her eminent piety, easiness, and condescension;[4] and as absolutely merits respect from all the world, as she does that passion and resignation she receives from your lordship; and which is, on her part, with so much tenderness returned. Methinks your tranquil lives are an image of the new-made and beautiful pair in paradise. And 'tis the prayers and wishes of all who have the honor to know you, that it may eternally so continue, with additions of all the blessings this world can give you.

My lord, the obligations I have to some of the great men of your nation, particularly to your lordship, gives me an ambition of making my acknowledgements by all the opportunities I can; and such humble fruits as my industry produces I lay at your lordship's feet. This is a true story, of a man

7. Talents.
8. Patrons, guardians.
9. Taste for.
1. Lack, stand in need of.
2. Augustine of Hippo (354–430) converted to Christianity in 386 at the age of thirty-one, renouncing his promiscuous, riotous ways.

3. Inconvenient. "Barrenness of your soil": Scotland's barrenness was often contrasted with England's fertility.
4. Courtesy to social inferiors. "A lady": Maitland's wife, Lady Anne, was daughter of Archibald Campbell, the ninth Earl of Argyle.

gallant enough to merit your protection, and, had he always been so fortunate, he had not made so inglorious an end. The Royal Slave I had the honor
to know in my travels to the other world; and though I had none above me in
that country, yet I wanted power to preserve this great man.[5] If there be anything that seems romantic,[6] I beseech your lordship to consider these countries do, in all things, so far differ from ours that they produce unconceivable
wonders; at least, they appear so to us, because new and strange. What I have
mentioned I have taken care should be truth, let the critical reader judge as
he pleases. 'Twill be no commendation to the book to assure your lordship I
writ it in a few hours, though it may serve to excuse some of its faults of connection, for I never rested my pen a moment for thought: 'Tis purely the merit
of my slave[7] that must render it worthy of the honor it begs; and the author of
that of subscribing herself,

My lord
Your Lordship's most obliged
and obedient Servant

A. Behn.

I do not pretend, in giving you the history of this royal slave, to entertain my
reader with the adventures of a feigned hero, whose life and fortunes fancy
may manage at the poet's pleasure; nor in relating the truth, design to adorn
it with any accidents but such as arrived in earnest to him. And it shall come
simply into the world, recommended by its own proper merits and natural
intrigues, there being enough of reality to support it, and to render it diverting, without the addition of invention.

I was myself an eyewitness to a great part of what you will find here set
down, and what I could not be witness of, I received from the mouth of the
chief actor in this history, the hero himself, who gave us the whole transactions of his youth; and though I shall omit for brevity's sake a thousand little
accidents of his life, which, however pleasant to us, where history was scarce
and adventures very rare, yet might prove tedious and heavy to my reader, in
a world where he finds diversions for every minute, new and strange. But we
who were perfectly charmed with the character of this great man were curious to gather every circumstance of his life.

The scene of the last part of his adventures lies in a colony in America
called Surinam,[8] in the West Indies.

But before I give you the story of this gallant slave, 'tis fit I tell you the
manner of bringing them to these new colonies, for those they make use of
there are not natives of the place; for those we live with in perfect amity,
without daring to command 'em, but on the contrary caress 'em with all the
brotherly and friendly affection in the world, trading with 'em for their fish,
venison, buffaloes, skins, and little rarities; as marmosets, a sort of monkey
as big as a rat or weasel but of a marvelous and delicate shape, and has face

5. Despite her high social standing in the South
American colony, Behn could not save Oroonoko's
life. "Other world": the New World, South America.
6. Like the fictions in a romance tale.

7. Oroonoko.
8. A British sugar colony on the South American
coast east of Venezuela; later Dutch Guiana,
now the Republic of Suriname.

and hands like a human creature, and *cousheries*,[9] a little beast in the form and fashion of a lion, as big as a kitten, but so exactly made in all parts like that noble beast, that it is it in miniature. Then for little parakeetoes, great parrots, macaws, and a thousand other birds and beasts of wonderful and surprising forms, shapes, and colors. For skins of prodigious snakes, of which there are some threescore yards in length, as is the skin of one that may be seen at his Majesty's antiquaries'; where are also some rare flies[1] of amazing forms and colors, presented to 'em by myself, some as big as my fist, some less, and all of various excellencies, such as art cannot imitate. Then we trade for feathers, which they order into all shapes, make themselves little short habits of 'em, and glorious wreaths for their heads, necks, arms and legs, whose tinctures are unconceivable. I had a set of these presented to me, and I gave 'em to the King's theater, and it was the dress of the Indian Queen,[2] infinitely admired by persons of quality, and were unimitable. Besides these, a thousand little knacks and rarities in nature, and some of art, as their baskets, weapons, aprons, et cetera. We dealt with 'em with beads of all colors, knives, axes, pins and needles, which they used only as tools to drill holes with in their ears, noses, and lips, where they hang a great many little things, as long beads, bits of tin, brass, or silver beat thin, and any shining trinket. The beads they weave into aprons about a quarter of an ell long, and of the same breadth,[3] working them very prettily in flowers of several colors of beads; which apron they wear just before 'em, as Adam and Eve did the fig leaves, the men wearing a long stripe of linen which they deal with us for. They thread these beads also on long cotton threads and make girdles to tie their aprons to, which come twenty times or more about the waist, and then cross, like a shoulder belt, both ways, and round their necks, arms, and legs. This adornment, with their long black hair, and the face painted in little specks or flowers here and there, makes 'em a wonderful figure to behold.

Some of the beauties which indeed are finely shaped, as almost all are, and who have pretty features, are very charming and novel; for they have all that is called beauty, except the color, which is a reddish yellow; or after a new oiling, which they often use to themselves, they are of the color of a new brick, but smooth, soft, and sleek. They are extreme[4] modest and bashful, very shy and nice of being touched. And though they are all thus naked, if one lives forever among 'em there is not to be seen an indecent action or glance; and being continually used to see one another so unadorned, so like our first parents before the Fall, it seems as if they had no wishes; there being nothing to heighten curiosity, but all you can see you see at once, and every moment see, and where there is no novelty there can be no curiosity. Not but I have seen a handsome young Indian dying for love of a very beautiful young Indian maid; but all his courtship was to fold his arms, pursue her with his eyes, and sighs were all his language; while she, as if no such lover were present, or rather, as if she desired none such, carefully guarded her eyes from beholding him, and never approached him but she looked down with all the blushing modesty I

9. A name appearing in local descriptions, but the animal is not clearly identified; probably the lion-headed marmoset or perhaps the *cujara* (Portuguese), a rodent known as the rice rat. "Buffaloes": wild oxen of various species.
1. Butterflies. "Antiquaries": probably the natural history museum of the Royal Society.

2. The title character in the 1664 heroic play by Sir Robert Howard and John Dryden, which was noted for its lavish production. There are contemporary records of "speckled plumes" and feather headdresses.
3. About a foot square.
4. Extremely.

have seen in the most severe and cautious of our world. And these people represented to me an absolute idea of the first state of innocence, before man knew how to sin. And 'tis most evident and plain that simple Nature is the most harmless, inoffensive, and virtuous mistress. 'Tis she alone, if she were permitted, that better instructs the world than all the inventions of man. Religion would here but destroy that tranquillity they possess by ignorance, and laws would but teach 'em to know offense, of which now they have no notion. They once made mourning and fasting for the death of the English governor, who had given his hand to come on such a day to 'em and neither came nor sent, believing when once a man's word was passed, nothing but death could or should prevent his keeping it. And when they saw he was not dead, they asked him what name they had for a man who promised a thing he did not do. The governor told them, such a man was a liar, which was a word of infamy to a gentleman. Then one of 'em replied, "Governor, you are a liar, and guilty of that infamy." They have a native justice which knows no fraud, and they understand no vice or cunning, but when they are taught by the white men. They have plurality of wives, which, when they grow old, they serve those that succeed 'em, who are young, but with a servitude easy and respected; and unless they take slaves in war, they have no other attendants.

Those on that continent where I was had no king, but the oldest war captain was obeyed with great resignation. A war captain is a man who has led them on to battle with conduct[5] and success, of whom I shall have occasion to speak more hereafter, and of some other of their customs and manners, as they fall in my way.

With these people, as I said, we live in perfect tranquillity and good understanding, as it behooves us to do, they knowing all the places where to seek the best food of the country and the means of getting it, and for very small and unvaluable trifles, supply us with what 'tis impossible for us to get; for they do not only in the wood and over the savannas, in hunting, supply the parts of hounds, by swiftly scouring through those almost impassable places, and by the mere activity of their feet run down the nimblest deer and other eatable beasts; but in the water one would think they were gods of the rivers, or fellow citizens of the deep, so rare an art they have in swimming, diving, and almost living in water, by which they command the less swift inhabitants of the floods. And then for shooting, what they cannot take, or reach with their hands, they do with arrows, and have so admirable an aim that they will split almost a hair; and at any distance that an arrow can reach, they will shoot down oranges and other fruit, and only touch the stalk with the dart's point, that they may not hurt the fruit. So that they being, on all occasions, very useful to us, we find it absolutely necessary to caress 'em as friends, and not to treat 'em as slaves; nor dare we do other, their numbers so far surpassing ours in that continent.

Those then whom we make use of to work in our plantations of sugar are Negroes, black slaves altogether, which are transported thither in this manner. Those who want slaves make a bargain with a master or captain of a ship and contract to pay him so much apiece, a matter of twenty pound a head for as many as he agrees for, and to pay for 'em when they shall be delivered on such a plantation. So that when there arrives a ship laden with

5. Capacity to lead.

slaves, they who have so contracted go aboard and receive their number by lot; and perhaps in one lot that may be for ten, there may happen to be three or four men, the rest women and children. Or be there more or less of either sex, you are obliged to be contented with your lot.

Coramantien,[6] a country of blacks so called, was one of those places in which they found the most advantageous trading for these slaves, and thither most of our great traders in that merchandise trafficked; for that nation is very warlike and brave, and having a continual campaign, being always in hostility with one neighboring prince or other, they had the fortune to take a great many captives; for all they took in battle were sold as slaves, at least those common men who could not ransom themselves. Of these slaves so taken, the general only has all the profit; and of these generals, our captains and masters of ships buy all their freights.

The King of Coramantien was himself a man of a hundred and odd years old, and had no son, though he had many beautiful black wives; for most certainly there are beauties that can charm of that color. In his younger years he had had many gallant men to his sons, thirteen of which died in battle, conquering when they fell; and he had only left him for his successor one grandchild, son to one of these dead victors, who, as soon as he could bear a bow in his hand and a quiver at his back, was sent into the field, to be trained up by one of the oldest generals to war; where, from his natural inclination to arms and the occasions given him, with the good conduct of the old general, he became, at the age of seventeen, one of the most expert captains and bravest soldiers that ever saw the field of Mars. So that he was adored as the wonder of all that world, and the darling of the soldiers. Besides, he was adorned with a native beauty so transcending all those of his gloomy race that he struck an awe and reverence even in those that knew not his quality; as he did in me, who beheld him with surprise and wonder, when afterwards he arrived in our world.

He had scarce arrived at his seventeenth year, when fighting by his side, the general was killed with an arrow in his eye, which the Prince Oroonoko (for so was this gallant Moor[7] called) very narrowly avoided; nor had he, if the general, who saw the arrow shot, and perceiving it aimed at the Prince, had not bowed his head between, on purpose to receive it in his own body rather than it should touch that of the Prince, and so saved him.

'Twas then, afflicted as Oroonoko was, that he was proclaimed general in the old man's place; and then it was, at the finishing of that war, which had continued for two years, that the Prince came to court, where he had hardly been a month together from the time of his fifth year to that of seventeen; and 'twas amazing to imagine where it was he learned so much humanity; or to give his accomplishments a juster name, where 'twas he got that real greatness of soul, those refined notions of true honor, that absolute generosity, and that softness that was capable of the highest passions of love and gallantry, whose objects were almost continually fighting men, or those mangled or dead; who heard no sounds but those of war and groans. Some

6. Not a country but a British-held fort and slave market on the Gold Coast of Africa, in modern-day Ghana. As the slave trade expanded, the slaves and workers shipped out from the region (who came to be called Cormantines) impressed many European observers by their beauty and bearing, their fierceness in war, and their extreme dignity under captivity or torture.
7. Loosely used for any dark-skinned person.

part of it we may attribute to the care of a Frenchman of wit and learning, who, finding it turn to very good account to be a sort of royal tutor to this young black, and perceiving him very ready, apt, and quick of apprehension, took a great pleasure to teach him morals, language, and science, and was for it extremely beloved and valued by him. Another reason was, he loved, when he came from war, to see all the English gentlemen that traded thither, and did not only learn their language but that of the Spaniards also, with whom he traded afterwards for slaves.

I have often seen and conversed with this great man, and been a witness to many of his mighty actions, and do assure my reader the most illustrious courts could not have produced a braver man, both for greatness of courage and mind, a judgment more solid, a wit more quick, and a conversation more sweet and diverting. He knew almost as much as if he had read much. He had heard of and admired the Romans; he had heard of the late civil wars in England, and the deplorable death of our great monarch,[8] and would discourse of it with all the sense and abhorrence of the injustice imaginable. He had an extreme good and graceful mien, and all the civility of a well-bred great man. He had nothing of barbarity in his nature, but in all points addressed himself as if his education had been in some European court.

This great and just character of Oroonoko gave me an extreme curiosity to see him, especially when I knew he spoke French and English, and that I could talk with him. But though I had heard so much of him, I was as greatly surprised when I saw him as if I had heard nothing of him, so beyond all report I found him. He came into the room and addressed himself to me, and some other women, with the best grace in the world. He was pretty tall, but of a shape the most exact that can be fancied. The most famous statuary[9] could not form the figure of a man more admirably turned from head to foot. His face was not of that brown, rusty black which most of that nation are, but a perfect ebony or polished jet. His eyes were the most awful that could be seen, and very piercing, the white of 'em being like snow, as were his teeth. His nose was rising and Roman, instead of African and flat; his mouth the finest shaped that could be seen, far from those great turned lips which are so natural to the rest of the Negroes. The whole proportion and air of his face was so noble and exactly formed that, bating[1] his color, there could be nothing in nature more beautiful, agreeable, and handsome. There was no one grace wanting that bears the standard of true beauty. His hair came down to his shoulders by the aids of art; which was by pulling it out with a quill and keeping it combed, of which he took particular care. Nor did the perfections of his mind come short of those of his person, for his discourse was admirable upon almost any subject; and whoever had heard him speak would have been convinced of their errors, that all fine wit is confined to the white men, especially to those of Christendom, and would have confessed that Oroonoko was as capable even of reigning well, and of governing

---

8. Charles I, beheaded in 1649 during the civil wars between Royalists and Parliamentarians. In 1688 this remark and others would have signaled Behn's ardent support of James II, the last of the Stuart kings, who would be forced into exile within the year.
9. Sculptor.

1. Except for. The singling out of Africans with European looks or moral values is by no means unique to Behn; for example, Edward Long's 1774 *History of Jamaica* reports of the Cormantines that "their features are very different from the rest of the African Negroes, being smaller, and more of the European turn."

as wisely, had as great a soul, as politic[2] maxims, and was as sensible of power, as any prince civilized in the most refined schools of humanity and learning, or the most illustrious courts.

This prince, such as I have described him, whose soul and body were so admirably adorned, was (while yet he was in the court of his grandfather), as I said, as capable of love as 'twas possible for a brave and gallant man to be; and in saying that, I have named the highest degree of love, for sure, great souls are most capable of that passion.

I have already said, the old general was killed by the shot of an arrow, by the side of this prince, in battle, and that Oroonoko was made general. This old dead hero had one only daughter left of his race, a beauty that, to describe her truly, one need say only she was female to the noble male, the beautiful black Venus to our young Mars, as charming in her person as he, and of delicate virtues. I have seen an hundred white men sighing after her, and making a thousand vows at her feet, all vain and unsuccessful. And she was, indeed, too great for any but a prince of her own nation to adore.

Oroonoko coming from the wars (which were now ended), after he had made his court to his grandfather, he thought in honor he ought to make a visit to Imoinda, the daughter of his foster-father, the dead general; and to make some excuses to her, because his preservation was the occasion of her father's death; and to present her with those slaves that had been taken in this last battle, as the trophies of her father's victories. When he came, attended by all the young soldiers of any merit, he was infinitely surprised at the beauty of this fair queen of night, whose face and person was so exceeding all he had ever beheld; that lovely modesty with which she received him; that softness in her look, and sighs, upon the melancholy occasion of this honor that was done by so great a man as Oroonoko, and a prince of whom she had heard such admirable things: the awfulness[3] wherewith she received him, and the sweetness of her words and behavior while he stayed, gained a perfect conquest over his fierce heart, and made him feel the victor could be subdued. So that having made his first compliments, and presented her a hundred and fifty slaves in fetters, he told her with his eyes that he was not insensible of her charms; while Imoinda, who wished for nothing more than so glorious a conquest, was pleased to believe she understood that silent language of newborn love, and from that moment put on all her additions to beauty.

The Prince returned to court with quite another humor than before; and though he did not speak much of the fair Imoinda, he had the pleasure to hear all his followers speak of nothing but the charms of that maid, insomuch that, even in the presence of the old king, they were extolling her and heightening, if possible, the beauties they had found in her. So that nothing else was talked of, no other sound was heard in every corner where there were whisperers, but "Imoinda! Imoinda!"

'Twill be imagined Oroonoko stayed not long before he made his second visit, nor, considering his quality, not much longer before he told her he adored her. I have often heard him say that he admired by what strange inspiration he came to talk things so soft and so passionate, who never knew love, nor was used to the conversation[4] of women; but (to use his own words)

---

2. Shrewd, sagacious.
3. Reverence.

4. Company. "Admired": marveled.

he said, most happily some new and till then unknown power instructed his heart and tongue in the language of love, and at the same time, in favor of him, inspired Imoinda with a sense of his passion. She was touched with what he said, and returned it all in such answers as went to his very heart, with a pleasure unknown before. Nor did he use those obligations[5] ill that love had done him, but turned all his happy moments to the best advantage; and as he knew no vice, his flame aimed at nothing but honor, if such a distinction may be made in love; and especially in that country, where men take to themselves as many as they can maintain, and where the only crime and sin with woman is to turn her off, to abandon her to want, shame, and misery. Such ill morals are only practiced in Christian countries, where they prefer the bare name of religion, and, without virtue or morality, think that's sufficient. But Oroonoko was none of those professors, but as he had right notions of honor, so he made her such propositions as were not only and barely such; but contrary to the custom of his country, he made her vows she should be the only woman he would possess while he lived; that no age or wrinkles should incline him to change, for her soul would be always fine and always young, and he should have an eternal idea in his mind of the charms she now bore, and should look into his heart for that idea when he could find it no longer in her face.

After a thousand assurances of his lasting flame, and her eternal empire over him, she condescended to receive him for her husband, or rather, received him as the greatest honor the gods could do her.

There is a certain ceremony in these cases to be observed, which I forgot to ask him how performed; but 'twas concluded on both sides that, in obedience to him, the grandfather was to be first made acquainted with the design, for they pay a most absolute resignation to the monarch, especially when he is a parent also.

On the other side, the old king, who had many wives and many concubines, wanted not court flatterers to insinuate in his heart a thousand tender thoughts for this young beauty, and who represented her to his fancy as the most charming he had ever possessed in all the long race of his numerous years. At this character his old heart, like an extinguished brand, most apt to take fire, felt new sparks of love and began to kindle; and now grown to his second childhood, longed with impatience to behold this gay thing, with whom, alas! he could but innocently play. But how he should be confirmed she was this wonder, before he used his power to call her to court (where maidens never came, unless for the King's private use), he was next to consider; and while he was so doing, he had intelligence brought him that Imoinda was most certainly mistress to the Prince Oroonoko. This gave him some chagrin; however, it gave him also an opportunity, one day when the Prince was a-hunting, to wait on a man of quality, as his slave and attendant, who should go and make a present to Imoinda as from the Prince; he should then, unknown, see this fair maid, and have an opportunity to hear what message she would return the Prince for his present, and from thence gather the state of her heart and degree of her inclination. This was put in execution, and the old monarch saw, and burned. He found her all he had heard,

5. Benefits.

and would not delay his happiness, but found he should have some obstacle to overcome her heart; for she expressed her sense of the present the Prince had sent her in terms so sweet, so soft and pretty, with an air of love and joy that could not be dissembled, insomuch that 'twas past doubt whether she loved Oroonoko entirely. This gave the old king some affliction, but he salved it with this, that the obedience the people pay their king was not at all inferior to what they paid their gods; and what love would not oblige Imoinda to do, duty would compel her to.

He was therefore no sooner got to his apartment but he sent the royal veil to Imoinda, that is, the ceremony of invitation: he sends the lady he has a mind to honor with his bed a veil, with which she is covered, and secured for the King's use; and 'tis death to disobey, besides held a most impious disobedience.

'Tis not to be imagined the surprise and grief that seized this lovely maid at this news and sight. However, as delays in these cases are dangerous and pleading worse than treason, trembling, and almost fainting, she was obliged to suffer herself to be covered and led away.

They brought her thus to court; and the King, who had caused a very rich bath to be prepared, was led into it, where he sat under a canopy, in state, to receive this longed-for virgin; whom he having commanded should be brought to him, they (after disrobing her) led her to the bath, and making fast the doors, left her to descend. The King, without more courtship, bade her throw off her mantle and come to his arms. But Imoinda, all in tears, threw herself on the marble, on the brink of the bath, and besought him to hear her. She told him, as she was a maid, how proud of the divine glory she should have been, of having it in her power to oblige her king; but as by the laws he could not, and from his royal goodness would not, take from any man his wedded wife, so she believed she should be the occasion of making him commit a great sin, if she did not reveal her state and condition, and tell him she was another's, and could not be so happy to be his.

The King, enraged at this delay, hastily demanded the name of the bold man that had married a woman of her degree without his consent. Imoinda, seeing his eyes fierce and his hands tremble (whether with age or anger, I know not, but she fancied the last), almost repented she had said so much, for now she feared the storm would fall on the Prince. She therefore said a thousand things to appease the raging of his flame, and to prepare him to hear who it was with calmness; but before she spoke, he imagined who she meant, but would not seem to do so, but commanded her to lay aside her mantle and suffer herself to receive his caresses; or by his gods, he swore that happy man whom she was going to name should die, though it were even Oroonoko himself. "Therefore," said he, "deny this marriage, and swear thyself a maid." "That," replied Imoinda, "by all our powers I do, for I am not yet known to my husband." "'Tis enough," said the King; "'tis enough to satisfy both my conscience and my heart." And rising from his seat, he went and led her into the bath, it being in vain for her to resist.

In this time the Prince, who was returned from hunting, went to visit his Imoinda, but found her gone; and not only so, but heard she had received the royal veil. This raised him to a storm, and in his madness they had much ado to save him from laying violent hands on himself. Force first prevailed, and then reason. They urged all to him that might oppose his rage, but nothing weighed so greatly with him as the King's old age, uncapable of injuring him with Imoinda. He would give way to that hope, because it pleased him most, and flattered best his heart. Yet this served not altogether to make him cease his different passions, which sometimes raged within him, and sometimes softened into showers. 'Twas not enough to appease him, to tell him his grandfather was old and could not that way injure him, while he retained that awful duty which the young men are used there to pay to their grave relations. He could not be convinced he had no cause to sigh and mourn for the loss of a mistress he could not with all his strength and courage retrieve. And he would often cry, "O my friends! Were she in walled cities or confined from me in fortifications of the greatest strength, did enchantments or monsters detain her from me, I would venture through any hazard to free her. But here, in the arms of a feeble old man, my youth, my violent love, my trade in arms, and all my vast desire of glory avail me nothing. Imoinda is as irrecoverably lost to me as if she were snatched by the cold arms of Death. Oh! she is never to be retrieved. If I would wait tedious years, till fate should bow the old king to his grave, even that would not leave me Imoinda free; but still that custom that makes it so vile a crime for a son to marry his father's wives or mistresses would hinder my happiness, unless I would either ignobly set an ill precedent to my successors, or abandon my country and fly with her to some unknown world, who never heard our story."

But it was objected to him that his case was not the same; for Imoinda being his lawful wife, by solemn contract, 'twas he was the injured man and might if he so pleased take Imoinda back, the breach of the law being on his grandfather's side; and that if he could circumvent him and redeem her from the Otan, which is the palace of the King's women, a sort of seraglio, it was both just and lawful for him so to do.

This reasoning had some force upon him, and he should have been entirely comforted, but for the thought that she was possessed by his grandfather. However, he loved so well that he was resolved to believe what most favored his hope, and to endeavor to learn from Imoinda's own mouth what only she could satisfy him in, whether she was robbed of that blessing which was only due to his faith and love. But as it was very hard to get a sight of the women (for no men ever entered into the Otan but when the King went to entertain himself with some one of his wives or mistresses, and 'twas death at any other time for any other to go in), so he knew not how to contrive to get a sight of her.

While Oroonoko felt all the agonies of love, and suffered under a torment the most painful in the world, the old king was not exempted from his share of affliction. He was troubled for having been forced by an irresistible passion to rob his son[6] of a treasure he knew could not but be extremely dear to him, since she was the most beautiful that ever had been seen, and had besides all the sweetness and innocence of youth and modesty, with a charm of wit surpassing all. He found that, however she was forced to expose her lovely person to his withered arms, she could only sigh and weep there, and think of Oroonoko; and oftentimes could not forbear speaking of him, though her life were, by custom, forfeited by owning her passion. But she spoke not of a lover only, but of a prince dear to him to whom she spoke, and

6. I.e., grandson.

of the praises of a man who, till now, filled the old man's soul with joy at every recital of his bravery, or even his name. And 'twas this dotage on our young hero that gave Imoinda a thousand privileges to speak of him without offending, and this condescension in the old king that made her take the satisfaction of speaking of him so very often.

Besides, he many times inquired how the Prince bore himself; and those of whom he asked, being entirely slaves to the merits and virtues of the Prince, still answered what they thought conduced best to his service; which was to make the old king fancy that the Prince had no more interest in Imoinda, and had resigned her willingly to the pleasure of the King; that he diverted himself with his mathematicians, his fortifications, his officers, and his hunting.

This pleased the old lover, who failed not to report these things again to Imoinda, that she might, by the example of her young lover, withdraw her heart, and rest better contented in his arms. But however she was forced to receive this unwelcome news, in all appearance with unconcern and content, her heart was bursting within, and she was only happy when she could get alone, to vent her griefs and moans with sighs and tears.

What reports of the Prince's conduct were made to the King, he thought good to justify as far as possibly he could by his actions, and when he appeared in the presence of the King, he showed a face not at all betraying his heart. So that in a little time, the old man being entirely convinced that he was no longer a lover of Imoinda, he carried him with him in his train to the Otan, often to banquet with his mistress. But as soon as he entered, one day, into the apartment of Imoinda with the King, at the first glance from her eyes, notwithstanding all his determined resolution, he was ready to sink in the place where he stood, and had certainly done so but for the support of Aboan, a young man who was next to him; which, with his change of countenance, had betrayed him, had the King chanced to look that way. And I have observed, 'tis a very great error, in those who laugh when one says a Negro can change color, for I have seen 'em as frequently blush, and look pale, and that as visibly as ever I saw in the most beautiful white. And 'tis certain that both these changes were evident, this day, in both these lovers. And Imoinda, who saw with some joy the change in the Prince's face, and found it in her own, strove to divert the King from beholding either by a forced caress, with which she met him, which was a new wound in the heart of the poor dying Prince. But as soon as the King was busied in looking on some fine thing of Imoinda's making, she had time to tell the Prince with her angry but love-darting eyes that she resented his coldness, and bemoaned her own miserable captivity. Nor were his eyes silent, but answered hers again, as much as eyes could do, instructed by the most tender and most passionate heart that ever loved. And they spoke so well and so effectually, as Imoinda no longer doubted but she was the only delight and the darling of that soul she found pleading in 'em its right of love, which none was more willing to resign than she. And 'twas this powerful language alone that in an instant conveyed all the thoughts of their souls to each other, that[7] they both found there wanted but opportunity to make them both entirely happy. But when he saw another door opened by Onahal, a former old wife of the King's

7. So that.

who now had charge of Imoinda, and saw the prospect of a bed of state made ready with sweets and flowers for the dalliance of the King, who immediately led the trembling victim from his sight into that prepared repose, what rage, what wild frenzies seized his heart! which forcing to keep within bounds, and to suffer without noise, it became the more insupportable, and rent his soul with ten thousand pains. He was forced to retire to vent his groans, where he fell down on a carpet and lay struggling a long time, and only breathing now and then, "—O Imoinda!"

When Onahal had finished her necessary affair within, shutting the door, she came forth to wait till the King called; and hearing someone sighing in the other room, she passed on, and found the Prince in that deplorable condition, which she thought needed her aid. She gave him cordials, but all in vain, till finding the nature of his disease by his sighs and naming Imoinda. She told him, he had not so much cause as he imagined to afflict himself, for if he knew the King so well as she did, he would not lose a moment in jealousy, and that she was confident that Imoinda bore, at this minute, part in his affliction. Aboan was of the same opinion, and both together persuaded him to reassume his courage; and all sitting down on the carpet, the Prince said so many obliging things to Onahal that he half persuaded her to be of his party. And she promised him she would thus far comply with his just desires, that she would let Imoinda know how faithful he was, what he suffered, and what he said.

This discourse lasted till the King called, which gave Oroonoko a certain satisfaction, and with the hope Onahal had made him conceive, he assumed a look as gay as 'twas possible a man in his circumstances could do; and presently after, he was called in with the rest who waited without. The King commanded music to be brought, and several of his young wives and mistresses came all together by his command to dance before him; where Imoinda performed her part with an air and grace so passing all the rest as her beauty was above 'em, and received the present ordained as a prize. The Prince was every moment more charmed with the new beauties and graces he beheld in this fair one. And while he gazed, and she danced, Onahal was retired to a window with Aboan.

This Onahal, as I said, was one of the cast mistresses of the old king; and 'twas these (now past their beauty) that were made guardians or governants[8] to the new and the young ones, and whose business it was to teach them all those wanton arts of love with which they prevailed and charmed heretofore in their turn; and who now treated the triumphing happy ones with all the severity, as to liberty and freedom, that was possible, in revenge of those honors they rob them of; envying them those satisfactions, those gallantries and presents, that were once made to themselves, while youth and beauty lasted, and which they now saw pass regardless by, and paid only to the bloomings. And certainly nothing is more afflicting to a decayed beauty than to behold in itself declining charms that were once adored, and to find those caresses paid to new beauties to which once she laid a claim; to hear 'em whisper as she passes by, "That once was a delicate woman." These abandoned ladies therefore endeavor to revenge all the despites[9] and decays

8. Female teachers or chaperones. "Cast": i.e., cast-off.
9. Insults.

of time on these flourishing happy ones. And 'twas this severity that gave
Oroonoko a thousand fears he should never prevail with Onahal to see
Imoinda. But, as I said, she was now retired to a window with Aboan.

This young man was not only one of the best quality,[1] but a man extremely
well made and beautiful; and coming often to attend the King to the Otan, he
had subdued the heart of the antiquated Onahal, which had not forgot how
pleasant it was to be in love. And though she had some decays in her face, she
had none in her sense and wit; she was there agreeable still, even to Aboan's
youth, so that he took pleasure in entertaining her with discourses of love.
He knew also that to make his court to these she-favorites was the way to be
great, these being the persons that do all affairs and business at court. He
had also observed that she had given him glances more tender and inviting
than she had done to others of his quality. And now, when he saw that her
favor could so absolutely oblige the Prince, he failed not to sigh in her ear and
to look with eyes all soft upon her, and give her hope that she had made some
impressions on his heart. He found her pleased at this, and making a thousand advances to him; but the ceremony ending and the King departing
broke up the company for that day, and his conversation.

Aboan failed not that night to tell the Prince of his success, and how
advantageous the service of Onahal might be to his amour with Imoinda.
The Prince was overjoyed with this good news and besought him, if it were
possible, to caress her so as to engage her entirely, which he could not fail
to do, if he complied with her desires. "For then," said the Prince, "her life
lying at your mercy, she must grant you the request you make in my behalf."
Aboan understood him, and assured him he would make love so effectually
that he would defy the most expert mistress of the art to find out whether
he dissembled it or had it really. And 'twas with impatience they waited the
next opportunity of going to the Otan.

The wars came on, the time of taking the field approached, and 'twas
impossible for the Prince to delay his going at the head of his army to
encounter the enemy. So that every day seemed a tedious year till he saw his
Imoinda, for he believed he could not live if he were forced away without
being so happy. 'Twas with impatience, therefore, that he expected the next
visit the King would make, and according to his wish, it was not long.

The parley of the eyes of these two lovers had not passed so secretly but
an old jealous lover could spy it; or rather, he wanted not flatterers who told
him they observed it. So that the Prince was hastened to the camp, and this
was the last visit he found he should make to the Otan; he therefore urged
Aboan to make the best of this last effort, and to explain himself so to Onahal that she, deferring her enjoyment of her young lover no longer, might
make way for the Prince to speak to Imoinda.

The whole affair being agreed on between the Prince and Aboan, they
attended the King, as the custom was, to the Otan, where, while the whole
company was taken up in beholding the dancing and antic postures the
women-royal made to divert the King, Onahal singled out Aboan, whom
she found most pliable to her wish. When she had him where she believed she
could not be heard, she sighed to him, and softly cried, "Ah, Aboan! When
will you be sensible of my passion? I confess it with my mouth, because I

1. Rank.

would not give my eyes the lie; and you have but too much already perceived they have confessed my flame. Nor would I have you believe that because I am the abandoned mistress of a king, I esteem myself altogether divested of charms. No, Aboan; I have still a rest[2] of beauty enough engaging, and have learned to please too well not to be desirable. I can have lovers still, but will have none but Aboan." "Madam," replied the half-feigning youth, "you have already, by my eyes, found you can still conquer, and I believe 'tis in pity of me you condescend to this kind confession. But, Madam, words are used to be so small a part of our country courtship, that 'tis rare one can get so happy an opportunity as to tell one's heart, and those few minutes we have are forced to be snatched for more certain proofs of love than speaking and sighing; and such I languish for."

He spoke this with such a tone that she hoped it true, and could not forbear believing it; and being wholly transported with joy, for having subdued the finest of all the King's subjects to her desires, she took from her ears two large pearls and commanded him to wear 'em in his. He would have refused 'em, crying, "Madam, these are not the proofs of your love that I expect; 'tis opportunity, 'tis a lone hour only, that can make me happy." But forcing the pearls into his hand, she whispered softly to him, "Oh! Do not fear a woman's invention, when love sets her a-thinking." And pressing his hand, she cried, "This night you shall be happy. Come to the gate of the orange groves behind the Otan, and I will be ready, about midnight, to receive you." 'Twas thus agreed, and she left him, that no notice might be taken of their speaking together.

The ladies were still dancing, and the King, laid on a carpet, with a great deal of pleasure was beholding them, especially Imoinda, who that day appeared more lovely than ever, being enlivened with the good tidings Onahal had brought her of the constant passion the Prince had for her. The Prince was laid on another carpet at the other end of the room, with his eyes fixed on the object of his soul; and as she turned or moved, so did they, and she alone gave his eyes and soul their motions. Nor did Imoinda employ her eyes to any other use than in beholding with infinite pleasure the joy she produced in those of the Prince. But while she was more regarding him than the steps she took, she chanced to fall, and so near him as that, leaping with extreme force from the carpet, he caught her in his arms as she fell; and 'twas visible to the whole presence[3] the joy wherewith he received her. He clasped her close to his bosom, and quite forgot that reverence that was due to the mistress of a king, and that punishment that is the reward of a boldness of this nature; and had not the presence of mind of Imoinda (fonder of his safety than her own) befriended him, in making her spring from his arms and fall into her dance again, he had at that instant met his death; for the old king, jealous to the last degree, rose up in rage, broke all the diversion, and led Imoinda to her apartment, and sent out word to the Prince to go immediately to the camp, and that if he were found another night in court he should suffer the death ordained for disobedient offenders.

You may imagine how welcome this news was to Oroonoko, whose unseasonable transport and caress of Imoinda was blamed by all men that loved

2. Remnant.   3. Company.

him; and now he perceived his fault, yet cried that for such another moment, he would be content to die.

All the Otan was in disorder about this accident; and Onahal was particularly concerned, because on the Prince's stay depended her happiness, for she could no longer expect that of Aboan. So that ere they departed, they contrived it so that the Prince and he should come both that night to the grove of the Otan, which was all of oranges and citrons, and that there they should wait her orders.

They parted thus, with grief enough, till night, leaving the King in possession of the lovely maid. But nothing could appease the jealousy of the old lover. He would not be imposed on, but would have it that Imoinda made a false step on purpose to fall into Oroonoko's bosom, and that all things looked like a design on both sides; and 'twas in vain she protested her innocence. He was old and obstinate, and left her more than half assured that his fear was true.

The King going to his apartment sent to know where the Prince was, and if he intended to obey his command. The messenger returned and told him, he found the Prince pensive and altogether unpreparing for the campaign, that he lay negligently on the ground, and answered very little. This confirmed the jealousy of the King, and he commanded that they should very narrowly and privately watch his motions, and that he should not stir from his apartment but one spy or other should be employed to watch him. So that the hour approaching wherein he was to go to the citron grove, and taking only Aboan along with him, he leaves his apartment, and was watched to the very gate of the Otan, where he was seen to enter, and where they left him, to carry back the tidings to the King.

Oroonoko and Aboan were no sooner entered but Onahal led the Prince to the apartment of Imoinda, who, not knowing anything of her happiness, was laid in bed. But Onahal only left him in her chamber, to make the best of his opportunity, and took her dear Aboan to her own, where he showed the heighth of complaisance for his prince, when, to give him an opportunity, he suffered himself to be caressed in bed by Onahal.

The Prince softly wakened Imoinda, who was not a little surprised with joy to find him there; and yet she trembled with a thousand fears. I believe he omitted saying nothing to this young maid that might persuade her to suffer him to seize his own, and take the rights of love; and I believe she was not long resisting those arms where she so longed to be; and having opportunity, night and silence, youth, love and desire, he soon prevailed, and ravished in a moment what his old grandfather had been endeavoring for so many months.

'Tis not to be imagined the satisfaction of these two young lovers; nor the vows she made him that she remained a spotless maid till that night, and that what she did with his grandfather had robbed him of no part of her virgin honor, the gods in mercy and justice having reserved that for her plighted lord, to whom of right it belonged. And 'tis impossible to express the transports he suffered, while he listened to a discourse so charming from her loved lips, and clasped that body in his arms for whom he had so long languished; and nothing now afflicted him but his sudden departure from her; for he told her the necessity and his commands, but should depart satisfied in this, that since the old king had hitherto not been able to deprive him of those enjoyments which only belonged to him, he believed for the future he would be less able to injure him; so that abating the scandal of the veil, which was no otherwise so than that she was wife to another, he believed her safe, even in the arms of the King, and innocent; yet would he have ventured at the conquest of the world, and have given it all, to have had her avoided that honor of receiving the royal veil. 'Twas thus, between a thousand caresses, that both bemoaned the hard fate of youth and beauty, so liable to that cruel promotion. 'Twas a glory that could well have been spared here, though desired and aimed at by all the young females of that kingdom.

But while they were thus fondly employed, forgetting how time ran on, and that the dawn must conduct him far away from his only happiness, they heard a great noise in the Otan, and unusual voices of men; at which the Prince, starting from the arms of the frighted Imoinda, ran to a little battle-ax he used to wear by his side, and having not so much leisure as to put on his habit, he opposed himself against some who were already opening the door; which they did with so much violence that Oroonoko was not able to defend it, but was forced to cry out with a commanding voice, "Whoever ye are that have the boldness to attempt to approach this apartment thus rudely, know that I, the Prince Oroonoko, will revenge it with the certain death of him that first enters. Therefore stand back, and know, this place is sacred to love and me this night; tomorrow 'tis the King's."

This he spoke with a voice so resolved and assured that they soon retired from the door, but cried, "'Tis by the King's command we are come; and being satisfied by thy voice, O Prince, as much as if we had entered, we can report to the King the truth of all his fears, and leave thee to provide for thy own safety, as thou art advised by thy friends."

At these words they departed, and left the Prince to take a short and sad leave of his Imoinda, who, trusting in the strength of her charms, believed she should appease the fury of a jealous king by saying she was surprised, and that it was by force of arms he got into her apartment. All her concern now was for his life, and therefore she hastened him to the camp, and with much ado prevailed on him to go. Nor was it she alone that prevailed; Aboan and Onahal both pleaded, and both assured him of a lie that should be well enough contrived to secure Imoinda. So that at last, with a heart sad as death, dying eyes, and sighing soul, Oroonoko departed and took his way to the camp.

It was not long after the King in person came to the Otan, where, beholding Imoinda with rage in his eyes, he upbraided her wickedness and perfidy, and threatening her royal lover, she fell on her face at his feet, bedewing the floor with her tears and imploring his pardon for a fault which she had not with her will committed, as Onahal, who was also prostrate with her, could testify; that unknown to her, he had broke into her apartment, and ravished her. She spoke this much against her conscience, but to save her own life 'twas absolutely necessary she should feign this falsity. She knew it could not injure the Prince, he being fled to an army that would stand by him against any injuries that should assault him. However, this last thought of Imoinda's being ravished changed the measures of his revenge; and whereas before he designed to be himself her executioner, he now resolved she should not die. But as it is the greatest crime in nature amongst 'em to touch a woman after having been possessed by a son, a father, or a brother, so now he looked on Imoinda as a polluted thing, wholly unfit for his embrace; nor would he resign her to his grandson, because she had received the royal veil. He therefore removes her from the Otan, with Onahal; whom he put into safe hands, with order they should be both sold off as slaves to another country, either Christian or heathen; 'twas no matter where.

This cruel sentence, worse than death, they implored might be reversed; but their prayers were vain, and it was put in execution accordingly, and that with so much secrecy that none, either without or within the Otan, knew anything of their absence or their destiny.

The old king, nevertheless, executed this with a great deal of reluctancy; but he believed he had made a very great conquest over himself, when he had once resolved, and had performed what he resolved. He believed now that his love had been unjust, and that he could not expect the gods, or Captain of the Clouds (as they call the unknown power), should suffer a better consequence from so ill a cause. He now begins to hold Oroonoko excused, and to say he had reason for what he did. And now everybody could assure the King how passionately Imoinda was beloved by the Prince; even those confessed it now, who said the contrary before his flame was abated. So that the King being old, and not able to defend himself in war, and having no sons of all his race remaining alive but only this, to maintain him on his throne; and looking on this as a man disobliged, first by the rape of his mistress, or rather wife; and now by depriving of him wholly of her, he feared, might make him desperate and do some cruel thing, either to himself or his old grandfather, the offender: he began to repent him extremely of the contempt he had, in his rage, put on Imoinda. Besides, he considered he ought in honor to have killed her for this offense, if it had been one. He ought to have had so much value and consideration for a maid of her quality as to have nobly put her to death, and not to have sold her like a common slave, the greatest revenge and the most disgraceful of any; and to which they a thousand times prefer death, and implore it, as Imoinda did, but could not obtain that honor. Seeing therefore it was certain that Oroonoko would highly resent this affront, he thought good to make some excuse for his rashness to him; and to that end he sent a messenger to the camp, with orders to treat with him about the matter, to gain his pardon, and to endeavor to mitigate his grief; but that by no means he should tell him she was sold, but secretly put to death, for he knew he should never obtain his pardon for the other.

When the messenger came, he found the Prince upon the point of engaging with the enemy; but as soon as he heard of the arrival of the messenger, he commanded him to his tent, where he embraced him and received him with joy; which was soon abated by the downcast looks of the messenger, who was instantly demanded the cause by Oroonoko, who, impatient of delay, asked a thousand questions in a breath, and all concerning Imoinda. But there needed little return, for he could almost answer himself of all he demanded, from his sighs and eyes. At last, the messenger casting himself at the Prince's feet, and kissing them with all the submission of a man that had something to implore which he dreaded to utter, he besought him to hear with calmness what he had to deliver to him, and to call up all his noble and heroic courage to encounter with his words, and defend himself against the ungrateful[4] things he must relate. Oroonoko replied, with a deep sigh and a

4. Offensive.

languishing voice, "I am armed against their worst efforts—; for I know they will tell me, Imoinda is no more—and after that, you may spare the rest." Then, commanding him to rise, he laid himself on a carpet, under a rich pavilion, and remained a good while silent, and was hardly heard to sigh. When he was come a little to himself, the messenger asked him leave to deliver that part of his embassy which the Prince had not yet divined. And the Prince cried, "I permit thee—." Then he told him the affliction the old king was in, for the rashness he had committed in his cruelty to Imoinda; and how he deigned to ask pardon for his offense, and to implore the Prince would not suffer that loss to touch his heart too sensibly, which now all the gods could not restore him, but might recompense him in glory, which he begged he would pursue; and that Death, that common revenger of all injuries, would soon even the account between him and a feeble old man.

Oroonoko bade him return his duty to his lord and master, and to assure him, there was no account of revenge to be adjusted between them; if there were, 'twas he was the aggressor, and that Death would be just and, maugre[5] his age, would see him righted; and he was contented to leave his share of glory to youths more fortunate and worthy of that favor from the gods. That henceforth he would never lift a weapon or draw a bow, but abandon the small remains of his life to sighs and tears, and the continual thoughts of what his lord and grandfather had thought good to send out of the world, with all that youth, that innocence, and beauty.

After having spoken this, whatever his greatest officers and men of the best rank could do, they could not raise him from the carpet, or persuade him to action and resolutions of life; but commanding all to retire, he shut himself into his pavilion all that day, while the enemy was ready to engage; and wondering at the delay, the whole body of the chief of the army then addressed themselves to him, and to whom they had much ado to get admittance. They fell on their faces at the foot of his carpet, where they lay and besought him with earnest prayers and tears to lead 'em forth to battle, and not let the enemy take advantages of them; and implored him to have regard to his glory, and to the world, that depended on his courage and conduct. But he made no other reply to all their supplications but this, that he had now no more business for glory; and for the world, it was a trifle not worth his care. "Go," continued he, sighing, "and divide it amongst you; and reap with joy what you so vainly prize, and leave me to my more welcome destiny."

They then demanded what they should do, and whom he would constitute in his room, that the confusion of ambitious youth and power might not ruin their order and make them a prey to the enemy. He replied, he would not give himself the trouble—; but wished 'em to choose the bravest man amongst 'em, let his quality or birth be what it would. "For, O my friends!" said he, "it is not titles make men brave or good, or birth that bestows courage and generosity, or makes the owner happy. Believe this, when you behold Oroonoko, the most wretched and abandoned by fortune of all the creation of the gods." So turning himself about, he would make no more reply to all they could urge or implore.

The army, beholding their officers return unsuccessful, with sad faces and ominous looks that presaged no good luck, suffered a thousand fears

---

5. In spite of. Oroonoko is saying that he will die before the king does.

to take possession of their hearts, and the enemy to come even upon 'em, before they would provide for their safety by any defense; and though they were assured by some, who had a mind to animate 'em, that they should be immediately headed by the Prince, and that in the meantime Aboan had orders to command as general, yet they were so dismayed for want of that great example of bravery that they could make but a very feeble resistance; and at last downright fled before the enemy, who pursued 'em to the very tents, killing 'em. Nor could all Aboan's courage, which that day gained him immortal glory, shame 'em into a manly defense of themselves. The guards that were left behind about the Prince's tent, seeing the soldiers flee before the enemy and scatter themselves all over the plain, in great disorder, made such outcries as roused the Prince from his amorous slumber, in which he had remained buried for two days without permitting any sustenance to approach him. But in spite of all his resolutions, he had not the constancy of grief to that degree, as to make him insensible of the danger of his army; and in that instant he leaped from his couch and cried, "—Come, if we must die, let us meet Death the noblest way; and 'twill be more like Oroonoko to encounter him at an army's head, opposing the torrent of a conquering foe, than lazily on a couch to wait his lingering pleasure, and die every moment by a thousand wrecking[6] thoughts; or be tamely taken by an enemy, and led a whining, lovesick slave to adorn the triumphs of Jamoan, that young victor, who already is entered beyond the limits I had prescribed him."

While he was speaking, he suffered his people to dress him for the field, and sallying out of his pavilion, with more life and vigor in his countenance than ever he showed, he appeared like some divine power descended to save his country from destruction; and his people had purposely put on him all things that might make him shine with most splendor, to strike a reverend awe into the beholders. He flew into the thickest of those that were pursuing his men, and being animated with despair, he fought as if he came on purpose to die, and did such things as will not be believed that human strength could perform, and such as soon inspired all the rest with new courage and new order. And now it was that they began to fight indeed, and so as if they would not be outdone even by their adored hero; who, turning the tide of the victory, changing absolutely the fate of the day, gained an entire conquest; and Oroonoko having the good fortune to single out Jamoan, he took him prisoner with his own hand, having wounded him almost to death.

This Jamoan afterwards became very dear to him, being a man very gallant and of excellent graces and fine parts; so that he never put him amongst the rank of captives, as they used to do, without distinction, for the common sale or market; but kept him in his own court, where he retained nothing of the prisoner but the name, and returned no more into his own country, so great an affection he took for Oroonoko; and by a thousand tales and adventures of love and gallantry flattered[7] his disease of melancholy and languishment, which I have often heard him say had certainly killed him, but for the conversation of this prince and Aboan, and the French governor he had from his childhood, of whom I have spoken before, and who was a man of admirable wit, great ingenuity and learning, all which he had infused into his young pupil. This Frenchman was banished out of his own country for

6. Racking. 7. Soothed.

some heretical notions he held, and though he was a man of very little religion, he had admirable morals and a brave soul.

After the total defeat of Jamoan's army, which all fled, or were left dead upon the place, they spent some time in the camp, Oroonoko choosing rather to remain a while there in his tents than enter into a palace or live in a court where he had so lately suffered so great a loss. The officers, therefore, who saw and knew his cause of discontent, invented all sorts of diversions and sports to entertain their prince; so that what with those amusements abroad and others at home, that is, within their tents, with the persuasions, arguments, and care of his friends and servants that he more peculiarly prized, he wore off in time a great part of that chagrin and torture of despair which the first efforts of Imoinda's death had given him. Insomuch as having received a thousand kind embassies from the King, and invitations to return to court, he obeyed, though with no little reluctancy; and when he did so, there was a visible change in him, and for a long time he was much more melancholy than before. But time lessens all extremes, and reduces 'em to mediums and unconcern; but no motives or beauties, though all endeavored it, could engage him in any sort of amour, though he had all the invitations to it, both from his own youth and others' ambitions and designs.

Oroonoko was no sooner returned from this last conquest, and received at court with all the joy and magnificence that could be expressed to a young victor, who was not only returned triumphant but beloved like a deity, when there arrived in the port an English ship.

This person[8] had often before been in these countries and was very well known to Oroonoko, with whom he had trafficked for slaves, and had used to do the same with his predecessors.

This commander was a man of a finer sort of address and conversation, better bred and more engaging than most of that sort of men are, so that he seemed rather never to have been bred out of a court than almost all his life at sea. This captain therefore was always better received at court than most of the traders to those countries were; and especially by Oroonoko, who was more civilized, according to the European mode, than any other had been, and took more delight in the white nations, and above all men of parts and wit. To this captain he sold abundance of his slaves, and for the favor and esteem he had for him, made him many presents, and obliged him to stay at court as long as possibly he could. Which the captain seemed to take as a very great honor done him, entertaining the Prince every day with globes and maps, and mathematical discourses and instruments; eating, drinking, hunting, and living with him with so much familiarity that it was not to be doubted but he had gained very greatly upon the heart of this gallant young man. And the captain, in return of all these mighty favors, besought the Prince to honor his vessel with his presence, some day or other, to dinner, before he should set sail; which he condescended to accept, and appointed his day. The captain, on his part, failed not to have all things in a readiness, in the most magnificent order he could possibly. And the day being come, the captain in his boat, richly adorned with carpets and velvet cushions, rowed to the shore to receive the Prince, with another longboat where was placed all his music and trumpets, with which Oroonoko was extremely delighted;

8. The ship's captain.

who met him on the shore attended by his French governor, Jamoan, Aboan, and about a hundred of the noblest of the youths of the court. And after they had first carried the Prince on board, the boats fetched the rest off; where they found a very splendid treat, with all sorts of fine wines, and were as well entertained as 'twas possible in such a place to be.

The Prince, having drunk hard of punch and several sorts of wine, as did all the rest (for great care was taken they should want nothing of that part of the entertainment), was very merry, and in great admiration of the ship, for he had never been in one before; so that he was curious of beholding every place where he decently might descend. The rest, no less curious, who were not quite overcome with drinking, rambled at their pleasure fore and aft, as their fancies guided 'em. So that the captain, who had well laid his design before, gave the word, and seized on all his guests; they clapping great irons suddenly on the Prince, when he was leaped down in the hold to view that part of the vessel, and locking him fast down, secured him. The same treachery was used to all the rest; and all in one instant, in several places of the ship, were lashed fast in irons, and betrayed to slavery. That great design over, they set all hands to work to hoise[9] sail; and with as treacherous and fair a wind, they made from the shore with this innocent and glorious prize, who thought of nothing less than such an entertainment.

Some have commended this act as brave in the captain; but I will spare my sense of it, and leave it to my reader to judge as he pleases.

It may be easily guessed in what manner the Prince resented this indignity, who may be best resembled to a lion taken in a toil; so he raged, so he struggled for liberty, but all in vain; and they had so wisely managed his fetters that he could not use a hand in his defense, to quit himself of a life that would by no means endure slavery, nor could he move from the place where he was tied to any solid part of the ship, against which he might have beat his head, and have finished his disgrace that way. So that being deprived of all other means, he resolved to perish for want of food. And pleased at last with that thought, and toiled and tired by rage and indignation, he laid himself down, and sullenly resolved upon dying, and refused all things that were brought him.

This did not a little vex the captain, and the more so because he found almost all of 'em of the same humor; so that the loss of so many brave slaves, so tall and goodly to behold, would have been very considerable. He therefore ordered one to go from him (for he would not be seen himself) to Oroonoko, and to assure him he was afflicted for having rashly done so unhospitable a deed, and which could not be now remedied, since they were far from shore; but since he resented it in so high a nature, he assured him he would revoke his resolution, and set both him and his friends ashore on the next land they should touch at; and of this the messenger gave him his oath, provided he would resolve to live. And Oroonoko, whose honor was such as he never had violated a word in his life himself, much less a solemn asseveration, believed in an instant what this man said, but replied, he expected for a confirmation of this to have his shameful fetters dismissed. This demand was carried to the captain, who returned him answer that the offense had been so great which he had put upon the Prince that he durst not trust him with liberty

9. Hoist.

while he remained in the ship, for fear lest by a valor natural to him, and a revenge that would animate that valor, he might commit some outrage fatal to himself and the King his master, to whom his vessel did belong. To this Oroonoko replied, he would engage his honor to behave himself in all friendly order and manner, and obey the command of the captain, as he was lord of the King's vessel and general of those men under his command.

This was delivered to the still doubting captain, who could not resolve to trust a heathen, he said, upon his parole,[1] a man that had no sense or notion of the God that he worshipped. Oroonoko then replied, he was very sorry to hear that the captain pretended to the knowledge and worship of any gods who had taught him no better principles than not to credit as he would be credited; but they told him the difference of their faith occasioned that distrust. For the captain had protested to him upon the word of a Christian, and sworn in the name of a great god, which if he should violate, he would expect eternal torment in the world to come. "Is that all the obligation he has to be just to his oath?" replied Oroonoko. "Let him know I swear by my honor; which to violate, would not only render me contemptible and despised by all brave and honest men, and so give myself perpetual pain, but it would be eternally offending and diseasing all mankind, harming, betraying, circumventing and outraging all men; but punishments hereafter are suffered by one's self, and the world takes no cognizances whether this god have revenged 'em or not, 'tis done so secretly and deferred so long. While the man of no honor suffers every moment the scorn and contempt of the honester world, and dies every day ignominiously in his fame, which is more valuable than life. I speak not this to move belief, but to show you how you mistake, when you imagine that he who will violate his honor will keep his word with his gods." So turning from him with a disdainful smile, he refused to answer him, when he urged him to know what answer he should carry back to his captain; so that he departed without saying any more.

The captain pondering and consulting what to do, it was concluded that nothing but Oroonoko's liberty would encourage any of the rest to eat, except the Frenchman, whom the captain could not pretend to keep prisoner, but only told him he was secured because he might act something in favor of the Prince, but that he should be freed as soon as they came to land. So that they concluded it wholly necessary to free the Prince from his irons, that he might show himself to the rest; that they might have an eye upon him, and that they could not fear a single man.

This being resolved, to make the obligation the greater, the captain himself went to Oroonoko; where after many compliments, and assurances of what he had already promised, he receiving from the Prince his parole and his hand for his good behavior, dismissed his irons and brought him to his own cabin; where after having treated and reposed him a while, for he had neither eat[2] nor slept in four days before, he besought him to visit those obstinate people in chains, who refused all manner of sustenance, and entreated him to oblige 'em to eat, and assure 'em of their liberty the first opportunity.

Oroonoko, who was too generous not to give credit to his words, showed himself to his people, who were transported with excess of joy at the sight of their darling prince, falling at his feet and kissing and embracing 'em,

1. Word of honor.　　　　　2. The past form of *eat*.

believing, as some divine oracle, all he assured 'em. But he besought 'em to bear their chains with that bravery that became those whom he had seen act so nobly in arms; and that they could not give him greater proofs of their love and friendship, since 'twas all the security the captain (his friend) could have, against the revenge, he said, they might possibly justly take for the injuries sustained by him. And they all with one accord assured him, they could not suffer enough, when it was for his repose and safety.

After this they no longer refused to eat, but took what was brought 'em, and were pleased with their captivity, since by it they hoped to redeem the Prince, who, all the rest of the voyage, was treated with all the respect due to his birth, though nothing could divert his melancholy; and he would often sigh for Imoinda, and think this a punishment due to his misfortune, in having left that noble maid behind him that fatal night, in the Otan, when he fled to the camp.

Possessed with a thousand thoughts of past joys with this fair young person, and a thousand griefs for her eternal loss, he endured a tedious voyage, and at last arrived at the mouth of the river of Surinam, a colony belonging to the King of England, and where they were to deliver some part of their slaves. There the merchants and gentlemen of the country going on board to demand those lots of slaves they had already agreed on, and, amongst those, the overseers of those plantations where I then chanced to be, the captain, who had given the word, ordered his men to bring up those noble slaves in fetters whom I have spoken of; and having put 'em some in one and some in other lots, with women and children (which they call pickaninnies), they sold 'em off as slaves to several merchants and gentlemen; not putting any two in one lot, because they would separate 'em far from each other, not daring to trust 'em together, lest rage and courage should put 'em upon contriving some great action, to the ruin of the colony.

Oroonoko was first seized on, and sold to our overseer, who had the first lot, with seventeen more of all sorts and sizes, but not one of quality with him. When he saw this, he found what they meant, for, as I said, he understood English pretty well; and being wholly unarmed and defenseless, so as it was in vain to make any resistance, he only beheld the captain with a look all fierce and disdainful, upbraiding him with eyes that forced blushes on his guilty cheeks; he only cried, in passing over the side of the ship, "Farewell, sir. 'Tis worth my suffering, to gain so true a knowledge both of you and of your gods by whom you swear." And desiring those that held him to forbear their pains, and telling 'em he would make no resistance, he cried, "Come, my fellow slaves; let us descend, and see if we can meet with more honor and honesty in the next world we shall touch upon." So he nimbly leaped into the boat, and showing no more concern, suffered himself to be rowed up the river with his seventeen companions.

The gentleman that bought him was a young Cornish gentleman whose name was Trefry, a man of great wit and fine learning, and was carried into those parts by the Lord ——, Governor,[3] to manage all his affairs. He reflecting on the last words of Oroonoko to the captain, and beholding the richness of his vest,[4] no sooner came into the boat but he fixed his eyes on him; and

---

3. Lord Willoughby of Parham, coproprietor of Surinam by royal grant. John Treffry, or Treffry, was his plantation overseer.

4. An outer garment or robe.

finding something so extraordinary in his face, his shape and mien, a great-ness of look and haughtiness in his air, and finding he spoke English, had a great mind to be inquiring into his quality and fortune; which, though Oroonoko endeavored to hide, by only confessing he was above the rank of common slaves, Trefry soon found he was yet something greater than he confessed, and from that moment began to conceive so vast an esteem for him that he ever after loved him as his dearest brother, and showed him all the civilities due to so great a man.

Trefry was a very good mathematician and a linguist, could speak French and Spanish; and in the three days they remained in the boat (for so long were they going from the ship to the plantation) he entertained Oroonoko so agreeably with his art and discourse, that he was no less pleased with Trefry than he was with the Prince; and he thought himself at least fortunate in this, that since he was a slave, as long as he would suffer himself to remain so, he had a man of so excellent wit and parts for a master. So that before they had finished their voyage up the river, he made no scruple of declaring to Trefry all his fortunes, and most part of what I have here related, and put himself wholly into the hands of his new friend, whom he found resenting all the injuries were done him, and was charmed with all the greatness of his actions; which were recited with that modesty and delicate sense as wholly vanquished him, and subdued him to his interest. And he promised him on his word and honor, he would find the means to reconduct him to his own country again, assuring him, he had a perfect abhorrence of so dishonorable an action, and that he would sooner have died than have been the author of such a perfidy. He found the Prince was very much concerned to know what became of his friends, and how they took their slavery; and Trefry promised to take care about the inquiring after their condition, and that he should have an account of 'em.

Though, as Oroonoko afterwards said, he had little reason to credit the words of a *backearary*,[5] yet he knew not why, but he saw a kind of sincerity and awful truth in the face of Trefry; he saw an honesty in his eyes, and he found him wise and witty enough to understand honor; for it was one of his maxims, a man of wit could not be a knave or villain.

In their passage up the river they put in at several houses for refreshment, and ever when they landed, numbers of people would flock to behold this man; not but their eyes were daily entertained with the sight of slaves, but the fame of Oroonoko was gone before him, and all people were in admiration of his beauty. Besides, he had a rich habit on, in which he was taken, so differ-ent from the rest, and which the captain could not strip him of, because he was forced to surprise his person in the minute he sold him. When he found his habit made him liable, as he thought, to be gazed at the more, he begged Trefry to give him something more befitting a slave, which he did, and took off his robes. Nevertheless, he shone through all; and his osenbrigs (a sort of brown holland[6] suit he had on) could not conceal the graces of his looks and mien, and he had no less admirers than when he had his dazzling habit on. The royal youth appeared in spite of the slave, and people could not help

---

5. White person or master; a variant of *backra*, from an Ibo word transported with the slaves to Surinam and the Caribbean.

6. Coarse cotton or linen, sometimes called osna-burg, after a German cloth-manufacturing town.

treating him after a different manner, without designing it. As soon as they approached him, they venerated and esteemed him; his eyes insensibly commanded respect, and his behavior insinuated it into every soul. So that there was nothing talked of but this young and gallant slave, even by those who yet knew not that he was a prince.

I ought to tell you that the Christians never buy any slaves but they give 'em some name of their own, their native ones being likely very barbarous and hard to pronounce; so that Mr. Trefry gave Oroonoko that of Caesar, which name will live in that country as long as that (scarce more) glorious one of the great Roman; for 'tis most evident, he wanted[7] no part of the personal courage of that Caesar, and acted things as memorable, had they been done in some part of the world replenished with people and historians that might have given him his due. But his misfortune was to fall in an obscure world, that afforded only a female pen to celebrate his fame; though I doubt not but it had lived from others' endeavors, if the Dutch, who immediately after his time took that country,[8] had not killed, banished, and dispersed all those that were capable of giving the world this great man's life, much better than I have done. And Mr. Trefry, who designed it, died before he began it, and bemoaned himself for not having undertook it in time.

For the future, therefore, I must call Oroonoko Caesar, since by that name only he was known in our western world, and by that name he was received on shore at Parham House, where he was destined a slave. But if the King himself (God bless him) had come ashore, there could not have been greater expectations by all the whole plantation, and those neighboring ones, than was on ours at that time; and he was received more like a governor than a slave. Notwithstanding, as the custom was, they assigned him his portion of land, his house, and his business, up in the plantation. But as it was more for form than any design to put him to his task, he endured no more of the slave but the name, and remained some days in the house, receiving all visits that were made him, without stirring towards that part of the plantation where the Negroes were.

At last he would needs go view his land, his house, and the business assigned him. But he no sooner came to the houses of the slaves, which are like a little town by itself, the Negroes all having left work, but they all came forth to behold him, and found he was that prince who had, at several times, sold most of 'em to these parts; and from a veneration they pay to great men, especially if they know 'em, and from the surprise and awe they had at the sight of him, they all cast themselves at his feet, crying out in their language, "Live, O King! Long live, O King!" and kissing his feet, paid him even divine homage.

Several English gentlemen were with him; and what Mr. Trefry had told 'em was here confirmed, of which he himself before had no other witness than Caesar himself. But he was infinitely glad to find his grandeur confirmed by the adoration of all the slaves.

Caesar, troubled with their over-joy and over-ceremony, besought 'em to rise and to receive him as their fellow slave, assuring them he was no better. At which they set up with one accord a most terrible and hideous mourning

---

7. Lacked.
8. In 1667 the Dutch attacked and conquered Surinam, and England ceded it by treaty in exchange for New York.

and condoling, which he and the English had much ado to appease; but at last they prevailed with 'em, and they prepared all their barbarous music, and everyone killed and dressed something of his own stock (for every family has their land apart, on which, at their leisure times, they breed all eatable things), and clubbing it together,[9] made a most magnificent supper, inviting their *Grandee Captain*, their prince, to honor it with his presence; which he did, and several English with him; where they all waited on him, some playing, others dancing before him all the time, according to the manners of their several nations, and with unwearied industry endeavoring to please and delight him.

While they sat at meat Mr. Trefry told Caesar that most of these young slaves were undone in love with a fine she-slave, whom they had had about six months on their land. The Prince, who never heard the name of love without a sigh, nor any mention of it without the curiosity of examining further into that tale, which of all discourses was most agreeable to him, asked how they came to be so unhappy as to be all undone for one fair slave. Trefry, who was naturally amorous and loved to talk of love as well as anybody, proceeded to tell him, they had the most charming black that ever was beheld on their plantation, about fifteen or sixteen years old, as he guessed; that for his part, he had done nothing but sigh for her ever since she came, and that all the white beauties he had seen never charmed him so absolutely as this fine creature had done; and that no man, of any nation, ever beheld her that did not fall in love with her; and that she had all the slaves perpetually at her feet, and the whole country resounded with the fame of Clemene, "for so," said he, "we have christened her. But she denies us all with such a noble disdain, that 'tis a miracle to see that she, who can give such eternal desires, should herself be all ice and all unconcern. She is adorned with the most graceful modesty that ever beautified youth; the softest sigher—that, if she were capable of love, one would swear she languished for some absent happy man; and so retired, as if she feared a rape even from the god of day,[1] or that the breezes would steal kisses from her delicate mouth. Her task of work some sighing lover every day makes it his petition to perform for her, which she accepts blushing and with reluctancy, for fear he will ask her a look for a recompense, which he dares not presume to hope, so great an awe she strikes into the hearts of her admirers." "I do not wonder," replied the Prince, "that Clemene should refuse slaves, being as you say so beautiful, but wonder how she escapes those who can entertain her as you can do; or why, being your slave, you do not oblige her to yield." "I confess," said Trefry, "when I have, against her will, entertained her with love so long as to be transported with my passion, even above decency, I have been ready to make use of those advantages of strength and force nature has given me. But oh! she disarms me with that modesty and weeping, so tender and so moving that I retire, and thank my stars she overcame me." The company laughed at his civility to a slave, and Caesar only applauded the nobleness of his passion and nature, since that slave might be noble or, what was better, have true notions of honor and virtue in her. Thus passed they this night, after having received from the slaves all imaginable respect and obedience.

9. Contributing jointly.   1. The sun.

The next day Trefry asked Caesar to walk, when the heat was allayed, and designedly carried him by the cottage of the fair slave, and told him she whom he spoke of last night lived there retired. "But," says he, "I would not wish you to approach, for I am sure you will be in love as soon as you behold her." Caesar assured him he was proof against all the charms of that sex, and that if he imagined his heart could be so perfidious to love again, after Imoinda, he believed he should tear it from his bosom. They had no sooner spoke, but a little shock dog[2] that Clemene had presented her, which she took great delight in, ran out; and she, not knowing anybody was there, ran to get it in again, and bolted out on those who were just speaking of her. When seeing them, she would have run in again, but Trefry caught her by the hand and cried, "Clemene, however you fly a lover, you ought to pay some respect to this stranger" (pointing to Caesar). But she, as if she had resolved never to raise her eyes to the face of a man again, bent 'em the more to the earth when he spoke, and gave the Prince the leisure to look the more at her. There needed no long gazing or consideration to examine who this fair creature was; he soon saw Imoinda all over her; in a minute he saw her face, her shape, her air, her modesty, and all that called forth his soul with joy at his eyes, and left his body destitute of almost life; it stood without motion, and for a minute knew not that it had a being; and I believe he had never come to himself, so oppressed he was with over-joy, if he had not met with this allay, that he perceived Imoinda fall dead in the hands of Trefry. This awakened him, and he ran to her aid and caught her in his arms, where by degrees she came to herself; and 'tis needless to tell with what transports, what ecstasies of joy, they both a while beheld each other, without speaking; then snatched each other to their arms; then gaze again, as if they still doubted whether they possessed the blessing they grasped; but when they recovered their speech, 'tis not to be imagined what tender things they expressed to each other, wondering what strange fate had brought 'em again together. They soon informed each other of their fortunes, and equally bewailed their fate; but at the same time they mutually protested that even fetters and slavery were soft and easy, and would be supported with joy and pleasure, while they could be so happy to possess each other and to be able to make good their vows. Caesar swore he disdained the empire of the world while he could behold his Imoinda; and she despised grandeur and pomp, those vanities of her sex, when she could gaze on Oroonoko. He adored the very cottage where she resided, and said that little inch of the world would give him more happiness than all the universe could do; and she vowed it was a palace, while adorned with the presence of Oroonoko.

Trefry was infinitely pleased with this novel,[3] and found this Clemene was the fair mistress of whom Caesar had before spoke; and was not a little satisfied that heaven was so kind to the Prince as to sweeten his misfortunes by so lucky an accident; and leaving the lovers to themselves, was impatient to come down to Parham House (which was on the same plantation) to give me an account of what had happened. I was as impatient to make these lovers a visit, having already made a friendship with Caesar, and from his own mouth learned what I have related; which was confirmed by his French-

---

2. A long-haired dog or poodle, especially associated with women of fashion.
3. I.e., novel event or piece of news.

man, who was set on shore to seek his fortunes, and of whom they could not make a slave, because a Christian, and he came daily to Parham Hill to see and pay his respects to his pupil prince. So that concerning and interesting myself in all that related to Caesar, whom I had assured of liberty as soon as the Governor arrived, I hasted presently to the place where the lovers were, and was infinitely glad to find this beautiful young slave (who had already gained all our esteems, for her modesty and her extraordinary prettiness) to be the same I had heard Caesar speak so much of. One may imagine then we paid her a treble respect; and though, from her being carved in fine flowers and birds all over her body, we took her to be of quality before, yet when we knew Clemene was Imoinda, we could not enough admire her.

I had forgot to tell you that those who are nobly born of that country are so delicately cut and rased[4] all over the forepart of the trunk of their bodies, that it looks as if it were japanned, the works being raised like high point round the edges of the flowers. Some are only carved with a little flower or bird at the sides of the temples, as was Caesar; and those who are so carved over the body resemble our ancient Picts,[5] that are figured in the chronicles, but these carvings are more delicate.

From that happy day Caesar took Clemene for his wife, to the general joy of all people; and there was as much magnificence as the country would afford at the celebration of this wedding: and in a very short time after she conceived with child, which made Caesar even adore her, knowing he was the last of his great race. This new accident made him more impatient of liberty, and he was every day treating with Trefry for his and Clemene's liberty, and offered either gold or a vast quantity of slaves, which should be paid before they let him go, provided he could have any security that he should go when his ransom was paid. They fed him from day to day with promises, and delayed him till the Lord Governor should come; so that he began to suspect them of falsehood, and that they would delay him till the time of his wife's delivery and make a slave of that too, for all the breed is theirs to whom the parents belong. This thought made him very uneasy, and his sullenness gave them some jealousies[6] of him; so that I was obliged, by some persons who feared a mutiny (which is very fatal sometimes in those colonies, that abound so with slaves that they exceed the whites in vast numbers), to discourse with Caesar, and to give him all the satisfaction I possibly could; they knew he and Clemene were scarce an hour in a day from my lodgings, that they eat with me, and that I obliged 'em in all things I was capable of. I entertained him with the lives of the Romans, and great men, which charmed him to my company, and her with teaching her all the pretty works[7] that I was mistress of, and telling her stories of nuns, and endeavoring to bring her to the knowledge of the true God. But of all discourses Caesar liked that the worst, and would never be reconciled to our notions of the Trinity, of which he ever made a jest; it was a riddle, he said, would turn his brain to conceive, and one could not make him understand what faith was. However, these conversations failed not altogether so well to divert him that he liked the company of us women much above the men, for he could

---

4. Incised. The carving is likened to figured lacquerwork in the Japanese style and to elaborate "high point" lace.
5. A North British people appearing in histories of England and Scotland.
6. Suspicions.
7. Decorative needlework or other handiwork.

not drink, and he is but an ill companion in that country that cannot. So that obliging him to love us very well, we had all the liberty of speech with him, especially myself, whom he called his Great Mistress; and indeed my word would go a great way with him. For these reasons, I had opportunity to take notice to him that he was not well pleased of late as he used to be; was more retired and thoughtful; and told him I took it ill he should suspect we would break our words with him, and not permit both him and Clemene to return to his own kingdom, which was not so long a way but when he was once on his voyage he would quickly arrive there. He made me some answers that showed a doubt in him, which made me ask him what advantage it would be to doubt. It would but give us a fear of him, and possibly compel us to treat him so as I should be very loath to behold; that is, it might occasion his confinement. Perhaps this was not so luckily spoke of me, for I perceived he resented that word, which I strove to soften again in vain. However, he assured me that whatsoever resolutions he should take, he would act nothing upon the white people; and as for myself and those upon that plantation where he was, he would sooner forfeit his eternal liberty, and life itself, than lift his hand against his greatest enemy on that place. He besought me to suffer no fears upon his account, for he could do nothing that honor should not dictate; but he accused himself for having suffered slavery so long; yet he charged that weakness on Love alone, who was capable of making him neglect even glory itself, and for which now he reproaches himself every moment of the day. Much more to this effect he spoke, with an air impatient enough to make me know he would not be long in bondage; and though he suffered only the name of a slave, and had nothing of the toil and labor of one, yet that was sufficient to render him uneasy; and he had been too long idle, who used to be always in action and in arms. He had a spirit all rough and fierce, and that could not be tamed to lazy rest; and though all endeavors were used to exercise himself in such actions and sports as this world afforded, as running, wrestling, pitching the bar, hunting and fishing, chasing and killing tigers of a monstrous size, which this continent affords in abundance, and wonderful snakes, such as Alexander is reported to have encountered at the river of Amazons,[8] and which Caesar took great delight to overcome, yet these were not actions great enough for his large soul, which was still panting after more renowned action.

Before I parted that day with him, I got, with much ado, a promise from him to rest yet a little longer with patience, and wait the coming of the Lord Governor, who was every day expected on our shore; he assured me he would, and this promise he desired me to know was given perfectly in complaisance to me, in whom he had an entire confidence.

After this, I neither thought it convenient to trust him much out of our view, nor did the country, who feared him; but with one accord it was advised to treat him fairly, and oblige him to remain within such a compass, and that he should be permitted as seldom as could be to go up to the plantations of the Negroes or, if he did, to be accompanied by some that should be rather in appearance attendants than spies. This care was for some time taken, and

8. Alexander the Great is supposed to have encountered both snakes and Amazons in a campaign against India. "Pitching the bar": game in which players compete in throwing a heavy bar or rod. "Tigers": wild cats, including the South American jaguar and cougar.

Caesar looked upon it as a mark of extraordinary respect, and was glad his discontent had obliged 'em to be more observant to him. He received new assurance from the overseer, which was confirmed to him by the opinion of all the gentlemen of the country, who made their court to him. During this time that we had his company more frequently than hitherto we had had, it may not be unpleasant to relate to you the diversions we entertained him with, or rather he us.

My stay was to be short in that country, because my father died at sea, and never arrived to possess the honor was designed him (which was lieutenant general of six and thirty islands, besides the continent[9] of Surinam) nor the advantages he hoped to reap by them; so that though we were obliged to continue on our voyage, we did not intend to stay upon the place. Though, in a word, I must say thus much of it, that certainly had his late Majesty, of sacred memory, but seen and known what a vast and charming world he had been master of in that continent, he would never have parted so easily with it to the Dutch. 'Tis a continent whose vast extent was never yet known, and may contain more noble earth than all the universe besides, for, they say, it reaches from east to west, one way as far as China and another to Peru. It affords all things both for beauty and use; 'tis there eternal spring, always the very months of April, May, and June; the shades are perpetual, the trees bearing at once all degrees of leaves and fruit, from blooming buds to ripe autumn: groves of oranges, lemons, citrons, figs, nutmegs, and noble aromatics, continually bearing their fragrancies. The trees appearing all like nosegays adorned with flowers of different kinds; some are all white, some purple, some scarlet, some blue, some yellow; bearing, at the same time, ripe fruit and blooming young, or producing every day new. The very wood of all these trees has an intrinsic value above common timber, for they are, when cut, of different colors, glorious to behold, and bear a price considerable, to inlay withal. Besides this they yield rich balm and gums, so that we make our candles of such an aromatic substance as does not only give a sufficient light, but, as they burn, they cast their perfumes all about. Cedar is the common firing, and all the houses are built with it. The very meat we eat, when set on the table, if it be native, I mean of the country, perfumes the whole room; especially a little beast called an armadilly, a thing which I can liken to nothing so well as a rhinoceros; 'tis all in white armor, so jointed that it moves as well in it as if it had nothing on; this beast is about the bigness of a pig of six weeks old. But it were endless to give an account of all the diverse wonderful and strange things that country affords, and which we took a very great delight to go in search of, though those adventures are oftentimes fatal and at least dangerous. But while we had Caesar in our company on these designs we feared no harm, nor suffered any.

As soon as I came into the country, the best house in it was presented me, called St. John's Hill. It stood on a vast rock of white marble, at the foot of which the river ran a vast depth down, and not to be descended on that side; the little waves still dashing and washing the foot of this rock made the softest murmurs and purlings in the world; and the opposite bank was adorned with such vast quantities of different flowers eternally blowing,[1] and

9. "Land not disjoined by the sea from other lands" (Johnson's *Dictionary*).
1. Blooming.

every day and hour new, fenced behind 'em with lofty trees of a thousand rare forms and colors, that the prospect was the most ravishing that fancy can create. On the edge of this white rock, towards the river, was a walk or grove of orange and lemon trees, about half the length of the Mall[2] here, whose flowery and fruit-bearing branches met at the top and hindered the sun, whose rays are very fierce there, from entering a beam into the grove; and the cool air that came from the river made it not only fit to entertain people in, at all the hottest hours of the day, but refreshed the sweet blossoms and made it always sweet and charming; and sure the whole globe of the world cannot show so delightful a place as this grove was. Not all the gardens of boasted Italy can produce a shade to outvie this, which nature had joined with art to render so exceeding fine; and 'tis a marvel to see how such vast trees, as big as English oaks, could take footing on so solid a rock and in so little earth as covered that rock; but all things by nature there are rare, delightful, and wonderful. But to our sports.

Sometimes we would go surprising,[3] and in search of young tigers in their dens, watching when the old ones went forth to forage for prey; and oftentimes we have been in great danger and have fled apace for our lives when surprised by the dams. But once, above all other times, we went on this design, and Caesar was with us, who had no sooner stolen a young tiger from her nest but, going off, we encountered the dam, bearing a buttock of a cow which he[4] had torn off with his mighty paw, and going with it towards his den. We had only four women, Caesar, and an English gentleman, brother to Harry Martin, the great Oliverian;[5] we found there was no escaping this enraged and ravenous beast. However, we women fled as fast as we could from it; but our heels had not saved our lives if Caesar had not laid down his cub, when he found the tiger quit her prey to make the more speed towards him, and taking Mr. Martin's sword, desired him to stand aside, or follow the ladies. He obeyed him, and Caesar met this monstrous beast of might, size, and vast limbs, who came with open jaws upon him; and fixing his awful stern eyes full upon those of the beast, and putting himself into a very steady and good aiming posture of defense, ran his sword quite through his breast down to his very heart, home to the hilt of the sword. The dying beast stretched forth her paw, and going to grasp his thigh, surprised with death in that very moment, did him no other harm than fixing her long nails in his flesh very deep, feebly wounded him, but could not grasp the flesh to tear off any. When he had done this, he hallooed to us to return, which, after some assurance of his victory, we did, and found him lugging out the sword from the bosom of the tiger, who was laid in her blood on the ground; he took up the cub, and with an unconcern that had nothing of the joy or gladness of a victory, he came and laid the whelp at my feet. We all extremely wondered at his daring, and at the bigness of the beast, which was about the heighth of a heifer but of mighty, great, and strong limbs.

Another time, being in the woods, he killed a tiger which had long infested that part, and borne away abundance of sheep and oxen, and other things

---

2. Fashionable walk in St. James's Park in London.
3. A military term for making sudden raids.
4. The jarring mixture of pronouns in the two accounts of the tigers (wild cats) may suggest a reluctance to use a feminine pronoun in moments of extreme violence. The first account was left uncorrected in all four 17th-century editions.
5. Supporter of Oliver Cromwell.

that were for the support of those to whom they belonged; abundance of people assailed this beast, some affirming they had shot her with several bullets quite through the body at several times, and some swearing they shot her through the very heart, and they believed she was a devil rather than a mortal thing. Caesar had often said he had a mind to encounter this monster, and spoke with several gentlemen who had attempted her, one crying, "I shot her with so many poisoned arrows," another with his gun in this part of her, and another in that; so that he, remarking all these places where she was shot, fancied still he should overcome her by giving her another sort of a wound than any had yet done; and one day said (at the table), "What trophies and garlands, ladies, will you make me, if I bring you home the heart of this ravenous beast that eats up all your lambs and pigs?" We all promised he should be rewarded at all our hands. So taking a bow, which he choosed out of a great many, he went up in the wood, with two gentlemen, where he imagined this devourer to be; they had not passed very far in it but they heard her voice, growling and grumbling, as if she were pleased with something she was doing. When they came in view, they found her muzzling in the belly of a new ravished sheep, which she had torn open; and seeing herself approached, she took fast hold of her prey with her forepaws and set a very fierce raging look on Caesar, without offering to approach him, for fear at the same time of losing what she had in possession. So that Caesar remained a good while, only taking aim, and getting an opportunity to shoot her where he designed; 'twas some time before he could accomplish it, and to wound her and not kill her would but have enraged her more, and endangered him. He had a quiver of arrows at his side, so that if one failed he could be supplied; at last, retiring a little, he gave her opportunity to eat, for he found she was ravenous, and fell to as soon as she saw him retire, being more eager of her prey than of doing new mischiefs. When he going softly to one side of her, and hiding his person behind certain herbage that grew high and thick, he took so good aim that, as he intended, he shot her just into the eye, and the arrow was sent with so good a will and so sure a hand that it stuck in her brain, and made her caper and become mad for a moment or two; but being seconded by another arrow, he fell dead upon the prey. Caesar cut him open with a knife, to see where those wounds were that had been reported to him, and why he did not die of 'em. But I shall now relate a thing that possibly will find no credit among men, because 'tis a notion commonly received with us, that nothing can receive a wound in the heart and live; but when the heart of this courageous animal was taken out, there were seven bullets of lead in it, and the wounds seamed up with great scars, and she lived with the bullets a great while, for it was long since they were shot. This heart the conqueror brought up to us, and 'twas a very great curiosity, which all the country came to see, and which gave Caesar occasion of many fine discourses, of accidents in war and strange escapes.

At other times he would go a-fishing; and discoursing on that diversion, he found we had in that country a very strange fish, called a numb eel[6] (an eel of which I have eaten), that while it is alive, it has a quality so cold, that those who are angling, though with a line of never so great a length with a rod at the end of it, it shall, in the same minute the bait is touched by this eel, seize

6. Electric eel.

him or her that holds the rod with benumbedness, that shall deprive 'em of sense for a while; and some have fallen into the water, and others dropped as dead on the banks of the rivers where they stood, as soon as this fish touches the bait. Caesar used to laugh at this, and believed it impossible a man could lose his force at the touch of a fish, and could not understand that philosophy,[7] that a cold quality should be of that nature. However, he had a great curiosity to try whether it would have the same effect on him it had on others, and often tried, but in vain. At last the sought for fish came to the bait, as he stood angling on the bank; and instead of throwing away the rod or giving it a sudden twitch out of the water, whereby he might have caught both the eel and have dismissed the rod, before it could have too much power over him, for experiment sake he grasped it but the harder, and fainting fell into the river; and being still possessed of the rod, the tide carried him, senseless as he was, a great way, till an Indian boat took him up, and perceived when they touched him a numbness seize them, and by that knew the rod was in his hand; which with a paddle (that is, a short oar) they struck away, and snatched it into the boat, eel and all. If Caesar were almost dead with the effect of this fish, he was more so with that of the water, where he had remained the space of going a league, and they found they had much ado to bring him back to life. But at last they did, and brought him home, where he was in a few hours well recovered and refreshed, and not a little ashamed to find he should be overcome by an eel, and that all the people who heard his defiance would laugh at him. But we cheered him up; and he being convinced, we had the eel at supper, which was a quarter of an ell about and most delicate meat, and was of the more value, since it cost so dear as almost the life of so gallant a man.

About this time we were in many mortal fears about some disputes the English had with the Indians, so that we could scarce trust ourselves, without great numbers, to go to any Indian towns or place where they abode, for fear they should fall upon us, as they did immediately after my coming away; and that it was in the possession of the Dutch, who used 'em not so civilly as the English, so that they cut in pieces all they could take, getting into houses and hanging up the mother and all her children about her, and cut a footman I left behind me all in joints, and nailed him to trees.

This feud began while I was there, so that I lost half the satisfaction I proposed, in not seeing and visiting the Indian towns. But one day, bemoaning of our misfortunes upon this account, Caesar told us we need not fear, for if we had a mind to go, he would undertake to be our guard. Some would, but most would not venture; about eighteen of us resolved and took barge, and after eight days arrived near an Indian town. But approaching it, the hearts of some of our company failed, and they would not venture on shore; so we polled who would and who would not. For my part, I said if Caesar would, I would go; he resolved; so did my brother and my woman, a maid of good courage. Now none of us speaking the language of the people, and imagining we should have a half diversion in gazing only and not knowing what they said, we took a fisherman that lived at the mouth of the river, who had been a long inhabitant there, and obliged him to go with us. But because he was known to the Indians, as trading among 'em, and being by long living

7. "Hypothesis or system upon which natural effects are explained" (Johnson's *Dictionary*).

there become a perfect Indian in color, we, who resolved to surprise 'em by making 'em see something they never had seen (that is, white people), resolved only myself, my brother and woman should go; so Caesar, the fisherman, and the rest, hiding behind some thick reeds and flowers that grew on the banks, let us pass on towards the town, which was on the bank of the river all along. A little distant from the houses, or huts, we saw some dancing, others busied in fetching and carrying of water from the river. They had no sooner spied us but they set up a loud cry, that frighted us at first; we thought it had been for those that should kill us, but it seems it was of wonder and amazement. They were all naked, and we were dressed so as is most commode for the hot countries, very glittering and rich, so that we appeared extremely fine; my own hair was cut short, and I had a taffety cap with black feathers on my head; my brother was in a stuff[8] suit, with silver loops and buttons and abundance of green ribbon. This was all infinitely surprising to them, and because we saw them stand still till we approached 'em, we took heart and advanced, came up to 'em, and offered 'em our hands; which they took, and looked on us round about, calling still for more company; who came swarming out, all wondering and crying out *"Tepeeme,"* taking their hair up in their hands and spreading it wide to those they called out to, as if they would say (as indeed it signified) "Numberless wonders," or not to be recounted, no more than to number the hair of their heads. By degrees they grew more bold, and from gazing upon us round, they touched us, laying their hands upon all the features of our faces, feeling our breasts and arms, taking up one petticoat, then wondering to see another; admiring our shoes and stockings, but more our garters, which we gave 'em, and they tied about their legs, being laced with silver lace at the ends, for they much esteem any shining things. In fine, we suffered 'em to survey us as they pleased, and we thought they would never have done admiring us. When Caesar and the rest saw we were received with such wonder, they came up to us; and finding the Indian trader whom they knew (for 'tis by these fishermen, called Indian traders, we hold a commerce with 'em, for they love not to go far from home, and we never go to them), when they saw him therefore they set up a new joy, and cried, in their language, "Oh! here's our *tiguamy,* and we shall now know whether those things can speak." So advancing to him, some of 'em gave him their hands and cried, *"Amora tiguamy,"* which is as much as, "How do you?" or "Welcome, friend," and all with one din began to gabble to him, and asked if we had sense and wit; if we could talk of affairs of life and war, as they could do; if we could hunt, swim, and do a thousand things they use. He answered 'em, we could. Then they invited us into their houses, and dressed venison and buffalo for us; and going out, gathered a leaf of a tree called a *sarumbo* leaf, of six yards long, and spread it on the ground for a tablecloth; and cutting another in pieces instead of plates, setting us on little bow Indian stools, which they cut out of one entire piece of wood and paint in a sort of japan work. They serve everyone their mess[9] on these pieces of leaves, and it was very good, but too high seasoned with pepper. When we had eat, my brother and I took out our flutes and played to 'em, which gave 'em new wonder; and I soon perceived, by an admiration that is natural to these people, and by the extreme ignorance and simplicity of 'em, it were not

---

8. Woven fabric, worsted. "Commode": suitable.   9. Meal.

difficult to establish any unknown or extravagant religion among them, and to impose any notions or fictions upon 'em. For seeing a kinsman of mine set some paper afire with a burning glass, a trick they had never before seen, they were like to have adored him for a god, and begged he would give them the characters or figures of his name, that they might oppose it against winds and storms; which he did, and they held it up in those seasons, and fancied it had a charm to conquer them, and kept it like a holy relic. They are very superstitious, and called him the great *Peeie,* that is, prophet. They showed us their Indian *Peeie,* a youth of about sixteen years old, as handsome as nature could make a man. They consecrate a beautiful youth from his infancy, and all arts are used to complete him in the finest manner, both in beauty and shape. He is bred to all the little arts and cunning they are capable of, to all the legerdemain tricks and sleight of hand, whereby he imposes upon the rabble, and is both a doctor in physic[1] and divinity; and by these tricks makes the sick believe he sometimes eases their pains, by drawing from the afflicted part little serpents, or odd flies, or worms, or any strange thing; and though they have besides undoubted good remedies for almost all their diseases, they cure the patient more by fancy than by medicines, and make themselves feared, loved, and reverenced. This young *Peeie* had a very young wife, who seeing my brother kiss her, came running and kissed me; after this they kissed one another, and made it a very great jest, it being so novel; and new admiration and laughing went round the multitude, that they never will forget that ceremony, never before used or known. Caesar had a mind to see and talk with their war captains, and we were conducted to one of their houses, where we beheld several of the great captains, who had been at council. But so frightful a vision it was to see 'em no fancy can create; no such dreams can represent so dreadful a spectacle. For my part I took 'em for hobgoblins or fiends rather than men; but however their shapes appeared, their souls were very humane and noble; but some wanted their noses, some their lips, some both noses and lips, some their ears, and others cut through each cheek with long slashes, through which their teeth appeared; they had other several formidable wounds and scars, or rather dismemberings. They had *comitias* or little aprons before 'em, and girdles of cotton, with their knives naked, stuck in it; a bow at their backs and a quiver of arrows on their thighs; and most had feathers on their heads of diverse colors. They cried *"Amora tiguamy"* to us at our entrance, and were pleased we said as much to 'em; they seated us, and gave us drink of the best sort, and wondered, as much as the others had done before, to see us. Caesar was marveling as much at their faces, wondering how they should all be so wounded in war; he was impatient to know how they all came by those frightful marks of rage or malice, rather than wounds got in noble battle. They told us, by our interpreter, that when any war was waging, two men chosen out by some old captain whose fighting was past, and who could only teach the theory of war, these two men were to stand in competition for the generalship, or great war captain; and being brought before the old judges, now past labor, they are asked what they dare do to show they are worthy to lead an army. When he who is first asked, making no reply, cuts off his nose, and throws it contemptibly[2] on the ground; and the other does something to

1. Medicine.   2. With contempt.

himself that he thinks surpasses him, and perhaps deprives himself of lips and an eye; so they slash on till one gives out, and many have died in this debate. And 'tis by a passive valor they show and prove their activity, a sort of courage too brutal to be applauded by our black hero; nevertheless he expressed his esteem of 'em.

In this voyage Caesar begot so good an understanding between the Indians and the English that there were no more fears or heart-burnings during our stay, but we had a perfect, open, and free trade with 'em. Many things remarkable and worthy reciting we met with in this short voyage, because Caesar made it his business to search out and provide for our entertainment, especially to please his dearly adored Imoinda, who was a sharer in all our adventures; we being resolved to make her chains as easy as we could, and to compliment the Prince in that manner that most obliged him.

As we were coming up again, we met with some Indians of strange aspects; that is, of a larger size and other sort of features than those of our country. Our Indian slaves that rowed us asked 'em some questions, but they could not understand us; but showed us a long cotton string with several knots on it, and told us, they had been coming from the mountains so many moons as there were knots. They were habited in skins of a strange beast, and brought along with 'em bags of gold dust, which, as well as they could give us to understand, came streaming in little small channels down the high mountains when the rains fell; and offered to be the convoy to any body or persons that would go to the mountains. We carried these men up to Parham, where they were kept till the Lord Governor came. And because all the country was mad to be going on this golden adventure, the Governor by his letters commanded (for they sent some of the gold to him) that a guard should be set at the mouth of the river of Amazons[3] (a river so called, almost as broad as the river of Thames) and prohibited all people from going up that river, it conducting to those mountains of gold. But we going off for England before the project was further prosecuted, and the Governor being drowned in a hurricane, either the design died, or the Dutch have the advantage of it. And 'tis to be bemoaned what his Majesty lost by losing that part of America.

Though this digression is a little from my story, however since it contains some proofs of the curiosity and daring of this great man, I was content to omit nothing of his character.

It was thus for some time we diverted him; but now Imoinda began to show she was with child, and did nothing but sigh and weep for the captivity of her lord, herself, and the infant yet unborn, and believed if it were so hard to gain the liberty of two, 'twould be more difficult to get that for three. Her griefs were so many darts in the great heart of Caesar; and taking his opportunity one Sunday when all the whites were overtaken in drink, as there were abundance of several trades and slaves for four years[4] that inhabited among the Negro houses, and Sunday was their day of debauch (otherwise they were a sort of spies upon Caesar), he went pretending out of goodness to 'em to feast amongst 'em; and sent all his music, and ordered a great treat for the whole gang, about three hundred Negroes; and about a hundred and fifty were able to bear arms, such as they had, which were

3. The mouth of the Amazon, in Brazil, is far distant from Surinam.

4. Whites who, for crimes or debt, were indentured for a fixed period. "Trades": tradesman.

sufficient to do execution[5] with spirits accordingly. For the English had none but rusty swords that no strength could draw from a scabbard, except the people of particular quality, who took care to oil 'em and keep 'em in good order. The guns also, unless here and there one, or those newly carried from England, would do no good or harm; for 'tis the nature of that country to rust and eat up iron, or any metals but gold and silver. And they are very unexpert at the bow, which the Negroes and Indians are perfect masters of.

Caesar, having singled out these men from the women and children, made an harangue to 'em of the miseries and ignominies of slavery, counting up all their toils and sufferings, under such loads, burdens, and drudgeries as were fitter for beasts than men, senseless brutes than human souls. He told 'em, it was not for days, months, or years, but for eternity; there was no end to be of their misfortunes. They suffered not like men, who might find a glory and fortitude in oppression, but like dogs that loved the whip and bell,[6] and fawned the more they were beaten. That they had lost the divine quality of men and were become insensible asses, fit only to bear; nay, worse: an ass, or dog, or horse, having done his duty, could lie down in retreat and rise to work again, and while he did his duty endured no stripes; but men, villainous, senseless men such as they, toiled on all the tedious week till Black Friday;[7] and then, whether they worked or not, whether they were faulty or meriting, they promiscuously, the innocent with the guilty, suffered the infamous whip, the sordid stripes, from their fellow slaves, till their blood trickled from all parts of their body, blood whose every drop ought to be revenged with a life of some of those tyrants that impose it. "And why," said he, "my dear friends and fellow sufferers, should we be slaves to an unknown people? Have they vanquished us nobly in fight? Have they won us in honorable battle? And are we by the chance of war become their slaves? This would not anger a noble heart, this would not animate a soldier's soul; no, but we are bought and sold like apes or monkeys, to be the sport of women, fools, and cowards, and the support of rogues, runagades,[8] that have abandoned their own countries for rapine, murders, thefts, and villainies. Do you not hear every day how they upbraid each other with infamy of life, below the wildest savages; and shall we render obedience to such a degenerate race, who have no one human virtue left to distinguish 'em from the vilest creatures? Will you, I say, suffer the lash from such hands?" They all replied, with one accord, "No, no, no; Caesar has spoke like a great captain, like a great king."

After this he would have proceeded, but was interrupted by a tall Negro of some more quality than the rest; his name was Tuscan; who bowing at the feet of Caesar, cried, "My lord, we have listened with joy and attention to what you have said, and, were we only men, would follow so great a leader through the world. But oh! consider, we are husbands and parents too, and have things more dear to us than life, our wives and children, unfit for travel in these unpassable woods, mountains, and bogs; we have not only difficult lands to overcome, but rivers to wade, and monsters to encounter, ravenous

---

5. Harm, slaughter.
6. Proverbial for something that distracts from comfort or pleasure, from the protective charm on chariots of triumphing generals in ancient Rome.

7. Here a day of customary beating; more widely, a Friday bringing some notable disaster, from students' slang for examination day.
8. Renegades or fugitives.

beasts of prey—." To this, Caesar replied that honor was the first principle in nature that was to be obeyed; but as no man would pretend to that, without all the acts of virtue, compassion, charity, love, justice, and reason, he found it not inconsistent with that to take an equal care of their wives and children as they would of themselves; and that he did not design, when he led them to freedom and glorious liberty, that they should leave that better part of themselves to perish by the hand of the tyrant's whip. But if there were a woman among them so degenerate from love and virtue to choose slavery before the pursuit of her husband, and with the hazard of her life to share with him in his fortunes, that such a one ought to be abandoned, and left as a prey to the common enemy.

To which they all agreed—and bowed. After this, he spoke of the impassable woods and rivers, and convinced 'em, the more danger, the more glory. He told them that he had heard of one Hannibal, a great captain, had cut his way through mountains of solid rocks;[9] and should a few shrubs oppose them, which they could fire before 'em? No, 'twas a trifling excuse to men resolved to die or overcome. As for bogs, they are with a little labor filled and hardened; and the rivers could be no obstacle, since they swam by nature, at least by custom, from their first hour of their birth. That when the children were weary they must carry them by turns, and the woods and their own industry would afford them food. To this they all assented with joy.

Tuscan then demanded what he would do. He said, they would travel towards the sea, plant a new colony, and defend it by their valor; and when they could find a ship, either driven by stress of weather or guided by Providence that way, they would seize it and make it a prize, till it had transported them to their own countries; at least, they should be made free in his kingdom, and be esteemed as his fellow sufferers, and men that had the courage and the bravery to attempt, at least, for liberty; and if they died in the attempt it would be more brave than to live in perpetual slavery.

They bowed and kissed his feet at this resolution, and with one accord vowed to follow him to death. And that night was appointed to begin their march; they made it known to their wives, and directed them to tie their hamaca[1] about their shoulder and under their arm like a scarf, and to lead their children that could go, and carry those that could not. The wives, who pay an entire obedience to their husbands, obeyed, and stayed for 'em where they were appointed. The men stayed but to furnish themselves with what defensive arms they could get; and all met at the rendezvous, where Caesar made a new encouraging speech to 'em, and led 'em out.

But as they could not march far that night, on Monday early, when the overseers went to call 'em all together to go to work, they were extremely surprised to find not one upon the place, but all fled with what baggage they had. You may imagine this news was not only suddenly spread all over the plantation, but soon reached the neighboring ones; and we had by noon about six hundred men they call the militia of the county, that came to assist us in the pursuit of the fugitives. But never did one see so comical an army march forth to war. The men of any fashion would not concern themselves, though it were almost the common cause; for such revoltings are very ill

9. The Carthaginian general and his troops literally hacked their way down the Alps into Italy to attack Rome.

1. Hammock.

examples, and have very fatal consequences oftentimes in many colonies. But they had a respect for Caesar, and all hands were against the Parhamites, as they called those of Parham plantation, because they did not, in the first place, love the Lord Governor, and secondly they would have it that Caesar was ill used, and baffled with;[2] and 'tis not impossible but some of the best in the country was of his counsel in this flight, and depriving us of all the slaves; so that they of the better sort would not meddle in the matter. The deputy governor,[3] of whom I have had no great occasion to speak, and who was the most fawning fair-tongued fellow in the world and one that pretended the most friendship to Caesar, was now the only violent man against him; and though he had nothing, and so need fear nothing, yet talked and looked bigger than any man. He was a fellow whose character is not fit to be mentioned with the worst of the slaves. This fellow would lead his army forth to meet Caesar, or rather to pursue him; most of their arms were of those sort of cruel whips they call cat with nine tails; some had rusty useless guns for show, others old basket hilts[4] whose blades had never seen the light in this age, and others had long staffs and clubs. Mr. Trefry went along, rather to be a mediator than a conqueror in such a battle; for he foresaw and knew, if by fighting they put the Negroes into despair, they were a sort of sullen fellows that would drown or kill themselves before they would yield; and he advised that fair means was best. But Byam was one that abounded in his own wit and would take his own measures.

It was not hard to find these fugitives; for as they fled they were forced to fire and cut the woods before 'em, so that night or day they pursued 'em by the light they made and by the path they had cleared. But as soon as Caesar found he was pursued, he put himself in a posture of defense, placing all the women and children in the rear, and himself with Tuscan by his side, or next to him, all promising to die or conquer. Encouraged thus, they never stood to parley, but fell on pell-mell upon the English, and killed some and wounded a good many, they having recourse to their whips as the best of their weapons. And as they observed no order, they perplexed the enemy so sorely with lashing 'em in the eyes; and the women and children seeing their husbands so treated, being of fearful cowardly dispositions, and hearing the English cry out, "Yield and live, yield and be pardoned," they all run in amongst their husbands and fathers, and hung about 'em, crying out, "Yield, yield; and leave Caesar to their revenge"; that by degrees the slaves abandoned Caesar, and left him only Tuscan and his heroic Imoinda; who, grown big as she was, did nevertheless press near her lord, having a bow and a quiver full of poisoned arrows, which she managed with such dexterity that she wounded several, and shot the governor[5] into the shoulder; of which wound he had like to have died, but that an Indian woman, his mistress, sucked the wound and cleansed it from the venom. But however, he stirred not from the place till he had parleyed with Caesar, who he found was resolved to die fighting, and would not be taken; no more would Tuscan, or Imoinda. But he, more thirsting after revenge of another sort than that of depriving him of life, now made use of all his art of talking and dissembling,

2. Cheated.
3. William Byam. There are recorded complaints against him for high-handedness and from him

about insubordination by settlers and slaves.
4. Swords with protective hilt guards.
5. I.e., Byam, the deputy governor.

and besought Caesar to yield himself upon terms which he himself should propose, and should be sacredly assented to and kept by him. He told him, it was not that he any longer feared him, or could believe the force of two men, and a young heroine, could overcome all them, with all the slaves now on their side also; but it was the vast esteem he had for his person, the desire he had to serve so gallant a man, and to hinder himself from the reproach hereafter of having been the occasion of the death of a prince whose valor and magnanimity deserved the empire of the world. He protested to him, he looked upon this action as gallant and brave, however tending to the prejudice of his lord and master, who would by it have lost so considerable a number of slaves; that this flight of his should be looked on as a heat of youth, and rashness of a too forward courage, and an unconsidered impatience of liberty, and no more; and that he labored in vain to accomplish that which they would effectually perform as soon as any ship arrived that would touch on his coast. "So that if you will be pleased," continued he, "to surrender yourself, all imaginable respect shall be paid you; and yourself, your wife, and child, if it be here born, shall depart free out of our land."

But Caesar would hear of no composition;[6] though Byam urged, if he pursued and went on in his design, he would inevitably perish, either by great snakes, wild beasts, or hunger; and he ought to have regard to his wife, whose condition required ease, and not the fatigues of tedious travel, where she could not be secured from being devoured. But Caesar told him, there was no faith in the white men or the gods they adored, who instructed 'em in principles so false that honest men could not live amongst 'em; though no people professed so much, none performed so little; that he knew what he had to do when he dealt with men of honor, but with them a man ought to be eternally on his guard, and never to eat and drink with Christians without his weapon of defense in his hand; and for his own security, never to credit one word they spoke. As for the rashness and inconsiderateness of his action, he would confess the governor is in the right; and that he was ashamed of what he had done, in endeavoring to make those free who were by nature slaves, poor wretched rogues, fit to be used as Christians' tools; dogs, treacherous and cowardly, fit for such masters; and they wanted only but to be whipped into the knowledge of the Christian gods to be the vilest of all creeping things, to learn to worship such deities as had not power to make 'em just, brave, or honest. In fine, after a thousand things of this nature, not fit here to be recited, he told Byam he had rather die than live upon the same earth with such dogs. But Trefry and Byam pleaded and protested together so much that Trefry, believing the governor to mean what he said, and speaking very cordially himself, generously put himself into Caesar's hands, and took him aside and persuaded him, even with tears, to live, by surrendering himself, and to name his conditions. Caesar was overcome by his wit and reasons, and in consideration of Imoinda; and demanding what he desired, and that it should be ratified by their hands in writing, because he had perceived that was the common way of contract between man and man, amongst the whites. All this was performed, and Tuscan's pardon was put in, and they surrender to the governor, who walked peaceably down into the plantation with 'em, after giving order to bury their dead. Caesar was very much toiled with the

6. Settlement.

bustle of the day, for he had fought like a fury; and what mischief was done he and Tuscan performed alone, and gave their enemies a fatal proof that they durst do anything and feared no mortal force.

But they were no sooner arrived at the place where all the slaves receive their punishments of whipping, but they laid hands on Caesar and Tuscan, faint with heat and toil; and surprising them, bound them to two several stakes, and whipped them in a most deplorable and inhuman manner, rending the very flesh from their bones; especially Caesar, who was not perceived to make any moan or to alter his face, only to roll his eyes on the faithless governor, and those he believed guilty, with fierceness and indignation; and to complete his rage, he saw every one of those slaves, who but a few days before adored him as something more than mortal, now had a whip to give him some lashes, while he strove not to break his fetters; though if he had, it were impossible. But he pronounced a woe and revenge from his eyes, that darted fire that 'twas at once both awful and terrible to behold.

When they thought they were sufficiently revenged on him, they untied him, almost fainting with loss of blood from a thousand wounds all over his body, from which they had rent his clothes, and led him bleeding and naked as he was, and loaded him all over with irons; and then rubbed his wounds, to complete their cruelty, with Indian pepper, which had like to have made him raving mad; and in this condition made him so fast to the ground that he could not stir, if his pains and wounds would have given him leave. They spared Imoinda, and did not let her see this barbarity committed towards her lord, but carried her down to Parham and shut her up; which was not in kindness to her, but for fear she should die with the sight, or miscarry, and then they should lose a young slave and perhaps the mother.

You must know, that when the news was brought on Monday morning that Caesar had betaken himself to the woods and carried with him all the Negroes, we were possessed with extreme fear, which no persuasions could dissipate, that he would secure himself till night, and then that he would come down and cut all our throats. This apprehension made all the females of us fly down the river, to be secured; and while we were away they acted this cruelty. For I suppose I had authority and interest enough there, had I suspected any such thing, to have prevented it; but we had not gone many leagues but the news overtook us that Caesar was taken and whipped like a common slave. We met on the river with Colonel Martin, a man of great gallantry, wit, and goodness, and whom I have celebrated in a character of my new comedy[7] by his own name, in memory of so brave a man. He was wise and eloquent and, from the fineness of his parts, bore a great sway over the hearts of all the colony. He was a friend to Caesar, and resented this false dealing with him very much. We carried him back to Parham, thinking to have made an accommodation; when we came, the first news we heard was that the governor was dead of a wound Imoinda had given him; but it was not so well. But it seems he would have the pleasure of beholding the revenge he took on Caesar, and before the cruel ceremony was finished, he dropped down; and then they perceived the wound he had on his shoulder was by a venomed arrow, which, as I said, his Indian mistress healed by sucking the wound.

---

7. *The Younger Brother; or, The Amorous Jilt*, not produced until 1696 despite this piece of promotion.

We were no sooner arrived but we went up to the plantation to see Caesar, whom we found in a very miserable and unexpressible condition; and I have a thousand times admired how he lived, in so much tormenting pain. We said all things to him that trouble, pity, and good nature could suggest, protesting our innocency of the fact and our abhorrence of such cruelties; making a thousand professions of services to him and begging as many pardons for the offenders, till we said so much that he believed we had no hand in his ill treatment; but told us he could never pardon Byam; as for Trefry, he confessed he saw his grief and sorrow for his suffering, which he could not hinder, but was like to have been beaten down by the very slaves for speaking in his defense. But for Byam, who was their leader, their head—and should, by his justice and honor, have been an example to 'em—for him, he wished to live, to take a dire revenge of him, and said, "It had been well for him if he had sacrificed me, instead of giving me the contemptible[8] whip." He refused to talk much, but begging us to give him our hands, he took 'em, and protested never to lift up his to do us any harm. He had a great respect for Colonel Martin, and always took his counsel like that of a parent, and assured him he would obey him in anything but his revenge on Byam. "Therefore," said he, "for his own safety, let him speedily dispatch me; for if I could dispatch myself I would not, till that justice were done to my injured person,[9] and the contempt of a soldier. No, I would not kill myself, even after a whipping, but will be content to live with that infamy, and be pointed at by every grinning slave, till I have completed my revenge; and then you shall see that Oroonoko scorns to live with the indignity that was put on Caesar." All we could do could get no more words from him; and we took care to have him put immediately into a healing bath to rid him of his pepper, and ordered a chirurgeon[1] to anoint him with healing balm, which he suffered; and in some time he began to be able to walk and eat. We failed not to visit him every day, and to that end had him brought to an apartment at Parham.

The governor was no sooner recovered, and had heard of the menaces of Caesar, but he called his council; who (not to disgrace them, or burlesque the government there) consisted of such notorious villains as Newgate[2] never transported; and possibly originally were such who understood neither the laws of God or man, and had no sort of principles to make 'em worthy the name of men; but at the very council table would contradict and fight with one another, and swear so bloodily that 'twas terrible to hear and see 'em. (Some of 'em were afterwards hanged when the Dutch took possession of the place, others sent off in chains.) But calling these special rulers of the nation together, and requiring their counsel in this weighty affair, they all concluded that (Damn 'em) it might be their own cases; and that Caesar ought to be made an example to all the Negroes, to fright 'em from daring to threaten their betters, their lords and masters; and at this rate no man was safe from his own slaves; and concluded, *nemine contradicente*,[3] that Caesar should be hanged.

Trefry then thought it time to use his authority, and told Byam his command did not extend to his lord's plantation, and that Parham was as much

---

exempt from the law as Whitehall,[4] and that they ought no more to touch the servants of the Lord—— (who there represented the King's person) than they could those about the King himself; and that Parham was a sanctuary; and though his lord were absent in person, his power was still in being there, which he had entrusted with him as far as the dominions of his particular plantations reached, and all that belonged to it; the rest of the country, as Byam was lieutenant to his lord, he might exercise his tyranny upon. Trefry had others as powerful, or more, that interested themselves in Caesar's life, and absolutely said he should be defended. So turning the governor and his wise council out of doors (for they sat at Parham House), they set a guard upon our landing place, and would admit none but those we called friends to us and Caesar.

The governor having remained wounded at Parham till his recovery was completed, Caesar did not know but he was still there; and indeed, for the most part his time was spent there, for he was one that loved to live at other people's expense; and if he were a day absent, he was ten present there, and used to play and walk and hunt and fish with Caesar. So that Caesar did not at all doubt, if he once recovered strength, but he should find an opportunity of being revenged on him. Though after such a revenge, he could not hope to live, for if he escaped the fury of the English mobile,[5] who perhaps would have been glad of the occasion to have killed him, he was resolved not to survive his whipping; yet he had, some tender hours, a repenting softness, which he called his fits of coward, wherein he struggled with Love for the victory of his heart, which took part with his charming Imoinda there; but for the most part his time was passed in melancholy thought and black designs. He considered, if he should do this deed and die, either in the attempt or after it, he left his lovely Imoinda a prey, or at best a slave, to the enraged multitude; his great heart could not endure that thought. "Perhaps," said he, "she may be first ravished by every brute, exposed first to their nasty lusts and then a shameful death." No; he could not live a moment under that apprehension, too insupportable to be borne. These were his thoughts and his silent arguments with his heart, as he told us afterwards; so that now resolving not only to kill Byam but all those he thought had enraged him, pleasing his great heart with the fancied slaughter he should make over the whole face of the plantation, he first resolved on a deed, that (however horrid it at first appeared to us all), when we had heard his reasons, we thought it brave and just. Being able to walk and, as he believed, fit for the execution of his great design, he begged Trefry to trust him into the air, believing a walk would do him good, which was granted him; and taking Imoinda with him, as he used to do in his more happy and calmer days, he led her up into a wood, where, after (with a thousand sighs, and long gazing silently on her face, while tears gushed, in spite of him, from his eyes) he told her his design first of killing her, and then his enemies, and next himself, and the impossibility of escaping, and therefore he told her the necessity of dying, he found the heroic wife faster pleading for death than he was to propose it, when she found his fixed resolution, and on her knees besought him not to leave her a prey to his enemies. He (grieved to death) yet pleased at her

4. The king's palace in London. Trefry stands as Lord Willoughby's deputy on his private land, Byam in the colony at large.

5. Common people or mob.

noble resolution, took her up, and embracing her with all the passion and languishment of a dying lover, drew his knife to kill this treasure of his soul, this pleasure of his eyes; while tears trickled down his cheeks, hers were smiling with joy she should die by so noble a hand, and be sent in her own country (for that's their notion of the next world) by him she so tenderly loved and so truly adored in this; for wives have a respect for their husbands equal to what any other people pay a deity, and when a man finds any occasion to quit his wife, if he love her, she dies by his hand; if not, he sells her, or suffers some other to kill her. It being thus, you may believe the deed was soon resolved on; and 'tis not to be doubted but the parting, the eternal leave-taking of two such lovers, so greatly born, so sensible,[6] so beautiful, so young, and so fond, must be very moving, as the relation of it was to me afterwards.

All that love could say in such cases being ended, and all the intermitting irreso-

C. Grignion, after J. Barralet, *Mr. Savigny in the Character of Oroonoko*; engraving, 1785. Through the 18th century, the story of *Oroonoko* was known mostly in a 1696 play adapted from Behn's work by Thomas Southerne. His version makes Imoinda white, as this scene from a 1775 production shows. The actor plays Oroonoko in blackface, here on the verge of killing Imoinda. In *Oroonoko. A tragedy. Written by Thomas Southern, Marked with the variations in the manager's book, at the Theatre-Royal in Drury-Lane* (1785).

lutions being adjusted, the lovely, young, and adored victim lays herself down before the sacrificer; while he, with a hand resolved and a heart breaking within, gave the fatal stroke; first cutting her throat, and then severing her yet smiling face from that delicate body, pregnant as it was with fruits of tenderest love. As soon as he had done, he laid the body decently on leaves and flowers, of which he made a bed, and concealed it under the same coverlid of nature; only her face he left yet bare to look on. But when he found she was dead and past all retrieve, never more to bless him with her eyes and soft language, his grief swelled up to rage; he tore, he raved, he roared, like some monster of the wood, calling on the loved name of Imoinda. A thousand times he turned the fatal knife that did the deed toward his own heart, with a resolution to go immediately after her; but dire revenge, which now was a

6. Sensitive.

thousand times more fierce in his soul than before, prevents him; and he would cry out, "No; since I have sacrificed Imoinda to my revenge, shall I lose that glory which I have purchased so dear as at the price of the fairest, dearest, softest creature that ever nature made? No, no!" Then, at her name, grief would get the ascendant of rage, and he would lie down by her side and water her face with showers of tears, which never were wont to fall from those eyes. And however bent he was on his intended slaughter, he had not power to stir from the sight of this dear object, now more beloved and more adored than ever.

He remained in this deploring condition for two days, and never rose from the ground where he had made his sad sacrifice. At last, rousing from her side, and accusing himself with living too long now Imoinda was dead, and that the deaths of those barbarous enemies were deferred too long, he resolved now to finish the great work; but offering to rise, he found his strength so decayed that he reeled to and fro, like boughs assailed by contrary winds; so that he was forced to lie down again, and try to summon all his courage to his aid. He found his brains turned round, and his eyes were dizzy, and objects appeared not the same to him they were wont to do; his breath was short, and all his limbs surprised with a faintness he had never felt before. He had not eat in two days, which was one occasion of this feebleness, but excess of grief was the greatest; yet still he hoped he should recover vigor to act his design, and lay expecting it yet six days longer, still mourning over the dead idol of his heart, and striving every day to rise, but could not.

In all this time you may believe we were in no little affliction for Caesar and his wife; some were of opinion he was escaped never to return; others thought some accident had happened to him. But however, we failed not to send out an hundred people several ways to search for him; a party of about forty went that way he took, among whom was Tuscan, who was perfectly reconciled to Byam. They had not gone very far into the wood but they smelt an unusual smell, as of a dead body; for stinks must be very noisome that can be distinguished among such a quantity of natural sweets as every inch of that land produces. So that they concluded they should find him dead, or somebody that was so. They passed on towards it, as loathsome as it was, and made such a rustling among the leaves that lie thick on the ground, by continual falling, that Caesar heard he was approached; and though he had during the space of these eight days endeavored to rise, but found he wanted strength, yet looking up and seeing his pursuers, he rose and reeled to a neighboring tree, against which he fixed his back; and being within a dozen yards of those that advanced and saw him, he called out to them and bid them approach no nearer, if they would be safe. So that they stood still, and hardly believing their eyes, that would persuade them that it was Caesar that spoke to 'em, so much was he altered, they asked him what he had done with his wife, for they smelt a stink that almost struck them dead. He, pointing to the dead body, sighing, cried, "Behold her there." They put off the flowers that covered her with their sticks, and found she was killed, and cried out, "Oh, monster! that hast murdered thy wife." Then asking him why he did so cruel a deed, he replied, he had no leisure to answer impertinent questions. "You may go back," continued he, "and tell the faithless governor he may thank fortune that I am breathing my last, and that my arm is too feeble to obey my heart in what it had designed him." But his tongue faltering, and trembling, he could scarce end what he was saying. The English, taking advantage by his weakness, cried, "Let us take him alive by all means." He heard 'em; and as if he had revived from a fainting, or a dream, he cried out, "No, gentlemen, you are deceived; you will find no more Caesars to be whipped, no more find a faith in me. Feeble as you think me, I have strength yet left to secure me from a second indignity." They swore all anew, and he only shook his head and beheld them with scorn. Then they cried out, "Who will venture on this single man? Will nobody?" They stood all silent while Caesar replied, "Fatal will be the attempt to the first adventurer, let him assure himself," and at that word, held up his knife in a menacing posture. "Look ye, ye faithless crew," said he, "'tis not life I seek, nor am I afraid of dying," and at that word cut a piece of flesh from his own throat, and threw it at 'em; "yet still I would live if I could, till I had perfected my revenge. But oh! it cannot be; I feel life gliding from my eyes and heart, and if I make not haste, I shall yet fall a victim to the shameful whip." At that, he ripped up his own belly, and took his bowels and pulled 'em out, with what strength he could; while some, on their knees imploring, besought him to hold his hand. But when they saw him tottering, they cried out, "Will none venture on him?" A bold English cried, "Yes, if he were the devil" (taking courage when he saw him almost dead); and swearing a horrid oath for his farewell to the world, he rushed on him; Caesar, with his armed hand, met him so fairly as stuck him to the heart, and he fell dead at his feet. Tuscan, seeing that, cried out, "I love thee, O Caesar, and therefore will not let thee die, if possible." And running to him, took him in his arms; but at the same time warding a blow that Caesar made at his bosom, he received it quite through his arm; and Caesar having not the strength to pluck the knife forth, though he attempted it, Tuscan neither pulled it out himself nor suffered it to be pulled out, but came down with it sticking in his arm; and the reason he gave for it was, because the air should not get into the wound. They put their hands across, and carried Caesar between six of 'em, fainted as he was, and they thought dead, or just dying; and they brought him to Parham, and laid him on a couch, and had the chirurgeon immediately to him, who dressed his wounds and sewed up his belly, and used means to bring him to life, which they effected. We ran all to see him, and if before we thought him so beautiful a sight, he was now so altered that his face was like a death's head blacked over, nothing but teeth and eyeholes. For some days we suffered nobody to speak to him, but caused cordials to be poured down his throat, which sustained his life; and in six or seven days he recovered his senses. For you must know that wounds are almost to a miracle cured in the Indies, unless wounds in the legs, which rarely ever cure.

When he was well enough to speak, we talked to him, and asked him some questions about his wife, and the reasons why he killed her; and he then told us what I have related of that resolution, and of his parting; and he besought us we would let him die, and was extremely afflicted to think it was possible he might live; he assured us if we did not dispatch him, he would prove very fatal to a great many. We said all we could to make him live, and gave him new assurances; but he begged we would not think so poorly of him, or of his love to Imoinda, to imagine we could flatter him to life again; but the chirurgeon assured him he could not live, and therefore he need not fear. We were all (but Caesar) afflicted at this news; and the sight was gashly;[7] his discourse was sad, and the earthly smell about him so strong that I was persuaded to leave the place for some time (being myself but sickly, and very apt to fall into fits of dangerous illness upon any extraordinary melancholy). The servants and Trefry and the chirurgeons promised all to take what possible care they could of the life of Caesar, and I, taking boat, went with other company to Colonel Martin's, about three days' journey down the river; but I was no sooner gone, but the governor taking Trefry about some pretended earnest business a day's journey up the river, having communicated his design to one Banister, a wild Irishman and one of the council, a fellow of absolute barbarity, and fit to execute any villainy, but was rich: he came up to Parham, and forcibly took Caesar, and had him carried to the same post where he was whipped; and causing him to be tied to it, and a great fire made before him, he told him he should die like a dog, as he was. Caesar replied, this was the first piece of bravery that ever Banister did, and he never spoke sense till he pronounced that word; and if he would keep it, he would declare, in the other world, that he was the only man of all the whites that ever he heard speak truth. And turning to the men that bound him, he said, "My friends, am I to die, or to be whipped?" And they cried, "Whipped! No, you shall not escape so well." And then he replied, smiling, "A blessing on thee," and assured them they need not tie him, for he would stand fixed like a rock, and endure death so as should encourage them to die. "But if you whip me," said he, "be sure you tie me fast."

He had learned to take tobacco; and when he was assured he should die, he desired they would give him a pipe in his mouth, ready lighted, which they did; and the executioner came, and first cut off his members,[8] and threw them into the fire; after that, with an ill-favored knife, they cut his ears, and his nose, and burned them; he still smoked on, as if nothing had touched him. Then they hacked off one of his arms, and still he bore up, and held his pipe; but at the cutting off the other arm, his head sunk, and his pipe dropped, and he gave up the ghost, without a groan or a reproach. My mother and sister were by him all the while, but not suffered to save him, so rude and wild were the rabble, and so inhuman were the justices, who stood by to see the execution, who after paid dearly enough for their insolence. They cut Caesar in quarters, and sent them to several of the chief plantations. One quarter was sent to Colonel Martin, who refused it, and swore he had rather see the quarters of Banister and the governor himself than those of Caesar on his plantations, and that he could govern his Negroes without terrifying and grieving them with frightful spectacles of a mangled king.

Thus died this great man, worthy of a better fate, and a more sublime wit than mine to write his praise; yet, I hope, the reputation of my pen is considerable enough to make his glorious name to survive to all ages, with that of the brave, the beautiful, and the constant Imoinda.

1688

---

7. Ghastly.   8. Genitals.

WILLIAM CONGREVE
1670–1729

Both of William Congreve's parents came from well-to-do and prominent county families. His father, a younger son, obtained a commission as lieutenant in the army and moved to Ireland in 1674. There the future playwright was educated at Kilkenny School and Trinity College, Dublin; at both places he was a younger contemporary of Swift. In 1691 he took rooms in the Middle Temple and began to study law, but soon found he preferred the wit of the coffeehouses and the theater. Within a year he had so distinguished himself at Will's Coffeehouse that he had become intimate with the great Dryden himself, and his brief career as a dramatist began shortly thereafter.

The success of *The Old Bachelor* (produced in 1693) immediately established him as the most promising young dramatist in London. It had the then phenomenally long run of fourteen days, and Dryden declared it the best first play he had ever read. *The Double Dealer* (produced in 1693) was a near failure, though it evoked one of Dryden's most graceful and gracious poems, in which he praised Congreve as the superior of Jonson and Fletcher and the equal of Shakespeare. *Love for Love* (produced in 1695) was an unqualified success and remains Congreve's most frequently revived play. In 1697 he brought out a well-received tragedy, *The Mourning Bride*. Congreve's most elegant comedy of manners, *The Way of the World*, received a brilliant production in 1700, but it did not have a long run. During the rest of his life he wrote no more plays. Instead he held a minor government post, which, although a Whig, he was allowed to keep during the Tory ministry of Oxford and Bolingbroke; after the accession of George I he was given a more lucrative government sinecure. Despite the political animosities of the first two decades of the century, he managed to remain on friendly terms with Swift and Pope, and Pope dedicated to him his translation of the *Iliad*. Congreve's final years were perplexed by poor health but were made bearable by the love of Henrietta, second duchess of Marlborough, whose last child, a daughter, was in all probability the playwright's.

The Way of the World is one of the wittiest plays ever written, a play to read slowly and savor. Like an expert jeweler, Congreve polished the Restoration comedy of manners to its ultimate sparkle and gloss. The dialogue is epigrammatic and brilliant, the plot is an intricate puzzle, and the characters shine with surprisingly complex facets. Yet the play is not all dazzling surface; it also has depths. Most Restoration comedies begin with the struggle for power, sex, and money and end with a marriage. In an age that viewed property, not romance, as the basis of marriage, the hero shows his prowess by catching an heiress. *The Way of the World* reflects that standard plot; it is a battle more over a legacy than over a woman, a battle in which sexual attraction is used as a weapon. Yet Congreve, writing after such conventions had been thoroughly explored, reveals the weakness of those who treat love as a war or a game: "each deceiver to his cost may find / That marriage frauds too oft are paid in kind." If "the way of the world" is cynical self-interest, it is also the worldly prudence that sees through the ruses of power and turns them to better ends. In this world generosity and affection win the day and true love conquers—with the help of some clever plotting.

At the center of the action are four fully realized characters—Mirabell and Millamant, the hero and heroine, and Fainall and Mrs. Marwood, the two villains—whose stratagems and relations move the play. Around them are characters who serve in one way or another as foils: Witwoud, the would-be wit, with whom we contrast the true wit of Mirabell and Millamant; Petulant, a "humor" character, who affects bluff candor and cynical realism, but succeeds only in being offensive; and Sir Wilfull Witwoud, the booby squire from the country, who serves with Petulant to throw into relief the high good breeding and fineness of nature of the hero and heroine. Finally there is one of Congreve's most striking creations, Lady Wishfort ("wish for it"), who though aging still longs for love, gallantry, and courtship and who is led by her appetites into the trap that Mirabell lays for her.

Because of the complexity of the plot, a summary of the situation at the rise of the curtain may prove helpful. Mirabell (a reformed rake) is sincerely in love with and wishes to marry Millamant, who, though a coquette and a highly sophisticated wit, is a virtuous woman. Mirabell some time before has married off his former mistress, the daughter of Lady Wishfort, to his friend Fainall. Fainall has grown tired of his wife and has been squandering her money on his mistress, Mrs. Marwood. In order to gain access to Millamant, Mirabell has pretended to pay court to the elderly and amorous Lady Wishfort, who is the guardian of Millamant and as such controls half her fortune. But his game has been spoiled by Mrs. Marwood, who nourishes a secret love for Mirabell and, to separate him from Millamant, has made Lady Wishfort aware of Mirabell's duplicity. Lady Wishfort now loathes Mirabell for making a fool of her—an awkward situation, because if Millamant should marry without her guardian's consent she would lose half her fortune, and Mirabell cannot afford to marry any but a rich wife. It is at this point that the action begins. Mirabell perfects a plot to get such power over Lady Wishfort as to force her to agree to the marriage, while Millamant continues to doubt whether she wishes to marry at all.

The Way of the World

DRAMATIS PERSONAE[1]

Men

FAINALL, *in love with* MRS. MARWOOD
MIRABELL, *in love with* MRS. MILLAMANT
WITWOUD } *followers of* MRS. MILLAMANT
PETULANT }
SIR WILFULL WITWOUD, *half brother to* WITWOUD, *and nephew to* LADY WISHFORT
WAITWELL, *servant to* MIRABELL

Women

LADY WISHFORT, *enemy to* MIRABELL, *for having falsely pretended love to her*
MRS. MILLAMANT, *a fine lady, niece to* LADY WISHFORT, *and loves* MIRABELL
MRS. MARWOOD, *friend to* MR. FAINALL, *and likes* MIRABELL
MRS. FAINALL, *daughter to* LADY WISHFORT, *and wife to* FAINALL, *formerly friend to* MIRABELL
FOIBLE, *woman to* LADY WISHFORT

1. As was conventional in the period's plays, the names of the principal characters reveal their dominant traits: e.g., Fainall would *fain* have *all*, with perhaps also the suggestion that he is the complete hypocrite, who *feigns*. Witwoud is the *would-be wit*. Wishfort suggests *wish for it*. Millamant is the lady with a thousand lovers (French *mille amants*). Marwood *would* willingly *mar* (injure) the lovers. Mincing has an air of affected gentility (i.e., she *minces*), which clashes with her vulgar English. "Mrs." is "Mistress," a title then used by young unmarried ladies as well as by the married Mrs. Fainall.

MINCING, *woman to* MRS. MILLAMANT
BETTY, *waitress at the chocolate house*
PEG, *under-servant to* LADY WISHFORT
DANCERS, FOOTMEN, *and* ATTENDANTS

SCENE—*London*

Prologue

SPOKEN BY MR. BETTERTON[2]

    Of those few fools, who with ill stars are cursed,
Sure scribbling fools, called poets, fare the worst:
For they're a sort of fools which Fortune makes,
And after she has made 'em fools, forsakes.
5   With nature's oafs 'tis quite a different case,
For Fortune favors all her idiot race.
In her own nest the cuckoo eggs we find,
O'er which she broods to hatch the changeling kind.[3]
No portion for her own she has to spare,
10   So much she dotes on her adopted care.
    Poets are bubbles,° by the town drawn in,   *dupes*
Suffered at first some trifling stakes to win:
But what unequal hazards do they run!
Each time they write they venture all they've won:
15 The squire that's buttered still,° is sure to be undone.   *constantly flattered*
This author, heretofore, has found your favor,
But pleads no merit from his past behavior;
To build on that might prove a vain presumption,
Should grants to poets made, admit resumption:[4]
20 And in Parnassus[5] he must lose his seat,
If that be found a forfeited estate.[6]
    He owns,° with toil he wrought the following scenes,   *admits*
But if they're naught ne'er spare him for his pains:
Damn him the more; have no commiseration
25 For dullness on mature deliberation.
He swears he'll not resent one hissed-off scene
Nor, like those peevish wits, his play maintain,°   *defend*
Who, to assert their sense, your taste arraign.
Some plot we think he has, and some new thought;
30 Some humor too, no farce; but that's a fault.
Satire, he thinks, you ought not to expect,
For so reformed a town,[7] who dares correct?
To please, this time, has been his sole pretense,
He'll not instruct, lest it should give offense.

2. Thomas Betterton (ca. 1635–1710), the greatest actor of the period, played Fainall in the original production of this play.
3. Simpletons; children supposed to have been secretly exchanged in infancy for others. The cuckoo lays its eggs in the nests of other birds.
4. The Crown could both grant and take back ("resume") estates.
5. Greek mountain sacred to the Muses.

6. *Seat* rhymed with *estate*; in the next couplet, *scenes* and *pains* rhymed. A few lines later *scene* is similarly pronounced to rhyme with *maintain*, and *fault* (the *l* being silent) is rhymed with *thought*.
7. A sarcasm, directed against the general movement to reform manners and morals and, more particularly, against Jeremy Collier's attack on actors and playwrights in his *Short View of the Profaneness and Immorality of the English Stage* (1698).

₃₅ Should he by chance a knave or fool expose,
That hurts none here; sure here are none of those.
In short, our play shall (with your leave to show it)
Give you one instance of a passive poet
Who to your judgments yields all resignation;
₄₀ So save or damn after your own discretion.

Act 1—*A chocolate house*

MIRABELL *and* FAINALL *rising from cards*, BETTY *waiting*.

MIRABELL   You are a fortunate man, Mr. Fainall.

FAINALL   Have we done?

MIRABELL   What you please. I'll play on to entertain you.

FAINALL   No, I'll give you your revenge another time, when you are not so indifferent; you are thinking of something else now, and play too negligently. The coldness of a losing gamester lessens the pleasure of the winner. I'd no more play with a man that slighted his ill fortune than I'd make love to a woman who undervalued the loss of her reputation.

MIRABELL   You have a taste extremely delicate, and are for refining on your pleasures.

FAINALL   Prithee, why so reserved? Something has put you out of humor.

MIRABELL   Not at all. I happen to be grave today, and you are gay; that's all.

FAINALL   Confess, Millamant and you quarreled last night after I left you; my fair cousin has some humors that would tempt the patience of a stoic. What, some coxcomb came in, and was well received by her, while you were by?

MIRABELL   Witwoud and Petulant; and what was worse, her aunt, your wife's mother, my evil genius; or to sum up all in her own name, my old Lady Wishfort came in.

FAINALL   O, there it is then—she has a lasting passion for you, and with reason. What, then my wife was there?

MIRABELL   Yes, and Mrs. Marwood and three or four more, whom I never saw before. Seeing me, they all put on their grave faces, whispered one another; then complained aloud of the vapors,[8] and after fell into a profound silence.

FAINALL   They had a mind to be rid of you.

MIRABELL   For which good reason I resolved not to stir. At last the good old lady broke through her painful taciturnity, with an invective against long visits. I would not have understood her, but Millamant joining in the argument, I rose and with a constrained smile told her I thought nothing was so easy as to know when a visit began to be troublesome. She reddened and I withdrew, without expecting[9] her reply.

FAINALL   You were to blame to resent what she spoke only in compliance with her aunt.

MIRABELL   She is more mistress of herself than to be under the necessity of such a resignation.

FAINALL   What? though half her fortune depends upon her marrying with my lady's approbation?

---

8. Melancholy.

9. Awaiting.

MIRABELL   I was then in such a humor that I should have been better pleased if she had been less discreet.

FAINALL   Now I remember, I wonder not they were weary of you: last night was one of their cabal[1] nights; they have 'em three times a week, and meet by turns, at one another's apartments, where they come together like the coroner's inquest, to sit upon the murdered reputations of the week. You and I are excluded; and it was once proposed that all the male sex should be excepted; but somebody moved that to avoid scandal there might be one man of the community; upon which Witwoud and Petulant were enrolled members.

MIRABELL   And who may have been the foundress of this sect? My Lady Wishfort, I warrant, who publishes her detestation of mankind, and full of the vigor of fifty-five, declares for a friend and ratafia;[2] and let posterity shift for itself, she'll breed no more.

FAINALL   The discovery of your sham addresses to her, to conceal your love to her niece, has provoked this separation. Had you dissembled better, things might have continued in the state of nature.[3]

MIRABELL   I did as much as man could, with any reasonable conscience: I proceeded to the very last act of flattery with her, and was guilty of a song in her commendation. Nay, I got a friend to put her into a lampoon and compliment her with the imputation of an affair with a young fellow, which I carried so far that I told her the malicious town took notice that she was grown fat of a sudden; and when she lay in of a dropsy, persuaded her she was reported to be in labor. The devil's in't, if an old woman is to be flattered further, unless a man should endeavor downright personally to debauch her; and that my virtue forbade me. But for the discovery of this amour, I am indebted to your friend, or your wife's friend, Mrs. Marwood.

FAINALL   What should provoke her to be your enemy, unless she has made you advances, which you have slighted? Women do not easily forgive omissions of that nature.

MIRABELL   She was always civil to me, till of late. I confess I am not one of those coxcombs who are apt to interpret a woman's good manners to her prejudice, and think that she who does not refuse 'em everything, can refuse 'em nothing.

FAINALL   You are a gallant man, Mirabell; and though you may have cruelty enough not to satisfy a lady's longing, you have too much generosity not to be tender of her honor. Yet you speak with an indifference which seems to be affected, and confesses you are conscious of a negligence.

MIRABELL   You pursue the argument with a distrust that seems to be unaffected, and confesses you are conscious of a concern for which the lady is more indebted to you than is your wife.

FAINALL   Fie, fie, friend, if you grow censorious I must leave you.—I'll look upon the gamesters in the next room.

MIRABELL   Who are they?

---

1. Secret organization designed for intrigue.
2. A liqueur flavored with fruit kernels (pronounced *rat-a-fé-a*).

3. Lady Wishfort's natural inclination for you would have continued.

FAINALL   Petulant and Witwoud. [*To* BETTY.] Bring me some chocolate. [*Exit* FAINALL.]

MIRABELL   Betty, what says your clock?

BETTY   Turned of the last canonical hour,[4] sir. [*Exit* BETTY.]

MIRABELL   How pertinently the jade answers me! Ha? almost one a clock! [*Looking on his watch.*]—O, y'are come—

[*Enter a* FOOTMAN.]

MIRABELL   Well, is the grand affair over? You have been something tedious.[5]

FOOTMAN   Sir, there's such coupling at Pancras[6] that they stand behind one another, as 'twere in a country dance. Ours was the last couple to lead up; and no hopes appearing of dispatch, besides, the parson growing hoarse, we were afraid his lungs would have failed before it came to our turn; so we drove around to Duke's Place, and there they were riveted in a trice.

MIRABELL   So, so, you are sure they are married?

FOOTMAN   Married and bedded, sir. I am witness.

MIRABELL   Have you the certificate?

FOOTMAN   Here it is, sir.

MIRABELL   Has the tailor brought Waitwell's clothes home, and the new liveries?

FOOTMAN   Yes, sir.

MIRABELL   That's well. Do you go home again, d'ye hear, and adjourn the consummation till farther order. Bid Waitwell shake his ears, and Dame Partlet rustle up her feathers, and meet me at one a clock by Rosamond's Pond, that I may see her before she returns to her lady: and as you tender your ears,[7] be secret. [*Exit* FOOTMAN.]

[*Re-enter* FAINALL, BETTY.]

FAINALL   Joy of your success, Mirabell; you look pleased.

MIRABELL   Aye, I have been engaged in a matter of some sort of mirth, which is not yet ripe for discovery. I am glad this is not a cabal night. I wonder, Fainall, that you who are married, and of consequence should be discreet, will suffer your wife to be of such a party.

FAINALL   Faith, I am not jealous. Besides, most who are engaged are women and relations; and for the men, they are of a kind too contemptible to give scandal.

MIRABELL   I am of another opinion. The greater the coxcomb, always the more the scandal: for a woman who is not a fool can have but one reason for associating with a man who is one.

FAINALL   Are you jealous as often as you see Witwoud entertained by Millamant?

MIRABELL   Of her understanding I am, if not of her person.

FAINALL   You do her wrong; for to give her her due, she has wit.

MIRABELL   She has beauty enough to make any man think so; and complaisance enough not to contradict him who shall tell her so.

---

4. The hours in which marriage can legally be performed in the Anglican Church, then eight to twelve noon.
5. Taken a long time.
6. The Church of St. Pancras, like that of St. James in Duke's Place (referred to later in the same speech), was notorious for a thriving trade in unlicensed marriages.
7. If you don't want your ears cropped. "Dame Partlet": Pertelote, the hen-wife of the cock Chauntecleer in Chaucer's *The Nun's Priest's Tale*. Rosamond's Pond is in St. James's Park.

FAINALL   For a passionate lover, methinks you are a man somewhat too discerning in the failings of your mistress.

MIRABELL   And for a discerning man, somewhat too passionate a lover; for I like her with all her faults, nay, like her for her faults. Her follies are so natural, or so artful, that they become her, and those affectations which in another woman would be odious, serve but to make her more agreeable. I'll tell thee, Fainall, she once used me with that insolence that in revenge I took her to pieces; sifted her, and separated her failings; I studied 'em, and got 'em by rote. The catalogue was so large that I was not without hopes, one day or other, to hate her heartily: to which end I so used myself to think of 'em that at length, contrary to my design and expectation, they gave me every hour less and less disturbance, till in a few days it became habitual to me to remember 'em without being displeased. They are now grown as familiar to me as my own frailties, and in all probability in a little time longer I shall like 'em as well.

FAINALL   Marry her, marry her; be half as well acquainted with her charms as you are with her defects, and my life on't, you are your own man again.

MIRABELL   Say you so?

FAINALL   Aye, aye, I have experience; I have a wife, and so forth.

[*Enter a* MESSENGER.]

MESSENGER   Is one Squire Witwoud here?

BETTY   Yes. What's your business?

MESSENGER   I have a letter for him, from his brother Sir Wilfull, which I am charged to deliver into his own hands.

BETTY   He's in the next room, friend—that way. [*Exit* MESSENGER.]

MIRABELL   What, is the chief of that noble family in town, Sir Wilfull Witwoud?

FAINALL   He is expected today. Do you know him?

MIRABELL   I have seen him. He promises to be an extraordinary person; I think you have the honor to be related to him.

FAINALL   Yes; he is half brother to this Witwoud by a former wife, who was sister to my Lady Wishfort, my wife's mother. If you marry Millamant, you must call cousins too.

MIRABELL   I had rather be his relation than his acquaintance.

FAINALL   He comes to town in order to equip himself for travel.

MIRABELL   For travel! Why the man that I mean is above forty.[8]

FAINALL   No matter for that; 'tis for the honor of England that all Europe should know that we have blockheads of all ages.

MIRABELL   I wonder there is not an Act of Parliament to save the credit of the nation, and prohibit the exportation of fools.

FAINALL   By no means, 'tis better as 'tis; 'tis better to trade with a little loss than to be quite eaten up with being overstocked.

MIRABELL   Pray, are the follies of this knight-errant, and those of the squire his brother, anything related?

8. The grand tour of the Continent was rapidly becoming a part of the education of gentlemen, but it was usually made in company with a tutor after a young man had graduated from a university, not after a man had passed the age of forty.

FAINALL   Not at all. Witwoud grows by the knight, like a medlar grafted on a crab.[9] One will melt in your mouth, and t'other set your teeth on edge; one is all pulp, and the other all core.

MIRABELL   So one will be rotten before he be ripe, and the other will be rotten without ever being ripe at all.

FAINALL   Sir Wilfull is an odd mixture of bashfulness and obstinacy. But when he's drunk, he's as loving as the monster in the *Tempest;*[1] and much after the same manner. To give t'other his due, he has something of good nature, and does not always want wit.

MIRABELL   Not always; but as often as his memory fails him, and his commonplace of comparisons.[2] He is a fool with a good memory, and some few scraps of other folks' wit. He is one whose conversation can never be approved, yet it is now and then to be endured. He has indeed one good quality, he is not exceptious,[3] for he so passionately affects the reputation of understanding raillery that he will construe an affront into a jest; and call downright rudeness and ill language, satire and fire.

FAINALL   If you have a mind to finish his picture, you have an opportunity to do it at full length. Behold the original.

[*Enter* WITWOUD.]

WITWOUD   Afford me your compassion, my dears; pity me, Fainall, Mirabell, pity me.

MIRABELL   I do from my soul.

FAINALL   Why, what's the matter?

WITWOUD   No letters for me, Betty?

BETTY   Did not a messenger bring you one but now, sir?

WITWOUD   Aye, but no other?

BETTY   No, sir.

WITWOUD   That's hard, that's very hard. A messenger, a mule, a beast of burden, he has brought me a letter from the fool my brother, as heavy as a panegyric in a funeral sermon, or a copy of commendatory verses from one poet to another. And what's worse, 'tis as sure a forerunner of the author as an epistle dedicatory.

MIRABELL   A fool, and your brother, Witwoud!

WITWOUD   Aye, aye, my half brother. My half brother he is, no nearer upon honor.

MIRABELL   Then 'tis possible he may be but half a fool.

WITWOUD   Good, good, Mirabell, *le drôle!*[4] Good, good. Hang him, don't let's talk of him. Fainall, how does your lady? Gad. I say anything in the world to get this fellow out of my head. I beg pardon that I should ask a man of pleasure and the town a question at once so foreign and domestic. But I talk like an old maid at a marriage, I don't know what I say: but she's the best woman in the world.

9. Crabapple. "Medlar": a fruit eaten when it is overripe.
1. Trinculo, in the adaptation of Shakespeare's *Tempest* by Sir William Davenant and Dryden (1667), having made Caliban drunk, says, "The poor monster is loving in his drink" (2.2).
2. One recognized sign of wit was the ability to quickly discover resemblances between objects apparently unlike. Witwoud specializes in this kind of wit, but Mirabell suggests that they are all obvious and collected from others, like observations copied in a notebook, or "commonplace" book.
3. Quarrelsome.
4. The witty fellow (French).

FAINALL 'Tis well you don't know what you say, or else your commendation would go near to make me either vain or jealous.

WITWOUD No man in town lives well with a wife but Fainall. Your judgment, Mirabell?

MIRABELL You had better step and ask his wife, if you would be credibly informed.

WITWOUD Mirabell.

MIRABELL Aye.

WITWOUD My dear, I ask ten thousand pardons—gad, I have forgot what I was going to say to you.

MIRABELL I thank you heartily, heartily.

WITWOUD No, but prithee excuse me—my memory is such a memory.

MIRABELL Have a care of such apologies, Witwoud—for I never knew a fool but he affected to complain, either of the spleen⁵ or his memory.

FAINALL What have you done with Petulant?

WITWOUD He's reckoning his money—my money it was.—I have no luck today.

FAINALL You may allow him to win of you at play—for you are sure to be too hard for him at repartee. Since you monopolize the wit that is between you, the fortune must be his of course.

MIRABELL I don't find that Petulant confesses the superiority of wit to be your talent, Witwoud.

WITWOUD Come, come, you are malicious now, and would breed debates.— Petulant's my friend, and a very honest fellow, and a very pretty fellow, and has a smattering—faith and troth a pretty deal of an odd sort of a small wit: nay, I'll do him justice. I'm his friend, I won't wrong him.— And if he had any judgment in the world—he would not be altogether contemptible. Come, come, don't detract from the merits of my friend.

FAINALL You don't take your friend to be over-nicely bred.

WITWOUD No, no, hang him, the rogue has no manners at all, that I must own—no more breeding than a bum-bailey,⁶ that I grant you.— 'Tis pity; the fellow has fire and life.

MIRABELL What, courage?

WITWOUD Hum, faith I don't know as to that—I can't say as to that.— Yes, faith, in a controversy he'll contradict anybody.

MIRABELL Though 'twere a man whom he feared, or a woman whom he loved.

WITWOUD Well, well, he does not always think before he speaks—we have all our failings; you are too hard upon him, you are, faith. Let me excuse him—I can defend most of his faults, except one or two. One he has, that's the truth on't, if he were my brother, I could not acquit him.—That indeed I could wish were otherwise.

MIRABELL Aye marry, what's that, Witwoud?

WITWOUD O, pardon me—expose the infirmities of my friend?—No, my dear, excuse me there.

FAINALL What, I warrant he's unsincere, or 'tis some such trifle.

---

5. Depression.   6. Bumbailiff, the lowest arresting officer.

WITWOUD   No, no, what if he be? 'Tis no matter for that, his wit will excuse that. A wit should no more be sincere than a woman constant; one argues a decay of parts[7] as t'other of beauty.

MIRABELL   Maybe you think him too positive?

WITWOUD   No, no, his being positive is an incentive to argument, and keeps up conversation.

FAINALL   Too illiterate.

WITWOUD   That! that's his happiness.—His want of learning gives him the more opportunities to show his natural parts.

MIRABELL   He wants words.

WITWOUD   Aye; but I like him for that now; for his want of words gives me the pleasure very often to explain his meaning.

FAINALL   He's impudent.

WITWOUD   No, that's not it.

MIRABELL   Vain.

WITWOUD   No.

MIRABELL   What, he speaks unseasonable truths sometimes, because he has not wit enough to invent an evasion.

WITWOUD   Truths! Ha, ha, ha! No, no, since you will have it—I mean, he never speaks truth at all—that's all. He will lie like a chambermaid, or a woman of quality's porter. Now that is a fault.

[*Enter* COACHMAN.]

COACHMAN   Is Master Petulant here, mistress?

BETTY   Yes.

COACHMAN   Three gentlewomen in a coach would speak with him.

FAINALL   O brave Petulant, three!

BETTY   I'll tell him.

COACHMAN   You must bring two dishes of chocolate and a glass of cinnamon water.

[*Exeunt* BETTY, COACHMAN.]

WITWOUD   That should be for two fasting strumpets, and a bawd troubled with wind. Now you may know what the three are.

MIRABELL   You are free with your friend's acquaintance.

WITWOUD   Aye, aye, friendship without freedom is as dull as love without enjoyment, or wine without toasting; but to tell you a secret, these are trulls[8] whom he allows coach-hire, and something more by the week, to call on him once a day at public places.

MIRABELL   How!

WITWOUD   You shall see he won't go to 'em because there's no more company here to take notice of him.—Why this is nothing to what he used to do, before he found out this way. I have known him call for himself.—

FAINALL   Call for himself? What dost thou mean?

WITWOUD   Mean? Why he would slip you out of this chocolate house, just when you had been talking to him.—As soon as your back was turned—whip he was gone—then trip to his lodging, clap on a hood and scarf, and a mask, slap into a hackney coach, and drive hither to the door again in a trice; where he would send in for himself, that I mean, call for him-

---

7. Talents.   8. Prostitutes.

self, wait for himself, nay and what's more, not finding himself, sometimes leave a letter for himself.

MIRABELL   I confess this is something extraordinary.—I believe he waits for himself now, he is so long a-coming. O, I ask his pardon.

[*Enter* PETULANT, BETTY.]

BETTY   Sir, the coach stays.

PETULANT   Well, well; I come.—'Sbud,[9] a man had as good be a professed midwife, as a professed whoremaster, at this rate; to be knocked up and raised at all hours, and in all places. Pox on 'em, I won't come.—D'ye hear, tell 'em I won't come.—Let 'em snivel and cry their hearts out.

FAINALL   You are very cruel, Petulant.

PETULANT   All's one, let it pass—I have a humor to be cruel.

MIRABELL   I hope they are not persons of condition[1] that you use at this rate.

PETULANT   Condition, condition's a dried fig, if I am not in humor.—By this hand, if they were your—a—a—your what-dee-call-'ems themselves, they must wait or rub off,[2] if I want appetite.

MIRABELL   What-de-call-ems! What are they, Witwoud?

WITWOUD   Empresses, my dear.—By your what-dee-call-'ems he means sultana queens.

PETULANT   Aye, Roxolanas.[3]

MIRABELL   Cry you mercy.

FAINALL   Witwoud says they are—

PETULANT   What does he say th' are?

WITWOUD   I? Fine ladies I say.

PETULANT   Pass on, Witwoud.—Harkee, by this light his relations—two coheiresses his cousins, and an old aunt, who loves caterwauling better than a conventicle.[4]

WITWOUD   Ha, ha, ha; I had a mind to see how the rogue would come off.—Ha, ha, ha; gad, I can't be angry with him, if he had said they were my mother and my sisters.

MIRABELL   No!

WITWOUD   No; the rogue's wit and readiness of invention charm me, dear Petulant.

BETTY   They are gone, sir, in great anger.

PETULANT   Enough, let 'em trundle.[5] Anger helps complexion, saves paint.[6]

FAINALL   This continence is all dissembled; this is in order to have something to brag of the next time he makes court to Millamant, and swear he had abandoned the whole sex for her sake.

MIRABELL   Have you not left off your impudent pretensions there yet? I shall cut your throat, sometime or other, Petulant, about that business.

PETULANT   Aye, aye, let that pass.—There are other throats to be cut.—

MIRABELL   Meaning mine, sir?

9. God's body.
1. High social standing.
2. Go away.
3. "Empresses," "sultana queens," and "Roxolanas" were terms for prostitutes. Roxolana is the

wife of the Sultan in Davenant's *Siege of Rhodes* (1656).
4. Nonconformist religious meeting.
5. Move along.
6. Makeup.

PETULANT   Not I—I mean nobody—I know nothing. But there are uncles and nephews in the world—and they may be rivals—What then? All's one for that—

MIRABELL   How! Harkee, Petulant, come hither—explain, or I shall call your interpreter.

PETULANT   Explain? I know nothing.—Why, you have an uncle, have you not, lately come to town, and lodges by my Lady Wishfort's?

MIRABELL   True.

PETULANT   Why, that's enough.—You and he are not friends; and if he should marry and have a child, you may be disinherited, ha?

MIRABELL   Where hast thou stumbled upon all this truth?

PETULANT   All's one for that; why, then, say I know something.

MIRABELL   Come, thou art an honest fellow, Petulant, and shalt make love to my mistress, thou sha't, faith. What hast thou heard of my uncle?

PETULANT   I, nothing, I. If throats are to be cut, let swords clash; snug's the word, I shrug and am silent.

MIRABELL   O raillery, raillery. Come, I know thou art in the women's secrets.—What, you're a cabalist. I know you stayed at Millamant's last night, after I went. Was there any mention made of my uncle or me? Tell me; if thou hadst but good nature equal to thy wit, Petulant, Tony Witwoud, who is now thy competitor in fame, would show as dim by thee as a dead whiting's eye by a pearl of Orient. He would no more be seen by thee than Mercury is by the sun: come, I'm sure thou wo't tell me.

PETULANT   If I do, will you grant me common sense then, for the future?

MIRABELL   Faith, I'll do what I can for thee, and I'll pray that Heaven may grant it thee in the meantime.

PETULANT   Well, harkee.

        [MIRABELL *and* PETULANT *talk privately.*]

FAINALL   Petulant and you both will find Mirabell as warm a rival as a lover.

WITWOUD   Pshaw, pshaw, that she laughs at Petulant is plain. And for my part—but that it is almost a fashion to admire her, I should—harkee—to tell you a secret, but let it go no further—between friends, I shall never break my heart for her.

FAINALL   How!

WITWOUD   She's handsome; but she's a sort of an uncertain woman.

FAINALL   I thought you had died for her.

WITWOUD   Umh—no—

FAINALL   She has wit.

WITWOUD   'Tis what she will hardly allow anybody else.—Now, demme,[7] I should hate that, if she were as handsome as Cleopatra. Mirabell is not so sure of her as he thinks for.

FAINALL   Why do you think so?

WITWOUD   We stayed pretty late there last night, and heard something of an uncle to Mirabell, who is lately come to town—and is between him and the best part of his estate. Mirabell and he are at some distance, as my Lady Wishfort has been told; and you know she hates Mirabell, worse

---

7. Damn me.

than a Quaker hates a parrot,[8] or than a fishmonger hates a hard frost. Whether this uncle has seen Mrs. Millamant or not, I cannot say; but there were items of such a treaty being in embryo; and if it should come to life, poor Mirabell would be in some sort unfortunately fobbed[9] i' faith.

FAINALL 'Tis impossible Millamant should harken to it.

WITWOUD Faith, my dear, I can't tell; she's a woman and a kind of a humorist.[1]

[MIRABELL, PETULANT *privately.*]

MIRABELL And this is the sum of what you could collect last night.

PETULANT The quintessence. Maybe Witwoud knows more, he stayed longer.—Besides they never mind him; they say anything before him.

MIRABELL I thought you had been the greatest favorite.

PETULANT Aye, *tête à tête;*[2] but not in public, because I make remarks.

MIRABELL You do?

PETULANT Aye, aye, pox, I'm malicious, man. Now he's soft, you know, they are not in awe of him.—The fellow's well bred, he's what you call a—what-d'ye-call-'em. A fine gentleman, but he's silly withal.

MIRABELL I thank you, I know as much as my curiosity requires. Fainall, are you for the Mall?[3]

FAINALL Aye, I'll take a turn before dinner.

WITWOUD Aye, we'll all walk in the park, the ladies talked of being there.

MIRABELL I thought you were obliged to watch for your brother Sir Wilfull's arrival.

WITWOUD No, no, he's come to his aunt's, my Lady Wishfort. Pox on him, I shall be troubled with him too. What shall I do with the fool?

PETULANT Beg him for his estate, that I may beg you afterwards, and so have but one trouble with you both.

WITWOUD O rare Petulant; thou art as quick as fire in a frosty morning; thou shalt to the Mall with us; and we'll be very severe.

PETULANT Enough, I'm in a humor to be severe.

MIRABELL Are you? Pray then walk by yourselves.—Let not us be accessory to your putting the ladies out of countenance with your senseless ribaldry, which you roar out aloud as often as they pass by you; and when you have made a handsome woman blush, then you think you have been severe.

PETULANT What, what? Then let 'em either show their innocence by not understanding what they hear, or else show their discretion by not hearing what they would not be thought to understand.

MIRABELL But hast not thou then sense enough to know that thou ought'st to be most ashamed thyself, when thou hast put another out of countenance?

PETULANT Not I, by this hand.—I always take blushing either for a sign of guilt, or ill breeding.

---

8. In his *Apology for the True Christian Divinity* (1678), the Quaker Robert Barclay says that professing belief in Christ without spiritual revelation is like "the prattling of a parrot."
9. Tricked.

1. A capricious person.
2. Face to face (French); i.e., in private.
3. A walk in St. James's Park, one of the fashionable public places of London.

MIRABELL   I confess you ought to think so. You are in the right, that you may plead the error of your judgment in defense of your practice.

Where modesty's ill manners, 'tis but fit
That impudence and malice pass for wit.

Act 2—St. James's Park

[*Enter* MRS. FAINALL *and* MRS. MARWOOD.]

MRS. FAINALL   Aye, aye, dear Marwood, if we will be happy, we must find the means in ourselves, and among ourselves. Men are ever in extremes; either doting or averse. While they are lovers, if they have fire and sense, their jealousies are insupportable: and when they cease to love (we ought to think at least) they loathe. They look upon us with horror and distaste; they meet us like the ghosts of what we were, and as from such, fly from us.

MRS. MARWOOD   True, 'tis an unhappy circumstance of life that love should ever die before us; and that the man so often should outlive the lover. But say what you will, 'tis better to be left than never to have been loved. To pass over youth in dull indifference, to refuse the sweets of life because they once must leave us, is as preposterous as to wish to have been born old, because we one day must be old. For my part, my youth may wear and waste, but it shall never rust in my possession.

MRS. FAINALL   Then it seems you dissemble an aversion to mankind only in compliance to my mother's humor.

MRS. MARWOOD   Certainly. To be free,[4] I have no taste of those insipid dry discourses with which our sex of force must entertain themselves apart from men. We may affect endearments to each other, profess eternal friendships, and seem to dote like lovers; but 'tis not in our natures long to persevere. Love will resume his empire in our breasts, and every heart, or soon or late, receive and readmit him as its lawful tyrant.

MRS. FAINALL   Bless me, how have I been deceived! Why, you profess[5] a libertine.

MRS. MARWOOD   You see my friendship by my freedom. Come, be as sincere, acknowledge that your sentiments agree with mine.

MRS. FAINALL   Never.

MRS. MARWOOD   You hate mankind?

MRS. FAINALL   Heartily, inveterately.

MRS. MARWOOD   Your husband?

MRS. FAINALL   Most transcendently; aye, though I say it, meritoriously.

MRS. MARWOOD   Give me your hand upon it.

MRS. FAINALL   There.

MRS. MARWOOD   I join with you. What I have said has been to try you.

MRS. FAINALL   Is it possible? Dost thou hate those vipers men?

MRS. MARWOOD   I have done hating 'em, and am now come to despise 'em; the next thing I have to do is eternally to forget 'em.

MRS. FAINALL   There spoke the spirit of an Amazon, a Penthesilea.[6]

4. To speak freely.
5. Talk like.

6. Queen of the Amazons (a legendary nation of women warriors).

MRS. MARWOOD   And yet I am thinking sometimes to carry my aversion further.

MRS. FAINALL   How?

MRS. MARWOOD   Faith, by marrying. If I could but find one that loved me very well, and would be thoroughly sensible of ill usage, I think I should do myself the violence of undergoing the ceremony.

MRS. FAINALL   You would not make him a cuckold?

MRS. MARWOOD   No; but I'd make him believe I did, and that's as bad.

MRS. FAINALL   Why had not you as good do it?

MRS. MARWOOD   O, if he should ever discover it, he would then know the worst, and be out of his pain; but I would have him ever to continue upon the rack of fear and jealousy.

MRS. FAINALL   Ingenious mischief! Would thou wert married to Mirabell.

MRS. MARWOOD   Would I were.

MRS. FAINALL   You change color.

MRS. MARWOOD   Because I hate him.

MRS. FAINALL   So do I; but I can hear him named. But what reason have you to hate him in particular?

MRS. MARWOOD   I never loved him; he is and always was insufferably proud.

MRS. FAINALL   By the reason you give for your aversion, one would think it dissembled; for you have laid a fault to his charge of which his enemies must acquit him.

MRS. MARWOOD   O then it seems you are one of his favorable enemies. Methinks you look a little pale, and now you flush again.

MRS. FAINALL   Do I? I think I am a little sick o' the sudden.

MRS. MARWOOD   What ails you?

MRS. FAINALL   My husband. Don't you see him? He turned short upon me unawares, and has almost overcome me.

[Enter FAINALL and MIRABELL.]

MRS. MARWOOD   Ha, ha, ha; he comes opportunely for you.

MRS. FAINALL   For you, for he has brought Mirabell with him.

FAINALL   My dear.

MRS. FAINALL   My soul.

FAINALL   You don't look well today, child.

MRS. FAINALL   D'ye think so?

MIRABELL   He is the only man that does, madam.

MRS. FAINALL   The only man that would tell me so at least; and the only man from whom I could hear it without mortification.

FAINALL   O my dear, I am satisfied of your tenderness; I know you cannot resent anything from me, especially what is an effect of my concern.

MRS. FAINALL   Mr. Mirabell, my mother interrupted you in a pleasant relation last night. I would fain hear it out.

MIRABELL   The persons concerned in that affair have yet a tolerable reputation.—I am afraid Mr. Fainall will be censorious.

MRS. FAINALL   He has a humor more prevailing than his curiosity, and will willingly dispense with the hearing of one scandalous story to avoid giving an occasion to make another by being seen to walk with his wife. This way, Mr. Mirabell, and I dare promise you will oblige us both.

[Exeunt MIRABELL and MRS. FAINALL.]

FAINALL Excellent creature! Well, sure if I should live to be rid of my wife, I should be a miserable man.

MRS. MARWOOD Aye!

FAINALL For having only that one hope, the accomplishment of it of consequence must put an end to all my hopes; and what a wretch is he who must survive his hopes! Nothing remains when that day comes but to sit down and weep like Alexander, when he wanted other worlds to conquer.

MRS. MARWOOD Will you not follow 'em?

FAINALL Faith, I think not.

MRS. MARWOOD Pray let us; I have a reason.

FAINALL You are not jealous?

MRS. MARWOOD Of whom?

FAINALL Of Mirabell.

MRS. MARWOOD If I am, is it inconsistent with my love to you that I am tender of your honor?

FAINALL You would intimate then, as if there were a fellow-feeling between my wife and him.

MRS. MARWOOD I think she does not hate him to that degree she would be thought.

FAINALL But he, I fear, is too insensible.[7]

MRS. MARWOOD It may be you are deceived.

FAINALL It may be so. I do now begin to apprehend it.

MRS. MARWOOD What?

FAINALL That I have been deceived, Madam, and you are false.

MRS. MARWOOD That I am false! What mean you?

FAINALL To let you know I see through all your little arts.—Come, you both love him; and both have equally dissembled your aversion. Your mutual jealousies of one another have made you clash till you have both struck fire. I have seen the warm confession reddening on your cheeks, and sparkling from your eyes.

MRS. MARWOOD You do me wrong.

FAINALL I do not.—'Twas for my ease to oversee[8] and willfully neglect the gross advances made him by my wife; that by permitting her to be engaged I might continue unsuspected in my pleasures; and take you oftener to my arms in full security. But could you think, because the nodding husband would not wake, that e'er the watchful lover slept?

MRS. MARWOOD And wherewithal can you reproach me?

FAINALL With infidelity, with loving another, with love of Mirabell.

MRS. MARWOOD 'Tis false. I challenge you to show an instance that can confirm your groundless accusation. I hate him.

FAINALL And wherefore do you hate him? He is insensible, and your resentment follows his neglect. An instance! The injuries you have done him are a proof: your interposing in his love. What cause had you to make discoveries of his pretended passion? To undeceive the credulous aunt, and be the officious obstacle of his match with Millamant?

7. Indifferent.　　　　8. Overlook.

MRS. MARWOOD   My obligations to my lady[9] urged me. I had professed a friendship to her, and could not see her easy nature so abused by that dissembler.

FAINALL   What, was it conscience then? Professed a friendship! O the pious friendships of the female sex!

MRS. MARWOOD   More tender, more sincere, and more enduring than all the vain and empty vows of men, whether professing love to us, or mutual faith to one another.

FAINALL   Ha, ha, ha; you are my wife's friend too.

MRS. MARWOOD   Shame and ingratitude! Do you reproach me? You, you upbraid me! Have I been false to her, through strict fidelity to you, and sacrificed my friendship to keep my love inviolate? And have you the baseness to charge me with the guilt, unmindful of the merit! To you it should be meritorious that I have been vicious: and do you reflect that guilt upon me, which should lie buried in your bosom?

FAINALL   You misinterpret my reproof. I meant but to remind you of the slight account you once could make of strictest ties, when set in competition with your love to me.

MRS. MARWOOD   'Tis false, you urged it with deliberate malice.—'Twas spoke in scorn, and I never will forgive it.

FAINALL   Your guilt, not your resentment, begets your rage. If yet you loved, you could forgive a jealousy, but you are stung to find you are discovered.

MRS. MARWOOD   It shall be all discovered. You too shall be discovered; be sure you shall. I can but be exposed.—If I do it myself, I shall prevent[1] your baseness.

FAINALL   Why, what will you do?

MRS. MARWOOD   Disclose it to your wife; own what has passed between us.

FAINALL   Frenzy!

MRS. MARWOOD   By all my wrongs I'll do't—I'll publish to the world the injuries you have done me, both in my fame and fortune: with both I trusted you, you bankrupt in honor, as indigent of wealth.

FAINALL   Your fame[2] I have preserved. Your fortune has been bestowed as the prodigality of your love would have it, in pleasures which we both have shared. Yet, had not you been false, I had e'er this repaid it.—'Tis true—had you permitted Mirabell with Millamant to have stolen their marriage, my lady had been incensed beyond all means of reconcilement: Millamant had forfeited the moiety[3] of her fortune, which then would have descended to my wife—and wherefore did I marry, but to make lawful prize of a rich widow's wealth, and squander it on love and you?

MRS. MARWOOD   Deceit and frivolous pretense.

FAINALL   Death, am I not married? What's pretense? Am I not imprisoned, fettered? Have I not a wife? Nay, a wife that was a widow, a young widow, a handsome widow; and would be again a widow, but that I have a heart of proof,[4] and something of a constitution to bustle through the ways of wedlock and this world. Will you yet be reconciled to truth and me?

---

9. Lady Wishfort.
1. Anticipate.
2. Good name.

3. Half.
4. I.e., a proved or tempered heart.

MRS. MARWOOD Impossible. Truth and you are inconsistent—I hate you, and shall forever.

FAINALL For loving you?

MRS. MARWOOD I loathe the name of love after such usage; and next to the guilt with which you would asperse me, I scorn you most. Farewell.

FAINALL Nay, we must not part thus.

MRS. MARWOOD Let me go.

FAINALL Come, I'm sorry.

MRS. MARWOOD I care not.—Let me go.—Break my hands, do—I'd leave 'em to get loose.

FAINALL I would not hurt you for the world. Have I no other hold to keep you here?

MRS. MARWOOD Well, I have deserved it all.

FAINALL You know I love you.

MRS. MARWOOD Poor dissembling!—O that—Well, it is not yet—

FAINALL What? What is it not? What is it not yet? It is not yet too late—

MRS. MARWOOD No, it is not yet too late—I have that comfort.

FAINALL It is, to love another.

MRS. MARWOOD But not to loathe, detest, abhor mankind, myself, and the whole treacherous world.

FAINALL Nay, this is extravagance.—Come, I ask your pardon.—No tears.—I was to blame. I could not love you and be easy in my doubts.—Pray forbear.—I believe you; I'm convinced I've done you wrong; and any way, every way will make amends.—I'll hate my wife yet more, damn her, I'll part with her, rob her of all she's worth, and we'll retire somewhere, anywhere, to another world. I'll marry thee.—Be pacified.—'Sdeath, they come, hide your face, your tears.—You have a mask,[5] wear it a moment. This way, this way, be persuaded. [*Exeunt* FAINALL *and* MRS. MARWOOD.]

    [*Enter* MIRABELL *and* MRS. FAINALL.]

MRS. FAINALL They are here yet.

MIRABELL They are turning into the other walk.

MRS. FAINALL While I only hated my husband, I could bear to see him, but since I have despised him, he's too offensive.

MIRABELL O, you should hate with prudence.

MRS. FAINALL Yes, for I have loved with indiscretion.

MIRABELL You should have just so much disgust for your husband as may be sufficient to make you relish your lover.

MRS. FAINALL You have been the cause that I have loved without bounds, and would you set limits to that aversion, of which you have been the occasion? Why did you make me marry this man?

MIRABELL Why do we daily commit disagreeable and dangerous actions? To save that idol, reputation. If the familiarities of our loves had produced that consequence, of which you were apprehensive, where could you have fixed a father's name with credit, but on a husband? I knew Fainall to be a man lavish of his morals, an interested and professing friend, a false and a designing lover; yet one whose wit and outward fair

5. Often worn in public places by fashionable women of the time to preserve their complexions; they were also useful to disguise a woman and so to protect her reputation when she was carrying on an illicit affair.

behavior have gained a reputation with the town, enough to make that woman stand excused who has suffered herself to be won by his addresses. A better man ought not to have been sacrificed to the occasion; a worse had not answered to the purpose. When you are weary of him, you know your remedy.

MRS. FAINALL I ought to stand in some degree of credit with you, Mirabell.

MIRABELL In justice to you, I have made you privy to my whole design, and put it in your power to ruin or advance my fortune.

MRS. FAINALL Whom have you instructed to represent your pretended uncle?

MIRABELL Waitwell, my servant.

MRS. FAINALL He is an humble servant to Foible,[6] my mother's woman, and may win her to your interest.

MIRABELL Care is taken for that.—She is won and worn by this time. They were married this morning.

MRS. FAINALL Who?

MIRABELL Waitwell and Foible. I would not tempt my servant to betray me by trusting him too far. If your mother, in hopes to ruin me, should consent to marry my pretended uncle, he might, like Mosca in *The Fox,* stand upon terms;[7] so I made him sure beforehand.

MRS. FAINALL So, if my poor mother is caught in a contract, you will discover the imposture betimes; and release her by producing a certificate of her gallant's former marriage.

MIRABELL Yes, upon condition that she consent to my marriage with her niece, and surrender the moiety of her fortune in her possession.

MRS. FAINALL She talked last night of endeavoring at a match between Millamant and your uncle.

MIRABELL That was by Foible's direction, and my instruction, that she might seem to carry it more privately.

MRS. FAINALL Well, I have an opinion of your success, for I believe my lady will do anything to get an husband; and when she has this, which you have provided for her, I suppose she will submit to anything to get rid of him.

MIRABELL Yes, I think the good lady would marry anything that resembled a man, though 'twere no more than what a butler could pinch out of a napkin.

MRS. FAINALL Female frailty! We must all come to it, if we live to be old, and feel the craving of a false appetite when the true is decayed.

MIRABELL An old woman's appetite is depraved like that of a girl—'tis the greensickness[8] of a second childhood; and like the faint offer of a latter spring, serves but to usher in the fall and withers in an affected bloom.

MRS. FAINALL Here's your mistress.

[*Enter* MRS. MILLAMANT, WITWOUD, *and* MINCING.]

---

6. He is Foible's lover.
7. To insist on conditions; here, to blackmail. "Mosca": the scheming parasite in Ben Jonson's *Volpone,* who in the end tries to blackmail

Volpone.
8. The anemia that sometimes affects girls at puberty.

MIRABELL Here she comes, i'faith, full sail, with her fan spread and streamers out, and a shoal of fools for tenders.—Ha, no, I cry her mercy.

MRS. FAINALL I see but one poor empty sculler, and he tows her woman after him.

MIRABELL You seem to be unattended, madam.—You used to have the *beau monde* throng after you; and a flock of gay fine perukes[9] hovering round you.

WITWOUD Like moths about a candle—I had like to have lost my comparison for want of breath.

MILLAMANT O, I have denied myself airs today. I have walked as fast through the crowd—

WITWOUD As a favorite just disgraced; and with as few followers.

MILLAMANT Dear Mr. Witwoud, truce with your similitudes: For I am as sick of 'em—

WITWOUD As a physician of a good air—I cannot help it, madam, though 'tis against myself.

MILLAMANT Yet again! Mincing, stand between me and his wit.

WITWOUD Do, Mrs. Mincing, like a screen before a great fire. I confess I do blaze today, I am too bright.

MRS. FAINALL But dear Millamant, why were you so long?

MILLAMANT Long! Lord, have I not made violent haste? I have asked every living thing I met for you; I have inquired after you, as after a new fashion.

WITWOUD Madam, truce with your similitudes.—No, you met her husband, and did not ask him for her.

MIRABELL By your leave, Witwoud, that were like inquiring after an old fashion, to ask a husband for his wife.

WITWOUD Hum, a hit, a hit, a palpable hit,[1] I confess it.

MRS. FAINALL You were dressed before I came abroad.

MILLAMANT Aye, that's true.—O, but then I had—Mincing, what had I? Why was I so long?

MINCING O mem, your la'ship stayed to peruse a packet of letters.

MILLAMANT O, aye, letters—I had letters—I am persecuted with letters—I hate letters.—Nobody knows how to write letters; and yet one has 'em, one does not know why.—They serve one to pin up one's hair.

WITWOUD Is that the way? Pray, madam, do you pin up your hair with all your letters? I find I must keep copies.

MILLAMANT Only with those in verse, Mr. Witwoud. I never pin up my hair with prose. I think I tried once, Mincing.

MINCING O mem, I shall never forget it.

MILLAMANT Aye, poor Mincing tiffed[2] and tiffed all the morning.

MINCING Till I had the cramp in my fingers, I'll vow, mem. And all to no purpose. But when your la'ship pins it up with poetry, it sits so pleasant the next day as anything, and is so pure and so crips.[3]

WITWOUD Indeed, so crips?

MINCING You're such a critic, Mr. Witwoud.

---

9. Periwigs, worn by fashionable men (cf. Pope's *Rape of the Lock* 1.101). "*Beau monde*": fashionable world (French).
1. An allusion to the dueling scene in *Hamlet*

5.2.
2. Dressed the hair.
3. A dialectal form of "crisp," curly.

MILLAMANT   Mirabell, did not you take exceptions last night? O, aye, and went away.—Now I think on't I'm angry.—No, now I think on't I'm pleased—for I believe I gave you some pain.

MIRABELL   Does that please you?

MILLAMANT   Infinitely; I love to give pain.

MIRABELL   You would affect a cruelty which is not in your nature; your true vanity is in the power of pleasing.

MILLAMANT   O, I ask your pardon for that—one's cruelty is one's power, and when one parts with one's cruelty, one parts with one's power; and when one has parted with that, I fancy one's old and ugly.

MIRABELL   Aye, aye, suffer your cruelty to ruin the object of your power, to destroy your lover.—And then how vain, how lost a thing you'll be! Nay, 'tis true: you are no longer handsome when you've lost your lover; your beauty dies upon the instant: for beauty is the lover's gift; 'tis he bestows your charms—your glass is all a cheat. The ugly and the old, whom the looking glass mortifies, yet after commendation can be flattered by it, and discover beauties in it: for that reflects our praises, rather than your face.

MILLAMANT   O, the vanity of these men! Fainall, d'ye hear him? If they did not commend us, we were not handsome! Now you must know they could not commend one, if one was not handsome. Beauty the lover's gift?—Lord, what is a lover, that it can give? Why, one makes lovers as fast as one pleases, and they live as long as one pleases, and they die as soon as one pleases: and then if one pleases one makes more.

WITWOUD   Very pretty. Why, you make no more of making of lovers, madam, than of making so many card-matches.[4]

MILLAMANT   One no more owes one's beauty to a lover than one's wit to an echo.—They can but reflect what we look and say; vain empty things if we are silent or unseen, and want a being.

MIRABELL   Yet, to those two vain empty things, you owe two of the greatest pleasures of your life.

MILLAMANT   How so?

MIRABELL   To your lover you owe the pleasure of hearing yourselves praised; and to an echo the pleasure of hearing yourselves talk.

WITWOUD   But I know a lady that loves talking so incessantly she won't give an echo fair play; she has that everlasting rotation of tongue, that an echo must wait till she dies before it can catch her last words.

MILLAMANT   O, fiction; Fainall, let us leave these men.

MIRABELL   [Aside to MRS. FAINALL.]   Draw off Witwoud.

MRS. FAINALL   Immediately; I have a word or two for Mr. Witwoud.

        [Exeunt WITWOUD and MRS. FAINALL.]

MIRABELL   I would beg a little private audience too.—You had the tyranny to deny me last night, though you knew I came to impart a secret to you that concerned my love.

MILLAMANT   You saw I was engaged.

MIRABELL   Unkind. You had the leisure to entertain a herd of fools, things who visit you from their excessive idleness, bestowing on your easiness that time, which is the encumbrance of their lives. How can

---

4. Matches made by dipping pieces of card in melted sulfur.

you find delight in such society? It is impossible they should admire you, they are not capable: or if they were, it should be to you as a mortification; for sure to please a fool is some degree of folly.

MILLAMANT   I please myself—besides, sometimes to converse with fools is for my health.

MIRABELL   Your health! Is there a worse disease than the conversation of fools?

MILLAMANT   Yes, the vapors; fools are physic for it, next to asafetida.[5]

MIRABELL   You are not in a course[6] of fools?

MILLAMANT   Mirabell, if you persist in this offensive freedom, you'll displease me. I think I must resolve after all not to have you.—We shan't agree.

MIRABELL   Not in our physic, it may be.

MILLAMANT   And yet our distemper in all likelihood will be the same, for we shall be sick of one another. I shan't endure to be reprimanded nor instructed; 'tis so dull to act always by advice, and so tedious to be told of one's faults.—I can't bear it. Well, I won't have you, Mirabell—I'm resolved—I think—you may go—ha, ha, ha. What would you give that you could help loving me?

MIRABELL   I would give something that you did not know I could not help it.

MILLAMANT   Come, don't look grave then. Well, what do you say to me?

MIRABELL   I say that a man may as soon make a friend by his wit, or a fortune by his honesty, as win a woman with plain-dealing and sincerity.

MILLAMANT   Sententious Mirabell! prithee don't look with that violent and inflexible wise face, like Solomon at the dividing of the child in an old tapestry hanging.[7]

MIRABELL   You are merry, madam, but I would persuade you for a moment to be serious.

MILLAMANT   What, with that face? No, if you keep your countenance, 'tis impossible I should hold mine. Well, after all, there is something very moving in a lovesick face. Ha, ha, ha.—Well I won't laugh, don't be peevish—heigho! Now I'll be melancholy, as melancholy as a watchlight.[8] Well, Mirabell, if ever you will win me, woo me now. Nay, if you are so tedious, fare you well; I see they are walking away.

MIRABELL   Can you not find in the variety of your disposition one moment—

MILLAMANT   To hear you tell me Foible's married and your plot like to speed.—No.

MIRABELL   But how you came to know it—

MILLAMANT   Without the help of the devil, you can't imagine; unless she should tell me herself. Which of the two it may have been, I will leave you to consider; and when you have done thinking of that, think of me.
    [*Exeunt* MILLAMANT *and* MINCING.]

MIRABELL   I have something more.—Gone!—Think of you! To think of a whirlwind, though 'twere in a whirlwind, were a case of more steady contemplation, a very tranquility of mind and mansion. A fellow that

5. An evil-smelling resin used for medicinal purposes.
6. Plan of medical treatment.

7. The Judgment of Solomon (1 Kings 3.16–27) was a favorite subject in painting and tapestry.
8. Nightlight.

lives in a windmill has not a more whimsical dwelling than the heart of a man that is lodged in a woman. There is no point of the compass to which they cannot turn, and by which they are not turned; and by one as well as another, for motion, not method, is their occupation. To know this, and yet continue to be in love, is to be made wise from the dictates of reason, and yet persevere to play the fool by the force of instinct. O, here come my pair of turtles[9]—what, billing so sweetly! Is not Valentine's Day over with you yet?

[*Enter* WAITWELL *and* FOIBLE.]

MIRABELL Sirrah[1] Waitwell, why sure you think you were married for your own recreation and not for my conveniency.

WAITWELL Your pardon, sir. With submission, we have indeed been solacing in lawful delights, but still with an eye to business, sir. I have instructed her as well as I could. If she can take your directions as readily as my instructions, sir, your affairs are in a prosperous way.

MIRABELL Give you joy, Mrs. Foible.

FOIBLE O-las, sir, I'm so ashamed—I'm afraid my lady has been in a thousand inquietudes for me. But I protest, sir, I made as much haste as I could.

WAITWELL That she did indeed, sir. It was my fault that she did not make more.

MIRABELL That I believe.

FOIBLE But I told my lady as you instructed me, sir. That I had a prospect of seeing Sir Rowland your uncle, and that I would put her ladyship's picture in my pocket to show him; which I'll be sure to say has made him so enamored of her beauty that he burns with impatience to lie at her ladyship's feet and worship the original.

MIRABELL Excellent, Foible! Matrimony has made you eloquent in love.

WAITWELL I think she has profited, sir. I think so.

FOIBLE You have seen Madam Millamant, sir?

MIRABELL Yes.

FOIBLE I told her, sir, because I did not know that you might find an opportunity; she had so much company last night.

MIRABELL Your diligence will merit more—in the meantime—

[*Gives money.*]

FOIBLE O dear sir, your humble servant.

WAITWELL Spouse.

MIRABELL Stand off, sir, not a penny. Go on and prosper, Foible. The lease shall be made good and the farm stocked if we succeed.[2]

FOIBLE I don't question your generosity, sir. And you need not doubt of success. If you have no more commands, sir, I'll be gone; I'm sure my lady is at her toilet,[3] and can't dress till I come. O dear, I'm sure that [*Looking out.*] was Mrs. Marwood that went by in a mask; if she has seen me with you I'm sure she'll tell my lady. I'll make haste home and prevent her.[4] Your servant, sir. B'w'y,[5] Waitwell. [*Exit* FOIBLE.]

9. I.e., turtledoves, remarkable for their affectionate billing and cooing. Birds were popularly supposed to choose their mates on St. Valentine's Day.
1. Form of address to an inferior.
2. Mirabell has promised to lease a farm for the couple for helping him.
3. Vanity, makeup table.
4. Arrive before she does.
5. A shortened form of "God be with you" (our word *good-bye*).

WAITWELL Sir Rowland, if you please. The jade's so pert upon her prefer-ment she forgets herself.

MIRABELL Come, sir, will you endeavor to forget yourself—and trans-form into Sir Rowland.

WAITWELL Why, sir, it will be impossible I should remember myself—married, knighted, and attended[6] all in one day! 'Tis enough to make any man forget himself. The difficulty will be how to recover my acquain-tance and familiarity with my former self; and fall from my transforma-tion to a reformation into Waitwell. Nay, I shan't be quite the same Waitwell neither—for now I remember me, I'm married and can't be my own man again.

Aye, there's my grief; that's the sad change of life;
To lose my title, and yet keep my wife.

Act 3—A room in LADY WISHFORT's house

LADY WISHFORT at her toilet, PEG waiting.

LADY WISHFORT Merciful, no news of Foible yet?

PEG No, madam.

LADY WISHFORT I have no more patience. If I have not fretted myself till I am pale again, there's no veracity in me. Fetch me the red—the red, do you hear, sweetheart? An errant ash color, as I'm a person. Look you how this wench stirs! Why dost thou not fetch me a little red? Didst thou not hear me, mopus?[7]

PEG The red ratafia does your ladyship mean, or the cherry brandy?

LADY WISHFORT Ratafia, fool. No, fool. Not the ratafia, fool. Grant me patience! I mean the Spanish paper,[8] idiot—complexion, darling. Paint, paint, paint, dost thou understand that, changeling, dangling thy hands like bobbins before thee? Why dost thou not stir, puppet? Thou wooden thing upon wires.

PEG Lord, madam, your ladyship is so impatient.—I cannot come at the paint, madam. Mrs. Foible has locked it up and carried the key with her.

LADY WISHFORT A pox take you both!—Fetch me the cherry brandy then. [Exit PEG.] I'm as pale and as faint, I look like Mrs. Qualmsick, the curate's wife, that's always breeding. Wench, come, come, wench, what art thou doing? Sipping? Tasting? Save thee, dost thou not know the bottle?
[Re-enter PEG with a bottle and china cup.]

PEG Madam, I was looking for a cup.

LADY WISHFORT A cup, save thee, and what a cup hast thou brought! Dost thou take me for a fairy, to drink out of an acorn? Why didst thou not bring thy thimble? Hast thou ne'er a brass thimble clinking in thy pocket with a bit of nutmeg? I warrant thee. Come, fill, fill.—So—again. See who that is.—[A knock is heard.]—Set down the bottle first. Here, here, under the table.—What, wouldst thou go with the bottle in thy hand like a tapster?[9] As I'm a person, this wench has lived in an inn upon

6. By servants.
7. Dull, stupid person.
8. Rouge.
9. Bartender.

the road before she came to me, like Maritornes the Asturian[1] in *Don Quixote*. No Foible yet?

PEG   No, madam, Mrs. Marwood.

LADY WISHFORT   O Marwood, let her come in. Come in, good Marwood.
   [*Enter* MRS. MARWOOD.]

MRS. MARWOOD   I'm surprised to find your ladyship in *deshabillé*[2] at this time of day.

LADY WISHFORT   Foible's a lost thing; has been abroad since morning, and never heard of since.

MRS. MARWOOD   I saw her but now, as I came masked through the park, in conference with Mirabell.

LADY WISHFORT   With Mirabell! you call my blood into my face, with mentioning that traitor. She durst not have the confidence. I sent her to negotiate an affair, in which if I'm detected I'm undone. If that wheedling villain has wrought upon Foible to detect me, I'm ruined. O my dear friend, I'm a wretch of wretches if I'm detected.

MRS. MARWOOD   O madam, you cannot suspect Mrs. Foible's integrity.

LADY WISHFORT   O, he carries poison in his tongue that would corrupt integrity itself. If she has given him an opportunity, she has as good as put her integrity into his hands. Ah dear Marwood, what's integrity to an opportunity? Hark! I hear her—dear friend, retire into my closet,[3] that I may examine her with more freedom. You'll pardon me, dear friend, I can make bold with you. There are books over the chimney—Quarles and Prynne, and the *Short View of the Stage*,[4] with Bunyan's works to entertain you. [*Exit* MRS. MARWOOD; *to* PEG.] Go, you thing, and send her in. [*Exit* PEG.]
   [*Enter* FOIBLE.]

LADY WISHFORT   O Foible, where hast thou been? What hast thou been doing?

FOIBLE   Madam, I have seen the party.

LADY WISHFORT   But what hast thou done?

FOIBLE   Nay, 'tis your ladyship has done, and are to do; I have only promised. But a man so enamored—so transported! Well, if worshiping of pictures be a sin—poor Sir Rowland, I say.

LADY WISHFORT   The miniature has been counted like[5]—but hast thou not betrayed me, Foible? Hast thou not detected me to that faithless Mirabell?—What hadst thou to do with him in the park? Answer me, has he got nothing out of thee?

FOIBLE [*Aside.*]   So, the devil has been beforehand with me. What shall I say?—Alas, madam, could I help it if I met that confident thing? Was I in fault? If you had heard how he used me, and all upon your ladyship's account, I'm sure you would not suspect my fidelity. Nay, if that had

---

1. The servant at the inn where Don Quixote and Sancho Panza are taken care of.
2. In her negligee (French).
3. Private room.
4. By Collier (see p. 189, n. 7). Francis Quarles (1592–1644), a religious poet, by 1700 regarded with contempt, but formerly greatly admired, especially among the Puritans. William Prynne

(1600–1669), Puritan pamphleteer, author of *Histriomastix* (1632), a violent attack on the stage. Congreve, who had been the object of much of Collier's vituperation, slyly identifies his enemy with Puritans and Nonconformists, whom Collier, an ardent High Churchman, despised.
5. Considered a good likeness.

been the worst I could have borne; but he had a fling at your ladyship too; and then I could not hold; but i' faith I gave him his own.

LADY WISHFORT   Me? What did the filthy fellow say?

FOIBLE   O madam; 'tis a shame to say what he said—with his taunts and his fleers,[6] tossing up his nose. Humh (says he) what, you are a-hatching some plot (says he) you are so early abroad, or catering (says he), ferreting for some disbanded[7] officer, I warrant—half pay is but thin subsistence (says he).—Well, what pension does your lady propose? Let me see (says he) what, she must come down pretty deep now, she's superannuated (says he) and—

LADY WISHFORT   Ods my life, I'll have him—I'll have him murdered. I'll have him poisoned. Where does he eat? I'll marry a drawer[8] to have him poisoned in his wine. I'll send for Robin from Locket's[9]—immediately.

FOIBLE   Poison him? Poisoning's too good for him. Starve him, madam, starve him; marry Sir Rowland, and get him disinherited. O, you would bless yourself, to hear what he said.

LADY WISHFORT   A villain!—superannuated!

FOIBLE   Humh (says he) I hear you are laying designs against me too (says he) and Mrs. Millamant is to marry my uncle; (he does not suspect a word of your ladyship) but (says he) I'll fit you for that, I warrant you (says he) I'll hamper you for that (says he) you and your old frippery[1] too (says he). I'll handle you—

LADY WISHFORT   Audacious villain! handle me, would he durst—frippery? old frippery! Was there ever such a foul-mouthed fellow? I'll be married tomorrow, I'll be contracted tonight.

FOIBLE   The sooner the better, madam.

LADY WISHFORT   Will Sir Rowland be here, say'st thou? When, Foible?

FOIBLE   Incontinently, madam. No new sheriff's wife expects the return of her husband after knighthood, with that impatience in which Sir Rowland burns for the dear hour of kissing your ladyship's hand after dinner.

LADY WISHFORT   Frippery! Superannuated frippery! I'll frippery the villain, I'll reduce him to frippery and rags. A tatterdemalion—I hope to see him hung with tatters, like a Long Lane penthouse,[2] or a gibbet-thief. A slander-mouthed railer—I warrant the spendthrift prodigal's in debt as much as the million lottery, or the whole court upon a birthday. I'll spoil his credit with his tailor. Yes, he shall have my niece with her fortune, he shall.

FOIBLE   He! I hope to see him lodge in Ludgate first, and angle into Blackfriars for brass farthings with an old mitten.[3]

LADY WISHFORT   Aye, dear Foible; thank thee for that, dear Foible. He has put me out of all patience. I shall never recompose my features to receive

---

6. Jeers.
7. When a regiment was "disbanded," its officers went on half pay, often for life. "Catering": procuring (i.e., pimping for Lady Wishfort).
8. One who draws wine from casks and serves it.
9. A fashionable tavern near Charing Cross.
1. Old, cast-off clothes; an insulting metaphor to apply to Lady Wishfort.

2. A shed, supported by the wall toward which it is inclined. "Tatterdemalion": ragamuffin. Long Lane was a street where old clothes were sold.
3. Prisoners begged by letting down a mitten on a string; passers-by dropped coins into it. Ludgate was a debtor's prison, adjoining the district of Blackfriars in London.

Sir Rowland with any economy of face. This wretch has fretted me that I am absolutely decayed. Look, Foible.

FOIBLE Your ladyship has frowned a little too rashly, indeed, madam. There are some cracks discernible in the white varnish.

LADY WISHFORT Let me see the glass.—Cracks, say'st thou? Why I am arrantly flayed—I look like an old peeled wall. Thou must repair me, Foible, before Sir Rowland comes, or I shall never keep up to my picture.

FOIBLE I warrant you, madam; a little art once made your picture like you and now a little of the same art must make you like your picture. Your picture must sit for you, madam.

LADY WISHFORT But art thou sure Sir Rowland will not fail to come? Or will a' not fail[4] when he does come? Will he be importunate, Foible, and push? For if he should not be importunate—I shall never break decorums.—I shall die with confusion, if I am forced to advance.—Oh, no, I can never advance.—I shall swoon if he should expect advances. No, I hope Sir Rowland is better bred than to put a lady to the necessity of breaking her forms. I won't be too coy neither—I won't give him despair—but a little disdain is not amiss; a little scorn is alluring.

FOIBLE A little scorn becomes your ladyship.

LADY WISHFORT Yes, but tenderness becomes me best.—A sort of dyingness—You see that picture has a sort of a—Ha, Foible? A swimmingness in the eyes—Yes, I'll look so—my niece affects it; but she wants features.[5] Is Sir Rowland handsome? Let my toilet be removed—I'll dress above. I'll receive Sir Rowland here. Is he handsome? Don't answer me. I won't know: I'll be surprised. I'll be taken by surprise.

FOIBLE By storm, madam. Sir Rowland's a brisk man.

LADY WISHFORT Is he! O, then he'll importune, if he's a brisk man, I shall save decorums if Sir Rowland importunes. I have a mortal terror at the apprehension of offending against decorums. O, I'm glad he's a brisk man. Let my things be removed, good Foible. [*Exit* LADY WISHFORT.]
[*Enter* MRS. FAINALL.][6]

MRS. FAINALL O Foible, I have been in a fright, lest I should come too late. That devil Marwood saw you in the park with Mirabell, and I'm afraid will discover it to my lady.

FOIBLE Discover what, madam?

MRS. FAINALL Nay, nay, put not on that strange face. I am privy to the whole design and know Waitwell, to whom thou wert this morning married, is to personate[7] Mirabell's uncle, and as such, winning my lady, to involve her in those difficulties from which Mirabell only must release her, by his making his conditions to have my cousin and her fortune left to her own disposal.

FOIBLE O dear madam, I beg your pardon. It was not my confidence in your ladyship that was deficient, but I thought the former good correspondence between your ladyship and Mr. Mirabell might have hindered his communicating this secret.

MRS. FAINALL Dear Foible, forget that.

---

4. I.e., will *he* not fail?
5. Lacks the looks for it.
6. The subsequent conversation is sometimes

staged to show Mrs. Marwood overhearing it.
7. I.e., impersonate.

FOIBLE   O dear madam, Mr. Mirabell is such a sweet winning gentleman— but your ladyship is the pattern of generosity. Sweet lady, to be so good! Mr. Mirabell cannot choose but to be grateful. I find your ladyship has his heart still. Now, madam, I can safely tell your ladyship our success. Mrs. Marwood had told my lady; but I warrant I managed myself. I turned it all for the better. I told my lady that Mr. Mirabell railed at her. I laid horrid things to his charge, I'll vow; and my lady is so incensed that she'll be contracted to Sir Rowland tonight, she says—I warrant I worked her up, that he may have her for asking for, as they say of a Welsh maidenhead.

MRS. FAINALL   O rare Foible!

FOIBLE   Madam, I beg your ladyship to acquaint Mr. Mirabell of his success. I would be seen as little as possible to speak to him—besides, I believe Madam Marwood watches me. She has a month's mind,[8] but I know Mr. Mirabell can't abide her. [*Calls.*] John, remove my lady's toilet. Madam, your servant. My lady is so impatient, I fear she'll come for me if I stay.

MRS. FAINALL   I'll go with you up the back stairs, lest I should meet her.

[*Exeunt* MRS. FAINALL, FOIBLE.]

[*Enter* MRS. MARWOOD.]

MRS. MARWOOD   Indeed, Mrs. Engine,[9] is it thus with you? Are you become a go-between of this importance? Yes, I shall watch you. Why, this wench is the *passe-partout*, a very master key to everybody's strongbox. My friend Fainall,[1] have you carried it so swimmingly? I thought there was something in it; but it seems it's over with you. Your loathing is not from a want of appetite, then, but from a surfeit. Else you could never be so cool to fall from a principal to be an assistant; to procure for him! A pattern of generosity, that I confess. Well, Mr. Fainall, you have met with your match. O, man, man! Woman, woman! The devil's an ass: If I were a painter, I would draw him like an idiot, a driveler with a bib and bells. Man should have his head and horns, and woman the rest of him. Poor simple fiend! Madam Marwood has a month's mind, but he can't abide her.—'Twere better for him you had not been his confessor in that affair without you could have kept his counsel closer. I shall not prove another pattern of generosity.—He has not obliged me to that with those excesses of himself; and now I'll have none of him. Here comes the good lady, panting ripe, with a heart full of hope and a head full of care, like any chemist upon the day of projection.[2]

[*Enter* LADY WISHFORT.]

LADY WISHFORT   O dear Marwood, what shall I say for this rude forgetfulness—but my dear friend is all goodness.

MRS. MARWOOD   No apologies, dear madam. I have been very well entertained.

LADY WISHFORT   As I'm a person I am in a very chaos to think I should so forget myself—but I have such an olio[3] of affairs really I know not what

---

8. An inclination (toward Mirabell).
9. A person who serves as an instrument or tool of others in an intrigue.
1. Mrs. Fainall.

2. An alchemical term denoting the final step in the transmutation of baser metals into gold.
3. Hodgepodge.

to do—[*Calls.*] Foible—I expect my nephew Sir Wilfull every moment too.—Why, Foible!—He means to travel for improvement.

MRS. MARWOOD Methinks Sir Wilfull should rather think of marrying than traveling at his years. I hear he is turned of forty.

LADY WISHFORT O, he's in less danger of being spoiled by his travels.—I am against my nephew's marrying too young. It will be time enough when he comes back and has acquired discretion to choose for himself.

MRS. MARWOOD Methinks Mrs. Millamant and he would make a very fit match. He may travel afterwards. 'Tis a thing very usual with young gentlemen.

LADY WISHFORT I promise you I have thought on't—and since 'tis your judgment, I'll think on't again. I assure you I will; I value your judgment extremely. On my word I'll propose it.
        [*Enter* FOIBLE.]

LADY WISHFORT Come, come Foible—I had forgot my nephew will be here before dinner.—I must make haste.

FOIBLE Mr. Witwoud and Mr. Petulant are come to dine with your ladyship.

LADY WISHFORT O dear, I can't appear till I am dressed. Dear Marwood, shall I be free with you again and beg you to entertain 'em? I'll make all imaginable haste. Dear friend, excuse me.
        [*Exeunt* LADY WISHFORT *and* FOIBLE.]
        [*Enter* MRS. MILLAMANT *and* MINCING.]

MILLAMANT Sure never anything was so unbred as that odious man.— Marwood, your servant.

MRS. MARWOOD You have a color. What's the matter?

MILLAMANT That horrid fellow Petulant has provoked me into a flame—I have broke my fan.—Mincing, lend me yours; is not all the powder out of my hair?

MRS. MARWOOD No. What has he done?

MILLAMANT Nay, he has done nothing; he has only talked.—Nay, he has said nothing neither; but he has contradicted everything that has been said. For my part, I thought Witwoud and he would have quarreled.

MINCING I vow, mem, I thought once they would have fit.[4]

MILLAMANT Well, 'tis a lamentable thing, I swear, that one has not the liberty of choosing one's acquaintance as one does one's clothes.

MRS. MARWOOD If we had that liberty, we should be as weary of one set of acquaintance, though never so good, as we are of one suit, though never so fine. A fool and a doily stuff[5] would now and then find days of grace, and be worn for variety.

MILLAMANT I could consent to wear 'em, if they would wear alike; but fools never wear out—they are such drap-de-Berry[6] things! Without one could give 'em to one's chambermaid after a day or two.

MRS. MARWOOD 'Twere better so indeed. Or what think you of the play house?[7] A fine gay glossy fool should be given there, like a new masking habit after the masquerade is over, and we have done with the disguise.

---

4. Fought. Millamant turns Mincing's word to refer to clothing in her next remark.
5. A woolen cloth.
6. Coarse woolen cloth, made in the Berry dis-

trict of France.
7. Fine gentlemen and ladies sometimes donated their old clothes to the playhouses.

For a fool's visit is always a disguise, and never admitted by a woman of wit, but to blind her affair with a lover of sense. If you would but appear barefaced now and own Mirabell, you might as easily put off Petulant and Witwoud as your hood and scarf. And indeed 'tis time, for the town has found it: the secret is grown too big for the pretense: 'tis like Mrs. Primly's great belly; she may lace it down before, but it burnishes[8] on her hips. Indeed, Millamant, you can no more conceal it than my Lady Strammel can her face, that goodly face, which in defiance of her Rhenish-wine tea will not be comprehended in a mask.[9]

MILLAMANT   I'll take my death, Marwood, you are more censorious than a decayed beauty, or a discarded toast.[1] Mincing, tell the men they may come up. My aunt is not dressing here; their folly is less provoking than your malice. [*Exit* MINCING.] "The town has found it." What has it found? That Mirabell loves me is no more a secret than it is a secret that you discovered it to my aunt, or than the reason why you discovered it is a secret.

MRS. MARWOOD   You are nettled.

MILLAMANT   You're mistaken. Ridiculous!

MRS. MARWOOD   Indeed, my dear, you'll tear another fan if you don't mitigate those violent airs.

MILLAMANT   O silly! Ha, ha, ha. I could laugh immoderately. Poor Mirabell! His constancy to me has quite destroyed his complaisance for all the world beside. I swear, I never enjoined it him, to be so coy.—If I had the vanity to think he would obey me, I would command him to show more gallantry.—'Tis hardly well bred to be so particular on one hand and so insensible on the other. But I despair to prevail, and so let him follow his own way. Ha, ha, ha. Pardon me, dear creature, I must laugh, ha, ha, ha; though I grant you 'tis a little barbarous, ha, ha, ha.

MRS. MARWOOD   What pity 'tis, so much fine raillery, and delivered with so significant gesture, should be so unhappily directed to miscarry.

MILLAMANT   Ha? Dear creature, I ask your pardon—I swear I did not mind you.

MRS. MARWOOD   Mr. Mirabell and you both may think it a thing impossible, when I shall tell him by telling you—

MILLAMANT   O dear, what? For it is the same thing, if I hear it—Ha, ha, ha.

MRS. MARWOOD   That I detest him, hate him, madam.

MILLAMANT   O madam, why so do I—and yet the creature loves me, ha, ha, ha. How can one forbear laughing to think of it?—I am a sibyl[2] if I am not amazed to think what he can see in me. I'll take my death, I think you are handsomer—and within a year or two as young. If you could but stay for me, I should overtake you.—But that cannot be.—Well, that thought makes me melancholy.—Now I'll be sad.

MRS. MARWOOD   Your merry note may be changed sooner than you think.

---

8. Spreads out.
9. Lady Strammel (the name means "a lean, ill-favored person") tries to lose weight by drinking Rhenish wine, but still her face is too large to be

contained ("comprehended") in a mask.
1. A lady to whom toasts are no longer drunk.
2. A prophetess.

MILLAMANT   D'ye say so? Then I'm resolved I'll have a song to keep up my
spirits.
       [*Enter* MINCING.]
MINCING   The gentlemen stay but to comb,[3] madam, and will wait on you.
MILLAMANT   Desire Mrs. ——[4] that is in the next room to sing the song I
would have learnt yesterday. You shall hear it, madam—not that there's
any great matter in it—But 'tis agreeable to my humor.

[*Song. Set by Mr. John Eccles*]

I

Love's but the frailty of the mind,
    When 'tis not with ambition joined;
A sickly flame, which if not fed expires;
And feeding, wastes in self-consuming fires.

2

'Tis not to wound a wanton boy
    Or amorous youth, that gives the joy;
But 'tis the glory to have pierced a swain,
For whom inferior beauties sighed in vain.

3

Then I alone the conquest prize,
    When I insult a rival's eyes:
If there's delight in love, 'tis when I see
That heart which others bleed for, bleed for me.

       [*Enter* PETULANT, WITWOUD.]
MILLAMANT   Is your animosity composed, gentlemen?
WITWOUD   Raillery, raillery, madam, we have no animosity. We hit off a
little wit now and then, but no animosity. The falling out of wits is like
the falling out of lovers—we agree in the main, like treble and bass. Ha,
Petulant!
PETULANT   Aye, in the main. But when I have a humor to contradict—
WITWOUD   Aye, when he has a humor to contradict, then I contradict too.
What, I know my cue. Then we contradict one another like two bat-
tledores,[5] for contradictions beget one another like Jews.
PETULANT   If he says black's black—if I have a humor to say 'tis blue—let
that pass.—All's one for that. If I have a humor to prove it, it must be
granted.
WITWOUD   Not positively must—but it may—it may.
PETULANT   Yes, it positively must, upon proof positive.
WITWOUD   Aye, upon proof positive it must; but upon proof presumptive
it only may. That's a logical distinction now, madam.

3. I.e., to comb their periwigs.
4. The name of the singer was to be inserted.
The music was by John Eccles (d. 1735), a popular composer for the theater.

5. Rackets used to strike the shuttlecock, or
bird, in the old game from which badminton is
descended.

MRS. MARWOOD   I perceive your debates are of importance and very learn-edly handled.

PETULANT   Importance is one thing, and learning's another; but a debate's a debate, that I assert.

WITWOUD   Petulant's an enemy to learning; he relies altogether on his parts.[6]

PETULANT   No, I'm no enemy to learning; it hurts not me.

MRS. MARWOOD   That's a sign indeed it's no enemy to you.

PETULANT   No, no, it's no enemy to anybody but them that have it.

MILLAMANT   Well, an illiterate man's my aversion. I wonder at the impu-dence of any illiterate man, to offer to make love.

WITWOUD   That I confess I wonder at too.

MILLAMANT   Ah! to marry an ignorant! that can hardly read or write.

PETULANT   Why should a man be any further from being married though he can't read than he is from being hanged. The ordinary's[7] paid for setting the Psalm, and the parish priest for reading the ceremony. And for the rest which is to follow in both cases, a man may do it without book.—So all's one for that.

MILLAMANT   D'ye hear the creature? Lord, here's company, I'll be gone.
        [Exeunt MILLAMANT and MINCING.]

WITWOUD   In the name of Bartlemew and his Fair, what have we here?[8]

MRS. MARWOOD   'Tis your brother, I fancy. Don't you know him?

WITWOUD   Not I.—Yes, I think it is he—I've almost forgot him; I have not seen him since the Revolution.[9]
        [Enter SIR WILFULL WITWOUD in riding clothes, and a FOOTMAN to LADY WISHFORT.]

FOOTMAN   Sir, my lady's dressing. Here's company; if you please to walk in, in the meantime.

SIR WILFULL   Dressing! What, it's but morning here, I warrant, with you in London; we should count it towards afternoon in our parts, down in Shropshire. Why, then belike my aunt han't dined yet—ha, friend?

FOOTMAN   Your aunt, Sir?

SIR WILFULL   My aunt, sir, yes, my aunt, sir, and your lady, sir; your lady is my aunt, sir.—Why, what do'st thou not know me, friend? Why, then send somebody hither that does. How long hast thou lived with thy lady, fellow, ha?

FOOTMAN   A week, sir; longer than anybody in the house, except my lady's woman.

SIR WILFULL   Why, then belike thou dost not know thy lady, if thou see'st her, ha, friend?

FOOTMAN   Why truly, sir, I cannot safely swear to her face in a morning, before she is dressed. 'Tis like I may give a shrewd guess at her by this time.

SIR WILFULL   Well, prithee try what thou canst do; if thou canst not guess, inquire her out, do'st hear, fellow? And tell her her nephew, Sir Wilfull Witwoud, is in the house.

FOOTMAN   I shall, sir.

SIR WILFULL   Hold ye, hear me, friend; a word with you in your ear. Prithee who are these gallants?

FOOTMAN   Really, sir, I can't tell; there come so many here, 'tis hard to know 'em all. [*Exit* FOOTMAN.]

SIR WILFULL   Oons,[1] this fellow knows less than a starling; I don't think a'knows his own name.

MRS. MARWOOD   Mr. Witwoud, your brother is not behind hand in forgetfulness—I fancy he has forgot you too.

WITWOUD   I hope so.—The devil take him that remembers first, I say.

SIR WILFULL   Save you, gentlemen and lady.

MRS. MARWOOD   For shame, Mr. Witwoud; why don't you speak to him?— And you, sir.

WITWOUD   Petulant, speak.

PETULANT   And you, sir.

SIR WILFULL   [*Salutes*[2] MARWOOD.]   No offense, I hope.

MRS. MARWOOD   No sure, sir.

WITWOUD   This is a vile dog, I see that already. No offense! Ha, ha, ha, to him; to him, Petulant, smoke him.[3]

PETULANT   [*Surveying him round.*]   It seems as if you had come a journey, sir. Hem, hem.

SIR WILFULL   Very likely, sir, that it may seem so.

PETULANT   No offense, I hope, sir.

WITWOUD   Smoke the boots, the boots, Petulant, the boots. Ha, ha, ha.

SIR WILFULL   Maybe not, sir; thereafter as 'tis meant, sir.

PETULANT   Sir, I presume upon the information of your boots.

SIR WILFULL   Why, 'tis like you may, sir: If you are not satisfied with the information of my boots, sir, if you will step to the stable, you may inquire further of my horse, sir.

PETULANT   Your horse, sir! Your horse is an ass, sir!

SIR WILFULL   Do you speak by way of offense, sir?

MRS. MARWOOD   The gentleman's merry, that's all, sir.—[*Aside.*] 'Slife,[4] we shall have a quarrel betwixt an horse and an ass, before they find one another out. [*Aloud.*] You must not take anything amiss from your friends, sir. You are among your friends, here, though it may be you don't know it.—If I am not mistaken, you are Sir Wilfull Witwoud.

SIR WILFULL   Right, lady; I am Sir Wilfull Witwoud, so I write myself; no offense to anybody, I hope; and nephew to the Lady Wishfort of this mansion.

MRS. MARWOOD   Don't you know this gentleman, sir?

SIR WILFULL   Hum! What, sure, 'tis not—yea by'r Lady, but 'tis—'sheart,[5] I know not whether 'tis or no.—Yea but 'tis, by the Wrekin.[6] Brother Antony! What, Tony, i'faith! What, do'st thou not know me? By'r Lady, nor I thee, thou art so becravated and so beperriwigged—'sheart, why do'st not speak? Art thou o'erjoyed?

WITWOUD   Odso, brother, is it you? Your servant, brother.

1. An uncouth oath: God's wounds.
2. Kisses.
3. Make fun of him.
4. God's life.
5. God's heart.
6. A solitary mountain peak in Shropshire, near the Welsh border.

SIR WILFULL Your servant! Why, yours, sir. Your servant again—'sheart, and your friend and servant to that—and a—[*Puff.*]—and a flapdragon for your service, sir: and a hare's foot, and a hare's scut[7] for your service, sir; an you be so cold and so courtly!

WITWOUD No offense, I hope, brother.

SIR WILFULL 'Sheart, sir, but there is, and much offense. A pox, is this your Inns o'Court[8] breeding, not to know your friends and your relations, your elders and your betters?

WITWOUD Why, Brother Wilfull of Salop, you may be as short as a Shrewsbury cake,[9] if you please. But I tell you 'tis not modish to know relations in town. You think you're in the country, where great lubberly brothers slabber and kiss one another when they meet, like a call of sergeants.[1]— 'Tis not the fashion here; 'tis not indeed, dear brother.

SIR WILFULL The fashion's a fool; and you're a fop, dear brother. 'Sheart, I've suspected this—by'r Lady, I conjectured you were a fop, since you began to change the style of your letters and write in a scrap of paper gilt round the edges, no bigger than a subpoena. I might expect this when you left off "Honored Brother" and "hoping you are in good health," and so forth—to begin with a "Rat me, knight, I'm so sick of a last night's debauch"—'od's heart, and then tell a familiar tale of a cock and bull, and a whore and a bottle, and so conclude—You could write news before you were out of your time, when you lived with honest Pumple-Nose, the attorney of Furnival's Inn[2]—You could entreat to be remembered then to your friends round the Wrekin. We could have gazettes then, and Dawks's *Letter,* and the Weekly Bill,[3] till of late days.

PETULANT 'Slife, Witwoud, were you ever an attorney's clerk? Of the family of the Furnivals. Ha, ha, ha!

WITWOUD Aye, aye, but that was but for a while. Not long, not long; pshaw, I was not in my own power then. An orphan, and this fellow was my guardian; aye, aye, I was glad to consent to that man to come to London. He had the disposal of me then. If I had not agreed to that, I might have been bound 'prentice to a felt-maker in Shrewsbury; this fellow would have bound me to a maker of felts.

SIR WILFULL 'Sheart, and better than to be bound to a maker of fops; where, I suppose, you have served your time; and now you may set up for yourself.

MRS. MARWOOD You intend to travel, sir, as I'm informed.

SIR WILFULL Belike I may, madam. I may chance to sail upon the salt seas, if my mind hold.

PETULANT And the wind serve.

---

7. Rabbit's tail. "Flapdragon": something worthless.
8. The buildings—Gray's Inn, Lincoln's Inn, the Inner Temple, the Middle Temple—housing the four legal societies that have the sole right to admit persons to the practice of law.
9. Shortcake, in the modern meaning of the term. Witwoud puns, using "short" also in the sense of "abrupt." "Salop": ancient name of Shropshire.
1. Witwoud refers to the mutual greetings and felicitations of a group of barristers ("sergeants") newly admitted to the bar. "Lubberly": loutish.
2. One of the inns of Chancery, attached to Lincoln's Inn. Attorneys were looked down on socially; hence Petulant's ill-natured mirth in his next speech. "Before you were out of your time": before you had served out your apprenticeship.
3. The official list of the deaths occurring in London. "Gazettes": newspapers. "Dawks's *Letter*": a popular source of news in the country.

SIR WILFULL   Serve or not serve, I shan't ask license of you, sir; nor the weather-cock[4] your companion. I direct my discourse to the lady, sir. 'Tis like my aunt may have told you, madam—Yes, I have settled my concerns, I may say now, and am minded to see foreign parts. If an' how that the peace[5] holds, whereby, that is, taxes abate.

MRS. MARWOOD   I thought you had designed for France at all adventures.[6]

SIR WILFULL   I can't tell that; 'tis like I may and 'tis like I may not. I am somewhat dainty in making a resolution, because when I make it I keep it, I don't stand shill I, shall I,[7] then; if I say't, I'll do't. But I have thoughts to tarry a small matter in town, to learn somewhat of your lingo first, before I cross the seas. I'd gladly have a spice of your French as they say, whereby to hold discourse in foreign countries.

MRS. MARWOOD   Here's an academy in town for that use.

SIR WILFULL   There is? 'Tis like there may.

MRS. MARWOOD   No doubt you will return very much improved.

WITWOUD   Yes, refined like a Dutch skipper from a whale-fishing.

[Enter LADY WISHFORT and FAINALL.]

LADY WISHFORT   Nephew, you are welcome.

SIR WILFULL   Aunt, your servant.

FAINALL   Sir Wilfull, your most faithful servant.

SIR WILFULL   Cousin Fainall, give me your hand.

LADY WISHFORT   Cousin Witwoud, your servant; Mr. Petulant, your servant.—Nephew, you are welcome again. Will you drink anything after your journey, nephew, before you eat? Dinner's almost ready.

SIR WILFULL   I'm very well, I thank you, aunt. However, I thank you for your courteous offer. 'Sheart, I was afraid you would have been in the fashion too, and have remembered to have forgot your relations. Here's your cousin Tony, belike, I mayn't call him brother for fear of offense.

LADY WISHFORT   O, he's a rallier, nephew—my cousin's a wit; and your great wits always rally their best friends to choose.[8] When you have been abroad, nephew, you'll understand raillery better.

[FAINALL and MRS. MARWOOD talk apart.]

SIR WILFULL   Why then let him hold his tongue in the meantime, and rail when that day comes.

[Enter MINCING.]

MINCING   Mem, I come to acquaint your la'ship that dinner is impatient.

SIR WILFULL   Impatient? Why then belike it won't stay till I pull off my boots. Sweetheart, can you help me to a pair of slippers?—My man's with his horses, I warrant.

LADY WISHFORT   Fie, fie, nephew, you would not pull off your boots here. Go down into the hall.—Dinner shall stay for you. My nephew's a little unbred; you'll pardon him, madam.—Gentlemen, will you walk? Marwood?

MRS. MARWOOD   I'll follow you, madam—before Sir Wilfull is ready.

[Exeunt all but MRS. MARWOOD, FAINALL.]

4. Weathervane.
5. The peace established by the Treaty of Ryswick in 1697, which concluded the war against France waged under the leadership of William III by England, the Empire, Spain, and Holland. It endured until the spring of 1702, when the War of the Spanish Succession began.
6. No matter what happens.
7. Shilly-shally. "Dainty": scrupulous, cautious.
8. By choice.

222 | WILLIAM CONGREVE

FAINALL   Why then Foible's a bawd, an errant, rank, match-making bawd. And I it seems am a husband, a rank husband; and my wife a very errant, rank wife—all in the way of the world. 'Sdeath, to be a cuckold by anticipation, a cuckold in embryo? Sure I was born with budding antlers like a young satyr, or a citizen's child.[9] 'Sdeath, to be outwitted, to be outjilted—outmatrimonied. If I had kept my speed like a stag, 'twere somewhat, but to crawl after, with my horns like a snail, and be outstripped by my wife—'tis scurvy wedlock.

MRS. MARWOOD   Then shake it off. You have often wished for an opportunity to part, and now you have it. But first prevent their plot.—The half of Millamant's fortune is too considerable to be parted with to a foe, to Mirabell.

FAINALL   Damn him, that had been mine—had you not made that fond[1] discovery.—That had been forfeited, had they been married. My wife had added luster to my horns. By that increase of fortune, I could have worn 'em tipped with gold, though my forehead had been furnished like a Deputy-Lieutenant's hall.[2]

MRS. MARWOOD   They may prove a cap of maintenance[3] to you still, if you can away with your wife. And she's no worse than when you had her—I dare swear she had given up her game, before she was married.

FAINALL   Hum! That may be—She might throw up her cards; but I'll be hanged if she did not put Pam[4] in her pocket.

MRS. MARWOOD   You married her to keep you, and if you can contrive to have her keep you better than you expected, why should you not keep her longer than you intended?

FAINALL   The means, the means.

MRS. MARWOOD   Discover to my lady your wife's conduct; threaten to part with her.—My lady loves her and will come to any composition to save her reputation. Take the opportunity of breaking it, just upon the discovery of this imposture. My lady will be enraged beyond bounds and sacrifice niece and fortune and all at that conjuncture. And let me alone to keep her warm; if she should flag in her part, I will not fail to prompt her.

FAINALL   Faith, this has an appearance.[5]

MRS. MARWOOD   I'm sorry I hinted to my lady to endeavor a match between Millamant and Sir Wilfull. That may be an obstacle.

FAINALL   O, for that matter leave me to manage him; I'll disable him for that; he will drink like a Dane; after dinner, I'll set his hand in.

MRS. MARWOOD   Well, how do you stand affected towards your lady?

FAINALL   Why, faith, I'm thinking of it. Let me see—I am married already; so that's over. My wife has played the jade with[6] me—well, that's over too. I never loved her, or if I had, why that would have been over too by this time. Jealous of her I cannot be, for I am certain; so there's an end of

9. A cuckold is said to wear horns. Because the wives of "citizens" (merchants living in the old city of London, not the fashionable suburbs) were regarded by the rakes as their natural and easy prey, a "citizen's child" was born to be cuckolded. "Satyr": a sylvan deity, usually represented with a goat's legs and horns.
1. Foolish. Fainall blames her for revealing to Lady Wishfort that Mirabell was not interested in her.
2. I.e., the great hall in the house of the deputy lieutenant of a shire. Fainall imagines it ornamented with numerous antlers taken from deer slain in the hunt.
3. In heraldry, a cap with two points like horns.
4. Jack of clubs, high card in the game of loo.
5. It's a promising scheme.
6. Cheated on.

jealousy. Weary of her I am and shall be—no, there's no end of that; no, no, that were too much to hope. Thus far concerning my repose. Now for my reputation. As to my own, I married not for it; so that's out of the question. And as to my part in my wife's—why, she had parted with hers before; so bringing none to me, she can take none from me; 'tis against all rule of play that I should lose to one who has not wherewithal to stake.

MRS. MARWOOD   Besides you forget, marriage is honorable.

FAINALL   Hum! Faith, and that's well thought on; marriage is honorable, as you say; and if so, wherefore should cuckoldom be a discredit, being derived from so honorable a root?

MRS. MARWOOD   Nay, I know not; if the root be honorable, why not the branches?[7]

FAINALL   So, so, why this point's clear.[8] Well, how do we proceed?

MRS. MARWOOD   I will contrive a letter which shall be delivered to my lady at the time when that rascal who is to act Sir Rowland is with her. It shall come as from an unknown hand—for the less I appear to know of the truth, the better I can play the incendiary. Besides, I would not have Foible provoked if I could help it, because you know she knows some passages—nay, I expect all will come out. But let the mine be sprung first, and then I care not if I am discovered.

FAINALL   If the worst come to the worst, I'll turn my wife to grass[9]—I have already a deed of settlement of the best part of her estate, which I wheedled out of her; and that you shall partake at least.

MRS. MARWOOD   I hope you are convinced that I hate Mirabell now: you'll be no more jealous?

FAINALL   Jealous, no—by this kiss.—Let husbands be jealous, but let the lover still believe. Or if he doubt, let it be only to endear his pleasure and prepare the joy that follows, when he proves his mistress true. But let husbands' doubts convert to endless jealousy; or if they have belief, let it corrupt to superstition and blind credulity. I am single, and will herd no more with 'em. True, I wear the badge, but I'll disown the order. And since I take my leave of 'em, I care not if I leave 'em a common motto to their common crest.

> All husbands must, or pain, or shame, endure;
> The wise too jealous are, fools too secure.

[*Exeunt* FAINALL *and* MRS. MARWOOD.]

Act 4—Scene continues

[*Enter* LADY WISHFORT *and* FOIBLE.]

LADY WISHFORT   Is Sir Rowland coming, say'st thou, Foible? and are things in order?

FOIBLE   Yes, madam. I have put wax lights in the sconces, and placed the footmen in a row in the hall, in their best liveries, with the coachman and postilion to fill up the equipage.

---

7. I.e., of the cuckold's horns.
8. Cleared up.

9. Turn out to pasture. A "grass widow" is divorced or separated from her husband.

LADY WISHFORT Have you pulvilled[1] the coachman and postilion, that they may not stink of the stable, when Sir Rowland comes by?

FOIBLE Yes, madam.

LADY WISHFORT And are the dancers and the music ready, that he may be entertained in all points with correspondence to his passion?

FOIBLE All is ready, madam.

LADY WISHFORT And—well—and how do I look, Foible?

FOIBLE Most killing well, madam.

LADY WISHFORT Well, and how shall I receive him? In what figure shall I give his heart the first impression? There is a great deal in the first impression. Shall I sit?—No, I won't sit—I'll walk.—Aye, I'll walk from the door upon his entrance; and then turn full upon him.—No, that will be too sudden. I'll lie—aye, I'll lie down—I'll receive him in my little dressing-room, there's a couch.—Yes, yes, I'll give the first impression on a couch.—I won't lie neither, but loll and lean upon one elbow; with one foot a little dangling off, jogging in a thoughtful way—yes—and then as soon as he appears, start, aye, start and be surprised, and rise to meet him in a pretty disorder—yes. O, nothing is more alluring than a levee[2] from a couch in some confusion. It shows the foot to advantage and furnishes with blushes and recomposing airs beyond comparison. Hark! There's a coach.

FOIBLE 'Tis he, madam.

LADY WISHFORT O dear, has my nephew made his addresses to Millamant? I ordered him.

FOIBLE Sir Wilfull is set in to drinking, madam, in the parlor.

LADY WISHFORT 'Ods my life, I'll send him to her. Call her down, Foible; bring her hither. I'll send him as I go.—When they are together, then come to me, Foible, that I may not be too long alone with Sir Rowland.
[Exit LADY WISHFORT.]
    [Enter MRS. MILLAMANT and MRS. FAINALL.]

FOIBLE Madam, I stayed here to tell your ladyship that Mr. Mirabell has waited this half hour for an opportunity to talk with you. Though my lady's orders were to leave you and Sir Wilfull together. Shall I tell Mr. Mirabell that you are at leisure?

MILLAMANT No—What would the dear man have? I am thoughtful and would amuse myself.—Bid him come another time.

There never yet was woman made,
Nor shall, but to be cursed.[3]

[Repeating and walking about.]
That's hard!

MRS. FAINALL You are very fond of Sir John Suckling today, Millamant, and the poets.

MILLAMANT He? Aye, and filthy verses—so I am.

FOIBLE Sir Wilfull is coming, madam. Shall I send Mr. Mirabell away?

1. Sprinkled with perfumed powder.
2. A rising.
3. The opening lines of a poem by Sir John Suckling. Impelled by her love to accept Mirabell, but reluctant to give herself, Millamant broods over poems that speak of the brief happiness of lovers and the falseness of men.

MILLAMANT   Aye, if you please, Foible, send him away—or send him hither, just as you will, dear Foible. I think I'll see him—Shall I? Aye, let the wretch come.

Thyrsis, a youth of the inspirèd train.[4]

[Repeating.]

Dear Fainall, entertain Sir Wilfull.—Thou hast philosophy to undergo a fool, thou art married and hast patience.—I would confer with my own thoughts.

MRS. FAINALL   I am obliged to you that you would make me your proxy in this affair, but I have business of my own.

[Enter SIR WILFULL.]

MRS. FAINALL   O Sir Wilfull; you are come at the critical instant. There's your mistress up to the ears in love and contemplation. Pursue your point, now or never.

SIR WILFULL   Yes; my aunt will have it so.—I would gladly have been encouraged with a bottle or two, because I'm somewhat wary at first, before I am acquainted; [This while MILLAMANT walks about repeating to herself.]—but I hope, after a time, I shall break my mind[5]—that is upon further acquaintance.—So for the present, cousin, I'll take my leave.—If so be you'll be so kind to make my excuse, I'll return to my company.—

MRS. FAINALL   O fie, Sir Wilfull! What, you must not be daunted.

SIR WILFULL   Daunted, no, that's not it; it is not so much for that—for if so be that I set on't, I'll do't. But only for the present, 'tis sufficient till further acquaintance, that's all.—Your servant.

MRS. FAINALL   Nay, I'll swear you shall never lose so favorable an opportunity if I can help it. I'll leave you together and lock the door. [Exit MRS. FAINFALL.]

SIR WILFULL   Nay, nay, cousin—I have forgot my gloves.—What d'ye do? 'Sheart, a'has locked the door indeed, I think.—Nay, cousin Fainall, open the door.—Pshaw, what a vixen trick is this? Nay, now a'has seen me too.—Cousin, I made bold to pass through, as it were.—I think this door's enchanted.—

MILLAMANT   [Repeating.]

I prithee spare me, gentle boy,
Press me no more for that slight toy.[6]

SIR WILFULL   Anan?[7] Cousin, your servant.

MILLAMANT.   —"That foolish trifle of a heart"—Sir Wilfull!

SIR WILFULL   Yes—your servant. No offense I hope, cousin.

MILLAMANT   [Repeating.]

I swear it will not do its part,
Though thou dost thine, employ'st thy power and art.

Natural, easy Suckling!

---

4. The first line of Edmund Waller's "The Story of Phoebus and Daphne Applied." In the flight of the virgin nymph from the embraces of the amorous god, Millamant finds an emblem of her relations with Mirabell.

5. Speak more openly.
6. The first lines of a song by Suckling, which she continues in her next lines.
7. How's that?

SIR WILFULL Anan? Suckling? No such suckling neither, cousin, nor stripling: I thank heaven I'm no minor.

MILLAMANT Ah rustic, ruder than Gothic.[8]

SIR WILFULL Well, well, I shall understand your lingo one of these days, cousin. In the meanwhile I must answer in plain English.

MILLAMANT Have you any business with me, Sir Wilfull?

SIR WILFULL Not at present, cousin.—Yes, I made bold to see, to come and know if that how you were disposed to fetch a walk this evening, if so be that I might not be troublesome, I would have sought a walk with you.

MILLAMANT A walk? What then?

SIR WILFULL Nay nothing—only for the walk's sake, that's all—

MILLAMANT I nauseate walking; 'tis a country diversion. I loathe the country and everything that relates to it.

SIR WILFULL Indeed! Hah! Look ye, look ye, you do? Nay, 'tis like you may.—Here are choice of pastimes here in town, as plays and the like; that must be confessed indeed.—

MILLAMANT Ah, l'étourdi.[9] I hate the town too.

SIR WILFULL Dear heart, that's much—Hah! that you should hate 'em both! Hah! 'tis like you may; there are some can't relish the town, and others can't away with the country—'tis like you may be one of those, cousin.

MILLAMANT Ha, ha, ha. Yes, 'tis like I may. You have nothing further to say to me?

SIR WILFULL Not at present, cousin. 'Tis like when I have an opportunity to be more private, I may break my mind in some measure.—I conjecture you partly guess—however, that's as time shall try; but spare to speak and spare to speed, as they say.

MILLAMANT If it is of no great importance, Sir Wilfull, you will oblige me to leave me. I have just now a little business.

SIR WILFULL Enough, enough, cousin. Yes, yes, all a case—when you're disposed, when you're disposed. Now's as well as another time; and another time as well as now. All's one for that.—Yes, yes, if your concerns call you, there's no haste; it will keep cold as they say.—Cousin, your servant. I think this door's locked.

MILLAMANT You may go this way, sir.

SIR WILFULL Your servant—then with your leave I'll return to my company.

[*Exit* SIR WILFULL.]

MILLAMANT Aye, aye. Ha, ha, ha.

Like Phoebus sung the no less amorous Boy.[1]

[*Enter* MIRABELL.]

MIRABELL

Like Daphne she, as lovely and as coy.

---

8. To the new age with its classical taste, medieval art, especially architecture, seemed crude ("rude").
9. Oh, the silly fellow (French); also the title of a comedy by Molière.
1. This, and the line that Mirabell caps it with, are also from Waller's "The Story of Phoebus and Daphne Applied."

Do you lock yourself up from me, to make my search more curious?[2] Or is this pretty artifice contrived to signify that here the chase must end, and my pursuit be crowned, for you can fly no further?

MILLAMANT Vanity! No—I'll fly and be followed to the last moment. Though I am upon the very verge of matrimony, I expect you should solicit me as much as if I were wavering at the grate of a monastery,[3] with one foot over the threshold. I'll be solicited to the very last, nay and afterwards.

MIRABELL What, after the last?

MILLAMANT O, I should think I was poor and had nothing to bestow, if I were reduced to an inglorious ease; and freed from the agreeable fatigues of solicitation.

MIRABELL But do not you know that when favors are conferred upon instant and tedious solicitation, that they diminish in their value and that both the giver loses the grace, and the receiver lessens his pleasure?

MILLAMANT It may be in things of common application, but never sure in love. O, I hate a lover that can dare to think he draws a moment's air, independent on the bounty of his mistress. There is not so impudent a thing in nature as the saucy look of an assured man, confident of success. The pedantic arrogance of a very husband has not so pragmatical[4] an air. Ah! I'll never marry, unless I am first made sure of my will and pleasure.

MIRABELL Would you have 'em both before marriage? Or will you be contented with the first now, and stay for the other till after grace?

MILLAMANT Ah, don't be impertinent.—My dear liberty, shall I leave thee? My faithful solitude, my darling contemplation, must I bid you then adieu? Ay-h adieu—My morning thoughts, agreeable wakings, indolent slumbers, all ye *douceurs, ye sommeils du matin*,[5] adieu.—I can't do't, 'tis more than impossible.—Positively, Mirabell, I'll lie abed in a morning as long as I please.

MIRABELL Then I'll get up in a morning as early as I please.

MILLAMANT Ah, idle creature, get up when you will.—and d'ye hear? I won't be called names after I'm married; positively I won't be called names.

MIRABELL Names!

MILLAMANT Aye, as wife, spouse, my dear, joy, jewel, love, sweetheart, and the rest of that nauseous cant, in which men and their wives are so fulsomely familiar—I shall never bear that.—Good Mirabell, don't let us be familiar or fond, nor kiss before folks, like my Lady Fadler[6] and Sir Francis; nor go to Hyde Park together the first Sunday in a new chariot, to provoke eyes and whispers; and then never be seen there together again, as if we were proud of one another the first week, and ashamed of one another ever after. Let us never visit together, nor go to a play together, but let us be very strange[7] and well bred; let us be as strange as if we had been married a great while; and as well bred as if we were not married at all.

---

2. Intricate, laborious.
3. The grated door of a convent.
4. Self-assured, conceited.

5. Soft (pleasures) and morning naps (French).
6. I.e., Fondler.
7. Reserved.

MIRABELL   Have you any more conditions to offer? Hitherto your demands are pretty reasonable.

MILLAMANT   Trifles—as liberty to pay and receive visits to and from whom I please; to write and receive letters, without interrogatories or wry faces on your part; to wear what I please; and choose conversation with regard only to my own taste; to have no obligation upon me to converse with wits that I don't like, because they are your acquaintance; or to be intimate with fools, because they may be your relations. Come to dinner when I please, dine in my dressing room when I'm out of humor, without giving a reason. To have my closet inviolate; to be sole empress of my tea table, which you must never presume to approach without first asking leave. And lastly, wherever I am, you shall always knock at the door before you come in. These articles subscribed, if I continue to endure you a little longer, I may by degrees dwindle into a wife.

MIRABELL   Your bill of fare is something advanced in this latter account. Well, have I liberty to offer conditions—that when you are dwindled into a wife, I may not be beyond measure enlarged into a husband?

MILLAMANT   You have free leave, propose your utmost, speak and spare not.

MIRABELL   I thank you. *Imprimis*[8] then, I covenant that your acquaintance be general; that you admit no sworn confidante or intimate of your own sex; no she-friend to screen her affairs under your countenance and tempt you to make trial of a mutual secrecy. No decoy duck to wheedle you a fop—scrambling to the play in a mask—then bring you home in a pretended fright, when you think you shall be found out—and rail at me for missing the play, and disappointing the frolic which you had to pick me up and prove my constancy.

MILLAMANT   Detestable *imprimis*! I go to the play in a mask!

MIRABELL   *Item*, I article,[9] that you continue to like your own face as long as I shall; and while it passes current with me, that you endeavor not to new coin it. To which end, together with all vizards for the day, I prohibit all masks for the night, made of oiled-skins and I know not what—hog's bones, hare's gall, pig water, and the marrow of a roasted cat.[1] In short, I forbid all commerce with the gentlewoman in what-d'ye-call-it court. *Item*, I shut my doors against all bawds with baskets, and pennyworths of muslin, china, fans, atlases,[2] etc. *Item*, when you shall be breeding—

MILLAMANT   Ah! Name it not.

MIRABELL   Which may be presumed, with a blessing on our endeavors—

MILLAMANT   Odious endeavors!

MIRABELL   I denounce against all strait lacing, squeezing for a shape, till you mold my boy's head like a sugar loaf; and instead of a man-child, make me father to a crooked billet.[3] Lastly, to the dominion of the tea table I submit.—But with proviso that you exceed not in your province; but restrain yourself to native and simple tea-table drinks, as tea, chocolate, and coffee. As likewise to genuine and authorized tea-table talk—such as mending of fashions, spoiling reputations, railing at absent

8. In the first place (Latin), as in legal documents.
9. I stipulate. *"Item"*: used to introduce each item in a list.
1. Cosmetics were made of materials as repulsive as those that Mirabell names. "Vizards": masks.
2. Rich silk fabrics.
3. I.e., a crooked piece of firewood.

friends, and so forth—but that on no account you encroach upon the men's prerogative, and presume to drink healths, or toast fellows; for prevention of which, I banish all foreign forces, all auxiliaries to the tea table, as orange brandy, all aniseed, cinnamon, citron and Barbados waters, together with ratafia and the most noble spirit of clary.[4]—But for cowslip-wine, poppy water, and all dormitives,[5] those I allow. These provisos admitted, in other things I may prove a tractable and complying husband.

MILLAMANT   O, horrid provisos! filthy strong waters! I toast fellows, odious men! I hate your odious provisos.

MIRABELL   Then we're agreed. Shall I kiss your hand upon the contract? And here comes one to be a witness to the sealing of the deed.

        [*Enter* MRS. FAINALL.]

MILLAMANT   Fainall, what shall I do? Shall I have him? I think I must have him.

MRS. FAINALL   Aye, aye, take him, take him. What should you do?

MILLAMANT   Well then—I'll take my death I'm in a horrid fright— Fainall, I shall never say it—well—I think—I'll endure you.

MRS. FAINALL   Fy, fy, have him, have him, and tell him so in plain terms: for I am sure you have a mind to him.

MILLAMANT   Are you? I think I have—and the horrid man looks as if he thought so too.—Well, you ridiculous thing you, I'll have you.—I won't be kissed, nor I won't be thanked.—Here kiss my hand though.—So, hold your tongue now, don't say a word.

MRS. FAINALL   Mirabell, there's a necessity for your obedience—you have neither time to talk nor stay. My mother is coming; and in my conscience if she should see you, would fall into fits, and maybe not recover, time enough to return to Sir Rowland; who, as Foible tells me, is in a fair way to succeed. Therefore spare your ecstasies for another occasion, and slip down the back stairs, where Foible waits to consult you.

MILLAMANT   Aye, go, go. In the meantime I suppose you have said something to please me.

MIRABELL   I am all obedience.

        [*Exit* MIRABELL.]

MRS. FAINALL   Yonder Sir Wilfull's drunk, and so noisy that my mother has been forced to leave Sir Rowland to appease him; but he answers her only with singing and drinking.—What they may have done by this time I know not, but Petulant and he were upon quarreling as I came by.

MILLAMANT   Well, if Mirabell should not make a good husband, I am a lost thing; for I find I love him violently.

MRS. FAINALL   So it seems, for you mind not what's said to you.—If you doubt him, you had best take up with Sir Wilfull.

MILLAMANT   How can you name that superannuated lubber? foh!

        [*Enter* WITWOUD *from drinking.*]

MRS. FAINALL   So, is the fray made up, that you have left 'em?

WITWOUD   Left 'em? I could stay no longer—I have laughed like ten christenings—I am tipsy with laughing.—If I had stayed any longer, I

4. A sweet liqueur made of wine, honey, and spices. "Aniseed, cinnamon, citron and Barbados   waters": alcoholic drinks.
5. Sedatives.

should have burst—I must have been let out and pieced in the sides like an unsized camlet.[6]—Yes, yes, the fray is composed; my lady came in like a *nolle prosequi*[7] and stopped the proceedings.

MILLAMANT What was the dispute?

WITWOUD That's the jest; there was no dispute. They could neither of 'em speak for rage; and so fell a-sputtering at one another like two roasting apples.

[*Enter* PETULANT *drunk.*]

WITWOUD Now, Petulant? All's over, all's well? Gad, my head begins to whim it about.—Why dost thou not speak? Thou art both as drunk and as mute as a fish.

PETULANT Look you, Mrs. Millamant—if you can love me, dear nymph—say it—and that's the conclusion—pass on, or pass off—that's all.

WITWOUD Thou hast uttered volumes, folios, in less than decimo sexto, my dear Lacedemonian.[8] Sirrah Petulant, thou art an epitomizer of words.

PETULANT Witwoud—You are an annihilator of sense.

WITWOUD Thou art a retailer of phrases, and dost deal in remnants of remnants, like a maker of pincushions. Thou art in truth (metaphorically speaking) a speaker of shorthand.

PETULANT Thou art (without a figure) just one-half of an ass, and Baldwin[9] yonder, thy half brother, is the rest.—A Gemini[1] of asses split, would make just four of you.

WITWOUD Thou dost bite, my dear mustard-seed; kiss me for that.

PETULANT Stand off—I'll kiss no more males.—I have kissed your twin yonder in a humor of reconciliation, till he—[*Hiccup.*]—rises upon my stomach like a radish.

MILLAMANT Eh! filthy creature.—What was the quarrel?

PETULANT There was no quarrel—there might have been a quarrel.

WITWOUD If there had been words enow between 'em to have expressed provocation, they had gone together by the ears like a pair of castanets.

PETULANT You were the quarrel.

MILLAMANT Me!

PETULANT If I have a humor to quarrel, I can make less matters conclude premises.[2]—If you are not handsome, what then, if I have a humor to prove it?—If I shall have my reward, say so; if not, fight for your face the next time yourself.—I'll go sleep.

WITWOUD Do, wrap thyself up like a woodlouse, and dream revenge—and hear me, if thou canst learn to write by tomorrow morning, pen me a challenge.—I'll carry it for thee.

PETULANT Carry your mistress's monkey a spider—go flea dogs, and read romances—I'll go to bed to my maid.[3]

MRS. FAINALL He's horridly drunk—how came you all in this pickle?

6. A fabric made by mixing wool and silk; "unsized" because not stiffened with some glutinous substance.
7. A Latin phrase indicating the withdrawal of a lawsuit.
8. Spartans; people of few words. "Folios": books of the largest size. "Decimo sexto": a book of the smallest size.
9. The name of the ass in the beast epic *Reynard the Fox* (ca. 1175–1250).

1. The two Roman deities, the twins Castor and Pollux, for whom one of the signs of the zodiac is named.
2. I can argue successfully about matters less significant than you.
3. Monkeys were supposed to eat spiders. Petulant scornfully contrasts what he imagines to be Witwoud's technique with his lady with his own more vigorous and direct program for the rest of the evening.

WITWOUD   A plot, a plot, to get rid of the knight—your husband's advice; but he sneaked off.

[*Enter* SIR WILFULL *drunk, and* LADY WISHFORT.]

LADY WISHFORT   Out upon't, out upon't! At years of discretion, and comport yourself at this rantipole[4] rate!

SIR WILFULL   No offense, aunt.

LADY WISHFORT   Offense? As I'm a person, I'm ashamed of you.—Fogh! how you stink of wine! D'ye think my niece will ever endure such a borachio![5] you're an absolute borachio.

SIR WILFULL   Borachio!

LADY WISHFORT   At a time when you should commence an amour, and put your best foot foremost—

SIR WILFULL   'Sheart, an you grutch[6] me your liquor, make a bill.—Give me more drink, and take my purse.

[*Sings.*]   Prithee fill me the glass
                 'Till it laugh in my face,
            With ale that is potent and mellow;
                 He that whines for a lass
                 Is an ignorant ass,
            For a bumper[7] has not its fellow.

But if you would have me marry my cousin—say the word and I'll do't— Wilfull will do't, that's the word—Wilfull will do't, that's my crest—my motto I have forgot.[8]

LADY WISHFORT   My nephew's a little overtaken, cousin—but 'tis with drinking your health—O' my word you are obliged to him—

SIR WILFULL   *In vino veritas,*[9] aunt.—If I drunk your health today, cousin—I am a borachio. But if you have a mind to be married, say the word, and send for the piper; Wilfull will do't. If not, dust[1] it away, and let's have t'other round.—Tony, 'ods heart, where's Tony?—Tony's an honest fellow, but he spits after a bumper, and that's a fault—

[*Sings.*]   We'll drink and we'll never ha' done, boys,
                 Put the glass then around with the sun, boys,
            Let Apollo's example invite us;
                 For he's drunk every night,
                 And that makes him so bright,
            That he's able next morning to light us.

The sun's a good pimple,[2] an honest soaker, he has a cellar at your Antipodes. If I travel, aunt, I touch at your Antipodes.—Your Antipodes are a good rascally sort of topsy-turvy fellows.—If I had a bumper, I'd stand upon my head and drink a health to 'em.—A match or no match, cousin, with the hard name?—aunt, Wilfull will do't. If she has her maidenhead, let her look to't; if she has not, let her keep her own counsel in the meantime, and cry out at the nine months' end.

---

4. Rakish.
5. Drunkard (Spanish).
6. Grudge.
7. A wineglass filled to the brim. The word comes from the custom of touching (bumping) glasses when drinking toasts.

8. A coat of arms had a crest—a helmet surmounting the shield—and a motto. In his drunkenness, Sir Wilfull confuses the two.
9. In wine [there is] truth (Latin).
1. Throw.
2. Fellow.

MILLAMANT   Your pardon, madam, I can stay no longer—Sir Wilfull grows very powerful. Egh! how he smells! I shall be overcome if I stay. Come, cousin.

[*Exeunt* MRS. MILLAMANT *and* MRS. FAINALL.]

LADY WISHFORT   Smells! he would poison a tallow-chandler[3] and his family. Beastly creature, I know not what to do with him. Travel, quoth a'; aye, travel, travel, get thee gone, get thee but far enough, to the Saracens, or the Tartars, or the Turks—for thou art not fit to live in a Christian commonwealth, thou beastly pagan.

SIR WILFULL   Turks, no; no Turks, aunt. Your Turks are infidels, and believe not in the grape.[4] Your Mahometan, your Mussulman is a dry stinkard.— No offense, aunt. My map says that your Turk is not so honest a man as your Christian.—I cannot find by the map that your Mufti[5] is orthodox— whereby it is a plain case, that orthodox is a hard word, aunt, and—[*Hiccup.*]—Greek for claret.

[*Sings.*]   To drink is a Christian diversion.
          Unknown to the Turk or the Persian:
              Let Mahometan fools
              Live by heathenish rules,
          And be damned over tea cups and coffee.
              But let British lads sing,
              Crown a health to the king,
          And a fig for your sultan and sophy.[6]

Ah, Tony!   [*Enter* FOIBLE, *and whispers to* LADY WISHFORT.]

LADY WISHFORT   Sir Rowland impatient? Good lack! what shall I do with this beastly tumbrel?[7]—Go lie down and sleep, you sot—or as I'm a person, I'll have you bastinadoed[8] with broomsticks. Call up the wenches with broomsticks. [*Exit* FOIBLE.]

SIR WILFULL   Ahay? Wenches, where are the wenches?

LADY WISHFORT   Dear cousin Witwoud, get him away, and you will bind me to you inviolably. I have an affair of moment that invades me with some precipitation—you will oblige me to all futurity.

WITWOUD   Come, knight.—Pox on him, I don't know what to say to him.— Will you go to a cockmatch?

SIR WILFULL   With a wench, Tony? Is she a shakebag,[9] sirrah? Let me bite your cheek for that.

WITWOUD   Horrible! He has a breath like a bagpipe.—Aye, aye, come, will you march, my Salopian?[1]

SIR WILFULL   Lead on, little Tony—I'll follow thee, my Anthony, my Tantony. Sirrah, thou shalt be my Tantony, and I'll be thy pig.[2]

—And a fig for your sultan and sophy.

---

3. Candle maker.
4. Muslims do not drink alcohol.
5. The Grand Mufti, head of the state religion of Turkey.
6. The shah of Persia.
7. Dung cart.

8. Punished by beating the soles of the feet.
9. Gamecock.
1. Inhabitant of Shropshire.
2. St. Anthony (hence "Tantony"), the patron of swineherds, was represented accompanied by a pig.

LADY WISHFORT This will never do. It will never make a match—at least before he has been abroad.

[*Exeunt* SIR WILFULL, *singing, and* WITWOUD.]

[*Enter* WAITWELL, *disguised as* SIR ROWLAND.]

LADY WISHFORT Dear Sir Rowland, I am confounded with confusion at the retrospection of my own rudeness—I have more pardons to ask than the Pope distributes in the Year of Jubilee. But I hope where there is likely to be so near an alliance—we may unbend the severity of decorum—and dispense with a little ceremony.

WAITWELL My impatience, madam, is the effect of my transport—and till I have the possession of your adorable person, I am tantalized on the rack; and do but hang, madam, on the tenter[3] of expectation.

LADY WISHFORT You have excess of gallantry, Sir Rowland; and press things to a conclusion, with a most prevailing vehemence.—But a day or two for decency of marriage.—

WAITWELL For decency of funeral, madam. The delay will break my heart—or if that should fail, I shall be poisoned. My nephew will get an inkling of my designs, and poison me—and I would willingly starve him before I die—I would gladly go out of the world with that satisfaction.—That would be some comfort to me, if I could but live so long as to be revenged on that unnatural viper.

LADY WISHFORT Is he so unnatural, say you? Truly I would contribute much both to the saving of your life and the accomplishment of your revenge—Not that I respect[4] myself; though he has been a perfidious wretch to me.

WAITWELL Perfidious to you!

LADY WISHFORT O Sir Rowland, the hours that he has died away at my feet, the tears that he has shed, the oaths that he has sworn, the palpitations that he has felt, the trances and the tremblings, the ardors and the ecstasies, the kneelings, and the risings, the heart-heavings and the hand-gripings, the pangs and the pathetic regards of his protesting eyes! Oh, no memory can register.

WAITWELL What, my rival! Is the rebel my rival? a'dies.

LADY WISHFORT No, don't kill him at once, Sir Rowland, starve him gradually inch by inch.

WAITWELL I'll do't. In three weeks he shall be barefoot; in a month out at knees with begging an alms—he shall starve upward and upward, till he has nothing living but his head, and then go out in a stink like a candle's end upon a saveall.[5]

LADY WISHFORT Well, Sir Rowland, you have the way.—You are no novice in the labyrinth of love—you have the clue—but as I am a person, Sir Rowland, you must not attribute my yielding to any sinister appetite, or indigestion of widowhood; nor impute my complacency to any lethargy of continence.—I hope you do not think me prone to any iteration of nuptials.—

3. A frame for stretching cloth on hooks so that it may dry without losing its original shape (cf. the phrase "to be on tenterhooks").

4. Consider.

5. A small pan inserted into a candlestick to catch the drippings of the candle.

WAITWELL Far be it from me—

LADY WISHFORT If you do, I protest I must recede—or think that I have made a prostitution of decorums, but in the vehemence of compassion, and to save the life of a person of so much importance—

WAITWELL I esteem it so—

LADY WISHFORT Or else you wrong my condescension—

WAITWELL I do no, I do not—

LADY WISHFORT Indeed you do.

WAITWELL I do not, fair shrine of virtue.

LADY WISHFORT If you think the least scruple of carnality was an ingredient—

WAITWELL Dear madam, no. You are all camphire[6] and frankincense, all chastity and odor.

LADY WISHFORT Or that—

[*Enter* FOIBLE.]

FOIBLE Madam, the dancers are ready, and there's one with a letter, who must deliver it into your own hands.

LADY WISHFORT Sir Rowland, will you give me leave? Think favorably, judge candidly, and conclude you have found a person who would suffer racks in honor's cause, dear Sir Rowland, and will wait on you incessantly.[7]

[*Exit* LADY WISHFORT.]

WAITWELL Fie, fie!—What a slavery have I undergone; spouse, hast thou any cordial? I want spirits.

FOIBLE What a washy rogue art thou, to pant thus for a quarter of an hour's lying and swearing to a fine lady?

WAITWELL O, she is the antidote to desire. Spouse, thou wilt fare the worse for't—I shall have no appetite for iteration of nuptials—this eight and forty hours—by this hand I'd rather be a chairman in the dog days[8]—than act Sir Rowland till this time tomorrow.

[*Re-enter* LADY WISHFORT, *with a letter.*]

LADY WISHFORT Call in the dancers.—Sir Rowland, we'll sit, if you please, and see the entertainment.

[*Dance.*]

Now with your permission, Sir Rowland, I will peruse my letter.—I would open it in your presence, because I would not make you uneasy. If it should make you uneasy, I would burn it—speak if it does—but you may see, the superscription is like a woman's hand.

FOIBLE [*To him.*] By heaven! Mrs. Marwood's, I know it—my heart aches—get it from her.—

WAITWELL A woman's hand? No, madam, that's no woman's hand, I see that already. That's somebody whose throat must be cut.

LADY WISHFORT Nay, Sir Rowland, since you give me a proof of your passion by your jealousy, I promise you I'll make a return, by a frank communication—you shall see it—we'll open it together—look you here.—[*Reads.*]—*Madam, though unknown to you* (Look you there, 'tis from nobody that I know.)—*I have that honor for your character, that I think myself obliged to let you know you are abused. He who pretends to be Sir Rowland is a cheat and a rascal*—O Heavens! what's this?

FOIBLE Unfortunate, all's ruined.

WAITWELL How, how, let me see, let me see—[*Reads.*]—*A rascal and disguised, and suborned for that imposture*—O villainy! O villainy!—*by the contrivance of*—

LADY WISHFORT I shall faint, I shall die, oh!

FOIBLE [*To him.*] Say, 'tis your nephew's hand.—Quickly, his plot, swear, swear it.—

WAITWELL Here's a villain! Madam, don't you perceive it, don't you see it?

LADY WISHFORT Too well, too well. I have seen too much.

WAITWELL I told you at first I knew the hand—A woman's hand? The rascal writes a sort of a large hand, your Roman hand—I saw there was a throat to be cut presently. If he were my son, as he is my nephew, I'd pistol him—

FOIBLE O treachery! But are you sure, Sir Rowland, it is his writing?

WAITWELL Sure? Am I here? Do I live? Do I love this pearl of India? I have twenty letters in my pocket from him in the same character.

LADY WISHFORT How!

FOIBLE O, what luck it is, Sir Rowland, that you were present at this juncture! This was the business that brought Mr. Mirabell disguised to Madam Millamant this afternoon. I thought something was contriving, when he stole by me and would have hid his face.

LADY WISHFORT How, how!—I heard the villain was in the house indeed; and now I remember, my niece went away abruptly, when Sir Wilfull was to have made his addresses.

FOIBLE Then, then, madam, Mr. Mirabell waited for her in her chamber; but I would not tell your ladyship to discompose you when you were to receive Sir Rowland.

WAITWELL Enough, his date is short.[9]

FOIBLE No, good Sir Rowland, don't incur the law.

WAITWELL Law! I care not for law. I can but die, and 'tis in a good cause—my lady shall be satisfied of my truth and innocence, though it cost me my life.

LADY WISHFORT No, dear Sir Rowland, don't fight. If you should be killed I must never show my face—or be hanged—O, consider my reputation, Sir Rowland—no, you shan't fight—I'll go and examine my niece; I'll make her confess. I conjure you, Sir Rowland, by all your love not to fight.

WAITWELL I am charmed, madam, I obey. But some proof you must let me give you—I'll go for a black box, which contains the writings of my whole estate, and deliver that into your hands.

LADY WISHFORT Aye, dear Sir Rowland, that will be some comfort. Bring the black box.

WAITWELL And may I presume to bring a contract to be signed this night? May I hope so far?

LADY WISHFORT Bring what you will; but come alive, pray come alive. O, this is a happy discovery.

---

9. He won't live long.

WAITWELL Dead or alive I'll come—and married we will be in spite of treachery; aye, and get an heir that shall defeat the last remaining glimpse of hope in my abandoned nephew. Come, my buxom widow:

> E'er long you shall substantial proof receive
> That I'm an arrant[1] knight——

FOIBLE   Or arrant knave.

Act 5—Scene continues

[*Enter* LADY WISHFORT *and* FOIBLE.]

LADY WISHFORT Out of my house, out of my house, thou viper, thou serpent, that I have fostered; thou bosom traitress, that I raised from nothing.—Begone, begone, begone, go, go—that I took from washing of old gauze and weaving of dead hair,[2] with a bleak blue nose over a chafing dish of starved embers, and dining behind a traverse rag,[3] in a shop no bigger than a bird cage—go, go, starve again, do, do.

FOIBLE Dear madam, I'll beg pardon on my knees.

LADY WISHFORT Away, out, out, go set up for yourself again.—Do, drive a trade, do, with your three-pennyworth of small ware, flaunting upon a packthread, under a brandy-seller's bulk or against a dead wall[4] by a ballad-monger. Go, hang out an old frisoneer-gorget, with a yard of yellow colberteen[5] again; do; an old gnawed mask, two rows of pins and a child's fiddle; a glass necklace with the beads broken, and a quilted nightcap with one ear. Go, go, drive a trade—these were your commodities, you treacherous trull, this was the merchandise you dealt in when I took you into my house, placed you next myself, and made you governante[6] of my whole family. You have forgot this, have you, now you have feathered your nest?

FOIBLE No, no, dear madam. Do but hear me, have but a moment's patience—I'll confess all. Mr. Mirabell seduced me; I am not the first that he has wheedled with his dissembling tongue. Your ladyship's own wisdom has been deluded by him, then how should I, a poor ignorant, defend myself? O madam, if you knew but what he promised me, and how he assured me your ladyship should come to no damage—or else the wealth of the Indies should not have bribed me to conspire against so good, so sweet, so kind a lady as you have been to me.

LADY WISHFORT No damage? What, to betray me, to marry me to a cast[7] servingman; to make me a receptacle, an hospital for a decayed pimp? No damage? O, thou frontless[8] impudence, more than a big-bellied actress.

FOIBLE Pray do but hear me, madam. He could not marry your ladyship, madam.—No, indeed, his marriage was to have been void in law; for he was married to me first, to secure your ladyship. He could not have bed-

---

1. The two words *errant* ("wandering," as in "knight-errant") and *arrant* ("thorough-going," "notorious") were originally the same and were still pronounced alike. This makes possible Foible's pun.
2. Foible had been a wigmaker.
3. A worn cloth, used to curtain off part of a room.

4. A continuous, unbroken wall. "Bulk": stall.
5. A French imitation of Italian lace. "Frisoneer-gorget": a woolen garment that covers the neck and breast.
6. Housekeeper.
7. Cast off, discharged.
8. Shameless.

ded your ladyship; for if he had consummated with your ladyship, he must have run the risk of the law, and been put upon his clergy.[9]—Yes, indeed, I inquired of the law in that case before I would meddle or make.[1]

LADY WISHFORT What, then I have been your property, have I? I have been convenient to you, it seems.—While you were catering for Mirabell, I have been broker for you? What, have you made a passive bawd of me?—This exceeds all precedent; I am brought to fine uses, to become a botcher of second-hand marriages between Abigails and Andrews![2] I'll couple you. Yes, I'll baste you together, you and your philander.[3] I'll Duke's-Place[4] you, as I'm a person. Your turtle is in custody already: you shall coo in the same cage, if there be constable or warrant in the parish. [*Exit* LADY WISHFORT.]

FOIBLE O, that ever I was born, O, that I was ever married.—A bride, aye, I shall be a Bridewell-bride.[5] Oh!
        [*Enter* MRS. FAINALL.]

MRS. FAINALL Poor Foible, what's the matter?

FOIBLE O madam, my lady's gone for a constable. I shall be had to a justice, and put to Bridewell to beat hemp; poor Waitwell's gone to prison already.

MRS. FAINALL Have a good heart, Foible. Mirabell's gone to give security for him. This is all Marwood's and my husband's doing.

FOIBLE Yes, yes, I know it, madam; she was in my lady's closet, and overheard all that you said to me before dinner. She sent the letter to my lady; and that missing effect,[6] Mr. Fainall laid this plot to arrest Waitwell, when he pretended to go for the papers; and in the meantime Mrs. Marwood declared all to my lady.

MRS. FAINALL Was there no mention made of me in the letter?—My mother does not suspect my being in the confederacy? I fancy Marwood has not told her, though she has told my husband.

FOIBLE Yes, madam; but my lady did not see that part. We stifled the letter before she read so far. Has that mischievous devil told Mr. Fainall of your ladyship then?

MRS. FAINALL Aye, all's out, my affair with Mirabell, everything discovered. This is the last day of our living together, that's my comfort.

FOIBLE Indeed, madam, and so 'tis a comfort if you knew all.—He has been even with your ladyship; which I could have told you long enough since, but I love to keep peace and quietness by my good will. I had rather bring friends together than set 'em at distance. But Mrs. Marwood and he are nearer related than ever their parents thought for!

MRS. FAINALL Say'st thou so, Foible? Canst thou prove this?

FOIBLE I can take my oath of it, madam. So can Mrs. Mincing; we have had many a fair word from Madam Marwood, to conceal something that

---

9. I.e., pleaded "benefit of clergy," originally the privilege of the clergy to be tried for felony before ecclesiastical, not secular, courts. By Congreve's time it had become the privilege to plead exemption from a penal sentence granted a person who could read and was a first offender.
1. A dialectal phrase; the two words mean approximately the same thing.
2. Generic names for maidservants and serving-

men. "Botcher": a mender of old clothes. Lady Wishfort means something like "a patcher-up of marriages."
3. Lover. "Baste": sew together loosely.
4. Notorious for its thriving trade in unlicensed marriages.
5. House of correction for women, in London.
6. Not working.

passed in our chamber one evening when you were at Hyde Park—and we were thought to have gone a-walking; but we went up unawares—though we were sworn to secrecy too; Madam Marwood took a book and swore us upon it, but it was but a book of poems.—So long as it was not a Bible-oath, we may break it with a safe conscience.

MRS. FAINALL This discovery is the most opportune thing I could wish. Now, Mincing?

[*Enter* MINCING.]

MINCING My lady would speak with Mrs. Foible, mem. Mr. Mirabell is with her; he has set your spouse at liberty, Mrs. Foible, and would have you hide yourself in my lady's closet, till my old lady's anger is abated. O, my old lady is in a perilous passion, at something Mr. Fainall has said; he swears, and my old lady cries. There's a fearful hurricane, I vow. He says, mem, how that he'll have my lady's fortune made over to him, or he'll be divorced.

MRS. FAINALL Does your lady or Mirabell know that?

MINCING Yes, mem, they have sent me to see if Sir Wilfull be sober, and to bring him to them. My lady is resolved to have him, I think, rather than lose such a vast sum as six thousand pound. O, come, Mrs. Foible, I hear my old lady.

MRS. FAINALL Foible, you must tell Mincing that she must prepare to vouch when I call her.

FOIBLE Yes, yes, madam.

MINCING O yes, mem, I'll vouch anything for your ladyship's service, be what it will. [*Exit* MINCING, FOIBLE.]

[*Enter* LADY WISHFORT *and* MRS. MARWOOD.]

LADY WISHFORT O my dear friend, how can I enumerate the benefit that I have received from your goodness? To you I owe the timely discovery of the false vows of Mirabell; to you I owe the detection of the imposter Sir Rowland. And now you are become an intercessor with my son-in-law, to save the honor of my house, and compound for the frailties of my daughter. Well, friend, you are enough to reconcile me to the bad world, or else I would retire to deserts and solitudes, and feed harmless sheep by groves and purling streams. Dear Marwood, let us leave the world and retire by ourselves and be shepherdesses.

MRS. MARWOOD Let us first dispatch the affair in hand, madam. We shall have leisure to think of retirement afterwards. Here is one who is concerned in the treaty.

LADY WISHFORT O daughter, daughter, is it possible thou should'st be my child, bone of my bone, and flesh of my flesh, and as I may say, another me, and yet transgress the most minute particle of severe virtue? Is it possible you should lean aside to iniquity, who have been cast in the direct mold of virtue? I have not only been a mold but a pattern for you, and a model for you, after you were brought into the world.

MRS. FAINALL I don't understand your ladyship.

LADY WISHFORT Not understand? Why, have you not been naught?[7] Have you not been sophisticated?[8] Not understand? Here I am ruined to com-

7. Wicked.   8. Corrupted.

pound[9] for your caprices and your cuckoldoms. I must pawn my plate and my jewels, and ruin my niece, and all little enough—

MRS. FAINALL   I am wronged and abused, and so are you. 'Tis a false accusation, as false as hell, as false as your friend there, aye, or your friend's friend, my false husband.

MRS. MARWOOD   My friend, Mrs. Fainall? Your husband my friend, what do you mean?

MRS. FAINALL   I know what I mean, madam, and so do you; and so shall the world at a time convenient.

MRS. MARWOOD   I am sorry to see you so passionate, madam. More temper[1] would look more like innocence. But I have done. I am sorry my zeal to serve your ladyship and family should admit of misconstruction, or make me liable to affront. You will pardon me, madam, if I meddle no more with an affair in which I am not personally concerned.

LADY WISHFORT   O dear friend, I am so ashamed that you should meet with such returns.—You ought to ask pardon on your knees, ungrateful creature; she deserves more from you than all your life can accomplish—O, don't leave me destitute in this perplexity—no, stick to me, my good genius.

MRS. FAINALL   I tell you, madam, you're abused—Stick to you? aye, like a leech, to suck your best blood—She'll drop off when she's full. Madam, you shan't pawn a bodkin, nor part with a brass counter, in composition for me.[2] I defy 'em all. Let 'em prove their aspersions; I know my own innocence, and dare stand a trial. [*Exit* MRS. FAINALL.]

LADY WISHFORT   Why, if she should be innocent, if she should be wronged after all, ha? I don't know what to think—and I promise you, her education has been unexceptionable—I may say it; for I chiefly made it my own care to initiate her very infancy in the rudiments of virtue, and to impress upon her tender years a young odium and aversion to the very sight of men.—Aye, friend, she would have shrieked if she had but seen a man, till she was in her teens. As I'm a person, 'tis true—she was never suffered to play with a male child, though but in coats.[3] Nay, her very babies[4] were of the feminine gender—O, she never looked a man in the face but her own father, or the chaplain, and him we made a shift to put upon her for a woman, by the help of his long garments, and his sleek face; till she was going in her fifteen.

MRS. MARWOOD   'Twas much she should be deceived so long.

LADY WISHFORT   I warrant you, or she would never have borne to have been catechized by him; and have heard his long lectures against singing and dancing, and such debaucheries; and going to filthy plays; and profane music-meetings, where the lewd trebles squeek nothing but bawdry, and the basses roar blasphemy. O, she would have swooned at the sight or name of an obscene play-book—and can I think after all this, that my daughter can be naught? What, a whore? And thought it excommunication to set her foot within the door of a playhouse? O dear friend, I can't believe it, no, no; as she says, let him prove it, let him prove it.

9. I.e., come to terms by making a monetary settlement.
1. Moderation.
2. To settle my debts. "Bodkin": ornamental hairpin. "Brass counter": an imitation coin, used in games of chance.
3. In the dress common to young children of both genders.
4. Dolls.

MRS. MARWOOD   Prove it, madam? What, and have your name prostituted in a public court; yours and your daughter's reputation worried at the bar by a pack of bawling lawyers? To be ushered in with an O *Yes* of scandal; and have your case opened by an old fumbler lecher in a quoif[5] like a man midwife, to bring your daughter's infamy to light; to be a theme for legal punsters, and quibblers by the statute; and become a jest, against a rule of court, where there is no precedent for a jest in any record, not even in Doomsday Book;[6] to discompose the gravity of the bench, and provoke naughty interrogatories in more naughty law-Latin; while the good judge, tickled with the proceeding, simpers under a gray beard, and fidges off and on his cushion as if he had swallowed cantharides, or sate upon cowhage.[7]

LADY WISHFORT   O, 'tis very hard!

MRS. MARWOOD   And then to have my young revelers of the Temple take notes, like 'prentices at a conventicle; and after talk it over again in commons,[8] or before drawers in an eating house.

LADY WISHFORT   Worse and worse.

MRS. MARWOOD   Nay, this is nothing; if it would end here 'twere well. But it must after this be consigned by the shorthand writers to the public press; and from thence be transferred to the hands, nay into the throats and lungs of hawkers, with voices more licentious than the loud flounderman's or the woman that cries gray peas;[9] and this you must hear till you are stunned; nay, you must hear nothing else for some days.

LADY WISHFORT   O, 'tis insupportable. No, no, dear friend, make it up, make it up; aye, aye, I'll compound. I'll give up all, myself and my all, my niece and her all—anything, everything for composition.

MRS. MARWOOD   Nay, madam, I advise nothing; I only lay before you, as a friend, the inconveniencies which perhaps you have overseen.[1] Here comes Mr. Fainall. If he will be satisfied to huddle up all in silence, I shall be glad. You must think I would rather congratulate than condole with you.

[*Enter* FAINALL.]

LADY WISHFORT   Aye, aye, I do not doubt it, dear Marwood. No, no, I do not doubt it.

FAINALL   Well, madam; I have suffered myself to be overcome by the importunity of this lady, your friend, and am content you shall enjoy your own proper estate during life; on condition you oblige yourself never to marry, under such penalty as I think convenient.

LADY WISHFORT   Never to marry?

FAINALL   No more Sir Rowlands—the next imposture may not be so timely detected.

MRS. MARWOOD   That condition, I dare answer, my lady will consent to, without difficulty; she has already but too much experienced the

---

5. The cap of a sergeant-at-law. "*O Yes*": The formula for opening court, a variant of Old French *Oyez*, "Hear ye."
6. Or Domesday Book, the survey of England made in 1085–86 by William the Conqueror.
7. A plant that causes intolerable itching. "Fidges": fidgets. "Cantharides": Spanish fly, an

irritant.
8. In the dining hall. "Revelers": here, law students. The Temple is one of the Inns of Court. "Conventicle": clandestine meeting of Protestant Dissenters.
9. Street vendors known for their stridency.
1. Overlooked.

perfidiousness of men. Besides, madam, when we retire to our pastoral solitude we shall bid adieu to all other thoughts.

LADY WISHFORT Aye, that's true; but in case of necessity; as of health, or some such emergency—

FAINALL O, if you are prescribed marriage, you shall be considered; I will only reserve to myself the power to choose for you. If your physic be wholesome, it matters not who is your apothecary. Next, my wife shall settle on me the remainder of her fortune, not made over already; and for her maintenance depend entirely on my discretion.

LADY WISHFORT This is most inhumanly savage; exceeding the barbarity of a Muscovite husband.

FAINALL I learned it from His Czarish Majesty's retinue,[2] in a winter evening's conference over brandy and pepper, amongst other secrets of matrimony and policy, as they are at present practiced in the northern hemisphere. But this must be agreed unto, and that positively. Lastly, I will be endowed, in right of my wife, with that six thousand pound, which is the moiety of Mrs. Millamant's fortune in your possession; and which she has forfeited (as will appear by the last will and testament of your deceased husband, Sir Jonathan Wishfort) by her disobedience in contracting herself against your consent or knowledge; and by refusing the offered match with Sir Wilfull Witwoud, which you, like a careful aunt, had provided for her.

LADY WISHFORT My nephew was *non compos*,[3] and could not make his addresses.

FAINALL I come to make demands—I'll hear no objections.

LADY WISHFORT You will grant me time to consider?

FAINALL Yes, while the instrument[4] is drawing, to which you must set your hand till more sufficient deeds can be perfected: which I will take care shall be done with all possible speed. In the meanwhile I will go for the said instrument, and till my return you may balance this matter in your own discretion. [*Exit* FAINALL.]

LADY WISHFORT This insolence is beyond all precedent, all parallel; must I be subject to this merciless villain?

MRS. MARWOOD 'Tis severe indeed, madam, that you should smart for your daughter's wantonness.

LADY WISHFORT 'Twas against my consent that she married this barbarian, but she would have him, though her year was not out.[5]—Ah! her first husband, my son Languish, would not have carried it thus. Well, that was my choice, this is hers; she is matched now with a witness[6]—I shall be mad, dear friend. Is there no comfort for me? Must I live to be confiscated at this rebel-rate?—Here comes two more of my Egyptian plagues,[7] too.

[*Enter* MRS. MILLAMANT *and* SIR WILFULL.]

SIR WILFULL Aunt, your servant.

LADY WISHFORT Out, caterpillar, call not me aunt; I know thee not.

---

2. Peter the Great of Russia visited London in 1698.
3. I.e., *non compos mentis* (of unsound mind, Latin).
4. Legal contract.
5. The conventional period of mourning for a widow was one year.
6. With a vengeance.
7. The plagues visited by God on Pharaoh until he agreed to release the Israelites from bondage (Exodus 7–12).

SIR WILFULL   I confess I have been a little in disguise,[8] as they say—
'Sheart! and I'm sorry for't. What would you have? I hope I committed no
offense, aunt—and if I did, I am willing to make satisfaction; and what
can a man say fairer? If I have broke anything, I'll pay for't, an' it cost a
pound. And so let that content for what's past, and make no more words.
For what's to come, to pleasure you I'm willing to marry my cousin. So,
pray, let's all be friends. She and I are agreed upon the matter before a
witness.

LADY WISHFORT   How's this, dear niece? Have I any comfort? Can this be
true?

MILLAMANT   I am content to be a sacrifice to your repose, madam; and to
convince you that I had no hand in the plot, as you were misinformed, I
have laid my commands on Mirabell to come in person, and be a witness that I give my hand to this flower of knighthood; and for the contract that passed between Mirabell and me, I have obliged him to make
a resignation of it in your ladyship's presence.—He is without, and waits
your leave for admittance.

LADY WISHFORT   Well, I'll swear I am something revived at this testimony
of your obedience; but I cannot admit that traitor—I fear I cannot fortify myself to support his appearance. He is as terrible to me as a Gorgon;[9] if I see him, I fear I shall turn to stone, petrify incessantly.

MILLAMANT   If you disoblige him, he may resent your refusal, and insist
upon the contract still. Then 'tis the last time he will be offensive to you.

LADY WISHFORT   Are you sure it will be the last time?—If I were sure of
that—Shall I never see him again?

MILLAMANT   Sir Wilfull, you and he are to travel together, are you not?

SIR WILFULL   'Sheart, the gentleman's a civil gentleman, aunt, let him
come in; why, we are sworn brothers and fellow travelers. We are to
be Pylades and Orestes,[1] he and I. He is to be my interpreter in foreign
parts. He has been overseas once already; and with proviso that I marry
my cousin, will cross 'em once again, only to bear my company.—'Sheart,
I'll call him in—an I set on't once, he shall come in; and see who'll hinder him. [*Exit* SIR WILFULL.]

MRS. MARWOOD   This is precious fooling, if it would pass; but I'll know
the bottom of it.

LADY WISHFORT   O dear Marwood, you are not going?

MARWOOD   Not far, madam; I'll return immediately. [*Exit* MRS. MARWOOD.]
    [*Re-enter* SIR WILFULL *and* MIRABELL.]

SIR WILFULL [*Aside.*]   Look up, man, I'll stand by you. 'Sbud an she do
frown, she can't kill you—besides—harkee, she dare not frown desperately, because her face is none of her own. 'Sheart, an she should her
forehead would wrinkle like the coat of a cream cheese; but mum for
that, fellow traveler.

MIRABELL   If a deep sense of the many injuries I have offered to so good
a lady, with a sincere remorse, and a hearty contrition, can but obtain
the least glance of compassion, I am too happy—Ah madam, there was

---

8. Drunk.
9. In Greek mythology, a hideous monster with
snakes in her hair. Her glance turned people to
stone.

1. Pylades was the constant friend who journeyed with Orestes, the son and avenger of the
murdered king Agamemnon.

a time—but let it be forgotten—I confess I have deservedly forfeited the high place I once held of sighing at your feet. Nay kill me not by turning from me in disdain—I come not to plead for favor—nay not for pardon. I am a suppliant only for pity—I am going where I never shall behold you more—

SIR WILFULL [*Aside.*] How, fellow traveler!—You shall go by yourself then.

MIRABELL Let me be pitied first, and afterwards forgotten—I ask no more.

SIR WILFULL By'r Lady a very reasonable request, and will cost you nothing, aunt.—Come, come, forgive and forget, aunt. Why you must, an you are a Christian.

MIRABELL Consider, madam, in reality you could not receive much prejudice; it was an innocent device, though I confess it had a face of guiltiness.—It was at most an artifice which love contrived—and errors which love produces have ever been accounted venial. At least think it is punishment enough that I have lost what in my heart I hold most dear, that to your cruel indignation, I have offered up this beauty, and with her my peace and quiet; nay, all my hopes of future comfort.

SIR WILFULL An he does not move me, would I may never be o' the quorum[2]—An it were not as good a deed as to drink, to give her to him again—I would I might never take shipping.—Aunt, if you don't forgive quickly I shall melt, I can tell you that. My contract went no farther than a little mouth glue,[3] and that's hardly dry.—One doleful sigh more from my fellow traveler and 'tis dissolved.

LADY WISHFORT Well, nephew, upon your account—Ah, he has a false insinuating tongue.—Well, sir, I will stifle my just resentment at my nephew's request. I will endeavor what I can to forget—but on proviso that you resign the contract with my niece immediately.

MIRABELL It is in writing and with papers of concern, but I have sent my servant for it and will deliver it to you, with all acknowledgements for your transcendent goodness.

LADY WISHFORT [*Aside.*] O, he has witchcraft in his eyes and tongue; when I did not see him I could have bribed a villain to his assassination; but his appearance rakes the embers which have so long lain smothered in my breast.—

[*Enter* FAINALL *and* MRS. MARWOOD.]

FAINALL Your date of deliberation, madam, is expired. Here is the instrument; are you prepared to sign?

LADY WISHFORT If I were prepared, I am not empowered. My niece exerts a lawful claim, having matched herself by my direction to Sir Wilfull.

FAINALL That sham is too gross to pass on me—though 'tis imposed on you, madam.

MILLAMANT Sir, I have given my consent.

MIRABELL And, sir, I have resigned my pretensions.

2. Justices of the peace, who were required to be present at the sessions of a court.
3. Literally, glue to be used by moistening with the tongue; but here, "glue made of mere words" and therefore not binding.

SIR WILFULL   And, sir, I assert my right; and will maintain it in defiance of you, sir, and of your instrument. 'Sheart, an you talk of an instrument, sir, I have an old fox by my thigh shall hack your instrument of ram vellum[4] to shreds, sir. It shall not be sufficient for a *mittimus*[5] or a tailor's measure; therefore withdraw your instrument, sir, or by'r Lady I shall draw mine.

LADY WISHFORT   Hold, nephew, hold.

MILLAMANT   Good Sir Wilfull, respite your valor.

FAINALL   Indeed? Are you provided of your guard, with your single beefeater[6] there? But I'm prepared for you; and insist upon my first proposal. You shall submit your own estate to my management and absolutely make over my wife's to my sole use, as pursuant to the purport and tenor of this other covenant. I suppose, madam, your consent is not requisite in this case; nor, Mr. Mirabell, your resignation; nor, Sir Wilfull, your right— You may draw your fox if you please, sir, and make a bear garden[7] flourish somewhere else: for here it will not avail. This, my Lady Wishfort, must be subscribed, or your darling daughter's turned adrift, like a leaky hulk to sink or swim, as she and the current of this lewd town can agree.

LADY WISHFORT   Is there no means, no remedy, to stop my ruin? Ungrateful wretch! Dost thou not owe thy being, thy subsistence to my daughter's fortune?

FAINALL   I'll answer you when I have the rest of it in my possession.

MIRABELL   But that you would not accept of a remedy from my hands—I own I have not deserved you should owe any obligation to me; or else perhaps I could advise—

LADY WISHFORT   O, what? what? to save me and my child from ruin, from want, I'll forgive all that's past; nay, I'll consent to anything to come, to be delivered from this tyranny.

MIRABELL   Aye, madam, but that is too late; my reward is intercepted. You have disposed of her who only could have made me a compensation for all my services; but be it as it may, I am resolved I'll serve you. You shall not be wronged in this savage manner.

LADY WISHFORT   How! Dear Mr. Mirabell, can you be so generous at last! But it is not possible. Harkee, I'll break my nephew's match, you shall have my niece yet, and all her fortune, if you can but save me from this imminent danger.

MIRABELL   Will you? I take you at your word. I ask no more. I must have leave for two criminals to appear.

LADY WISHFORT   Aye, aye, anybody, anybody.

MIRABELL   Foible is one, and a penitent.

[*Enter* MRS. FAINALL, FOIBLE, *and* MINCING.]

MRS. MARWOOD   O, my shame! These corrupt things are brought hither to expose me.

[MIRABELL *and* LADY WISHFORT *go to* MRS. FAINALL *and* FOIBLE.]

---

4. The legal instrument to be signed is written on vellum. "Fox": a kind of sword.
5. A warrant, committing a felon to jail.

6. Yeoman of the guard.
7. The place for bear baiting, frequented by a vulgar and unruly crowd. "Draw": track by scent.

FAINALL If it must all come out, why let 'em know it, 'tis but *the way of the world*. That shall not urge me to relinquish or abate one tittle of my terms; no, I will insist the more.

FOIBLE Yes, indeed, madam, I'll take my Bible-oath of it.

MINCING And so will I, mem.

LADY WISHFORT O Marwood, Marwood, art thou false? My friend deceive me? Hast thou been a wicked accomplice with that profligate man?

MRS. MARWOOD Have you so much ingratitude and injustice, to give credit against your friend to the aspersions of two such mercenary trulls?

MINCING Mercenary, mem? I scorn your words. 'Tis true we found you and Mr. Fainall in the blue garret; by the same token, you swore us to secrecy upon Messalina's[8] poems. Mercenary? No, if we would have been mercenary, we should have held our tongues; you would have bribed us sufficiently.

FAINALL Go, you are an insignificant thing. Well, what are you the better for this! Is this Mr. Mirabell's expedient? I'll be put off no longer. You, thing that was a wife, shall smart for this. I will not leave thee where-withal to hide thy shame: your body shall be naked as your reputation.

MRS. FAINALL I despise you and defy your malice.—You have aspersed me wrongfully.—I have proved your falsehood.—Go, you and your treacher-ous—I will not name it, but starve together—perish.

FAINALL Not while you are worth a groat, indeed, my dear. Madam, I'll be fooled no longer.

LADY WISHFORT Ah, Mr. Mirabell, this is small comfort, the detection of this affair.

MIRABELL O, in good time—Your leave for the other offender and peni-tent to appear, madam.

[*Enter* WAITWELL *with a box of writings.*]

LADY WISHFORT O Sir Rowland—Well, rascal.

WAITWELL What your ladyship pleases—I have brought the black box at last, madam.

MIRABELL Give it me. Madam, you remember your promise.

LADY WISHFORT Aye, dear sir.

MIRABELL Where are the gentlemen?

WAITWELL At hand, sir, rubbing their eyes, just risen from sleep.

FAINALL 'Sdeath, what's this to me? I'll not wait your private concerns.

[*Enter* PETULANT *and* WITWOUD.]

PETULANT How now? What's the matter? Whose hand's out?[9]

WITWOUD Heyday! What, are you all got together, like players at the end of the last act?

MIRABELL You may remember, gentlemen, I once requested your hands as witnesses to a certain parchment.

WITWOUD Aye, I do, my hand I remember—Petulant set his mark.

MIRABELL You wrong him, his name is fairly written, as shall appear. You do not remember, gentlemen, anything of what that parchment contained—[*Undoing the box.*]

---

8. Mincing means *Miscellany*, a collection of poems by various writers, such as Dryden's popu-lar *Miscellanies*. Messalina was the viciously debauched wife of the Roman emperor Claudius. 9. I.e., Whose game's over?

WITWOUD   No.

PETULANT   Not I. I writ, I read nothing.

MIRABELL   Very well, now you shall know. Madam, your promise.

LADY WISHFORT   Aye, aye, sir, upon my honor.

MIRABELL   Mr. Fainall, it is now time that you should know that your lady, while she was at her own disposal, and before you had by your insinuations wheedled her out of a pretended settlement of the greatest part of her fortune—

FAINALL   Sir! Pretended!

MIRABELL   Yes, sir. I say that this lady while a widow, having, it seems, received some cautions respecting your inconstancy and tyranny of temper, which from her own partial opinion and fondness of you she could never have suspected—she did, I say, by the wholesome advice of friends and of sages learned in the laws of this land, deliver this same as her act and deed to me in trust, and to the uses within mentioned. You may read if you please—[*Holding out the parchment.*]—though perhaps what is written on the back may serve your occasions.

FAINALL   Very likely, sir. What's here? Damnation!—[*Reads.*] *A deed of conveyance of the whole estate real of Arabella Languish, widow, in trust to Edward Mirabell.* Confusion!

MIRABELL   Even so, sir, 'tis the way of the world, sir; of the widows of the world. I suppose this deed may bear an elder date than what you have obtained from your lady.

FAINALL   Perfidious fiend! Then thus I'll be revenged.

[*Offers to run at* MRS. FAINALL.]

SIR WILFULL   Hold, sir, now you may make your bear garden flourish somewhere else, sir.

FAINALL   Mirabell, you shall hear of this, sir, be sure you shall. Let me pass, oaf. [*Exit* FAINALL.]

MRS. FAINALL   Madam, you seem to stifle your resentment: you had better give it vent.

MRS. MARWOOD   Yes, it shall have vent—and to your confusion, or I'll perish in the attempt. [*Exit* MRS. MARWOOD.]

LADY WISHFORT   O daughter, daughter, 'tis plain thou hast inherited thy mother's prudence.

MRS. FAINALL   Thank Mr. Mirabell, a cautious friend, to whose advice all is owing.

LADY WISHFORT   Well, Mr. Mirabell, you have kept your promise and I must perform mine. First I pardon for your sake Sir Rowland there and Foible.—The next thing is to break the matter to my nephew—and how to do that—

MIRABELL   For that, madam, give yourself no trouble—let me have your consent.—Sir Wilfull is my friend; he has had compassion upon lovers, and generously engaged a volunteer in this action, for our service; and now designs to prosecute his travels.

SIR WILFULL   'Sheart, aunt, I have no mind to marry. My cousin's a fine lady, and the gentleman loves her, and she loves him, and they deserve one another. My resolution is to see foreign parts—I have set on't—and when I'm set on't, I must do't. And if these two gentlemen would travel too, I think they may be spared.

PETULANT   For my part, I say little—I think things are best off or on.

WITWOUD   Igad, I understand nothing of the matter—I'm in a maze yet; like a dog in a dancing school.

LADY WISHFORT   Well, sir, take her, and with her all the joy I can give you.

MILLAMANT   Why does not the man take me? Would you have me give myself to you over again?

MIRABELL   Aye, and over and over again—[*Kisses her hand.*]—I would have you as often as possibly I can. Well, Heaven grant I love you not too well, that's all my fear.

SIR WILFULL   'Sheart, you'll have time enough to toy after you're married; or if you will toy now, let us have a dance in the meantime; that we who are not lovers may have some other employment, besides looking on.

MIRABELL   With all my heart, dear Sir Wilfull. What shall we do for music?

FOIBLE   O, sir, some that were provided for Sir Rowland's entertainment are yet within call.

[A DANCE.]

LADY WISHFORT   As I am a person I can hold out no longer.—I have wasted my spirits so today already, that I am ready to sink under the fatigue; and I cannot but have some fears upon me yet, that my son Fainall will pursue some desperate course.

MIRABELL   Madam, disquiet not yourself on that account; to my knowledge his circumstances are such, he must of force comply. For my part, I will contribute all that in me lies to a reunion: in the meantime, madam—[*To* MRS. FAINALL.]—let me before these witnesses restore to you this deed of trust; it may be a means, well managed, to make you live easily together.

> From hence let those be warned, who mean to wed;
> Lest mutual falsehood stain the bridal bed:
> For each deceiver to his cost may find,
> That marriage frauds too oft are paid in kind.

[*Exeunt omnes.*]

Epilogue

SPOKEN BY MRS. BRACEGIRDLE[1]

> After our Epilogue this crowd dismisses,
> I'm thinking how this play'll be pulled to pieces.
> But pray consider, e'er you doom its fall,
> How hard a thing 'twould be to please you all.
> 5 There are some critics so with spleen diseased,
> They scarcely come inclining to be pleased;
> And sure he must have more than mortal skill,
> Who pleases anyone against his will.
> Then, all bad poets we are sure are foes,
> 10 And how their number's swelled the town well knows:

---

1. Anne Bracegirdle (ca. 1663–1748), the most brilliant actress of her generation. She created the role of Millamant. Congreve loved her, and it was rumored that they were secretly married.

In shoals, I've marked 'em judging in the pit; }
Though they're on no pretence for judgment fit, }
But that they have been damned for want of wit. }
Since when, they by their own offenses taught
15 Set up for spies on plays, and finding fault.
Others there are whose malice we'd prevent; }
Such, who watch plays, with scurrilous intent }
To mark out who by characters are meant. }
And though no perfect likeness they can trace,
20 Yet each pretends to know the copied face.
These, with false glosses feed their own ill-nature,
And turn to libel, what was meant a *satire*.[2]
May such malicious fops this fortune find,
To think themselves alone the fools designed:
25 If any are so arrogantly vain, }
To think they singly can support a scene, }
And furnish fool enough to entertain. }
For well the learn'd and the judicious know, }
That satire scorns to stoop so meanly low, }
30 As any one abstracted° fop to show. }   separated
For, as when painters form a matchless face,
They from each fair one catch some different grace,
And shining features in one portrait blend,
To which no single beauty must pretend:
35 So poets oft do in one piece expose
Whole *belles assemblées* of coquettes and beaux.

1700

2. Pronounced *nā-ter* and *sā-ter*.

MARY ASTELL
1666–1731

Daughter of a Newcastle merchant, Mary Astell was encouraged and educated by her uncle, a clergyman. She never forgot what he taught her: a confidence in her own reason and a religious faith entirely compatible with reason. In her twenties she moved to Chelsea, on the outskirts of London, where she spent the rest of her life. There she championed the causes of women and the Church of England, and her vigorous way of arguing (not only in print but in person) won her many admirers, both male and female. Her political and religious polemics also put her at odds with many important writers, including John Locke and Daniel Defoe (for her response to Lockean arguments for political liberty, see p. 965). One of her best-known works, *A Serious Proposal to the Ladies* (1694), was, like the rest of her writings, published anonymously ("by a Lover of her Sex"). It advocates the founding of a monastic school or retreat for women, where a rigorous, wide-ranging education could be combined with moral and religious discipline. Though the idea was never carried out, it had a broad influence on later plans for educating women as well as on literature. At the end of Johnson's *Rasselas*, both Pekuah's dream of leading a religious order and Nekayah's desire to found a college of learned women owe something to Astell.

To question the customs and laws of marriage is to question society itself, its distribution of money and power and love. During the eighteenth century many of the terms of marriage were renegotiated. The older view of the wife as a chattel, bound by contract to a husband whom others had chosen for her and whom she was sworn to obey, was hotly debated and challenged. The witty arguments of Congreve's *The Way of the World* (1700) reflect this growing debate between the sexes. Another work published in the same year, *Some Reflections upon Marriage*, takes a more independent position. Marriage, according to Astell, is all too often a trap. She insists that a woman should be guided by reason, not only in choosing a mate but in choosing whether or not to marry at all (Astell herself never married). So long as the institution of marriage perpetuates inequality rather than a true partnership of minds, women had better beware of flattery and look to themselves or to God, not to men, for the hope of a better life. The debate on marriage continued throughout the century in works such as Defoe's *Roxana*, Hogarth's *Marriage A-la-Mode*, the novels of Samuel Richardson, *Rasselas*, and eventually the writings of Mary Wollstonecraft and William Godwin. It still continues today. In her sharp, lively style and the pertinent questions she raised, Astell has come to be seen as ahead of her time.

From Some Reflections upon Marriage[1]

If marriage be such a blessed state, how comes it, may you say, that there are so few happy marriages? Now in answer to this, it is not to be wondered that so few succeed; we should rather be surprised to find so many do, considering how imprudently men engage, the motives they act by, and the very strange conduct they observe throughout.

For pray, what do men propose to themselves in marriage? What qualifications do they look after in a spouse? What will she bring? is the first enquiry: How many acres? Or how much ready coin? Not that this is altogether an unnecessary question, for marriage without a competency, that is, not only a bare subsistence, but even a handsome and plentiful provision, according to the quality[2] and circumstances of the parties, is no very comfortable condition. They who marry for love, as they call it, find time enough to repent their rash folly, and are not long in being convinced, that whatever fine speeches might be made in the heat of passion, there could be no *real kindness* between those who can agree to make each other miserable. But as an estate is to be considered, so it should not be the *main*, much less the *only* consideration; for happiness does not depend on wealth.

* * *

But suppose a man does not marry for money, though for one that does not, perhaps there are thousands that do; suppose he marries for love, an heroic action, which makes a mighty noise in the world, partly because of its

1. The text is from the first edition.
2. Social position. "Competency": sufficient income.

rarity, and partly in regard of its extravagancy, and what does his marrying for love amount to? There's no great odds between his marrying for the love of money, or for the love of beauty; the man does not act according to reason in either case, but is governed by irregular appetites. But he loves her wit perhaps, and this, you'll say, is more spiritual, more refined: not at all, if you examine it to the bottom. For what is that which nowadays passes under the name of wit? A bitter and ill-natured raillery, a pert repartee, or a confident talking at all; and in such a multitude of words, it's odds if something or other does not pass that is surprising, though every thing that surprises does not please; some things are wondered at for their ugliness, as well as others for their beauty. True wit, durst one venture to describe it, is quite another thing; it consists in such a sprightliness of imagination, such a reach and turn of thought, so properly expressed, as strikes and pleases a judicious taste.[3]

*   *   *

Thus, whether it be wit or beauty that a man's in love with, there's no great hopes of a lasting happiness; beauty, with all the helps of art, is of no very lasting date; the more it is helped, the sooner it decays; and he, who only or chiefly chose for beauty, will in a little time find the same reason for another choice. Nor is that sort of wit which he prefers, of a more sure tenure; or allowing it to last, it will not always please. For that which has not a real excellency and value in itself entertains no longer than that giddy humor which recommended it to us holds; and when we can like on no just, or on very little ground, 'tis certain a dislike will arise, as lightly and as unaccountably. And it is not improbable that such a husband may in a little time, by ill usage, provoke such a wife to exercise her wit, that is, her spleen[4] on him, and then it is not hard to guess how very agreeable it will be to him.

*   *   *

But do the women never choose amiss? Are the men only in fault? That is not pretended; for he who will be just must be forced to acknowledge that neither sex is always in the right. A woman, indeed, can't properly be said to choose; all that is allowed her, is to refuse or accept what is offered. And when we have made such reasonable allowances as are due to the sex, perhaps they may not appear so much in fault as one would at first imagine, and a generous spirit will find more occasion to pity than to reprove. But sure I transgress—it must not be supposed that the ladies can do amiss! He is but an ill-bred fellow who pretends that they need amendment! They are, no doubt on't, always in the right, and most of all when they take pity on distressed lovers; whatever they *say* carries an authority that no reason can resist, and all that they *do* must needs be exemplary! This is the modish language, nor is there a man of honor amongst the whole tribe that would not venture his life, nay and his salvation too, in their defense, if any but himself attempts to injure them. But I must ask pardon if I can't come up to these heights, nor flatter them with the having no faults, which is only a malicious way of continuing and increasing their mistakes.

3. Cf. Pope's *An Essay on Criticism* 2.297–304 (pp. 496–97).
4. Bad temper.

* * *

But, alas! what poor woman is ever taught that she should have a higher design than to get her a husband? Heaven will fall in of course; and if she make but an obedient and dutiful wife, she cannot miss of it. A husband indeed is thought by both sexes so very valuable, that scarce a man who can keep himself clean and make a bow, but thinks he is good enough to pretend[5] to any woman; no matter for the difference of birth or fortune, a husband is such a wonder-working name as to make an equality, or something more, whenever it is pronounced.

* * *

To wind up this matter: if a woman were duly principled and taught to know the world, especially the true sentiments that men have of her, and the traps they lay for her under so many gilded compliments, and such a seemingly great respect, that disgrace would be prevented which is brought upon too many families; women would marry more discreetly, and demean[6] themselves better in a married state than some people say they do.

* * *

But some sage persons may perhaps object, that were women allowed to improve themselves, and not, amongst other discouragements, driven back by the wise jests and scoffs that are put upon a woman of sense or learning, a philosophical lady, as she is called by way of ridicule, they would be too wise, and too good for the men. I grant it, for vicious and foolish men. Nor is it to be wondered that he is afraid he should not be able to govern them were their understandings improved, who is resolved not to take too much pains with his own. But these, 'tis to be hoped, are no very considerable number, the foolish at least; and therefore this is so far from being an argument against their improvement, that it is a strong one for it, if we do but suppose the men to be as capable of improvement as the women; but much more if, according to tradition, we believe they have greater capacities. This, if anything, would stir them up to be what they ought, not permit them to waste their time and abuse their faculties in the service of their irregular appetites and unreasonable desires, and so let poor contemptible women, who have been their slaves, excel them in all that is truly excellent. This would make them blush at employing an immortal mind no better than in making provision for the flesh to fulfill the lusts thereof, since women, by a wiser conduct, have brought themselves to such a reach of thought, to such exactness of judgment, such clearness and strength of reasoning, such purity and elevation of mind, such command of their passions, such regularity of will and affection, and, in a word, to such a pitch of perfection as the human soul is capable of attaining even in this life by the grace of God; such true wisdom, such real greatness, as though it does not qualify them to make a noise in this world, to found or overturn empires, yet it qualifies them for what is infinitely better, a Kingdom that cannot be moved, an incorruptible crown of glory.

---

5. Aspire or lay claim.   6. Behave.

* * *

Again, it may be said, if a wife's case be as it is here represented, it is not good for a woman to marry, and so there's an end of human race. But this is no fair consequence, for all that can justly be inferred from hence is that a woman has no mighty obligations to the man who makes love to her; she has no reason to be fond of being a wife, or to reckon it a piece of preferment when she is taken to be a man's upper-servant;[7] it is no advantage to her in this world; if rightly managed it may prove one as to the next. For she who marries purely to do good, to educate souls for heaven, who can be so truly mortified as to lay aside her own will and desires, to pay such an entire submission for life, to one whom she cannot be sure will always deserve it, does certainly perform a more heroic action than all the famous masculine heroes can boast of; she suffers a continual martyrdom to bring glory to God, and benefit to mankind; which consideration indeed may carry her through all difficulties, I know not what else can, and engage her to love him who proves perhaps so much worse than a brute, as to make this condition yet more grievous than it needed to be. She has need of a strong reason, of a truly Christian and well-tempered spirit, of all the assistance the best education can give her, and ought to have some good assurance of her own firmness and virtue, who ventures on such a trial; and for this reason 'tis less to be wondered at that women marry off in haste, for perhaps if they took time to consider and reflect upon it, they seldom would.

1700

7. High-ranking servant. "Preferment": advancement in rank.

ANNE FINCH, COUNTESS OF WINCHILSEA
1661–1720

Born into an ancient country family, Anne Kingsmill became a maid of honor at the court of Charles II. There she met Colonel Heneage Finch; in 1684 they married. During the short reign of James II they prospered at court, but at the king's fall in 1688 they were forced to retire, eventually settling on a beautiful family estate at Eastwell, in Kent, near the south coast of England. Here Colonel Finch became, in 1712, earl of Winchilsea, and here Anne Finch wrote most of her poems, influenced, she said, by "the solitude and security of the country," and by "objects naturally inspiring soft and poetical imaginations." Her *Miscellany Poems on Several Occasions, Written by a Lady* were published in 1713. One poem, "The Spleen," a description of the mysterious melancholic illness from which she and many other fashionable people suffered, achieved some fame; Pope seems to refer to it when he invokes the goddess Spleen in *The Rape of the Lock*. But Finch's larger reputation began only a century later, when Wordsworth praised her for keeping her eye on external nature and for a style "often admirable, chaste, tender, and vigorous."

Three things conspired to keep Finch's poems in the shade: she was an aristocrat, her nature was retiring, and she was a woman. Any one of these might have made her shrink from exposing herself to the jeers that still, at the turn of the century, greeted any effort by a "scribbling lady." Many of her best poems, for instance "The Petition for an Absolute Retreat," celebrate the joys of solitude. Nevertheless, remarkably, she chose to publish. The reason for Finch's push to publish may be found in her contempt for the notion that women are fit for nothing but trivial pursuits. In "The Introduction" (to her poems) she insists that women are "education's, more than nature's fools," and she often comments on the damaging exclusion of half the human race from public life. But Finch is her own best example of what a woman can be: keen-eyed and self-sufficient and a poet.

A Nocturnal Reverie

In such a night,[1] when every louder wind
Is to its distant cavern safe confined;
And only gentle Zephyr fans his wings,
And lonely Philomel,° still waking, sings;   *nightingale*
5   Or from some tree, famed for the owl's delight,
She, hollowing clear, directs the wanderer right:
In such a night, when passing clouds give place,
Or thinly veil the heavens' mysterious face;
When in some river, overhung with green,
10 The waving moon and trembling leaves are seen;
When freshened grass now bears itself upright,
And makes cool banks to pleasing rest invite,
Whence springs the woodbind, and the bramble-rose,
And where the sleepy cowslip sheltered grows;
15 Whilst now a paler hue the foxglove takes,
Yet checkers still with red the dusky brakes:°   *thickets*
When scattered glow-worms, but in twilight fine,
Show trivial beauties watch their hour to shine;
Whilst Salisbury[2] stands the test of every light,
20 In perfect charms, and perfect virtue bright:
When odors, which declined repelling day,
Through temperate air uninterrupted stray;
When darkened groves their softest shadows wear,
And falling waters we distinctly hear;
25 When through the gloom more venerable shows
Some ancient fabric,° awful in repose,   *edifice*
While sunburnt hills their swarthy looks conceal,
And swelling haycocks thicken up the vale:
When the loosed horse now, as his pasture leads,
30 Comes slowly grazing through the adjoining meads,
Whose stealing pace, and lengthened shade we fear,
Till torn-up forage in his teeth we hear:

1. This phrase, repeated twice in this poem, echoes the same repeated phrase in the night piece that opens act 5 of *The Merchant of Venice.*
2. Probably Lady Salisbury, the daughter of a friend. The sense is that this lady differs from others more trivial, who like glowworms look fine only one hour a day.

When nibbling sheep at large pursue their food,
And unmolested kine rechew the cud;
35 When curlews cry beneath the village walls,
And to her straggling brood the partridge calls;
Their shortlived jubilee the creatures keep,
Which but endures, whilst tyrant man does sleep;
When a sedate content the spirit feels,
40 And no fierce light disturbs, whilst it reveals;
But silent musings urge the mind to seek
Something, too high for syllables to speak;
Till the free soul to a composedness charmed,
Finding the elements of rage disarmed,
45 O'er all below a solemn quiet grown,
Joys in the inferior world,[3] and thinks it like her own:
In such a night let me abroad remain,
Till morning breaks, and all's confused again;
Our cares, our toils, our clamors are renewed,
50 Or pleasures, seldom reached, again pursued.

1713

3. The world of nature (compared to the world of the soul).

JONATHAN SWIFT
1667–1745

Jonathan Swift was born of English parents in Dublin. His father, a lawyer, died seven months before he was born, and his mother and sister went to live with relations in the English Midlands. An uncle helped see Jonathan through an excellent education at preeminent institutions in Ireland, Kilkenny School and then Trinity College, Dublin. Before he could fix on a career, the troubles that followed upon James II's abdication and subsequent invasion of Ireland drove Swift along with other Anglo-Irish to England. Between 1689 and 1699 he was more or less continuously a member of the household of his kinsman Sir William Temple, an urbane, civilized man, a retired diplomat, and a friend of King William III, who took the throne in 1689. During these years Swift read widely, rather reluctantly decided on the church as a career and so took orders, and discovered his astonishing gifts as a satirist. In 1696–97 he wrote his powerful satires on corruptions in religion and learning, A Tale of a Tub and The Battle of the Books, which were published in 1704 and reached their final form only in the fifth edition of 1710. When, at the age of thirty-two, he returned to Ireland as chaplain to the lord justice, the earl of Berkeley, he had a clear sense of his genius.

For the rest of his life, Swift devoted his talents to politics and religion—not clearly separated at the time—and most of his works in prose were written to further a specific cause. As a clergyman, a spirited controversialist, and a devoted supporter of the Anglican Church, he was hostile to all who seemed to threaten it: Deists, freethinkers, Roman Catholics, Nonconformists, or merely Whig politicians. In 1710 he abandoned the Whigs because he opposed their indifference to the welfare of the Anglican Church in Ireland and their desire to repeal the Test Act, which required all holders of offices of state to take the Sacrament according to the Anglican rites, thus excluding Roman Catholics and Dissenters. Welcomed by the Tories, he became the most brilliant political journalist of the day, serving the government of Oxford and Bolingbroke as editor of the party organ, the *Examiner,* and as author of its most powerful articles. He also wrote longer pamphlets in support of important policies, such as that favoring the Peace of Utrecht (1713). He was greatly valued by the two ministers, who admitted him to social intimacy, although never to their counsels. The reward of his services was not the English bishopric that he felt he deserved but the deanship of St. Patrick's Cathedral in Dublin, which came to him in 1713, a year before the death of Queen Anne and the fall of the Tories put an end to all his hopes of preferment in England.

In Ireland, where he lived unwillingly, he became not only an efficient ecclesiastical administrator but also, in 1724, the leader of Irish resistance to English oppression. Under the pseudonym "M. B. Drapier," he published the famous series of public letters that aroused the country to refuse to accept £100,000 in new copper coins (minted in England by William Wood, who had obtained his patent through court corruption), which, it was feared, would further debase the coinage of the already poverty-stricken kingdom. Although the authorship of the letters was known to all Dublin, no one could be found to earn the £300 offered by the government for information as to the identity of the drapier. Swift is still venerated in Ireland as a national hero. He earned the right to refer to himself in the epitaph that he wrote for his tomb as a vigorous defender of liberty.

His last years were less happy. Swift had suffered most of his adult life from what we now recognize as Ménière's disease, which affects the inner ear, causing dizziness, nausea, and deafness. After 1739, when he was seventy-two years old, his infirmities cut him off from his duties as dean, and from then on his social life dwindled. In 1742 guardians were appointed to administer his affairs, and his last three years were spent in gloom and lethargy. But this dark ending should not put his earlier life, so full of energy and humor, into a shadow. The writer of the satires was a man in full control of great intellectual powers.

He also had a gift for friendship. Swift was admired and loved by many of the distinguished men of his time. His friendships with Joseph Addison, Alexander Pope, John Arbuthnot, John Gay, Matthew Prior, Lord Oxford, and Lord Bolingbroke, not to mention those in his less brilliant but amiable Irish circle, bear witness to his moral integrity and social charm. He also had intense, tender, emotionally complicated relationships with women, especially Esther Johnson (whom he called "Stella" in his letters and poetry). She was the daughter of Temple's steward, and when Swift first knew her, she was little more than a child. He mentored her as she grew up and came to love her as he was to love no other person. After Temple's death she moved to Dublin, where she and Swift met constantly, but never alone. While working with the Tories in London, he wrote letters to her, later published as *The Journal to Stella* (1766), and they exchanged poems as well. Whether they were secretly married or never married—and in either case why—has been often debated. A marriage of any sort seems most unlikely; and however perplexing their relationship was to others, it seems to have satisfied them. Not even the violent passion that Swift awakened, no doubt unwittingly, in the much younger woman Esther Van Homrigh (pronounced *Van Úm-mery*)—with her pleadings and reproaches and early death—could unsettle his devotion to Stella. An enigmatic account of his relations with "Vanessa," as he called Van Homrigh, is given in his poem "Cadenus and Vanessa."

For all his involvement in public affairs, Swift seems to stand apart from his contemporaries—a striking figure among the statesmen of the time, a writer who towered above others by reason of his imagination, mordant wit, and emotional intensity. He has been called a misanthrope, a hater of humanity, and *Gulliver's Travels* has been considered an expression of savage misanthropy. It is true that Swift proclaimed himself a misanthrope in a letter to Pope, declaring that, though he loved individuals, he hated "that animal called man" in general and offering a new definition of the species not as *animal rationale* ("a rational animal") but as merely *animal rationis capax* ("an animal *capable* of reason"). This, he declared, is the "great foundation" on which his "misanthropy" was erected. Swift was stating not his hatred of his fellow creatures but his antagonism to the current optimistic view that human nature is essentially good. To the "philanthropic" flattery that sentimentalism and Deistic rationalism were paying to human nature, Swift opposed a more ancient view: that human nature is deeply and permanently flawed and that we can do nothing with or for the human race until we recognize its moral and intellectual limitations. In his epitaph he spoke of the "fierce indignation" that had torn his heart, an indignation that found superb expression in his greatest satires. It was provoked by the constant spectacle of creatures capable of reason, and therefore of reasonable conduct, steadfastly refusing to live up to their capabilities.

Swift is a master of prose. He defined a good style as "proper words in proper places," a more complex goal, and more difficult to attain, than it may appear. Much of his writing vigorously embraces concreteness and clarity. Yet he is also a master mimic, infusing diverse tones and mannerisms into his prose as his fictions demand, from the breathless, relentlessly elaborated sentences of *A Tale of a Tub* to Gulliver's subtle flickering between credulity and wry skepticism, joined and heightened into outrage by the end of the *Travels*, to the statistically fortified deadpan of "A Modest Proposal." A love of bluntness also animates his poems, which shock us with their hard look at the facts of life and the body. It is unpoetic poetry, devoid of, indeed as often as not mocking at, inspiration, romantic love, cosmetic beauty, easily assumed literary attitudes, and conventional poetic language. Like the prose, it is predominantly satiric in purpose, but not without its moments of comedy and lightheartedness, though most often written less to divert than to agitate the reader.

A Description of a City Shower

Careful observers may foretell the hour
(By sure prognostics) when to dread a shower:
While rain depends,[1] the pensive cat gives o'er
Her frolics, and pursues her tail no more.
5 Returning home at night, you'll find the sink°   *sewer*
Strike your offended sense with double stink.
If you be wise, then go not far to dine;
You'll spend in coach hire more than save in wine.
A coming shower your shooting corns presage,
10 Old achés throb, your hollow tooth will rage.
Sauntering in coffeehouse is Dulman[2] seen;
He damns the climate and complains of spleen.[3]
    Meanwhile the South, rising with dabbled wings,

1. Impends, is imminent. An example of elevated diction used frequently throughout the poem.
2. A type name (from "dull man"), like Congreve's "Petulant" or "Witwoud."
3. The English tendency to melancholy ("the spleen") was often attributed to the rainy climate.

A sable cloud athwart the welkin flings,
15 That swilled more liquor than it could contain,
And, like a drunkard, gives it up again.
Brisk Susan whips her linen from the rope,
While the first drizzling shower is borne aslope:
Such is that sprinkling which some careless quean°   *wench, slut*
20 Flirts on you from her mop, but not so clean:
You fly, invoke the gods; then turning, stop
To rail; she singing, still whirls on her mop.
Not yet the dust had shunned the unequal strife,
But, aided by the wind, fought still for life,
25 And wafted with its foe by violent gust,
'Twas doubtful which was rain and which was dust.
Ah! where must needy poet seek for aid,
When dust and rain at once his coat invade?
Sole coat, where dust cemented by the rain
30 Erects the nap,[4] and leaves a mingled stain.
     Now in contiguous drops the flood comes down,
Threatening with deluge this devoted town.
To shops in crowds the daggled° females fly,   *mud-spattered*
Pretend to cheapen° goods, but nothing buy.   *bargain for*
35 The Templar spruce, while every spout's abroach,[5]
Stays till 'tis fair, yet seems to call a coach.
The tucked-up sempstress walks with hasty strides,
While streams run down her oiled umbrella's sides.
Here various kinds, by various fortunes led,
40 Commence acquaintance underneath a shed.
Triumphant Tories and desponding Whigs
Forget their feuds,[6] and join to save their wigs.
Boxed in a chair° the beau impatient sits,   *sedan chair*
While spouts run clattering o'er the roof by fits,
45 And ever and anon with frightful din
The leather sounds;[7] he trembles from within.
So when Troy chairmen bore the wooden steed,
Pregnant with Greeks impatient to be freed
(Those bully Greeks, who, as the moderns do,
50 Instead of paying chairmen, run them through),[8]
Laocoön struck the outside with his spear,
And each imprisoned hero quaked for fear.[9]
     Now from all parts the swelling kennels[1] flow,
And bear their trophies with them as they go:
55 Filth of all hues and odors seem to tell
What street they sailed from, by their sight and smell.
They, as each torrent drives with rapid force,
From Smithfield or St. Pulchre's shape their course,

4. Stiffens the coat's surface.
5. Pouring out water. "The Templar": a young man engaged in studying law.
6. The Whig ministry had just fallen, and the Tories, led by Harley and St. John, were forming the government with which Swift was to be closely associated until the death of the queen in

1714.
7. The roof of the sedan chair was made of leather.
8. I.e., with their swords.
9. *Aeneid* 2.40–53.
1. The open gutters in the middle of the street.

258 | JONATHAN SWIFT

And in huge confluence joined at Snow Hill ridge,
60   Fall from the conduit prone to Holborn Bridge.[2]
Sweepings from butchers' stalls, dung, guts, and blood,
Drowned puppies, stinking sprats,[3] all drenched in mud,
Dead cats, and turnip tops, come tumbling down the flood.[4]   }

                                                              1710

Verses on the Death of Dr. Swift

Occasioned by Reading a Maxim in Rochefoucauld[1]

*Dans l'adversité de nos meilleurs amis nous trouvons toujours quelque
chose, qui ne nous déplaît pas.*[2]

        As Rochefoucauld his maxims drew
        From nature, I believe 'em true:
        They argue no corrupted mind
        In him; the fault is in mankind.
5   This maxim more than all the rest
        Is thought too base for human breast:
        "In all distresses of our friends
        We first consult our private ends,
        While Nature, kindly bent to ease us,
10   Points out some circumstance to please us."
        If this perhaps your patience move,°   *should agitate*
        Let reason and experience prove.
        We all behold with envious eyes
        Our equal raised above our size.
15   Who would not at a crowded show
        Stand high himself, keep others low?
        I love my friend as well as you,
        But why should he obstruct my view?
        Then let me have the higher post;
20   I ask but for an inch at most.
        If in a battle you should find
        One, whom you love of all mankind,
        Had some heroic action done,
        A champion killed, or trophy won;
25   Rather than thus be overtopped,

---

2. An accurate description of the drainage system of this part of London—the eastern edge of Holborn and West Smithfield, which lie outside the old walls west and east of Newgate. The great cattle and sheep markets were in Smithfield. The church of St. Sepulchre ("St. Pulchre's") stood opposite Newgate Prison. Holborn Conduit was at the foot of Snow Hill. It drained into Fleet Ditch, an evil-smelling open sewer, at Holborn Bridge.
3. Small herrings.
4. In George Faulkner's edition of Swift's *Works* (Dublin, 1735) a note almost certainly suggested by Swift points to the concluding triplet, with its resonant final alexandrine, as a burlesque of a mannerism of Dryden and other Restoration poets and claims that Swift's ridicule banished the triplet from contemporary poetry.
1. François de la Rochefoucauld (1613–1680), writer of witty, cynical maxims. Writing to Pope (November 26, 1725), Swift, opposing the optimistic philosophy that Pope and Bolingbroke (see p. 259, n. 5) were at that time developing, professed to have founded his whole character on these maxims.
2. In the misfortune of our best friends we always find something that does not displease us (French).

Would you not wish his laurels cropped?
    Dear honest Ned is in the gout,
Lies racked with pain, and you without:
How patiently you hear him groan!
How glad the case is not your own!
    What poet would not grieve to see
His brethren write as well as he?
But rather than they should excel,
He'd wish his rivals all in hell.
    Her end when Emulation misses,
She turns to envy, stings, and hisses:
The strongest friendship yields to pride,
Unless the odds be on our side.
    Vain humankind! fantastic race!
Thy various follies who can trace?
Self-love, ambition, envy, pride,
Their empire in our hearts divide.
Give others riches, power, and station;
'Tis all on me an usurpation;
I have no title to aspire,
Yet, when you sink, I seem the higher.
In Pope I cannot read a line,
But with a sigh I wish it mine:
When he can in one couplet fix
More sense than I can do in six,
It gives me such a jealous fit,
I cry, "Pox take him and his wit!"
    I grieve to be outdone by Gay[3]
In my own humorous biting way.
Arbuthnot[4] is no more my friend,
Who dares to irony pretend,
Which I was born to introduce,
Refined it first, and showed its use.
St. John, as well as Pulteney,[5] knows
That I had some repute for prose;
And, till they drove me out of date,
Could maul a minister of state.
If they have mortified my pride,
And made me throw my pen aside;
If with such talents Heaven hath blessed 'em,
Have I not reason to detest 'em?
    To all my foes, dear Fortune, send
Thy gifts, but never to my friend:
I tamely can endure the first,

Line numbers: 30, 35, 40, 45, 50, 55, 60, 65

3. The author of *The Beggar's Opera* and an intimate friend of Swift and Pope. His *Trivia, or the Art of Walking the Streets of London* (1716) owes something to Swift's "City Shower."
4. A physician and wit, friend of Swift and Pope (see Pope's *Epistle to Dr. Arbuthnot*, p. 542).
5. Henry St. John, Lord Bolingbroke (see headnote to *An Essay on Man*, p. 534), though debarred from the House of Lords and from public office, had become the center of a group of Tories and discontented young Whigs (of whom William Pulteney was one) who united in opposing Sir Robert Walpole, the chief minister. They published a political periodical, the *Craftsman*, thus rivaling Swift in his role of political pamphleteer and enemy of Sir Robert.

70   But this with envy makes me burst.
          Thus much may serve by way of proem;
      Proceed we therefore to our poem.
          The time is not remote, when I
      Must by the course of nature die;
75   When, I foresee, my special friends
      Will try to find their private ends:
      Though it is hardly understood
      Which way my death can do them good;
      Yet thus, methinks, I hear 'em speak:
80   "See how the Dean begins to break!
      Poor gentleman! he droops apace!
      You plainly find it in his face.
      That old vertigo⁶ in his head
      Will never leave him till he's dead.
85   Besides, his memory decays;
      He recollects not what he says;
      He cannot call his friends to mind;
      Forgets the place where last he dined;
      Plies you with stories o'er and o'er,
90   He told them fifty times before.
      How does he fancy we can sit
      To hear his out-of-fashion'd wit?
      But he takes up with younger folks,
      Who for his wine will bear his jokes.
95   Faith, he must make his stories shorter,
      Or change his comrades once a quarter;
      In half the time, he talks them round;
      There must another set be found.
          "For poetry, he's past his prime;
100   He takes an hour to find a rhyme;
      His fire is out, his wit decayed,
      His fancy sunk, his Muse a jade.⁷
      I'd have him throw away his pen—
      But there's no talking to some men."
105   And then their tenderness appears
      By adding largely to my years:
      "He's older than he would be reckoned,
      And well remembers Charles the Second.
      He hardly drinks a pint of wine;
110   And that, I doubt, is no good sign.
      His stomach, too, begins to fail;
      Last year we thought him strong and hale;
      But now he's quite another thing;
      I wish he may hold out till spring."
115   Then hug themselves, and reason thus:
      "It is not yet so bad with us."
          In such a case they talk in tropes,°   *figures of speech*

---

6. Johnson in his *Dictionary* authorizes Swift's pronunciation: *ver-ti-go*.
7. A worn-out horse, in contrast to Pegasus, the winged horse of Greek mythology, emblem of poetic inspiration.

And by their fears express their hopes.
Some great misfortune to portend
120   No enemy can match a friend.
With all the kindness they profess,
The merit of a lucky guess
(When daily how-d'ye's come of course,
And servants answer, "Worse and worse!")
125   Would please 'em better, than to tell
That God be praised! the Dean is well.
Then he who prophesied the best,
Approves his foresight to the rest:
"You know I always feared the worst,
130   And often told you so at first."
He'd rather choose that I should die,
Than his prediction prove a lie.
Not one foretells I shall recover,
But all agree to give me over.
135   Yet, should some neighbor feel a pain
Just in the parts where I complain,
How many a message would he send?
What hearty prayers that I should mend?
Inquire what regimen I kept;
140   What gave me ease, and how I slept,
And more lament, when I was dead,
Than all the snivelers round my bed.
    My good companions, never fear;
For though you may mistake a year,
145   Though your prognostics run too fast,
They must be verified at last.
    Behold the fatal day arrive!
"How is the Dean?"—"He's just alive."
Now the departing prayer is read.
150   "He hardly breathes"—"The Dean is dead."
Before the passing bell begun,
The news through half the town has run.
"Oh! may we all for death prepare!
What has he left? and who's his heir?"
155   "I know no more than what the news is;
'Tis all bequeathed to public uses."
"To public use! a perfect whim!
What had the public done for him?
Mere envy, avarice, and pride:
160   He gave it all—but first he died.
And had the Dean in all the nation
No worthy friend, no poor relation?
So ready to do strangers good,
Forgetting his own flesh and blood?"
165   Now Grub Street[8] wits are all employed;
With elegies the town is cloyed;

8. Originally a street in London largely inhabited by hack writers; later, a generic term applied to all such writers.

Some paragraph in every paper
To curse the Dean, or bless the Drapier.[9]
The doctors, tender of their fame,
170   Wisely on me lay all the blame.
"We must confess his case was nice;[1]
But he would never take advice.
Had he been ruled, for aught appears,
He might have lived these twenty years:
175   For, when we opened him, we found,
That all his vital parts were sound."
    From Dublin soon to London spread,
'Tis told at court, "The Dean is dead."
Kind Lady Suffolk, in the spleen,[2]
180   Runs laughing up to tell the Queen.
The Queen, so gracious, mild and good,
Cries, "Is he gone? 'tis time he should.
He's dead, you say; why, let him rot:
I'm glad the medals were forgot.[3]
185   I promised him, I own; but when?
I only was the Princess then;
But now, as consort of the King,
You know, 'tis quite a different thing."
    Now Chartres, at Sir Robert's[4] levee,°   *morning reception*
190   Tells with a sneer the tidings heavy:
"Why, is he dead without his shoes?"
Cries Bob, "I'm sorry for the news:
Oh, were the wretch but living still,
And in his place my good friend Will![5]
195   Or had a miter on his head,
Provided Bolingbroke were dead!"
    Now Curll[6] his shop from rubbish drains:
Three genuine tomes of Swift's remains.
And then, to make them pass the glibber,
200   Revised by Tibbalds, Moore, and Cibber.[7]
He'll treat me as he does my betters,
Publish my will, my life, my letters;
Revive the libels born to die,
Which Pope must bear, as well as I.
205   Here shift the scene, to represent
How those I love, my death lament.

---

9. It was in the character of M. B., a Dublin dra-pier, that Swift aroused the Irish people to resis-tance against the importation of Wood's halfpence (see headnote, p. 254).
1. Delicate; hence demanding careful diagnosis and treatment.
2. In low spirits. The phrase is ironic, as "laugh-ing" (line 180) makes clear. Lady Suffolk was George II's mistress, with whom Swift became friendly during his visit to Pope in 1726.
3. Queen Caroline had promised Swift some medals when she was Princess of Wales during the same year.
4. Sir Robert Walpole. Colonel Francis Chartres was a debauchee, often satirized by Pope.

5. William Pulteney (see p. 259, n. 5).
6. Edmund Curll, shrewd and disreputable book-seller, published pirated works, scandalous biog-raphies, and works falsely ascribed to notable writers of the time.
7. Colley Cibber (1671–1757), comic actor, play-wright, and supremely untalented poet laureate. He succeeded Theobald as king of the Dunces in Pope's *The Dunciad* of 1743. Lewis Theobald (1688–1744), Shakespeare scholar and editor, already enthroned as king of the Dunces in *The Dunciad* of 1728. Like Pope, Swift spells the name phonetically. James Moore Smythe, poetas-ter and playwright, an enemy of Pope.

Poor Pope will grieve a month, and Gay
A week, and Arbuthnot a day.
   St. John himself will scarce forbear
210 To bite his pen, and drop a tear.
The rest will give a shrug, and cry,
"I'm sorry—but we all must die."
   Indifference clad in wisdom's guise
All fortitude of mind supplies:
215 For how can stony bowels melt
In those who never pity felt?
When *we* are lashed, *they* kiss the rod,
Resigning to the will of God.
   The fools, my juniors by a year,
220 Are tortured with suspense and fear;
Who wisely thought my age a screen,
When death approached, to stand between:
The screen removed, their hearts are trembling;
They mourn for me without dissembling.
225   My female friends, whose tender hearts
Have better learned to act their parts,
Receive the news in doleful dumps:
"The Dean is dead (and what is trumps?)
Then, Lord have mercy on his soul!
230 (Ladies, I'll venture for the vole.)[8]
Six deans, they say, must bear the pall.
(I wish I knew what king to call.)
Madam, your husband will attend
The funeral of so good a friend?"
235 "No, madam, 'tis a shocking sight;
And he's engaged tomorrow night:
My Lady Club would take it ill,
If he should fail her at quadrille.
He loved the Dean—(I lead a heart)
240 But dearest friends, they say, must part.
His time was come; he ran his race;
We hope he's in a better place."
   Why do we grieve that friends should die?
No loss more easy to supply.
245 One year is past; a different scene;
No further mention of the Dean,
Who now, alas! no more is missed,
Than if he never did exist.
Where's now this favorite of Apollo?[9]
250 Departed—and his works must follow,
Must undergo the common fate;
His kind of wit is out of date.
   Some country squire to Lintot[1] goes,
Inquires for *Swift* in verse and prose.

---

8. The equivalent in the card game quadrille of bidding a grand slam in bridge.
9. Poet who is inspired by the god of poetry (Apollo).
1. Bernard Lintot, a bookseller and the publisher of Pope's Homer and some of his early poems.

255   Says Lintot, "I have heard the name;
      He died a year ago."—"The same."
      He searches all his shop in vain.
      "Sir, you may find them in Duck Lane:[2]
      I sent them, with a load of books,
260   Last Monday to the pastry-cook's.[3]
      To fancy they could live a year!
      I find you're but a stranger here.
      The Dean was famous in his time,
      And had a kind of knack at rhyme.
265   His way of writing now is past:
      The town has got a better taste.
      I keep no antiquated stuff;
      But spick and span I have enough.
      Pray do but give me leave to show 'em:
270   Here's Colley Cibber's birthday poem.[4]
      This ode you never yet have seen
      By Stephen Duck[5] upon the Queen.
      Then here's a letter finely penned
      Against the *Craftsman*[6] and his friend;
275   It clearly shows that all reflection
      On ministers is disaffection.
      Next, here's Sir Robert's vindication,[7]
      And Mr. Henley's[8] last oration.
      The hawkers have not got 'em yet:
280   Your honor please to buy a set?
          "Here's Woolston's[9] tracts, the twelfth edition;
      'Tis read by every politician:
      The country members, when in town,
      To all their boroughs send them down;
285   You never met a thing so smart;
      The courtiers have them all by heart;
      Those maids of honor (who can read)
      Are taught to use them for their creed.
      The reverend author's good intention
290   Has been rewarded with a pension.
      He does an honor to his gown,
      By bravely running priestcraft down;
      He shows, as sure as God's in Gloucester,[1]
      That Jesus was a grand impostor;
295   That all his miracles were cheats,
      Performed as jugglers do their feats:
      The Church had never such a writer;

2. London street where secondhand books and publishers' remainders were sold.
3. To be used as waste paper for lining baking dishes and wrapping parcels.
4. The laureate Cibber was obliged to celebrate each of the king's birthdays with a poem.
5. "The Thresher Poet," an agricultural laborer whose verse brought him to the notice and patronage of Queen Caroline.
6. See p. 259, n. 5.
7. Walpole hires a string of party scribblers who do nothing else but write in his defense [Swift's note].
8. "Orator" John Henley, an Independent preacher who dazzled unlearned audiences with his oratory and who wrote treatises on elocution.
9. Thomas Woolston (1670–1733), a Cambridge scholar (hence wearing a "gown" in line 291) whose *Discourses on the Miracles of Our Saviour* had recently earned him notoriety.
1. Proverbially, Gloucestershire was full of monks.

A shame he hath not got a miter!"
    Suppose me dead; and then suppose
300 A club assembled at the Rose;[2]
Where, from discourse of this and that,
I grow the subject of their chat:
And while they toss my name about,
With favor some, and some without,
305 One, quite indifferent in the cause,
My character impartial draws:
    "The Dean, if we believe report,
Was never ill received at court.
As for his works in verse and prose,
310 I own myself no judge of those;
Nor can I tell what critics thought 'em:
But this I know, all people bought 'em,
As with a moral view designed
To cure the vices of mankind.
315   "His vein, ironically grave,
Exposed the fool and lashed the knave;
To steal a hint was never known,
But what he writ was all his own.[3]
    "He never thought an honor done him,
320 Because a duke was proud to own him;
Would rather slip aside and choose
To talk with wits in dirty shoes;
Despised the fools with stars and garters,[4]
So often seen caressing Chartres.
325 He never courted men in station,
Nor persons held in admiration;
Of no man's greatness was afraid,
Because he sought for no man's aid.
Though trusted long in great affairs,
330 He gave himself no haughty airs;
Without regarding private ends,
Spent all his credit for his friends;
And only chose the wise and good;
No flatterers, no allies in blood;
335 But succored virtue in distress,
And seldom failed of good success;
As numbers in their hearts must own,
Who, but for him, had been unknown.
    "With princes kept a due decorum,
340 But never stood in awe before 'em.
He followed David's lesson just;
In princes never put thy trust:[5]
And would you make him truly sour,
Provoke him with a slave in power.
345 The Irish senate if you named,

---

2. A fashionable tavern in Covent Garden.
3. A near exact copy of line 30 of John Denham's "On Mr. Abraham Cowley" (1667): "Yet what he wrote was all his own."
4. Emblems of knighthood.
5. Psalms 146.3.

With what impatience he declaimed!
Fair Liberty was all his cry,
For her he stood prepared to die;
For her he boldly stood alone;
350 For her he oft exposed his own.
Two kingdoms, just as faction led,
Had set a price upon his head,
But not a traitor could be found,
To sell him for six hundred pound.[6]
355 "Had he but spared his tongue and pen,
He might have rose like other men;
But power was never in his thought,
And wealth he valued not a groat:
Ingratitude he often found,
360 And pitied those who meant the wound;
But kept the tenor of his mind,
To merit well of human kind:
Nor made a sacrifice of those
Who still were true, to please his foes.
365 He labored many a fruitless hour,
To reconcile his friends in power;
Saw mischief by a faction brewing,
While they pursued each other's ruin.
But, finding vain was all his care,
370 He left the court in mere despair.[7]
"And, oh! how short are human schemes!
Here ended all our golden dreams.
What St. John's skill in state affairs,
What Ormonde's[8] valor, Oxford's cares,
375 To save their sinking country lent,
Was all destroyed by one event.[9]
Too soon that precious life was ended,
On which alone our weal depended.
When up a dangerous faction starts,[1]
380 With wrath and vengeance in their hearts;
By solemn League and Covenant bound,
To ruin, slaughter, and confound;
To turn religion to a fable,
And make the government a Babel;
385 Pervert the laws, disgrace the gown,
Corrupt the senate, rob the crown;
To sacrifice old England's glory,

6. In 1714 the government offered £300 for the discovery of the author of Swift's "Public Spirit of the Whigs," and in 1724 the Irish government offered a similar amount for the discovery of the author of the fourth of Swift's *Drapier's Letters*.
7. The antagonism between the two chief ministers (his dear friends), Robert Harley, earl of Oxford, and Bolingbroke, paralyzed the Tory ministry in the crucial last months of Queen Anne's life and drove Swift to retirement in Ireland, whence he returned in 1714 to make a final effort to heal the breach and save the government, which failed.
8. James Butler, duke of Ormond, who succeeded to the command of the English armies on the Continent when, in 1711, the duke of Marlborough was stripped of his offices by Anne. He went into exile in 1714 and was active in Jacobite intrigue.
9. The death of Queen Anne.
1. Swift feared the policies of the "dangerous faction" (the Whig party) because its toleration of Dissenters threatened the Church of England.

And make her infamous in story:
When such a tempest shook the land,
390 How could unguarded Virtue stand?
With horror, grief, despair, the Dean
Beheld the dire destructive scene:
His friends in exile, or the Tower,[2]
Himself within the frown of power,
395 Pursued by base envenomed pens,
Far to the land of slaves and fens;°   *Ireland*
A servile race in folly nursed,
Who truckle most, when treated worst.
    "By innocence and resolution,
400 He bore continual persecution;
While numbers to preferment rose,
Whose merits were to be his foes;
When even his own familiar friends,
Intent upon their private ends,
405 Like renegadoes now he feels,
Against him lifting up their heels.
    "The Dean did, by his pen, defeat
An infamous destructive cheat;[3]
Taught fools their interest how to know,
410 And gave them arms to ward the blow.
Envy has owned it was his doing,
To save that hapless land from ruin;
While they who at the steerage[4] stood,
And reaped the profit, sought his blood.
415   "To save them from their evil fate,
In him was held a crime of state.
A wicked monster on the bench,[5]
Whose fury blood could never quench;
As vile and profligate a villain,
420 As modern Scroggs, or old Tresilian;[6]
Who long all justice had discarded,
Nor feared he God, nor man regarded;
Vowed on the Dean his rage to vent,
And make him of his zeal repent:
425 But Heaven his innocence defends,
The grateful people stand his friends;
Not strains of law, nor judge's frown,
Nor topics° brought to please the crown,   *arguments*

2. Bolingbroke was in exile. Oxford was sent to the Tower of London by the Whigs.
3. The scheme to introduce Wood's copper halfpence into Ireland in 1723–24.
4. Literally the steering of a ship. Here the direction and management of public affairs in Ireland.
5. William Whitshed, lord chief justice of the King's Bench of Ireland. In 1720, when the jury refused to find Swift's anonymous pamphlet "Proposal for the Universal Use of Irish Manufacture" wicked and seditious, Whitshed sent them back nine times, hoping to force them to another ver-

dict. In 1724 he presided over the trial of Harding, the printer of the fourth of Swift's *Drapier's Letters,* but again was unable, despite bullying, to force a verdict of guilty.
6. In 1381, Sir Robert Tresilian punished with great severity men who had participated in the Peasants' Revolt; he was impeached and in 1387 was hanged. Sir William Scroggs, lord chief justice of England at the time of the Popish Plot, 1678 (see Dryden's *Absalom and Achitophel,* p. 38), was impeached for his misdemeanors in office in 1680.

Nor witness hired, nor jury picked,
430 Prevail to bring him in convict.
    "In exile, with a steady heart,
He spent his life's declining part;
Where folly, pride, and faction sway,
Remote from St. John, Pope, and Gay.
435   "His friendships there, to few confined,
Were always of the middling kind;
No fools of rank, a mongrel breed,
Who fain would pass for lords indeed:
Where titles give no right or power,
440 And peerage is a withered flower;
He would have held it a disgrace,
If such a wretch had known his face.
On rural squires, that kingdom's bane,
He vented oft his wrath in vain;
445 Biennial squires[7] to market brought:
Who sell their souls and votes for naught;
The nation stripped, go joyful back,
To rob the church, their tenants rack,
Go snacks° with rogues and rapparees;°   *shares / highwaymen*
450 And keep the peace to pick up fees;
In every job to have a share,
A jail or barrack to repair;
And turn the tax for public roads
Commodious to their own abodes.
455   "Perhaps I may allow the Dean
Had too much satire in his vein;
And seemed determined not to starve it,
Because no age could more deserve it.
Yet malice never was his aim;
460 He lashed the vice, but spared the name;
No individual could resent,
Where thousands equally were meant;
His satire points at no defect,
But what all mortals may correct;
465 For he abhorred that senseless tribe
Who call it humor when they gibe:
He spared a hump, or crooked nose,
Whose owners set not up for beaux.
True genuine dullness moved his pity,
470 Unless it offered to be witty.
Those who their ignorance confessed,
He ne'er offended with a jest;
But laughed to hear an idiot quote
A verse from Horace learned by rote.
475   "He knew an hundred pleasant stories,
With all the turns of Whigs and Tories:
Was cheerful to his dying day;
And friends would let him have his way.

7. Members of the Irish Parliament.

"He gave the little wealth he had
480 To build a house for fools and mad;[8]
And showed by one satiric touch,
No nation wanted it so much.
That kingdom he hath left his debtor,
I wish it soon may have a better."

1731   1739

From A Tale of a Tub

A Digression Concerning the Original, the Use, and Improvement of Madness in a Commonwealth[1]

Nor shall it any ways detract from the just reputation of this famous sect,[2] that its rise and institution are owing to such an author as I have described Jack to be, a person whose intellectuals were overturned, and his brain shaken out of its natural position; which we commonly suppose to be a distemper, and call by the name of madness or frenzy. For, if we take a survey of the greatest actions that have been performed in the world, under the influence of single men, which are the establishment of new empires by conquest, the advance and progress of new schemes in philosophy, and the contriving, as well as the propagating, of new religions, we shall find the authors of them all to have been persons whose natural reason had admitted great revolutions from their diet, their education, the prevalency of some certain temper, together with the particular influence of air and climate. Besides, there is something individual in human minds, that easily kindles at the accidental approach and collision of certain circumstances, which, though of paltry and mean appearance, do often flame out into the greatest emergencies of life. For great turns are not always given by strong hands, but by lucky adaption, and at proper seasons; and it is of no import where the fire was kindled, if the vapor has once got up into the brain. For the upper region of man is furnished like the middle region of the air; the materials are formed from causes of the widest difference, yet produce at last the same substance and effect. Mists arise from the earth, steams from dunghills, exhalations from the sea, and smoke from fire; yet all clouds are the same in composition as well as consequences, and the fumes issuing from a jakes[3] will furnish as comely and useful a vapor as incense from an altar. Thus far,

8. Swift left funds to endow a hospital for the insane.
1. *A Tale of a Tub*, Swift's first major work, recounts the adventures of three brothers: Peter (Roman Catholicism), Martin (Luther, here regarded as inspiring the Church of England), and Jack (Calvin, the spirit of Protestant dissent). But the most memorable character of the book is its narrator, who interrupts the story with numerous digressions (including even "A Digression in Praise of Digressions") and whose pride in learning and lack of common sense represent the zealous modern insanity that Swift takes as his target for satire. "A Digression Concerning Madness,"

this narrator's masterpiece, is based on Swift's ironic doctrine of "the mechanical operation of the spirit": the notion that all spiritual and mental states derive from physical causes—in this case, the ascent of "vapors" to the brain. Beneath his whimsy, however, the author raises a fearful question: what right has any human being to trust that he or she is sane?
2. The Aeolists, who "maintain the original cause of all things to be wind," are equated by Swift with religious dissenters who believe themselves to be inspired by the Holy Spirit.
3. Latrine.

I suppose, will easily be granted me; and then it will follow, that as the face of nature never produces rain but when it is overcast and disturbed, so human understanding, seated in the brain, must be troubled and overspread by vapors, ascending from the lower faculties to water the invention and render it fruitful. Now, although these vapors (as it hath been already said) are of as various original as those of the skies, yet the crop they produce differs both in kind and degree, merely according to the soil. I will produce two instances to prove and explain what I am now advancing.

A certain great prince[4] raised a mighty army, filled his coffers with infinite treasures, provided an invincible fleet, and all this without giving the least part of his design to his greatest ministers or his nearest favorites. Immediately the whole world was alarmed; the neighboring crowns in trembling expectation towards what point the storm would burst; the small politicians everywhere forming profound conjectures. Some believed he had laid a scheme for universal monarchy; others, after much insight, determined the matter to be a project for pulling down the Pope, and setting up the reformed religion, which had once been his own. Some again, of a deeper sagacity, sent him into Asia to subdue the Turk, and recover Palestine. In the midst of all these projects and preparations, a certain state-surgeon,[5] gathering the nature of the disease by these symptoms, attempted the cure, at one blow performed the operation, broke the bag, and out flew the vapor; nor did anything want to render it a complete remedy, only that the prince unfortunately happened to die in the performance. Now, is the reader exceeding curious to learn whence this vapor took its rise, which had so long set the nations at a gaze? What secret wheel, what hidden spring, could put into motion so wonderful an engine? It was afterwards discovered that the movement of this whole machine had been directed by an absent female, whose eyes had raised a protuberancy, and before emission, she was removed into an enemy's country. What should an unhappy prince do in such ticklish circumstances as these? He tried in vain the poet's never-failing receipt of *corpora quaeque*;[6] for,

> *Idque petit corpus mens unde est saucia amore:*
> *Unde feritur, eo tendit, gestitque coire.*[7]—Lucretius

Having to no purpose used all peaceable endeavors, the collected part of the semen, raised and inflamed, became adust,[8] converted to choler, turned head upon the spinal duct, and ascended to the brain. The very same principle that influences a bully to break the windows of a whore who has jilted him, naturally stirs up a great prince to raise mighty armies, and dream of nothing but sieges, battles, and victories.

> ——*Teterrima belli*
> *Causa*[9]——

4. "This was Harry the Great of France" [Swift's note]. Henry IV (1553–1610), infatuated with the princesse de Condé, whose husband had removed her to the Spanish Netherlands, prepared an expedition to bring her back.
5. Ravillac, who stabbed Henry the Great in his coach [Swift's note].
6. Any available bodies (Latin). "Receipt": recipe.

7. The body strives for that which sickens the mind with love. . . . Stretches out toward that which smites it, and yearns to couple (Latin; *De Rerum Natura* 4.1048ff.).
8. Burned up.
9. "The most abominable cause of war" (Latin) in olden days, according to Horace, *Satires* 1.3.107–08, was a whore.

The other instance is what I have read somewhere in a very ancient author, of a mighty king,[1] who, for the space of above thirty years, amused himself to take and lose towns, beat armies, and be beaten, drive princes out of their dominions; fright children from their bread and butter; burn, lay waste, plunder, dragoon, massacre subject and stranger, friend and foe, male and female. 'Tis recorded, that the philosophers of each country were in grave dispute upon causes natural, moral, and political, to find out where they should assign an original solution of this phenomenon. At last the vapor or spirit, which animated the hero's brain, being in perpetual circulation, seized upon that region of the human body, so renowned for furnishing the *zibeta occidentalis*,[2] and gathering there into a tumor, left the rest of the world for that time in peace. Of such mighty consequence it is where those exhalations fix, and of so little from whence they proceed. The same spirits which, in their superior progress, would conquer a kingdom, descending upon the anus, conclude in a fistula.[3]

Let us next examine the great introducers of new schemes in philosophy, and search till we can find from what faculty of the soul the disposition arises in mortal man, of taking it into his head to advance new systems with such an eager zeal, in things agreed on all hands impossible to be known; from what seeds this disposition springs, and to what quality of human nature these grand innovators have been indebted for their number of disciples. Because it is plain, that several of the chief among them, both ancient and modern, were usually mistaken by their adversaries, and indeed by all except their own followers, to have been persons crazed, or out of their wits; having generally proceeded, in the common course of their words and actions, by a method very different from the vulgar dictates of unrefined reason; agreeing for the most part in their several models, with their present undoubted successors in the academy of modern Bedlam[4] (whose merits and principles I shall farther examine in due place). Of this kind were *Epicurus, Diogenes, Apollonius, Lucretius, Paracelsus, Descartes*,[5] and others, who, if they were now in the world, tied fast, and separate from their followers, would, in this our undistinguishing age, incur manifest danger of phlebotomy,[6] and whips, and chains, and dark chambers, and straw. For what man, in the natural state or course of thinking, did ever conceive it in his power to reduce the notions of all mankind exactly to the same length, and breadth, and height of his own? Yet this is the first humble and civil design of all innovators in the empire of reason. Epicurus modestly hoped, that one time or other a certain fortuitous concourse of all men's opinions, after perpetual justlings, the sharp with the smooth, the light and the heavy, the round and the square, would by certain *clinamina*[7] unite in the notions of atoms and void, as these did in the originals of all things. Cartesius reckoned to see,

1. This is meant of the present French king [Louis XIV] [Swift's note].
2. Paracelsus, who was so famous for chemistry, tried an experiment upon human excrement, to make a perfume of it, which when he had brought to perfection, he called *zibeta occidentalis*, or western-civet, the back parts of man . . . being the west [Swift's note].
3. Ulcer shaped like a pipe.
4. Bethlehem hospital, London's lunatic asylum.

5. Each of these famous speculative thinkers was known as a materialist, hence suspected by Swift of encouraging atheism.
6. Medical bloodletting.
7. Swerves. The Greek philosopher Epicurus held that the universe was formed by atoms swerving together. Swift implies that a similar miracle would be required for people to join in agreement with Epicurus.

before he died, the sentiments of all philosophers, like so many lesser stars in his romantic system, wrapped and drawn within his own vortex.[8] Now, I would gladly be informed, how it is possible to account for such imaginations as these in particular men without recourse to my phenomenon of vapors, ascending from the lower faculties to overshadow the brain, and there distilling into conceptions for which the narrowness of our mother-tongue has not yet assigned any other name beside that of madness or frenzy. Let us therefore now conjecture how it comes to pass, that none of these great prescribers do ever fail providing themselves and their notions with a number of implicit disciples. And, I think, the reason is easy to be assigned: for there is a peculiar string in the harmony of human understanding, which in several individuals is exactly of the same tuning. This, if you can dexterously screw up to its right key, and then strike gently upon it, whenever you have the good fortune to light among those of the same pitch, they will, by a secret necessary sympathy, strike exactly at the same time. And in this one circumstance lies all the skill or luck of the matter; for if you chance to jar the string among those who are either above or below your own height, instead of subscribing to your doctrine, they will tie you fast, call you mad, and feed you with bread and water. It is therefore a point of the nicest conduct to distinguish and adapt this noble talent, with respect to the differences of persons and of times. Cicero understood this very well, when writing to a friend in England, with a caution, among other matters, to beware of being cheated by our hackney-coachmen (who, it seems, in those days were as arrant rascals as they are now), has these remarkable words: *Est quod gaudeas te in ista loca venisse, ubi aliquid sapere viderere.*[9] For, to speak a bold truth, it is a fatal miscarriage so ill to order affairs, as to pass for a fool in one company, when in another you might be treated as a philosopher. Which I desire some certain gentlemen of my acquaintance to lay up in their hearts, as a very seasonable *innuendo.*

This, indeed, was the fatal mistake of that worthy gentleman, my most ingenious friend, Mr. W—tt—n,[1] a person, in appearance, ordained for great designs, as well as performances; whether you will consider his notions or his looks. Surely no man ever advanced into the public with fitter qualifications of body and mind, for the propagation of a new religion. Oh, had those happy talents, misapplied to vain philosophy, been turned into their proper channels of dreams and visions, where distortion of mind and countenance are of such sovereign use, the base detracting world would not then have dared to report that something is amiss, that his brain has undergone an unlucky shake; which even his brother modernists themselves, like ungrates, do whisper so loud, that it reaches up to the very garret I am now writing in.

Lastly, whosoever pleases to look into the fountains of enthusiasm,[2] from whence, in all ages, have eternally proceeded such fattening streams, will find the springhead to have been as troubled and muddy as the current. Of

---

8. The physics of René Descartes (1596–1650) is based on a theory of vortices. Swift considered the theory pure romance.
9. It is ground for rejoicing that you have come to such places, where anyone can seem wise (Latin; Cicero's *Familiar Epistles* 7.10).
1. William Wotton (who had championed modern authors against Swift's patron, Sir William Temple, a spokesman for the ancients) is ridiculed in Swift's *The Battle of the Books,* published in the same volume as *A Tale of a Tub* (1704).
2. For much of the 18th century the word *enthusiasm* (literally, "possessed by a god") signified a deluded belief in personal revelation.

such great emolument is a tincture of this vapor, which the world calls madness, that without its help, the world would not only be deprived of those two great blessings, conquests and systems, but even all mankind would unhappily be reduced to the same belief in things invisible. Now, the former *postulatum* being held, that it is of no import from what originals this vapor proceeds, but either in what angles it strikes and spreads over the understanding, or upon what species of brain it ascends; it will be a very delicate point to cut the feather, and divide the several reasons to a nice and curious reader, how this numerical difference in the brain can produce effects of so vast a difference from the same vapor, as to be the sole point of individuation between Alexander the Great, Jack of Leyden[3] and Monsieur Descartes. The present argument is the most abstracted that ever I engaged in; it strains my faculties to their highest stretch; and I desire the reader to attend with utmost perpensity;[4] for I now proceed to unravel this knotty point.

There is in mankind a certain[5] •   •   •   •   •
•   •   •   •   •   •   •   •   •   •
Hic multa   •   •   •   •   •   •
desiderantur.[6]   •   •   •   •   •   •
•   •   •   •   •   • And this I take to be a
clear solution of the matter.

Having therefore so narrowly passed through this intricate difficulty, the reader will, I am sure, agree with me in the conclusion, that if the moderns mean by madness, only a disturbance or transposition of the brain, by force of certain vapors issuing up from the lower faculties, then has this madness been the parent of all those mighty revolutions that have happened in empire, in philosophy, and in religion. For the brain, in its natural position and state of serenity, disposeth its owner to pass his life in the common forms, without any thought of subduing multitudes to his own power, his reasons, or his visions; and the more he shapes his understanding by the pattern of human learning, the less he is inclined to form parties after his particular notions, because that instructs him in his private infirmities, as well as in the stubborn ignorance of the people. But when a man's fancy gets astride on his reason, when imagination is at cuffs[7] with the senses, and common understanding, as well as common sense, is kicked out of doors, the first proselyte he makes is himself; and when that is once compassed, the difficulty is not so great in bringing over others; a strong delusion always operating from without as vigorously as from within. For cant[8] and vision are to the ear and the eye, the same that tickling is to the touch. Those entertainments and pleasures we most value in life, are such as dupe and play the wag with the senses. For, if we take an examination of what is generally understood by happiness, as it has respect either to the understanding or the senses, we shall find all its properties and adjuncts will herd under

3. John of Leyden, a tailor and prophet, briefly established a revolutionary Anabaptist community, the "New Jerusalem," in the city of Münster early in the 16th century.
4. Consideration.
5. Here is another defect in the manuscript, but I think the author did wisely, and that the matter which thus strained his faculties, was not worth a solution; and it were well if all metaphysical cob-

web problems were no otherwise answered" [Swift's note].
6. Much is missing here (Latin), indicating a gap in the text Swift pretends to be "editing."
7. In conflict.
8. "Sudden exclamations, whining, unusual tones, and in fine all praying and preaching like the unlearned of the Presbyterians" (*Spectator* 147).

this short definition, that it is a perpetual possession of being well deceived. And first, with relation to the mind or understanding, 'tis manifest what mighty advantages fiction has over truth; and the reason is just at our elbow, because imagination can build nobler scenes, and produce more wonderful revolutions, than fortune or nature will be at expense to furnish. Nor is mankind so much to blame in his choice thus determining him, if we consider that the debate merely lies between things past and things conceived; and so the question is only this: whether things that have place in the imagination, may not as properly be said to exist, as those that are seated in the memory; which may be justly held in the affirmative, and very much to the advantage of the former, since this is acknowledged to be the womb of things, and the other allowed to be no more than the grave. Again, if we take this definition of happiness, and examine it with reference to the senses, it will be acknowledged wonderfully adapt. How fading and insipid do all objects accost us, that are not conveyed in the vehicle of delusion! How shrunk is everything, as it appears in the glass of nature! So that if it were not for the assistance of artificial mediums, false lights, refracted angles, varnish, and tinsel, there would be a mighty level in the felicity and enjoyments of mortal men. If this were seriously considered by the world, as I have a certain reason to suspect it hardly will, men would no longer reckon among their high points of wisdom, the art of exposing weak sides, and publishing infirmities; an employment, in my opinion, neither better nor worse than that of unmasking, which, I think, has never been allowed[9] fair usage, either in the world, or the playhouse.

In the proportion that credulity is a more peaceful possession of the mind than curosity, so far preferable is that wisdom, which converses about the surface, to that pretended philosophy which enters into the depth of things, and then comes gravely back with informations and discoveries, that in the inside they are good for nothing. The two senses, to which all objects first address themselves, are the sight and the touch; these never examine farther than the color, the shape, the size, and whatever other qualities dwell, or are drawn by art upon the outward of bodies; and then comes reason officiously with tools for cutting, and opening, and mangling, and piercing, offering to demonstrate, that they are not of the same consistence quite through. Now I take all this to be the last degree of perverting nature; one of whose eternal laws it is, to put her best furniture forward. And therefore, in order to save the charges of all such expensive anatomy for the time to come, I do here think fit to inform the reader, that in such conclusions as these, reason is certainly in the right, and that in most corporeal beings, which have fallen under my cognizance, the outside has been infinitely preferable to the in; whereof I have been farther convinced from some late experiments. Last week I saw a woman flayed, and you will hardly believe how much it altered her person for the worse. Yesterday I ordered the carcass of a beau to be stripped in my presence; when we were all amazed to find so many unsuspected faults under one suit of clothes. Then I laid open his brain, his heart, and his spleen; but I plainly perceived at every operation, that the farther we proceeded, we found the defects increase upon us in number and bulk; from all which, I justly formed this conclusion to myself: that whatever philoso-

9. Admitted to be.

pher or projector[1] can find out an art to solder and patch up the flaws and imperfections of nature, will deserve much better of mankind, and teach us a more useful science, than that so much in present esteem, of widening and exposing them (like him who held anatomy to be the ultimate end of physic[2]). And he, whose fortunes and dispositions have placed him in a convenient station to enjoy the fruits of this noble art; he that can with Epicurus content his ideas with the films and images that fly off upon his senses from the superficies[3] of things; such a man, truly wise, creams off nature, leaving the sour and the dregs for philosophy and reason to lap up. This is the sublime and refined point of felicity, called the possession of being well deceived; the serene peaceful state of being a fool among knaves.

But to return to madness. It is certain, that according to the system I have above deduced, every species thereof proceeds from a redundancy of vapors; therefore, as some kinds of frenzy give double strength to the sinews, so there are of other species, which add vigor, and life, and spirit to the brain. Now, it usually happens, that these active spirits, getting possession of the brain, resemble those that haunt other waste and empty dwellings, which for want of business, either vanish, and carry away a piece of the house, or else stay at home and fling it all out of the windows. By which are mystically displayed the two principal branches of madness, and which some philosophers, not considering so well as I, have mistaken to be different in their causes, over-hastily assigning the first to deficiency, and the other to redundance.

I think it therefore manifest, from what I have here advanced, that the main point of skill and address is to furnish employment for this redundancy of vapor, and prudently to adjust the season of it; by which means it may certainly become of cardinal and catholic emolument, in a commonwealth. Thus one man, choosing a proper juncture, leaps into a gulf, from thence proceeds a hero, and is called the saver of his country; another achieves the same enterprise, but unluckily timing it, has left the brand of madness fixed as a reproach upon his memory; upon so nice a distinction, are we taught to repeat the name of Curtius with reverence and love, that of Empedocles[4] with hatred and contempt. Thus also it is usually conceived, that the elder Brutus only personated the fool and madman for the good of the public; but this was nothing else than a redundancy of the same vapor long misapplied, called by the Latins, *ingenium par negotiis;*[5] or (to translate it as nearly as I can) a sort of frenzy, never in its right element, till you take it up in business of the state.

Upon all which, and many other reasons of equal weight, though not equally curious, I do here gladly embrace an opportunity I have long sought for, of recommending it as a very noble undertaking to Sir Edward Seymour, Sir Christopher Musgrave, Sir John Bowls, John How, Esq.,[6] and other patriots concerned, that they would move for leave to bring in a bill for appointing

1. Someone given to speculative experiments.
2. Medical practice.
3. Surfaces. Epicurus considered the senses, directly affected by objects, more trustworthy than reason.
4. Committed suicide by leaping into the crater of Mount Etna. The Roman hero Marcus Curtius appeased the gods by hurling himself into an ominous crack in the earth of the Forum.
5. A talent for business (Latin). Lucius Junius Brutus, like Hamlet, pretended madness to deceive his murderous uncle, Tarquin the Proud.
6. Members of Parliament.

commissioners to inspect into Bedlam, and the parts adjacent; who shall be empowered to send for persons, papers, and records, to examine into the merits and qualifications of every student and professor, to observe with utmost exactness their several dispositions and behavior, by which means, duly distinguishing and adapting their talents, they might produce admirable instruments for the several offices in a state, . . . ,[7] civil, and military, proceeding in such methods as I shall here humbly propose. And I hope the gentle reader will give some allowance to my great solicitudes in this important affair, upon account of the high esteem I have borne that honorable society, whereof I had some time the happiness to be an unworthy member.

Is any student tearing his straw in piece-meal, swearing and blaspheming, biting his grate, foaming at the mouth, and emptying his piss-pot in the spectators' faces? Let the right worshipful the commissioners of inspection give him a regiment of dragoons, and send him into Flanders among the rest. Is another eternally talking, sputtering, gaping, bawling in a sound without period or article? What wonderful talents are here mislaid! Let him be furnished immediately with a green bag and papers, and threepence in his pocket,[8] and away with him to Westminster Hall. You will find a third gravely taking the dimensions of his kennel, a person of foresight and insight, though kept quite in the dark; forwhy, like Moses, *ecce cornuta erat ejus facies.*[9] He walks duly in one pace, entreats your penny with due gravity and ceremony, talks much of hard times, and taxes, and the whore of Babylon, bars up the wooden window of his cell constantly at eight o'clock, dreams of fire, and shoplifters, and court-customers, and privileged places. Now, what a figure would all these acquirements amount to, if the owner were sent into the city[1] among his brethren! Behold a fourth, in much and deep conversation with himself, biting his thumbs at proper junctures, his countenance checkered with business and design, sometimes walking very fast, with his eyes nailed to a paper that he holds in his hands; a great saver of time, somewhat thick of hearing, very short of sight, but more of memory; a man ever in haste, a great hatcher and breeder of business, and excellent at the famous art of whispering nothing; a huge idolator of monosyllables and procrastination, so ready to give his word to everybody, that he never keeps it; one that has forgot the common meaning of words, but an admirable retainer of the sound; extremely subject to the looseness,[2] for his occasions are perpetually calling him away. If you approach his grate in his familiar intervals, "Sir," says he, "give me a penny, and I'll sing you a song; but give me the penny first." (Hence comes the common saying, and commoner practice, of parting with money for a song.) What a complete system of court skill is here described in every branch of it, and all utterly lost with wrong application! Accost the hole of another kennel, first stopping your nose, you will behold a surly, gloomy, nasty, slovenly mortal, raking in his own dung, and dabbling in his urine. The best part of his diet is the

7. Swift omits the third office, ecclesiastical. "Instruments": useful persons.
8. A lawyer's coach-hire [Swift's note] from the Inns of Court to Westminster. Most lawyers carried green bags.
9. Cornutus is either horned or shining, and by this term, Moses is described in the vulgar

Latin of the Bible [Swift's note]. Swift puns on the Latin phrase (behold his face was shining) by suggesting someone kept in the dark through being "horned," i.e., a cuckold. "Forwhy": because.
1. The commercial center of London.
2. Diarrhea.

reversion of his own ordure, which expiring into steams, whirls perpetually about, and at last re-infunds.[3] His complexion is of a dirty yellow, with a thin scattered beard, exactly agreeable to that of his diet upon its first declination, like other insects, who having their birth and education in an excrement, from thence borrow their color and their smell. The student of this apartment is very sparing of his words, but somewhat over-liberal of his breath; he holds his hand out ready to receive your penny, and immediately upon receipt withdraws to his former occupations. Now, is it not amazing to think, the society of Warwick-lane[4] should have no more concern for the recovery of so useful a member, who, if one may judge from these appearances, would become the greatest ornament to that illustrious body? Another student struts up fiercely to your teeth, puffing with his lips, half squeezing out his eyes, and very graciously holds you out his hand to kiss. The keeper desires you not to be afraid of this professor, for he will do you no hurt; to him alone is allowed the liberty of the antechamber, and the orator of the place gives you to understand, that this solemn person is a tailor run mad with pride. This considerable student is adorned with many other qualities, upon which at present I shall not farther enlarge.————*Hark in your ear*[5]————I am strangely mistaken, if all his address, his motions, and his airs, would not then be very natural, and in their proper element.

I shall not descend so minutely, as to insist upon the vast number of beaux, fiddlers, poets, and politicians, that the world might recover by such a reformation; but what is more material, besides the clear gain redounding to the commonwealth, by so large an acquisition of persons to employ, whose talents and acquirements, if I may be so bold as to affirm it, are now buried, or at least misapplied; it would be a mighty advantage accruing to the public from this inquiry, that all these would very much excel, and arrive at great perfection in their several kinds; which, I think, is manifest from what I have already shown, and shall enforce by this one plain instance: that even I myself, the author of these momentous truths, am a person, whose imaginations are hard-mouthed,[6] and exceedingly disposed to run away with his reason, which I have observed from long experience to be a very light rider, and easily shook off; upon which account, my friends will never trust me alone, without a solemn promise to vent my speculations in this, or the like manner, for the universal benefit of human kind; which perhaps the gentle, courteous, and candid reader, brimful of that modern charity and tenderness usually annexed to his office, will be very hardly persuaded to believe.

1704

---

3. Pours in again.
4. Royal College of Physicians.
5. I cannot conjecture what the author means here, or how this chasm could be filled, though it is capable of more than one interpretation [Swift's note].
6. (Of a horse) apt to reject control by the bit.

Gulliver's Travels

Gulliver's Travels is Swift's most enduring satire. Although full of allusions to recent and current events, it still rings true today, for its objects are human failings and the defective political, economic, and social institutions that they call into being. Swift adopts an ancient satirical device: the imaginary voyage. Lemuel Gulliver, the narrator, is a ship's surgeon, a moderately well educated man, kindly, resourceful, cheerful, inquiring, patriotic, truthful, and rather unimaginative—in short, a reasonably decent example of humanity, with whom a reader can readily identify. He undertakes four voyages, all of which end disastrously among "several remote nations of the world." In the first, Gulliver is shipwrecked in the empire of Lilliput, where he finds himself a giant among a diminutive people, charmed by their miniature city and amused by their toylike prettiness. But in the end they prove to be treacherous, malicious, ambitious, vengeful, and cruel. As we read we grow disenchanted with the inhabitants of this fanciful kingdom, and then gradually we begin to recognize our likeness to them, especially in the disproportion between our natural pettiness and our boundless and destructive passions. In the second voyage, Gulliver is abandoned by his shipmates in Brobdingnag, a land of giants, creatures ten times as large as Europeans. Though he fears that such monsters must be brutes, the reverse proves to be the case. Brobdingnag is something of a utopia, governed by a humane and enlightened prince who is the embodiment of moral and political wisdom. In the long interview in which Gulliver pridefully enlarges on the glories of England and its political institutions, the king reduces him to resentful silence by asking questions that reveal the difference between what England is and what it ought to be. In Brobdingnag, Gulliver finds himself a Lilliputian, his pride humbled by his helpless state and his human vanity diminished by the realization that his body must have seemed as disgusting to the Lilliputians as do the bodies of the Brobdingnagians to him.

Part 3 differs from the other parts of the *Travels*, each of which describes a single, distinct society that challenges Gulliver's sense of his own humanity by landing him among bodies very different from his. In Part 3, Gulliver instead visits many places—Laputa, Balnibarbi, Glubbdubdrib, Luggnagg, and (jarringly adding a real nation to the fantastic itinerary) Japan—and the inhabitants all at least look like normal human beings. This allows Swift to mock a variety of targets, including extremes of abstract reasoning in science, politics, and economics as well as commonly received ideas about history and human happiness. Much of this voyage reflects on political and cultural life under the administration of the Whig minister Sir Robert Walpole. The final voyage sets Gulliver between a race of horses, Houyhnhnms (pronounced *Hwín-ims*), who live entirely by reason except for a few well-controlled and muted social affections, and their slaves, the Yahoos, whose bodies are obscene caricatures of the human body and who have no glimmer of reason but are mere creatures of appetite and passion.

When *Gulliver's Travels* first appeared, everyone read it—children for the story and politicians for the satire of current affairs—and ever since it has retained a hold on readers of every kind. Almost unique in world literature, it is simple enough for children, complex enough to carry adults beyond their depth. Swift's art works on many levels. First of all, there is the sheer playfulness of the narrative. Through Gulliver's eyes, we gaze on marvel after marvel: a tiny girl who threads an invisible needle with invisible silk or a white mare who threads a needle between pastern and hoof. The travels, like a fairy story, transport us to imaginary worlds that function with a perfect, fantastic logic different from our own; Swift exercises our sense of vision. But beyond that, he exercises our perceptions of meaning. In *Gulliver's Travels,* things are seldom what they seem; irony, probing or corrosive, underlies almost every word. In the last chapter, Gulliver insists that the example of the Houyhnhnms has made him incapable of telling a lie—but the oath he swears is quoted from Sinon, whose lies to the Trojans persuaded them to accept the Trojan *horse.* Swift trains us to read alertly, to look beneath the surface. Yet on its deepest level, the book does not offer final meanings, but a question: What is a human being? Voyaging through imag-

the original manuscript is all destroyed, since the publication of my book. Neither have I any copy left; however, I have sent you some corrections, which you may insert, if ever there should be a second edition; and yet I cannot stand to them, but shall leave that matter to my judicious and candid readers, to adjust it as they please.

I hear some of our sea Yahoos find fault with my sea language, as not proper in many parts, nor now in use. I cannot help it. In my first voyages, while I was young, I was instructed by the oldest mariners, and learned to speak as they did. But I have since found that the sea Yahoos are apt, like the land ones, to become new fangled in their words; which the latter change every year; insomuch, as I remember upon each return to mine own country, their old dialect was so altered, that I could hardly understand the new. And I observe, when any Yahoo comes from London out of curiosity to visit me at mine own house, we neither of us are able to deliver our conceptions in a manner intelligible to the other.[6]

If the censure of Yahoos could any way affect me, I should have great reason to complain that some of them are so bold as to think my book of travels a mere fiction out of mine own brain; and have gone so far as to drop hints that the Houyhnhnms, and Yahoos have no more existence than the inhabitants of Utopia.

Indeed I must confess that as to the people of Lilliput, Brobdingrag (for so the word should have been spelled, and not erroneously Brobdingnag) and Laputa, I have never yet heard of any Yahoo so presumptuous as to dispute their being, or the facts I have related concerning them; because the truth immediately strikes every reader with conviction. And, is there less probability in my account of the Houyhnhnms or Yahoos, when it is manifest as to the latter, there are so many thousands even in this city, who only differ from their brother brutes in Houyhnhnmland, because they use a sort of a jabber, and do not go naked. I wrote for their amendment, and not their approbation. The united praise of the whole race would be of less consequence to me, than the neighing of those two degenerate Houyhnhnms I keep in my stable; because, from these, degenerate as they are, I still improve in some virtues, without any mixture of vice.

Do these miserable animals presume to think that I am so far degenerated as to defend my veracity; Yahoo as I am, it is well known through all Houyhnhnmland, that by the instructions and example of my illustrious master, I was able in the compass of two years (although I confess with the utmost difficulty) to remove that infernal habit of lying, shuffling, deceiving, and equivocating, so deeply rooted in the very souls of all my species; especially the Europeans.

I have other complaints to make upon this vexatious occasion; but I forbear troubling myself or you any further. I must freely confess that since my last return, some corruptions of my Yahoo nature have revived in me by conversing with a few of your species, and particularly those of mine own family, by an unavoidable necessity; else I should never have attempted so absurd a project as that of reforming the Yahoo race in this kingdom; but I have now done with all such visionary schemes for ever.

1727?   1735

6. Swift was the inveterate enemy of slang.

The Publisher to the Reader

The author of these travels, Mr. Lemuel Gulliver, is my ancient and intimate friend; there is likewise some relation between us by the mother's side. About three years ago Mr. Gulliver, growing weary of the concourse of curious people coming to him at his house in Redriff,[7] made a small purchase of land, with a convenient house, near Newark, in Nottinghamshire, his native country; where he now lives retired, yet in good esteem among his neighbors.

Although Mr. Gulliver were born in Nottinghamshire, where his father dwelt, yet I have heard him say his family came from Oxfordshire; to confirm which, I have observed in the churchyard at Banbury, in that county, several tombs and monuments of the Gullivers.

Before he quitted Redriff, he left the custody of the following papers in my hands, with the liberty to dispose of them as I should think fit. I have carefully perused them three times; the style is very plain and simple; and the only fault I find is that the author, after the manner of travelers, is a little too circumstantial. There is an air of truth apparent through the whole; and indeed the author was so distinguished for his veracity, that it became a sort of proverb among his neighbors at Redriff, when anyone affirmed a thing, to say, it was as true as if Mr. Gulliver had spoke it.

By the advice of several worthy persons, to whom, with the author's permission, I communicated these papers, I now venture to send them into the world; hoping they may be, at least for some time, a better entertainment to our young noblemen, than the common scribbles of politics and party.

This volume would have been at least twice as large, if I had not made bold to strike out innumerable passages relating to the winds and tides, as well as to the variations and bearings in the several voyages; together with the minute descriptions of the management of the ship in storms, in the style of sailors; likewise the account of the longitudes and latitudes, wherein I have reason to apprehend that Mr. Gulliver may be a little dissatisfied; but I was resolved to fit the work as much as possible to the general capacity of readers. However, if my own ignorance in sea affairs shall have led me to commit some mistakes, I alone am answerable for them; and if any traveler hath a curiosity to see the whole work at large, as it came from the hand of the author, I will be ready to gratify him.

As for any further particulars relating to the author, the reader will receive satisfaction from the first pages of the book.

RICHARD SYMPSON

Part 1. A Voyage to Lilliput

CHAPTER 1. *The author gives some account of himself and family; his first inducements to travel. He is shipwrecked, and swims for his life; gets safe on shore in the country of Lilliput; is made a prisoner, and carried up the country.*

My father had a small estate in Nottinghamshire; I was the third of five sons. He sent me to Emanuel College in Cambridge, at fourteen years old,

---

7. Rotherhithe, a district in southern London, below Tower Bridge, then frequented by sailors.

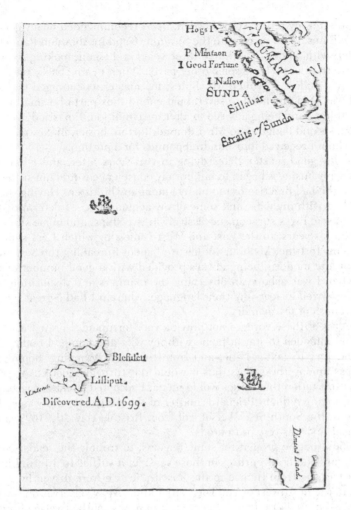

where I resided three years, and applied myself close to my studies: but the charge of maintaining me (although I had a very scanty allowance) being too great for a narrow fortune, I was bound apprentice to Mr. James Bates, an eminent surgeon in London, with whom I continued four years; and my father now and then sending me small sums of money, I laid them out in learning navigation, and other parts of the mathematics, useful to those who intend to travel, as I always believed it would be some time or other my fortune to do. When I left Mr. Bates, I went down to my father; where, by the assistance of him and my uncle John, and some other relations, I got forty pounds, and a promise of thirty pounds a year to maintain me at Leyden:[8] there I studied physic two years and seven months, knowing it would be useful in long voyages.

8. The University of Leyden, in Holland, was a center for the study of medicine ("physic").

Soon after my return from Leyden, I was recommended by my good master Mr. Bates, to be surgeon to the *Swallow,* Captain Abraham Pannell commander; with whom I continued three years and a half, making a voyage or two into the Levant[9] and some other parts. When I came back, I resolved to settle in London, to which Mr. Bates, my master, encouraged me; and by him I was recommended to several patients. I took part of a small house in the Old Jury; and being advised to alter my condition, I married Mrs.[1] Mary Burton, second daughter to Mr. Edmond Burton, hosier, in Newgate Street, with whom I received four hundred pounds for a portion.

But, my good master Bates dying in two years after, and I having few friends, my business began to fail; for my conscience would not suffer me to imitate the bad practice of too many among my brethren. Having therefore consulted with my wife, and some of my acquaintance, I determined to go again to sea. I was surgeon successively in two ships, and made several voyages, for six years, to the East and West Indies; by which I got some addition to my fortune. My hours of leisure I spent in reading the best authors, ancient and modern, being always provided with a good number of books; and when I was ashore, in observing the manners and dispositions of the people, as well as learning their language; wherein I had a great facility by the strength of my memory.

The last of these voyages not proving very fortunate, I grew weary of the sea, and intended to stay at home with my wife and family. I removed from the Old Jury to Fetter Lane, and from thence to Wapping, hoping to get business among the sailors; but it would not turn to account. After three years' expectation that things would mend, I accepted an advantageous offer from Captain William Prichard, master of the *Antelope,* who was making a voyage to the South Sea. We set sail from Bristol, May 4th, 1699, and our voyage at first was very prosperous.

It would not be proper, for some reasons, to trouble the reader with the particulars of our adventures in those seas: let it suffice to inform him, that in our passage from thence to the East Indies we were driven by a violent storm to the northwest of Van Diemen's Land.[2] By an observation, we found ourselves in the latitude of 30 degrees 2 minutes south. Twelve of our crew were dead by immoderate labor, and ill food, the rest were in a very weak condition. On the fifth of November, which was the beginning of summer in those parts, the weather being very hazy, the seamen spied a rock, within half a cable's length[3] of the ship; but the wind was so strong, that we were driven directly upon it, and immediately split. Six of the crew, of whom I was one, having let down the boat into the sea, made a shift to get clear of the ship, and the rock. We rowed by my computation about three leagues, till we were able to work no longer, being already spent with labor while we were in the ship. We therefore trusted ourselves to the mercy of the waves; and in about half an hour the boat was overset by a sudden flurry from the north. What became of my companions in the boat, as well as of those who escaped on the rock, or were left in the vessel, I cannot tell; but conclude they were all lost. For my own part, I swam as fortune directed me, and was pushed

9. The eastern Mediterranean.
1. The title (pronounced *mistress*) designated any woman, married or unmarried. "Old Jury": a street (once "Old Jewry") in the City of London.
2. Tasmania.
3. A cable is about six hundred feet (one hundred fathoms).

forward by wind and tide. I often let my legs drop, and could feel no bottom; but when I was almost gone, and able to struggle no longer, I found myself within my depth; and by this time the storm was much abated. The declivity was so small, that I walked near a mile before I got to the shore, which I conjectured was about eight o'clock in the evening. I then advanced forward near half a mile, but could not discover any sign of houses or inhabitants; at least I was in so weak a condition, that I did not observe them. I was extremely tired, and with that, and the heat of the weather, and about half a pint of brandy that I drank as I left the ship, I found myself much inclined to sleep. I lay down on the grass, which was very short and soft, where I slept sounder than ever I remember to have done in my life, and as I reckoned, above nine hours; for when I awaked, it was just daylight. I attempted to rise, but was not able to stir: for as I happened to lie on my back, I found my arms and legs were strongly fastened on each side to the ground; and my hair, which was long and thick, tied down in the same manner. I likewise felt several slender ligatures across my body, from my armpits to my thighs. I could only look upwards; the sun began to grow hot, and the light offended my eyes. I heard a confused noise about me, but in the posture I lay, could see nothing except the sky. In a little time I felt something alive moving on my left leg, which advancing gently forward over my breast, came almost up to my chin; when bending my eyes downwards as much as I could, I perceived it to be a human creature not six inches high,[4] with a bow and arrow in his hands, and a quiver at his back. In the meantime, I felt at least forty more of the same kind (as I conjectured) following the first. I was in the utmost astonishment, and roared so loud, that they all ran back in a fright; and some of them, as I was afterwards told, were hurt with the falls they got by leaping from my sides upon the ground. However, they soon returned; and one of them, who ventured so far as to get a full sight of my face, lifting up his hands and eyes by way of admiration,[5] cried out in a shrill, but distinct voice, *Hekinah Degul*: the others repeated the same words several times, but I then knew not what they meant. I lay all this while, as the reader may believe, in great uneasiness; at length, struggling to get loose, I had the fortune to break the strings, and wrench out the pegs that fastened my left arm to the ground; for, by lifting it up to my face, I discovered the methods they had taken to bind me; and, at the same time, with a violent pull, which gave me excessive pain, I a little loosened the strings that tied down my hair on the left side; so that I was just able to turn my head about two inches. But the creatures ran off a second time, before I could seize them; whereupon there was a great shout in a very shrill accent; and after it ceased, I heard one of them cry aloud, *Tolgo phonac*; when in an instant I felt above an hundred arrows discharged on my left hand, which pricked me like so many needles; and besides they shot another flight into the air, as we do bombs in Europe, whereof many, I suppose, fell on my body (though I felt them not) and some on my face, which I immediately covered with my left hand. When this shower of arrows was over, I fell a groaning with grief and pain; and then striving again to get loose, they discharged another volley larger than the first, and some of them attempted with spears to stick me in the

4. Lilliput is scaled, fairly consistently, at one-twelfth of Gulliver's world.

5. Wonderment.

sides; but, by good luck, I had on me a buff jerkin,[6] which they could not pierce. I thought it the most prudent method to lie still; and my design was to continue so till night, when, my left hand being already loose, I could easily free myself: and as for the inhabitants, I had reason to believe I might be a match for the greatest armies they could bring against me, if they were all of the same size with him that I saw. But fortune disposed otherwise of me. When the people observed I was quiet, they discharged no more arrows: but by the noise increasing, I knew their numbers were greater; and about four yards from me, over-against my right ear, I heard a knocking for above an hour, like people at work; when turning my head that way, as well as the pegs and strings would permit me, I saw a stage erected about a foot and a half from the ground, capable of holding four of the inhabitants, with two or three ladders to mount it: from whence one of them, who seemed to be a person of quality, made me a long speech, whereof I understood not one syllable. But I should have mentioned, that before the principal person began his oration, he cried out three times, *Langro Dehul san*: (these words and the former were afterwards repeated and explained to me). Whereupon immediately about fifty of the inhabitants came, and cut the strings that fastened the left side of my head, which gave me the liberty of turning it to the right, and of observing the person and gesture of him who was to speak. He appeared to be of a middle age, and taller than any of the other three who attended him; whereof one was a page who held up his train, and seemed to be somewhat longer than my middle finger; the other two stood one on each side to support him. He acted every part of an orator, and I could observe many periods[7] of threatenings, and others of promises, pity and kindness. I answered in a few words, but in the most submissive manner, lifting up my left hand and both my eyes to the sun, as calling him for a witness; and being almost famished with hunger, having not eaten a morsel for some hours before I left the ship, I found the demands of nature so strong upon me, that I could not forbear showing my impatience (perhaps against the strict rules of decency) by putting my finger frequently on my mouth, to signify that I wanted food. The *Hurgo* (for so they call a great lord, as I afterwards learned) understood me very well. He descended from the stage, and commanded that several ladders should be applied to my sides, on which above an hundred of the inhabitants mounted, and walked towards my mouth, laden with baskets full of meat, which had been provided and sent thither by the King's orders upon the first intelligence he received of me. I observed there was the flesh of several animals, but could not distinguish them by the taste. There were shoulders, legs, and loins shaped like those of mutton, and very well dressed, but smaller than the wings of a lark. I eat them by two or three at a mouthful, and took three loaves at a time, about the bigness of musket bullets. They supplied me as fast as they could, showing a thousand marks of wonder and astonishment at my bulk and appetite. I then made another sign that I wanted drink. They found by my eating that a small quantity would not suffice me; and being a most ingenious people, they slung up with great dexterity one of their largest hogsheads; then rolled it towards my hand, and beat out the top; I drank it off at a draught,

6. Leather jacket.
7. In rhetoric, complete, well-constructed sentences.

which I might well do, for it hardly held half a pint, and tasted like a small wine of Burgundy, but much more delicious. They brought me a second hogshead, which I drank in the same manner, and made signs for more, but they had none to give me. When I had performed these wonders, they shouted for joy, and danced upon my breast, repeating several times as they did at first, *Hekinah Degul.* They made me a sign that I should throw down the two hogsheads, but first warned the people below to stand out of the way, crying aloud, *Borach Mivola,* and when they saw the vessels in the air, there was an universal shout of *Hekinah Degul.* I confess I was often tempted, while they were passing backwards and forwards on my body, to seize forty or fifty of the first that came in my reach, and dash them against the ground. But the remembrance of what I had felt, which probably might not be the worst they could do; and the promise of honor I made them, for so I interpreted my submissive behavior, soon drove out those imaginations. Besides, I now considered myself as bound by the laws of hospitality to a people who had treated me with so much expense and magnificence. However, in my thoughts I could not sufficiently wonder at the intrepidity of these diminutive mortals, who durst venture to mount and walk on my body, while one of my hands was at liberty, without trembling at the very sight of so prodigious a creature as I must appear to them. After some time, when they observed that I made no more demands for meat, there appeared before me a person of high rank from his Imperial Majesty. His Excellency, having mounted on the small of my right leg, advanced forwards up to my face, with about a dozen of his retinue. And producing his credentials under the Signet Royal, which he applied[8] close to my eyes, spoke about ten minutes, without any signs of anger, but with a kind of determinate resolution; often pointing forwards, which, as I afterwards found, was towards the capital city, about half a mile distant, whither it was agreed by his Majesty in council that I must be conveyed. I answered in a few words, but to no purpose, and made a sign with my hand that was loose, putting it to the other (but over his Excellency's head, for fear of hurting him or his train) and then to my own head and body, to signify that I desired my liberty. It appeared that he understood me well enough; for he shook his head by way of disapprobation, and held his hand in a posture to show that I must be carried as a prisoner. However, he made other signs to let me understand that I should have meat and drink enough, and very good treatment. Whereupon I once more thought of attempting to break my bonds; but again, when I felt the smart of their arrows upon my face and hands, which were all in blisters, and many of the darts still sticking in them; and observing likewise that the number of my enemies increased; I gave tokens to let them know that they might do with me what they pleased. Upon this the *Hurgo* and his train withdrew, with much civility and cheerful countenances. Soon after I heard a general shout, with frequent repetitions of the words, *Peplom Selan,* and I felt great numbers of the people on my left side relaxing the cords to such a degree, that I was able to turn upon my right, and to ease myself with making water; which I very plentifully did, to the great astonishment of the people, who conjecturing by my motions what I was going to do, immediately opened to the right and left on that side, to avoid the torrent which fell with such noise and

8. Brought.

violence from me. But before this, they had daubed my face and both my hands with a sort of ointment very pleasant to the smell, which in a few minutes removed all the smart of their arrows. These circumstances, added to the refreshment I had received by their victuals and drink, which were very nourishing, disposed me to sleep. I slept about eight hours, as I was afterwards assured; and it was no wonder; for the physicians, by the Emperor's order, had mingled a sleeping potion in the hogsheads of wine.

It seems that upon the first moment I was discovered sleeping on the ground after my landing, the Emperor had early notice of it by an express; and determined in council that I should be tied in the manner I have related (which was done in the night while I slept), that plenty of meat and drink should be sent me, and a machine prepared to carry me to the capital city.

This resolution perhaps may appear very bold and dangerous, and I am confident would not be imitated by any prince in Europe on the like occasion; however, in my opinion it was extremely prudent as well as generous. For supposing these people had endeavored to kill me with their spears and arrows while I was asleep; I should certainly have awaked with the first sense of smart, which might so far have roused my rage and strength, as to enable me to break the strings wherewith I was tied; after which, as they were not able to make resistance, so they could expect no mercy.

These people are most excellent mathematicians, and arrived to a great perfection in mechanics by the countenance and encouragement of the Emperor, who is a renowned patron of learning. This prince hath several machines fixed on wheels, for the carriage of trees and other great weights. He often builds his largest men of war, whereof some are nine foot long, in the woods where the timber grows, and has them carried on these engines[9] three or four hundred yards to the sea. Five hundred carpenters and engineers were immediately set at work to prepare the greatest engine they had. It was a frame of wood raised three inches from the ground, about seven foot long and four wide, moving upon twenty-two wheels. The shout I heard was upon the arrival of this engine, which it seems set out in four hours after my landing. It was brought parallel to me as I lay. But the principal difficulty was to raise and place me in this vehicle. Eighty poles, each of one foot high, were erected for this purpose, and very strong cords of the bigness of packthread were fastened by hooks to many bandages, which the workmen had girt round my neck, my hands, my body, and my legs. Nine hundred of the strongest men were employed to draw up these cords by many pulleys fastened on the poles; and thus, in less than three hours, I was raised and slung into the engine, and there tied fast. All this I was told, for while the whole operation was performing, I lay in a profound sleep, by the force of that soporiferous[1] medicine infused into my liquor. Fifteen hundred of the Emperor's largest horses, each about four inches and a half high, were employed to draw me towards the metropolis, which, as I said, was half a mile distant.

About four hours after we began our journey, I awaked by a very ridiculous accident; for, the carriage being stopped a while to adjust something that was out of order, two or three of the young natives had the curiosity to see how I looked when I was asleep; they climbed up into the engine, and

9. Contrivances.   1. Inducing unnatural sleep.

advancing very softly to my face, one of them, an officer in the guards, put the sharp end of his half-pike a good way up into my left nostril, which tickled my nose like a straw, and made me sneeze violently: whereupon they stole off unperceived, and it was three weeks before I knew the cause of my awaking so suddenly. We made a long march the remaining part of the day, and rested at night with five hundred guards on each side of me half with torches, and half with bows and arrows, ready to shoot me if I should offer to stir. The next morning at sunrise we continued our march, and arrived within two hundred yards of the city gates about noon. The Emperor and all his court came out to meet us, but his great officers would by no means suffer his Majesty to endanger his person by mounting on my body.

At the place where the carriage stopped, there stood an ancient temple, esteemed to be the largest in the whole kingdom, which having been polluted some years before by an unnatural murder,[2] was, according to the zeal of those people, looked on as profane, and therefore had been applied to common use, and all the ornaments and furniture carried away. In this edifice it was determined I should lodge. The great gate fronting to the north was about four foot high, and almost two foot wide, through which I could easily creep. On each side of the gate was a small window not above six inches from the ground: into that on the left side, the King's smiths conveyed fourscore and eleven chains, like those that hang to a lady's watch in Europe, and almost as large, which were locked to my left leg with six and thirty padlocks. Over against this temple, on the other side of the great highway, at twenty foot distance, there was a turret at least five foot high. Here the Emperor ascended with many principal lords of his court, to have an opportunity of viewing me, as I was told, for I could not see them. It was reckoned that above an hundred thousand inhabitants came out of the town upon the same errand; and in spite of my guards, I believe there could not be fewer than ten thousand, at several times, who mounted upon my body by the help of ladders. But a proclamation was soon issued to forbid it upon pain of death. When the workmen found it was impossible for me to break loose, they cut all the strings that bound me; whereupon I rose up with as melancholy a disposition as ever I had in my life. But the noise and astonishment of the people at seeing me rise and walk are not to be expressed. The chains that held my left leg were about two yards long, and gave me not only the liberty of walking backwards and forwards in a semicircle; but, being fixed within four inches of the gate, allowed me to creep in, and lie at my full length in the temple.

CHAPTER 2. *The Emperor of Lilliput, attended by several of the nobility, comes to see the author in his confinement. The Emperor's person and habit described. Learned men appointed to teach the author their language. He gains favor by his mild disposition. His pockets are searched, and his sword and pistols taken from him.*

When I found myself on my feet, I looked about me, and must confess I never beheld a more entertaining prospect. The country round appeared like

---

2. Presumably a reference to the execution of Charles I, who was sentenced in Westminster Hall.

a continued garden, and the inclosed fields, which were generally forty foot square, resembled so many beds of flowers. These fields were intermingled with woods of half a stang,[3] and the tallest trees, as I could judge, appeared to be seven foot high. I viewed the town on my left hand, which looked like the painted scene of a city in a theater.

I had been for some hours extremely pressed by the necessities of nature; which was no wonder, it being almost two days since I had last disburthened myself. I was under great difficulties between urgency and shame. The best expedient I could think on, was to creep into my house, which I accordingly did; and shutting the gate after me, I went as far as the length of my chain would suffer; and discharged my body of that uneasy load. But this was the only time I was ever guilty of so uncleanly an action; for which I cannot but hope the candid reader will give some allowance, after he hath maturely and impartially considered my case, and the distress I was in. From this time my constant practice was, as soon as I rose, to perform that business in open air, at the full extent of my chain, and due care was taken every morning before company came, that the offensive matter should be carried off in wheelbarrows by two servants appointed for that purpose. I would not have dwelt so long upon a circumstance, that perhaps at first sight may appear not very momentous, if I had not thought it necessary to justify my character in point of cleanliness to the world; which I am told some of my maligners have been pleased, upon this and other occasions, to call in question.

When this adventure was at an end, I came back out of my house, having occasion for fresh air. The Emperor was already descended from the tower, and advancing on horseback towards me, which had like to have cost him dear; for the beast, although very well trained, yet wholly unused to such a sight, which appeared as if a mountain moved before him, reared up on his hinder feet: but that prince, who is an excellent horseman, kept his seat, until his attendants ran in, and held the bridle, while his Majesty had time to dismount. When he alighted, he surveyed me round with great admiration, but kept beyond the length of my chains. He ordered his cooks and butlers, who were already prepared, to give me victuals and drink, which they pushed forward in a sort of vehicles upon wheels until I could reach them. I took these vehicles, and soon emptied them all; twenty of them were filled with meat, and ten with liquor; each of the former afforded me two or three good mouthfuls, and I emptied the liquor of ten vessels, which was contained in earthen vials, into one vehicle, drinking it off at a draught; and so I did with the rest. The Empress, and young princes of the blood, of both sexes, attended by many ladies, sat at some distance in their chairs; but upon the accident that happened to the Emperor's horse, they alighted, and came near his person; which I am now going to describe. He is taller, by almost the breadth of my nail, than any of his court, which alone is enough to strike an awe into the beholders. His features are strong and masculine, with an Austrian lip, and arched nose, his complexion olive, his countenance[4] erect, his body and limbs well proportioned, all his motions graceful, and his deportment majestic. He was then past his prime, being twenty-eight years

3. A quarter of an acre.
4. Bearing, appearance. Swift may be satirically idealizing George I, whom most of the British thought gross.

and three quarters old, of which he had reigned about seven, in great felicity, and generally victorious. For the better convenience of beholding him, I
lay on my side, so that my face was parallel to his, and he stood but three
yards off: however, I have had him since many times in my hand, and therefore cannot be deceived in the description. His dress was very plain and
simple, the fashion of it between the Asiatic and the European; but he had
on his head a light helmet of gold, adorned with jewels, and a plume on the
crest. He held his sword drawn in his hand, to defend himself, if I should
happen to break loose; it was almost three inches long, the hilt and scabbard
were gold enriched with diamonds. His voice was shrill, but very clear
and articulate, and I could distinctly hear it when I stood up. The ladies and
courtiers were all most magnificently clad, so that the spot they stood upon
seemed to resemble a petticoat spread on the ground, embroidered with figures of gold and silver. His Imperial Majesty spoke often to me, and I
returned answers, but neither of us could understand a syllable. There were
several of his priests and lawyers present (as I conjectured by their habits)
who were commanded to address themselves to me, and I spoke to them in
as many languages as I had the least smattering of, which were High and
Low Dutch, Latin, French, Spanish, Italian, and Lingua Franca;[5] but all to
no purpose. After about two hours the court retired, and I was left with a
strong guard, to prevent the impertinence, and probably the malice of the
rabble, who were very impatient to crowd about me as near as they durst;
and some of them had the impudence to shoot their arrows at me as I sat on
the ground by the door of my house, whereof one very narrowly missed my
left eye. But the colonel ordered six of the ringleaders to be seized, and
thought no punishment so proper as to deliver them bound into my hands,
which some of his soldiers accordingly did, pushing them forwards with the
butt-ends of their pikes into my reach; I took them all in my right hand, put
five of them into my coat-pocket; and as to the sixth, I made a countenance
as if I would eat him alive. The poor man squalled terribly, and the colonel
and his officer were in much pain, especially when they saw me take out my
penknife: but I soon put them out of fear; for, looking mildly, and immediately cutting the strings he was bound with, I set him gently on the ground,
and away he ran. I treated the rest in the same manner, taking them one by
one out of my pocket, and I observed both the soldiers and people were
highly obliged at this mark of my clemency, which was represented very
much to my advantage at court.

Towards night I got with some difficulty into my house, where I lay on the
ground, and continued to do so about a fortnight; during which time the
Emperor gave orders to have a bed prepared for me. Six hundred beds of
the common measure were brought in carriages, and worked up in my house;
an hundred and fifty of their beds sewn together made up the breadth
and length, and these were four double, which however kept me but very
indifferently from the hardness of the floor, that was of smooth stone. By
the same computation they provided me with sheets, blankets, and cover-
lets, tolerable enough for one who had been so long enured to hardships
as I.

5. A jargon, based on Italian, used by traders in the Mediterranean. "High and Low Dutch": German and
Dutch, respectively.

As the news of my arrival spread through the kingdom, it brought prodigious numbers of rich, idle, and curious people to see me; so that the villages were almost emptied, and great neglect of tillage and household affairs must have ensued, if his Imperial Majesty had not provided by several proclamations and orders of state against this inconveniency. He directed that those who had already beheld me should return home, and not presume to come within fifty yards of my house without license from court; whereby the secretaries of state got considerable fees.

In the mean time, the Emperor held frequent councils to debate what course should be taken with me; and I was afterwards assured by a particular friend, a person of great quality, who was as much in the secret as any, that the court was under many difficulties concerning me. They apprehended[6] my breaking loose, that my diet would be very expensive, and might cause a famine. Sometimes they determined to starve me, or at least to shoot me in the face and hands with poisoned arrows, which would soon dispatch me: but again they considered, that the stench of so large a carcass might produce a plague in the metropolis, and probably spread through the whole kingdom. In the midst of these consultations, several officers of the army went to the door of the great council chamber; and two of them being admitted, gave an account of my behavior to the six criminals above-mentioned; which made so favorable an impression in the breast of his Majesty, and the whole board, in my behalf, that an imperial commission was issued out, obliging all the villages nine hundred yards round the city to deliver in every morning six beeves, forty sheep, and other victuals for my sustenance; together with a proportionable quantity of bread and wine, and other liquors: for the due payment of which his Majesty gave assignments[7] upon his treasury. For this prince lives chiefly upon his own demesnes; seldom except upon great occasions raising any subsidies upon his subjects, who are bound to attend him in his wars at their own expense. An establishment was also made of six hundred persons to be my domestics, who had board-wages allowed for their maintenance, and tents built for them very conveniently on each side of my door. It was likewise ordered, that three hundred tailors should make me a suit of clothes after the fashion of the country: that six of his Majesty's greatest scholars should be employed to instruct me in their language: and, lastly, that the Emperor's horses, and those of the nobility, and troops of guards, should be exercised in my sight, to accustom themselves to me. All these orders were duly put in execution; and in about three weeks I made a great progress in learning their language; during which time the Emperor frequently honored me with his visits, and was pleased to assist my masters in teaching me. We began already to converse together in some sort; and the first words I learned, were to express my desire that he would please to give me my liberty; which I every day repeated on my knees.[8] His answer, as I could apprehend, was, that this must be a work of time, not to be thought on without the advice of his council; and that first I must *Lumos kelmin pesso desmar lon emposo*; that is, swear a peace with him and his kingdom. However, that I should be used with all kindness; and he advised

---

6. Anticipated with fear.
7. Formal mandates of revenue.
8. Gulliver's plea for liberty and the threat of starvation or rebellion he represents to his captors suggest the situation of Ireland with respect to England.

me to acquire by my patience and discreet behavior, the good opinion of himself and his subjects. He desired I would not take it ill, if he gave orders to certain proper officers to search me; for probably I might carry about me several weapons, which must needs be dangerous things, if they answered the bulk of so prodigious a person.[9] I said, his Majesty should be satisfied, for I was ready to strip myself, and turn up my pockets before him. This I delivered part in words, and part in signs. He replied, that by the laws of the kingdom, I must be searched by two of his officers; that he knew this could not be done without my consent and assistance; that he had so good an opinion of my generosity and justice, as to trust their persons in my hands; that whatever they took from me should be returned when I left the country, or paid for at the rate which I would set upon them. I took up the two officers in my hands, put them first into my coat-pockets, and then into every other pocket about me, except my two fobs, and another secret pocket which I had no mind should be searched, wherein I had some little necessaries of no consequence to any but myself. In one of my fobs there was a silver watch, and in the other a small quantity of gold in a purse. These gentlemen, having pen, ink, and paper about them, made an exact inventory of everything they saw; and when they had done, desired I would set them down, that they might deliver it to the Emperor. This inventory I afterwards translated into English, and is word for word as follows.

Imprimis,[1] In the right coat-pocket of the Great Man-Mountain (for so I interpret the words *Quinbus Flestrin*) after the strictest search, we found only one great piece of coarse cloth, large enough to be a foot-cloth for your Majesty's chief room of state. In the left pocket, we saw a huge silver chest, with a cover of the same metal, which we the searchers were not able to lift. We desired it should be opened; and one of us, stepping into it, found himself up to the mid leg in a sort of dust, some part whereof flying up to our faces, set us both a sneezing for several times together. In his right waistcoat-pocket, we found a prodigious bundle of white thin substances, folded one over another, about the bigness of three men, tied with a strong cable, and marked with black figures; which we humbly conceive to be writings; every letter almost half as large as the palm of our hands. In the left there was a sort of engine, from the back of which were extended twenty long poles, resembling the palisados[2] before your Majesty's court; wherewith we conjecture the Man-Mountain combs his head; for we did not always trouble him with questions, because we found it a great difficulty to make him understand us. In the large pocket on the right side of his middle cover (so I translate the word *ranfu-lo,* by which they meant my breeches) we saw a hollow pillar of iron, about the length of a man, fastened to a strong piece of timber, larger than the pillar; and upon one side of the pillar were huge pieces of iron sticking out, cut into strange figures; which we know not what to make of. In the left pocket, another engine of the same kind. In the smaller pocket on the right side, were several round flat pieces of

9. When the Whigs came into power in 1715, the leading Tories, who included Swift's friends Oxford and Bolingbroke (Robert Harley and Henry St. John) as well as Swift himself, were investigated by a committee of secrecy.
1. In the first place (Latin).
2. Fences of stakes.

white and red metal, of different bulk; some of the white, which seemed to be silver, were so large and heavy, that my comrade and I could hardly lift them. In the left pocket were two black pillars irregularly shaped: we could not, without difficulty, reach the top of them as we stood at the bottom of his pocket. One of them was covered, and seemed all of a piece; but at the upper end of the other, there appeared a white round substance, about twice the bigness of our heads. Within each of these was inclosed a prodigious plate of steel; which, by our orders, we obliged him to show us, because we apprehended they might be dangerous engines. He took them out of their cases, and told us, that in his own country his practice was to shave his beard with one of these, and to cut his meat with the other. There were two pockets which we could not enter: these he called his fobs; they were two large slits cut into the top of his middle cover, but squeezed close by the pressure of his belly. Out of the right fob hung a great silver chain, with a wonderful kind of engine at the bottom. We directed him to draw out whatever was at the end of the chain, which appeared to be a globe, half silver, and half of some transparent metal: for on the transparent side we saw certain strange figures circularly drawn, and thought we could touch them, until we found our fingers stopped with that lucid substance. He put this engine to our ears, which made an incessant noise like that of a watermill. And we conjecture it is either some unknown animal, or the god that he worships: but we are more inclined to the latter opinion, because he assured us (if we understood him right, for he expressed himself very imperfectly), that he seldom did any thing without consulting it. He called it his oracle, and said it pointed out the time for every action of his life. From the left fob he took out a net almost large enough for a fisherman, but contrived to open and shut like a purse, and served him for the same use: we found therein several massy pieces of yellow metal, which if they be of real gold, must be of immense value.

Having thus, in obedience to your Majesty's commands, diligently searched all his pockets, we observed a girdle[3] about his waist made of the hide of some prodigious animal; from which, on the left side, hung a sword of the length of five men; and on the right, a bag or pouch divided into cells; each cell capable of holding three of your Majesty's subjects. In one of these cells were several globes or balls of a most ponderous metal, about the bigness of our heads, and required a strong hand to lift them: the other cell contained a heap of certain black grains, but of no great bulk or weight, for we could hold above fifty of them in the palms of our hands.

This is an exact inventory of what we found about the body of the Man-Mountain; who used us with great civility, and due respect to your Majesty's commission. Signed and sealed on the fourth day of the eighty-ninth moon of your Majesty's auspicious reign.

CLEFREN FRELOCK, MARSI FRELOCK.

---

3. Belt.

When this inventory was read over to the Emperor, he directed me to deliver up the several particulars. He first called for my scimitar, which I took out, scabbard and all. In the meantime he ordered three thousand of his choicest troops (who then attended him) to surround me at a distance, with their bows and arrows just ready to discharge: but I did not observe it; for my eyes were wholly fixed upon his Majesty. He then desired me to draw my scimitar, which, although it had got some rust by the sea water, was in most parts exceeding bright. I did so, and immediately all the troops gave a shout between terror and surprise; for the sun shone clear, and the reflection dazzled their eyes, as I waved the scimitar to and fro in my hand. His Majesty, who is a most magnanimous[4] prince, was less daunted than I could expect; he ordered me to return it into the scabbard, and cast it on the ground as gently as I could, about six foot from the end of my chain. The next thing he demanded was one of the hollow iron pillars, by which he meant my pocket-pistols. I drew it out, and at his desire, as well as I could, expressed to him the use of it, and charging it only with powder, which by the closeness of my pouch happened to escape wetting in the sea (an inconvenience that all prudent mariners take special care to provide against), I first cautioned the Emperor not to be afraid; and then I let it off in the air. The astonishment here was much greater than at the sight of my scimitar. Hundreds fell down as if they had been struck dead; and even the Emperor, although he stood his ground, could not recover himself in some time. I delivered up both my pistols in the same manner as I had done my scimitar, and then my pouch of powder and bullets; begging him that the former might be kept from fire; for it would kindle with the smallest spark, and blow up his imperial palace into the air. I likewise delivered up my watch, which the Emperor was very curious to see; and commanded two of his tallest yeomen of the guards to bear it on a pole upon their shoulders, as draymen in England do a barrel of ale. He was amazed at the continual noise it made, and the motion of the minute-hand, which he could easily discern; for their sight is much more acute than ours: he asked the opinions of his learned men about him, which were various and remote, as the reader may well imagine without my repeating; although indeed I could not very perfectly understand them. I then gave up my silver and copper money, my purse with nine large pieces of gold, and some smaller ones; my knife and razor, my comb and silver snuffbox, my handkerchief and journal book. My scimitar, pistols, and pouch, were conveyed in carriages to his Majesty's stores; but the rest of my goods were returned me.

I had, as I before observed, one private pocket which escaped their search, wherein there was a pair of spectacles (which I sometimes use for the weakness of my eyes), a pocket perspective,[5] and several other little conveniences; which, being of no consequence to the Emperor, I did not think myself bound in honor to discover, and I apprehended they might be lost or spoiled if I ventured them out of my possession.

---

4. Courageous, great-spirited.   5. Telescope.

CHAPTER 3. *The author diverts the Emperor and his nobility of both sexes in a very uncommon manner. The diversions of the court of Lilliput described. The author hath his liberty granted him upon certain conditions.*

My gentleness and good behavior had gained so far on the Emperor and his court, and indeed upon the army and people in general, that I began to conceive hopes of getting my liberty in a short time. I took all possible methods to cultivate this favorable disposition. The natives came by degrees to be less apprehensive of any danger from me. I would sometimes lie down, and let five or six of them dance on my hand. And at last the boys and girls would venture to come and play at hide-and-seek in my hair. I had now made a good progress in understanding and speaking their language. The Emperor had a mind one day to entertain me with several of the country shows; wherein they exceed all nations I have known, both for dexterity and magnificence. I was diverted with none so much as that of the rope-dancers, performed upon a slender white thread, extended about two foot, and twelve inches from the ground. Upon which I shall desire liberty, with the reader's patience, to enlarge a little.

This diversion is only practiced by those persons who are candidates for great employments, and high favor, at court. They are trained in this art from their youth, and are not always of noble birth, or liberal education. When a great office is vacant either by death or disgrace (which often happens) five or six of those candidates petition the Emperor to entertain his Majesty and the court with a dance on the rope; and whoever jumps the highest without falling, succeeds in the office. Very often the chief ministers themselves are commanded to show their skill, and to convince the Emperor that they have not lost their faculty. Flimnap,[6] the Treasurer, is allowed to cut a caper on the strait rope, at least an inch higher than any other lord in the whole empire. I have seen him do the summerset several times together upon a trencher[7] fixed on the rope, which is no thicker than a common packthread in England. My friend Reldresal, Principal Secretary for Private Affairs, is, in my opinion, if I am not partial, the second after the Treasurer; the rest of the great officers are much upon a par.

These diversions are often attended with fatal accidents, whereof great numbers are on record. I myself have seen two or three candidates break a limb. But the danger is much greater when the ministers themselves are commanded to show their dexterity; for, by contending to excel themselves and their fellows, they strain so far, that there is hardly one of them who hath not received a fall; and some of them two or three. I was assured, that a year or two before my arrival, Flimnap would have infallibly broke his neck, if one of the King's cushions,[8] that accidentally lay on the ground, had not weakened the force of his fall.

There is likewise another diversion, which is only shown before the Emperor and Empress, and first minister, upon particular occasions. The Emperor lays on a table three fine silken threads of six inches long. One is blue, the other red, and the third green.[9] These threads are proposed as

---

6. Sir Robert Walpole, the Whig head of the government, was notorious in Swift's circle for his political acrobatics.
7. Plate. "Summerset": somersault.

8. A mistress of George I was supposed to have helped restore Walpole to office in 1721.
9. The Orders of the Garter, the Bath, and the Thistle, conferred for services to the king.

prizes for those persons whom the Emperor hath a mind to distinguish by a peculiar mark of his favor. The ceremony is performed in his Majesty's great chamber of state; where the candidates are to undergo a trial of dexterity very different from the former, and such as I have not observed the least resemblance of in any other country of the old or the new world. The Emperor holds a stick in his hands, both ends parallel to the horizon, while the candidates, advancing one by one, sometimes leap over the stick, sometimes creep under it backwards and forwards several times, according as the stick is advanced or depressed. Sometimes the Emperor holds one end of the stick, and his first minister the other; sometimes the minister has it entirely to himself. Whoever performs his part with most agility, and holds out the longest in *leaping* and *creeping*, is rewarded with the blue-colored silk; the red is given to the next, and the green to the third, which they all wear girt twice round about the middle; and you see few great persons about this court who are not adorned with one of these girdles.

The horses of the army, and those of the royal stables, having been daily led before me, were no longer shy, but would come up to my very feet, without starting. The riders would leap them over my hand as I held it on the ground; and one of the Emperor's huntsmen, upon a large courser, took[1] my foot, shoe and all; which was indeed a prodigious leap. I had the good fortune to divert the Emperor one day after a very extraordinary manner. I desired he would order several sticks of two foot high, and the thickness of an ordinary cane, to be brought me; whereupon his Majesty commanded the master of his woods to give directions accordingly; and the next morning six woodmen arrived with as many carriages, drawn by eight horses to each. I took nine of these sticks, and fixing them firmly in the ground in a quadrangular figure, two foot and a half square, I took four other sticks, and tied them parallel at each corner, about two foot from the ground; then I fastened my handkerchief to the nine sticks that stood erect, and extended it on all sides till it was as tight as the top of a drum; and the four parallel sticks, rising about five inches higher than the handkerchief, served as ledges on each side. When I had finished my work, I desired the Emperor to let a troop of his best horse, twenty-four in number, come and exercise upon this plain. His Majesty approved of the proposal, and I took them up one by one in my hands, ready mounted and armed, with the proper officers to exercise them. As soon as they got into order, they divided into two parties, performed mock skirmishes, discharged blunt arrows, drew their swords, fled and pursued, attacked and retired; and in short discovered the best military discipline I ever beheld. The parallel sticks secured them and their horses from falling over the stage; and the Emperor was so much delighted, that he ordered this entertainment to be repeated several days; and once was pleased to be lifted up, and give the word of command; and, with great difficulty, persuaded even the Empress herself to let me hold her in her close chair[2] within two yards of the stage, from whence she was able to take a full view of the whole performance. It was my good fortune that no ill accident happened in these entertainments, only once a fiery horse that belonged to one of the captains pawing with his hoof struck a hole in my handkerchief, and his foot slipping, he overthrew his rider and himself; but I immediately

1. Jumped over.   2. An enclosed or sedan chair.

relieved them both; for covering the hole with one hand, I set down the troop with the other, in the same manner as I took them up. The horse that fell was strained in the left shoulder, but the rider got no hurt, and I repaired my handkerchief as well as I could; however, I would not trust to the strength of it any more in such dangerous enterprises.

About two or three days before I was set at liberty, as I was entertaining the court with these kinds of feats, there arrived an express to inform his Majesty that some of his subjects, riding near the place where I was first taken up, had seen a great black substance lying on the ground, very oddly shaped, extending its edges round as wide as his Majesty's bedchamber, and rising up in the middle as high as a man; that it was no living creature, as they at first apprehended, for it lay on the grass without motion, and some of them had walked round it several times; that by mounting upon each other's shoulders, they had got to the top, which was flat and even; and stamping upon it they found it was hollow within; that they humbly conceived it might be some-thing belonging to the Man-Mountain, and if his Majesty pleased, they would undertake to bring it with only five horses. I presently³ knew what they meant; and was glad at heart to receive this intelligence. It seems upon my first reaching the shore after our shipwreck, I was in such confusion, that before I came to the place where I went to sleep, my hat, which I had fastened with a string to my head while I was rowing, and had stuck on all the time I was swimming, fell off after I came to land; the string, as I conjecture, breaking by some accident which I never observed, but thought my hat had been lost at sea. I intreated his Imperial Majesty to give orders it might be brought to me as soon as possible, describing to him the use and the nature of it: and the next day the wagoners arrived with it, but not in a very good condition; they had bored two holes in the brim, within an inch and half of the edge, and fastened two hooks in the holes; these hooks were tied by a long cord to the harness, and thus my hat was dragged along for above half an English mile: but the ground in that country being extremely smooth and level, it received less damage than I expected.

Two days after this adventure, the Emperor, having ordered that part of his army which quarters in and about his metropolis to be in a readiness, took a fancy of diverting himself in a very singular manner. He desired I would stand like a colossus, with my legs as far asunder as I conveniently could. He then commanded his general (who was an old experienced leader, and a great patron of mine) to draw up the troops in close order, and march them under me; the foot⁴ by twenty-four in a breast, and the horse by sixteen, with drums beating, colors flying, and pikes advanced. This body consisted of three thou-sand foot, and a thousand horse. His Majesty gave orders, upon pain of death, that every soldier in his march should observe the strictest decency with regard to my person; which, however, could not prevent some of the younger officers from turning up their eyes as they passed under me. And, to confess the truth, my breeches were at that time in so ill a condition, that they afforded some opportunities for laughter and admiration.

I had sent so many memorials and petitions for my liberty, that his Majesty at length mentioned the matter first in the cabinet, and then in a full council;

3. Immediately.
4. Foot soldiers or infantry.

5. The earl of Nottingham, an enemy of Swift.

where it was opposed by none, except Skyresh Bolgolam,[5] who was pleased, without any provocation, to be my mortal enemy. But it was carried against him by the whole board, and confirmed by the Emperor. That minister was *Galbet*, or Admiral of the Realm; very much in his master's confidence, and a person well versed in affairs, but of a morose and sour complexion.[6] However, he was at length persuaded to comply; but prevailed that the articles and conditions upon which I should be set free, and to which I must swear, should be drawn up by himself. These articles were brought to me by Skyresh Bolgolam in person, attended by two under-secretaries, and several persons of distinction. After they were read, I was demanded to swear to the performance of them; first in the manner of my own country, and afterwards in the method prescribed by their laws; which was to hold my right foot in my left hand, to place the middle finger of my right hand on the crown of my head, and my thumb on the tip of my right ear. But because the reader may perhaps be curious to have some idea of the style and manner of expression peculiar to that people, as well as to know the articles upon which I recovered my liberty, I have made a translation of the whole instrument,[7] word for word, as near as I was able; which I here offer to the public.

GOLBASTO MOMAREN EVLAME GURDILO SHEFIN MULLY ULLY GUE, most mighty Emperor of Lilliput, delight and terror of the universe, whose dominions extend five thousand blustrugs (about twelve miles in circumference) to the extremities of the globe; Monarch of all Monarchs; taller than the sons of men; whose feet press down to the center, and whose head strikes against the sun; at whose nod the princes of the earth shake their knees; pleasant as the spring, comfortable as the summer, fruitful as autumn, dreadful as winter. His most sublime Majesty proposeth to the Man-Mountain, lately arrived at our celestial dominions, the following articles, which by a solemn oath he shall be obliged to perform.

First, The Man-Mountain shall not depart from our dominions, without our license under our great seal.

Secondly, He shall not presume to come into our metropolis, without our express order; at which time the inhabitants shall have two hours warning, to keep within their doors.

Thirdly, The said Man-Mountain shall confine his walks to our principal high roads; and not offer to walk or lie down in a meadow, or field of corn.

Fourthly, As he walks the said roads, he shall take the utmost care not to trample upon the bodies of any of our loving subjects, their horses, or carriages, nor take any of our said subjects into his hands, without their own consent.

Fifthly, If an express require extraordinary dispatch, the Man-Mountain shall be obliged to carry in his pocket the messenger and horse, a six days' journey once in every moon, and return the said messenger back (if so required) safe to our Imperial Presence.

Sixthly, He shall be our ally against our enemies in the island of Blefuscu, and do his utmost to destroy their fleet, which is now preparing to invade us.

---

6. Disposition.   7. A formal legal document.

Seventhly, That the said Man-Mountain shall, at his times of leisure, be aiding and assisting to our workmen, in helping to raise certain great stones, towards covering the wall of the principal park, and other our royal buildings.

Eighthly, That the said Man-Mountain shall, in two moons' time, deliver in an exact survey of the circumference of our dominions by a computation of his own paces round the coast.

Lastly, That upon his solemn oath to observe all the above articles, the said Man-Mountain shall have a daily allowance of meat and drink sufficient for the support of 1,728 of our subjects; with free access to our Royal Person, and other marks of our favor. Given at our palace at Belfaborac the twelfth day of the ninety-first moon of our reign.

I swore and subscribed to these articles with great cheerfulness and content, although some of them were not so honorable as I could have wished; which proceeded wholly from the malice of Skyresh Bolgolam the High Admiral: whereupon my chains were immediately unlocked, and I was at full liberty: the Emperor himself in person did me the honor to be by at the whole ceremony. I made my acknowledgements by prostrating myself at his Majesty's feet: but he commanded me to rise; and after many gracious expressions, which, to avoid the censure of vanity, I shall not repeat, he added, that he hoped I should prove a useful servant, and well deserve all the favors he had already conferred upon me, or might do for the future.

The reader may please to observe, that in the last article for the recovery of my liberty, the Emperor stipulates to allow me a quantity of meat and drink, sufficient for the support of 1,728 Lilliputians. Some time after, asking a friend at court how they came to fix on that determinate number, he told me, that his Majesty's mathematicians, having taken the height of my body by the help of a quadrant, and finding it to exceed theirs in the proportion of twelve to one, they concluded from the similarity of their bodies, that mine must contain at least 1,728 of theirs, and consequently would require as much food as was necessary to support that number of Lilliputians. By which, the reader may conceive an idea of the ingenuity of that people, as well as the prudent and exact economy of so great a prince.

CHAPTER 4. *Mildendo, the metropolis of Lilliput, described, together with the Emperor's palace. A conversation between the author and a principal secretary, concerning the affairs of that empire; the author's offers to serve the Emperor in his wars.*

The first request I made after I had obtained my liberty, was, that I might have license to see Mildendo, the metropolis; which the Emperor easily granted me, but with a special charge to do no hurt, either to the inhabitants, or their houses. The people had notice by proclamation of my design to visit the town. The wall which encompassed it is two foot and an half high, and at least eleven inches broad, so that a coach and horses may be driven very safely round it; and it is flanked with strong towers at ten foot distance.

I stepped over the great western gate, and passed very gently, and sideling[8] through the two principal streets, only in my short waistcoat, for fear of damaging the roofs and eaves of the houses with the skirts of my coat. I walked with the utmost circumspection, to avoid treading on any stragglers, who might remain in the streets, although the orders were very strict, that all people should keep in their houses, at their own peril. The garret windows and tops of houses were so crowded with spectators, that I thought in all my travels I had not seen a more populous place. The city is an exact square, each side of the wall being five hundred foot long. The two great streets, which run cross and divide it into four quarters, are five foot wide. The lanes and alleys, which I could not enter, but only viewed them as I passed, are from twelve to eighteen inches. The town is capable of holding five hundred thousand souls. The houses are from three to five stories. The shops and markets well provided.

The Emperor's palace is in the center of the city, where the two great streets meet. It is enclosed by a wall of two foot high, and twenty foot distant from the buildings. I had his Majesty's permission to step over this wall; and the space being so wide between that and the palace, I could easily view it on every side. The outward court is a square of forty foot, and includes two other courts: in the inmost are the royal apartments, which I was very desirous to see, but found it extremely difficult; for the great gates, from one square into another, were but eighteen inches high, and seven inches wide. Now the buildings of the outer court were at least five foot high; and it was impossible for me to stride over them, without infinite damage to the pile, although the walls were strongly built of hewn stone, and four inches thick. At the same time the Emperor had a great desire that I should see the magnificence of his palace; but this I was not able to do till three days after, which I spent in cutting down with my knife some of the largest trees in the royal park, about an hundred yards distance from the city. Of these trees I made two stools, each about three foot high, and strong enough to bear my weight. The people having received notice a second time, I went again through the city to the palace, with my two stools in my hands. When I came to the side of the outer court, I stood upon one stool, and took the other in my hand: this I lifted over the roof, and gently set it down on the space between the first and second court, which was eight foot wide. I then stepped over the buildings very conveniently from one stool to the other, and drew up the first after me with a hooked stick. By this contrivance I got into the inmost court; and lying down upon my side, I applied my face to the windows of the middle stories, which were left open on purpose, and discovered the most splendid apartments that can be imagined. There I saw the Empress, and the young princes in their several lodgings, with their chief attendants about them. Her Imperial Majesty was pleased to smile very graciously upon me and gave me out of the window her hand to kiss.

But I shall not anticipate the reader with farther descriptions of this kind, because I reserve them for a greater work, which is now almost ready for the press; containing a general description of this empire, from its first

8. Sideways.

erection, through a long series of princes, with a particular account of their wars and politics, laws, learning, and religion; their plants and animals, their peculiar manners and customs, with other matters very curious and useful; my chief design at present being only to relate such events and transactions as happened to the public, or to myself, during a residence of about nine months in that empire.

One morning, about a fortnight after I had obtained my liberty, Reldresal, Principal Secretary (as they style him) of Private Affairs, came to my house, attended only by one servant. He ordered his coach to wait at a distance, and desired I would give him an hour's audience; which I readily consented to, on account of his quality, and personal merits, as well as of the many good offices he had done me during my solicitations at court. I offered to lie down, that he might the more conveniently reach my ear; but he chose rather to let me hold him in my hand during our conversation. He began with compliments on my liberty, said he might pretend to some merit in it; but, however, added, that if it had not been for the present situation of things at court, perhaps I might not have obtained it so soon. For, said he, as flourishing a condition as we appear to be in to foreigners, we labor under two mighty evils; a violent faction at home, and the danger of an invasion by a most potent enemy from abroad. As to the first, you are to understand, that for above seventy moons past, there have been two struggling parties in the empire, under the names of *Tramecksan*, and *Slamecksan*,[9] from the high and low heels on their shoes, by which they distinguish themselves.

It is alleged indeed, that the high heels are most agreeable to our ancient constitution: but however this be, his Majesty hath determined to make use of only low heels in the administration of the government and all offices in the gift of the crown; as you cannot but observe; and particularly, that his Majesty's imperial heels are lower at least by a *drurr* than any of his court; (*drurr* is a measure about the fourteenth part of an inch). The animosities between these two parties run so high, that they will neither eat nor drink, nor talk with each other. We compute the *Tramecksan*, or High-Heels, to exceed us in number; but the power is wholly on our side. We apprehend his Imperial Highness, the heir to the crown, to have some tendency towards the High-Heels; at least we can plainly discover one of his heels higher than the other, which gives him a hobble in his gait.[1] Now, in the midst of these intestine disquiets, we are threatened with an invasion from the island of Blefuscu,[2] which is the other great empire of the universe, almost as large and powerful as this of his Majesty. For as to what we have heard you affirm, that there are other kingdoms and states in the world, inhabited by human creatures as large as yourself, our philosophers are in much doubt; and would rather conjecture that you dropped from the moon, or one of the stars; because it is certain, that an hundred mortals of your bulk would, in a short time, destroy all the fruits and cattle of his Majesty's dominions. Besides, our histories of six thousand moons make no mention of any other

9. Tory (High Church) and Whig (Low Church), respectively.
1. The prince of Wales (later George II) had

friends in both parties.
2. France.

regions, than the two great empires of Lilliput and Blefuscu. Which two mighty powers have, as I was going to tell you, been engaged in a most obstinate war for six and thirty moons past. It began upon the following occasion. It is allowed on all hands, that the primitive way of breaking eggs before we eat them, was upon the larger end: but his present Majesty's grandfather, while he was a boy, going to eat an egg, and breaking it according to the ancient practice, happened to cut one of his fingers. Whereupon the Emperor his father published an edict, commanding all his subjects, upon great penalties, to break the smaller end of their eggs. The people so highly resented this law, that our histories tell us there have been six rebellions raised on that account; wherein one emperor lost his life, and another his crown.[3] These civil commotions were constantly fomented by the monarchs of Blefuscu; and when they were quelled, the exiles always fled for refuge to that empire. It is computed, that eleven thousand persons have, at several times, suffered death, rather than submit to break their eggs at the smaller end. Many hundred large volumes have been published upon this controversy: but the books of the Big-Endians have been long forbidden, and the whole party rendered incapable by law of holding employments.[4] During the course of these troubles, the emperors of Blefuscu did frequently expostulate by their ambassadors, accusing us of making a schism in religion, by offending against a fundamental doctrine of our great prophet Lustrog, in the fifty-fourth chapter of the *Brundecral* (which is their Alcoran[5]). This, however, is thought to be a mere strain upon the text: for the words are these; *That all true believers shall break their eggs at the convenient end:* and which is the convenient end, seems, in my humble opinion, to be left to every man's conscience, or at least in the power of the chief magistrate[6] to determine. Now the Big-Endian exiles have found so much credit in the Emperor of Blefuscu's court, and so much private assistance and encouragement from their party here at home, that a bloody war hath been carried on between the two empires for six and thirty moons with various success;[7] during which time we have lost forty capital ships, and a much greater number of smaller vessels, together with thirty thousand of our best seamen and soldiers; and the damage received by the enemy is reckoned to be somewhat greater than ours. However, they have now equipped a numerous fleet, and are just preparing to make a descent upon us; and his Imperial Majesty, placing great confidence in your valor and strength, hath commanded me to lay this account of his affairs before you.

I desired the Secretary to present my humble duty to the Emperor, and to let him know, that I thought it would not become me, who was a foreigner, to interfere with parties; but I was ready, with the hazard of my life, to defend his person and state against all invaders.

---

3. Swift's satirical allegory of the strife between Catholics (Big-Endians) and Protestants (Little-Endians) touches on Henry VIII (who "broke" with the Pope), Charles I (who lost his life), and James II (who lost his crown).
4. The Test Act (1673) prevented Catholics and Nonconformists from holding office unless they accepted the Anglican Sacrament.
5. Koran.
6. Ruler, sovereign. Swift himself accepted the right of the king to determine religious observances.
7. Reminiscent of the War of the Spanish Succession (1702–13).

CHAPTER 5. *The author by an extraordinary stratagem prevents an invasion. A high title of honor is conferred upon him. Ambassadors arrive from the Emperor of Blefuscu, and sue for peace. The Empress's apartment on fire by an accident; the author instrumental in saving the rest of the palace.*

The empire of Blefuscu is an island situated to the north north-east side of Lilliput, from whence it is parted only by a channel of eight hundred yards wide. I had not yet seen it, and upon this notice of an intended invasion, I avoided appearing on that side of the coast, for fear of being discovered by some of the enemy's ships, who had received no intelligence of me; all intercourse between the two empires having been strictly forbidden during the war, upon pain of death; and an embargo laid by our Emperor upon all vessels whatsoever. I communicated to his Majesty a project I had formed of seizing the enemy's whole fleet; which, as our scouts assured us, lay at anchor in the harbor ready to sail with the first fair wind. I consulted the most experienced seamen upon the depth of the channel, which they had often plumbed; who told me, that in the middle at high water it was seventy *glumgluffs* deep, which is about six foot of European measure; and the rest of it fifty *glumgluffs* at most. I walked to the northeast coast over against Blefuscu; where, lying down behind a hillock, I took out my small pocket perspective glass, and viewed the enemy's fleet at anchor, consisting of about fifty men of war, and a great number of transports: I then came back to my house, and gave order (for which I had a warrant) for a great quantity of the strongest cable and bars of iron. The cable was about as thick as packthread and the bars of the length and size of a knitting-needle. I trebled the cable to make it stronger, and for the same reason I twisted three of the iron bars together, bending the extremities into a hook. Having thus fixed fifty hooks to as many cables, I went back to the northeast coast, and putting off my coat, shoes, and stockings, walked into the sea in my leathern jerkin, about half an hour before high water. I waded with what haste I could, and swam in the middle about thirty yards until I felt the ground; I arrived at the fleet in less than half an hour. The enemy was so frighted when they saw me, that they leaped out of their ships, and swam to shore, where there could not be fewer than thirty thousand souls. I then took my tackling, and fastening a hook to the hole at the prow of each, I tied all the cords together at the end. While I was thus employed, the enemy discharged several thousand arrows, many of which stuck in my hands and face; and besides the excessive smart, gave me much disturbance in my work. My greatest apprehension was for my eyes, which I should have infallibly lost, if I had not suddenly thought of an expedient. I kept, among other little necessaries, a pair of spectacles in a private pocket, which, as I observed before, had escaped the Emperor's searchers. These I took out, and fastened as strongly as I could upon my nose; and thus armed went on boldly with my work in spite of the enemy's arrows; many of which struck against the glasses of my spectacles, but without any other effect, further than a little to discompose them. I had now fastened all the hooks, and taking the knot in my hand, began to pull; but not a ship would stir, for they were all too fast by their anchors, so that the boldest part of my enterprise remained. I therefore let go the cord, and leaving the hooks fixed to the ships, I resolutely cut with my knife the cables that fastened the anchors, receiving about two hundred shots in my face and hands; then I took up the knotted end of the cables to which my hooks were tied; and with great ease drew fifty of the enemy's largest men-of-war after me.

The Blefuscudians, who had not the least imagination of what I intended, were at first confounded with astonishment. They had seen me cut the cables, and thought my design was only to let the ships run adrift, or fall foul on each other: but when they perceived the whole fleet moving in order, and saw me pulling at the end, they set up such a scream of grief and despair, that it is almost impossible to describe or conceive. When I had got out of danger, I stopped a while to pick out the arrows that stuck in my hands and face, and rubbed on some of the same ointment that was given me at my first arrival, as I have formerly mentioned. I then took off my spectacles, and waiting about an hour until the tide was a little fallen, I waded through the middle with my cargo, and arrived safe at the royal port of Lilliput.

The Emperor and his whole court stood on the shore, expecting the issue of this great adventure. They saw the ships move forward in a large half-moon, but could not discern me, who was up to my breast in water. When I advanced to the middle of the channel, they were yet more in pain, because I was under water to my neck. The Emperor concluded me to be drowned, and that the enemy's fleet was approaching in a hostile manner: but he was soon eased of his fears, for the channel growing shallower every step I made, I came in a short time within hearing; and holding up the end of the cable by which the fleet was fastened, I cried in a loud voice, Long live the most puissant Emperor of Lilliput! This great prince received me at my landing with all possible encomiums, and created me a *Nardac* upon the spot, which is the highest title of honor among them.

His Majesty desired I would take some other opportunity of bringing all the rest of his enemy's ships into his ports. And so unmeasurable is the ambition of princes, that he seemed to think of nothing less than reducing the whole empire of Blefuscu into a province, and governing it by a viceroy; of destroying the Big-Endian exiles, and compelling that people to break the smaller end of their eggs, by which he would remain sole monarch of the whole world. But I endeavored to divert him from this design, by many arguments drawn from the topics of policy as well as justice: and I plainly protested, that I would never be an instrument of bringing a free and brave people into slavery. And when the matter was debated in council, the wisest part of the ministry were of my opinion.

This open bold declaration of mine was so opposite to the schemes and politics of his Imperial Majesty, that he could never forgive me; he mentioned it in a very artful manner at council, where I was told that some of the wisest appeared, at least by their silence, to be of my opinion; but others, who were my secret enemies, could not forbear some expressions, which by a side-wind[8] reflected on me. And from this time began an intrigue between his Majesty and a junta of ministers maliciously bent against me, which broke out in less than two months, and had like to have ended in my utter destruction. Of so little weight are the greatest services to princes, when put into the balance with a refusal to gratify their passions.[9]

8. Indirectly.
9. After a series of British naval victories, the Treaty of Utrecht (1713) had ended the war with France, but the Tory ministers who engineered the peace were subsequently accused of having sold out to the enemy.

About three weeks after this exploit, there arrived a solemn embassy from Blefuscu, with humble offers of a peace; which was soon concluded upon conditions very advantageous to our Emperor; wherewith I shall not trouble the reader. There were six ambassadors, with a train of about five hundred persons; and their entry was very magnificent, suitable to the grandeur of their master, and the importance of their business. When their treaty was finished, wherein I did them several good offices by the credit I now had, or at least appeared to have at court, their Excellencies, who were privately told how much I had been their friend, made me a visit in form. They began with many compliments upon my valor and generosity; invited me to that kingdom in the Emperor their master's name; and desired me to show them some proofs of my prodigious strength, of which they had heard so many wonders; wherein I readily obliged them, but shall not interrupt the reader with the particulars.

When I had for some time entertained their Excellencies to their infinite satisfaction and surprise, I desired they would do me the honor to present my most humble respects to the Emperor their master, the renown of whose virtues had so justly filled the whole world with admiration, and whose royal person I resolved to attend before I returned to my own country. Accordingly, the next time I had the honor to see our Emperor, I desired his general license to wait on the Blefuscudian monarch, which he was pleased to grant me, as I could plainly perceive, in a very cold manner; but could not guess the reason, till I had a whisper from a certain person, that Flimnap and Bolgolam had represented my intercourse with those ambassadors as a mark of disaffection, from which I am sure my heart was wholly free. And this was the first time I began to conceive some imperfect idea of courts and ministers.

It is to be observed, that these ambassadors spoke to me by an interpreter; the languages of both empires differing as much from each other as any two in Europe, and each nation priding itself upon the antiquity, beauty, and energy of their own tongues, with an avowed contempt for that of their neighbor; yet our Emperor, standing upon the advantage he had got by the seizure of their fleet, obliged them to deliver their credentials, and make their speech, in the Lilliputian tongue. And it must be confessed, that from the great intercourse of trade and commerce between both realms, from the continual reception of exiles, which is mutual among them, and from the custom in each empire to send their young nobility and richer gentry to the other, in order to polish themselves, by seeing the world, and understanding men and manners, there are few persons of distinction, or merchants, or seamen, who dwell in the maritime parts, but what can hold conversation in both tongues; as I found some weeks after, when I went to pay my respects to the Emperor of Blefuscu, which in the midst of great misfortunes, through the malice of my enemies, proved a very happy adventure to me, as I shall relate in its proper place.

The reader may remember, that when I signed those articles upon which I recovered my liberty, there were some which I disliked upon account of their being too servile, neither could any thing but an extreme necessity have forced me to submit. But being now a *Nardac*, of the highest rank in that empire, such offices[1] were looked upon as below my dignity, and the Emperor (to do him justice) never once mentioned them to me. However, it

1. Duties.

was not long before I had an opportunity of doing his Majesty, at least as I then thought, a most signal service. I was alarmed at midnight with the cries of many hundred people at my door; by which being suddenly awaked, I was in some kind of terror. I heard the word *burglum* repeated incessantly; several of the Emperor's court, making their way through the crowd, intreated me to come immediately to the palace, where her Imperial Majesty's apartment was on fire, by the carelessness of a maid of honor, who fell asleep while she was reading a romance. I got up in an instant; and orders being given to clear the way before me, and it being likewise a moonshine night, I made a shift to get to the palace without trampling on any of the people. I found they had already applied ladders to the walls of the apartment, and were well provided with buckets, but the water was at some distance. These buckets were about the size of a large thimble, and the poor people supplied me with them as fast as they could; but the flame was so violent, that they did little good. I might easily have stifled it with my coat, which I unfortunately left behind me for haste, and came away only in my leathern jerkin. The case seemed wholly desperate and deplorable; and this magnificent palace would have infallibly been burnt down to the ground, if, by a presence of mind, unusual to me, I had not suddenly thought of an expedient. I had the evening before drank plentifully of a most delicious wine, called *glimigrim* (the Blefuscudians call it *flunec*, but ours is esteemed the better sort), which is very diuretic. By the luckiest chance in the world, I had not discharged myself of any part of it. The heat I had contracted by coming very near the flames, and by my laboring to quench them, made the wine begin to operate by urine; which I voided in such a quantity, and applied so well to the proper places, that in three minutes the fire was wholly extinguished; and the rest of that noble pile, which had cost so many ages in erecting, preserved from destruction.

It was now daylight, and I returned to my house, without waiting to congratulate with the Emperor; because, although I had done a very eminent piece of service, yet I could not tell how his Majesty might resent the manner by which I had performed it: for, by the fundamental laws of the realm, it is capital[2] in any person, of what quality soever, to make water within the precincts of the palace. But I was a little comforted by a message from his Majesty, that he would give orders to the Grand Justiciary for passing my pardon in form; which, however, I could not obtain. And I was privately assured, that the Empress, conceiving the greatest abhorrence of what I had done,[3] removed to the most distant side of the court, firmly resolved that those buildings should never be repaired for her use; and, in the presence of her chief confidents, could not forbear vowing revenge.

CHAPTER 6. *Of the inhabitants of Lilliput; their learning, laws, and customs, the manner of educating their children. The author's way of living in that country. His vindication of a great lady.*

Although I intend to leave the description of this empire to a particular treatise, yet in the mean time I am content to gratify the curious reader with

---

2. Punishable by death.
3. Queen Anne, whom Swift called "a royal prude," strongly objected to the coarseness of *A Tale of a Tub.*

some general ideas. As the common size of the natives is somewhat under six inches, so there is an exact proportion in all other animals, as well as plants and trees: for instance, the tallest horses and oxen are between four and five inches in height, the sheep an inch and a half, more or less; their geese about the bigness of a sparrow; and so the several gradations downwards, till you come to the smallest, which, to my sight, were almost invisible; but nature hath adapted the eyes of the Lilliputians to all objects proper for their view: they see with great exactness, but at no great distance. And to show the sharpness of their sight towards objects that are near, I have been much pleased with observing a cook pulling[4] a lark, which was not so large as a common fly; and a young girl threading an invisible needle with invisible silk. Their tallest trees are about seven foot high; I mean some of those in the great royal park, the tops whereof I could but just reach with my fist clinched. The other vegetables[5] are in the same proportion; but this I leave to the reader's imagination.

I shall say but little at present of their learning, which for many ages hath flourished in all its branches among them: but their manner of writing is very peculiar; being neither from the left to the right, like the Europeans; nor from the right to the left, like the Arabians; nor from up to down, like the Chinese; nor from down to up, like the Cascagians;[6] but aslant from one corner of the paper to the other, like ladies in England.

They bury their dead with their heads directly downwards; because they hold an opinion that in eleven thousand moons they are all to rise again; in which period, the earth (which they conceive to be flat) will turn upside down, and by this means they shall, at their resurrection, be found ready standing on their feet. The learned among them confess the absurdity of this doctrine; but the practice still continues, in compliance to the vulgar.[7]

There are some laws and customs in this empire very peculiar; and if they were not so directly contrary to those of my own dear country, I should be tempted to say a little in their justification. It is only to be wished, that they were as well executed. The first I shall mention relateth to informers. All crimes against the state are punished here with the utmost severity; but if the person accused make his innocence plainly to appear upon his trial, the accuser is immediately put to an ignominious death; and out of his goods or lands, the innocent person is quadruply recompensed for the loss of his time, for the danger he underwent, for the hardship of his imprisonment, and for all the charges he hath been at in making his defense. Or, if that fund be deficient, it is largely[8] supplied by the crown. The Emperor doth also confer on him some public mark of his favor; and proclamation is made of his innocence through the whole city.

They look upon fraud as a greater crime than theft, and therefore seldom fail to punish it with death; for they allege, that care and vigilance, with a very common understanding, may preserve a man's goods from thieves; but honesty hath no fence against superior cunning: and since it is necessary that there should be a perpetual intercourse of buying and selling, and dealing upon credit, where fraud is permitted or connived at, or hath no law to

---

4. Plucking.
5. Plants.
6. Swift's invention.

7. The (beliefs of the) common people.
8. Fully.

punish it, the honest dealer is always undone, and the knave gets the advantage. I remember when I was once interceding with the King for a criminal who had wronged his master of a great sum of money, which he had received by order, and ran away with; and happening to tell his Majesty, by way of extenuation, that it was only a breach of trust, the Emperor thought it monstrous in me to offer, as a defense, the greatest aggravation of the crime: and truly, I had little to say in return, farther than the common answer, that different nations had different customs; for, I confess, I was heartily ashamed.

Although we usually call reward and punishment the two hinges upon which all government turns, yet I could never observe this maxim to be put in practice by any nation, except that of Lilliput. Whoever can there bring sufficient proof that he hath strictly observed the laws of his country for seventy-three moons, hath a claim to certain privileges, according to his quality[9] and condition of life, with a proportionable sum of money out of a fund appropriated for that use: he likewise acquires the title of *Snilpall*, or *Legal*, which is added to his name, but doth not descend to his posterity. And these people thought it a prodigious defect of policy among us, when I told them that our laws were enforced only by penalties, without any mention of reward. It is upon this account that the image of Justice, in their courts of judicature, is formed with six eyes, two before, as many behind, and on each side one, to signify circumspection; with a bag of gold open in her right hand, and a sword sheathed in her left, to show she is more disposed to reward than to punish.

In choosing persons for all employments, they have more regard to good morals than to great abilities; for, since government is necessary to mankind, they believe that the common size of human understandings is fitted to some station or other; and that Providence never intended to make the management of public affairs a mystery, to be comprehended only by a few persons of sublime genius, of which there seldom are three born in an age: but they suppose truth, justice, temperance, and the like, to be in every man's power; the practice of which virtues, assisted by experience and a good intention, would qualify any man for the service of his country, except where a course of study is required. But they thought the want of moral virtues was so far from being supplied by superior endowments of the mind, that employments could never be put into such dangerous hands as those of persons so qualified; and at least, that the mistakes committed by ignorance in a virtuous disposition would never be of such fatal consequence to the public weal, as the practices of a man whose inclinations led him to be corrupt, and had great abilities to manage, to multiply, and defend his corruptions.

In like manner, the disbelief of a divine Providence renders a man uncapable of holding any public station; for since kings avow themselves to be the deputies of Providence, the Lilliputians think nothing can be more absurd than for a prince to employ such men as disown the authority under which he acteth.

In relating these and the following laws, I would only be understood to mean the original institutions, and not the most scandalous corruptions into which these people are fallen by the degenerate nature of man. For as to that infamous practice of acquiring great employments by dancing on the ropes, or badges of favor and distinction by leaping over sticks, and creeping under

9. Social position.

them, the reader is to observe, that they were first introduced by the grand-father of the Emperor now reigning; and grew to the present height by the gradual increase of party and faction.

Ingratitude is among them a capital crime, as we read it to have been in some other countries; for they reason thus, that whoever makes ill returns to his benefactor, must needs be a common enemy to the rest of mankind, from whom he hath received no obligation; and therefore such a man is not fit to live.

Their notions relating to the duties of parents and children differ extremely from ours. For, since the conjunction of male and female is founded upon the great law of nature, in order to propagate and continue the species, the Lilliputians will needs have it, that men and women are joined together like other animals, by the motives of concupiscence; and that their tenderness towards their young proceedeth from the like natural principle: for which reason they will never allow, that a child is under any obligation to his father for begetting him, or to his mother for bringing him into the world; which, considering the miseries of human life, was neither a benefit in itself, nor intended so by his parents, whose thoughts in their love-encounters were otherwise employed. Upon these, and the like reasonings, their opinion is, that parents are the last of all others to be trusted with the education of their own children: and therefore they have in every town public nurseries, where all parents, except cottagers[1] and laborers, are obliged to send their infants of both sexes to be reared and educated when they come to the age of twenty moons; at which time they are supposed to have some rudiments of docility. These schools are of several kinds, suited to different qualities, and to both sexes. They have certain professors[2] well skilled in preparing children for such a condition of life as befits the rank of their parents, and their own capacities as well as inclinations. I shall first say something of the male nurseries, and then of the female.

The nurseries for males of noble or eminent birth are provided with grave and learned professors, and their several deputies. The clothes and food of the children are plain and simple. They are bred up in the principles of honor, justice, courage, modesty, clemency, religion, and love of their country; they are always employed in some business, except in the times of eating and sleeping, which are very short, and two hours for diversions, consisting of bodily exercises. They are dressed by men until four years of age, and then are obliged to dress themselves, although their quality be ever so great; and the women attendants, who are aged proportionably to ours at fifty, perform only the most menial offices. They are never suffered to converse with ser-vants, but go together in small or greater numbers to take their diversions, and always in the presence of a professor, or one of his deputies; whereby they avoid those early bad impressions of folly and vice to which our children are subject. Their parents are suffered to see them only twice a year; the visit is not to last above an hour; they are allowed to kiss the child at meeting and parting; but a professor, who always standeth by on those occasions, will not suffer them to whisper, or use any fondling expressions, or bring any presents of toys, sweetmeats, and the like.

1. Agricultural workers, peasants.
2. Professional teachers.

The pension from each family for the education and entertainment[3] of a child, upon failure of due payment, is levied by the Emperor's officers.

The nurseries for children of ordinary gentlemen, merchants, traders, and handicrafts, are managed proportionably after the same manner; only those designed for trades are put out apprentices at seven years old; whereas those of persons of quality continue in their exercises until fifteen, which answers to one and twenty with us: but the confinement is gradually lessened for the last three years.

In the female nurseries, the young girls of quality are educated much like the males, only they are dressed by orderly servants of their own sex, but always in the presence of a professor or deputy, until they come to dress themselves, which is at five years old. And if it be found that these nurses ever presume to entertain the girls with frightful or foolish stories, or the common follies practiced by chambermaids among us, they are publicly whipped thrice about the city, imprisoned for a year, and banished for life to the most desolate parts of the country. Thus the young ladies there are as much ashamed of being cowards and fools as the men; and despise all personal ornaments beyond decency and cleanliness: neither did I perceive any difference in their education, made by their difference of sex, only that the exercises of the females were not altogether so robust; and that some rules were given them relating to domestic life, and a smaller compass of learning was enjoined them: for their maxim is, that among people of quality, a wife should be always a reasonable and agreeable companion, because she cannot always be young. When the girls are twelve years old, which among them is the marriageable age, their parents or guardians take them home, with great expressions of gratitude to the professors, and seldom without tears of the young lady and her companions.

In the nurseries of females of the meaner sort, the children are instructed in all kinds of works proper for their sex, and their several degrees:[4] those intended for apprentices are dismissed at seven years old, the rest are kept to eleven.

The meaner families who have children at these nurseries are obliged, besides their annual pension, which is as low as possible, to return to the steward of the nursery a small monthly share of their gettings, to be a portion for the child; and therefore all parents are limited in their expenses by the law. For the Lilliputians think nothing can be more unjust, than that people, in subservience to their own appetites, should bring children into the world, and leave the burthen of supporting them on the public. As to persons of quality, they give security to appropriate a certain sum for each child, suitable to their condition; and these funds are always managed with good husbandry, and the most exact justice.

The cottagers and laborers keep their children at home, their business being only to till and cultivate the earth; and therefore their education is of little consequence to the public; but the old and diseased among them are supported by hospitals: for begging is a trade unknown in this empire.

And here it may perhaps divert the curious reader, to give some account of my domestic,[5] and my manner of living in this country, during a residence of

---

3. Sustenance.   5. Household.
4. Various social ranks.

nine months and thirteen days. Having a head mechanically turned, and being likewise forced by necessity, I had made for myself a table and chair convenient enough, out of the largest trees in the royal park. Two hundred sempstresses were employed to make me shirts, and linen for my bed and table, all of the strongest and coarsest kind they could get; which, however, they were forced to quilt together in several folds; for the thickest was some degrees finer than lawn. Their linen is usually three inches wide, and three foot make a piece. The sempstresses took my measure as I lay on the ground, one standing at my neck, and another at my mid-leg, with a strong cord extended, that each held by the end, while the third measured the length of the cord with a rule of an inch long. Then they measured my right thumb, and desired no more; for by a mathematical computation, that twice round the thumb is one round the wrist, and so on to the neck and the waist; and by the help of my old shirt, which I displayed on the ground before them for a pattern, they fitted me exactly. Three hundred tailors were employed in the same manner to make me clothes; but they had another contrivance for taking my measure. I kneeled down, and they raised a ladder from the ground to my neck; upon this ladder one of them mounted, and let fall a plumb-line from my collar to the floor, which just answered the length of my coat; but my waist and arms I measured myself. When my clothes were finished, which was done in my house (for the largest of theirs would not have been able to hold them), they looked like the patchwork made by the ladies in England, only that mine were all of a color.

I had three hundred cooks to dress my victuals, in little convenient huts built about my house, where they and their families lived, and prepared me two dishes apiece. I took up twenty waiters in my hand, and placed them on the table; an hundred more attended below on the ground, some with dishes of meat, and some with barrels of wine, and other liquors, slung on their shoulders; all which the waiters above drew up as I wanted, in a very ingenious manner, by certain cords, as we draw the bucket up a well in Europe. A dish of their meat was a good mouthful, and a barrel of their liquor a reasonable draught. Their mutton yields to ours, but their beef is excellent. I have had a sirloin so large, that I have been forced to make three bites of it; but this is rare. My servants were astonished to see me eat it bones and all, as in our country we do the leg of a lark. Their geese and turkeys I usually eat at a mouthful, and I must confess they far exceed ours. Of their smaller fowl I could take up twenty or thirty at the end of my knife.

One day his Imperial Majesty, being informed of my way of living, desired that himself and his royal consort, with the young princes of the blood of both sexes, might have the happiness (as he was pleased to call it) of dining with me. They came accordingly, and I placed them upon chairs of state on my table, just over against me, with their guards about them. Flimnap the Lord High Treasurer attended there likewise, with his white staff; and I observed he often looked on me with a sour countenance, which I would not seem to regard, but eat more than usual, in honor to my dear country, as well as to fill the court with admiration. I have some private reasons to believe, that this visit from his Majesty gave Flimnap an opportunity of doing me ill offices to his master. That minister had always been my secret enemy, although he outwardly caressed me more than was usual to the moroseness of his nature. He represented to the Emperor the low condition of his treasury; that he was forced to take up money at great discount; that exchequer bills[6] would not circulate under nine per cent below par; that I had cost his Majesty above a million and a half of *sprugs* (their greatest gold coin, about the bigness of a spangle); and upon the whole, that it would be advisable in the Emperor to take the first fair occasion of dismissing me.

I am here obliged to vindicate the reputation of an excellent lady, who was an innocent sufferer upon my account. The Treasurer took a fancy to be jealous of his wife, from the malice of some evil tongues, who informed him that her Grace had taken a violent affection for my person; and the court-scandal ran for some time that she once came privately to my lodging. This I solemnly declare to be a most infamous falsehood, without any grounds, farther than that her Grace was pleased to treat me with all innocent marks of freedom and friendship. I own she came often to my house, but always publicly, nor ever without three more in the coach, who were usually her sister and young daughter, and some particular acquaintance; but this was common to many other ladies of the court. And I still appeal to my servants round, whether they at any time saw a coach at my door without knowing what persons were in it. On those occasions, when a servant had given me notice, my custom was to go immediately to the door; and, after paying my respects, to take up the coach and two horses very carefully in my hands (for if there were six horses, the postillion always unharnessed four) and place them on a table, where I had fixed a moveable rim quite round, of five inches high, to prevent accidents. And I have often had four coaches and horses at once on my table full of company, while I sat in my chair leaning my face towards them; and when I was engaged with one set, the coachmen would gently drive the others round my table. I have passed many an afternoon very agreeably in these conversations. But I defy the Treasurer, or his two inform-ers (I will name them, and let them make their best of it) Clustril and Drunlo, to prove that any person ever came to me *incognito*, except the Secretary Rel-dresal, who was sent by express command of his Imperial Majesty, as I have before related. I should not have dwelt so long upon this particular, if it had not been a point wherein the reputation of a great lady is so nearly concerned, to say nothing of my own; although I had the honor to be a *Nardac*, which the Treasurer himself is not; for all the world knows he is only a *Clumglum*, a title inferior by one degree, as that of a marquis is to a duke in England; yet I allow he preceded me in right of his post. These false informations, which I after-wards came to the knowledge of, by an accident not proper to mention, made the Treasurer show his lady for some time an ill countenance, and me a worse; for although he was at last undeceived and reconciled to her, yet I lost all credit with him; and found my interest decline very fast with the Emperor himself, who was indeed too much governed by that favorite.

CHAPTER 7. *The author, being informed of a design to accuse him of high treason, makes his escape to Blefuscu. His reception there.*

Before I proceed to give an account of my leaving this kingdom, it may be proper to inform the reader of a private intrigue which had been for two months forming against me.

6. Government bills of credit. Walpole was noted as a canny financier.

I had been hitherto all my life a stranger to courts, for which I was unqualified by the meanness of my condition. I had indeed heard and read enough of the dispositions of great princes and ministers; but never expected to have found such terrible effects of them in so remote a country, governed, as I thought, by very different maxims from those in Europe.

When I was just preparing to pay my attendance on the Emperor of Blefuscu, a considerable person at court (to whom I had been very serviceable at a time when he lay under the highest displeasure of his Imperial Majesty) came to my house very privately at night in a close chair, and without sending his name, desired admittance. The chairmen were dismissed; I put the chair, with his Lordship in it, into my coat-pocket; and giving orders to a trusty servant to say I was indisposed and gone to sleep, I fastened the door of my house, placed the chair on the table, according to my usual custom, and sat down by it. After the common salutations were over, observing his Lordship's countenance full of concern, and enquiring into the reason, he desired I would hear him with patience, in a matter that highly concerned my honor and my life. His speech was to the following effect, for I took notes of it as soon as he left me.

You are to know, said he, that several committees of council have been lately called in the most private manner on your account: and it is but two days since his Majesty came to a full resolution.

You are very sensible that Skyresh Bolgolam (*Galbet*, or High Admiral) hath been your mortal enemy almost ever since your arrival. His original reasons I know not; but his hatred is much increased since your great success against Blefuscu, by which his glory, as Admiral, is obscured. This lord, in conjunction with Flimnap the High Treasurer, whose enmity against you is notorious on account of his lady, Limtoc the General, Lalcon the Chamberlain, and Balmuff the Grand Justiciary, have prepared articles of impeachment against you, for treason, and other capital crimes.[7]

This preface made me so impatient, being conscious of my own merits and innocence, that I was going to interrupt; when he entreated me to be silent, and thus proceeded.

Out of gratitude for the favors you have done me, I procured information of the whole proceedings, and a copy of the articles, wherein I venture my head for your service.

Articles of Impeachment against Quinbus Flestrin (*the* Man-Mountain).

ARTICLE 1

Whereas, by a statute made in the reign of his Imperial Majesty Calin Deffar Plune, it is enacted, that whoever shall make water within the precincts of the royal palace shall be liable to the pains and penalties of high treason: notwithstanding, the said Quinbus Flestrin, in open breach of the said law, under color of extinguishing the fire kindled in the apartment of his Majesty's most dear imperial consort, did mali-

---

7. After the Whigs had investigated Oxford and Bolingbroke, both were impeached for high treason, on charges of being sympathetic to the Jacobites and the French.

ciously, traitorously, and devilishly, by discharge of his urine, put out the said fire kindled in the said apartment, lying and being within the precincts of the said royal palace; against the statute in that case provided, etc., against the duty, etc.

ARTICLE 2

That the said Quinbus Flestrin, having brought the imperial fleet of Blefuscu into the royal port, and being afterwards commanded by his Imperial Majesty to seize all the other ships of the said empire of Blefuscu, and reduce that empire to a province, to be governed by a viceroy from hence; and to destroy and put to death not only all the Big-Endian exiles, but likewise all the people of that empire who would not immediately forsake the Big-Endian heresy: he, the said Flestrin, like a false traitor against his most auspicious, serene, Imperial Majesty, did petition to be excused from the said service, upon pretense of unwillingness to force the consciences, or destroy the liberties and lives of an innocent people.

ARTICLE 3

That, whereas certain ambassadors arrived from the court of Blefuscu to sue for peace in his Majesty's court: he the said Flestrin did, like a false traitor, aid, abet, comfort, and divert the said ambassadors; although he knew them to be servants to a prince who was lately an open enemy to his Imperial Majesty, and in open war against his said Majesty.

ARTICLE 4

That the said Quinbus Flestrin, contrary to the duty of a faithful subject, is now preparing to make a voyage to the court and empire of Blefuscu, for which he hath received only verbal license from his Imperial Majesty; and under color of the said license, doth falsely and traitorously intend to take the said voyage, and thereby to aid, comfort, and abet the Emperor of Blefuscu, so late an enemy, and in open war with his Imperial Majesty aforesaid.

There are some other articles, but these are the most important, of which I have read you an abstract.

In the several debates upon this impeachment, it must be confessed that his Majesty gave many marks of his great *lenity*; often urging the services you had done him, and endeavoring to extenuate your crimes. The Treasurer and Admiral insisted that you should be put to the most painful and ignominious death, by setting fire on your house at night; and the General was to attend with twenty thousand men armed with poisoned arrows, to shoot you on the face and hands. Some of your servants were to have private orders to strew a poisonous juice on your shirts and sheets, which would soon make you tear your own flesh, and die in the utmost torture. The General came into the same opinion; so that for a long time there was a majority against you. But his Majesty resolving, if possible, to spare your life, at last brought off[8] the Chamberlain.

8. Won over.

Upon this incident, Reldresal, Principal Secretary for Private Affairs, who always approved[9] himself your true friend, was commanded by the Emperor to deliver his opinion, which he accordingly did; and therein justified the good thoughts you have of him. He allowed your crimes to be great; but that still there was room for mercy, the most commendable virtue in a prince, and for which his Majesty was so justly celebrated. He said, the friendship between you and him was so well known to the world, that perhaps the most honorable board might think him partial: however, in obedience to the command he had received, he would freely offer his sentiments. That if his Majesty, in consideration of your services, and pursuant to his own merciful disposition, would please to spare your life, and only give order to put out both your eyes, he humbly conceived, that by this expedient justice might in some measure be satisfied, and all the world would applaud the *lenity* of the Emperor, as well as the fair and generous proceedings of those who have the honor to be his counselors. That the loss of your eyes would be no impediment to your bodily strength, by which you might still be useful to his Majesty. That blindness is an addition to courage, by concealing dangers from us; that the fear you had for your eyes was the greatest difficulty in bringing over the enemy's fleet; and it would be sufficient for you to see by the eyes of the ministers, since the greatest princes do no more.

This proposal was received with the utmost disapprobation by the whole board. Bolgolam, the Admiral, could not preserve his temper; but rising up in fury, said, he wondered how the Secretary durst presume to give his opinion for preserving the life of a traitor: that the services you had performed were, by all true reasons of state, the great aggravation of your crimes; that you, who were able to extinguish the fire by discharge of urine in her Majesty's apartment (which he mentioned with horror), might, at another time, raise an inundation by the same means, to drown the whole palace; and the same strength which enabled you to bring over the enemy's fleet might serve, upon the first discontent, to carry it back: that he had good reasons to think you were a Big-Endian in your heart; and as treason begins in the heart before it appears in overt acts, so he accused you as a traitor on that account, and therefore insisted you should be put to death.

The Treasurer was of the same opinion; he showed to what straits his Majesty's revenue was reduced by the charge of maintaining you, which would soon grow insupportable: that the Secretary's expedient of putting out your eyes was so far from being a remedy against this evil, that it would probably increase it; as it is manifest from the common practice of blinding some kind of fowl, after which they fed the faster, and grew sooner fat: that his sacred Majesty, and the council, who are your judges, were in their own consciences fully convinced of your guilt; which was a sufficient argument to condemn you to death, without the formal proofs required by the strict letter of the law.

But his Imperial Majesty, fully determined against capital punishment, was graciously pleased to say, that since the council thought the loss of your eyes too easy a censure, some other may be inflicted hereafter. And your friend the Secretary humbly desiring to be heard again, in answer to what the Treasurer had objected concerning the great charge his Majesty was at in maintaining you, said, that his Excellency, who had the sole disposal of

9. Proved.

the Emperor's revenue, might easily provide against this evil, by gradually lessening your establishment; by which, for want of sufficient food, you would grow weak and faint, and lose your appetite, and consequently decay and consume in a few months; neither would the stench of your carcass be then so dangerous, when it should become more than half diminished; and immediately upon your death, five or six thousand of his Majesty's subjects might, in two or three days, cut your flesh from your bones, take it away by cart-loads, and bury it in distant parts to prevent infection; leaving the skeleton as a monument of admiration to posterity.

Thus by the great friendship of the Secretary, the whole affair was compromised. It was strictly enjoined, that the project of starving you by degrees should be kept a secret; but the sentence of putting out your eyes was entered on the books; none dissenting except Bolgolam the Admiral, who being a creature of the Empress, was perpetually instigated by her Majesty to insist upon your death; she having borne perpetual malice against you, on account of that infamous and illegal method you took to extinguish the fire in her apartment.

In three days your friend the Secretary will be directed to come to your house, and read before you the articles of impeachment; and then to signify the great lenity and favor of his Majesty and council; whereby you are only condemned to the loss of your eyes, which his Majesty doth not question you will gratefully and humbly submit to; and twenty of his Majesty's surgeons will attend, in order to see the operation well performed, by discharging very sharp-pointed arrows into the balls of your eyes, as you lie on the ground.

I leave to your prudence what measures you will take; and to avoid suspicion, I must immediately return in as private a manner as I came.

His Lordship did so, and I remained alone, under many doubts and perplexities of mind.

It was a custom introduced by this prince and his ministry (very different, as I have been assured, from the practices of former times), that after the court had decreed any cruel execution, either to gratify the monarch's resentment, or the malice of a favorite, the Emperor always made a speech to his whole council, expressing his great lenity and tenderness, as qualities known and confessed by all the world. This speech was immediately published through the kingdom; nor did any thing terrify the people so much as those encomiums on his Majesty's mercy; because it was observed, that the more these praises were enlarged and insisted on, the more inhuman was the punishment, and the sufferer more innocent. Yet as to myself, I must confess, having never been designed for a courtier, either by my birth or education, I was so ill a judge of things, that I could not discover the lenity and favor of this sentence, but conceived it (perhaps erroneously) rather to be rigorous than gentle. I sometimes thought of standing my trial; for although I could not deny the facts alleged in the several articles, yet I hoped they would admit of some extenuations. But having in my life perused many state trials, which I ever observed to terminate as the judges thought fit to direct, I durst not rely on so dangerous a decision, in so critical a juncture, and against such powerful enemies. Once I was strongly bent upon resistance: for while I had liberty, the whole strength of that empire could hardly subdue me, and I might easily with stones pelt the metropolis to pieces; but I soon rejected that project with horror, by remembering the oath I had made to the Emperor, the favors I received from him, and the high title of *Nardac* he conferred upon me. Neither had I so soon learned the gratitude of courtiers, to persuade myself that his Majesty's present severities acquitted me of all past obligations.

At last I fixed upon a resolution, for which it is probable I may incur some censure, and not unjustly; for I confess I owe the preserving my eyes, and consequently my liberty, to my own great rashness and want of experience: because if I had then known the nature of princes and ministers, which I have since observed in many other courts, and their methods of treating criminals less obnoxious than myself, I should with great alacrity and readiness have submitted to so *easy* a punishment. But hurried on by the precipitancy of youth, and having his Imperial Majesty's license to pay my attendance upon the Emperor of Blefuscu, I took this opportunity, before the three days were elapsed, to send a letter to my friend the Secretary, signifying my resolution of setting out that morning for Blefuscu,[1] pursuant to the leave I had got; and without waiting for an answer, I went to that side of the island where our fleet lay. I seized a large man of war, tied a cable to the prow, and lifting up the anchors, I stripped myself, put my clothes (together with my coverlet, which I carried under my arm) into the vessel; and drawing it after me, between wading and swimming, arrived at the royal port of Blefuscu, where the people had long expected me. They lent me two guides to direct me to the capital city, which is of the same name; I held them in my hands until I came within two hundred yards of the gate; and desired them to signify my arrival to one of the secretaries, and let him know, I there waited his Majesty's commands. I had an answer in about an hour, that his Majesty, attended by the royal family, and great officers of the court, was coming out to receive me. I advanced a hundred yards; the Emperor, and his train, alighted from their horses, the Empress and ladies from their coaches; and I did not perceive they were in any fright or concern. I lay on the ground to kiss his Majesty's and the Empress's hand. I told his Majesty that I was come according to my promise, and with the license of the Emperor my master, to have the honor of seeing so mighty a monarch, and to offer him any service in my power, consistent with my duty to my own prince; not mentioning a word of my disgrace, because I had hitherto no regular information of it, and might suppose myself wholly ignorant of any such design; neither could I reasonably conceive that the Emperor would discover the secret while I was out of his power: wherein, however, it soon appeared I was deceived.

I shall not trouble the reader with the particular account of my reception at this court, which was suitable to the generosity of so great a prince; nor of the difficulties I was in for want of a house and bed, being forced to lie on the ground, wrapped up in my coverlet.

CHAPTER 8. *The author, by a lucky accident, finds means to leave Blefuscu; and, after some difficulties, returns safe to his native country.*

Three days after my arrival, walking out of curiosity to the northeast coast of the island, I observed, about half a league off, in the sea, somewhat that looked like a boat overturned. I pulled off my shoes and stockings, and

1. Before his trial for treason could be held, Bolingbroke had escaped to France.

wading two or three hundred yards, I found the object to approach nearer by force of the tide; and then plainly saw it to be a real boat, which I supposed might, by some tempest, have been driven from a ship. Whereupon I returned immediately towards the city, and desired his Imperial Majesty to lend me twenty of the tallest vessels he had left after the loss of his fleet, and three thousand seamen under the command of his Vice Admiral. This fleet sailed round, while I went back the shortest way to the coast where I first discovered the boat; I found the tide had driven it still nearer; the seamen were all provided with cordage, which I had beforehand twisted to a sufficient strength. When the ships came up, I stripped myself, and waded till I came within an hundred yards of the boat; after which I was forced to swim till I got up to it. The seamen threw me the end of the cord, which I fastened to a hole in the forepart of the boat, and the other end to a man of war: but I found all my labor to little purpose; for being out of my depth, I was not able to work. In this necessity, I was forced to swim behind, and push the boat forwards as often as I could, with one of my hands; and the tide favoring me, I advanced so far, that I could just hold up my chin and feel the ground. I rested two or three minutes, and then gave the boat another shove, and so on till the sea was no higher than my armpits. And now the most laborious part being over, I took out my other cables which were stowed in one of the ships, and fastening them first to the boat, and then to nine of the vessels which attended me, the wind being favorable, the seamen towed, and I shoved till we arrived within forty yards of the shore; and waiting till the tide was out, I got dry to the boat, and by the assistance of two thousand men, with ropes and engines, I made a shift to turn it on its bottom, and found it was but little damaged.

I shall not trouble the reader with the difficulties I was under by the help of certain paddles, which cost me ten days making, to get my boat to the royal port of Blefuscu; where a mighty concourse of people appeared upon my arrival, full of wonder at the sight of so prodigious a vessel. I told the Emperor that my good fortune had thrown this boat in my way, to carry me to some place from whence I might return into my native country; and begged his Majesty's orders for getting materials to fit it up, together with license to depart; which, after some kind expostulations, he was pleased to grant.

I did very much wonder, in all this time, not to have heard of any express relating to me from our Emperor to the court of Blefuscu. But I was afterwards given privately to understand, that his Imperial Majesty, never imagining I had the least notice of his designs, believed I was only gone to Blefuscu in performance of my promise, according to the license he had given me, which was well known at our court; and would return in a few days when that ceremony was ended. But he was at last in pain at my long absence; and, after consulting with the Treasurer, and the rest of that cabal, a person of quality was dispatched with the copy of the articles against me. This envoy had instructions to represent to the monarch of Blefuscu the great lenity of his master, who was content to punish me no further than with the loss of my eyes; that I had fled from justice, and if I did not return in two hours, I should be deprived of my title of *Nardac*, and declared a traitor. The envoy further added, that in order to maintain the peace and amity between both empires, his master expected, that his brother of Blefuscu would give orders to have me sent back to Lilliput, bound hand and foot, to be punished as a traitor.

The Emperor of Blefuscu, having taken three days to consult, returned an answer consisting of many civilities and excuses. He said, that as for sending me bound, his brother knew it was impossible; that although I had deprived him of his fleet, yet he owed great obligations to me for many good offices I had done him in making the peace. That however, both their Majesties would soon be made easy; for I had found a prodigious vessel on the shore, able to carry me on the sea, which he had given order to fit up with my own assistance and direction; and he hoped in a few weeks both empires would be freed from so insupportable an incumbrance.

With this answer the envoy returned to Lilliput, and the monarch of Blefuscu related to me all that had passed, offering me at the same time (but under the strictest confidence) his gracious protection, if I would continue in his service; wherein although I believed him sincere, yet I resolved never more to put any confidence in princes or ministers, where I could possibly avoid it; and therefore, with all due acknowledgements for his favorable intentions, I humbly begged to be excused. I told him, that since fortune, whether good or evil, had thrown a vessel in my way, I was resolved to venture myself in the ocean, rather than be an occasion of difference between two such mighty monarchs. Neither did I find the Emperor at all displeased; and I discovered by a certain accident, that he was very glad of my resolution, and so were most of his ministers.

These considerations moved me to hasten my departure somewhat sooner than I intended; to which the court, impatient to have me gone, very readily contributed. Five hundred workmen were employed to make two sails to my boat, according to my directions, by quilting thirteen fold of their strongest linen together. I was at the pains of making ropes and cables, by twisting ten, twenty or thirty of the thickest and strongest of theirs. A great stone that I happened to find, after a long search by the seashore, served me for an anchor. I had the tallow of three hundred cows for greasing my boat, and other uses. I was at incredible pains in cutting down some of the largest timber trees for oars and masts, wherein I was, however, much assisted by his Majesty's ship-carpenters, who helped me in smoothing them, after I had done the rough work.

In about a month, when all was prepared, I sent to receive his Majesty's commands, and to take my leave. The Emperor and royal family came out of the palace; I lay down on my face to kiss his hand, which he very graciously gave me: so did the Empress, and young princes of the blood. His Majesty presented me with fifty purses of two hundred *sprugs* apiece, together with his picture at full length, which I put immediately into one of my gloves, to keep it from being hurt. The ceremonies at my departure were too many to trouble the reader with at this time.

I stored the boat with the carcasses of an hundred oxen, and three hundred sheep, with bread and drink proportionable, and as much meat ready dressed as four hundred cooks could provide. I took with me six cows and two bulls alive, with as many ewes and rams, intending to carry them into my own country, and propagate the breed. And to feed them on board, I had a good bundle of hay, and a bag of corn.[2] I would gladly have taken a dozen of the natives; but this was a thing the Emperor would by no means permit;

2. Generic term for any cereal or grain crop (here, wheat).

and besides a diligent search into my pockets, his Majesty engaged my honor not to carry away any of his subjects, although with their own consent and desire.

Having thus prepared all things as well as I was able, I set sail on the twenty-fourth day of September, 1701, at six in the morning; and when I had gone about four leagues to the northward, the wind being at southeast, at six in the evening, I descried a small island about half a league to the northwest. I advanced forward, and cast anchor on the lee-side of the island, which seemed to be uninhabited. I then took some refreshment, and went to my rest. I slept well, and as I conjecture at least six hours; for I found the day broke in two hours after I awaked. It was a clear night; I eat my breakfast before the sun was up; and heaving anchor, the wind being favorable, I steered the same course that I had done the day before, wherein I was directed by my pocket compass. My intention was to reach, if possible, one of those islands which I had reason to believe lay to the northeast of Van Diemen's Land. I discovered nothing all that day; but upon the next, about three in the afternoon, when I had by my computation made twenty-four leagues from Blefuscu, I descried a sail steering to the southeast; my course was due east. I hailed her, but could get no answer; yet I found I gained upon her, for the wind slackened. I made all the sail I could, and in half an hour she spied me, then hung out her ancient,[3] and discharged a gun. It is not easy to express the joy I was in upon the unexpected hope of once more seeing my beloved country, and the dear pledges[4] I had left in it. The ship slackened her sails, and I came up with her between five and six in the evening, September 26; but my heart leapt within me to see her English colors. I put my cows and sheep into my coat-pockets and got on board with all my little cargo of provisions. The vessel was an English merchantman, returning from Japan by the North and South Seas;[5] the captain, Mr. John Biddel of Deptford, a very civil man, and an excellent sailor. We were now in the latitude of 30 degrees south; there were about fifty men in the ship; and here I met an old comrade of mine, one Peter Williams, who gave me a good character to the captain. This gentleman treated me with kindness, and desired I would let him know what place I came from last, and whither I was bound; which I did in few words; but he thought I was raving, and that the dangers I underwent had disturbed my head; whereupon I took my black cattle and sheep out of my pocket, which, after great astonishment, clearly convinced him of my veracity. I then showed him the gold given me by the Emperor of Blefuscu, together with his Majesty's picture at full length, and some other rarities of that country. I gave him two purses of two hundred *sprugs* each, and promised, when we arrived in England, to make him a present of a cow and a sheep big with young.

I shall not trouble the reader with a particular account of this voyage; which was very prosperous for the most part. We arrived in the Downs[6] on the 13th of April, 1702. I had only one misfortune, that the rats on board carried away one of my sheep; I found her bones in a hole, picked clean from the flesh. The rest of my cattle I got safe on shore, and set them a grazing in a

3. Flag.
4. Hostages (i.e., his family).
5. North and South Pacific.

6. A rendezvous for ships off the southeast coast of England.

bowling-green at Greenwich, where the fineness of the grass made them feed very heartily, though I had always feared the contrary; neither could I possibly have preserved them in so long a voyage, if the captain had not allowed me some of his best biscuit, which rubbed to powder, and mingled with water, was their constant food. The short time I continued in England, I made a considerable profit by showing my cattle to many persons of quality, and others: and before I began my second voyage, I sold them for six hundred pounds. Since my last return, I find the breed is considerably increased, especially the sheep; which I hope will prove much to the advantage of the woolen manufacture, by the fineness of the fleeces.

I stayed but two months with my wife and family; for my insatiable desire of seeing foreign countries would suffer me to continue no longer. I left fifteen hundred pounds with my wife, and fixed her in a good house at Redriff. My remaining stock I carried with me, part in money, and part in goods, in hopes to improve my fortunes. My eldest uncle, John, had left me an estate in land, near Epping, of about thirty pounds a year; and I had a long lease of the Black Bull in Fetter Lane, which yielded me as much more: so that I was not in any danger of leaving my family upon the parish.[7] My son Johnny, named so after his uncle, was at the grammar school, and a towardly[8] child. My daughter Betty (who is now well married, and has children) was then at her needlework. I took leave of my wife, and boy and girl, with tears on both sides; and went on board the *Adventure*, a merchant-ship of three hundred tons, bound for Surat, Captain John Nicholas of Liverpool, Commander. But my account of this voyage must be referred to the second part of my *Travels*.

Part 2. A Voyage to Brobdingnag

CHAPTER 1. *A great storm described. The longboat sent to fetch water; the Author goes with it to discover the country. He is left on shore, is seized by one of the natives, and carried to a farmer's house. His reception there, with several accidents that happened there. A description of the inhabitants.*

Having been condemned by nature and fortune to an active and restless life, in ten months after my return I again left my native country, and took shipping in the Downs on the 20th day of June, 1702, in the *Adventure*, Captain John Nicholas, a Cornish man, Commander, bound for Surat.[9] We had a very prosperous gale till we arrived at the Cape of Good Hope, where we landed for fresh water, but discovering a leak we unshipped our goods and wintered there; for the Captain falling sick of an ague, we could not leave the Cape till the end of March. We then set sail, and had a good voyage till we passed the Straits of Madagascar; but having got northward of that island, and to about five degrees south latitude, the winds, which in those seas are

7. On welfare (living on charity given by the parish).
8. Promising.
9. In India. The geography of the voyage (described next) is simple: The *Adventure*, after sailing up the east coast of Africa to about five degrees south of the equator (the "Line"), is blown past India into the Malay Archipelago, north of the islands of Buru and Ceram. The storm then drives the ship northward and eastward, away from the coast of Siberia ("Great Tartary") into the northeast Pacific, at that time unexplored. Brobdingnag lies somewhere in the vicinity of Alaska.

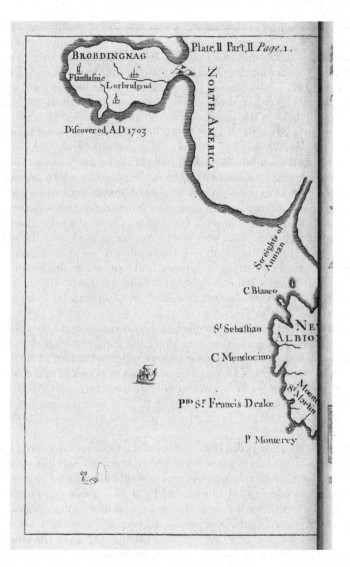

observed to blow a constant equal gale between the north and west from the beginning of December to the beginning of May, on the 19th of April began to blow with much greater violence and more westerly than usual, continuing so far twenty days together, during which time we were driven a little to the east of the Molucca Islands and about three degrees northward of the Line, as our Captain found by an observation he took the 2nd of May, at which time the wind ceased, and it was a perfect calm, whereat I was not a little rejoiced. But he, being a man well experienced in the navigation of those seas, bid us all prepare against a storm, which accordingly happened the day following: for a southern wind, called the southern monsoon, began to set in.

Finding it was likely to overblow,[1] we took in our spritsail, and stood by to hand the foresail; but making foul weather, we looked the guns were all fast, and handed the mizzen. The ship lay very broad off, so we thought it better spooning before the sea, than trying or hulling. We reefed the foresail and set him, we hauled aft the foresheet; the helm was hard aweather. The ship wore bravely. We belayed the fore-downhaul; but the sail was split, and we hauled down the yard and got the sail into the ship, and unbound all the things clear of it. It was a very fierce storm; the sea broke strange and dangerous. We hauled off upon the lanyard of the whipstaff, and helped the man at helm. We would not get down our topmast, but let all stand, because she scudded before the sea very well, and we knew that the topmast being aloft, the ship was the wholesomer, and made better way through the sea, seeing we had searoom. When the storm was over, we set foresail and mainsail, and brought the ship to. Then we set the mizzen, main topsail and the fore topsail. Our course was east-northeast, the wind was at southwest. We got the starboard tacks aboard, we cast off our weather braces and lifts; we set in the lee braces, and hauled forward by the weather bowlings, and hauled them tight, and belayed them, and hauled over the mizzen tack to windward, and kept her full and by as near as she would lie.

During this storm, which was followed by a strong wind west-southwest, we were carried by my computation about five hundred leagues to the east, so that the oldest sailor on board could not tell in what part of the world we were. Our provisions held out well, our ship was staunch, and our crew all in good health; but we lay in the utmost distress for water. We thought it best to hold on the same course rather than turn more northerly, which might have brought us to the northwest parts of Great Tartary, and into the frozen sea.

On the 16th day of June, 1703, a boy on the topmast discovered land. On the 17th we came in full view of a great island or continent (for we knew not whether) on the south side whereof was a small neck of land jutting out into the sea, and a creek[2] too shallow to hold a ship of above one hundred tons. We cast anchor within a league of this creek, and our Captain sent a dozen of his men well armed in the longboat, with vessels for water if any could be found. I desired his leave to go with them that I might see the country and make what discoveries I could. When we came to land we saw no river or spring, nor any sign of inhabitants. Our men therefore wandered on the shore to find out some fresh water near the sea, and I walked alone about a mile on the other side, where I observed the country all barren and rocky. I now began to be weary, and seeing nothing to entertain my curiosity, I returned gently down towards the creek; and the sea being full in my view, I saw our men already got into the boat, and rowing for life to the ship. I was going to hollow after them, although it had been to little purpose, when I observed a huge creature walking after them in the sea as fast as he could; he waded not much deeper than his knees and took prodigious strides, but our men had the start of him half a league, and the sea thereabouts being full of sharp-pointed

---

1. This paragraph is taken almost literally from Samuel Sturmy's *Mariner's Magazine* (1669). Swift is ridiculing the use of technical terms by writers of popular voyages.
2. A small bay or cove, affording anchorage.

rocks, the monster was not able to overtake the boat. This I was afterwards told, for I durst not stay to see the issue of that adventure, but ran as fast as I could the way I first went, and then climbed up a steep hill, which gave me some prospect of the country. I found it fully cultivated; but that which first surprised me was the length of the grass, which, in those grounds that seemed to be kept for hay, was about twenty foot high.[3]

I fell into a highroad, for so I took it to be, although it served to the inhabitants only as a footpath through a field of barley. Here I walked on for some time, but could see little on either side, it being now near harvest, and the corn[4] rising at least forty foot. I was an hour walking to the end of this field, which was fenced in with a hedge of at least one hundred and twenty foot high, and the trees so lofty that I could make no computation of their altitude. There was a stile to pass from this field into the next: it had four steps, and a stone to cross over when you came to the utmost. It was impossible for me to climb this stile, because every step was six foot high, and the upper stone above twenty. I was endeavoring to find some gap in the hedge when I discovered one of the inhabitants in the next field advancing towards the stile, of the same size with him whom I saw in the sea pursuing our boat. He appeared as tall as an ordinary spire-steeple, and took about ten yards at every stride, as near as I could guess. I was struck with the utmost fear and astonishment, and ran to hide myself in the corn, from whence I saw him at the top of the stile, looking back into the next field on the right hand; and heard him call in a voice many degrees louder than a speaking trumpet; but the noise was so high in the air that at first I certainly thought it was thunder. Whereupon seven monsters like himself came towards him with reaping hooks in their hands, each hook about the largeness of six scythes. These people were not so well clad as the first, whose servants or laborers they seemed to be. For, upon some words he spoke, they went to reap the corn in the field where I lay. I kept from them at as great a distance as I could, but was forced to move with extreme difficulty, for the stalks of the corn were sometimes not above a foot distant, so that I could hardly squeeze my body betwixt them. However, I made a shift to go forward till I came to a part of the field where the corn had been laid by the rain and wind; here it was impossible for me to advance a step, for the stalks were so interwoven that I could not creep through, and the beards of the fallen ears so strong and pointed that they pierced through my clothes into my flesh. At the same time I heard the reapers not above an hundred yards behind me. Being quite dispirited with toil, and wholly overcome by grief and despair, I lay down between two ridges and heartily wished I might there end my days. I bemoaned my desolate widow and fatherless children; I lamented my own folly and willfulness in attempting a second voyage against the advice of all my friends and relations. In this terrible agitation of mind, I could not forbear thinking of Lilliput, whose inhabitants looked upon me as the greatest prodigy that ever appeared in the world; where I was able to draw an imperial fleet in my hand, and perform those other actions which will be recorded forever in the chronicles of that empire, while posterity shall hardly believe them, although

3. Swift's intention, not always carried out accurately, is that everything in Brobdingnag should be, in relation to our familiar world, on a scale of ten to one.

4. Here, barley.

attested by millions. I reflected what a mortification it must prove to me to appear as inconsiderable in this nation as one single Lilliputian would be among us. But this I conceived was to be the least of my misfortunes; for as human creatures are observed to be more savage and cruel in proportion to their bulk, what could I expect but to be a morsel in the mouth of the first among these enormous barbarians who should happen to seize me? Undoubtedly philosophers are in the right when they tell us that nothing is great or little otherwise than by comparison. It might have pleased fortune to let the Lilliputians find some nation where the people were as diminutive with respect to them as they were to me. And who knows but that even this prodigious race of mortals might be equally overmatched in some distant part of the world, whereof we have yet no discovery?

Scared and confounded as I was, I could not forbear going on with these reflections; when one of the reapers approaching within ten yards of the ridge where I lay, made me apprehend that with the next step I should be squashed to death under his foot, or cut in two with his reaping hook. And therefore when he was again about to move, I screamed as loud as fear could make me. Whereupon the huge creature trod short, and looking round about under him for some time, at last espied me as I lay on the ground. He considered a while with the caution of one who endeavors to lay hold on a small dangerous animal in such a manner that it shall not be able either to scratch or to bite him, as I myself have sometimes done with a weasel in England. At length he ventured to take me up behind by the middle between his forefinger and thumb, and brought me within three yards of his eyes, that he might behold my shape more perfectly. I guessed his meaning, and my good fortune gave me so much presence of mind that I resolved not to struggle in the least as he held me in the air about sixty foot from the ground, although he grievously pinched my sides, for fear I should slip through his fingers. All I ventured was to raise mine eyes towards the sun, and place my hands together in a supplicating posture, and to speak some words in an humble melancholy tone, suitable to the condition I then was in. For I apprehended every moment that he would dash me against the ground, as we usually do any little hateful animal which we have a mind to destroy. But my good star would have it that he appeared pleased with my voice and gestures, and began to look upon me as a curiosity, much wondering to hear me pronounce articulate words, although he could not understand them. In the meantime I was not able to forbear groaning and shedding tears and turning my head towards my sides, letting him know, as well as I could, how cruelly I was hurt by the pressure of his thumb and finger. He seemed to apprehend my meaning; for, lifting up the lappet[5] of his coat, he put me gently into it, and immediately ran along with me to his master, who was a substantial farmer, and the same person I had first seen in the field.

The farmer having (as I supposed by their talk) received such an account of me as his servant could give him, took a piece of a small straw about the size of a walking staff, and therewith lifted up the lappets of my coat, which it seems he thought to be some kind of covering that nature had given me. He blew my hairs aside to take a better view of my face. He called his hinds[6]

5. Flap or fold.   6. Farm servants.

about him, and asked them (as I afterwards learned) whether they had ever seen in the fields any little creature that resembled me. He then placed me softly on the ground upon all four; but I got immediately up, and walked slowly backwards and forwards, to let those people see I had no intent to run away. They all sat down in a circle about me, the better to observe my motions. I pulled off my hat, and made a low bow towards the farmer; I fell on my knees, and lifted up my hands and eyes, and spoke several words as loud as I could; I took a purse of gold out of my pocket, and humbly presented it to him. He received it on the palm of his hand, then applied it close to his eye to see what it was, and afterwards turned it several times with the point of a pin (which he took out of his sleeve), but could make nothing of it. Whereupon I made a sign that he should place his hand on the ground; I then took the purse, and opening it, poured all the gold into his palm. There were six Spanish pieces of four pistoles each, beside twenty or thirty smaller coins. I saw him wet the tip of his little finger upon his tongue, and take up one of my largest pieces, and then another; but he seemed to be wholly ignorant what they were. He made me a sign to put them again into my purse, and the purse again into my pocket, which after offering to him several times, I thought it best to do.

The farmer by this time was convinced I must be a rational creature. He spoke often to me, but the sound of his voice pierced my ears like that of a water mill, yet his words were articulate enough. I answered as loud as I could in several languages, and he often laid his ear within two yards of me, but all in vain, for we were wholly unintelligible to each other. He then sent his servants to their work, and taking his handkerchief out of his pocket, he doubled and spread it on his hand, which he placed flat on the ground with the palm upwards, making me a sign to step into it, as I could easily do, for it was not above a foot in thickness. I thought it my part to obey, and for fear of falling, laid myself at full length upon the handkerchief, with the remainder of which he lapped me up to the head for further security, and in this manner carried me home to his house. There he called his wife, and showed me to her; but she screamed and ran back as women in England do at the sight of a toad or a spider. However, when she had a while seen my behavior, and how well I observed the signs her husband made, she was soon reconciled, and by degrees grew extremely tender of me.

It was about twelve at noon, and a servant brought in dinner. It was only one substantial dish of meat (fit for the plain condition of an husbandman) in a dish of about four-and-twenty foot diameter. The company were the farmer and his wife, three children, and an old grandmother. When they were sat down, the farmer placed me at some distance from him on the table, which was thirty foot high from the floor. I was in a terrible fright, and kept as far as I could from the edge, for fear of falling. The wife minced a bit of meat, then crumbled some bread on a trencher, and placed it before me. I made her a low bow, took out my knife and fork, and fell to eat; which gave them exceeding delight. The mistress sent her maid for a small dram cup, which held about two gallons, and filled it with drink; I took up the vessel with much difficulty in both hands, and in a most respectful manner drank to her ladyship's health, expressing the words as loud as I could in English; which made the company laugh so heartily that I was almost deafened with the noise. This liquor tasted like a small cider,[7] and was not unpleasant. Then the master made me a sign to come to his trencher side; but as I walked on the table, being in great surprise all the time, as the indulgent reader will easily conceive and excuse, I happened to stumble against a crust, and fell flat on my face, but received no hurt. I got up immediately, and observing the good people to be in much concern, I took my hat (which I held under my arm out of good manners) and waving it over my head, made three huzzas to show I had got no mischief by my fall. But advancing forwards toward my master (as I shall henceforth call him), his youngest son who sat next him, an arch boy of about ten years old, took me up by the legs, and held me so high in the air that I trembled every limb; but his father snatched me from him, and at the same time gave him such a box on the left ear as would have felled an European troop of horse to the earth, ordering him to be taken from the table. But being afraid the boy might owe me a spite, and well remembering how mischievous all children among us naturally are to sparrows, rabbits, young kittens, and puppy dogs, I fell on my knees, and pointing to the boy, made my master to understand, as well as I could, that I desired his son might be pardoned. The father complied, and the lad took his seat again; whereupon I went to him and kissed his hand, which my master took, and made him stroke me gently with it.

In the midst of dinner, my mistress's favorite cat leaped into her lap. I heard a noise behind me like that of a dozen stocking weavers at work; and turning my head, I found it proceeded from the purring of this animal, who seemed to be three times larger than an ox, as I computed by the view of her head and one of her paws, while her mistress was feeding and stroking her. The fierceness of this creature's countenance altogether discomposed me, although I stood at the farther end of the table, about fifty foot off, and although my mistress held her fast for fear she might give a spring and seize me in her talons. But it happened there was no danger, for the cat took not the least notice of me when my master placed me within three yards of her. And as I have been always told, and found true by experience in my travels, that flying or discovering[8] fear before a fierce animal is a certain way to make it pursue or attack you, so I resolved in this dangerous juncture to show no manner of concern. I walked with intrepidity five or six times before the very head of the cat, and came within half a yard of her; whereupon she drew herself back, as if she were more afraid of me. I had less apprehension concerning the dogs, whereof three or four came into the room, as it is usual in farmers' houses; one of which was a mastiff, equal in bulk to four elephants, and a greyhound, somewhat taller than the mastiff, but not so large.

When dinner was almost done, the nurse came in with a child of a year old in her arms, who immediately spied me, and began a squall that you might have heard from London Bridge to Chelsea, after the usual oratory of infants, to get me for a plaything. The mother out of pure indulgence took me up, and put me towards the child, who presently seized me by the middle, and got my head in his mouth, where I roared so loud that the urchin was frighted and let me drop; and I should infallibly have broke my neck if the mother had not

7. I.e., weak cider.
8. Revealing.

held her apron under me. The nurse to quiet her babe made use of a rattle, which was a kind of hollow vessel filled with great stones, and fastened by a cable to the child's waist: but all in vain, so that she was forced to apply the last remedy by giving it suck. I must confess no object ever disgusted me so much as the sight of her monstrous breast, which I cannot tell what to compare with so as to give the curious reader an idea of its bulk, shape, and color. It stood prominent six foot, and could not be less than sixteen in circumference. The nipple was about half the bigness of my head, and the hue both of that and the dug so varified with spots, pimples, and freckles that nothing could appear more nauseous: for I had a near sight of her, she sitting down the more conveniently to give suck, and I standing on the table. This made me reflect upon the fair skins of our English ladies, who appear so beautiful to us, only because they are of our own size, and their defects not to be seen but through a magnifying glass, where we find by experiment that the smoothest and whitest skins look rough and coarse and ill colored.

I remember when I was at Lilliput, the complexion of those diminutive people appeared to me the fairest in the world; and talking upon this subject with a person of learning there, who was an intimate friend of mine, he said that my face appeared much fairer and smoother when he looked on me from the ground than it did upon a nearer view when I took him up in my hand and brought him close, which he confessed was at first a very shocking sight. He said he could discover great holes in my skin; that the stumps of my beard were ten times stronger than the bristles of a boar, and my complexion made up of several colors altogether disagreeable: although I must beg leave to say for myself that I am as fair as most of my sex and country and very little sunburnt by all my travels. On the other side, discoursing of the ladies in that Emperor's court, he used to tell me one had freckles, another too wide a mouth, a third too large a nose; nothing of which I was able to distinguish. I confess this reflection was obvious enough; which however I could not forbear, lest the reader might think those vast creatures were actually deformed: for I must do them justice to say they are a comely race of people; and particularly the features of my master's countenance, although he were but a farmer, when I beheld him from the height of sixty foot, appeared very well proportioned.

When dinner was done, my master went out to his laborers; and as I could discover by his voice and gesture, gave his wife a strict charge to take care of me. I was very much tired and disposed to sleep, which my mistress perceiving, she put me on her own bed, and covered me with a clean white handkerchief, but larger and coarser than the mainsail of a man-of-war.

I slept about two hours, and dreamed I was at home with my wife and children, which aggravated my sorrows when I awaked and found myself alone in a vast room, between two and three hundred foot wide, and above two hundred high, lying in a bed twenty yards wide. My mistress was gone about her household affairs, and had locked me in. The bed was eight yards from the floor. Some natural necessities required me to get down; I durst not presume to call, and if I had, it would have been in vain with such a voice as mine at so great a distance from the room where I lay to the kitchen where the family kept. While I was under these circumstances, two rats crept up the curtains, and ran smelling backwards and forwards on the bed. One of them came up almost to my face; whereupon I rose in a fright, and drew out my hanger[9] to defend myself. These horrible animals had the boldness to attack me on both sides, and one of them held his forefeet at my collar; but I had the good fortune to rip up his belly before he could do me any mischief. He fell down at my feet; and the other seeing the fate of his comrade, made his escape, but not without one good wound on the back, which I gave him as he fled, and made the blood run trickling from him. After this exploit I walked gently to and fro on the bed, to recover my breath and loss of spirits. These creatures were of the size of a large mastiff, but infinitely more nimble and fierce; so that if I had taken off my belt before I went to sleep, I must have infallibly been torn to pieces and devoured. I measured the tail of the dead rat, and found it to be two yards long, wanting an inch; but it went against my stomach to drag the carcass off the bed, where it lay still bleeding; I observed it had yet some life, but with a strong slash cross the neck, I thoroughly dispatched it.

Soon after, my mistress came into the room, who seeing me all bloody, ran and took me up in her hand. I pointed to the dead rat, smiling and making other signs to show I was not hurt, whereat she was extremely rejoiced, calling the maid to take up the dead rat with a pair of tongs, and throw it out of the window. Then she set me on a table, where I showed her my hanger all bloody, and wiping it on the lappet of my coat, returned it to the scabbard. I was pressed to do more than one thing, which another could not do for me, and therefore endeavored to make my mistress understand that I desired to be set down on the floor; which after she had done, my bashfulness would not suffer me to express myself farther than by pointing to the door, and bowing several times. The good woman with much difficulty at last perceived what I would be at, and taking me up again in her hand, walked into the garden, where she set me down. I went on one side about two hundred yards; and beckoning to her not to look or to follow me, I hid myself between two leaves of sorrel, and there discharged the necessities of nature.

I hope the gentle reader will excuse me for dwelling on these and the like particulars, which however insignificant they may appear to groveling vulgar minds, yet will certainly help a philosopher[1] to enlarge his thoughts and imagination, and apply them to the benefit of public as well as private life, which was my sole design in presenting this and other accounts of my travels to the world; wherein I have been chiefly studious of truth, without affecting any ornaments of learning or of style. But the whole scene of this voyage made so strong an impression on my mind, and is so deeply fixed in my memory, that in committing it to paper I did not omit one material circumstance; however, upon a strict review, I blotted out several passages of less moment which were in my first copy, for fear of being censured as tedious and trifling, whereof travelers are often, perhaps not without justice, accused.

9. A short, broad sword.
1. Scientist, in contrast to the "vulgar" (commonplace, uncultivated).

CHAPTER 2. *A description of the farmer's daughter. The Author carried to a market town, and then to the metropolis. The particulars of his journey.*

My mistress had a daughter of nine years old, a child of towardly parts for her age, very dexterous at her needle, and skillful in dressing her baby.[2] Her mother and she contrived to fit up the baby's cradle for me against night: the cradle was put into a small drawer of a cabinet, and the drawer placed upon a hanging shelf for fear of the rats. This was my bed all the time I stayed with those people, although made more convenient by degrees as I began to learn their language, and make my wants known. This young girl was so handy, that after I had once or twice pulled off my clothes before her, she was able to dress and undress me, although I never gave her that trouble when she would let me do either myself. She made me seven shirts, and some other linen of as fine cloth as could be got, which indeed was coarser than sackcloth, and these she constantly washed for me with her own hands. She was likewise my schoolmistress to teach me the language: when I pointed to anything, she told me the name of it in her own tongue, so that in a few days I was able to call for whatever I had a mind to. She was very good-natured, and not above forty foot high, being little for her age. She gave me the name of *Grildrig*, which the family took up, and afterwards the whole kingdom. The word imports what the Latins call *nanunculus*, the Italian *homunceletino*, and the English *mannikin*.[3] To her I chiefly owe my preservation in that country: we never parted while I was there; I called her my *Glumdalclitch*, or little nurse: and I should be guilty of great ingratitude if I omitted this honorable mention of her care and affection towards me, which I heartily wish it lay in my power to requite as she deserves, instead of being the innocent but unhappy instrument of her disgrace, as I have too much reason to fear.

It now began to be known and talked of in the neighborhood that my master had found a strange animal in the field, about the bigness of a *splacknuck*, but exactly shaped in every part like a human creature, which it likewise imitated in all its actions: seemed to speak in a little language of its own, had already learned several words of theirs, went erect upon two legs, was tame and gentle, would come when it was called, do whatever it was bid, had the finest limbs in the world, and a complexion fairer than a nobleman's daughter of three years old. Another farmer who lived hard by, and was a particular friend of my master, came on a visit on purpose to inquire into the truth of this story. I was immediately produced, and placed upon a table, where I walked as I was commanded, drew my hanger, put it up again, made my reverence to my master's guest, asked him in his own language how he did, and told him he was welcome, just as my little nurse had instructed me. This man, who was old and dimsighted, put on his spectacles to behold me better, at which I could not forbear laughing very heartily, for his eyes appeared like the full moon shining into a chamber at two windows. Our people, who discovered the cause of my mirth, bore me company in laughing, at which the old fellow was fool enough to be angry and out of counte-

---

2. Doll. "Towardly parts": promising abilities.
3. Little man, dwarf. The Latin and Italian words are Swift's own coinages, as, of course, are the various words from the Brobdingnagian language.

332 I JONATHAN SWIFT

nance. He had the character of a great miser, and to my misfortune he well deserved it by the cursed advice he gave my master to show me as a sight upon a market day in the next town, which was half an hour's riding, about two and twenty miles from our house. I guessed there was some mischief contriving when I observed my master and his friend whispering long together, sometimes pointing at me; and my fears made me fancy that I overheard and understood some of their words. But the next morning Glumdalclitch, my little nurse, told me the whole matter, which she had cunningly picked out from her mother. The poor girl laid me on her bosom, and fell a weeping with shame and grief. She apprehended some mischief would happen to me from rude vulgar folks, who might squeeze me to death, or break one of my limbs by taking me in their hands. She had also observed how modest I was in my nature, how nicely I regarded my honor, and what an indignity I should conceive it to be exposed for money as a public spectacle to the meanest of the people. She said her papa and mamma had promised that Grildrig should be hers; but now she found they meant to serve her as they did last year, when they pretended to give her a lamb, and yet, as soon as it was fat, sold it to a butcher. For my own part, I may truly affirm that I was less concerned than my nurse. I had a strong hope, which never left me, that I should one day recover my liberty; and as to the ignominy of being carried about for a monster, I considered myself to be a perfect stranger in the country, and that such a misfortune could never be charged upon me as a reproach, if ever I should return to England; since the King of Great Britain himself, in my condition, must have undergone the same distress.

My master, pursuant to the advice of his friend, carried me in a box the next market day to the neighboring town, and took along with him his little daughter, my nurse, upon a pillion[4] behind him. The box was close on every side, with a little door for me to go in and out, and a few gimlet holes to let in air. The girl had been so careful to put the quilt of her baby's bed into it, for me to lie down on. However, I was terribly shaken and discomposed in this journey, although it were but of half an hour. For the horse went about forty foot at every step, and trotted so high that the agitation was equal to the rising and falling of a ship in a great storm, but much more frequent. Our journey was somewhat further than from London to St. Albans.[5] My master alighted at an inn which he used to frequent; and after consulting a while with the innkeeper, and making some necessary preparations, he hired the *Grultrud*, or crier, to give notice through the town of a strange creature to be seen at the Sign of the Green Eagle, not so big as a *splacknuck* (an animal in that country very finely shaped, about six foot long), and in every part of the body resembling an human creature; could speak several words and perform an hundred diverting tricks.

I was placed upon a table in the largest room of the inn, which might be near three hundred foot square. My little nurse stood on a low stool close to the table, to take care of me, and direct what I should do. My master, to avoid a crowd, would suffer only thirty people at a time to see me. I walked about on the table as the girl commanded; she asked me questions as far as she knew my understanding of the language reached, and I answered them

4. A pad attached to the hinder part of a saddle, on which a second person, usually a woman, could ride.
5. About twenty miles.

as loud as I could. I turned about several times to the company, paid my humble respects, said they were welcome, and used some other speeches I had been taught. I took up a thimble filled with liquor, which Glumdalclitch had given me for a cup, and drank their health. I drew out my hanger, and flourished with it after the manner of fencers in England. My nurse gave me part of a straw, which I exercised as pike, having learned the art in my youth. I was that day shown to twelve sets of company, and as often forced to go over again with the same fopperies, till I was half dead with weariness and vexation. For those who had seen me made such wonderful reports that the people were ready to break down the doors to come in. My master for his own interest would not suffer anyone to touch me except my nurse; and, to prevent danger, benches were set round the table at such a distance as put me out of everybody's reach. However, an unlucky schoolboy aimed a hazel-nut directly at my head, which very narrowly missed me; otherwise, it came with so much violence that it would have infallibly knocked out my brains, for it was almost as large as a small pumpion:[6] but I had the satisfaction to see the young rogue well beaten, and turned out of the room.

My master gave public notice that he would show me again the next market day, and in the meantime he prepared a more convenient vehicle for me, which he had reason enough to do; for I was so tired with my first journey, and with entertaining company for eight hours together, that I could hardly stand upon my legs or speak a word. It was at least three days before I recovered my strength; and that I might have no rest at home, all the neighboring gentlemen from an hundred miles round, hearing of my fame, came to see me at my master's own house. There could not be fewer than thirty persons with their wives and children (for the country is very populous); and my master demanded the rate of a full room whenever he showed me at home, although it were only to a single family. So that for some time I had but little ease every day of the week (except Wednesday, which is their Sabbath) although I were not carried to the town.

My master finding how profitable I was like to be, resolved to carry me to the most considerable cities of the kingdom. Having therefore provided himself with all things necessary for a long journey, and settled his affairs at home, he took leave of his wife; and upon the 17th of August, 1703, about two months after my arrival, we set out for the metropolis, situated near the middle of that empire, and about three thousand miles distance from our house. My master made his daughter Glumdalclitch ride behind him. She carried me on her lap in a box tied about her waist. The girl had lined it on all sides with the softest cloth she could get, well quilted underneath, furnished it with her baby's bed, provided me with linen and other necessaries, and made everything as convenient as she could. We had no other company but a boy of the house, who rode after us with the luggage.

My master's design was to show me in all the towns by the way, and to step out of the road for fifty or an hundred miles to any village or person of quality's house where he might expect custom. We made easy journeys of not above seven or eight score miles a day: for Glumdalclitch, on purpose to spare me, complained she was tired with the trotting of the horse. She often took me out of my box at my own desire, to give me air and show me the

6. Pumpkin.

country, but always held me fast by leading strings.[7] We passed over five or six rivers many degrees broader and deeper than the Nile or the Ganges; and there was hardly a rivulet so small as the Thames at London Bridge. We were ten weeks in our journey, and I was shown in eighteen large towns, besides many large villages and private families.

On the 26th day of October, we arrived at the metropolis, called in their language *Lorbrulgrud*, or Pride of the Universe. My master took a lodging in the principal street of the city, not far from the royal palace, and put out bills in the usual form, containing an exact description of my person and parts. He hired a large room between three and four hundred foot wide. He provided a table sixty foot in diameter, upon which I was to act my part, and palisadoed it round three foot from the edge, and as many high, to prevent my falling over. I was shown ten times a day to the wonder and satisfaction of all people. I could now speak the language tolerably well, and perfectly understood every word that was spoken to me. Besides, I had learned their alphabet, and could make a shift to explain a sentence here and there; for Glumdalclitch had been my instructor while we were at home, and at leisure hours during our journey. She carried a little book in her pocket, not much larger than a Sanson's *Atlas*;[8] it was a common treatise for the use of young girls, giving a short account of their religion: out of this she taught me my letters, and interpreted the words.

CHAPTER 3. *The Author sent for to Court. The Queen buys him of his master, the farmer, and presents him to the King. He disputes with his Majesty's great scholars. An apartment at Court provided for the Author. He is in high favor with the Queen. He stands up for the honor of his own country. His quarrels with the Queen's dwarf.*

The frequent labors I underwent every day made in a few weeks a very considerable change in my health: the more my master got by me, the more unsatiable he grew. I had quite lost my stomach, and was almost reduced to a skeleton. The farmer observed it, and concluding I soon must die, resolved to make as good a hand of me as he could. While he was thus reasoning and resolving with himself, a *Slardral*, or Gentleman Usher, came from Court, commanding my master to carry me immediately thither for the diversion of the Queen and her ladies. Some of the latter had already been to see me and reported strange things of my beauty, behavior, and good sense. Her Majesty and those who attended her were beyond measure delighted with my demeanor. I fell on my knees and begged the honor of kissing her Imperial foot; but this gracious princess held out her little finger towards me (after I was set on a table), which I embraced in both my arms, and put the tip of it, with the utmost respect, to my lip. She made me some general questions about my country and my travels, which I answered as distinctly and in as few words as I could. She asked whether I would be content to live at Court. I bowed down to the board of the table, and humbly answered that I was my master's slave, but if I were at my own disposal, I should be proud to devote my life to her Majesty's service. She then asked my master whether he were

---

7. Used to guide children learning to walk.
8. I.e., over two feet long and about two feet wide.

willing to sell me at a good price. He, who apprehended I could not live a month, was ready enough to part with me, and demanded a thousand pieces of gold, which were ordered him on the spot, each piece being about the bigness of eight hundred moidores;[9] but, allowing for the proportion of all things between that country and Europe, and the high price of gold among them, was hardly so great a sum as a thousand guineas would be in England. I then said to the Queen, since I was now her Majesty's most humble creature and vassal, I must beg the favor that Glumdalclitch, who had always tended me with so much care and kindness, and understood to do it so well, might be admitted into her service, and continue to be my nurse and instructor. Her Majesty agreed to my petition, and easily got the farmer's consent, who was glad enough to have his daughter preferred at Court; and the poor girl herself was not able to hide her joy. My late master withdrew, bidding me farewell, and saying he had left me in a good service; to which I replied not a word, only making him a slight bow.

The Queen observed my coldness, and when the farmer was gone out of the apartment, asked me the reason. I made bold to tell her Majesty that I owed no other obligation to my late master than his not dashing out the brains of a poor harmless creature found by chance in his field; which obligation was amply recompensed by the gain he had made in showing me through half the kingdom, and the price he had now sold me for. That the life I had since led was laborious enough to kill an animal of ten times my strength. That my health was much impaired by the continual drudgery of entertaining the rabble every hour of the day; and that if my master had not thought my life in danger, her Majesty perhaps would not have got so cheap a bargain. But as I was out of all fear of being ill treated under the protection of so great and good an Empress, the Ornament of Nature, the Darling of the World, the Delight of her Subjects, the Phoenix of the Creation; so I hoped my late master's apprehensions would appear to be groundless, for I already found my spirits to revive by the influence of her most august presence.

This was the sum of my speech, delivered with great improprieties and hesitation; the latter part was altogether framed in the style peculiar to that people, whereof I learned some phrases from Glumdalclitch, while she was carrying me to Court.

The Queen, giving great allowance for my defectiveness in speaking, was however surprised at so much wit and good sense in so diminutive an animal. She took me in her own hand, and carried me to the King, who was then retired to his cabinet.[1] His Majesty, a prince of much gravity, and austere countenance, not well observing my shape at first view, asked the Queen after a cold manner how long it was since she grew fond of a *splacknuck*; for such it seems he took me to be, as I lay upon my breast in her Majesty's right hand. But this princess, who hath an infinite deal of wit and humor, set me gently on my feet upon the scrutore,[2] and commanded me to give his Majesty an account of myself, which I did in a very few words; and Glumdalclitch, who attended at the cabinet door, and could not endure I should be out of her sight, being admitted, confirmed all that had passed from my arrival at her father's house.

9. Portuguese coins.
1. Private apartment.

2. Writing desk.

The King, although he be as learned a person as any in his dominions, had been educated in the study of philosophy and particularly mathematics; yet when he observed my shape exactly, and saw me walk erect, before I began to speak, conceived I might be a piece of clockwork (which is in that country arrived to a very great perfection) contrived by some ingenious artist. But when he heard my voice, and found what I delivered to be regular and rational, he could not conceal his astonishment. He was by no means satisfied with the relation I gave him of the manner I came into his kingdom, but thought it a story concerted between Glumdalclitch and her father, who had taught me a set of words to make me sell at a higher price. Upon this imagination he put several other questions to me, and still received rational answers, no otherwise defective than by a foreign accent, and an imperfect knowledge in the language, with some rustic phrases which I had learned at the farmer's house, and did not suit the polite style of a court.

His Majesty sent for three great scholars who were then in their weekly waiting (according to the custom in that country). These gentlemen, after they had a while examined my shape with much nicety, were of different opinions concerning me. They all agreed that I could not be produced according to the regular laws of nature, because I was not framed with a capacity of preserving my life, either by swiftness, or climbing of trees, or digging holes in the earth. They observed by my teeth, which they viewed with great exactness, that I was a carnivorous animal; yet most quadrupeds being an overmatch for me, and field mice, with some others, too nimble, they could not imagine how I should be able to support myself, unless I fed upon snails and other insects; which they offered, by many learned arguments, to evince that I could not possibly do. One of them seemed to think that I might be an embryo, or abortive birth. But this opinion was rejected by the other two, who observed my limbs to be perfect and finished, and that I had lived several years, as it was manifested from my beard, the stumps whereof they plainly discovered through a magnifying glass. They would not allow me to be a dwarf, because my littleness was beyond all degrees of comparison; for the Queen's favorite dwarf, the smallest ever known in that kingdom, was nearly thirty foot high. After much debate, they concluded unanimously that I was only *relplum scalcath*, which is interpreted literally, *lusus naturae*; a determination exactly agreeable to the modern philosophy of Europe, whose professors, disdaining the old evasion of *occult causes*, whereby the followers of Aristotle endeavor in vain to disguise their ignorance, have invented this wonderful solution of all difficulties, to the unspeakable advancement of human knowledge.[3]

After this decisive conclusion, I entreated to be heard a word or two. I applied myself to the King, and assured his Majesty that I came from a country which abounded with several millions of both sexes, and of my own stature, where the animals, trees, and houses were all in proportion, and where by consequence I might be as able to defend myself, and to find sustenance, as any of his Majesty's subjects could do here; which I took for a full

3. Swift had contempt for both the medieval Schoolmen, who discussed "occult causes," the unknown causes of observable effects, and modern scientists, who, he believed, often concealed their ignorance by using equally meaningless terms. "*Lusus naturae*": one of nature's sports, or, roughly, freaks.

answer to those gentlemen's arguments. To this they only replied with a smile of contempt, saying that the farmer had instructed me very well in my lesson. The King, who had a much better understanding, dismissing his learned men, sent for the farmer, who by good fortune was not yet gone out of town; having therefore first examined him privately, and then confronted him with me and the young girl, his Majesty began to think that what we told him might possibly be true. He desired the Queen to order that a particular care should be taken of me, and was of opinion that Glumdalclitch should still continue in her office of tending me, because he observed we had a great affection for each other. A convenient apartment was provided for her at Court; she had a sort of governess appointed to take care of her education, a maid to dress her, and two other servants for menial offices; but the care of me was wholly appropriated to herself. The Queen commanded her own cabinetmaker to contrive a box that might serve me for a bedchamber, after the model that Glumdalclitch and I should agree upon. This man was a most ingenious artist, and according to my directions, in three weeks finished for me a wooden chamber of sixteen foot square and twelve high, with sash windows, a door, and two closets, like a London bedchamber. The board that made the ceiling was to be lifted up and down by two hinges, to put in a bed ready furnished by her Majesty's upholsterer, which Glumdalclitch took out every day to air, made it with her own hands, and letting it down at night, locked up the roof over me. A nice[4] workman, who was famous for little curiosities, undertook to make me two chairs, with backs and frames, of a substance not unlike ivory, and two tables, with a cabinet to put my things in. The room was quilted on all sides, as well as the floor and the ceiling, to prevent any accident from the carelessness of those who carried me, and to break the force of a jolt when I went in a coach. I desired a lock for my door to prevent rats and mice from coming in: the smith, after several attempts, made the smallest that ever was seen among them, for I have known a larger at the gate of a gentleman's house in England. I made a shift[5] to keep the key in a pocket of my own, fearing Glumdalclitch might lose it. The Queen likewise ordered the thinnest silks that could be gotten, to make me clothes, not much thicker than an English blanket, very cumbersome till I was accustomed to them. They were after the fashion of the kingdom, partly resembling the Persian, and partly the Chinese, and are a very grave, decent habit.

The Queen became so fond of my company that she could not dine without me. I had a table placed upon the same at which her Majesty ate, just at her left elbow, and a chair to sit on. Glumdalclitch stood upon a stool on the floor, near my table, to assist and take care of me. I had an entire set of silver dishes and plates, and other necessaries, which, in proportion to those of the Queen, were not much bigger than what I have seen of the same kind in a London toyshop,[6] for the furniture of a baby-house: these my little nurse kept in her pocket in a silver box and gave me at meals as I wanted them, always cleaning them herself. No person dined with the Queen but the two Princesses Royal, the elder sixteen years old, and the younger at that time thirteen and a month. Her Majesty used to put a bit of meat upon one of my

4. Exact.
5. Contrived.

6. A shop for selling knickknacks.

dishes, out of which I carved for myself; and her diversion was to see me eat in miniature. For the Queen (who had indeed but a weak stomach) took up at one mouthful as much as a dozen English farmers could eat at a meal, which to me was for some time a very nauseous sight. She would craunch the wing of a lark, bones and all, between her teeth, although it were nine times as large as that of a full-grown turkey; and put a bit of bread into her mouth as big as two twelve-penny loaves. She drank out of a golden cup, above a hogshead at a draught. Her knives were twice as long as a scythe set straight upon the handle. The spoons, forks, and other instruments were all in the same proportion. I remember when Glumdalclitch carried me out of curiosity to see some of the tables at Court, where ten or a dozen of these enormous knives and forks were lifted up together, I thought I had never till then beheld so terrible a sight.

It is the custom that every Wednesday (which, as I have before observed, was their Sabbath) the King and Queen, with the royal issue of both sexes, dine together in the apartment of his Majesty, to whom I was now become a favorite; and at these times my little chair and table were placed at his left hand, before one of the salt-cellars. This prince took a pleasure in conversing with me, inquiring into the manners, religion, laws, government, and learning of Europe; wherein I gave him the best account I was able. His apprehension was so clear, and his judgment so exact, that he made very wise reflections and observations upon all I said. But I confess that after I had been a little too copious in talking of my own beloved country, of our trade and wars by sea and land, of our schisms in religion and parties in the state, the prejudices of his education prevailed so far that he could not forbear taking me up in his right hand, and stroking me gently with the other, after an hearty fit of laughing, asked me whether I were a Whig or a Tory. Then turning to his first minister, who waited behind him with a white staff, near as tall as the mainmast of the *Royal Sovereign*,[7] he observed how contemptible a thing was human grandeur, which could be mimicked by such diminutive insects as I: "and yet," said he, "I dare engage, these creatures have their titles and distinctions of honor; they contrive little nests and burrows, that they call houses and cities; they make a figure in dress and equipage; they love, they fight, they dispute, they cheat, they betray." And thus he continued on, while my color came and went several times with indignation to hear our noble country, the mistress of arts and arms, the scourge of France, the arbitress of Europe, the seat of virtue, piety, honor, and truth, the pride and envy of the world, so contemptuously treated.

But as I was not in a condition to resent injuries, so, upon mature thoughts, I began to doubt whether I were injured or no. For, after having been accustomed several months to the sight and converse of this people, and observed every object upon which I cast my eyes to be of proportionable magnitude, the horror I had first conceived from their bulk and aspect was so far worn off that if I had then beheld a company of English lords and ladies in their finery and birthday clothes,[8] acting their several parts in the most courtly manner of strutting and bowing and prating, to say the truth, I should have

---

7. One of the largest ships in the Royal Navy. "White staff": at the English court borne by the lord treasurer as the symbol of his office.

8. Courtiers dressed with special splendor on the monarch's birthday.

been strongly tempted to laugh as much at them as this King and his grandees did at me. Neither indeed could I forbear smiling at myself when the Queen used to place me upon her hand towards a looking glass, by which both our persons appeared before me in full view together; and there could be nothing more ridiculous than the comparison; so that I really began to imagine myself dwindled many degrees below my usual size.

Nothing angered and mortified me so much as the Queen's dwarf, who being of the lowest stature that was ever in that country (for I verily think he was not full thirty foot high) became so insolent at seeing a creature so much beneath him that he would always affect to swagger and look big as he passed by me in the Queen's antechamber, while I was standing on some table talking with the lords or ladies of the court; and he seldom failed of a smart word or two upon my littleness, against which I could only revenge myself by calling him brother, challenging him to wrestle, and such repartees as are usual in the mouths of Court pages. One day at dinner this malicious little cub was so nettled with something I had said to him that, raising himself upon the frame of Her Majesty's chair, he took me up by the middle, as I was sitting down, not thinking any harm, and let me drop into a large silver bowl of cream, and then ran away as fast as he could. I fell over head and ears, and if I had not been a good swimmer, it might have gone very hard with me; for Glumdalclitch in that instant happened to be at the other end of the room, and the Queen was in such a fright that she wanted presence of mind to assist me. But my little nurse ran to my relief, and took me out, after I had swallowed above a quart of cream. I was put to bed; however, I received no other damage than the loss of a suit of clothes, which was utterly spoiled. The dwarf was soundly whipped, and as further punishment, forced to drink up the bowl of cream into which he had thrown me; neither was he ever restored to favor: for soon after the Queen bestowed him to a lady of high quality, so that I saw him no more, to my very great satisfaction; for I could not tell to what extremity such a malicious urchin might have carried his resentment.

He had before served me a scurvy trick, which set the Queen a laughing, although at the same time she were heartily vexed, and would have immediately cashiered him, if I had not been so generous as to intercede. Her Majesty had taken a marrow bone upon her plate, and after knocking out the marrow, placed the bone again in the dish, erect as it stood before; the dwarf watching his opportunity, while Glumdalclitch was gone to the sideboard, mounted upon the stool she stood on to take care of me at meals, took me up in both hands, and squeezing my legs together, wedged them into the marrow bone above my waist, where I stuck for some time, and made a very ridiculous figure. I believe it was near a minute before anyone knew what was become of me, for I thought it below me to cry out. But, as princes seldom get their meat hot, my legs were not scalded, only my stockings and breeches in a sad condition. The dwarf at my entreaty had no other punishment than a sound whipping.

I was frequently rallied by the Queen upon account of my fearfulness, and she used to ask me whether the people of my country were as great cowards as myself. The occasion was this. The kingdom is much pestered with flies in summer, and these odious insects, each of them as big as a Dunstable lark, hardly gave me any rest while I sat at dinner, with their continual humming and buzzing about my ears. They would sometimes alight upon my victuals, and leave their loathsome excrement or spawn behind, which to me was very visible, although not to the natives of that country, whose large optics were not so acute as mine in viewing smaller objects. Sometimes they would fix upon my nose or forehead, where they stung me to the quick, smelling very offensively; and I could easily trace that viscous matter, which our naturalists tell us enables those creatures to walk with their feet upwards upon a ceiling. I had much ado to defend myself against these detestable animals, and could not forbear starting when they came on my face. It was the common practice of the dwarf to catch a number of these insects in his hand, as schoolboys do among us, and let them out suddenly under my nose, on purpose to frighten me, and divert the Queen. My remedy was to cut them in pieces with my knife as they flew in the air, wherein my dexterity was much admired.

I remember one morning when Glumdalclitch had set me in my box upon a window, as she usually did in fair days to give me air (for I durst not venture to let the box be hung on a nail out of the window, as we do with cages in England), after I had lifted up one of my sashes, and sat down at my table to eat a piece of sweet cake for my breakfast, above twenty wasps, allured by the smell, came flying into the room, humming louder than the drones of as many bagpipes. Some of them seized my cake, and carried it piecemeal away; others flew about my head and face, confounding me with the noise, and putting me in the utmost terror of their stings. However, I had the courage to rise and draw my hanger, and attack them in the air. I dispatched four of them, but the rest got away, and I presently shut my window. These insects were as large as partridges; I took out their stings, found them an inch and a half long, and as sharp as needles. I carefully preserved them all, and having since shown them with some other curiosities in several parts of Europe, upon my return to England I gave three of them to Gresham College,[9] and kept the fourth for myself.

CHAPTER 4. *The country described. A proposal for correcting modern maps. The King's palace, and some account of the metropolis. The Author's way of traveling. The chief temple described.*

I now intend to give the reader a short description of this country, as far as I had traveled in it, which was not above two thousand miles round Lorbrulgrud the metropolis. For the Queen, whom I always attended, never went further when she accompanied the King in his progresses, and there stayed till his Majesty returned from viewing his frontiers. The whole extent of this prince's dominions reacheth about six thousand miles in length, and from three to five in breadth. From whence I cannot but conclude that our geographers of Europe are in a great error by supposing nothing but sea between Japan and California: for it was ever my opinion that there must be a balance of earth to counterpoise the great continent of Tartary; and therefore they ought to correct their maps and charts by joining this vast tract of land to the northwest parts of America, wherein I shall be ready to lend them my assistance.

9. The Royal Society, in its earliest years, met in Gresham College.

The kingdom is a peninsula, terminated to the northeast by a ridge of mountains thirty miles high, which are altogether impassable by reason of the volcanoes upon the tops. Neither do the most learned know what sort of mortals inhabit beyond those mountains, or whether they be inhabited at all. On the three other sides it is bounded by the ocean. There is not one seaport in the whole kingdom; and those parts of the coasts into which the rivers issue are so full of pointed rocks, and the sea generally so rough, that there is no venturing with the smallest of their boats; so that these people are wholly excluded from any commerce with the rest of the world. But the large rivers are full of vessels, and abound with excellent fish, for they seldom get any from the sea, because the sea fish are of the same size with those in Europe, and consequently not worth catching; whereby it is manifest that nature, in the production of plants and animals of so extraordinary a bulk, is wholly confined to this continent, of which I leave the reasons to be determined by philosophers. However, now and then they take a whale that happens to be dashed against the rocks, which the common people feed on heartily. These whales I have known so large that a man could hardly carry one upon his shoulders; and sometimes for curiosity they are brought in hampers to Lorbrulgrud: I saw one of them in a dish at the King's table, which passed for a rarity, but I did not observe he was fond of it; for I think indeed the bigness disgusted him, although I have seen one somewhat larger in Greenland.

The country is well inhabited, for it contains fifty-one cities, near an hundred walled towns, and a great number of villages. To satisfy my curious reader, it may be sufficient to describe Lorbrulgrud. This city stands upon almost two equal parts on each side the river that passes through. It contains above eight thousand houses, and about six hundred thousand inhabitants. It is in length three *glonglungs* (which make about fifty-four English miles) and two and a half in breadth, as I measured it myself in the royal map made by the King's order, which was laid on the ground on purpose for me, and extended an hundred feet; I paced the diameter and circumference several times barefoot, and computing by the scale, measured it pretty exactly.

The King's palace is no regular edifice, but an heap of buildings about seven miles round: the chief rooms are generally two hundred and forty foot high, and broad and long in proportion. A coach was allowed to Glumdalclitch and me, wherein her governess frequently took her out to see the town, go among the shops; and I was always of the party, carried in my box, although the girl at my own desire would often take me out, and hold me in her hand, that I might more conveniently view the houses and the people as we passed along the streets. I reckoned our coach to be about a square of Westminster Hall,[1] but not altogether so high; however, I cannot be very exact. One day the governess ordered our coachman to stop at several shops, where the beggars, watching their opportunity, crowded to the sides of the coach, and gave me the most horrible spectacles that ever an English eye beheld. There was a woman with a cancer in her breast, swelled to a monstrous size, full of holes, in two or three of which I could have easily crept, and covered my whole body. There was a fellow with a wen in his neck, larger

---

1. The ancient hall, now incorporated into the Houses of Parliament, where the law courts then sat. Swift presumably means the square of its breadth (just under sixty-eight feet).

than five woolpacks, and another with a couple of wooden legs, each about twenty foot high. But the most hateful sight of all was the lice crawling on their clothes. I could see distinctly the limbs of these vermin with my naked eye, much better than those of an European louse through a microscope, and their snouts with which they rooted like swine. They were the first I had ever beheld; and I should have been curious enough to dissect one of them if I had proper instruments (which I unluckily left behind me in the ship), although indeed the sight was so nauseous that it perfectly turned my stomach.

Besides the large box in which I was usually carried, the Queen ordered a smaller one to be made for me, of about twelve foot square and ten high, for the convenience of traveling, because the other was somewhat too large for Glumdalclitch's lap, and cumbersome in the coach; it was made by the same artist, whom I directed in the whole contrivance. This traveling closet was an exact square with a window in the middle of three of the squares, and each window was latticed with iron wire on the outside, to prevent accidents in long journeys. On the fourth side, which had no windows, two strong staples were fixed, through which the person that carried me, when I had a mind to be on horseback, put in a leathern belt, and buckled it about his waist. This was always the office of some grave trusty servant in whom I could confide, whether I attended the King and Queen in their progresses, or were disposed to see the gardens, or pay a visit to some great lady or minister of state in the court, when Glumdalclitch happened to be out of order: for I soon began to be known and esteemed among the greatest officers, I suppose more upon account of their Majesties' favor than any merit of my own. In journeys, when I was weary of the coach, a servant on horseback would buckle my box, and place it on a cushion before him; and there I had a full prospect of the country on three sides from my three windows. I had in this closet a field bed[2] and a hammock hung from the ceiling, two chairs and a table, neatly screwed to the floor to prevent being tossed about by the agitation of the horse or the coach. And having been long used to sea voyages, those motions, although sometimes very violent, did not much discompose me.

When I had a mind to see the town, it was always in my traveling closet, which Glumdalclitch held in her lap in a kind of open sedan, after the fashion of the country, borne by four men, and attended by two others in the Queen's livery. The people, who had often heard of me, were very curious to crowd about the sedan; and the girl was complaisant enough to make the bearers stop, and to take me in her hand that I might be more conveniently seen.

I was very desirous to see the chief temple, and particularly the tower belonging to it, which is reckoned the highest in the kingdom. Accordingly one day my nurse carried me thither, but I may truly say I came back disappointed; for the height is not above three thousand foot, reckoning from the ground to the highest pinnacle top; which, allowing for the difference between the size of those people and us in Europe, is no great matter for admiration, nor at all equal in proportion (if I rightly remember) to Salisbury steeple.[3] But, not to detract from a nation to which during my life I shall

---

2. Folding bed, cot.
3. One of the most beautiful Gothic steeples in

England is that of Salisbury Cathedral, 404 feet high.

acknowledge myself extremely obliged, it must be allowed that whatever this famous tower wants in height is amply made up in beauty and strength. For the walls are near an hundred foot thick, built of hewn stone, whereof each is about forty foot square, and adorned on all sides with statues of gods and emperors cut in marble larger than the life, placed in their several niches. I measured a little finger which had fallen down from one of these statues, and lay unperceived among some rubbish, and found it exactly four foot and an inch in length. Glumdalclitch wrapped it up in a handkerchief, and carried it home in her pocket to keep among other trinkets, of which the girl was very fond, as children at her age usually are.

The King's kitchen is indeed a noble building, vaulted at top, and about six hundred foot high. The great oven is not so wide by ten paces as the cupola at St. Paul's:[4] for I measured the latter on purpose after my return. But if I should describe the kitchen grate, the prodigious pots and kettles, the joints of meat turning on the spits, with many other particulars, perhaps I should be hardly believed; at least a severe critic would be apt to think I enlarged a little, as travelers are often suspected to do. To avoid which censure, I fear I have run too much into the other extreme, and that if this treatise should happen to be translated into the language of Brobdingnag (which is the general name of that kingdom) and transmitted thither, the King and his people would have reason to complain that I had done them an injury by a false and diminutive representation.

His Majesty seldom keeps above six hundred horses in his stables: they are generally from fifty-four to sixty foot high. But when he goes abroad on solemn days, he is attended for state by a militia guard of five hundred horse, which indeed I thought was the most splendid sight that could be ever beheld, till I saw part of his army in battalia,[5] whereof I shall find another occasion to speak.

CHAPTER 5. *Several adventures that happened to the Author. The execution of a criminal. The Author shows his skill in navigation.*

I should have lived happy enough in that country if my littleness had not exposed me to several ridiculous and troublesome accidents, some of which I shall venture to relate. Glumdalclitch often carried me into the gardens of the court in my smaller box, and would sometimes take me out of it and hold me in her hand, or set me down to walk. I remember, before the dwarf left the Queen, he followed us one day into those gardens; and my nurse having set me down, he and I being close together near some dwarf apple trees, I must needs show my wit by a silly allusion between him and the trees, which happens to hold in their language as it doth in ours. Whereupon, the malicious rogue watching his opportunity, when I was walking under one of them, shook it directly over my head, by which a dozen apples, each of them near as large as a Bristol barrel, came tumbling about my ears; one of them hit me on the back as I chanced to stoop, and knocked me down flat on my face, but I received no other hurt; and the dwarf was pardoned at my desire, because I had given the provocation.

4. The cupola of St. Paul's Cathedral in London is 108 feet in diameter.
5. Battle array.

Another day Glumdalclitch left me on a smooth grassplot to divert myself while she walked at some distance with her governess. In the meantime there suddenly fell such a violent shower of hail that I was immediately by the force of it struck to the ground: and when I was down, the hailstones gave me such cruel bangs all over the body as if I had been pelted with tennis balls;[6] however I made a shift to creep on all four, and shelter myself by lying on my face on the lee side of a border of lemon thyme, but so bruised from head to foot that I could not go abroad in ten days. Neither is this at all to be wondered at, because nature in that country observing the same proportion through all her operations, a hailstone is near eighteen hundred times as large as one in Europe; which I can assert upon experience, having been so curious to weigh and measure them.

But a more dangerous accident happened to me in the same garden when my little nurse, believing she had put me in a secure place, which I often entreated her to do that I might enjoy my own thoughts, and having left my box at home to avoid the trouble of carrying it, went to another part of the garden with her governess and some ladies of her acquaintance. While she was absent and out of hearing, a small white spaniel belonging to one of the chief gardeners, having got by accident into the garden, happened to range near the place where I lay. The dog following the scent, came directly up, and taking me in his mouth, ran straight to his master, wagging his tail, and set me gently on the ground. By good fortune he had been so well taught that I was carried between his teeth without the least hurt, or even tearing my clothes. But the poor gardener, who knew me well, and had a great kindness for me, was in a terrible fright. He gently took me up in both his hands, and asked me how I did; but I was so amazed and out of breath that I could not speak a word. In a few minutes I came to myself, and he carried me safe to my little nurse, who by this time had returned to the place where she left me, and was in cruel agonies when I did not appear nor answer when she called; she severely reprimanded the gardener on account of his dog. But the thing was hushed up and never known at court; for the girl was afraid of the Queen's anger; and truly, as to myself, I thought it would not be for my reputation that such a story should go about.

This accident absolutely determined Glumdalclitch never to trust me abroad for the future out of her sight. I had been long afraid of this resolution, and therefore concealed from her some little unlucky adventures that happened in those times when I was left by myself. Once a kite hovering over the garden made a stoop[7] at me, and if I had not resolutely drawn my hanger, and run under a thick espalier, he would have certainly carried me away in his talons. Another time walking to the top of a fresh molehill, I fell to my neck in the hole through which that animal had cast up the earth, and coined some lie, not worth remembering, to excuse myself for spoiling my clothes. I likewise broke my right shin against the shell of a snail, which I happened to stumble over, as I was walking alone, and thinking on poor England.

I cannot tell whether I were more pleased or mortified to observe in those solitary walks that the smaller birds did not appear to be at all afraid of me;

---

6. Eighteenth-century tennis balls, unlike the modern, were very hard.
7. Swoop. "Kite": a bird of prey.

but would hop about within a yard distance, looking for worms and other food with as much indifference and security as if no creature at all were near them. I remember a thrush had the confidence to snatch out of my hand with his bill a piece of cake that Glumdalclitch had just given me for my breakfast. When I attempted to catch any of these birds, they would boldly turn against me, endeavoring to pick my fingers, which I durst not venture within their reach; and then they would hop back unconcerned to hunt for worms or snails, as they did before. But one day I took a thick cudgel, and threw it with all my strength so luckily at a linnet that I knocked him down, and seizing him by the neck with both my hands, ran with him in triumph to my nurse. However, the bird, who had only been stunned, recovering himself, gave me so many boxes with his wings on both sides of my head and body, though I held him at arm's length, and was out of the reach of his claws, that I was twenty times thinking to let him go. But I was soon relieved by one of our servants, who wrung off the bird's neck, and I had him next day for dinner, by the Queen's command. This linnet, as near as I can remember, seemed to be somewhat larger than an English swan.

The Maids of Honor often invited Glumdalclitch to their apartments, and desired she would bring me along with her, on purpose to have the pleasure of seeing and touching me. They would often strip me naked from top to toe and lay me at full length in their bosoms; wherewith I was much disgusted, because, to say the truth, a very offensive smell came from their skins, which I do not mention or intend to the disadvantage of those excellent ladies, for whom I have all manner of respect; but I conceive that my sense was more acute in proportion to my littleness, and that those illustrious persons were no more disagreeable to their lovers, or to each other, than people of the same quality are with us in England. And, after all, I found their natural smell was much more supportable than when they used perfumes, under which I immediately swooned away. I cannot forget that an intimate friend of mine in Lilliput took the freedom in a warm day, when I had used a good deal of exercise, to complain of a strong smell about me, although I am as little faulty that way as most of my sex: but I suppose his faculty of smelling was as nice with regard to me as mine was to that of this people. Upon this point, I cannot forbear doing justice to the Queen, my mistress, and Glumdalclitch, my nurse, whose persons were as sweet as those of any lady in England.

That which gave me most uneasiness among these Maids of Honor, when my nurse carried me to visit them, was to see them use me without any manner of ceremony, like a creature who had no sort of consequence. For they would strip themselves to the skin and put on their smocks in my presence, while I was placed on their toilet[8] directly before their naked bodies; which, I am sure, to me was very far from being a tempting sight, or from giving me any other emotions than those of horror and disgust. Their skins appeared so coarse and uneven, so variously colored, when I saw them near, with a mole here and there as broad as a trencher, and hairs hanging from it thicker than packthreads, to say nothing further concerning the rest of their persons. Neither did they at all scruple, while I was by, to discharge what they had drunk, to the quantity of at least two hogsheads, in a vessel that

8. Toilet table.

held above three tuns. The handsomest among these Maids of Honor, a pleasant frolicsome girl of sixteen, would sometimes set me astride upon one of her nipples, with many other tricks, wherein the reader will excuse me for not being over particular. But I was so much displeased that I entreated Glumdalclitch to contrive some excuse for not seeing that young lady any more.

One day a young gentleman, who was nephew to my nurse's governess, came and pressed them both to see an execution. It was of a man who had murdered one of that gentleman's intimate acquaintance. Glumdalclitch was prevailed on to be of the company, very much against her inclination, for she was naturally tender-hearted: and as for myself, although I abhorred such kind of spectacles, yet my curiosity tempted me to see something that I thought must be extraordinary. The malefactor was fixed in a chair upon a scaffold erected for the purpose, and his head cut off at a blow with a sword of about forty foot long. The veins and arteries spouted up such a prodigious quantity of blood, and so high in the air, that the great *jet d'eau* at Versailles was not equal for the time it lasted; and the head, when it fell on the scaffold floor, gave such a bounce,[9] as made me start, although I were at least half an English mile distant.

The Queen, who often used to hear me talk of my sea voyages, and took all occasions to divert me when I was melancholy, asked me whether I understood how to handle a sail or an oar, and whether a little exercise of rowing might not be convenient for my health. I answered that I understood both very well. For although my proper employment had been to be surgeon or doctor to the ship, yet often, upon a pinch, I was forced to work like a common mariner. But I could not see how this could be done in their country, where the smallest wherry was equal to a first-rate man-of-war among us, and such a boat as I could manage would never live in any of their rivers. Her Majesty said, if I would contrive a boat, her own joiner should make it, and she would provide a place for me to sail in. The fellow was an ingenious workman and, by my instructions, in ten days finished a pleasure boat with all its tackling, able conveniently to hold eight Europeans. When it was finished, the Queen was so delighted that she ran with it in her lap to the King, who ordered it to be put in a cistern full of water, with me in it, by way of trial; where I could not manage my two sculls, or little oars, for want of room. But the Queen had before contrived another project. She ordered the joiner to make a wooden trough of three hundred foot long, fifty broad, and eight deep; which being well pitched to prevent leaking, was placed on the floor along the wall in an outer room of the palace. It had a cock near the bottom to let out the water when it began to grow stale, and two servants could easily fill it in half an hour. Here I often used to row for my own diversion, as well as that of the Queen and her ladies, who thought themselves well entertained with my skill and agility. Sometimes I would put up my sail, and then my business was only to steer, while the ladies gave me a gale with their fans; and when they were weary, some of the pages would blow my sail forward with their breath, while I showed my art by steering starboard or larboard as I pleased. When I had done, Glumdalclitch always carried my boat into her closet, and hung it on a nail to dry.

9. A sudden noise. "*Jet d'eau* at Versailles": this fountain rose over forty feet in the air.

In this exercise I once met an accident which had like to have cost me my life. For one of the pages having put my boat into the trough, the governess who attended Glumdalclitch very officiously lifted me up to place me in the boat; but I happened to slip through her fingers, and should have infallibly fallen down forty foot upon the floor, if by the luckiest chance in the world I had not been stopped by a corking-pin that stuck in the good gentlewoman's stomacher;[1] the head of the pin passed between my shirt and the waistband of my breeches, and thus I was held by the middle in the air until Glumdalclitch ran to my relief.

Another time, one of the servants, whose office it was to fill my trough every third day with fresh water, was so careless to let a huge frog (not perceiving it) slip out of his pail. The frog lay concealed till I was put into my boat, but then seeing a resting place, climbed up, and made it lean so much on one side that I was forced to balance it with all my weight on the other, to prevent overturning. When the frog was got in, it hopped at once half the length of the boat, and then over my head, backwards and forwards, daubing my face and clothes with its odious slime. The largeness of its features made it appear the most deformed animal that can be conceived. However, I desired Glumdalclitch to let me deal with it alone. I banged it a good while with one of my sculls, and at last forced it to leap out of the boat.

But the greatest danger I ever underwent in that kingdom was from a monkey, who belonged to one of the clerks of the kitchen. Glumdalclitch had locked me up in her closet, while she went somewhere upon business or a visit. The weather being very warm, the closet window was left open, as well as the windows in the door of my bigger box, in which I usually lived, because of its largeness and conveniency. As I sat quietly meditating at my table, I heard something bounce in at the closet window, and skip about from one side to the other, whereat, although I was much alarmed, yet I ventured to look out, but stirred not from my seat; and then I saw this frolicsome animal, frisking and leaping up and down, till at last he came to my box, which he seemed to view with great pleasure and curiosity, peeping in at the door and every window. I retreated to the farther corner of my room, or box, but the monkey looking in at every side, put me into such a fright that I wanted presence of mind to conceal myself under the bed, as I might easily have done. After some time spent in peeping, grinning, and chattering, he at last espied me, and reaching one of his paws in at the door, as a cat does when she plays with a mouse, although I often shifted place to avoid him, he at length seized the lappet of my coat (which, being made of that country cloth, was very thick and strong) and dragged me out. He took me up in his right forefoot, and held me as a nurse does a child she is going to suckle, just as I have seen the same sort of creature do with a kitten in Europe: and when I offered to struggle, he squeezed me so hard that I thought it more prudent to submit. I have good reason to believe that he took me for a young one of his own species, by his often stroking my face very gently with his other paw. In these diversions he was interrupted by a noise at the closet door, as if somebody were opening it, whereupon he suddenly leaped up to the window at which he had come in, and thence upon the leads and gutters, walking upon three

---

1. An ornamental covering for the front and upper part of the body. "Officiously": kindly, dutifully. "Corking-pin": a pin of the largest size.

legs, and holding me in the fourth, till he clambered up to a roof that was next to ours. I heard Glumdalclitch give a shriek at the moment he was carrying me out. The poor girl was almost distracted: that quarter of the palace was all in an uproar; the servants ran for ladders; the monkey was seen by hundreds in the court, sitting upon the ridge of a building, holding me like a baby in one of his forepaws and feeding me with the other, by cramming into my mouth some victuals he had squeezed out of the bag on one side of his chaps, and patting me when I would not eat; whereat many of the rabble below could not forebear laughing; neither do I think they justly ought to be blamed, for without question the sight was ridiculous enough to everybody but myself. Some of the people threw up stones, hoping to drive the monkey down; but this was strictly forbidden, or else very probably my brains had been dashed out.

The ladders were now applied, and mounted by several men; which the monkey observing, and finding himself almost encompassed, not being able to make speed enough with his three legs, let me drop on a ridge tile, and made his escape. Here I sat for some time three hundred yards from the ground, expecting every moment to be blown down by the wind, or to fall by my own giddiness, and come tumbling over and over from the ridge to the eaves. But an honest lad, one of my nurse's footmen, climbed up, and putting me into his breeches pocket, brought me down safe.

I was almost choked with the filthy stuff the monkey had crammed down my throat; but my dear little nurse picked it out of my mouth with a small needle, and then I fell a vomiting, which gave me great relief. Yet I was so weak and bruised in the sides with the squeezes given me by this odious animal that I was forced to keep my bed a fortnight. The King, Queen, and all the Court sent every day to inquire after my health, and her Majesty made me several visits during my sickness. The monkey was killed, and an order made that no such animal should be kept about the palace.

When I attended the King after my recovery, to return him thanks for his favors, he was pleased to rally me a good deal upon this adventure. He asked me what my thoughts and speculations were while I lay in the monkey's paw, how I liked the victuals he gave me, his manner of feeding, and whether the fresh air on the roof had sharpened my stomach. He desired to know what I would have done upon such an occasion in my own country. I told his Majesty that in Europe we had no monkeys, except such as were brought for curiosities from other places, and so small that I could deal with a dozen of them together, if they presumed to attack me. And as for that monstrous animal with whom I was so lately engaged (it was indeed as large as an elephant), if my fears had suffered me to think so far as to make use of my hanger (looking fiercely and clapping my hand upon the hilt as I spoke) when he poked his paw into my chamber, perhaps I should have given him such a wound as would have made him glad to withdraw it with more haste than he put it in. This I delivered in a firm tone, like a person who was jealous lest his courage should be called in question. However, my speech produced nothing else besides a loud laughter, which all the respect due to his Majesty from those about him could not make them contain. This made me reflect how vain an attempt it is for a man to endeavor doing himself honor among those who are out of all degree of equality or comparison with him. And yet I have seen the moral of my own behavior very frequent in England since my return, where a little contemptible varlet, without the least title to birth, person, wit, or common sense, shall presume to look with importance, and put himself upon a foot with the greatest persons of the kingdom.

I was every day furnishing the court with some ridiculous story; and Glumdalclitch, although she loved me to excess, yet was arch enough to inform the Queen whenever I committed any folly that she thought would be diverting to her Majesty. The girl, who had been out of order,[2] was carried by her governess to take the air about an hour's distance, or thirty miles from town. They alighted out of the coach near a small footpath in a field, and Glumdalclitch setting down my traveling box, I went out of it to walk. There was a cow dung in the patch, and I must needs try my activity by attempting to leap over it. I took a run, but unfortunately jumped short, and found myself just in the middle up to my knees. I waded through with some difficulty, and one of the footmen wiped me as clean as he could with his handkerchief; for I was filthily bemired, and my nurse confined me to my box till we returned home, where the Queen was soon informed of what had passed and the footmen spread it about the Court, so that all the mirth, for some days, was at my expense.

CHAPTER 6. *Several contrivances of the Author to please the King and Queen. He shows his skill in music. The King inquires into the state of Europe, which the Author relates to him. The King's observations thereon.*

I used to attend the King's levee once or twice a week, and had often seen him under the barber's hand, which indeed was at first very terrible to behold. For the razor was almost twice as long as an ordinary scythe. His Majesty, according to the custom of the country, was only shaved twice a week. I once prevailed on the barber to give me some of the suds or lather, out of which I picked forty or fifty of the strongest stumps of hair. I then took a piece of fine wood, and cut it like the back of a comb, making several holes in it at equal distance with as small a needle as I could get from Glumdalclitch. I fixed in the stumps so artificially,[3] scraping and sloping them with my knife towards the points, that I made a very tolerable comb; which was a seasonable supply, my own being so much broken in the teeth that it was almost useless; neither did I know any artist in that country so nice and exact as would undertake to make me another.

And this puts me in mind of an amusement wherein I spent many of my leisure hours. I desired the Queen's woman to save for me the combings of her Majesty's hair, whereof in time I got a good quantity; and consulting with my friend the cabinetmaker, who had received general orders to do little jobs for me, I directed him to make two chair frames, no larger than those I had in my box, and then to bore little holes with a fine awl round those parts where I designed the backs and seats; through these holes I wove the strongest hairs I could pick out, just after the manner of cane chairs in England. When they were finished, I made a present of them to her Majesty, who kept them in her cabinet, and used to show them for curiosities, as indeed they were the wonder of every one that beheld them. The

2. Not feeling well.   3. Skillfully.

Queen would have made me sit upon one of these chairs, but I absolutely refused to obey her, protesting I would rather die a thousand deaths than place a dishonorable part of my body on those precious hairs that once adorned her Majesty's head. Of these hairs (as I had always a mechanical genius) I likewise made a neat little purse above five foot long, with her Majesty's name deciphered in gold letters, which I gave to Glumdalclitch by the Queen's consent. To say the truth, it was more for show than use, being not of strength to bear the weight of the larger coins; and therefore she kept nothing in it but some little toys[4] that girls are fond of.

The King, who delighted in music, had frequent consorts[5] at court, to which I was sometimes carried, and set in my box on a table to hear them; but the noise was so great that I could hardly distinguish the tunes. I am confident that all the drums and trumpets of a royal army, beating and sounding together just at your ears, could not equal it. My practice was to have my box removed from the places where the performers sat, as far as I could, then to shut the doors and windows of it, and draw the window curtains, after which I found their music not disagreeable.

I had learned in my youth to play a little upon the spinet. Glumdalclitch kept one in her chamber, and a master attended twice a week to teach her: I call it a spinet, because it somewhat resembled that instrument, and was played upon in the same manner. A fancy came into my head that I would entertain the King and Queen with an English tune upon this instrument. But this appeared extremely difficult: for the spinet was near sixty foot long, each key being almost a foot wide; so that, with my arms extended, I could not reach to above five keys, and to press them down required a good smart stroke with my fist, which would be too great a labor and to no purpose. The method I contrived was this: I prepared two round sticks about the bigness of common cudgels; they were thicker at one end than the other, and I covered the thicker ends with a piece of a mouse's skin, that by rapping on them I might neither damage the tops of the keys, nor interrupt the sound. Before the spinet a bench was placed, about four foot below the keys, and I was put upon the bench. I ran sideling upon it that way and this, as fast as I could, banging the proper keys with my two sticks; and made a shift to play a jig, to the great satisfaction of both their Majesties: but it was the most violent exercise I ever underwent, and yet I could not strike above sixteen keys, nor, consequently, play the bass and treble together, as other artists do; which was a great disadvantage to my performance.

The King, who, as I before observed, was a prince of excellent understanding, would frequently order that I should be brought in my box and set upon the table in his closet. He would then command me to bring one of my chairs out of the box, and sit down within three yards distance upon the top of the cabinet, which brought me almost to a level with his face. In this manner I had several conversations with him. I one day took the freedom to tell his Majesty that the contempt he discovered towards Europe, and the rest of the world, did not seem answerable to those excellent qualities of mind that he was master of. That reason did not extend itself with the bulk of the body: on the contrary, we observed in our country that the tallest persons were usually

4. Trifles.   5. Concerts.

least provided with it. That among other animals, bees and ants had the reputation of more industry, art, and sagacity than many of the larger kinds; and that, as inconsiderable as he took me to be, I hoped I might live to do his Majesty some signal service. The King heard me with attention, and began to conceive a much better opinion of me than he had before. He desired I would give him as exact an account of the government of England as I possibly could; because, as fond as princes commonly are of their own customs (for so he conjectured of other monarchs, by my former discourses), he should be glad to hear of anything that might deserve imitation.

Imagine with thyself, courteous reader, how often I then wished for the tongue of Demosthenes or Cicero,[6] that might have enabled me to celebrate the praise of my own dear native country in a style equal to its merits and felicity.

I began my discourse by informing his Majesty that our dominions consisted of two islands, which composed three mighty kingdoms under one sovereign, beside our plantations in America. I dwelt long upon the fertility of our soil, and the temperature[7] of our climate. I then spoke at large upon the constitution of an English Parliament, partly made up of an illustrious body called the House of Peers,[8] persons of the noblest blood, and of the most ancient and ample patrimonies. I described that extraordinary care always taken of their education in arts and arms, to qualify them for being counselors born to the king and kingdom; to have a share in the legislature, to be members of the highest Court of Judicature, from whence there could be no appeal; and to be champions always ready for the defense of their prince and country, by their valor, conduct, and fidelity. That these were the ornament and bulwark of the kingdom, worthy followers of their most renowned ancestors, whose honor had been the reward of their virtue, from which their posterity were never once known to degenerate. To these were joined several holy persons, as part of that assembly, under the title of Bishops, whose peculiar business it is to take care of religion, and of those who instruct the people therein. These were searched and sought out through the whole nation, by the prince and his wisest counselors, among such of the priesthood as were most deservedly distinguished by the sanctity of their lives and the depth of their erudition, who were indeed the spiritual fathers of the clergy and the people.

That the other part of the Parliament consisted of an assembly called the House of Commons, who were all principal gentlemen, freely picked and culled out by the people themselves, for their great abilities and love of their country, to represent the wisdom of the whole nation. And these two bodies make up the most august assembly in Europe, to whom, in conjunction with the prince, the whole legislature is committed.

I then descended to the Courts of Justice, over which the Judges, those venerable sages and interpreters of the law, presided, for determining the disputed rights and properties of men, as well as for the punishment of vice, and protection of innocence. I mentioned the prudent management of our treasury, the valor and achievements of our forces by sea and land. I computed the number of our people, by reckoning how many millions there

6. Great orators of Athens and Rome, respectively.
7. Temperateness.
8. The House of Lords.

might be of each religious sect, or political party among us. I did not omit even our sports and pastimes, or any other particular which I thought might redound to the honor of my country. And I finished all with a brief historical account of affairs and events in England for about an hundred years past.

This conversation was not ended under five audiences, each of several hours, and the King heard the whole with great attention, frequently taking notes of what I spoke, as well as memorandums of several questions he intended to ask me.

When I had put an end to these long discourses, his Majesty in a sixth audience consulting his notes, proposed many doubts, queries, and objections, upon every article. He asked what methods were used to cultivate the minds and bodies of our young nobility, and in what kind of business they commonly spent the first and teachable part of their lives. What course was taken to supply that assembly when any noble family became extinct. What qualifications were necessary in those who were to be created new lords. Whether the humor[9] of the prince, a sum of money to a Court lady or a prime minister, or a design of strengthening a party opposite to the public interest, ever happened to be motives in those advancements. What share of knowledge these lords had in the laws of their country, and how they came by it, so as to enable them to decide the properties of their fellow subjects in the last resort. Whether they were always so free from avarice, partialities, or want that a bribe or some other sinister view could have no place among them. Whether those holy lords I spoke of were constantly promoted to that rank upon account of their knowledge in religious matters, and the sanctity of their lives; had never been compliers with the times while they were common priests, or slavish prostitute chaplains to some nobleman, whose opinions they continued servilely to follow after they were admitted into that assembly.

He then desired to know what arts were practiced in electing those whom I called Commoners. Whether a stranger with a strong purse might not influence the vulgar voters to choose him before their own landlord or the most considerable gentleman in the neighborhood. How it came to pass that people were so violently bent upon getting into this assembly, which I allowed to be a great trouble and expense, often to the ruin of their families, without any salary or pension: because this appeared such an exalted strain of virtue and public spirit that his Majesty seemed to doubt it might possibly not be always sincere; and he desired to know whether such zealous gentlemen could have any views of refunding themselves for the charges and trouble they were at, by sacrificing the public good to the designs of a weak and vicious prince in conjunction with a corrupted ministry. He multiplied his questions, and sifted me thoroughly upon every part of this head, proposing numberless inquiries and objections, which I think it not prudent or convenient to repeat.

Upon what I said in relation to our Courts of Justice, his Majesty desired to be satisfied in several points: and this I was the better able to do, having been formerly almost ruined by a long suit in chancery, which was decreed for me with costs. He asked what time was usually spent in determining between right and wrong, and what degree of expense. Whether advocates and orators

9. Whim.

had liberty to plead in causes manifestly known to be unjust, vexatious, or oppressive. Whether party in religion or politics were observed to be of any weight in the scale of justice. Whether those pleading orators were persons educated in the general knowledge of equity, or only in provincial, national, and other local customs. Whether they or their judges had any part in penning those laws which they assumed the liberty of interpreting and glossing upon at their pleasure. Whether they had ever at different times pleaded for and against the same cause, and cited precedents to prove contrary opinions. Whether they were a rich or a poor corporation. Whether they received any pecuniary reward for pleading or delivering their opinions. And particularly whether they were ever admitted as members in the lower senate.

He fell next upon the management of our treasury, and said he thought my memory had failed me, because I computed our taxes at about five or six millions a year, and when I came to mention the issues,[1] he found they sometimes amounted to more than double, for the notes he had taken were very particular in this point; because he hoped, as he told me, that the knowledge of our conduct might be useful to him, and he could not be deceived in his calculations. But if what I told him were true, he was still at a loss how a kingdom could run out of its estate like a private person. He asked me, who were our creditors? and where we should find money to pay them? He wondered to hear me talk of such chargeable and extensive wars; that certainly we must be a quarrelsome people, or live among very bad neighbors, and that our generals must needs be richer than our kings.[2] He asked what business we had out of our own islands, unless upon the score of trade or treaty or to defend the coasts with our fleet. Above all, he was amazed to hear me talk of a mercenary standing army[3] in the midst of peace, and among a free people. He said if we were governed by our own consent in the persons of our representatives, he could not imagine of whom we were afraid, or against whom we were to fight; and would hear my opinion whether a private man's house might not better be defended by himself, his children, and family, than by half a dozen rascals picked up at a venture[4] in the streets for small wages, who might get an hundred times more by cutting their throats.

He laughed at my odd kind of arithmetic (as he was pleased to call it) in reckoning the numbers of our people by a computation drawn from the several sects among us in religion and politics. He said he knew no reason why those who entertain opinions prejudicial to the public should be obliged to change, or should not be obliged to conceal them. And as it was tyranny in any government to require the first, so it was weakness not to enforce the second: for a man may be allowed to keep poisons in his closet, but not to vend them about for cordials.[5]

He observed that among the diversions of our nobility and gentry I had mentioned gaming. He desired to know at what age this entertainment was usually taken up, and when it was laid down; how much of their time it

1. Expenditures.
2. An allusion to the enormous fortune gained by the duke of Marlborough, formerly captain-general of the army, whom Swift detested.
3. Since the declaration of the Bill of Rights (1689), a standing army without authorization by

Parliament had been illegal. Swift and the Tories in general were vigilant in their opposition to such an army.
4. By chance.
5. Medicines to stimulate the heart, or, equally commonly, liquers.

employed; whether it ever went so high as to affect their fortunes; whether mean, vicious people, by their dexterity in that art, might not arrive at great riches, and sometimes keep our very nobles in dependence, as well as habituate them to vile companions, wholly take them from the improvement of their minds, and force them, by the losses they received, to learn and practice that infamous dexterity upon others.

He was perfectly astonished with the historical account I gave him of our affairs during the last century, protesting it was only an heap of conspiracies, rebellions, murders, massacres, revolutions, banishments, the very worst effects that avarice, faction, hypocrisy, perfidiousness, cruelty, rage, madness, hatred, envy, lust, malice, or ambition could produce.

His Majesty in another audience was at the pains to recapitulate the sum of all I had spoken; compared the questions he made with the answers I had given; then taking me into his hands, and stroking me gently, delivered himself in these words, which I shall never forget, nor the manner he spoke them in. "My little friend Grildrig, you have made a most admirable panegyric upon your country. You have clearly proved that ignorance, idleness, and vice are the proper ingredients for qualifying a legislator. That laws are best explained, interpreted, and applied by those whose interests and abilities lie in perverting, confounding, and eluding them. I observe among you some lines of an institution which in its original might have been tolerable; but these half erased, and the rest wholly blurred and blotted by corruptions. It doth not appear from all you have said how any one virtue is required towards the procurement of any one station among you; much less that men are ennobled on account of their virtue, that priests are advanced for their piety or learning, soldiers for their conduct or valor, judges for their integrity, senators for the love of their country, or counselors for their wisdom. As for yourself," continued the King, "who have spent the greatest part of your life in traveling, I am well disposed to hope you may hitherto have escaped many vices of your country. But by what I have gathered from your own relation, and the answers I have with much pains wringed and extorted from you, I cannot but conclude the bulk of your natives to be the most pernicious race of little odious vermin that nature ever suffered to crawl upon the surface of the earth."

CHAPTER 7. *The Author's love of his country. He makes a proposal of much advantage to the King; which is rejected. The King's great ignorance in politics. The learning of that country very imperfect and confined. Their laws, and military affairs, and parties in the State.*

Nothing but an extreme love of truth could have hindered me from concealing this part of my story. It was in vain to discover my resentments, which were always turned into ridicule: and I was forced to rest with patience while my noble and most beloved country was so injuriously treated. I am heartily sorry as any of my readers can possibly be that such an occasion was given, but this prince happened to be so curious and inquisitive upon every particular that it could not consist either with gratitude or good manners to refuse giving him what satisfaction I was able. Yet thus much I may be allowed to say in my own vindication: that I artfully eluded many of his questions, and gave to every point a more favorable turn by many degrees than the strictness of truth would allow. For I have always borne that laudable partiality to my own country, which Dionysius Halicarnassensis[6] with so much justice recommends to an historian. I would hide the frailties and deformities of my political mother, and place her virtues and beauties in the most advantageous light. This was my sincere endeavor in those many discourses I had with that mighty monarch, although it unfortunately failed of success.

But great allowances should be given to a King who lives wholly secluded from the rest of the world, and must therefore be altogether unacquainted with the manners and customs that most prevail in other nations: the want of which knowledge will ever produce many *prejudices*, and a certain *narrowness of thinking*, from which we and the politer countries of Europe are wholly exempted. And it would be hard indeed if so remote a prince's notions of virtue and vice were to be offered as a standard for all mankind.

To confirm what I have now said, and further to show the miserable effects of a *confined education*, I shall here insert a passage which will hardly obtain belief. In hopes to ingratiate myself farther into his Majesty's favor, I told him of an invention discovered between three and four hundred years ago, to make a certain powder, into an heap of which the smallest spark of fire falling would kindle the whole in a moment, although it were as big as a mountain, and make it all fly up in the air together, with a noise and agitation greater than thunder. That a proper quantity of this powder rammed into an hollow tube of brass or iron, according to its bigness, would drive a ball of iron or lead with such violence and speed as nothing was able to sustain its force. That the largest balls thus discharged would not only destroy whole ranks of an army at once, but batter the strongest walls to the ground; sink down ships with a thousand men in each, to the bottom of the sea; and, when linked together by a chain, would cut through masts and rigging; divide hundreds of bodies in the middle, and lay all waste before them. That we often put this powder into large hollow balls of iron, and discharged them by an engine into some city we were besieging; which would rip up the pavements, tear the houses to pieces, burst and throw splinters on every side, dashing out the brains of all who came near. That I knew the ingredients very well, which were cheap and common; I understood the manner of compounding them, and could direct his workmen how to make those tubes of a size proportionable to all other things in his Majesty's kingdom, and the largest need not be above two hundred foot long; twenty or thirty of which tubes, charged with the proper quantity of powder and balls, would batter down the walls of the strongest town in his dominions in a few hours; or destroy the whole metropolis, if ever it should pretend to dispute his absolute commands. This I humbly, offered to his Majesty as a small tribute of acknowledgement in return of so many marks that I had received of his royal favor and protection.

The King was struck with horror at the description I had given of those terrible engines and the proposal I had made. He was amazed how so impotent and groveling an insect as I (these were his expressions) could entertain such inhuman ideas, and in so familiar a manner as to appear wholly unmoved at all the scenes of blood and desolation which I had painted as the

6. A Greek rhetorician and historian, who flourished ca. 25 B.C.E. His history of Rome was written to reconcile the Greeks to their Roman masters.

common effects of those destructive machines; whereof he said some evil genius, enemy to mankind, must have been the first contriver. As for himself, he protested that although few things delighted him so much as new discoveries in art or in nature, yet he would rather lose half his kingdom than be privy to such a secret, which he commanded me, as I valued my life, never to mention any more.

A strange effect of *narrow principles* and *short views!* that a prince possessed of every quality which procures veneration, love, and esteem; of strong parts, great wisdom, and profound learning; endued with admirable talents for government, and almost adored by his subjects; should from a *nice, unnecessary scruple,* whereof in Europe we can have no conception, let slip an opportunity put into his hands that would have made him absolute master of the lives, the liberties, and the fortunes of his people. Neither do I say this with the least intention to detract from the many virtues of that excellent King, whose character I am sensible will on this account be very much lessened in the opinion of an English reader: but I take this defect among them to have risen from their ignorance; they not having hitherto reduced politics into a science, as the more acute wits of Europe have done. For I remember very well, in a discourse one day with the King, when I happened to say there were several thousand books among us written upon the art of government, it gave him (directly contrary to my intention) a very mean opinion of our understandings. He professed both to abominate and despise all *mystery, refinement,* and *intrigue,* either in a prince or a minister. He could not tell what I meant by *secrets of state,* where an enemy or some rival nation were not in the case. He confined the knowledge of governing within very *narrow bounds:* to common sense and reason, to justice and lenity, to the speedy determination of civil and criminal causes, with some other obvious topics which are not worth considering. And he gave it for his opinion that whoever could make two ears of corn or two blades of grass to grow upon a spot of ground where only one grew before would deserve better of mankind and do more essential service to his country than the whole race of politicians[7] put together.

The learning of this people is very defective, consisting only in morality, history, poetry, and mathematics; wherein they must be allowed to excel. But the last of these is wholly applied to what may be useful in life, to the improvement of agriculture and all mechanical arts; so that among us it would be little esteemed. And as to ideas, entities, abstractions, and transcendentals,[8] I could never drive the least conception into their heads.

No law of that country must exceed in words the number of letters in their alphabet, which consists only in two and twenty. But indeed few of them extend even to that length. They are expressed in the most plain and simple terms, wherein those people are not mercurial enough to discover above one interpretation. And to write a comment upon any law is a capital crime. As to the decision of civil causes, or proceedings against criminals, their precedents are so few that they have little reason to boast of any extraordinary skill in either.

They have had the art of printing as well as the Chinese, time out of mind. But their libraries are not very large; for that of the King's, which is reck-

---

7. Swift means something like our modern political scientists or theorists.

8. In Swift's time, *transcendental* was practically synonymous with *metaphysical.*

oned the biggest, doth not amount to above a thousand volumes, placed in a gallery of twelve hundred foot long, from whence I had liberty to borrow what books I pleased. The Queen's joiner had contrived in one of the Glumdalclitch's rooms a kind of wooden machine five and twenty foot high, formed like a standing ladder; the steps were each fifty foot long. It was indeed a movable pair of stairs, the lowest end placed at ten foot distance from the wall of the chamber. The book I had a mind to read was put up leaning against the wall. I first mounted to the upper step of the ladder, and turning my face towards the book began at the top of the page, and so walking to the right and left about eight or ten paces according to the length of the lines, till I had gotten a little below the level of mine eyes, and then descending gradually till I came to the bottom: after which I mounted again, and began the other page in the same manner, and so turned over the leaf, which I could easily do with both my hands, for it was as thick and stiff as a pasteboard, and in the largest folios not above eighteen or twenty foot long.

Their style is clear, masculine, and smooth, but not florid; for they avoid nothing more than multiplying unnecessary words or using various expressions. I have perused many of their books, especially those in history and morality. Among the rest, I was much diverted with a little old treatise, which always lay in Glumdalclitch's bedchamber, and belonged to her governess, a grave elderly gentlewoman, who dealt in writings of morality and devotion. The book treats of the weakness of human kind, and is in little esteem, except among the women and the vulgar. However, I was curious to see what an author of that country could say upon such a subject. This writer went through all the usual topics of European moralists: showing how diminutive, contemptible, and helpless an animal was man in his own nature; how unable to defend himself from the inclemencies of the air, or the fury of wild beasts; how much he was excelled by one creature in strength, by another in speed, by a third in foresight, by a fourth in industry. He added that nature was degenerated in these latter declining ages of the world, and could now produce only small abortive births in comparison of those in ancient times. He said it was very reasonable to think, not only that the species of men were originally much larger, but also that there must have been giants in former ages; which, as it is asserted by history and tradition, so it hath been confirmed by huge bones and skulls casually dug up in several parts of the kingdom, far exceeding the common dwindled race of man in our days. He argued that the very laws of nature absolutely required we should have been made in the beginning of a size more large and robust, not so liable to destruction from every little accident of a tile falling from a house, or a stone cast from the hand of a boy, or of being drowned in a little brook. From this way of reasoning, the author drew several moral applications useful in the conduct of life, but needless here to repeat. For my own part, I could not avoid reflecting how universally this talent was spread, of drawing lectures in morality, or indeed rather matter of discontent and repining, from the quarrels we raise with nature. And I believe, upon a strict inquiry, those quarrels might be shown as ill grounded among us as they are among that people.

As to their military affairs, they boast that the King's army consists of an hundred and seventy-six thousand foot and thirty-two thousand horse: if that may be called an army which is made up of tradesmen in the several cities, and farmers in the country, whose commanders are only the nobility and gentry, without pay or reward. They are indeed perfect enough in their exercises, and under very good discipline, wherein I saw no great merit; for how should it be otherwise, where every farmer is under the command of his own landlord, and every citizen under that of the principal men in his own city, chosen after the manner of Venice by ballot?

I have often seen the militia of Lorbrulgrud drawn out to exercise in a great field near the city, of twenty miles square. They were in all not above twenty-five thousand foot, and six thousand horse; but it was impossible for me to compute their number, considering the space of ground they took up. A cavalier mounted on a large steed might be about an hundred foot high. I have seen this whole body of horse, upon a word of command, draw their swords at once, and brandish them in the air. Imagination can figure nothing so grand, so surprising, and so astonishing. It looked as if ten thousand flashes of lightning were darting at the same time from every quarter of the sky.

I was curious to know how this prince, to whose dominions there is no access from any other country, came to think of armies, or to teach his people the practice of military discipline. But I was soon informed, both by conversation and reading their histories. For in the course of many ages they have been troubled with the same disease to which the whole race of mankind is subject: the nobility often contending for power, the people for liberty, and the King for absolute dominion. All which, however happily tempered by the laws of the kingdom, have been sometimes violated by each of the three parties, and have more than once occasioned civil wars, the last whereof was happily put an end to by this prince's grandfather in a general composition;[9] and the militia, then settled with common consent, hath been ever since kept in the strictest duty.

CHAPTER 8. *The King and Queen make a progress to the frontiers. The Author attends them. The manner in which he leaves the country very particularly related. He returns to England.*

I had always a strong impulse that I should some time recover my liberty, though it were impossible to conjecture by what means, or to form any project with the least hope of succeeding. The ship in which I sailed was the first ever known to be driven within sight of that coast; and the King had given strict orders that if at any time another appeared, it should be taken ashore, and with all its crew and passengers brought in a tumbrel[1] to Lorbrulgrud. He was strongly bent to get me a woman of my own size, by whom I might propagate the breed: but I think I should rather have died than undergone the disgrace of leaving a posterity to be kept in cages like tame canary birds, and perhaps in time sold about the kingdom to persons of quality for curiosities. I was indeed treated with much kindness: I was the favorite of a great King and Queen, and the delight of the whole Court, but it was upon such a foot as ill became the dignity of human kind. I could never forget those domestic pledges I had left behind me. I wanted to be among people with

9. A political settlement based on general agreement of all parties.
1. A farm wagon.

whom I could converse upon even terms, and walk about the streets and fields without fear of being trod to death like a frog or a young puppy. But my deliverance came sooner than I expected, and in a manner not very common; the whole story and circumstances of which I shall faithfully relate.

I had now been two years in this country; and about the beginning of the third, Glumdalclitch and I attended the King and Queen in progress to the south coast of the kingdom. I was carried as usual in my traveling box, which, as I have already described, was a very convenient closet of twelve foot wide. I had ordered a hammock to be fixed by silken ropes from the four corners at the top, to break the jolts when a servant carried me before him on horseback, as I sometimes desired; and would often sleep in my hammock while we were upon the road. On the roof of my closet, set not directly over the middle of the hammock, I ordered the joiner to cut out a hole of a foot square to give me air in hot weather as I slept, which hole I shut at pleasure with a board that drew backwards and forwards through a groove.

When we came to our journey's end, the King thought proper to pass a few days at a palace he hath near Flanflasnic, a city within eighteen English miles of the seaside. Glumdalclitch and I were much fatigued; I had gotten a small cold, but the poor girl was so ill as to be confined to her chamber. I longed to see the ocean, which must be the only scene of my escape, if ever it should happen. I pretended to be worse than I really was, and desired leave to take the fresh air of the sea with a page whom I was very fond of, and who had sometimes been trusted with me. I shall never forget with what unwillingness Glumdalclitch consented, nor the strict charge she gave the page to be careful of me, bursting at the same time into a flood of tears, as if she had some foreboding of what was to happen. The boy took me out in my box about half an hour's walk from the palace, towards the rocks on the seashore. I ordered him to set me down, and lifting up one of my sashes, cast many a wistful melancholy look towards the sea. I found myself not very well, and told the page that I had a mind to take a nap in my hammock, which I hoped would do me good. I got in, and the boy shut the window close down, to keep out the cold. I soon fell asleep: and all I can conjecture is that while I slept, the page, thinking no danger could happen, went among the rocks to look for birds' eggs; having before observed him from my window searching about, and picking up one or two in the clefts. Be that as it will, I found myself suddenly awaked with a violent pull upon the ring which was fastened at the top of my box for the conveniency of carriage. I felt my box raised very high in the air, and then borne forward with prodigious speed. The first jolt had like to have shaken me out of my hammock, but afterwards the motion was easy enough. I called out several times as loud as I could raise my voice, but all to no purpose. I looked towards my windows, and could see nothing but the clouds and sky. I heard a noise just over my head like the clapping of wings, and then began to perceive the woeful condition I was in; that some eagle had got the ring of my box in his beak, with an intent to let it fall on a rock, like a tortoise in a shell, and then pick out my body and devour it. For the sagacity and smell of this bird enable him to discover his quarry at a great distance, although better concealed than I could be within a two-inch board.

In a little time I observed the noise and flutter of wings to increase very fast, and my box was tossed up and down like a signpost in a windy day. I heard several bangs or buffets, as I thought, given to the eagle (for such I am

certain it must have been that held the ring of my box in his beak), and then
all on a sudden felt myself falling perpendicularly down for above a minute,
but with such incredible swiftness that I almost lost my breath. My fall was
topped by a terrible squash, that sounded louder to mine ears than the cataract of Niagara; after which I was quite in the dark for another minute, and
then my box began to rise so high that I could see light from the tops of my
windows. I now perceived that I was fallen into the sea. My box, by the
weight of my body, the goods that were in, and the broad plates of iron fixed
for strength at the four corners of the top and bottom, floated above five foot
deep in water. I did then and do now suppose that the eagle which flew away
with my box was pursued by two or three others, and forced to let me drop
while he was defending himself against the rest, who hoped to share in the
prey. The plates of iron fastened at the bottom of the box (for those were the
strongest) preserved the balance while it fell, and hindered it from being
broken on the surface of the water. Every joint of it was well grooved, and
the door did not move on hinges, but up and down like a sash; which kept
my closet so tight that very little water came in. I got with much difficulty
out of my hammock, having first ventured to draw back the slip-board on the
roof already mentioned, contrived on purpose to let in air, for want of which
I found myself almost stifled.

How often did I then wish myself with my dear Glumdalclitch, from
whom one single hour had so far divided me! And I may say with truth that
in the midst of my own misfortune, I could not forbear lamenting my poor
nurse, the grief she would suffer for my loss, the displeasure of the Queen,
and the ruin of her fortune. Perhaps many travelers have not been under
greater difficulties and distress than I was at this juncture, expecting every
moment to see my box dashed in pieces, or at least overset by the first violent
blast or a rising wave. A breach in one single pane of glass would have been
immediate death, nor could anything have preserved the windows but the
strong lattice wires placed on the outside against accidents in traveling. I
saw the water ooze in at several crannies, although the leaks were not considerable, and I endeavored to stop them as well as I could. I was not able to
lift up the roof of my closet, which otherwise I certainly should have done,
and sat on the top of it, where I might at least preserve myself from being
shut up, as I may call it, in the hold. Or, if I escaped these dangers for a day
or two, what could I expect but a miserable death of cold and hunger! I was
four hours under these circumstances, expecting and indeed wishing every
moment to be my last.

I have already told the reader that there were two strong staples fixed
upon that side of my box which had no window and into which the servant,
who used to carry me on horseback, would put a leathern belt, and buckle
it about his waist. Being in this disconsolate state, I heard, or at least thought
I heard, some kind of grating noise on that side of my box where the staples
were fixed; and soon after I began to fancy that the box was pulled or towed
along in the sea; for I now and then felt a sort of tugging, which made the
waves rise near the tops of my windows, leaving me almost in the dark. This
gave me some faint hopes of relief, although I was not able to imagine how it
could be brought about. I ventured to unscrew one of my chairs, which were
always fastened to the floor; and having made a hard shift to screw it down
again directly under the slipping-board that I had lately opened, I mounted

on the chair, and putting my mouth as near as I could to the hole, I called for help in a loud voice, and in all the languages I understood. I then fastened my handkerchief to a stick I usually carried, and thrusting it up the hole, waved it several times in the air, that if any boat or ship were near, the seamen might conjecture some unhappy mortal to be shut up in the box.

I found no effect from all I could do, but plainly perceived my closet to be moved along; and in the space of an hour or better, that side of the box where the staples were, and had no window, struck against something that was hard. I apprehended it to be a rock, and found myself tossed more than ever. I plainly heard a noise upon the cover of my closet, like that of a cable, and the grating of it as it passed through the ring. I then found myself hoisted up by degrees at least three foot higher than I was before. Whereupon I again thrust up my stick and handkerchief, calling for help till I was almost hoarse. In return to which, I heard a great shout repeated three times, giving me such transports of joy as are not to be conceived but by those who feel them. I now heard a trampling over my head, and somebody calling through the hole with a loud voice in the English tongue: "If there be anybody below, let them speak." I answered, I was an Englishman, drawn by ill fortune into the greatest calamity that ever any creature underwent, and begged, by all that was moving, to be delivered out of the dungeon I was in. The voice replied, I was safe, for my box was fastened to their ship; and the carpenter should immediately come and saw an hole in the cover, large enough to pull me out. I answered, that was needless and would take up too much time, for there was no more to be done but let one of the crew put his finger into the ring, and take the box out of the sea into the ship, and so into the captain's cabin. Some of them, upon hearing me talk so wildly, thought I was mad; others laughed; for indeed it never came into my head that I was now got among people of my own stature and strength. The carpenter came, and in a few minutes sawed a passage about four foot square; then let down a small ladder, upon which I mounted, and from thence was taken into the ship in a very weak condition.

The sailors were all in amazement, and asked me a thousand questions, which I had no inclination to answer. I was equally confounded at the sight of so many pygmies, for such I took them to be, after having so long accustomed my eyes to the monstrous objects I had left. But the Captain, Mr. Thomas Wilcocks, an honest, worthy Shropshire man, observing I was ready to faint, took me into his cabin, gave me a cordial to comfort me, and made me turn in upon his own bed, advising me to take a little rest, of which I had great need. Before I went to sleep I gave him to understand that I had some valuable furniture in my box, too good to be lost, a fine hammock, an handsome field bed, two chairs, a table, and a cabinet; that my closet was hung on all sides, or rather quilted with silk and cotton; that if he would let one of the crew bring my closet into his cabin, I would open it before him and show him my goods. The Captain, hearing me utter these absurdities, concluded I was raving; however (I suppose to pacify me), he promised to give order as I desired, and going upon deck, sent some of his men down into my closet, from whence (as I afterwards found) they drew up all my goods and stripped off the quilting; but the chairs, cabinet, and bedstead, being screwed to the floor, were much damaged by the ignorance of the seamen, who tore them up by force. Then they knocked off some of the boards for the use of the ship; and when they had got all they had a mind for, let the hulk drop into the sea, which, by reason of many breaches made in the bottom and sides, sunk to rights.[2] And indeed I was glad not to have been a spectator of the havoc they made, because I am confident it would have sensibly touched me, by bringing former passages into my mind, which I had rather forget.

I slept some hours, but perpetually disturbed with dreams of the place I had left, and the dangers I had escaped. However, upon waking, I found myself much recovered. It was now about eight o'clock at night, and the Captain ordered supper immediately, thinking I had already fasted too long. He entertained me with great kindness, observing me not to look wildly, or talk inconsistently; and when we were left alone, desired I would give him a relation of my travels, and by what accident I came to be set adrift in that monstrous wooden chest. He said that about twelve o'clock at noon, as he was looking through his glass, he spied it at a distance, and thought it was a sail, which he had a mind to make,[3] being not much out of his course, in hopes of buying some biscuit, his own beginning to fall short. That, upon coming nearer, and finding his error, he sent out his longboat to discover what I was; that his men came back in a fright, swearing they had seen a swimming house. That he laughed at their folly, and went himself in the boat, ordering his men to take a strong cable along with them. That the weather being calm, he rowed round me several times, observed my windows, and the wire lattices that defended them. That he discovered two staples upon one side, which was all of boards, without any passage for light. He then commanded his men to row up to that side, and fastening a cable to one of the staples, ordered his men to tow my chest (as he called it) towards the ship. When it was there, he gave directions to fasten another cable to the ring fixed in the cover, and to raise up my chest with pulleys, which all the sailors were not able to do above two or three foot. He said they saw my stick and handkerchief thrust out of the hole, and concluded that some unhappy man must be shut up in the cavity. I asked whether he or the crew had seen any prodigious birds in the air about the time he first discovered me. To which he answered that, discoursing this matter with the sailors while I was asleep, one of them said he had observed three eagles flying towards the north, but remarked nothing of their being larger than the usual size (which I suppose must be imputed to the great height they were at), and he could not guess the reason of my question. I then asked the Captain how far he reckoned we might be from land; he said, by the best computation he could make, we were at least an hundred leagues. I assured him that he must be mistaken by almost half; for I had not left the country from whence I came above two hours before I dropped into the sea. Whereupon he began again to think that my brain was disturbed, of which he gave me a hint, and advised me to go to bed in a cabin he had provided. I assured him I was well refreshed with his good entertainment and company, and as much in my senses as ever I was in my life. He then grew serious and desired to ask me freely whether I were not troubled in mind by the consciousness of some enormous crime, for which I was punished at the command of some prince, by exposing me in that chest, as great criminals in other countries have been forced to sea in a leaky vessel without provisions; for although he should be sorry to have taken so

2. At once, altogether.   3. Overtake.

ill[4] a man into his ship, yet he would engage his word to set me safe on shore in the first port where we arrived. He added that his suspicions were much increased by some very absurd speeches I had delivered at first to the sailors, and afterwards to himself, in relation to my closet or chest, as well as by my odd looks and behavior while I was at supper.

I begged his patience to hear me tell my story, which I faithfully did from the last time I left England to the moment he first discovered me. And as truth always forceth its way into rational minds, so this honest, worthy gentleman, who had some tincture of learning, and very good sense, was immediately convinced of my candor and veracity. But further to confirm all I had said, I entreated him to give order that my cabinet should be brought, of which I kept the key in my pocket (for he had already informed me how the seamen disposed of my closet). I opened it in his presence and showed him the small collection of rarities I made in the country from whence I had been so strangely delivered. There was the comb I had contrived out of the stumps of the King's beard, and another of the same materials, but fixed into a paring of her Majesty's thumbnail, which served for the back. There was a collection of needles and pins from a foot to half a yard long; four wasp-stings, like joiners' tacks; some combings of the Queen's hair; a gold ring which one day she made me a present of in a most obliging manner, taking it from her little finger, and throwing it over my head like a collar. I desired the Captain would please to accept this ring in return for his civilities, which he absolutely refused. I showed him a corn that I had cut off with my own hand from a Maid of Honor's toe; it was about the bigness of a Kentish pippin, and grown so hard that, when I returned to England, I got it hollowed into a cup and set in silver. Lastly, I desired him to see the breeches I had then on, which were made of a mouse's skin.

I could force nothing on him but a footman's tooth, which I observed him to examine with great curiosity, and found he had a fancy for it. He received it with abundance of thanks, more than such a trifle could deserve. It was drawn by an unskillful surgeon in a mistake from one of Glumdalclitch's men, who was afflicted with the toothache; but it was as sound as any in his head. I got it cleaned, and put it into my cabinet. It was about a foot long, and four inches in diameter.

The Captain was very well satisfied with this plain relation I had given him, and said he hoped when we returned to England I would oblige the world by putting it in paper and making it public. My answer was that I thought we were already overstocked with books of travels; that nothing could now pass which was not extraordinary; wherein I doubted some authors less consulted truth than their own vanity or interest, or the diversion of ignorant readers. That my story could contain little besides common events, without those ornamental descriptions of strange plants, trees, birds, and other animals, or the barbarous customs and idolatry of savage people, with which most writers abound. However, I thanked him for his good opinion, and promised to take the matter into my thoughts.

He said he wondered at one thing very much, which was to hear me speak so loud, asking me whether the King or Queen of that country were thick of hearing. I told him it was what I had been used to for above two years past,

4. Evil.

and that I admired[5] as much at the voices of him and his men, who seemed to me only to whisper, and yet I could hear them well enough. But, when I spoke in that country, it was like a man talking in the street to another looking out from the top of a steeple, unless when I was placed on a table, or held in any person's hand. I told him I had likewise observed another thing: that when I first got into the ship, and the sailors stood all about me, I thought they were the most little contemptible creatures I had ever beheld. For indeed while I was in that prince's country, I could never endure to look in a glass after my eyes had been accustomed to such prodigious objects, because the comparison gave me so despicable a conceit[6] of myself. The Captain said that while we were at supper he observed me to look at everything with a sort of wonder, and that I often seemed hardly able to contain my laughter; which he knew not well how to take, but imputed it to some disorder in my brain. I answered, it was very true; and I wondered how I could forbear, when I saw his dishes of the size of a silver threepence, a leg of pork hardly a mouthful, a cup not so big as a nutshell; and so I went on, describing the rest of his household stuff and provisions after the same manner. For, although the Queen had ordered a little equipage of all things necessary for me while I was in her service, yet my ideas were wholly taken up with what I saw on every side of me, and I winked at my own littleness, as people do at their own faults. The Captain understood my raillery very well, and merrily replied with the old English proverb, that he doubted[7] my eyes were bigger than my belly, for he did not observe my stomach so good, although I had fasted all day; and continuing in his mirth, protested he would have gladly given an hundred pounds to have seen my closet in the eagle's bill, and afterwards in its fall from so great an height into the sea; which would certainly have been a most astonishing object, worthy to have the description of it transmitted to future ages: and the comparison of Phaeton[8] was so obvious, that he could not forbear applying it, although I did not much admire the conceit.

The Captain having been at Tonquin,[9] was in his return to England driven northeastward to the latitude of 44 degrees, and of longitude 143. But meeting a trade wind two days after I came on board him, we sailed southward a long time, and coasting New Holland[1] kept our course west-southwest, and then south-southwest till we doubled the Cape of Good Hope. Our voyage was very prosperous, but I shall not trouble the reader with a journal of it. The Captain called in at one or two ports, and sent in his longboat for provisions and fresh water; but I never went out of the ship till we came into the Downs, which was on the third day of June, 1706, about nine months after my escape. I offered to leave my goods in security for payment of my freight; but the Captain protested he would not receive one farthing. We took kind leave of each other, and I made him promise he would come to see me at my house in Redriff. I hired a horse and guide for five shillings, which I borrowed of the Captain.

As I was on the road, observing the littleness of the houses, the trees, the cattle, and the people, I began to think myself in Lilliput. I was afraid of

5. Wondered.
6. Notion.
7. Feared.
8. Son of Helios, the sun god, whose unsuccessful attempt to drive his father's chariot led to his death, when he lost control and was hurled by Zeus from the sky, falling into the river Eridanus, where he drowned.
9. Tonkin, now in Vietnam.
1. Australia.

trampling on every traveler I met, and often called aloud to have them stand out of the way, so that I had like to have gotten one or two broken heads for my impertinence.

When I came to my own house, for which I was forced to inquire, one of the servants opening the door, I bent down to go in (like a goose under a gate) for fear of striking my head. My wife ran out to embrace me, but I stooped lower than her knees, thinking she could otherwise never be able to reach my mouth. My daughter kneeled to ask my blessing, but I could not see her till she arose, having been so long used to stand with my head and eyes erect to above sixty foot; and then I went to take her up with one hand by the waist. I looked down upon the servants and one or two friends who were in the house, as if they had been pygmies and I a giant. I told my wife she had been too thrifty; for I found she had starved herself and her daughter to nothing. In short, I behaved myself so unaccountably that they were all of the Captain's opinion when he first saw me, and concluded I had lost my wits. This I mention as an instance of the great power of habit and prejudice.

In a little time I and my family and friends came to a right understanding; but my wife protested I should never go to sea any more, although my evil destiny so ordered that she had not power to hinder me; as the reader may know hereafter. In the meantime I here conclude the second part of my unfortunate voyages.

Part 3. A Voyage to Laputa, Balnibarbi, Glubbdubdrib, Luggnagg, and Japan

CHAPTER 1. *The author sets out on his third voyage. Is taken by pirates. The malice of a Dutchman. His arrival at an island. He is received into Laputa.*

I had not been at home above ten days, when Captain William Robinson, a Cornish man, commander of the Hopewell, a stout ship of three hundred tons, came to my house. I had formerly been surgeon of another ship where he was master, and a fourth part owner, in a voyage to the Levant. He had always treated me more like a brother than an inferior officer; and, hearing of my arrival, made me a visit, as I apprehended only out of friendship, for nothing passed more than what is usual after long absence. But repeating his visits often, expressing his joy to find me in good health, asking whether I were now settled for life, adding that he intended a voyage to the East Indies in two months, at last he plainly invited me, although with some apologies, to be surgeon of the ship. That I should have another surgeon under me, besides our two mates; that my salary should be double to the usual pay; and that having experienced my knowledge in sea-affairs to be at least equal to his, he would enter into any engagement to follow my advice, as much as if I had share in the command.

He said so many other obliging things, and I knew him to be so honest a man, that I could not reject this proposal; the thirst I had of seeing the world, notwithstanding my past misfortunes, continuing as violent as ever. The only difficulty that remained was to persuade my wife, whose consent however I at last obtained, by the prospect of advantage she proposed to her children.

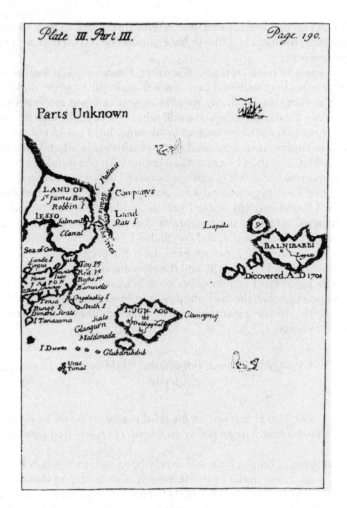

We set out the 5th day of August, 1706, and arrived at Fort St. George[2] the 11th of April, 1707. We stayed there three weeks to refresh our crew, many of whom were sick. From thence we went to Tonquin, where the captain resolved to continue some time, because many of the goods he intended to buy were not ready, nor could he expect to be dispatched[3] in several months. Therefore in hopes to defray some of the charges he must be at, he bought a sloop, loaded it with several sorts of goods wherewith the Tonquinese usually trade to the neighboring islands, and putting fourteen men on board, whereof three were of the country, he appointed me master of the sloop, and gave me power to traffic,[4] while he transacted his affairs at Tonquin.

We had not sailed above three days when a great storm arising, we were driven five days to the north-northeast, and then to the east: after which we

2. British fortress in South Asia founded in 1644, around which the city of Madras, now Chennai, grew.

3. To have his business settled.
4. Trade.

had fair weather, but still with a pretty strong gale from the west. Upon the tenth day we were chased by two pirates, who soon overtook us; for my sloop was so deep loaden, that she sailed very slow; neither were we in a condition to defend ourselves.

We were boarded about the same time by both the pirates, who entered furiously at the head of their men; but finding us all prostrate upon our faces (for so I gave order), they pinioned us with strong ropes, and setting guard upon us, went to search the sloop.

I observed among them a Dutchman, who seemed to be of some authority, although he were not commander of either ship. He knew us by our countenances to be Englishmen, and jabbering to us in his own language, swore we should be tied back to back and thrown into the sea. I spoke Dutch tolerably well; I told him who we were, and begged him, in consideration of our being Christians and Protestants, of neighboring countries in strict alliance,[5] that he would move the captains to take some pity on us. This inflamed his rage; he repeated his threatenings, and turning to his companions, spoke with great vehemence in the Japanese language, as I suppose, often using the word *Christianos.*[6]

The largest of the two pirate ships was commanded by a Japanese captain, who spoke a little Dutch, but very imperfectly. He came up to me, and after several questions, which I answered in great humility, he said we should not die. I made the captain a very low bow, and then, turning to the Dutchman, said I was sorry to find more mercy in a heathen, than in a brother Christian. But I had soon reason to repent those foolish words; for that malicious reprobate, having often endeavored in vain to persuade both the captains that I might be thrown into the sea (which they would not yield to, after the promise made me that I should not die), however prevailed so far as to have a punishment inflicted on me worse in all human appearance than death itself. My men were sent by an equal division into both the pirate ships, and my sloop new manned. As to myself, it was determined that I should be set adrift in a small canoe, with paddles and a sail, and four days' provisions; which last the Japanese captain was so kind to double out of his own stores, and would permit no man to search me. I got down into the canoe, while the Dutchman, standing upon the deck, loaded me with all the curses and injurious terms his language could afford.

About an hour before we saw the pirates I had taken an observation, and found we were in the latitude of 46 N. and of longitude 183.[7] When I was at some distance from the pirates, I discovered by my pocket-glass several islands to the southeast. I set up my sail, the wind being fair, with a design to reach the nearest of those islands, which I made a shift[8] to do in about three hours. It was all rocky; however I got many birds' eggs; and striking fire, I kindled some heath and dry seaweed, by which I roasted my eggs. I ate no other supper, being resolved to spare my provisions as much as I could. I passed the night under the shelter of a rock, strowing some heath under me, and slept pretty well.

---

5. The Dutch and English were then allied against the French, though the passage perhaps reflects Swift's animosity against the Dutch, in part for their extensive religious toleration.

6. Christians (Greek).
7. East of Japan and south of the westernmost Aleutian Islands.
8. Made an effort.

The next day I sailed to another island, and thence to a third and fourth, sometimes using my sail, and sometimes my paddles. But not to trouble the reader with a particular account of my distresses, let it suffice, that on the fifth day I arrived at the last island in my sight, which lay south-southeast to the former.

This island was at a greater distance than I expected, and I did not reach it in less than five hours. I encompassed it almost round before I could find a convenient place to land in, which was a small creek, about three times the wideness of my canoe. I found the island to be all rocky, only a little intermingled with tufts of grass, and sweet-smelling herbs. I took out my small provisions, and after having refreshed myself, I secured the remainder in a cave, whereof there were great numbers. I gathered plenty of eggs upon the rocks, and got a quantity of dry seaweed, and parched grass, which I designed to kindle the next day, and roast my eggs as well as I could. (For I had about me my flint, steel, match, and burning-glass.) I lay all night in the cave where I had lodged my provisions. My bed was the same dry grass and seaweed which I intended for fuel. I slept very little, for the disquiets of my mind prevailed over my weariness, and kept me awake. I considered how impossible it was to preserve my life in so desolate a place, and how miserable my end must be. Yet I found myself so listless and desponding that I had not the heart to rise; and before I could get spirits enough to creep out of my cave, the day was far advanced. I walked awhile among the rocks, the sky was perfectly clear, and the sun so hot, that I was forced to turn my face from it: when all on a sudden it became obscure, as I thought, in a manner very different from what happens by the interposition of a cloud. I turned back, and perceived a vast opaque body between me and the sun, moving forwards towards the island. It seemed to be about two miles high, and hid the sun six or seven minutes, but I did not observe the air to be much colder, or the sky more darkened, than if I had stood under the shade of a mountain. As it approached nearer over the place where I was, it appeared to be a firm substance, the bottom flat, smooth, and shining very bright from the reflection of the sea below. I stood upon a height about two hundred yards from the shore, and saw this vast body descending almost to a parallel with me, at less than an English mile distance. I took out my pocket perspective, and could plainly discover numbers of people moving up and down the sides of it, which appeared to be sloping, but what those people where doing I was not able to distinguish.

The natural love of life gave me some inward motions of joy; and I was ready to entertain a hope that this adventure might some way or other help to deliver me from the desolate place and condition I was in. But at the same time the reader can hardly conceive my astonishment to behold an island in the air, inhabited by men, who were able (as it should seem) to raise or sink or put it into progressive motion, as they pleased. But not being at that time in a disposition to philosophize upon this phenomenon, I rather chose to observe what course the island would take, because it seemed for a while to stand still. Yet soon after it advanced nearer, and I could see the sides of it encompassed with several gradations of galleries and stairs, at certain intervals, to descend from one to the other. In the lowest gallery, I beheld some people fishing with long angling rods, and others looking on. I waved my cap (for my hat was long since worn out) and my handkerchief toward the island; and upon its nearer approach, I called and shouted with the utmost strength of my voice; and then looking circumspectly, I beheld a crowd gather to that side which was most in my view. I found by their pointing towards me and to each other that they plainly discovered me, although they made no return to my shouting. But I could see four or five men running in great haste up the stairs to the top of the island, who then disappeared. I happened rightly to conjecture, that these were sent for orders to some person in authority upon this occasion.

The number of people increased, and in less than half an hour, the island was moved and raised in such a manner, that the lowest gallery appeared in a parallel of less than a hundred yards distance from the height where I stood. I then put myself in the most supplicating postures, and spoke in the humblest accent, but received no answer. Those who stood nearest over against me seemed to be persons of distinction, as I supposed by their habit.[9] They conferred earnestly with each other, looking often upon me. At length one of them called out in a clear, polite, smooth dialect, not unlike in sound to the Italian; and therefore I returned an answer in that language, hoping at least that the cadence might be more agreeable to his ears. Although neither of us understood the other, yet my meaning was easily known, for the people saw the distress I was in.

They made signs for me to come down from the rock, and go towards the shore, which I accordingly did; and the flying island being raised to a convenient height, the verge directly over me, a chain was let down from the lowest gallery, with a seat fastened to the bottom, to which I fixed myself, and was drawn up by pulleys.

CHAPTER 2. *The humors and dispositions of the Laputans described. An account of their learning. Of the King and his court. The author's reception there. The inhabitants subject to fears and disquietudes. An account of the women.*

At my alighting I was surrounded by a crowd of people, but those who stood nearest seemed to be of better quality. They beheld me with all the marks and circumstances of wonder; neither indeed was I much in their debt, having never till then seen a race of mortals so singular in their shapes, habits, and countenances. Their heads were all reclined to the right, or the left; one of their eyes turned inward, and the other directly up to the zenith. Their outward garments were adorned with the figures of suns, moons, and stars, interwoven with those of fiddles, flutes, harps, trumpets, guitars, harpsichords, and many more instruments of music, unknown to us in Europe.[1] I observed here and there many in the habits of servants, with a blown bladder fastened like a flail to the end of a short stick, which they carried in their hands. In each bladder was a small quantity of dried pease or little pebbles (as I was afterwards informed). With these bladders they now and then flapped the mouths and ears of those who stood near them, of which practice

9. Dress.
1. The Laputans represent contemporary speculation, deplored by Swift, about abstract theories of science, mathematics, and music. Both the Royal Society and Sir Isaac Newton took an interest in the mathematical basis of music.

I could not then conceive the meaning. It seems, the minds of these people are so taken up with intense speculations, that they neither can speak, or attend to the discourses of others, without being roused by some external taction[2] upon the organs of speech and hearing; for which reason those persons who are able to afford it always keep a flapper (the original is *clime-nole*) in their family, as one of their domestics; nor ever walk abroad or make visits without him. And the business of this officer is, when two or more persons are in company, gently to strike with his bladder the mouth of him who is to speak, and the right ear of him or them to whom the speaker addresseth himself. This flapper is likewise employed diligently to attend his master in his walks, and upon occasion to give him a soft flap on his eyes, because he is always so wrapped up in cogitation, that he is in manifest danger of falling down every precipice, and bouncing his head against every post; and in the streets, of jostling others, or being jostled himself into the kennel.[3]

It was necessary to give the reader this information, without which he would be at the same loss with me, to understand the proceedings of these people, as they conducted me up the stairs to the top of the island, and from thence to the royal palace. While we were ascending, they forgot several times what they were about, and left me to myself, till their memories were again roused by their flappers; for they appeared altogether unmoved by the sight of my foreign habit and countenance, and by the shouts of the vulgar, whose thoughts and minds were more disengaged.

At last we entered the palace, and proceeded into the chamber of presence; where I saw the King seated on his throne, attended on each side by persons of prime quality. Before the throne was a large table filled with globes and spheres, and mathematical instruments of all kinds. His Majesty took not the least notice of us, although our entrance was not without sufficient noise, by the concourse of all persons belonging to the court. But he was then deep in a problem, and we attended at least an hour before he could solve it. There stood by him on each side a young page, with flaps in their hands, and when they saw he was at leisure, one of them gently struck his mouth, and the other his right ear; at which he started like one awaked on the sudden, and looking towards me, and the company I was in, recollected the occasion of our coming, whereof he had been informed before. He spoke some words, whereupon immediately a young man with a flap came up to my side, and flapped me gently on the right ear; but I made signs as well as I could, that I had no occasion for such an instrument; which as I afterwards found gave his Majesty and the whole court a very mean opinion of my understanding. The King, as far as I could conjecture, asked me several questions, and I addressed myself to him in all the languages I had. When it was found that I could neither understand nor be understood, I was conducted by his order to an apartment in his palace (this prince being distinguished above all his predecessors for his hospitality to strangers),[4] where two servants were appointed to attend me. My dinner was brought, and four persons of quality, whom I remembered to have

2. Touch.
3. Gutter.
4. George I, a patron of music and science, had filled his court with Hanoverians when he came to England in 1714.

seen very near the King's person, did me the honor to dine with me. We had two courses, of three dishes each. In the first course there was a shoulder of mutton, cut into an equilateral triangle; a piece of beef into a rhomboid; and a pudding into a cycloid. The second course was two ducks, trussed up into the form of fiddles; sausages and pudding resembling flutes and haut-boys,[5] and a breast of veal in the shape of a harp. The servants cut our bread into cones, cylinders, parallelograms, and several other mathematical figures.

While we were at dinner, I made bold to ask the names of several things in their language, and those noble persons, by the assistance of their flappers, delighted to give me answers, hoping to raise my admiration of their great abilities, if I could be brought to converse with them. I was soon able to call for bread and drink, or whatever else I wanted.

After dinner my company withdrew, and a person was sent to me by the King's order, attended by a flapper. He brought with him pen, ink, and paper, and three or four books; giving me to understand by signs, that he was sent to teach me the language. We sat together four hours, in which time I wrote down a great number of words in columns, with the translations over against them. I likewise made a shift to learn several short sentences. For my tutor would order one of my servants to fetch something, to turn about, to make a bow, to sit, or stand, or walk, and the like. Then I took down the sentence in writing. He showed me also in one of his books the figures of the sun, moon, and stars, the zodiac, the tropics and polar circles, together with the denominations of many figures of planes and solids. He gave me the names and descriptions of all the musical instruments, and the general terms of art in playing on each of them. After he had left me, I placed all my words with their interpretations in alphabetical order. And thus in a few days, by the help of a very faithful memory, I got some insight into their language.

The word, which I interpret the *Flying* or *Floating Island,* is in the original *Laputa;* whereof I could never learn the true etymology. *Lap* in the old obsolete language signifieth *high,* and *untuh* a *governor;* from which they say by corruption was derived *Laputa,* from *Lapuntuh.* But I do not approve of this derivation, which seems to be a little strained. I ventured to offer to the learned among them a conjecture of my own, that *Laputa* was *quasi Lap outed; Lap* signifying properly the dancing of the sunbeams in the sea, and *outed* a wing, which however I shall not obtrude, but submit to the judicious reader.[6]

Those to whom the King had entrusted me, observing how ill I was clad, ordered a tailor to come next morning, and take my measure for a suit of clothes. This operator did his office after a different manner from those of his trade in Europe. He first took my altitude by a quadrant, and then, with rule and compasses, described the dimensions and outlines of my whole body; all which he entered upon paper, and in six days brought my clothes very ill made, and quite out of shape, by happening to mistake a figure in the calculation. But my comfort was, that I observed such accidents very frequent, and little regarded.

---

5. Oboes.
6. Gulliver overlooks a likelier etymology: Spanish *la puta,* "the whore."

During my confinement for want of clothes, and by an indisposition that held me some days longer, I much enlarged my dictionary; and when I went next to court, was able to understand many things the King spoke, and to return him some kind of answers. His Majesty had given orders that the island should move northeast and by east, to the vertical point over Lagado, the metropolis of the whole kingdom, below upon the firm earth. It was about ninety leagues distant, and our voyage lasted four days and a half. I was not in the least sensible of the progressive motion made in the air by the island. On the second morning, about eleven o'clock, the King himself in person, attended by his nobility, courtiers, and officers, having prepared all their musical instruments, played on them for three hours without intermission, so that I was quite stunned with the noise; neither could I possibly guess the meaning, till my tutor informed me. He said, that the people of their island had their ears adapted to hear the music of the spheres, which always played at certain periods; and the court was now prepared to bear their part in whatever instrument they most excelled.

In our journey towards Lagado, the capital city, his Majesty ordered that the island should stop over certain towns and villages, from whence he might receive the petitions of his subjects. And to this purpose, several pack-threads were let down with small weights at the bottom. On these pack-threads the people strung their petitions, which mounted up directly like the scraps of paper fastened by schoolboys at the end of the string that holds their kite.[7] Sometimes we received wine and victuals from below, which were drawn up by pulleys.

The knowledge I had in mathematics gave me great assistance in acquiring their phraseology, which depended much upon that science and music; and in the latter I was not unskilled. Their ideas are perpetually conversant in lines and figures. If they would, for example, praise the beauty of a woman, or any other animal, they describe it by rhombs, circles, parallelograms, ellipses, and other geometrical terms; or else by words of art drawn from music, needless here to repeat. I observed in the King's kitchen all sorts of mathematical and musical instruments, after the figures of which they cut up the joints that were served to his Majesty's table.

Their houses are very ill built, the walls bevil, without one right angle in any apartment; and this defect ariseth from the contempt they bear for practical geometry; which they despise as vulgar and mechanic, those instructions they give being too refined for the intellectuals of their workmen; which occasions perpetual mistakes. And although they are dextrous enough upon a piece of paper, in the management of the rule, the pencil, and the divider, yet in the common actions and behavior of life I have not seen a more clumsy, awkward, and unhandy people, nor so slow and perplexed in their conceptions upon all other subjects, except those of mathematics and music. They are very bad reasoners, and vehemently given to opposition, unless when they happen to be of the right opinion, which is seldom their case. Imagination, fancy, and invention, they are wholly strangers to, nor have any words in their language by which those ideas can be

---

7. Petitioners, that is, might as well go fly a kite. Throughout this section Swift satirizes the "distance" of George I (who spent much of his time in Hanover) from his British subjects.

expressed; the whole compass of their thoughts and mind being shut up within the two forementioned sciences.

Most of them, and especially those who deal in the astronomical part, have great faith in judicial astrology, although they are ashamed to own it publicly. But what I chiefly admired,[8] and thought altogether unaccountable, was the strong disposition I observed in them towards news and politics; perpetually enquiring into public affairs, giving their judgments in matters of state; and passionately disputing every inch of a party opinion. I have indeed observed the same disposition among most of the mathematicians I have known in Europe; although I could never discover the least analogy between the two sciences; unless those people suppose, that because the smallest circle hath as many degrees as the largest, therefore the regulation and management of the world require no more abilities than the handling and turning of a globe. But I rather take this quality to spring from a very common infirmity of human nature, inclining us to be more curious and conceited in matters where we have least concern, and for which we are least adapted either by study or nature.

These people are under continual disquietudes, never enjoying a minute's peace of mind; and their disturbances proceed from causes which very little affect the rest of mortals. Their apprehensions arise from several changes they dread in the celestial bodies. For instance; that the earth, by the continual approaches of the sun towards it, must in course of time be absorbed or swallowed up. That the face of the sun will by degrees be encrusted with its own effluvia,[9] and give no more light to the world. That the earth very narrowly escaped a brush from the tail of the last comet, which would have infallibly reduced it to ashes; and that the next, which they have calculated for one and thirty years hence, will probably destroy us.[1] For, if in its perihelion it should approach within a certain degree of the sun (as by their calculations they have reason to dread), it will conceive a degree of heat ten thousand times more intense than that of red-hot glowing iron; and in its absence from the sun, carry a blazing tail ten hundred thousand and fourteen miles long; through which if the earth should pass at the distance of one hundred thousand miles from the nucleus, or main body of the comet, it must in its passage be set on fire, and reduced to ashes. That the sun daily spending its rays without any nutriment to supply them, will at last be wholly consumed and annihilated; which must be attended with the destruction of this earth, and of all the planets that receive their light from it.

They are so perpetually alarmed with the apprehensions of these and the like impending dangers, that they can neither sleep quietly in their beds, nor have any relish for the common pleasures or amusements of life. When they meet an acquaintance in the morning, the first question is about the sun's health, how he looked at his setting and rising, and what hopes they have to avoid the stroke of the approaching comet. This conversation they are apt to run into with the same temper that boys discover in delighting to hear

8. Wondered at.
9. Sunspots.
1. Halley's comet, some astronomers had feared, might strike the earth on its next appearance

(1758). All the disasters that disquiet the Laputans had occurred to English scientists as possible implications of Newtonian theory.

terrible stories of sprites and hobgoblins, which they greedily listen to, and dare not go to bed for fear.

The women of the island have abundance of vivacity; they contemn their husbands, and are exceedingly fond of strangers, whereof there is always a considerable number from the continent below, attending at court, either upon affairs of the several towns and corporations, or their own particular occasions; but are much despised, because they want[2] the same endowments. Among these the ladies choose their gallants: but the vexation is, that they act with too much ease and security; for the husband is always so rapt in speculation, that the mistress and lover may proceed to the greatest familiarities before his face, if he be but provided with paper and implements, and without his flapper at his side.

The wives and daughters lament their confinement to the island, although I think it the most delicious spot of ground in the world; and although they live here in the greatest plenty and magnificence, and are allowed to do whatever they please, they long to see the world, and take the diversions of the metropolis, which they are not allowed to do without a particular license from the King; and this is not easy to be obtained, because the people of quality have found by frequent experience, how hard it is to persuade their women to return from below. I was told that a great court lady, who had several children, is married to the prime minister, the richest subject in the kingdom, a very graceful person, extremely fond of her, and lives in the finest palace of the island, went down to Lagado, on the pretense of health, there hid herself for several months, till the King sent a warrant to search for her, and she was found in an obscure eating-house all in rags, having pawned her clothes to maintain an old deformed footman, who beat her every day, and in whose company she was taken much against her will. And although her husband received her with all possible kindness, and without the least reproach, she soon after contrived to steal down again with all her jewels, to the same gallant, and hath not been heard of since.

This may perhaps pass with the reader rather for an European or English story, than for one of a country so remote. But he may please to consider, that the caprices of womankind are not limited by any climate or nation; and that they are much more uniform than can be easily imagined.

In about a month's time I had made a tolerable proficiency in their language, and was able to answer most of the King's questions, when I had the honor to attend him. His Majesty discovered not the least curiosity to enquire into the laws, government, history, religion, or manners of the countries where I had been; but confined his questions to the state of mathematics, and received the account I gave him with great contempt and indifference, though often roused by his flapper on each side.

2. Lack. "Corporations": municipal authorities.

CHAPTER 3. *A phenomenon solved by modern philosophy and astronomy. The Laputians' great improvements in the latter. The king's method of suppressing insurrections.*

I desired leave of this prince to see the curiosities of the island, which he was graciously pleased to grant, and ordered my tutor to attend me. I chiefly wanted to know to what cause in art or in nature it owed its several motions; whereof I will now give a philosophical account to the reader.

The flying or floating island is exactly circular, its diameter 7837 yards, or about four miles and a half, and consequently contains ten thousand acres. It is three hundred yards thick. The bottom, or under surface, which appears to those who view it from below, is one even regular plate of adamant,[3] shooting up to the height of about two hundred yards. Above it lie the several minerals in their usual order, and over all is a coat of rich mould[4] ten or twelve foot deep. The declivity of the upper surface from the circumference to the center is the natural cause why all the dews and rains which fall upon the island are conveyed in small rivulets toward the middle, where they are emptied into four large basins, each of about half a mile in circuit, and two hundred yards distant from the center. From these basins the water is continually exhaled[5] by the sun in the daytime, which effectually prevents their overflowing. Besides, as it is in the power of the monarch to raise the island above the region of clouds and vapors, he can prevent the falling of dews and rains whenever he pleases. For the highest clouds cannot rise above two miles, as naturalists agree;[6] at least they were never known to do so in that country.

At the center of the island there is a chasm about fifty yards in diameter, from whence the astronomers descend into a large dome, which is therefore called *Flandona Gagnole*, or the astronomer's cave, situated at the depth of an hundred yards beneath the upper surface of the adamant. In this cave are twenty lamps continually burning, which from the reflection of the adamant cast a strong light into every part. The place is stored with great variety of sextants, quadrants, telescopes, astrolabes, and other astronomical instruments. But the greatest curiosity, upon which the fate of the island depends, is a loadstone[7] of a prodigious size, in shape resembling a weaver's shuttle. It is in length six yards, and in the thickest part at least three yards over.[8] This magnet is sustained by a very strong axle of adamant passing through its middle, upon which it plays,[9] and is poised so exactly that the weakest hand can turn it. It is hooped round with a hollow cylinder of adamant, four feet deep, as many thick, and twelve yards in diameter, placed horizontally, and supported by eight adamantine feet, each six yards high. In the middle of the concave side there is a groove twelve inches deep, in which the extremities of the axle are lodged, and turned round as there is occasion.

This stone cannot be moved from its place by any force, because the hoop and its feet are one continued piece with that body of adamant which constitutes the bottom of the island.

---

3. An extremely hard mineral, not identified otherwise.
4. Soil.
5. Evaporated.
6. The altitude of clouds of course extends considerably higher, but "naturalists" in Swift's time set the limit at two miles.
7. Magnet.
8. Across.
9. Turns freely.

By means of this loadstone, the island is made to rise and fall, and move from one place to another. For with respect to that part of the earth over which the monarch presides, the stone is endued at one of its sides with an attractive power, and at the other with a repulsive. Upon placing the magnet erect with its attracting end towards the earth, the island descends; but when the repelling extremity points downwards, the island mounts directly upwards. When the position of the stone is oblique, the motion of the island is so too: for in this magnet, the forces always act in lines parallel to its direction.

By this oblique motion the island is conveyed to different parts of the monarch's dominions. To explain the manner of its progress, let A B represent a line drawn cross the dominions of Balnibarbi, let the line c d represent the loadstone, of which let d be the repelling end, and c the attracting end, the island being over C: let the stone be placed in position c d, with its repelling end downwards; then the island will be driven upwards obliquely towards D. When it is arrived at D, let the stone be turned upon its axle till its attracting end points towards E, and then the island will be carried obliquely towards E; where if the stone be again turned upon its axle till it stands in the position E F, with its repelling point downwards, the island will rise obliquely towards F, where by directing the attracting end towards G, the island may be carried to G, and from G to H, by turning the stone, so as to make its repelling extremity to point directly downwards. And thus by changing the situation of the stone as often as there is occasion, the island is made to rise and fall by turns in an oblique direction, and by those alternate risings and fallings (the obliquity being not considerable) is conveyed from one part of the dominions to the other.

But it must be observed, that this island cannot move beyond the extent of the dominions below, nor can it rise above the height of four miles. For which the astronomers (who have written large systems[1] concerning the stone) assign the following reason: that the magnetic virtue does not extend beyond the distance of four miles, and that the mineral which acts upon the stone in the bowels of the earth, and in the sea about six leagues distant from the shore, is not diffused through the whole globe, but terminated with the limits of the king's dominions. And it was easy, from the great advantage of such a superior situation, for a prince to bring under his obedience whatever country lay within the attraction of that magnet.

When the stone is put parallel to the plane of the horizon, the island standeth still; for in that case the extremities of it, being at equal distance from the earth, act with equal force, the one in drawing downwards, the other in pushing upwards, and consequently no motion can ensue.

This loadstone is under the care of certain astronomers, who from time to time give it such positions as the monarch directs. They spend the greatest part of their lives in observing the celestial bodies, which they do by the assistance of glasses,[2] far excelling ours in goodness. For although their largest telescopes do not exceed three feet, they magnify much more than those of a hundred with us, and show the stars with greater clearness. This advantage hath enabled them to extend their discoveries much farther than our astronomers in Europe. They have made a catalogue of ten thousand fixed stars,

---

1. Lengthy theoretical works.   2. Telescopes.

whereas the largest of ours do not contain above one third part of that number. They have likewise discovered two lesser stars, or satellites, which revolve about Mars; whereof the innermost is distant from the center of the primary planet exactly three of his diameters, and the outermost, five; the former revolves in the space of ten hours, and the latter in twenty-one and a half; so that the squares of their periodical times are very near in the same proportion with the cubes of their distance from the center of Mars; which evidently shows them to be governed by the same law of gravitation that influences the other heavenly bodies.

They have observed ninety-three different comets, and settled their periods[3] with great exactness. If this be true (and they affirm it with great confidence), it is much to be wished that their observations were made public, whereby the theory of comets, which at present is very lame and defective, might be brought to the same perfection with other parts of astronomy.

The king would be the most absolute prince in the universe, if he could but prevail on a ministry to join with him; but these having their estates below on the continent, and considering that the office of a favorite hath a very uncertain tenure, would never consent to the enslaving of their country.[4]

If any town should engage in rebellion or mutiny, fall into violent factions, or refuse to pay the usual tribute, the king hath two methods of reducing them to obedience. The first and the mildest course is by keeping the island hovering over such a town, and the lands about it, whereby he can deprive them of the benefit of the sun and the rain, and consequently afflict the inhabitants with dearth and diseases: and if the crime deserve it, they are at the same time pelted from above with great stones, against which they have no defense but by creeping into cellars or caves, while the roofs of their houses are beaten to pieces. But if they still continue obstinate, or offer to raise insurrections, he proceeds to the last remedy, by letting the island drop directly upon their heads, which makes a universal destruction both of houses and men. However, this is an extremity to which the prince is seldom driven, neither indeed is he willing to put it in execution; nor dare his ministers advise him to an action, which as it would render them odious to the people, so it would be a great damage to their own estates that lie all below; for the island is the king's demesne.[5]

But there is still indeed a more weighty reason why the kings of this country have been always averse from executing so terrible an action unless upon the utmost necessity. For if the town intended to be destroyed should have in it any tall rocks, as it generally falls out in the larger cities, a situation probably chosen at first with a view to prevent such a catastrophe; or if it abound in high spires or pillars of stone, a sudden fall might endanger the bottom or under surface of the island, which although it consist as I have said, of one entire adamant two hundred yards thick, might happen to crack by too great a shock, or burst by approaching too near the fires from the houses below, as the backs both of iron and stone will often do in our chimneys. Of all this the people are well apprised, and understand how far to carry their obstinacy, where their liberty or property is concerned. And the king, when he is highest

3. The times from one appearance to the next.
4. A reflection on Robert Walpole, prime minister of Britain who, Swift thought, too readily secured parliamentary support for George I and so gave him close to absolute power.
5. The king has no estate other than the island.

provoked, and most determined to press a city to rubbish, orders the island to descend with great gentleness, out of a pretense of tenderness to his people, but indeed for fear of breaking the adamantine bottom; in which case it is the opinion of all their philosophers, that the loadstone could no longer hold it up, and the whole mass would fall to the ground.

By a fundamental law of this realm, neither the king nor either of his two eldest sons are permitted to leave the island; nor the queen till she is past child-bearing.

CHAPTER 4. *The author leaves Laputa, is conveyed to Balnibarbi, arrives at the metropolis. A description of the metropolis and the country adjoining. The author hospitably received by a great lord. His conversation with that lord.*

Although I cannot say that I was ill treated in this island, yet I must confess I thought myself too much neglected, not without some degree of contempt. For neither prince nor people appeared to be curious in any part of knowledge, except mathematics and music, wherein I was far their inferior, and upon that account very little regarded.

On the other side, after having seen all the curiosities of the island, I was very desirous to leave it, being heartily weary of those people. They were indeed excellent in two sciences for which I have great esteem, and wherein I am not unversed; but at the same time so abstracted and involved in speculation that I never met with such disagreeable companions. I conversed only with women, tradesmen, flappers, and court-pages, during two months of my abode there; by which at last I rendered myself extremely contemptible; yet these were the only people from whom I could ever receive a reasonable answer.

I had obtained by hard study a good degree of knowledge in their language: I was weary of being confined to an island where I received so little countenance,[6] and resolved to leave it with the first opportunity.

There was a great lord at court, nearly related to the king, and for that reason alone used[7] with respect. He was universally reckoned the most ignorant and stupid person among them. He had performed many eminent services for the crown, had great natural and acquired parts,[8] adorned with integrity and honor; but so ill an ear for music, that his detractors reported he had been often known to beat time in the wrong place; neither could his tutors without extreme difficulty teach him to demonstrate the most easy proposition in the mathematics. He was pleased to show me many marks of favor, often did me the honor of a visit, desired to be informed in the affairs of Europe, the laws and customs, the manners and learning of the several countries where I had travelled. He listened to me with great attention, and made very wise observations on all I spoke. He had two flappers attending him for state,[9] but never made use of them except at court and in visits of ceremony, and would always command them to withdraw when we were alone together.

6. Respect.
7. Treated.
8. Talents.
9. Ceremonial purposes.

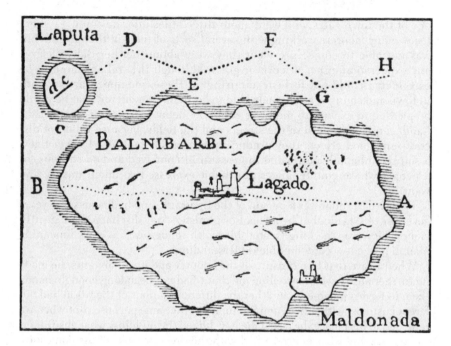

I entreated this illustrious person to intercede in my behalf with his majesty for leave to depart; which he accordingly did, as he was pleased to tell me, with regret. For indeed he had made me several offers very advantageous, which however I refused with expressions of the highest acknowledgment.

On the 16th day of February, I took leave of his majesty and the court. The king made me a present to the value of about two hundred pounds English, and my protector his kinsman as much more, together with a letter of recommendation to a friend of his in Lagado, the metropolis. The island being then hovering over a mountain about two miles from it, I was let down from the lowest gallery, in the same manner as I had been taken up.

The continent, as far as it is subject to the monarch of the flying island, passes under the general name of *Balnibarbi*; and the metropolis, as I said before, is called *Lagado*. I felt some little satisfaction in finding myself on firm ground. I walked to the city without any concern, being clad like one of the natives, and sufficiently instructed to converse with them. I soon found out the person's house to whom I was recommended, presented my letter from his friend the grandee in the island, and was received with much kindness. This great lord, whose name was Munodi, ordered me an apartment in his own house, where I continued during my stay, and was entertained in a most hospitable manner.

The next morning after my arrival he took me in his chariot to see the town, which is about half the bigness of London; but the houses very strangely built, and most of them out of repair. The people in the streets walked fast, looked wild, their eyes fixed, and were generally in rags. We passed through one of the town gates, and went about three miles into the country, where I saw many laborers working with several sorts of tools in the ground, but was not able to conjecture what they were about: neither did I observe any expectation either of corn or grass, although the soil appeared to be excellent. I could not forbear admiring[1] at these odd appearances, both in town and country; and I made bold to desire my conductor, that he would be pleased to explain to me what could be meant by so many busy heads, hands, and faces, both in the streets and the fields, because I did not discover any good effects they produced; but on the contrary, I never knew a soil so unhappily cultivated, houses so ill contrived and so ruinous, or a people whose countenances and habit expressed so much misery and want.

This lord Munodi was a person of the first rank, and had been some years governor of Lagado; but by a cabal of ministers was discharged for insufficiency. However the king treated him with tenderness, as a well-meaning man, but of a low contemptible understanding.

When I gave that free censure of the country and its inhabitants, he made no further answer than by telling me that I had not been long enough among them to form a judgment; and that the different nations of the world had different customs; with other common topics to the same purpose. But when we returned to his palace, he asked me how I liked the building, what absurdities I observed, and what quarrel I had with the dress or looks of his domestics. This he might safely do; because every thing about him was magnificent, regular, and polite. I answered, that his excellency's prudence, quality, and fortune had exempted him from those defects which folly and beggary had produced in others. He said if I would go with him to his country house about twenty miles distant, where his estate lay, there would be more leisure for this kind of conversation. I told his excellency that I was entirely at his disposal; and accordingly we set out next morning.

During our journey, he made me observe the several methods used by farmers in managing their lands, which to me were wholly unaccountable. For except in some very few places, I could not discover one ear of corn or blade of grass. But in three hours travelling, the scene was wholly altered; we came into a most beautiful country; farmers' houses, at small distances, neatly built, the fields enclosed, containing vineyards, corn-grounds, and meadows. Neither do I remember to have seen a more delightful prospect. His excellency observed my countenance to clear up; he told me, with a sigh, that there his estate began, and would continue the same till we should come to his house; that his countrymen ridiculed and despised him for managing his affairs no better, and for setting so ill an example to the kingdom; which however was followed by very few, such as were old and willful, and weak like himself.

We came at length to the house, which was indeed a noble structure, built according to the best rules of ancient architecture. The fountains, gardens, walks, avenues, and groves were all disposed with exact judgment and taste. I gave due praises to every thing I saw, whereof his excellency took not the least notice till after supper; when, there being no third companion, he told me with a very melancholy air that he doubted[2] he must throw down his

1. Wondering.   2. Feared.

houses in town and country, to rebuild them after the present mode; destroy all his plantations, and cast others into such a form as modern usage required, and give the same directions to all his tenants, unless he would submit to incur the censure of pride, singularity, affectation, ignorance, caprice, and perhaps increase his majesty's displeasure.

That the admiration I appeared to be under would cease or diminish when he had informed me of some particulars, which probably I never heard of at court, the people there being too much taken up in their own speculations, to have regard to what passed here below.

The sum of his discourse was to this effect. That about forty years ago, certain persons went up to Laputa, either upon business or diversion; and after five months' continuance, came back with a very little smattering in mathematics, but full of volatile spirits acquired in that airy region: that these persons, upon their return, began to dislike the management of every thing below, and fell into schemes of putting all arts, sciences, languages, and mechanics[3] upon a new foot. To this end they procured a royal patent for erecting an Academy of Projectors[4] in Lagado; and the humor prevailed so strongly among the people, that there is not a town of any consequence in the kingdom without such an academy. In these colleges, the professors contrive new rules and methods of agriculture and building, and new instruments and tools for all trades and manufactures; whereby, as they undertake,[5] one man shall do the work of ten; a palace may be built in a week, of materials so durable as to last forever without repairing. All the fruits of the earth shall come to maturity at whatever season we think fit to choose, and increase a hundred-fold more than they do at present; with innumerable other happy proposals. The only inconvenience is that none of these projects are yet brought to perfection; and in the meantime, the whole country lies miserably waste, the houses in ruins, and the people without food or clothes. By all which, instead of being discouraged, they are fifty times more violently bent upon prosecuting their schemes, driven equally on by hope and despair: that as for himself, being not of an enterprising spirit, he was content to go on in the old forms, to live in the houses his ancestors had built, and act as they did, in every part of life without innovation. That some few other persons of quality and gentry had done the same, but were looked on with an eye of contempt and ill will, as enemies to art, ignorant, and ill commonwealth's men,[6] preferring their own ease and sloth before the general improvement of their country.

His lordship added that he would not by any further particulars prevent the pleasure I should certainly take in viewing the grand academy, whither he was resolved I should go. He only desired me to observe a ruined building upon the side of a mountain about three miles distant, of which he gave me this account. That he had a very convenient mill within half a mile of his house, turned by a current from a large river, and sufficient for his own family as well as a great number of his tenants. That about seven years ago, a club of those projectors came to him with proposals to destroy this mill, and build another on the side of that mountain, on the long ridge whereof a long canal must be cut for a repository of water, to be conveyed up by pipes and

3. Mechanical engineering.
4. Those who promote (often worthless) projects.
5. Promise.
6. Bad citizens.

engines to supply the mill, because the wind and air upon a height agitated the water, and thereby made it fitter for motion; and because the water descending down a declivity would turn the mill with half the current of a river whose course is more upon a level. He said that being then not very well with the court, and pressed by many of his friends, he complied with the proposal; and after employing a hundred men for two years, the work miscarried, the projectors went off, laying the blame entirely upon him, railing at him ever since, and putting others upon the same experiment, with equal assurance of success, as well as equal disappointment.

In a few days we came back to town; and his excellency, considering the bad character he had in the academy, would not go with me himself, but recommended me to a friend of his to bear me company thither. My lord was pleased to represent me as a great admirer of projects, and a person of much curiosity and easy belief; which indeed was not without truth; for I had myself been a sort of projector in my younger days.

CHAPTER 5. *The author permitted to see the grand academy of Lagado. The academy largely described. The arts wherein the professors employ themselves.*

This academy is not an entire single building, but a continuation of several houses on both sides of a street, which growing waste, was purchased and applied to that use.[7]

I was received very kindly by the warden, and went for many days to the academy. Every room hath in it one or more projectors; and I believe I could not be in fewer than five hundred rooms.

The first man I saw was of a meager aspect, with sooty hands and face, his hair and beard long, ragged, and singed in several places. His clothes, shirt, and skin were all of the same color. He had been eight years upon a project for extracting sunbeams out of cucumbers, which were to be put in vials hermetically sealed, and let out to warm the air in raw inclement summers. He told me he did not doubt in eight years more, he should be able to supply the governor's gardens with sunshine at a reasonable rate; but he complained that his stock was low, and entreated me to give him something as an encouragement to ingenuity, especially since this had been a very dear season for cucumbers. I made him a small present, for my lord had furnished me with money on purpose, because he knew their practice of begging from all who go to see them.

I went into another chamber, but was ready to hasten back, being almost overcome with a horrible stink. My conductor pressed me forward, conjuring me in a whisper to give no offence, which would be highly resented; and therefore I durst not so much as stop my nose. The projector of this cell was the most ancient student of the academy; his face and beard were of a pale yellow; his hands and clothes daubed over with filth. When I was presented to him, he gave me a very close embrace (a compliment I could well have excused). His

---

7. Swift here satirizes the Royal Society for Improving Natural Knowledge, the English academy founded in 1660 to promote scientific research, but the layout of the Academy of Lagado more resembles the government buildings at Whitehall than Crane Court, which housed the Royal Society from 1710 to 1780.

employment from his first coming into the academy was an operation to reduce human excrement to its original food, by separating the several parts, removing the tincture which it receives from the gall,[8] making the odor exhale, and scumming off the saliva. He had a weekly allowance from the society, of a vessel filled with human ordure, about the bigness of a Bristol barrel.

I saw another at work to calcine[9] ice into gunpowder; who likewise showed me a treatise he had written concerning the malleability of fire, which he intended to publish.

There was a most ingenious architect who had contrived a new method for building houses by beginning at the roof, and working downwards to the foundation; which he justified to me by the like practice of those two prudent insects, the bee and the spider.

There was a man born blind, who had several apprentices in his own condition: their employment was to mix colors for painters, which their master taught them to distinguish by feeling and smelling. It was indeed my misfortune to find them at that time not very perfect in their lessons; and the professor himself happened to be generally mistaken. This artist is much encouraged and esteemed by the whole fraternity.

In another apartment I was highly pleased with a projector who had found a device of plowing the ground with hogs, to save the charges of plows, cattle, and labor. The method is this: in an acre of ground you bury at six inches distance, and eight deep, a quantity of acorns, dates, chestnuts, and other masts[1] or vegetables whereof these animals are fondest; then you drive six hundred or more of them into the field, where in a few days, they will root up the whole ground in search of their food, and make it fit for sowing, at the same time manuring it with their dung. It is true, upon experiment they found the charge and trouble very great, and they had little or no crop. However it is not doubted that this invention may be capable of great improvement.

I went into another room, where the walls and ceiling were all hung round with cobwebs, except a narrow passage for the artist to go in and out. At my entrance, he called aloud to me not to disturb his webs. He lamented the fatal mistake the world had been so long in of using silkworms, while we had such plenty of domestic insects, who infinitely excelled the former, because they understood how to weave as well as spin. And he proposed farther, that by employing spiders, the charge of dyeing silks should be wholly saved; whereof I was fully convinced when he showed me a vast number of flies[2] most beautifully colored, wherewith he fed his spiders, assuring us that the webs would take a tincture from them; and as he had them of all hues, he hoped to fit everybody's fancy, as soon as he could find proper food for the flies, of certain gums, oils, and other glutinous matter, to give a strength and consistence to the threads.

There was an astronomer who had undertaken to place a sundial upon the great weathercock on the townhouse,[3] by adjusting the annual and diurnal motions of the earth and sun, so as to answer and coincide with all accidental turnings of the wind.

8. Bile, secretion of the liver.
9. "To reduce to quick-lime, or to an analogous substance, by roasting or burning" (Johnson).

1. Nuts used as food for pigs.
2. Butterflies.
3. Town hall.

I was complaining of a small fit of the colic,[4] upon which my conductor led me into a room where a great physician resided, who was famous for curing that disease by contrary operations from the same instrument. He had a large pair of bellows, with a long slender muzzle of ivory. This he conveyed eight inches up the anus, and drawing in the wind, he affirmed he could make the guts as lank as a dried bladder. But when the disease was more stubborn and violent, he let in the muzzle while the bellows was full of wind, which he discharged into the body of the patient; then withdrew the instrument to replenish it, clapping his thumb strongly against the orifice of the fundament;[5] and this being repeated three or four times, the adventitious wind would rush out, bringing the noxious along with it (like water put into a pump) and the patient recovers. I saw him try both experiments upon a dog, but could not discern any effect from the former. After the latter, the animal was ready to burst, and made so violent a discharge as was very offensive to me and my companion. The dog died on the spot, and we left the doctor endeavoring to recover him by the same operation.

I visited many other apartments, but shall not trouble my reader with all the curiosities I observed, being studious of brevity.

I had hitherto seen only one side of the academy, the other being appropriated to the advancers of speculative learning; of whom I shall say something when I have mentioned one illustrious person more, who is called among them *the universal artist*. He told us he had been thirty years employing his thoughts for the improvement of human life. He had two large rooms full of wonderful curiosities, and fifty men at work. Some were condensing air into a dry tangible substance, by extracting the nitre, and letting the aqueous or fluid particles percolate; others softening marble for pillows and pincushions; others petrifying the hoofs of a living horse, to preserve them from foundering.[6] The artist himself was at that time busy upon two great designs; the first, to sow land with chaff, wherein he affirmed the true seminal virtue[7] to be contained, as he demonstrated by several experiments which I was not skillful enough to comprehend. The other was, by a certain composition of gums, minerals, and vegetables, outwardly applied to prevent the growth of wool upon two young lambs; and he hoped in a reasonable time to propagate the breed of naked sheep all over the kingdom.

We crossed a walk to the other part of the academy, where, as I have already said, the projectors in speculative learning resided.

The first professor I saw was in a very large room, with forty pupils about him. After salutation, observing me to look earnestly upon a frame, which took up the greatest part of both the length and breadth of the room, he said, perhaps I might wonder to see him employed in a project for improving speculative knowledge by practical and mechanical operations. But the world would soon be sensible[8] of its usefulness, and he flattered himself that a more noble, exalted thought never sprang in any other man's head. Everyone knew how laborious the usual method is of attaining to arts and sciences;

4. Stomach pains.
5. Buttocks.
6. Succumbing to painful inflammation in the hoof's layers. "Nitre": sodium or potassium nitrate; saltpeter.
7. Power of the seed.
8. Aware.

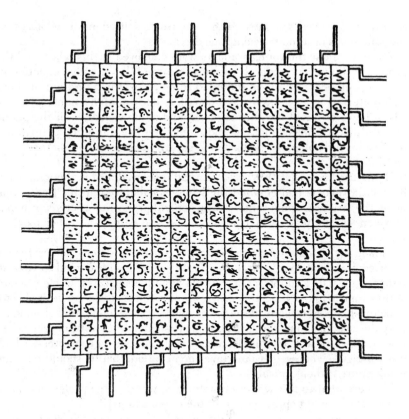

whereas by his contrivance the most ignorant person at a reasonable charge, and with a little bodily labor, may write books in philosophy, poetry, politics, law, mathematics, and theology, without the least assistance from genius or study. He then led me to the frame, about the sides whereof all his pupils stood in ranks. It was twenty foot square, placed in the middle of the room. The superficies[9] was composed of several bits of wood, about the bigness of a die, but some larger than others. They were all linked together by slender wires. These bits of wood were covered on every square with papers pasted on them; and on these papers were written all the words of their language in their several moods, tenses, and declensions, but without any order. The professor then desired me to observe, for he was going to set his engine at work. The pupils at his command took each of them hold of an iron handle, whereof there were forty fixed round the edges of the frame; and giving them a sudden turn, the whole disposition[1] of the words was entirely changed. He then commanded six and thirty of the lads to read the several lines softly as they appeared upon the frame; and where they found three or four words together that might make part of a sentence, they dictated to the four remaining boys who were scribes. This work was repeated three or four times, and at every

9. Surface.   1. Arrangement.

turn the engine was so contrived that the words shifted into new places, as the square bits of wood moved upside down.

Six hours a day the young students were employed in this labor; and the professor showed me several volumes in large folio already collected, of broken sentences, which he intended to piece together, and out of those rich materials to give the world a complete body of all arts and sciences; which however might be still improved, and much expedited, if the public would raise a fund for making and employing five hundred such frames in Lagado, and oblige the managers to contribute in common their several[2] collections.

He assured me, that this invention had employed all his thoughts from his youth, that he had emptied the whole vocabulary into his frame, and made the strictest computation of the general proportion there is in books between the numbers of particles, nouns, and verbs, and other parts of speech.

I made my humblest acknowledgments to this illustrious person for his great communicativeness, and promised if ever I had the good fortune to return to my native country, that I would do him justice, as the sole inventor of this wonderful machine; the form and contrivance of which I desired leave to delineate upon paper as in the figure here annexed. I told him, although it were the custom of our learned in Europe to steal inventions from each other, who had thereby at least this advantage, that it became a controversy which was the right owner, yet I would take such caution, that he should have the honor entire without a rival.

We next went to the school of languages, where three professors sat in consultation upon improving that of their own country.[3]

The first project was to shorten discourse by cutting polysyllables into one, and leaving out verbs and participles, because in reality all things imaginable are but nouns.

The other was a scheme for entirely abolishing all words whatsoever; and this was urged as a great advantage in point of health as well as brevity. For it is plain, that every word we speak is in some degree a diminution of our lungs by corrosion, and consequently contributes to the shortening of our lives. An expedient was therefore offered, that since words are only names for *things*, it would be more convenient for all men to carry about them such *things* as were necessary to express the particular business they are to discourse on. And this invention would certainly have taken place, to the great ease as well as health of the subject, if the women in conjunction with the vulgar and illiterate had not threatened to raise a rebellion, unless they might be allowed the liberty to speak with their tongues, after the manner of their forefathers. Such constant irreconcilable enemies to science[4] are the common people. However, many of the most learned and wise adhere to the new scheme of expressing themselves by *things*, which hath only this inconvenience attending it, that if a man's business be very great, and of various kinds, he must be obliged in proportion to carry a greater bundle of *things* upon his back, unless

2. Separate.
3. Many contemporary scientists had proposed a philosophical language that would eliminate the treacherous disparity between words and things and thus allow accurate scientific discourse.
4. Knowledge.

he can afford one or two strong servants to attend him. I have often beheld two of those sages almost sinking under the weight of their packs, like pedlars among us, who when they met in the streets would lay down their loads, open their sacks, and hold conversation for an hour together, then put up their implements, help each other to resume their burdens, and take their leave.

But for short conversations a man may carry implements in his pockets and under his arms, enough to supply him, and in his house he cannot be at a loss; therefore the room where company meet who practice this art is full of all *things* ready at hand, requisite to furnish matter for this kind of artificial converse.[5]

Another great advantage proposed by this invention was that it would serve as an universal language to be understood in all civilized nations, whose goods and utensils are generally of the same kind, or nearly resembling, so that their uses might easily be comprehended. And thus, ambassadors would be qualified to treat with foreign princes or ministers of state to whose tongues they were utter strangers.

I was at the mathematical school, where the master taught his pupils after a method scarce imaginable to us in Europe. The proposition and demonstration were fairly written on a thin wafer, with ink composed of a cephalic tincture.[6] This the student was to swallow upon a fasting stomach, and for three days following eat nothing but bread and water. As the wafer digested, the tincture mounted to his brain, bearing the proposition along with it. But the success hath not hitherto been answerable, partly by some error in the *quantum* or composition, and partly by the perverseness of lads, to whom this bolus[7] is so nauseous that they generally steal aside, and discharge it upwards before it can operate; neither have they been yet persuaded to use so long an abstinence as the prescription requires.

CHAPTER 6. *A further account of the academy. The author proposeth some improvements, which are honorably received.*

In the school of political projectors, I was but ill entertained; the professors appearing in my judgment wholly out of their senses, which is a scene that never fails to make me melancholy. These unhappy people were proposing schemes for persuading monarchs to choose favorites upon the score of their wisdom, capacity, and virtue; of teaching ministers to consult the public good; of rewarding merit, great abilities, and eminent services; of instructing princes to know their true interest, by placing it on the same foundation with that of their people; of choosing for employments persons qualified to exercise them; with many other wild impossible chimeras, that never entered before into the heart of man to conceive; and confirmed in me the old observation, that there is nothing so extravagant and irrational which some philosophers have not maintained for truth.

---

5. The Royal Society had sponsored a collection intended to contain one specimen of every thing in the world.

6. A solution or dye directed toward the head.

7. A large pill. *"Quantum"*: amount.

But, however, I shall so far do justice to this part of the Academy, as to acknowledge that all of them were not so visionary. There was a most ingenious doctor who seemed to be perfectly versed in the whole nature and system of government. This illustrious person had very usefully employed his studies in finding out effectual remedies for all diseases and corruptions to which the several kinds of public administration are subject by the vices or infirmities of those who govern, as well as by the licentiousness of those who are to obey. For instance: whereas all writers and reasoners have agreed that there is a strict universal resemblance between the natural and the political body; can there be anything more evident than that the health of both must be preserved, and the diseases cured, by the same prescriptions? It is allowed that senates and great councils are often troubled with redundant, ebullient, and other peccant humors;[8] with many diseases of the head, and more of the heart; with strong convulsions, with grievous contractions of the nerves and sinews in both hands, but especially the right;[9] with spleen, flatus, vertigos, and deliriums; with scrofulous tumors full of fetid purulent matter; with sour frothy ructations: with canine[1] appetites and crudeness of digestion, besides many others needless to mention. This doctor therefore proposed that upon the meeting of a senate, certain physicians should attend at the three first days of their sitting, and at the close of each day's debate feel the pulses of every senator; after which having maturely considered and consulted upon the nature of the several maladies, and the methods of cure, they should on the fourth day return to the senate house, attended by their apothecaries stored with proper medicines; and before the members sat, administer to each of them lenitives, aperitives, abstersives, corrosives, restringents, palliatives, laxatives, cephalalgics, icterics, apophlegmatics, acoustics,[2] as their several cases required; and according as these medicines should operate, repeat, alter, or omit them at the next meeting.

This project could not be of any great expense to the public; and might in my poor opinion be of much use for the dispatch of business in those countries where senates have any share in the legislative power; beget unanimity, shorten debates, open a few mouths which are now closed, and close many more which are now open; curb the petulancy of the young, and correct the positiveness[3] of the old; rouse the stupid, and damp the pert.

Again, because it is a general complaint that the favorites of princes are troubled with short and weak memories, the same doctor proposed that whoever attended a first minister, after having told his business with the utmost brevity, and in the plainest words, should at his departure give the said minister a tweak by the nose, or a kick in the belly, or tread on his corns, or lug him thrice by both ears, or run a pin into his breech;

---

8. Swift uses terms pertaining to the humors, the system of fluids understood as the basis for bodily health and disease. "Ebullient": agitated, as if by boiling. "Peccant": causing disease.
9. The hand that takes bribes.
1. Greedily hungry. "Ructations": belchings.
2. Medicines to improve hearing. "Lenitives": laxatives. "Aperitives": medicines that open the bowels. "Abstersives": medicinal purges. "Corrosives": substances that burn tissue. "Restringents": medicines that prevent flow of bodily fluids. "Palliatives": any agents that improve symptoms. "Cephalalgics": headache treatments. "Icterics": cures for jaundice. "Apophlegmatics": removers of phlegm.
3. Dogmatic inflexibility.

or pinch his arm black and blue, to prevent forgetfulness; and at every levee day[4] repeat the same operation, till the business were done or absolutely refused.

He likewise directed that every senator in the great council of a nation, after he had delivered his opinion and argued in the defense of it, should be obliged to give his vote directly contrary; because if that were done, the result would infallibly terminate in the good of the public.

When parties in a state are violent,[5] he offered a wonderful contrivance to reconcile them. The method is this. You take an hundred leaders of each party; you dispose them into couples of such whose heads are nearest of a size; then let two nice operators saw off the occiput[6] of each couple at the same time, in such a manner that the brain may be equally divided. Let the occiputs thus cut off be interchanged, applying each to the head of his opposite party-man. It seems indeed to be a work that requireth some exactness, but the professor assured us that if it were dexterously performed, the cure would be infallible. For he argued thus, that the two half brains being left to debate the matter between themselves within the space of one skull, would soon come to a good understanding, and produce that moderation as well as regularity of thinking, so much to be wished for in the heads of those who imagine they came into the world only to watch and govern its motion: and as to the difference of brains in quantity or quality, among those who are directors in faction, the doctor assured us, from his own knowledge, that it was a perfect trifle.

I heard a very warm debate between two professors about the most commodious and effectual ways and means of raising money without grieving the subject. The first affirmed the justest method would be to lay a certain tax upon vices and folly; and the sum fixed upon every man to be rated after the fairest manner by a jury of his neighbors. The second was of an opinion directly contrary: to tax those qualities of body and mind for which men chiefly value themselves, the rate to be more or less according to the degrees of excelling; the decision whereof should be left entirely to their own breast. The highest tax was upon men who are the greatest favorites of the other sex, and the assessments according to the number and natures of the favors they have received; for which they are allowed to be their own vouchers. Wit, valor, and politeness were likewise proposed to be largely taxed and collected in the same manner, by every person giving his own word for the quantum of what he possessed. But as to honor, justice, wisdom, and learning, they should not be taxed at all; because they are qualifications of so singular a kind that no man will either allow them in his neighbor or value them in himself.

The women were proposed to be taxed according to their beauty and skill in dressing, wherein they had the same privilege with the men, to be determined by their own judgment. But constancy, chastity, good sense, and good nature were not rated, because they would not bear the charge of collecting.[7]

---

4. Day on which meetings are conducted. "Lug": tug.
5. When politics is highly partisan.
6. Back part of the head. "Nice operators": pre-

cise surgeons.
7. Raise enough to pay for the cost of collecting the tax.

To keep senators in the interest of the crown, it was proposed that the members should raffle for employments; every man first taking an oath and giving security that he would vote for the court, whether he won or no; after which the losers had in their turn the liberty of raffling upon the next vacancy. Thus hope and expectation would be kept alive; none would complain of broken promises, but impute their disappointments wholly to fortune, whose shoulders are broader and stronger than those of a ministry.

Another professor showed me a large paper of instructions for discovering plots and conspiracies against the government. He advised great statesmen to examine into the diet of all suspected persons; their times of eating; upon which side they lay in bed; with which hand they wipe their posteriors; to take a strict view of their excrements and from the color, the odor, the taste, the consistence, the crudeness or maturity of digestion, form a judgment of their thoughts and designs; because men are never so serious, thoughtful, and intent, as when they are at stool, which he found by frequent experiment; for in such conjunctures, when he used merely as a trial to consider which was the best way of murdering the king, his ordure would have a tincture of green; but quite different when he thought only of raising an insurrection, or burning the metropolis.[8]

The whole discourse was written with great acuteness, containing many observations, both curious and useful for politicians; but as I conceived not altogether complete. This I ventured to tell the author, and offered if he pleased to supply him with some additions. He received my proposition with more compliance than is usual among writers, especially those of the projecting species, professing he would be glad to receive farther information.

I told him that in the kingdom of Tribnia, by the natives called Langden,[9] where I had long sojourned, the bulk of the people consisted wholly of discoverers, witnesses, informers, accusers, prosecutors, evidences, swearers, together with their several subservient and subaltern instruments, all under the colors, the conduct,[1] and pay of ministers and their deputies. The plots in that kingdom are usually the workmanship of those persons who desire to raise their own characters of profound politicians; to restore new vigor to a crazy[2] administration; to stifle or divert general discontents; to fill their coffers with forfeitures;[3] and raise or sink the opinion of public credit,[4] as either shall best answer their private advantage. It is first agreed and settled among them what suspected persons shall be accused of a plot. Then effectual care is taken to secure all their letters and other papers, and put the owners in chains. These papers are delivered to a set of artists[5] very dexterous in finding out the mysterious meanings of words, syllables, and letters: for instance, they can decipher a close stool to signify a privy council;[6] a flock of geese, a senate; a

8. When Bishop Francis Atterbury was tried in 1722 for participating a Jacobite plot, part of the evidence against him were letters in code (which his friend Swift thought were spurious) supposedly found in his toilet.
9. Anagram for *England*. "Tribina": anagram for *Britain*.
1. Direction. Colors: allegiances.

2. Unsound. "Characters of": reputations as.
3. Property or money forfeited to the government as punishment for crimes.
4. Price of government bonds.
5. Skilled persons. Swift alludes to government agents who discover, as in the Atterbury trial, hidden meanings in private correspondence.
6. Advisers to the king. "Close stool": toilet.

lame dog, an invader; the plague, a standing army;[7] a buzzard, a minister; the gout, a high priest; a gibbet, a secretary of state; a chamber pot, a committee of grandees; a sieve, a court lady; a broom, a revolution; a mouse-trap, an employment; a bottomless pit, a treasury; a sink, a court; a cap and bells, a favorite; a broken reed, a court of justice; an empty tun,[8] a general; a running sore, the administration.

When this method fails, they have two others more effectual, which the learned among them call acrostics and anagrams. First, they can decipher all initial letters into political meanings. Thus N shall signify a plot; B, a regiment of horse; L, a fleet at sea. Or, secondly, by transposing the letters of the alphabet in any suspected paper, they can lay open the deepest designs of a discontented party. So, for example, if I should say in a letter to a friend, "Our brother Tom hath just got the piles,"[9] a man of skill in this art would discover how the same letters which compose that sentence, may be analyzed into the following words: "Resist—a plot is brought home—The tour." And this is the anagrammatic method.

The professor made me great acknowledgments for communicating these observations, and promised to make honorable mention of me in his treatise.

I saw nothing in this country that could invite me to a longer continuance, and began to think of returning home to England.

CHAPTER 7. *The author leaves Lagado: arrives at Maldonada.[1] No ship ready. He takes a short voyage to Glubbdubdrib. His reception by the governor.*

The continent of which this kingdom is a part extends itself, as I have reason to believe, eastward to that unknown tract of America westward of California, and north to the Pacific Ocean, which is not above an hundred and fifty miles from Lagado; where there is a good port and much commerce with the great island of Luggnagg, situated to the northwest about 29 degrees north latitude, and 140 longitude. This island of Luggnagg stands southeastwards of Japan, about an hundred leagues distant. There is a strict alliance between the Japanese emperor and the king of Luggnagg, which affords frequent opportunities of sailing from one island to the other. I determined therefore to direct my course this way, in order to my return to Europe. I hired two mules with a guide to show me the way, and carry my small baggage. I took leave of my noble protector, who had shown me so much favor, and made me a generous present at my departure.

My journey was without any accident or adventure worth relating. When I arrived at the port of Maldonada (for so it is called) there was no ship in the harbor bound for Luggnagg, nor like to be in some time. The town is about as large as Portsmouth. I soon fell into some acquaintance, and was very hospitably received. A gentleman of distinction said to me, that since the ships bound for Luggnagg could not be ready in less than a month, it might be no disagreeable amusement for me to take a trip to the little island of Glubbdubdrib, about five leagues off to the southwest. He offered himself and a friend

---

7. An army of full-time paid soldiers, as opposed to a militia. "Lame dog": Atterbury's dog, Harlequin, a gift from his wife in France (where the Old Pretender resided), was used in evidence against him at trial.
8. Cask.
9. Hemorrhoids.
1. Ill-favored (Spanish).

to accompany me, and that I should be provided with a small convenient bark for the voyage.

Glubbdubdrib, as nearly as I can interpret the word, signifies the Island of Sorcerers or Magicians. It is about one third as large as the Isle of Wight,[2] and extremely fruitful: it is governed by the head of a certain tribe, who are all magicians. This tribe marries only among each other, and the eldest in succession is prince or governor. He hath a noble palace, and a park of about three thousand acres, surrounded by a wall of hewn stone twenty foot high. In this park are several small enclosures for cattle, corn, and gardening.

The governor and his family are served and attended by domestics of a kind somewhat unusual. By his skill in necromancy he hath a power of calling whom he pleaseth from the dead, and commanding their service for twenty-four hours, but no longer; nor can he call the same persons up again in less than three months, except upon very extraordinary occasions.

When we arrived at the island, which was about eleven in the morning, one of the gentlemen who accompanied me went to the governor, and desired admittance for a stranger, who came on purpose to have the honor of attending on his highness. This was immediately granted, and we all three entered the gate of the palace between two rows of guards, armed and dressed after a very antic[3] manner, and with something in their countenances that made my flesh creep with a horror I cannot express. We passed through several apartments between servants of the same sort, ranked on each side as before, till we came to the chamber of presence, where after three profound obeisances,[4] and a few general questions, we were permitted to sit on three stools near the lowest step of his highness's throne. He understood the language of Balnibarbi, although it were different from that of his island. He desired me to give him some account of my travels; and to let me see that I should be treated without ceremony, he dismissed all his attendants with a turn of his finger; at which to my great astonishment they vanished in an instant, like visions in a dream, when we awake on a sudden. I could not recover myself in some time, till the governor assured me that I should receive no hurt: and observing my two companions to be under no concern, who had been often entertained in the same manner, I began to take courage, and related to his highness a short history of my several adventures; yet not without some hesitation, and frequently looking behind me to the place where I had seen those domestic specters. I had the honor to dine with the governor, where a new set of ghosts served up the meat, and waited at table. I now observed myself to be less terrified than I had been in the morning. I stayed till sunset, but humbly desired his highness to excuse me for not accepting his invitation of lodging in the palace. My two friends and I lay at a private house in the town adjoining, which is the capital of this little island; and the next morning we returned to pay our duty to the governor, as he was pleased to command us.

After this manner we continued in the island for ten days, most part of every day with the governor, and at night in our lodging. I soon grew so

2. Off the southern coast of England with an area of 148 square miles.

3. Bizarre.

4. Bows.

familiarized to the sight of spirits, that after the third or fourth time they gave me no emotion at all; or if I had any apprehensions left, my curiosity prevailed over them. For his highness the governor ordered me to call up whatever persons I would choose to name, and in whatever numbers among all the dead from the beginning of the world to the present time, and command them to answer any questions I should think fit to ask; with this condition, that my questions must be confined within the compass of the times they lived in. And one thing I might depend upon, that they would certainly tell me truth, for lying was a talent of no use in the lower world.

I made my humble acknowledgments to his highness for so great a favor. We were in a chamber, from whence there was a fair prospect into the park. And because my first inclination was to be entertained with scenes of pomp and magnificence, I desired to see Alexander the Great at the head of his army just after the battle of Arbela: which upon a motion of the governor's finger immediately appeared in a large field under the window where we stood. Alexander was called up into the room: it was with great difficulty that I understood his Greek, and had but little of my own. He assured me upon his honor that he was not poisoned, but died of a fever by excessive drinking.[5]

Next, I saw Hannibal passing the Alps, who told me he had not a drop of vinegar in his camp.[6]

I saw Caesar and Pompey at the head of their troops just ready to engage.[7] I saw the former in his last great triumph. I desired that the senate of Rome might appear before me in one large chamber, and a modern representative,[8] in counterview, in another. The first seemed to be an assembly of heroes and demigods; the other a knot of peddlers, pickpockets, highwaymen, and bullies.

The governor at my request gave the sign for Caesar and Brutus to advance towards us. I was struck with a profound veneration at the sight of Brutus,[9] and could easily discover the most consummate virtue, the greatest intrepidity and firmness of mind, the truest love of his country, and general benevolence for mankind, in every lineament of his countenance. I observed with much pleasure that these two persons were in good intelligence[1] with each other; and Caesar freely confessed to me, that the greatest actions of his own life were not equal by many degrees to the glory of taking it away. I had the honor to have much conversation with Brutus; and was told that his ancestor Junius, Socrates, Epaminondas, Cato the younger, Sir Thomas More, and himself were perpetually together: a sextumvirate[2] to which all the ages of the world cannot add a seventh.

---

5. Various theories, including the one Gulliver mentions, have been proposed as the cause of death of Alexander the Great (356–323 B.C.E.). He won the Battle of Arbela (also called the Battle of Gaugamela), against forces of the Persian empire in 331 B.C.E.
6. According to Roman historian Livy (59 B.C.E.–17 C.E.), the Carthaginian general Hannibal (247–181 B.C.E.) used vinegar and fire to break through a rockslide in the Alps as his army marched toward Rome.
7. In the Battle of Pharsalus (48 B.C.E.) during the Roman civil war, Julius Caesar (100–44 B.C.E.) decisively defeated Pompey (106–48 B.C.E.).

8. Assembly, representative body.
9. Marcus Junius Brutus (85 B.C.E.–42 B.C.E.) assassinated Julius Caesar to preserve the Roman Republic.
1. On good terms.
2. Group of six men (Latin). Lucius Junius Brutus, known as Junius, founder of the Roman Republic in 509 B.C.E. Socrates (470–399 B.C.E.), Greek philosopher. Epaminondas (4th century B.C.E.), Theban general and statesman. Marcus Porcius Cato Uticensis, known as Cato the Younger (95–46 B.C.E.), Roman statesman. More (1478–1535), English lawyer, statesman, and author.

It would be tedious to trouble the reader with relating what vast numbers of illustrious persons were called up to gratify that insatiable desire I had to see the world in every period of antiquity placed before me. I chiefly fed mine eyes with beholding the destroyers of tyrants and usurpers, and the restorers of liberty to oppressed and injured nations. But it is impossible to express the satisfaction I received in my own mind, after such a manner as to make it a suitable entertainment to the reader.

CHAPTER 8. *A further account of Glubbdubdrib. Ancient and modern history corrected.*

Having a desire to see those ancients who were most renowned for wit and learning, I set apart one day on purpose. I proposed that Homer and Aristotle might appear at the head of all their commentators; but these were so numerous, that some hundreds were forced to attend in the court and outward rooms of the palace. I knew and could distinguish those two heroes at first sight, not only from the crowd, but from each other. Homer was the taller and comelier person of the two, walked very erect for one of his age, and his eyes were the most quick and piercing I ever beheld.[3] Aristotle stooped much, and made use of a staff. His visage was meager, his hair lank and thin, and his voice hollow. I soon discovered that both of them were perfect strangers to the rest of the company, and had never seen or heard of them before; and I had a whisper from a ghost who shall be nameless, that these commentators always kept in the most distant quarters from their principals in the lower world, through a consciousness of shame and guilt, because they had so horribly misrepresented the meaning of those authors to posterity. I introduced Didymus and Eustathius[4] to Homer, and prevailed on him to treat them better than perhaps they deserved, for he soon found they wanted a genius to enter into the spirit of a poet. But Aristotle was out of all patience with the account I gave him of Scotus and Ramus,[5] as I presented them to him; and he asked them whether the rest of the tribe were as great dunces[6] as themselves.

I then desired the governor to call up Descartes and Gassendi,[7] with whom I prevailed to explain their systems to Aristotle. This great philosopher freely acknowledged his own mistakes in natural philosophy, because he proceeded in many things upon conjecture, as all men must do; and he found that Gassendi, who had made the doctrine of Epicurus as palatable as he could, and the vortices[8] of Descartes, were equally exploded. He predicted the same fate to *attraction*,[9] whereof the present learned are such

3. Tradition has it that Homer was blind.
4. Greek bishop (ca. 1115–1195), author of commentaries on Homer's epics: Didymus Chalcenterus (ca. 63 B.C.E.–10 C.E.), Greek scholar and grammarian.
5. Petrus Ramus (1515–1572), French humanist and critic of Aristotlean scholasticism. John Duns Scotus (ca. 1266–1308), Scottish philosopher and theologian, commentator on Aristotle.
6. The word *dunce* derives from Duns Scotus's name, used by 16th-century humanists as synonymous with useless scholarship and unsound

reasoning.
7. René Descartes (1596–1650) and Pierre Gassendi (1592–1655), French philosophers.
8. Descartes's physics defined vortices as circling bands of material particles that, among other things, explained the motions of celestial bodies. Epicurus (341–270 B.C.E.), Greek philosopher whose doctrine that the universe consists of atoms and void was revived by Gassendi, who sought to reconcile it with Christianity.
9. The theory of gravity of Isaac Newton (1642–1727).

zealous asserters. He said that new systems of nature were but new fashions, which would vary in every age; and even those who pretend to demonstrate them from mathematical principles would flourish but a short period of time, and be out of vogue when that was determined.[1]

I spent five days in conversing with many others of the ancient learned. I saw most of the first Roman emperors. I prevailed on the governor to call up Eliogabalus's cooks[2] to dress us a dinner, but they could not show us much of their skill, for want of materials. A helot of Agesilaus made us a dish of Spartan broth,[3] but I was not able to get down a second spoonful.

The two gentlemen who conducted me to the island were pressed by their private affairs to return in three days, which I employed in seeing some of the modern dead, who had made the greatest figure for two or three hundred years past in our own and other countries of Europe; and having been always a great admirer of old illustrious families, I desired the governor would call up a dozen or two of kings with their ancestors in order for eight or nine generations. But my disappointment was grievous and unexpected. For instead of a long train with royal diadems, I saw in one family two fiddlers, three spruce[4] courtiers, and an Italian prelate. In another, a barber, an abbot, and two cardinals. I have too great a veneration for crowned heads to dwell any longer on so nice[5] a subject. But as to counts, marquises, dukes, earls, and the like, I was not so scrupulous. And I confess it was not without some pleasure that I found myself able to trace the particular features by which certain families are distinguished up to their originals. I could plainly discover whence one family derives a long chin;[6] why a second hath abounded with knaves for two generations, and fools for two more; why a third happened to be crack-brained, and a fourth to be sharpers.[7] Whence it came, what Polydore Virgil says of a certain great house, *Nec vir fortis, nec foemina casta*;[8] how cruelty, falsehood, and cowardice grew to be characteristics by which certain families are distinguished as much as by their coat of arms; who first brought the pox[9] into a noble house, which hath lineally descended in scrofulous tumors to their posterity. Neither could I wonder at all this, when I saw such an interruption of lineages by pages, lackeys, valets, coachmen, gamesters, fiddlers, players, captains, and pickpockets.

I was chiefly disgusted with modern history. For having strictly examined all the persons of greatest name in the courts of princes for a hundred years past, I found how the world had been misled by prostitute writers to ascribe the greatest exploits in war to cowards, the wisest counsel to fools, sincerity to flatterers, Roman virtue to betrayers of their country, piety to atheists, chastity to sodomites, truth to informers. How many innocent and excellent persons had

---

1. When that period of time came to an end.
2. Roman emperor Heliogabalus or Elagabalus (ca. 203–222 C.E.) was notorious for overindulgence.
3. Unappetizing black broth eaten by Spartan armies. "Helot": one of the subordinated population of ancient Sparta. Agesilaus II (ca. 444–ca. 360 B.C.E.), king of Sparta.
4. Dapper.
5. Delicate.

6. The Hapsburgs, the family whose members occupied the throne of the Holy Roman Empire, were noted for their large chins.
7. Cheats. "Crack-brained": intellectually impaired.
8. Not a man was brave, nor a woman chaste (Latin). Polydore Vergil (ca. 1470–1555), Italian humanist scholar who spent most of his life in England.
9. Syphilis.

396 | JONATHAN SWIFT

been condemned to death or banishment by the practicing of great ministers upon the corruption of judges, and the malice of factions. How many villains had been exalted to the highest places of trust, power, dignity, and profit: how great a share in the motions and events of courts, councils, and senates might be challenged by bawds, whores, pimps, parasites, and buffoons. How low an opinion I had of human wisdom and integrity, when I was truly informed of the springs and motives of great enterprises and revolutions in the world, and of the contemptible accidents to which they owed their success.

Here I discovered the roguery and ignorance of those who pretend to write anecdotes, or secret history;[1] who send so many kings to their graves with a cup of poison; will repeat the discourse between a prince and chief minister, where no witness was by; unlock the thoughts and cabinets of ambassadors and secretaries of state; and have the perpetual misfortune to be mistaken. Here I discovered the true causes of many great events that have surprised the world; how a whore can govern the back stairs,[2] the back stairs a council, and the council a senate. A general confessed in my presence that he got a victory purely by the force of cowardice and ill conduct; and an admiral that, for want of proper intelligence, he beat the enemy to whom he intended to betray the fleet. Three kings protested to me that in their whole reigns they never did once prefer any person of merit, unless by mistake or treachery of some minister in whom they confided. Neither would they do it if they were to live again: and they showed with great strength of reason that the royal throne could not be supported without corruption, because that positive, confident, restive temper which virtue infused into man was a perpetual clog to public business.

I had the curiosity to inquire in a particular manner by what methods great numbers had procured to themselves high titles of honor and prodigious estates; and I confined my inquiry to a very modern period: however, without grating upon present times, because I would be sure to give no offence even to foreigners (for I hope the reader need not be told that I do not in the least intend my own country in what I say upon this occasion). A great number of persons concerned were called up; and, upon a very slight examination, discovered such a scene of infamy, that I cannot reflect upon it without some seriousness. Perjury, oppression, subornation, fraud, panderism,[3] and the like infirmities were amongst the most excusable arts they had to mention; and for these I gave, as it was reasonable, due allowance. But when some confessed they owed their greatness and wealth to sodomy or incest; others, to the prostituting of their own wives and daughters; others, to the betraying of their country or their prince; some to poisoning, more to the perverting of justice in order to destroy the innocent; I hope I may be pardoned if these discoveries inclined me a little to abate of that profound veneration which I am naturally apt to pay to persons of high rank, who ought to be treated with the utmost respect due to their sublime dignity, by us their inferiors.

I had often read of some great services done to princes and states, and desired to see the persons by whom those services were performed. Upon

1. Gossipy narratives of scandal, often with fictionalized names meant to be decoded.
2. Private intrigues of the powerful.
3. Pimping.

inquiry I was told that their names were to be found on no record, except a few of them whom history hath represented as the vilest rogues and traitors. As to the rest, I had never once heard of them. They all appeared with dejected looks, and in the meanest habit; most of them telling me they died in poverty and disgrace, and the rest on a scaffold or a gibbet.

Among others there was one person whose case appeared a little singular. He had a youth about eighteen years old standing by his side. He told me he had for many years been commander of a ship; and in the sea fight at Actium,[4] had the good fortune to break through the enemy's great line of battle, sink three of their capital ships, and take a fourth, which was the sole cause of Antony's flight, and of the victory that ensued; that the youth standing by him, his only son, was killed in the action. He added that upon the confidence of some merit, the war being at an end, he went to Rome, and solicited at the court of Augustus to be preferred to a greater ship whose commander had been killed; but, without any regard to his pretensions, it was given to a boy who had never seen the sea, the son of a libertina,[5] who waited on one of the emperor's mistresses. Returning back to his own vessel, he was charged with neglect of duty, and the ship given to a favorite page of Publicola[6] the vice-admiral; whereupon he retired to a poor farm at a great distance from Rome, and there ended his life. I was so curious to know the truth of this story, that I desired Agrippa[7] might be called, who was admiral in that fight. He appeared and confirmed the whole account, but with much more advantage to the captain, whose modesty had extenuated or concealed a great part of his merit.

I was surprised to find corruption grown so high and so quick in that empire, by the force of luxury so lately introduced; which made me less wonder at many parallel cases in other countries, where vices of all kinds have reigned so much longer, and where the whole praise, as well as pillage, hath been engrossed by the chief commander, who perhaps had the least title to either.

As every person called up made exactly the same appearance he had done in the world, it gave me melancholy reflections to observe how much the race of human kind was degenerate among us within these hundred years past; how the pox under all its consequences and denominations had altered every lineament of an English countenance; shortened the size of bodies, unbraced[8] the nerves, relaxed the sinews and muscles, introduced a sallow complexion, and rendered the flesh loose and rancid.

I descended so low as to desire some English yeoman of the old stamp might be summoned to appear; once so famous for the simplicity of their manners, diet, and dress; for justice in their dealings; for their true spirit of liberty; for their valor and love of their country. Neither could I be wholly unmoved after comparing the living with the dead, when I considered how all these pure native virtues were prostituted for a piece of money by

---

4. Naval battle of 31 B.C.E. at which Mark Antony and Cleopatra were defeated by Octavian, later called Augustus.
5. A freedwoman, a former slave; prostitutes normally belonged to this class in ancient Rome.
6. Lucius Gellius Publicola, Roman consul (36 B.C.E.), though rewarded here by Augustus, commanded some of Antony's forces at Actium.
7. Marcus Vipsanius Agrippa (64/63–12 B.C.E.), Roman general credited for securing Octavian's victory at Actium.
8. Slackened.

their grandchildren; who in selling their votes and managing at[9] elections, have acquired every vice and corruption that can possibly be learned in a court.

CHAPTER 9. *The author returns to Maldonada. Sails to the kingdom of Lug-gnagg. The author confined. He is sent for to court. The manner of his admittance. The king's great lenity to his subjects.*

The day of our departure being come, I took leave of his highness, the Governor of Glubbdubdrib, and returned with my two companions to Maldonada, where after a fortnight's waiting, a ship was ready to sail for Luggnagg. The two gentlemen and some others were so generous and kind as to furnish me with provisions, and see me on board. I was a month in this voyage. We had one violent storm, and were under a necessity of steering westward to get into the trade wind, which holds for above sixty leagues. On the 21st of April, 1708, we sailed into the river of Clumegnig, which is a seaport town, at the southeast point of Luggnagg. We cast anchor within a league of the town, and made a signal for a pilot. Two of them came on board in less than half an hour, by whom we were guided between certain shoals and rocks, which are very dangerous in the passage, to a large basin, where a fleet may ride in safety within a cable's length of the town wall.

Some of our sailors, whether out of treachery or inadvertence, had informed the pilots that I was a stranger and great traveller, whereof these gave notice to a custom-house officer, by whom I was examined very strictly upon my landing. This officer spoke to me in the language of Balnibarbi, which by the force of much commerce is generally understood in that town, especially by seamen and those employed in the customs. I gave him a short account of some particulars, and made my story as plausible and consistent as I could; but I thought it necessary to disguise my country, and call myself a Hollander; because my intentions were for Japan, and I knew the Dutch were the only Europeans permitted to enter into that kingdom. I therefore told the officer, that having been shipwrecked on the coast of Balnibarbi, and cast on a rock, I was received up into Laputa, or the flying island (of which he had often heard), and was now endeavoring to get to Japan, whence I might find a convenience of returning to my own country. The officer said I must be confined till he could receive orders from court, for which he would write immediately, and hoped to receive an answer in a fortnight. I was carried to a convenient lodging with a sentry placed at the door; however, I had the liberty of a large garden, and was treated with humanity enough, being maintained all the time at the king's charge. I was invited by several persons, chiefly out of curiosity, because it was reported that I came from countries very remote, of which they had never heard.

I hired a young man who came in the same ship to be an interpreter; he was a native of Luggnagg, but had lived some years at Maldonada, and was a perfect master of both languages. By his assistance, I was able to hold a conversation with those who came to visit me; but this consisted only of their questions and my answers.

9. Corruptly influencing.

The dispatch came from court about the time we expected. It contained a warrant for conducting me and my retinue to *Traldragdubh*, or *Trildrogdrib* (for it is pronounced both ways as near as I can remember), by a party of ten horse. All my retinue was that poor lad for an interpreter, whom I persuaded into my service. At my humble request we had each of us a mule to ride on. A messenger was dispatched half a day's journey before us, to give the king notice of my approach, and to desire that his majesty would please to appoint a day and hour, when it would be his gracious pleasure that I might have the honor to lick the dust before his footstool. This is the court style, and I found it to be more than matter of form. For upon my admittance two days after my arrival, I was commanded to crawl upon my belly, and lick the floor as I advanced; but on account of my being a stranger, care was taken to have it made so clean that the dust was not offensive. However, this was a peculiar grace, not allowed to any but persons of the highest rank, when they desire an admittance. Nay, sometimes the floor is strewed with dust on purpose, when the person to be admitted happens to have powerful enemies at court. And I have seen a great lord with his mouth so crammed, that when he had crept to the proper distance from the throne, he was not able to speak a word. Neither is there any remedy, because it is capital[1] for those who receive an audience to spit or wipe their mouths in his majesty's presence. There is indeed another custom, which I cannot altogether approve of. When the king hath a mind to put any of his nobles to death in a gentle indulgent manner, he commands to have the floor strowed with a certain brown powder of a deadly composition, which being licked up infallibly kills him in twenty-four hours. But in justice to this prince's great clemency, and the care he hath of his subjects' lives (wherein it were much to be wished that the monarchs of Europe would imitate him), it must be mentioned for his honor that strict orders are given to have the infected parts of the floor well washed after every such execution, which if his domestics neglect, they are in danger of incurring his royal displeasure. I myself heard him give directions that one of his pages should be whipped whose turn it was to give notice about washing the floor after an execution, but maliciously had omitted it; by which neglect a young lord of great hopes coming to an audience was unfortunately poisoned, although the king at that time had no design against his life. But this good prince was so gracious as to forgive the poor page his whipping, upon promise that he would do so no more, without special orders.

To return from this digression. When I had crept within four yards of the throne, I raised myself gently upon my knees, and then striking my forehead seven times against the ground, I pronounced the following words, as they had been taught me the night before, *Ickpling Gloffthrobb Squutserumm blhiop Mlashnalt Zwin tnodbalkguffh Slhiophad Gurdlubh Asht*. This is the compliment established by the laws of the land for all persons admitted to the king's presence. It may be rendered into English thus: "May your celestial majesty outlive the sun, eleven moons and an half." To this the king returned some answer, which although I could not understand, yet I replied as I had been directed: *Fluft drin Yalerick Dwuldum prastrad mirplush*, which properly signifies, "My tongue is in the mouth of my friend;" and by this expression was meant that I desired leave to bring my interpreter; whereupon the

---

1. Punishable by death.

young man already mentioned was accordingly introduced; by whose intervention I answered as many questions as his majesty could put in above an hour. I spoke in the Balnibarbian tongue, and my interpreter delivered my meaning in that of Luggnagg.

The king was much delighted with my company, and ordered his *Bliffmarklub* or high chamberlain to appoint a lodging in the court for me and my interpreter; with a daily allowance for my table, and a large purse of gold for my common expenses.

I stayed three months in this country out of perfect obedience to his majesty, who was pleased highly to favor me, and made me very honorable offers. But I thought it more consistent with prudence and justice to pass the remainder of my days with my wife and family.

CHAPTER 10. *The Luggnaggians commended. A particular description of the struldbruggs, with many conversations between the author and some eminent persons upon that subject.*

The Luggnaggians are a polite[2] and generous people, and although they are not without some share of that pride which is peculiar to all eastern countries, yet they show themselves courteous to strangers, especially such who are countenanced by the court. I had many acquaintance among persons of the best fashion, and being always attended by my interpreter, the conversation we had was not disagreeable.

One day in much good company, I was asked by a person of quality, whether I had seen any of their *struldbruggs* or *immortals*. I said I had not; and desired he would explain to me what he meant by such an appellation, applied to a mortal creature. He told me, that sometimes, although very rarely, a child happened to be born in a family with a red circular spot in the forehead, directly over the left eyebrow, which was an infallible mark that it should never die. The spot, as he described it, was about the compass of a silver threepence, but in the course of time grew larger, and changed its color; for at twelve years old it became green, so continued till five and twenty, then turned to a deep blue; at five and forty it grew coal black, and as large as an English shilling; but never admitted any farther alteration. He said these births were so rare, that he did not believe there could be above eleven hundred *struldbruggs* of both sexes in the whole kingdom, of which he computed about fifty in the metropolis, and among the rest a young girl born about three years ago. That these productions were not peculiar to any family, but a mere effect of chance; and the children of the *struldbruggs* themselves were equally mortal with the rest of the people.

I freely own myself to have been struck with inexpressible delight upon hearing this account: and the person who gave it me happening to understand the Balnibarbian language, which I spoke very well, I could not forbear breaking out into expressions perhaps a little too extravagant. I cried out as in a rapture: Happy nation, where every child hath at least a chance for being immortal! Happy people who enjoy so many living examples of ancient virtue, and have masters ready to instruct them in the wisdom of all former ages! But happiest beyond all comparison are those excellent *struldbruggs*, who being

2. Refined, cultivated.

born exempt from that universal calamity of human nature, have their minds free and disengaged, without the weight and depression of spirits caused by the continual apprehension of death. I discovered my admiration that I had not observed any of these illustrious persons at court; the black spot on the forehead being so remarkable a distinction, that I could not have easily overlooked it; and it was impossible that his Majesty, a most judicious prince, should not provide himself with a good number of such wise and able counselors. Yet perhaps the virtue of those reverend sages was too strict for the corrupt and libertine manners of a court. And we often find by experience that young men are too opinionative[3] and volatile to be guided by the sober dictates of their seniors. However, since the King was pleased to allow me access to his royal person, I was resolved upon the very first occasion to deliver my opinion to him on this matter freely, and at large by the help of my interpreter; and whether he would please to take my advice or no, yet in one thing I was determined, that his Majesty having frequently offered me an establishment in this country, I would with great thankfulness accept the favor, and pass my life here in the conversation of those superior beings the *struldbruggs*, if they would please to admit me.

The gentleman to whom I addressed my discourse, because (as I have already observed) he spoke the language of Balnibarbi, said to me with a sort of a smile, which usually ariseth from pity to the ignorant, that he was glad of any occasion to keep me among them, and desired my permission to explain to the company what I had spoke. He did so; and they talked together for some time in their own language, whereof I understood not a syllable, neither could I observe by their countenances what impression my discourse had made on them. After a short silence the same person told me, that his friends and mine (so he thought fit to express himself) were very much pleased with the judicious remarks I had made on the great happiness and advantages of immortal life; and they were desirous to know in a particular manner, what scheme of living I should have formed to myself, if it had fallen to my lot to have been born a *struldbrugg*.

I answered, it was easy to be eloquent on so copious and delightful a subject, especially to me who have been often apt to amuse myself with visions of what I should do if I were a king, a general, or a great lord; and upon this very case I had frequently run over the whole system how I should employ myself, and pass the time if I were sure to live forever.

That, if it had been my good fortune to come into the world a *struldbrugg*, as soon as I could discover my own happiness by understanding the difference between life and death, I would first resolve by all arts and methods whatsoever to procure myself riches: in the pursuit of which, by thrift and management, I might reasonably expect in about two hundred years to be the wealthiest man in the kingdom. In the second place, I would from my earliest youth apply myself to the study of arts and sciences, by which I should arrive in time to excel all others in learning. Lastly, I would carefully record every action and event of consequence that happened in the public, impartially draw the characters of the several successions of princes, and great ministers of state; with my own observations on every point. I would exactly set down the several changes in customs, languages, fashions of dress, diet and diver-

3. Speculative, impractical.

sions. By all which acquirements, I should be a living treasury of knowledge and wisdom, and certainly become the oracle of the nation.

I would never marry after threescore, but live in an hospitable manner, yet still on the saving side. I would entertain myself in forming and directing the minds of hopeful young men, by convincing them from my own remembrance, experience and observation, fortified by numerous examples, of the usefulness of virtue in public and private life. But my choice and constant companions should be a set of my own immortal brotherhood, among whom I would elect a dozen from the most ancient down to my own contemporaries. Where any of these wanted fortunes, I would provide them with convenient lodges round my own estate, and have some of them always at my table, only mingling a few of the most valuable among you mortals, whom length of time would harden me to lose with little or no reluctance, and treat your posterity after the same manner; just as a man diverts himself with the annual succession of pinks and tulips in his garden, without regretting the loss of those which withered the preceding year.

These *struldbruggs* and I would mutually communicate our observations and memorials[4] through the course of time; remark the several gradations by which corruption steals into the world, and oppose it in every step, by giving perpetual warning and instruction to mankind; which, added to the strong influence of our own example, would probably prevent that continual degeneracy of human nature, so justly complained of in all ages.

Add to all this, the pleasure of seeing the various revolutions of states and empires; the changes in the lower and upper world;[5] ancient cities in ruins; and obscure villages become the seats of kings. Famous rivers lessening into shallow brooks; the ocean leaving one coast dry, and overwhelming another; the discovery of many countries yet unknown. Barbarity overrunning the politest nations, and the most barbarous becoming civilized. I should then see the discovery of the longitude, the perpetual motion, the universal medicine,[6] and many other great inventions brought to the utmost perfection.

What wonderful discoveries should we make in astronomy, by outliving and confirming our own predictions, by observing the progress and returns of comets, with the changes of motion in the sun, moon and stars.

I enlarged upon many other topics, which the natural desire of endless life and sublunary happiness could easily furnish me with. When I had ended, and the sum of my discourse had been interpreted as before to the rest of the company, there was a good deal of talk among them in the language of the country, not without some laughter at my expense. At last the same gentleman who had been my interpreter said, he was desired by the rest to set me right in a few mistakes, which I had fallen into through the common imbecility[7] of human nature, and upon that allowance was less answerable for them. That this breed of *struldbruggs* was peculiar to their country, for there were no such people either in Balnibarbi or Japan, where he had the honor to be ambassador from his Majesty, and found the natives in both those kingdoms very hard to believe that the fact was possible; and it appeared from my astonishment when he first mentioned the matter to me,

4. Memories.
5. Earth and heaven; figuratively, common people and the ruling class. "Revolutions": cycles.
6. The *elixir vitae*, an alchemical formula to pre-serve life forever, was considered by Swift an impossible dream, like a method for calculating longitude at sea or a perpetual motion machine.
7. Weakness.

that I received it as a thing wholly new, and scarcely to be credited. That in the two kingdoms above mentioned, where during his residence he had conversed very much, he observed long life to be the universal desire and wish of mankind. That whoever had one foot in the grave was sure to hold back the other as strongly as he could. That the oldest had still hopes of living one day longer, and looked on death as the greatest evil, from which nature always prompted him to retreat; only in this island of Luggnagg the appetite for living was not so eager, from the continual example of the *struldbruggs* before their eyes.

That the system of living contrived by me was unreasonable and unjust, because it supposed a perpetuity of youth, health, and vigor, which no man could be so foolish to hope, however extravagant he might be in his wishes. That the question therefore was not whether a man would choose to be always in the prime of youth, attended with prosperity and health; but how he would pass a perpetual life under all the usual disadvantages which old age brings along with it. For although few men will avow their desires of being immortal upon such hard conditions, yet in the two kingdoms before mentioned of Balnibarbi and Japan, he observed that every man desired to put off death for some time longer, let it approach ever so late; and he rarely heard of any man who died willingly, except he were incited by the extremity of grief or torture. And he appealed to me whether in those countries I had traveled, as well as my own, I had not observed the same general disposition.

After this preface he gave me a particular account of the *struldbruggs* among them. He said they commonly acted like mortals, till about thirty years old, after which by degrees they grew melancholy and dejected, increasing in both till they came to fourscore. This he learned from their own confession; for otherwise there not being above two or three of that species born in an age, they were too few to form a general observation by. When they came to fourscore years, which is reckoned the extremity of living in this country, they had not only all the follies and infirmities of other old men, but many more which arose from the dreadful prospect of never dying. They were not only opinionative, peevish, covetous, morose, vain, talkative; but uncapable of friendship, and dead to all natural affection, which never descended below their grandchildren. Envy and impotent desires are their prevailing passions. But those objects against which their envy seems principally directed, are the vices of the younger sort, and the deaths of the old. By reflecting on the former, they find themselves cut off from all possibility of pleasure; and whenever they see a funeral, they lament and repine that others are gone to an harbor of rest, to which they themselves never can hope to arrive. They have no remembrance of anything but what they learned and observed in their youth and middle age, and even that is very imperfect. And for the truth or particulars of any fact, it is safer to depend on common traditions than upon their best recollections. The least miserable among them appear to be those who turn to dotage, and entirely lose their memories; these meet with more pity and assistance, because they want many bad qualities which abound in others.

If a *struldbrugg* happen to marry one of his own kind, the marriage is dissolved of course by the courtesy of the kingdom, as soon as the younger of the two comes to be fourscore. For the law thinks it a reasonable indulgence, that those who are condemned without any fault of their own to a perpetual continuance in the world, should not have their misery doubled by the load of a wife.

As soon as they have completed the term of eighty years, they are looked on as dead in law; their heirs immediately succeed to their estates, only a small pittance is reserved for their support; and the poor ones are maintained at the public charge. After that period they are held incapable of any employment of trust or profit; they cannot purchase land, or take leases, neither are they allowed to be witnesses in any cause, either civil or criminal, not even for the decision of meers[8] and bounds.

At ninety they lose their teeth and hair; they have at that age no distinction of taste, but eat and drink whatever they can get, without relish or appetite. The diseases they were subject to still continue without increasing or diminishing. In talking they forget the common appellation of things, and the names of persons, even of those who are their nearest friends and relations. For the same reason they never can amuse themselves with reading, because their memory will not serve to carry them from the beginning of a sentence to the end, and by this defect they are deprived of the only entertainment whereof they might otherwise be capable.

The language of this country being always upon the flux, the *struldbruggs* of one age do not understand those of another; neither are they able after two hundred years to hold any conversation (farther than by a few general words) with their neighbors the mortals; and thus they lie under the disadvantage of living like foreigners in their own country.

This was the account given me of the *struldbruggs,* as near as I can remember. I afterwards saw five or six of different ages, the youngest not above two hundred years old, who were brought to me at several times by some of my friends; but although they were told that I was a great traveler, and had seen all the world, they had not the least curiosity to ask me a question; only desired I would give them *slumskudask,* or a token of remembrance; which is a modest way of begging, to avoid the law that strictly forbids it, because they are provided for by the public, although indeed with a very scanty allowance.

They are despised and hated by all sorts of people; when one of them is born, it is reckoned ominous, and their birth is recorded very particularly; so that you may know their age by consulting the registry, which however hath not been kept above a thousand years past, or at least hath been destroyed by time or public disturbances. But the usual way of computing how old they are, is by asking them what kings or great persons they can remember, and then consulting history; for infallibly the last prince in their mind did not begin his reign after they were fourscore years old.

They were the most mortifying sight I ever beheld; and the women more horrible than the men. Besides the usual deformities in extreme old age, they acquired an additional ghastliness in proportion to their number of years, which is not to be described; and among half a dozen I soon distinguished which was the oldest, although there were not above a century or two between them.

The reader will easily believe, that from what I had heard and seen, my keen appetite for perpetuity of life was much abated. I grew heartily ashamed

---

8. Boundaries.

of the pleasing visions I had formed; and thought no tyrant could invent a death into which I would not run with pleasure from such a life. The King heard of all that had passed between me and my friends upon this occasion, and rallied[9] me very pleasantly; wishing I would send a couple of *struldbruggs* to my own country, to arm our people against the fear of death; but this it seems is forbidden by the fundamental laws of the kingdom; or else I should have been well content with the trouble and expense of transporting them.

I could not but agree, that the laws of this kingdom relating to the *struldbruggs*, were founded upon the strongest reasons, and such as any other country would be under the necessity of enacting in the like circumstances. Otherwise, as avarice is the necessary consequent of old age, those immortals would in time become proprietors of the whole nation, and engross[1] the civil power; which, for want of abilities to manage, must end in the ruin of the public.

CHAPTER 11. *The author leaves Luggnagg and sails to Japan. From thence he returns in a Dutch ship to Amsterdam, and from Amsterdam to England.*

I thought this account of the *struldbruggs* might be some entertainment to the reader, because it seems to be a little out of the common way; at least I do not remember to have met the like in any book of travels that hath come to my hands. And if I am deceived, my excuse must be that it is necessary for travellers who describe the same country very often to agree in dwelling on the same particulars, without deserving the censure of having borrowed or transcribed from those who wrote before them.

There is indeed a perpetual commerce between this kingdom and the great empire of Japan; and it is very probable that the Japanese authors may have given some account of the *struldbruggs*; but my stay in Japan was so short, and I was so entirely a stranger to the language, that I was not qualified to make any inquiries. But I hope the Dutch upon this notice will be curious and able enough to supply my defects.

His majesty having often pressed me to accept some employment in his court, and finding me absolutely determined to return to my native country, was pleased to give me his license to depart; and honored me with a letter of recommendation under his own hand to the Emperor of Japan. He likewise presented me with four hundred and forty-four large pieces of gold (this nation delighting in even numbers) and a red diamond which I sold in England for eleven hundred pounds.

On the 6th of May, 1709, I took a solemn leave of his majesty, and all my friends. This prince was so gracious as to order a guard to conduct me to Glanguenstald, which is a royal port to the southwest part of the island. In six days I found a vessel ready to carry me to Japan, and spent fifteen days in the voyage. We landed at a small port-town called Xamoschi,[2] situated on the southeast part of Japan. The town lies on the western part, where there is a narrow strait leading northward into a long arm of the sea, upon the northwest part of which Yedo,[3] the metropolis, stands. At landing I showed

9. Ridiculed.
1. Absorb, monopolize.
2. Swift's name for the ancient province of

Shimōsa, on the eastern coast of Japan.
3. Edo, former name of Tokyo.

the custom-house officers my letter from the king of Luggnagg to his imperial majesty. They knew the seal perfectly well; it was as broad as the palm of my hand. The impression was, *A king lifting up a lame beggar from the earth*. The magistrates of the town, hearing of my letter, received me as a public minister. They provided me with carriages and servants, and bore my charges to Yedo, where I was admitted to an audience, and delivered my letter, which was opened with great ceremony, and explained to the Emperor by an interpreter, who then gave me notice, by his majesty's order, that I should signify my request, and, whatever it were, it should be granted for the sake of his royal brother of Luggnagg. This interpreter was a person employed to transact affairs with the Hollanders. He soon conjectured by my countenance that I was an European, and therefore repeated his majesty's commands in Low Dutch, which he spoke perfectly well. I answered (as I had before determined) that I was a Dutch merchant, shipwrecked in a very remote country, from whence I travelled by sea and land to Luggnagg, and then took shipping for Japan, where I knew my countrymen often traded, and with some of these I hoped to get an opportunity of returning into Europe. I therefore most humbly entreated his royal favor to give order that I should be conducted in safety to Nangasac.[4] To this I added another petition, that for the sake of my patron the king of Luggnagg, his majesty would condescend to excuse my performing the ceremony imposed on my countrymen, of trampling upon the crucifix:[5] because I had been thrown into his kingdom by my misfortunes, without any intention of trading. When this latter petition was interpreted to the Emperor, he seemed a little surprised; and said he believed I was the first of my countrymen who ever made any scruple in this point; and that he began to doubt, whether I was a real Hollander, or not; but rather suspected I must be a Christian.[6] However, for the reasons I had offered, but chiefly to gratify the king of Luggnagg by an uncommon mark of his favor, he would comply with the singularity of my humor; but the affair must be managed with dexterity, and his officers should be commanded to let me pass as it were by forgetfulness. For he assured me that if the secret should be discovered by my countrymen the Dutch, they would cut my throat in the voyage. I returned my thanks by the interpreter for so unusual a favor; and some troops being at that time on their march to Nangasac, the commanding officer had orders to convey me safe thither, with particular instructions about the business of the crucifix.

On the 9th day of June, 1709, I arrived at Nangasac, after a very long and troublesome journey. I soon fell into the company of some Dutch sailors belonging to the *Amboyna*,[7] of Amsterdam, a stout ship of 450 tons. I had lived long in Holland, pursuing my studies at Leyden, and I spoke Dutch well. The seamen soon knew from whence I came last: they were curious to inquire into my voyages and course of life. I made up a story as short and probable as I could, but concealed the greatest part. I knew many persons in Holland. I was able to invent names for my parents, whom I pretended to be obscure people in the province of Gelderland.[8] I would have given the captain (one

4. Nagasaki, where the Dutch often traded.
5. A test said to be used against Japanese Christians.
6. Another swipe by Swift against the Dutch, whose traders were said to accept the Japanese prohibition against outward demonstration their religion.

7. Ship named after Ambon Island (now Maluku, Indonesia) in the East Indies, where the Dutch traded, and where they tortured and executed English traders in 1623, despite treaties granting the English trading rights.
8. The largest province of the Netherlands, in the eastern center of the country.

Theodorus Vangrult) what he pleased to ask for my voyage to Holland; but understanding I was a surgeon, he was contented to take half the usual rate, on condition that I would serve him in the way of my calling. Before we took shipping, I was often asked by some of the crew, whether I had performed the ceremony above mentioned? I evaded the question by general answers, that I had satisfied the Emperor and court in all particulars. However, a malicious rogue of a skipper[9] went to an officer, and pointing to me, told him I had not yet trampled on the crucifix. But the other, who had received instructions to let me pass, gave the rascal twenty strokes on the shoulders with a bamboo; after which I was no more troubled with such questions.

Nothing happened worth mentioning in this voyage. We sailed with a fair wind to the Cape of Good Hope, where we stayed only to take in fresh water. On the 10th of April, 1710, we arrived safe at Amsterdam, having lost only three men by sickness in the voyage, and a fourth, who fell from the foremast into the sea, not far from the coast of Guinea. From Amsterdam I soon after set sail for England, in a small vessel belonging to that city.

On the 16th of April we put in at the Downs. I landed the next morning, and saw once more my native country after an absence of five years and six months complete. I went straight to Redriff, where I arrived the same day at two in the afternoon, and found my wife and family in good health.

Part 4. A Voyage to the Country of the Houyhnhnms[1]

CHAPTER 1. *The Author sets out as Captain of a ship. His men conspire against him, confine him a long time to his cabin, set him on shore in an unknown land. He travels up into the country. The Yahoos, a strange sort of animal, described. The Author meets two Houyhnhnms.*

I continued at home with my wife and children about five months in a very happy condition, if I could have learned the lesson of knowing when I was well. I left my poor wife big with child, and accepted an advantageous offer made me to be Captain of the *Adventure,* a stout merchantman of 350 tons; for I understood navigation well, and being grown weary of a surgeon's employment at sea, which however I could exercise upon occasion, I took a skillful young man of that calling, one Robert Purefoy, into my ship. We set sail from Portsmouth upon the 7th day of September, 1710; on the 14th we met with Captain Pocock of Bristol, at Tenariff, who was going to the Bay of Campeachy[2] to cut logwood. On the 16th he was parted from us by a storm; I heard since my return that his ship foundered and none escaped, but one cabin boy. He was an honest man and a good sailor, but a little too positive in his own opinions, which was the cause of his destruction, as it hath been of several others. For if he had followed my advice, he might at this time have been safe at home with his family as well as myself.

9. Seaman.
1. Pronounced *hwin-ims.* The word suggests the neigh characteristic of a horse.

2. Campeche, in the Gulf of Mexico. Teneriffe is one of the Canary Islands.

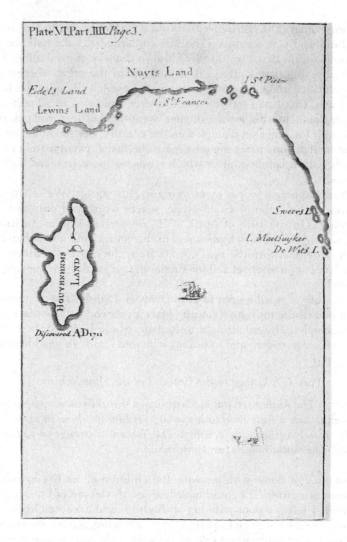

Plate VI.Part.IIII.*Page*.1.

Nuyts Land

Edels Land

Lewins Land

I. S.t Francesi

I S.t Pieter

Sweers I.

l. Maelsuyker

De Wits I.

HOUYHNHNMS LAND

Difcovered AD 1711

I had several men died in my ship of calentures,[3] so that I was forced to get recruits out of Barbadoes and the Leeward Islands, where I touched by the direction of the merchants who employed me; which I had soon too much cause to repent, for I found afterwards that most of them had been buccaneers. I had fifty hands on board; and my orders were that I should trade with the Indians in the South Sea, and make what discoveries I could. These rogues whom I had picked up debauched my other men, and they all formed a conspiracy to seize the ship and secure me; which they did one morning, rushing into my cabin, and binding me hand and foot, threatening

3. "A distemper peculiar to sailors, in hot climates; wherein they imagine the sea to be green fields, and will throw themselves into it, if not restrained" (Johnson's *Dictionary*).

to throw me overboard, if I offered to stir. I told them I was their prisoner, and would submit. This they made me swear to do, and then unbound me, only fastening one of my legs with a chain near my bed, and placed a sentry at my door with his piece charged, who was commanded to shoot me dead if I attempted my liberty. They sent me down victuals and drink, and took the government of the ship to themselves. Their design was to turn pirates and plunder the Spaniards, which they could not do, till they got more men. But first they resolved to sell the goods in the ship, and then go to Madagascar for recruits, several among them having died since my confinement. They sailed many weeks, and traded with the Indians; but I knew not what course they took, being kept close prisoner in my cabin, and expecting nothing less than to be murdered, as they often threatened me.

Upon the 9th day of May, 1711, one James Welch came down to my cabin; and said he had orders from the Captain to set me ashore. I expostulated with him, but in vain; neither would he so much as tell me who their new Captain was. They forced me into the longboat, letting me put on my best suit of clothes, which were as good as new, and a small bundle of linen, but no arms except my hanger; and they were so civil as not to search my pockets, into which I conveyed what money I had, with some other little necessaries. They rowed about a league, and then set me down on a strand. I desired them to tell me what country it was; they all swore, they knew no more than myself, but said that the Captain (as they called him) was resolved, after they had sold the lading, to get rid of me in the first place where they discovered land. They pushed off immediately, advising me to make haste, for fear of being overtaken by the tide, and bade me farewell.

In this desolate condition I advanced forward, and soon got upon firm ground, where I sat down on a bank to rest myself, and consider what I had best to do. When I was a little refreshed, I went up into the country, resolving to deliver myself to the first savages I should meet, and purchase my life from them by some bracelets, glass rings, and other toys, which sailors usually provide themselves with in those voyages, and whereof I had some about me. The land was divided by long rows of trees, not regularly planted, but naturally growing; there was great plenty of grass, and several fields of oats. I walked very circumspectly for fear of being surprised, or suddenly shot with an arrow from behind, or on either side. I fell into a beaten road, where I saw many tracks of human feet, and some of cows, but most of horses. At last I beheld several animals in a field, and one or two of the same kind sitting in trees. Their shape was very singular, and deformed, which a little discomposed me, so that I lay down behind a thicket to observe them better. Some of them coming forward near the place where I lay, gave me an opportunity of distinctly marking their form. Their heads and breasts were covered with a thick hair, some frizzled and others lank; they had beards like goats, and a long ridge of hair down their backs, and the fore parts of their legs and feet; but the rest of their bodies were bare, so that I might see their skins, which were of a brown buff color. They had no tails, nor any hair at all on their buttocks, except about the anus; which, I presume Nature had placed there to defend them as they sat on the ground; for this posture they used, as well as lying down, and often stood on their hind feet. They climbed high trees, as nimbly as a squirrel, for they had strong extended claws before and behind, terminating in sharp points, and hooked. They would often spring, and bound, and leap with prodigious agility. The females were not so large as the males; they had long lank hair on their heads, and only a sort of down on the rest of their bodies, except about the anus, and pudenda. Their dugs hung between their forefeet, and often reached almost to the ground as they walked. The hair of both sexes was of several colors, brown, red, black, and yellow. Upon the whole, I never beheld in all my travels so disagreeable an animal, or one against which I naturally conceived so strong an antipathy. So that thinking I had seen enough, full of contempt and aversion, I got up and pursued the beaten road, hoping it might direct me to the cabin of some Indian. I had not gone far when I met one of these creatures full in my way, and coming up directly to me. The ugly monster, when he saw me, distorted several ways every feature of his visage, and stared as at an object he had never seen before; then approaching nearer, lifted up his forepaw, whether out of curiosity or mischief, I could not tell; but I drew my hanger, and gave him a good blow with the flat side of it; for I durst not strike him with the edge, fearing the inhabitants might be provoked against me, if they should come to know that I had killed or maimed any of their cattle. When the beast felt the smart, he drew back, and roared so loud, that a herd of at least forty came flocking about me from the near field, howling and making odious faces; but I ran to the body of a tree, and leaning my back against it, kept them off, by waving my hanger. Several of this cursed brood getting hold of the branches behind, leaped up into the tree, from whence they began to discharge their excrements on my head; however, I escaped pretty well, by sticking close to the stem of the tree, but was almost stifled with the filth, which fell about me on every side.

In the midst of this distress, I observed them all to run away on a sudden as fast as they could; at which I ventured to leave the tree, and pursue the road, wondering what it was that could put them into this fright. But looking on my left hand, I saw a horse walking softly in the field; which my persecutors having sooner discovered, was the cause of their flight. The horse started a little when he came near me, but soon recovering himself, looked full in my face with manifest tokens of wonder; he viewed my hands and feet, walking round me several times. I would have pursued my journey, but he placed himself directly in the way, yet looking with a very mild aspect, never offering the least violence. We stood gazing at each other for some time; at last I took the boldness, to reach my hand towards his neck, with a design to stroke it; using the common style and whistle of jockies when they are going to handle a strange horse. But this animal, seeming to receive my civilities with disdain, shook his head, and bent his brows, softly raising up his left forefoot to remove my hand. Then he neighed three or four times, but in so different a cadence, that I almost began to think he was speaking to himself in some language of his own.

While he and I were thus employed, another horse came up; who applying himself to the first in a very formal manner, they gently struck each other's right hoof before, neighing several times by turns, and varying the sound, which seemed to be almost articulate. They went some paces off, as if it were to confer together, walking side by side, backward and forward, like persons deliberating upon some affair of weight; but often turning their eyes towards me, as it were to watch that I might not escape. I was amazed to see such actions and behavior in brute beasts; and concluded with myself that if the inhabitants of this country were endued with a proportionable degree of reason, they must needs be the wisest people upon earth. This thought gave me so much comfort, that I resolved to go forward until I could discover some house or village, or meet with any of the natives, leaving the two horses to discourse together as they pleased. But the first, who was a dapple grey, observing me to steal off, neighed after me in so expressive a tone that I fancied myself to understand what he meant; whereupon I turned back, and came near him, to expect his farther commands; but concealing my fear as much as I could; for I began to be in some pain, how this adventure might terminate; and the reader will easily believe I did not much like my present situation.

The two horses came up close to me, looking with great earnestness upon my face and hands. The grey steed rubbed my hat all round with his right fore hoof, and discomposed it so much that I was forced to adjust it better, by taking it off, and settling it again; whereat both he and his companion (who was a brown bay) appeared to be much surprised; the latter felt the lappet of my coat, and finding it to hang loose about me, they both looked with new signs of wonder. He stroked my right hand, seeming to admire the softness, and color; but he squeezed it so hard between his hoof and his pastern, that I was forced to roar; after which they both touched me with all possible tenderness. They were under great perplexity about my shoes and stockings, which they felt very often, neighing to each other, and using various gestures, not unlike those of a philosopher, when he would attempt to solve some new and difficult phenomenon.

Upon the whole, the behavior of these animals was so orderly and rational, so acute and judicious, that I at last concluded, they must needs be magicians, who had thus metamorphosed themselves upon some design; and seeing a stranger in the way, were resolved to divert themselves with him; or perhaps were really amazed at the sight of a man so very different in habit, feature, and complexion from those who might probably live in so remote a climate. Upon the strength of this reasoning, I ventured to address them in the following manner: "Gentlemen, if you be conjurers, as I have good cause to believe, you can understand any language; therefore I make bold to let your worships know that I am a poor distressed Englishman, driven by his misfortunes upon your coast; and I entreat one of you, to let me ride upon his back, as if he were a real horse, to some house or village, where I can be relieved. In return of which favor, I will make you a present of this knife and bracelet" (taking them out of my pocket). The two creatures stood silent while I spoke, seeming to listen with great attention; and when I had ended, they neighed frequently towards each other, as if they were engaged in serious conversation. I plainly observed, that their language expressed the passions very well, and the words might with little pains be resolved into an alphabet more easily than the Chinese.

I could frequently distinguish the word *Yahoo*,[4] which was repeated by each of them several times; and although it were impossible for me to con-

---

4. Perhaps compounded from two expressions of disgust, *yah* and *ugh* (or *hoo*), common in the 18th century.

jecture what it meant, yet while the two horses were busy in conversation, I endeavored to practice this word upon my tongue; and as soon as they were silent, I boldly pronounced "Yahoo" in a loud voice, imitating, at the same time, as near as I could, the neighing of a horse; at which they were both visibly surprised, and the grey repeated the same word twice, as if he meant to teach me the right accent, wherein I spoke after him as well as I could, and found myself perceivably to improve every time, although very far from any degree of perfection. Then the bay tried me with a second word, much harder to be pronounced; but reducing it to the English orthography, may be spelt thus, *Houyhnhnm*. I did not succeed in this so well as the former, but after two or three farther trials, I had better fortune; and they both appeared amazed at my capacity.

After some farther discourse, which I then conjectured might relate to me, the two friends took their leaves, with the same compliment of striking each other's hoof; and the grey made me signs that I should walk before him; wherein I thought it prudent to comply, till I could find a better director. When I offered to slacken my pace, he would cry, "Hhuun, Hhuun"; I guessed his meaning, and gave him to understand, as well as I could that I was weary, and not able to walk faster; upon which, he would stand a while to let me rest.

CHAPTER 2. *The Author conducted by a Houyhnhnm to his house. The house described. The Author's reception. The food of the Houyhnhnms. The Author in distress for want of meat is at last relieved. His manner of feeding in that country.*

Having traveled about three miles, we came to a long kind of building, made of timber, stuck in the ground, and wattled across; the roof was low, and covered with straw. I now began to be a little comforted, and took out some toys, which travelers usually carry for presents to the savage Indians of America and other parts, in hopes the people of the house would be thereby encouraged to receive me kindly. The horse made me a sign to go in first; it was a large room with a smooth clay floor, and a rack and manger extending the whole length on one side. There were three nags, and two mares, not eating, but some of them sitting down upon their hams, which I very much wondered at; but wondered more to see the rest employed in domestic business. The last seemed but ordinary cattle; however this confirmed my first opinion, that a people who could so far civilize brute animals must needs excel in wisdom all the nations of the world. The grey came in just after, and thereby prevented any ill treatment, which the others might have given me. He neighed to them several times in a style of authority, and received answers.

Beyond this room there were three others, reaching the length of the house, to which you passed through three doors, opposite to each other, in the manner of a vista; we went through the second room towards the third; here the grey walked in first, beckoning me to attend.[5] I waited in the second room, and got ready my presents, for the master and mistress of the house; they were two knives, three bracelets of false pearl, a small looking glass and

5. To wait. "Vista": a long, open corridor.

a bead necklace. The horse neighed three or four times, and I waited to hear some answers in a human voice, but I heard no other returns than in the same dialect, only one or two a little shriller than his. I began to think that this house must belong to some person of great note among them, because there appeared so much ceremony before I could gain admittance. But, that a man of quality should be served all by horses, was beyond my comprehension. I feared my brain was disturbed by my sufferings and misfortunes; I roused myself, and looked about me in the room where I was left alone; this was furnished as the first, only after a more elegant manner. I rubbed my eyes often, but the same objects still occurred. I pinched my arms and sides, to awaken myself, hoping I might be in a dream. I then absolutely concluded that all these appearances could be nothing else but necromancy and magic. But I had no time to pursue these reflections; for the grey horse came to the door, and made me a sign to follow him into the third room; where I saw a very comely mare, together with a colt and foal, sitting on their haunches, upon mats of straw, not unartfully made, and perfectly neat and clean.

The mare soon after my entrance, rose from her mat, and coming up close, after having nicely observed my hands and face, gave me a most contemptuous look; then turning to the horse, I heard the word *Yahoo* often repeated betwixt them; the meaning of which word I could not then comprehend, although it were the first I had learned to pronounce; but I was soon better informed, to my everlasting mortification: for the horse beckoning to me with his head, and repeating the word, "Hhuun, Hhuun," as he did upon the road, which I understood was to attend him, led me out into a kind of court, where was another building at some distance from the house. Here we entered, and I saw three of those detestable creatures, which I first met after my landing, feeding upon roots, and the flesh of some animals, which I afterwards found to be that of asses and dogs, and now and then a cow dead by accident or disease. They were all tied by the neck with strong withes,[6] fastened to a beam; they held their food between the claws of their forefeet, and tore it with their teeth.

The master horse ordered a sorrel nag, one of his servants, to untie the largest of these animals, and take him into a yard. The beast and I were brought close together; and our countenances diligently compared, both by master and servant, who thereupon repeated several times the word *Yahoo*. My horror and astonishment are not to be described, when I observed, in this abominable animal, a perfect human figure; the face of it indeed was flat and broad, the nose depressed, the lips large, and the mouth wide; but these differences are common to all savage nations, where the lineaments of the countenance are distorted by the natives suffering their infants to lie groveling on the earth, or by carrying them on their backs, nuzzling with their face against the mother's shoulders. The forefeet of the Yahoo differed from my hands in nothing else but the length of the nails, the coarseness and brownness of the palms, and the hairiness on the backs. There was the same resemblance between our feet, with the same differences, which I knew very well, although the horses did not, because of my shoes and stockings;

6. Slender, flexible branches.

the same in every part of our bodies, except as to hairiness and color, which I have already described.

The great difficulty that seemed to stick with the two horses was to see the rest of my body so very different from that of a Yahoo, for which I was obliged to my clothes, whereof they had no conception; the sorrel nag offered me a root, which he held (after their manner, as we shall describe in its proper place) between his hoof and pastern; I took it in my hand, and having smelled it, returned it to him again as civilly as I could. He brought out of the Yahoo's kennel a piece of ass's flesh, but it smelled so offensively that I turned from it with loathing; he then threw it to the Yahoo, by whom it was greedily devoured. He afterwards showed me a wisp of hay, and a fetlock full of oats; but I shook my head, to signify that neither of these were food for me. And indeed, I now apprehended that I must absolutely starve, if I did not get to some of my own species; for as to those filthy Yahoos, although there were few greater lovers of mankind, at that time, than myself, yet I confess I never saw any sensitive being so detestable on all accounts; and the more I came near them, the more hateful they grew, while I stayed in that country. This the master horse observed by my behavior, and therefore sent the Yahoo back to his kennel. He then put his forehoof to his mouth, at which I was much surprised, although he did it with ease, and with a motion that appeared perfectly natural; and made other signs to know what I would eat; but I could not return him such an answer as he was able to apprehend; and if he had understood me, I did not see how it was possible to contrive any way for finding myself nourishment. While we were thus engaged, I observed a cow passing by; whereupon I pointed to her, and expressed a desire to let me go and milk her. This had its effect; for he led me back into the house, and ordered a mare-servant to open a room, where a good store of milk lay in earthen and wooden vessels, after a very orderly and cleanly manner. She gave me a large bowl full, of which I drank very heartily, and found myself well refreshed.

About noon I saw coming towards the house a kind of vehicle, drawn like a sledge by four Yahoos. There was in it an old steed, who seemed to be of quality; he alighted with his hind feet forward, having by accident got a hurt in his left forefoot. He came to dine with our horse, who received him with great civility. They dined in the best room, and had oats boiled in milk for the second course, which the old horse eat warm, but the rest cold. Their mangers were placed circular in the middle of the room, and divided into several partitions, round which they sat on their haunches upon bosses[7] of straw. In the middle was a large rack with angles answering to every partition of the manger. So that each horse and mare eat their own hay, and their own mash of oats and milk, with much decency and regularity. The behavior of the young colt and foal appeared very modest; and that of the master and mistress extremely cheerful and complaisant to their guest. The grey ordered me to stand by him; and much discourse passed between him and his friend concerning me, as I found by the stranger's often looking on me, and the frequent repetition of the word *Yahoo*.

I happened to wear my gloves; which the master grey observing, seemed perplexed; discovering signs of wonder what I had done to my forefeet; he

---

7. Seats of bundled grasses.

put his hoof three or four times to them, as if he would signify, that I should reduce them to their former shape, which I presently did, pulling off both my gloves, and putting them into my pocket. This occasioned farther talk, and I saw the company was pleased with my behavior, whereof I soon found the good effects. I was ordered to speak the few words I understood; and while they were at dinner, the master taught me the names for oats, milk, fire, water, and some others which I could readily pronounce after him, having from my youth a great facility in learning languages.

When dinner was done, the master horse took me aside, and by signs and words made me understand the concern he was in that I had nothing to eat. Oats in their tongue are called *hlunnh*. This word I pronounced two or three times; for although I had refused them at first, yet upon second thoughts, I considered that I could contrive to make a kind of bread, which might be sufficient with milk to keep me alive, till I could make my escape to some other country, and to creatures of my own species. The horse immediately ordered a white mare-servant of his family to bring me a good quantity of oats in a sort of wooden tray. These I heated before the fire as well as I could, and rubbed them till the husks came off, which I made a shift to winnow from the grain; I ground and beat them between two stones, then took water, and made them into a paste or cake, which I toasted at the fire, and eat warm with milk. It was at first a very insipid diet, although common enough in many parts of Europe, but grew tolerable by time; and having been often reduced to hard fare in my life, this was not the first experiment I had made how easily nature is satisfied. And I cannot but observe that I never had one hour's sickness, while I staid in this island. It is true, I sometimes made a shift to catch a rabbit, or bird, by springes[8] made of Yahoos' hairs; and I often gathered wholesome herbs, which I boiled, or eat as salads with my bread; and now and then, for a rarity, I made a little butter, and drank the whey. I was at first at a great loss for salt; but custom soon reconciled the want of it; and I am confident that the frequent use of salt among us is an effect of luxury, and was first introduced only as a provocative to drink; except where it is necessary for preserving of flesh in long voyages, or in places remote from great markets. For we observe no animal to be fond of it but man;[9] and as to myself, when I left this country, it was a great while before I could endure the taste of it in anything that I eat.

This is enough to say upon the subject of my diet, wherewith other travelers fill their books, as if the readers were personally concerned whether we fare well or ill. However, it was necessary to mention this matter, lest the world should think it impossible that I could find sustenance for three years in such a country, and among such inhabitants.

When it grew towards evening, the master horse ordered a place for me to lodge in; it was but six yards from the house, and separated from the stable of the Yahoos. Here I got some straw, and covering myself with my own clothes, slept very sound. But I was in a short time better accommodated, as the reader shall know hereafter, when I come to treat more particularly about my way of living.

---

8. Snares.
9. Gulliver is, of course, in error; many animals require salt.

CHAPTER 3. *The Author studious to learn the language, the Houyhnhnm his master assists in teaching him. The language described. Several Houyhnhnms of quality come out of curiosity to see the Author. He gives his master a short account of his voyage.*

My principal endeavor was to learn the language, which my master (for so I shall henceforth call him) and his children, and every servant of his house were desirous to teach me. For they looked upon it as a prodigy, that a brute animal should discover such marks of a rational creature. I pointed to everything, and enquired the name of it, which I wrote down in my journal book when I was alone, and corrected my bad accent, by desiring those of the family to pronounce it often. In this employment, a sorrel nag, one of the under servants, was very ready to assist me.

In speaking, they pronounce through the nose and throat, and their language approaches nearest to the High Dutch or German, of any I know in Europe; but is much more graceful and significant. The Emperor Charles V made almost the same observation, when he said, that if he were to speak to his horse, it should be in High Dutch.[1]

The curiosity and impatience of my master were so great, that he spent many hours of his leisure to instruct me. He was convinced (as he afterwards told me) that I must be a Yahoo, but my teachableness, civility, and cleanliness astonished him; which were qualities altogether so opposite to those animals. He was most perplexed about my clothes, reasoning sometimes with himself whether they were a part of my body; for I never pulled them off till the family were asleep, and got them on before they waked in the morning. My master was eager to learn from whence I came; how I acquired those appearances of reason, which I discovered in all my actions; and to know my story from my own mouth, which he hoped he should soon do by the great proficiency I made in learning and pronouncing their words and sentences. To help my memory, I formed all I learned into the English alphabet, and writ the words down with the translations. This last, after some time, I ventured to do in my master's presence. It cost me much trouble to explain to him what I was doing; for the inhabitants have not the least idea of books or literature.

In about ten weeks time I was able to understand most of his questions; and in three months could give him some tolerable answers. He was extremely curious to know from what part of the country I came, and how I was taught to imitate a rational creature; because the Yahoos (whom he saw I exactly resembled in my head, hands, and face, that were only visible) with some appearance of cunning, and the strongest disposition to mischief, were observed to be the most unteachable of all brutes. I answered that I came over the sea, from a far place, with many others of my own kind, in a great hollow vessel made of the bodies of trees; that my companions forced me to land on this coast, and then left me to shift for myself. It was with some difficulty, and by the help of many signs, that I brought him to understand me. He replied that I must needs be mistaken, or that I *said the thing which was not.* (For they have no word in their language to express lying or falsehood.)

---

1. The emperor is supposed to have said that he would speak to his God in Spanish, to his mistress in Italian, and to his horse in German.

He knew it was impossible that there could be a country beyond the sea, or that a parcel of brutes could move a wooden vessel whither they pleased upon water. He was sure no Houyhnhnm alive could make such a vessel, or would trust Yahoos to manage it.

The word Houyhnhnm, in their tongue, signifies a Horse; and in its etymology, the Perfection of Nature. I told my master that I was at a loss for expression, but would improve as fast as I could; and hoped in a short time I should be able to tell him wonders. He was pleased to direct his own mare, his colt, and foal, and the servants of the family to take all opportunities of instructing me; and every day for two or three hours, he was at the same pains himself. Several horses and mares of quality in the neighborhood came often to our house, upon the report spread of a wonderful Yahoo, that could speak like a Houyhnhnm, and seemed in his words and actions to discover some glimmerings of reason. These delighted to converse with me; they put many questions, and received such answers as I was able to return. By all which advantages, I made so great a progress, that in five months from my arrival, I understood whatever was spoke, and could express myself tolerably well.

The Houyhnhnms who came to visit my master, out of a design of seeing and talking with me, could hardly believe me to be a right Yahoo, because my body had a different covering from others of my kind. They were astonished to observe me without the usual hair or skin, except on my head, face, and hands; but I discovered that secret to my master, upon an accident, which happened about a fortnight before.

I have already told the reader, that every night when the family were gone to bed, it was my custom to strip and cover myself with my clothes; it happened one morning early, that my master sent for me, by the sorrel nag, who was his valet; when he came, I was fast asleep, my clothes fallen off on one side, and my shirt above my waist. I awaked at the noise he made, and observed him to deliver his message in some disorder; after which he went to my master, and in a great fright gave him a very confused account of what he had seen. This I presently discovered; for going as soon as I was dressed, to pay my attendance upon his honor, he asked me the meaning of what his servant had reported; that I was not the same thing when I slept as I appeared to be at other times; that his valet assured him, some part of me was white, some yellow, at least not so white, and some brown.

I had hitherto concealed the secret of my dress, in order to distinguish myself as much as possible, from that cursed race of Yahoos; but now I found it in vain to do so any longer. Besides, I considered that my clothes and shoes would soon wear out, which already were in a declining condition, and must be supplied by some contrivance from the hides of Yahoos, or other brutes; whereby the whole secret would be known. I therefore told my master, that in the country from whence I came, those of my kind always covered their bodies with the hairs of certain animals prepared by art, as well for decency, as to avoid inclemencies of air both hot and cold; of which, as to my own person I would give him immediate conviction, if he pleased to command me; only desiring his excuse, if I did not expose those parts that Nature taught us to conceal. He said, my discourse was all very strange, but especially the last part; for he could not understand why Nature should teach us to conceal what Nature had given. That neither himself nor family were ashamed of any parts of their bodies; but however I might do as I pleased. Whereupon, I first unbuttoned my coat, and pulled it off. I did the same with my waistcoat; I drew off my shoes, stockings, and breeches. I let my shirt down to my waist, and drew up the bottom, fastening it like a girdle about my middle to hide my nakedness.

My master observed the whole performance with great signs of curiosity and admiration. He took up all my clothes in his pastern, one piece after another, and examined them diligently; he then stroked my body very gently, and looked round me several times; after which he said, it was plain I must be a perfect Yahoo; but that I differed very much from the rest of my species, in the whiteness and smoothness of my skin, my want of hair in several parts of my body, the shape and shortness of my claws behind and before, and my affectation of walking continually on my two hinder feet. He desired to see no more; and gave me leave to put on my clothes again, for I was shuddering with cold.

I expressed my uneasiness at his giving me so often the appellation of Yahoo, an odious animal, for which I had so utter an hatred and contempt. I begged he would forbear applying that word to me, and take the same order in his family, and among his friends whom he suffered to see me. I requested likewise, that the secret of my having a false covering to my body might be known to none but himself, at least as long as my present clothing should last; for as to what the sorrel nag his valet had observed, his honor might command him to conceal it.

All this my master very graciously consented to; and thus the secret was kept till my clothes began to wear out, which I was forced to supply by several contrivances, that shall hereafter be mentioned. In the meantime, he desired I would go on with my utmost diligence to learn their language, because he was more astonished at my capacity for speech and reason, than at the figure of my body, whether it were covered or no; adding that he waited with some impatience to hear the wonders which I promised to tell him.

From thenceforward he doubled the pains he had been at to instruct me; he brought me into all company, and made them treat me with civility, because, as he told them privately, this would put me into good humor, and make me more diverting.

Every day when I waited on him, beside the trouble he was at in teaching, he would ask me several questions concerning myself, which I answered as well as I could; and by those means he had already received some general ideas, although very imperfect. It would be tedious to relate the several steps, by which I advanced to a more regular conversation, but the first account I gave of myself in any order and length was to this purpose:

That, I came from a very far country, as I already had attempted to tell him, with about fifty more of my own species; that we traveled upon the seas, in a great hollow vessel made of wood, and larger than his honor's house. I described the ship to him in the best terms I could; and explained by the help of my handkerchief displayed, how it was driven forward by the wind. That, upon a quarrel among us, I was set on shore on this coast, where I walked forward without knowing whither, till he delivered me from the persecution of those execrable Yahoos. He asked me who made the ship, and how it was possible that the Houyhnhnms of my country would leave it to the management of brutes? My answer was that I durst proceed no farther in my relation, unless he would give me his word and honor that he would not be offended; and then I would tell him the wonders I had so often promised. He agreed; and I went on by assuring him, that the ship was made by creatures like myself, who in all the countries I had traveled, as well as in my own, were the only governing, rational animals; and that upon my arrival hither, I was as much astonished to see the Houyhnhnms act like rational beings, as he or his friends could be in finding some marks of reason in a creature he was pleased to call a Yahoo; to which I owned my resemblance in every part, but could not account for their degenerate and brutal nature. I said farther, that if good fortune ever restored me to my native country, to relate my travels hither, as I resolved to do, everybody would believe that I *said the thing which was not,* that I invented the story out of my own head; and with all possible respect to himself, his family, and friends, and under his promise of not being offended, our countrymen would hardly think it probable, that a Houyhnhnm should be the presiding creature of a nation, and a Yahoo the brute.

CHAPTER 4. *The Houyhnhnms' notion of truth and falsehood. The Author's discourse disapproved by his master. The Author gives a more particular account of himself, and the accidents of his voyage.*

My master heard me with great appearances of uneasiness in his countenance; because *doubting* or *not believing* are so little known in this country, that the inhabitants cannot tell how to behave themselves under such circumstances. And I remember in frequent discourses with my master concerning the nature of manhood, in other parts of the world, having occasion to talk of *lying* and *false representation,* it was with much difficulty that he comprehended what I meant; although he had otherwise a most acute judgment. For he argued thus: that the use of speech was to make us understand one another, and to receive information of facts; now if anyone *said the thing which was not,* these ends were defeated; because I cannot properly be said to understand him; and I am so far from receiving information, that he leaves me worse than in ignorance; for I am led to believe a thing *black* when it is *white,* and *short* when it is *long.* And these were all the notions he had concerning the faculty of *lying,* so perfectly well understood, and so universally practiced among human creatures.

To return from this digression; when I asserted that the Yahoos were the only governing animals in my country, which my master said was altogether past his conception, he desired to know, whether we had Houyhnhnms among us, and what was their employment. I told him we had great numbers; that in summer they grazed in the fields, and in winter were kept in houses, with hay and oats, where Yahoo servants were employed to rub their skins smooth, comb their manes, pick their feet, serve them with food, and make their beds. "I understand you well," said my master; "it is now very plain from all you have spoken, that whatever share of reason the Yahoos pretend to, the Houyhnhnms are your masters; I heartily wish our Yahoos would be so tractable." I begged his honor would please to excuse me from proceeding any farther, because I was very certain that the account he expected from me would be highly displeasing. But he insisted in commanding me to let him know the best and the worst; I told him he should be obeyed. I owned that the Houyhnhnms among us, whom we called Horses, were the most generous[2] and comely animal we had; that they excelled in strength and swiftness; and when they belonged to persons of quality, employed in traveling, racing, and drawing chariots, they were treated with much kindness and care, till they fell into diseases, or became foundered in the feet; but then they were sold, and used to all kind of drudgery till they died; after which their skins were stripped and sold for what they were worth, and their bodies left to be devoured by dogs and birds of prey. But the common race of horses had not so good fortune, being kept by farmers and carriers, and other mean people, who put them to greater labor, and feed them worse. I described as well as I could, our way of riding; the shape and use of a bridle, a saddle, a spur, and a whip; of harness and wheels. I added, that we fastened plates of a certain hard substance called iron at the bottom of their feet, to preserve their hoofs from being broken by the stony ways on which we often traveled.

My master, after some expressions of great indignation, wondered how we dared to venture upon a Houyhnhnm's back; for he was sure, that the weakest servant in his house would be able to shake off the strongest Yahoo; or by lying down, and rolling upon his back, squeeze the brute to death. I answered that our horses were trained up from three or four years old to the several uses we intended them for; that if any of them proved intolerably vicious, they were employed for carriages; that they were severely beaten while they were young for any mischievous tricks; that the males, designed for the common use of riding or draught, were generally castrated about two years after their birth, to take down their spirits, and make them more tame and gentle; that they were indeed sensible of rewards and punishments; but his honor would please to consider that they had not the least tincture of reason any more than the Yahoos in this country.

It put me to the pains of many circumlocutions to give my master a right idea of what I spoke; for their language doth not abound in variety of words, because their wants and passions are fewer than among us. But it is impossible to express his noble resentment at our savage treatment of the Houyhnhnm race; particularly after I had explained the manner and use of castrating horses among us, to hinder them from propagating their kind, and to render them more servile. He said, if it were possible there could be any country where Yahoos alone were endued with reason, they certainly must be the governing animal, because reason will in time always prevail against brutal strength. But, considering the frame of our bodies, and especially of mine, he thought no creature of equal bulk was so ill-contrived for employing that reason in the common offices of life; whereupon he desired to know whether those among whom I lived resembled me or the Yahoos of his country. I assured him that I was as well shaped as most of my age; but the younger and the females were much more soft and tender, and the skins of the latter generally as white as milk. He said I differed indeed from other Yahoos, being much more cleanly, and not altogether so deformed; but in point of real advantage, he thought I differed for the worse. That my nails were of no use either to my fore or hinder feet; as to my forefeet, he could not properly call them by that name, for he never observed me to walk upon them; that they were too soft to bear the ground; that I generally went with them uncovered, neither was the covering I sometimes wore on them of the same shape, or so

2. Noble.

strong as that on my feet behind. That I could not walk with any security; for if either of my hinder feet slipped, I must inevitably fall. He then began to find fault with other parts of my body; the flatness of my face, the prominence of my nose, my eyes placed directly in front, so that I could not look on either side without turning my head; that I was not able to feed myself without lifting one of my forefeet to my mouth; and therefore nature had placed those joints to answer that necessity. He knew not what could be the use of those several clefts and divisions in my feet behind; that these were too soft to bear the hardness and sharpness of stones without a covering made from the skin of some other brute; that my whole body wanted a fence against heat and cold, which I was forced to put on and off every day with tediousness and trouble. And lastly, that he observed every animal in his country naturally to abhor the Yahoos, whom the weaker avoided, and the stronger drove from them. So that supposing us to have the gift of reason, he could not see how it were possible to cure that natural antipathy which every creature discovered against us; nor consequently, how we could tame and render them serviceable. However, he would (as he said) debate the matter no farther, because he was more desirous to know my own story, the country where I was born, and the several actions and events of my life before I came hither.

I assured him how extremely desirous I was that he should be satisfied in every point; but I doubted much whether it would be possible for me to explain myself on several subjects whereof his honor could have no conception, because I saw nothing in his country to which I could resemble them. That however, I would do my best, and strive to express myself by similitudes, humbly desiring his assistance when I wanted proper words; which he was pleased to promise me.

I said, my birth was of honest parents, in an island called England, which was remote from this country, as many days journey as the strongest of his honor's servants could travel in the annual course of the sun. That I was bred a surgeon, whose trade it is to cure wounds and hurts in the body, got by accident or violence. That my country was governed by a female man, whom we called a queen. That I left it to get riches, whereby I might maintain myself and family when I should return. That in my last voyage, I was Commander of the ship and had about fifty Yahoos under me, many of which died at sea, and I was forced to supply them by others picked out from several nations. That our ship was twice in danger of being sunk; the first time by a great storm, and the second, by striking against a rock. Here my master interposed, by asking me, how I could persuade strangers out of different countries to venture with me, after the losses I had sustained, and the hazards I had run. I said, they were fellows of desperate fortunes, forced to fly from the places of their birth, on account of their poverty or their crimes. Some were undone by lawsuits; others spent all they had in drinking, whoring, and gaming; others fled for treason; many for murder, theft, poisoning, robbery, perjury, forgery, coining false money; for committing rapes or sodomy; for flying from their colors, or deserting to the enemy; and most of them had broken prison. None of these durst return to their native countries for fear of being hanged, or of starving in a jail; and therefore were under a necessity of seeking a livelihood in other places.

During this discourse, my master was pleased often to interrupt me. I had made use of many circumlocutions in describing to him the nature of the several crimes, for which most of our crew had been forced to fly their country. This labor took up several days conversation before he was able to comprehend me. He was wholly at a loss to know what could be the use or necessity of practicing those vices. To clear up which I endeavored to give him some ideas of the desire of power and riches; of the terrible effects of lust, intemperance, malice, and envy. All this I was forced to define and describe by putting of cases, and making suppositions. After which, like one whose imagination was struck with something never seen or heard of before, he would lift up his eyes with amazement and indignation. Power, government, war, law, punishment, and a thousand other things had no terms, wherein that language could express them; which made the difficulty almost insuperable to give my master any conception of what I meant; but being of an excellent understanding, much improved by contemplation and converse, he at last arrived at a competent knowledge of what human nature in our parts of the world is capable to perform; and desired I would give him some particular account of that land, which we call Europe, especially, of my own country.

CHAPTER 5. *The Author, at his master's commands, informs him of the state of England. The causes of war among the princes of Europe. The Author begins to explain the English Constitution.*

The reader may please to observe that the following extract of many conversations I had with my master contains a summary of the most material points, which were discoursed at several times for above two years; his honor often desiring fuller satisfaction as I farther improved in the Houyhnhnm tongue. I laid before him, as well as I could, the whole state of Europe; I discoursed of trade and manufactures, of arts and sciences; and the answers I gave to all the questions he made, as they arose upon several subjects, were a fund of conversation not to be exhausted. But I shall here only set down the substance of what passed between us concerning my own country, reducing it into order as well as I can, without any regard to time or other circumstances, while I strictly adhere to truth. My only concern is that I shall hardly be able to do justice to my master's arguments and expressions; which must needs suffer by my want of capacity, as well as by a translation into our barbarous English.

In obedience therefore to his honor's commands, I related to him the Revolution under the Prince of Orange; the long war with France entered into by the said Prince, and renewed by his successor the present queen; wherein the greatest powers of Christendom were engaged, and which still continued. I computed at his request, that about a million of Yahoos might have been killed in the whole progress of it; and perhaps a hundred or more cities taken, and five times as many ships burned or sunk.[3]

He asked me what were the usual causes or motives that made one country to go to war with another. I answered, they were innumerable; but I should only mention a few of the chief. Sometimes the ambition of princes, who never think they have land or people enough to govern; sometimes the

---

3. Gulliver relates recent English history: the Glorious Revolution (1688–89) and the War of Spanish Succession (1701–13). He greatly exaggerates the casualties in the war.

corruption of ministers, who engage their master in a war in order to stifle or divert the clamor of the subjects against their evil administration. Difference in opinions hath cost many millions of lives; for instance, whether flesh be bread, or bread be flesh; whether the juice of a certain berry be blood or wine; whether whistling be a vice or a virtue; whether it be better to kiss a post, or throw it into the fire; what is the best color for a coat, whether black, white, red, or grey; and whether it should be long or short, narrow or wide, dirty or clean;[4] with many more. Neither are any wars so furious and bloody, or of so long continuance, as those occasioned by difference in opinion, especially if it be in things indifferent.[5]

Sometimes the quarrel between two princes is to decide which of them shall dispossess a third of his dominions, where neither of them pretend to any right. Sometimes one prince quarreleth with another, for fear the other should quarrel with him. Sometimes a war is entered upon, because the enemy is too strong, and sometimes because he is too weak. Sometimes our neighbors want the things which we have, or have the things which we want; and we both fight, till they take ours or give us theirs. It is a very justifiable cause of war to invade a country after the people have been wasted by famine, destroyed by pestilence, or embroiled by factions amongst themselves. It is justifiable to enter into a war against our nearest ally, when one of his towns lies convenient for us, or a territory of land, that would render our dominions round and compact. If a prince send forces into a nation, where the people are poor and ignorant, he may lawfully put half of them to death, and make slaves of the rest, in order to civilize and reduce them from their barbarous way of living. It is a very kingly, honorable, and frequent practice, when one prince desires the assistance of another to secure him against an invasion, that the assistant, when he hath driven out the invader, should seize on the dominions himself, and kill, imprison, or banish the prince he came to relieve. Alliance by blood or marriage is a sufficient cause of war between princes; and the nearer the kindred is, the greater is their disposition to quarrel. Poor nations are hungry, and rich nations are proud; and pride and hunger will ever be at variance. For these reasons, the trade of a soldier is held the most honorable of all others: because a soldier is a Yahoo hired to kill in cold blood as many of his own species, who have never offended him, as possibly he can.

There is likewise a kind of beggarly princes in Europe, not able to make war by themselves, who hire out their troops to richer nations for so much a day to each man; of which they keep three fourths to themselves, and it is the best part of their maintenance; such are those in many northern parts of Europe.[6]

"What you have told me," said my master, "upon the subject of war, doth indeed discover most admirably the effects of that reason you pretend to. However, it is happy that the shame is greater than the danger; and that Nature hath left you utterly uncapable of doing much mischief; for your mouths lying flat with your faces, you can hardly bite each other to any pur-

---

4. Gulliver refers to the religious controversies of the Reformation and Counter-Reformation: the doctrine of transubstantiation, the use of music in church services, the veneration of the crucifix, and the wearing of priestly vestments.
5. Of little consequence.
6. A satiric glance at George I, who, as elector of Hanover, had dealt in this trade.

pose, unless by consent. Then, as to the claws upon your feet before and behind, they are so short and tender, that one of our Yahoos would drive a dozen of yours before him. And therefore in recounting the numbers of those who have been killed in battle, I cannot but think that you have *said the thing which is not.*"

I could not forbear shaking my head and smiling a little at his ignorance. And, being no stranger to the art of war, I gave him a description of cannons, culverins, muskets, carabines, pistols, bullets, powder, swords, bayonets, battles, sieges, retreats, attacks, undermines, countermines, bombardments, sea fights; ships sunk with a thousand men; twenty thousand killed on each side; dying groans, limbs flying in the air; smoke, noise, confusion, trampling to death under horses' feet; flight, pursuit, victory; fields strewed with carcasses left for food to dogs, and wolves, and birds of prey; plundering, stripping, ravishing, burning, and destroying. And, to set forth the valor of my own dear countrymen, I assured him that I had seen them blow up a hundred enemies at once in a siege, and as many in a ship; and beheld the dead bodies drop down in pieces from the clouds, to the great diversion of all the spectators.

I was going on to more particulars, when my master commanded me silence. He said, whoever understood the nature of Yahoos might easily believe it possible for so vile an animal, to be capable of every action I had named, if their strength and cunning equaled their malice. But, as my discourse had increased his abhorrence of the whole species, so he found it gave him a disturbance in his mind, to which he was wholly a stranger before. He thought his ears being used to such abominable words, might by degrees admit them with less detestation. That, although he hated the Yahoos of this country, yet he no more blamed them for their odious qualities, than he did a *gnnayh* (a bird of prey) for its cruelty, or a sharp stone for cutting his hoof. But, when a creature pretending to reason could be capable of such enormities, he dreaded lest the corruption of that faculty might be worse than brutality itself. He seemed therefore confident, that instead of reason, we were only possessed of some quality fitted to increase our natural vices; as the reflection from a troubled stream returns the image of an ill-shapen body, not only larger, but more distorted.

He added that he had heard too much upon the subject of war, both in this and some former discourses. There was another point which a little perplexed him at present. I had said that some of our crew left their country on account of being ruined by law: that I had already explained the meaning of the word; but he was at a loss how it should come to pass, that the law which was intended for every man's preservation, should be any man's ruin. Therefore he desired to be farther satisfied what I meant by law, and the dispensers thereof, according to the present practice in my own country; because he thought Nature and Reason were sufficient guides for a reasonable animal, as we pretended to be, in showing us what we ought to do, and what to avoid.

I assured his honor that law was a science wherein I had not much conversed, further than by employing advocates, in vain, upon some injustices that had been done me. However, I would give him all the satisfaction I was able.

I said there was a society of men among us, bred up from their youth in the art of proving by words multiplied for the purpose, that white is black, and black is white, according as they are paid. To this society all the rest of the people are slaves.

"For example. If my neighbor hath a mind to my cow, he hires a lawyer to prove that he ought to have my cow from me. I must then hire another to defend my right; it being against all rules of law that any man should be allowed to speak for himself. Now in this case, I who am the true owner lie under two great disadvantages. First, my lawyer being practiced almost from his cradle in defending falsehood is quite out of his element when he would be an advocate for justice, which as an office unnatural, he always attempts with great awkwardness, if not with ill-will. The second disadvantage is that my lawyer must proceed with great caution, or else he will be reprimanded by the judges, and abhorred by his brethren, as one who would lessen the practice of the law. And therefore I have but two methods to preserve my cow. The first is to gain over my adversary's lawyer with a double fee; who will then betray his client, by insinuating that he hath justice on his side. The second way is for my lawyer to make my cause appear as unjust as he can; by allowing the cow to belong to my adversary; and this if it be skillfully done, will certainly bespeak the favor of the bench.

"Now, your honor is to know that these judges are persons appointed to decide all controversies of property, as well as for the trial of criminals; and picked out from the most dextrous lawyers who are grown old or lazy; and having been biased all their lives against truth and equity, lie under such a fatal necessity of favoring fraud, perjury, and oppression, that I have known some of them to have refused a large bribe from the side where justice lay, rather than injure the faculty,[7] by doing anything unbecoming their nature or their office.

"It is a maxim among these lawyers, that whatever hath been done before may legally be done again; and therefore they take special care to record all the decisions formerly made against common justice and the general reason of mankind. These, under the name of *precedents*, they produce as authorities to justify the most iniquitous opinions; and the judges never fail of directing accordingly.

"In pleading, they studiously avoid entering into the merits of the cause; but are loud, violent, and tedious in dwelling upon all circumstances which are not to the purpose. For instance, in the case already mentioned, they never desire to know what claim or title my adversary hath to my cow; but whether the said cow were red or black; her horns long or short; whether the field I graze her in be round or square; whether she were milked at home or abroad; what diseases she is subject to, and the like. After which they consult precedents, adjourn the cause, from time to time, and in ten, twenty, or thirty years come to an issue.

"It is likewise to be observed, that this society hath a peculiar cant and jargon of their own, that no other mortal can understand, and wherein all their laws are written, which they take special care to multiply; whereby they have wholly confounded the very essence of truth and falsehood, of right and wrong; so that it will take thirty years to decide whether the field, left me by my ancestors for six generations, belong to me, or to a stranger three hundred miles off.

7. Profession.

"In the trial of persons accused for crimes against the state, the method is much more short and commendable: the judge first sends to sound the disposition of those in power; after which he can easily hang or save the criminal, strictly preserving all the forms of law."

Here my master interposing said it was a pity that creatures endowed with such prodigious abilities of mind as these lawyers, by the description I gave of them, must certainly be, were not rather encouraged to be instructors of others in wisdom and knowledge. In answer to which, I assured his honor that in all points out of their own trade, they were usually the most ignorant and stupid generation among us, the most despicable in common conversation, avowed enemies to all knowledge and learning; and equally disposed to pervert the general reason of mankind, in every other subject of discourse as in that of their own profession.

CHAPTER 6. *A continuation of the state of England, under Queen Anne. The character of a first minister in the courts of Europe.*

My master was yet wholly at a loss to understand what motives could incite this race of lawyers to perplex, disquiet, and weary themselves by engaging in a confederacy of injustice, merely for the sake of injuring their fellow animals; neither could he comprehend what I meant in saying they did it for hire. Whereupon I was at much pains to describe to him the use of money, the materials it was made of, and the value of the metals; that when a Yahoo had got a great store of this precious substance, he was able to purchase whatever he had a mind to; the finest clothing, the noblest houses, great tracts of land, the most costly meats and drinks; and have his choice of the most beautiful females. Therefore since money alone was able to perform all these feats, our Yahoos thought they could never have enough of it to spend or to save, as they found themselves inclined from their natural bent either to profusion or avarice. That the rich man enjoyed the fruit of the poor man's labor, and the latter were a thousand to one in proportion to the former. That the bulk of our people was forced to live miserably, by laboring every day for small wages to make a few live plentifully. I enlarged myself much on these and many other particulars to the same purpose, but his honor was still to seek,[8] for he went upon a supposition that all animals had a title to their share in the productions of the earth; and especially those who presided over the rest. Therefore he desired I would let him know what these costly meats were, and how any of us happened to want them. Whereupon I enumerated as many sorts as came into my head, with the various methods of dressing them, which could not be done without sending vessels by sea to every part of the world, as well for liquors to drink, as for sauces, and innumerable other conveniencies. I assured him, that this whole globe of earth must be at least three times gone round, before one of our better female Yahoos could get her breakfast, or a cup to put it in. He said, "That must needs be a miserable country which cannot furnish food for its own inhabitants." But what he chiefly wondered at, was how such vast tracts of ground as I described, should be wholly without fresh water, and the people put to the necessity of sending over the sea for drink. I replied that England (the dear place of my nativity)

8. Still did not understand.

was computed to produce three times the quantity of food, more than its inhabitants are able to consume, as well as liquors extracted from grain, or pressed out of the fruit of certain trees, which made excellent drink; and the same proportion in every other convenience of life. But, in order to feed the luxury and intemperance of the males, and the vanity of the females, we sent away the greatest part of our necessary things to other countries, from whence in return we brought the materials of diseases, folly, and vice, to spend among ourselves. Hence it follows of necessity, that vast numbers of our people are compelled to seek their livelihood by begging, robbing, stealing, cheating, pimping, forswearing, flattering, suborning, forging, gaming, lying, fawning, hectoring, voting, scribbling, star gazing, poisoning, whoring, canting, libeling, freethinking, and the like occupations; every one of which terms, I was at much pains to make him understand.

That, wine was not imported among us from foreign countries, to supply the want of water or other drinks, but because it was a sort of liquid which made us merry, by putting us out of our senses; diverted all melancholy thoughts, begat wild extravagant imaginations in the brain, raised our hopes, and banished our fears; suspended every office of reason for a time, and deprived us of the use of our limbs, until we fell into a profound sleep; although it must be confessed, that we always awaked sick and dispirited; and that the use of this liquor filled us with diseases, which made our lives uncomfortable and short.

But beside all this, the bulk of our people supported themselves by furnishing the necessities or conveniencies of life to the rich, and to each other. For instance, when I am at home and dressed as I ought to be, I carry on my body the workmanship of an hundred tradesmen; the building and furniture of my house employ as many more; and five times the number to adorn my wife.

I was going on to tell him of another sort of people, who get their livelihood by attending the sick; having upon some occasions informed his honor that many of my crew had died of diseases. But here it was with the utmost difficulty that I brought him to apprehend what I meant. He could easily conceive that a Houyhnhnm grew weak and heavy a few days before his death; or by some accident might hurt a limb. But that nature, who worketh all things to perfection, should suffer any pains to breed in our bodies, he thought impossible; and desired to know the reason of so unaccountable an evil. I told him, we fed on a thousand things which operated contrary to each other; that we eat when we were not hungry, and drank without the provocation of thirst; that we sat whole nights drinking strong liquors without eating a bit, which disposed us to sloth, inflamed our bodies, and precipitated or prevented digestion. That, prostitute female Yahoos acquired a certain malady, which bred rottenness in the bones of those who fell into their embraces; that this and many other diseases were propagated from father to son; so that great numbers come into the world with complicated maladies upon them; that it would be endless to give him a catalogue of all diseases incident to human bodies; for they could not be fewer than five or six hundred, spread over every limb, and joint; in short, every part, external and intestine, having diseases appropriated to each. To remedy which, there was a sort of people bred up among us, in the profession or pretense of curing the sick. And because I had some skill in the faculty, I would in gratitude to his honor let him know the whole mystery and method by which they proceed.

Their fundamental is that all diseases arise from repletion; from whence they conclude, that a great evacuation of the body is necessary, either through the natural passage, or upwards at the mouth. Their next business is, from herbs, minerals, gums, oils, shells, salts, juices, seaweed, excrements, barks of trees, serpents, toads, frogs, spiders, dead men's flesh and bones, birds, beasts and fishes, to form a composition for smell and taste the most abominable, nauseous, and detestable, that they can possibly contrive, which the stomach immediately rejects with loathing, and this they call a vomit. Or else from the same storehouse, with some other poisonous additions, they command us to take in at the orifice above or below (just as the physician then happens to be disposed) a medicine equally annoying and disgustful to the bowels; which relaxing the belly, drives down all before it; and this they call a purge, or a clyster. For nature (as the physicians allege) having intended the superior anterior orifice only for the intromission of solids and liquids, and the inferior posterior for ejection, these artists ingeniously considering that in all diseases nature is forced out of her seat; therefore to replace her in it, the body must be treated in a manner directly contrary, by interchanging the use of each orifice; forcing solids and liquids in at the anus, and making evacuations at the mouth.

But, besides real diseases, we are subject to many that are only imaginary, for which the physicians have invented imaginary cures; these have their several names, and so have the drugs that are proper for them; and with these our female Yahoos are always infested.

One great excellency in this tribe is their skill at prognostics, wherein they seldom fail; their predictions in real diseases, when they rise to any degree of malignity, generally portending death, which is always in their power, when recovery is not, and therefore, upon any unexpected signs of amendment, after they have pronounced their sentence, rather than be accused as false prophets, they know how to approve[9] their sagacity to the world by a seasonable dose.

They are likewise of special use to husbands and wives, who are grown weary of their mates; to eldest sons, to great ministers of state, and often to princes.

I had formerly upon occasion discoursed with my master upon the nature of government in general, and particularly of our own excellent constitution, deservedly the wonder and envy of the whole world. But having here accidently mentioned a minister of state, he commanded me some time after to inform him what species of Yahoo I particularly meant by that appellation.

I told him that a first or chief minister of state, whom I intended to describe, was a creature wholly exempt from joy and grief, love and hatred, pity and anger; at least makes use of no other passions but a violent desire of wealth, power, and titles; that he applies his words to all uses, except to the indication of his mind; that he never tells a truth, but with an intent that you should take it for a lie; nor a lie, but with a design that you should take it for a truth; that those he speaks worst of behind their backs are in the surest way to preferment; and whenever he begins to praise you to others or to

9. Prove.

yourself, you are from that day forlorn. The worst mark you can receive is a promise, especially when it is confirmed with an oath; after which every wise man retires, and gives over all hopes.

There are three methods by which a man may rise to be chief minister: the first is by knowing how with prudence to dispose of a wife, a daughter, or a sister; the second, by betraying or undermining his predecessor; and the third is by a furious zeal in public assemblies against the corruptions of the court. But a wise prince would rather choose to employ those who practice the last of these methods; because such zealots prove always the most obsequious and subservient to the will and passions of their master. That, these ministers having all employments at their disposal, preserve themselves in power by bribing the majority of a senate or great council; and at last by an expedient called an Act of Indemnity[1] (whereof I described the nature to him) they secure themselves from after reckonings, and retire from the public, laden with the spoils of the nation.

The palace of a chief minister is a seminary to breed up others in his own trade; the pages, lackies, and porter, by imitating their master, become ministers of state in their several districts, and learn to excel in the three principal ingredients, of insolence, lying, and bribery. Accordingly, they have a subaltern court paid to them by persons of the best rank; and sometimes by the force of dexterity and impudence, arrive through several gradations to be successors to their lord.

He is usually governed by a decayed wench, or favorite footman, who are the tunnels through which all graces are conveyed, and may properly be called, in the last resort, the governors of the kingdom.

One day, my master, having heard me mention the nobility of my country, was pleased to make me a compliment which I could not pretend to deserve: that, he was sure, I must have been born of some noble family, because I far exceeded in shape, color, and cleanliness, all the Yahoos of his nation, although I seemed to fail in strength, and agility, which must be imputed to my different way of living from those other brutes; and besides, I was not only endowed with the faculty of speech, but likewise with some rudiments of reason, to a degree, that with all his acquaintance I passed for a prodigy.

He made me observe, that among the Houyhnhnms, the white, the sorrel, and the iron grey were not so exactly shaped as the bay, the dapple grey, and the black; nor born with equal talents of mind, or a capacity to improve them; and therefore continued always in the condition of servants, without ever aspiring to match out of their own race, which in that country would be reckoned monstrous and unnatural.

I made his honor my most humble acknowledgments for the good opinion he was pleased to conceive of me; but assured him at the same time, that my birth was of the lower sort, having been born of plain, honest parents, who were just able to give me a tolerable education; that, nobility among us was altogether a different thing from the idea he had of it; that, our young noblemen are bred from their childhood in idleness and luxury; that, as soon as years will permit, they consume their vigor, and contract odious diseases among lewd females; and when their fortunes are almost ruined, they marry

1. An act passed at each session of Parliament to protect ministers of state who in good faith might have acted illegally.

some woman of mean birth, disagreeable person, and unsound constitution, merely for the sake of money, whom they hate and despise. That, the productions of such marriages are generally scrofulous, rickety or deformed children; by which means the family seldom continues above three generations, unless the wife take care to provide a healthy father among her neighbors, or domestics, in order to improve and continue the breed. That a weak diseased body, a meager countenance, and sallow complexion are the true marks of noble blood; and a healthy robust appearance is so disgraceful in a man of quality, that the world concludes his real father to have been a groom or a coachman. The imperfections of his mind run parallel with those of his body; being a composition of spleen, dullness, ignorance, caprice, sensuality, and pride.

Without the consent of this illustrious body, no law can be enacted, repealed, or altered, and these nobles have likewise the decision of all our possessions without appeal.

CHAPTER 7. *The Author's great love of his native country. His master's observations upon the constitution and administration of England, as described by the Author, with parallel cases and comparisons. His master's observations upon human nature.*

The reader may be disposed to wonder how I could prevail on myself to give so free a representation of my own species, among a race of mortals who were already too apt to conceive the vilest opinion of humankind, from that entire congruity betwixt me and their Yahoos. But I must freely confess that the many virtues of those excellent quadrupeds placed in opposite view to human corruptions had so far opened my eyes, and enlarged my understanding, that I began to view the actions and passions of man in a very different light; and to think the honor of my own kind not worth managing;[2] which, besides, it was impossible for me to do before a person of so acute a judgment as my master, who daily convinced me of a thousand faults in myself, whereof I had not the least perception before, and which with us would never be numbered even among human infirmities. I had likewise learned from his example an utter detestation of all falsehood or disguise; and truth appeared so amiable to me, that I determined upon sacrificing everything to it.

Let me deal so candidly with the reader as to confess that there was yet a much stronger motive for the freedom I took in my representation of things. I had not been a year in this country, before I contracted such a love and veneration for the inhabitants, that I entered on a firm resolution never to return to humankind, but to pass the rest of my life among these admirable Houyhnhnms in the contemplation and practice of every virtue; where I could have no example or incitement to vice. But it was decreed by fortune, my perpetual enemy, that so great a felicity should not fall to my share. However, it is now some comfort to reflect that in what I said of my countrymen, I extenuated their faults as much as I durst before so strict an examiner; and upon every article, gave as favorable a turn as the matter would bear. For, indeed, who is there alive that will not be swayed by his bias and partiality to the place of his birth?

2. Defending.

I have related the substance of several conversations I had with my master, during the greatest part of the time I had the honor to be in his service; but have indeed for brevity sake omitted much more than is here set down.

When I had answered all his questions, and his curiosity seemed to be fully satisfied; he sent for me one morning early, and commanding me to sit down at some distance (an honor which he had never before conferred upon me), he said he had been very seriously considering my whole story, as far as it related both to myself and my country; that, he looked upon us as a sort of animals to whose share, by what accident he could not conjecture, some small pittance of reason had fallen, whereof we made no other use than by its assistance to aggravate our natural corruptions, and to acquire new ones which nature had not given us. That we disarmed ourselves of the few abilities she had bestowed; had been very successful in multiplying our original wants, and seemed to spend our whole lives in vain endeavors to supply them by our own inventions. That, as to myself, it was manifest I had neither the strength or agility of a common Yahoo; that I walked infirmly on my hinder feet; had found out a contrivance to make my claws of no use or defense, and to remove the hair from my chin, which was intended as a shelter from the sun and the weather. Lastly, that I could neither run with speed, nor climb trees like my brethren (as he called them) the Yahoos in this country.

That our institutions of government and law were plainly owing to our gross defects in reason, and by consequence, in virtue; because reason alone is sufficient to govern a rational creature; which was therefore a character we had no pretense to challenge, even from the account I had given of my own people; although he manifestly perceived, that in order to favor them, I had concealed many particulars, and often *said the thing which was not.*

He was the more confirmed in this opinion, because he observed that I agreed in every feature of my body with other Yahoos, except where it was to my real disadvantage in point of strength, speed, and activity, the shortness of my claws, and some other particulars where Nature had no part; so, from the representation I had given him of our lives, our manners, and our actions, he found as near a resemblance in the disposition of our minds. He said the Yahoos were known to hate one another more than they did any different species of animals; and the reason usually assigned was the odiousness of their own shapes, which all could see in the rest, but not in themselves. He had therefore begun to think it not unwise in us to cover our bodies, and by that invention, conceal many of our deformities from each other, which would else be hardly supportable. But he now found he had been mistaken; and that the dissensions of those brutes in his country were owing to the same cause with ours, as I had described them. For, if (said he) you throw among five Yahoos as much food as would be sufficient for fifty, they will instead of eating peaceably, fall together by the ears, each single one impatient to have all to itself; and therefore a servant was usually employed to stand by while they were feeding abroad, and those kept at home were tied at a distance from each other. That, if a cow died of age or accident, before a Houyhnhnm could secure it for his own Yahoos, those in the neighborhood would come in herds to seize it, and then would ensue such a battle as I had described, with terrible wounds made by their claws on both sides, although they seldom were able to kill one another, for want of such convenient instruments of death as we had invented. At other times the like battles have been fought between the Yahoos of several neighbor-hoods without any visible cause; those of one district watching all opportu-nities to surprise the next before they are prepared. But if they find their project hath miscarried, they return home, and for want of enemies, engage in what I call a civil war among themselves.

That, in some fields of his country, there are certain shining stones of several colors, whereof the Yahoos are violently fond; and when part of these stones are fixed in the earth, as it sometimes happeneth, they will dig with their claws for whole days to get them out, and carry them away, and hide them by heaps in their kennels; but still looking round with great cau-tion, for fear their comrades should find out their treasure. My master said he could never discover the reason of this unnatural appetite, or how these stones could be of any use to a Yahoo; but now he believed it might proceed from the same principle of avarice, which I had ascribed to mankind. That he had once, by way of experiment, privately removed a heap of these stones from the place where one of his Yahoos had buried it, whereupon, the sordid animal missing his treasure, by his loud lamenting brought the whole herd to the place, there miserably howled, then fell to biting and tearing the rest; began to pine away, would neither eat nor sleep, nor work, till he ordered a servant privately to convey the stones into the same hole, and hide them as before; which when his Yahoo had found, he presently recovered his spirits and good humor; but took care to remove them to a better hiding place; and hath ever since been a very serviceable brute.

My master farther assured me, which I also observed myself, that in the fields where these shining stones abound, the fiercest and most frequent bat-tles are fought, occasioned by perpetual inroads of the neighboring Yahoos.

He said it was common when two Yahoos discovered such a stone in a field, and were contending which of them should be the proprietor, a third would take the advantage, and carry it away from them both; which my mas-ter would needs contend to have some resemblance with our suits at law; wherein I thought it for our credit not to undeceive him; since the decision he mentioned was much more equitable than many decrees among us; because the plaintiff and defendant there lost nothing beside the stone they contended for; whereas our courts of equity would never have dismissed the cause while either of them had anything left.

My master continuing his discourse said there was nothing that rendered the Yahoos more odious, than their undistinguished appetite to devour everything that came in their way, whether herbs, roots, berries, corrupted flesh of animals, or all mingled together; and it was peculiar in their temper, that they were fonder of what they could get by rapine or stealth at a greater distance, than much better food provided for them at home. If their prey held out, they would eat till they were ready to burst, after which nature had pointed out to them a certain root that gave them a general evacuation.

There was also another kind of root very juicy, but something rare and difficult to be found, which the Yahoos sought for with much eagerness, and would suck it with great delight; it produced the same effects that wine hath upon us. It would make them sometimes hug, and sometimes tear one another; they would howl and grin, and chatter, and reel, and tumble, and then fall asleep in the mud.

I did indeed observe that the Yahoos were the only animals in this country subject to any diseases; which however, were much fewer than horses have among us, and contracted not by any ill treatment they meet with, but by the nastiness and greediness of that sordid brute. Neither has their language any more than a general appellation for those maladies; which is borrowed from the name of the beast, and called *Hnea Yahoo,* or the Yahoo's Evil; and the cure prescribed is a mixture of their own dung and urine, forcibly put down the Yahoo's throat. This I have since often known to have been taken with success, and do here freely recommend it to my countrymen, for the public good, as an admirable specific[3] against all diseases produced by repletion.

As to learning, government, arts, manufactures, and the like, my master confessed he could find little or no resemblance between the Yahoos of that country and those in ours. For he only meant to observe what parity there was in our natures. He had heard indeed some curious Houyhnhnms observe that in most herds there was a sort of ruling Yahoo (as among us there is generally some leading or principal stag in a park) who was always more deformed in body, and mischievous in disposition, than any of the rest. That this leader had usually a favorite as like himself as he could get, whose employment was to lick his master's feet and posteriors, and drive the female Yahoos to his kennel; for which he was now and then rewarded with a piece of ass's flesh. This favorite is hated by the whole herd; and therefore to protect himself, keeps always near the person of his leader. He usually continues in office till a worse can be found; but the very moment he is discarded, his successor, at the head of all the Yahoos in that district, young and old, male and female, come in a body, and discharge their excrements upon him from head to foot. But how far this might be applicable to our courts and favorites, and ministers of state, my master said I could best determine.

I durst make no return to this malicious insinuation, which debased human understanding below the sagacity of a common hound, who hath judgment enough to distinguish and follow the cry of the ablest dog in the pack, without being ever mistaken.

My master told me there were some qualities remarkable in the Yahoos, which he had not observed me to mention, or at least very slightly, in the accounts I had given him of humankind. He said, those animals, like other brutes, had their females in common; but in this they differed, that the she-Yahoo would admit the male while she was pregnant; and that the hes would quarrel and fight with the females as fiercely as with each other. Both which practices were such degrees of infamous brutality, that no other sensitive creature ever arrived at.

Another thing he wondered at in the Yahoos was their strange disposition to nastiness and dirt; whereas there appears to be a natural love of cleanliness in all other animals. As to the two former accusations, I was glad to let them pass without any reply, because I had not a word to offer upon them in defense of my species, which otherwise I certainly had done from my own inclinations. But I could have easily vindicated humankind from the imputation of singularity upon the last article, if there had been any swine in that country (as unluckily for me there were not) which although it may be a

3. Remedy.

sweeter quadruped than a Yahoo, cannot I humbly conceive in justice pretend to more cleanliness; and so his honor himself must have owned, if he had seen their filthy way of feeding, and their custom of wallowing and sleeping in the mud.

My master likewise mentioned another quality, which his servants had discovered in several Yahoos, and to him was wholly unaccountable. He said, a fancy would sometimes take a Yahoo, to retire into a corner, to lie down and howl, and groan, and spurn away all that came near him, although he were young and fat, and wanted neither food nor water; nor did the servants imagine what could possibly ail him. And the only remedy they found was to set him to hard work, after which he would infallibly come to himself. To this I was silent out of partiality to my own kind; yet here I could plainly discover the true seeds of spleen,[4] which only seizeth on the lazy, the luxurious, and the rich; who, if they were forced to undergo the same regimen, I would undertake for the cure.

His Honor had farther observed, that a female Yahoo would often stand behind a bank or a bush, to gaze on the young males passing by, and then appear, and hide, using many antic gestures and grimaces; at which time it was observed, that she had a most offensive smell; and when any of the males advanced, would slowly retire, looking back, and with a counterfeit show of fear, run off into some convenient place where she knew the male would follow her.

At other times, if a female stranger came among them, three or four of her own sex would get about her, and stare and chatter, and grin, and smell her all over; and then turn off with gestures that seemed to express contempt and disdain.

Perhaps my master might refine a little in these speculations, which he had drawn from what he observed himself, or had been told by others; however, I could not reflect without some amazement, and much sorrow, that the rudiments of lewdness, coquetry, censure, and scandal, should have place by instinct in womankind.

I expected every moment that my master would accuse the Yahoos of those unnatural appetites in both sexes, so common among us. But Nature it seems hath not been so expert a schoolmistress; and these politer pleasures are entirely the productions of art and reason, on our side of the globe.

CHAPTER 8. *The Author relateth several particulars of the Yahoos. The great virtues of the Houyhnhnms. The education and exercises of their youth. Their general assembly.*

As I ought to have understood human nature much better than I supposed it possible for my master to do, so it was easy to apply the character he gave of the Yahoos to myself and my countrymen; and I believed I could yet make farther discoveries from my own observation. I therefore often begged his honor to let me go among the herds of Yahoos in the neighborhood; to which he always very graciously consented, being perfectly convinced that the hatred I bore those brutes would never suffer me to be corrupted by them; and his honor ordered one of his servants, a strong sorrel nag, very honest

4. Depression.

and good-natured, to be my guard; without whose protection I durst not undertake such adventures. For I have already told the reader how much I was pestered by those odious animals upon my first arrival. I afterwards failed very narrowly three or four times of falling into their clutches, when I happened to stray at any distance without my hanger. And I have reason to believe, they had some imagination that I was of their own species, which I often assisted myself, by stripping up my sleeves, and shewing my naked arms and breast in their sight, when my protector was with me; at which times they would approach as near as they durst, and imitate my actions after the manner of monkeys, but ever with great signs of hatred; as a tame jackdaw with cap and stockings is always persecuted by the wild ones, when he happens to be got among them.

They are prodigiously nimble from their infancy; however, I once caught a young male of three years old, and endeavored by all marks of tenderness to make it quiet; but the little imp fell a squalling, and scratching, and biting with such violence, that I was forced to let it go; and it was high time, for a whole troop of old ones came about us at the noise; but finding the cub was safe (for away it ran) and my sorrel nag being by, they durst not venture near us. I observed the young animal's flesh to smell very rank, and the stink was somewhat between a weasel and a fox, but much more disagreeable. I forgot another circumstance (and perhaps I might have the reader's pardon, if it were wholly omitted) that while I held the odious vermin in my hands, it voided its filthy excrements of a yellow liquid substance, all over my clothes; but by good fortune there was a small brook hard by, where I washed myself as clean as I could; although I durst not come into my master's presence until I were sufficiently aired.

By what I could discover, the Yahoos appear to be the most unteachable of all animals, their capacities never reaching higher than to draw or carry burdens. Yet I am of opinion, this defect ariseth chiefly from a perverse, restive disposition. For they are cunning, malicious, treacherous and revengeful. They are strong and hardy, but of a cowardly spirit, and by consequence insolent, abject, and cruel. It is observed that the red-haired of both sexes are more libidinous and mischievous than the rest, whom yet they much exceed in strength and activity.

The Houyhnhnms keep the Yahoos for present use in huts not far from the house; but the rest are sent abroad to certain fields, where they dig up roots, eat several kinds of herbs, and search about for carrion, or sometimes catch weasels and *luhimuhs* (a sort of wild rat) which they greedily devour. Nature hath taught them to dig deep holes with their nails on the side of a rising ground, wherein they lie by themselves; only the kennels of the females are larger, sufficient to hold two or three cubs.

They swim from their infancy like frogs, and are able to continue long under water, where they often take fish, which the females carry home to their young. And upon this occasion, I hope the reader will pardon my relating an odd adventure.

Being one day abroad with my protector the sorrel nag, and the weather exceeding hot, I entreated him to let me bathe in a river that was near. He consented, and I immediately stripped myself stark naked, and went down softly into the stream. It happened that a young female Yahoo standing behind a bank, saw the whole proceeding; and inflamed by desire, as the nag and I conjectured, came running with all speed, and leaped into the water within five yards of the place where I bathed. I was never in my life so terribly frighted; the nag was grazing at some distance, not suspecting any harm. She embraced me after a most fulsome manner; I roared as loud as I could, and the nag came galloping towards me, whereupon she quitted her grasp, with the utmost reluctancy, and leaped upon the opposite bank, where she stood gazing and howling all the time I was putting on my clothes.

This was matter of diversion to my master and his family, as well as of mortification to myself. For now I could no longer deny that I was a real Yahoo, in every limb and feature, since the females had a natural propensity to me as one of their own species; neither was the hair of this brute of a red color (which might have been some excuse for an appetite a little irregular) but black as a sloe, and her countenance did not make an appearance altogether so hideous as the rest of the kind; for I think, she could not be above eleven years old.

Having already lived three years in this country, the reader I suppose will expect that I should, like other travelers, give him some account of the manners and customs of its inhabitants, which it was indeed my principal study to learn.

As these noble Houyhnhnms are endowed by Nature with a general disposition to all virtues, and have no conceptions or ideas of what is evil in a rational creature; so their grand maxim is to cultivate reason, and to be wholly governed by it. Neither is reason among them a point problematical as with us, where men can argue with plausibility on both sides of a question; but strikes you with immediate conviction; as it must needs do where it is not mingled, obscured, or discolored by passion and interest. I remember it was with extreme difficulty that I could bring my master to understand the meaning of the word "opinion," or how a point could be disputable; because reason taught us to affirm or deny only where we are certain; and beyond our knowledge we cannot do either. So that controversies, wranglings, disputes, and positiveness in false or dubious propositions are evils unknown among the Houyhnhnms. In the like manner when I used to explain to him our several systems of natural philosophy,[5] he would laugh that a creature pretending to reason should value itself upon the knowledge of other people's conjectures, and in things, where that knowledge, if it were certain, could be of no use. Wherein he agreed entirely with the sentiments of Socrates, as Plato delivers them, which I mention as the highest honor I can do that prince of philosophers. I have often since reflected what destruction such a doctrine would make in the libraries of Europe; and how many paths to fame would be then shut up in the learned world.

Friendship and benevolence are the two principal virtues among the Houyhnhnms; and these not confined to particular objects, but universal to the whole race. For a stranger from the remotest part is equally treated with the nearest neighbor, and wherever he goes, looks upon himself as at home. They preserve decency and civility in the highest degrees, but are altogether ignorant of ceremony. They have no fondness for their colts or foals; but the care they take in educating them proceedeth entirely from the dictates of reason. And I observed my master to show the same affection to his neigh-

5. Science.

bor's issue that he had for his own. They will have it that Nature teaches them to love the whole species, and it is reason only that maketh a distinction of persons, where there is a superior degree of virtue.

When the matron Houyhnhnms have produced one of each sex, they no longer accompany with their consorts, except they lose one of their issue by some casualty, which very seldom happens; but in such a case they meet again; or when the like accident befalls a person whose wife is past bearing, some other couple bestows on him one of their own colts, and then go together a second time, until the mother be pregnant. This caution is necessary to prevent the country from being overburdened with numbers. But the race of inferior Houyhnhnms bred up to be servants is not so strictly limited upon this article; these are allowed to produce three of each sex, to be domestics in the noble families.

In their marriages they are exactly careful to choose such colors as will not make any disagreeable mixture in the breed. Strength is chiefly valued in the male, and comeliness in the female; not upon the account of love, but to preserve the race from degenerating; for, where a female happens to excel in strength, a consort is chosen with regard to comeliness. Courtship, love, presents, jointures, settlements, have no place in their thoughts, or terms whereby to express them in their language. The young couple meet and are joined, merely because it is the determination of their parents and friends; it is what they see done every day; and they look upon it as one of the necessary actions in a reasonable being. But the violation of marriage, or any other unchastity, was never heard of; and the married pair pass their lives with the same friendship and mutual benevolence that they bear to all others of the same species who come in their way, without jealousy, fondness, quarreling, or discontent.

In educating the youth of both sexes, their method is admirable, and highly deserveth our imitation. These are not suffered to taste a grain of oats, except upon certain days, till eighteen years old; nor milk, but very rarely; and in summer they graze two hours in the morning, and as many in the evening, which their parents likewise observe; but the servants are not allowed above half that time; and a great part of the grass is brought home, which they eat at the most convenient hours when they can be best spared from work.

Temperance, industry, exercise, and cleanliness are the lessons equally enjoined to the young ones of both sexes; and my master thought it monstrous in us to give the females a different kind of education from the males, except in some articles of domestic management; whereby, as he truly observed, one half of our natives were good for nothing but bringing children into the world; and to trust the care of their children to such useless animals, he said was yet a greater instance of brutality.

But the Houyhnhnms train up their youth to strength, speed, and hardiness, by exercising them in running races up and down steep hills, or over hard stony grounds; and when they are all in a sweat, they are ordered to leap over head and ears into a pond or a river. Four times a year the youth of certain districts meet to show their proficiency in running, and leaping, and other feats of strength or agility; where the victor is rewarded with a song made in his or her praise. On this festival the servants drive a herd of Yahoos into the field, laden with hay, and oats, and milk for a repast to the Houyhnhnms; after which these brutes are immediately driven back again, for fear of being noisome to the assembly.

Every fourth year, at the vernal equinox, there is a representative council of the whole nation, which meets in a plain about twenty miles from our house, and continueth about five or six days. Here they inquire into the state and condition of the several districts; whether they abound or be deficient in hay or oats, or cows or Yahoos? And wherever there is any want (which is but seldom) it is immediately supplied by unanimous consent and contribution. Here likewise the regulation of children is settled: as for instance, if a Houyhnhnm hath two males, he changeth one of them with another who hath two females, and when a child hath been lost by any casualty, where the mother is past breeding, it is determined what family in the district shall breed another to supply the loss.

CHAPTER 9. *A grand debate at the general assembly of the Houyhnhnms, and how it was determined. The learning of the Houyhnhnms. Their buildings. Their manner of burials. The defectiveness of their language.*

One of these grand assemblies was held in my time, about three months before my departure, whither my master went as the representative of our district. In this council was resumed their old debate, and indeed, the only debate that ever happened in their country; whereof my master after his return gave me a very particular account.

The question to be debated was whether the Yahoos should be exterminated from the face of the earth. One of the members for the affirmative offered several arguments of great strength and weight, alleging that, as the Yahoos were the most filthy, noisome, and deformed animal which nature ever produced, so they were the most restive and indocible,[6] mischievous, and malicious; they would privately suck the teats of the Houyhnhnms' cows; kill and devour their cats, trample down their oats and grass, if they were not continually watched; and commit a thousand other extravagancies. He took notice of a general tradition, that Yahoos had not been always in their country, but that many ages ago, two of these brutes appeared together upon a mountain; whether produced by the heat of the sun upon corrupted mud and slime, or from the ooze and froth of the sea, was never known. That these Yahoos engendered, and their brood in a short time grew so numerous as to overrun and infest the whole nation. That the Houyhnhnms to get rid of this evil, made a general hunting, and at last enclosed the whole herd; and destroying the older, every Houyhnhnm kept two young ones in a kennel, and brought them to such a degree of tameness as an animal so savage by nature can be capable of acquiring, using them for draught and carriage. That there seemed to be much truth in this tradition, and that those creatures could not be *ylnhniamshy* (or aborigines of the land) because of the violent hatred the Houyhnhnms as well as all other animals bore them; which although their evil disposition sufficiently deserved, could never have arrived at so high a degree, if they had been aborigines, or else they would have long since been rooted out. That the inhabitants taking a fancy to use the service of the Yahoos, had very imprudently neglected to cultivate the breed of asses, which were a comely animal, easily kept, more tame and orderly, without any offensive smell, strong enough for labor, although they

6. Unteachable.

yield to the other in agility of body; and if their braying be no agreeable sound, it is far preferable to the horrible howlings of the Yahoos.

Several others declared their sentiments to the same purpose, when my master proposed an expedient to the assembly, whereof he had indeed borrowed the hint from me. He approved of the tradition, mentioned by the honorable member, who spoke before; and affirmed, that the two Yahoos said to be first seen among them, had been driven thither over the sea; that coming to land, and being forsaken by their companions, they retired to the mountains, and degenerating by degrees, became in process of time much more savage than those of their own species in the country from whence these two originals came. The reason of his assertion was that he had now in his possession a certain wonderful Yahoo (meaning myself) which most of them had heard of, and many of them had seen. He then related to them how he first found me; that my body was all covered with an artificial composure of the skins and hairs of other animals; that I spoke in a language of my own, and had thoroughly learned theirs; that I had related to him the accidents which brought me thither; that when he saw me without my covering, I was an exact Yahoo in every part, only of a whiter color, less hairy and with shorter claws. He added how I had endeavored to persuade him that in my own and other countries the Yahoos acted as the governing, rational animal, and held the Houyhnhnms in servitude; that he observed in me all the qualities of a Yahoo, only a little more civilized by some tincture of reason, which however was in a degree as far inferior to the Houyhnhnm race as the Yahoos of their country were to me; that among other things, I mentioned a custom we had of castrating Houyhnhnms when they were young, in order to render them tame; that the operation was easy and safe; that it was no shame to learn wisdom from brutes, as industry is taught by the ant, and building by the swallow (for so I translate the world *lyhannh,* although it be a much larger fowl). That this invention might be practiced upon the younger Yahoos here, which, besides rendering them tractable and fitter for use, would in an age put an end to the whole species without destroying life. That in the meantime the Houyhnhnms should be exhorted to cultivate the breed of asses, which, as they are in all respects more valuable brutes, so they have this advantage, to be fit for service at five years old, which the other are not till twelve.

This was all my master thought fit to tell me at that time, of what passed in the grand council. But he was pleased to conceal one particular, which related personally to myself, whereof I soon felt the unhappy effect, as the reader will know in its proper place, and from whence I date all the succeeding misfortunes of my life.

The Houyhnhnms have no letters, and consequently, their knowledge is all traditional. But there happening few events of any moment among a people so well united, naturally disposed to every virtue, wholly governed by reason, and cut off from all commerce with other nations, the historical part is easily preserved without burdening their memories. I have already observed that they are subject to no diseases, and therefore can have no need of physicians. However, they have excellent medicines composed of herbs, to cure accidental bruises and cuts in the pastern or frog[7] of the foot by sharp stones, as well as other maims and hurts in the several parts of the body.

7. Sole.

They calculate the year by the revolution of the sun and the moon, but use no subdivisions into weeks. They are well enough acquainted with the motions of those two luminaries, and understand the nature of eclipses; and this is the utmost progress of their astronomy.

In poetry they must be allowed to excel all other mortals; wherein the justness of their similes, and the minuteness, as well as exactness of their descriptions, are indeed inimitable. Their verses abound very much in both of these, and usually contain either some exalted notions of friendship and benevolence, or the praises of those who were victors in races and other bodily exercises. Their buildings, although very rude and simple, are not inconvenient, but well contrived to defend them from all injuries of cold and heat. They have a kind of tree, which at forty years old loosens in the root, and falls with the first storm; it grows very straight, and being pointed like stakes with a sharp stone (for the Houyhnhnms know not the use of iron), they stick them erect in the ground about ten inches asunder, and then weave in oat straw, or sometimes wattles, betwixt them. The roof is made after the same manner, and so are the doors.

The Houyhnhnms use the hollow part between the pastern and the hoof of their forefeet as we do our hands, and this with greater dexterity than I could at first imagine. I have seen a white mare of our family thread a needle (which I lent her on purpose) with that joint. They milk their cows, reap their oats, and do all the work which requires hands in the same manner. They have a kind of hard flints, which by grinding against other stones they form into instruments that serve instead of wedges, axes, and hammers. With tools made of these flints, they likewise cut their hay, and reap their oats, which there groweth naturally in several fields. The Yahoos draw home the sheaves in carriages, and the servants tread them in certain covered huts, to get out the grain, which is kept in stores. They make a rude kind of earthen and wooden vessels, and bake the former in the sun.

If they can avoid casualties, they die only of old age, and are buried in the obscurest places that can be found, their friends and relations expressing neither joy nor grief at their departure; nor does the dying person discover the least regret that he is leaving the world, any more than if he were upon returning home from a visit to one of his neighbors; I remember my master having once made an appointment with a friend and his family to come to his house upon some affair of importance; on the day fixed, the mistress and her two children came very late; she made two excuses, first for her husband, who, as she said, happened that very morning to *lhnuwnh*. The word is strongly expressive in their language, but not easily rendered into English; it signifies, *to retire to his first Mother*. Her excuse for not coming sooner was that her husband dying late in the morning, she was a good while consulting her servants about a convenient place where his body should be laid; and I observed she behaved herself at our house, as cheerfully as the rest. She died about three months after.

They live generally to seventy or seventy-five years, very seldom to fourscore; some weeks before their death they feel a gradual decay, but without pain. During this time they are much visited by their friends, because they cannot go abroad with their usual ease and satisfaction. However, about ten days before their death, which they seldom fail in computing, they return the visits that have been made by those who are nearest in the neighbor-hood, being carried in a convenient sledge drawn by Yahoos; which vehicle they use, not only upon this occasion, but when they grow old, upon long journeys, or when they are lamed by any accident. And therefore when the dying Houyhnhnms return those visits, they take a solemn leave of their friends, as if they were going to some remote part of the country, where they designed to pass the rest of their lives.

I know not whether it may be worth observing, that the Houyhnhnms have no word in their language to express anything that is evil, except what they borrow from the deformities or ill qualities of the Yahoos. Thus they denote the folly of a servant, an omission of a child, a stone that cuts their feet, a continuance of foul or unseasonable weather, and the like, by adding to each the epithet of Yahoo. For instance, *hhnm Yahoo, whnaholm Yahoo, ynlhmnd-wihlma Yahoo,* and an ill-contrived house, *ynholmhnmrohlnw Yahoo.*

I could with great pleasure enlarge farther upon the manners and virtues of this excellent people; but intending in a short time to publish a volume by itself expressly upon that subject, I refer the reader thither. And in the meantime, proceed to relate my own sad catastrophe.

CHAPTER 10. *The Author's economy, and happy life among the Houyhnhnms. His great improvement in virtue, by conversing with them. Their conversa-tions. The Author hath notice given him by his master that he must depart from the country. He falls into a swoon for grief, but submits. He contrives and finishes a canoe, by the help of a fellow servant, and puts to sea at a venture.*

I had settled my little economy to my own heart's content. My master had ordered a room to be made for me after their manner, about six yards from the house; the sides and floors of which I plastered with clay, and covered with rush mats of my own contriving; I had beaten hemp, which there grows wild, and made of it a sort of ticking; this I filled with the feathers of several birds I had taken with springes made of Yahoos' hairs, and were excellent food. I had worked two chairs with my knife, the sorrel nag helping me in the grosser and more laborious part. When my clothes were worn to rags, I made myself others with the skins of rabbits, and of a certain beautiful animal about the same size, called *nnuhnoh,* the skin of which is covered with a fine down. Of these I likewise made very tolerable stockings. I soled my shoes with wood which I cut from a tree, and fitted to the upper leather, and when this was worn out, I supplied it with the skins of Yahoos, dried in the sun. I often got honey out of hollow trees, which I mingled with water, or eat it with my bread. No man could more verify the truth of these two maxims, that *Nature is very easily satisfied;* and, that *Necessity is the mother of invention.* I enjoyed perfect health of body, and tranquility of mind; I did not feel the treachery or inconstancy of a friend, nor the inquiries of a secret or open enemy. I had no occasion of bribing, flattering, or pimping to procure the favor of any great man, or of his minion. I wanted no fence against fraud or oppression; here was neither physician to destroy my body, nor lawyer to ruin my fortune; no informer to watch my words and actions, or forge accusations against me for hire; here were no gibers, censurers, backbiters, pickpockets, highwaymen, housebreakers, attorneys, bawds, buffoons, gamesters, politicians, wits, splenetics, tedious talkers, controvertists, ravishers, murderers, robbers, virtuosos;[8] no leaders or followers of party and faction; no encouragers to vice, by seducement or examples; no dungeons, axes, gibbets, whipping posts, or pillories; no cheating shopkeepers or mechanics; no pride, vanity or affectation; no fops, bullies, drunkards, strolling whores, or poxes; no ranting, lewd, expensive wives; no stupid, proud pedants; no importunate, overbearing, quarrelsome, noisy, roaring, empty, conceited, swearing companions; no scoundrels raised from the dust upon the merit of their vices; or nobility thrown into it on account of their virtues; no lords, fiddlers, judges, or dancing masters.

I had the favor of being admitted to several Houyhnhnms, who came to visit or dine with my master; where his honor graciously suffered me to wait in the room, and listen to their discourse. Both he and his company would often descend to ask me questions, and receive my answers. I had also sometimes the honor of attending my master in his visits to others. I never presumed to speak, except in answer to a question; and then I did it with inward regret, because it was a loss of so much time for improving myself; but I was infinitely delighted with the station of an humble auditor in such conversations, where nothing passed but what was useful, expressed in the fewest and most significant words; where (as I have already said) the greatest decency was observed, without the least degree of ceremony; where no person spoke without being pleased himself, and pleasing his companions; where there was no interruption, tediousness, heat, or difference of sentiments. They have a notion, that when people are met together, a short silence doth much improve conversation; this I found to be true; for during those little intermissions of talk, new ideas would arise in their minds, which very much enlivened the discourse. Their subjects are generally on friendship and benevolence; on order and economy; sometimes upon the visible operations of nature, or ancient traditions; upon the bounds and limits of virtue; upon the unerring rules of reason; or upon some determinations, to be taken at the next great assembly; and often upon the various excellencies of poetry. I may add, without vanity, that my presence often gave them sufficient matter for discourse, because it afforded my master an occasion of letting his friends into the history of me and my country, upon which they were all pleased to descant in a manner not very advantageous to human kind; and for that reason I shall not repeat what they said; only I maybe allowed to observe that his honor, to my great admiration, appeared to understand the nature of Yahoos much better than myself. He went through all our vices and follies, and discovered many which I had never mentioned to him; by only supposing what qualities a Yahoo of their country, with a small proportion of reason, might be capable of exerting; and concluded, with too much probability, how vile as well as miserable such a creature must be.

I freely confess, that all the little knowledge I have of any value was acquired by the lectures I received from my master, and from hearing the discourses of him and his friends; to which I should be prouder to listen, than to dictate to the greatest and wisest assembly in Europe. I admired the strength, comeliness, and speed of the inhabitants; and such a constellation of virtues in such amiable persons produced in me the highest veneration. At

8. Those who pursue special interests in the arts or sciences.

first, indeed, I did not feel that natural awe which the Yahoos and all other animals bear towards them; but it grew upon me by degrees, much sooner than I imagined, and was mingled with a respectful love and gratitude, that they would condescend to distinguish me from the rest of my species.

When I thought of my family, my friends, my countrymen, or human race in general, I considered them as they really were, Yahoos in shape and disposition, perhaps a little more civilized, and qualified with the gift of speech; but making no other use of reason than to improve and multiply those vices, whereof their brethren in this country had only the share that nature allotted them. When I happened to behold the reflection of my own form in a lake or fountain, I turned away my face in horror and detestation of myself, and could better endure the sight of a common Yahoo than of my own person. By conversing with the Houyhnhnms, and looking upon them with delight, I fell to imitate their gait and gesture, which is now grown into a habit; and my friends often tell me in a blunt way, that I trot like a horse; which, however, I take for a great compliment. Neither shall I disown, that in speaking I am apt to fall into the voice and manner of the Houyhnhnms, and hear myself ridiculed on that account without the least mortification.

In the midst of this happiness, when I looked upon myself to be fully settled for life, my master sent for me one morning a little earlier than his usual hour. I observed by his countenance that he was in some perplexity, and at a loss how to begin what he had to speak. After a short silence, he told me, he did not know how I would take what he was going to say; that, in the last general assembly, when the affair of the Yahoos was entered upon, the representatives had taken offense at his keeping a Yahoo (meaning myself) in his family more like a Houyhnhnm than a brute animal. That he was known frequently to converse with me, as if he could receive some advantage of pleasure in my company; that such a practice was not agreeable to reason or nature, or a thing ever heard of before among them. The assembly did therefore exhort him, either to employ me like the rest of my species, or command me to swim back to the place from whence I came. That the first of these expedients was utterly rejected by all the Houyhnhnms who had ever seen me at his house or their own; for, they alleged, that because I had some rudiments of reason, added to the natural pravity[9] of those animals, it was to be feared, I might be able to seduce them into the woody and mountainous parts of the country, and bring them in troops by night to destroy the Houyhnhnms' cattle, as being naturally of the ravenous kind, and averse from labor.

My master added that he was daily pressed by the Houyhnhnms of the neighborhood to have the assembly's exhortation executed, which he could not put off much longer. He doubted[1] it would be impossible for me to swim to another country; and therefore wished I would contrive some sort of vehicle resembling those I had described to him, that might carry me on the sea; in which work I should have the assistance of his own servants, as well as those of his neighbors. He concluded that for his own part he could have been content to keep me in his service as long as I lived; because he found I had cured myself of some bad habits and dispositions, by endeavoring, as far as my inferior nature was capable, to imitate the Houyhnhnms.

9. Corruption.   1. Feared.

I should here observe to the reader, that a decree of the general assembly in this country is expressed by the word *hnhloayn*, which signifies an exhortation, as near as I can render it; for they have no conception how a rational creature can be compelled, but only advised, or exhorted; because no person can disobey reason without giving up his claim to be a rational creature.

I was struck with the utmost grief and despair at my master's discourse; and being unable to support the agonies I was under, I fell into a swoon at his feet; when I came to myself, he told me that he concluded I had been dead (for these people are subject to no such imbecilities of nature). I answered, in a faint voice, that death would have been too great an happiness; that although I could not blame the assembly's exhortation, or the urgency of his friends; yet in my weak and corrupt judgment, I thought it might consist with reason to have been less rigorous. That I could not swim a league, and probably the nearest land to theirs might be distant above an hundred; that many materials, necessary for making a small vessel to carry me off, were wholly wanting in this country, which, however, I would attempt in obedience and gratitude to his honor, although I concluded the thing to be impossible, and therefore looked on myself as already devoted[2] to destruction. That the certain prospect of an unnatural death was the least of my evils; for, supposing I should escape with life by some strange adventure, how could I think with temper[3] of passing my days among Yahoos, and relapsing into my old corruptions, for want of examples to lead and keep me within the paths of virtue. That I knew too well upon what solid reasons all the determinations of the wise Houyhnhnms were founded, not to be shaken by arguments of mine, a miserable Yahoo; and therefore after presenting him with my humble thanks for the offer of his servants' assistance in making a vessel, and desiring a reasonable time for so difficult a work, I told him I would endeavor to preserve a wretched being; and, if ever I returned to England, was not without hopes of being useful to my own species by celebrating the praises of the renowned Houyhnhnms, and proposing their virtues to the imitation of mankind.

My master in a few words made me a very gracious reply, allowed me the space of two months to finish my boat, and ordered the sorrel nag, my fellow servant (for so at this distance I may presume to call him), to follow my instructions, because I told my master that his help would be sufficient, and I knew he had a tenderness for me.

In his company my first business was to go to that part of the coast where my rebellious crew had ordered me to be set on shore. I got upon a height, and looking on every side into the sea, fancied I saw a small island towards the northeast; I took out my pocket glass, and could then clearly distinguish it about five leagues off, as I computed; but it appeared to the sorrel nag to be only a blue cloud; for, as he had no conception of any country besides his own, so he could not be as expert in distinguishing remote objects at sea, as we who so much converse in that element.

After I had discovered this island, I considered no farther; but resolved, it should, if possible, be the first place of my banishment, leaving the consequence to fortune.

I returned home, and consulting with the sorrel nag, we went into a copse at some distance, where I with my knife, and he with a sharp flint fastened

2. Doomed.   3. Equanimity.

very artificially,[4] after their manner, to a wooden handle, cut down several oak wattles about the thickness of a walking staff, and some larger pieces. But I shall not trouble the reader with a particular description of my own mechanics; let it suffice to say, that in six weeks time, with the help of the sorrel nag, who performed the parts that required most labor, I finished a sort of Indian canoe; but much larger, covering it with the skins of Yahoos, well stitched together, with hempen threads of my own making. My sail was likewise composed of the skins of the same animal; but I made use of the youngest I could get, the older being too tough and thick; and I likewise provided myself with four paddles. I laid in a stock of boiled flesh, of rabbits and fowls; and took with me two vessels, one filled with milk, and the other with water.

I tried my canoe in a large pond near my master's house, and then corrected in it what was amiss, stopping all the chinks with Yahoo's tallow, till I found it staunch, and able to bear me and my freight. And when it was as complete as I could possibly make it, I had it drawn on a carriage very gently by Yahoos, to the seaside, under the conduct of the sorrel nag and another servant.

When all was ready, and the day came for my departure, I took leave of my master and lady, and the whole family, my eyes flowing with tears and my heart quite sunk with grief.[5] But his honor, out of curiosity, and perhaps (if I may speak it without vanity) partly out of kindness, was determined to see me in my canoe; and got several of his neighboring friends to accompany him. I was forced to wait above an hour for the tide, and then observing the wind very fortunately bearing towards the island to which I intended to steer my course, I took a second leave of my master; but as I was going to prostrate myself to kiss his hoof, he did me the honor to raise it gently to my mouth. I am not ignorant how much I have been censured for mentioning this last particular. Detractors are pleased to think it improbable that so illustrious a person should descend to give so great a mark of distinction to a creature so inferior as I. Neither have I forgot how apt some travelers are to boast of extraordinary favors they have received. But, if these censurers were better acquainted with the noble and courteous disposition of the Houyhnhnms, they would soon change their opinion. I paid my respects to the rest of the Houyhnhnms in his honor's company; then getting into my canoe, I pushed off from shore.

CHAPTER 11. *The Author's dangerous voyage. He arrives at New Holland, hoping to settle there. Is wounded with an arrow by one of the natives. Is seized and carried by force into a Portuguese ship. The great civilities of the Captain. The Author arrives at England.*

I began this desperate voyage on February 15, 1714/5,[6] at 9 o'clock in the morning. The wind was very favorable; however, I made use at first only of my paddles; but considering I should soon be weary, and that the wind might probably chop about, I ventured to set up my little sail, and thus, with the help

---

4. Artfully.
5. For a depiction of this scene by Sawrey Gilpin, see the color insert in this volume.

6. I.e., 1715, by modern dating. The year began on March 25.

of the tide, I went at the rate of a league and a half an hour, as near as I could guess. My master and his friends continued on the shore, till I was almost out of sight; and I often heard the sorrel nag (who always loved me) crying out, *"Hnuy illa nyha maiah Yahoo"* ("Take care of thyself, gentle Yahoo").

My design was, if possible, to discover some small island uninhabited, yet sufficient by my labor to furnish me with necessaries of life, which I would have thought a greater happiness than to be first minister in the politest court of Europe, so horrible was the idea I conceived of returning to live in the society and under the government of Yahoos. For in such a solitude as I desired, I could at least enjoy my own thoughts, and reflect with delight on the virtues of those inimitable Houyhnhnms, without any opportunity of degenerating into the vices and corruptions of my own species.

The reader may remember what I related when my crew conspired against me, and confined me to my cabin, how I continued there several weeks, without knowing what course we took; and when I was put ashore in the longboat, how the sailors told me with oaths, whether true or false, that they knew not in what part of the world we were. However, I did then believe us to be about 10 degrees southward of the Cape of Good Hope, or about 45 degrees southern latitude, as I gathered from some general words I overheard among them, being I supposed to the southeast in their intended voyage to Madagascar. And although this were but little better than conjecture, yet I resolved to steer my course eastward, hoping to reach the southwest coast of New Holland, and perhaps some such island as I desired, lying westward of it. The wind was full west, and by six in the evening I computed I had gone eastward at least eighteen leagues; when I spied a very small island about half a league off, which I soon reached. It was nothing but a rock with one creek, naturally arched by the force of tempests. Here I put in my canoe, and climbing a part of the rock, I could plainly discover land to the east, extending from south to north. I lay all night in my canoe; and repeating my voyage early in the morning, I arrived in seven hours to the southeast point of New Holland. This confirmed me in the opinion I have long entertained, that the maps and charts place this country at least three degrees more to the east than it really is; which thought I communicated many years ago to my worthy friend Mr. Herman Moll,[7] and gave him my reasons for it, although he hath rather chosen to follow other authors.

I saw no inhabitants in the place where I landed; and being unarmed, I was afraid of venturing far into the country. I found some shellfish on the shore, and eat them raw, not daring to kindle a fire, for fear of being discovered by the natives. I continued three days feeding on oysters and limpets, to save my own provisions; and I fortunately found a brook of excellent water, which gave me great relief.

On the fourth day, venturing out early a little too far, I saw twenty or thirty natives upon a height, not above five hundred yards from me. They were stark naked, men, women, and children round a fire, as I could discover by the smoke. One of them spied me, and gave notice to the rest; five of them advanced towards me, leaving the women and children at the fire. I made what haste I could to the shore, and getting into my canoe, shoved off; the savages observing me retreat, ran after me; and before I could get far enough

---

7. A famous contemporary map maker.

into the sea, discharged an arrow, which wounded me deeply on the inside of my left knee. (I shall carry the mark to my grave.) I apprehended the arrow might be poisoned; and paddling out of the reach of their darts (being a calm day) I made a shift to suck the wound, and dress it as well as I could.

I was at a loss what to do, for I durst not return to the same landing place, but stood to the north, and was forced to paddle; for the wind, although very gentle, was against me, blowing northwest. As I was looking about for a secure landing place, I saw a sail to the north northeast, which appearing every minute more visible, I was in some doubt whether I should wait for them or no; but at last my detestation of the Yahoo race prevailed; and turning my canoe, I sailed and paddled together to the south, and got into the same creek from whence I set out in the morning, choosing rather to trust myself among these barbarians than live with European Yahoos. I drew up my canoe as close as I could to the shore, and hid myself behind a stone by the little brook, which, as I have already said, was excellent water.

The ship came within half a league of this creek, and sent out her longboat with vessels to take in fresh water (for the place it seems was very well known), but I did not observe it until the boat was almost on shore; and it was too late to seek another hiding place. The seamen at their landing observed my canoe, and rummaging it all over, easily conjectured that the owner could not be far off. Four of them well armed searched every cranny and lurking hole, till at last they found me flat on my face behind the stone. They gazed a while in admiration at my strange uncouth dress; my coat made of skins, my wooden-soled shoes, and my furred stockings; from whence, however, they concluded I was not a native of the place, who all go naked. One of the seamen in Portuguese bid me rise, and asked who I was. I understood that language very well, and getting upon my feet, said I was a poor Yahoo, banished from the Houyhnhnms, and desired they would please to let me depart. They admired to hear me answer them in their own tongue, and saw by my complexion I must be an European; but were at a loss to know what I meant by Yahoos and Houyhnhnms, and at the same time fell a laughing at my strange tone in speaking, which resembled the neighing of a horse. I trembled all the while betwixt fear and hatred; I again desired leave to depart, and was gently moving to my canoe; but they laid hold on me, desiring to know what country I was of? whence I came? with many other questions. I told them I was born in England, from whence I came about five years ago, and then their country and ours was at peace. I therefore hoped they would not treat me as an enemy, since I meant them no harm, but was a poor Yahoo, seeking some desolate place where to pass the remainder of his unfortunate life.

When they began to talk, I thought I never heard or saw any thing so unnatural; for it appeared to me as monstrous as if a dog or a cow should speak in England, or a Yahoo in Houyhnhnmland. The honest Portuguese were equally amazed at my strange dress, and the odd manner of delivering my words, which however they understood very well. They spoke to me with great humanity, and said they were sure their Captain would carry me *gratis* to Lisbon, from whence I might return to my own country; that two of the seamen would go back to the ship, to inform the Captain of what they had seen, and receive his orders; in the meantime, unless I would give my solemn oath not to fly, they would secure me by force. I thought it best to comply with their proposal. They were very curious to know my story, but I gave them very little satisfaction; and they all conjectured, that my misfortunes had impaired my reason. In two hours the boat, which went laden with vessels of water, returned with the Captain's commands to fetch me on board. I fell on my knees to preserve my liberty; but all was in vain, and the men having tied me with cords, heaved me into the boat, from whence I was taken into the ship, and from thence into the Captain's cabin.

His name was Pedro de Mendez; he was a very courteous and generous person; he entreated me to give some account of myself, and desired to know what I would eat or drink; said I should be used as well as himself, and spoke so many obliging things, that I wondered to find such civilities from a Yahoo. However, I remained silent and sullen; I was ready to faint at the very smell of him and his men. At last I desired something to eat out of my own canoe; but he ordered me a chicken and some excellent wine, and then directed that I should be put to bed in a very clean cabin. I would not undress myself, but lay on the bedclothes; and in half an hour stole out, when I thought the crew was at dinner; and getting to the side of the ship, was going to leap into the sea, and swim for my life, rather than continue among Yahoos. But one of the seamen prevented me, and having informed the Captain, I was chained to my cabin.

After dinner Don Pedro came to me, and desired to know my reason for so desperate an attempt; assured me he only meant to do me all the service he was able; and spoke so very movingly, that at last I descended to treat him like an animal which had some little portion of reason. I gave him a very short relation of my voyage; of the conspiracy against me by my own men; of the country where they set me on shore, and of my five years residence there. All which he looked upon as if it were a dream or a vision; whereat I took great offense; for I had quite forgot the faculty of lying, so peculiar to Yahoos in all countries where they preside, and consequently the disposition of suspecting truth in others of their own species. I asked him whether it were the custom of his country to *say the thing that was not?* I assured him I had almost forgot what he meant by falsehood; and if I had lived a thousand years in Houyhnhnmland, I should never have heard a lie from the meanest servant. That I was altogether indifferent whether he believed me or no; but however, in return for his favors, I would give so much allowance to the corruption of his nature, as to answer any objection he would please to make; and he might easily discover the truth.

The Captain, a wise man, after many endeavors to catch me tripping in some part of my story, at last began to have a better opinion of my veracity. But he added that since I professed so inviolable an attachment to truth, I must give him my word of honor to bear him company in this voyage without attempting anything against my life; or else he would continue me a prisoner till we arrived at Lisbon. I gave him the promise he required; but at the same time protested that I would suffer the greatest hardships rather than return to live among Yahoos.

Our voyage passed without any considerable accident. In gratitude to the Captain I sometimes sat with him at his earnest request, and strove to conceal my antipathy against humankind, although it often broke out; which he suffered to pass without observation. But the greatest part of the day, I confined myself to my cabin, to avoid seeing any of the crew. The Captain had often entreated me to strip myself of my savage dress, and offered to lend me the best suit of clothes he had. This I would not be prevailed on to accept, abhorring to cover myself with anything that had been on the back of a Yahoo. I only desired he would lend me two clean shirts, which having been washed since he wore them, I believed would not so much defile me. These I changed every second day, and washed them myself.

We arrived at Lisbon, Nov. 5, 1715. At our landing, the Captain forced me to cover myself with his cloak, to prevent the rabble from crowding about me. I was conveyed to his own house; and at my earnest request, he led me up to the highest room backwards.[8] I conjured him to conceal from all persons what I had told him of the Houyhnhnms; because the least hint of such a story would not only draw numbers of people to see me, but probably put me in danger of being imprisoned, or burned by the Inquisition. The Captain persuaded me to accept a suit of clothes newly made; but I would not suffer the tailor to take my measure; however, Don Pedro being almost of my size, they fitted me well enough. He accoutered me with other necessaries, all new, which I aired for twenty-four hours before I would use them.

The Captain had no wife, nor above three servants, none of which were suffered to attend at meals; and his whole deportment was so obliging, added to very good human understanding, that I really began to tolerate his company. He gained so far upon me, that I ventured to look out of the back window. By degrees I was brought into another room, from whence I peeped into the street, but drew my head back in a fright. In a week's time he seduced me down to the door. I found my terror gradually lessened, but my hatred and contempt seemed to increase. I was at last bold enough to walk the street in his company, but kept my nose well stopped with rue, or sometimes with tobacco.

In ten days, Don Pedro, to whom I had given some account of my domestic affairs, put it upon me as a point of honor and conscience that I ought to return to my native country, and live at home with my wife and children. He told me there was an English ship in the port just ready to sail, and he would furnish me with all things necessary. It would be tedious to repeat his arguments, and my contradictions. He said it was altogether impossible to find such a solitary island as I had desired to live in; but I might command in my own house, and pass my time in a manner as recluse as I pleased.

I complied at last, finding I could not do better. I left Lisbon the 24th day of November, in an English merchantman, but who was the Master I never inquired. Don Pedro accompanied me to the ship, and lent me twenty pounds. He took kind leave of me, and embraced me at parting; which I bore as well as I could. During this last voyage I had no commerce with the Master, or any of his men; but pretending I was sick kept close in my cabin. On the fifth of December, 1715, we cast anchor in the Downs about nine in the morning, and at three in the afternoon I got safe to my house at Redriff.

My wife and family received me with great surprise and joy, because they concluded me certainly dead; but I must freely confess, the sight of them filled me only with hatred, disgust, and contempt; and the more, by reflecting on the near alliance I had to them. For although since my unfortunate

8. At the rear.

exile from the Houyhnhnm country, I had compelled myself to tolerate the sight of Yahoos, and to converse with Don Pedro de Mendez; yet my memory and imaginations were perpetually filled with the virtues and ideas of those exalted Houyhnhnms. And when I began to consider that by copulating with one of the Yahoo species, I had become a parent of more, it struck me with the utmost shame, confusion, and horror.

As soon as I entered the house, my wife took me in her arms, and kissed me; at which, having not been used to the touch of that odious animal for so many years, I fell in a swoon for almost an hour. At the time I am writing, it is five years since my last return to England. During the first year I could not endure my wife or children in my presence, the very smell of them was intolerable; much less could I suffer them to eat in the same room. To this hour they dare not presume to touch my bread, or drink out of the same cup; neither was I ever able to let one of them take me by the hand. The first money I laid out was to buy two young stone-horses,[9] which I keep in a good stable, and next to them the groom is my greatest favorite; for I feel my spirits revived by the smell he contracts in the stable. My horses understand me tolerably well; I converse with them at least four hours every day. They are strangers to bridle or saddle; they live in great amity with me, and friendship to each other.

CHAPTER 12. *The Author's veracity. His design in publishing this work. His censure of those travelers who swerve from the truth. The Author clears himself from any sinister ends in writing. His native country commended. The right of the crown to those countries described by the Author is justified. The difficulty of conquering them. The Author takes his last leave of the reader; proposeth his manner of living for the future; gives good advice, and concludeth.*

Thus gentle reader, I have given thee a faithful history of my travels for sixteen years, and above seven months; wherein I have not been so studious of ornament as of truth. I could perhaps like others have astonished thee with strange improbable tales; but I rather chose to relate plain matter of fact in the simplest manner and style; because my principal design was to inform, and not to amuse thee.

It is easy for us who travel into remote countries, which are seldom visited by Englishmen or other Europeans, to form descriptions of wonderful animals both at sea and land. Whereas a traveler's chief aim should be to make men wiser and better, and to improve their minds by the bad as well as good example of what they deliver concerning foreign places.

I could heartily wish a law were enacted, that every traveler, before he were permitted to publish his voyages, should be obliged to make oath before the Lord High Chancellor that all he intended to print was absolutely true to the best of his knowledge; for then the world would no longer be deceived as it usually is, while some writers, to make their works pass the better upon the public, impose the grossest falsities on the unwary reader. I have perused several books of travels with great delight in my younger days; but, having since gone over most parts of the globe, and been able to contradict many fabulous accounts from my own observation, it hath given me a great disgust against this part of reading, and some indignation to see the credulity of

9. Stallions.

mankind so impudently abused. Therefore, since my acquaintance were pleased to think my poor endeavors might not be unacceptable to my country, I imposed on myself as a maxim, never to be swerved from, that I would *strictly adhere to truth;* neither indeed can I be ever under the least temptation to vary from it, while I retain in my mind the lectures and example of my noble master, and the other illustrious Houyhnhnms, of whom I had so long the honor to be an humble hearer.

> ——*Nec si miserum Fortuna Sinonem*
> *Finxit, vanum etiam, mendacemque improba finget.*[1]

I know very well how little reputation is to be got by writings which require neither genius nor learning, nor indeed any other talent, except a good memory, or an exact journal. I know likewise, that writers of travels, like dictionary-makers, are sunk into oblivion by the weight and bulk of those who come last, and therefore lie uppermost. And it is highly probable that such travelers who shall hereafter visit the countries described in this work of mine, may be detecting my errors (if there be any) and adding many new discoveries of their own, jostle me out of vogue, and stand in my place, making the world forget that ever I was an author. This indeed would be too great a mortification if I wrote for fame; but, as my sole intention was the PUBLIC GOOD, I cannot be altogether disappointed. For, who can read the virtues I have mentioned in the glorious Houyhnhnms, without being ashamed of his own vices, when he considers himself as the reasoning, governing animal of his country? I shall say nothing of those remote nations where Yahoos preside; amongst which the least corrupted are the Brobdingnagians, whose wise maxims in morality and government it would be our happiness to observe. But I forbear descanting further, and rather leave the judicious reader to his own remarks and applications.

I am not a little pleased that this work of mine can possibly meet with no censurers; for what objections can be made against a writer who relates only plain facts that happened in such distant countries, where we have not the least interest with respect either to trade or negotiations? I have carefully avoided every fault with which common writers of travels are often too justly charged. Besides, I meddle not the least with any party, but write without passion, prejudice, or ill-will against any man or number of men whatsoever. I write for the noblest end, to inform and instruct mankind, over whom I may, without breach of modesty, pretend to some superiority, from the advantages I received by conversing so long among the most accomplished Houyhnhnms. I write without any view towards profit or praise. I never suffer a word to pass that may look like a reflection,[2] or possibly give the least offense even to those who are most ready to take it. So that, I hope, I may with justice pronounce myself an Author perfectly blameless; against whom the tribes of answerers, considerers, observers, reflectors, detecters, remarkers will never be able to find matter for exercising their talents.

I confess it was whispered to me that I was bound in duty as a subject of England, to have given in a memorial[3] to a secretary of state, at my first com-

---

1. Nor if Fortune had molded Sinon for misery, will she also in spite mold him as false and lying (Latin; Virgil's *Aeneid* 2.79–80).

2. Censure, criticism.
3. Statement of facts for government use.

ing over; because, whatever lands are discovered by a subject, belong to the Crown. But I doubt whether our conquests in the countries I treat of would be as easy as those of Ferdinando Cortez over the naked Americans. The Lilliputians, I think, are hardly worth the charge of a fleet and army to reduce them; and I question whether it might be prudent or safe to attempt the Brobdingnagians; or, whether an English army would be much at their ease with the Flying Island over their heads. The Houyhnhnms, indeed, appear not to be so well prepared for war, a science to which they are perfect strangers, and especially against missive weapons. However, supposing myself to be a minister of state, I could never give my advice for invading them. Their prudence, unanimity, unacquaintedness with fear, and their love of their country would amply supply all defects in the military art. Imagine twenty thousand of them breaking into the midst of an European army, confounding the ranks, overturning the carriages, battering the warriors' faces into mummy, by terrible yerks from their hinder hoofs: for they would well deserve the character given to Augustus, *Recalcitrat undique tutus.*[4] But instead of proposals for conquering that magnanimous nation, I rather wish they were in a capacity or disposition to send a sufficient number of their inhabitants for civilizing Europe; by teaching us the first principles of Honor, Justice, Truth, Temperance, Public Spirit, Fortitude, Chastity, Friendship, Benevolence, and Fidelity. The names of all which virtues are still retained among us in most languages, and are to be met with in modern as well as ancient authors, which I am able to assert from my own small reading.

But I had another reason which made me less forward to enlarge his majesty's dominions by my discoveries: to say the truth, I had conceived a few scruples with relation to the distributive justice of princes upon those occasions. For instance, a crew of pirates are driven by a storm they know not whither; at length a boy discovers land from the topmast; they go on shore to rob and plunder; they see an harmless people, are entertained with kindness, they give the country a new name, they take formal possession of it for the king, they set up a rotten plank or a stone for a memorial, they murder two or three dozen of the natives, bring away a couple more by force for a sample, return home, and get their pardon. Here commences a new dominion acquired with a title by Divine Right. Ships are sent with the first opportunity; the natives driven out or destroyed, their princes tortured to discover their gold; a free license given to all acts of inhumanity and lust; the earth reeking with the blood of its inhabitants: and this execrable crew of butchers employed in so pious an expedition is a *modern colony* sent to convert and civilize an idolatrous and barbarous people.

But this description, I confess, doth by no means affect the British nation, who may be an example to the whole world for their wisdom, care, and justice in planting colonies; their liberal endowments for the advancement of religion and learning; their choice of devout and able pastors to propagate Christianity; their caution in stocking their provinces with people of sober lives and conversations from this the Mother Kingdom; their strict regard to the distribution of justice, in supplying the civil administration through all their colonies with officers of the greatest abilities, utter strangers to corrup-

4. He kicks backward, at every point on his guard (Latin; Horace's *Satires* 2.1.20). "Mummy": pulp. "Yerks": kicks.

tion: and to crown all, by sending the most vigilant and virtuous governors, who have no other views than the happiness of the people over whom they preside, and the honor of the king their master.

But, as those countries which I have described do not appear to have any desire of being conquered, and enslaved, murdered, or driven out by colonies, nor abound either in gold, silver, sugar, or tobacco, I did humbly conceive they were by no means proper objects of our zeal, our valor, or our interest. However, if those whom it may concern, think fit to be of another opinion, I am ready to depose, when I shall be lawfully called, that no European did ever visit these countries before me. I mean, if the inhabitants ought to be believed.

But, as to the formality of taking possession in my sovereign's name, it never came once into my thoughts; and if it had, yet as my affairs then stood, I should perhaps in point of prudence and self-preservation have put it off to a better opportunity.

Having thus answered the only objection that can be raised against me as a traveler, I here take a final leave of my courteous readers, and return to enjoy my own speculations in my little garden at Redriff; to apply those excellent lessons of virtue which I learned among the Houyhnhnms; to instruct the Yahoos of my own family as far as I shall find them docible animals; to behold my figure often in a glass, and thus if possible habituate myself by time to tolerate the sight of a human creature; to lament the brutality of Houyhnhnms in my own country, but always treat their persons with respect, for the sake of my noble master, his family, his friends, and the whole Houyhnhnm race, whom these of ours have the honor to resemble in all their lineaments, however their intellectuals came to degenerate.

I began last week to permit my wife to sit at dinner with me, at the farthest end of a long table; and to answer (but with the utmost brevity) the few questions I ask her. Yet the smell of a Yahoo continuing very offensive, I always keep my nose well stopped with rue, lavender, or tobacco leaves. And although it be hard for a man late in life to remove old habits, I am not altogether out of hopes in some time to suffer a neighbor Yahoo in my company, without the apprehensions I am yet under of his teeth or his claws.

My reconcilement to the Yahoo kind in general might not be so difficult, if they would be content with those vices and follies only which nature hath entitled them to. I am not in the least provoked at the sight of a lawyer, a pickpocket, a colonel, a fool, a lord, a gamester, a politician, a whoremonger, a physician, an evidence,[5] a suborner, an attorney, a traitor, or the like: this is all according to the due course of things. But when I behold a lump of deformity, and diseases both in body and mind, smitten with *pride*, it immediately breaks all the measures of my patience; neither shall I be ever able to comprehend how such an animal and such a vice could tally together. The wise and virtuous Houyhnhnms, who abound in all excellencies that can adorn a rational creature, have no name for this vice in their language, which hath no terms to express anything that is evil, except those whereby they describe the detestable qualities of their Yahoos, among which they were not able to distinguish this of pride, for want of thoroughly understanding human nature, as it showeth itself in other countries, where that animal presides. But I, who had more experience, could plainly observe some rudiments of it among the wild Yahoos.

5. Witness.

But the Houyhnhnms, who live under the government of reason, are no more proud of the good qualities they possess, than I should be for not wanting a leg or an arm, which no man in his wits would boast of, although he must be miserable without them. I dwell the longer upon this subject from the desire I have to make the society of an English Yahoo by any means not insupportable; and therefore I here entreat those who have any tincture of this absurd vice, that they will not presume to appear in my sight.

1726, 1735

A Modest Proposal[1]

FOR PREVENTING THE CHILDREN OF POOR PEOPLE IN IRELAND FROM BEING A BURDEN TO THEIR PARENTS OR COUNTRY, AND FOR MAKING THEM BENEFICIAL TO THE PUBLIC

It is a melancholy object to those who walk through this great town[2] or travel in the country, when they see the streets, the roads, and cabin doors, crowded with beggars of the female sex, followed by three, four, or six children, all in rags and importuning every passenger for an alms. These mothers, instead of being able to work for their honest livelihood, are forced to employ all their time in strolling to beg sustenance for their helpless infants, who, as they grow up, either turn thieves for want of work, or leave their dear native country to fight for the Pretender in Spain, or sell themselves to the Barbadoes.[3]

I think it is agreed by all parties that this prodigious number of children in the arms, or on the backs, or at the heels of their mothers, and frequently of their fathers, is in the present deplorable state of the kingdom a very great additional grievance; and therefore whoever could find out a fair, cheap, and easy method of making these children sound, useful members of the commonwealth would deserve so well of the public as to have his statue set up for a preserver of the nation.

But my intention is very far from being confined to provide only for the children of professed beggars; it is of a much greater extent, and shall take in the whole number of infants at a certain age who are born of parents in effect as little able to support them as those who demand our charity in the streets.

1. "A Modest Proposal" is an example of Swift's favorite satiric devices used with superb effect. Irony (from the deceptive adjective *modest* in the title to the very last sentence) pervades the piece. A rigorous logic deduces ghastly arguments from a premise so quietly assumed that readers assent before they are aware of what that assent implies. Parody, at which Swift is adept, allows him to glance sardonically at the by then familiar figure of the benevolent humanitarian (forerunner of the modern sociologist, social worker, and economic planner) concerned to correct a social evil by means of a theoretically conceived plan. The proposer, as naive as he is apparently logical and kindly, ignores and therefore emphasizes for the reader the enormity of his plan. The whole is an elaboration of a rather trite metaphor: "The English are devouring the Irish." But there is nothing trite about the pamphlet, which expresses in Swift's most controlled style his revulsion at the contemporary state of Ireland and his indignation at the rapacious English absentee landlords, who were bleeding the country white with the silent approbation of Parliament, ministers, and the crown.

2. Dublin.

3. James Francis Edward Stuart (1688–1766), the son of James II, was claimant ("Pretender") to the throne of England from which the Glorious Revolution had barred his succession. Catholic Ireland was loyal to him, and Irishmen joined him in his exile on the Continent. Because of the poverty in Ireland, many Irish emigrated to the West Indies and other British colonies in America; they paid their passage by binding themselves to work for a stated period for one of the planters.

As to my own part, having turned my thoughts for many years upon this important subject, and maturely weighed the several schemes of other projectors,[4] I have always found them grossly mistaken in their computation. It is true, a child just dropped from its dam may be supported by her milk for a solar year, with little other nourishment; at most not above the value of two shillings, which the mother may certainly get, or the value in scraps, by her lawful occupation of begging; and it is exactly at one year old that I propose to provide for them in such a manner as instead of being a charge upon their parents or the parish, or wanting food and raiment for the rest of their lives, they shall on the contrary contribute to the feeding, and partly to the clothing, of many thousands.

There is likewise another great advantage in my scheme, that it will prevent those voluntary abortions, and that horrid practice of women murdering their bastard children, alas, too frequent among us, sacrificing the poor innocent babes, I doubt, more to avoid the expense than the shame, which would move tears and pity in the most savage and inhuman breast.

The number of souls in this kingdom[5] being usually reckoned one million and a half, of these I calculate there may be about two hundred thousand couple whose wives are breeders; from which number I subtract thirty thousand couples who are able to maintain their own children, although I apprehend there cannot be so many under the present distresses of the kingdom; but this being granted, there will remain an hundred and seventy thousand breeders. I again subtract fifty thousand for those women who miscarry, or whose children die by accident or disease within the year. There only remain an hundred and twenty thousand children of poor parents annually born. The question therefore is, how this number shall be reared and provided for, which, as I have already said, under the present situation of affairs, is utterly impossible by all the methods hitherto proposed. For we can neither employ them in handicraft or agriculture; we neither build houses (I mean in the country) nor cultivate land. They can very seldom pick up a livelihood by stealing till they arrive at six years old, except where they are of towardly parts;[6] although I confess they learn the rudiments much earlier, during which time they can however be looked upon only as probationers, as I have been informed by a principal gentleman in the county of Cavan, who protested to me that he never knew above one or two instances under the ages of six, even in a part of the kingdom so renowned for the quickest proficiency in that art.

I am assured by our merchants that a boy or a girl before twelve years old is no salable commodity; and even when they come to this age they will not yield above three pounds, or three pounds and half a crown at most on the Exchange; which cannot turn to account either to the parents or the kingdom, the charge of nutriment and rags having been at least four times that value.

I shall now therefore humbly propose my own thoughts, which I hope will not be liable to the least objection.

I have been assured by a very knowing American of my acquaintance in London, that a young healthy child well nursed is at a year old a most delicious, nourishing, and wholesome food, whether stewed, roasted, baked, or boiled; and I make no doubt that it will equally serve in a fricassee or a ragout.[7]

4. Devisers of schemes.
5. Ireland.

6. Promising abilities.
7. A highly seasoned meat stew.

I do therefore humbly offer it to public consideration that of the hundred and twenty thousand children, already computed, twenty thousand may be reserved for breed, whereof only one fourth part to be males, which is more than we allow to sheep, black cattle, or swine; and my reason is that these children are seldom the fruits of marriage, a circumstance not much regarded by our savages, therefore one male will be sufficient to serve four females. That the remaining hundred thousand may at a year old be offered in sale to the persons of quality and fortune through the kingdom, always advising the mother to let them suck plentifully in the last month, so as to render them plump and fat for a good table. A child will make two dishes at an entertainment for friends; and when the family dines alone, the fore or hind quarter will make a reasonable dish, and seasoned with a little pepper or salt will be very good boiled on the fourth day, especially in winter.

I have reckoned upon a medium that a child just born will weigh twelve pounds, and in a solar year if tolerably nursed increaseth to twenty-eight pounds.

I grant this food will be somewhat dear, and therefore very proper for landlords, who, as they have already devoured most of the parents, seem to have the best title to the children.

Infant's flesh will be in season throughout the year, but more plentiful in March, and a little before and after. For we are told by a grave author, an eminent French physician,[8] that fish being a prolific diet, there are more children born in Roman Catholic countries about nine months after Lent than at any other season; therefore, reckoning a year after Lent, the markets will be more glutted than usual, because the number of popish infants is at least three to one in this kingdom; and therefore it will have one other collateral advantage, by lessening the number of Papists among us.

I have already computed the charge of nursing a beggar's child (in which list I reckon all cottagers, laborers, and four fifths of the farmers) to be about two shillings per annum, rags included; and I believe no gentleman would repine to give ten shillings for the carcass of a good fat child, which, as I have said, will make four dishes of excellent nutritive meat, when he hath only some particular friend or his own family to dine with him. Thus the squire will learn to be a good landlord, and grow popular among the tenants; the mother will have eight shillings net profit, and be fit for the work till she produces another child.

Those who are more thrifty (as I must confess the times require) may flay the carcass; the skin of which artificially[9] dressed will make admirable gloves for ladies, and summer boots for fine gentlemen.

As to our city of Dublin, shambles[1] may be appointed for this purpose in the most convenient parts of it, and butchers we may be assured will not be wanting; although I rather recommend buying the children alive, and dressing them hot from the knife as we do roasting pigs.

A very worthy person, a true lover of his country, and whose virtues I highly esteem, was lately pleased in discoursing on this matter to offer a refinement upon my scheme. He said that many gentlemen of this kingdom, having of late destroyed their deer, he conceived that the want of venison

---

8. François Rabelais (ca. 1494–1553), a humorist and satirist, by no means grave.

9. Skillfully.
1. Slaughterhouses.

might be well supplied by the bodies of young lads and maidens, not exceeding fourteen years of age nor under twelve, so great a number of both sexes in every county being now ready to starve for want of work and service; and these to be disposed of by their parents, if alive, or otherwise by their nearest relations. But with due deference to so excellent a friend and so deserving a patriot, I cannot be altogether in his sentiments; for as to the males, my American acquaintance assured me from frequent experience that their flesh was generally tough and lean, like that of our schoolboys, by continual exercise, and their taste disagreeable; and to fatten them would not answer the charge. Then as to the females, it would, I think with humble submission, be a loss to the public, because they soon would become breeders themselves; and besides, it is not improbable that some scrupulous people might be apt to censure such a practice (although indeed very unjustly) as a little bordering upon cruelty; which I confess, hath always been with me the strongest objection against any project, how well soever intended.

But in order to justify my friend, he confessed that this expedient was put into his head by the famous Psalmanazar,[2] a native of the island Formosa, who came from thence to London above twenty years ago, and in conversation told my friend that in his country when any young person happened to be put to death, the executioner sold the carcass to persons of quality as a prime dainty; and that in his time the body of a plump girl of fifteen, who was crucified for an attempt to poison the emperor, was sold to his Imperial Majesty's prime minister of state, and other great mandarins of the court, in joints from the gibbet, at four hundred crowns. Neither indeed can I deny that if the same use were made of several plump young girls in this town, who without one single groat to their fortunes cannot stir abroad without a chair, and appear at the playhouse and assemblies in foreign fineries which they never will pay for, the kingdom would not be the worse.

Some persons of a desponding spirit are in great concern about that vast number of poor people who are aged, diseased, or maimed, and I have been desired to employ my thoughts what course may be taken to ease the nation of so grievous an encumbrance. But I am not in the least pain upon that matter, because it is very well known that they are every day dying and rotting by cold and famine, and filth and vermin, as fast as can be reasonably expected. And as to the younger laborers, they are now in almost as hopeful a condition. They cannot get work, and consequently pine away for want of nourishment to a degree that if at any time they are accidentally hired to common labor, they have not strength to perform it; and thus the country and themselves are happily delivered from the evils to come.

I have too long digressed, and therefore shall return to my subject. I think the advantages by the proposal which I have made are obvious and many, as well as of the highest importance.

For first, as I have already observed, it would greatly lessen the number of Papists, with whom we are yearly overrun, being the principal breeders of the nation as well as our most dangerous enemies; and who stay at home on purpose to deliver the kingdom to the Pretender, hoping to take their

2. George Psalmanazar (ca. 1679–1763), a famous impostor. A Frenchman, he imposed himself on English bishops, noblemen, and scientists as a Formosan. He wrote an entirely fictitious account of Formosa, in which he described human sacrifices and cannibalism.

advantage by the absence of so many good Protestants, who have chosen rather to leave their country than stay at home and pay tithes against their conscience to an Episcopal curate.[3]

Secondly, the poorer tenants will have something valuable of their own, which by law may be made liable to distress,[4] and help to pay their landlord's rent, their corn and cattle being already seized and money a thing unknown.

Thirdly, whereas the maintenance of an hundred thousand children, from two years old and upwards, cannot be computed at less than ten shillings a piece per annum, the nation's stock will be thereby increased fifty thousand pounds per annum, besides the profit of a new dish introduced to the tables of all gentlemen of fortune in the kingdom who have any refinement in taste. And the money will circulate among ourselves, the goods being entirely of our own growth and manufacture.

Fourthly, the constant breeders, besides the gain of eight shillings sterling per annum by the sale of their children, will be rid of the charge of maintaining them after the first year.

Fifthly, this food would likewise bring great custom to taverns, where the vintners will certainly be so prudent as to procure the best receipts[5] for dressing it to perfection, and consequently have their houses frequented by all the fine gentlemen, who justly value themselves upon their knowledge in good eating; and a skillful cook, who understands how to oblige his guests, will contrive to make it as expensive as they please.

Sixthly, this would be a great inducement to marriage, which all wise nations have either encouraged by rewards or enforced by laws and penalties. It would increase the care and tenderness of mothers toward their children, when they were sure of a settlement for life to the poor babes, provided in some sort by the public, to their annual profit instead of expense. We should see an honest emulation among the married women, which of them could bring the fattest child to the market. Men would become as fond of their wives during the time of their pregnancy as they are now of their mares in foal, their cows in calf, or sows when they are ready to farrow; nor offer to beat or kick them (as is too frequent a practice) for fear of a miscarriage.

Many other advantages might be enumerated. For instance, the addition of some thousand carcasses in our exportation of barreled beef, the propagation of swine's flesh, and improvement in the art of making good bacon, so much wanted among us by the great destruction of pigs, too frequent at our tables, which are no way comparable in taste or magnificence to a well-grown, fat, yearling child, which roasted whole will make a considerable figure at a lord mayor's feast or any other public entertainment. But this and many others I omit, being studious of brevity.

Supposing that one thousand families in this city would be constant customers for infants' flesh, besides others who might have it at merry meetings, particularly weddings and christenings, I compute that Dublin would take off annually about twenty thousand carcasses, and the rest of the kingdom (where probably they will be sold somewhat cheaper) the remaining eighty thousand.

3. Ireland had many Protestant sectarians who did not support the "Episcopal" (Anglican) Church of Ireland.
4. Distraint, i.e., the seizing, through legal action, of property for the payment of debts and other obligations. "Corn": grain.
5. Recipes.

I can think of no one objection that will probably be raised against this proposal, unless it should be urged that the number of people will be thereby much lessened in the kingdom. This I freely own, and it was indeed one principal design in offering it to the world. I desire the reader will observe, that I calculate my remedy for this one individual kingdom of Ireland and for no other that ever was, is, or I think ever can be upon earth. Therefore let no man talk to me of other expedients: of taxing our absentees at five shillings a pound: of using neither clothes nor household furniture except what is of our own growth and manufacture: of utterly rejecting the materials and instruments that promote foreign luxury: of curing the expensiveness of pride, vanity, idleness, and gaming in our women: of introducing a vein of parsimony, prudence, and temperance: of learning to love our country, in the want of which we differ even from Laplanders and the inhabitants of Topinamboo:[6] of quitting our animosities and factions, nor acting any longer like the Jews, who were murdering one another at the very moment their city was taken:[7] of being a little cautious not to sell our country and conscience for nothing: of teaching landlords to have at least one degree of mercy toward their tenants: lastly, of putting a spirit of honesty, industry, and skill into our shopkeepers; who, if a resolution could now be taken to buy only our native goods, would immediately unite to cheat and exact upon us in the price, the measure, and the goodness, nor could ever yet be brought to make one fair proposal of just dealing, though often and earnestly invited to it.[8]

Therefore I repeat, let no man talk to me of these and the like expedients, till he hath at least some glimpse of hope that there will ever be some hearty and sincere attempt to put them in practice.

But as to myself, having been wearied out for many years with offering vain, idle, visionary thoughts, and at length utterly despairing of success, I fortunately fell upon this proposal, which, as it is wholly new, so it hath something solid and real, of no expense and little trouble, full in our own power, and whereby we can incur no danger in disobliging England. For this kind of commodity will not bear exportation, the flesh being of too tender a consistence to admit a long continuance in salt, although perhaps I could name a country which would be glad to eat up our whole nation without it.[9]

After all, I am not so violently bent upon my own opinion as to reject any offer proposed by wise men, which shall be found equally innocent, cheap, easy, and effectual. But before something of that kind shall be advanced in contradiction to my scheme, and offering a better, I desire the author or authors will be pleased maturely to consider two points. First, as things now stand, how they will be able to find food and raiment for an hundred thousand useless mouths and backs. And secondly, there being a round million of creatures in human figure throughout this kingdom, whose sole subsistence put into a common stock would leave them in debt two millions of pounds sterling, adding those who are beggars by profession to the bulk of farmers, cottagers, and laborers, with their wives and children who are beggars in

---

6. I.e., even Laplanders love their frozen, infertile country and the tribes of Brazil love their jungle more than the Anglo-Irish love Ireland.
7. During the siege of Jerusalem by the Roman Titus (later emperor), who captured and destroyed the city in 70 C.E., bloody fights broke out between

fanatical factions among the defenders.
8. Swift himself had made all these proposals in various pamphlets. In editions printed during his lifetime the various proposals were italicized to indicate Swift's support for them.
9. England.

effect; I desire those politicians who dislike my overture, and may perhaps be so bold to attempt an answer, that they will first ask the parents of these mortals whether they would not at this day think it a great happiness to have been sold for food at a year old in the manner I prescribe, and thereby have avoided such a perpetual sense of misfortunes as they have since gone through by the oppression of landlords, the impossibility of paying rent without money or trade, the want of common sustenance, with neither house nor clothes to cover them from the inclemencies of the weather, and the most inevitable prospect of entailing the like or greater miseries upon their breed forever.

I profess, in the sincerity of my heart, that I have not the least personal interest in endeavoring to promote this necessary work, having no other motive than the public good of my country, by advancing our trade, providing for infants, relieving the poor, and giving some pleasure to the rich. I have no children by which I can propose to get a single penny; the youngest being nine years old, and my wife past childbearing.

1729

JOSEPH ADDISON *and* SIR RICHARD STEELE
1672–1719   1672–1729

The friendship of Joseph Addison and Richard Steele began when they were schoolboys together in London. Their careers ran parallel courses and brought them for a while into fruitful collaboration. Addison, although charming when among friends, was by nature reserved, calculating, and prudent. Steele was impulsive and rakish when young (but ardently devoted to his wife), often imprudent, and frequently in want of money. Addison never stumbled in his progress to financial security, a late marriage to a widowed countess, and a successful political career; walking less surely, Steele experienced many vicissitudes and faced serious financial problems during his last years.

Both men attended Oxford, where Addison took his degree, won a fellowship, and gained a reputation for Latin verse; the less scholarly Steele left the university before earning a degree to take a commission in the army. For a while he cut a dashing figure in London, even, to his horror, seriously wounding a man in a duel. Both men enjoyed the patronage of the great Whig magnates; and except during the last four years of Queen Anne's reign, when the Tories were in the ascendancy, they were generously treated. Steele edited and wrote the *London Gazette*, an official newspaper that normally appeared twice a week, listing government appointments and reporting domestic and foreign news—much like a modern paper. He served in Parliament, was knighted by George I, and later became manager of the Theatre Royal, Drury Lane. Addison held more important positions: he was secretary to the lord lieutenant of Ireland and later an undersecretary of state; finally, toward the end of his life, he became secretary of state. Both men wrote plays: Addison's *Cato*, a frigid and very "correct" tragedy, had great success in 1713, and Steele's later plays at Drury Lane (especially *The Conscious Lovers*, 1722) were instrumental in establishing the popularity of sentimental comedy throughout the eighteenth century.

Steele's debts and Addison's loss of office in 1710 drove them to journalistic enter-prises, through which they developed one of the most characteristic types of eighteenth-century literature, the periodical essay. Steele's experience as gazetteer had involved him in journalism and, in need of money, in 1709 he launched the *Tatler* under the pseudonym Isaac Bickerstaff. He sought to attract the largest pos-sible audience: the title was a bid for female readers, and the mixture of news with personal reflections soon became popular in coffeehouses and at breakfast tables. The paper appeared three times a week from April 1709 to January 1711. Steele wrote by far the greater number of *Tatlers*, but Addison contributed helpfully, as did other friends. When the *Spectator* began its run two months after the last *Tatler*, the new periodical drew on and expanded the readership Steele had reached and influenced. The *Spectator* appeared daily except Sunday from March 1711 to December 1712 (and was briefly resumed by Addison in 1714). It was the joint undertaking of the two friends, although it was dominated by Addison. Both the *Spectator* and the *Tatler* had many imitators in their own day and throughout the rest of the century. There was a *Female Tatler* and a *Female Spectator*, as well as Samuel Johnson's *Rambler* and *Idler* and Oliver Goldsmith's brief *Bee*.

The periodical writing of Addison and Steele is remarkable for its comprehensive attention to diverse aspects of English life—good manners, daily happenings in London, going to church, shopping, investing in the stock market, the fascinations of trade and commerce, proper gender roles and relations, the personality types found in society, the town's offerings of high and low entertainment, tastes in lit-erature and luxury goods, philosophical speculations—and the seamless way all were shown to be elements of a single vast, agreeable world. In this unifying spirit, both Steele and Addison set the divisive political battles of the day, so vigorously fought in other periodicals and newspapers, at a distance: they portray the ardor for political dispute more as a personal quirk than as a provocation to true civil unrest. Less formal and didactic than the essays of Francis Bacon, less personal than those of Charles Lamb and William Hazlitt in the next century, these essays promote morality among their readers by praising and enacting sociability and set standards of good taste and polite behavior with a light but firm and unwavering grace. They thereby sought to establish a new social-literary ethos transcending the narrowness of Puritan morality and the exorbitance of the fashionable court culture of the last century.

In the *Spectator*, Steele and especially Addison set out to break down the distinc-tion between educating their readers and entertaining them with winning charac-ters, vivid scenes, and even playfully visionary allegories. In the second number, Steele introduces us to the members of Mr. Spectator's Club: a man about town, a student of law and literature, a churchman, a soldier, a Tory country squire, and—interestingly enough—a London merchant. The development of these characters shows how the very manner in which the *Spectator* makes distinctions tends to smooth away conflict. As a Whig, Steele sympathized with the new moneyed class in London and evidently intended to pit the merchant Sir Andrew Freeport, the repre-sentative of the new order, against the Tory Sir Roger de Coverley, representative of the one passing away. Addison, however, preferred to present Sir Roger in episodes set in town and in country as an endearing, eccentric character, often absurd but always amiable and innocent. He is a prominent ancestor of a long line of similar characters in fiction in the following two centuries. Addison's scholarly interests broadened the material to include not only social criticism but the popularization of current philosophical and scientific notions. He wrote important critical papers dis-tinguishing true and false wit; an extended series of Saturday essays evaluating *Par-adise Lost*; and an influential series on "the pleasures of the imagination," which treated the visual effect of beautiful, "great," and uncommon objects in nature and art. Altogether, the *Spectator* fulfilled his ambition (outlined in "The Aims of the Spectator") to be considered an agreeable modern Socrates.

The best description of Addison's prose is Samuel Johnson's in his *Life of Addison*: "His prose is the model of the middle style; on grave subjects not formal, on light occasions not groveling; pure without scrupulosity, and exact without apparent elaboration; always equable, and always easy, without glowing words or pointed sentences." And he concludes: "Whoever wishes to attain an English style, familiar but not coarse, and elegant but not ostentatious, must give his days and nights to the volumes of Addison"—a course of study that a good many aspiring writers during the century seem to have undertaken.

THE PERIODICAL ESSAY: MANNERS, SOCIETY, GENDER

STEELE: [The Spectator's Club]

The Spectator, *No. 2, Friday, March 2, 1711*

——*Ast alii sex*
Et plures uno conclamant ore.[1]
—JUVENAL, *Satire* 7.167–68

The first of our society is a gentleman of Worcestershire, of ancient descent, a baronet, his name Sir Roger de Coverley. His great-grandfather was inventor of that famous country-dance which is called after him. All who know the shire are very well acquainted with the parts and merits of Sir Roger. He is a gentleman that is very singular in his behavior, but his singularities proceed from his good sense, and are contradictions to the manners of the world only as he thinks the world is in the wrong. However, this humor creates him no enemies, for he does nothing with sourness or obstinacy; and his being unconfined to modes and forms[2] makes him but the readier and more capable to please and oblige all who know him. When he is in town, he lives in Soho Square. It is said he keeps himself a bachelor by reason he was crossed in love by a perverse, beautiful widow of the next county to him. Before this disappointment, Sir Roger was what you call a fine gentleman, had often supped with my Lord Rochester and Sir George Etherege, fought a duel upon his first coming to town, and kicked Bully Dawson[3] in a public coffeehouse for calling him "youngster." But being ill used by the above-mentioned widow, he was very serious for a year and a half; and though, his temper being naturally jovial, he at last got over it, he grew careless of himself, and never dressed afterwards. He continues to wear a coat and doublet of the same cut that were in fashion at the time of his repulse, which, in his merry humors, he tells us, has been in and out twelve times since he first wore it. 'Tis said Sir Roger grew humble in his desires after he had forgot this cruel beauty, insomuch that it is reported he has frequently offended in point of chastity with beggars and gypsies; but this is looked upon by his friends rather as matter of raillery than truth. He is now in his fifty-sixth year, cheerful, gay, and hearty; keeps a good house both in town and country; a great lover of mankind; but there is such a mirthful cast in his behavior that he is rather beloved than esteemed. His

1. Six more at least join their consenting voice (Latin).
2. Social conventions.
3. Notorious cardsharp of the period. John

Wilmot, second earl of Rochester (1647–1680), British poet; Etherege (ca. 1634–1691), playwright, rake, and close companion of the king and Rochester.

tenants grow rich, his servants look satisfied, all the young women profess love to him, and the young men are glad of his company; when he comes into a house he calls the servants by their names, and talks all the way upstairs to a visit. I must not omit that Sir Roger is a justice of the quorum, that he fills the chair at a quarter-session with great abilities; and, three months ago, gained universal applause by explaining a passage in the Game Act.[4]

The gentleman next in esteem and authority among us is another bachelor, who is a member of the Inner Temple; a man of great probity, wit, and understanding; but he has chosen his place of residence rather to obey the direction of an old humorsome[5] father, than in pursuit of his own inclinations. He was placed there to study the laws of the land, and is the most learned of any of the house in those of the stage. Aristotle and Longinus are much better understood by him than Littleton or Coke.[6] The father sends up, every post, questions relating to marriage articles, leases, and tenures, in the neighborhood; all which questions he agrees with an attorney to answer and take care of in the lump. He is studying the passions themselves, when he should be inquiring into the debates among men which arise from them. He knows the argument of each of the orations of Demosthenes and Tully,[7] but not one case in the reports of our own courts. No one ever took him for a fool, but none, except his intimate friends, know he has a great deal of wit. This turn makes him at once both disinterested and agreeable; as few of his thoughts are drawn from business, they are most of them fit for conversation. His taste of books is a little too just[8] for the age he lives in; he has read all, but approves of very few. His familiarity with the customs, manners, actions, and writings of the ancients makes him a very delicate observer of what occurs to him in the present world. He is an excellent critic, and the time of the play is his hour of business; exactly at five he passes through New Inn, crosses through Russell Court, and takes a turn at Will's till the play begins; he has his shoes rubbed and his periwig powdered at the barber's as you go into the Rose.[9] It is for the good of the audience when he is at a play, for the actors have an ambition to please him.

The person of next consideration is Sir Andrew Freeport, a merchant of great eminence in the city of London, a person of indefatigable industry, strong reason, and great experience. His notions of trade are noble and generous, and (as every rich man has usually some sly way of jesting which would make no great figure were he not a rich man) he calls the sea the British Common. He is acquainted with commerce in all its parts, and will tell you that it is a stupid and barbarous way to extend dominion by arms; for true power is to be got by arts and industry. He will often argue that if this part of our trade

4. In 1671 the act gave the gentry (Sir Roger's class) broad legal powers to prevent poaching and hence granted them a virtual monopoly on hunting. "Justice of the quorum": a country justice of the peace, presiding over quarterly sessions of the court.
5. Temperamental. "Inner Temple": one of the Inns of Court, where lawyers resided or had their offices and where students studied law.
6. In other words, he is more familiar with the laws of literature than those of England. The *Poetics* of Aristotle and the Greek treatise *On the Sublime* (reputedly by Longinus) were in high favor

among the critics of the time. Sir Thomas Littleton, 15th-century jurist, was author of a renowned treatise on *Tenures*. Sir Edward Coke (1552–1634) was the judge and writer whose *Reports* and *Institutes of the Laws of England* (known as *Coke upon Littleton*) have exerted a great influence on the interpretation of English law.
7. Marcus Tullius Cicero.
8. Exact.
9. A tavern near Drury Lane. "Will's": the coffee-house in Covent Garden associated with literature and criticism since Dryden had begun to frequent it in the 1660s.

were well cultivated, we should gain from one nation; and if another, from another. I have heard him prove that diligence makes more lasting acquisitions than valor, and that sloth has ruined more nations than the sword. He abounds in several frugal maxims, among which the greatest favorite is, "A penny saved is a penny got." A general trader of good sense is pleasanter company than a general scholar; and Sir Andrew having a natural unaffected eloquence, the perspicuity of his discourse gives the same pleasure that wit would in another man. He has made his fortunes himself, and says that England may be richer than other kingdoms by as plain methods as he himself is richer than other men; though at the same time I can say this of him, that there is not a point in the compass but blows home a ship in which he is an owner.

Next to Sir Andrew in the clubroom sits Captain Sentry, a gentleman of great courage, good understanding, but invincible modesty. He is one of those that deserve very well, but are very awkward at putting their talents within the observation of such as should take notice of them. He was some years a captain, and behaved himself with great gallantry in several engagements and at several sieges; but having a small estate of his own, and being next heir to Sir Roger, he has quitted a way of life in which no man can rise suitably to his merit who is not something of a courtier as well as a soldier. I have heard him often lament that in a profession where merit is placed in so conspicuous a view, impudence should get the better of modesty. When he has talked to this purpose I never heard him make a sour expression, but frankly confess that he left the world because he was not fit for it. A strict honesty and an even, regular behavior are in themselves obstacles to him that must press through crowds who endeavor at the same end with himself—the favor of a commander. He will, however, in his way of talk, excuse generals for not disposing according to men's desert, or inquiring into it, "for," says he, "that great man who has a mind to help me, has as many to break through to come at me as I have to come at him"; therefore he will conclude that the man who would make a figure, especially in a military way, must get over all false modesty, and assist his patron against the importunity of other pretenders by a proper assurance in his own vindication. He says it is a civil cowardice to be backward in asserting[1] what you ought to expect, as it is a military fear to be slow in attacking when it is your duty. With this candor does the gentleman speak of himself and others. The same frankness runs through all his conversation. The military part of his life has furnished him with many adventures, in the relation of which he is very agreeable to the company; for he is never overbearing, though accustomed to command men in the utmost degree below him; nor ever too obsequious from an habit of obeying men highly above him.

But that our society may not appear a set of humorists[2] unacquainted with the gallantries and pleasures of the age, we have among us the gallant Will Honeycomb, a gentleman who, according to his years, should be in the decline of his life, but having ever been very careful of his person, and always had a very easy fortune, time has made but very little impression either by wrinkles on his forehead or traces in his brain. His person is well turned, of a good height. He is very ready at that sort of discourse with which men usually entertain women. He has all his life dressed very well, and remembers habits[3] as

1. Claiming.   3. Clothes.
2. Eccentrics.

others do men. He can smile when one speaks to him, and laughs easily. He knows the history of every mode, and can inform you from which of the French king's wenches our wives and daughters had this manner of curling their hair, that way of placing their hoods; whose frailty was covered by such a sort of petticoat, and whose vanity to show her foot made that part of the dress so short in such a year. In a word, all his conversation and knowledge has been in the female world. As other men of his age will take notice to you what such a minister said upon such and such an occasion, he will tell you when the Duke of Monmouth[4] danced at court such a woman was then smitten, another was taken with him at the head of his troop in the Park. In all these important relations, he has ever about the same time received a kind glance or a blow of a fan from some celebrated beauty, mother of the present Lord Such-a-one. If you speak of a young commoner that said a lively thing in the House, he starts up: "He has good blood in his veins; Tom Mirabell begot him, the rogue cheated me in that affair; that young fellow's mother used me more like a dog than any woman I ever made advances to." This way of talking of his very much enlivens the conversation among us of a more sedate turn; and I find there is not one of the company but myself, who rarely speak at all, but speaks of him as of that sort of man who is usually called a well-bred, fine gentleman. To conclude his character, where women are not concerned he is an honest, worthy man.

I cannot tell whether I am to account him whom I am next to speak of as one of our company, for he visits us but seldom; but when he does, it adds to every man else a new enjoyment of himself. He is a clergyman, a very philosophic man, of general learning, great sanctity of life, and the most exact good breeding. He has the misfortune to be of a very weak constitution, and consequently cannot accept of such cares and business as preferments in his function would oblige him to; he is therefore among divines what a chamber-counselor[5] is among lawyers. The probity of his mind and the integrity of his life create him followers, as being eloquent or loud advances others. He seldom introduces the subject he speaks upon; but we are so far gone in years that he observes, when he is among us, an earnestness to have him fall on some divine topic, which he always treats with much authority, as one who has no interest in this world, as one who is hastening to the object of all his wishes and conceives hope from his decays and infirmities. These are my ordinary companions.

ADDISON: [The Aims of the *Spectator*]

The Spectator, *No. 10, Monday, March 12, 1711*

> *Non aliter quam qui adverso vix flumine lembum*
> *Remigiis subigit, si bracchia forte remisit,*
> *Atque illum in præceps prono rapit alveus amni.*[1]
> —VIRGIL, *Georgics* 1.201–3

It is with much satisfaction that I hear this great city inquiring day by day after these my papers, and receiving my morning lectures with a becoming seriousness and attention. My publisher tells me that there are already three

---

4. The illegitimate son of Charles II, the ill-fated Absalom of Dryden's *Absalom and Achitophel*.
5. A lawyer who gives opinions in private, not in court.

1. Like him whose oars can hardly force his boat against the current, if by chance he relaxes his arms, the boat sweeps him headlong down the stream (Latin).

thousand of them distributed every day. So that if I allow twenty readers to every paper, which I look upon as a modest computation, I may reckon about three-score thousand disciples in London and Westminster, who I hope will take care to distinguish themselves from the thoughtless herd of their ignorant and unattentive brethren. Since I have raised to myself so great an audience, I shall spare no pains to make their instruction agreeable, and their diversion useful. For which reasons I shall endeavor to enliven morality with wit, and to temper wit with morality, that my readers may, if possible, both ways find their account in the speculation of the day. And to the end that their virtue and discretion may not be short, transient, intermitting starts of thought, I have resolved to refresh their memories from day to day, till I have recovered them out of that desperate state of vice and folly into which the age is fallen. The mind that lies fallow but a single day sprouts up in follies that are only to be killed by a constant and assiduous culture. It was said of Socrates that he brought philosophy down from heaven, to inhabit among men; and I shall be ambitious to have it said of me that I have brought philosophy out of closets[2] and libraries, schools and colleges, to dwell in clubs and assemblies, at tea tables and in coffeehouses.

I would therefore in a very particular manner recommend these my speculations to all well-regulated families that set apart an hour in every morning for tea and bread and butter; and would earnestly advise them for their good to order this paper to be punctually served up, and to be looked upon as a part of the tea equipage.

Sir Francis Bacon observes that a well-written book, compared with its rivals and antagonists, is like Moses's serpent, that immediately swallowed up and devoured those of the Egyptians.[3] I shall not be so vain as to think that where *The Spectator* appears the other public prints will vanish; but shall leave it to my reader's consideration whether is it not much better to be let into the knowledge of one's self, than to hear what passes in Muscovy or Poland; and to amuse ourselves with such writings as tend to the wearing out of ignorance, passion, and prejudice, than such as naturally conduce to inflame hatreds, and make enmities irreconcilable?

In the next place, I would recommend this paper to the daily perusal of those gentlemen whom I cannot but consider as my good brothers and allies, I mean the fraternity of spectators who live in the world without having anything to do in it; and either by the affluence of their fortunes or laziness of their dispositions have no other business with the rest of mankind but to look upon them. Under this class of men are comprehended all contemplative tradesmen, titular physicians, fellows of the Royal Society, Templars[4] that are not given to be contentious, and statesmen that are out of business; in short, everyone that considers the world as a theater, and desires to form a right judgment of those who are the actors on it.

There is another set of men that I must likewise lay a claim to, whom I have lately called the blanks of society, as being altogether unfurnished with ideas, till the business and conversation of the day has supplied them. I have often considered these poor souls with an eye of great commiseration, when

2. Private rooms, studies.
3. In *The Advancement of Learning* 2, "To the King." But it was the rod of Aaron, not of Moses, that turned into a devouring serpent (Exodus 7.10–12).

4. Lawyers or students of the law who live or have their offices ("chambers") in the Middle or Inner Temple, one of the Inns of Court.

I have heard them asking the first man they have met with, whether there was any news stirring? and by that means gathering together materials for thinking. These needy persons do not know what to talk of till about twelve o'clock in the morning; for by that time they are pretty good judges of the weather, know which way the wind sits, and whether the Dutch mail[5] be come in. As they lie at the mercy of the first man they meet, and are grave or impertinent all the day long, according to the notions which they have imbibed in the morning, I would earnestly entreat them not to stir out of their chambers till they have read this paper, and do promise them that I will daily instil into them such sound and wholesome sentiments as shall have a good effect on their conversation for the ensuing twelve hours.

But there are none to whom this paper will be more useful than to the female world. I have often thought there has not been sufficient pains taken in finding out proper employments and diversions for the fair ones. Their amusements seem contrived for them, rather as they are women, than as they are reasonable creatures; and are more adapted to the sex than to the species. The toilet[6] is their great scene of business, and the right adjusting of their hair the principal employment of their lives. The sorting of a suit of ribbons is reckoned a very good morning's work; and if they make an excursion to a mercer's or a toyshop,[7] so great a fatigue makes them unfit for anything else all the day after. Their more serious occupations are sewing and embroidery, and their greatest drudgery the preparation of jellies and sweetmeats. This, I say, is the state of ordinary women; though I know there are multitudes of those of a more elevated life and conversation, that move in an exalted sphere of knowledge and virtue, that join all the beauties of the mind to the ornaments of dress, and inspire a kind of awe and respect, as well as love, into their male beholders. I hope to increase the number of these by publishing this daily paper, which I shall always endeavor to make an innocent if not improving entertainment, and by that means at least divert the minds of my female readers from greater trifles. At the same time, as I would fain give some finishing touches to those which are already the most beautiful pieces in human nature, I shall endeavor to point all those imperfections that are the blemishes, as well as those virtues which are the embellishments, of the sex. In the meanwhile I hope these my gentle readers, who have so much time on their hands, will not grudge throwing away a quarter of an hour in a day on this paper, since they may do it without any hindrance to business.

I know several of my friends and well-wishers are in great pain for me, lest I should not be able to keep up the spirit of a paper which I oblige myself to furnish every day: but to make them easy in this particular, I will promise them faithfully to give it over as soon as I grow dull. This I know will be matter of great raillery to the small wits; who will frequently put me in mind of my promise, desire me to keep my word, assure me that it is high time to give over, with many other little pleasantries of the like nature, which men of a little smart genius cannot forbear throwing out against their best friends, when they have such a handle given them of being witty. But let them remember that I do hereby enter my caveat against this piece of raillery.

5. Bringing the latest war news.
6. Dressing table.
7. A shop where baubles and trifles are sold. "Suit

of ribbons": A set of ribbons to be worn together. "Mercer": a seller of such notions as tape, ribbon, and fringe.

STEELE: [Inkle and Yarico]

The Spectator, No. 11, Tuesday, March 13, 1711

Dat veniam corvis, vexat censura columbas.[1]
—JUVENAL, *Satire* 2.63

Arietta is visited by all persons of both sexes who have any pretence to wit and gallantry. She is in that time of life which is neither affected with the follies of youth or infirmities of age; and her conversation is so mixed with gaiety and prudence that she is agreeable both to the young and the old. Her behavior is very frank without being in the least blamable; as she is out of the tract[2] of any amorous or ambitious pursuits of her own, her visitants entertain her with accounts of themselves very freely, whether they concern their passions or their interests. I made her a visit this afternoon, having been formerly introduced to the honor of her acquaintance by my friend Will Honeycomb, who has prevailed upon her to admit me sometimes into her assembly as a civil, inoffensive man. I found her accompanied with one person only, a commonplace talker who upon my entrance arose and after a very slight civility sat down again; then turning to Arietta pursued his discourse, which I found was upon the old topic of constancy in love. He went on with great facility in repeating what he talks every day of his life; and with the ornaments of insignificant laughs and gestures enforced his arguments by quotations out of plays and songs which allude to the perjuries of the fair and the general levity[3] of women. Methought he strove to shine more than ordinarily in his talkative way that he might insult my silence, and distinguish himself before a woman of Arietta's taste and understanding. She had often an inclination to interrupt him but could find no opportunity, till the larum ceased of itself; which it did not till he had repeated and murdered the celebrated story of the Ephesian Matron.[4]

Arietta seemed to regard this piece of raillery as an outrage done to her sex, as indeed I have always observed that women, whether out of a nicer regard to their honor or what other reason I cannot tell, are more sensibly touched with those general aspersions which are cast upon their sex than men are by what is said of theirs.

When she had a little recovered her self from the serious anger she was in, she replied in the following manner.

Sir, when I consider how perfectly new all you have said on this subject is, and that the story you have given us is not quite two thousand years old, I cannot but think it a piece of presumption to dispute with you. But your quotations put in me in mind of the fable of the Lion and the Man.[5] The man walking with that noble animal showed him, in the ostentation of human superiority, a sign of a man killing a lion. Upon which the lion said very justly, "We lions are none of us painters, else we could show a hundred men killed by lions, for one lion killed by a man." You men are writers and can represent us women as unbecoming as you please in your works, while

1. Censure acquits the raven, but pursues the dove (Latin).
2. Course, way of acting.
3. Frivolity.
4. A story from Petronius's *Satyricon*, satirizing a supposedly grieving widow who allows a soldier to seduce her and to steal her husband's body. Cf. Haywood's *Fantomina*, p. 609. "Larum": clamor.
5. Attributed to Aesop, the name under which a body of beast fables from Greek antiquity and later are collected. Cf. Chaucer, *The Wife of Bath's Prologue*, line 698.

we are unable to return the injury. You have twice or thrice observed in your discourse that hypocrisy is the very foundation of our education; and that an ability to dissemble our affections is a professed part of our breeding. These and such other reflections are sprinkled up and down the writings of all ages by authors who leave behind them memorials of their resentment against the scorn of particular women in invectives against the whole sex. Such a writer, I doubt not, was the celebrated Petronius, who invented the pleasant aggravations of the frailty of the Ephesian Lady; but when we consider this question between the sexes, which has been either a point of dispute or raillery ever since there were men and women, let us take facts from plain people, and from such as have not either ambition or capacity to embellish their narrations with any beauties of imagination. I was the other day amusing myself with Ligon's account of Barbados; and in answer to your well-wrought tale, I will give you (as it dwells upon my memory) out of that honest traveler, in his fifty fifth page, the history of Inkle and Yarico.[6]

Mr. Thomas Inkle of London, aged twenty years, embarked in the Downs[7] on the good ship called the Achilles, bound for the West Indies, on the 16th of June 1647, in order to improve his fortune by trade and merchandise. Our adventurer was the third son of an eminent citizen,[8] who had taken particular care to instill into his mind an early love of gain by making him a perfect master of numbers, and consequently giving him a quick view of loss and advantage, and preventing the natural impulses of his passions by prepossession towards his interests. With a mind thus turned, young Inkle had a person[9] every way agreeable, a ruddy vigor in his countenance, strength in his limbs, with ringlets of fair hair loosely flowing on his shoulders. It happened in the course of the voyage that the Achilles, in some distress, put into a creek on the main[1] of America in search of provisions. The youth, who is the hero of my story, among others went ashore on this occasion. From their first landing they were observed by a party of Indians who hid themselves in the woods for that purpose. The English unadvisedly marched a great distance from the shore into the country, and were intercepted by the natives, who slew the greatest number of them. Our adventurer escaped among others by flying into a forest. Upon his coming into a remote and pathless part of the wood, he threw himself, tired and breathless, on a little hillock, when an Indian maid rushed from a thicket behind him. After the first surprise, they appeared mutually agreeable to each other. If the European was highly charmed with the limbs, features, and wild graces of the naked American, the American was no less taken with the dress, complexion, and shape of an European, covered from head to foot. The Indian grew immediately enamored of him, and consequently solicitous for his preservation. She therefore conveyed him to a cave, where she gave him a delicious repast of fruits, and led him to a stream to slake his thirst. In the midst of these good offices, she would sometimes play with his hair and delight in the opposition of its color to that of her fingers; then open his bosom, then laugh at him for covering it. She was, it seems, a person of distinction, for she every day came to him in a different dress of the most beautiful shells,

6. In A True and Exact History of the Island of Barbados (1657), Richard Ligon tells the first version of this story, which was retold throughout the 18th century. Steele invents the names of the lovers and many incidental details.
7. An anchorage off the southeast coast of England.
8. Inhabitant of a city (especially London), often identified as "a man of trade, not a gentleman" (Johnson's Dictionary).
9. Physical appearance.
1. Mainland.

bugles and bredes.[2] She likewise brought him a great many spoils which her other lovers had presented to her; so that his cave was richly adorned with all the spotted skins of beasts and most parti-colored feathers of fowls which that world afforded. To make his confinement more tolerable, she would carry him in the dusk of the evening or by the favor of moonlight to unfrequented groves and solitudes, and show him where to lie down in safety and sleep amidst the falls of waters and melody of nightingales. Her part was to watch and hold him awake in her arms for fear of her countrymen, and wake him on occasions to consult his safety. In this manner did the lovers pass away their time, till they had learned a language of their own in which the voyager communicated to his mistress how happy he should be to have her in his country, where she should be clothed in such silks as his waistcoat was made of and be carried in houses drawn by horses, without being exposed to wind or weather. All this he promised her the enjoyment of, without such fears and alarms as they were there tormented with. In this tender correspondence these lovers lived for several months, when Yarico, instructed by her lover, discovered a vessel on the coast, to which she made signals, and in the night, with the utmost joy and satisfaction, accompanied him to a ships' crew of his countrymen bound for Barbados. When a vessel from the main arrives in that island, it seems the planters come down to the shore, where there is an immediate market of the Indians and other slaves, as with us of horses and oxen.

To be short, Mr. Thomas Inkle, now coming into English territories, began seriously to reflect upon his loss of time and to weigh with himself how many days' interest of his money he had lost during his stay with Yarico. This thought made the young man very pensive and careful what account he should be able to give his friends[3] of his voyage. Upon which considerations, the prudent and frugal young man sold Yarico to a Barbadian merchant; notwithstanding that the poor girl, to incline him to commiserate her condition, told him that she was with child by him. But he only made use of that information to rise in his demands upon the purchaser.

I was so touched with this story (which I think should be always a counterpart to the Ephesian Matron) that I left the room with tears in my eyes; which a woman of Arietta's good sense did, I am sure, take for greater applause than any compliments I could make her.

---

2. Tube-shaped glass beads and braided or interwoven ornaments.
3. Family members and other connections.

ADDISON: [The Royal Exchange]

The Spectator, No. 69, Saturday, May 19, 1711

Hic segetes, illic veniunt felicius uvae:
Arborei foetus alibi, atque injussa virescunt
Gramina. Nonne vides, croceos ut Tmolus odores,
India mittit ebur, molles sua thura Saboei?
At Chalybes nudi ferrum, virosaque Pontus
Castorea, Eliadum palmas Epirus equarum?
Continuo has leges aeternaque foedera certis
Imposuit Natura locis[1] . . .
—VIRGIL, *Georgics* 1.54–61

There is no place in the town which I so much love to frequent as the Royal Exchange.[2] It gives me a secret satisfaction, and in some measure gratifies my vanity as I am an Englishman, to see so rich an assembly of countrymen and foreigners consulting together upon the private business of mankind, and making this metropolis a kind of emporium for the whole earth. I must confess I look upon High Change[3] to be a great council in which all considerable nations have their representatives. Factors[4] in the trading world are what ambassadors are in the politic world; they negotiate affairs, conclude treaties, and maintain a good correspondence between those wealthy societies of men that are divided from one another by seas and oceans or live on the different extremities of a continent. I have often been pleased to hear disputes adjusted between an inhabitant of Japan and an alderman of London, or to see a subject of the Great Mogul entering into a league with one of the Czar of Muscovy.[5] I am infinitely delighted in mixing with these several ministers of commerce as they are distinguished by their different walks[6] and different languages. Sometimes I am justled among a body of Armenians; sometimes I am lost in a crowd of Jews; and sometimes make one in a group of Dutchmen. I am a Dane, Swede, or Frenchman at different times; or rather fancy myself like the old philosopher,[7] who upon being asked what countryman he was, replied that he was a citizen of the world.

Though I very frequently visit this busy multitude of people, I am known to nobody there but my friend Sir Andrew, who often smiles upon me as he sees me bustling in the crowd, but at the same time connives[8] at my presence without taking any further notice of me. There is indeed a merchant of Egypt who just knows me by sight, having formerly remitted me some money to Grand Cairo; but as I am not versed in the modern Coptic,[9] our conferences go no further than a bow and a grimace.

1. Here grain, there grapes grow more successfully, and elsewhere young trees and grasses sprout up spontaneously. Don't you see how Tmolus sends us fragrant saffron, India sends ivory, the soft Sabaeans send frankincense; but the naked Chalybes offer us iron, Pontus the pungent beaver-oil, and Epirus their award-winning horses? From the beginning, nature imposed these laws, and made eternal covenants with particular places (Latin).
2. A financial institution in the City of London near the Bank of England; a center where businessmen gathered and around two hundred shops and private companies were assembled.
Opened in 1570, its first buildings were burned in the Great Fire of 1666: Addison discusses the Exchange as it was rebuilt in 1669.
3. The time of day when trading is most active.
4. Agents who buy and sell for other people.
5. Russia. The Great Mogul was the European name for the emperor of Delhi, whose dominions extended throughout most of Hindustan.
6. Ways of life.
7. Diogenes the Cynic (4th century B.C.E.).
8. Winks.
9. Language of the Copts, a sect of Egyptian Christians.

The bustle of the **Royal Exchange** in the 18th century. Etching 1788a by Francesco Bartolozzi.

This grand scene of business gives me an infinite variety of solid and substantial entertainments. As I am a great lover of mankind, my heart naturally overflows with pleasure at the sight of a prosperous and happy multitude, insomuch that at many public solemnities I cannot forbear expressing my joy with tears that have stolen down my cheeks. For this reason I am wonderfully delighted to see such a body of men thriving in their own private fortunes and at the same time promoting the public stock; or in other words, raising estates for their own families by bringing into their country whatever is wanting, and carrying out of it whatever is superfluous.

Nature seems to have taken a particular care to disseminate her blessings among the different regions of the world with an eye to this mutual intercourse and traffic among mankind, that the natives of the several parts of the globe might have a kind of dependence upon one another and be united together by their common interest. Almost every degree[1] produces something peculiar to it. The food often grows in one country and the sauce in another. The fruits of Portugal are corrected by the products of Barbados; the infusion of a China plant sweetened with the pith of an Indian cane. The Philippick Islands[2] give a flavor to our European bowls. The single dress of a woman of quality is often the product of an hundred climates. The muff and the fan come together from the different ends of the earth. The scarf is sent from the torrid zone and the tippet[3] from beneath the pole. The brocade petticoat rises out of the mines of Peru and the diamond necklace out of the bowels of Indostan.[4]

1. Here, a degree of latitude, hence a particular position on the earth's surface.
2. The Philippines.
3. A cape or other hanging part of a woman's dress.
4. India.

If we consider our own country in its natural prospect without any of the benefits and advantages of commerce, what a barren uncomfortable spot of earth falls to our share! Natural historians tell us that no fruit grows originally among us besides hips and haws, acorns and pig-nuts, with other delicacies of the like nature; that our climate of itself and without the assistances of art can make no further advances towards a plum than to a sloe and carries an apple to no greater a perfection than a crab;[5] that our melons, our peaches, our figs, our apricots, and cherries are strangers among us, imported in different ages and naturalized in our English gardens; and that they would all degenerate and fall away into the trash of our own country, if they were wholly neglected by the planter and left to the mercy of our sun and soil. Nor has traffic[6] more enriched our vegetable world than it has improved the whole face of nature among us. Our ships are laden with the harvest of every climate; our tables are stored with spices, and oils, and wines; our rooms are filled with pyramids of China and adorned with the workmanship of Japan; our morning's draught comes to us from the remotest corners of the earth. We repair our bodies by the drugs of America and repose ourselves under Indian canopies. My friend Sir Andrew calls the vineyards of France our gardens; the Spice-Islands our hot-beds; the Persians our silk-weavers, and the Chinese our potters. Nature indeed furnishes us with the bare necessaries of life, but traffic gives us great variety of what is useful, and at the same time supplies us with every thing that is convenient and ornamental. Nor is it the least part of this our happiness that whilst we enjoy the remotest products of the north and south, we are free from those extremities of weather which give them birth; that our eyes are refreshed with the green fields of Britain at the same time that our palates are feasted with fruits that rise between the tropics.

For these reasons there are no more useful members in a commonwealth than merchants. They knit mankind together in a mutual intercourse of good offices, distribute the gifts of nature, find work for the poor, add wealth to the rich, and magnificence to the great. Our English merchant converts the tin of his own country into gold and exchanges his wool for rubies. The Mahometans are clothed in our British manufacture and the inhabitants of the frozen zone warmed with the fleeces of our sheep.

When I have been upon the 'Change, I have often fancied one of our old kings standing in person where he is represented in effigy, and looking down upon the wealthy concourse of people with which that place is every day filled. In this case, how would he be surprised to hear all the languages of Europe spoken in this little spot of his former dominions, and to see so many private men, who in his time would have been the vassals of some powerful baron, negotiating like princes for greater sums of money than were formerly to be met with in the Royal Treasury! Trade, without enlarging the British territories, has given us a kind of additional empire. It has multiplied the number of the rich, made our landed estates infinitely more valuable than they were formerly, and added to them an accession of other estates as valuable as the lands themselves.

---

5. Crabapple. "Hips and haws": rosehips and the berries of the hawthorn tree. "Pig-nuts": or groundnuts, the tuber of *Bunium flexuosum*.
6. Trade.

THE PERIODICAL ESSAY: IDEAS

ADDISON: [Wit: True, False, Mixed]

The Spectator, No. 62, Friday, March 11, 1711

Scribendi recte sapere est et principium et fons.[1]
—HORACE, *Ars Poetica* 309

Mr. Locke has an admirable reflection upon the difference of wit and judgment, whereby he endeavors to show the reason why they are not always the talents of the same person. His words are as follow: "And hence, perhaps, may be given some reason of that common observation, that men who have a great deal of wit and prompt memories, have not always the clearest judgment, or deepest reason. For wit lying most in the assemblage of ideas, and putting those together with quickness and variety, wherein can be found any resemblance or congruity, thereby to make up pleasant pictures and agreeable visions in the fancy; judgment, on the contrary, lies quite on the other side, in separating carefully one from another, ideas wherein can be found the least difference, thereby to avoid being misled by similitude, and by affinity to take one thing for another. This is a way of proceeding quite contrary to metaphor and allusion; wherein, for the most part, lies that entertainment and pleasantry of wit which strikes so lively on the fancy, and is therefore so acceptable to all people."[2]

This is, I think, the best and most philosophical account that I have ever met with of wit, which generally, though not always, consists in such a resemblance and congruity of ideas as this author mentions. I shall only add to it, by way of explanation, that every resemblance of ideas is not that which we call wit, unless it be such an one that gives delight and surprise to the reader. These two properties seem essential to wit, more particularly the last of them. In order therefore that the resemblance in the ideas be wit, it is necessary that the ideas should not lie too near one another in the nature of things; for where the likeness is obvious, it gives no surprise. To compare one man's singing to that of another, or to represent the whiteness of any object by that of milk and snow, or the variety of its colors by those of the rainbow, cannot be called wit, unless, besides this obvious resemblance, there be some further congruity discovered in the two ideas that is capable of giving the reader some surprise. Thus when a poet tells us, the bosom of his mistress is as white as snow, there is no wit in the comparison; but when he adds, with a sigh, that it is as cold too, it then grows into wit. Every reader's memory may supply him with innumerable instances of the same nature. For this reason, the similitudes in heroic poets, who endeavor rather to fill the mind with great conceptions, than to divert it with such as are new and surprising, have seldom anything in them that can be called wit. Mr. Locke's account of wit, with this short explanation, comprehends most of the species of wit, as metaphors, similitudes, allegories, enigmas, mottoes, parables, fables, dreams, visions, dramatic writings, burlesque, and all the methods of allusion:[3] as there are many other pieces of wit (how

1. Discernment is the source and fount of writing well (Latin).
2. John Locke's *An Essay Concerning Human*

Understanding 2.11.2.
3. Wordplay; more broadly, any covert or symbolic use of language.

remote soever they may appear at first sight from the foregoing description) which upon examination will be found to agree with it.

As true wit generally consists in this resemblance and congruity of ideas, false wit chiefly consists in the resemblance and congruity sometimes of single letters, as in anagrams, chronograms, lipograms, and acrostics; sometimes of syllables, as in echoes and doggerel rhymes; sometimes of words, as in puns and quibbles; and sometimes of whole sentences or poems, cast into the figures of eggs, axes, or altars:[4] nay, some carry the notion of wit so far, as to ascribe it even to external mimicry; and to look upon a man as an ingenious person, that can resemble the tone, posture, or face of another.

As true wit consists in the resemblance of ideas, and false wit in the resemblance of words, according to the foregoing instances; there is another kind of wit which consists partly in the resemblance of ideas, and partly in the resemblance of words; which for distinction's sake I shall call mixed wit. This kind of wit is that which abounds in Cowley, more than in any author that ever wrote. Mr. Waller has likewise a great deal of it. Mr. Dryden is very sparing in it. Milton had a genius much above it. Spenser is in the same class with Milton. The Italians, even in their epic poetry, are full of it. Monsieur Boileau,[5] who formed himself upon the ancient poets, has everywhere rejected it with scorn. If we look after mixed wit among the Greek writers, we shall find it nowhere but in the epigrammatists. There are indeed some strokes of it in the little poem ascribed to Musaeus,[6] which by that, as well as many other marks, betrays itself to be a modern composition. If we look into the Latin writers, we find none of this mixed wit in Virgil, Lucretius, or Catullus; very little in Horace, but a great deal of it in Ovid, and scarce anything else in Martial.

Out of the innumerable branches of mixed wit, I shall choose one instance which may be met with in all the writers of this class. The passion of love in its nature has been thought to resemble fire; for which reason the words fire and flame are made use of to signify love. The witty poets therefore have taken an advantage from the doubtful meaning of the word fire, to make an infinite number of witticisms. Cowley, observing the cold regard of his mistress's eyes,[7] and at the same time their power of producing love in him, considers them as burning-glasses made of ice; and finding himself able to live in the greatest extremities of love, concludes the torrid zone to be habitable. When his mistress has read his letter written in juice of lemon by holding it to the fire, he desires her to read it over a second time by love's flames. When she weeps, he wishes it were inward heat that distilled those drops from the limbec.[8] When she is absent he is beyond eighty, that is, thirty degrees nearer the pole than when she is with him. His ambitious love is a fire that naturally mounts upwards; his happy love is the beams of heaven, and his unhappy love flames of hell. When it does not let him sleep, it is a flame that sends up no smoke; when it is opposed by counsel and advice, it is a fire that rages the more by the wind's blowing upon it. Upon the dying of a tree in which he had

4. E.g., George Herbert's "The Altar" and "Easter Wings." "Chronogram": phrase in which certain letters express a date; e.g., "LorD haVe MerCIe Vpon Vs"; the capital letters (in Roman numerals) add up to 1666, the *annus mirabilis* of fire, plague, and war. "Lipograms": compositions omitting all words that contain a certain letter or letters.
5. Nicolas Boileau (1636–1711), French neoclas-
sicist who wrote a verse *Art of Poetry* (1674), which was translated by Dryden.
6. A poem called *Hero and Leander*, attributed to the ancient Greek poet Musaeus, was first published in 1635.
7. In *The Mistress, or Several Copies of Love-Verses* (1647).
8. Or alembic, an apparatus used in distilling.

cut his loves, he observes that his written flames had burned up and withered the tree. When he resolves to give over his passion, he tells us that one burnt like him for ever dreads the fire. His heart is an Aetna, that instead of Vulcan's shop[9] encloses Cupid's forge in it. His endeavoring to drown his love in wine is throwing oil upon the fire. He would insinuate to his mistress that the fire of love, like that of the sun (which produces so many living creatures), should not only warm but beget. Love in another place cooks pleasure at his fire. Sometimes the poet's heart is frozen in every breast, and sometimes scorched in every eye. Sometimes he is drowned in tears, and burnt in love, like a ship set on fire in the middle of the sea.

The reader may observe in every one of these instances that the poet mixes the qualities of fire with those of love; and in the same sentence speaking of it both as a passion, and as real fire, surprises the reader with those seeming resemblances or contradictions that make up all the wit in this kind of writing. Mixed wit therefore is a composition of pun and true wit, and is more or less perfect as the resemblance lies in the ideas or in the words. Its foundations are laid partly in falsehood and partly in truth: reason puts in her claim for one half of it, and extravagance for the other. The only province therefore for this kind of wit is epigram, or those little occasional poems that in their own nature are nothing else but a tissue of epigrams. I cannot conclude this head of mixed wit without owning that the admirable poet out of whom I have taken the examples of it had as much true wit as any author that ever writ; and indeed all other talents of an extraordinary genius.

It may be expected, since I am upon this subject, that I should take notice of Mr. Dryden's definition of wit; which, with all the deference that is due to the judgment of so great a man, is not so properly a definition of wit, as of good writing in general. Wit, as he defines it, is "a propriety of words and thoughts adapted to the subject."[1] If this be a true definition of wit, I am apt to think that Euclid[2] was the greatest wit that ever set pen to paper: it is certain there never was a greater propriety of words and thoughts adapted to the subject than what that author has made use of in his elements. I shall only appeal to my reader, if this definition agrees with any notion he has of wit: if it be a true one, I am sure Mr. Dryden was not only a better poet, but a greater wit than Mr. Cowley; and Virgil a much more facetious man than either Ovid or Martial.

Bouhours,[3] whom I look upon to be the most penetrating of all the French critics, has taken pains to show that it is impossible for any thought to be beautiful which is not just, and has not its foundation in the nature of things; that the basis of all wit is truth; and that no thought can be valuable, of which good sense is not the groundwork. Boileau has endeavored to inculcate the same notion in several parts of his writings, both in prose and verse. This is that natural way of writing, that beautiful simplicity, which we so much admire in the compositions of the ancients; and which nobody deviates from, but those who want strength of genius to make a thought shine in its own natural beauties. Poets who want this strength of genius to give that majestic simplicity to nature, which we so much admire in the works of the ancients,

9. Mount Etna was supposed to be the workshop of Vulcan, the Roman god of fire and metalworking.
1. Adapted from Dryden's "Apology for Heroic Poetry."
2. Hellenic mathematician (ca. 300 B.C.E.).
3. Dominique Bouhours (1628–1702), who wrote Art of Criticism.

are forced to hunt after foreign ornaments, and not to let any piece of wit of what kind soever escape them. I look upon these writers as Goths in poetry, who, like those in architecture, not being able to come up to the beautiful simplicity of the old Greeks and Romans, have endeavored to supply its place with all the extravagances of an irregular fancy. Mr. Dryden makes a very handsome observation on Ovid's writing a letter from Dido to Aeneas, in the following words:[4] "Ovid" (says he, speaking of Virgil's fiction of Dido and Aeneas) "takes it up after him, even in the same age, and makes an ancient heroine of Virgil's new-created Dido; dictates a letter for her just before her death to the ungrateful fugitive; and, very unluckily for himself, is for mea-suring a sword with a man so much superior in force to him, on the same subject. I think I may be judge of this, because I have translated both. The famous author of the Art of Love[5] has nothing of his own; he borrows all from a greater master in his own profession, and, which is worse, improves nothing which he finds: nature fails him, and being forced to his old shift, he has recourse to witticism. This passes indeed with his soft admirers, and gives him the preference to Virgil in their esteem."

Were not I supported by so great an authority as that of Mr. Dryden, I should not venture to observe that the taste of most of our English poets, as well as readers, is extremely Gothic. He quotes Monsieur Segrais for a threefold distinction of the readers of poetry: in the first of which he com-prehends the rabble of readers, whom he does not treat as such with regard to their quality,[6] but to their numbers and the coarseness of their taste. His words are as follow: "Segrais has distinguished the readers of poetry, according to their capacity of judging, into three classes. [He might have said the same of writers too, if he had pleased.] In the lowest form he places those whom he calls *les petits esprits*,[7] such things as are our upper-gallery audience in a play-house; who like nothing but the husk and rind of wit, pre-fer a quibble, a conceit, an epigram, before solid sense and elegant expres-sion: these are mob-readers. If Virgil and Martial stood for parliament-men, we know already who would carry it.[8] But though they make the greatest appearance in the field, and cry the loudest, the best on 't is they are but a sort of French Huguenots, or Dutch boors,[9] brought over in herds, but not naturalized; who have not lands of two pounds per annum in Parnassus, and therefore are not privileged to poll.[1] Their authors are of the same level, fit to represent them on a mountebank's stage, or to be masters of the ceremonies in a bear-garden:[2] yet these are they who have the most admirers. But it often happens, to their mortification, that as their readers improve their stock of sense (as they may by reading better books, and by conversa-tion with men of judgment), they soon forsake them."

I must not dismiss this subject without observing, that as Mr. Locke in the passage above-mentioned has discovered the most fruitful source of wit, so there is another of a quite contrary nature to it, which does likewise branch

4. From Dryden's dedication to his translation of the *Aeneid* (1697).
5. Ovid.
6. Social standing. Jean Regnauld de Segrais (1624–1701), who had translated Virgil into French, is quoted extensively by Dryden.
7. The small minded (French).
8. I.e., the witty Martial would easily defeat the weighty Virgil in an election.

9. Peasants. Huguenots and the Dutch were the largest class of immigrants in England. "On 't": that one can say.
1. Vote. Only freeholders worth £2 a year could go to the polls, and these readers of little taste hold no land in Parnassus (where the Muses live).
2. Place for bearbaiting and other violent exhibi-tions.

itself out into several kinds. For not only the resemblance but the opposition of ideas does very often produce wit; as I could show in several little points, turns, and antitheses, that I may possibly enlarge upon in some future speculation.[3]

ADDISON: [*Paradise Lost*: General Critical Remarks]

The Spectator, No. 267, Saturday, January 5, 1712

Cedite Romani scriptores, cedite Graii.[1]
—PROPERTIUS, *Elegies* 2.34.65

There is nothing in nature so irksome as general discourses, especially when they turn chiefly upon words. For this reason I shall waive the discussion of that point which was started some years since, Whether Milton's *Paradise Lost* may be called an heroic poem? Those who will not give it that title may call it (if they please) a *divine poem*. It will be sufficient to its perfection, if it has in it all the beauties of the highest kind of poetry; and as for those who allege it is not an heroic poem, they advance no more to the diminution of it, than if they should say Adam is not Aeneas, nor Eve Helen.

I shall therefore examine it by the rules of epic poetry,[2] and see whether it falls short of the *Iliad* or *Aeneid*, in the beauties which are essential to that kind of writing. The first thing to be considered in an epic poem is the fable,[3] which is perfect or imperfect, according as the action which it relates is more or less so. This action should have three qualifications in it. First, it should be but one action. Secondly, it should be an entire action; and thirdly, it should be a great action. To consider the action of the *Iliad, Aeneid,* and *Paradise Lost,* in these three several lights. Homer to preserve the unity of his action hastens into the midst of things, as Horace has observed:[4] had he gone up to Leda's egg, or begun much later, even at the rape of Helen, or the investing of Troy, it is manifest that the story of the poem would have been a series of several actions. He therefore opens his poem with the discord of his princes, and with great art interweaves in the several succeeding parts of it, an account of everything material which relates to them and had passed before that fatal dissension. After the same manner Aeneas makes his first appearance in the Tyrrhene seas, and within sight of Italy, because the action proposed to be celebrated was that of his settling himself in Latium.[5] But because it was necessary for the reader to know what had happened to him in the taking of Troy, and in the preceding parts of his voyage, Virgil makes his hero

3. For such an "enlargement," see Samuel Johnson's remarks on wit in the life of Cowley (p. 817).
1. Yield place, ye Roman and ye Grecian writers, yield (Latin).
2. The rules for the conduct of an epic poem—derived out of the poems of Homer and Virgil, the *Poetics* of Aristotle, and the *Art of Poetry* of Horace—had been given their most systematic and complete statement in Père René Le Bossu's *Traité du poème épique* (1675), which was immediately absorbed into English critical thought. Addison writes of *Paradise Lost* with Le Bossu well in sight, but he is no slavish disciple.

3. The plot of a drama or poem.
4. *Art of Poetry,* 147–49. Helen, whose abduction from her husband Menelaus by the Trojan prince Paris brought on the Trojan War, was the daughter of Leda, who was visited by Zeus in the guise of a swan.
5. The kingdom of the Latini, where Aeneas was hospitably received when he landed at the mouth of the Tiber. He married Lavinia, the daughter of King Latinus, and later ruled the kingdom. The Tyrrhene seas are that part of the Mediterranean west of Italy, bounded by the islands of Sicily, Sardinia, and Corsica.

relate it by way of episode[6] in the second and third books of the *Aeneid*. The contents of both which books come before those of the first book in the thread of the story, though for preserving of this unity of action, they follow them in the disposition of the poem. Milton, in imitation of these two great poets, opens his *Paradise Lost* with an infernal council plotting the fall of man, which is the action he proposed to celebrate; and as for those great actions which preceded in point of time, the battle of the angels, and the creation of the world (which would have entirely destroyed the unity of his principal action, had he related them in the same order that they happened), he cast them into the fifth, sixth, and seventh books, by way of episode to this noble poem.

Aristotle himself allows that Homer has nothing to boast of as to the unity of his fable, though at the same time that great critic and philosopher endeavors to palliate this imperfection in the Greek poet, by imputing it in some measure to the very nature of an epic poem. Some have been of opinion that the *Aeneid* labors also in this particular, and has episodes which may be looked upon as excrescences rather than as parts of the action. On the contrary, the poem which we have now under our consideration hath no other episodes than such as naturally arise from the subject, and yet is filled with such a multitude of astonishing incidents that it gives us at the same time a pleasure of the greatest variety, and of the greatest simplicity.

I must observe also that as Virgil, in the poem which was designed to celebrate the original of the Roman Empire, has described the birth of its great rival, the Carthaginian commonwealth, Milton with the like art in his poem on the Fall of Man, has related the fall of those angels who are his professed enemies. Besides the many other beauties in such an episode, its running parallel with the great action of the poem hinders it from breaking the unity so much as another episode would have done that had not so great an affinity with the principal subject. In short, this is the same kind of beauty which the critics admire in the *Spanish Friar, or The Double Discovery*,[7] where the two different plots look like counterparts and copies of one another.

The second qualification required in the action of an epic poem is that it should be an *entire* action. An action is entire when it is complete in all its parts; or as Aristotle describes it, when it consists of a beginning, a middle, and an end. Nothing should go before it, be intermixed with it, or follow after it, that is not related to it. As on the contrary, no single step should be omitted in that just and regular process which it must be supposed to take from its original to its consummation. Thus, we see the anger of Achilles in its birth, its continuance, and effects; and Aeneas's settlement in Italy, carried on through all the oppositions in his way to it both by sea and land. The action in Milton excels (I think) both the former in this particular: we see it contrived in hell, executed upon earth, and punished by heaven. The parts of it are told in the most distinct manner, and grow out of one another in the most natural method.

The third qualification of an epic poem is its *greatness*. The anger of Achilles was of such consequence that it embroiled the kings of Greece, destroyed the heroes of Troy, and engaged all the gods in factions. Aeneas's settlement in Italy produced the Caesars, and gave birth to the Roman Empire. Milton's

---

6. An incidental narration or digression in an epic that arises naturally from the subject but is separable from the main action.

7. A comedy by Dryden.

subject was still greater than either of the former; it does not determine the fate of single persons or nations, but of a whole species. The united powers of hell are joined together for the destruction of mankind, which they effected in part, and would have completed, had not Omnipotence itself interposed. The principal actors are man in his greatest perfection, and woman in her highest beauty. Their enemies are the fallen angels: the Messiah their friend, and the Almighty their protector. In short, everything that is great in the whole circle of being, whether within the verge of nature, or out of it, has a proper part assigned it in this noble poem.

In poetry, as in architecture, not only the whole, but the principal members, and every part of them, should be great. I will not presume to say, that the book of games in the *Aeneid*, or that in the *Iliad*, are not of this nature, nor to reprehend Virgil's simile of the top,[8] and many other of the same nature in the *Iliad*, as liable to any censure in this particular; but I think we may say, without derogating from those wonderful performances, that there is an unquestionable magnificence in every part of *Paradise Lost*, and indeed a much greater than could have been formed upon any pagan system.

But Aristotle, by the greatness of the action, does not only mean that it should be great in its nature, but also in its duration, or in other words, that it should have a due length in it, as well as what we properly call greatness. The just measure of the kind of magnitude he explains by the following similitude. An animal no bigger than a mite cannot appear perfect to the eye, because the sight takes it in at once, and has only a confused idea of the whole, and not a distinct idea of all its parts: if on the contrary you should suppose an animal of ten thousand furlongs in length, the eye would be so filled with a single part of it, that it would not give the mind an idea of the whole. What these animals are to the eye, a very short or a very long action would be to the memory. The first would be, as it were, lost and swallowed up by it, and the other difficult to be contained in it. Homer and Virgil have shown their principal art in this particular; the action of the *Iliad*, and that of the *Aeneid*, were in themselves exceeding short, but are so beautifully extended and diversified by the invention of episodes, and the machinery[9] of gods, with the like poetical ornaments, that they make up an agreeable story sufficient to employ the memory without overcharging it. Milton's action is enriched with such a variety of circumstances that I have taken as much pleasure in reading the contents of his books as in the best invented story I ever met with. It is possible that the traditions on which the *Iliad* and *Aeneid* were built had more circumstances in them than the history of the Fall of Man, as it is related in Scripture. Besides it was easier for Homer and Virgil to dash the truth with fiction, as they were in no danger of offending the religion of their country by it. But as for Milton, he had not only a very few circumstances upon which to raise his poem, but was also obliged to proceed with the greatest caution in everything that he added out of his own invention. And, indeed, notwithstanding all the restraints he was under, he has filled his story with so many surprising incidents, which bear so close an

8. In book VII of the *Aeneid*, Virgil compares Amata, enraged at the engagement of her daughter to Aeneas, to a top whipped by young boys.
9. The technical term (from *deus ex machina*) in critical theory for the supernatural beings who oversee and intervene in the affairs of the characters in epic poems.

analogy with what is delivered in Holy Writ, that it is capable of pleasing the most delicate reader, without giving offense to the most scrupulous.

The modern critics have collected from several hints in the *Iliad* and *Aeneid* the space of time which is taken up by the action of each of these poems; but as a great part of Milton's story was transacted in regions that lie out of the reach of the sun and the sphere of day, it is impossible to gratify the reader with such a calculation, which indeed would be more curious than instructive; none of the critics, either ancient or modern, having laid down rules to circumscribe the action of an epic poem with any determined number of years, days, or hours.

This Piece of Criticism on Milton's Paradise Lost *shall be carried on in the following Saturdays' papers.*[1]

ADDISON: [The Pleasures of the Imagination]

The Spectator, No. 411, Saturday, June 21, 1712

> *Avia Pieridum peragro loca, nullius ante*
> *Trita solo; juvat integros accedere fonts [fonteis];*
> *Atque haurire:*[1] . . .
> —LUCRETIUS, *De Rerum Natura*, 1.926–8

Our sight is the most perfect and most delightful of all our senses. It fills the mind with the largest variety of ideas, converses with its objects at the greatest distance, and continues the longest in action without being tired or satiated with its proper enjoyments. The sense of feeling can indeed give us a notion of extension, shape, and all other ideas that enter at the eye, except colors; but at the same time it is very much straitened and confined in its operations, to the number, bulk, and distance of its particular objects. Our sight seems designed to supply all these defects, and may be considered as a more delicate and diffusive kind of touch, that spreads itself over an infinite multitude of bodies, comprehends the largest figures, and brings into our reach some of the most remote parts of the universe.

It is this sense which furnishes the imagination with its ideas; so that by the pleasures of the imagination or fancy (which I shall use promiscuously[2]) I here mean such as arise from visible objects, either when we have them actually in our view or when we call up their ideas into our minds by paintings, statues, descriptions, or any the like occasion. We cannot indeed have a single image in the fancy that did not make its first entrance through the sight; but we have the power of retaining, altering, and compounding those images which we have once received into all the varieties of picture and vision that are most agreeable to the imagination; for by this faculty a man in a dungeon is capable of entertaining himself with scenes and landscapes more beautiful than any that can be found in the whole compass of nature.

There are few words in the English language which are employed in a more loose and uncircumscribed sense than those of the fancy and the imagination. I therefore thought it necessary to fix and determine the notion of these

---

1. The series on *Paradise Lost* contains eighteen essays.
1. I wander paths of the Pierides [muses] not traveled before and joy to be the first to drink at untasted springs (Latin).
2. Without discriminating between them.

two words, as I intend to make use of them in the thread of my following speculations, that the reader may conceive rightly what is the subject which I proceed upon. I must therefore desire him to remember that by the pleasures of the imagination I mean only such pleasures as arise originally from sight, and that I divide these pleasures into two kinds: my design being first of all to discourse of those primary pleasures of the imagination which entirely proceed from such objects as are before our eyes; and in the next place to speak of those secondary pleasures of the imagination which flow from the ideas of visible objects when the objects are actually before the eye, but are called up into our memories, or formed into agreeable visions of things that are either absent or fictitious.

The pleasures of the imagination taken in their full extent are not so gross as those of sense nor so refined as those of the understanding. The last are indeed more preferable, because they are founded on some new knowledge or improvement in the mind of man; yet it must be confessed that those of the imagination are as great and as transporting as the other. A beautiful prospect delights the soul as much as a demonstration; and a description in Homer has charmed more readers than a chapter in Aristotle. Besides, the pleasures of the imagination have this advantage above those of the understanding, that they are more obvious and more easy to be acquired. It is but opening the eye, and the scene enters. The colors paint themselves on the fancy with very little attention of thought or application of mind in the beholder. We are struck, we know not how, with the symmetry of any thing we see, and immediately assent to the beauty of an object without enquiring into the particular causes and occasions of it.

A man of a polite imagination is let into a great many pleasures that the vulgar[3] are not capable of receiving. He can converse with a picture and find an agreeable companion in a statue. He meets with a secret refreshment in a description, and often feels a greater satisfaction in the prospect of fields and meadows than another does in the possession. It gives him indeed a kind of property in everything he sees, and makes the most rude, uncultivated parts of nature administer to his pleasure; so that he looks upon the world, as it were, in another light, and discovers in it a multitude of charms that conceal themselves from the generality of mankind.

There are indeed but very few who know how to be idle and innocent, or have a relish of any pleasures that are not criminal; every diversion they take is at the expense of some one virtue or another, and their very first step out of business is into vice or folly. A man should endeavor, therefore, to make the sphere of his innocent pleasures as wide as possible, that he may retire into them with safety, and find in them such a satisfaction as a wise man would not blush to take. Of this nature are those of the imagination, which do not require such a bent of thought as is necessary to our more serious employments, nor at the same time suffer the mind to sink into that negligence and remissness which are apt to accompany our more sensual delights, but, like a gentle exercise to the faculties, awaken them from sloth and idleness without putting them upon any labor or difficulty.

We might here add that the pleasures of the fancy are more conducive to health than those of the understanding, which are worked out by dint of

3. The ordinary sort of person. "Polite": cultivated, refined.

thinking and attended with too violent a labor of the brain. Delightful scenes, whether in nature, painting, or poetry, have a kindly influence on the body as well as the mind, and not only serve to clear and brighten the imagination but are able to disperse grief and melancholy, and to set the animal spirits[4] in pleasing and agreeable motions. For this reason Sir Francis Bacon in his Essay upon Health[5] has not thought it improper to prescribe to his reader a poem or a prospect, where he particularly dissuades him from knotty and subtle disquisitions, and advises him to pursue studies that fill the mind with splendid and illustrious objects, as histories, fables, and contemplations of nature.

I have in this paper, by way of introduction, settled the notion of those pleasures of the imagination which are the subject of my present undertaking, and endeavored by several considerations to recommend to my reader the pursuit of those pleasures. I shall in my next paper examine the several sources from whence these pleasures are derived.[6]

ADDISON: [On the Scale of Being]

The Spectator, No. 519, October 25, 1712

Inde hominum pecudumque genus, vitaeque volantum,
Et quae marmoreo fert monstra sub aequore pontus.[1]
—VIRGIL, *Aeneid* 6.728–29

Though there is a great deal of pleasure in contemplating the material world, by which I mean that system of bodies into which nature has so curiously wrought the mass of dead matter, with the several relations which those bodies bear to one another, there is still, methinks, something more wonderful and surprising in contemplations on the world of life, by which I mean all those animals with which every part of the universe is furnished. The material world is only the shell of the universe: the world of life are its inhabitants.

If we consider those parts of the material world which lie the nearest to us and are, therefore, subject to our observations and inquiries, it is amazing to consider the infinity of animals with which it is stocked. Every part of matter is peopled. Every green leaf swarms with inhabitants. There is scarce a single humor in the body of a man, or of any other animal, in which our glasses[2] do not discover myriads of living creatures. The surface of animals is also covered with other animals which are, in the same manner, the basis of other animals that live upon it; nay, we find in the most solid bodies, as in marble itself, innumerable cells and cavities that are crowded with such imperceptible inhabitants as are too little for the naked eye to discover. On the other hand, if we look into the more bulky parts of nature, we see the seas, lakes, and rivers teeming with numberless kinds of living creatures. We find every mountain and marsh, wilderness and wood, plentifully stocked with birds and beasts, and every part of matter affording proper necessaries and conveniences for the livelihood of multitudes which inhabit it.

4. Principle of animating bodily energy.
5. Bacon's Essay 30, "Of Regiment of Health," appeared in his *Essays* (1597).
6. Addison wrote eleven papers on various aspects of the pleasures of the imagination (*Spectator*

nos. 411–21), of which this is first.
1. Thence the race of men and beasts, the life of flying creatures, and the monsters that ocean bears beneath her smooth surface (Latin).
2. Microscopes. "Humor": fluid.

The author of *The Plurality of Worlds*[3] draws a very good argument upon this consideration for the peopling of every planet, as indeed it seems very probable from the analogy of reason that, if no part of matter which we are acquainted with lies waste and useless, those great bodies, which are at such a distance from us, should not be desert and unpeopled, but rather that they should be furnished with beings adapted to their respective situations.

Existence is a blessing to those beings only which are endowed with perception and is, in a manner, thrown away upon dead matter any further than as it is subservient to beings which are conscious of their existence. Accordingly, we find from the bodies which lie under our observation that matter is only made as the basis and support of animals and that there is no more of the one than what is necessary for the existence of the other.

Infinite Goodness is of so communicative a nature that it seems to delight in the conferring of existence upon every degree of perceptive being. As this is a speculation which I have often pursued with great pleasure to myself, I shall enlarge farther upon it, by considering that part of the scale of beings which comes within our knowledge.

There are some living creatures which are raised but just above dead matter. To mention only that species of shellfish, which are formed in the fashion of a cone, that grow to the surface of several rocks and immediately die upon their being severed from the place where they grow. There are many other creatures but one remove from these, which have no other sense besides that of feeling and taste. Others have still an additional one of hearing; others of smell, and others of sight. It is wonderful to observe by what a gradual progress the world of life advances through a prodigious variety of species before a creature is formed that is complete in all its senses; and, even among these, there is such a different degree of perfection in the sense which one animal enjoys, beyond what appears in another, that, though the sense in different animals be distinguished by the same common denomination, it seems almost of a different nature. If after this we look into the several inward perfections of cunning and sagacity, or what we generally call instinct, we find them rising after the same manner, imperceptibly, one above another, and receiving additional improvements, according to the species in which they are implanted. This progress in nature is so very gradual that the most perfect of an inferior species comes very near to the most imperfect of that which is immediately above it.

The exuberant and overflowing goodness of the Supreme Being, whose mercy extends to all his works, is plainly seen, as I have before hinted, from his having made so very little matter, at least what falls within our knowledge, that does not swarm with life. Nor is his goodness less seen in the diversity than in the multitude of living creatures. Had he only made one species of animals, none of the rest would have enjoyed the happiness of existence; he has, therefore, *specified* in his creation every degree of life, every capacity of being. The whole chasm in nature, from a plant to a man, is filled up with diverse kinds of creatures, rising one over another by such a gentle and easy ascent that the little transitions and deviations from one

3. Bernard de Fontenelle (1657–1757). This popular book, a series of dialogues between a scientist and a countess concerning the possibility of other inhabited planets and the new astrophysics in general, was published in 1686 in France and was translated in 1688 by both John Glanvill and Aphra Behn.

species to another are almost insensible. This intermediate space is so well husbanded and managed that there is scarce a degree of perception which does not appear in some one part of the world of life. Is the goodness or wisdom of the Divine Being more manifested in this his proceeding?

There is a consequence, besides those I have already mentioned, which seems very naturally deducible from the foregoing considerations. If the scale of being rises by such a regular progress so high as man, we may by a parity of reason[4] suppose that it still proceeds gradually through those beings which are of a superior nature to him, since there is an infinitely greater space and room for different degrees of perfection between the Supreme Being and man than between man and the most despicable insect. This consequence of so great a variety of beings which are superior to us, from that variety which is inferior to us, is made by Mr. Locke[5] in a passage which I shall here set down after having premised that, notwithstanding there is such infinite room between man and his Maker for the creative power to exert itself in, it is impossible that it should ever be filled up, since there will be still an infinite gap or distance between the highest created being and the Power which produced him:

> That there should be more species of intelligent creatures above us than there are of sensible and material below, is probable to me from hence: That in all the visible corporeal world we see no chasms or no gaps. All quite down from us, the descent is by easy steps and a continued series of things that, in each remove, differ very little from the other. There are fishes that have wings and are not strangers to the airy region; and there are some birds that are inhabitants of the water, whose blood is cold as fishes and their flesh so like in taste that the scrupulous are allowed them on fish days.[6] There are animals so near of kin both to birds and beasts that they are in the middle between both: amphibious animals link the terrestrial and aquatic together; seals live at land and at sea, and porpoises have the warm blood and entrails of a hog, not to mention what is confidently reported of mermaids or seamen. There are some brutes that seem to have as much knowledge and reason as some that are called men; and the animal and vegetable kingdoms are so nearly joined that, if you will take the lowest of one and the highest of the other, there will scarce be perceived any great difference between them; and so on, till we come to the lowest and the most inorganical parts of matter, we shall find everywhere that the several species are linked together and differ but in almost insensible degrees. And when we consider the infinite power and wisdom of the Maker, we have reason to think that it is suitable to the magnificent harmony of the universe and the great design and infinite goodness of the Architect, that the species of creatures should also, by gentle degrees, ascend upward from us toward his infinite perfection, as we see they gradually descend from us downward; which, if it be probable, we have reason to be persuaded that there are far more species of creatures above us than there are beneath, we being in degrees of perfection much more remote from the infinite being of God than we are from the lowest state of being

---

4. A reasonable analogy or equivalence.
5. John Locke, in his *Essay Concerning Human Understanding*, 3.6.12.

6. Days of religious observance when fish instead of meat is eaten.

and that which approaches nearest to nothing. And yet of all those distinct species we have no clear distinct ideas.

In this system of being, there is no creature so wonderful in its nature, and which so much deserves our particular attention, as man, who fills up the middle space between the animal and intellectual nature, the visible and invisible world, and is that link in the chain of beings which has been often termed the *nexus utriusque mundi*.[7] So that he who, in one respect, is associated with angels and archangels, may look upon a Being of infinite perfection as his father, and the highest order of spirits as his brethren, may, in another respect, say to corruption, "Thou art my father," and to the worm, "Thou art my mother and my sister."[8]

7. The binding together of both worlds (Latin).   8. Job 17.14.

ALEXANDER POPE
1688–1744

Alexander Pope is the only important writer of his generation who was solely a man of letters. Because he could not, as a Roman Catholic, attend a university, vote, or hold public office, he was excluded from the sort of patronage that was bestowed by statesmen on many writers during the reign of Anne. This disadvantage he turned into a positive good, for the translation of Homer's *Iliad* and *Odyssey*, which he undertook for profit as well as for fame, gave him ample means to live the life of an independent suburban gentleman. After 1718 he lived hospitably in his villa by the Thames at Twickenham (then pronounced *Twit'nam*), entertaining his friends and converting his five acres of land into a diminutive landscape garden. Almost exactly a century earlier, William Shakespeare had earned enough to retire to a country estate at Stratford—but he had been an actor-manager as well as a playwright; Pope was the first English writer to build a lucrative, lifelong career by publishing his works.

Ill health plagued Pope almost from birth. Crippled early by tuberculosis of the bone, he never grew taller than four and a half feet. In later life he suffered from violent headaches and required constant attention from servants. But Pope did not allow his infirmities to hold him back; he was always a master at making the best of what he had. Around 1700 his father, a well-to-do, retired London merchant, moved to a small property at Binfield in Windsor Forest. There, in rural surroundings, young Pope completed his education by reading whatever he pleased, "like a boy gathering flowers in the woods and fields just as they fall in his way"; and there, encouraged by his father, he began to write verse. He was already an accomplished poet in his teens; no English poet has ever been more precocious.

Pope's first striking success as a poet was *An Essay on Criticism* (1711), which brought him Joseph Addison's approval and an intemperate personal attack from the critic John Dennis, who was angered by a casual reference to himself in the poem. *The Rape of the Lock,* both in its original shorter version of 1712 and in its more elaborate version of 1714, proved the author a master not only of metrics and of language but also of witty, urbane satire. In *An Essay on Criticism,* Pope had excelled all his predecessors in writing a didactic poem after the example of Horace; in the *Rape,* he had written the most brilliant mock epic in the language. But there was another vein in Pope's youthful poetry, a tender concern with natural beauty and love. The *Pastorals* (1709), his first publication, and *Windsor Forest* (1713; much of it was written earlier) abound in visual imagery and descriptive passages of ideally ordered nature; they remind us that Pope was an amateur painter. The "Elegy to the Memory of an Unfortunate Lady" and *Eloisa to Abelard,* published in the collected poems of 1717, dwell on the pangs of unhappy lovers (Pope himself never married). And even the long task of translating Homer, the "dull duty" of editing Shakespeare, and, in middle age, his dedication to ethical and satirical poetry did not make less fine his keen sense of beauty in nature and art.

Pope's early poetry brought him to the attention of literary men, with whom he began to associate in the masculine world of coffeehouse and tavern, where he liked to play the rake. Between 1706 and 1711 he came to know, among many others, William Congreve; William Walsh, the critic and poet; and Richard Steele and Joseph Addison. As it happened, all were Whigs. Pope could readily ignore politics in the excitement of taking his place among the leading wits of the town. But after the fall of the Whigs in 1710 and the formation of the Tory government under Robert Harley (later the earl of Oxford) and Henry St. John (later Viscount Bolingbroke), party loyalties bred bitterness among the wits as among the politicians. By 1712, Pope had made the acquaintance of another group of writers, all Tories, who were soon his intimate friends: Jonathan Swift, by then the close associate of Harley and St. John and the principal propagandist for their policies; Dr. John Arbuthnot, physician to the queen, a learned scientist, a wit, and a man of humanity and integrity; John Gay, the poet, who in 1728 was to create *The Beggar's Opera,* the greatest theatrical success of the century; and the poet Thomas Parnell. Through them he became the friend and admirer of Oxford and later the intimate of Bolingbroke. In 1714 this group, at the instigation of Pope, formed a club for satirizing all sorts of false learning. The friends proposed to write jointly the biography of a learned fool whom they named Martinus Scriblerus (Martin the Scribbler), whose life and opinions would be a running commentary on educated nonsense. Some amusing episodes were later rewritten and published as the *Memoirs of Martinus Scriblerus* (1741). The real importance of the club, however, is that it fostered a satiric temper that would be expressed in such mature works of the friends as *Gulliver's Travels, The Beggar's Opera,* and *The Dunciad.*

"The life of a wit is a warfare on earth," said Pope, generalizing from his own experience. His very success as a poet (and his astonishing precocity brought him success very early) made enemies who were to plague him in pamphlets, verse satires, and squibs in the journals throughout his entire literary career. He was attacked for his writings, his religion, and his physical deformity. Although he smarted under the jibes of his detractors, he was a fighter who struck back, always giving better than he got. Pope's literary warfare began in 1713, when he announced his intention of translating the *Iliad* and sought subscribers to a deluxe edition of the work. Subscribers came in droves, but the Whig writers who surrounded Addison at Button's Coffee House did all they could to discredit the venture. The eventual success of the first published installment of his *Iliad* in 1715 did not obliterate Pope's resentment against Addison and his "little senate"; and he took his revenge in the damaging portrait of Addison (under the name of Atticus), which was later included in the *Epistle to Dr. Arbuthnot* (1735), lines 193–214. The not unjustified attacks on Pope's edition of Shakespeare (1725) by the learned Shakespeare scholar Lewis Theobald (Pope always spelled and pronounced the name "Tibbald" in his satires) led to Theobald's appearance as king of the dunces in *The Dunciad* (1728). In this impressive poem Pope stigmatized his literary enemies as agents of all that he disliked and feared in the tendencies of his time—the vulgarization of taste and the arts consequent on the rapid growth of the reading public and the development of journalism, magazines, and other popular and cheap publications, which spread scandal, sensationalism, and political partisanship—in short the new commercial spirit of the nation that was corrupting not only the arts but, as Pope saw it, the national life itself.

In the 1730s Pope moved on to philosophical, ethical, and political subjects in *An Essay on Man*, the *Epistles to Several Persons*, and the *Imitations of Horace*. The reigns of George I and George II appeared to him, as to Swift and other Tories, a period of rapid moral, political, and cultural deterioration. The agents of decay fed on the rise of moneyed (as opposed to landed) wealth, which accounted for the political corruption encouraged by Sir Robert Walpole and the court party and the corruption of all aspects of the national life by a vulgar class of *nouveaux riches*. Pope assumed the role of the champion of traditional values: of right reason, humanistic learning, sound art, good taste, and public virtue. It was fortunate that many of his enemies happened to illustrate various degrees of unreason, pedantry, bad art, vulgar taste, and at best, indifferent morals.

The satirist traditionally deals in generally prevalent evils and generally observable human types, not with particular individuals. So too with Pope; the bulk of his satire can be read and enjoyed without much biographical information. Usually he used fictional or type names, although he most often had an individual in mind—Sappho, Atossa, Atticus, Sporus—and when he named individuals (as he consistently did in *The Dunciad*), his purpose was to raise his victims to emblems of folly and vice. To judge and censure the age, Pope also created the *I* of the satires (not identical with Alexander Pope of Twickenham). This semifictional figure is the detached observer, somewhat removed from the city, town, and court, the centers of corruption; he is the friend of the virtuous, whose friendship for him testifies to his integrity; he is fond of peace, country life, the arts, morality, and truth; and he detests their opposites that flourish in the great world. In such an age, Pope implies, it is impossible for such a man—honest, truthful, blunt—not to write satire.

Pope was a master of style. From first to last, his verse is notable for its rhythmic variety, despite the apparently rigid metrical unit—the heroic couplet—in which he wrote; for the precision of meaning and the harmony (or expressive disharmony) of his language; and for the union of maximum conciseness with maximum complexity. The passages as marked below suggest how the subtle metrical effects of Pope's verse spring from the page, inviting us to embody them vocally in a living, dramatic reading. The first, lines 71–76 of the pastoral poem "Summer" (1709), is so lyrical that composer G. H. Handel used it in his operatic entertainment *Semele* (1744). Accents mark where the rhetorical stress departs from normal iambic rhythm, often because of the slight emphasis to be given to "you," Summer, the addressee, on the off beat. Strong pauses inside the lines are marked with double bars, alliteration and assonance by italics.

> Óh déign to visit our *f*or*s*aken *s*eats,
>
> The mossy *f*ountains ‖ and the *g*reen retreats!
>
> Where'er yóu wálk ‖ cóol gáles shall *f*an the glade,
>
> Trées whére yóu sít ‖ shall crowd into a shade:
>
> Where'er yóu tréad ‖ the blushing *f*lowers shall rise,
>
> And all things *f*lóurish where yóu túrn your eyes.

Pope has attained metrical variety by the free substitution of trochees and spondees for the normal iambs; he has achieved rhythmic variety by arranging phrases and clauses (units of syntax and logic) of different lengths within single lines and couplets, so that the passage moves with the sinuous fluency of thought and feeling; and he not only has chosen musical combinations of words but has also subtly modulated the harmony of the passage by unobtrusive patterns of alliteration and assonance.

Contrast with this pastoral passage lines 16–25 of the "Epilogue to the Satires, Dialogue 2" (1738), in which Pope is not making music but imitating actual conversation so realistically that the metrical pattern and the integrity of the couplet and individual line seem to be destroyed (although in fact they remain in place). As above, double bars indicate where strong pauses might fall in the middle of lines in a live, vocal performance; here, possible lesser pauses are marked by single bars. In a dialogue with a friend who warns him that his satire is too personal, indeed mere libel, the poet-satirist replies:

> Yé státesmen, | priests of one religion all!
>
> Yé trádesmen vile || in army, court, or hall!
>
> Yé réverend atheists. || F. Scandal! | name them, | Who?
>
> P. Why that's the thing you bid me not to do.
>
> Whó stárved a sister, || who foreswore a debt,
>
> Í néver named; || the town's inquiring yet.
>
> The poisoning dame—| F. Yóu méan—| P. I don't—| F. Yóu dó.
>
> P. Sée, nów Í kéep the secret, || and nót yóu!
>
> The bribing statesman—| F. Hóld, || tóo hígh you go.
>
> P. The bribed elector—|| F. There you stoop tóo lów.

In such a passage the language and rhythms of poetry merge with the language and rhythms of impassioned living speech.

A fine example of Pope's ability to derive the maximum of meaning from the most economic use of language and image is the description of the manor house in which lives old Cotta, the miser (*Epistle to Lord Bathurst*, lines 187–96):

> Like some lone Chartreuse stands the good old Hall,
> Silence without, and fasts within the wall;
> No raftered roofs with dance and tabor sound,
> No noontide bell invites the country round;
> Tenants with sighs the smokeless towers survey,
> And turn the unwilling steeds another way;
> Benighted wanderers, the forest o'er,
> Curse the saved candle and unopening door;
> While the gaunt mastiff growling at the gate,
> Affrights the beggar whom he longs to eat.

The first couplet of this passage associates the "Hall," symbol of English rural hospitality, with the Grande Chartreuse, the monastery in the French Alps, which, although a place of "silence" and "fasts" for the monks, afforded food and shelter to all travelers. Then the dismal details of Cotta's miserly dwelling provide a stark contrast, and the meaning of the scene is concentrated in the grotesque image of the last couplet: the half-starved watchdog and the frightened beggar confronting each other in mutual hunger.

But another sort of variety derives from Pope's respect for the idea that the different kinds of literature have their different and appropriate styles. Thus *An Essay on Criticism*, an informal discussion of literary theory, is written, like Horace's *Art of Poetry* (a similarly didactic poem), in a plain style, the easy language of well-bred talk. *The Rape of the Lock*, "a heroi-comical poem" (that is, a comic poem that treats trivial material in an epic style), employs the lofty heroic language that John Dryden had perfected in his translation of Virgil and introduces amusing parodies of passages in *Paradise Lost*, parodies later raised to truly Miltonic sublimity and complexity by the conclusion of *The Dunciad. Eloisa to Abelard* renders the brooding, passionate voice of its heroine in a declamatory language, given to sudden outbursts and shifts of tone, that recalls the stage. The grave epistles that make up *An Essay on Man,* a philosophical discussion of such majestic themes as the Creator and His creation, the universe, human nature, society, and happiness, are written in a stately forensic language and tone and constantly employ the traditional rhetorical figures. The *Imitations of Horace* and, above all, the *Epistle to Dr. Arbuthnot,* his finest poem "in the Horatian way," reveal Pope's final mastery of the plain style of Horace's epistles and satires and support his image of himself as the heir of the Roman poet. In short, no other poet of the century can equal Pope in the range of his materials, the diversity of his poetic styles, and the wizardry of his technique.

An Essay on Criticism   There is no more pleasant introduction to the canons of taste in the English Augustan age than Pope's *An Essay on Criticism.* As Addison said in his review in *Spectator* 253, it assembles the "most known and most received observations on the subject of literature and criticism." Pope was attempting to do for his time what Horace, in his *Art of Poetry,* and what Nicolas Boileau (French poet, of the age of Louis XIV), in his *L'Art Poétique,* had done for theirs. Horace is Pope's model not only for principles of criticism but also for style, especially in the simple, conversational language and the tone of well-bred ease.

In framing his critical creed, Pope did not try for novelty: he wished merely to give to generally accepted doctrines pleasing and memorable expression and make them useful to modern poets. Here one meets the key words of neoclassical criticism: *wit, Nature, ancients, rules,* and *genius. Wit* in the poem is a word of many meanings—a clever remark or the person who makes it, a conceit, liveliness of mind, inventiveness, fancy, genius, a genius, and poetry itself, among others. *Nature* is an equally ambiguous word, meaning not "things out there" or "the outdoors" but most important that which is representative, universal, permanent in human experience as opposed to the idiosyncratic, the individual, the temporary. In line 21, *Nature* comes close to meaning "intuitive knowledge." In line 52, it means that half-personified power manifested in the cosmic order, which in its modes of working is a model for art. The reverence felt by most Augustans for the great writers of ancient Greece and Rome raised the question how far the authority of these *ancients* extended. Were their works to be received as models to be conscientiously imitated? Were the *rules* received from them or deducible from their works to be accepted as prescriptive laws or merely convenient guides? Was individual *genius* to be bound by what has been conventionally held to be *Nature,* by the authority of the *ancients,* and by the legalistic pedantry of *rules?* Or could it go its own way?

In part 1 of the *Essay,* Pope constructs a harmonious system in which he effects a compromise among all these conflicting forces—a compromise that is typical of his times. Part 2 analyzes the causes of faulty criticism. Part 3 characterizes the good critic and praises the great critics of the past.

An Essay on Criticism

Part 1

'Tis hard to say, if greater want of skill
Appear in writing or in judging ill;
But of the two less dangerous is the offense
To tire our patience than mislead our sense.

5 Some few in that, but numbers err in this,
  Ten censure° wrong for one who writes amiss;   *judge*
  A fool might once himself alone expose,
  Now one in verse makes many more in prose.
   'Tis with our judgments as our watches, none
10 Go just alike, yet each believes his own.
  In poets as true genius is but rare,
  True taste as seldom is the critic's share;
  Both must alike from Heaven derive their light,
  These born to judge, as well as those to write.
15 Let such teach others who themselves excel,
  And censure freely who have written well.
  Authors are partial to their wit, 'tis true,
  But are not critics to their judgment too?
   Yet if we look more closely, we shall find
20 Most have the seeds of judgment in their mind:
  Nature affords at least a glimmering light;
  The lines, though touched but faintly, are drawn right.
  But as the slightest sketch, if justly traced, ⎤
  Is by ill coloring but the more disgraced, ⎬
25 So by false learning is good sense defaced: ⎦
  Some are bewildered in the maze of schools,
  And some made coxcombs[1] Nature meant but fools.
  In search of wit these lose their common sense,
  And then turn critics in their own defense:
30 Each burns alike, who can, or cannot write,
  Or with a rival's or an eunuch's spite.
  All fools have still an itching to deride,
  And fain would be upon the laughing side.
  If Maevius[2] scribble in Apollo's spite,
35 There are who judge still worse than he can write.
   Some have at first for wits, then poets passed,
  Turned critics next, and proved plain fools at last.
  Some neither can for wits nor critics pass,
  As heavy mules are neither horse nor ass.
40 Those half-learn'd witlings, numerous in our isle,
  As half-formed insects on the banks of Nile;[3]
  Unfinished things, one knows not what to call,
  Their generation's so equivocal:
  To tell° them would a hundred tongues require,   *reckon, count*
45 Or one vain wit's, that might a hundred tire.
   But you who seek to give and merit fame,
  And justly bear a critic's noble name,
  Be sure yourself and your own reach to know,
  How far your genius, taste, and learning go;
50 Launch not beyond your depth, but be discreet,
  And mark that point where sense and dullness meet.
   Nature to all things fixed the limits fit,
  And wisely curbed proud man's pretending° wit.   *aspiring*

1. Superficial pretenders to learning.
2. A silly poet alluded to contemptuously by Virgil in *Eclogue* 3 and by Horace in *Epode* 10.

3. The ancients believed that many forms of life were spontaneously generated in the fertile mud of the Nile.

As on the land while here the ocean gains,
55 In other parts it leaves wide sandy plains;
Thus in the soul while memory prevails,
The solid power of understanding fails;
Where beams of warm imagination play,
The memory's soft figures melt away.
60 One science° only will one genius fit,   *branch of learning*
So vast is art, so narrow human wit.
Not only bounded to peculiar arts,
But oft in those confined to single parts.
Like kings we lose the conquests gained before,
65 By vain ambition still to make them more;
Each might his several province well command,
Would all but stoop to what they understand.
    First follow Nature, and your judgment frame
By her just standard, which is still the same;
70 Unerring Nature, still divinely bright,
One clear, unchanged, and universal light,
Life, force, and beauty must to all impart,
At once the source, and end, and test of art.
Art from that fund each just supply provides,
75 Works without show, and without pomp presides.
In some fair body thus the informing soul
With spirits feeds, with vigor fills the whole,
Each motion guides, and every nerve sustains;
Itself unseen, but in the effects remains.
80 Some, to whom Heaven in wit has been profuse,
Want as much more to turn it to its use;
For wit and judgment often are at strife,
Though meant each other's aid, like man and wife.
'Tis more to guide than spur the Muse's steed,
85 Restrain his fury than provoke his speed;
The wingèd courser,[4] like a generous° horse,   *spirited, highly bred*
Shows most true mettle when you check his course.
    Those rules of old discovered, not devised,
Are Nature still, but Nature methodized;
90 Nature, like liberty, is but restrained
By the same laws which first herself ordained.
    Hear how learn'd Greece her useful rules indites,
When to repress and when indulge our flights:
High on Parnassus' top her sons she showed,
95 And pointed out those arduous paths they trod;
Held from afar, aloft, the immortal prize,
And urged the rest by equal steps to rise.
Just precepts thus from great examples given,
She drew from them what they derived from Heaven.
100 The generous critic fanned the poet's fire,
And taught the world with reason to admire.
Then criticism the Muse's handmaid proved,
To dress her charms, and make her more beloved:
But following wits from that intention strayed,

---

4. Pegasus, associated with the Muses and poetic inspiration.

105 Who could not win the mistress, wooed the maid;
    Against the poets their own arms they turned,
    Sure to hate most the men from whom they learned.
    So modern 'pothecaries, taught the art
    By doctors's bills° to play the doctor's part,   *prescriptions*
110 Bold in the practice of mistaken rules,
    Prescribe, apply, and call their masters fools.
    Some on the leaves of ancient authors prey,
    Nor time nor moths e'er spoiled so much as they.
    Some dryly plain, without invention's aid,
115 Write dull receipts[5] how poems may be made.
    These leave the sense their learning to display,
    And those explain the meaning quite away.
        You then whose judgment the right course would steer,
    Know well each ancient's proper character;
120 His fable,[6] subject, scope° in every page;   *aim, purpose*
    Religion, country, genius of his age:
    Without all these at once before your eyes,
    Cavil you may, but never criticize.
    Be Homer's works your study and delight,
125 Read them by day, and meditate by night;
    Thence form your judgment, thence your maxims bring,
    And trace the Muses upward to their spring.
    Still with itself compared, his text peruse;
    And let your comment be the Mantuan Muse.
130   When first young Maro[7] in his boundless mind
    A work to outlast immortal Rome designed,
    Perhaps he seemed above the critic's law,
    And but from Nature's fountains scorned to draw;
    But when to examine every part he came,
135 Nature and Homer were, he found, the same.
    Convinced, amazed, he checks the bold design, ⎤
    And rules as strict his labored work confine   ⎬
    As if the Stagirite[8] o'erlooked each line.   ⎦
    Learn hence for ancient rules a just esteem;
140 To copy Nature is to copy them.
        Some beauties yet no precepts can declare,
    For there's a happiness as well as care.[9]
    Music resembles poetry, in each   ⎤
    Are nameless graces which no methods teach, ⎬
145 And which a master hand alone can reach.   ⎦
    If, where the rules not far enough extend
    (Since rules were made but to promote their end)
    Some lucky license answers to the full
    The intent proposed, that license is a rule.

5. Formulas for preparing a dish; recipes. Pope himself wrote an amusing burlesque, "Receipt to Make an Epic Poem," first published in the *Guardian* 78 (1713).
6. Plot or story of a play or poem.
7. Virgil, who was born in a village adjacent to Mantua in Italy, hence "Mantuan Muse." His epic, the *Aeneid*, was modeled on Homer's *Iliad* and *Odyssey* and was considered to be a refinement of the Greek poems. Thus it could be thought of as a commentary ("comment") on Homer's poems.
8. Aristotle, a native of Stagira, from whose *Poetics* later critics formulated strict rules for writing tragedy and the epic.
9. I.e., no rules ("precepts") can explain ("declare") some beautiful effects in a work of art that can be the result only of inspiration or good luck ("happiness"), not of painstaking labor ("care").

150 Thus Pegasus, a nearer way to take,
      May boldly deviate from the common track.
      Great wits sometimes may gloriously offend,
      And rise to faults true critics dare not mend;
      From vulgar bounds with brave disorder part,
155 And snatch a grace beyond the reach of art,
      Which, without passing through the judgment, gains
      The heart, and all its end at once attains.
      In prospects thus, some objects please our eyes, ⎫
      Which out of Nature's common order rise, ⎬
160 The shapeless rock, or hanging precipice. ⎭
      But though the ancients thus their rules invade°   *violate*
      (As kings dispense with laws themselves have made)
      Moderns, beware! or if you must offend
      Against the precept, ne'er transgress its end;
165 Let it be seldom, and compelled by need;
      And have at least their precedent to plead.
      The critic else proceeds without remorse,
      Seizes your fame, and puts his laws in force.
          I know there are, to whose presumptuous thoughts
170 Those freer beauties, even in them, seem faults.[1]
      Some figures monstrous and misshaped appear,
      Considered singly, or beheld too near,
      Which, but proportioned to their light or place,
      Due distance reconciles to form and grace.
175 A prudent chief not always must display
      His powers in equal ranks and fair array,
      But with the occasion and the place comply,
      Conceal his force, nay seem sometimes to fly.
      Those oft are stratagems which errors seem,
180 Nor is it Homer nods, but we that dream.
          Still green with bays each ancient altar stands
      Above the reach of sacrilegious hands,
      Secure from flames, from envy's fiercer rage,
      Destructive war, and all-involving age.
185 See, from each clime the learn'd their incense bring!
      Here in all tongues consenting° paeans ring!   *agreeing, concurring*
      In praise so just let every voice be joined,[2]
      And fill the general chorus of mankind.
      Hail, bards triumphant! born in happier days,
190 Immortal heirs of universal praise!
      Whose honors with increase of ages grow,
      As streams roll down, enlarging as they flow;
      Nations unborn your mighty names shall sound,
      And worlds applaud that must not yet be found!
195 Oh, may some spark of your celestial fire,
      The last, the meanest of your sons inspire
      (That on weak wings, from far, pursues your flights,
      Glows while he reads, but trembles as he writes)
      To teach vain wits a science little known,
200 To admire superior sense, and doubt their own!

---

1. Pronounced *fawts*.   2. Pronounced *jined*.

Part 2

Of all the causes which conspire to blind
Man's erring judgment, and misguide the mind,
What the weak head with strongest bias rules,
Is pride, the never-failing vice of fools.
205   Whatever Nature has in worth denied,
She gives in large recruits° of needful pride;   *supplies*
For as in bodies, thus in souls, we find
What wants in blood and spirits, swelled with wind:
Pride, where wit fails, steps in to our defense,
210   And fills up all the mighty void of sense.
If once right reason drives that cloud away,
Truth breaks upon us with resistless day.
Trust not yourself: but your defects to know,
Make use of every friend—and every foe.
215   A little learning is a dangerous thing;
Drink deep, or taste not the Pierian spring.[3]
There shallow draughts intoxicate the brain,
And drinking largely sobers us again.
Fired at first sight with what the Muse imparts,
220   In fearless youth we tempt° the heights of arts,   *attempt*
While from the bounded level of our mind
Short views we take, nor see the lengths behind;
But more advanced, behold with strange surprise
New distant scenes of endless science rise!
225   So pleased at first the towering Alps we try,
Mount o'er the vales, and seem to tread the sky,
The eternal snows appear already past,
And the first clouds and mountains seem the last;
But, those attained, we tremble to survey
230   The growing labors of the lengthened way,
The increasing prospect tires our wandering eyes,
Hills peep o'er hills, and Alps on Alps arise!
        A perfect judge will read each work of wit
With the same spirit that its author writ:
235   Survey the whole, nor seek slight faults to find
Where Nature moves, and rapture warms the mind;
Nor lose, for that malignant dull delight,
The generous pleasure to be charmed with wit.
But in such lays as neither ebb nor flow,
240   Correctly cold, and regularly low,
That, shunning faults, one quiet tenor keep,
We cannot blame indeed—but we may sleep.
In wit, as nature, what affects our hearts
Is not the exactness of peculiar° parts;   *particular*
245   'Tis not a lip, or eye, we beauty call,
But the joint force and full result of all.
Thus when we view some well-proportioned dome[4]
(The world's just wonder, and even thine, O Rome!),
No single parts unequally surprise,

3. The spring in Pieria on Mount Olympus, sacred to the Muses.

4. The dome of St. Peter's, designed by Michelangelo.

250   All comes united to the admiring eyes:
No monstrous height, or breadth, or length appear;
The whole at once is bold and regular.
    Whoever thinks a faultless piece to see,
Thinks what ne'er was, nor is, nor e'er shall be.
255   In every work regard the writer's end,
Since none can compass more than they intend;
And if the means be just, the conduct true,
Applause, in spite of trivial faults, is due.
As men of breeding, sometimes men of wit,
260   To avoid great errors must the less commit,
Neglect the rules each verbal critic lays,
For not to know some trifles is a praise.
Most critics, fond of some subservient art,
Still make the whole depend upon a part:
265   They talk of principles, but notions prize,
And all to one loved folly sacrifice.
    Once on a time La Mancha's knight,[5] they say,
A certain bard encountering on the way,
Discoursed in terms as just, with looks as sage,
270   As e'er could Dennis,[6] of the Grecian stage;
Concluding all were desperate sots and fools
Who durst depart from Aristotle's rules.
Our author, happy in a judge so nice,
Produced his play, and begged the knight's advice;
275   Made him observe the subject and the plot,
The manners, passions, unities; what not?
All which exact to rule were brought about,
Were but a combat in the lists left out.
"What! leave the combat out?" exclaims the knight.
280   "Yes, or we must renounce the Stagirite."
"Not so, by Heaven!" he answers in a rage,
"Knights, squires, and steeds must enter on the stage."
"So vast a throng the stage can ne'er contain."
"Then build a new, or act it in a plain."
285   Thus critics of less judgment than caprice,
Curious,° not knowing, not exact, but nice,°   *laborious / fussy*
Form short ideas, and offend in arts
(As most in manners), by a love to parts.
    Some to conceit[7] alone their taste confine,
290   And glittering thoughts struck out at every line;
Pleased with a work where nothing's just or fit,
One glaring chaos and wild heap of wit.
Poets, like painters, thus unskilled to trace
The naked nature and the living grace,
295   With gold and jewels cover every part,
And hide with ornaments their want of art.
True wit is Nature to advantage dressed,

---

5. Don Quixote. The story comes not from Cervantes's novel, but from a spurious sequel to it by Don Alonzo Fernandez de Avellaneda.
6. John Dennis (1657–1734), although one of the leading critics of the time, was frequently ridiculed by the wits for his irascibility and pomposity. Pope apparently did not know Dennis personally, but his jibe at him in part 3 of this poem made him a bitter enemy.
7. Pointed wit, ingenuity, and extravagance, or affectation in the use of figures, especially similes and metaphors.

What oft was thought, but ne'er so well expressed;
Something whose truth convinced at sight we find,
300 That gives us back the image of our mind.
As shades more sweetly recommend the light,
So modest plainness sets off sprightly wit;
For works may have more wit than does them good,
As bodies perish through excess of blood.
305   Others for language all their care express,
And value books, as women men, for dress.
Their praise is still—the style is excellent;
The sense they humbly take upon contènt.°   *mere acquiescence*
Words are like leaves; and where they most abound,
310 Much fruit of sense beneath is rarely found.
False eloquence, like the prismatic glass,
Its gaudy colors spreads on every place;[8]
The face of Nature we no more survey,
All glares alike, without distinction gay.
315 But true expression, like the unchanging sun,⎤
Clears and improves whate'er it shines upon; ⎬
It gilds all objects, but it alters none.   ⎦
Expression is the dress of thought, and still
Appears more decent as more suitable.
320 A vile conceit in pompous words expressed
Is like a clown° in regal purple dressed: *country bumpkin*
For different styles with different subjects sort,
As several garbs with country, town, and court.
Some by old words to fame have made pretense,
325 Ancients in phrase, mere moderns in their sense.
Such labored nothings, in so strange a style,
Amaze the unlearn'd, and make the learned smile;
Unlucky as Fungoso[9] in the play,   ⎤
These sparks with awkward vanity display ⎬
330 What the fine gentleman wore yesterday; ⎦
And but so mimic ancient wits at best,
As apes our grandsires in their doublets dressed.
In words as fashions the same rule will hold,
Alike fantastic if too new or old:
335 Be not the first by whom the new are tried,
Nor yet the last to lay the old aside.
    But most by numbers° judge a poet's song,   *versification*
And smooth or rough with them is right or wrong.
In the bright Muse though thousand charms conspire,
340 Her voice is all these tuneful fools admire,
Who haunt Parnassus but to please their ear, ⎤
Not mend their minds; as some to church repair, ⎬
Not for the doctrine, but the music there.   ⎦
These equal syllables alone require,
345 Though oft the ear the open vowels tire,[1]

8. A very up-to-date scientific reference. Newton's *Opticks*, which dealt with the prism and the
spectrum, had been published in 1704, although
his theories had been known earlier.
9. A character in Ben Jonson's comedy *Every*

Man out of His Humor (1599).
1. In lines 345–57 Pope cleverly contrives to make
his own metrics or diction illustrate the faults
that he is exposing.

While expletives[2] their feeble aid do join,
And ten low words oft creep in one dull line:
While they ring round the same unvaried chimes,
With sure returns of still expected rhymes;
350 Where'er you find "the cooling western breeze,"
In the next line, it "whispers through the trees";
If crystal streams "with pleasing murmurs creep,"
The reader's threatened (not in vain) with "sleep";
Then, at the last and only couplet fraught
355 With some unmeaning thing they call a thought,
A needless Alexandrine[3] ends the song
That, like a wounded snake, drags its slow length along.
Leave such to tune their own dull rhymes, and know
What's roundly smooth or languishingly slow;
360 And praise the easy vigor of a line
Where Denham's strength and Waller's sweetness join.[4]
True ease in writing comes from art, not chance,
As those move easiest who have learned to dance.
'Tis not enough no harshness gives offense,
365 The sound must seem an echo to the sense.
Soft is the strain when Zephyr gently blows,
And the smooth stream in smoother numbers flows;
But when loud surges lash the sounding shore,
The hoarse, rough verse should like the torrent roar.
370 When Ajax strives some rock's vast weight to throw,
The line too labors, and the words move slow;
Not so when swift Camilla[5] scours the plain,
Flies o'er the unbending corn, and skims along the main.
Hear how Timotheus'[6] varied lays surprise,
375 And bid alternate passions fall and rise!
While at each change the son of Libyan Jove°   *Alexander the Great*
Now burns with glory, and then melts with love;
Now his fierce eyes with sparkling fury glow,
Now sighs steal out, and tears begin to flow:
380 Persians and Greeks like turns of nature[7] found
And the world's victor stood subdued by sound!
The power of music all our hearts allow,
And what Timotheus was, is Dryden now.
    Avoid extremes; and shun the fault of such
385 Who still are pleased too little or too much.
At every trifle scorn to take offense:
That always shows great pride, or little sense.
Those heads, as stomachs, are not sure the best,
Which nauseate all, and nothing can digest.
390 Yet let not each gay turn thy rapture move;
For fools admire,° but men of sense approve:[8]   *wonder*

---

2. Words used merely to achieve the necessary number of feet in a line of verse.
3. A line of verse containing six iambic feet; it is illustrated in the next line.
4. Dryden, whom Pope echoes here, considered Sir John Denham (1615–1669) and Edmund Waller (1606–1687) to have been the principal shapers of the closed pentameter couplet. He had distinguished the "strength" of the one and the "sweetness" of the other.
5. Fleet-footed virgin warrior (*Aeneid* 7, 11).
6. The musician in Dryden's "Alexander's Feast." Pope retells the story of that poem in the following lines.
7. Alternations of feelings.
8. Judge favorably only after due deliberation.

As things seem large which we through mists descry,
Dullness is ever apt to magnify.
    Some foreign writers, some our own despise;
395 The ancients only, or the moderns prize.
Thus wit, like faith, by each man is applied
To one small sect, and all are damned beside.
Meanly they seek the blessing to confine,
And force that sun but on a part to shine,
400 Which not alone the southern wit sublimes,°   *raises up, purifies*
But ripens spirits in cold northern climes;
Which from the first has shone on ages past,
Enlights the present, and shall warm the last;
Though each may feel increases and decays,
405 And see now clearer and now darker days.
Regard not then if wit be old or new,
But blame the false and value still the true.
    Some ne'er advance a judgment of their own,
But catch the spreading notion of the town;
410 They reason and conclude by precedent,
And own° stale nonsense which they ne'er invent.   *lay claim to*
Some judge of authors' names, not works, and then
Nor praise nor blame the writings, but the men.
Of all this servile herd the worst is he
415 That in proud dullness joins with quality,[9]
A constant critic at the great man's board,
To fetch and carry nonsense for my lord.
What woeful stuff this madrigal would be
In some starved hackney sonneteer° or me!   *hireling poet*
420 But let a lord once own the happy lines,
How the wit brightens! how the style refines!
Before his sacred name flies every fault,
And each exalted stanza teems with thought!
    The vulgar thus through imitation err;
425 As oft the learn'd by being singular;
So much they scorn the crowd, that if the throng
By chance go right, they purposely go wrong.
So schismatics[1] the plain believers quit,
And are but damned for having too much wit.
430 Some praise at morning what they blame at night,
But always think the last opinion right.
A Muse by these is like a mistress used,
This hour she's idolized, the next abused;
While their weak heads like towns unfortified,
435 'Twixt sense and nonsense daily change their side.
Ask them the cause; they're wiser still, they say;
And still tomorrow's wiser than today.
We think our fathers fools, so wise we grow;
Our wiser sons, no doubt, will think us so.
440 Once school divines[2] this zealous isle o'erspread;

9. People of high rank.
1. Those who have divided the church on points of theology. Pope stressed the first syllable, the pronunciation approved by Johnson in his *Dic-* *tionary.*
2. The medieval theologians, such as the followers of Duns Scotus and St. Thomas Aquinas, mentioned in line 444.

Who knew most sentences[3] was deepest read.
Faith, Gospel, all seemed made to be disputed,
And none had sense enough to be confuted.
Scotists and Thomists now in peace remain
445   Amidst their kindred cobwebs in Duck Lane.[4]
If faith itself has different dresses worn,
What wonder modes in wit should take their turn?
Oft, leaving what is natural and fit,
The current folly proves the ready wit;
450   And authors think their reputation safe,
Which lives as long as fools are pleased to laugh.
    Some valuing those of their own side or mind,
Still make themselves the measure of mankind:
Fondly° we think we honor merit then,   *foolishly*
455   When we but praise ourselves in other men.
Parties in wit attend on those of state,
And public faction doubles private hate.
Pride, Malice, Folly against Dryden rose,
In various shapes of parsons, critics, beaux;
460   But sense survived, when merry jests were past;
For rising merit will buoy up at last.
Might he return and bless once more our eyes,
New Blackmores and new Milbourns[5] must arise.
Nay, should great Homer lift his awful head,
465   Zoilus[6] again would start up from the dead.
Envy will merit, as its shade, pursue,
But like a shadow, proves the substance true;
For envied wit, like Sol eclipsed, makes known
The opposing body's grossness, not its own.
470   When first that sun too powerful beams displays,
It draws up vapors which obscure its rays;
But even those clouds at last adorn its way,
Reflect new glories, and augment the day.
    Be thou the first true merit to befriend;
475   His praise is lost who stays till all commend.
Short is the date, alas! of modern rhymes,
And 'tis but just to let them live betimes.°   *for a brief time*
No longer now that golden age appears,
When patriarch wits survived a thousand years:
480   Now length of fame (our second life) is lost,
And bare threescore is all even that can boast;
Our sons their fathers' failing language see,
And such as Chaucer is, shall Dryden be.[7]
So when the faithful pencil has designed
485   Some bright idea of the master's mind,

3. Allusion to Peter Lombard's *Book of Sentences*, a book esteemed by Scholastic philosophers.
4. Street where publishers' remainders and secondhand books were sold.
5. Luke Milbourn had attacked Dryden's translation of Virgil. Sir Richard Blackmore, physician and poet, had attacked Dryden for the immorality of his plays.

6. A Greek critic of the 4th century B.C.E. who wrote a book of carping criticism of Homer.
7. The radical changes that took place in the English language between the death of Chaucer in 1400 and the death of Dryden in 1700 suggested that in another three hundred years Dryden would be unintelligible.

Where a new world leaps out at his command,
And ready Nature waits upon his hand;
When the ripe colors soften and unite,
And sweetly melt into just shade and light;
490 When mellowing years their full perfection give,
And each bold figure just begins to live,
The treacherous colors the fair art betray,
And all the bright creation fades away!
    Unhappy° wit, like most mistaken things,   *ill-fated*
495 Atones not for that envy which it brings.
In youth alone its empty praise we boast,
But soon the short-lived vanity is lost;
Like some fair flower the early spring supplies,
That gaily blooms, but even in blooming dies.
500 What is this wit, which must our cares employ?
The owner's wife, that other men enjoy;
Then most our trouble still when most admired,
And still the more we give, the more required;
Whose fame with pains we guard, but lose with ease,
505 Sure some to vex, but never all to please;
'Tis what the vicious fear, the virtuous shun,
By fools 'tis hated, and by knaves undone!
    If wit so much from ignorance undergo,
Ah, let not learning too commence its foe!
510 Of old those met rewards who could excel,
And such were praised who but endeavored well;
Though triumphs were to generals only due,
Crowns were reserved to grace the soldiers too.[8]
Now they who reach Parnassus' lofty crown
515 Employ their pains to spurn° some others down;   *kick*
And while self-love each jealous writer rules,
Contending wits become the sport of fools;
But still the worst with most regret commend,
For each ill author is as bad a friend.
520 To what base ends, and by what abject ways,
Are mortals urged through sacred° lust of praise![9]   *accursed*
Ah, ne'er so dire a thirst of glory boast,
Nor in the critic let the man be lost!
Good nature and good sense must ever join;
525 To err is human, to forgive divine.
    But if in noble minds some dregs remain
Not yet purged off, of spleen° and sour disdain,   *rancor*
Discharge that rage on more provoking crimes,
Nor fear a dearth in these flagitious° times.   *scandalously wicked*
530 No pardon vile obscenity should find,
Though wit and art conspire to move your mind;
But dullness with obscenity must prove
As shameful sure as impotence in love.
In the fat age of pleasure, wealth, and ease

8. To celebrate Roman victories, valiant soldiers were decorated with a variety of crowns.

9. The phrase imitates Virgil's *auri sacra famis*, "accursed hunger for gold" (*Aeneid* 3.57).

535   Sprung the rank weed, and thrived with large increase:
When love was all an easy monarch's[1] care,
Seldom at council, never in a war;
Jilts[2] ruled the state, and statesmen farces writ;
Nay, wits had pensions, and young lords had wit;
540   The fair sat panting at a courtier's play,
And not a mask[3] went unimproved away;
The modest fan was lifted up no more,
And virgins smiled at what they blushed before.
The following license of a foreign reign
545   Did all the dregs of bold Socinus[4] drain;
Then unbelieving priests reformed the nation,
And taught more pleasant methods of salvation;
Where Heaven's free subjects might their rights dispute,
Lest God himself should seem too absolute;
550   Pulpits their sacred satire learned to spare,
And Vice admired° to find a flatterer there!   *wondered*
Encouraged thus, wit's Titans braved the skies,
And the press groaned with licensed blasphemies.
These monsters, critics! with your darts engage,
555   Here point your thunder, and exhaust your rage!
Yet shun their fault, who, scandalously nice,°   *subtle*
Will needs mistake an author into vice;
All seems infected that the infected spy,
As all looks yellow to the jaundiced eye.

Part 3

560   Learn then what morals critics ought to show,
For 'tis but half a judge's task, to know.
'Tis not enough, taste, judgment, learning, join;
In all you speak, let truth and candor° shine: *kindness, impartiality*
That not alone what to your sense is due
565   All may allow; but seek your friendship too.
    Be silent always when you doubt your sense;
And speak, though sure, with seeming diffidence:
Some positive, persisting fops we know,
Who, if once wrong, will needs be always so;
570   But you, with pleasure own your errors past,
And make each day a critic° on the last.   *critique*
    'Tis not enough, your counsel still be true;
Blunt truths more mischief than nice falsehoods do;
Men must be taught as if you taught them not,
575   And things unknown proposed as things forgot.
Without good breeding, truth is disapproved;
That only makes superior sense beloved.
    Be niggards of advice on no pretense;

1. Charles II. The concluding lines of part 2 discuss the corruption of wit and poetry under this monarch.
2. Mistresses of the king.
3. A woman wearing a mask.

4. The name of two Italian theologians of the 16th century who denied the divinity of Jesus. Pope charges that freethinkers attained the upper hand during the "foreign reign" of William III, a Dutchman.

For the worst avarice is that of sense.
580 With mean complacence[5] ne'er betray your trust,
Nor be so civil as to prove unjust.
Fear not the anger of the wise to raise;
Those best can bear reproof, who merit praise.
    'Twere well might critics still this freedom take;
585 But Appius reddens at each word you speak,
And stares, tremendous! with a threatening eye,
Like some fierce tyrant in old tapestry.[6]
Fear most to tax an honorable fool,
Whose right it is, uncensured to be dull;
590 Such, without wit, are poets when they please,
As without learning they can take degrees.[7]
Leave dangerous truths to unsuccessful satyrs,°   satires
And flattery to fulsome dedicators,
Whom, when they praise, the world believes no more,
595 Than when they promise to give scribbling o'er.
'Tis best sometimes your censure to restrain,
And charitably let the dull be vain:
Your silence there is better than your spite,
For who can rail so long as they can write?
600 Still humming on, their drowsy course they keep,
And lashed so long, like tops, are lashed asleep.[8]
False steps but help them to renew the race,
As, after stumbling, jades° will mend their pace.   worn-out horses
What crowds of these, impenitently bold,
605 In sounds and jingling syllables grown old,
Still run on poets, in a raging vein,
Even to the dregs and squeezings of the brain,
Strain out the last dull droppings of their sense,
And rhyme with all the rage of impotence.
610   Such shameless bards we have, and yet 'tis true,
There are as mad, abandoned critics too.
The bookful blockhead, ignorantly read,
With loads of learned lumber° in his head,   rubbish
With his own tongue still edifies his ears,
615 And always listening to himself appears.
All books he reads, and all he reads assails,
From Dryden's Fables down to Durfey's Tales.[9]
With him, most authors steal their works, or buy;
Garth did not write his own Dispensary.[1]
620 Name a new play, and he's the poet's friend,
Nay showed his faults—but when would poets mend?
No place so sacred from such fops is barred,

5. Softness of manners; desire of pleasing.
6. "This picture was taken to himself by John
Dennis, a furious old critic by profession, who,
upon no other provocation, wrote against this
Essay and its author, in a manner perfectly lunatic" [Pope's note, 1744]. Pope *did* intend to ridicule
Dennis, whose *Appius and Virginia* had failed on
the stage in 1709 and who was known for his stare
and his use of the word *tremendous* (see line 270).
7. Honorary degrees were granted to unqualified

men of rank.
8. Tops "sleep" when they spin so rapidly that
they seem not to move.
9. Thomas D'Urfey's *Tales* (1704) were notorious
potboilers. Dryden's *Fables* (1700), a set of translations, were among his most admired works.
1. Samuel Garth (1661–1719), who had been
accused of plagiarizing his mock-epic poem *The
Dispensary* (1699), was admired and defended by
Pope.

Nor is Paul's church more safe than Paul's churchyard:[2]
Nay, fly to altars; *there* they'll talk you dead:
625   For fools rush in where angels fear to tread.
Distrustful sense with modest caution speaks, ⎫
It still looks home, and short excursions makes; ⎬
But rattling nonsense in full volleys breaks, ⎭
And never shocked, and never turned aside,
630   Bursts out, resistless, with a thundering tide.
    But where's the man, who counsel can bestow,
Still pleased to teach, and yet not proud to know?
Unbiased, or° by favor, or by spite: *either*
Not dully prepossessed, nor blindly right;
635   Though learned, well-bred; and though well-bred, sincere;
Modestly bold, and humanly severe:
Who to a friend his faults can freely show,
And gladly praise the merit of a foe?
Blessed with a taste exact, yet unconfined;
640   A knowledge both of books and humankind;
Gen'rous converse;[3] a soul exempt from pride;
And love to praise, with reason on his side?
    Such once were critics; such the happy few,
Athens and Rome in better ages knew.
645   The mighty Stagirite° first left the shore,   *Aristotle*
Spread all his sails, and durst the deeps explore;
He steered securely, and discovered far,
Led by the light of the Maeonian star.[4]
Poets, a race long unconfined, and free,
650   Still fond and proud of savage liberty,
Received his laws; and stood convinced 'twas fit,
Who conquered nature, should preside o'er wit.
    Horace still charms with graceful negligence,
And without method talks us into sense;
655   Will, like a friend, familiarly convey
The truest notions in the easiest° way.   *least formal*
He, who supreme in judgment, as in wit,
Might boldly censure, as he boldly writ,
Yet judged with coolness, though he sung with fire;
660   His precepts teach but what his works inspire.
Our critics take a contrary extreme,
They judge with fury, but they write with fle'me.°   *phlegmatically*
Nor suffers Horace more in wrong translations
By wits, than critics[5] in as wrong quotations.
665   See Dionysius[6] Homer's thoughts refine,
And call new beauties forth from every line!
    Fancy and art in gay Petronius[7] please,
The scholar's learning, with the courtier's ease.

2. Booksellers' district near St. Paul's Cathedral, whose aisles were used as a place to meet
and do business.
3. Well-bred conversation.
4. Homer, who was supposed to have been born
in Maeonia.

5. I.e., than by critics. Phrases from Horace's
Art of Poetry were quoted incessantly by critics.
6. Dionysius of Halicarnassus (1st century
B.C.E.) wrote an important treatise on the artistic
arrangement of words.
7. Author of the *Satyricon* (1st century C.E.).

In grave Quintilian's[8] copious work, we find
670 The justest rules, and clearest method joined:
Thus useful arms in magazines° we place,   *storehouses, arsenals*
All ranged in order, and disposed with grace,
But less to please the eye, than arm the hand,
Still fit for use, and ready at command.
675   Thee, bold Longinus![9] all the nine° inspire,   *Muses*
And bless their critic with a poet's fire.
An ardent judge, who, zealous in his trust,
With warmth gives sentence, yet is always just;
Whose own example strengthens all his laws,
680 And is himself that great sublime he draws.
        Thus long succeeding critics justly reigned,
License repressed, and useful laws ordained.
Learning and Rome alike in empire grew;
And arts still followed where her eagles[1] flew;
685 From the same foes, at last, both felt their doom,
And the same age saw learning fall, and Rome.
With tyranny, then superstition joined,
As that the body, this enslaved the mind;
Much was believed, but little understood,
690 And to be dull was construed to be good;
A second deluge learning thus o'errun,
And the monks finished what the Goths begun.[2]
        At length Erasmus, that great, injured name
(The glory of the priesthood, and the shame!),[3]
695 Stemmed the wild torrent of a barb'rous age,
And drove those holy Vandals off the stage.
        But see! each Muse, in Leo's golden days,
Starts from her trance, and trims her withered bays![4]
Rome's ancient Genius, o'er its ruins spread,
700 Shakes off the dust, and rears his reverend head.
Then sculpture and her sister-arts revive;
Stones leaped to form, and rocks began to live;
With sweeter notes each rising temple rung;
A Raphael painted, and a Vida[5] sung.
705 Immortal Vida: on whose honored brow
The poet's bays and critic's ivy grow:
Cremona now shall ever boast thy name,
As next in place to Mantua, next in fame![6]
        But soon by impious arms from Latium[7] chased,

8. Author of the *Institutio Oratorio* (ca. 95 C.E.), a famous treatise on rhetoric. Here as elsewhere, Pope's terms of praise are drawn from the author he is praising.
9. Supposed author of the influential treatise *On the Sublime* (1st century C.E.), greatly in vogue at the time of Pope.
1. Emblems on the standards of the Roman army.
2. Pope thought that the Scholastic theologians of the Middle Ages were "holy Vandals" who had "sacked" learning as the Goths and Vandals had sacked Rome.
3. Erasmus (1466–1536), the great humanist scholar, was the "glory of the priesthood" because

of his goodness and learning and its "shame" because he was persecuted.
4. The wreath of poetry. Leo X, pope from 1513 to 1521, was notable for his encouragement of artists.
5. "M. Hieronymus Vida, an excellent Latin poet, who writ an Art of Poetry in verse. He flourished in the time of Leo the Tenth" [Pope's note]. Raphael (1483–1520) painted many of his greatest works under the patronage of Leo X.
6. Vida came from Cremona, near Mantua, the birthplace of Virgil, his favorite poet.
7. Italy. German and Spanish troops sacked Rome in 1527.

710 Their ancient bounds the banished Muses passed;
     Thence arts o'er all the northern world advance,
     But critic-learning flourished most in France:
     The rules a nation, born to serve, obeys;
     And Boileau still in right of Horace sways.[8]
715 But we, brave Britons, foreign laws despised,
     And kept unconquered—and uncivilized;
     Fierce for the liberties of wit, and bold,
     We still defied the Romans, as of old.
     Yet some there were, among the sounder few
720 Of those who less presumed, and better knew,
     Who durst assert the juster ancient cause,
     And here restored wit's fundamental laws.
     Such was the Muse, whose rules and practice tell,
     "Nature's chief masterpiece is writing well."[9]
725 Such was Roscommon,[1] not more learned than good,
     With manners gen'rous as his noble blood;
     To him the wit of Greece and Rome was known,
     And every author's merit, but his own.
     Such late was Walsh—the Muse's[2] judge and friend,
730 Who justly knew to blame or to commend;
     To failings mild, but zealous for desert;
     The clearest head, and the sincerest heart.
     This humble praise, lamented shade! receive,
     This praise at least a grateful Muse may give:
735 The Muse, whose early voice you taught to sing,
     Prescribed her heights, and pruned her tender wing,
     (Her guide now lost) no more attempts to rise,
     But in low numbers° short excursions tries: *humble verses*
     Content, if hence the unlearned their wants may view,
740 The learned reflect on what before they knew:
     Careless of° censure, nor too fond of fame;   *unconcerned at*
     Still pleased to praise, yet not afraid to blame;
     Averse alike to flatter, or offend;
     Not free from faults, nor yet too vain to mend.

1709   1711

The Rape of the Lock

The Rape of the Lock is based on an actual episode that provoked a quarrel between two prominent Catholic families. Pope's friend John Caryll, to whom the poem is addressed (line 3), suggested that Pope write it, in the hope that a little laughter might serve to soothe ruffled tempers. Lord Petre had cut off a lock of hair from the head of the lovely Arabella Fermor (often spelled "Farmer" and doubtless so pronounced), much to the indignation of the lady and her relatives. In its original version of two cantos and 334 lines, published in 1712, *The Rape of the Lock* was a great success. In 1713 a new version was undertaken

8. Boileau's *L'Art Poétique* (1674) regularized and modernized the lessons of Horace's *Art of Poetry*.
9. Quoted from an *Essay on Poetry* by John Sheffield, duke of Buckingham (1648–1721), who had befriended the young Pope.
1. Wentworth Dillon, earl of Roscommon, wrote the important *Essay on Translated Verse* (1684).
2. Here, Pope himself. William Walsh (1663–1708), whom Dryden once called "the best critic of our nation," had advised Pope to work at becoming the first great "correct" poet in English.

against the advice of Addison, who considered the poem perfect as it was first written. Pope greatly expanded the earlier version, adding the delightful "machinery" (i.e., the supernatural agents in epic action) of the Sylphs, Belinda's toilet, the card game, and the visit to the Cave of Spleen in canto 4. In 1717, with the addition of Clarissa's speech on good humor, the poem assumed its final form.

With delicate fancy and playful wit, Pope elaborated the trivial episode that occasioned the poem into the semblance of an epic in miniature, the most nearly perfect heroicomical poem in English. The verse abounds in parodies and echoes of the *Iliad*, the *Aeneid*, and *Paradise Lost*, thus constantly forcing the reader to compare small things with great. The familiar devices of epic are observed, but the incidents or characters are beautifully proportioned to the scale of mock epic. The *Rape* tells of war, but it is the drawing-room war between the sexes; it has its heroes and heroines, but they are beaux and belles; it has its supernatural characters ("machinery"), but they are Sylphs (borrowed, as Pope tells us in his dedicatory letter, from Rosicrucian lore)—creatures of the air, the souls of dead coquettes (surprisingly given male pronouns), with tasks appropriate to their nature—or the Gnome Umbriel, once a prude on earth; it has its epic game, played on the "velvet plain" of the card table, its feasting heroes, who sip coffee and gossip, and its battle, fought with the clichés of compliment and conceits, with frowns and angry glances, with snuff and bodkin; it has the traditional epic journey to the underworld—here the Cave of Spleen, emblematic of the ill nature of female hypochondriacs. And Pope creates a world in which these actions take place, a world that is dense with beautiful objects: brocades, ivory and tortoiseshell, cosmetics and diamonds, lacquered furniture, silver teapot, delicate chinaware. It is a world that is constantly in motion and that sparkles and glitters with light, whether the light of the sun or of Belinda's eyes or that light into which the "fluid" bodies of the Sylphs seem to dissolve as they flutter in shrouds and around the mast of Belinda's ship. Pope laughs at this world, its ritualized triviality, its irrational, upper-class women and feminized men—and remembers that a grimmer, darker world surrounds it (3.19–24 and 5.145–48); but he also makes us aware of its beauty and charm.

The epigraph may be translated, "I was unwilling, Belinda, to ravish your locks; but I rejoice to have conceded this to your prayers" (Martial's *Epigrams* 12.84.1–2). Pope substituted his heroine for Martial's Polytimus. The epigraph is intended to suggest that the poem was published at Miss Fermor's request.

The Rape of the Lock

An Heroi-Comical Poem

Nolueram, Belinda, tuos violare capillos;
sed juvat hoc precibus me tribuisse tuis.
—MARTIAL

TO MRS. ARABELLA FERMOR

MADAM,

It will be in vain to deny that I have some regard for this piece, since I dedicate it to you. Yet you may bear me witness, it was intended only to divert a few young ladies, who have good sense and good humor enough to laugh not only at their sex's little unguarded follies, but at their own. But as it was communicated with the air of a secret, it soon found its way into the world. An imperfect copy having been offered to a bookseller, you had the good nature for my sake to consent to the publication of one more correct; this I was forced to, before I had executed half my design, for the machinery was entirely wanting to complete it.

The machinery, Madam, is a term invented by the critics, to signify that part which the deities, angels, or demons are made to act in a poem; for the ancient poets are in one respect like many modern ladies: let an action be never so trivial in itself, they always make it appear of the utmost importance. These machines I determined to raise on a very new and odd foundation, the Rosicrucian[1] doctrine of spirits.

I know how disagreeable it is to make use of hard words before a lady; but 'tis so much the concern of a poet to have his works understood, and particularly by your sex, that you must give me leave to explain two or three difficult terms.

The Rosicrucians are a people I must bring you acquainted with. The best account I know of them is in a French book called *Le Comte de Gabalis*,[2] which both in its title and size is so like a novel, that many of the fair sex have read it for one by mistake. According to these gentlemen, the four elements are inhabited by spirits, which they call Sylphs, Gnomes, Nymphs, and Salamanders. The Gnomes or Demons of earth delight in mischief; but the Sylphs, whose habitation is in the air, are the best-conditioned creatures imaginable. For they say, any mortals may enjoy the most intimate familiarities with these gentle spirits, upon a condition very easy to all true adepts, an inviolate preservation of chastity.

As to the following cantos, all the passages of them are as fabulous as the vision at the beginning, or the transformation at the end (except the loss of your hair, which I always mention with reverence). The human persons are as fictitious as the airy ones; and the character of Belinda, as it is now managed, resembles you in nothing but in beauty.

If this poem had as many graces as there are in your person, or in your mind, yet I could never hope it should pass through the world half so uncensured as you have done. But let its fortune be what it will, mine is happy enough, to have given me this occasion of assuring you that I am, with the truest esteem,

MADAM,
Your most obedient, humble servant,
A. POPE

Canto 1

What dire offense from amorous causes springs,
What mighty contests rise from trivial things,
I sing—This verse to Caryll, Muse! is due:
This, even Belinda may vouchsafe to view:
5   Slight is the subject, but not so the praise,
If she inspire, and he approve my lays.
Say what strange motive, Goddess! could compel
A well-bred lord to assault a gentle belle?
Oh, say what stranger cause, yet unexplored,
10   Could make a gentle belle reject a lord?

1. A system of arcane philosophy introduced into England from Germany in the 17th century.   2. By the Abbé de Montfaucon de Villars, published in 1670.

In tasks so bold can little men engage,
And in soft bosoms dwells such mighty rage?
   Sol through white curtains shot a timorous ray,
And oped those eyes that must eclipse the day.
15 Now lapdogs give themselves the rousing shake,
And sleepless lovers, just at twelve, awake:
Thrice rung the bell, the slipper knocked the ground,[3]
And the pressed watch[4] returned a silver sound.
Belinda still her downy pillow pressed,
20 Her guardian Sylph prolonged the balmy rest.
'Twas he had summoned to her silent bed
The morning dream that hovered o'er her head.
A youth more glittering than a birthnight beau[5]
(That even in slumber caused her cheek to glow)
25 Seemed to her ear his winning lips to lay,
And thus in whispers said, or seemed to say:
   "Fairest of mortals, thou distinguished care
Of thousand bright inhabitants of air!
If e'er one vision touched thy infant thought,
30 Of all the nurse and all the priest have taught,
Of airy elves by moonlight shadows seen,
The silver token, and the circled green,[6]
Or virgins visited by angel powers,
With golden crowns and wreaths of heavenly flowers,
35 Hear and believe! thy own importance know,
Nor bound thy narrow views to things below.
Some secret truths, from learned pride concealed,
To maids alone and children are revealed:
What though no credit doubting wits may give?
40 The fair and innocent shall still believe.
Know, then, unnumbered spirits round thee fly,
The light militia of the lower sky:
These, though unseen, are ever on the wing,
Hang o'er the box, and hover round the Ring.[7]
45 Think what an equipage thou hast in air,
And view with scorn two pages and a chair.°   *sedan chair*
As now your own, our beings were of old,
And once enclosed in woman's beauteous mold;
Thence, by a soft transition, we repair
50 From earthly vehicles to these of air.
Think not, when woman's transient breath is fled,
That all her vanities at once are dead:
Succeeding vanities she still regards,
And though she plays no more, o'erlooks the cards.
55 Her joy in gilded chariots, when alive,
And love of ombre,[8] after death survive.

3. Summons to a maid.
4. A watch that chimes the hour and the quarter hour when the stem is pressed down.
5. Courtiers wore especially fine clothes on the sovereign's birthday.
6. Rings of bright green grass, which are common in England even in winter, were held to be caused by the round dances of fairies. According to popular belief, fairies skim off the cream from jugs of milk left standing overnight and leave a coin ("silver token") in payment.
7. The "box" in the theater and the fashionable circular drive ("Ring") in Hyde Park.
8. A popular card game (see p. 515, n. 3).

For when the Fair in all their pride expire,
To their first elements[9] their souls retire:
The sprites of fiery termagants[1] in flame
60   Mount up, and take a Salamander's[2] name.
Soft yielding minds to water glide away,
And sip, with Nymphs, their elemental tea.[3]
The graver prude sinks downward to a Gnome,
In search of mischief still on earth to roam.
65   The light coquettes in Sylphs aloft repair,
And sport and flutter in the fields of air.
    "Know further yet; whoever fair and chaste
Rejects mankind, is by some Sylph embraced:
For spirits, freed from mortal laws, with ease
70   Assume what sexes and what shapes they please.[4]
What guards the purity of melting maids,
In courtly balls, and midnight masquerades,
Safe from the treacherous friend, the daring spark,
The glance by day, the whisper in the dark,
75   When kind occasion prompts their warm desires,
When music softens, and when dancing fires?
'Tis but their Sylph, the wise Celestials° know,   *heavenly beings*
Though Honor is the word with men below.
    "Some nymphs[5] there are, too conscious of their face,
80   For life predestined to the Gnomes' embrace.
These swell their prospects and exalt their pride,
When offers are disdained, and love denied:
Then gay ideas° crowd the vacant brain,   *showy images*
While peers, and dukes, and all their sweeping train,
85   And garters, stars, and coronets[6] appear,
And in soft sounds, 'your Grace'° salutes their ear.   *a duchess*
'Tis these that early taint the female soul,
Instruct the eyes of young coquettes to roll,
Teach infant cheeks a bidden blush to know,
90   And little hearts to flutter at a beau.
    "Oft, when the world imagine women stray,
The Sylphs through mystic mazes guide their way,
Through all the giddy circle they pursue,
And old impertinence° expel by new.   *trifle*
95   What tender maid but must a victim fall
To one man's treat, but for another's ball?
When Florio speaks, what virgin could withstand,
If gentle Damon did not squeeze her hand?
With varying vanities, from every part,
100   They shift the moving toyshop[7] of their heart;

9. The four elements out of which all things were believed to have been made were fire, water, earth, and air. One or another of these elements was supposed to be predominant in both the physical and the psychological makeup of each human being. In this context they are spoken of as "humors."
1. Shrewish or overbearing women.
2. A lizardlike animal, in antiquity believed to live in fire. Each element was inhabited by a spirit, as the following lines explain.
3. Pronounced *tay*.
4. Cf. *Paradise Lost* 1.427–31; this is one of many allusions to that poem in the *Rape*.
5. Here and after, a fanciful name for a young woman, to be distinguished from the "Nymphs" (water spirits) in line 62.
6. Emblems of nobility.
7. A shop stocked with baubles and trifles.

Where wigs with wigs, with sword-knots sword-knots strive,
Beaux banish beaux, and coaches coaches drive.
This erring mortals levity may call;
Oh, blind to truth! the Sylphs contrive it all.
105   "Of these am I, who thy protection claim,
A watchful sprite, and Ariel is my name.
Late, as I ranged the crystal wilds of air,
In the clear mirror of thy ruling star
I saw, alas! some dread event impend,
110   Ere to the main this morning sun descend,
But Heaven reveals not what, or how, or where:
Warned by thy Sylph, O pious maid, beware!
This to disclose is all thy guardian can:
Beware of all, but most beware of Man!"
115   He said; when Shock,[8] who thought she slept too long,
Leaped up, and waked his mistress with his tongue.
'Twas then, Belinda, if report say true,
Thy eyes first opened on a billet-doux;
Wounds, charms, and ardors were no sooner read,
120   But all the vision vanished from thy head.
   And now, unveiled, the toilet stands displayed,
Each silver vase in mystic order laid.
First, robed in white, the nymph intent adores,
With head uncovered, the cosmetic powers.
125   A heavenly image in the glass appears;
To that she bends, to that her eyes she rears.
The inferior priestess, at her altar's side,
Trembling begins the sacred rites of Pride.
Unnumbered treasures ope at once, and here
130   The various offerings of the world appear;
From each she nicely culls with curious toil,
And decks the goddess with the glittering spoil.
This casket India's glowing gems unlocks,
And all Arabia breathes from yonder box.
135   The tortoise here and elephant unite,
Transformed to combs, the speckled and the white.
Here files of pins extend their shining rows,
Puffs, powders, patches, Bibles,[9] billet-doux.
Now awful° Beauty puts on all its arms;   *awe-inspiring*
140   The fair each moment rises in her charms,
Repairs her smiles, awakens every grace,
And calls forth all the wonders of her face;
Sees by degrees a purer blush arise,
And keener lightnings quicken in her eyes.
145   The busy Sylphs surround their darling care,
These set the head, and those divide the hair,
Some fold the sleeve, whilst others plait the gown;
And Betty's[1] praised for labors not her own.

8. A long-haired poodle, Belinda's lapdog.
9. It has been suggested that Pope intended here
not "Bibles," but "bibelots" (trinkets), but this
interpretation has not gained wide acceptance.
1. Belinda's maid, the "inferior priestess" mentioned in line 127.

Canto 2

Not with more glories, in the ethereal plain,
The sun first rises o'er the purpled main,
Than, issuing forth, the rival of his beams
Launched on the bosom of the silver Thames.
5 Fair nymphs and well-dressed youths around her shone,
But every eye was fixed on her alone.
On her white breast a sparkling cross she wore,
Which Jews might kiss, and infidels adore.
Her lively looks a sprightly mind disclose,
10 Quick as her eyes, and as unfixed as those:
Favors to none, to all she smiles extends;
Oft she rejects, but never once offends.
Bright as the sun, her eyes the gazers strike,
And, like the sun, they shine on all alike.
15 Yet graceful ease, and sweetness void of pride,
Might hide her faults, if belles had faults to hide:
If to her share some female errors fall,
Look on her face, and you'll forget 'em all.
This nymph, to the destruction of mankind,
20 Nourished two locks which graceful hung behind
In equal curls, and well conspired to deck
With shining ringlets her smooth ivory neck.
Love in these labyrinths his slaves detains,
And mighty hearts are held in slender chains.
25 With hairy springes² we the birds betray,
Slight lines of hair surprise the finny prey,
Fair tresses man's imperial race ensnare,
And beauty draws us with a single hair.
The adventurous Baron the bright locks admired,
30 He saw, he wished, and to the prize aspired.
Resolved to win, he meditates the way,
By force to ravish, or by fraud betray;
For when success a lover's toil attends,
Few ask if fraud or force attained his ends.
35 For this, ere Phoebus° rose, he had implored   *the sun*
Propitious Heaven, and every power adored,
But chiefly Love—to Love an altar built,
Of twelve vast French romances, neatly gilt.
There lay three garters, half a pair of gloves,
40 And all the trophies of his former loves.
With tender billet-doux he lights the pyre,
And breathes three amorous sighs to raise the fire.
Then prostrate falls, and begs with ardent eyes
Soon to obtain, and long possess the prize:
45 The powers gave ear, and granted half his prayer,
The rest the winds dispersed in empty air.
But now secure the painted vessel glides,
The sunbeams trembling on the floating tides,

---

2. Snares (pronounced *sprìn-jez*).

While melting music steals upon the sky,
50 And softened sounds along the waters die.
Smooth flow the waves, the zephyrs gently play,
Belinda smiled, and all the world was gay.
All but the Sylph—with careful thoughts oppressed,
The impending woe sat heavy on his breast.
55 He summons straight his denizens of air;
The lucid squadrons round the sails repair:
Soft o'er the shrouds aërial whispers breathe
That seemed but zephyrs to the train beneath.
Some to the sun their insect-wings unfold,
60 Waft on the breeze, or sink in clouds of gold.
Transparent forms too fine for mortal sight,
Their fluid bodies half dissolved in light,
Loose to the wind their airy garments flew,
Thin glittering textures of the filmy dew,
65 Dipped in the richest tincture of the skies,
Where light disports in ever-mingling dyes,
While every beam new transient colors flings,
Colors that change whene'er they wave their wings.
Amid the circle, on the gilded mast,
70 Superior by the head was Ariel placed;
His purple[3] pinions opening to the sun,
He raised his azure wand, and thus begun:
    "Ye Sylphs and Sylphids, to your chief give ear!
Fays, Fairies, Genïi, Elves, and Daemons, hear!
75 Ye know the spheres and various tasks assigned
By laws eternal to the aërial kind.
Some in the fields of purest ether play,
And bask and whiten in the blaze of day.
Some guide the course of wandering orbs on high,
80 Or roll the planets through the boundless sky.
Some less refined, beneath the moon's pale light
Pursue the stars that shoot athwart the night,
Or suck the mists in grosser air below,
Or dip their pinions in the painted bow,°   rainbow
85 Or brew fierce tempests on the wintry main,
Or o'er the glebe° distill the kindly rain.   cultivated field
Others on earth o'er human race preside,
Watch all their ways, and all their actions guide:
Of these the chief the care of nations own,
90 And guard with arms divine the British Throne.
    "Our humbler province is to tend the Fair,
Not a less pleasing, though less glorious care:
To save the powder from too rude a gale,
Nor let the imprisoned essences° exhale;   perfumes
95 To draw fresh colors from the vernal flowers;
To steal from rainbows e'er they drop in showers
A brighter wash;° to curl their waving hairs,   cosmetic lotion

3. In 18th-century poetic diction the word might mean bloodred, purple, or simply (as is likely here) brightly colored. The word derives from Virgil's Eclogue 9.40, *purpureum*, and is an example of the Latinate nature of some poetic diction of the period.

Assist their blushes, and inspire their airs,
Nay oft, in dreams invention we bestow,
100 To change a flounce, or add a furbelow.
  "This day black omens threat the brightest fair,
That e'er deserved a watchful spirit's care;
Some dire disaster, or by force or slight,
But what, or where, the Fates have wrapped in night:
105 Whether the nymph shall break Diana's[4] law,
Or some frail china jar receive a flaw,
Or stain her honor, or her new brocade,
Forget her prayers, or miss a masquerade,
Or lose her heart, or necklace, at a ball;
110 Or whether Heaven has doomed that Shock must fall.
Haste, then, ye spirits! to your charge repair:
The fluttering fan be Zephyretta's care;
The drops[5] to thee, Brillante, we consign;
And, Momentilla, let the watch be thine;
115 Do thou, Crispissa,[6] tend her favorite Lock;
Ariel himself shall be the guard of Shock.
  "To fifty chosen Sylphs, of special note,
We trust the important charge, the petticoat;
Oft have we known that sevenfold fence to fail,
120 Though stiff with hoops, and armed with ribs of whale.[7]
Form a strong line about the silver bound,
And guard the wide circumference around.
  "Whatever spirit, careless of his charge,
His post neglects, or leaves the fair at large,
125 Shall feel sharp vengeance soon o'ertake his sins,
Be stopped in vials, or transfixed with pins,
Or plunged in lakes of bitter washes lie,
Or wedged whole ages in a bodkin's[8] eye;
Gums and pomatums shall his flight restrain,
130 While clogged he beats his silken wings in vain,
Or alum styptics with contracting power
Shrink his thin essence like a riveled[9] flower:
Or, as Ixion[1] fixed, the wretch shall feel
The giddy motion of the whirling mill,
135 In fumes of burning chocolate shall glow,
And tremble at the sea that froths below!"
  He spoke; the spirits from the sails descend;
Some, orb in orb, around the nymph extend;
Some thread the mazy ringlets of her hair;
140 Some hang upon the pendants of her ear:
With beating hearts the dire event they wait,
Anxious, and trembling for the birth of Fate.

---

4. Diana was the goddess of chastity.
5. Diamond earrings. Observe the appropriateness of the names of the Sylphs to their assigned functions.
6. From Latin *crispere*, "to curl."
7. Corsets and the hoops of hoopskirts were made of whalebone.
8. A blunt needle with a large eye used for drawing ribbon through eyelets in the edging of women's garments.
9. To "rivel" is to "contract into wrinkles and corrugations" (Johnson's *Dictionary*).
1. In the Greek myth, he was punished in the underworld by being bound on an everturning wheel.

Canto 3

Close by those meads, forever crowned with flowers,
Where Thames with pride surveys his rising towers,
There stands a structure of majestic frame,
Which from the neighboring Hampton² takes its name.
5 Here Britain's statesmen oft the fall foredoom
Of foreign tyrants and of nymphs at home;
Here thou, great Anna! whom three realms obey,
Dost sometimes counsel take—and sometimes tea.
   Hither the heroes and the nymphs resort,
10 To taste awhile the pleasures of a court;
In various talk the instructive hours they passed,
Who gave the ball, or paid the visit last;
One speaks the glory of the British Queen,
And one describes a charming Indian screen;
15 A third interprets motions, looks, and eyes;
At every word a reputation dies.
Snuff, or the fan, supply each pause of chat,
With singing, laughing, ogling, and all that.
   Meanwhile, declining from the noon of day,
20 The sun obliquely shoots his burning ray;
The hungry judges soon the sentence sign,
And wretches hang that jurymen may dine;
The merchant from the Exchange returns in peace,
And the long labors of the toilet cease.
25 Belinda now, whom thirst of fame invites,
Burns to encounter two adventurous knights,
At ombre³ singly to decide their doom,
And swells her breast with conquests yet to come.
Straight the three bands prepare in arms to join,
30 Each band the number of the sacred nine.
Soon as she spreads her hand, the aërial guard
Descend, and sit on each important card:
First Ariel perched upon a Matadore,
Then each according to the rank they bore;
35 For Sylphs, yet mindful of their ancient race,
Are, as when women, wondrous fond of place.
   Behold, four Kings in majesty revered,
With hoary whiskers and a forky beard;
And four fair Queens whose hands sustain a flower,
40 The expressive emblem of their softer power;
Four Knaves in garbs succinct,° a trusty band,   *girded up*
Caps on their heads, and halberts in their hand;

2. Hampton Court, the royal palace, about fifteen miles up the Thames from London.
3. The game of ombre that Belinda plays against the baron and another young man is too complicated for complete explication here. Pope has carefully arranged the cards so that Belinda wins. The baron's hand is strong enough to be a threat, but the third player's is of little account. The hand is played exactly according to the rules of ombre, and Pope's description of the cards is equally accurate. Each player holds nine cards (line 30). The "Matadores" (line 33), when spades are trump, are "Spadillio" (line 49), the ace of spades; "Manillio" (line 51), the two of spades; and "Basto" (line 53), the ace of clubs. Belinda holds all three of these. (For a more complete description of ombre, see *The Rape of the Lock and Other Poems*, ed. Geoffrey Tillotson, in the Twickenham Edition of Pope's poems, vol. 2, Appendix C.)

And parti-colored troops, a shining train,
Draw forth to combat on the velvet plain.
45   The skillful nymph reviews her force with care;
"Let Spades be trumps!" she said, and trumps they were.
    Now move to war her sable Matadores,
In show like leaders of the swarthy Moors.
Spadillio first, unconquerable lord!
50   Led off two captive trumps, and swept the board.
As many more Manillio forced to yield,
And marched a victor from the verdant field.
Him Basto followed, but his fate more hard
Gained but one trump and one plebeian card.
55   With his broad saber next, a chief in years,
The hoary Majesty of Spades appears,
Puts forth one manly leg, to sight revealed,
The rest his many-colored robe concealed.
The rebel Knave, who dares his prince engage,
60   Proves the just victim of his royal rage.
Even mighty Pam,[4] that kings and queens o'erthrew
And mowed down armies in the fights of loo,
Sad chance of war! now destitute of aid,
Falls undistinguished by the victor Spade.
65   Thus far both armies to Belinda yield;
Now to the Baron fate inclines the field.
His warlike amazon her host invades,
The imperial consort of the crown of Spades.
The Club's black tyrant first her victim died,
70   Spite of his haughty mien and barbarous pride.
What boots° the regal circle on his head,   avails
His giant limbs, in state unwieldy spread?
That long behind he trails his pompous robe,
And of all monarchs only grasps the globe?[5]
75   The Baron now his Diamonds pours apace;
The embroidered King who shows but half his face,
And his refulgent Queen, with powers combined,
Of broken troops an easy conquest find.
Clubs, Diamonds, Hearts, in wild disorder seen,
80   With throngs promiscuous strew the level green.
Thus when dispersed a routed army runs,
Of Asia's troops, and Afric's sable sons,
With like confusion different nations fly,
Of various habit, and of various dye,
85   The pierced battalions disunited fall
In heaps on heaps; one fate o'erwhelms them all.
    The Knave of Diamonds tries his wily arts,
And wins (oh, shameful chance!) the Queen of Hearts.
At this, the blood the virgin's cheek forsook,
90   A livid paleness spreads o'er all her look;
She sees, and trembles at the approaching ill,

4. The knave of clubs, the highest trump in the game of loo.

5. In the English deck, only the king of clubs holds an imperial orb.

Just in the jaws of ruin, and Codille.[6]
And now (as oft in some distempered state)
On one nice trick depends the general fate.
95 An Ace of Hearts steps forth: the King unseen
Lurked in her hand, and mourned his captive Queen.
He springs to vengeance with an eager pace,
And falls like thunder on the prostrate Ace.
The nymph exulting fills with shouts the sky,
100 The walls, the woods, and long canals reply.
    O thoughtless mortals! ever blind to fate,
Too soon dejected, and too soon elate:
Sudden these honors shall be snatched away,
And cursed forever this victorious day.
105   For lo! the board with cups and spoons is crowned,
The berries crackle, and the mill turns round;[7]
On shining altars of Japan[8] they raise
The silver lamp; the fiery spirits blaze:
From silver spouts the grateful liquors glide,
110 While China's earth receives the smoking tide.
At once they gratify their scent and taste,
And frequent cups prolong the rich repast.
Straight hover round the fair her airy band;
Some, as she sipped, the fuming liquor fanned,
115 Some o'er her lap their careful plumes displayed,
Trembling, and conscious of the rich brocade.
Coffee (which makes the politician wise,
And see through all things with his half-shut eyes)
Sent up in vapors to the Baron's brain
120 New stratagems, the radiant Lock to gain.
Ah, cease, rash youth! desist ere 'tis too late,
Fear the just Gods, and think of Scylla's[9] fate!
Changed to a bird, and sent to flit in air,
She dearly pays for Nisus' injured hair!
125   But when to mischief mortals bend their will,
How soon they find fit instruments of ill!
Just then, Clarissa drew with tempting grace
A two-edged weapon from her shining case:
So ladies in romance assist their knight,
130 Present the spear, and arm him for the fight.
He takes the gift with reverence, and extends
The little engine on his fingers' ends;
This just behind Belinda's neck he spread,
As o'er the fragrant steams she bends her head.
135 Swift to the Lock a thousand sprites repair,
A thousand wings, by turns, blow back the hair,
And thrice they twitched the diamond in her ear,

6. The term applied to losing a hand at cards.
7. Coffee is roasted and ground.
8. Small, lacquered tables. "Altars": suggests the ritualistic character of coffee drinking in Belinda's world.
9. Scylla, daughter of Nisus, was turned into a sea bird because, for the sake of her love for Minos of Crete, who was besieging her father's city of Megara, she cut from her father's head the purple lock on which his safety depended. She is not the Scylla of "Scylla and Charybdis."

Thrice she looked back, and thrice the foe drew near.
Just in that instant, anxious Ariel sought
140 The close recesses of the virgin's thought;
As on the nosegay in her breast reclined,
He watched the ideas rising in her mind,
Sudden he viewed, in spite of all her art,
An earthly lover lurking at her heart.
145 Amazed, confused, he found his power expired,
Resigned to fate, and with a sigh retired.
    The Peer now spreads the glittering forfex° wide,   *scissors*
To enclose the Lock; now joins it, to divide.
Even then, before the fatal engine closed,
150 A wretched Sylph too fondly interposed;
Fate urged the shears, and cut the Sylph in twain
(But airy substance soon unites again):
The meeting points the sacred hair dissever
From the fair head, forever and forever!
155   Then flashed the living lightning from her eyes,
And screams of horror rend the affrighted skies.
Not louder shrieks to pitying heaven are cast,
When husbands, or when lapdogs breathe their last;
Or when rich china vessels fallen from high,
160 In glittering dust and painted fragments lie!
"Let wreaths of triumph now my temples twine,"
The victor cried, "the glorious prize is mine!
While fish in streams, or birds delight in air,
Or in a coach and six the British fair,
165 As long as *Atalantis*[1] shall be read,
Or the small pillow grace a lady's bed,
While visits shall be paid on solemn days,
When numerous wax-lights in bright order blaze,
While nymphs take treats,° or assignations give,   *free refreshments*
170 So long my honor, name, and praise shall live!
    "What time would spare, from steel receives its date,
And monuments, like men, submit to fate!
Steel could the labor of the Gods destroy,
And strike to dust the imperial towers of Troy;
175 Steel could the works of mortal pride confound,
And hew triumphal arches to the ground.
What wonder then, fair nymph! thy hairs should feel,
The conquering force of unresisted steel?"

Canto 4

But anxious cares the pensive nymph oppressed,
And secret passions labored in her breast.
Not youthful kings in battle seized alive,
Not scornful virgins who their charms survive,
5 Not ardent lovers robbed of all their bliss,

---

1. Delarivier Manley's *New Atalantis* (1709) was notorious for its thinly concealed allusions to contemporary scandals.

Not ancient ladies when refused a kiss,
Not tyrants fierce that unrepenting die,
Not Cynthia when her manteau's° pinned awry,　　　　　*wrap*
E'er felt such rage, resentment, and despair,
10　As thou, sad virgin! for thy ravished hair.
　　　For, that sad moment, when the Sylphs withdrew
And Ariel weeping from Belinda flew,
Umbriel,[2] a dusky, melancholy sprite
As ever sullied the fair face of light,
15　Down to the central earth, his proper scene,
Repaired to search the gloomy Cave of Spleen.°　　　*Ill Humor*
　　　Swift on his sooty pinions flits the Gnome,
And in a vapor reached the dismal dome.
No cheerful breeze this sullen region knows,
20　The dreaded east is all the wind that blows.
Here in a grotto, sheltered close from air,
And screened in shades from day's detested glare,
She sighs forever on her pensive bed,
Pain at her side, and Megrim° at her head.　　　　　*headache*
25　　Two handmaids wait the throne: alike in place
But differing far in figure and in face.
Here stood Ill-Nature like an ancient maid,
Her wrinkled form in black and white arrayed;
With store of prayers for mornings, nights, and noons,
30　Her hand is filled; her bosom with lampoons.
　　　There Affectation, with a sickly mien,
Shows in her cheek the roses of eighteen,
Practiced to lisp, and hang the head aside,
Faints into airs, and languishes with pride,
35　On the rich quilt sinks with becoming woe,
Wrapped in a gown, for sickness and for show.
The fair ones° feel such maladies as these,　　　　　*women*
When each new nightdress gives a new disease.
　　　A constant vapor[3] o'er the palace flies,
40　Strange phantoms rising as the mists arise;
Dreadful as hermit's dreams in haunted shades,
Or bright as visions of expiring maids.
Now glaring fiends, and snakes on rolling spires,°　　*coils*
Pale specters, gaping tombs, and purple fires;
45　Now lakes of liquid gold, Elysian scenes,
And crystal domes, and angels in machines.[4]
　　　Unnumbered throngs on every side are seen
Of bodies changed to various forms by Spleen.
Here living teapots stand, one arm held out,
50　One bent; the handle this, and that the spout:
A pipkin° there, like Homer's tripod,[5] walks;　　　*earthen pot*
Here sighs a jar, and there a goose pie talks;

2. The name suggests shade and darkness.
3. Emblematic of "the vapors," a fashionable
hypochondria, melancholy, or peevishness.
4. Mechanical devices used in the theaters for
spectacular effects. The catalog of hallucina-
tions draws on the sensational stage effects popular with contemporary audiences.
5. In the *Iliad* (18.373–77), Vulcan furnishes the
gods with self-propelling "tripods" (three-legged
stools).

Men prove with child, as powerful fancy works,
And maids, turned bottles, call aloud for corks.
55   Safe passed the Gnome through this fantastic band,
A branch of healing spleenwort[6] in his hand.
Then thus addressed the Power: "Hail, wayward Queen!
Who rule the sex to fifty from fifteen:
Parent of vapors and of female wit,
60 Who give the hysteric or poetic fit,
On various tempers act by various ways,
Make some take physic,° others scribble plays;   *medicine*
Who cause the proud their visits to delay,
And send the godly in a pet to pray.
65 A nymph there is that all your power disdains,
And thousands more in equal mirth maintains.
But oh! if e'er thy Gnome could spoil a grace,
Or raise a pimple on a beauteous face,
Like citron-waters[7] matrons' cheeks inflame,
70 Or change complexions at a losing game;
If e'er with airy horns[8] I planted heads,
Or rumpled petticoats, or tumbled beds,
Or caused suspicion when no soul was rude,
Or discomposed the headdress of a prude,
75 Or e'er to costive lapdog gave disease,
Which not the tears of brightest eyes could ease,
Hear me, and touch Belinda with chagrin:°   *ill humor*
That single act gives half the world the spleen."
    The Goddess with a discontented air
80 Seems to reject him though she grants his prayer.
A wondrous bag with both her hands she binds,
Like that where once Ulysses held the winds;[9]
There she collects the force of female lungs,
Sighs, sobs, and passions, and the war of tongues.
85 A vial next she fills with fainting fears,
Soft sorrows, melting griefs, and flowing tears.
The Gnome rejoicing bears her gifts away,
Spreads his black wings, and slowly mounts to day.
    Sunk in Thalestris'[1] arms the nymph he found,
90 Her eyes dejected and her hair unbound.
Full o'er their heads the swelling bag he rent,
And all the Furies issued at the vent.
Belinda burns with more than mortal ire,
And fierce Thalestris fans the rising fire.
95 "O wretched maid!" she spread her hands, and cried
(While Hampton's echoes, "Wretched maid!" replied),

---

6. An herb, efficacious against diseases of the spleen. Pope alludes to the golden bough that Aeneas and the Cumaean sibyl carry with them for protection into the underworld in *Aeneid* 6.
7. Brandy flavored with orange or lemon peel.
8. The symbol of the cuckold, the man whose wife has been unfaithful to him; here "airy," because they exist only in the jealous suspicions of the husband, the victim of the mischievous Umbriel.

9. Aeolus (later conceived of as god of the winds) gave Ulysses a bag containing all the winds adverse to his voyage home. When his ship was in sight of Ithaca, his companions opened the bag and the storms that ensued drove Ulysses far away (*Odyssey* 10.19ff.).
1. The name is borrowed from a queen of the Amazons, hence a fierce and warlike woman.

"Was it for this you took such constant care
The bodkin, comb, and essence to prepare?
For this your locks in paper durance bound,
100   For this with torturing irons wreathed around?
For this with fillets strained your tender head,
And bravely bore the double loads of lead?[2]
Gods! shall the ravisher display your hair,
While the fops envy, and the ladies stare!
105   Honor forbid! at whose unrivaled shrine
Ease, pleasure, virtue, all, our sex resign.
Methinks already I your tears survey,
Already hear the horrid things they say,
Already see you a degraded toast,
110   And all your honor in a whisper lost!
How shall I, then, your helpless fame defend?
'Twill then be infamy to seem your friend!
And shall this prize, the inestimable prize,
Exposed through crystal to the gazing eyes,
115   And heightened by the diamond's circling rays,
On that rapacious hand forever blaze?
Sooner shall grass in Hyde Park Circus grow,
And wits take lodgings in the sound of Bow;[3]
Sooner let earth, air, sea, to chaos fall,
120   Men, monkeys, lapdogs, parrots, perish all!"
    She said; then raging to Sir Plume repairs,
And bids her beau demand the precious hairs
(Sir Plume of amber snuffbox justly vain,
And the nice conduct of a clouded° cane).   *marbled, veined*
125   With earnest eyes, and round unthinking face,
He first the snuffbox opened, then the case,
And thus broke out—"My Lord, why, what the devil!
Z—ds! damn the lock! 'fore Gad, you must be civil!
Plague on 't! 'tis past a jest—nay prithee, pox!
130   Give her the hair"—he spoke, and rapped his box.
    "It grieves me much," replied the Peer again,
"Who speaks so well should ever speak in vain.
But by this Lock, this sacred Lock I swear
(Which never more shall join its parted hair;
135   Which never more its honors shall renew,
Clipped from the lovely head where late it grew),
That while my nostrils draw the vital air,
This hand, which won it, shall forever wear."
He spoke, and speaking, in proud triumph spread
140   The long-contended honors[4] of her head.
    But Umbriel, hateful Gnome, forbears not so;
He breaks the vial whence the sorrows flow.
Then see! the nymph in beauteous grief appears,
Her eyes half languishing, half drowned in tears;

2. The frame on which the elaborate coiffures of the day were arranged.
3. A person born within sound of the bells of St. Mary-le-Bow in Cheapside is said to be a cock- ney. No fashionable wit would have so vulgar an address.
4. Ornaments, hence locks; a Latinism.

₁₄₅ On her heaved bosom hung her drooping head,
Which with a sigh she raised, and thus she said:
  "Forever cursed be this detested day,
Which snatched my best, my favorite curl away!
Happy! ah, ten times happy had I been,
₁₅₀ If Hampton Court these eyes had never seen!
Yet am not I the first mistaken maid,
By love of courts to numerous ills betrayed.
Oh, had I rather unadmired remained
In some lone isle, or distant northern land;
₁₅₅ Where the gilt chariot never marks the way,
Where none learn ombre, none e'er taste bohea!⁵
There kept my charms concealed from mortal eye,
Like roses that in deserts bloom and die.
What moved my mind with youthful lords to roam?
₁₆₀ Oh, had I stayed, and said my prayers at home!
'Twas this the morning omens seemed to tell;
Thrice from my trembling hand the patch box⁶ fell;
The tottering china shook without a wind,
Nay, Poll sat mute, and Shock was most unkind!
₁₆₅ A Sylph too warned me of the threats of fate,
In mystic visions, now believed too late!
See the poor remnants of these slighted hairs!
My hands shall rend what e'en thy rapine spares.
These in two sable ringlets taught to break,
₁₇₀ Once gave new beauties to the snowy neck.
The sister lock now sits uncouth, alone,
And in its fellow's fate foresees its own;
Uncurled it hangs, the fatal shears demands,
And tempts once more thy sacrilegious hands.
₁₇₅ Oh, hadst thou, cruel! been content to seize
Hairs less in sight, or any hairs but these!"

Canto 5

  She said: the pitying audience melt in tears.
But Fate and Jove had stopped the Baron's ears.
In vain Thalestris with reproach assails,
For who can move when fair Belinda fails?
₅ Not half so fixed the Trojan⁷ could remain,
While Anna begged and Dido raged in vain.
Then grave Clarissa graceful waved her fan;
Silence ensued, and thus the nymph began:
  "Say, why are beauties praised and honored most,
₁₀ The wise man's passion, and the vain man's toast?
Why decked with all that land and sea afford,
Why angels called, and angel-like adored?
Why round our coaches crowd the white-gloved beaux,

5. A costly sort of tea.
6. To hold the ornamental patches of court plaster worn on the face by both sexes.
7. Aeneas, who forsook Dido at the bidding of the gods, despite her reproaches and the supplications of her sister Anna. Virgil compares him to a steadfast oak that withstands a storm (*Aeneid* 4.437–43).

Why bows the side box from its inmost rows?
15 How vain are all these glories, all our pains,
Unless good sense preserve what beauty gains;
That men may say when we the front box grace,
'Behold the first in virtue as in face!'
Oh! if to dance all night, and dress all day,
20 Charmed the smallpox, or chased old age away,
Who would not scorn what housewife's cares produce,
Or who would learn one earthly thing of use?
To patch, nay ogle, might become a saint,
Nor could it sure be such a sin to paint.
25 But since, alas! frail beauty must decay,
Curled or uncurled, since locks will turn to gray;
Since painted, or not painted, all shall fade,
And she who scorns a man must die a maid;
What then remains but well our power to use,
30 And keep good humor still whate'er we lose?
And trust me, dear, good humor can prevail
When airs, and flights, and screams, and scolding fail.
Beauties in vain their pretty eyes may roll;
Charms strike the sight, but merit wins the soul."[8]
35   So spoke the dame, but no applause ensued;
Belinda frowned, Thalestris called her prude.
"To arms, to arms!" the fierce virago cries,
And swift as lightning to the combat flies.
All side in parties, and begin the attack;
40 Fans clap, silks rustle, and tough whalebones crack;
Heroes' and heroines' shouts confusedly rise,
And bass and treble voices strike the skies.
No common weapons in their hands are found,
Like Gods they fight, nor dread a mortal wound.
45   So when bold Homer makes the Gods engage,
And heavenly breasts with human passions rage;
'Gainst Pallas, Mars; Latona, Hermes arms;
And all Olympus rings with loud alarms:
Jove's thunder roars, heaven trembles all around,
50 Blue Neptune storms, the bellowing deeps resound:
Earth shakes her nodding towers, the ground gives way,
And the pale ghosts start at the flash of day!
    Triumphant Umbriel on a sconce's[9] height
Clapped his glad wings, and sat to view the fight:
55 Propped on the bodkin spears, the sprites survey
The growing combat, or assist the fray.
    While through the press enraged Thalestris flies,
And scatters death around from both her eyes,
A beau and witling perished in the throng,
60 One died in metaphor, and one in song.
"O cruel nymph! a living death I bear,"
Cried Dapperwit, and sunk beside his chair.

8. The speech is a close parody of Pope's own
translation of the speech of Sarpedon to Glau-
cus, first published in 1709 and slightly revised
in his version of the *Iliad* (12.371–96).
9. A candlestick fastened on the wall.

A mournful glance Sir Fopling upwards cast,
"Those eyes are made so killing"—was his last.
65 Thus on Maeander's flowery margin lies
The expiring swan,[1] and as he sings he dies.
        When bold Sir Plume had drawn Clarissa down,
Chloe stepped in, and killed him with a frown;
She smiled to see the doughty hero slain,
70 But, at her smile, the beau revived again.
        Now Jove suspends his golden scales in air,
Weighs the men's wits against the lady's hair;
The doubtful beam long nods from side to side;
At length the wits mount up, the hairs subside.
75 See, fierce Belinda on the Baron flies,
With more than usual lightning in her eyes;
Nor feared the chief the unequal fight to try,
Who sought no more than on his foe to die.
        But this bold lord with manly strength endued,
80 She with one finger and a thumb subdued:
Just where the breath of life his nostrils drew,
A charge of snuff the wily virgin threw;
The Gnomes direct, to every atom just,
The pungent grains of titillating dust.
85 Sudden, with starting tears each eye o'erflows,
And the high dome re-echoes to his nose.
        "Now meet thy fate," incensed Belinda cried,
And drew a deadly bodkin[2] from her side.
(The same, his ancient personage to deck,
90 Her great-great-grandsire wore about his neck,
In three seal rings; which after, melted down,
Formed a vast buckle for his widow's gown:
Her infant grandame's whistle next it grew,
The bells she jingled, and the whistle blew;
95 Then in a bodkin graced her mother's hairs,
Which long she wore, and now Belinda wears.)
        "Boast not my fall," he cried, "insulting foe!
Thou by some other shalt be laid as low.
Nor think to die dejects my lofty mind:
100 All that I dread is leaving you behind!
Rather than so, ah, let me still survive,
And burn in Cupid's flames—but burn alive."
        "Restore the Lock!" she cries; and all around
"Restore the Lock!" the vaulted roofs rebound.
105 Not fierce Othello in so loud a strain
Roared for the handkerchief that caused his pain.[3]
But see how oft ambitious aims are crossed,
And chiefs contend till all the prize is lost!
The lock, obtained with guilt, and kept with pain,
110 In every place is sought, but sought in vain:
With such a prize no mortal must be blessed,

1. The Maeander, a river in what is now Turkey,
was famous for its swans.

2. Here, an ornamental hairpin shaped like a
dagger.
3. *Othello* 3.4.

So Heaven decrees! with Heaven who can contest?
   Some thought it mounted to the lunar sphere,
Since all things lost on earth are treasured there.
115 There heroes' wits are kept in ponderous vases,
And beaux' in snuffboxes and tweezer cases.
There broken vows and deathbed alms are found,
And lovers' hearts with ends of riband bound,
The courtier's promises, and sick man's prayers,
120 The smiles of harlots, and the tears of heirs,
Cages for gnats, and chains to yoke a flea,
Dried butterflies, and tomes of casuistry.
   But trust the Muse—she saw it upward rise,
Though marked by none but quick, poetic eyes
125 (So Rome's great founder to the heavens withdrew,[4]
To Proculus alone confessed in view);
A sudden star, it shot through liquid air,
And drew behind a radiant trail of hair.
Not Berenice's locks first rose so bright,[5]
130 The heavens bespangling with disheveled light.
The Sylphs behold it kindling as it flies,
And pleased pursue its progress through the skies.
   This the beau monde shall from the Mall[6] survey,
And hail with music its propitious ray.
135 This the blest lover shall for Venus take,
And send up vows from Rosamonda's Lake.[7]
This Partridge[8] soon shall view in cloudless skies,
When next he looks through Galileo's eyes;°   *telescope*
And hence the egregious wizard shall foredoom
140 The fate of Louis, and the fall of Rome.
   Then cease, bright nymph! to mourn thy ravished hair,
Which adds new glory to the shining sphere!
Not all the tresses that fair head can boast
Shall draw such envy as the Lock you lost.
145 For, after all the murders of your eye,
When, after millions slain, yourself shall die:
When those fair suns shall set, as set they must,
And all those tresses shall be laid in dust,
This Lock the Muse shall consecrate to fame,
150 And 'midst the stars inscribe Belinda's name.

1712   1714, 1717

4. Romulus, the "founder" and first king of Rome, was snatched to heaven in a storm cloud while reviewing his army in the Campus Martius (Livy 1.16).
5. The wife of Ptolemy III dedicated a lock of her hair to the gods to ensure her husband's safe return from war. It was turned into a constellation.
6. A walk laid out by Charles II in St. James's Park (London), a resort for strollers of all sorts.
7. In St. James's Park; associated with unhappy lovers.
8. John Partridge, an astrologer whose annually published predictions (among them that Louis XIV and the Catholic Church would fall) had been amusingly satirized by Swift and other wits in 1708.

Eloisa to Abelard   Like Ovid's *Sappho to Phaon*, which Pope had translated in his teens, *Eloisa to Abelard* is a heroic epistle: strictly defined, a versified love letter, involving historical persons, which dramatizes the feelings of a woman who has been forsaken. Pope took his subject from one of the most famous affairs of history. Peter Abelard (1079–1142), a brilliant Scholastic theologian, seduced a young girl, his pupil Heloise; eventually she bore him a child, and they were secretly married. Enraged at the betrayal of trust, and what he regarded as the casting off of Heloise, her uncle Fulbert revenged himself by having Abelard castrated. The lovers separated; each of them entered a monastery and went on to a distinguished career in the church. Yet their greatest fame derives from the letters they are supposed to have exchanged late in their lives (some scholars have cast doubt on the authenticity of Heloise's letters). It is this correspondence, made newly popular by French and English translations of the original Latin, that inspired Pope's poem.

The heroic epistle challenges authors in two ways: they must exert historical imagination, projecting themselves into another time and place; and they must enter the mind and passions of a woman, acting her part, and showing everything from her point of view. Historically, Pope draws on his knowledge of Roman Catholic ritual to envelop Eloisa in a rich medieval atmosphere. The dark Gothic convent, situated in an imaginary landscape of grottos, mountains, and pine forests, embodies the eighteenth-century sense of the romantic: fantastic, legendary, and extravagant. Here Eloisa is cloistered, not only physically but mentally, by religious mysticism that surrounds her with a melancholy as palpable as the image of her lover. The greatest triumph of the poem, however, is psychological. In *Eloisa*, for the only time in his career, Pope tells a story wholly in another's voice. Confused and tormented, the heroine tosses between two kinds of love: an erotic passion for the earthly lover whose memory she cannot quell and the divine, chaste love that must content a nun. Abelard and God, within her fantasy, compete for her soul. Pope brings these internal struggles to the surface by externalizing them in bold dramatic rhetoric, formal and intense as an aria in an opera (the poem was long a favorite for reading aloud). Eloisa views herself theatrically, if only because, in the letter, she is trying to make Abelard visualize the pathos of her situation. There is literally no way out for her, and at the end of the poem, she can break the static circle of desire and loneliness only by picturing herself in the peace of death. Yet the high reputation of the work, well into the Romantic era, owes less to its theatrics than to its convincing image of a mind in pain. "If you search for passion," Lord Byron wrote more than a century later, "where is it to be found stronger than in the Epistle from Eloisa to Abelard?"

For a depiction of an incident in this famous love story, see Angelika Kauffmann's painting *The Parting of Abelard from Heloise* (ca. 1778), in the color insert in this volume.

Eloisa to Abelard

The Argument

Abelard and Eloisa flourished in the twelfth century; they were two of the most distinguished persons of their age in learning and beauty, but for nothing more famous than for their unfortunate passion. After a long course of calamities, they retired each to a several[1] convent, and consecrated the remainder of their days to religion. It was many years after this separation,

---

1. Separate.

that a letter of Abelard's to a friend which contained the history of his misfortune, fell into the hands of Eloisa. This awakening all her tenderness, occasioned those celebrated letters (out of which the following is partly extracted)[2] which give so lively a picture of the struggles of grace and nature, virtue and passion.

In these deep solitudes and awful cells,
Where heavenly-pensive contemplation dwells,
And ever-musing melancholy reigns;
What means this tumult in a vestal's[3] veins?
5   Why rove my thoughts beyond this last retreat?
Why feels my heart its long-forgotten heat?
Yet, yet I love!—From Abelard it[4] came,
And Eloisa yet must kiss the name.
    Dear fatal name! rest ever unrevealed,
10 Nor pass these lips in holy silence sealed.
Hide it, my heart, within that close disguise,
Where mixed with God's, his loved idea° lies.   mental image
O write it not, my hand—the name appears
Already written—wash it out, my tears!
15 In vain lost Eloisa weeps and prays,
Her heart still dictates, and her hand obeys.
    Relentless walls! whose darksome round contains
Repentant sighs, and voluntary pains:
Ye rugged rocks! which holy knees have worn;
20 Ye grots and caverns shagged with horrid° thorn!   bristling
Shrines! where their vigils pale-eyed virgins keep,
And pitying saints, whose statues learn to weep![5]
Tho' cold like you, unmoved, and silent grown,
I have not yet forgot myself to stone.
25 All is not Heaven's while Abelard has part,
Still rebel nature holds out half my heart;
Nor prayers nor fasts its stubborn pulse restrain,
Nor tears, for ages taught to flow in vain.
    Soon as thy letters trembling I unclose,
30 That well-known name awakens all my woes.
Oh name for ever sad! for ever dear!
Still breathed in sighs, still ushered with a tear.
I tremble too, where'er my own I find,
Some dire misfortune follows close behind.
35 Line after line my gushing eyes o'erflow,
Led through a sad variety of woe:
Now warm in love, now withering in my bloom,
Lost in a convent's solitary gloom!
There stern religion quenched the unwilling flame,
40 There died the best of passions, love and fame.
    Yet write, oh write me all, that I may join

2. Pope's source was a highly romanticized English version of the letters by John Hughes, published in 1713.
3. Nun's. Here, as elsewhere, Eloisa substitutes a pagan form for a Christian; nor is she in fact a virgin (vestal).
4. The letter to which Eloisa is replying.
5. In damp places, stone "weeps" through condensation.

Griefs to thy griefs, and echo sighs to thine.
Nor foes nor fortune take this power away.
And is my Abelard less kind than they?
45 Tears still are mine, and those I need not spare,
Love but demands what else were shed in prayer;
No happier task these faded eyes pursue,
To read and weep is all they now can do.
    Then share thy pain, allow that sad relief;
50 Ah, more than share it! give me all thy grief.
Heaven first taught letters for some wretch's aid,
Some banished lover, or some captive maid;
They live, they speak, they breathe what love inspires,
Warm from the soul, and faithful to its fires,
55 The virgin's wish without her fears impart,
Excuse the blush, and pour out all the heart,
Speed the soft intercourse from soul to soul,
And waft a sigh from Indus to the Pole.[6]
    Thou knowest how guiltless first I met thy flame,
60 When love approached me under friendship's name;
My fancy formed thee of angelic kind,
Some emanation of the all-beauteous Mind.[7]
Those smiling eyes, attempering° every ray,   moderating, assuaging
Shone sweetly lambent with celestial day:
65 Guiltless I gazed; heaven listened while you sung;
And truths divine came mended from that tongue.[8]
From lips like those what precept failed to move?
Too soon they taught me 'twas no sin to love.
Back through the paths of pleasing sense I ran,
70 Nor wished an angel whom I loved a man.
Dim and remote the joys of saints I see,
Nor envy them, that heaven I lose for thee.
    How oft, when pressed to marriage, have I said,
Curse on all laws but those which love has made!
75 Love, free as air, at sight of human ties,
Spreads his light wings, and in a moment flies.
Let wealth, let honor, wait the wedded dame,
August her deed, and sacred be her fame;
Before true passion all those views remove,°   depart
80 Fame, wealth, and honor! what are you to love?
The jealous god, when we profane his fires,
Those restless passions in revenge inspires,
And bids them make mistaken mortals groan,
Who seek in love for aught but love alone.
85 Should at my feet the world's great master fall,
Himself, his throne, his world, I'd scorn 'em all:
Nor Caesar's empress would I deign to prove;°   try
No, make me mistress to the man I love;
If there be yet another name more free,

6. From the Indus River, in South Asia, to the North Pole.
7. God, conceived (as is proper to a student of

philosophy) in Platonic terms.
8. He was her preceptor in philosophy and divinity [Pope's note].

90 More fond than mistress, make me that to thee!
Oh happy state! when souls each other draw,
When love is liberty, and nature, law:
All then is full, possessing, and possessed,
No craving void left aching in the breast:
95 Even thought meets thought ere from the lips it part,
And each warm wish springs mutual from the heart.
This sure is bliss (if bliss on earth there be)
And once the lot of Abelard and me.
　　Alas how changed! what sudden horrors rise!
100 A naked lover bound and bleeding lies!
Where, where was Eloise? her voice, her hand,
Her poniard,° had opposed the dire command.　　　　　*dagger*
Barbarian, stay! that bloody stroke restrain;
The crime was common,° common be the pain.°　　*shared / punishment*
105 I can no more; by shame, by rage suppressed,
Let tears, and burning blushes speak the rest.
　　Canst thou forget that sad, that solemn day,
When victims at yon altar's foot we lay?
Canst thou forget what tears that moment fell,
110 When, warm in youth, I bade the world farewell?
As with cold lips I kissed the sacred veil,
The shrines all trembled, and the lamps grew pale:
Heaven scarce believed the conquest it surveyed,
And saints with wonder heard the vows I made.
115 Yet then, to those dread altars as I drew,
Not on the Cross my eyes were fixed, but you;
Not grace, or zeal, love only was my call,
And if I lose thy love, I lose my all.
Come! with thy looks, thy words, relieve my woe;
120 Those still at least are left thee to bestow.
Still on that breast enamored let me lie,
Still drink delicious poison from thy eye,
Pant on thy lip, and to thy heart be pressed;
Give all thou canst—and let me dream the rest.
125 Ah no! instruct me other joys to prize,
With other beauties charm my partial[9] eyes,
Full in my view set all the bright abode,
And make my soul quit Abelard for God.
　　Ah think at least thy flock deserves thy care,
130 Plants of thy hand, and children of thy prayer.
From the false world in early youth they fled,
By thee to mountains, wilds, and deserts led.
You raised these hallowed walls;[1] the desert smiled,
And paradise was opened in the wild.
135 No weeping orphan saw his father's stores
Our shrines irradiate,[2] or emblaze the floors;
No silver saints, by dying misers given,

---

9. Fond; seeing only a part.
1. He founded the monastery [Pope's note]. Abelard erected the "Paraclete," a modest oratory
near Troyes, in 1122; seven years later, when the

nunnery of which Heloise was prioress was
evicted from its property, he ceded the lands of
the Paraclete to her.
2. Adorn with splendor.

Here bribed the rage of ill-requited heaven:
But such plain roofs as piety could raise,
140 And only vocal with the Maker's[3] praise.
In these lone walls (their day's eternal bound)
These moss-grown domes with spiry turrets crowned,
Where awful arches make a noon-day night,
And the dim windows shed a solemn light,
145 Thy eyes diffused a reconciling ray,
And gleams of glory brightened all the day.
But now no face divine contentment wears,
'Tis all blank sadness, or continual tears.
See how the force of others' prayers I try,
150 (O pious fraud of amorous charity!)
But why should I on others' prayers depend?
Come thou, my father, brother, husband, friend!
Ah let thy handmaid, sister, daughter move,
And all those tender names in one, thy love!
155 The darksome pines that o'er yon rocks reclined
Wave high, and murmur to the hollow wind,
The wandering streams that shine between the hills,
The grots that echo to the tinkling rills,
The dying gales that pant upon the trees,
160 The lakes that quiver to the curling breeze;
No more these scenes my meditation aid,
Or lull to rest the visionary[4] maid.
But o'er the twilight groves and dusky caves,
Long-sounding isles,[5] and intermingled graves,
165 Black Melancholy sits, and round her throws
A death-like silence, and a dread repose:
Her gloomy presence saddens all the scene,
Shades every flower, and darkens every green,
Deepens the murmur of the falling floods,
170 And breathes a browner horror on the woods.[6]
    Yet here for ever, ever must I stay;
Sad proof how well a lover can obey!
Death, only death, can break the lasting chain;
And here, even then, shall my cold dust remain,
175 Here all its frailties, all its flames resign,
And wait, till 'tis no sin to mix with thine.
    Ah wretch! believed the spouse of God in vain,
Confessed within the slave of love and man.
Assist me, heaven! but whence arose that prayer?
180 Sprung it from piety, or from despair?
Even here, where frozen chastity retires,
Love finds an altar for forbidden fires.
I ought to grieve, but cannot what I ought;
I mourn the lover, not lament the fault;

---

3. God's or Abelard's.
4. Given to visions.
5. Sounds reverberate over water as in the *aisles* of a church.
6. The image of the Goddess Melancholy sitting over the convent, and, as it were, expanding her dreadful wings over its whole circuit, and diffusing her gloom all around it, is truly sublime, and strongly conceived [Joseph Warton's note].

185   I view my crime, but kindle at the view,
          Repent old pleasures, and solicit new;
          Now turned to heaven, I weep my past offense,
          Now think of thee, and curse my innocence.
          Of all affliction taught a lover yet,
190   'Tis sure the hardest science° to forget!   *knowledge*
          How shall I lose the sin, yet keep the sense,[7]
          And love the offender, yet detest the offense?
          How the dear object from the crime remove,
          Or how distinguish penitence from love?
195   Unequal task! a passion to resign,
          For hearts so touched, so pierced, so lost as mine.
          Ere such a soul regains its peaceful state,
          How often must it love, how often hate!
          How often hope, despair, resent, regret,
200   Conceal, disdain—do all things but forget.
          But let heaven seize it, all at once 'tis fired,
          Not touched, but rapt; not wakened, but inspired![8]
          Oh come! oh teach me nature to subdue,
          Renounce my love, my life, my self—and you.
205   Fill my fond heart with God alone, for he
          Alone can rival, can succeed to thee.
             How happy is the blameless vestal's lot!
          The world forgetting, by the world forgot.
          Eternal sun-shine of the spotless mind!
210   Each prayer accepted, and each wish resigned;
          Labor and rest, that equal periods keep;
          "Obedient slumbers that can wake and weep;"[9]
          Desires composed, affections ever even;
          Tears that delight, and sighs that waft to heaven.
215   Grace shines around her with serenest beams,
          And whispering angels prompt her golden dreams.
          For her the unfading rose of Eden blooms,
          And wings of seraphs shed divine perfumes,
          For her the Spouse prepares the bridal ring,
220   For her white virgins hymenaeals[1] sing,
          To sounds of heavenly harps she dies away,
          And melts in visions of eternal day.
             Far other dreams my erring soul employ,
          Far other raptures, of unholy joy:
225   When at the close of each sad, sorrowing day,
          Fancy restores what vengeance snatched away,
          Then conscience sleeps, and leaving nature free,
          All my loose soul unbounded springs to thee.
          O curst, dear horrors of all-conscious night![2]
230   How glowing guilt exalts the keen delight!
          Provoking daemons all restraint remove,

7. Both perception and sensation.
8. I.e., when touched, at once rapt; when wakened, at once inspired.
9. From *Description of a Religious House* (1648), by Richard Crashaw.

1. Wedding hymns. Every nun is the bride of Christ, her spouse.
2. The night knows everything, and Eloisa is conscious (guiltily aware) all through the night.

And stir within me every source of love.
I hear thee, view thee, gaze o'er all thy charms,
And round thy phantom glue my clasping arms.
235 I wake—no more I hear, no more I view,
The phantom flies me, as unkind as you.
I call aloud; it hears not what I say;
I stretch my empty arms; it glides away:
To dream once more I close my willing eyes;
240 Ye soft illusions, dear deceits, arise!
Alas, no more!—methinks we wandering go
Through dreary wastes, and weep each other's woe;
Where round some moldering tower pale ivy creeps,
And low-browed rocks hang nodding o'er the deeps.
245 Sudden you mount! you beckon from the skies;
Clouds interpose, waves roar, and winds arise.
I shriek, start up, the same sad prospect find,
And wake to all the griefs I left behind.
  For thee the fates, severely kind, ordain
250 A cool suspense° from pleasure and from pain;   suspension
Thy life a long dead calm of fixed repose;
No pulse that riots, and no blood that glows.
Still as the sea, ere winds were taught to blow,
Or moving spirit bade the waters flow;
255 Soft as the slumbers of a saint forgiven,
And mild as opening gleams of promised heaven.
  Come, Abelard! for what hast thou to dread?
The torch of Venus burns not for the dead.
Nature stands checked; religion disapproves;
260 Even thou art cold—yet Eloisa loves.
Ah hopeless, lasting flames! like those that burn
To light the dead, and warm the unfruitful urn.[3]
  What scenes appear where'er I turn my view?
The dear ideas, where I fly, pursue,
265 Rise in the grove, before the altar rise,
Stain all my soul, and wanton in my eyes!
I waste the matin lamp in sighs for thee,
Thy image steals between my God and me,
Thy voice I seem in every hymn to hear,
270 With every bead I drop too soft a tear.
When from the censer clouds of fragrance roll,
And swelling organs lift the rising soul,
One thought of thee puts all the pomp to flight,
Priests, tapers, temples, swim before my sight:
275 In seas of flame° my plunging soul is drowned,   love or hell
While altars blaze, and angels tremble round.
  While prostrate here in humble grief I lie,
Kind, virtuous drops just gathering in my eye,
While praying, trembling, in the dust I roll,
280 And dawning grace is opening on my soul:
Come, if thou dar'st, all charming as thou art!

---

3. Perpetual fires were placed in Roman tombs.

Oppose thyself to heaven; dispute° my heart;   *contend for*
Come, with one glance of those deluding eyes
Blot out each bright idea of the skies.
285 Take back that grace, those sorrows, and those tears,
Take back my fruitless penitence and prayers,
Snatch me, just mounting, from the blest abode,
Assist the fiends and tear me from my God!
    No, fly me, fly me! far as pole from pole;
290 Rise Alps between us! and whole oceans roll!
Ah come not, write not, think not once of me,
Nor share one pang of all I felt for thee.
Thy oaths I quit,° thy memory resign,   *absolve*
Forget, renounce me, hate whate'er was mine.
295 Fair eyes, and tempting looks (which yet I view!)
Long loved, adored ideas! all adieu!
O grace serene! oh virtue heavenly fair!
Divine oblivion of low-thoughted care!
Fresh blooming hope, gay daughter of the sky!
300 And faith, our early immortality!
Enter, each mild, each amicable guest;
Receive, and wrap me in eternal rest!
    See in her cell sad Eloisa spread,
Propped on some tomb, a neighbor of the dead!
305 In each low wind methinks a spirit calls,
And more than echoes talk along the walls.
Here, as I watched the dying lamps around,
From yonder shrine I heard a hollow sound.
"Come, sister, come! (it said, or seemed to say)
310 Thy place is here, sad sister, come away!
Once like thyself, I trembled, wept, and prayed,
Love's victim then, tho' now a sainted maid:
But all is calm in this eternal sleep;
Here grief forgets to groan, and love to weep,
315 Even superstition loses every fear:
For God, not man, absolves our frailties here."
    I come, I come! prepare your roseate bowers,
Celestial palms, and ever-blooming flowers.
Thither, where sinners may have rest, I go,
320 Where flames refined in breasts seraphic glow.
Thou, Abelard! the last sad office pay,
And smooth my passage to the realms of day;
See my lips tremble, and my eyeballs roll,
Suck my last breath, and catch my flying soul!
325 Ah no—in sacred vestments may'st thou stand,
The hallowed taper trembling in thy hand,
Present the Cross before my lifted eye,
Teach me at once, and learn of° me to die.   *from*
Ah then, thy once-loved Eloisa see!
330 It will be then no crime to gaze on me.
See from my cheek the transient roses fly!
See the last sparkle languish in my eye!
Till every motion, pulse, and breath be o'er;

And even my Abelard be loved no more.
335 O death all-eloquent! you only prove
What dust we doat on, when 'tis man we love.
    Then too, when fate shall thy fair frame destroy,
    (That cause of all my guilt, and all my joy)
    In trance ecstatic may thy pangs be drowned,
340 Bright clouds descend, and angels watch thee round,
From opening skies may streaming glories shine,
And saints embrace thee with a love like mine.
    May one kind grave unite each hapless name,[4]
    And graft my love immortal on thy fame!
345 Then, ages hence, when all my woes are o'er,
When this rebellious heart shall beat no more;
If ever chance two wandering lovers brings
To Paraclete's white walls, and silver springs,
O'er the pale marble shall they join their heads,
350 And drink the falling tears each other sheds,
Then sadly say, with mutual pity moved,
"Oh may we never love as these have loved!"
From the full choir when loud Hosannas rise,
And swell the pomp of dreadful sacrifice,[5]
355 Amid that scene if some relenting eye
Glance on the stone where our cold relics lie,
Devotion's self shall steal a thought from heaven,
One human tear shall drop, and be forgiven.
And sure if fate some future bard shall join
360 In sad similitude of griefs to mine,
Condemned whole years in absence to deplore,[6]
And image° charms he must behold no more,   imagine, depict
Such if there be, who loves so long, so well,
Let him our sad, our tender story tell;
365 The well-sung woes will sooth my pensive ghost;
He best can paint 'em, who shall feel 'em most.

1717

An Essay on Man

Pope's philosophical poem *An Essay on Man* represents the beginnings of an ambitious but never completed plan for what he called his "ethic work," intended to be a large survey of human nature, society, and morals. He dedicated the *Essay* to Henry St. John (pronounced *Sín-jun*), Viscount Bolingbroke (1678–1751), the brilliant, erratic secretary of state in the Tory ministry of 1710–14. After the accession of George I, Bolingbroke fled to France, but he was allowed to return in 1723, settling near Pope at Dawley Farm. The two formed a close friendship and talked through the ideas expressed in the *Essay* and in Bolingbroke's own philosophical writings (some of which are addressed to Pope). But

---

4. Abelard and Eloisa were interred in the same grave, or in monuments adjoining, in the monastery of the Paraclete [Pope's note].
5. The celebration of the Eucharist (mass).
6. Lament. Pope, imagining himself imagined by Eloisa, hints that he too is separated from a loved

one, perhaps Lady Mary Wortley Montagu, who was in Turkey. Pope and Montagu later quarreled, and she appears as Sappho in Epistle 2, *To a Lady*, in the *Epistle to Dr. Arbuthnot*, and in other places in his work.

Pope's poem has many sources in the thought of his times and the philosophical tradition at large, and he says himself in the poem's little preface that his intention is to formulate a widely acceptable system of obvious, familiar truths. Pope's "optimism"—his insistence that everything must be "RIGHT" in a universe created and superintended by God—skips over the tragic elements of experience that much great literary, philosophical, and religious expression confronts. But the strains and contradictions of the poem are themselves deeply revealing about the thinking of Pope and his age, as he both presents and withholds a comprehensive view of the universe and reasons out reason's drastic limitations.

Pope's purpose is to "vindicate the ways of God to man," a phrase that consciously echoes *Paradise Lost* 1.26. Like John Milton, Pope faces the problem of the existence of evil in a world presumed to be the creation of a good god. *Paradise Lost* is biblical in content, Christian in doctrine; *An Essay on Man* avoids all specifically Christian doctrines, not because Pope disbelieved them but because "man," the subject of the poem, includes millions who never heard of Christianity and Pope is concerned with the universal. Milton tells a Judeo-Christian story. Pope writes in abstract terms.

The *Essay* is divided into four epistles. In the first Pope asserts the essential order and goodness of the universe and the rightness of our place in it. The other epistles deal with how we may emulate in our nature and in society the cosmic harmony revealed in the first epistle. The second seeks to show how we may attain a psychological harmony that can become the basis of a virtuous life through the cooperation of self-love and the passions (both necessary to our complete humanity) with reason, the controller and director. The third is concerned with the individual in society, which, it teaches, was created through the cooperation of self-love (the egoistic drives that motivate us) and social love (our dependence on others, our inborn benevolence). The fourth is concerned with happiness, which lies within the reach of all for it is dependent on virtue, which becomes possible when—though only when—self-love is transmuted into love of others and love of God. Such, in brief summary, are Pope's main ideas, expressed in many phrases so memorable that they have detached themselves from the poem and become part of daily speech.

From An Essay on Man

TO HENRY ST. JOHN, LORD BOLINGBROKE

Epistle 1. Of the Nature and State of Man,
with Respect to the Universe

Awake, my St. John! leave all meaner things
To low ambition, and the pride of kings.
Let us (since life can little more supply
Than just to look about us and to die)
5　Expatiate free° o'er all this scene of man;   *range freely*
A mighty maze! but not without a plan;
A wild, where weeds and flowers promiscuous shoot,
Or garden, tempting with forbidden fruit.
Together let us beat this ample field,[1]
10　Try what the open, what the covert yield;
The latent tracts, the giddy heights, explore

1. Pope and Bolingbroke will try to drive truth into the open, like hunters beating the bushes for game.

Of all who blindly creep, or sightless soar;
Eye Nature's walks, shoot folly as it flies,
And catch the manners living as they rise;
15 Laugh where we must, be candid° where we can;   favorably disposed
But vindicate the ways of God to man.

    1. Say first, of God above, or man below,
What can we reason, but from what we know?
Of man, what see we but his station here,
20 From which to reason, or to which refer?
Through worlds unnumbered though the God be known,
'Tis ours to trace him only in our own.
He, who through vast immensity can pierce,
See worlds on worlds compose one universe,
25 Observe how system into system runs,
What other planets circle other suns,
What varied being peoples every star,
May tell why Heaven has made us as we are.
But of this frame° the bearings, and the ties,   the universe
30 The strong connections, nice dependencies,
Gradations just, has thy pervading soul
Looked through? or can a part contain the whole?
    Is the great chain, that draws all to agree,
And drawn supports, upheld by God, or thee?[2]

35   2. Presumptuous man! the reason wouldst thou find,
Why formed so weak, so little, and so blind?
First, if thou canst, the harder reason guess,
Why formed no weaker, blinder, and no less!
Ask of thy mother earth, why oaks are made
40 Taller or stronger than the weeds they shade?
Or ask of yonder argent fields above,
Why Jove's satellites[3] are less than Jove?
    Of systems possible, if 'tis confessed
That Wisdom Infinite must form the best,
45 Where all must full or not coherent be,
And all that rises, rise in due degree;
Then, in the scale of reasoning life, 'tis plain,
There must be, somewhere, such a rank as man:
And all the question (wrangle e'er so long)
50 Is only this, if God has placed him wrong?
    Respecting man, whatever wrong we call,
May, must be right, as relative to all.
In human works, though labored on with pain,
A thousand movements scarce one purpose gain;
55 In God's, one single can its end produce;
Yet serves to second too some other use.
So man, who here seems principal alone,
Perhaps acts second to some sphere unknown,

2. For the chain of being, see Addison's *The Spectator* 519 (p. 483) and lines 207–58.

3. In his *Dictionary,* Johnson notes and condemns Pope's giving this word four syllables, as in Latin.

Touches some wheel, or verges to some goal;
60 'Tis but a part we see, and not a whole.
   When the proud steed shall know why man restrains
His fiery course, or drives him o'er the plains;
When the dull ox, why now he breaks the clod,
Is now a victim, and now Egypt's god:[4]
65 Then shall man's pride and dullness comprehend
His actions', passions', being's use and end;
Why doing, suffering, checked, impelled; and why
This hour a slave, the next a deity.
   Then say not man's imperfect, Heaven in fault;
70 Say rather, man's as perfect as he ought;
His knowledge measured to his state and place,
His time a moment, and a point his space.
If to be perfect in a certain sphere,[5]
What matter, soon or late, or here or there?
75 The blest today is as completely so,
As who began a thousand years ago.

   3. Heaven from all creatures hides the book of Fate,
All but the page prescribed, their present state:
From brutes what men, from men what spirits know:
80 Or who could suffer being here below?
The lamb thy riot° dooms to bleed today,   feast
Had he thy reason, would he skip and play?
Pleased to the last, he crops the flowery food,
And licks the hand just raised to shed his blood.
85 O blindness to the future! kindly given,
That each may fill the circle marked by Heaven:
Who sees with equal eye, as God of all,
A hero perish, or a sparrow fall,
Atoms or systems° into ruin hurled,   solar systems
90 And now a bubble burst, and now a world.
   Hope humbly then; with trembling pinions soar;
Wait the great teacher Death, and God adore!
What future bliss, he gives not thee to know,
But gives that hope to be thy blessing now.
95 Hope springs eternal in the human breast:
Man never is, but always to be blest:
The soul, uneasy and confined from home,
Rests and expatiates in a life to come.
   Lo! the poor Indian, whose untutored mind
100 Sees God in clouds, or hears him in the wind;
His soul proud Science never taught to stray
Far as the solar walk, or milky way;
Yet simple Nature to his hope has given,
Behind the cloud-topped hill, an humbler heaven;
105 Some safer world in depth of woods embraced,
Some happier island in the watery waste,
Where slaves once more their native land behold,

4. The Egyptians worshiped a bull called Apis.   5. I.e., in one's "state and place."

No fiends torment, no Christians thirst for gold!
To be, contents his natural desire,
110 He asks no angel's wing, no seraph's fire;
But thinks, admitted to that equal° sky,   *impartial*
His faithful dog shall bear him company.

4. Go, wiser thou! and, in thy scale of sense,
Weigh thy opinion against Providence;
115 Call imperfection what thou fancy'st such,
Say, here he gives too little, there too much;
Destroy all creatures for thy sport or gust,[6]
Yet cry, if man's unhappy, God's unjust;
If man alone engross not Heaven's high care,
120 Alone made perfect here, immortal there:
Snatch from his hand the balance and the rod,[7]
Rejudge his justice, be the God of God!
In pride, in reasoning pride, our error lies;
All quit their sphere, and rush into the skies.
125 Pride still is aiming at the blest abodes,
Men would be angels, angels would be gods.
Aspiring to be gods, if angels fell,
Aspiring to be angels, men rebel:
And who but wishes to invert the laws
130 Of order, sins against the Eternal Cause.

5. Ask for what end the heavenly bodies shine,
Earth for whose use? Pride answers, " 'Tis for mine:
For me kind Nature wakes her genial power,
Suckles each herb, and spreads out every flower;
135 Annual for me, the grape, the rose renew
The juice nectareous, and the balmy dew;
For me, the mine a thousand treasures brings;
For me, health gushes from a thousand springs;
Seas roll to waft me, suns to light me rise;
140 My footstool earth, my canopy the skies."
But errs not Nature from this gracious end,
From burning suns when livid deaths descend,
When earthquakes swallow, or when tempests sweep
Towns to one grave, whole nations to the deep?
145 "No," 'tis replied, "the first Almighty Cause
Acts not by partial, but by general laws;
The exceptions few; some change since all began,
And what created perfect?"—Why then man?
If the great end be human happiness,
150 Then Nature deviates; and can man do less?
As much that end a constant course requires
Of showers and sunshine, as of man's desires;
As much eternal springs and cloudless skies,
As men forever temperate, calm, and wise.
155 If plagues or earthquakes break not Heaven's design,

6. "Sense of tasting" (Johnson's *Dictionary*).   7. Symbols of judgment and punishment.

Why then a Borgia, or a Catiline?[8]
Who knows but he whose hand the lightning forms,
Who heaves old ocean, and who wings the storms,
Pours fierce ambition in a Caesar's mind,
160   Or turns young Ammon[9] loose to scourge mankind?
From pride, from pride, our very reasoning springs;
Account for moral, as for natural things:
Why charge we Heaven in those, in these acquit?
In both, to reason right is to submit.
165   Better for us, perhaps, it might appear,
Were there all harmony, all virtue here;
That never air or ocean felt the wind;
That never passion discomposed the mind:
But ALL subsists by elemental strife;
170   And passions are the elements of life.
The general ORDER, since the whole began,
Is kept in Nature, and is kept in man.

    6. What would this man? Now upward will he soar,
And little less than angel, would be more;
175   Now looking downwards, just as grieved appears
To want the strength of bulls, the fur of bears.
Made for his use all creatures if he call,
Say what their use, had he the powers of all?
Nature to these, without profusion, kind,
180   The proper organs, proper powers assigned;
Each seeming want compènsated of course,°   *as a matter of course*
Here with degrees of swiftness, there of force;
All in exact proportion to the state;
Nothing to add, and nothing to abate.
185   Each beast, each insect, happy in its own;
Is Heaven unkind to man, and man alone?
Shall he alone, whom rational we call,
Be pleased with nothing, if not blessed with all?
    The bliss of man (could pride that blessing find)
190   Is not to act or think beyond mankind;
No powers of body or of soul to share,
But what his nature and his state can bear.
Why has not man a microscopic eye?
For this plain reason, man is not a fly.
195   Say what the use, were finer optics given,
To inspect a mite, not comprehend the heaven?
Or touch, if tremblingly alive all o'er,
To smart and agonize at every pore?
Or quick effluvia[1] darting through the brain,

8. Lucius Sergius Catiline (ca. 108–62 B.C.E.), an ambitious, greedy, and cruel conspirator against the Roman state, was denounced in Cicero's famous orations before the senate and in the Forum. The Italian Renaissance family the Borgias was notorious for its ruthless lust for power, cruelty, rapaciousness, treachery, and murder (especially by poisoning). Cesare Borgia (1476–1507), son of Pope Alexander VI, is here referred to.
9. I.e., Alexander the Great.
1. According to the philosophy of Epicurus (adopted by Robert Boyle, the chemist, and other 17th-century scientists), the senses are stirred to perception by being bombarded through the pores by steady streams of "effluvia," incredibly thin

200 Die of a rose in aromatic pain?
  If nature thundered in his opening ears,
  And stunned him with the music of the spheres,
  How would he wish that Heaven had left him still
  The whispering zephyr, and the purling rill?
205 Who finds not Providence all good and wise,
  Alike in what it gives, and what denies?

   7. Far as creation's ample range extends,
  The scale of sensual,° mental powers ascends: *sensory*
  Mark how it mounts, to man's imperial race,
210 From the green myriads in the peopled grass:
  What modes of sight betwixt each wide extreme,
  The mole's dim curtain, and the lynx's beam:[2]
  Of smell, the headlong lioness between,
  And hound sagacious° on the tainted green: *quick of scent*
215 Of hearing, from the life that fills the flood,
  To that which warbles through the vernal wood:
  The spider's touch, how exquisitely fine!
  Feels at each thread, and lives along the line:
  In the nice° bee, what sense so subtly true   *exact, accurate*
220 From poisonous herbs extracts the healing dew:
  How instinct varies in the groveling swine,
  Compared, half-reasoning elephant, with thine!
  'Twixt that, and reason, what a nice barrier,[3]
  Forever separate, yet forever near!
225 Remembrance and reflection how allied;
  What thin partitions sense from thought divide:
  And middle natures, how they long to join,
  Yet never pass the insuperable line!
  Without this just gradation, could they be
230 Subjected, these to those, or all to thee?
  The powers of all subdued by thee alone,
  Is not thy reason all these powers in one?

   8. See, through this air, this ocean, and this earth,
  All matter quick, and bursting into birth.
235 Above, how high progressive life may go!
  Around, how wide! how deep extend below!
  Vast Chain of Being! which from God began,
  Natures ethereal, human, angel, man,
  Beast, bird, fish, insect, what no eye can see,
240 No glass can reach! from Infinite to thee,
  From thee to nothing.—On superior powers
  Were we to press, inferior might on ours:
  Or in the full creation leave a void,
  Where, one step broken, the great scale's destroyed:
245 From Nature's chain whatever link you strike,
  Tenth or ten thousandth, breaks the chain alike.

---

and tiny—but material—images of the objects
that surround us.
2. One of several early theories of vision held

that the eye casts a beam of light that makes
objects visible.
3. Pronounced *ba-réer*.

And, if each system in gradation roll
Alike essential to the amazing whole,
The least confusion but in one, not all
250 That system only, but the whole must fall.
Let earth unbalanced from her orbit fly,
Planets and suns run lawless through the sky,
Let ruling angels from their spheres be hurled,
Being on being wrecked, and world on world,
255 Heaven's whole foundations to their center nod,
And Nature tremble to the throne of God:
All this dread ORDER break—for whom? for thee?
Vile worm!—oh, madness, pride, impiety!

9. What if the foot, ordained the dust to tread,
260 Or hand, to toil, aspired to be the head?
What if the head, the eye, or ear repined
To serve mere engines to the ruling Mind?[4]
Just as absurd, for any part to claim
To be another, in this general frame.
265 Just as absurd, to mourn the tasks or pains,
The great directing MIND of ALL ordains.
All are but parts of one stupendous whole,
Whose body Nature is, and God the soul;
That, changed through all, and yet in all the same,
270 Great in the earth, as in the ethereal frame,
Warms in the sun, refreshes in the breeze,
Glows in the stars, and blossoms in the trees,
Lives through all life, extends through all extent,
Spreads undivided, operates unspent,
275 Breathes in our soul, informs our mortal part,
As full, as perfect, in a hair as heart;
As full, as perfect, in vile man that mourns,
As the rapt seraph that adores and burns;
To him no high, no low, no great, no small;
280 He fills, he bounds, connects, and equals all.

10. Cease then, nor ORDER imperfection name:
Our proper bliss depends on what we blame.
Know thy own point: this kind, this due degree
Of blindness, weakness, Heaven bestows on thee.
285 Submit—In this, or any other sphere,
Secure to be as blest as thou canst bear:
Safe in the hand of one disposing Power,
Or in the natal, or the mortal hour.
All Nature is but art, unknown to thee;
290 All chance, direction, which thou canst not see;
All discord, harmony not understood;
All partial evil, universal good:
And, spite of pride, in erring reason's spite,
One truth is clear: Whatever IS, is RIGHT.

4. Cf. 1 Corinthians 12.14–26.

From *Epistle 2. Of the Nature and State of Man with Respect to Himself, as an Individual*

1. Know then thyself, presume not God to scan;°   *judge*
The proper study of mankind is Man.
Placed on this isthmus of a middle state,
A being darkly wise, and rudely great:
5   With too much knowledge for the skeptic side,
With too much weakness for the Stoic's pride,
He hangs between; in doubt to act, or rest,
In doubt to deem himself a god, or beast;
In doubt his mind or body to prefer,
10 Born but to die, and reasoning but to err;
Alike in ignorance, his reason such,
Whether he thinks too little, or too much:
Chaos of thought and passion, all confused;
Still by himself abused, or disabused;
15 Created half to rise, and half to fall;
Great lord of all things, yet a prey to all;
Sole judge of truth, in endless error hurled:
The glory, jest, and riddle of the world!

*   *   *

1733

Epistle to Dr. Arbuthnot

Dr. John Arbuthnot (1667–1735), to whom Pope addressed his best-known verse epistle, was distinguished both as a physician and as a man of wit. He had been one of the liveliest members of the Martinus Scriblerus Club, helping his friends create the character and shape the career of the learned pedant whose memoirs the club had undertaken to write.

Pope had long been meditating such a poem, which was to be both an attack on his detractors and a defense of his own character and career. In his usual way, he had jotted down hints, lines, couplets, and fragments over a period of two decades, but the poem might never have been completed had it not been for two events: Arbuthnot, from his deathbed, wrote to urge Pope to continue his abhorrence of vice and to express it in his writings and, during 1733, Pope was the victim of two bitter attacks by "persons of rank and fortune," as the Advertisement has it. The "Verses Addressed to the Imitator of Horace" was the work of Lady Mary Wortley Montagu, helped by her friend Lord Hervey (pronounced *Harvey*), a close friend and confidant of Queen Caroline. "An Epistle to a Doctor of Divinity from a Nobleman at Hampton Court" was the work of Lord Hervey alone. Montagu had provocation enough, especially in Pope's recent reference to her in "The First Satire of the Second Book of Horace," lines 83–84; but Hervey had little to complain of beyond occasional covert references to him as "Lord Fanny." At any rate, the two scurrilous attacks goaded Pope into action, and he completed the poem by the end of the summer of 1734.

The *Epistle* is the most brilliant and daring execution of the techniques that Pope used in many of the autobiographical poems of the 1730s. He presents himself in a theatrical array of postures: the comically exaggerating complainer, the admired man of genius, the true friend, the unpretentiously honest man, the satirist-hero of his country, the "manly" defender of virtue, the tender son mothering his own mother. Part of what cements this mixture is the verve with which he modulates from role to role, implying that none of them exhaustively defines him. Pope tries to force the reader to take sides, for him and what he claims to represent, or against him. Thus reading becomes an ethical exercise; readers must make up their own minds about his moral superiority, his exquisitely crafted portraits of his enemies, his social self-positioning, or his self-righteous politics. Pope solicits our judgment of his character and his professed ideals, and no other poet in English does so with so much artistic energy, resourcefulness, and success.

It is not clear that Pope intended the poem to be thought of as a dialogue, as it has usually been printed since Warburton's edition of 1751. The original edition, while suggesting interruptions in the flow of the monologue, kept entirely to the form of a letter. The introduction of the friend, who speaks from time to time, converts the original letter into a dramatic dialogue.

Epistle to Dr. Arbuthnot

Advertisement

TO THE FIRST PUBLICATION OF THIS *Epistle*

This paper is a sort of bill of complaint, begun many years since, and drawn up by snatches, as the several occasions offered. I had no thoughts of publishing it, till it pleased some persons of rank and fortune (the authors of *Verses to the Imitator of Horace*, and of an *Epistle to a Doctor of Divinity from a Nobleman at Hampton Court*) to attack, in a very extraordinary manner, not only my writings (of which, being public, the public is judge) but my person, morals, and family, whereof, to those who know me not, a truer information may be requisite. Being divided between the necessity to say something of myself, and my own laziness to undertake so awkward a task, I thought it the shortest way to put the last hand to[1] this epistle. If it have anything pleasing, it will be that by which I am most desirous to please, the truth and the sentiment; and if anything offensive, it will be only to those I am least sorry to offend, the vicious or the ungenerous.

Many will know their own pictures in it, there being not a circumstance but what is true; but I have, for the most part, spared their names, and they may escape being laughed at, if they please.

I would have some of them know, it was owing to the request of the learned and candid friend to whom it is inscribed, that I make not as free use of theirs as they have done of mine. However, I shall have this advantage, and honor, on my side, that whereas, by their proceeding, any abuse may be directed at any man, no injury can possibly be done by mine, since a nameless character can never be found out, but by its truth and likeness. P.

    P. Shut, shut the door, good John![2] (fatigued, I said),
    Tie up the knocker, say I'm sick, I'm dead.
    The Dog Star[3] rages! nay 'tis past a doubt
    All Bedlam,[4] or Parnassus, is let out:
5 Fire in each eye, and papers in each hand,

---

1. Finish.
2. John Serle, Pope's gardener.
3. Sirius, associated with the period of greatest heat (and hence of madness) because it sets with

the sun in late summer. August, in ancient Rome, was the season for reciting poetry.
4. Bethlehem Hospital for the insane, in London.

They rave, recite, and madden round the land.
   What walls can guard me, or what shades can hide?
They pierce my thickets, through my grot[5] they glide,
By land, by water, they renew the charge,
10 They stop the chariot, and they board the barge.
No place is sacred, not the church is free;
Even Sunday shines no Sabbath day to me:
Then from the Mint[6] walks forth the man of rhyme,
Happy! to catch me just at dinner time.
15   Is there a parson, much bemused in beer,
A maudlin poetess, a rhyming peer,
A clerk foredoomed his father's soul to cross,
Who pens a stanza when he should engross?[7]
Is there who, locked from ink and paper,[8] scrawls
20 With desperate charcoal round his darkened walls?
All fly to Twit'nam,[9] and in humble strain
Apply to me to keep them mad or vain.
Arthur,[1] whose giddy son neglects the laws,
Imputes to me and my damned works the cause:
25 Poor Cornus[2] sees his frantic wife elope,
And curses wit, and poetry, and Pope.
   Friend to my life (which did not you prolong,
The world had wanted° many an idle song)   *missed*
What drop or nostrum° can this plague remove?   *medicine*
30 Or which must end me, a fool's wrath or love?
A dire dilemma! either way I'm sped,°   *killed*
If foes, they write, if friends, they read me dead.
Seized and tied down to judge, how wretched I!
Who can't be silent, and who will not lie.
35 To laugh were want of goodness and of grace,
And to be grave exceeds all power of face.
I sit with sad civility, I read
With honest anguish and an aching head,
And drop at last, but in unwilling ears,
40 This saving counsel, "Keep your piece nine years."[3]
   "Nine years!" cries he, who high in Drury Lane,[4]
Lulled by soft zephyrs through the broken pane,
Rhymes ere he wakes, and prints before term[5] ends,
Obliged by hunger and request of friends:
45 "The piece, you think, is incorrect? why, take it,
I'm all submission, what you'd have it, make it."
   Three things another's modest wishes bound,

---

5. The subterranean passage under the road that separated his house at Twickenham from his garden became, in Pope's hands, a romantic grotto ornamented with shells and mirrors.
6. A place in Southwark where debtors were free from arrest (they could not be arrested anywhere on Sundays)..
7. Write out legal documents.
8. Is there some madman who, locked up without ink or paper . . . ?
9. I.e., Twickenham, Pope's villa on the bank of the Thames; a few miles above Hampton Court.
1. Arthur Moore, whose son, James Moore

Smythe, dabbled in literature. Moore Smythe had earned Pope's enmity by using in one of his plays some unpublished lines from Pope's "Epistle 2. To a Lady" in spite of Pope's objections.
2. Latin for "horn," the traditional emblem of the cuckold.
3. The advice of Horace in *Art of Poetry* (line 388).
4. I.e., living in a garret in Drury Lane, site of one of the theaters and the haunt of the profligate.
5. One of the four annual periods in which the law courts are in session and with which the publishing season coincided.

My friendship, and a prologue,[6] and ten pound.
    Pitholeon[7] sends to me: "You know his Grace,
50 I want a patron; ask him for a place."
Pitholeon libeled me—"but here's a letter
Informs you, sir, 'twas when he knew no better.
Dare you refuse him? Curll[8] invites to dine,
He'll write a *Journal*, or he'll turn divine."[9]
55 Bless me! a packet.—"'Tis a stranger sues,°   *asks for help*
A virgin tragedy, an orphan Muse."
If I dislike it, "Furies, death, and rage!"
If I approve, "Commend it to the stage."
There (thank my stars) my whole commission ends,
60 The players and I are, luckily, no friends.
Fired that the house° reject him, "'Sdeath, I'll print it, *playhouse*
And shame the fools—Your interest, sir, with Lintot!"[1]
Lintot, dull rogue, will think your price too much.
"Not, sir, if you revise it, and retouch."
65 All my demurs but double his attacks;
At last he whispers, "Do; and we go snacks."°   *shares*
Glad of a quarrel, straight I clap the door,
"Sir, let me see your works and you no more."
    'Tis sung, when Midas' ears began to spring
70 (Midas, a sacred person and a king),
His very minister who spied them first,
(Some say his queen) was forced to speak, or burst.[2]
And is not mine, my friend, a sorer case,
When every coxcomb perks them in my face?
75   A. Good friend, forbear! you deal in dangerous things.
I'd never name queens, ministers, or kings;
Keep close to ears,° and those let asses prick;   *whisper*
'Tis nothing——P. Nothing? if they bite and kick?
Out with it, *Dunciad*! let the secret pass,
80 That secret to each fool, that he's an ass:
The truth once told (and wherefore should we lie?)
The queen of Midas slept, and so may I.
    You think this cruel? take it for a rule,
No creature smarts so little as a fool.
85 Let peals of laughter, Codrus![3] round thee break,
Thou unconcerned canst hear the mighty crack.
Pit, box, and gallery in convulsions hurled,
Thou stand'st unshook amidst a bursting world.
Who shames a scribbler? break one cobweb through,

---

6. Famous poets helped playwrights by contributing prologues to their plays.
7. "A foolish poet of Rhodes, who pretended much to Greek" [Pope's note]. He is Leonard Welsted, who translated Longinus and had attacked and slandered Pope (see line 375).
8. Edmund Curll, shrewd and disreputable bookseller, published pirated works, works falsely ascribed to reputable writers, scandalous biographies, and other ephemera. Pope had often attacked him and had assigned him a low role in *The Dunciad*.
9. I.e., he will attack Pope in the *London Journal*

or write a treatise on theology, as Welsted in fact did.
1. Bernard Lintot, publisher of Pope's Homer and other early works.
2. Midas, king of ancient Lydia, had the bad taste to prefer the flute-playing of Pan to that of Apollo, whereupon the god endowed him with ass's ears. It was his barber (not his wife or his minister) who discovered the secret and whispered it into a hole in the earth. The reference to "queen" and "minister" makes it plain that Pope is alluding to George II, Queen Caroline, and Walpole.
3. Poet ridiculed by Virgil and Juvenal.

90 He spins the slight, self-pleasing thread anew:
Destroy his fib or sophistry, in vain;
The creature's at his dirty work again,
Throned in the center of his thin designs,
Proud of a vast extent of flimsy lines.
95 Whom have I hurt? has poet yet or peer
Lost the arched eyebrow or Parnassian sneer?
And has not Colley[4] still his lord and whore?
His butchers Henley?[5] his freemasons Moore?
Does not one table Bavius still admit?
100 Still to one bishop Philips[6] seem a wit?
Still Sappho[7]——A. Hold! for god's sake—you'll offend.
No names—be calm—learn prudence of a friend.
I too could write, and I am twice as tall;
But foes like these!——P. One flatterer's worse than all.
105 Of all mad creatures, if the learn'd are right,
It is the slaver kills, and not the bite.
A fool quite angry is quite innocent:
Alas! 'tis ten times worse when they repent.

One dedicates in high heroic prose,
110 And ridicules beyond a hundred foes;
One from all Grub Street[8] will my fame defend,
And, more abusive, calls himself my friend.
This prints my letters,[9] that expects a bribe,
And others roar aloud, "Subscribe, subscribe!"[1]
115 There are, who to my person pay their court:
I cough like Horace,[2] and, though lean, am short;
Ammon's great son[3] one shoulder had too high,
Such Ovid's nose,[4] and "Sir! you have an eye—"
Go on, obliging creatures, make me see
120 All that disgraced my betters met in me.
Say for my comfort, languishing in bed,
"Just so immortal Maro° held his head":   Virgil
And when I die, be sure you let me know
Great Homer died three thousand years ago.

125 Why did I write? what sin to me unknown
Dipped me in ink, my parents', or my own?
As yet a child, nor yet a fool to fame,
I lisped in numbers,° for the numbers came.   verses

4. Colley Cibber, the poet laureate.
5. John Henley, known as "Orator" Henley, an independent preacher of marked eccentricity, was popular among the common people, especially for his elocution.
6. The "bishop" is Hugh Boulter, bishop of Armagh. He had employed as his secretary Ambrose Philips (1674–1749), whose insipid simplicity of manner in poetry earned him the nickname of "Namby-Pamby." Bavius, the bad poet alluded to in Virgil's *Eclogue* 3.
7. Lady Mary Wortley Montagu.
8. A term denoting the whole society of literary, political, and journalistic hack writers.
9. In 1726 Curll had surreptitiously acquired and published without permission some of Pope's letters to Henry Cromwell.
1. To ensure the financial success of a work, wealthy readers were often asked to "subscribe" to it before printing was undertaken. Pope's Homer was published in this manner.
2. Horace, who mentions a cough in a few poems, was plump and short.
3. Alexander the Great, whose head inclined to his left shoulder, resembling Pope's hunchback.
4. Ovid's family name, Naso, suggests the Latin word *nasus* ("nose"), hence the pun.

The Restoration and the Eighteenth Century (1660–1785)

Landscape with Apollo and the Muses, Claude Lorrain, 1652

Claude's poetic landscapes inspired many British landscape gardens. In this painting, a river god sprawls by the Castalian spring under Mount Parnassus; the white swans are sacred to Apollo. On the terrace to the left, Apollo plays his lyre, surrounded by the nine Muses, while four poets approach through the woods. At the upper left, below a temple, the fountain of Hippocrene pours forth its inspiring waters. The dreamlike distance of the figures in this mysterious, luminous scene is intended to draw the viewer in. Similarly, in landscape gardens visitors were invited to stroll amid temples, inscriptions, swans, and statues, gradually comprehending the master plan.

Great Fire of London,
Dutch school, 1666

The fire of London, described by Dryden in *Annus Mirabilis* and by Pepys in his diary, destroyed most of the central city. In the foreground of this panorama, huddled refugees carry their goods away from the city. Under a pall of smoke across the Thames, St. Paul's Cathedral blazes in the center, with London Bridge on the far left and the Tower on the far right. The fire raged for four days, after which a new city eventually rose from the ashes.

Embarkment for Cythera,
Jean Antoine Watteau, 1717

Cythera is one of the names of Venus, and in this painting elegant pilgrims visit an island of love to pay homage to Venus (whose statue is on the far right). Paired off, these lovers pass through a romantic, erotic dream-scape, related to the visionary landscape of Pope's *Eloisa to Abelard* (lines 155 ff., p. 530). A ship of love waits on the left to carry the couples away. Are they going or coming to Cythera? In the grip of love, is the prevailing mood one of joy and anticipation, or of melancholy and surfeit? Critics differ; this painting does not reveal all its secrets.

Bristol Docks and Quay, anonymous, early eighteenth century

Bristol, in southwest England, profited enormously from the expansion of the slave trade. From this port, merchants sent trinkets, guns, and rum to West Africa in exchange for slaves, who were transported to North America and the West Indies in exchange for money and sugar. This painting shows a bustling metropolis whose trade makes possible the busy shops the right and the great houses in the backgrou▮

Gulliver Taking Leave of the Houyhnhnms, Sawrey Gilpin, 1769

In part 4 of *Gulliver's Travels* (pp. 407 ff.), Swift cleverly makes use of the eighteenth-century British love of horses. Gulliver's infatuation with the dignity and nobility of the Houyhnhnms reflects the feelings of many hunters mounted for the chase or of gentlefolk promenading in the park; some preferred horses to human beings. Commercially, "horse painters" found eager and wealthy buyers, while Sawrey Gilpin tried to elevate horse painting by placing his horses against rich landscapes and in historical settings.

The Beggar's Opera, act 3, scene 11, William Hogarth, 1729

The highwayman Macheath, in leg irons, stands at the center, flanked by the women between whom he cannot choose. To the left, Lucy kneels before the jailer Lockit; to the right, Polly kneels before her father, Peachum. In the rear, a group of prisoners waits for its cue. But the setting is not so much a prison as the theater; spectators are seated on each side of the stage. Hogarth connects the audience with the actors just as *The Beggar's Opera* does, suggesting corruption "through all the employments of life." Behind Peachum, John Gay confers with his producer, John Rich. Below them, seated at the far right, the duke of Bolton (note his Star of the Garter) exchanges a rapt gaze with Polly; a satyr points down at him. On opening night, the duke fell in love with the actor who played Polly, Lavinia Fenton. He returned every night, until she became his mistress—and, two decades later, his wife.

Garrick between Tragedy and Comedy, Joshua Reynolds, 1762

Sir Joshua Reynolds specialized in portraits that characterized his subject by alluding to classical literature and art. Here, the great actor David Garrick is torn between Comedy, on the left, and Tragedy, on the right. The picture parodies a well-known image, *Hercules between Virtue and Pleasure,* and alludes to Guido Reni (Tragedy) and Correggio (Comedy). Exalted Tragedy urges Garrick to follow her, but darling Comedy drags him away

A Philosopher Giving That Lecture on the Orrery, in Which a Lamp Is Put in Place of the Sun, Joseph Wright, 1766

Joseph Wright came from the English Midlands, where an intense interest in science helped spark the industrial revolution. The orrery, a mechanism that represents the movements of the planets around the sun, was one of many devices that taught the public to appreciate the wonders and pleasures of science. In this picture, the philosopher at the center bears a striking resemblance to portraits of Sir Isaac Newton, who had cast light on the solar system. Wright specialized in "candlelight pictures." Strong effects of light and shade play over the faces around the lamp, as if to reflect the literal meaning of enlightenment.

The Death of General Wolfe, Benjamin West, 1771

History painting—pictures that represent a famous legend or historical event—was the most prestigious genre of eighteenth-century art. West's painting of Wolfe, who fell on the day that he captured Quebec, revolutionized the genre by dressing the figures in contemporary clothes, not classical togas. Twelve years after his death, Wolfe had become an icon; the composition draws on images of mourners around the dead Christ. The poetic shading is also appropriate to Wolfe. The night before he died, he is supposed to have said of Gray's "Elegy" (p. 998) that he "would rather have been the author of that piece than beat the French tomorrow"; and in his copy of the poem, he marked one passage: "The paths of glory lead but to the grave."

The Parting of Abelard from Heloise, Angelika Kauffmann, ca. 1778

Angelika Kauffmann, born in Switzerland in 1741, was a child prodigy; at eleven she made a name in Italy for her portraits. From 1766 to 1781 she lived in England, where she was admired both as a singer and as a painter. During the eighteenth century the affair of Abelard and Heloise, which Pope depicted as a struggle between God and Eros, softened into a sentimental love story. Rousseau's novel *The New Heloise* (1761) helped transform the heroine into a saint of love. In an Age of Sensibility, Kauffmann portrays a youthful and feminized Abelard, not a wounded middle-aged scholar, and pathos, not repentance, marks this tender parting.

The Cottage Door, Thomas Gainsborough (ca. 1780)

The great British portraitist and landscape painter Thomas Gainsborough (1727–1788) composed many versions of this scene of a peasant family outside a rustic dwelling in the countryside, which came to be called *The Cottage Door*. In the second half of the eighteenth century, artists and writers confronted the lives of the rural poor, with increasing vividness and varying degrees of idealization, from Thomas Gray's deeply pondered musings on the poor's deprivations and uncorrupted purity of life in "Elegy Written in a Country Churchyard" (1751), to Oliver Goldsmith's *The Deserted Village* (1770), which mourns the depopulation and loss of innocence of the countryside, to *The Village* (1783) by George Crabbe, which takes a harder view of the difficulties of rural life. Gainsborough's painting is suffused with "sensibility," as it tenderly and dramatically presents motherhood and innocent children in a glowing group, surrounded by darker, expressive, wild natural forms.

Illustration for Gray's "Ode on the Death of a Favourite Cat," William Blake, 1798

In 1797, as a birthday gift for his wife, Nancy, the sculptor John Flaxman commissioned Blake to illustrate Gray's poems. These designs, in pen and watercolor, view the art of Gray through Blake's own vision. The charm of Gray's ode depends on picturing Selima both as a cat who tumbles for goldfish and as a "nymph" or "maid" who falls for gold. Blake mixes the two together in a cat and turns the goldfish (or "genii of the stream") into fleeing, finny human forms. Meanwhile, a lurking Fate cuts the thread of Selima's life, reminding us, in this interpretation of Gray, that perverted desires can be deadly.

I left no calling for this idle trade,
130 No duty broke, no father disobeyed.
The Muse but served to ease some friend, not wife,
To help me through this long disease, my life,
To second, Arbuthnot! thy art and care,
And teach the being you preserved, to bear.°   *endure*
135   A. But why then publish? P. Granville the polite,
And knowing Walsh, would tell me I could write;
Well-natured Garth inflamed with early praise,
And Congreve loved, and Swift endured my lays;
The courtly Talbot, Somers, Sheffield, read;
140 Even mitered Rochester would nod the head,
And St. John's self (great Dryden's friends before)
With open arms received one poet more.[5]
Happy my studies, when by these approved!
Happier their author, when by these beloved!
145 From these the world will judge of men and books,
Not from the Burnets, Oldmixons, and Cookes.[6]
    Soft were my numbers; who could take offense
While pure description held the place of sense?
Like gentle Fanny's[7] was my flowery theme,
150 A painted mistress, or a purling stream.
Yet then did Gildon draw his venal quill;[8]
I wished the man a dinner, and sat still.
Yet then did Dennis[9] rave in furious fret;
I never answered, I was not in debt.
155 If want provoked, or madness made them print,
I waged no war with Bedlam or the Mint.
    Did some more sober critic come abroad?
If wrong, I smiled; if right, I kissed the rod.
Pains, reading, study are their just pretense,
160 And all they want is spirit, taste, and sense.
Commas and points they set exactly right,
And 'twere a sin to rob them of their mite.
Yet ne'er one sprig of laurel graced these ribalds,
From slashing Bentley down to piddling Tibbalds.[1]
165 Each wight who reads not, and but scans and spells,
Each word-catcher that lives on syllables,
Even such small critics some regard may claim,

5. The purpose of this list is to establish Pope as the successor of Dryden and thus to place him far above his Grub Street persecutors. George Granville, Lord Lansdowne, poet, and statesman. William Walsh, poet and critic. Sir Samuel Garth, physician and mock-epic poet. William Congreve, the playwright. Charles Talbot, duke of Shrewsbury, Lord Sommers. John Sheffield, duke of Buckinghamshire. Francis Atterbury, bishop of Rochester, statesman. All had been associated with Dryden in his later years and all had encouraged the young Pope.
6. Thomas Burnet, John Oldmixon, and Thomas Cooke: Pope identifies them in a note as "authors of secret and scandalous history."
7. John, Lord Hervey, whom Pope satirizes in the character of Sporus (lines 305–33).

8. Charles Gildon, minor critic and scribbler, who, Pope believed, early attacked him at the instigation of Addison; hence "venal quill."
9. John Dennis (see *An Essay on Criticism*, p. 503, n. 6).
1. Lewis Theobald (1688–1744), whose minute learning in Elizabethan literature had enabled him to expose Pope's defects as an editor of Shakespeare in 1726. Pope made him king of the Dunces in *The Dunciad* of 1728. Richard Bentley (1662–1742), the eminent classical scholar, seemed to both Pope and Swift the perfect type of the pedant: he is called "slashing" because, in his edition of *Paradise Lost* (1732), he had set in square brackets all passages that he disliked on the grounds that they had been slipped into the poem without the blind poet's knowledge.

Preserved in Milton's or in Shakespeare's name.
Pretty! in amber to observe the forms
170 Of hairs, or straws, or dirt, or grubs, or worms!
The things, we know, are neither rich nor rare,
But wonder how the devil they got there.
    Were others angry? I excused them too;
Well might they rage; I gave them but their due.
175 A man's true merit 'tis not hard to find;
But each man's secret standard in his mind,
That casting weight[2] pride adds to emptiness,
This, who can gratify? for who can guess?
The bard[3] whom pilfered pastorals renown,
180 Who turns a Persian tale for half a crown,
Just writes to make his barrenness appear,
And strains from hard-bound brains eight lines a year:
He, who still wanting, though he lives on theft,
Steals much, spends little, yet has nothing left;
185 And he who now to sense, now nonsense leaning,
Means not, but blunders round about a meaning:
And he whose fustian's so sublimely bad,
It is not poetry, but prose run mad:
All these, my modest satire bade translate,
190 And owned that nine such poets made a Tate.[4]
How did they fume, and stamp, and roar, and chafe!
And swear, not Addison himself was safe.
    Peace to all such! but were there one whose fires
True Genius kindles, and fair Fame inspires;
195 Blessed with each talent and each art to please,
And born to write, converse, and live with ease:
Should such a man, too fond to rule alone,
Bear, like the Turk, no brother near the throne;[5]
View him with scornful, yet with jealous eyes,
200 And hate for arts that caused himself to rise;
Damn with faint praise, assent with civil leer,
And without sneering, teach the rest to sneer;
Willing to wound, and yet afraid to strike,
Just hint a fault, and hesitate dislike;
205 Alike reserved to blame or to commend,
A timorous foe, and a suspicious friend;
Dreading even fools; by flatterers besieged,
And so obliging that he ne'er obliged;
Like Cato, give his little senate[6] laws,
210 And sit attentive to his own applause;

2. The weight that turns the scale; here, the "deciding factor."
3. Philips, Pope's rival in pastoral poetry in 1709, when their pastorals were published in Tonson's 6th *Miscellany*. Philips had also translated some Persian tales (see line 100 and p. 546, n. 6).
4. Nahum Tate, poet laureate from 1692 to 1715. His popular rewriting of Shakespeare's *King Lear* provided a happy ending; he wrote most of part 2 of *Absalom and Achitophel*. The line refers to the old adage that it takes nine tailors to make one man.

5. Turkish monarchs proverbially killed off their nearest rivals.
6. Addison's tragedy *Cato* had been a sensational success in 1713. Pope had written the prologue, in which occurs the line, "While Cato gives his little senate laws." The satirical reference here is to Addison in the role of arbiter of taste among his friends and admirers, mostly Whigs, at Button's Coffee House. This group worked against the success of Pope's Homer.

While wits and Templars° every sentence raise,   *law students*
And wonder with a foolish face of praise—
Who but must laugh, if such a man there be?
Who would not weep, if Atticus[7] were he?
215   What though my name stood rubric° on the walls   *in red letters*
Or plastered posts, with claps,° in capitals?   *posters*
Or smoking forth, a hundred hawkers' load,
On wings of winds came flying all abroad?
I sought no homage from the race that write;
220   I kept, like Asian monarchs, from their sight:
Poems I heeded (now berhymed so long)
No more than thou, great George! a birthday song.
I ne'er with wits or witlings passed my days
To spread about the itch of verse and praise;
225   Nor like a puppy daggled through the town
To fetch and carry sing-song up and down;
Nor at rehearsals sweat, and mouthed, and cried,
With handkerchief and orange at my side;
But sick of fops, and poetry, and prate,
230   To Bufo left the whole Castalian[8] state.
    Proud as Apollo on his forkèd hill,[9]
Sat full-blown Bufo, puffed° by every quill;°   *flattered / pen*
Fed with soft dedication all day long,
Horace and he went hand in hand in song.
235   His library (where busts of poets dead
And a true Pindar stood without a head)
Received of wits an undistinguished race,
Who first his judgment asked, and then a place:
Much they extolled his pictures, much his seat,[1]
240   And flattered every day, and some days eat:
Till grown more frugal in his riper days,
He paid some bards with port, and some with praise;
To some a dry rehearsal was assigned,
And others (harder still) he paid in kind.
245   Dryden alone (what wonder?) came not nigh;
Dryden alone escaped this judging eye:
But still the great have kindness in reserve;
He helped to bury whom he helped to starve.
    May some choice patron bless each gray goose quill!
250   May every Bavius have his Bufo still!
So when a statesman wants a day's defense,
Or envy holds a whole week's war with sense,
Or simple pride for flattery makes demands,
May dunce by dunce be whistled off my hands!
255   Blessed be the great! for those they take away,
And those they left me—for they left me Gay;[2]

7. Pope's satiric pseudonym for Addison. Atticus (109–32 B.C.E.), a wealthy man of letters and a friend of Cicero, was known as wise and disinterested.
8. The Castalian spring on Mount Parnassus was sacred to Apollo and the Muses. "Bufo": a type of tasteless patron of the arts. (*Bufo* means "toad" in Latin.)
9. Mount Parnassus had two peaks, one sacred to Apollo, one to Bacchus.
1. Estate. Pronounced *sate* and rhymed in next line with "eat" (*ate*).
2. John Gay (1685–1732), author of *The Beggar's Opera*, dear friend of Swift and Pope. His failure

Left me to see neglected genius bloom,
Neglected die, and tell it on his tomb;
Of all thy blameless life the sole return
260 My verse, and Queensberry weeping o'er thy urn!
Oh, let me live my own, and die so too!
("To live and die is all I have to do")[3]
Maintain a poet's dignity and ease,
And see what friends, and read what books I please;
265 Above a patron, though I condescend
Sometimes to call a minister my friend.
I was not born for courts or great affairs;
I pay my debts, believe, and say my prayers,
Can sleep without a poem in my head,
270 Nor know if Dennis be alive or dead.
　　Why am I asked what next shall see the light?
Heavens! was I born for nothing but to write?
Has life no joys for me? or (to be grave)
Have I no friend to serve, no soul to save?
275 "I found him close with Swift"—"Indeed? no doubt"
Cries prating Balbus,[4] "something will come out."
'Tis all in vain, deny it as I will.
"No, such a genius never can lie still,"
And then for mine obligingly mistakes
280 The first lampoon Sir Will or Bubo[5] makes.
Poor guiltless I! and can I choose but smile,
When every coxcomb knows me by my style?
　　Cursed be the verse, how well soe'er it flow,
That tends to make one worthy man my foe,
285 Give virtue scandal, innocence a fear,
Or from the soft-eyed virgin steal a tear!
But he who hurts a harmless neighbor's peace,
Insults fallen worth, or beauty in distress,
Who loves a lie, lame slander helps about,
290 Who writes a libel, or who copies out:
That fop whose pride affects a patron's name,
Yet absent, wounds an author's honest fame;
Who can your merit selfishly approve,
And show the sense of it without the love;
295 Who has the vanity to call you friend,
Yet wants the honor, injured, to defend;
Who tells whate'er you think, whate'er you say,
And, if he lie not, must at least betray:
Who to the dean and silver bell can swear,
300 And sees at Cannons what was never there:[6]

---

to obtain patronage from the court intensified
Pope's hostility to the Whig administration and
the queen. Gay spent the last years of his life
under the protection of the duke and duchess of
Queensberry. Pope wrote his epitaph.
3. A quotation from John Denham's poem "Of
Prudence."
4. Latin for *stammering*.
5. George Bubb ("Bubo") Dodington, a Whig

patron of letters. Sir William Yonge, Whig politician and poetaster.
6. Pope's enemies had accused him of satirizing
Cannons, the ostentatious estate of the duke of
Chandos, in his description of Timon's villa in
the *Epistle to Burlington*. This Pope quite justly
denied. The bell of Timon's chapel was of silver,
and there preached a dean who "never mentions
Hell to ears polite."

Who reads but with a lust to misapply,
Make satire a lampoon, and fiction, lie:
A lash like mine no honest man shall dread,
But all such babbling blockheads in his stead.

305   Let Sporus[7] tremble——A. What? that thing of silk,
Sporus, that mere white curd of ass's milk?[8]
Satire or sense, alas! can Sporus feel?
Who breaks a butterfly upon a wheel?
    P. Yet let me flap this bug with gilded wings,

310   This painted child of dirt, that stinks and stings;
Whose buzz the witty and the fair annoys,
Yet wit ne'er tastes, and beauty ne'er enjoys;
So well-bred spaniels civilly delight
In mumbling of the game they dare not bite.

315   Eternal smiles his emptiness betray,
As shallow streams run dimpling all the way.
Whether in florid impotence he speaks,
And, as the prompter breathes, the puppet squeaks;
Or at the ear of Eve,[9] familiar toad,

320   Half froth, half venom, spits himself abroad,
In puns, or politics, or tales, or lies,
Or spite, or smut, or rhymes, or blasphemies.
His wit all seesaw between *that* and *this*,
Now high, now low, now master up, now miss,

325   And he himself one vile antithesis.
Amphibious thing! that acting either part,
The trifling head or the corrupted heart,
Fop at the toilet, flatterer at the board,
Now trips a lady, and now struts a lord.

330   Eve's tempter thus the rabbins[1] have expressed,
A cherub's face, a reptile all the rest;
Beauty that shocks you, parts that none will trust,
Wit that can creep, and pride that licks the dust.
    Not fortune's worshiper, nor fashion's fool,

335   Not lucre's madman, nor ambition's tool,
Not proud, nor servile, be one poet's praise,
That if he pleased, he pleased by manly ways:
That flattery, even to kings, he held a shame,
And thought a lie in verse or prose the same:

340   That not in fancy's maze he wandered long,
But stooped[2] to truth, and moralized his song:
That not for fame, but virtue's better end,
He stood the furious foe, the timid friend,
The damning critic, half approving wit,

345   The coxcomb hit, or fearing to be hit;

---

7. John, Lord Hervey, effeminate courtier and confidant of Queen Caroline (see headnote, p. 542). The original Sporus was a boy, whom the emperor Nero publicly married (see Suetonius's life of Nero in *The Twelve Caesars*).
8. Drunk by invalids.
9. The queen; the allusion is to *Paradise Lost* (4.799–809).
1. Scholars of and authorities on Jewish law and doctrine.
2. The falcon is said to "stoop" to its prey when it swoops down and seizes it in flight.

Laughed at the loss of friends he never had,
The dull, the proud, the wicked, and the mad;
The distant threats of vengeance on his head,
The blow unfelt, the tear he never shed;
350 The tale revived, the lie so oft o'erthrown,
The imputed trash, and dullness not his own;
The morals blackened when the writings 'scape,
The libeled person, and the pictured shape;[3]
Abuse on all he loved, or loved him, spread,
355 A friend in exile, or a father dead;
The whisper, that to greatness still too near,
Perhaps yet vibrates on his Sovereign's ear—
Welcome for thee, fair virtue! all the past:
For thee, fair virtue! welcome even the last!
360 A. But why insult the poor, affront the great?
P. A knave's a knave to me in every state:
Alike my scorn, if he succeed or fail,
Sporus at court, or Japhet[4] in a jail,
A hireling scribbler, or a hireling peer,
365 Knight of the post[5] corrupt, or of the shire,
If on a pillory, or near a throne,
He gain his prince's ear, or lose his own.[6]
    Yet soft by nature, more a dupe than wit,
Sappho° can tell you how this man was bit:°   *Montagu / deceived*
370 This dreaded satirist Dennis will confess
Foe to his pride, but friend to his distress:[7]
So humble, he has knocked at Tibbald's door,
Has drunk with Cibber, nay, has rhymed for Moore.
Full ten years slandered, did he once reply?
375 Three thousand suns went down on Welsted's lie.[8]
To please a mistress one aspersed his life;
He lashed him not, but let her be his wife.
Let Budgell charge low Grub Street on his quill,
And write whate'er he pleased, except his will;[9]
380 Let the two Curlls of town and court,[1] abuse
His father, mother, body, soul, and muse.
Yet why? that father held it for a rule,
It was a sin to call our neighbor fool;
That harmless mother thought no wife a whore:
385 Hear this, and spare his family, James Moore!
Unspotted names, and memorable long,
If there be force in virtue, or in song.

---

3. Pope's deformity was frequently ridiculed and occasionally caricatured.
4. Japhet Crook, a notorious forger.
5. One who lives by selling false evidence.
6. Those punished in the pillory often also had their ears cropped.
7. Pope wrote the prologue to Cibber's *Provoked Husband* (1728) when that play was performed for Dennis's benefit, shortly before the old critic died.

8. "This man had the impudence to tell in print that Mr. P. had occasioned a Lady's death, and to name a person he had never heard of" [Pope's note].
9. Eustace Budgell attacked the *Grub Street Journal* for publishing what he took to be a squib by Pope charging him with having forged the will of Dr. Matthew Tindal.
1. I.e., the publisher and Lord Hervey.

Of gentle blood (part shed in honor's cause,
While yet in Britain honor had applause)
390 Each parent sprung——A. What fortune, pray?——P. Their own,
And better got than Bestia's[2] from the throne.
Born to no pride, inheriting no strife,
Nor marrying discord in a noble wife,
Stranger to civil and religious rage,
395 The good man walked innoxious through his age.
No courts he saw, no suits would ever try,
Nor dared an oath,[3] nor hazarded a lie.
Unlearn'd, he knew no schoolman's subtle art,
No language but the language of the heart.
400 By nature honest, by experience wise,
Healthy by temperance, and by exercise;
His life, though long, to sickness passed unknown,
His death was instant, and without a groan.
Oh, grant me thus to live, and thus to die!
405 Who sprung from kings shall know less joy than I.
    O friend! may each domestic bliss be thine!
Be no unpleasing melancholy mine:
Me, let the tender office long engage,
To rock the cradle of reposing age,
410 With lenient arts extend a mother's breath,
Make languor smile, and smooth the bed of death,
Explore the thought, explain the asking eye,
And keep a while one parent from the sky![4]
On cares like these if length of days attend,
415 May Heaven, to bless those days, preserve my friend,
Preserve him social, cheerful, and serene,
And just as rich as when he served a Queen![5]
    A. Whether that blessing be denied or given,
Thus far was right—the rest belongs to Heaven.

1735

2. Probably the duke of Marlborough, whose vast fortune was made through the favor of Queen Anne. The actual Bestia was a corrupt Roman consul.
3. As a Catholic, Pope's father refused to take the Oaths of Allegiance and Supremacy and the oath against the pope. He thus rendered himself vulnerable to the many repressive anti-Catholic laws then in force.
4. Pope was a tender and devoted son. His mother had died in 1733. The earliest version of these lines dates from 1731, when the poet was nursing her through a serious illness.
5. Pope alludes to the fact that Arbuthnot, a man of strict probity, left the queen's service no wealthier than when he entered it.

The Dunciad: Book the Fourth   The fourth book of *The Dunciad*, Pope's last major work, was originally intended as a continuation of *An Essay on Man*. To Jonathan Swift, the spiritual ancestor of the poem, Pope confided in 1736 that he was at work on a series of epistles on the uses of human reason and learning, to conclude with "a satire against the misapplication of all these, exemplified by pictures, characters, and examples." But the epistles never appeared; instead, the satire grew until it took their place. As Pope surveyed England in his last years, the complex literary and social order that had sustained him seemed to be crumbling. It was a time for desperate measures, for satire. And the means of retribution was at hand, in the structure of Pope's own *Dunciad,* the long work that had already impaled so many enemies.

The first *Dunciad*, published in three books in 1728, is a mock-epic reply to Pope's critics and other petty authors. Its hero and victim, Lewis Theobald, had attacked Pope's edition of Shakespeare (1725); other victims had offended Pope either by personal abuse or simply by ineptitude. Inspired by Dryden's "Mac Flecknoe," *The Dunciad* celebrates the triumph of the hordes of Grub Street. Indeed, so many obscure hacks were mentioned that a *Dunciad Variorum* (1729) was soon required, in which mock-scholarly notes identify the victims, "since it is only in this monument that they must expect to survive." But a modern reader need not catch every reference to enjoy the dazzling wit of the poem, or the sheer sense of fun with which Pope remakes the London literary world into a tiny insane fairground of his own.

The New Dunciad (1742), however, plays a far more serious game: here Pope takes aim at the rot of the whole social fabric. The satire goes deep and works at many levels, which for convenience may be divided into four. (1) Politics: From 1721 to 1742 England had been ruled by the Whig supremacy of Robert Walpole, first minister. To Pope and his circle, the immensely powerful Walpole (no friend of poets) seemed crass and greedy, like his monarch George II. It is no accident, in the kingdom of *The Dunciad,* that Dulness personified sits on a throne. (2) Society: Just as the action of the *Aeneid* had been the removal of the empire of Troy to Latium, the action of *The Dunciad,* according to Pope, is "the removal of the empire of Dulness from the City of London to the polite world, Westminster"; that is, the abdication of civility in favor of commerce and financial interests. In modern England, authors write for money, and ministers govern for profit; conspicuous consumption (especially the consumption of paper by scribblers) has replaced the old values of the yeoman and the aristocrat. In 1743 Pope revised the original *Dunciad*, substituting the actor and poet laureate Colley Cibber for Theobald as the hero and incorporating *The New Dunciad* as the fourth book (the version printed here). Dulness, he implies, has achieved her final triumph; Cibber is laureate in England. (3) Education: The word *dunce* is derived from the Scholastic philosopher John Duns Scotus (ca. 1265–1308), whose name had come to stand for silly and useless subtlety, logical hairsplitting. Pope, as an heir of the Renaissance, believes that the central subject of education must always be its relevance for human behavior: "The proper study of mankind is Man," and moral philosophy, the relation of individuals to each other and to the world, should be the teacher's first and last concern. By contrast, Dunces waste their time on grammar (words alone) or the "science" of the collector (things alone); they never comprehend that word and thing, like spirit and matter, are essentially dead unless they join. (4) Religion: At its deepest level, the subject of *The Dunciad* is the undoing of God's creation. Many passages from the fourth book echo *Paradise Lost,* and one of Pope's starting places seems to be Satan's threat to return the world to its original darkness, chaos, and ancient night (*Paradise Lost* 2.968–87). *The Dunciad* ends in a great apocalypse, with a yawn that signals the death of *Logos;* as words have become meaningless, so has the whole creation, which the Lord called forth with words. Here Pope invokes, with sublime intensity, the old idea that God was the first poet, one whose poem was the world, and suggests that the sickness of the word has infected all nature. Such a cosmic collapse allows Pope to realize in full the aim of his satirical poetry: to depict the evil of his enemies in all its excessive might and magnitude. As matter without spirit and substance without essence prevail in the final *Dunciad* over Pope's own ideals, the poem perversely confirms his poetic power, and the destruction of art permits his ultimate artistic triumph.

From The Dunciad

From *Book the Fourth*

[INVOCATION, THE GODDESS IN HER MAJESTY]

Yet, yet a moment, one dim ray of light
Indulge, dread Chaos, and eternal Night!
Of darkness visible[1] so much be lent,
As half to show, half veil the deep intent.
5   Ye Powers![2] whose mysteries restored I sing,
To whom Time bears me on his rapid wing,
Suspend a while your force inertly strong,
Then take at once the poet and the song.
     Now flamed the Dog-star's[3] unpropitious ray,
10 Smote every brain, and withered every bay,[4]
Sick was the sun, the owl forsook his bower,
The moon-struck prophet felt the madding hour:
Then rose the seed[5] of Chaos, and of Night,
To blot out Order, and extinguish Light,
15 Of dull and venal a new world to mold,
And bring Saturnian days of lead and gold.[6]
     She mounts the throne: her head a cloud concealed,
In broad effulgence all below revealed,
('Tis thus aspiring Dulness ever shines)
20 Soft on her lap her Laureate son[7] reclines.
     Beneath her foot-stool, Science groans in chains,
And Wit dreads exile, penalties and pains.
There foamed rebellious Logic, gagged and bound,
There, stripped, fair Rhetoric languished on the ground;
25 His blunted arms by Sophistry are borne,
And shameless Billingsgate[8] her robes adorn.
Morality, by her false guardians drawn,
Chicane in furs, and Casuistry in lawn,[9]
Gasps, as they straighten at each end the cord,
30 And dies, when Dulness gives her Page[1] the word.

* * *

1. Cf. *Paradise Lost* 1.63.
2. Chaos and Night, invoked in place of the Muse, because "the restoration of their empire is the action of the poem" [Pope's note].
3. Sirius, associated with the heat of summer and the madness of poets (see *Epistle to Dr. Arbuthnot*, p. 543, line 3).
4. The laurel, whose garlands are bestowed on poets.
5. The Goddess Dulness.
6. Saturn ruled during the golden age; the new age of "gold" will be reestablished by the dull and venal.
7. Colley Cibber, the poet laureate.
8. Fishmarket slang, which now covers the noble science of rhetoric.
9. Chicanery (legal trickery) wears the ermine robe of a judge. Casuistry wears the linen ("lawn") sleeves of a bishop.
1. Sir Francis Page, a notorious hanging judge; or court page, used to strangle criminals in Turkey; or page of writing on which a dull author "kills" moral sentiments.

[THE EDUCATOR]

135   Now crowds on crowds around the Goddess press,
       Each eager to present the first address.[2]
       Dunce scorning dunce beholds the next advance,
       But fop shows fop superior complaisance.
       When lo! a specter[3] rose, whose index-hand
140   Held forth the virtue of the dreadful wand;
       His beavered brow a birchen garland wears,[4]
       Dropping with infant's blood, and mother's tears.
       O'er every vein a shuddering horror runs;
       Eton and Winton shake through all their sons.
145   All flesh is humbled, Westminster's bold race[5]
       Shrink, and confess the Genius[6] of the place:
       The pale boy-Senator yet tingling stands,
       And holds his breeches close with both his hands.
          Then thus. "Since Man from beast by words is known,
150   Words are Man's province, words we teach alone.
       When reason doubtful, like the Samian letter,[7]
       Points him two ways, the narrower is the better.
       Placed at the door of learning, youth to guide,
       We never suffer it to stand too wide.
155   To ask, to guess, to know, as they commence,
       As fancy opens the quick springs of sense,
       We ply the memory, we load the brain,
       Bind rebel wit, and double chain on chain,
       Confine the thought, to exercise the breath;[8]
160   And keep them in the pale of words till death.
       Whate'er the talents, or howe'er designed,
       We hang one jingling padlock on the mind:
       A poet the first day, he dips his quill;
       And what the last? a very poet still.
165   Pity! the charm works only in our wall,
       Lost, lost too soon in yonder House or Hall."[9]

                    *   *   *

[THE CARNATION AND THE BUTTERFLY]

       Then thick as locusts blackening all the ground,
       A tribe,[1] with weeds and shells fantastic crowned,
       Each with some wondrous gift approached the Power,
400   A nest, a toad, a fungus, or a flower.
       But far the foremost, two, with earnest zeal,

2. The goddess, newly enthroned, is receiving petitions and congratulations.
3. The ghost of Dr. Busby, stern headmaster of Westminster School.
4. He wears a hat (beaver) and a garland of birch twigs, used for flogging. "Wand": cane used for beating.
5. Alumni of Westminster School, with a play on the justices and members of Parliament who meet at Westminster Hall.
6. I.e., admit that Dr. Busby is the presiding deity (Genius).
7. The letter Y, which Pythagoras (a native of Samos) used as an emblem of the different roads of virtue and vice.
8. Students are taught only to recite the classic poets by heart.
9. The House of Commons and Westminster Hall, where law cases were heard. The eloquence learned by rote disappears on occasions for public speaking.
1. The Virtuosi, or amateur scientists and collectors.

And aspect ardent to the throne appeal.
　　The first thus opened: "Hear thy suppliant's call,
Great Queen, and common mother of us all!
405　Fair from its humble bed I reared this flower,
Suckled, and cheer'd, with air, and sun, and shower,
Soft on the paper ruff its leaves I spread,
Bright with the gilded button tipped its head,
Then throned in glass, and named it CAROLINE:[2]
410　Each maid cried, charming! and each youth, divine!
Did Nature's pencil ever blend such rays,
Such varied light in one promiscuous blaze?
Now prostrate! dead! behold that Caroline:
No maid cries, charming! and no youth, divine!
415　And lo the wretch! whose vile, whose insect lust
Laid this gay daughter of the Spring in dust.
Oh punish him, or to th' Elysian shades
Dismiss my soul, where no carnation fades."
　　He ceased, and wept. With innocence of mien,
420　The accused stood forth, and thus addressed the Queen.
　　"Of all th' enameled race,° whose silvery wing　　　　*colored insects*
Waves to the tepid zephyrs of the spring,
Or swims along the fluid atmosphere,
Once brightest shined this child of heat and air.
425　I saw, and started from its vernal bower
The rising game, and chased from flower to flower.
It fled, I followed; now in hope, now pain;
It stopped, I stopped; it moved, I moved again.
At last it fixed, 'twas on what plant it pleased,
430　And where it fixed, the beauteous bird° I seized:　　　*flying creature*
Rose or carnation was below my care;
I meddle, Goddess! only in my sphere.
I tell the naked fact without disguise,
And, to excuse it, need but show the prize;
435　Whose spoils this paper offers to your eye,
Fair even in death! this peerless Butterfly."
　　"My sons!" she answered, "both have done your parts;
Live happy both, and long promote our arts.
But hear a mother, when she recommends
440　To your fraternal care, our sleeping friends.
The common soul, of heaven's more frugal make,
Serves but to keep fools pert, and knaves awake:
A drowsy watchman, that just gives a knock,
And breaks our rest, to tell us what's a clock.[3]
445　Yet by some object every brain is stirred;
The dull may waken to a hummingbird;
The most recluse, discreetly opened, find
Congenial matter in the cockle-kind;[4]

2. Queen Caroline, an enthusiastic gardener, is an appropriate choice to lend her name to the perfect carnation.
3. In the 18th century, watchmen kept guard in the streets and announced the hours.
4. Cockleshells, popular with collectors, as were hummingbirds and varieties of moss.

The mind, in metaphysics at a loss,
450 May wander in a wilderness of moss;
The head that turns at super-lunar things,
Poised with a tail, may steer on Wilkins' wings.[5]
"O! would the Sons of Men once think their eyes
And reason given them but to study *flies!*[6]
455 See Nature in some partial narrow shape,
And let the Author of the whole escape:
Learn but to trifle; or, who most observe,
To wonder at their Maker, not to serve."

* * *

[THE TRIUMPH OF DULNESS]

Then blessing all,[7] "Go children of my care!
580 To practice now from theory repair.
All my commands are easy, short, and full:
My sons! be proud, be selfish, and be dull.
Guard my prerogative, assert my throne:
This nod confirms each privilege your own.
585 The cap and switch be sacred to his Grace;[8]
With staff and pumps[9] the Marquis lead the race;
From stage to stage the licensed[1] Earl may run,
Paired with his fellow-charioteer the sun;
The learned baron butterflies design,
590 Or draw to silk Arachne's subtle line;°   *spiderweb*
The Judge to dance his brother Sergeant[2] call;
The Senator at cricket urge the ball;
The Bishop stow (pontific luxury!)
An hundred souls of turkeys in a pie;[3]
595 The sturdy squire to Gallic masters° stoop,   *French chefs*
And drown his lands and manors in a soup.
Others import yet nobler arts from France,
Teach kings to fiddle, and make senates dance.
Perhaps more high some daring son may soar,[4]
600 Proud to my list to add one monarch more;
And nobly conscious, Princes are but things
Born for First Ministers, as slaves for kings,
Tyrant supreme! shall three estates command,
And MAKE ONE MIGHTY DUNCIAD OF THE LAND!"
605 More she had spoke, but yawned—All Nature nods:
What mortal can resist the yawn of Gods?

5. John Wilkins (1614–1672), one of the founders of the Royal Society, had speculated "that a man may be able to fly, by the application of wings to his own body."
6. Cf. *An Essay on Man* 1.189–96 (p. 539).
7. Having conferred her titles, Dulness bids each eminent dunce to indulge in the triviality closest to his heart.
8. His Grace, a duke who loves horse racing, is to use the cap and switch of a jockey.
9. Footmen, who wore pumps (low-cut shoes for

running), were matched in races.
1. The license required by the owner of a stage-coach; also privileged or licentious.
2. A lawyer or legislative officer. Formal ceremonies at the Inns of Court are said to have resembled a country dance.
3. According to Pope, a hundred turkeys had been "not unfrequently deposited in one Pye in the Bishopric of Durham."
4. A bold, direct attack on Walpole.

Churches and chapels instantly it reached;
(St. James's first, for leaden Gilbert[5] preached)
Then catched the schools; the Hall scarce kept awake;
610 The Convocation gaped,[6] but could not speak:
Lost was the Nation's Sense,° nor could be found,   Parliament
While the long solemn unison went round:
Wide, and more wide, it spread o'er all the realm;
Even Palinurus[7] nodded at the helm:
615 The vapor mild o'er each committee crept;
Unfinished treaties in each office slept;
And chiefless armies dozed out the campaign;
And navies yawned for orders on the main.
      O Muse! relate (for you can tell alone,
620 Wits have short memories, and dunces none)
Relate, who first, who last resigned to rest;
Whose heads she partly, whose completely blessed;
What charms could faction, what ambition lull,
The venal quiet, and entrance the dull;
625 'Till drowned was sense, and shame, and right, and wrong—
O sing, and hush the nations with thy song!
· ·
In vain, in vain,—the all-composing Hour
Resistless falls: The Muse obeys the Power.
She comes! she comes![8] the sable throne behold
630 Of Night primeval, and of Chaos old!
Before her, Fancy's gilded clouds decay,
And all its varying rainbows die away.
Wit shoots in vain its momentary fires,
The meteor drops, and in a flash expires.
635 As one by one, at dread Medea's strain,
The sickening stars fade off the ethereal plain;[9]
As Argus' eyes by Hermes' wand oppressed,
Closed one by one to everlasting rest;[1]
Thus at her felt approach, and secret might,
640 Art after Art goes out, and all is Night.
See skulking Truth to her old cavern fled,[2]
Mountains of casuistry heaped o'er her head!
Philosophy, that leaned on Heaven before,
Shrinks to her second cause,[3] and is no more.
645 Physic[4] of Metaphysic begs defense,
And Metaphysic calls for aid on Sense!
See Mystery[5] to Mathematics fly!

---

5. Dr. John Gilbert, dean of Exeter.
6. The Convocation, an assembly of clergy consulting on ecclesiastical affairs, had been adjourned since 1717.
7. The pilot of Aeneas's ship; here Walpole.
8. Having triumphed in the contemporary world of affairs, Dulness (like her antitype Christ) has a Second Coming, a prophetic vision in which she extinguishes the light of the arts and sciences.
9. In Seneca's *Medea,* the stars obey the curse of Medea, a magician and an avenger.
1. Argus, Hera's hundred-eyed watchman, was charmed to sleep and slain by Hermes.
2. Alluding to the saying of Democritus, that Truth lay at the bottom of a deep well [Pope's note].
3. Science (philosophy) no longer accepts God as the first cause or final explanation of how all things came to be; instead, it accepts only the second or material cause and tries to account for all things by physical principles alone.
4. Natural science in general.
5. A religious truth known only through divine revelation.

In vain! they gaze, turn giddy, rave, and die.
Religion blushing veils her sacred fires,
650 And unawares Morality expires.
Nor public flame, nor private, dares to shine;
Nor human spark is left, nor glimpse divine!
Lo! thy dread Empire, CHAOS! is restored;
Light dies before thy uncreating word:[6]
655 Thy hand, great Anarch! lets the curtain fall;
And Universal Darkness buries All.

1743

6. Cf. God's first creating words in Genesis, "Let there be light."

Print Culture and the
Rise of the Novel

The origins of English literature's most popular form, the novel, have long been seen to lie in the eighteenth century. Critics have traced a great tradition arising from the fictions of Daniel Defoe, Samuel Richardson, Henry Fielding, and others, carrying forward to the nineteenth century in the work of Jane Austen and Walter Scott, George Eliot and Charles Dickens, to the outstanding experiments in fiction in the twentieth, and the diverse novelistic voices heard in English in the twenty-first. Yet there have been prose fictions in literature for millennia, from works of antiquity such as the *Satyricon* by the Roman author Petronius (ca. 27–66 C.E.) to *Don Quixote* (1605, 1616) by the Spanish master Miguel de Cervantes (1547–1616). As far back as the sixteenth century, English fictions were sometimes called "novels" on their title pages (a term, initially signifying a short story about love, taken from continental Europe). And many eighteenth-century works now classified as novels first appeared under other labels: tale, history, secret history, romance, "the life of," or "the adventures of." Why does this period's fiction feel more novelistic to readers of English now than the romances, fables, and other narratives that appeared centuries before? What changes in the conventions and subject matter of fictional prose, in literature's social contexts, and in modes of literary production and consumption led to the emergence in the eighteenth century of the novel as many now recognize it?

Scholars confronting these questions must face the sheer variety of eighteenth-century fictions. Autobiographical adventures that claim to be true, such as Aphra Behn's *Oroonoko* (1688; see p. 139) and Defoe's *Robinson Crusoe* (1719; see p. 566), and parodies of such stories like Swift's *Gulliver's Travels* (1726; see p. 278), draw one strand of fictional narrative through outdoor settings as expansive as the globe. But more intimate stories of desire, seduction, and resistance also proliferated in the period, from tales of disguise and sexual curiosity such as Eliza Haywood's *Fantomina* (1725; see p. 609) to Samuel Richardson's revelations of private domestic spaces and the inner recesses of his characters' minds. Henry Fielding's flair for theatrical comedy and intricate plots, and his self-consciously literary style, enliven his masterpieces *Joseph Andrews* (1742) and *Tom Jones* (1749). After midcentury, the novel haunted Gothic castles or flowed with the tears and passions of sensibility, though often with ironic twists, as in Laurence Sterne's *Tristram Shandy* (1759–67) and *A Sentimental Journey* (1768; see p. 865). Frances Burney's novels interweave emotional plots of courtship with keen satirical accounts of elegant social mingling (or attempts at it), while those of Tobias Smollett practice a rougher satire and barrel through less-refined settings. Fiction could also offer opportunities for explicit reflections on the meaning of life, as in Samuel Johnson's *Rasselas* (p. 734). As the selection of works in the present volume shows, the eighteenth-century novel takes in so much—from the fantastic to the everyday, the narratively propulsive to the philosophically meditative, the talk of ordinary people to the sophisticated language of the great or the learned—that it has been a challenge to say what one thing it essentially is or does.

One distinctive feature noticed by some novel writers themselves about their works is the closeness of their plots and characters to readers' experiences of real life. Novels "come near us," William Congreve says in his essay early in this section, and are "not so distant from our belief" as the marvelous tales of romance that dominated prose fiction in earlier times. The critic Ian Watt, in his classic scholarly work *The Rise of the Novel* (1957), saw believability as the modern novel's dominant trait and called the ensemble of techniques that achieved it "formal realism," suited especially, he thought, to the practical tastes of a growing readership among the middle ranks of commercial Britain. Scholars of the novel in the decades after Watt's book have supplemented, qualified, and questioned his view by finding other motives shaping the novel form. Defoe's fictions not only grapple with life's hard, empirical facts but also heed the supernatural whisper of Providence and seek spiritual redemption; the scandalous tales and secret histories by writers such as Delarivier Manley (ca. 1670–1724) present the intrigues of the fabulously rich and powerful, not ordinary people. And the conventions of romance—a love requiring implausible coincidences to prevail, a birthmark that reveals the hero's true identity—never quite go away. The eighteenth-century novel includes a range of impulses much broader than what Watt's theory of formal realism first took into account. Celebrity gossip, religious inspiration, true (or half-true) crime, political allegories, ghost stories, and patterns for proper conduct variously "come near us" by engaging our aspirations, fears, and excited imaginations.

But the understanding in recent decades of the origins of the modern novel has most decisively been enhanced by recognizing the contributions of women authors to its success, widening Watt's focus on Defoe, Richardson, and Fielding. As novelists, women shaped the course of literature as they never had before. From Aphra Behn's fictions at the end of the seventeenth century, a tradition of British women's writing arose, including Manley and Haywood, Penelope Aubin (1679?–1738), Mary Davys (1674–1732), Elizabeth Rowe (1674–1737), Sarah Fielding (1710–1768), Sarah Scott (1720–1795), Charlotte Lennox (1730/31?–1804), and Burney—this list could be much expanded. Offering more than mere romantic tales, women fiction writers treated politics and religion, delivered tough-minded satire of women's credulity, men's cruelty, and the culture's unfair gender standards, and surveyed social ills and opportunities. Women authors helped establish the novel's unparalleled flexibility of theme and style, and their works sold at least as well as those of men.

The novel's success in the eighteenth century was buoyed by a growing industry that included booksellers (ancestors of present-day publishers), printers and all the labors associated with printing, and authors, catering to an increasingly literate populace of a Britain growing ever more prosperous. The publishing of works of all kinds dramatically increased: while a mere six thousand separate printed titles were published in the 1630s, the 1710s saw twenty-two thousand, and by the 1790s, about sixty thousand appeared. Readers not only bought but also borrowed books, from new institutions such as subscription libraries and circulating libraries (which both charged sometimes hefty membership fees). These terms were often used interchangeably, but the former tended to cultivate their collections to suit subscribers' tastes, and the latter bought and sold off their books as public demand changed—and hence offered many novels. (Free public libraries were virtually nonexistent.) A tale of multiple risings—of the middle classes, of literacy, of the book trades, and of new ways to disseminate books to the public—has provided a background for plotting the rise of the novel. And increasing literacy rates among women ensured they were decisively important as consumers of novels as well as producers—a fact often noted with alarm by commentators of the period. In his popular *Sermons to Young Women* (1766), James Fordyce inveighs that the preponderance of novels are "in their nature so shameful, in their tendency so pestiferous, and contain such rank treason against the royalty of Virtue, such horrible violation of all decorum, that she who can bear to peruse them must in her soul be a prostitute, let her reputation in life be what it will." The vigor of such denunciations testifies to a sense that the novel's power over women was growing.

Yet a complete picture of the novel's production, consumption, breadth of appeal, and social effects contains some surprising facts. Based on sales data and extant records from circulating libraries, we know men read novels at least as much as women, including ones with putatively "feminine" themes like love and courtship. Scholars have also challenged the idea that the "middling sort"—shopkeepers, apprentices, small tradesmen, and others connected with commerce—constituted the novel's

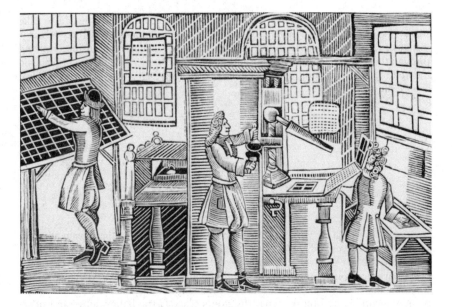

An eighteenth-century printer's shop. Woodcut, British library.

principal readership. The gentry, and clergymen and professional men and their families, bought and borrowed the most novels. The rate of new novels' publication rose and fell unevenly through the century. Though Watt concentrated on novelists from the first half, a real surge of new novels came in the late 1780s, and bigger ones followed. And as copious as the publication of novels was in the period, it amounted to only a small proportion of booksellers' and libraries' offerings. Readers seemed to gravitate even more to sermons and other works of religious devotion, histories, legal and medical works, and especially periodicals.

A vibrant print culture nonetheless provided the energy and promise of financial gain that the novel needed to flourish. A form that arose "from below," inspired by readers' curiosities and the demands of a growing marketplace, the novel only slowly gained respectability and was by many considered merely an ephemeral entertainment. Unlike high, ancient genres like epic and tragedy, the novel did not have a tradition of learned criticism and commentary to draw on. Many of the most revealing remarks on the theory and practice of novelistic writing appear in what book historians call the paratext of published novels: prefaces, introductions, letters to the reader, dedications, and other matter ancillary to the main text. Outstanding examples of this kind of writing in the cluster that follows help bring the literary aspirations and professional and personal difficulties of the period's novelists to life. In them, authors beckon to their readers, anticipate criticisms, praise their own invention, and at times lie by insisting they are offering a true story. Some play with familiar literary labels when explaining what they seek to achieve in fiction, as when Fielding calls his *Joseph Andrews* "a comic epic-poem in prose"; others like Richardson extol their work's high moral purpose.

As the century advanced, periodicals devoted to reviewing newly published works, including novels, were founded, such as *The Monthly Review* (1749–1845) and *The Critical Review* (1756–1817), of which Smollett was first editor. Other periodical essays, outstanding among them Samuel Johnson's *Rambler* 4 (see p. 723), theorize about the nature and value of fiction. The first full-length book in English discussing the history and significant examples of prose fiction, *The Progress of Romance* by Clara Reeve (see p. 601), appeared in 1785. As a result of the work of critics and literary historians such as Reeve, the English novel as we know it began to take shape: its canon of great early texts, its foundational oppositions (between, for instance, feeling Richardson and ribald Fielding), its special relationship, evolving through the century, to women as authors and readers, and its grip on an enthusiastic if not always discriminating reading public. No form of English literature would have a more illustrious future.

WILLIAM CONGREVE

William Congreve (1670–1729) is famous for comedies that have been admired by audiences and readers since their first performances, such as *Love for Love* (see in the NAEL Archive) and *The Way of the World* (see p. 188). But his first publication was *Incognita; or, Love and Duty Reconciled: A Novel* (1692), which appeared when he was twenty-two under a pastoral pseudonym, Cleophil. After the title page proudly identifies its literary type, the preface extols the believability and nearness to ordinary human concerns of novels, in contrast to romances. Yet Congreve's remarks also exemplify the novel's way of leaning on other, more traditionally prestigious genres—in this case, comic drama—to gain literary credit for itself. The setting of *Incognita* in Italy and its love intrigues, masks, and mistaken identities recall motifs common in English stage comedy of the sixteenth and seventeenth centuries. Though elegantly crafted, *Incognita* never entered the canon of English fiction—in his "Life of Congreve" (1779), Samuel Johnson remarked, "I would rather praise it than read it." But its preface offers a vivid sense of how writers understood what the novel is, decades before the more celebrated fictions of Defoe, Fielding, and Richardson.

From Incognita; or, Love and Duty Reconciled: A Novel

The Preface to the Reader

Reader,

Some authors are so fond of a preface, that they will write one though there be nothing more in it than an apology[1] for itself. But to show thee that I am not one of those, I will make no apology for this, but do tell thee that I think it necessary to be prefixed to this trifle, to prevent thy overlooking some little pains which I have taken in the composition of the following story. Romances are generally composed of the constant loves and invincible courages of heroes, heroines, kings and queens, mortals of the first rank, and so forth; where lofty language, miraculous contingencies, and impossible performances elevate and surprise the reader into a giddy delight, which leaves him flat upon the ground whenever he gives off,[2] and vexes him to think how he has suffered himself to be pleased and transported, concerned and afflicted at the several passages which he has read, viz. these knights' success to their

1. Justification.
2. Stops reading.

damsels' misfortunes, and such like, when he is forced to be very well convinced that 'tis all a lie. Novels are of a more familiar nature; come near us, and represent to us intrigues in practice,[3] delight us with accidents and odd events, but not such as are wholly unusual or unprecedented, such which not being so distant from our belief bring also the pleasure nearer us. Romances give more of wonder, novels more delight. And with reverence be it spoken, and the parallel kept at a due distance, there is something of equality in the proportion which they bear in reference to one another, with that between comedy and tragedy; but the drama is the long extracted from[4] romance and history: 'tis the midwife to industry, and brings forth alive the conceptions of the brain. Minerva walks upon the stage before us, and we are more assured of the real presence of wit when it is delivered viva voce[5] —

> Segnius irritant animos demissa per aurem,
> Quam quae sunt oculis subjecta fidelibus, & quae
> Ipse sibi tradit spectator.[6]—Horace.

Since all traditions must indisputably give place to[7] the drama, and since there is no possibility of giving that life to the writing or repetition of a story which it has in the action, I resolved in another beauty[8] to imitate dramatic writing, namely, in the design, contexture and result of the plot. I have not observed it before in a novel. Some I have seen begin with an unexpected accident, which has been the only surprising part of the story, cause enough to make the sequel[9] look flat, tedious, and insipid; for 'tis but reasonable the reader should expect it not to rise, at least to keep upon a level in the entertainment; for so he may be kept on in hopes that at some time or other it may mend; but the other is such a balk[1] to a man, 'tis carrying him up stairs to show him the dining room, and after forcing him to make a meal in the kitchen. This I have not only endeavored to avoid, but also have used a method for the contrary purpose. The design of the novel is obvious, after the first meeting of Aurelian and Hippolito with Incognita and Leonora,[2] and the difficulty is in bringing it to pass, maugre[3] all apparent obstacles, within the compass of two days. How many probable casualties[4] intervene in opposition to the main design, viz. of marrying two couple so oddly engaged in an intricate amour, I leave the reader at his leisure to consider; as also whether every obstacle does not in the progress of the story act as subservient to that purpose, which at first it seems to oppose. In a comedy this would be called the unity of action;[5] here it may pretend to no more than an unity of contrivance. The scene is continued in Florence from the commencement of the amour; and the time from first to last is but three days.[6] If there be any thing more in particular resembling the

3. As they (really) are performed.
4. Is very far from (superior to).
5. In a living voice (Latin). Minerva is the Roman goddess of wisdom.
6. That which enters through the ears affects the mind more languidly than that which is subjected to our faithful eyes, and which a spectator brings to himself (Latin), from "The Art of Poetry," lines 180–82, by the Roman poet Horace (65–8 B.C.E.).
7. Concede the preeminence of. "Traditions": all other genres of literature.
8. Another element of my fiction. "In the action": in an acted play.
9. The rest of the story after the beginning.
1. Obstacle. "The other": starting off a story on a

high note only to offer little afterward.
2. The two men and two women who pair up in the love plot of Congreve's novel.
3. Despite.
4. Occurrences.
5. One of the three "unities" which, by the neoclassic rules for drama derived from Aristotle, a comedy should adhere to: the unity of action was the connection, causal or otherwise, of all the incidents in a plot.
6. The other two unities, of place and of time, would also be (more or less) maintained by Congreve's selection of a single setting and compressed time frame for his plot.

copy which I imitate (as the curious reader will soon perceive) I leave it to show itself, being very well satisfied how much more proper it had been for him to have found out this himself, than for me to prepossess him with an opinion of something extraordinary in an essay[7] began and finished in the idler hours of a fortnight's time: for I can only esteem it a laborious idleness, which is parent to so inconsiderable a birth. I have gratified the bookseller in pretending an occasion for a preface; the other two persons concerned are the reader and myself, and if he be but pleased with what was produced for that end, my satisfaction follows of course,[8] since it will be proportioned to his approbation or dislike.

1692

7. Compositional effort.   8. As a consequence.

DANIEL DEFOE

Daniel Defoe (1660–1731) had many careers and wrote in many forms and styles before he began, at the age of nearly sixty, to publish the sequence of works for which he is best remembered: prose "autobiographies" of figures with sensational lives, all claiming to be true, all eventually called novels by later generations of grateful readers. He was raised as a Presbyterian and educated at a Dissenting academy at Newington Green in north London. (Not conforming to the doctrines of the Church of England, he could not attend Cambridge or Oxford.) Through the 1680s and early 1690s, he pursued high-stakes business ventures and made risky investments, going bankrupt in 1692 for the spectacular sum of £17,000, and ended up in debtors' prison. After his release, publishing his work took an increasingly large place among his business enterprises. His long, very popular satirical poem *The True-Born Englishman* (1701) defended his hero, the Protestant and Dutch king of England, William III, by pointing out that people of many faiths and nations have helped create English identity. His satire *The Shortest Way with the Dissenters* (1702) impersonated the bigotry against nonconformists effectively enough to anger both sides: he endured prison and the pillory for it. In 1704, he launched *The Review*, a journal that criticized the government and commented on other topics of public interest, which he ran almost single-handedly until 1713. Soon, however, he was drafted into government service, working as a spy in England and Scotland. For the remainder of the 1710s, he wrote a lot—conduct books, political pamphlets, scandalous "secret histories"—though more was attributed to him, he complained, than he ever wrote. (Correctly identifying Defoe's writings, many published anonymously, remains a thorny problem for scholars.)

In 1719, *The Life and Strange Surprising Adventures of Robinson Crusoe* appeared, "Written by Himself," the title page informs us. Defoe had recognized the popularity of travel writing in his time and gave the public more of what it wanted, basing *Crusoe* on stories of famous actual castaways such as Alexander Selkirk. But a pamphlet almost immediately identified Defoe's tale as untrue and attributed it to him. His most famous fictional work thus entered the world not as a novel—a story acknowledging itself as invented, to be admired for its plot's probability and lifelike characters—but rather as something like a fraud (though the preface seems to say its exact relation to the truth does not much matter). The sequel, *The Farther Adventures of Robinson Cru-*

soe, came out the same year, and a final installment, *The Serious Reflections of Robinson Crusoe* (1720), offered mostly contemplative and religious musings. After *Crusoe*, Defoe produced more "autobiographies" that would come to be seen as classic English novels: *Moll Flanders* (1722), *A Journal of the Plague Year* (1722), and *Roxana* (1724), among others. But *Robinson Crusoe* remained his most popular work in Britain and worldwide, never receding from the public consciousness: by some measures, it was the best-selling novel of the 1750s, some twenty years after his death, running to six editions in that decade. In the 1770s and 1780s, booksellers and circulating libraries began openly designating Defoe's first-person biographies as imaginative fiction, and as his: the canon of his novels began to take shape, though scholars have occasionally doubted his authorship of nearly all of them except *Crusoe*.

The power of *Robinson Crusoe*, in its long history as a classic of world literature, lies in its way of connecting Crusoe's extraordinary circumstances to readers' ordinary fantasies and fears and in the large, near-mythic meanings that this connection suggests. Washing up on an uninhabited island, he excites the reader's basic sense of what is needed to survive in the world, any world, alone. He eventually creates, or imitates, a comfortable mode of life by assuming a range of roles—landowner and farm laborer, builder, tailor, cobbler, potter, soldier, miller of wheat and baker of bread—usually performed by an entire society. Economists from the eighteenth century on have used him as an allegory of, or foil to, society's division of labor, its production and consumption of commodities, and so on. After building his world, he realizes he is not alone. First a single human footprint on the beach, then a scene of natives of the islands that terrifies him, then his violent attack on them and acquisition from among them of his "man" and friend, Friday: all this has served as a parable of British colonialism and encounters with indigenous peoples. Throughout, Crusoe's hauntingly solitary spirituality, his straining to hear the voice of Providence and assure himself of his salvation, offers an image of religious experience in which readers have recognized themselves. Defoe sustains these large meanings not with lofty, learned disquisitions but with a propulsive style personalized to Crusoe. The prose builds and pushes forward like the wave that carries his body to his island. The momentum of the sentences and their sometimes chaotic way of taking in everything moving across the focus of narration— Crusoe's immediate consciousness—carry readers forward also, immersing them in his fictional yet vivid world. Often its details are so concretely haphazard that it seems the only motive to include them must be that they are true—like the "two shoes that were not fellows" washed ashore among his mates' former possessions. Due to Defoe's magnificently full realization of him and his predicament, Crusoe has become the rarest of literary creations: a symbol of the most broadly significant cultural and historical forces, and a unique personage, dynamic, individual, and vivid.

From The Life and Strange Surprising Adventures of Robinson Crusoe[1]

Written by Himself

Preface

If ever the story of any private man's adventures in the world were worth making public, and were acceptable when published, the editor of this account thinks this will be so.

1. The complete title on the title page runs, *The Life and Strange Surprising Adventures of Robinson Crusoe, of York, Mariner, Who Lived Eight and Twenty Years, all alone in an un-inhabited Island on the Coast of America, near the Mouth of the Great River of Oroonoque* [i.e., the Orinoco, that runs mostly through present-day Venezuela]; *Having been cast on Shore by Shipwreck, wherein all the Men perished but himself. With An Account how he was at last as strangely deliver'd by Pirates.*

The wonders of this man's life exceed all that (he thinks) is to be found extant; the life of one man being scarce capable of a greater variety.

The story is told with modesty, with seriousness, and with a religious application of events to the uses to which wise men always apply them, viz. to the instruction of others by this example, and to justify and honor the wisdom of Providence in all the variety of our circumstances, let them happen how they will.

The editor believes the thing to be a just history of fact; neither is there any appearance of fiction in it. And however thinks, because all such things are dispatched,[2] that the improvement of it, as well to the diversion, as to the instruction of the reader, will be the same; and as such, he thinks, without farther compliments to the world, he does them a great service in the publication.

Crusoe. Frontispiece of *The Life and Strange Surprising Adventures of Robinson Crusoe*, 1719, artist unknown. John Clark and John Pine, engravers.

[*Crusoe Washes Ashore*]

Nothing can describe the confusion of thought which I felt when I sunk into the water;[3] for though I swam very well, yet I could not deliver myself from the waves so as to draw breath, till that wave having driven me, or rather carried me a vast way on towards the shore, and having spent itself, went back, and left me upon the land almost dry, but half dead with the water I took in. I had so much presence of mind as well as breath left, that seeing myself nearer the mainland[4] than I expected, I got upon my feet, and endeavored to make on towards the land as fast as I could before another wave should return and take me up again. But I soon found it was impossible to avoid it; for I saw the sea come after me as high as a great hill, and as furious as an enemy, which I had no means or strength to contend with: my business was to hold my breath, and raise myself upon the water, if I could; and so, by swimming to preserve my breathing, and pilot myself towards the shore, if possible; my greatest concern now being that the sea, as it

2. Read quickly. From the third (1719) edition on, the word used is *disputed*.
3. Near the beginning of the novel, a ferocious storm runs the ship on which Crusoe is a crew member onto a sandbar, and he and ten others

desperately escape in a lifeboat, which is soon swamped by a huge wave. The selection reprinted here begins at this moment.
4. The body of land that is the island.

would carry me a great way towards the shore when it came on, might not carry me back again with it when it gave back towards the sea.

The wave that came upon me again buried me at once twenty or thirty foot deep in its own body, and I could feel myself carried with a mighty force and swiftness towards the shore a very great way; but I held my breath, and assisted myself to swim still forward with all my might. I was ready to burst with holding my breath, when, as I felt myself rising up, so, to my immediate relief, I found my head and hands shoot out above the surface of the water; and though it was not two seconds of time that I could keep myself so, yet it relieved me greatly, gave me breath and new courage. I was covered again with water a good while, but not so long but I held it out; and finding the water had spent itself, and began to return, I strook forward against the return of the waves, and felt ground again with my feet. I stood still a few moments to recover breath, and till the water went from me, and then took to my heels, and run with what strength I had farther towards the shore. But neither would this deliver me from the fury of the sea, which came pouring in after me again; and twice more I was lifted up by the waves and carried forwards as before, the shore being very flat.

The last time of these two had well near been fatal to me; for the sea having hurried me along as before, landed me, or rather dashed me against a piece of rock, and that with such force, as it left me senseless, and indeed helpless, as to my own deliverance; for the blow taking my side and breast, beat the breath as it were quite out of my body; and had it returned again immediately, I must have been strangled in the water; but I recovered a little before the return of the waves, and seeing I should be covered again with the water, I resolved to hold fast by a piece of the rock, and so to hold my breath, if possible, till the wave went back; now as the waves were not so high as at first, being nearer land, I held my hold till the wave abated, and then fetched another run, which brought me so near the shore that the next wave, though it went over me, yet did not so swallow me up as to carry me away; and the next run I took, I got to the mainland, where, to my great comfort, I clambered up the clifts of the shore and sat me down upon the grass, free from danger, and quite out of the reach of the water.

I was now landed, and safe on shore, and began to look up and thank God that my life was saved, in a case wherein there was some minutes before scarce any room to hope. I believe it is impossible to express to the life[5] what the ecstasies and transports of the soul are, when it is so saved, as I may say, out of the very grave; and I do not wonder now at that custom, *viz.* that when a malefactor, who has the halter about his neck, is tied up, and just going to be turned off,[6] and has a reprieve brought to him: I say, I do not wonder that they bring a surgeon with it, to let him blood that very moment they tell him of it, that the surprise may not drive the animal spirits[7] from the heart, and overwhelm him:

> For sudden joys, like griefs, confound at first.[8]

---

5. In an accurately vivid way.
6. Hanged.
7. Vital principle animating the body. "Let him blood": open a vein to discharge his blood.

8. From Robert Wild, *Poetica Licentia, A Gratulatory Poem upon His Majesties Gracious Declaration for Liberty of Conscience, with a Friendly Debate betwixt Con and Non* (1672).

I walked about on the shore lifting up my hands, and my whole being, as I may say, wrapped up in the contemplation of my deliverance; making a thousand gestures and motions which I cannot describe; reflecting upon all my comrades that were drowned, and that there should not be one soul saved but myself; for, as for them, I never saw them afterwards, or any sign of them, except three of their hats, one cap, and two shoes that were not fellows.

I cast my eyes to the stranded vessel, when the breach and froth of the sea being so big, I could hardly see it, it lay so far off, and considered, Lord! how was it possible I could get on shore?

After I had solaced my mind with the comfortable part of my condition, I began to look round me to see what kind of place I was in, and what was next to be done; and I soon found my comforts abate, and that in a word I had a dreadful deliverance; for I was wet, had no clothes to shift me,[9] nor anything either to eat or drink to comfort me, neither did I see any prospect before me but that of perishing with hunger, or being devoured by wild beasts; and that which was particularly afflicting to me was that I had no weapon either to hunt and kill any creature for my sustenance, or to defend myself against any other creature that might desire to kill me for theirs. In a word, I had nothing about me but a knife, a tobacco-pipe, and a little tobacco in a box; this was all my provision; and this threw me into terrible agonies of mind, that for a while I run about like a madman. Night coming upon me, I began with a heavy heart to consider what would be my lot if there were any ravenous beasts in that country, seeing at night they always come abroad for their prey.

All the remedy that offered to my thoughts at that time was to get up into a thick bushy tree like a fir, but thorny, which grew near me, and where I resolved to set all night, and consider the next day what death I should die, for as yet I saw no prospect of life. I walked about a furlong[1] from the shore, to see if I could find any fresh water to drink, which I did, to my great joy; and having drank and put a little tobacco into my mouth to prevent hunger, I went to the tree, and getting up into it, endeavored to place myself so, as that if I should sleep I might not fall; and having cut me a short stick, like a truncheon, for my defense, I took up my lodging, and having been excessively fatigued, I fell fast asleep, and slept as comfortably as, I believe, few could have done in my condition, and found myself more refreshed with it, than I think I ever was on such an occasion.

When I waked it was broad day, the weather clear, and the storm abated, so that the sea did not rage and swell as before. But that which surprised me most was that the ship was lifted off in the night from the sand where she lay, by the swelling of the tide, and was driven up almost as far as the rock which I at first mentioned, where I had been so bruised by the wave dashing me against it; this being within about a mile from the shore where I was, and the ship seeming to stand upright still, I wished myself on board, that at least I might save some necessary things for my use.

When I came down from my apartment in the tree, I looked about me again, and the first thing I found was the boat,[2] which lay as the wind and the sea had tossed her up upon the land, about two miles on my right hand. I walked as far as I could upon the shore to have got to her; but found a

---

9. To allow me to change out of my wet ones.
1. A furlong is 220 yards.

2. The lifeboat in which Crusoe and the other crew members left the ship.

neck or inlet of water between me and the boat which was about half a mile broad; so I came back for the present, being more intent upon getting at the ship, where I hoped to find something for my present subsistence.

A little after noon I found the sea very calm, and the tide ebbed so far out, that I could come within a quarter of a mile of the ship; and here I found a fresh renewing of my grief; for I saw evidently, that if we had kept on board we had been all safe, that is to say, we had all got safe on shore, and I had not been so miserable as to be left entirely destitute of all comfort and company as I now was; this forced tears from my eyes again, but as there was little relief in that, I resolved, if possible, to get to the ship, so I pulled off my clothes, for the weather was hot to extremity, and took the water; but when I came to the ship, my difficulty was still greater to know how to get on board, for as she lay aground, and high out of the water, there was nothing within my reach to lay hold of. I swam round her twice, and the second time I spied a small piece of rope, which I wondered I did not see at first, hang down by the fore-chains so low, as that with great difficulty I got hold of it, and by the help of that rope I got up into the forecastle of the ship. Here I found that the ship was bulged,[3] and had a great deal of water in her hold, but that she lay so on the side of a bank of hard sand, or rather earth, that her stern lay lifted up upon the bank, and her head low almost to the water; by this means all her quarter[4] was free, and all that was in that part was dry; for you may be sure my first work was to search and to see what was spoiled and what was free; and first I found that all the ship's provisions were dry and untouched by the water, and being very well disposed to eat, I went to the bread room and filled my pockets with biscuit, and eat it as I went about other things, for I had no time to lose. I also found some rum in the great cabin, of which I took a large dram,[5] and which I had indeed need enough of to spirit me for what was before me. Now I wanted nothing but a boat to furnish myself with many things which I foresaw would be very necessary to me.

It was in vain to sit still and wish for what was not to be had, and this extremity roused my application; we had several spare yards, and two or three large spars[6] of wood, and a spare topmast or two in the ship; I resolved to fall to work with these, and I flung as many of them overboard as I could manage for their weight, tying every one with a rope that they might not drive away; when this was done I went down the ship's side, and pulling them to me, I tied four of them fast together at both ends as well as I could in the form of a raft, and laying two or three short pieces of plank upon them crossways, I found I could walk upon it very well, but that it was not able to bear any great weight, the pieces being too light; so I went to work, and with the carpenter's saw I cut a spare topmast into three lengths, and added them to my raft, with a great deal of labor and pains, but hope of furnishing myself with necessaries encouraged me to go beyond what I should have been able to have done upon another occasion.

My raft was now strong enough to bear any reasonable weight; my next care was what to load it with, and how to preserve what I laid upon it from the surf of the sea; but I was not long considering this. I first laid all the

3. Fractured in the hull.
4. Upper part of the side of a ship behind the center beam, where the ship is broadest. "Stern": the ship's rear. "Head": front of the ship.
5. A swallow, a swig.
6. Lengths of wood used for masts, booms, etc., on a ship. "Yards": comparatively slender spars.

plank or boards upon it that I could get, and having considered well what I most wanted, I first got three of the seamen's chests, which I had broken open and emptied, and lowered them down upon my raft; the first of these I filled with provision—viz. bread, rice, three Dutch cheeses, five pieces of dried goat's flesh which we lived much upon, and a little remainder of European corn,[7] which had been laid by for some fowls which we brought to sea with us, but the fowls were killed. There had been some barley and wheat together, but to my great disappointment, I found afterwards that the rats had eaten or spoiled it all. As for liquors, I found several cases of bottles belonging to our skipper, in which were some cordial waters, and in all about five or six gallons of rack.[8] These I stowed by themselves, there being no need to put them into the chest, nor no room for them. While I was doing this, I found the tide began to flow, though very calm; and I had the mortification to see my coat, shirt, and waistcoat, which I had left on shore, upon the sand swim away. As for my breeches, which were only linen and open-kneed, I swam on board in them and my stockings. However this put me upon rummaging for clothes, of which I found enough, but took no more than I wanted for present use, for I had others things which my eye was more upon, as first tools to work with on shore, and it was after long searching that I found out the carpenter's chest, which was indeed a very useful prize to me, and much more valuable than a ship-loading of gold would have been at that time; I got it down to my raft, even whole as it was, without losing time to look into it, for I knew in general what it contained.

My next care was for some ammunition and arms; there were two very good fowling-pieces[9] in the great cabin, and two pistols. These I secured first, with some powder-horns, and a small bag of shot, and two old rusty swords. I knew there were three barrels of powder in the ship, but knew not where our gunner had stowed them; but with much search I found them, two of them dry and good, the third had taken water; those two I got to my raft with the arms, and now I thought myself pretty well freighted, and began to think how I should get to shore with them, having neither sail, oar, or rudder, and the least capful of wind would have overset all my navigation.

I had three encouragements, 1. A smooth, calm sea, 2. The tide rising and setting in to the shore, 3. What little wind there was blew me towards the land. And thus, having found two or three broken oars belonging to the boat and besides the tools which were in the chest, I found two saws, an axe, and a hammer; and with this cargo I put to sea. For a mile or thereabouts my raft went very well, only that I found it drive a little distant from the place where I had landed before; by which I perceived that there was some indraft of the water, and consequently I hoped to find some creek or river there, which I might make use of as a port to get to land with my cargo.

As I imagined, so it was, there appeared before me a little opening of the land, and I found a strong current of the tide set into it; so I guided my raft as well as I could to keep in the middle of the stream. But here I had like to have suffered a second shipwreck, which, if I had, I think verily would have broken

---

7. Generic term for grain.
8. Arrack, "a spirituous liquor imported from the East Indies, used by way of dram and in punch"

(Johnson's *Dictionary*). "Cordial waters": alcoholic drinks for medicinal purposes.
9. Light shotguns for hunting fowl.

my heart, for knowing nothing of the coast, my raft run aground at one end of it upon a shoal, and not being aground at the other end, it wanted but[1] a little that all my cargo had slipped off towards the end that was afloat, and so fallen into the water. I did my utmost by setting my back against the chests, to keep them in their places, but could not thrust off the raft with all my strength, neither durst I stir from the posture I was in, but holding up the chests with all my might, stood in that manner near half an hour, in which time the rising of the water brought me a little more upon a level, and a little after, the water still rising, my raft floated again, and I thrust her off with the oar I had, into the channel, and then driving up higher, I at length found myself in the mouth of a little river, with land on both sides, and a strong current of tide running up. I looked on both sides for a proper place to get to shore, for I was not willing to be driven too high up the river, hoping in time to see some ship at sea, and therefore resolved to place myself as near the coast as I could.

At length I spied a little cove on the right shore of the creek, to which with great pain and difficulty I guided my raft, and at last got so near as that, reaching ground with my oar, I could thrust her directly in. But here I had like to have dipped all my cargo in the sea again; for that shore lying pretty steep, that is to say sloping, there was no place to land, but where one end of my float, if it run on shore, would lie so high, and the other sink lower as before, that it would endanger my cargo again. All that I could do was to wait till the tide was at the highest, keeping the raft with my oar like an anchor to hold the side of it fast to the shore, near a flat piece of ground, which I expected the water would flow over; and so it did. As soon as I found water enough, for my raft drew about a foot water,[2] I thrust her on upon that flat piece of ground, and there fastened or moored her by sticking my two broken oars into the ground, one on one side near the one end, and one on the other side near the other end; and thus I lay till the water ebbed away, and left my raft and all my cargo safe on shore.

My next work was to view the country, and seek a proper place for my habitation, and where to stow my goods to secure them from whatever might happen; where I was I yet knew not, whether on the continent or on an island, whether inhabited or not inhabited, whether in danger of wild beasts or not. There was a hill not above a mile from me, which rose up very steep and high, and which seemed to overtop some other hills which lay as in a ridge from it northward. I took out one of the fowling pieces, and one of the pistols, and a horn of powder; and thus armed I travelled for discovery up to the top of that hill, where after I had with great labor and difficulty got to the top, I saw my fate to my great affliction, (viz.) that I was in an island environed every way with the sea, no land to be seen, except some rocks which lay a great way off; and two small islands less than this, which lay about three leagues[3] to the west.

I found also that the island I was in was barren, and, as I saw good reason to believe, uninhabited, except by wild beasts, of whom however I saw none, yet I saw abundance of fowls, but knew not their kinds, neither when I killed them could I tell what was fit for food, and what not; at my coming

1. It would have taken only.
2. Required about a foot of water to float.
3. A league is about three miles.

back, I shot at a great bird which I saw sitting upon a tree on the side of a great wood. I believe it was the first gun that had been fired there since the creation of the world; I had no sooner fired, but from all parts of the wood there arose an innumerable number of fowls of many sorts, making a confused screaming, and crying every one according to his usual note, but not one of them of any kind that I knew. As for the creature I killed, I took it to be a kind of a hawk, its color and beak resembling it, but had no talons or claws more than common; its flesh was carrion, and fit for nothing.

Contented with this discovery, I came back to my raft, and fell to work to bring my cargo on shore, which took me up the rest of that day, and what to do with myself at night I knew not, nor indeed where to rest; for I was afraid to lie down on the ground, not knowing but some wild beast might devour me, though, as I afterwards found, there was really no need for those fears.

However, as well as I could, I barricadoed myself round with the chests and boards that I had brought on shore, and made a kind of hut for that night's lodging; as for food, I yet saw not which way to supply myself, except that I had seen two or three creatures like hares run out of the wood where I shot the fowl.

I now began to consider, that I might yet get a great many things out of the ship, which would be useful to me, and particularly some of the rigging, and sails, and such other things as might come to land; and I resolved to make another voyage on board the vessel, if possible; and as I knew that the first storm that blew must necessarily break her all in pieces, I resolved to set all other things apart,[4] till I got everything out of the ship that I could get; then I called a council, that is to say, in my thoughts, whether I should take back the raft; but this appeared impracticable: so I resolved to go as before, when the tide was down; and I did so, only that I stripped before I went from my hut, having nothing on but a checkered shirt, a pair of linen drawers, and a pair of pumps[5] on my feet.

I got on board the ship, as before, and prepared a second raft; and having had experience of the first, I neither made this so unwieldy, nor loaded it so hard, but yet I brought away several things very useful to me; as first, in the carpenter's stores I found two or three bags full of nails and spikes, a great screw-jack, a dozen or two of hatchets, and above all, that most useful thing called a grindstone.[6] All these I secured together with several things belonging to the gunner, particularly two or three iron crows,[7] and two barrels of musket bullets, seven muskets, another fowling-piece, with some small quantity of powder more; a large bagful of small shot, and a great roll of sheet-lead. But this last was so heavy I could not hoise it up to get it over the ship's side.

Besides these things, I took all the men's clothes that I could find, and a spare fore-topsail, a hammock and some bedding; and with this I loaded my second raft, and brought them all safe on shore to my very great comfort.

I was under some apprehensions during my absence from the land, that at least my provisions might be devoured on shore: but when I came back, I

---

4. Put everything else aside.
5. Low-heeled shoes.
6. A stone disk on an axle, for grinding and sharp-

ening. "Screw-jack": a jack, for lifting heavy objects.
7. Crowbars.

found no sign of any visitor, only there sat a creature like a wild cat upon one of the chests, which when I came towards it, ran away a little distance, and then stood still; she sat very composed, and unconcerned, and looked full in my face, as if she had a mind to be acquainted with me. I presented[8] my gun at her, but as she did not understand it, she was perfectly unconcerned at it, nor did she offer to stir away; upon which I tossed her a bit of biscuit, though by the way I was not very free of it, for my store was not great: however, I spared her a bit, I say, and she went to it, smelled of it, and ate it, and looked (as pleased) for more, but I thanked her, and could spare no more; so she marched off.

Having got my second cargo on shore, though I was fain to open the barrels of powder, and bring them by parcels, for they were too heavy, being large casks, I went to work to make me a little tent with the sail and some poles which I cut for that purpose, and into this tent I brought everything that I knew would spoil, either with rain or sun, and I piled all the empty chests and casks up in a circle round the tent, to fortify it from any sudden attempt, either from man or beast.

When I had done this I blocked up the door of the tent with some boards within, and an empty chest set up on end without, and spreading one of the beds upon the ground, laying my two pistols just at my head, and my gun at length by me, I went to bed for the first time, and slept very quietly all night, for I was very weary and heavy, for the night before I had slept little, and had labored very hard all day, as well to fetch all those things from the ship, as to get them on shore.

I had the biggest magazine[9] of all kinds now that ever were laid up, I believe, for one man: but I was not satisfied still; for while the ship sat upright in that posture, I thought I ought to get everything out of her that I could; so every day at low water I went on board, and brought away something or other; but particularly the third time I went, I brought away as much of the rigging as I could, as also all the small ropes and rope-twine I could get, with a piece of spare canvas, which was to mend the sails upon occasion,[1] and the barrel of wet gunpowder. In a word, I brought away all the sails first and last, only that I was fain to cut them in pieces, and bring as much at a time as I could, for they were no more useful to be sails, but as mere canvas only.

But that which comforted me more still was that last of all, after I had made five or six such voyages as these, and thought I had nothing more to expect from the ship that was worth my meddling with, I say, after all this, I found a great hogshead of bread, three large runlets[2] of rum or spirits, a box of sugar, and a barrel of fine flour; this was surprising to me, because I had given over expecting any more provisions, except what was spoiled by the water. I soon emptied the hogshead of that bread, and wrapped it up parcel by parcel in pieces of the sails, which I cut out; and, in a word, I got all this safe on shore also.

The next day I made another voyage; and now having plundered the ship of what was portable and fit to hand out, I began with the cables; and cutting the great cable into pieces, such as I could move, I got two cables and a hawser on shore, with all the ironwork I could get; and having cut down the spritsail-yard,

---

8. Pointed.
9. Store of goods.

1. When necessary.
2. Casks. "Hogshead": large cask.

and the mizzen-yard,[3] and everything I could to make a large raft, I loaded it with all those heavy goods, and came away; but my good luck began now to leave me; for this raft was so unwieldy, and so overladen, that after I was entered the little cove, where I had landed the rest of my goods, not being able to guide it so handily as I did the other, it overset, and threw me and all my cargo into the water; as for myself, it was no great harm, for I was near the shore; but as to my cargo, it was a great part of it lost, especially the iron, which I expected would have been of great use to me; however, when the tide was out, I got most of the pieces of the cable ashore, and some of the iron, though with infinite labor; for I was fain to dip[4] for it into the water, a work which fatigued me very much. After this, I went every day on board, and brought away what I could get.

I had been now thirteen days on shore, and had been eleven times on board the ship; in which time I had brought away all that one pair of hands could well be supposed capable to bring, though I believe verily, had the calm weather held, I should have brought away the whole ship piece by piece. But preparing the twelfth time to go on board, I found the wind begin to rise: however, at low water I went on board, and though I thought I had rummaged the cabin so effectually as that nothing more could be found, yet I discovered a locker with drawers in it, in one of which I found two or three razors, and one pair of large scissors, with some ten or a dozen of good knives and forks: in another I found about thirty-six pounds value in money, some European coin, some Brazil, some pieces of eight, some gold, some silver.

I smiled to myself at the sight of this money. "O drug!" said I aloud, "what art thou good for? Thou art not worth to me, no not the taking off of the ground, one of those knives is worth all this heap, I have no manner of use for thee, e'en remain where thou art, and go to the bottom as a creature whose life is not worth saving." However upon second thoughts, I took it away; and wrapping all this in a piece of canvas, I began to think of making another raft, but while I was preparing this, I found the sky overcast, and the wind began to rise, and in a quarter of an hour it blew a fresh gale from the shore; it presently occurred to me that it was in vain to pretend[5] to make a raft with the wind off shore, and that it was my business to be gone before the tide of flood began, otherwise I might not be able to reach the shore at all. Accordingly I let myself down into the water, and swam across the channel, which lay between the ship and the sands, and even that with difficulty enough, partly with the weight of the things I had about me, and partly the roughness of the water, for the wind rose very hastily, and before it was quite high water, it blew a storm.

But I was gotten home to my little tent, where I lay with all my wealth about me very secure. It blew very hard all that night, and in the morning when I looked out, behold no more ship was to be seen; I was a little surprised, but recovered myself with the satisfactory reflection, viz. that I had lost no time, nor abated no diligence to get everything out of her that could be useful to me, and that indeed there was little left in her that I was able to bring away if I had had more time.

3. The yards are wood pieces that support different sails.
4. Dive.
5. Attempt.

I now gave over any more thoughts of the ship, or of anything out of her, except what might drive on shore from her wreck, as indeed divers pieces of her afterwards did; but those things were of small use to me.

* * *

1719

From The Farther Adventures of Robinson Crusoe

The Preface

The success the former part of this work has met with in the world has yet been no other than is acknowledged to be due to the surprising variety of the subject, and to the agreeable manner of the performance.

All the endeavors of envious people to reproach it with being a romance,[1] to search it for errors in geography, inconsistency in the relation, and contradictions in the fact, have proved abortive, and as impotent as malicious.

The just application of every incident, the religious and useful inferences drawn from every part, are so many testimonies to the good design of making it public, and must legitimate all the part that may be called invention, or parable in the story.

The second part, if the editor's opinion may pass, is (contrary to the usage of[2] second parts) every way as entertaining as the first, contains as strange and surprising incidents, and as great a variety of them; nor is the application less serious, or suitable; and doubtless will, to the sober, as well as ingenious reader, be every way as profitable and diverting: and this makes the abridging this work as scandalous as it is knavish and ridiculous,[3] seeing, while to shorten the book, that they may seem to reduce the value, they strip it of all those reflections, as well religious as moral, which are not only the greatest beauties of the work, but are calculated for the infinite advantage of the reader.

By this they leave the work naked of its brightest ornaments; and if they would at the same time pretend that the author has supplied the story out of his invention, they take from it the improvement, which alone recommends that invention to wise and good men.

The injury these men do to the proprietor of this work is a practice all honest men abhor; and he believes he may challenge them to show the difference between that and robbing on the highway, or breaking open a house.

If they can't show any difference in the crime, they will find it hard to show why there should be any difference in the punishment: And he will answer for it, that nothing shall be wanting on his part, to do them justice.

1719

1. A fanciful, fictional tale.
2. What is usual with. "The second part": the current volume, *The Farther Adventures*.
3. Abridgements of *The Life and Surprising*

Adventures of Robinson Crusoe appeared the year it was published and were a flourishing enterprise throughout the remainder of the century.

MARY DAVYS

Mary Davys (1674–1732) was born in Ireland and married a Dublin clergyman, a college friend of Jonathan Swift. Her husband died after just four years of marriage; their first daughter died before, their second just after him. Nearly destitute, she moved to London in 1700, published two works of fiction, then moved to York. Her play, *The Northern Heiress*, was staged there in 1715, and in London the next year. It earned money enough for her to open a coffeehouse in Cambridge in 1718, where she lived the rest of her life. Her best fiction, which displays her talent for deft plotting, colorful, concrete dialogue, and humorous situations, appeared in the 1720s. *The Reform'd Coquet* (1725), a comic novel about a vain young woman who learns to value the right man, sold well enough to inspire the publication of *The Works of Mary Davys* (also 1725), which contained plays, poems, and fiction. Her final novel, *The Accomplish'd Rake* (1727) takes a satirical view of the dissolute ways of fashionable London life. The preface to her *Works* offers an important perspective on both the theory and the practice of novel writing. She defines novels as "probable feigned stories," noting their decline in sales compared to histories and travels—perhaps thinking, among other works, of the success of Defoe's *Robinson Crusoe* (1719), which would not commonly be called a novel until decades later. She also reflects on her tough literary career, as "a woman left to her own endeavors for twenty-seven years together," battling back against undeserved censures for bawdiness. (Late in her life, in 1731, *The Grub-Street Journal* published another such attack, and again she replied, "the novels may e'ne fight their own battles . . . they are too unfashionable to have one word of bawdy in them, the readers are the best judges and to them I appeal.") Though literary historians now recognize how the success of Davys and other women writers of her time shaped the history of the novel, her story reminds us it never came easy.

From The Works of Mary Davys

The Preface

'Tis now for some time that those sort of writings called novels have been a great deal out of use and fashion, and that the ladies (for whose service they were chiefly designed) have been taken up with amusements of more use and improvement: I mean history and travels: with which the relation of probable feigned stories can by no means stand in competition. However, these are not without their advantages, and those considerable too; and it is very likely the chief reason that put them out of vogue was the world's being surfeited with such as were either flat and insipid, or offensive to modesty and good manners; or that they found them only a circle or repetition of the same adventures.

The French, who have dealt most in this kind, have, I think, chiefly contributed to put them out of countenance:[1] who, though upon all occasions,

---

1. Make them unpopular.

and where they pretend to write true history, give themselves the utmost liberty of feigning, are too tedious and dry in their matter, and so impertinent in their harangues, that the readers can hardly keep themselves awake over them. I have read a French novel of four hundred pages without the least variety of events, or any issue[2] in the conclusion, either to please or amuse the reader, yet all fiction and romance; and the commonest matters of fact, truly told, would have been much more entertaining. Now this is to lose the only advantage of invention, which gives us room to order accidents[3] better than fortune will be at the pains to do; so to work upon the reader's passions, sometimes keep him in suspense between fear and hope, and at last send him satisfied away. This I have endeavored to do in the following sheets.[4] I have in every novel proposed one entire scheme or plot, and the other adventures are only incident or collateral to it; which is the great rule prescribed by the critics, not only in tragedy, and other heroic poems, but in comedy too. The adventures, as far as I could order them, are wonderful[5] and probable; and I have with the utmost justice rewarded virtue, and punished vice. *The Lady's Tale* was writ in the year 1700, and was the effect of my first flight to the muses, it was sent about the world as naked as it came into it, having not so much as one page of preface to keep it in countenance.[6] What success it met with, I never knew; for as some unnatural parents sell their offspring to beggars, in order to see them no more, I took three guineas for the brat of my brain, and then went a hundred and fifty miles northward,[7] to which place it was not very likely its fame should follow. But meeting with it some time ago, I found it in a sad ragged condition, and had so much pity for it, as to take it home, and get it into better clothes, that when it made a second sally,[8] it might with more assurance appear before its betters.

My whole design both in that and *The Cousins*[9] is to endeavor to restore the purity and empire of love, and correct the vile abuses of it; which, could I do, it would be an important service to the public: for since passions will ever have a place in the actions of men, and love a principal one, what cannot be removed or subdued ought at least to be regulated; and if the reformation would once begin from our sex, the men would follow it in spite of their hearts; for it is we have given up our empire, betrayed by rebels among ourselves.

The two plays I leave to fight their own battles; and I shall say no more than that I never was so vain as to think they deserved a place in the first rank, or so humble as to resign them to the last.

I have been so anxious for the credit of my *Modern Poet*[1] that I showed it to several of my friends, and earnestly begged their impartial opinion of it. Every one separately told me his objection, but not two among them agreed in any one particular; so that I found, to remove all the faults, would be to leave nothing behind, and I could not help thinking my case parallel with the man in the fable, whose two wives disliking, one his gray hairs, and the other his black, picked both out, till they left him nothing but a bald pate.

2. Outcome.
3. Incidents in a story.
4. Pages.
5. Full of wonders.
6. To give it support.
7. Davys moved to York from London in 1704.

8. When published a second time, in this edition.
9. Another short novel in volume 2 of Davys's *Works*.
1. A long poem in couplets that concludes volume 1 of Davys's *Works*.

Perhaps it may be objected against me, by some more ready to give reproach than relief, that as I am the relict of a clergyman, and in years,[2] I ought not to publish plays, &c. But I beg of such to suspend their uncharitable opinions, till they have read what I have writ, and if they find anything there offensive either to God or Man, anything either to shock their morals or their modesty, 'tis then time enough to blame. And let them farther consider, that a woman left to her own endeavors for twenty-seven years together, may well be allowed to catch at any opportunity for that bread, which they that condemn her would very probably deny to give her.

1725

2. Davys was fifty-one when she published her works. "Relict": widow.

HENRY FIELDING

Writing novels was a second literary career for Henry Fielding (1707–1754), who first became famous as the preeminent comic playwright of his time. The need to make money motivated both. He was from a family with high social connections, a relation of earls and second cousin to Lady Mary Wortley Montagu, and he received a classical education (1719–24) at England's most elite school, Eton, forming friendships with the nation's future leaders. But his prodigal father, an army colonel who would rise to the rank of general, squandered the fortune that Henry needed to live the life of a gentleman he thought he deserved. Early on, Fielding determined on a career as a writer to maintain this life, seeing his first comedy staged in London when he was twenty. After some time studying literature at the University of Leiden in Holland, he returned to England and wrote for the theater, specializing in farces, ballad operas, and political satires. These last were so successful that the ministry of Robert Walpole passed the Licensing Act of 1737, which subjected all new plays to government censorship and closed the Haymarket Theatre where Fielding's plays were produced, effectively ending his theatrical career. He studied law and was admitted to the bar in 1740.

That year also he aimed his talent for parody at the greatest sensation in fiction of the day, *Pamela, or Virtue Rewarded* (1740) by Samuel Richardson. Fielding's *Shamela* makes fun of that novel's epistolary style and of its heroine's way of using her chastity to her advantage. He extends the joke in his next fictional work, *Joseph Andrews* (1742), which follows Pamela's brother, a footman employed by a lady who attempts to seduce him. But Fielding now aspired to be much more than a parodist of Richardson, acknowledging Cervantes' great *Don Quixote* (1605, 1616) as a model even as he remarks in the preface on his own originality. Seven years later, he asserted this claim yet more strongly in his masterpiece *Tom Jones* (1749), in which he declares himself "founder of a new province of writing." He concluded his novelistic career with *Amelia* (1751), which disappointed some readers as it indulged sentiments reminiscent of Richardson's own idiom. (One wit in response advertised a nonexistent novel called *Shamelia*.)

· Despite his initial contempt, Fielding had sent Richardson a letter warm with praise for *Clarissa*: "beyond any thing I have ever read," he said of one affecting part. Though gratified, Richardson remained hostile and would never miss a chance to deplore the bad morals of *Tom Jones*. From their rivalry, a multilayered contrast arose in commentary on novelistic fiction that strongly influenced later understandings of the form's possibilities. Richardson's excellences—his moral, psychological, and emotional intensity, his preference for feminine protagonists and intimate domestic settings, his orchestration of narrative through the first-person voices of correspondents—seemed incompatible with Fielding's strengths: a comic vigor and well-populated plots that open out into the countryside and twist through chaotic scenes at public inns, overseen in the third person by an ironic, sociable author-narrator who smiles at the lapses of basically good-hearted heroes.

The preface to *Joseph Andrews* asserts not only the novelty of Fielding's fictional enterprise but also its potential as high literary art. Fielding notices its deep connection to ancient and exalted literary forms, comedy and epic. His techniques also compare, he says, with those of his friend, "the comic history painter" William Hogarth, whose art represents the ridiculous in human nature without falling into unrealistic exaggeration and caricature. The theory of the ridiculous in the preface considers not only the undistorted representation of fictional characters but also realities of human motivation and morality. Fielding's intent here to tell the reader what to think about his work will enter the body of this and his other novels, as his narrator points out details of the plot, moralizes on his characters' behavior, and theorizes on the nature of fiction. In *Joseph Andrews*, he will depict the vicissitudes that finally bring the hero Joseph, virtuous but warmly in love with a young woman of his own social station, Fanny Goodwill, to a happy end. The resolution of the plot, which includes Joseph's discovery of his true identity, employs some conventions of romance; and the preface applies that term to *Joseph Andrews* without embarrassment, though it contrasts this novel with the vast French prose romances of the seventeenth century. Fielding seems most taken with his creation of Parson Abraham Adams, who accompanies Joseph and Fanny on their adventures and sponsors their match—a character the likes of whom, Fielding says, is "not to be found in any book now extant." Readers have concurred with this sense of Adams's uniqueness, a result of his pleasing (if at times maddening and puzzling) power to elicit both ridicule and affection. The success of Adams as a literary creation points to a feature typical of novels in the future: their construction of what the twentieth-century novelist E. M. Forster would call "round" characters. Instead of presenting simplifications of human beings, novels introduce characters that seem to breathe, feel, and think. Fielding's power to raise affection for such characters while also comprehensively surveying an entire social world lies at the heart of his achievement.

From The History of the Adventures of Joseph Andrews[1]

Preface

As it is possible the mere English reader may have a different idea of romance with the author of these little volumes,[2] and may consequently expect a kind of entertainment not to be found, nor which was even intended, in the following pages, it may not be improper to premise a few words concerning this kind of writing, which I do not remember to have seen hitherto attempted in our language.

The epic as well as the drama is divided into tragedy and comedy. Homer, who was the father of this species of poetry, gave us a pattern of both these,

---

1. The entire title on the title page runs, *The History of the Adventures of Joseph Andrews, and his Friend, Mr. Abraham Adams, Written in Imitation* *of the Manner of Cervantes, Author of Don Quixote.* 2. *Joseph Andrews* was originally published to two duodecimo (small) volumes.

though that of the latter kind is entirely lost; which Aristotle tells us bore the same relation to comedy which his *Iliad* bears to tragedy.[3] And perhaps, that we have no more instances of it among the writers of antiquity, is owing to the loss of this great pattern, which, had it survived, would have found its imitators equally with the other poems of this great original.

And farther, as this poetry may be tragic or comic, I will not scruple to say it may be likewise either in verse or prose: for though it wants one particular, which the critic[4] enumerates in the constituent parts of an epic poem, namely meter; yet, when any kind of writing contains all its other parts, such as fable, action, characters, sentiments, and diction,[5] and is deficient in meter only; it seems, I think, reasonable to refer it to the epic; at least, as no critic hath thought proper to range it under any other head, or to assign it a particular name to itself.

Thus the *Telemachus* of the archbishop of Cambray appears to me of the epic kind, as well as[6] the *Odyssey* of Homer; indeed, it is much fairer and more reasonable to give it a name common with that species from which it differs only in a single instance, than to confound it with those which it resembles in no other. Such are those voluminous works, commonly called romances, namely, *Clelia, Cleopatra, Astraea, Cassandra,* the *Grand Cyrus,*[7] and innumerable others, which contain, as I apprehend, very little instruction or entertainment.

Now a comic romance is a comic epic-poem in prose; differing from comedy, as the serious epic from tragedy: its action being more extended and comprehensive; containing a much larger circle of incidents, and introducing a greater variety of characters. It differs from the serious romance in its fable and action, in this: that as in the one these are grave and solemn, so in the other they are light and ridiculous: it differs in its characters by introducing persons of inferior rank, and consequently of inferior manners, whereas the grave romance sets the highest before us: lastly in its sentiments and diction; by preserving the ludicrous instead of the sublime.[8] In the diction, I think, burlesque[9] itself may be sometimes admitted; of which many instances will occur in this work, as in the description of the battles, and some other places, not necessary to be pointed out to the classical reader, for whose entertainment those parodies or burlesque imitations are chiefly calculated.

But though we have sometimes admitted this in our diction, we have carefully excluded it from our sentiments and characters; for there it is never properly introduced, unless in writings of the burlesque kind, which this is not intended to be. Indeed, no two species of writing can differ more widely than the comic and the burlesque; for as the latter is ever the exhibition of what is monstrous and unnatural, and where our delight, if we examine it, arises from the surprising absurdity, as in appropriating the manners of the

---

3. In the *Poetics* (ca. 335 B.C.E.), Aristotle mentions a comic mock-epic of Homer's, the *Margites*, which is now lost.
4. Aristotle. "Wants": lacks.
5. Epic poetry shares this list of elements with tragedy, according to Aristotle. "Fable": story, plot. "Sentiments": thoughts.
6. Just as much as. François de Salignac de Mothe Fénelon (1651–1715) published the prose epic *Telemachus* in French in 1699.

7. All popular, multivolume French romances of the 17th century. Madeleine de Scudéry (1607–1701) wrote *Clélie* (1654–60) and *Artamène, ou le Grand Cyrus* (1647–58). Gautier de Costes de la Calprenède (ca. 1610–1663) wrote *Cléopatre* (1647–58) and *Cassandre* (1642–45). Honoré d'Urfé (1567–1625) wrote *L'Astrée* (1607–27).
8. Lofty ideas and language.
9. Comically exaggerated imitation.

highest to the lowest, or *è converso;*[1] so in the former we should ever confine ourselves strictly to nature, from the just imitation of which will flow all the pleasure we can this way convey to a sensible reader. And perhaps there is one reason why a comic writer should of all others be the least excused for deviating from nature, since it may not be always so easy for a serious poet to meet with the great and the admirable; but life everywhere furnishes an accurate observer with the ridiculous.

I have hinted this little concerning burlesque; because I have often heard that name given to performances which have been truly of the comic kind, from the author's having sometimes admitted it in his diction only; which, as it is the dress of poetry, doth like the dress of men establish characters (the one of the whole poem, and the other of the whole man) in vulgar opinion, beyond any of their greater excellencies. But surely a certain drollery in style, where the characters and sentiments are perfectly natural, no more constitutes the burlesque, than an empty pomp and dignity of words, where everything else is mean and low, can entitle any performance to the appellation of the true sublime.

And I apprehend my Lord Shaftesbury's opinion of mere burlesque agrees with mine, when he asserts, "There is no such thing to be found in the writings of the ancients."[2] But perhaps I have less abhorrence than he professes for it; and that not because I have had some little success on the stage this way,[3] but rather as it contributes more to exquisite mirth and laughter than any other; and these are probably more wholesome physic for the mind, and conduce better to purge away spleen,[4] melancholy, and ill affections, than is generally imagined. Nay, I will appeal to common observation, whether the same companies are not found more full of good-humor and benevolence, after they have been sweetened for two or three hours with entertainments of this kind, than when soured by a tragedy or a grave lecture.

But to illustrate all this by another science, in which, perhaps, we shall see the distinction more clearly and plainly: let us examine the works of a comic history painter,[5] with those performances which the Italians call *caricatura,* where we shall find the true excellence of the former to consist in the exactest copy of nature; insomuch that a judicious eye instantly rejects anything *outré,* any liberty which the painter hath taken with the features of that *alma mater.*[6]—Whereas in the *caricatura* we allow all license. Its aim is to exhibit monsters, not men; and all distortions and exaggerations whatever are within its proper province.

Now, what *caricatura* is in painting, burlesque is in writing; and in the same manner the comic writer and painter correlate to each other. And here I shall observe, that as in the former the painter seems to have the advantage; so it is in the latter infinitely on the side of the writer; for the monstrous is much easier to paint than describe, and the ridiculous to describe than paint.

---

1. To the contrary (Latin); i.e., vice versa.
2. This idea is delivered in *Sensus Communis: An Essay on the Freedom of Wit and Humor* (1709) by Anthony Ashley Cooper, third earl of Shaftesbury (1671–1713), though not exactly in these words.
3. Fielding's plays of the 1730s, including *The Tragedy of Tragedies, or the Life and Death of Tom Thumb the Great* (1731), frequently offered burlesque and parody.
4. Bad temper. "Physic": medical treatment.
5. William Hogarth (1697–1764), English artist and Fielding's friend, praised in the next paragraph.
6. Bounteous mother (Latin); here nature. "*Caricatura*": caricature (Italian); the art of exaggerated portraiture.

And though perhaps this latter species doth not in either science so strongly affect and agitate the muscles as the other; yet it will be owned, I believe, that a more rational and useful pleasure arises to us from it. He who should call the ingenious Hogarth a burlesque painter, would, in my opinion, do him very little honor; for sure it is much easier, much less the subject of admiration, to paint a man with a nose or any other feature, of a preposterous size, or to expose him in some absurd or monstrous attitude, than to express the affections of men on canvas. It hath been thought a vast commendation of a painter to say his figures seem to breathe; but surely it is a much greater and nobler applause, that they appear to think.

But to return. The ridiculous only, as I have before said, falls within my province in the present work. Nor will some explanation of this word be thought impertinent by the reader, if he considers how wonderfully it hath been mistaken, even by writers who have professed it: for to what but such a mistake can we attribute the many attempts to ridicule the blackest villainies, and, what is yet worse, the most dreadful calamities? What could exceed the absurdity of an author, who should write the comedy of Nero, with the merry incident of ripping up his mother's belly?[7] or what would give a greater shock to humanity than an attempt to expose the miseries of poverty and distress to ridicule? And yet the reader will not want much learning to suggest such instances to himself.

Besides, it may seem remarkable that Aristotle, who is so fond and free of definitions, hath not thought proper to define the ridiculous. Indeed, where he tells us it is proper to comedy, he hath remarked that villainy is not its object: but he hath not, as I remember, positively asserted what is. Nor doth the Abbé Bellegarde, who hath written a treatise on this subject,[8] though he shows us many species of it, once trace it to its fountain.

The only source of the true ridiculous (as it appears to me) is affectation. But though it arises from one spring only, when we consider the infinite streams into which this one branches, we shall presently cease to admire[9] at the copious field it affords to an observer. Now, affectation proceeds from one of these two causes, vanity or hypocrisy: for as vanity puts us on affecting false characters, in order to purchase applause; so hypocrisy sets us on an endeavor to avoid censure, by concealing our vices under an appearance of their opposite virtues. And though these two causes are often confounded (for there is some difficulty in distinguishing them), yet, as they proceed from very different motives, so they are as clearly distinct in their operations: for indeed, the affectation which arises from vanity is nearer to truth than the other, as it hath not that violent repugnancy of nature to struggle with, which that of the hypocrite hath. It may be likewise noted, that affectation doth not imply an absolute negation of those qualities which are affected; and, therefore, though, when it proceeds from hypocrisy, it be nearly allied to deceit; yet when it comes from vanity only, it partakes of the nature of ostentation: for instance, the affectation of liberality in a vain man differs visibly from the same affectation in the avaricious; for though the vain man is not what he would appear, or hath not the virtue he

7. According to some accounts, the assassins sent by Roman emperor Nero (37–68) to kill his mother stabbed her in the womb.
8. This work (1696) by Jean Baptiste Morvan de Bellegarde (1648–1734) was translated as *Reflexions upon Ridicule, or What It Is that Makes a Man Ridiculous, and How to Avoid It* (1706).
9. Wonder.

affects, to the degree he would be thought to have it; yet it sits less awkwardly on him than on the avaricious man, who is the very reverse of what he would seem to be.

From the discovery of this affectation arises the ridiculous, which always strikes the reader with surprise and pleasure; and that in a higher and stronger degree when the affectation arises from hypocrisy, than when from vanity; for to discover any one to be the exact reverse of what he affects, is more surprising, and consequently more ridiculous, than to find him a little deficient in the quality he desires the reputation of. I might observe that our Ben Jonson,[1] who of all men understood the ridiculous the best, hath chiefly used the hypocritical affectation.

Now from affectation only, the misfortunes and calamities of life, or the imperfections of nature, may become the objects of ridicule. Surely he hath a very ill-framed mind who can look on ugliness, infirmity, or poverty, as ridiculous in themselves: nor do I believe any man living, who meets a dirty fellow riding through the streets in a cart, is struck with an idea of the ridiculous from it; but if he should see the same figure descend from his coach and six, or bolt from his chair[2] with his hat under his arm, he would then begin to laugh, and with justice. In the same manner, were we to enter a poor house and behold a wretched family shivering with cold and languishing with hunger, it would not incline us to laughter (at least we must have very diabolical natures if it would); but should we discover there a grate, instead of coals, adorned with flowers, empty plate or china dishes on the sideboard, or any other affectation of riches and finery, either on their persons or in their furniture, we might then indeed be excused for ridiculing so fantastical an appearance. Much less are natural imperfections the object of derision; but when ugliness aims at the applause of beauty, or lameness endeavors to display agility, it is then that these unfortunate circumstances, which at first moved our compassion, tend only to raise our mirth.

The poet carries this very far:

> None are for being what they are in fault,
> But for not being what they would be thought.[3]

Where if the meter would suffer the word "ridiculous" to close the first line, the thought would be rather more proper. Great vices are the proper objects of our detestation, smaller faults, of our pity; but affectation appears to me the only true source of the ridiculous.

But perhaps it may be objected to me that I have against my own rules introduced vices, and of a very black kind, into this work. To which I shall answer: first, that it is very difficult to pursue a series of human actions, and keep clear from them. Secondly, that the vices to be found here are rather the accidental consequences of some human frailty or foible, than causes habitually existing in the mind. Thirdly, that they are never set forth as the objects of ridicule, but detestation. Fourthly, that they are never the principal figure at that time on the scene: and, lastly they never produce the intended evil.

Having thus distinguished *Joseph Andrews* from the productions of romance writers on the one hand and burlesque writers on the other, and

---

1. English dramatist and poet (ca. 1572–1637).
2. Sedan chair, a closed cabin for one passenger carried by two bearers.

3. From "Of Pleasing: An Epistle to Sir William Temple," lines 63–4, by William Congreve (1670–1729).

given some few very short hints (for I intended no more) of this species of writing, which I have affirmed to be hitherto unattempted in our language; I shall leave to my good-natured reader to apply my piece to my observations, and will detain him no longer than with a word concerning the characters in this work.

And here I solemnly protest I have no intention to vilify or asperse any one; for though everything is copied from the book of nature, and scarce a character or action produced which I have not taken from my own observations and experience; yet I have used the utmost care to obscure the persons by such different circumstances, degrees, and colors, that it will be impossible to guess at them with any degree of certainty; and if it ever happens otherwise, it is only where the failure characterized is so minute, that it is a foible only which the party himself may laugh at as well as any other.

As to the character of Adams,[4] as it is the most glaring in the whole, so I conceive it is not to be found in any book now extant. It is designed a character of perfect simplicity; and as the goodness of his heart will recommend him to the good-natured, so I hope it will excuse me to the gentlemen of his cloth;[5] for whom, while they are worthy of their sacred order, no man can possibly have a greater respect. They will therefore excuse me, notwithstanding the low adventures in which he is engaged, that I have made him a clergyman; since no other office could have given him so many opportunities of displaying his worthy inclinations.

1742

4. A principal character in the novel, whose innocence and simplemindedness are intended to elicit both affection and laughter.
5. Clergymen.

SARAH FIELDING

Sarah Fielding (1710–1768), sister of Henry Fielding, significantly contributed to mid-eighteenth-century fiction. Her novels won her recognition and success, especially her first, The Adventures of David Simple (1744), anonymously published and initially attributed to her brother, despite its self-identification as "the work of a woman." (He would support her career by providing prefaces to David Simple's second edition and to its epistolary continuation, 1747.) Her Remarks on Clarissa (1749) influenced Samuel Richardson's revisions in later editions of his great novel, which she deeply admired. In the "Advertisement" of David Simple, she expresses the tentativeness of a woman author embarking on a literary career out of financial distress, yet her designation of her novel as a "moral romance" stakes out her own terrain, distinct from both her brother's and Richardson's rival conceptions of novelistic fiction.

From The Adventures of David Simple[1]

Advertisement to the Reader

The following moral romance (or whatever title the reader shall please to give it) is the work of a woman, and her first essay;[2] which, to the good-natured and candid reader will, it is hoped, be a sufficient apology for the many inaccuracies he will find in the style, and other faults of the composition.

Perhaps the best excuse that can be made for a woman's venturing to write at all, is that which really produced this book: distress in her circumstances; which she could not so well remove by any other means in her power.

If it should meet with success, it will be the only good fortune she ever has known; but as she is very sensible, that must chiefly depend upon the entertainment the world will find in the book itself, and not upon what she can say in the preface, either to move their compassion, or bespeak their good-will, she will detain them from it no longer.

1744

---

1. The original title page reads *The Adventures of David Simple: Containing an Account of his Travels through the Cities of London and Westminster,* *in the Search of a Real Friend*, by a Lady.
2. Attempt (at fiction).

SAMUEL RICHARDSON

The novels of Samuel Richardson (1689–1761) emerged not from a genteel literary world of elite education and social privilege but from a London culture of printing presses, paper, type, and ink. He came to his position as one of the two most celebrated masters of eighteenth-century fiction with (in his words) "only common school-learning," without Latin or Greek, starting in the book trades as a printer's apprentice in London. He held that position for seven years, then worked for his former master as a compositor and corrector, and finally in 1722 gained the livery of the Stationer's Company, the guild of London printers, that licensed him to set up his own printing business, at the age of thirty-three. Through the 1720s and 1730s this business thrived, as he printed documents for the government, periodicals, and many kinds of books and also did work as an editor, a bookseller, and occasionally an author.

In 1739 he was composing a book of sample letters to serve as models for correspondence when one pair of them, an exchange about a master's violent sexual harassment of a servant girl, sparked an idea. In two months, he wrote his first novel, *Pamela, or Virtue Rewarded* (1740)—published, like all the miscellaneous work he had previously written, anonymously (though his authorship soon became known). In a 1741 letter, he would describe it as representing a "new species of writing" that did not traffic in "the improbable and marvelous, with which novels general abound." *Pamela* elaborated on the situation in the letter manual and was itself an epistolary novel, composed entirely in letters, mostly written by the servant, Pamela Andrews, to her parents. She is "rewarded" near the end with a proposal of marriage from her finally reformed master Mr. B, which she accepts. The novel was a vast success, running to five editions in a year, inspiring rapturous praise and censures of its erotic content and disruption of social hierarchy, continuations by other writers, theatrical adaptations, prints and other visual representations, and parodies, notably Henry Fielding's *Shamela* (1740) and Eliza Haywood's *Anti-Pamela* (1741). Richardson himself wrote a sequel in 1741, but his greatest achievement as a novelist would appear in 1747 and 1748, in seven volumes: *Clarissa, or the History of a Young Lady*, also composed of letters, nearly a million words long, follows the trials of Clarissa Harlowe, young, pious, rich, and beautiful, whose family cruelly forces her toward a financially advantageous marriage to an odious man. Clarissa is deceived into accepting the aid of a handsome libertine of high station, Lovelace, her great antagonist, bent on possessing and destroying her. Richardson's final novel, *The History of Sir Charles Grandison* (1753–54) portrays a truly good man, as an antidote to the specious appeal of men such as his own villain Lovelace and Fielding's comical hero Tom Jones, whom he thought far from harmless. Also notably prolix (seven volumes long) and also an epistolary novel, *Grandison* has not lived in readers' imaginations quite as *Pamela* and *Clarissa* have done, though its portrayal of intimate rhythms of domestic life (if not of male virtue) captivated later masters of fiction such as Jane Austen.

Richardson did not invent epistolary fiction—Aphra Behn's *Love-Letters between a Nobleman and His Sister* (three volumes, 1684–87) is a substantial earlier example—but his works did more for the prestige of the form in European literature than those of any other author. A skeptical reader such as Henry Fielding can find aspects of the epistolary form that strain credulity. How do the authors of so very many letters find time to live the lives they so copiously write about? Where are these letters, who has them, and how did this "editor" get them from correspondents who are estranged or widely distant from each other, or dead? Yet the documentary illusion of the form, its consisting of "real" physical objects—actual letters—that may not only be read but also hidden, stolen, passed secretly from hand to hand, helps overcome its artificiality, both for eighteenth-century readers used to sharing their own (often voluminous) correspondence, and readers now.

In Richardson's preface to *Clarissa*, posing as the editor who has overseen the letters' transformation from handwriting to print, he describes the technique's power, its way of depicting characters' emotions at the very moment they write, in the midst of the plot, not knowing the outcome. This close scrutiny of the motions of consciousness would be seen as a hallmark of the novel form in general. But epistolary fiction, Richardson knew, had its dangers. Giving ample space to self-justifying, plausible villains such as Lovelace, without authorial correction, could trap readers in the wrong sympathies. Before the final volumes of *Clarissa* had appeared, Richardson's devotees urged him to reform Lovelace for a happy ending; he felt they missed the point. The preface printed here, from the third, 1751 edition, testifies to his anxiety about controlling readers' wayward reactions. As editor, he "restores" (in fact invents) more epistolary material to this third edition, making the novel yet longer, much of which serves to discredit Lovelace further. The preface also addresses mundane problems that Richardson the printer knew mattered: the size of the type, the "spoilers" in the previous edition's outline. The epistolary form that Richardson mastered did not immediately take off; it came into greatest vogue in the 1770s (when Frances Burney's *Evelina* appeared) and 1780s, when the French author Pierre Choderlos de Laclos published his epistolary classic *Les Liaisons dangereuses* (1782). Though only occasionally revived in later fiction, the epistolary method allowed Richardson to create an intimacy between characters and the reader that remains at the heart of the novel's power.

From Clarissa[1]

Preface

The following history is given in a series of letters written principally in a double yet separate correspondence;

Between two young ladies of virtue and honor, bearing an inviolable friendship for each other, and writing not merely for amusement, but upon the most *interesting*[2] subjects; in which every private family, more or less, may find itself concerned; and,

Between two gentlemen[3] of free lives; one of them glorying in his talents for stratagem and invention, and communicating to the other, in confidence, all the secret purposes of an intriguing head and resolute heart.

But here it will be proper to observe, for the sake of such as may apprehend hurt to the morals of youth, from the more freely written letters, that the gentlemen, though professed libertines as to the female sex, and making it one of their wicked maxims, to keep no faith with any of the individuals of it, who are thrown into their power, are not, however, either infidels or scoffers;[4] nor yet such as think themselves freed from the observance of those other moral duties which bind man to man.

On the contrary, it will be found, in the progress of the work, that they very often make such reflections upon each other, and each upon himself and his own actions, as reasonable beings *must* make, who disbelieve not a future state of rewards and punishments,[5] and who one day propose to reform— One of them actually reforming,[6] and by that means giving an opportunity to censure the freedoms which fall from the gayer pen and lighter heart of the other.

And yet that other, although in unbosoming himself to a select friend, he discovers[7] wickedness enough to entitle him to general detestation, preserves a decency, as well in his images as in his language, which is not always to be found in the works of some of the most celebrated modern writers, whose subjects and characters have less warranted the liberties they have taken.

In the letters of the two young ladies, it is presumed will be found not only the highest exercise of a reasonable and *practicable* friendship, between minds endowed with the noblest principles of virtue and religion, but occasionally interspersed, such delicacy of sentiments, particularly with regard to the other sex; such instances of impartiality, each freely, as a fundamental principle of their friendship, blaming, praising, and setting right the other, as are strongly to be recommended to the observation of the *younger* part (more especially) of the female readers.

---

1. The title page of the first edition reads *Clarissa, or, the History of a Young Lady: Comprehending the Most Important Concerns of Private Life and Particularly Shewing, the Distresses that May Attend the Misconduct Both of Parents and Children, in Relation to Marriage. Published by the Editor of Pamela.* (The text of the preface here is from the third edition.)
2. Touching, involving. "Two young ladies": Clarissa Harlowe, the heroine of the novel, and her confidante, Anna Howe.
3. Robert Lovelace, the novel's villain obsessed with seducing Clarissa, and his friend and fellow libertine, John Belford.
4. At religion or morality.
5. Heaven for the righteous, hell for sinners.
6. As the novel advances, Belford converts to a moral life, inspired by Clarissa's example.
7. Reveals. "Unbosoming himself": confessing his secret thoughts.

The principal of these two young ladies is proposed as an exemplar to her sex. Nor is it any objection to her being so, that she is not in all respects a perfect character. It was not only natural, but it was necessary, that she should have some faults, were it only to show the reader how laudably she could mistrust and blame herself, and carry to her own heart, divested of self-partiality, the censure which arose from her own convictions, and that even to the acquittal of those, because revered characters,[8] whom no one else would acquit, and to whose much greater faults her errors were owing, and not to a weak or reproachable heart. As far as it is consistent with human frailty, and as far as she could be perfect, considering the people she had to deal with, and those with whom she was inseparably connected, she *is* perfect. To have been impeccable must have left nothing for the divine grace and a purified state to do, and carried our idea of her from woman to angel. As such is she often esteemed by the man[9] whose *heart* was so corrupt that he could hardly believe human nature capable of the purity, which, on every trial or temptation, shone out in *hers*.

Besides the four principal persons, several others are introduced, whose letters are characteristic:[1] and it is presumed that there will be found in some of them, but more especially in those of the chief character among the men, and the second character among the women,[2] such strokes of gayety, fancy, and humor, as will entertain and divert; and at the same time both warn and instruct.

All the letters are written while the hearts of the writers must be supposed to be wholly engaged in their subjects (the events at the time generally dubious[3]): so that they abound not only with critical situations, but with what may be called *instantaneous* descriptions and reflections (proper to be brought home to the breast of the youthful reader); as also with affecting conversations; many of them written in the dialogue or dramatic way.

"*Much more* lively and affecting," says one of the principal characters (Vol. VII, p. 73),[4] "must be the style of those who write in the height of a *present* distress; the mind tortured by the pangs of uncertainty (the events then hidden in the womb of fate;) *than* the dry, narrative, unanimated style of a person relating difficulties and dangers surmounted, can be; the relater perfectly at ease; and if himself unmoved by his own story, not likely greatly to affect the reader."

What will be found to be more particularly aimed at in the following work is—To warn the inconsiderate and thoughtless of the one sex, against the base arts and designs of specious contrivers of the other—To caution parents against the undue exercise of their natural authority over their children in the great article of marriage—To warn children against preferring a man of pleasure to a man of probity, upon that dangerous but too commonly received notion, *that a reformed rake makes the best husband*—But above all, to investigate the highest and most important doctrines not only of morality, but of Christianity, by showing them thrown into action in the conduct of the

---

8. Clarissa censures herself to excuse her vindictive family members, whom she reveres.
9. Lovelace frequently calls Clarissa an angel through the novel.
1. Suit and reveal their characters.

2. Lovelace and Howe, respectively.
3. Their outcomes uncertain.
4. The comments appear in a letter of John Belford toward the end of the novel, slightly misquoted here.

worthy characters; while the *unworthy*, who set those doctrines at defiance, are condignly, and, as may be said, consequentially punished.

From what has been said, considerate readers will not enter upon the perusal of the piece before them as if it were designed *only* to divert and amuse. It will probably be thought tedious to all such as *dip* into it, expecting a *light novel*, or *transitory romance*; and look upon story in it (interesting as that is generally allowed to be) as its *sole end*, rather than as a vehicle to the instruction.

It is proper to observe, with regard to the *present edition*,[5] that it has been thought fit to restore many passages, and several letters, which were omitted in the former merely for shortening-sake;[6] and which some friends to the work thought equally necessary and entertaining. These are distinguished by dots or inverted full-points.[7] And will be printed separately in justice to the purchasers of the former editions.

Fault having been found, particularly by elderly readers, and by some who have weak eyes, with the smallness of the type, on which some part of the three last volumes were printed (which was done in order to bring the work, that had extended to an undesirable length, into as small a compass as possible), the present edition is uniformly printed on the larger-sized letter of the three made use of before. But the doing this, together with the additions above-mentioned, has unavoidably run the seven volumes into eight.

The work having been originally published at three different times, and a greater distance than was intended having passing between the first publication and the second; a preface was thought proper to be affixed to the third and fourth volumes; being the second publication.[8] A very learned and eminent hand was so kind as to favor the editor, at his request, with one. But the occasion of inserting it being *temporary*, and the editor having been left at liberty to do with it as he pleased, it was omitted in the second edition, when the whole work came to be printed together; as was, for the same reason, the preface to the first volume; and a short advertisement to the reader inserted instead of both. That advertisement being also temporary, the present address to the reader is substituted in its place.

In the second edition an ample table of contents to the *whole* work was prefixed to the first volume: but that having in some measure anticipated the catastrophe, and been thought to detain the reader too long from entering upon the history, it has been judged advisable to *add* (and that rather than *prefix*) to *each* volume its *particular* contents; which will serve not only as an index, but as a brief recapitulation of the most material passages contained in it; and which will enable the reader to connect in his mind the perused volume with that which follows; and more clearly show the characters and views of the particular correspondents.

An ingenious gentleman[9] having made a collection of many of the moral and instructive sentiments in this history, and presented it to the editor, he

5. The third, 1751.
6. Richardson, in his guise as "editor" of the correspondences contained in *Clarissa*, claims to "restore" passages and letters that were in fact newly composed for the third edition.
7. Suspended period marks.
8. The first edition of *Clarissa* appeared over a period of fourteen months from 1747 through 1748. The second installment, volumes 3 and 4 (1748), had a preface by English bishop and scholar William Warburton (1698–1779), which Richardson cut in subsequent editions.
9. Solomon Lowe, a friend of Richardson's.

thought the design and usefulness of the work could not be more strikingly exhibited, than by inserting it (greatly enlarged) at the end of the last volume. The reader will accordingly find it there, digested under proper heads, with references to the pages where each caution, aphorism, reflection, or observation, is to be found, either wrought into the *practice* of the respective correspondents, or recommended by them as useful *theory* to the youth of both sexes.

Different persons, as might be expected, have been of different opinions, in relation to the conduct of the heroine in particular situations; and several worthy persons have objected to the general catastrophe,[1] and other parts of the history. Whatever is thought material of these shall be taken notice of by way of postscript, at the conclusion of the history; for this work being addressed to the public as a history of *life* and *manners*, those parts of it which are proposed to carry with them the force of an example, ought to be as unobjectionable as is consistent with the *design of the whole*, and with *human nature*.

1747–48, 1751

1. What becomes of Clarissa at the end.

FRANCES BURNEY

"I believe it has not before been executed, though it seems a fair field open for the Novelist"—so Frances Burney, at the age of twenty-six, pitched the idea for her first novel, *Evelina* (1778), to the bookseller who would publish it. She did not divulge her identity to him, nor confide in anybody except two siblings and a cousin about her composition of it, nor put her name on the title page when the novel appeared. But *Evelina* did not come out of nowhere. Her family's London social circle included famous artists, writers, actors, and musicians, friends of her father, Charles Burney, a prominent musician himself and historian of music. Though she was shy, and not encouraged by him as much as her sisters, Burney educated herself and honed her intellect and observational skill among this cultured elite. She also learned the book business by helping her father prepare his own work for the press. As a teenager, she had drafted a version (now lost) of *Evelina*'s backstory.

When she came to write *Evelina* itself, then, she was prepared to make the claim for its originality in the letter to the bookseller and, more cautiously yet palpably, at the end of the novel's preface. The claim also relies on her deep understanding of her most distinguished predecessors in novel writing, including Fielding, Richardson, Smollett, and the Burney family friend, Samuel Johnson, whose philosophical fable *Rasselas* (see p. 734) showed how fiction could present sober satirical truths. While noting the lowly situation of "the humble novelist," the preface of *Evelina* performs an act of canonization, claiming a unique place for itself among a select, illustrious tradition. Early reviewers agreed. The *Critical Review*, not knowing the author's name and mistaking her gender, saw *Evelina* as a fresh combination of Richardsonian moral sensibility and a bright comic vein. For the rest of her career as the most formidable

English novelist of the late eighteenth century, Burney would continue to test the novel's range: *Cecilia* (1782) expanded her satirical and sentimental scope to present the fashionable world of London as a kind of wasteland; the immensely popular *Camilla* (1796) again mixed comedy and romantic feeling to portray the trials in love and life of a family's siblings; and her final novel, *The Wanderer* (1814), explored the possibilities of historical fiction, employing Gothic touches against a background of the French Revolution.

Many nineteenth-century readers viewed Burney's brilliant memoirs (see p. 941) as her principal achievement, but now her power as a novelist has been more fully recognized, and *Evelina* is her most popular work. In it she describes, as the novel's subtitle says, her heroine's "entrance into the world," that is, the world of London high society. Evelina, a beautiful ingénue from the country, stumbles in learning the codes that govern conduct at public resorts and private parties and that shape taste, desire, and love. The selections reprinted here include the preface and one episode from early in the novel, in which Evelina attends a ball and learns, to her cost, how rules of politeness often serve as vehicles for aggression. But she also sees how these rules trap their practitioners in absurdities. The novel employs Richardson's form of epistolary fiction (that is, it is presented as a series of letters), which enjoyed its greatest vogue in the 1770s, some thirty years after his *Pamela* appeared. (Burney's subsequent novels dropped the epistolary style and used a detached, sometimes severe third-person narrator.) It may be tempting to draw parallels between Burney's inexperienced first heroine and Burney herself at her literary debut—as the novel's preface and other introductory material encourage—but they only go so far. Though *Evelina* widened Burney's acquaintance and buoyed her confidence with praise from the best minds of her time, she did not begin her career artlessly and seemed to comprehend her own genius from the beginning.

From Evelina[1]

Preface

In the republic of letters, there is no member of such inferior rank, or who is so much disdained by his brethren of the quill,[2] as the humble novelist; nor is his fate less hard in the world at large, since, among the whole class of writers, perhaps not one can be named of which the votaries are more numerous but less respectable.

Yet, while in the annals of those few of our predecessors, to whom this species of writing is indebted for being saved from contempt, and rescued from depravity, we can trace such names as Rousseau, Johnson,[3] Marivaux, Fielding, Richardson, and Smollett, no man need blush at starting from the same post, though many, nay, most men, may sigh at finding themselves distanced.[4]

The following letters are presented to the public—for such, by novel writers, novel readers will be called,—with a very singular mixture of timidity

1. The complete title on the title page is *Evelina, or, A Young Lady's Entrance into the World, in a Series of Letters*.
2. Fellow writers.
3. However superior the capacities in which these great writers deserve to be considered, they must pardon me that, for the dignity of my subject, I here rank the authors of *Rasselas* and *Eloise* as Novelists [Burney's note]. Burney refers to Jean-

Jacques Rousseau (1712–1778), French philosopher and author of the novel *Julie, or the New Heloise* (1761), along with Samuel Johnson (see *Rasselas*, p. 734). Filling out her list of respectable novelists are Pierre Carlet de Chamblain de Marivaux (1688–1763), Henry Fielding (see p. 580), Samuel Richardson (see p. 587), and Scottish writer Tobias Smollett (1721–1771).
4. Outrun. "Post": starting line.

and confidence, resulting from the peculiar situation of the editor;[5] who, though trembling for their success from a consciousness of their imperfections, yet fears not being involved in their disgrace, while happily wrapped up in a mantle of impenetrable obscurity.

To draw characters from nature, though not from life,[6] and to mark the manners of the times, is the attempted plan of the following letters. For this purpose, a young female, educated in the most secluded retirement, makes, at the age of seventeen, her first appearance upon the great and busy stage of life; with a virtuous mind, a cultivated understanding, and a feeling heart, her ignorance of the forms,[7] and inexperience in the manners of the world, occasion all the little incidents which these volumes record, and which form the natural progression of the life of a young woman of obscure birth, but conspicuous beauty, for the first six months after her *entrance into the world*.

Perhaps were it possible to effect the total extirpation of novels, our young ladies in general, and boarding-school damsels in particular, might profit from their annihilation; but since the distemper they have spread seems incurable, since their contagion bids defiance to the medicine of advice or reprehension, and since they are found to baffle all the mental art of physic, save what is prescribed by the slow regimen of time, and bitter diet of experience, surely all attempts to contribute to the number of those which may be read, if not with advantage, at least without injury, ought rather to be encouraged than contemned.

Let me, therefore, prepare for disappointment those who, in the perusal of these sheets, entertain the gentle expectation of being transported to the fantastic regions of romance, where fiction is colored by all the gay tints of luxurious imagination, where reason is an outcast, and where the sublimity of the *marvelous* rejects all aid from sober probability. The heroine of these memoirs, young, artless, and inexperienced, is

No faultless Monster that the world ne'er saw;[8]

but the offspring of nature, and of nature in her simplest attire.

In all the arts, the value of copies can only be proportioned to the scarcity of originals: among sculptors and painters, a fine statue, or a beautiful picture, of some great master, may deservedly employ the imitative talents of younger and inferior artists, that their appropriation to one spot may not wholly prevent the more general expansion of their excellence;[9] but among authors, the reverse is the case, since the noblest productions of literature are almost equally attainable with the meanest. In books, therefore, imitation cannot be shunned too sedulously; for the very perfection of a model which is frequently seen, serves but more forcibly to mark the inferiority of a copy.

To avoid what is common, without adopting what is unnatural, must limit the ambition of the vulgar herd of authors: however zealous, therefore, my veneration of the great writers I have mentioned, however I may feel myself enlightened by the knowledge of Johnson, charmed with the eloquence of Rousseau, softened by the pathetic[1] powers of Richardson, and exhilarated

---

5. Burney strikes the Richardsonian pose as "editor" of the letters composing *Evelina*, though she also acknowledges that they and the characters who wrote them are fictional.
6. *Evelina*'s characters represent human nature but not real people.

7. Etiquette, rules of behavior.
8. John Sheffield, duke of Buckingham, *An Essay upon Poetry* (1682), line 235.
9. So that the master's single copy will not confine his talent to a single place.
1. Passionately moving.

by the wit of Fielding and humor of Smollett, I yet presume not to attempt pursuing the same ground which they have tracked; whence, though they may have cleared the weeds, they have also culled the flowers; and, though they have rendered the path plain, they have left it barren.

The candor of my readers I have not the impertinence to doubt, and to their indulgence I am sensible I have no claim; I have, therefore, only to entreat, that my own words may not pronounce my condemnation; and that what I have here ventured to say in regard to imitation, may be understood as it is meant, in a general sense, and not be imputed to an opinion of my own originality, which I have not the vanity, the folly, or the blindness, to entertain.

Whatever may be the fate of these letters, the editor is satisfied they will meet with justice; and commits them to the press, though hopeless of fame, yet not regardless of censure.

Volume I, Letter XI[1]

Queen-Ann-Street,[2] April 5, Tuesday morning.

I have a vast deal to say, and shall give all this morning to my pen. As to my plan of writing every evening the adventures of the day, I find it impracticable; for the diversions here are so very late, that if I begin my letters after them, I could not go to bed at all.

We passed a most extraordinary evening. A *private* ball this was called, so I expected to have seen about four or five couple; but Lord! my dear Sir, I believe I saw half the world! Two very large rooms were full of company; in one were cards for the elderly ladies, and in the other were the dancers. My mamma Mirvan,[3] for she always calls me her child, said she would sit with Maria and me till we were provided with partners, and then join the card-players.

The gentlemen, as they passed and re-passed, looked as if they thought we were quite at their disposal, and only waiting for the honor of their commands; and they sauntered about, in a careless indolent manner, as if with a view to keep us in suspense. I don't speak of this in regard to Miss Mirvan and myself only, but to the ladies in general: and I thought it so provoking, that I determined in my own mind that, far from humoring such airs, I would rather not dance at all, than with any one who would seem to think me ready to accept the first partner who would condescend to take me.

Not long after, a young man, who had for some time looked at us with a kind of negligent impertinence, advanced, on tiptoe, towards me; he had a set smile on his face, and his dress was so foppish, that I really believed he even wished to be stared at; and yet he was very ugly.

Bowing almost to the ground with a sort of swing, and waving his hand with the greatest conceit, after a short and silly pause, he said, "Madam— may I presume?"—and stopped, offering to take my hand. I drew it back, but could scarce forbear laughing. "Allow me, Madam," continued he, affectedly breaking off every half moment, "the honor and happiness—if I am not so unhappy as to address you too late—to have the happiness and honor—"

1. Early in volume 1, Evelina, wide-eyed and naive, recounts her experiences of London social life in letters like this one to her guardian in the country, the Reverend Arthur Villars.
2. The residence rented by Evelina's hosts, the Mirvan family, on Queen Anne Street was in a fashionable district in the west of London, now called Marylebone.
3. Mrs. Mirvan, mother of Evelina's friend Maria, chaperones the young women during their stay in London.

Again he would have taken my hand, but bowing my head, I begged to be excused, and turned to Miss Mirvan to conceal my laughter. He then desired to know if I had already engaged myself to some more fortunate man? I said No, and that I believed I should not dance at all. He would keep himself, he told me, disengaged, in hopes I should relent; and then, uttering some ridiculous speeches of sorrow and disappointment, though his face still wore the same invariable smile, he retreated.

It so happened, as we have since recollected, that during this little dialogue, Mrs. Mirvan was conversing with the lady of the house. And very soon after, another gentleman, who seemed about six-and-twenty years old, gaily but not foppishly dressed, and indeed extremely handsome, with an air of mixed politeness and gallantry, desired to know if I was engaged, or would honor him with my hand. So he was pleased to say, though I am sure I know not what honor he could receive from me; but these sort of expressions, I find, are used as words of course,[4] without any distinction of persons, or study of propriety.

Well, I bowed, and I am sure I colored; for indeed I was frightened at the thoughts of dancing before so many people, all strangers, and, which was worse, *with* a stranger; however, that was unavoidable, for though I looked round the room several times, I could not see one person that I knew. And so he took my hand, and led me to join in the dance.

The minuets were over[5] before we arrived, for we were kept late by the milliner's making us wait for our things.

He seemed very desirous of entering into conversation with me; but I was seized with such a panic, that I could hardly speak a word, and nothing but the shame of so soon changing my mind prevented my returning to my seat, and declining to dance at all.

He appeared to be surprised at my terror, which I believe was but too apparent: however, he asked no questions, though I fear he must think it very strange, for I did not choose to tell him it was owing to my never before dancing but with a school-girl.

His conversation was sensible and spirited; his air and address were open and noble; his manners gentle, attentive, and infinitely engaging; his person is all elegance, and his countenance the most animated and expressive I have ever seen.

In a short time we were joined by Miss Mirvan, who stood next couple to us. But how I was startled when she whispered me that my partner was a nobleman! This gave me a new alarm: how will he be provoked, thought I, when he finds what a simple rustic[6] he has honored with his choice! one whose ignorance of the world makes her perpetually fear doing something wrong!

That he should be so much my superior in every way quite disconcerted me; and you will suppose my spirits were not much raised, when I heard a lady, in passing us, say, "This is the most difficult dance I ever saw."

"O dear, then," cried Maria to her partner, "with your leave, I'll sit down till the next."

"So will I too, then," cried I, "for I am sure I can hardly stand."

"But you must speak to your partner first," answered she; for he had turned aside to talk with some gentlemen. However, I had not sufficient courage to

4. Formulaic phrases.
5. Balls often began with minuets, rather formal and difficult dances, and then usually gave way to

less demanding country dances.
6. Country girl.

address him, and so away we all three tripped,[7] and seated ourselves at another end of the room.

But, unfortunately for me, Miss Mirvan soon after suffered herself to be prevailed upon to attempt the dance; and just as she rose to go, she cried, "My dear, yonder is your partner, Lord Orville walking about the room in search of you."

"Don't leave me then, dear girl!" cried I; but she was obliged to go. And now I was more uneasy than ever; I would have given the world to have seen Mrs. Mirvan, and begged of her to make my apologies; for what, thought I, can I possibly say to him in excuse for running away? He must either conclude me a fool, or half mad; for any one brought up in the great world, and accustomed to its ways, can have no idea of such sort of fears as mine.

My confusion increased when I observed that he was everywhere seeking me, with apparent perplexity and surprise; but when, at last, I saw him move towards the place where I sat, I was ready to sink with shame and distress. I found it absolutely impossible to keep my seat, because I could not think of a word to say for myself, and so I rose, and walked hastily towards the card-room, resolving to stay with Mrs. Mirvan the rest of the evening, and not to dance at all. But before I could find her, Lord Orville saw and approached me.

He begged to know if I was not well? You may easily imagine how much I was embarrassed. I made no answer; but hung my head like a fool, and looked on my fan.

He then, with an air the most respectfully serious, asked if he had been so unhappy as to offend me?

"No, indeed!" cried I; and, in hopes of changing the discourse, and preventing his further inquiries, I desired to know if he had seen the young lady who had been conversing with me?

No;—but would I honor him with any commands to her?

"O, by no means!"

Was there any other person with whom I wished to speak?

I said *no*, before I knew I had answered at all.

Should he have the pleasure of bringing me any refreshment?

I bowed, almost involuntarily. And away he flew.

I was quite ashamed of being so troublesome, and so much *above* myself as these seeming airs made me appear; but indeed I was too much confused to think or act with any consistency.

If he had not been swift as lightning, I don't know whether I should not have stolen away again; but he returned in a moment. When I had drank a glass of lemonade, he hoped, he said, that I would again honor him with my hand, as a new dance was just begun. I had not the presence of mind to say a single word, and so I let him once more lead me to the place I had left.

Shocked to find how silly, how childish a part I had acted, my former fears of dancing before such a company, and with such a partner, returned more forcibly than ever. I suppose he perceived my uneasiness, for he entreated me to sit down again, if dancing was disagreeable to me. But I was quite satisfied with the folly I had already shown; and therefore declined his offer, though I was really scarce able to stand.

7. Stepped lightly.

Under such conscious disadvantages, you may easily imagine, my dear Sir, how ill I acquitted myself. But, though I both expected and deserved to find him very much mortified and displeased at his ill fortune in the choice he had made, yet, to my very great relief, he appeared to be even contented, and very much assisted and encouraged me. These people in high life have too much presence of mind, I believe, to *seem* disconcerted, or out of humor, however they may feel: for had I been the person of the most consequence in the room, I could not have met with more attention and respect.

When the dance was over, seeing me still very much flurried, he led me to a seat, saying that he would not suffer me to fatigue myself from politeness.

And then, if my capacity, or even if my spirits had been better, in how animated a conversation I might have been engaged! It was then I saw that the rank of Lord Orville was his least recommendation, his understanding and his manners being far more distinguished. His remarks upon the company in general were so apt, so just, so lively, I am almost surprised myself that they did not reanimate me; but indeed I was too well convinced of the ridiculous part I had myself played before so nice[8] an observer, to be able to enjoy his pleasantry: so self-compassion gave me feeling for others. Yet I had not the courage to attempt either to defend them or to rally in my turn; but listened to him in silent embarrassment.

When he found this, he changed the subject, and talked of public places, and public performers; but he soon discovered that I was totally ignorant of them.

He then, very ingeniously, turned the discourse to the amusements and occupations of the country.

It now struck me that he was resolved to try whether or not I was capable of talking upon *any* subject. This put so great a constraint upon my thoughts, that I was unable to go further than a monosyllable, and not ever so far, when I could possibly avoid it.

We were sitting in this manner, he conversing with all gaiety, I looking down with all foolishness, when that fop who had first asked me to dance, with a most ridiculous solemnity approached, and, after a profound bow or two, said, "I humbly beg pardon, Madam,—and of you too, my Lord,—for breaking in upon such agreeable conversation—which must, doubtless, be much more delectable—than what I have the honor to offer—but—"

I interrupted him—I blush for my folly—with laughing; yet I could not help it; for, added to the man's stately foppishness, (and he actually took snuff between every three words) when I looked around at Lord Orville, I saw such extreme surprise in his face,—the cause of which appeared so absurd, that I could not for my life preserve my gravity.

I had not laughed before from the time I had left Miss Mirvan, and I had much better have cried then; Lord Orville actually stared at me; the beau, I know not his name, looked quite enraged. "Refrain—Madam," said he, with an important air, "a few moments refrain!—I have but a sentence to trouble you with.—May I know to what accident I must attribute not having the honor of your hand?"

"Accident, Sir!" repeated I, much astonished.

---

8. Exact.

"Yes, accident, Madam;—for surely,—I must take the liberty to observe—pardon me, Madam,—it ought to be no common one—that should tempt a lady—so young a one too—to be guilty of ill-manners."

A confused idea now for the first time entered my head, of something I had heard of the rules of an assembly; but I was never at one before—I have only danced at school—and so giddy and heedless I was, that I had not once considered the impropriety of refusing one partner, and afterwards accepting another. I was thunderstruck at the recollection: but, while these thoughts were rushing into my head, Lord Orville with some warmth, said, "This lady, Sir, is incapable of meriting such an accusation!"

The creature—for I am very angry with him—made a low bow and with a grin the most malicious I ever saw, "My Lord," said he, "far be it from me to *accuse* the lady, for having the discernment to distinguish and prefer—the superior attractions of your Lordship."

Again he bowed, and walked off.

Was ever any thing so provoking? I was ready to die with shame. "What a coxcomb!" exclaimed Lord Orville: while I, without knowing what I did, rose hastily, and moving off, "I can't imagine," cried I, "where Mrs. Mirvan has hid herself!"

"Give me leave to see," answered he. I bowed and sat down again, not daring to meet his eyes; for what must he think of me, between my blunder, and the supposed preference?

He returned in a moment, and told me that Mrs. Mirvan was at cards, but would be glad to see me; and I went immediately. There was but one chair vacant; so, to my great relief, Lord Orville presently left us. I then told Mrs. Mirvan my disasters; and she good-naturedly blamed herself for not having better instructed me; but said she had taken it for granted that I must know such common customs. However, the man may, I think, be satisfied with his pretty speech, and carry his resentment no farther.

In a short time, Lord Orville returned. I consented, with the best grace I could, to go down another dance, for I had had time to recollect myself; and therefore resolved to use some exertion, and, if possible, to appear less a fool than I had hitherto done; for it occurred to me, that, insignificant as I was, compared to a man of his rank and figure, yet, since he had been so unfortunate as to make choice of me for a partner, why I should endeavor to make the best of it.

The dance, however, was short, and he spoke very little; so I had no opportunity of putting my resolution in practice. He was satisfied, I suppose, with his former successless efforts to draw me out; or, rather, I fancied he had been inquiring *who I was*. This again disconcerted me; and the spirits I had determined to exert, again failed me. Tired, ashamed, and mortified, I begged to sit down till we returned home, which we did soon after. Lord Orville did me the honor to hand me to the coach, talking all the way of the honor *I* had done *him!* O these fashionable people!

Well, my dear Sir, was it not a strange evening? I could not help being thus particular, because, to me, every thing is so new. But it is now time to conclude. I am, with all love and duty, your

EVELINA

1778

CLARA REEVE

L ike many successful women writers of the eighteenth century, Clara Reeve (1729–1807) wrote out of financial necessity, but unlike most, she did not move in metropolitan circles. Reeve's most discussed works now, the Gothic novel *The Old English Baron* (1777, 1778) and her literary history *The Progress of Romance* (1785), were first printed in the town of Colchester, near her home in Ipswich. The printing of books, pamphlets, and catalogs had increasingly spread to urban centers outside London as the century wore on, though the capital remained the undisputed center of the literary world. Never marrying, Reeve managed her literary career herself, corresponding with the booksellers in London to see nearly all of her works into print there, including novels, poems, and a treatise on women's education. Her provincial origins and life did not prevent Reeve from becoming famous. For over a century, *The Old English Baron* was read as a classic English novel, often printed together with her inspiration for it, Horace Walpole's Gothic novel *The Castle of Otranto* (1764)—though Reeve aims, as she says in her preface to her work, to surpass Walpole by avoiding supernatural extravagances.

Unlike *The Old English Baron*, Reeve's *Progress of Romance* did not initially attract much attention and remained mostly unnoticed even by scholars until recently. It presents a learned history of prose fictional narrative, from ancient Greek romances (which she calls "the parents of the rest") to the novels of the eighteenth century. Reeve asserts the comprehensiveness and rigor of her scholarship: "while many eminent writers," she says in the preface, have "skimmed over the surface of this subject, it seemed to me that none of them had sounded the depths of it." Written as a dialogue between two women and a man—a form intended to enliven what otherwise might be a dry discourse—*The Progress* says romances are "neither so contemptible, nor so dangerous a kind of reading" as is commonly supposed, compares them favorably to epic poems, and recognizes their antiquity, giving examples from not only Greek but also Arabic and even Egyptian literature. (She appends an Egyptian tale, "The History of Charoba, Queen of Egypt," to the second volume of *The Progress*.) While firmly distinguishing romances from the modern novel in the first excerpt reprinted here, she does so not to denigrate the former, as in many other efforts to define the novel in the period, but to identity two species of the same genus. She also offers suggestive remarks on the novel's special power over the minds of readers.

In Reeve's account, the lineaments of later critical histories of the novel already appear. She describes the tradition of women writers starting with Aphra Behn as crucial to the modern novel's early development. Within this account, she offers what would become a common narrative: early women novelists such as Behn and Delarivier Manley were scandalous and sexually improper, she says, but by the mid-eighteenth century a more morally edifying kind of women's fiction began to hold sway—a transition exemplified in the career of Eliza Haywood, who redeemed herself in her final works. (Recently scholars have told a more complex story, noting that women novelists from the beginning presented the public with works at diverse points on the scale of sexual morality.) Reeve also provides illuminating terms in which to distinguish "the two most eminent writers of our country," Richardson and Fielding—a contrast inescapable in taxonomies of English novels in the coming centuries. The final selection recognizes not only the dangers of indiscriminate reading in the collections of circulating libraries but also how impracticable any attempt to ban fiction would be, given the prevalence of fictional stories throughout the best literature, ancient and modern. Reeve supports the reading of novels as long as it is subject to parental and other culturally authoritative monitors, and to a well-developed moral monitor within.

From The Progress of Romance[1]

From *Evening VII*[2]

* * *

Euphrasia. * * * The word *novel* in all languages signifies something new. It was first used to distinguish these works from romance, though they have lately been confounded together and are frequently mistaken for each other.

Sophronia. But how will you draw the line of distinction, so as to separate them effectually, and prevent future mistakes?

Euphrasia. I will attempt this distinction, and I presume if it is properly done it will be followed—if not, you are but where you were before. The romance is an heroic fable, which treats of fabulous persons and things.—The novel is a picture of real life and manners, and of the times in which it is written. The romance in lofty and elevated language describes what never happened nor is likely to happen.—The novel gives a familiar relation of such things as pass every day before our eyes, such as may happen to our friend, or to ourselves; and the perfection of it is to represent every scene in so easy and natural a manner, and to make them appear so probable, as to deceive us into a persuasion (at least while we are reading) that all is real, until we are affected by the joys or distresses of the persons in the story, as if they were our own.

Hortensius. You have well distinguished, and it is necessary to make this distinction.—I clearly perceive the difference between the romance and novel, and am surprised they should be confounded together.

Euphrasia. I have sometimes thought it has been done insidiously, by those who endeavor to render all writings of both kinds contemptible.

Sophronia. I have generally observed that men of learning have spoken of them with the greatest disdain, especially collegians.[3]

Euphrasia. Take care what you say my friend, they are a set of men who are not to be offended with impunity. Yet they deal in romances, though of a different kind.—Some have taken up an opinion[4] upon trust in others whose judgment they prefer to their own.—Others having seen a few of the worst or dullest among them,[5] have judged of all the rest by them;—just as some men affect to despise our sex, because they have only conversed with the worst part of it.

---

1. The complete title on the title page is *The Progress of Romance, through Times, Countries, and Manners, with Remarks on the Good and Bad Effects of It, on Them Respectively; in a Course of Evening Conversations.*
2. As the title indicates, Reeve's work takes the form of a dialogue between three participants, two women (Euphrasia and Sophronia) and a man (Hortensius), held on a series of evenings.
3. Scholars affiliated with the colleges of Oxford and Cambridge universities.
4. That novels deserve contempt.
5. Novels.

Hortensius. Your sex knows how to retort upon ours, and to punish us for our offenses against you.—Proceed however.[6]

* * *

Euphrasia. * * * Let us next consider some of the early novels of our own country.

We had early translations of the best novels of all other countries, but for a long time produced very few of our own. One of the earliest I know of is the *Cyprian Academy,* by Robert Baron[7] in the reign of Charles the First.—Among our early novel-writers we must reckon Mrs. Behn.[8]—There are strong marks of genius in all this lady's works, but unhappily, there are some parts of them very improper to be read by or recommended to virtuous minds, and especially to youth.—She wrote in an age, and to a court of licentious manners,[9] and perhaps we ought to ascribe to these causes the loose turn of her stories.—Let us do justice to her merits, and cast the veil of compassion over her faults.—She died in the year 1689, and lies buried in the cloisters of Westminster Abbey.[1]—The inscription will show how high she stood in estimation at that time.

Hortensius. Are you not partial to the sex of this genius?—when you excuse in her, what you would not to a man?

Euphrasia. Perhaps I may, and you must excuse me if I am so, especially as this lady had many fine and amiable qualities, besides her genius for writing.

Sophronia. Pray let her rest in peace—you were speaking of the inscription on her monument, I do not remember it.

Euphrasia. It is as follows:

> Mrs. Aphra Behn, 1689.
> Here lies a proof that wit can never be
> Defense enough against mortality.

Let me add that Mrs. Behn will not be forgotten, so long as the tragedy of *Oroonoko* is acted; it was from her story of that illustrious African, that Mr. Southerne[2] wrote that play, and the most affecting parts of it are taken almost literally from her.

Hortensius. Peace be to her *manes!*[3] I shall not disturb her, or her works.

Euphrasia. I shall not recommend them to your perusal, Hortensius.

The next female writer of this class is Mrs. Manley,[4] whose works are still more exceptionable than Mrs. Behn's, and as much inferior to them in point of merit.—She hoarded up all the public and private scandal within her reach, and poured it forth, in a work too well known in the last age,

---

6. Euphrasia proceeds to identify Renaissance Italian writers such as Giovanni Boccaccio (1313–1375) as the first modern novelists, then describes the novels of Spanish master Miguel de Cervantes (1547–1616), and the more realistic French fiction of the 17th century.
7. The *Erotopaignion; or, The Cyprian Academy* (1647) by Robert Baron (1630–1658) was written in both prose and verse and later became notorious for its wholesale copying of passages from Milton, Shakespeare, and other famous writers.
8. Aphra Behn (ca. 1640–1689), playwright and author of *Oroonoko* (p. 139).
9. The court of the Restoration era (1660–88) was

often denounced for its sexual license.
1. Gothic church in the city of Westminster, London, where English royalty and many famous writers are buried.
2. Thomas Southerne (1660–1746), Irish playwright, whose tragedy *Oroonoko* (1696) was based on Behn's novel.
3. Borrowed from Latin, a fanciful name of the deified or otherwise respected spirit of the dead.
4. Delarivier Manley (ca. 1670–1724), whose "too well known" work of satirical fiction, *The New Atalantis* (1709), portrayed the scandalous doings of prominent Whigs.

though almost forgotten in the present; a work that partakes of the style of the romance, and the novel. I forbear the name, and further observations on it, as Mrs. Manley's works are sinking gradually into oblivion. I am sorry to say they were once in fashion, which obliges me to mention them, otherwise I had rather be spared the pain of disgracing an author of my own sex.

Sophronia. It must be confessed that these books of the last age were of worse tendency than any of those of the present.

Euphrasia. My dear friend, there were bad books at all times, for those who sought them.—Let us pass them over in silence.

Hortensius. No not yet.—Let me help your memory to one more lady-author of the same class.—Mrs. Haywood.[5] She has the same claim upon you as those you have last mentioned.

Euphrasia. I had intended to have mentioned Mrs. Haywood though in a different way, but I find you will not suffer any part of her character to escape you.

Hortensius. Why should she be spared any more than the others?

Euphrasia. Because she repented of her faults, and employed the latter part of her life in expiating the offences of the former.[6]—There is reason to believe that the examples of the two ladies we have spoken of seduced Mrs. Haywood into the same track; she certainly wrote some amorous novels in her youth, and also two books of the same kind as Mrs. Manley's capital work,[7] all of which I hope are forgotten.

Hortensius. I fear they will not be so fortunate, they will be known to posterity by the infamous immortality conferred upon them by Pope in his *Dunciad.*[8]

Euphrasia. Mr. Pope was severe in his castigations, but let us be just to merit of every kind. Mrs. Haywood had the singular good fortune to recover a lost reputation, and the yet greater honor to atone for her errors.—She devoted the remainder of her life and labors to the service of virtue. Mrs. Haywood was one of the most voluminous female writers that ever England produced, none of her latter works are destitute of merit, though they do not rise to the highest pitch of excellence.—*Betsy Thoughtless* is reckoned her best novel; but those works by which she is most likely to be known to posterity are the *Female Spectator* and the *Invisible Spy.*[9] This lady died so lately as the year 1758.[1]

Sophronia. I have heard it often said that Mr. Pope was too severe in his treatment of this lady; it was supposed that she had given him some private offense, which he resented publicly as was too much his way.

Hortensius. That is very likely, for he was not of a forgiving disposition.—If I have been too severe also, you ladies must forgive me in behalf of your sex.

---

5. Eliza Haywood (1693–1756), prolific author of fiction, including *Fantomina* (see p. 609).
6. Haywood's later works such as *The History of Miss Betsy Thoughtless* (1751) took a more moral turn than her earlier ones.
7. Reeve probably means Haywood's *Memoirs of a Certain Island, Adjacent to Utopia* (1724) and *The Secret History of the Present Intrigues of the Court of Caramania* (1727) both of which satirically reflected on contemporary British politics by presenting fictionalized parallel "histories," in the manner of *The New Atalantis.*
8. Alexander Pope's mockery of the book trade in his poem *The Dunciad* (1728, 1743) makes Haywood the prize in a pissing contest between booksellers.
9. The former is a periodical for women (1744–1746) treating philosophical and social topics, the latter a work of fiction (1754) full of political and cultural reflections.
1. Reeve misstates Haywood's date of death, which is 1756.

Euphrasia. Truth is sometimes severe.—Mrs. Haywood's wit and ingenuity were never denied. I would be the last to vindicate her faults, but the first to celebrate her return to virtue, and her atonement for them.

Sophronia. May her first writings be forgotten, and the last survive to do her honor!

* * *

From *Evening VIII*

Hortensius. You have not yet made mention of the most eminent writers of our country, Richardson and Fielding.

Euphrasia. I hope you did not think it possible for me to forget them. Mr. Richardson published his works at a considerable distance of time from each other. *Pamela*[2] was the first; it met with a very warm reception, as it well deserved to do.—I remember my mother and aunts being shut up in the parlor reading *Pamela*, and I took it very hard that I was excluded.—I have since seen it put into the hands of children, so much are their understandings riper than mine, or so much are our methods of education improved since that time.

Sophronia. It is a general[3] mistake in regard to the youth of our time, they are put too forward in all respects. Let us return to *Pamela*, I can remember the time when this book was the fashion, the person that had not read *Pamela* was disqualified for conversation, of which it was the principal subject for a long time.—You will give us your opinion of this, and the other words of Mr. Richardson?

Euphrasia. To praise the works of Mr. Richardson is to hold a candle to the sun, their merits are well understood in other countries besides our own; they have been translated into French, Italian, and German, and they are read in English frequently, by the people of the first rank in all the politest countries in Europe.

A lady of quality in France sent an epigram to one of Mr. Richardson's family soon after his death, which I will give you here. * * *[4]

> Richardson is now no more!
> Then may the human heart deplore[5]
> Its most profound investigator,
> Its patron, friend, and regulator,
> And its most perfect legislator.

Hortensius. Very close indeed to the original.

Sophronia. But your remarks on Richardson's works?

Euphrasia. I will hazard a few remarks on them, which perhaps I may be allowed, because no person whatever has read them over with more pleasure and delight than myself.

It seems that *Pamela* is the *chef d'oeuvre*[6] of Mr. Richardson.—The originality, the beautiful simplicity of the manners and language of the charming

---

2. Published in 1740, *Pamela, or Virtue Rewarded*, tells the story, in letters, of a young servant woman harassed by her employer, whom she resists and eventually marries.
3. Widespread.

4. Euphrasia quotes the passage in French, then provides her own literal translation.
5. Grieve over, lament the loss of.
6. Masterpiece.

maid, are interesting past expression; and find a short way to the heart, which it engages by its best and noblest feelings.—There needs no other proof of a bad and corrupted heart, than its being insensible to the distresses, and incapable[7] to the rewards of virtue.—I should want no other criterion of a *good* or a *bad* heart, than the manner in which a young person was affected by reading *Pamela*.

Hortensius. Your plaudit is a warm one.—But Richardson is a writer all your own; your sex are more obliged to him and Addison,[8] than to all other men-authors.

Euphrasia. I deny that.—We have many other redoubtable champions as I shall bring proof enough,—and no man is degraded by defending us, for the female cause is the cause of virtue.

Hortensius. I mean not to degrade your champions or their cause.—But let us hear your critique on Mr. Richardson's other works?

Euphrasia. It was yourself who digressed from the subject. I have but little more to say of them; that all are of capital merit is indisputable; but it seems to me that *Pamela* has the most originality.—*Grandison* the greatest regularity and equality.—*Clarissa* the highest graces, and most defects.[9]

Mr. Richardson was besides the first who wrote novels in the epistolary style, and he was truly an original writer.

* * *

Euphrasia. The next author upon the list, and whom Hortensius feared I should forget, is Henry Fielding, Esq., whose works are universally known and admired.—As I consider wit only as a secondary merit, I must beg leave to observe that his writings are as much inferior to Richardson's in morals and exemplary characters, as they are superior in wit and learning.—Young men of warm passions and not strict principles are always desirous to shelter themselves under the sanction of mixed characters, wherein virtue is allowed to be predominant.—In this light the character of Tom Jones is capable of doing much mischief; and for this reason a translation of this book was prohibited in France.[1]—On the contrary no harm can possibly arise from the imitation of a perfect character, though the attempt should fail of the original.

Sophronia. This is an indisputable truth—there are many objectionable scenes in Fielding's works, which I think Hortensius will not defend.

Hortensius. My objections were in character, and yours are so likewise; as you have defended Richardson, so I will defend Fielding. I allow there is some foundation for your remarks, nevertheless in all Fielding's works, virtue has always the superiority she ought to have, and challenges the honors that are justly due to her, the general tenor of them is in her favor, and it were happy for us, if our language had no greater cause of complaint in her behalf.

Euphrasia. There we will agree with you.—Have you any further observations to make upon Fielding's writings?

7. Insusceptible.
8. Joseph Addison (1672–1719), author, with Richard Steele, of the periodical *The Spectator* (1711–14, see p. 462).
9. The two novels Richardson wrote after *Pamela*: *Clarissa* (1748, see p. 589), and *The History of Sir Charles Grandison* (1753), which tells the story of a virtuous aristocrat who honors women and defends them against wicked men.
1. A French translation of Fielding's masterpiece, *The History of Tom Jones, a Foundling* (1749), was suppressed when it was discovered that the bookseller who published it did not have permission from an official censor to do so.

Hortensius. Since you refer this part of your task to me, I will offer a few more remarks.—Fielding's *Amelia*[2] is in much lower estimation than his *Joseph Andrews*, or *Tom Jones*; which have both received the stamp of public applause. He likewise wrote several dramatic pieces of various merits,[3] but these and his other works have no place in our present retrospect.—Lest you should think me too partial to the merits of this writer, I will give you the sentence of an historian upon him. "The genius of Cervantes" (says Dr. Smollett) "was transfused into the novels of Fielding, who painted the characters, and ridiculed the follies of life, with equal strength, humor, and propriety."[4]

Euphrasia. We are willing to join with you in paying the tribute due to Fielding's genius, humor, and knowledge of mankind, but he certainly painted human nature as *it is*, rather than as *it ought to be*.

* * *

From *Evening XII*

Euphrasia. A circulating library[5] is indeed a great evil—young people are allowed to subscribe to them, and to read indiscriminately all they contain; and thus both food and poison are conveyed to the young mind together.

Hortensius. I should suppose that if books of the worst kind were excluded, still there would be enough to lay a foundation of idleness and folly.—A person used to this kind of reading will be disgusted with everything serious or solid, as a weakened and depraved stomach rejects plain and wholesome food.

Sophronia. There is truth and justice in your observation—but how to prevent it?

Hortensius. There are yet more and greater evils behind. The seeds of vice and folly are sown in the heart—the passions are awakened—false expectations are raised.—A young woman is taught to expect adventures and intrigues—she expects to be addressed in the style of these books, with the language of flattery and adulation.—If a plain man addresses her in rational terms and pays her the greatest of compliments—that of desiring to spend his life with her—that is not sufficient, her vanity is disappointed, she expects to meet a hero in romance.

Euphrasia. No, Hortensius—not a hero in romance, but a fine gentleman in a novel—you will not make the distinction.

Hortensius. I ask your pardon, I agreed to the distinction and therefore ought to observe it.

Euphrasia. I would not have interrupted you on this punctilio;[6] but let us walk into the house, and pursue the subject in the library.

Hortensius. Now[7] you are armed with your extracts, you think yourself invulnerable.

Euphrasia. I will not attempt to contradict you, unless I have good reason for it.—I beg you to proceed with your remarks.

---

2. His last novel, published in 1751.
3. Fielding was a prolific comic dramatist in the 1730s.
4. From Tobias Smollett's *Continuation of the Complete History of England*, vol. 4 (1761).
5. New in the 18th century, libraries required families to subscribe by paying a fee for access to the latest books, including novels.
6. Minor point.
7. We are to imagine some elapsed time as the dialogists move indoors to the library, though the text does not represent it.

Hortensius. From this kind of reading, young people fancy themselves capable of judging of men and manners, and that they are knowing, while involved[8] in the profoundest ignorance. They believe themselves wiser than their parents and guardians, whom they treat with contempt and ridicule.— Thus armed with ignorance, conceit, and folly, they plunge into the world and its dissipations, and who can wonder if they become its victims? For such as the foundation is, such will be the superstructure.

Euphrasia. All this is undoubtedly true, but at the same time would you exclude all works of fiction from the young reader?—In this case you would deprive him of the pleasure and improvement he might receive from works of genius, taste, and morality.

Hortensius. Yes, I would serve them as the priest did *Don Quixote*'s library, burn the good ones for being found in bad company.[9]

Euphrasia. That is being very severe, especially if you consider how far your execution would extend.—If you would prohibit reading *all* works of fiction, what will become of your favorites the great ancients, as well as the most ingenious and enlightened modern writers?

Sophronia. Surely this is carrying the prohibition too far, and though it may sound well in theory, it would be utterly impracticable.

Hortensius. I do not deny that.—There are many things to be wished, that are not to be hoped. I see no way to cure this vice of the times, but by extirpating the cause of it.

Euphrasia. Pray Hortensius, is all this severity in behalf of our sex or your own?

Hortensius. Of both.—Yet yours are most concerned in my remonstrance for they read more of these books than ours, and consequently are most hurt by them.

Euphrasia. You will then become a knight errant, to combat with the windmills, which your imagination represents as giants;[1] while in the mean time you leave a side unguarded.

Hortensius. And you have found it out.—Pray tell me without metaphors your meaning in plain English?

Euphrasia. It seems to me that you are unreasonably severe upon these books, which you suppose to be appropriated to our sex (which however is not the case)—not considering how many books of worse tendency are put into the hands of the youth of your own, without scruple.

Hortensius. Indeed! how will you bring proofs of that assertion?

Euphrasia. I will not go far for them. I will fetch them from the school books, that generally make a part of the education of young men.—They are taught the history—the mythology—the morals—of the great ancients, whom you and all learned men revere.—But with these, they learn also—their idolatry—their follies—their vices—and everything that is shocking to virtuous manners. Lucretius teaches them that fear first made gods[2]—that men grew out of the earth like trees, and that the indulgence of the passions and

8. Enfolded.
9. In chapter 6 of part one of *Don Quixote*, a priest and a barber resolve to burn Don Quixote's books of chivalry.
1. Euphrasia evokes the famous episode of Don Quixote tilting at windmills.

2. The line "first of all, fear created the gods" comes from the *Thebiad* by Roman poet, Statius (ca. 45–ca. 96 C.E.), though the poem *Of the Nature of Things* by Lucretius (ca. 99–ca. 55 B.C.E.) offers that and the other tenets of Epicurean philosophy here listed.

appetites is the truest wisdom. Juvenal and Persius[3] describe such scenes as I may venture to affirm that romance and novel writers of any credit would blush at—and Virgil, the modest and delicate Virgil, informs them of many things, they had better be ignorant of.—As a woman I cannot give this argument its full weight—but a hint is sufficient—and I presume you will not deny the truth of my assertion.

Hortensius. I am astonished—admonished—and convinced!—I cannot deny the truth of what you have advanced, I confess that a reformation is indeed wanting in the mode of education of the youth of our sex.

Sophronia. Of both sexes you may say.—We will not condemn yours and justify our own.—You are convinced, and Euphrasia will use her victory generously I am certain.

Euphrasia. You judge rightly.—I do not presume to condemn indiscriminately the books used in the education of youth; but surely they might be better selected, and some omitted, without any disadvantage.—I fear there is little prospect of such a general reformation as Hortensius generously wishes for. If any method can be found to alleviate these evils, it must be lenient—gradual—and practicable.—Let us then try to find out some expedient, with respect to those kind of books, which are our proper subject.

As this kind of reading is so common, and so much in everybody's power, it is the more incumbent on parents and guardians to give young people a good taste for reading, and above all to lay the foundation of good principles from their very infancy; to make them read what is really good, and by forming their taste teach to despise paltry books of every kind. When they come to maturity of reason, they will scorn to run over[4] a circulating library, but will naturally aspire to read the best books of all kinds.

1785

---

3. Persius (34–62 C.E.) and Juvenal (late 1st–early 2nd century C.E.), Roman satirical poets.
4. Read indiscriminately in.

ELIZA HAYWOOD
1693?–1756

Not much is known about the early life of Elizabeth Fowler or about the "unfortunate marriage," as she described it, that made her Eliza Haywood. She first came before the public as an actress in 1714 in Dublin, then moved to London. But "the stage not answering my expectation," as she later confessed, soon "made me turn my genius another way," to the life of a professional writer. Her first novel, the racy, best-selling *Love in Excess; or, The Fatal Inquiry* (1719), launched her long career as one of the most popular, prolific, and versatile authors of her time. She retailed gossip and also was gossiped about, becoming involved with the poet Richard Savage—a friend of Pope and later of Samuel Johnson—and with William

Hatchett, a playwright and actor who seems to have been her longtime companion. Pope mocked her scandal mongering, and her two illegitimate children, in his own scandal-mongering *Dunciad* (1728), and Fielding caricatured her as "Mrs. Novel." But nothing could keep her from writing. In addition to many kinds of fiction, she produced poems, translations, plays, political satires, essays, criticism, and books of advice and conduct—whatever might sell. In the 1730s she returned to the stage, as a playwright and actress, until the government cracked down on the theater in 1737. From 1744 to 1746 she had another great success with the *Female Spectator*, a wide-ranging periodical written for women. Later, *The History of Miss Betsy Thoughtless* (1751), the story of an indiscreet charmer who eventually reforms and finds her Mr. Trueworth, proved how well Haywood could adjust to the new style of edifying novels. And right up to the moment of her death she continued to work.

Fantomina first appeared among Haywood's *Secret Histories, Novels, and Poems* (1725), and the title page calls it "A Secret History of an Amour between Two Persons of Condition." The popular genre of "secret histories" promised a peep at what went on behind the scenes of fashionable society; and even though Haywood's story is obviously made up, it suggests that private lives, and especially love lives, are very different from what the public sees. Right at the start, the aristocratic heroine (whose name we never learn) is fascinated by the dalliance between "respectable" gentlemen and loose women of the town. She soon becomes a player herself. Cleverly switching roles, she gratifies her own desire by exploiting her lover's fickle passions. The story unsettles conventional views of social position, identity, morality, and gender. But most of all it shows that love is not only an irresistible impulse but also a risky, exciting game.

Fantomina; or, Love in a Maze

> *In love the victors from the vanquished fly.*
> *They fly that wound, and they pursue that die.*
> —Waller[1]

A young lady of distinguished birth, beauty, wit, and spirit, happened to be in a box one night at the playhouse; where, though there were a great number of celebrated toasts,[2] she perceived several gentlemen extremely pleased themselves with entertaining a woman who sat in a corner of the pit and, by her air and manner of receiving them, might easily be known to be one of those who come there for no other purpose, than to create acquaintance with as many as seem desirous of it. She could not help testifying her contempt of men who, regardless either of the play or circle, threw away their time in such a manner, to some ladies that sat by her. But they, either less surprised by being more accustomed to such sights than she who had been bred for the most part in the country, or not of a disposition to consider anything very deeply, took but little notice of it. She still thought of it, however; and the longer she reflected on it, the greater was her wonder that men, some of whom she knew were accounted to have wit, should have tastes so very depraved.—This excited a curiosity in her to know in what manner these creatures were addressed.—She was young, a stranger to the world, and consequently to the dangers of it; and having nobody in town, at that time, to whom she was obliged to be accountable for her actions, did in everything as her inclina-

---

1. Edmund Waller, "To A. H., of the different successes of their loves" (1645).
2. Women to whose charms men drink.

tions or humors rendered most agreeable to her: therefore thought it not in the least a fault to put in practice a little whim which came immediately into her head, to dress herself as near as she could in the fashion of those women who make sale of their favors, and set herself in the way of being accosted as such a one, having at that time no other aim than the gratification of an innocent curiosity.—She no sooner designed this frolic than she put it in execution; and muffling her hoods over her face, went the next night into the gallery-box, and practicing, as much as she had observed at that distance, the behavior of that woman, was not long before she found her disguise had answered the ends she wore it for.—A crowd of purchasers of all degrees and capacities were in a moment gathered about her, each endeavoring to outbid the other, in offering her a price for her embraces.—She listened to 'em all, and was not a little diverted in her mind at the disappointment she should give to so many, each of which thought himself secure of gaining her.—She was told by 'em all, that she was the most lovely woman in the world; and some cried, *Gad, she is mighty like my fine Lady Such-a-one*—naming her own name. She was naturally vain, and received no small pleasure in hearing herself praised, though in the person of another, and a supposed prostitute; but she dispatched as soon as she could all that had hitherto attacked her, when she saw the accomplished *Beauplaisir*[3] was making his way through the crowd as fast as he was able, to reach the bench she sat on. She had often seen him in the drawing-room, had talked with him; but then her quality[4] and reputed virtue kept him from using her with that freedom she now expected he would do, and had discovered something in him which had made her often think she should not be displeased, if he would abate some part of his reserve.—Now was the time to have her wishes answered.—He looked in her face, and fancied, as many others had done, that she very much resembled that lady whom she really was; but the vast disparity there appeared between their characters prevented him from entertaining even the most distant thought that they could be the same.—He addressed her at first with the usual salutations of her pretended profession, as, *Are you engaged, Madam?—Will you permit me to wait on you home after the play?—By Heaven, you are a fine girl!—How long have you used this house?*—and such like questions; but perceiving she had a turn of wit, and a genteel manner in her raillery, beyond what is frequently to be found among those wretches, who are for the most part gentlewomen but by necessity, few of 'em having had an education suitable to what they affect to appear, he changed the form of his conversation, and showed her it was not because he understood no better, that he had made use of expressions so little polite.—In fine, they were infinitely charmed with each other. He was transported to find so much beauty and wit in a woman who he doubted not but on very easy terms he might enjoy; and she found a vast deal of pleasure in conversing with him in this free and unrestrained manner. They passed their time all the play with an equal satisfaction; but when it was over, she found herself involved in a difficulty which before never entered into her head, but which she knew not well how to get over.—The passion he professed for her was not of that humble nature which can be content with distant adorations.—He resolved not to part from her

3. Fine pleasure (French).
4. Social standing.

without the gratifications of those desires she had inspired; and presuming on the liberties which her supposed function allowed of, told her she must either go with him to some convenient house of his procuring, or permit him to wait on her to her own lodgings.—Never had she been in such a *dilemma*. Three or four times did she open her mouth to confess her real quality; but the influence of her ill stars prevented it, by putting an excuse into her head which did the business as well, and at the same time did not take from her the power of seeing and entertaining him a second time with the same freedom she had done this.—She told him, she was under obligations to a man who maintained her, and whom she durst not disappoint, having promised to meet him that night at a house hard by.—This story, so like what those ladies sometimes tell, was not at all suspected, by *Beauplaisir*; and assuring her he would be far from doing her a prejudice,[5] desired that in return for the pain he should suffer in being deprived of her company that night, that she would order her affairs so as not to render him unhappy the next. She gave a solemn promise to be in the same box on the morrow evening, and they took leave of each other; he to the tavern to drown the remembrance of his disappointment; she in a hackney-chair[6] hurried home to indulge contemplation on the frolic she had taken, designing nothing less on her first reflections than to keep the promise she had made him, and hugging herself with joy, that she had the good luck to come off undiscovered.

But these cogitations were but of a short continuance, they vanished with the hurry of her spirits, and were succeeded by others vastly different and ruinous.—All the charms of *Beauplaisir* came fresh into her mind; she languished, she almost died for another opportunity of conversing with him; and not all the admonitions of her discretion were effectual to oblige her to deny laying hold of that which offered itself the next night.—She depended on the strength of her virtue to bear her fate through trials more dangerous than she apprehended this to be, and never having been addressed by him as Lady—, was resolved to receive his devoirs as a town-mistress,[7] imagining a world of satisfaction to herself in engaging him in the character of such a one and in observing the surprise he would be in to find himself refused by a woman who he supposed granted her favors without exception.—Strange and unaccountable were the whimsies she was possessed of—wild and incoherent her desires—unfixed and undetermined her resolutions, but in that of seeing *Beauplaisir* in the manner she had lately done. As for her proceedings with him, or how a second time to escape him without discovering who she was, she could neither assure herself, nor whether or not in the last extremity she would do so.—Bent, however, on meeting him, whatever should be the consequence, she went out some hours before the time of going to the playhouse, and took lodgings in a house not very far from it, intending, that if he should insist on passing some part of the night with her, to carry him there, thinking she might with more security to her honor entertain him at a place where she was mistress than at any of his own choosing.

The appointed hour being arrived, she had the satisfaction to find his love in his assiduity. He was there before her; and nothing could be more tender than the manner in which he accosted her. But from the first moment she

5. Harm.
6. A small hired coach, carried by two men.
7. Prostitute. "Devoirs": dutiful compliments.

came in, to that of the play being done, he continued to assure her no consideration should prevail with him to part from her again, as she had done the night before; and she rejoiced to think she had taken that precaution of providing herself with a lodging, to which she thought she might invite him without running any risk, either of her virtue or reputation.—Having told him she would admit of his accompanying her home, he seemed perfectly satisfied; and leading her to the place, which was not above twenty houses distant, would have ordered a collation to be brought after them. But she would not permit it, telling him she was not one of those who suffered themselves to be treated at their own lodgings; and as soon she was come in, sent a servant belonging to the house to provide a very handsome supper and wine, and everything was served to table in a manner which showed the director neither wanted money, nor was ignorant how it should be laid out.

This proceeding, though it did not take from him the opinion that she was what she appeared to be, yet it gave him thoughts of her which he had not before.—He believed her a *mistress,* but believed her to be one of a superior rank, and began to imagine the possession of her would be much more expensive than at first he had expected. But not being of a humor to grudge anything for his pleasures, he gave himself no farther trouble than what were occasioned by fears of not having money enough to reach her price about him.

Supper being over, which was intermixed with a vast deal of amorous conversation, he began to explain himself more than he had done; and both by his words and behavior let her know he would not be denied that happiness the freedoms she allowed had made him hope.—It was in vain; she would have retracted the encouragement she had given.—In vain she endeavored to delay, till the next meeting, the fulfilling of his wishes.—She had now gone too far to retreat.—*He* was bold;—he was resolute. *She* fearful—confused, altogether unprepared to resist in such encounters, and rendered more so by the extreme liking she had to him.—Shocked, however, at the apprehension of really losing her honor, she struggled all she could, and was just going to reveal the whole secret of her name and quality, when the thoughts of the liberty he had taken with her, and those he still continued to prosecute, prevented her, with representing the danger of being exposed, and the whole affair made a theme for public ridicule.—Thus much, indeed, she told him, that she was a virgin, and had assumed this manner of behavior only to engage him. But that he little regarded, or if he had, would have been far from obliging him to desist;—nay, in the present burning eagerness of desire, 'tis probable, that had he been acquainted both with who and what she really was, the knowledge of her birth would not have influenced him with respect sufficient to have curbed the wild exuberance of his luxurious wishes, or made him in that longing, that impatient moment, change the form of his addresses. In fine, she was undone; and he gained a victory, so highly rapturous, that had he known over whom, scarce could he have triumphed more. Her tears, however, and the distraction she appeared in, after the ruinous ecstasy was past, as it heightened his wonder, so it abated his satisfaction.—He could not imagine for what reason a woman, who, if she intended not to be a *mistress,* had counterfeited the part of one, and taken so much pains to engage him, should lament a consequence which she could not but expect, and till the last test, seemed inclinable to grant; and was both surprised and troubled at the mystery.—He omitted nothing that he thought might make her easy; and still retaining an opinion that the hope of interest[8] had been the chief motive which had led her to act in the manner she had done, and believing that she might know so little of him as to suppose, now she had nothing left to give, he might not make that recompense she expected for her favors: to put her out of that pain, he pulled out of his pocket a purse of gold, entreating her to accept of that as an earnest of what he intended to do for her; assuring her, with ten thousand protestations, that he would spare nothing which his whole estate could purchase, to procure her content and happiness. This treatment made her quite forget the part she had assumed, and throwing it from her with an air of disdain, Is this a reward (*said she*) for condescensions,[9] such as I have yielded to?—Can all the wealth you are possessed of make a reparation for my loss of honor?—Oh! no, I am undone beyond the power of heaven itself to help me!—She uttered many more such exclamations; which the amazed *Beauplaisir* heard without being able to reply to, till by degrees sinking from that rage of temper, her eyes resumed their softening glances, and guessing at the consternation he was in, No, my dear *Beauplaisir*, (*added she*) your love alone can compensate for the shame you have involved me in; be you sincere and constant, and I hereafter shall, perhaps, be satisfied with my fate, and forgive myself the folly that betrayed me to you.

Beauplaisir thought he could not have a better opportunity than these words gave him of inquiring who she was, and wherefore she had feigned herself to be of a profession which he was now convinced she was not; and after he had made her a thousand vows of an affection as inviolable and ardent as she could wish to find in him, entreated she would inform him by what means his happiness had been brought about, and also to whom he was indebted for the bliss he had enjoyed.—Some remains of yet unextinguished modesty, and sense of shame, made her blush exceedingly at this demand; but recollecting herself in a little time, she told him so much of the truth, as to what related to the frolic she had taken of satisfying her curiosity in what manner *mistresses*, of the sort she appeared to be, were treated by those who addressed them; but forbore discovering her true name and quality, for the reasons she had done before, resolving, if he boasted of this affair, he should not have it in his power to touch her character. She therefore said she was the daughter of a country gentleman, who was come to town to buy clothes, and that she was called *Fantomina*. He had no reason to distrust the truth of this story, and was therefore satisfied with it; but did not doubt by the beginning of her conduct, but that in the end she would be in reality the thing she so artfully had counterfeited; and had good nature enough to pity the misfortunes he imagined would be her lot. But to tell her so, or offer his advice in that point, was not his business, at least as yet.

They parted not till towards morning; and she obliged him to a willing vow of visiting her the next day at three in the afternoon. It was too late for her to go home that night, therefore she contented herself with lying there. In the morning she sent for the woman of the house to come up to her; and easily perceiving, by her manner, that she was a woman who might be influenced by gifts, made her a present of a couple of broad pieces,[1] and desired

8. Profit.
9. Humiliations.

1. Gold coins.

her, that if the gentleman who had been there the night before should ask any questions concerning her, that he should be told, she was lately come out of the country, had lodged there about a fortnight, and that her name was *Fantomina*. I shall (*also added she*) lie but seldom here; nor, indeed, ever come but in those times when I expect to meet him. I would, therefore, have you order it so, that he may think I am but just gone out, if he should happen by any accident to call when I am not here; for I would not, for the world, have him imagine I do not constantly lodge here. The landlady assured her she would do everything as she desired, and gave her to understand she wanted not[2] the gift of secrecy.

Everything being ordered at this home for the security of her reputation, she repaired to the other, where she easily excused to an unsuspecting aunt, with whom she boarded, her having been abroad all night, saying, she went with a gentleman and his lady in a barge to a little country seat of theirs up the river, all of them designing to return the same evening; but that one of the bargemen happening to be taken ill on the sudden, and no other waterman to be got that night, they were obliged to tarry till morning. Thus did this lady's wit and vivacity assist her in all but where it was most needful.— She had discernment to foresee and avoid all those ills which might attend the loss of her *reputation,* but was wholly blind to those of the ruin of her *virtue;* and having managed her affairs so as to secure the *one,* grew perfectly easy with the remembrance she had forfeited the *other.*—The more she reflected on the merits of *Beauplaisir,* the more she excused herself for what she had done; and the prospect of that continued bliss she expected to share with him took from her all remorse for having engaged in an affair which promised her so much satisfaction, and in which she found not the least danger of misfortune.—If he is really (*said she, to herself*) the faithful, the constant lover he has sworn to be, how charming will be our amour?—And if he should be false, grow satiated, like other men, I shall but, at the worst, have the private vexation of knowing I have lost him;—the intrigue being a secret, my disgrace will be so too.—I shall hear no whispers as I pass,—She is forsaken.—The odious word *forsaken* will never wound my ears; nor will my wrongs excite either the mirth or pity of the talking world.—It would not be even in the power of my undoer himself to triumph over me; and while he laughs at, and perhaps despises the fond, the yielding *Fantomina,* he will revere and esteem the virtuous, the reserved lady.—In this manner did she applaud her own conduct, and exult with the imagination that she had more prudence than all her sex beside. And it must be confessed, indeed, that she preserved an economy[3] in the management of this intrigue beyond what almost any woman but herself ever did: in the first place, by making no person in the world a confidant in it; and in the next, in concealing from *Beauplaisir* himself the knowledge who she was; for though she met him three or four days in a week at that lodging she had taken for that purpose, yet as much as he employed her time and thoughts, she was never missed from any assembly she had been accustomed to frequent.—The business of her love has engrossed her till six in the evening, and before seven she has been dressed in a different habit, and in another place.—Slippers, and a nightgown loosely flowing, has been the garb in which he has left the languishing

2. Did not lack.   3. Careful regulation.

Fantomina;—laced and adorned with all the blaze of jewels has he, in less than an hour after, beheld at the royal chapel, the palace gardens, drawing-room, opera, or play, the haughty awe-inspiring lady.—A thousand times has he stood amazed at the prodigious likeness between his little mistress and this court beauty; but was still as far from imagining they were the same as he was the first hour he had accosted her in the playhouse, though it is not impossible but that her resemblance to this celebrated lady might keep his inclination alive something longer than otherwise they would have been; and that it was to the thoughts of this (as he supposed) unenjoyed charmer she owed in great measure the vigor of his latter caresses.

But he varied not so much from his sex as to be able to prolong desire to any great length after possession. The rifled charms of *Fantomina* soon lost their poignancy,[4] and grew tasteless and insipid; and when the season of the year inviting the company to the *Bath*,[5] she offered to accompany him, he made an excuse to go without her. She easily perceived his coldness, and the reason why he pretended her going would be inconvenient, and endured as much from the discovery as any of her sex could do. She dissembled it, however, before him, and took her leave of him with the show of no other concern than his absence occasioned. But this she did to take from him all suspicion of her following him, as she intended, and had already laid a scheme for.—From her first finding out that he designed to leave her behind, she plainly saw it was for no other reason than that being tired of her conversation, he was willing to be at liberty to pursue new conquests; and wisely considering that complaints, tears, swoonings, and all the extravagancies which women make use of in such cases have little prevalence over a heart inclined to rove, and only serve to render those who practice them more contemptible, by robbing them of that beauty which alone can bring back the fugitive lover, she resolved to take another course; and remembering the height of transport she enjoyed when the agreeable *Beauplaisir* kneeled at her feet, imploring her first favors, she longed to prove the same again. Not but a woman of her beauty and accomplishments might have beheld a thousand in that condition *Beauplaisir* had been; but with her sex's modesty, she had not also thrown off another virtue equally valuable, though generally unfortunate, *constancy*. She loved *Beauplaisir*; it was only he whose solicitations could give her pleasure; and had she seen the whole species despairing, dying for her sake, it might, perhaps, have been a satisfaction to her pride, but none to her more tender inclination.—Her design was once more to engage him; to hear him sigh, to see him languish, to feel the strenuous pressures of his eager arms, to be compelled, to be sweetly forced to what she wished with equal ardor, was what she wanted, and what she had formed a stratagem to obtain, in which she promised herself success.

She no sooner heard he had left the town, than making a pretense to her aunt that she was going to visit a relation in the country, went towards *Bath*, attended but by two servants, who she found reasons to quarrel with on the road and discharged. Clothing herself in a habit she had brought with her, she forsook the coach and went into a wagon, in which equipage she arrived at *Bath*. The dress she was in was a round-eared cap, a short red petticoat,

---

4. Pungency.
5. A fashionable resort, one hundred miles west of London.

and a little jacket of gray stuff; all the rest of her accoutrements were answerable to[6] these, and joined with a broad country dialect, a rude unpolished air, which she, having been bred in these parts, knew very well how to imitate, with her hair and eye-brows blacked, made it impossible for her to be known, or taken for any other than what she seemed. Thus disguised did she offer herself to service in the house where *Beauplaisir* lodged, having made it her business to find out immediately where he was. Notwithstanding this metamorphosis she was still extremely pretty; and the mistress of the house happening at that time to want a maid, was very glad of the opportunity of taking her. She was presently[7] received into the family; and had a post in it (such as she would have chose, had she been left at her liberty), that of making the gentlemen's beds, getting them their breakfasts, and waiting on them in their chambers. Fortune in this exploit was extremely on her side; there were no others of the male sex in the house than an old gentleman who had lost the use of his limbs with the rheumatism, and had come thither for the benefit of the waters, and her beloved *Beauplaisir*; so that she was in no apprehensions of any amorous violence, but where she wished to find it. Nor were her designs disappointed. He was fired with the first sight of her; and though he did not presently take any farther notice of her than giving her two or three hearty kisses, yet she, who now understood that language but too well, easily saw they were the prelude to more substantial joys.—Coming the next morning to bring his chocolate, as he had ordered, he catched her by the pretty leg, which the shortness of her petticoat did not in the least oppose; then pulling her gently to him, asked her, how long she had been at service?—How many sweethearts she had? If she had ever been in love? and many other such questions, befitting one of the degree[8] she appeared to be. All which she answered with such seeming innocence, as more enflamed the amorous heart of him who talked to her. He compelled her to sit in his lap; and gazing on her blushing beauties, which, if possible, received addition from her plain and rural dress, he soon lost the power of containing himself.—His wild desires burst out in all his words and actions: he called her little angel, cherubim, swore he must enjoy her, though death were to be the consequence, devoured her lips, her breasts with greedy kisses, held to his burning bosom her half-yielding, half-reluctant body, nor suffered her to get loose till he had ravaged all, and glutted each rapacious sense with the sweet beauties of the pretty *Celia*, for that was the name she bore in this second expedition.— Generous as liberality itself to all who gave him joy this way, he gave her a handsome sum of gold, which she durst not now refuse, for fear of creating some mistrust, and losing the heart she so lately had regained; therefore taking it with an humble curtsy, and a well counterfeited show of surprise and joy, cried, O law, Sir! what must I do for all this? He laughed at her simplicity, and kissing her again, though less fervently than he had done before, bad her not be out of the way when he came home at night. She promised she would not, and very obediently kept her word.

His stay at *Bath* exceeded not a month; but in that time his supposed country lass had persecuted him so much with her fondness that in spite of the eagerness with which he first enjoyed her, he was at last grown more weary of

6. In harmony with.
7. Immediately.

8. Social class.

her than he had been of *Fantomina*: which she perceiving, would not be troublesome, but quitting her service remained privately in the town till she heard he was on his return; and in that time provided herself of another disguise to carry on a third plot, which her inventing brain had furnished her with, once more to renew his twice-decayed ardors. The dress she had ordered to be made was such as widows wear in their first mourning, which, together with the most afflicted and penitential countenance that ever was seen, was no small alteration to her who used to seem all gaiety.—To add to this, her hair, which she was accustomed to wear very loose, both when *Fantomina* and *Celia*, was now tied back so straight, and her pinners[9] coming so very forward, that there was none of it to be seen. In fine, her habit and her air were so much changed, that she was not more difficult to be known in the rude country *girl*, than she was now in the sorrowful *widow*.

She knew that *Beauplaisir* came alone in his chariot to the *Bath*, and in the time of her being servant in the house where he lodged, heard nothing of anybody that was to accompany him to *London*, and hoped he would return in the same manner he had gone. She therefore hired horses and a man to attend her to an inn about ten miles on this side *Bath*, where having discharged them, she waited till the chariot should come by; which when it did, and she saw that he was alone in it, she called to him that drove it to stop a moment, and going to the door saluted the master with these words:

The distressed and wretched, Sir (*said she*), never fail to excite compassion in a generous mind; and I hope I am not deceived in my opinion that yours is such.—You have the appearance of a gentleman, and cannot, when you hear my story, refuse that assistance which is in your power to give to an unhappy woman, who without it may be rendered the most miserable of all created beings.

It would not be very easy to represent the surprise so odd an address created in the mind of him to whom it was made.—She had not the appearance of one who wanted charity; and what other favor she required he could not conceive; but telling her she might command anything in his power, gave her encouragement to declare herself in this manner. You may judge (*resumed she*), by the melancholy garb I am in, that I have lately lost all that ought to be valuable to womankind; but it is impossible for you to guess the greatness of my misfortune, unless you had known my husband, who was master of every perfection to endear him to a wife's affections.—But, notwithstanding I look on myself as the most unhappy of my sex in out-living him, I must so far obey the dictates of my discretion as to take care of the little fortune he left behind him, which being in the hands of a brother of his in *London*, will be all carried off to *Holland*, where he is going to settle; if I reach not the town before he leaves it, I am undone for ever.—To which end I left *Bristol*, the place where we lived, hoping to get a place in the stage[1] at *Bath*, but they were all taken up before I came; and being, by a hurt I got in a fall, rendered incapable of traveling any long journey on horseback, I have no way to go to *London*, and must be inevitably ruined in the loss of all I have on earth, without[2] you have good nature enough to admit me to take part of your chariot.

---

9. Long flaps on the sides of a cap worn by women of rank.

1. Stagecoach.
2. Unless.

Here the feigned widow ended her sorrowful tale, which had been several times interrupted by a parenthesis of sighs and groans; and *Beauplaisir*, with a complaisant and tender air, assured her of his readiness to serve her in things of much greater consequence than what she desired of him; and told her it would be an impossibility of denying a place in his chariot to a lady, who he could not behold without yielding one in his heart. She answered the compliments he made her but with tears, which seemed to stream in such abundance from her eyes that she could not keep her handkerchief from her face one moment. Being come into the chariot, *Beauplaisir* said a thousand handsome things to persuade her from giving way to so violent a grief, which, he told her, would not only be destructive to her beauty, but likewise her health. But all his endeavors for consolement appeared ineffectual, and he began to think he should have but a dull journey, in the company of one who seemed so obstinately devoted to the memory of her dead husband that there was no getting a word from her on any other theme.—But bethinking himself of the celebrated story of the *Ephesian* matron,[3] it came into his head to make trial, she who seemed equally susceptible of *sorrow*, might not also be so too of *love*: and having began a discourse on almost every other topic, and finding her still incapable of answering, resolved to put it to the proof, if this would have no more effect to rouse her sleeping spirits.—With a gay air, therefore, though accompanied with the greatest modesty and respect, he turned the conversation, as though without design, on that joy-giving passion, and soon discovered that was indeed the subject she was best pleased to be entertained with; for on his giving her a hint to begin upon, never any tongue run more voluble than hers, on the prodigious power it had to influence the souls of those possessed of it, to actions even the most distant from their intentions, principles, or humors.—From that she passed to a description of the happiness of mutual affection;—the unspeakable ecstasy of those who meet with equal ardency; and represented it in colors so lively, and disclosed by the gestures with which her words were accompanied, and the accent of her voice so true a feeling of what she said, that *Beauplaisir*, without being as stupid as he was really the contrary, could not avoid perceiving there were seeds of fire not yet extinguished in this fair widow's soul, which wanted but the kindling breath of tender sighs to light into a blaze.—He now thought himself as fortunate, as some moments before he had the reverse; and doubted not but that before they parted, he should find a way to dry the tears of this lovely mourner, to the satisfaction of them both. He did not, however, offer, as he had done to *Fantomina* and *Celia*, to urge his passion directly to her, but by a thousand little softening artifices, which he well knew how to use, gave her leave to guess he was enamored. When they came to the inn where they were to lie, he declared himself somewhat more freely, and perceiving she did not resent it past forgiveness, grew more encroaching still.—He now took the liberty of kissing away her tears, and catching the sighs as they issued from her lips; telling her if grief was infectious, he was resolved to have his share; protesting he would gladly exchange passions with her, and be content to bear her load of *sorrow*, if she

---

3. In Petronius's *Satyricon*, a grieving widow who watches over her husband's burial vault is seduced by a soldier. When one of the bodies he was sup- posed to be guarding is stolen, she lets him replace it with her husband's.

would as willingly ease the burden of his *love*.—She said little in answer to the strenuous pressures with which at last he ventured to enfold her, but not thinking it decent, for the character she had assumed, to yield so suddenly, and unable to deny both his and her own inclinations, she counterfeited a fainting, and fell motionless upon his breast.—He had no great notion that she was in a real fit, and the room they supped in happening to have a bed in it, he took her in his arms and laid her on it, believing that whatever her distemper was, that was the most proper place to convey her to.—He laid himself down by her, and endeavored to bring her to herself; and she was too grateful to her kind physician at her returning sense, to remove from the posture he had put her in, without his leave.

It may, perhaps, seem strange that *Beauplaisir* should in such near intimacies continue still deceived. I know there are men who will swear it is an impossibility, and that no disguise could hinder them from knowing a woman they had once enjoyed. In answer to these scruples, I can only say, that besides the alteration which the change of dress made in her, she was so admirably skilled in the art of feigning that she had the power of putting on almost what face she pleased, and knew so exactly how to form her behavior to the character she represented that all the comedians[4] at both playhouses are infinitely short of her performances. She could vary her very glances, tune her voice to accents the most different imaginable from those in which she spoke when she appeared herself.—These aids from nature, joined to the wiles of art, and the distance between the places where the imagined *Fantomina* and *Celia* were, might very well prevent his having any thought that they were the same, or that the fair *widow* was either of them. It never so much as entered his head, and though he did fancy he observed in the face of the latter, features which were not altogether unknown to him, yet he could not recollect when or where he had known them;—and being told by her, that from her birth she had never removed from *Bristol*, a place where he never was, he rejected the belief of having seen her, and supposed his mind had been deluded by an idea of some other, whom she might have a resemblance of.

They passed the time of their journey in as much happiness as the most luxurious gratification of wild desires could make them; and when they came to the end of it, parted not without a mutual promise of seeing each other often.—He told her to what place she should direct a letter to him; and she assured him she would send to let him know where to come to her, as soon as she was fixed in lodgings.

She kept her promise; and charmed with the continuance of his eager fondness, went not home but into private lodgings, whence she wrote to him to visit her the first opportunity, and inquire for the Widow *Bloomer*.—She had no sooner dispatched this billet[5] than she repaired to the house where she had lodged as *Fantomina*, charging the people if *Beauplaisir* should come there, not to let him know she had been out of town. From thence she wrote to him, in a different hand, a long letter of complaint, that he had been so cruel in not sending one letter to her all the time he had been absent, entreated to see him, and concluded with subscribing herself his

4. Actors.
5. Letter.

unalterably affectionate *Fantomina*. She received in one day answers to both these. The first contained these lines:

To the Charming Mrs. BLOOMER,

It would be impossible, my Angel! for me to express the thousandth part of that infinity of transport, the sight of your dear letter gave me.—Never was woman formed to charm like you: never did any look like you,—write like you,—bless like you;—nor did ever man adore as I do.—Since yesterday we parted, I have seemed a body without a soul; and had you not by this inspiring billet, gave me new life, I know not what by tomorrow I should have been.—I will be with you this evening about five.—O, 'tis an age till then!—But the cursed formalities of duty oblige me to dine with my lord—who never rises from table till that hour;—therefore adieu till then sweet lovely mistress of the soul and all the faculties of

Your most faithful,
BEAUPLAISIR.

The other was in this manner:

To the Lovely FANTOMINA,

If you were half so sensible as you ought of your own power of charming, you would be assured, that to be unfaithful or unkind to you would be among the things that are in their very natures impossibilities.—It was my misfortune, not my fault, that you were not persecuted every post with a declaration of my unchanging passion; but I had unluckily forgot the name of the woman at whose house you are, and knew not how to form a direction that it might come safe to your hands.—And, indeed, the reflection how you might misconstrue my silence, brought me to town some weeks sooner than I intended—If you knew how I have languished to renew those blessings I am permitted to enjoy in your society, you would rather pity than condemn

Your ever faithful,
BEAUPLAISIR.

P.S. I fear I cannot see you till tomorrow; some business has unluckily fallen out that will engross my hours till then.—Once more, my dear, Adieu.

Traitor! (*cried she*) as soon as she had read them, 'tis thus our silly, fond, believing sex are served when they put faith in man. So had I been deceived and cheated, had I like the rest believed, and sat down mourning in absence, and vainly waiting recovered tendernesses.—How do some women (*continued she*) make their life a hell, burning in fruitless expectations, and dreaming out their days in hopes and fears, then wake at last to all the horror of despair?—But I have outwitted even the most subtle of the deceiving kind, and while he thinks to fool me, is himself the only beguiled person.

She made herself, most certainly, extremely happy in the reflection on the success of her stratagems; and while the knowledge of his inconstancy and levity of nature kept her from having that real tenderness for him she would else have had, she found the means of gratifying the inclination she had for his agreeable person in as full a manner as she could wish. She had all the sweets of love, but as yet had tasted none of the gall, and was in a state of contentment which might be envied by the more delicate.

When the expected hour arrived, she found that her lover had lost no part of the fervency with which he had parted from her; but when the next day she received him as *Fantomina*, she perceived a prodigious difference; which led her again into reflections on the unaccountableness of men's fancies, who still[6] prefer the last conquest, only because it is the last.—Here was an evident proof of it; for there could not be a difference in merit, because they were the same person; but the Widow *Bloomer* was a more new acquaintance than *Fantomina*, and therefore esteemed more valuable. This, indeed, must be said of *Beauplaisir*, that he had a greater share of good nature than most of his sex, who, for the most part, when they are weary of an intrigue, break it entirely off, without any regard to the despair of the abandoned nymph. Though he retained no more than a bare pity and complaisance[7] for *Fantomina*, yet believing she loved him to an excess, would not entirely forsake her, though the continuance of his visits was now become rather a penance than a pleasure.

The Widow *Bloomer* triumphed some time longer over the heart of this inconstant, but at length her sway was at an end, and she sunk in this character to the same degree of tastelessness as she had done before in that of *Fantomina* and *Celia*.—She presently perceived it, but bore it as she had always done; it being but what she expected, she had prepared herself for it, and had another project in *embryo* which she soon ripened into action. She did not, indeed, complete it altogether so suddenly as she had done the others, by reason there must be persons employed in it; and the aversion she had to any *confidants* in her affairs, and the caution with which she had hitherto acted, and which she was still determined to continue, made it very difficult for her to find a way without breaking through that resolution to compass what she wished.—She got over the difficulty at last, however, by proceeding in a manner, if possible, more extraordinary than all her former behavior.—Muffling herself up in her hood one day, she went into the park about the hour when there are a great many necessitous gentlemen, who think themselves above doing what they call little things for a maintenance, walking in the *Mall*, to take a *Camelion* treat,[8] and fill their stomachs with air instead of meat. Two of those, who by their physiognomy she thought most proper for her purpose, she beckoned to come to her; and taking them into a walk more remote from company, began to communicate the business she had with them in these words: I am sensible, gentlemen (*said she*), that, through the blindness of fortune and partiality of the world, merit frequently goes unrewarded, and that those of the best pretensions meet with the least encouragement.—I ask your pardon (*continued she*), perceiving they seemed surprised, if I am mistaken in the notion that you two may, perhaps, be of the number of those who have reason to complain of the injustice of fate; but if you are such as I take you for, I have a proposal to make you which may be of some little advantage to you. Neither of them made any immediate answer, but appeared buried in consideration for some moments. At length, We should, doubtless, madam (*said one of them*), willingly come into any measures to oblige you, provided they are such as may

6. Always.
7. Indulgence.

8. Chameleons supposedly fed on air. The Mall is a fashionable promenade in St. James's Park.

bring us into no danger, either as to our persons or reputations. That which I require of you (*resumed she*), has nothing in it criminal. All that I desire is *secrecy* in what you are entrusted, and to disguise yourselves in such a manner as you cannot be known, if hereafter seen by the person on whom you are to impose.—In fine, the business is only an innocent frolic, but if blazed abroad might be taken for too great a freedom in me.—Therefore, if you resolve to assist me, here are five pieces to drink my health and assure you, that I have not discoursed you on an affair I design not to proceed in; and when it is accomplished fifty more lie ready for your acceptance. These words, and above all the money, which was a sum which, 'tis probable, they had not seen of a long time, made them immediately assent to all she desired, and press for the beginning of their employment. But things were not yet ripe for execution; and she told them that the next day they should be let into the secret, charging them to meet her in the same place at an hour she appointed. 'Tis hard to say, which of these parties went away best pleased; *they*, that fortune had sent them so unexpected a windfall; or *she*, that she had found persons who appeared so well qualified to serve her.

Indefatigable in the pursuit of whatsoever her humor was bent upon, she had no sooner left her new-engaged emissaries than she went in search of a house for the completing her project.—She pitched on one very large and magnificently furnished, which she hired by the week, giving them the money beforehand to prevent any inquiries. The next day she repaired to the park, where she met the punctual squires of low degree; and ordering them to follow her to the house she had taken, told them they must condescend to appear like servants, and gave each of them a very rich livery. Then writing a letter to *Beauplaisir*, in a character vastly different from either of those she had made use of as *Fantomina*, or the fair Widow *Bloomer*, ordered one of them to deliver it into his own hands, to bring back an answer, and to be careful that he sifted out nothing of the truth.—I do not fear (*said she*), that you should discover to him who I am, because that is a secret of which you yourselves are ignorant; but I would have you be so careful in your replies, that he may not think the concealment springs from any other reasons than your great integrity to your trust.—Seem therefore to know my whole affairs; and let your refusing to make him partaker in the secret appear to be only the effect of your zeal for my interest and reputation. Promises of entire fidelity on the one side, and reward on the other, being past, the messenger made what haste he could to the house of *Beauplaisir*; and being there told where he might find him, performed exactly the injunction that had been given him. But never astonishment exceeding that which *Beauplaisir* felt at the reading this billet, in which he found these lines:

To the All-conquering BEAUPLAISIR.

I imagine not that 'tis a new thing to you, to be told you are the greatest charm in nature to our sex. I shall therefore, not to fill up my letter with any impertinent praises on your wit or person, only tell you that I am infinite in love with both, and if you have a heart not too deeply engaged, should think myself the happiest of my sex in being capable of inspiring it with some tenderness.— There is but one thing in my power to refuse you, which is the knowledge of my name, which believing the sight of my face will render no secret, you must not take it ill that I conceal from you.—The bearer of this is a person I can trust; send by him your answer; but endeavor not to dive into the meaning of this mystery, which will be impossible for you to unravel, and at the same time very much disoblige me.—But that you may be in no apprehensions of being imposed on by a woman unworthy of your regard, I will venture to assure you, the first and greatest men in the kingdom would think themselves blessed to have that influence over me you have, though unknown to yourself acquired.—But I need not go about to raise your curiosity, by giving you any idea of what my person is; if you think fit to be satisfied, resolve to visit me tomorrow about three in the afternoon; and though my face is hid, you shall not want sufficient demonstration that she who takes these unusual measures to commence a friendship with you is neither old, nor deformed. Till then I am,

Yours,
INCOGNITA.

He had scarce come to the conclusion before he asked the person who brought it, from what place he came;—the name of the lady he served;—if she were a wife, or widow, and several other questions directly opposite to the directions of the letter; but silence would have availed him as much as did all those testimonies of curiosity. No *Italian Bravo*,[9] employed in a business of the like nature, performed his office with more artifice; and the impatient inquirer was convinced, that nothing but doing as he was desired could give him any light into the character of the woman who declared so violent a passion for him; and little fearing any consequence which could ensue from such an encounter, resolved to rest satisfied till he was informed of everything from herself, not imagining this *Incognita* varied so much from the generality of her sex as to be able to refuse the knowledge of anything to the man she loved with that transcendency of passion she professed, and which his many successes with the ladies gave him encouragement enough to believe. He therefore took pen and paper, and answered her letter in terms tender enough for a man who had never seen the person to whom he wrote. The words were as follows:

To the Obliging and Witty INCOGNITA.

Though to tell me I am happy enough to be liked by a woman such, as by your manner of writing, I imagine you to be, is an honor which I can never sufficiently acknowledge, yet I know not how I am able to content myself with admiring the wonders of your wit alone. I am certain a soul like yours must shine in your eyes with a vivacity which must bless all they look on.—I shall, however, endeavor to restrain myself in those bounds you are pleased to set me, till by the knowledge of my inviolable fidelity, I may be thought worthy of gazing on that heaven I am now but to enjoy in contemplation.—You need not doubt my glad compliance with your obliging summons. There is a charm in your lines which gives too sweet an idea of their lovely author to be resisted.—I am all impatient for the blissful moment which is to throw me at your feet, and give me an opportunity of convincing you that I am,

Your everlasting slave,
BEAUPLAISIR.

9. Ruffian for hire.

Nothing could be more pleased than she to whom it was directed, at the receipt of this letter; but when she was told how inquisitive he had been concerning her character and circumstances, she could not forbear laughing heartily to think of the tricks she had played him, and applauding her own strength of genius and force of resolution, which by such unthought-of ways could triumph over her lover's inconstancy, and render that very temper,[1] which to other women is the greatest curse, a means to make herself more blessed.—Had he been faithful to me (*said she, to herself*), either as *Fantomina*, or *Celia*, or the Widow *Bloomer*, the most violent passion, if it does not change its object, in time will wither. Possession naturally abates the vigor of desire, and I should have had, at best, but a cold, insipid, husband-like lover in my arms; but by these arts of passing on him as a new mistress whenever the ardor, which alone makes love a blessing, begins to diminish for the former one, I have him always raving, wild, impatient, longing, dying.—O that all neglected wives and fond abandoned nymphs would take this method!—Men would be caught in their own snare, and have no cause to scorn our easy, weeping, wailing sex! Thus did she pride herself as if secure she never should have any reason to repent the present gaiety of her humor. The hour drawing near in which he was to come, she dressed herself in as magnificent a manner as if she were to be that night at a ball at court, endeavoring to repair the want of those beauties which the vizard[2] should conceal, by setting forth the others with the greatest care and exactness. Her fine shape, and air, and neck appeared to great advantage; and by that which was to be seen of her, one might believe the rest to be perfectly agreeable. *Beauplaisir* was prodigiously charmed, as well with her appearance as with the manner she entertained him. But though he was wild with impatience for the sight of a face which belonged to so exquisite a body, yet he would not immediately press for it, believing before he left her he should easily obtain that satisfaction.—A noble collation being over, he began to sue for the performance of her promise of granting everything he could ask, excepting the sight of her face, and knowledge of her name. It would have been a ridiculous piece of affectation in her to have seemed coy in complying with what she herself had been the first in desiring. She yielded without even a show of reluctance: and if there be any true felicity in an amour such as theirs, both here enjoyed it to the full. But not in the height of all their mutual raptures could he prevail on her to satisfy his curiosity with the sight of her face. She told him that she hoped he knew so much of her as might serve to convince him she was not unworthy of his tenderest regard; and if he could not content himself with that which she was willing to reveal, and which was the conditions of their meeting, dear as he was to her, she would rather part with him for ever than consent to gratify an inquisitiveness which, in her opinion, had no business with his love. It was in vain that he endeavored to make her sensible of her mistake; and that this restraint was the greatest enemy imaginable to the happiness of them both. She was not to be persuaded, and he was obliged to desist his solicitations, though determined in his mind to compass what he so ardently desired, before he left the house. He then turned the discourse wholly on the violence of the passion he had for her; and expressed the greatest discontent in the

1. Habit of mind (inconstancy).
2. Mask.

world at the apprehensions of being separated;—swore he could dwell for ever in her arms, and with such an undeniable earnestness pressed to be permitted to tarry with her the whole night, that had she been less charmed with his renewed eagerness of desire, she scarce would have had the power of refusing him; but in granting this request, she was not without a thought that he had another reason for making it besides the extremity of his passion, and had it immediately in her head how to disappoint him.

The hours of repose being arrived, he begged she would retire to her chamber; to which she consented, but obliged him to go to bed first; which he did not much oppose, because he supposed she would not lie in her mask, and doubted not but the morning's dawn would bring the wished discovery.—The two imagined servants ushered him to his new lodging; where he lay some moments in all the perplexity imaginable at the oddness of this adventure. But she suffered not these cogitations to be of any long continuance. She came, but came in the dark; which being no more than he expected by the former part of her proceedings, he said nothing of; but as much satisfaction as he found in her embraces, nothing ever longed for the approach of day with more impatience than he did. At last it came; but how great was his disappointment, when by the noises he heard in the street, the hurry of the coaches, and the cries of penny-merchants,[3] he was convinced it was night nowhere but with him? He was still in the same darkness as before; for she had taken care to blind the windows in such a manner that not the least chink was left to let in day.—He complained of her behavior in terms that she would not have been able to resist yielding to, if she had not been certain it would have been the ruin of her passion.—She therefore answered him only as she had done before; and getting out of the bed from him, flew out of the room with too much swiftness for him to have overtaken her, if he had attempted it. The moment she left him, the two attendants entered the chamber, and plucking down the implements which had screened him from the knowledge of that which he so much desired to find out, restored his eyes once more to day.—They attended to assist him in dressing, brought him tea, and by their obsequiousness, let him see there was but one thing which the mistress of them would not gladly oblige him in.—He was so much out of humor, however, at the disappointment of his curiosity, that he resolved never to make a second visit.—Finding her in an outer room, he made no scruple of expressing the sense he had of the little trust she reposed in him, and at last plainly told her, he could not submit to receive obligations from a lady who thought him uncapable of keeping a secret, which she made no difficulty of letting her servants into.—He resented,—he once more entreated,—he said all that man could do, to prevail on her to unfold the mystery; but all his adjurations were fruitless; and he went out of the house determined never to re-enter it, till she should pay the price of his company with the discovery of her face and circumstances.— She suffered him to go with this resolution, and doubted not but he would recede from it, when he reflected on the happy moments they had passed together; but if he did not, she comforted herself with the design of forming some other stratagem, with which to impose on him a fourth time.

She kept the house and her gentlemen-equipage for about a fortnight, in which time she continued to write to him as *Fantomina* and the Widow

3. Street vendors.

Bloomer, and received the visits he sometimes made to each; but his behavior to both was grown so cold, that she began to grow as weary of receiving his now insipid caresses as he was of offering them. She was beginning to think in what manner she should drop these two characters, when the sudden arrival of her mother, who had been some time in a foreign country, obliged her to put an immediate stop to the course of her whimsical adventures.—That lady, who was severely virtuous, did not approve of many things she had been told of the conduct of her daughter; and though it was not in the power of any person in the world to inform her of the truth of what she had been guilty of, yet she heard enough to make her keep her afterwards in a restraint, little agreeable to her humor, and the liberties to which she had been accustomed.

But this confinement was not the greatest part of the trouble of this now afflicted lady. She found the consequences of her amorous follies would be, without almost a miracle, impossible to be concealed.—She was with child; and though she would easily have found means to have screened even this from the knowledge of the world, had she been at liberty to have acted with the same unquestionable authority over herself as she did before the coming of her mother, yet now all her invention was at a loss for a stratagem to impose on a woman of her penetration.—By eating little, lacing prodigious straight, and the advantage of a great hoop-petticoat, however, her bigness was not taken notice of, and, perhaps, she would not have been suspected till the time of her going into the country, where her mother designed to send her, and from whence she intended to make her escape to some place where she might be delivered with secrecy, if the time of it had not happened much sooner than she expected.—A ball being at court, the good old lady was willing she should partake of the diversion of it as a farewell to the town.—It was there she was seized with those pangs, which none in her condition are exempt from.—She could not conceal the sudden rack[4] which all at once invaded her; or had her tongue been mute, her wildly rolling eyes, the distortion of her features, and the convulsions which shook her whole frame, in spite of her, would have revealed she labored under some terrible shock of nature.—Everybody was surprised, everybody was concerned, but few guessed at the occasion.—Her mother grieved beyond expression, doubted not but she was struck with the hand of death; and ordered her to be carried home in a chair,[5] while herself followed in another.—A physician was immediately sent for; but he presently perceiving what was her distemper, called the old lady aside and told her, it was not a doctor of his sex, but one of her own, her daughter stood in need of.—Never was astonishment and horror greater than that which seized the soul of this afflicted parent at these words. She could not for a time believe the truth of what she heard; but he insisting on it, and conjuring her to send for a midwife, she was at length convinced of it.—All the pity and tenderness she had been for some moment before possessed of now vanished, and were succeeded by an adequate[6] shame and indignation.—She flew to the bed where her daughter was lying, and telling her what she had been informed of, and which she was now far from doubting, commanded her to reveal the name of the person whose insinuations[7] had drawn her to this dishonor.—It was a great while before she could be

4. Intense pain.
5. Carriage.
6. Equal.
7. Artful ways of winding into someone's favor.

brought to confess anything, and much longer before she could be prevailed on to name the man whom she so fatally had loved; but the rack of nature growing more fierce, and the enraged old lady protesting no help should be afforded her while she persisted in her obstinacy, she, with great difficulty and hesitation in her speech, at last pronounced the name of *Beauplaisir*. She had no sooner satisfied her weeping mother, than that sorrowful lady sent messengers at the same time for a midwife, and for that gentleman who had occasioned the other's being wanted.—He happened by accident to be at home, and immediately obeyed the summons, though prodigiously surprised what business a lady so much a stranger to him could have to impart.—But how much greater was his amazement, when taking him into her closet,[8] she there acquainted him with her daughter's misfortune, of the discovery she had made, and how far he was concerned in it?—All the idea one can form of wild astonishment was mean to what he felt.—He assured her that the young lady her daughter was a person whom he had never, more than at a distance, admired;—that he had indeed spoke to her in public company, but that he never had a thought which tended to her dishonor.—His denials, if possible, added to the indignation she was before enflamed with.—She had no longer patience; and carrying him into the chamber, where she was just delivered of a fine girl, cried out, I will not be imposed on: the truth by one of you shall be revealed.—*Beauplaisir* being brought to the bedside, was beginning to address himself to the lady in it, to beg she would clear the mistake her mother was involved in; when she, covering herself with the clothes, and ready to die a second time with the inward agitations of her soul, shrieked out, Oh, I am undone!—I cannot live, and bear this shame!—But the old lady believing that now or never was the time to dive into the bottom of this mystery, forcing her to rear her head, told her she should not hope to escape the scrutiny of a parent she had dishonored in such a manner, and pointing to *Beauplaisir*, Is this the gentleman (*said she*), to whom you owe your ruin? or have you deceived me by a fictitious tale? Oh! no (*resumed the trembling creature*), he is indeed the innocent cause of my undoing.—Promise me your pardon (*continued she*), and I will relate the means. Here she ceased, expecting what she would reply, which, on hearing *Beauplaisir* cry out, What mean you, madam? I your undoing, who never harbored the least design on you in my life, she did in these words: Though the injury you have done your family (*said she*) is of a nature which cannot justly hope forgiveness, yet be assured, I shall much sooner excuse you when satisfied of the truth than while I am kept in a suspense, if possible, as vexatious as the crime itself is to me. Encouraged by this she related the whole truth. And 'tis difficult to determine if *Beauplaisir*, or the lady, were most surprised at what they heard; he, that he should have been blinded so often by her artifices; or she, that so young a creature should have the skill to make use of them. Both sat for some time in a profound reverie; till at length she broke it first in these words: Pardon, sir (*said she*), the trouble I have given you. I must confess it was with a design to oblige you to repair the supposed injury you had done this unfortunate girl, by marrying her, but now I know not what to say.—The blame is wholly hers, and I have nothing to request further of you, than that you will not divulge the distracted folly she has been guilty of.—He answered her in

8. Private room.

terms perfectly polite; but made no offer of that which, perhaps, she expected, though could not, now informed of her daughter's proceedings, demand. He assured her, however, that if she would commit the newborn lady to his care, he would discharge it faithfully. But neither of them would consent to that; and he took his leave, full of cogitations, more confused than ever he had known in his whole life. He continued to visit there, to inquire after her health every day; but the old lady perceiving there was nothing likely to ensue from these civilities but, perhaps, a renewing of the crime, she entreated him to refrain; and as soon as her daughter was in a condition, sent her to a monastery in *France*, the abbess of which had been her particular friend. And thus ended an intrigue which, considering the time it lasted, was as full of variety as any, perhaps, that many ages has produced.

1725

LADY MARY WORTLEY MONTAGU
1689–1762

In her early teens Lady Mary Pierrepont did something that well-bred young women were not supposed to do: she secretly taught herself Latin. The act reveals many of the traits that would also characterize her as a mature woman: curiosity, love of learning, intelligence, ambition, and independence of mind. The eldest daughter of a wealthy Whig peer (he later became marquess of Dorchester), she grew up amid a glittering London circle that included Addison, Steele, Congreve, and later Pope and Gay. But she was not content to live the life of a dutiful aristocratic daughter. Unlike most women in her time, she married for love, and when her husband, Edward Wortley Montagu, was appointed ambassador to Constantinople in 1716, she took advantage of the opportunity by traveling through Europe and studying the language and customs of Turkey. Returning home in 1718, she spent unhappy years that included bitter political quarrels with Pope and the gradual failure of her marriage. Then, in middle age, she fell in love with a young Italian author, Francesco Algarotti. In 1739 she traveled to Italy hoping to see him; but the passion that had kindled in their letters was soon quenched when he failed to join her. The rest of her life was passed abroad, in Avignon, France, and in Brescia and Venice, Italy. She died soon after her return to London, in 1762.

In a century that included many of the great letter writers in English—Gray, Horace Walpole, William Cowper, and others—Montagu is one of the greatest. She had saved her correspondence from 1716 to 1718, which centered on her experiences in the Ottoman Empire, and in the year before she died, she deposited a manuscript version with a Protestant clergyman, intending it to be published. *Letters . . . Written during Her Travels* appeared, posthumously, in 1763. "What fire, what ease, what knowledge of Europe and Asia!" the eminent historian Edward Gibbon exclaimed of the work. Montagu had traveled as a young woman with the deliberate ambition to gain such knowledge. Before arriving in Turkey, she undertook the project of understanding its culture in conversations with an Islamic scholar in Belgrade, and her curiosity led her to a multitude of revealing, provocative situations, on which she reflects with acuity and wit. She approvingly describes the liberties given to women by Turkish customs and institutions, such as the veils that rendered a woman incognito in the street (the better, she thought, to conduct secret love affairs). Letter XXXI explains the technique of smallpox inoculation in Turkey. Montagu would earn a place in medical history for her brave introduction of the practice to Britain on her return (her son and daughter were among the first to be inoculated), arousing resistance from doctors (as she predicts) and from fearful people in general. The admiring frankness of Montagu's description of the communal nudity of women in Turkish baths, in Letter XXVI, disturbed and shocked readers when the letters were finally published. Her correspondence presents two subjects to which many British readers at the time were unaccustomed: a complex, formidable civilization beyond Europe's borders, and the independent, brilliant perceptions of a woman able to view the norms of her own society critically in light of those of another.

From an early age Montagu had tried her hand at other literary forms as well: essays, poems, fiction, and even a translated play. In her own time she was especially admired as a poet. When Pope, after their quarrel, gave her the name "Sappho" (see *Epistle 2. To a Lady*, lines 24–26, p. 644), he was doubtless betraying the nervousness that many men felt in the presence of intelligent women (the Greek poet Sappho, after all, preferred women to men); yet Pope was also associating her with the classic author of lyric verse. Montagu's poems, although often casual, reveal the mind of a woman who is not willing to accept the stereotypes imposed upon her by men. Like her friend Mary Astell, Montagu puts her trust in education and reason, not in the opinions of others, and she insists on preserving her freedom of choice. A woman, Montagu's poems suggest, need not defer to a man who is less than her equal; she must look to her own satisfaction before she looks to his, and she retains the right to say no. The verse demands respect by virtue of its sexual candor and punishing wit. Like Montagu herself, it is never dull, and at its best it places her in that ideal community defined by E. M. Forster: "Not an aristocracy of power, based upon rank and influence, but an aristocracy of the sensitive, the considerate, and the plucky."

From Letters . . . Written during Her Travels [The Turkish Embassy Letters][1]

Letter XXVI, To Lady ———, *Adrianople,*[2] *1 April 1717*

["THE WOMEN'S COFFEE HOUSE"; OR, THE TURKISH BATHS]

I am now got into a new world, where every thing I see appears to me a change of scene; and I write to your ladyship with some content of mind, hoping, at least, that you will find the charm of novelty in my letters, and no longer reproach me that I tell you nothing extraordinary. I won't trouble you with a relation of our tedious journey; but I must not omit what I saw remarkable at Sophia,[3] one of the most beautiful towns in the Turkish empire and famous for its hot baths, that are resorted to both for diversion and health. I stopped here one day on purpose to see them; and designing to go *incognito*, I hired a

---

1. The complete title runs, *Letters of the Right Honourable Lady M——y W——y M——e: written, during her travels in Europe, Asia and Africa, to persons of distinction, Men of Letters, &c. in different parts of Europe, which contain, among other curious relations, Accounts of the Policy and Man-* ners of the Turks; Drawn from Sources that have been inaccessible to other Travellers.
2. A city in western Turkey, named after the Roman emperor Hadrian and now called Edirne.
3. Sofia, now the capital of Bulgaria.

Unknown artist, *Mary Wortley Montagu in the Turkish Bath*, 1781. The scene in Montagu's *Letters* that most fascinated her European readers: the visit to the Turkish baths. From the frontispiece of *Letters . . . written during her travels in Europe, Asia and Africa, to persons of distinction, men of letters, &c. . . . which contain . . . Accounts of the Policy and Manners of the Turks* (Berlin, 1781).

Turkish coach. These voitures[4] are not at all like ours, but much more convenient for the country, the heat being so great that glasses[5] would be very troublesome. They are made a good deal in the manner of the Dutch coaches, having wooden lattices painted and gilded; the inside being painted with baskets and nosegays of flowers, intermixed commonly with little poetical mottos. They are covered all over with scarlet cloth, lined with silk, and very often richly embroidered and fringed. This covering entirely hides the persons in them, but may be thrown back at pleasure, and thus permit the ladies to peep through the lattices. They hold four people very conveniently, seated on cushions, but not raised.

In one of these covered wagons, I went to the bagnio[6] about ten o'clock. It was already full of women. It is built of stone, in the shape of a dome, with no windows but in the roof, which gives light enough. There were five of these domes joined together, the outmost being less[7] than the rest, and serving only as a hall, where the portress stood at the door. Ladies of quality generally give this woman the value of a crown or ten shillings, and I did not forget that ceremony. The next room is a very large one, paved with marble, and all round it raised two sofas of marble, one above another. There were four fountains of cold water in this room, falling first into marble basins, and then

4. Carriages.
5. Windowpanes.

6. Bathhouse.
7. Smaller.

running on the floor in little channels made for that purpose, which carried the streams into the next room, something less than this, with the same sort of marble sofas, but so hot with steams of sulphur proceeding from the baths joining to it, 'twas impossible to stay there with one's clothes on. The two other domes were the hot baths, one of which had cocks[8] of cold water turning into it, to temper it to what degree of warmth the bathers pleased to have.

I was in my traveling habit, which is a riding dress, and certainly appeared very extraordinary to them. Yet there was not one of them that showed the least surprise or impertinent curiosity, but received me with all the obliging civility possible. I know no European court where the ladies would have behaved themselves in so polite a manner to such a stranger. I believe, upon the whole, there were two hundred women, and yet none of those disdainful smiles or satirical whispers that never fail in our assemblies when anybody appears that is not dressed exactly in fashion. They repeated over and over to me, "Uzelle, pek uzelle," which is nothing but "charming, very charming."—The first sofas were covered with cushions and rich carpets, on which sat the ladies; and on the second, their slaves behind them, but without any distinction of rank by their dress, all being in the state of nature, that is, in plain English, stark naked, without any beauty or defect concealed. Yet there was not the least wanton smile or immodest gesture amongst them. They walked and moved with the same majestic grace which Milton describes our General Mother[9] with. There were many amongst them as exactly proportioned as ever any goddess was drawn by the pencil of Guido or Titian,[1] and most of their skins shiningly white, only adorned by their beautiful hair, divided into many tresses hanging on their shoulders, braided either with pearl or ribbon, perfectly representing the figures of the graces.[2]

I was here convinced of the truth of a reflection I had often made, that if it were the fashion to go naked, the face would be hardly observed. I perceived that the ladies of the most delicate skins and finest shapes had the greatest share of my admiration, though their faces were sometimes less beautiful than those of their companions. To tell you the truth, I had wickedness enough to wish secretly that Mr. Gervase[3] could have been there invisible. I fancy it would have very much improved his art to see so many fine women naked in different postures, some in conversation, some working, others drinking coffee or sherbet, and many negligently lying on their cushions while their slaves (generally pretty girls of seventeen or eighteen) were employed in braiding their hair in several pretty fancies. In short, 'tis the women's coffee house, where all the news of the town is told, scandal invented, etc. They generally take this diversion once a week, and stay there at least four or five hours without getting cold, by immediate coming out of the hot bath into the cool room, which was very surprising to me. The lady that seemed the most considerable amongst them entreated me to sit by her, and would fain have undressed me for the bath. I excused myself with some difficulty. They being however all so earnest in persuading me, I was at last forced to open my skirt and show them

---

8. Faucets.
9. Eve. See *Paradise Lost*, 4.492 and 8.42–43.
1. Italian painter (ca. 1488–1576). Guido Reni, Italian painter (1575–1642).
2. Three goddesses, daughters of Zeus, personifying grace and beauty.
3. Charles Jervas (1675–1739), English portrait painter, friend of Montagu, Pope, and Swift.

my stays,[4] which satisfied them very well, for I saw they believed I was locked up in that machine, and that it was not in my own power to open it, which contrivance they attributed to my husband. I was charmed with their civility and beauty and should have been very glad to pass more time with them, but Mr. W[ortley] resolving to pursue his journey the next morning early, I was in haste to see the ruins of Justinian's church,[5] which did not afford me so agreeable a prospect as I had left, being little more than a heap of stones.

Adieu, Madam. I am sure I have now entertained you with an account of such a sight as you never saw in your life, and what no book of travels could inform you of, as 'tis no less than death for a man to be found in one of these places.

Letter XXXI, To Mrs. S. C. [Sarah Chiswell], Adrianople, 1 April 1717

[THE TURKISH METHOD OF INOCULATION FOR THE SMALL POX]

* * *

Apropos of distempers,[6] I am going to tell you a thing that will make you wish yourself here. The small pox, so fatal and so general amongst us, is here entirely harmless by the invention of engrafting, which is the term they give it. There is a set of old women who make it their business to perform the operation, every autumn, in the month of September, when the great heat is abated. People send to one another to know if any of their family has a mind to have the small pox; they make parties for this purpose, and when they are met (commonly fifteen or sixteen together) the old woman comes with a nutshell full of the matter of the best sort of small pox,[7] and asks what veins you please to have opened. She immediately rips open that you offer to her, with a large needle (which gives you no more pain than a common scratch) and puts into the vein as much matter as can lie upon the head of her needle, and after that, binds up the little wound with a hollow bit of shell, and in this manner opens four or five veins. The Grecians have commonly the superstition of opening one in the middle of the forehead, one in each arm, and one on the breast to mark the sign of the cross; but this has a very ill effect, all these wounds leaving little scars, and is not done by those that are not superstitious, who choose to have them in the legs, or that part of the arm that is concealed. The children or young patients play together all the rest of the day and are in perfect health to the eighth. Then the fever begins to seize them, and they keep their beds two days, very seldom three. They have very rarely above twenty or thirty in their faces, which never mark, and in eight days' time they are as well as before their illness. Where they are wounded, there remains running sores during the distemper, which I don't doubt is a great relief to it. Every year thousands undergo this operation, and the French ambassador says pleasantly that they take the small pox here by way of diversion, as they take the waters in other countries. There is no

---

4. Corset stiffened with strips of whalebone.
5. Roman emperor Justinian (483–565) built St. Sofia Church in the middle of the 6th century.
6. Montagu has just described a mild outbreak of

the plague in the area.
7. In inoculation or variolation, the milder form of the smallpox virus (*Variola minor*) is introduced to the skin of a healthy person; the localized nature

example of anyone that has died in it, and you may believe I am very well satisfied of the safety of this experiment, since I intend to try it on my dear little son. I am patriot enough to take pains to bring this useful invention into fashion in England, and I should not fail to write to some of our doctors very particularly about it, if I knew any one of them that I thought had virtue enough to destroy such a considerable branch of their revenue, for the good of mankind. But that distemper is too beneficial to them, not to expose to all their resentment the hardy wight[8] that should undertake to put an end to it. Perhaps if I live to return, I may, however, have courage to war with them. Upon this occasion, admire the heroism in the heart of your friend, etc.

1717   1763

Epistle from Mrs. Yonge to Her Husband[1]

Think not this paper comes with vain pretense
To move your pity, or to mourn th' offense.
Too well I know that hard obdurate heart;
No softening mercy there will take my part,
5 Nor can a woman's arguments prevail,
When even your patron's wise example fails.[2]
But this last privilege I still retain;
Th' oppressed and injured always may complain.
    Too, too severely laws of honor bind
10 The weak submissive sex of womankind.
If sighs have gained or force compelled our hand,
Deceived by art, or urged by stern command,
Whatever motive binds the fatal tie,
The judging world expects our constancy.
15   Just heaven! (for sure in heaven does justice reign,
Though tricks below that sacred name profane)
To you appealing I submit my cause,
Nor fear a judgment from impartial laws.
All bargains but conditional° are made;   *only conditionally*
20 The purchase void, the creditor unpaid;
Defrauded servants are from service free;

---

of this infection stimulates the immune system in time for the body both to terminate it and to protect itself against the virus in the future.
8. Person (archaic), often implying misfortune.
1. In 1724 the notorious libertine William Yonge, separated from his wife, Mary, discovered that she (like him) had committed adultery. He sued her lover, Colonel Norton, for damages and collected £1500. Later that year, according to the law of the time, he petitioned the Houses of Parliament for a divorce. The case was tried in public, Mary Yonge's love letters were read aloud, and two men testified that they had found her and Norton "together in naked bed." William Yonge was granted the divorce, his wife's dowry, and the greater part of her fortune.
    Although the "Epistle" is obviously based on this sensational affair, it is also a work of imagination.

Like Pope's *Eloisa to Abelard*—to which the author himself called Montagu's attention—it takes the form of a heroic epistle, the passionate outcry of an abandoned woman. The poet, entering into the feelings of Mary Yonge, justifies her conduct with reasons both of the heart and of the head. The objects of her attack include the institution of marriage, which binds wives in "eternal chains"; the double standard of morality, which requires chastity from women but not men; the hypocrisy of society, which condemns the very behavior it secretly lusts after; and the craven greed and cruelty of the husband himself. But 18th-century women seldom dared to speak like this in public, and the "Epistle" was not published until the 1970s.
2. Sir Robert Walpole, William Yonge's friend at court, was rumored to tolerate his own wife's infidelities.

A wounded slave regains his liberty.
For wives ill used no remedy remains,
To daily racks condemned, and to eternal chains.
25   From whence is this unjust distinction grown?
Are we not formed with passions like your own?
Nature with equal fire our souls endued,
Our minds as haughty, and as warm our blood;
O'er the wide world your pleasures you pursue, ⎫
30   The change is justified by something new;   ⎬
But we must sigh in silence—and be true.   ⎭
Our sex's weakness you expose and blame
(Of every prattling fop the common theme),
Yet from this weakness you suppose is due
35   Sublimer virtue than your Cato³ knew.
Had heaven designed us trials so severe,
It would have formed our tempers them to bear.
    And I have borne (oh what have I not borne!)
The pang of jealousy, the insults of scorn.
40   Wearied at length, I from your sight remove,
And place my future hopes in secret love.
In the gay bloom of glowing youth retired,
I quit the woman's joy to be admired,
With that small pension your hard heart allows,
45   Renounce your fortune, and release your vows.
To custom (though unjust) so much is due;
I hide my frailty from the public view.
My conscience clear, yet sensible of shame,
My life I hazard, to preserve my fame.
50   And I prefer this low inglorious state   ⎫
To vile dependence on the thing I hate—   ⎬
But you pursue me to this last retreat.   ⎭
Dragged into light, my tender crime is shown
And every circumstance of fondness known.
55   Beneath the shelter of the law you stand,
And urge my ruin with a cruel hand,
While to my fault thus rigidly severe,
Tamely submissive to the man you fear.⁴
    This wretched outcast, this abandoned wife,
60   Has yet this joy to sweeten shameful life:
By your mean conduct, infamously loose,
You are at once my accuser and excuse.
Let me be damned by the censorious prude
(Stupidly dull, or spiritually lewd),
65   My hapless case will surely pity find
From every just and reasonable mind.
When to the final sentence I submit,
The lips condemn me, but their souls acquit.

3. The asceticism and self-discipline of the Roman statesman Cato were emphasized in Addison's famous tragedy *Cato* (1713).

4. I.e., Walpole. Montagu suggests that the whole political establishment of England takes sides against Mary Yonge.

No more my husband, to your pleasures go,
70   The sweets of your recovered freedom know.
Go: court the brittle friendship of the great,
Smile at his board,° or at his levee[5] wait;   *dining table*
And when dismissed, to madam's toilet[6] fly,
More than her chambermaids, or glasses,° lie,   *mirrors*
75   Tell her how young she looks, how heavenly fair,
Admire the lilies and the roses there.
Your high ambition may be gratified,
Some cousin of her own be made your bride,
And you the father of a glorious race
80   Endowed with Ch—l's strength and Low—r's face.[7]

1724   1972

5. Morning reception of visitors.
6. It was fashionable for women like Lady Walpole to receive visitors during the last stages of dressing (their "toilet").
7. General Churchill was rumored to have had an affair with Lady Walpole. Antony Lowther was a notorious gallant. The author implies that William Yonge's next wife may be as untrue as his first. Mary Yonge remarried immediately after her divorce; five years later William Yonge himself (whose divorce had made him rich) married the daughter of a baron.

Debating Women:
Arguments in Verse

atires on women are an ancient tradition. In many cultures, male writers have defined the nature of women, distinguished them sharply from men, laughed at their faults, looked into their hearts, and told them how to behave; and female writers such as Christine de Pisan (1363?–1431) have countered by pointing out the virtues of women and the unfairness of men. But the argument intensified in seventeenth- and eighteenth-century Britain. As literacy increased to unprecedented numbers, much of the reading public began to consist of women, whose concerns were addressed directly by Mary Astell and other women as well as by men. New forms of writing—the periodical essay, the conduct book, and above all the novel—developed to give women rules and models for living. But the early eighteenth century was also a great age of satire. Male satirists could not resist the urge to reflect on, or try to reform, women's follies; nor could female satirists resist the urge to reply that men were just as bad or worse and did not know what they were talking about. This led to a lively exchange in which women were not only the subject of the debate but also agents who spoke for themselves.

Jonathan Swift and Alexander Pope, who were lifelong bachelors and friends as well as brilliant satirists, represent two different positions. Swift's misogyny is part of his misanthropy. As a Christian he hates human pride, or the illusion that we can rise above the sinfulness and frailty that are our nature as impure, fallen creatures; and he never misses a chance to shatter that illusion. Hence women, associated romantically with beauty and love, must be dragged down to earth and have their cosmetics rubbed off. To Swift's admirers, this is realism; to his detractors, woman-hating. His focus on bodily functions in works like "The Lady's Dressing Room" has often been ascribed to a personal fixation or frustrated desire, as in Lady Mary Wortley Montagu's counterattack. It might also be regarded as the fury of an idealist when he looks at the world as it is.

Pope was far more comfortable with illusions; when he writes about a lady's dressing room, in *The Rape of the Lock,* it sparkles with glamour. Many readers have thought he had a feminine sensibility. Despite his patronizing attitude toward women, he certainly took a strong interest in female psychology; and his pleasure in delicate things and domestic arrangements appealed to many women. Anne Irwin and Mary Leapor argue with Pope's *Characters of Women,* but they are clearly influenced by the way he sees their world as well as by his poetic style. In this respect his satire might be thought more insidious than Swift's. The sympathy he expresses for women lends plausibility to his analysis of their flaws, and his distinctions between the sexes seem rooted in nature, not merely in custom. Thus Pope's shrewd portraits of the ways that women waste their lives can be very chilling.

Yet women could also write satire. The poets who respond to Swift and Pope poke fun at the smug assumption that men can tell women what women are thinking and feeling. Montagu's parody, one of many answers to Swift's poem, turns the tables on his disgust at the body; here the *man's* body falls short. (Some women agreed that men were Yahoos, though women were not.) Irwin suggests that Pope is the problem, not the solution: because lack of education makes all the difference between women and men, a truly good poet would devote himself to educating women, not to ridiculing faults they cannot help. Similarly, Leapor regards satire of women as blaming the victim; her characters resemble Pope's, but what dooms them is not the bad choices they make but the lack of any good choice in a man's world that turns all their dreams against them. The female satirists in this debate do not belong to any set, nor do they agree with each other's diagnoses. They do agree, however, on one main point: when the ways of women come into question, women must speak for themselves.

JONATHAN SWIFT

"The Lady's Dressing Room" is the first in a series of "excremental" poems in which Swift looks below the surface of women's allure. If one object of satire is the grossness of Celia, "the goddess," the romantic illusions of Strephon, her disabused lover, are far more absurd.

The Lady's Dressing Room

Five hours (and who can do it less in?)
By haughty Celia spent in dressing,
The goddess from her chamber issues,
Arrayed in lace, brocade, and tissues.
5   Strephon, who found the room was void,
And Betty otherwise employed,
Stole in, and took a strict survey
Of all the litter as it lay;
Whereof, to make the matter clear,
10 An inventory follows here.
    And first a dirty smock appeared,
Beneath the armpits well besmeared.
Strephon, the rogue, displayed it wide,
And turned it round on every side.
15 In such a case few words are best,
And Strephon bids us guess the rest;
But swears how damnably the men lie,
In calling Celia sweet and cleanly.
    Now listen while he next produces
20 The various combs for various uses,
Filled up with dirt so closely fixed,
No brush could force a way betwixt;
A paste of composition rare,
Sweat, dandruff, powder, lead, and hair;
25 A forehead cloth with oil upon't
To smooth the wrinkles on her front;
Here alum flower° to stop the steams   *styptic powder*
Exhaled from sour unsavory streams;
There night-gloves made of Tripsy's hide,

30   Bequeathed by Tripsy when she died,
        With puppy water,[1] beauty's help,
        Distilled from Tripsy's darling whelp;
        Here gallipots° and vials placed,   *small pots*
        Some filled with washes, some with paste,
35   Some with pomatum,° paints, and slops,   *pomade*
        And ointments good for scabby chops.
        Hard by a filthy basin stands,
        Fouled with the scouring of her hands;
        The basin takes whatever comes,
40   The scraping of her teeth and gums,
        A nasty compound of all hues,
        For here she spits, and here she spews.
           But oh! it turned poor Strephon's bowels,
        When he beheld and smelt the towels,
45   Begummed, bemattered, and beslimed,
        With dirt, and sweat, and earwax grimed.
        No object Strephon's eye escapes;
        Here petticoats in frowzy heaps,
        Nor be the handkerchiefs forgot,
50   All varnished o'er with snuff and snot.
        The stockings why should I expose,
        Stained with the marks of stinking toes,
        Or greasy coifs and pinners° reeking,   *nightcaps*
        Which Celia slept at least a week in?
55   A pair of tweezers next he found
        To pluck her brows in arches round,
        Or hairs that sink the forehead low,
        Or on her chin like bristles grow.
           The virtues we must not let pass
60   Of Celia's magnifying glass.
        When frighted Strephon cast his eye on't,
        It showed the visage of a giant—
        A glass that can to sight disclose
        The smallest worm in Celia's nose,
65   And faithfully direct her nail
        To squeeze it out from head to tail;
        For catch it nicely by the head,
        It must come out alive or dead.
           Why Strephon will you tell the rest?
70   And must you needs describe the chest?
        That careless wench! no creature warn her
        To move it out from yonder corner,
        But leave it standing full in sight,
        For you to exercise your spite.
75   In vain the workman showed his wit
        With rings and hinges counterfeit
        To make it seem in this disguise
        A cabinet to vulgar eyes;
        For Strephon ventured to look in,

---

1. A cosmetic made from the internal organs of a puppy (here from the whelp of Celia's former lapdog).

80   Resolved to go through thick and thin;
     He lifts the lid, there needs no more,
     He smelt it all the time before.
       As from within Pandora's box,
     When Epimetheus oped the locks,
85   A sudden universal crew
     Of human evils upward flew,
     He still was comforted to find
     That Hope at last remained behind;[2]
     So Strephon, lifting up the lid
90   To view what in the chest was hid,
     The vapors flew from out the vent,
     But Strephon cautious never meant
     The bottom of the pan to grope,
     And foul his hands in search of Hope.
95   Oh never may such vile machine
     Be once in Celia's chamber seen!
     Oh may she better learn to keep
     "Those secrets of the hoary deep"![3]
       As mutton cutlets, prime of meat,
100 Which though with art you salt and beat,
     As laws of cookery require,
     And roast them at the clearest fire,
     If from adown the hopeful chops
     The fat upon a cinder drops,
105 To stinking smoke it turns the flame,
     Poisoning the flesh from whence it came,
     And thence exhales a greasy stench,
     For which you curse the careless wench;
     So things which must not be expressed,
110 When plumped into the reeking chest,
     Send up an excremental smell
     To taint the parts from which they fell,
     The petticoats and gown perfume,
     And waft a stink round every room.
115   Thus finishing his grand survey,
     The swain disgusted slunk away,
     Repeating in his amorous fits,
     "Oh! Celia, Celia, Celia shits!"
       But Vengeance, goddess never sleeping,
120 Soon punished Strephon for his peeping.
     His foul imagination links
     Each dame he sees with all her stinks,
     And, if unsavory odors fly,
     Conceives a lady standing by.
125 All women his description fits,
     And both ideas jump like wits,[4]

---

2. Despite the warnings of his brother Prometheus, Epimetheus married Pandora, the first woman (according to Greek mythology). When the box that Zeus had given her was opened, all evils flew out into the world, and only hope remained.
3. *Paradise Lost* 2.891.
4. Coincide; after the proverb "Good wits jump" (i.e., great minds think alike).

By vicious fancy coupled fast,
And still appearing in contrast.
   I pity wretched Strephon, blind
130 To all the charms of womankind.
Should I the queen of love refuse
Because she rose from stinking ooze?[5]
To him that looks behind the scene,
Statira's but some pocky quean.[6]
135 When Celia in her glory shows,
If Strephon would but stop his nose,
Who now so impiously blasphemes
Her ointments, daubs, and paints, and creams,
Her washes, slops, and every clout°   *rag*
140 With which she makes so foul a rout,
He soon would learn to think like me,
And bless his ravished eyes to see
Such order from confusion sprung,
Such gaudy tulips raised from dung.

1732

5. The goddess Venus rose out of the sea.
6. Strumpet, with a pun on Nathaniel Lee's *Rival* *Queens* (1677), a play in which Statira was a heroine.

LADY MARY WORTLEY MONTAGU

Montagu did not like Swift. She objected to his politics (he worked for Tories, she was a Whig), his friendship with Pope (with whom she had bitterly quarreled), his vanity (especially at knowing important people), and his defiant indecency (which she considered not only inappropriate for a clergyman but also a sign of low breeding). Her reply to "The Lady's Dressing Room" mimics its style, but substitutes vulgar names for its mock-pastoral (Betty instead of Celia) and personal pique for its moralistic conclusions. The poem was originally published anonymously in 1734 under the title "The Dean's Provocation for Writing the Lady's Dressing Room"; the version reprinted here is from a fair copy in Montagu's hand.

The Reasons That Induced Dr. Swift to Write a Poem Called the Lady's Dressing Room

The Doctor in a clean starched band,°   *clerical collar*
His golden snuff box in his hand,
With care his diamond ring displays
And artful shows its various rays,
5 While grave he stalks down ——— Street,
His dearest Betty ——— to meet.
   Long had he waited for this hour,

Nor gained admittance to the bower,
Had joked and punned, and swore and writ,
10   Tried all his gallantry and wit,
Had told her oft what part he bore
In Oxford's[1] schemes in days of yore,
But bawdy, politics, nor satyr[2]
Could move this dull hard-hearted creature.
15   Jenny her maid could taste a rhyme
And grieved to see him lose his time,
Had kindly whispered in his ear,
"For twice two pound you enter here;
My lady vows without that sum
20   It is in vain you write or come."
    The destined offering now he brought
And in a paradise of thought
With a low bow approached the dame
Who smiling heard him preach his flame.
25   His gold she takes (such proofs as these
Convince most unbelieving shes)
And in her trunk rose up to lock it
(Too wise to trust it in her pocket)
And then, returned with blushing grace,
30   Expects the Doctor's warm embrace.
    But now this is the proper place
Where morals stare me in the face
And for the sake of fine expression
I'm forced to make a small digression.
35   Alas for wretched humankind,
With learning mad, with wisdom blind!
The ox thinks he's for saddle fit
(As long ago friend Horace writ)[3]
And men their talents still mistaking,
40   The stutterer fancies his is speaking.
With admiration oft we see
Hard features heightened by toupée,
The beau affects° the politician,   *poses as*
Wit is the citizen's[4] ambition,
45   Poor Pope philosophy displays on
With so much rhyme and little reason,
And though he argues ne'er so long
That all is right, his head is wrong.[5]
    None strive to know their proper merit
50   But strain for wisdom, beauty, spirit,
And lose the praise that is their due
While they've the impossible in view.
So have I seen the injudicious heir
To add one window the whole house impair.
55   Instinct the hound does better teach

---

1. Robert Harley, earl of Oxford, headed the government from 1710 to 1714.
2. Satire (pronounced *say'tir*).
3. *Epistles* 1.14.43.

4. "A townsman; a man of trade; not a gentleman" (Johnson's *Dictionary*).
5. A parody of Pope's *Essay on Man* 1.292, which had just been published.

Who never undertook to preach;
The frighted hare from dogs does run
But not attempts to bear a gun.
Here many noble thoughts occur
60 But I prolixity abhor,
And will pursue the instructive tale
To show the wise in some things fail.
   The reverend lover with surprise ⎫
Peeps in her bubbies, and her eyes, ⎬
65 And kisses both, and tries—and tries. ⎭
The evening in this hellish play,
Beside his guineas thrown away,
Provoked the priest to that degree
He swore, "The fault is not in me.
70 Your damned close stool so near my nose,
Your dirty smock, and stinking toes,
Would make a Hercules as tame
As any beau that you can name."
   The nymph grown furious roared, "By God!
75 The blame lies all in sixty odd,"
And scornful pointing to the door
Cried, "Fumbler, see my face no more."
"With all my heart I'll go away,
But nothing done, I'll nothing pay.
80 Give back the money."—"How," cried she,
"Would you palm such a cheat on me!
For poor four pound to roar and bellow,
Why sure you want some new Prunella?"[6]
"I'll be revenged, you saucy quean"°   *strumpet*
85 (Replies the disappointed Dean),
"I'll so describe your dressing room
The very Irish shall not come."[7]
She answered short, "I'm glad you'll write,
You'll furnish paper when I shite."

1734

6. A name for a prostitute and a worsted cloth worn by clergymen.

7. A gibe at the supposed crassness of Irishmen (like Swift himself).

ALEXANDER POPE

"Epistle 2. To a Lady" is one of four poems that Pope grouped together under the title *Epistles to Several Persons* but that have usually been known by the less appropriate title *Moral Essays*. They were conceived as parts of Pope's ambitious "ethic work," of which only the first part, *An Essay on Man*, was completed. "Epistle 1" treats the characters of men and "Epistle 2," the characters of women. The other two epistles are concerned with the use of riches, a subject that engaged Pope's attention during the 1730s, because he distrusted the influence on private morals and public life of the rapidly growing wealth of England under the first Hanoverians.

"Epistle 2" combines two literary forms: the satire on women and the verse letter to a particular person—here Martha Blount (1690–1763), Pope's closest female friend, whose remark in line 2 sets the theme of the poem. The first section (to line 198) sketches a portrait gallery of ladies that illustrates their inconsistency and volatility. As an amateur painter, Pope is fascinated by the problem of catching such contrary types: the affected, the soft-natured, the cunning, the whimsical, the witty, and the silly. The next part of the poem (lines 199–248) develops Pope's favorite theory of the ruling passion—the idea that each person is driven by a single irresistible desire—and argues that women are limited to two passions: love of pleasure and love of power. The final part (line 249 to the end) describes an ideal woman, good-natured, sensible, and well balanced, who is identified with Blount herself.

Like every satire on women, "Epistle 2" is shaped by stereotypes: women are fickle, frail, and subordinate to men. Yet much of the poem undermines those prejudices by showing the real difficulties of women's lives. "By man's oppression cursed," they waste their talents on trivial pursuits and "die of nothing but a rage to live." The poem shares that restlessness. If women are full of contradictions, so are Pope's couplets, torn between sympathy and satiric bite. The poet finds himself strangely attracted to what he disapproves, and many female readers, then and now, have felt the same way about the poem.

Epistle 2. To a Lady

Of the Characters of Women

Nothing so true as what you once let fall,
"Most women have no characters at all."
Matter too soft a lasting mark to bear,
And best distinguished by black, brown, or fair.
5   How many pictures[1] of one nymph we view,
All how unlike each other, all how true!
Arcadia's countess, here, in ermined pride,
Is, there, Pastora by a fountain side.
Here Fannia, leering on her own good man,
10 And there, a naked Leda with a swan.[2]
Let then the fair one beautifully cry,
In Magdalen's loose hair and lifted eye,
Or dressed in smiles of sweet Cecilia shine,[3]
With simpering angels, palms, and harps divine;
15 Whether the charmer sinner it, or saint it,
If folly grow romantic,° I must paint it.   *extravagant*
    Come then, the colors and the ground[4] prepare!
Dip in the rainbow, trick° her off in air;   *sketch*
Choose a firm cloud, before it fall, and in it
20 Catch, ere she change, the Cynthia[5] of this minute.

1. Ladies of the 17th and 18th centuries were often painted in the costumes and attitudes of fanciful, mythological, or historical characters.
2. Leda was seduced by Zeus, who approached her in the form of a swan.
3. St. Mary Magdalen and St. Cecilia were often

painted in the manner described.
4. The first coatings of paint on the canvas before the figures in the picture are sketched in.
5. One of the names of Diana, goddess of the moon, a notoriously changeable heavenly body.

Rufa, whose eye quick-glancing o'er the park,
Attracts each light gay meteor of a spark,°   beau
Agrees as ill with Rufa studying Locke,
As Sappho's diamonds with her dirty smock,
25   Or Sappho at her toilet's greasy task,[6]
With Sappho fragrant at an evening masque:
So morning insects that in muck begun,
Shine, buzz, and flyblow[7] in the setting sun.
How soft is Silia! fearful to offend,
30   The frail one's advocate, the weak one's friend:
To her, Calista proved her conduct nice,°   refined
And good Simplicius asks of her advice.
Sudden, she storms! she raves! You tip the wink,°   look knowing
But spare your censure; Silia does not drink.
35   All eyes may see from what the change arose,
All eyes may see—a pimple on her nose.
Papillia,[8] wedded to her amorous spark,
Sighs for the shades—"How charming is a park!"
A park is purchased, but the fair he sees
40   All bathed in tears—"Oh, odious, odious trees!"
Ladies, like variegated tulips, show;
'Tis to their changes half their charms we owe;
Their happy spots the nice admirer take,°   captivate
Fine by defect, and delicately weak.
45   'Twas thus Calypso[9] once each heart alarmed,
Awed without virtue, without beauty charmed;
Her tongue bewitched as oddly as her eyes,
Less wit than mimic, more a wit than wise;
Strange graces still, and stranger flights she had,
50   Was just not ugly, and was just not mad;
Yet ne'er so sure our passion to create,
As when she touched the brink of all we hate.
Narcissa's[1] nature, tolerably mild,
To make a wash,° would hardly stew a child;   cosmetic lotion
55   Has even been proved to grant a lover's prayer,
And paid a tradesman once to make him stare,
Gave alms at Easter, in a Christian trim,
And made a widow happy, for a whim.
Why then declare good nature is her scorn,
60   When 'tis by that alone she can be borne?
Why pique all mortals, yet affect a name?
A fool to pleasure, yet a slave to fame:
Now deep in Taylor and the *Book of Martyrs*,[2]

---

6. Lady Mary Wortley Montagu, although beautiful as a young woman, became notorious for her slatternly appearance and personal uncleanliness. Both Sappho and Montagu were poets.
7. Deposit their eggs.
8. From Latin for "butterfly."
9. The name is borrowed from the fascinating goddess who detained Odysseus on his island for seven years after the fall of Troy, thus preventing his return to his kingdom, Ithaca.

1. Type of extreme self-love. Narcissus, a beautiful youth, fell in love with his own image when he saw it reflected in a fountain.
2. John Foxe's *Acts and Monuments*, usually referred to as Foxe's *Book of Martyrs*, was a household book in most Protestant families in the 17th and 18th centuries. Jeremy Taylor was a 17th-century Anglican divine whose *Holy Living and Holy Dying* was often reprinted in the 18th century.

Now drinking citron with his Grace and Chartres.[3]
65   Now conscience chills her, and now passion burns;
And atheism and religion take their turns;
A very heathen in the carnal part,
Yet still a sad, good Christian at her heart.
     See Sin in state, majestically drunk;
70   Proud as a peeress, prouder as a punk;°   *harlot*
Chaste to her husband, frank° to all beside,   *licentious*
A teeming mistress, but a barren bride.
What then? let blood and body bear the fault,
Her head's untouched, that noble seat of thought:
75   Such this day's doctrine—in another fit
She sins with poets through pure love of wit.
What has not fired her bosom or her brain?
Caesar and Tallboy, Charles[4] and Charlemagne.
As Helluo,[5] late dictator of the feast,
80   The nose of hautgout,[6] and the tip of taste,
Criticked your wine, and analyzed your meat,
Yet on plain pudding deigned at home to eat;
So Philomedé,[7] lecturing all mankind
On the soft passion, and the taste refined,
85   The address, the delicacy—stoops at once,
And makes her hearty meal upon a dunce.
     Flavia's a wit, has too much sense to pray;
To toast our wants and wishes, is her way;
Nor asks of God, but of her stars, to give
90   The mighty blessing, "while we live, to live."
Then all for death, that opiate of the soul!
Lucretia's dagger, Rosamonda's bowl.[8]
Say, what can cause such impotence of mind?
A spark too fickle, or a spouse too kind.
95   Wise wretch! with pleasures too refined to please,
With too much spirit to be e'er at ease,
With too much quickness ever to be taught,
With too much thinking to have common thought:
You purchase pain with all that joy can give,
100 And die of nothing but a rage to live.
     Turn then from wits; and look on Simo's mate,
No ass so meek, no ass so obstinate:
Or her, that owns her faults, but never mends,
Because she's honest, and the best of friends:
105 Or her, whose life the Church and scandal share,
Forever in a passion, or a prayer:
Or her, who laughs at hell, but (like her Grace)

3. Francis Charters was a debauchee often mentioned by Pope. "Citron": i.e., citron water; brandy flavored with lemon or orange peel. "His Grace" is usually said to be the duke of Wharton, an old enemy of Swift's and a notorious libertine.
4. A generic name for a footman in the period. "Tallboy": a crude young man in Richard Brome's comedy *The Jovial Crew* (1641) or the opera adapted from the play (1731).
5. Glutton (Latin).
6. "Anything with a strong relish or strong scent, as overkept venison" (Johnson's *Dictionary*).
7. The name is Pope's adaptation of a Greek epithet meaning "laughter-loving," frequently applied to Aphrodite; the goddess of love.
8. According to tradition, the "fair Rosamonda," mistress of Henry II, was forced by Queen Eleanor to drink poison. Lucretia, violated by a son of Tarquin, committed suicide.

Cries, "Ah! how charming, if there's no such place!"
Or who in sweet vicissitude appears
110 Of mirth and opium, ratafie[9] and tears,
The daily anodyne, and nightly draught,
To kill those foes to fair ones, time and thought.
Woman and fool are two hard things to hit,
For true no-meaning puzzles more than wit.
115   But what are these to great Atossa's[1] mind?
Scarce once herself, by turns all womankind!
Who, with herself, or others, from her birth
Finds all her life one warfare upon earth:
Shines in exposing knaves, and painting fools,
120 Yet is whate'er she hates and ridicules.
No thought advances, but her eddy brain
Whisks it about, and down it goes again.
Full sixty years the world has been her trade,
The wisest fool much time has ever made.
125 From loveless youth to unrespected age,
No passion gratified except her rage.
So much the fury still outran the wit,
The pleasure missed her, and the scandal hit.
Who breaks with her, provokes revenge from hell,
130 But he's a bolder man who dares be well:°   *in her favor*
Her every turn with violence pursued,
Nor more a storm her hate than gratitude:
To that each passion turns, or soon or late,
Love, if it makes her yield, must make her hate:
135 Superiors? death! and equals? what a curse!
But an inferior not dependent? worse.
Offend her, and she knows not to forgive;
Oblige her, and she'll hate you while you live:
But die, and she'll adore you—Then the bust
140 And temple rise—then fall again to dust.
Last night, her lord was all that's good and great;
A knave this morning, and his will a cheat.
Strange! by the means defeated of the ends,
By spirit robbed of power, by warmth of friends,
145 By wealth of followers! without one distress
Sick of herself through very selfishness!
Atossa, cursed with every granted prayer,
Childless with all her children,[2] wants an heir.
To heirs unknown descends the unguarded store,
150 Or wanders, Heaven-directed, to the poor.
    Pictures like these, dear Madam, to design,
Asks no firm hand, and no unerring line;
Some wandering touches, some reflected light,
Some flying stroke alone can hit 'em right:
155 For how should equal colors do the knack?°   *do the trick*

9. "A fine liquor, prepared from the kernels of
apricots and spirits" (Johnson's *Dictionary*).
1. Atossa, daughter of Cyrus, emperor of Persia
(d. 529 B.C.E.). If the duchess of Buckinghamshire

is alluded to, the name is appropriate, for she was
the natural daughter of James II.
2. The duchess's five children died before she
did.

Chameleons who can paint in white and black?
"Yet Chloe sure was formed without a spot—"
Nature in her then erred not, but forgot.
"With every pleasing, every prudent part,
160   Say, what can Chloe want?"—She wants a heart.
She speaks, behaves, and acts just as she ought;
But never, never, reached one generous thought.
Virtue she finds too painful an endeavor,
Content to dwell in decencies forever.
165   So very reasonable, so unmoved,
As never yet to love, or to be loved.
She, while her lover pants upon her breast,
Can mark° the figures on an Indian chest;   *pay attention to*
And when she sees her friend in deep despair,
170   Observes how much a chintz exceeds mohair.
Forbid it Heaven, a favor or a debt
She e'er should cancel—but she may forget.
Safe is your secret still in Chloe's ear;
But none of Chloe's shall you ever hear.
175   Of all her dears she never slandered one,
But cares not if a thousand are undone.
Would Chloe know if you're alive or dead?
She bids her footman put it in her head.
Chloe is prudent—Would you too be wise?
180   Then never break your heart when Chloe dies.
    One certain portrait may (I grant) be seen,
Which Heaven has varnished out, and made a *Queen:*
The same forever! and described by all
With truth and goodness, as with crown and ball.
185   Poets heap virtues, painters gems at will,
And show their zeal, and hide their want of skill.[3]
'Tis well—but, artists! who can paint or write,
To draw the naked is your true delight.
That robe of quality so struts and swells,
190   None see what parts of Nature it conceals:
The exactest traits of body or of mind,
We owe to models of an humble kind.
If Queensberry[4] to strip there's no compelling,
'Tis from a handmaid we must take a Helen.
195   From peer or bishop 'tis no easy thing
To draw the man who loves his God, or king:
Alas! I copy (or my draft would fail)
From honest Mah'met or plain Parson Hale.[5]
    But grant, in public men sometimes are shown,
200   A woman's seen in private life alone:
Our bolder talents in full light displayed;
Your virtues open fairest in the shade.
Bred to disguise, in public 'tis you hide;

3. Pope did not admire Queen Caroline.
4. The duchess of Queensberry, whom Pope valued because of her kindness to his friend John Gay, had been a famous beauty.

5. Dr. Stephen Hales, an Anglican clergyman and friend of Pope. Mahomet was a Turkish servant of George I.

There, none distinguish 'twixt your shame or pride,
205 Weakness or delicacy; all so nice,
That each may seem a virtue, or a vice.
    In men, we various ruling passions find;
In women, two almost divide the kind;
Those, only fixed, they first or last obey,
210 The love of pleasure, and the love of sway.
    That, Nature gives;[6] and where the lesson taught
Is but to please, can pleasure seem a fault?
Experience, this; by man's oppression cursed,
They seek the second not to lose the first.
215   Men, some to business, some to pleasure take;
But every woman is at heart a rake;
Men, some to quiet, some to public strife;
But every lady would be queen for life.
    Yet mark the fate of a whole sex of queens!
220 Power all their end, but beauty all the means:
In youth they conquer, with so wild a rage,
As leaves them scarce a subject in their age:
For foreign glory, foreign joy, they roam;
No thought of peace or happiness at home.
225 But wisdom's triumph is well-timed retreat,
As hard a science to the fair as great![7]
Beauties, like tyrants, old and friendless grown,
Yet hate repose, and dread to be alone,
Worn out in public, weary every eye,
230 Nor leave one sigh behind them when they die.
    Pleasures the sex, as children birds, pursue,
Still out of reach, yet never out of view,
Sure, if they catch, to spoil the toy at most,
To covet flying, and regret when lost:
235 At last, to follies youth could scarce defend,
It grows their age's prudence to pretend;
Ashamed to own they gave delight before,
Reduced to feign it, when they give no more:
As hags hold sabbaths,[8] less for joy than spite,
240 So these their merry, miserable night;[9]
Still round and round the ghosts of beauty glide,
And haunt the places where their honor died.
    See how the world its veterans rewards!
A youth of frolics, an old age of cards;
245 Fair to no purpose, artful to no end,
Young without lovers, old without a friend;
A fop their passion, but their prize a sot;
Alive, ridiculous, and dead, forgot!
    Ah friend! to dazzle let the vain design;
250 To raise the thought, and touch the heart be thine!

---

6. Women naturally love pleasure. Lines 213–14 say that experience teaches them a love of power ("sway").
7. Retreating is as hard for women to learn as it is for great soldiers or statesmen.
8. Obscene rites popularly supposed to be held by witches ("hags").
9. I.e., evenings on which ladies entertained guests.

That charm shall grow, while what fatigues the Ring[1]
Flaunts and goes down, an unregarded thing:
So when the sun's broad beam has tired the sight,
All mild ascends the moon's more sober light,
255　Serene in virgin modesty she shines,
And unobserved the glaring orb declines.
　　　Oh! blest with temper, whose unclouded ray
Can make tomorrow cheerful as today;
She, who can love a sister's charms, or hear
260　Sighs for a daughter with unwounded ear;
She, who ne'er answers till a husband cools,
Or, if she rules him, never shows she rules;
Charms by accepting, by submitting sways,
Yet has her humor most, when she obeys;
265　Lets fops or fortune fly which way they will;
Disdains all loss of tickets° or Codille;[2]　　　　　　*lottery tickets*
Spleen, vapors, or smallpox, above them all,
And mistress of herself, though China[3] fall.
　　　And yet, believe me, good as well as ill,
270　Woman's at best a contradiction still.
Heaven, when it strives to polish all it can
Its last best work, but forms a softer man;
Picks from each sex, to make the favorite blest,
Your love of pleasure, our desire of rest:
275　Blends, in exception to all general rules,
Your taste of follies, with our scorn of fools:
Reserve with frankness, art with truth allied,
Courage with softness, modesty with pride;
Fixed principles, with fancy ever new;
280　Shakes all together, and produces—you.
　　　Be this a woman's fame: with this unblest,
Toasts live a scorn, and queens may die a jest.
This Phoebus promised (I forget the year)
When those blue eyes first opened on the sphere;
285　Ascendant Phoebus watched that hour with care,
Averted half your parents' simple prayer;
And gave you beauty, but denied the pelf
That buys your sex a tyrant o'er itself.
The generous god, who wit and gold refines,
290　And ripens spirits as he ripens mines,[4]
Kept dross for duchesses, the world shall know it,
To you gave sense, good humor, and a poet.

1735, 1744

1. The fashionable drive in Hyde Park.
2. The loss of a hand at the card games of ombre or quadrille.
3. Pope refers punningly to the chinaware that fashionable women collected enthusiastically.

4. Phoebus Apollo, as god of poetry, "ripens wit"; as god of the sun, he "ripens mines," for respectable scientific theory held that the sun's rays mature precious metals in the earth.

ANNE INGRAM, VISCOUNTESS IRWIN

Lady Anne Howard (ca. 1696–1764) was raised on the Yorkshire estate of her father, third Earl of Carlisle; many years later she paid tribute to it and him in a poem, *Castle Howard* (1732). In 1717 she married Richard Ingram, fifth Viscount Irwin; and after he died of smallpox in 1721, she mourned him so long that she was reproached for it in verse by Lady Mary Wortley Montagu. Although the two women were friends, Irwin said that Montagu's "principles are as corrupt as her wit is entertaining"; and Montagu, who liked Irwin's good nature, was also amused by her "vanity and false pretensions." Irwin showed her independence by traveling alone in Holland and France in 1730. Later she served the Princess of Wales as a lady-in-waiting, but court life did not satisfy her; Pope's and Addison's works were "antidotes to preserve me from the contagion." In 1737, against the strong opposition of her family, she married Colonel William Douglas; he died in 1748. A young woman who knew her afterward was impressed by her learning and wit: "she wrote poetry, and every body was afraid of her." She died, in 1764, after a party at cards.

"An Epistle to Mr. Pope" reveals Irwin's keen attention to Pope's work as a whole, not only to his "Epistle 2. To a Lady"; it turns his verse technique as well as many of his principles against him. While many of Pope's couplets sharply contrast women's characters with men's, Irwin adapts the couplet form to emphasize what they have in common. In fact both sexes, she argues, want the same thing: love of power motivates them both. If women often trifle away their lives, the reason is poor education; not even Pope has taught them how to live. Irwin provides some positive models. Addressing Pope as an equal, in verse much like his own, she proves that men and women can think alike.

An Epistle to Mr. Pope,

Occasioned by his Characters of Women

Nec rude quid prosit video ingenium.[1]

By custom doomed to folly, sloth and ease,
No wonder Pope such female triflers sees.
But would the satirist confess the truth,
Nothing so like as male and female youth,
5   Nothing so like as man and woman old,
Their joys, their loves, their hates, if truly told.
Though different acts seem different sex's growth,
'Tis the same principle impels them both.
    View daring men stung with ambition's fire,
10   The conquering hero, or the youthful 'squire,
By different deeds aspire to deathless fame,
One murthers° man, the other murthers game.   murders
View a fair nymph blest with superior charms,
Whose tempting form the coldest bosom warms;
15   No eastern monarch more despotic reigns

---

1. Nor can I see what good can come from untrained talent (Latin; Horace's *Art of Poetry* 410).

Than this fair tyrant of the Cyprian plains.[2]
Whether a crown or bauble we desire,
Whether to learning or to dress aspire,
Whether we wait with joy the trumpet's call,
20   Or wish to shine the fairest at a ball,
In either sex the appetite's the same,
For love of power is still° the love of fame.[3]   *always*
Women must in a narrow orbit move,
But power alike both males and females love.
25   What makes the difference then, you may inquire,
Between the hero and the rural 'squire,
Between the maid bred up with courtly care,
Or she who earns by toil her daily fare?
Their power is stinted, but not so their will;
30   Ambitious thoughts the humblest cottage fill;
Far as they can they push their little fame,
And try to leave behind a deathless name.
In education all the difference lies;
Women, if taught, would be as bold and wise
35   As haughty man, improved by art and rules;
Where God makes one, neglect makes twenty fools.
And though *Nugatrixes*° are daily found,   *female triflers*
Flutt'ring *Nugators*° equally abound;   *male triflers*
Such heads are toyshops,[4] filled with trifling ware,
40   And can each folly with each female share.
     A female mind like a rude fallow lies;
No seed is sown, but weeds spontaneous rise.
As well might we expect, in winter, spring,
As land untilled a fruitful crop should bring;
45   As well might we expect Peruvian ore
We should possess, yet dig not for the store.
Culture° improves all fruits, all sorts we find,   *cultivation, tillage*
Wit, judgment, sense—fruits of the human mind.
     Ask the rich merchant, conversant in trade,
50   How nature operates in the growing blade;
Ask the philosopher the price of stocks,
Ask the gay courtier how to manage flocks;
Inquire the dogmas of the learned schools
(From Aristotle down to Newton's rules),
55   Of the rough soldier, bred to boisterous war,
Or one still rougher, a true British tar:
They'll all reply, unpracticed in such laws,
The effect they know, though ignorant of the cause.
The sailor may perhaps have equal parts°   *abilities*
60   With him bred up to sciences and arts;
And he who at the helm or stern is seen,
Philosopher or hero might have been.
The whole in application is comprised,

---

2. Love. Aphrodite was worshiped on Cyprus.
3. Cf. Pope's "Epistle 2," lines 207–10.
4. A shop stocked with baubles and trifles (see

Pope's *Rape of the Lock*, Canto 1, line 100, p. 510).

Reason's not reason, if not exercised;
65 Use, not possession, real good affords;
No miser's rich that dares not touch his hoards.
   Can female youth, left to weak woman's care,
Misled by custom (folly's fruitful heir),
Told that their charms a monarch may enslave,
70 That beauty like the gods can kill or save;
Taught the arcanas,[5] the mysterious art
By ambush dress to catch unwary hearts;
If wealthy born, taught to lisp French and dance,
Their morals left (Lucretius-like) to chance;[6]
75 Strangers to reason and reflection made,
Left to their passions, and by them betrayed;
Untaught the noble end of glorious truth,
Bred to deceive even from their earliest youth;
Unused to books, nor virtue taught to prize;
80 Whose mind a savage waste unpeopled lies,
Which to supply, trifles fill up the void,
And idly busy, to no end employed—
Can these, from such a school, more virtue show,
Or tempting vice treat like a common foe?
85 Can they resist, when soothing pleasure woos;
Preserve their virtue, when their fame° they lose?   *reputation*
Can they on other themes converse or write,
Than what they hear all day, and dream all night?
   Not so the Roman female fame was spread;
90 Not so was Clelia, or Lucretia bred;
Not so such heroines true glory sought;
Not so was Portia, or Cornelia[7] taught.
Portia! the glory of the female race;
Portia! more lovely by her mind than face.
95 Early informed by truth's unerring beam,
What to reject, what justly to esteem.
Taught by philosophy all moral good,
How to repel in youth the impetuous blood,
How her most favorite passions to subdue,
100 And fame through virtue's avenues pursue,
She tries herself, and finds even dolorous pain
Can't the close secret from her breast obtain.
To Cato born, to noble Brutus joined,
She shines invincible in form and mind.
105   No more such generous sentiments we trace
In the gay moderns of the female race,
No more, alas! heroic virtue's shown;

5. Profound secrets, as in alchemy. *Arcana* is the plural of the Latin *arcanum*, but some English writers added an *s*.
6. The Roman poet Lucretius was known as a materialist and atheist who taught that everything in the world results from the chance convergence of atoms.
7. Famous Roman paragons of virtue. Clelia (or Cloelia), given as a hostage to an enemy, Lars Porsenna, escaped to Rome by swimming the Tiber and was later set free by Porsenna for her bravery. Lucretia was raped by a son of King Tarquin and committed suicide, kindling a revolt that overthrew the Tarquins. Portia, the daughter of Cato and wife of Brutus, stabbed herself in the thigh to prove she was strong enough to keep her husband's secrets. Cornelia, mother of the Gracchi, was a model of maternal self-sacrifice.

Since knowledge ceased, philosophy's unknown.
No more can we expect our modern wives
110   Heroes should breed, who lead such useless lives.
Would you, who know the arcana of the soul,
The secret springs which move and guide the whole,
Would you, who can instruct as well as please,
Bestow some moments of your darling ease,
115   To rescue woman from this Gothic[8] state,
New passions raise, their minds anew create,
Then for the Spartan virtue[9] we might hope;
For who stands unconvinced by generous Pope?
Then would the British fair perpetual bloom,
120   And vie in fame with ancient Greece and Rome.

1736

8. Barbaric, as opposed to Greek or Roman. Cf. Pope's *Essay on Criticism* 3.692 (p. 505).

9. Spartan women were known for their courage and contempt of pleasure.

MARY LEAPOR

A gardener's daughter, Mary Leapor (1722–1746) spent her short life in or near the small town of Brackley in Northamptonshire. When she was ten or eleven "she would often be scribbling," and poetry turned into a consuming interest. One of her poems describes her sitting "whole evenings, reading wicked plays" by candlelight; according to another, she lost employment as a cook-maid because she would not stop writing, even in the kitchen. Passed around the neighborhood, her verse impressed Bridget Freemantle, the daughter of a former Oxford don; she became Leapor's best friend and mentor. Together they planned to publish Leapor's work. A play was sent to Colley Cibber, the impresario and poet laureate, but it was returned stained by wine. Leapor's health was rarely good, and she died of measles at age twenty-four; she had never seen any of her poems in print. But Freemantle arranged an edition of Leapor's *Poems upon Several Occasions* (1748), with six hundred subscribers, and it was warmly received. Samuel Richardson admired the "sweetly easy poems" so much that he published a second volume; later, William Cowper thought they showed "more marks of a true poetical talent than I remember to have observed in the verses of any, whether male or female, so disadvantageously circumstanced." Recently Leapor's work has attracted renewed attention for its wit and skill as well as its sharp observations about the life of a working-class woman.

The preface to Leapor's *Poems* reports that "the author she most admired was Mr. Pope, whom she chiefly endeavored to imitate." "An Essay on Woman," like Irwin's epistle, reflects careful study of Pope's epistle on the "Characters of Women." But its view of female predicaments is very much darker. If women are living contradictions, as Pope had asserted, the reason is that whatever they are and whatever they do can be turned against them. Beauty will be betrayed, wit and learning will be shunned, and the pursuit of wealth will shrink the soul. Leapor's own situation gives her satire bite. As a gardener's daughter, she knows that the flower of womanhood costs money to cultivate and does not last; as someone witty, poor, infirm, and unattractive, she sees through romantic myths. In "An Epistle to a Lady" (another Popean title), she more autobiographically reflects on education, the main avenue of advancement for women proposed by reformers throughout the period (including Astell, Defoe, Addison, Irwin, and Johnson). Leapor's experience makes her pessimistic: her learning merely allows her to depict her bleak place in the world on an astronomically expanded scale; and homely, tattered images must intrude on her dreams of the wealth and leisure that she knows a genteel education and a poetic vocation require. But despite Leapor's stress on her frustrating social position and on the softness and weakness of women in general, her verse is strong. This poet never stops fighting against the traps in which she is caught.

An Essay on Woman

WOMAN—a pleasing but a short-lived flower,
Too soft for business and too weak for power:
A wife in bondage, or neglected maid;
Despised if ugly; if she's fair—betrayed.
5 'Tis wealth alone inspires every grace,
And calls the raptures to her plenteous[1] face.
What numbers for those charming features pine,
If blooming acres[2] round her temples twine?
Her lip the strawberry, and her eyes more bright
10 Than sparkling Venus in a frosty night;
Pale lilies fade and, when the fair appears,
Snow turns a negro[3] and dissolves in tears,
And where the charmer treads her magic toe,
On English ground Arabian odors grow;
15 Till mighty Hymen[4] lifts his sceptred rod,
And sinks her glories with a fatal nod,
Dissolves her triumphs, sweeps her charms away,
And turns the goddess to her native clay.
But, Artemisia,[5] let your servant sing
20 What small advantage wealth and beauties bring.
Who would be wise, that knew Pamphilia's fate?
Or who be fair, and joined to Sylvia's mate?
Sylvia, whose cheeks are fresh as early day,
As evening mild, and sweet as spicy May;
25 And yet that face her partial husband tires,
And those bright eyes, that all the world admires.
Pamphilia's wit who does not strive to shun,
Like death's infection or a dog-day's sun?
The damsels view her with malignant eyes,
30 The men are vexed to find a nymph so wise,
And wisdom only serves to make her know
The keen sensation of superior woe.
The secret whisper and the listening ear,
The scornful eyebrow and the hated sneer,

1. Not only blooming but wealthy.
2. Not only hair but property.
3. Black, when set against the fair one's skin. The hyperbolic comparisons throughout this passage are intentionally ironic, as in Shakespeare's Sonnet 130.
4. The god of marriage.
5. Bridget Freemantle, given the name of an ancient patron of the arts.

35 The giddy censures of her babbling kind,
  With thousand ills that grate a gentle mind,
  By her are tasted in the first degree,
  Though overlooked by Simplicus and me.
  Does thirst of gold a virgin's heart inspire,
40 Instilled by nature or a careful sire?
  Then let her quit extravagance and play,
  The brisk companion and expensive tea,
  To feast with Cordia in her filthy sty
  On stewed potatoes or on mouldy pie;
45 Whose eager° eyes stare ghastly at the poor,   *fierce*
  And fright the beggars from the hated door;
  In greasy clouts she wraps her smoky chin,
  And holds that pride's a never-pardoned sin.
   If this be wealth, no matter where it falls;
50 But save, ye Muses, save your Mira's⁶ walls:
  Still give me pleasing indolence and ease,
  A fire to warm me and a friend to please.
   Since, whether sunk in avarice or pride,
  A wanton virgin or a starving bride,
55 Or wondering crowds attend her charming tongue,
  Or deemed an idiot, ever speaks the wrong;
  Though nature armed us for the growing ill
  With fraudful cunning and a headstrong will,
  Yet, with ten thousand follies to her charge,
60 Unhappy woman's but a slave at large.

                1751

An Epistle to a Lady¹

  In vain, dear Madam, yes, in vain you strive,
  Alas! to make your luckless Mira thrive;
  For Tycho and Copernicus² agree,
  No golden planet bent its rays on me.³

5 'Tis twenty winters, if it is no more,
  To speak the truth it may be twenty four:
  As many springs their 'pointed° space have run, *appointed*
  Since Mira's eyes first opened on the sun.
  'Twas when the flocks on slabby° hillocks lie,   *muddy*
10 And the cold fishes rule the watery sky;⁴
  But though these eyes the learned page explore,
  And turn the ponderous volumes o'er and o'er,

6. Leapor's pen name.
1. The poem addresses her friend and patron, Bridget Freemantle.
2. Polish founder of modern astronomy (1473–1543), who thought the Earth circled the sun. Tycho Brahe (1546–1601), Danish astronomer who thought the sun and moon revolved around the stationary Earth.
3. A "golden planet" would have marked Leapor's birth as auspicious.
4. Leapor was born in late winter, under the sign of Pisces (the "fishes").

I find no comfort from their systems flow,[5]
But am dejected more as more I know.
15 Hope shines a while, but like a vapor flies
(The fate of all the curious and the wise)
For, ah! cold Saturn[6] triumphed on that day,
And frowning Sol denied his golden ray.

You see I'm learned, and I show't the more,
20 That none may wonder when they find me poor.
Yet Mira dreams, as slumbering poets may,
And rolls in treasures till the breaking day:
While books and pictures in bright order rise,
And painted parlors swim before her eyes;
25 Till the shrill clock impertinently rings,
And the soft visions move their shining wings;
Then Mira wakes—her pictures are no more,
And through her fingers slides the vanished ore.
Convinced too soon, her eye unwilling falls
30 On the blue curtains and the dusty walls;
She wakes, alas! to business and to woes,
To sweep her kitchen, and to mend her clothes.[7]

But see pale sickness with her languid eyes,
At whose appearance all delusion flies:
35 The world recedes, its vanities decline,
Clorinda's features seem as faint as mine;
Gay robes no more the aching sight admires,
Wit grates the ear, and melting music tires;
Its wonted pleasures with each sense decay,
40 Books please no more, and paintings fade away,
The sliding joys in misty vapors end;
Yet let me still, ah! let me grasp a friend;
And when each joy, when each loved object flies,
Be you the last that leaves my closing eyes.

45 But how will this dismantled° soul appear,   *unclothed*
When stripped of all it lately held so dear,
Forced from its prison of expiring clay,
Afraid and shivering at the doubtful way?

Yet did these eyes a dying parent[8] see,
50 Loosed from all cares except a thought for me,
Without a tear resign her shortening breath,
And dauntless meet the lingering stroke of death.
Then at th'Almighty's sentence shall I mourn:
"Of dust thou art, to dust shalt thou return";[9]
55 Or shall I wish to stretch the line of fate,

5. I.e., no comfort flows from either the "systems" (bodies of doctrine) contained in books or the systems of stars and planets in the heavens.
6. The planet Saturn was thought to influence gloomy (hence "saturnine") temperaments.
7. Cf. Pope, *Eloisa to Abelard* 223–48.
8. Leapor's mother, Anne, died around 1742.
9. Genesis 3.19.

That the dull years may bear a longer date,
To share the follies of succeeding times
With more vexations and with deeper crimes?
Ah no—though Heav'n brings near the final day,
60   For such a life I will not, dare not pray;
But let the tear for future mercy flow,
And fall resigned beneath the mighty blow.
Nor I alone—for through the spacious ball,°   *Earth*
With me will numbers of all ages fall:
65   And the same day that Mira yields her breath,
Thousands may enter through the gates of death.

1748

JOHN GAY
1685–1732

The career of John Gay encompasses most of the ways that a talented but indigent writer of the early eighteenth century could try to make a living: publication, patronage, odd jobs at court, and the theater. After a good education at school in Devon, he went to London at seventeen to try his luck as apprentice to a dealer in silks. Five years later he became secretary to a friend from school, the writer and entrepreneur Aaron Hill, who introduced him to the publishing world and literary circles. Eventually, leading authors in London adopted Gay as a favorite; with Pope, Swift, Arbuthnot, and Thomas Parnell, he founded the Scriblerus Club, famous for its literary satires and practical jokes. Friends like these helped him obtain the patrons and political appointments that supported him. The same Scriblerian influence shaped the mixture of high Virgilian style and rustic humor in his first successful poem, *The Shepherd's Week* (1714), a burlesque pastoral. Here and in his other verse Gay shows off his special gifts: lightness of touch, a keen eye for homely details, and an irony that exposes the disparity between high poetic expectations and the coarse reality of the way people live. Two years later a mock georgic, *Trivia, or the Art of Walking the Streets of London,* revealed that the town could be as rough as the country, and far more corrupting. Gay's hopes for affluence were blasted by the collapse of South Sea stock in 1721. His popularity and financial security rose to new heights, however, with the phenomenal success of his verse *Fables* (1727; a second set was published posthumously in 1738) and above all *The Beggar's Opera* (1728), which made him rich. But he did not enjoy his prosperity for long. A sequel, *Polly* (1729), was banned from the stage by Walpole; and although the printed version sold very well, the tension may have precipitated the illness that led a few years later to his death.

Audiences have always loved *The Beggar's Opera*. Nothing quite like it had ever been seen on the London stage; when Congreve read the script, he said, "It would either take greatly, or be damned confoundedly." On opening night, according to Pope, Gay's friends were anxious, "till we were very much encouraged by overhearing the Duke of Argyle, who sat in the next box to us, say, 'It will do—it must do! I see it in the eyes of them.'" The duke was right. The play quickly became the talk of the town, it ran for a record sixty-two performances, and during the rest of the century it kept being revived. At first the shock of pleasure must have been sparked by daring thrusts at people and things in the news. Italian opera is one obvious target. Although it was preposterously artificial and costly, with lavish scenery and imported stars, opera had been the rage of fashionable London. Now Gay turned the music over to beggars, or actors playing thieves and whores, and gave them popular British tunes to sing instead of showy foreign arias.

On this stage, moreover, the underworld rose to the surface. Crime was a constant, brutal threat in early eighteenth-century London, and stories about notorious criminals (such as Moll Flanders) poured from the press. In the corrupt legal system, which rewarded racketeers for informing on (or "peaching") less powerful felons, the line between those who broke the law and those who enforced it was often smudged. Jonathan Wild, the "Thief-Taker General of Great Britain and Ireland," became rich and famous by manipulating this system (before the executioner caught up with him); he serves as a model for Peachum. By comparison, a forthright highwayman and killer like Macheath might seem rather gallant. But the electricity of the play comes from its superimposition of these criminals on heads of state, especially the prime minister, Robert Walpole. Playgoers recognized Walpole everywhere. In Act 2, scene 10, for instance, when Peachum and Lockit argue and conspire—"like great statesmen, we encourage those who betray their friends"— the audience roared at the allusion to Walpole and Lord Townshend, his ally and brother-in-law (at an early performance, Walpole himself is said to have won over the crowd by calling for an encore). Spectators saw a picture of their own times on the stage: a society driven by greed, where everything, including justice and love, was for sale.

Yet *The Beggar's Opera* has lasted beyond its age. The parallel between high life and low life turned out to be more than a trick; it still rings true when audiences reflect on those who hold power today. Brecht's and Weill's famous *Threepenny Opera* adapted Gay's story to the sinister conditions of Germany in the 1920s; gang lords, fascists, and capitalistic bosses all seem the same. Little people go to jail, the high ones get away. That worldly and cynical message, seasoned with wit, continues to make sense to people who compare their ideals of government, society, and law to things as they are.

Pope's epitaph on Gay, inscribed in Westminster Abbey, begins this way:

> Of manners gentle, of affections mild;
> In wit, a man; simplicity, a child;
> With native humor tempering virtuous rage,
> Formed to delight at once and lash the age.

But Gay's own epitaph is far less pious:

> Life is a jest, and all things show it;
> I thought so once, but now I know it.

The Beggar's Opera

DRAMATIS PERSONAE[1]

Men

PEACHUM	ROBIN OF BAGSHOT
LOCKIT	NIMMING NED
MACHEATH	HARRY PADDINGTON
FILCH	MATT OF THE MINT
JEMMY TWITCHER	BEN BUDGE
CROOK-FINGERED JACK	BEGGAR
WAT DREARY	PLAYER
CONSTABLES, DRAWER, TURNKEY, ETC.	

Women

MRS. PEACHUM	MRS. VIXEN
POLLY PEACHUM	BETTY DOXY
LUCY LOCKIT	JENNY DIVER
DIANA TRAPES	MRS. SLAMMEKIN
MRS. COAXER	SUKY TAWDRY
DOLLY TRULL	MOLLY BRAZEN

Introduction

BEGGAR, PLAYER

BEGGAR   If poverty be a title to poetry, I am sure nobody can dispute mine. I own myself of the Company of Beggars; and I make one at their weekly festivals at St. Giles's.[2] I have a small yearly salary for my catches,[3] and am welcome to a dinner there whenever I please, which is more than most poets can say.

PLAYER   As we live by the Muses, 'tis but gratitude in us to encourage poetical merit wherever we find it. The Muses, contrary to all other ladies, pay no distinction to dress, and never partially mistake the pertness of embroidery for wit, nor the modesty of want for dullness. Be the author who he will, we push his play as far as it will go. So (though you are in want) I wish you success heartily.

BEGGAR   This piece I own was originally writ for the celebrating the marriage of James Chanter and Moll Lay, two most excellent ballad singers. I have introduced the similes that are in all your celebrated operas: the swallow, the moth, the bee, the ship, the flower, etc. Besides, I have a prison scene, which the ladies always reckon charmingly pathetic. As to the parts, I have observed such a nice impartiality to our two ladies, that

---

1. The names of characters reflect their trades. Peachum ("peach 'em") is an informer, Lockit a jailer, Macheath a "son of the heath" or highwayman, Twitcher and Diver pickpockets, Nimming Ned a thief, Budge a burglar, Trull and Doxy harlots. Dreary ("gory") suggests a cutthroat; Bagshot Heath was known for highway robberies; Paddington ("pad," a highwayman) was where criminals were hanged; the Mint was a sanctuary for outlaws. Trapes and Slammekin are slatterns.
2. A slum named after the patron saint of beggars and lepers.
3. Rounds, in which one singer follows or chases the words of another.

it is impossible for either of them to take offense.[4] I hope I may be forgiven, that I have not made my opera throughout unnatural, like those in vogue; for I have no recitative.[5] Excepting this, as I have consented to have neither prologue nor epilogue, it must be allowed an opera in all its forms. The piece indeed hath been heretofore frequently represented by ourselves in our great room at St. Giles's, so that I cannot too often acknowledge your charity in bringing it now on the stage.

PLAYER But I see 'tis time for us to withdraw; the actors are preparing to begin. Play away the overture.   [*Exeunt.*]

Act 1

SCENE 1 *Peachum's house*

PEACHUM *sitting at a table with a large book of accounts before him.*

AIR 1. An old woman clothed in gray[6]

Through all the employments of life
Each neighbor abuses his brother;
Whore and rogue they call husband and wife;
All professions be-rogue one another.
The priest calls the lawyer a cheat,
The lawyer be-knaves the divine;
And the statesman, because he's so great,
Thinks his trade as honest as mine.

A lawyer is an honest employment, so is mine. Like me too he acts in a double capacity, both against rogues and for 'em; for 'tis but fitting that we should protect and encourage cheats, since we live by them.

SCENE 2

PEACHUM, FILCH

FILCH Sir, Black Moll hath sent word her trial comes on in the afternoon, and she hopes you will order matters so as to bring her off.

PEACHUM Why, she may plead her belly[7] at worst; to my knowledge she hath taken care of that security. But as the wench is very active and industrious, you may satisfy her that I'll soften the evidence.

FILCH Tom Gagg, sir, is found guilty.

PEACHUM A lazy dog! When I took him the time before, I told him what he would come to if he did not mend his hand. This is death without reprieve. I may venture to book him. [*Writes.*] For Tom Gagg, forty pounds.[8] Let Betty Sly know that I'll save her from transportation,[9] for I can get more by her staying in England.

---

4. Two famous divas, Faustina and Cuzzoni, had recently feuded on stage.
5. Operatic declamation, midway between singing and speaking.
6. The name of the ballad whose tune Peachum sings.

7. Claim to be pregnant, hence not at risk of execution.
8. The reward when informing resulted in execution.
9. Criminals were sentenced to banishment abroad.

FILCH Betty hath brought more goods into our lock to-year[1] than any five of the gang; and in truth, 'tis a pity to lose so good a customer.

PEACHUM If none of the gang take her off,[2] she may, in the common course of business, live a twelve-month longer. I love to let women scape. A good sportsman always lets the hen partridges fly, because the breed of the game depends upon them. Besides, here the law allows us no reward; there is nothing to be got by the death of women—except our wives.

FILCH Without dispute, she is a fine woman! 'Twas to her I was obliged for my education, and (to say a bold word) she hath trained up more young fellows to the business than the gaming-table.

PEACHUM Truly, Filch, thy observation is right. We and the surgeons are more beholden to women than all the professions besides.[3]

AIR 2. The bonny gray-eyed morn

FILCH
> 'Tis woman that seduces all mankind,
>   By her we first were taught the wheedling arts:
> Her very eyes can cheat; when most she's kind,
>   She tricks us of our money with our hearts.
> For her, like wolves by night we roam for prey,
>   And practise every fraud to bribe her charms;
> For suits of love, like law, are won by pay,
>   And beauty must be fee'd into our arms.

PEACHUM But make haste to Newgate,[4] boy, and let my friends know what I intend; for I love to make them easy one way or other.

FILCH When a gentleman is long kept in suspense, penitence may break his spirit ever after. Besides, certainty gives a man a good air upon his trial, and makes him risk another without fear or scruple. But I'll away, for 'tis a pleasure to be the messenger of comfort to friends in affliction.

SCENE 3

PEACHUM

But 'tis now high time to look about me for a decent execution against next Sessions.[5] I hate a lazy rogue, by whom one can get nothing 'till he is hanged. A register of the gang, [reading] Crook-fingered Jack. A year and a half in the service; let me see how much the stock owes to his industry: one, two, three, four, five gold watches, and seven silver ones. A mighty clean-handed fellow! Sixteen snuff-boxes, five of them of true gold. Six dozen of handkerchiefs, four silver-hilted swords, half a dozen of shirts, three tye-perriwigs, and a piece of broad cloth. Considering these are only the fruits of his leisure hours, I don't know a prettier fellow, for no man alive hath a more engaging presence of mind upon the road. Wat Dreary, alias Brown Will, an irregular dog, who hath an underhand way of disposing of his goods. I'll try him only for a Sessions or two longer upon his good behavior. Harry Paddington, a poor petty-larceny rascal, without the least genius; that fellow, though he were to live these six months, will

---

1. This year. "Lock": a house where stolen goods are kept.
2. Inform on her.

3. Surgeons treated venereal diseases.
4. The chief London prison.
5. Trials of criminals, held eight times a year.

never come to the gallows with any credit. Slippery Sam; he goes off the next Sessions, for the villain hath the impudence to have views of following his trade as a tailor, which he calls an honest employment. Matt of the Mint; listed[6] not above a month ago, a promising sturdy fellow, and diligent in his way; somewhat too bold and hasty, and may raise good contributions on the public, if he does not cut himself short by murder. Tom Tipple, a guzzling soaking sot, who is always too drunk to stand himself, or to make others stand.[7] A cart[8] is absolutely necessary for him. Robin of Bagshot, alias Gorgon, alias Bluff Bob, alias Carbuncle, alias Bob Booty.[9]

SCENE 4

PEACHUM, MRS. PEACHUM

MRS. PEACHUM What of Bob Booty, husband? I hope nothing bad hath betided him. You know, my dear, he's a favorite customer of mine. 'Twas he made me a present of this ring.

PEACHUM I have set his name down in the black-list, that's all, my dear; he spends his life among women, and as soon as his money is gone, one or other of the ladies will hang him for the reward, and there's forty pound lost to us forever.

MRS. PEACHUM You know, my dear, I never meddle in matters of death; I always leave those affairs to you. Women indeed are bitter bad judges in these cases, for they are so partial to the brave that they think every man handsome who is going to the camp or the gallows.

AIR 3. Cold and raw

If any wench Venus's girdle wear,
Though she be never so ugly;
Lilies and roses will quickly appear,
And her face look wond'rous smugly.
Beneath the left ear so fit but a cord,
(A rope so charming a zone is!)
The youth in his cart hath the air of a lord,
And we cry, "There dies an Adonis!"[1]

But really, husband, you should not be too hard hearted, for you never had a finer, braver set of men than at present. We have not had a murder among them all, these seven months. And truly, my dear, that is a great blessing.

PEACHUM What a dickens is the woman always a-whimpering about murder for? No gentleman is ever looked upon the worse for killing a man in his own defense; and if business cannot be carried on without it, what would you have a gentleman do?

MRS. PEACHUM If I am in the wrong, my dear, you must excuse me, for nobody can help the frailty of an over-scrupulous conscience.

PEACHUM Murder is as fashionable a crime as a man can be guilty of. How many fine gentlemen have we in Newgate every year, purely upon

6. Enlisted.
7. Stand still; i.e., when held up.
8. Carriage to the gallows.
9. This became a nickname for Walpole.

1. Venus's lover. The magic powers of Venus's belt ("girdle"), which could make any woman sexy, are associated with the rope or belt ("zone") around a condemned man's neck.

that article! If they have wherewithal to persuade the jury to bring it in manslaughter, what are they the worse for it? So, my dear, have done upon this subject. Was Captain Macheath here this morning, for the bank notes he left with you last week?

MRS. PEACHUM   Yes, my dear; and though the bank hath stopped payment, he was so cheerful and so agreeable! Sure there is not a finer gentleman upon the road than the Captain! If he comes from Bagshot at any reasonable hour he hath promised to make one this evening with Polly and me, and Bob Booty, at a party of quadrille.[2] Pray, my dear, is the Captain rich?

PEACHUM   The Captain keeps too good company ever to grow rich. Marybone and the chocolate-houses[3] are his undoing. The man that proposes to get money by play should have the education of a fine gentleman, and be trained up to it from his youth.

MRS. PEACHUM   Really, I am sorry upon Polly's account the Captain hath not more discretion. What business hath he to keep company with lords and gentlemen? He should leave them to prey upon one another.

PEACHUM   Upon Polly's account! What, a plague, does the woman mean? Upon Polly's account!

MRS. PEACHUM   Captain Macheath is very fond of the girl.

PEACHUM   And what then?

MRS. PEACHUM   If I have any skill in the ways of women, I am sure Polly thinks him a very pretty man.

PEACHUM   And what then? You would not be so mad to have the wench marry him! Gamesters and highwaymen are generally very good to their whores, but they are very devils to their wives.

MRS. PEACHUM   But if Polly should be in love, how should we help her, or how can she help herself? Poor girl, I am in the utmost concern about her.

AIR 4.   Why is your faithful slave disdained?

If love the virgin's heart invade,
How, like a moth, the simple maid
    Still plays about the flame!
If soon she be not made a wife,
Her honor's singed, and then for life,
    She's—what I dare not name.

PEACHUM   Look ye, wife. A handsome wench in our way of business is as profitable as at the bar of a Temple[4] coffee-house, who looks upon it as her livelihood to grant every liberty but one. You see I would indulge the girl as far as prudently we can. In anything but marriage! After that, my dear, how shall we be safe? Are we not then in her husband's power? For a husband hath the absolute power over all a wife's secrets but her own. If the girl had the discretion of a court lady, who can have a dozen young fellows at her ear without complying with one, I should not matter it;[5] but Polly is tinder, and a spark will at once set her on a flame. Married! If the

---

2. A card game.
3. Popular haunts for gambling.

4. London college for lawyers.
5. Think it important.

wench does not know her own profit, sure she knows her own pleasure better than to make herself a property![6] My daughter to me should be, like a court lady to a minister of state, a key to the whole gang. Married! If the affair is not already done, I'll terrify her from it, by the example of our neighbors.

MRS. PEACHUM Mayhap, my dear, you may injure the girl. She loves to imitate the fine ladies, and she may only allow the Captain liberties in the view of interest.

PEACHUM But 'tis your duty, my dear, to warn the girl against her ruin, and to instruct her how to make the most of her beauty. I'll go to her this moment, and sift her. In the meantime, wife, rip out the coronets and marks of these dozen of cambric handkerchiefs, for I can dispose of them this afternoon to a chap in the City.

SCENE 5

MRS. PEACHUM

Never was a man more out of the way in an argument than my husband! Why must our Polly, forsooth, differ from her sex, and love only her husband? And why must Polly's marriage, contrary to all observation, make her the less followed by other men? All men are thieves in love, and like a woman the better for being another's property.

AIR 5. Of all the simple things we do

A maid is like the golden ore,
Which hath guineas intrinsical in't,
Whose worth is never known, before
It is tried and impressed in the Mint.
A wife's like a guinea in gold,
Stamped with the name of her spouse:
Now here, now there, is bought, or is sold,
And is current in every house.

SCENE 6

MRS. PEACHUM, FILCH

MRS. PEACHUM Come hither, Filch. I am as fond of this child, as though my mind misgave me he were my own. He hath as fine a hand at picking a pocket as a woman, and is as nimble-fingered as a juggler. If an unlucky Session does not cut the rope of thy life, I pronounce, boy, thou wilt be a great man in history. Where was your post last night, my boy?

FILCH I plied at the opera, madam; and considering 'twas neither dark nor rainy, so that there was no great hurry in getting chairs and coaches, made a tolerable hand on't. These seven handkerchiefs, madam.

MRS. PEACHUM Colored ones, I see. They are of sure sale from our warehouse at Redriff among the seamen.

FILCH And this snuffbox.

---

6. A husband had legal title to everything his wife possessed.

MRS. PEACHUM Set in gold! A pretty encouragement this to a young beginner.

FILCH I had a fair tug at a charming gold watch. Pox take the tailors for making the fobs so deep and narrow! It stuck by the way, and I was forced to make my escape under a coach. Really, madam, I fear I shall be cut off in the flower of my youth, so that every now and then (since I was pumped)[7] I have thoughts of taking up and going to sea.

MRS. PEACHUM You should go to Hockley in the Hole,[8] and to Marybone, child, to learn valor. These are the schools that have bred so many brave men. I thought, boy, by this time, thou hadst lost fear as well as shame. Poor lad! How little does he know as yet of the Old Bailey![9] For the first fact I'll insure thee from being hanged; and going to sea, Filch, will come time enough upon a sentence of transportation. But now, since you have nothing better to do, even go to your book, and learn your catechism, for really a man makes but an ill figure in the Ordinary's paper,[1] who cannot give a satisfactory answer to his questions. But, hark you, my lad. Don't tell me a lie; for you know I hate a liar. Do you know of anything that hath passed between Captain Macheath and our Polly?

FILCH I beg you, madam, don't ask me; for I must either tell a lie to you or to Miss Polly; for I promised her I would not tell.

MRS. PEACHUM But when the honor of our family is concerned—

FILCH I shall lead a sad life with Miss Polly, if ever she come to know that I told you. Besides, I would not willingly forfeit my own honor by betraying anybody.

MRS. PEACHUM Yonder comes my husband and Polly. Come, Filch, you shall go with me into my own room, and tell me the whole story. I'll give thee a glass of a most delicious cordial that I keep for my own drinking.

SCENE 7

PEACHUM, POLLY

POLLY I know as well as any of the fine ladies how to make the most of myself and of my man too. A woman knows how to be mercenary, though she hath never been in a court or at an assembly.[2] We have it in our natures, papa. If I allow Captain Macheath some trifling liberties, I have this watch and other visible marks of his favor to show for it. A girl who cannot grant some things, and refuse what is most material, will make but a poor hand of her beauty, and soon be thrown upon the common.[3]

AIR 6. What shall I do to show how much I love her

> Virgins are like the fair flower in its luster,
>   Which in the garden enamels the ground;
> Near it the bees in play flutter and cluster,
>   And gaudy butterflies frolic around.
> But, when once plucked, 'tis no longer alluring,

---

7. When pickpockets were caught, they were doused with water.
8. A place for brutal sports such as bear-baiting.
9. London's criminal court.
1. First offenders could escape the death sentence by pleading "benefit of clergy" if they passed a literacy test given by the ordinary or chaplain of Newgate.
2. A public social affair.
3. Common land; common law; and a name for a prostitute.

*To Covent Garden*⁴ *'tis sent (as yet sweet),*
There fades, and shrinks, and grows past all enduring,
Rots, stinks, and dies, and is trod under feet.

PEACHUM You know, Polly, I am not against your toying and trifling with
a customer in the way of business, or to get out a secret, or so. But if
I find out that you have played the fool and are married, you jade you,
I'll cut your throat, hussy. Now you know my mind.

SCENE 8

PEACHUM, POLLY, MRS. PEACHUM

AIR 7. Oh London is a fine town

MRS. PEACHUM [*In a very great passion.*]
Our Polly is a sad slut! nor heeds what we have taught her.
I wonder any man alive will ever rear a daughter!
For she must have both hoods and gowns, and hoops to swell her pride,
With scarfs and stays, and gloves and lace; and she will have men beside;
And when she's dressed with care and cost, all-tempting, fine and gay,
*As men should serve a cowcumber,*⁵ *she flings herself away.*
Our Polly is a sad slut, etc.

You baggage! You hussy! You inconsiderate jade! Had you been hanged,
it would not have vexed me, for that might have been your misfortune;
but to do such a mad thing by choice! The wench is married, husband.

PEACHUM Married! The Captain is a bold man, and will risk anything for
money; to be sure he believes her a fortune. Do you think your mother
and I should have lived comfortably so long together, if ever we had been
married? Baggage!

MRS. PEACHUM I knew she was always a proud slut; and now the wench
hath played the fool and married, because forsooth she would do like the
gentry. Can you support the expense of a husband, hussy, in gaming,
drinking and whoring? Have you money enough to carry on the daily
quarrels of man and wife about who shall squander most? There are not
many husbands and wives who can bear the charges of plaguing one
another in a handsome way. If you must be married, could you introduce
nobody into our family but a highwayman? Why, thou foolish jade, thou
wilt be as ill-used, and as much neglected, as if thou hadst married a
lord!

PEACHUM Let not your anger, my dear, break through the rules of
decency, for the Captain looks upon himself in the military capacity, as
a gentleman by his profession. Besides what he hath already, I know he
is in a fair way of getting,⁶ or of dying; and both these ways, let me tell
you, are most excellent chances for a wife. Tell me hussy, are you ruined
or no?

MRS. PEACHUM With Polly's fortune, she might very well have gone off to
a person of distinction. Yes, that you might, you pouting slut!

---

4. A market where produce and prostitutes were
bought.

5. Cucumber.
6. Acquiring wealth.

PEACHUM   What, is the wench dumb? Speak, or I'll make you plead by squeezing out an answer from you. Are you really bound wife to him, or are you only upon liking?[7] [*Pinches her.*]

POLLY   Oh! [*Screaming.*]

MRS. PEACHUM   How the mother is to be pitied who hath handsome daughters! Locks, bolts, bars, and lectures of morality are nothing to them; they break through them all. They have as much pleasure in cheating a father and mother as in cheating at cards.

PEACHUM   Why, Polly, I shall soon know if you are married, by Macheath's keeping from our house.

AIR 8.   Grim king of the ghosts

POLLY
Can love be controlled by advice?
Will Cupid our mothers obey?
Though my heart were as frozen as ice,
At his flame 'twould have melted away.
When he kissed me so closely he pressed,
'Twas so sweet that I must have complied;
So I thought it both safest and best
To marry, for fear you should chide.

MRS. PEACHUM   Then all the hopes of our family are gone for ever and ever!

PEACHUM   And Macheath may hang his father and mother-in-law, in hope to get into their daughter's fortune.

POLLY   I did not marry him (as 'tis the fashion) coolly and deliberately for honor or money. But I love him.

MRS. PEACHUM   Love him! Worse and worse! I thought the girl had been better bred. O husband, husband! Her folly makes me mad! My head swims! I'm distracted! I can't support myself—O! [*Faints.*]

PEACHUM   See, wench, to what a condition you have reduced your poor mother! A glass of cordial, this instant. How the poor woman takes it to heart! [POLLY *goes out, and returns with it.*] Ah hussy, now this is the only comfort your mother has left!

POLLY   Give her another glass, sir; my mama drinks double the quantity whenever she is out of order. This, you see, fetches[8] her.

MRS. PEACHUM   The girl shows such a readiness, and so much concern, that I could almost find in my heart to forgive her.

AIR 9.   O Jenny, O Jenny, where hast thou been

MRS. PEACHUM
Oh Polly, you might have toyed and kissed.
By keeping men off, you keep them on.

POLLY
But he so teased me,
And he so pleased me,
What I did, you must have done.

MRS. PEACHUM   Not with a highwayman. You sorry slut!

PEACHUM   A word with you, wife. 'Tis no new thing for a wench to take man without consent of parents. You know 'tis the frailty of woman, my dear.

---

7. On approval.   8. Revives.

MRS. PEACHUM   Yes, indeed, the sex is frail. But the first time a woman is frail, she should be somewhat nice[9] methinks, for then or never is the time to make her fortune. After that, she hath nothing to do but to guard herself from being found out, and she may do what she pleases.

PEACHUM   Make yourself a little easy; I have a thought shall soon set all matters again to rights. Why so melancholy, Polly? Since what is done cannot be undone, we must all endeavor to make the best of it.

MRS. PEACHUM   Well, Polly, as far as one woman can forgive another, I forgive thee. Your father is too fond of you, hussy.

POLLY   Then all my sorrows are at an end.

MRS. PEACHUM   A mighty likely speech in troth, for a wench who is just married!

AIR 10.   Thomas, I cannot

POLLY

I, like a ship in storms, was tossed,
Yet afraid to put in to land;
For seized in the port the vessel's lost,
Whose treasure is contraband.
   The waves are laid,
    My duty's paid.
O joy beyond expression!
   Thus, safe ashore,
    I ask no more,
My all is in my possession.

PEACHUM   I hear customers in t'other room. Go, talk with 'em, Polly; but come to us again as soon as they are gone. But, hark ye, child, if 'tis the gentleman who was here yesterday about the repeating-watch,[1] say, you believe we can't get intelligence of it, till tomorrow, for I lent it to Suky Straddle, to make a figure with it tonight at a tavern in Drury Lane. If t'other gentleman calls for the silver-hilted sword, you know beetle-browed Jemmy hath it on, and he doth not come from Tunbridge till Tuesday night, so that it cannot be had till then.

SCENE 9

PEACHUM, MRS. PEACHUM

PEACHUM   Dear wife, be a little pacified. Don't let your passion run away with your senses. Polly, I grant you, hath done a rash thing.

MRS. PEACHUM   If she had had only an intrigue with the fellow, why the very best families have excused and huddled up a frailty of that sort. 'Tis marriage, husband, that makes it a blemish.

PEACHUM   But money, wife, is the true fuller's earth[2] for reputations, there is not a spot or a stain but what it can take out. A rich rogue nowadays is fit company for any gentleman; and the world, my dear, hath not such a contempt for roguery as you imagine. I tell you, wife, I can make this match turn to our advantage.

9. Choosy.
1. A watch that strikes the hour and quarter

hour when a button is pressed.
2. Clay used for cleaning fabrics.

MRS. PEACHUM   I am very sensible,[3] husband, that Captain Macheath is worth money, but I am in doubt whether he hath not two or three wives already, and then if he should die in a Session or two, Polly's dower would come into dispute.

PEACHUM   That, indeed, is a point which ought to be considered.

AIR 11.   A soldier and a sailor

> *A fox may steal your hens, sir,*
> *A whore your health and pence, sir,*
> *Your daughter rob your chest, sir,*
> *Your wife may steal your rest, sir,*
>   *A thief your goods and plate.*
> *But this is all but picking,*
> *With rest, pence, chest, and chicken;*
> *It ever was decreed, sir,*
> *If lawyer's hand is fee'd, sir,*
>   *He steals your whole estate.*

The lawyers are bitter enemies to those in our way. They don't care that anybody should get a clandestine livelihood but themselves.

SCENE 10

MRS. PEACHUM, PEACHUM, POLLY

POLLY   'Twas only Nimming Ned. He brought in a damask window curtain, a hoop-petticoat, a pair of silver candlesticks, a perriwig, and one silk stocking, from the fire that happened last night.

PEACHUM   There is not a fellow that is cleverer in his way, and saves more goods out of the fire than Ned. But now, Polly, to your affair; for matters must not be left as they are. You are married then, it seems?

POLLY   Yes, sir.

PEACHUM   And how do you propose to live, child?

POLLY   Like other women, sir, upon the industry of my husband.

MRS. PEACHUM   What, is the wench turned fool? A highwayman's wife, like a soldier's, hath as little of his pay as of his company.

PEACHUM   And had not you the common views of a gentlewoman in your marriage, Polly?

POLLY   I don't know what you mean, sir.

PEACHUM   Of a jointure,[4] and of being a widow.

POLLY   But I love him, sir. How then could I have thoughts of parting with him?

PEACHUM   Parting with him! Why, that is the whole scheme and intention of all marriage articles. The comfortable estate of widowhood is the only hope that keeps up a wife's spirits. Where is the woman who would scruple to be a wife, if she had it in her power to be a widow whenever she pleased? If you have any views of this sort, Polly, I shall think the match not so very unreasonable.

3. Aware.
4. Property jointly held by a couple, hence inherited by the wife if her husband died.

POLLY   How I dread to hear your advice! Yet I must beg you to explain yourself.

PEACHUM   Secure what he hath got, have him peached the next Sessions, and then at once you are made a rich widow.

POLLY   What, murder the man I love! The blood runs cold at my heart with the very thought of it.

PEACHUM   Fie, Polly! What hath murder to do in the affair? Since the thing sooner or later must happen, I dare say, the Captain himself would like that we should get the reward for his death sooner than a stranger. Why, Polly, the Captain knows that as 'tis his employment to rob, so 'tis ours to take robbers; every man in his business. So that there is no malice in the case.

MRS. PEACHUM   Ay, husband, now you have nicked the matter.[5] To have him peached is the only thing could ever make me forgive her.

AIR 12.   Now Ponder well, ye parents dear

POLLY

> O, ponder well! be not severe;
>   So save a wretched wife!
> For on the rope that hangs my dear
>   Depends poor Polly's life.

MRS. PEACHUM   But your duty to your parents, hussy, obliges you to hang him. What would many a wife give for such an opportunity!

POLLY   What is a jointure, what is widowhood to me? I know my heart. I cannot survive him.

AIR 13.   Le printemps rappelle aux armes[6]

> The turtle[7] thus with plaintive crying,
>   Her lover dying,
> The turtle thus with plaintive crying,
>   Laments her dove.
> Down she drops quite spent with sighing,
> Paired in death, as paired in love.

Thus, sir, it will happen to your poor Polly.

MRS. PEACHUM   What, is the fool in love in earnest then? I hate thee for being particular.[8] Why, wench, thou art a shame to thy very sex.

POLLY   But hear me, mother. If you ever loved—

MRS. PEACHUM   Those cursed playbooks she reads have been her ruin. One word more, hussy, and I shall knock your brains out, if you have any.

PEACHUM   Keep out of the way, Polly, for fear of mischief, and consider of what is proposed to you.

MRS. PEACHUM   Away, hussy. Hang your husband, and be dutiful.

SCENE 11

MRS. PEACHUM, PEACHUM [POLLY *listening*]

MRS. PEACHUM   The thing, husband, must and shall be done. For the sake of intelligence[9] we must take other measures, and have him peached the

---

5. Hit the mark.
6. The spring calls to arms (French).
7. Turtledove.

8. Attached to one person; freakish.
9. Secret information.

next Session without her consent. If she will not know her duty, we know ours.

PEACHUM   But really, my dear, it grieves one's heart to take off a great man. When I consider his personal bravery, his fine stratagem,[1] how much we have already got by him, and how much more we may get, methinks I can't find in my heart to have a hand in his death. I wish you could have made Polly undertake it.

MRS. PEACHUM   But in a case of necessity—our own lives are in danger.

PEACHUM   Then, indeed, we must comply with the customs of the world, and make gratitude give way to interest. He shall be taken off.

MRS. PEACHUM   I'll undertake to manage Polly.

PEACHUM   And I'll prepare matters for the Old Bailey.

SCENE 12

POLLY

Now I'm a wretch, indeed. Methinks I see him already in the cart, sweeter and more lovely than the nosegay in his hand! I hear the crowd extolling his resolution and intrepidity! What volleys of sighs are sent from the windows of Holborn,[2] that so comely a youth should be brought to disgrace! I see him at the tree! The whole circle are in tears! Even butchers weep! Jack Ketch[3] himself hesitates to perform his duty, and would be glad to lose his fee, by a reprieve. What then will become of Polly! As yet I may inform him of their design, and aid him in his escape. It shall be so. But then he flies, absents himself, and I bar my self from his dear dear conversation![4] That too will distract me. If he keep out of the way, my papa and mama may in time relent, and we may be happy. If he stays, he is hanged, and then he is lost forever! He intended to lie concealed in my room, 'till the dusk of the evening. If they are abroad, I'll this instant let him out, lest some accident should prevent him.

[*Exit, and returns.*]

SCENE 13

POLLY, MACHEATH

AIR 14.   Pretty parrot, say

MACHEATH   *Pretty Polly, say,*
                When I was away,
        Did your fancy never stray
            To some newer lover?

POLLY   *Without disguise,*
                Heaving sighs,
                Doating eyes,
        My constant heart discover.
            Fondly let me loll!

MACHEATH   *O pretty, pretty Poll.*

1. Guile.
2. The street that connects Newgate to the gallows ("tree") at Tyburn.
3. The hangman (after a famous 17th-century executioner).
4. Intimate contact.

POLLY And are *you* as fond as ever, my dear?

MACHEATH Suspect my honor, my courage, suspect anything but my love. May my pistols misfire, and my mare slip her shoulder while I am pursued, if I ever forsake thee!

POLLY Nay, my dear, I have no reason to doubt you, for I find in the romance you lent me, none of the great heroes were ever false in love.

AIR 15. Pray, fair one, be kind

MACHEATH

My heart was so free,
It roved like the bee,
'Till Polly my passion requited;
I sipped each flower,
I changed every hour,
But here every flower is united.

POLLY Were you sentenced to transportation, sure, my dear, you could not leave me behind you—could you?

MACHEATH Is there any power, any force that could tear me from thee? You might sooner tear a pension out of the hands of a courtier, a fee from a lawyer, a pretty woman from a looking glass, or any woman from quadrille. But to tear me from thee is impossible!

AIR 16. Over the hills and far away

MACHEATH *Were I laid on Greenland's coast,*
And in my arms embraced my lass;
Warm amidst eternal frost,
Too soon the half year's night would pass.
POLLY *Were I sold on Indian soil,*
Soon as the burning day was closed,
I could mock the sultry toil,
When on my charmer's breast reposed.
MACHEATH *And I would love you all the day,*
POLLY *Every night would kiss and play,*
MACHEATH *If with me you'd fondly stray*
POLLY *Over the hills and far away.*

Yes, I would go with thee. But oh! How shall I speak it? I must be torn from thee. We must part.

MACHEATH How? Part?

POLLY We must, we must. My papa and mama are set against thy life. They now, even now, are in search after thee. They are preparing evidence against thee. Thy life depends upon a moment.

AIR 17. Gin thou wert mine awn thing

Oh what pain it is to part!
Can I leave thee, can I leave thee?
Oh what pain it is to part!
Can thy Polly ever leave thee?
But lest death my love should thwart,
And bring thee to the fatal cart,

> *Thus I tear thee from my bleeding heart!*
> *Fly hence, and let me leave thee.*

One kiss and then—one kiss—begone—farewell.

MACHEATH   My hand, my heart, my dear, is so riveted to thine, that I cannot unloose my hold.

POLLY   But my papa may intercept thee, and then I should lose the very glimmering of hope. A few weeks, perhaps, may reconcile us all. Shall thy Polly hear from thee?

MACHEATH   Must I then go?

POLLY   And will not absence change your love?

MACHEATH   If you doubt it, let me stay—and be hanged.

POLLY   Oh how I fear! How I tremble! Go—but when safety will give you leave, you will be sure to see me again; for 'till then Polly is wretched.

AIR 18.   Oh the broom

[Parting, and looking back at each other with fondness; he at one door, she at the other.]

MACHEATH
> *The miser thus a shilling sees,*
> *Which he's obliged to pay,*
> *With sighs resigns it by degrees,*
> *And fears 'tis gone for aye.*

POLLY
> *The boy, thus, when his sparrow's flown,*
> *The bird in silence eyes;*
> *But soon as out of sight 'tis gone,*
> *Whines, whimpers, sobs, and cries.*

Act 2

SCENE 1 *A tavern near Newgate*

JEMMY TWITCHER, CROOK-FINGERED JACK, WAT DREARY, ROBIN OF BAGSHOT, NIMMING NED, HENRY PADDINGTON, MATT OF THE MINT, BEN BUDGE, *and the rest of the gang, at the table, with wine, brandy, and tobacco.*

BEN   But prithee, Matt, what is become of thy brother Tom? I have not seen him since my return from transportation.

MATT   Poor brother Tom had an accident this time twelve-month, and so clever a made fellow he was, that I could not save him from those flaying rascals the surgeons; and now, poor man, he is among the otamies[5] at Surgeon's Hall.

BEN   So it seems, his time was come.

JEMMY   But the present time is ours, and nobody alive hath more. Why are the laws levelled at us? Are we more dishonest than the rest of mankind? What we win, gentlemen, is our own by the law of arms and the right of conquest.

JACK   Where shall we find such another set of practical philosophers, who to a man are above the fear of death?

---

5. Skeletons ("anatomies"). "Had an accident": was hanged. "Clever a made": well-made.

WAT Sound men, and true!

ROBIN Of tried courage, and indefatigable industry!

NED Who is there here that would not die for his friend?

HARRY Who is there here that would betray him for his interest?

MATT Show me a gang of courtiers that can say as much.

BEN We are for a just partition of the world, for every man hath a right to enjoy life.

MATT We retrench the superfluities of mankind. The world is avaricious, and I hate avarice. A covetous fellow, like a jackdaw, steals what he was never made to enjoy, for the sake of hiding it. These are the robbers of mankind, for money was made for the free-hearted and generous, and where is the injury of taking from another what he hath not the heart to make use of?

JEMMY Our several stations[6] for the day are fixed. Good luck attend us all. Fill the glasses.

AIR 19. Fill every glass

MATT
> *Fill every glass, for wine inspires us,*
> *And fires us*
> *With courage, love, and joy.*
> *Women and wine should life employ.*
> *Is there ought else on earth desirous?*

CHORUS
> *Fill every glass, etc.*

SCENE 2

To them enter MACHEATH

MACHEATH Gentlemen, well met. My heart hath been with you this hour; but an unexpected affair hath detained me. No ceremony, I beg you.

MATT We were just breaking up to go upon duty. Am I to have the honor of taking the air with you, sir, this evening upon the heath? I drink a dram now and then with the stagecoachmen in the way of friendship and intelligence; and I know that about this time there will be passengers upon the Western Road, who are worth speaking with.

MACHEATH I was to have been of that party, but—

MATT But what, sir?

MACHEATH Is there any man who suspects my courage?

MATT We have all been witnesses of it.

MACHEATH My honor and truth to the gang?

MATT I'll be answerable for it.

MACHEATH In the division of our booty, have I ever shown the least marks of avarice or injustice?

MATT By these questions something seems to have ruffled you. Are any of us suspected?

MACHEATH I have a fixed confidence, gentlemen, in you all, as men of honor, and as such I value and respect you. Peachum is a man that is useful to us.

6. Individual posts.

MATT Is he about to play us any foul play? I'll shoot him through the head.

MACHEATH I beg you, gentlemen, act with conduct and discretion. A pistol is your last resort.

MATT He knows nothing of this meeting.

MACHEATH Business cannot go on without him. He is a man who knows the world, and is a necessary agent to us. We have had a slight difference, and till it is accommodated I shall be obliged to keep out of his way. Any private dispute of mine shall be of no ill consequence to my friends. You must continue to act under his direction, for the moment we break loose from him, our gang is ruined.

MATT As a bawd to a whore, I grant you, he is to us of great convenience.

MACHEATH Make him believe I have quitted the gang, which I can never do but with life. At our private quarters I will continue to meet you. A week or so will probably reconcile us.

MATT Your instructions shall be observed. 'Tis now high time for us to repair to our several duties; so till the evening at our quarters in Moorfields[7] we bid you farewell.

MACHEATH I shall wish myself with you. Success attend you. [*Sits down melancholy at the table.*]

AIR 20. March in Rinaldo,[8] with drums and trumpets

MATT

> *Let us take the road.*
> *Hark I hear the sound of coaches!*
> *The hour of attack approaches,*
> *To your arms, brave boys, and load.*
> *See the ball I hold!*
> *Let the chemists[9] toil like asses,*
> *Our fire their fire surpasses,*
> *And turns all our lead to gold.*

[*The gang, ranged in the front of the stage, load their pistols, and stick them under their girdles; then go off singing the first part in chorus.*]

SCENE 3

MACHEATH

What a fool is a fond wench! Polly is most confoundedly bit.[1] I love the sex. And a man who loves money might as well be contented with one guinea, as I with one woman. The town perhaps hath been as much obliged to me for recruiting it with free-hearted ladies, as to any recruiting officer in the army. If it were not for us and the other gentlemen of the sword, Drury Lane[2] would be uninhabited.

---

7. A district known as a "seminary of vice."
8. Opera by Handel.
9. Alchemists.

1. Taken in.
2. Associated with prostitutes.

AIR 21.   Would you have a young virgin

If the heart of a man is depressed with cares,
The mist is dispelled when a woman appears;
Like the notes of a fiddle, she sweetly, sweetly
Raises the spirits, and charms our ears,
  Roses and lilies her cheeks disclose,
  But her ripe lips are more sweet than those.
    Press her,
    Caress her,
    With blisses,
    Her kisses
Dissolve us in pleasure, and soft repose.

I must have women. There is nothing unbends the mind like them. Money is not so strong a cordial for the time. Drawer! [*Enter* DRAWER.] Is the porter gone for all the ladies, according to my directions?

DRAWER   I expect him back every minute. But you know, sir, you sent him as far as Hockley in the Hole, for three of the ladies, for one in Vinegar Yard, and for the rest of them somewhere about Lewkner's Lane. Sure some of them are below, for I hear the bar bell. As they come I will show them up. Coming, coming.

SCENE 4

MACHEATH, MRS. COAXER, DOLLY TRULL, MRS. VIXEN, BETTY DOXY, JENNY
DIVER, MRS. SLAMMEKIN, SUKY TAWDRY, *and* MOLLY BRAZEN

MACHEATH   Dear Mrs. Coaxer, you are welcome. You look charmingly today. I hope you don't want the repairs of quality, and lay on paint.[3] Dolly Trull! Kiss me, you slut; are you as amorous as ever, hussy? You are always so taken up with stealing hearts, that you don't allow yourself time to steal anything else. Ah Dolly, thou wilt ever be a coquette! Mrs. Vixen, I'm yours, I always loved a woman of wit and spirit; they make charming mistresses, but plaguey wives. Betty Doxy! Come hither, hussy. Do you drink as hard as ever? You had better stick to good wholesome beer; for in troth, Betty, strong waters[4] will in time ruin your constitution. You should leave those to your betters. What! and my pretty Jenny Diver too! As prim and demure as ever! There is not any prude, though ever so high bred, hath a more sanctified look, with a more mischievous heart. Ah! Thou art a dear artful hypocrite. Mrs. Slammekin! As careless and genteel as ever! All you fine ladies, who know your own beauty, affect an undress.[5] But see, here's Suky Tawdry come to contradict what I was saying. Everything she gets one way she lays out upon her back. Why, Suky, you must keep at least a dozen tallymen.[6] Molly Brazen! [*She kisses him.*] That's well done. I love a free-hearted wench. Thou hast a most agreeable assurance, girl, and art as willing as a turtle. But hark! I hear music. The harper is at the door. "If music be the food of love, play on."[7] E'er you seat yourselves,

---

3. Cosmetics. "Quality": women of high social position.
4. Spirits.

5. Prefer casual clothes.
6. Suppliers of clothes on credit.
7. The opening line of Shakespeare's *Twelfth Night*.

ladies, what think you of a dance? Come in. [*Enter* HARPER.] Play the French tune that Mrs. Slammekin was so fond of.

[*A dance a la ronde in the French manner; near the end of it this song and chorus.*]

AIR 22.   Cotillon

MACHEATH *Youth's the season made for joys,*
　　　　　　Love is then our duty,
　　　　　She alone who that employs,
　　　　　　Well deserves her beauty.
　　　　　　　Let's be gay,
　　　　　　　While we may,
　　　　　　　Beauty's a flower despised in decay.

CHORUS　　　*Youth's the season etc.*

MACHEATH　*Let us drink and sport today,*
　　　　　　Ours is not tomorrow.
　　　　　Love with youth flies swift away,
　　　　　　Age is nought but sorrow.
　　　　　　　Dance and sing,
　　　　　　　Time's on the wing,
　　　　　　　Life never knows the return of spring.

CHORUS　　　*Let us drink etc.*

MACHEATH Now, pray ladies, take your places. Here, fellow. [*Pays the* HARPER.] Bid the drawer bring us more wine. [*Exit* HARPER.] If any of the ladies choose gin, I hope they will be so free to call for it.

JENNY You look as if you meant me. Wine is strong enough for me. Indeed, sir, I never drink strong waters, but when I have the colic.

MACHEATH Just the excuse of the fine ladies! Why, a lady of quality is never without the colic. I hope, Mrs. Coaxer, you have had good success of late in your visits among the mercers.[8]

MRS. COAXER We have so many interlopers.[9] Yet with industry, one may still have a little picking. I carried a silver flowered lute string and a piece of black padesoy[1] to Mr. Peachum's lock but last week.

MRS. VIXEN There's Molly Brazen hath the ogle of a rattlesnake. She riveted a linen draper's eye so fast upon her that he was nicked of three pieces of cambric before he could look off.

MOLLY BRAZEN Oh dear madam! But sure nothing can come up to your handling of laces! And then you have such a sweet deluding tongue. To cheat a man is nothing; but the woman must have fine parts indeed who cheats a woman!

MRS. VIXEN Lace, madam, lies in a small compass, and is of easy conveyance. But you are apt, madam, to think too well of your friends.

MRS. COAXER If any woman hath more art than another, to be sure, 'tis Jenny Diver. Though her fellow be never so agreeable, she can pick his pocket as coolly, as if money were her only pleasure. Now that is a command of the passions uncommon in a woman!

---

8. Dealers in fabrics.　　　　　　　　1. Expensive silk.
9. I.e., competitors in thievery.

JENNY I never go to the tavern with a man, but in the view of business. I have other hours, and other sort of men, for my pleasure. But had I your address,[2] madam—

MACHEATH Have done with your compliments, ladies; and drink about. You are not so fond of me, Jenny, as you use to be.

JENNY 'Tis not convenient, sir, to show my fondness among so many rivals. 'Tis your own choice, and not the warmth of my inclination, that will determine you.

AIR 23. All in a misty morning

> Before the barn door crowing,
>   The cock by hens attended,
> His eyes around him throwing,
>   Stands for a while suspended.
> Then one he singles from the crew,
>   And cheers the happy hen;
> With how do you do, and how do you do,
>   And how do you do again.

MACHEATH Ah Jenny! Thou art a dear slut.

DOLLY Pray, madam, were you ever in keeping?[3]

SUKY I hope, madam, I ha'nt been so long upon the town, but I have met with some good fortune as well as my neighbors.

DOLLY Pardon me, madam, I meant no harm by the question; 'twas only in the way of conversation.

SUKY Indeed, madam, if I had not been a fool, I might have lived very handsomely with my last friend. But upon his missing five guineas, he turned me off. Now I never suspected he had counted them.

MRS. SLAMMEKIN Who do you look upon, madam, as your best sort of keepers?

DOLLY That, madam, is thereafter as they be.[4]

MRS. SLAMMEKIN I, madam, was once kept by a Jew; and bating[5] their religion, to women they are a good sort of people.

SUKY Now for my part, I own I like an old fellow, for we always make them pay for what they can't do.

MRS. VIXEN A spruce prentice, let me tell you, ladies, is no ill thing, they bleed[6] freely. I have sent at least two or three dozen of them in my time to the plantations.[7]

JENNY But to be sure, sir, with so much good fortune as you have had upon the road, you must be grown immensely rich.

MACHEATH The road, indeed, hath done me justice, but the gaming table hath been my ruin.

AIR 24. When once I lay with another man's wife

JENNY *The gamesters and lawyers are jugglers[8] alike,*
    If they meddle your all is in danger.
    Like gypsies, if once they can finger a souse,[9]

2. Adroitness.
3. A kept mistress.
4. Depends on their behavior.
5. Except for.

6. Spend.
7. The colonies, where convicts were transported.
8. Tricksters.
9. A negligible coin.

> *Your pockets they pick, and they pilfer your house,*
> *And give your estate to a stranger.*

A man of courage should never put anything to the risk but his life. These are the tools of a man of honor. Cards and dice are only fit for cowardly cheats, who prey upon their friends. [*She takes up his pistol.* SUKY *takes up the other.*]

SUKY   This, sir, is fitter for your hand. Besides your loss of money, 'tis a loss to the ladies. Gaming takes you off from women. How fond could I be of you! But before company, 'tis ill bred.

MACHEATH   Wanton hussies!

JENNY   I must and will have a kiss to give my wine a zest.
   [*They take him about the neck, and make signs to* PEACHUM *and the constables, who rush in upon him.*]

SCENE 5

To them, PEACHUM *and constables*

PEACHUM   I seize you, sir, as my prisoner.

MACHEATH   Was this well done, Jenny? Women are decoy ducks; who can trust them! Beasts, jades, jilts, harpies, furies, whores!

PEACHUM   Your case, Mr. Macheath, is not particular. The greatest heroes have been ruined by women. But, to do them justice, I must own they are a pretty sort of creatures, if we could trust them. You must now, sir, take your leave of the ladies, and if they have a mind to make you a visit, they will be sure to find you at home. The gentleman, ladies, lodges in Newgate. Constables, wait upon the Captain to his lodgings.

AIR 25.   When first I laid siege to my Chloris

MACHEATH   *At the tree I shall suffer with pleasure,*
   At the tree I shall suffer with pleasure,
   Let me go where I will,
   In all kinds of ill,
   I shall find no such Furies as these are.

PEACHUM   Ladies, I'll take care the reckoning shall be discharged.
   [*Exit* MACHEATH, *guarded, with* PEACHUM *and the constables.*]

SCENE 6

The women remain

MRS. VIXEN   Look ye, Mrs. Jenny, though Mr. Peachum may have made a private bargain with you and Suky Tawdry for betraying the Captain, as we were all assisting, we ought all to share alike.

MRS. COAXER   I think Mr. Peachum, after so long an acquaintance, might have trusted me as well as Jenny Diver.

MRS. SLAMMEKIN   I am sure at least three men of his hanging, and in a year's time too (if he did me justice), should be set down to my account.

DOLLY   Mrs. Slammekin, that is not fair. For you know one of them was taken in bed with me.

JENNY   As far as a bowl of punch or a treat, I believe Mrs. Suky will join with me. As for anything else, ladies, you cannot in conscience expect it.

MRS. SLAMMEKIN Dear madam—
DOLLY I would not for the world[1]—
MRS. SLAMMEKIN 'Tis impossible for me—
DOLLY As I hope to be saved, madam—
MRS. SLAMMEKIN Nay, then I must stay here all night—
DOLLY Since you command me.

[Exeunt with great ceremony.]

SCENE 7 *Newgate*

LOCKIT, *turnkeys*, MACHEATH, *constables*

LOCKIT Noble Captain, you are welcome. You have not been a lodger of mine this year and half. You know the custom, sir. Garnish,[2] Captain, garnish. Hand me down those fetters there.
MACHEATH Those, Mr. Lockit, seem to be the heaviest of the whole set. With your leave, I should like the further pair better.
LOCKIT Look ye, Captain, we know what is fittest for our prisoners. When a gentleman uses me with civility, I always do the best I can to please him. Hand them down I say. We have them of all prices, from one guinea to ten, and 'tis fitting every gentleman should please himself.
MACHEATH I understand you, sir. [*Gives money.*] The fees here are so many, and so exorbitant, that few fortunes can bear the expense of getting off handsomely, or of dying like a gentleman.
LOCKIT Those, I see, will fit the Captain better. Take down the further pair. Do but examine them, sir. Never was better work. How genteelly they are made! They will sit as easy as a glove, and the nicest man in England might not be ashamed to wear them. [*He puts on the chains.*] If I had the best gentleman in the land in my custody, I could not equip him more handsomely. And so, sir, I now leave you to your private meditations.

SCENE 8

MACHEATH

AIR 26. Courtiers, courtiers think it no harm

Man may escape from rope and gun;
Nay, some have outlived the doctor's pill;
Who takes a woman must he undone,
That basilisk[3] is sure to kill.
The fly that sips treacle is lost in the sweets,
So he that tastes woman, woman, woman,
He that tastes woman, ruin meets.

To what a woeful plight have I brought myself! Here must I (all day long, 'till I am hanged) be confined to hear the reproaches of a wench who lays her ruin at my door. I am in the custody of her father, and to be sure if he knows of the matter, I shall have a fine time on't betwixt this and my execution. But I promised the wench marriage. What signifies a promise

1. With exaggerated politeness, each gestures for the other to leave the room first.
2. Jailer's fee or bribe.

3. Mythical reptile whose breath and look were fatal.

to a woman? Does not man in marriage itself promise a hundred things that he never means to perform? Do all we can, women will believe us, for they look upon a promise as an excuse for following their own inclinations. But here comes Lucy, and I cannot get from her. Would I were deaf!

SCENE 9

MACHEATH, LUCY

LUCY You base man you! How can you look me in the face after what hath passed between us? See here, perfidious wretch, how I am forced to bear about the load of infamy[4] you have laid upon me. O Macheath! Thou hast robbed me of my quiet. To see thee tortured would give me pleasure!

AIR 27.   A lovely lass to a friar came

Thus when a good huswife sees a rat
In her trap in the morning taken,
With pleasure her heart goes pit a pat,
In revenge for her loss of bacon.
Then she throws him
To the dog or cat,
To be worried, crushed and shaken.

MACHEATH   Have you no bowels,[5] no tenderness, my dear Lucy, to see a husband in these circumstances?
LUCY A husband!
MACHEATH   In every respect but the form, and that, my dear, may be said over us at any time. Friends should not insist upon ceremonies. From a man of honor, his word is as good as his bond.
LUCY 'Tis the pleasure of all you fine men to insult the women you have ruined.

AIR 28.   'Twas when the sea was roaring

How cruel are the traitors,
Who lie and swear in jest,
To cheat unguarded creatures
Of virtue, fame, and rest!
Whoever steals a shilling,
Through shame the guilt conceals;
In love the perjured villain
With boasts the theft reveals.

MACHEATH   The very first opportunity, my dear (have but patience), you shall be my wife in whatever manner you please.
LUCY Insinuating monster! And so you think I know nothing of the affair of Miss Polly Peachum. I could tear thy eyes out!
MACHEATH   Sure Lucy, you can't be such a fool as to be jealous of Polly!
LUCY Are you not married to her, you brute, you?

4. Pregnancy.   5. Pity.

MACHEATH Married! Very good. The wench gives it out only to vex thee, and to ruin me in thy good opinion. 'Tis true, I go to the house; I chat with the girl, I kiss her, I say a thousand things to her (as all gentlemen do) that mean nothing, to divert myself; and now the silly jade hath set it about that I am married to her, to let me know what she would be at. Indeed, my dear Lucy, these violent passions may be of ill consequence to a woman in your condition.

LUCY Come, come, Captain, for all your assurance, you know that Miss Polly hath put it out of your power to do me the justice you promised me.

MACHEATH A jealous woman believes everything her passion suggests. To convince you of my sincerity, if we can find the Ordinary,[6] I shall have no scruples of making you my wife; and I know the consequence of having two at a time.

LUCY That you are only to be hanged, and so get rid of them both.

MACHEATH I am ready, my dear Lucy, to give you satisfaction—if you think there is any in marriage. What can a man of honor say more?

LUCY So then it seems you are not married to Miss Polly.

MACHEATH You know, Lucy, the girl is prodigiously conceited. No man can say a civil thing to her, but (like other fine ladies) her vanity makes her think he's her own for ever and ever.

AIR 29. The sun had loosed his weary teams

> *The first time at the looking-glass*
> *The mother sets her daughter,*
> *The image strikes the smiling lass*
> *With self-love ever after.*
> *Each time she looks, she, fonder grown,*
> *Thinks every charm grows stronger.*
> *But alas, vain maid, all eyes but your own*
> *Can see you are not younger.*

When women consider their own beauties, they are all alike unreasonable in their demands; for they expect their lovers should like them as long as they like themselves.

LUCY Yonder is my father. Perhaps this way we may light upon the Ordinary, who shall try if you will be as good as your word. For I long to be made an honest woman.

SCENE 10

PEACHUM, LOCKIT *with an account book*

LOCKIT In this last affair, Brother Peachum, we are agreed. You have consented to go halves in Macheath.

PEACHUM We shall never fall out about an execution. But as to that article, pray how stands our last year's account?

LOCKIT If you will run your eye over it, you'll find 'tis fair and clearly stated.

PEACHUM This long arrear[7] of the Government is very hard upon us! Can it be expected that we should hang our acquaintance for nothing, when

---

6. Chaplain.

7. Overdue reward money.

our betters will hardly save theirs without being paid for it. Unless the people in employment pay better, I promise them for the future, I shall let other rogues live besides their own.

LOCKIT Perhaps, brother, they are afraid these matters may be carried too far. We are treated too by them with contempt, as if our profession were not reputable.

PEACHUM In one respect indeed, our employment may be reckoned dishonest, because, like great statesmen, we encourage those who betray their friends.

LOCKIT Such language, brother, anywhere else, might turn to your prejudice. Learn to be more guarded, I beg you.

AIR 30. How happy are we

When you censure the age,
Be cautious and sage,
Lest the courtiers offended should be:
If you mention vice or bribe,
'Tis so pat to all the tribe,
Each cries, "That was leveled at me!"

PEACHUM Here's poor Ned Clincher's name, I see. Sure, brother Lockit, there was a little unfair proceeding in Ned's case; for he told me in the condemned hold,[8] that for value received, you had promised him a Session or two longer without molestation.

LOCKIT Mr. Peachum, this is the first time my honor was ever called in question.

PEACHUM Business is at an end if once we act dishonorably.

LOCKIT Who accuses me?

PEACHUM You are warm, brother.

LOCKIT He that attacks my honor, attacks my livelihood. And this usage, sir, is not to be born.

PEACHUM Since you provoke me to speak, I must tell you too that Mrs. Coaxer charges you with defrauding her of her information money, for the apprehending of curl-pated Hugh. Indeed, indeed, brother, we must punctually pay our spies, or we shall have no information.

LOCKIT Is this language to me, sirrah, who have saved you from the gallows, sirrah! [*Collaring each other.*]

PEACHUM If I am hanged, it shall be for ridding the world of an arrant rascal.

LOCKIT This hand shall do the office of the halter[9] you deserve, and throttle you—you dog!

PEACHUM Brother, brother, we are both in the wrong. We shall be both losers in the dispute—for you know we have it in our power to hang each other. You should not be so passionate.

LOCKIT Nor you so provoking.

PEACHUM 'Tis our mutual interest; 'tis for the interest of the world we should agree. If I said anything, brother, to the prejudice of your character, I ask pardon.

8. Prison cell.   9. Noose.

684 | JOHN GAY

LOCKIT Brother Peachum, I can forgive as well as resent. Give me your hand. Suspicion does not become a friend.

PEACHUM I only meant to give you occasion to justify yourself. But I must now step home, for I expect the gentleman about this snuffbox, that Filch nimmed[1] two nights ago in the park. I appointed him at this hour.

SCENE 11

LOCKIT, LUCY

LOCKIT Whence come you, hussy?

LUCY My tears might answer that question.

LOCKIT You have then been whimpering and fondling, like a spaniel, over the fellow that hath abused you.

LUCY One can't help love; one can't cure it. 'Tis not in my power to obey you, and hate him.

LOCKIT Learn to bear your husband's death like a reasonable woman. 'Tis not the fashion, nowadays, so much as to affect sorrow upon these occasions. No woman would ever marry, if she had not the chance of mortality for a release. Act like a woman of spirit, hussy, and thank your father for what he is doing.

AIR 31.   Of a noble race was Shenkin

LUCY

Is then his fate decreed, sir?
Such a man can I think of quitting?
When first we met, so moves me yet,
Oh see how my heart is splitting!

LOCKIT Look ye, Lucy, there is no saving him. So I think you must even do like other widows: buy yourself weeds,[2] and be cheerful.

AIR 32.   You'll think e'er many days ensue

You'll think e'er many days ensue
This sentence not severe;
I hang your husband, child, 'tis true,
But with him hang your care.
Twang dang dillo dee.

Like a good wife, go moan over your dying husband. That, child, is your duty. Consider, girl, you can't have the man and the money too. So make yourself as easy as you can, by getting all you can from him.

SCENE 12

LUCY, MACHEATH

LUCY Though the Ordinary was out of the way today, I hope; my dear, you will, upon the first opportunity, quiet my scruples. Oh sir! My father's hard heart is not to be softened, and I am in the utmost despair.

MACHEATH But if I could raise a small sum—would not twenty guineas, think you, move him? Of all the arguments in the way of business, the

1. Stole.   2. Mourning clothes.

perquisite[3] is the most prevailing. Your father's perquisites for the escape of prisoners must amount to a considerable sum in the year. Money well timed, and properly applied, will do any thing.

AIR 33.   London ladies

> *If you at an office solicit your due,*
>   *And would not have matters neglected,*
> *You must quicken the clerk with the perquisite too,*
>   *To do what his duty directed.*
> *Or would you the frowns of a lady prevent,*
>   *She too has this palpable failing,*
> *The perquisite softens her into consent;*
>   *That reason with all is prevailing.*

LUCY   What love or money can do shall be done; for all my comfort depends upon your safety.

SCENE 13

LUCY, MACHEATH, POLLY

POLLY   Where is my dear husband? Was a rope ever intended for this neck! Oh let me throw my arms about it, and throttle thee with love! Why dost thou turn away from me? 'Tis thy Polly! 'Tis thy wife!

MACHEATH   Was ever such an unfortunate rascal as I am!

LUCY   Was there ever such another villain!

POLLY   Oh Macheath! Was it for this we parted? Taken! Imprisoned! Tried! Hanged! Cruel reflection! I'll stay with thee 'till death. No force shall tear thy dear wife from thee now.—What means my love? Not one kind word! Not one kind look! Think what thy Polly suffers to see thee in this condition.

AIR 34.   All in the downs

> *Thus when the swallow, seeking prey,*
>   *Within the sash[4] is closely pent,*
> *His consort, with bemoaning lay,*
>   *Without sits pining for th' event.*
> *Her chattering lovers all around her skim;*
> *She heeds them not (poor bird!), her soul's with him.*

MACHEATH [*Aside.*]   I must disown her. The wench is distracted.

LUCY   Am I then bilked of my virtue? Can I have no reparation? Sure men were born to lie, and women to believe them! Oh villain! Villain!

POLLY   Am I not thy wife? Thy neglect of me, thy aversion to me, too severely proves it. Look on me. Tell me, am I not thy wife?

LUCY   Perfidious wretch!

POLLY   Barbarous husband!

LUCY   Hadst thou been hanged five months ago, I had been happy.

POLLY   And I too. If you had been kind to me 'till death, it would not have vexed me—and that's no very unreasonable request (though from a wife) to a man who hath not above seven or eight days to live.

3. Tip or bribe.   4. Window.

LUCY   Art thou then married to another? Hast thou two wives, monster?
MACHEATH   If women's tongues can cease for an answer, hear me.
LUCY   I won't. Flesh and blood can't bear my usage.
POLLY   Shall I not claim my own? Justice bids me speak.

AIR 35.   Have you heard of a frolicsome ditty

MACHEATH

How happy could I be with either,
Were t'other dear charmer away!
But while you thus tease me together,
To neither a word will I say,
But tol de rol, etc.

POLLY   Sure, my dear, there ought to be some preference shown to a wife. At least she may claim the appearance of it. He must be distracted with his misfortunes, or he could not use me thus!
LUCY   Oh villain, villain! Thou hast deceived me. I could even inform against thee with pleasure. Not a prude wishes more heartily to have facts[5] against her intimate acquaintance, than I now wish to have facts against thee. I would have her satisfaction, and they should all out.

AIR 36.   Irish trot

POLLY   *I'm bubbled.*[6]
LUCY   *I'm bubbled.*
POLLY   *O how I am troubled!*
LUCY   *Bamboozled, and bit!*
POLLY   *My distresses are doubled.*
LUCY   *When you come to the tree, should the hangman refuse,*
       These fingers, with pleasure, could fasten the noose.
POLLY   *I'm bubbled, etc.*

MACHEATH   Be pacified, my dear Lucy. This is all a fetch[7] of Polly's, to make me desperate with you in case I get off. If I am hanged, she would fain have the credit of being thought my widow. Really, Polly, this is no time for a dispute of this sort; for whenever you are talking of marriage, I am thinking of hanging.
POLLY   And hast thou the heart to persist in disowning me?
MACHEATH   And hast thou the heart to persist in persuading me that I am married? Why, Polly, dost thou seek to aggravate my misfortunes?
LUCY   Really, Miss Peachum, you but expose yourself. Besides, 'tis barbarous in you to worry a gentleman in his circumstances.

AIR 37.

POLLY

Cease your funning;
Force or cunning
Never shall my heart trapan.[8]
All these sallies
Are but malice
To seduce my constant man.

5. Incriminating information.
6. Cheated.
7. Ruse.
8. Beguile.

'Tis most certain,
By their flirting
Women oft have envy shown;
Pleased to ruin
Others wooing,
Never happy in their own!

Decency, madam, methinks might teach you to behave yourself with some reserve with the husband, while his wife is present.

MACHEATH   But seriously, Polly, this is carrying the joke a little too far.

LUCY   If you are determined, madam, to raise a disturbance in the prison, I shall be obliged to send for the turnkey to show you the door. I am sorry, madam, you force me to be so ill-bred.

POLLY   Give me leave to tell you, madam, these forward airs don't become you in the least, madam. And my duty, madam, obliges me to stay with my husband, madam.

AIR 38.   Good morrow, gossip Joan

LUCY   *Why how now, Madam Flirt?*
                  If you thus must chatter;
               And are for flinging dirt,
                  Let's try who best can spatter,
                              Madam Flirt!

POLLY   *Why how now, saucy jade?*
                  Sure the wench is tipsy!
[*To him.*]   *How can you see me made*
                  The scoff of such a gipsy?
[*To her.*]   *Saucy jade!*

SCENE 14

LUCY, MACHEATH, POLLY, PEACHUM

PEACHUM   Where's my wench? Ah hussy! Hussy! Come you home, you slut; and when your fellow is hanged, hang yourself, to make your family some amends.

POLLY   Dear, dear father, do not tear me from him. I must speak; I have more to say to him—Oh! Twist thy fetters about me, that he may not haul me from thee!

PEACHUM   Sure all women are alike! If ever they commit the folly, they are sure to commit another by exposing themselves. Away, not a word more. You are my prisoner now, hussy.

AIR 39.   Irish howl

POLLY   *No power on earth can e'er divide*
               The knot that sacred love hath tied.
               When parents draw against our mind,
               The true-love's knot they faster bind.
                  Oh, oh ray, oh Amborah—oh, oh, etc.

[*Holding* MACHEATH, PEACHUM *pulling her.*]

SCENE 15

LUCY, MACHEATH

MACHEATH   I am naturally compassionate, wife, so that I could not use the wench as she deserved; which made you at first suspect there was something in what she said.

LUCY   Indeed, my dear, I was strangely puzzled.

MACHEATH   If that had been the case, her father would never have brought me into this circumstance. No, Lucy, I had rather die than be false to thee.

LUCY   How happy am I, if you say this from your heart! For I love thee so, that I could sooner bear to see thee hanged than in the arms of another.

MACHEATH   But couldst thou bear to see me hanged?

LUCY   O Macheath, I can never live to see that day.

MACHEATH   You see, Lucy, in the account of love you are in my debt, and you must now be convinced that I rather choose to die than be another's. Make me, if possible, love thee more, and let me owe my life to thee. If you refuse to assist me, Peachum and your father will immediately put me beyond all means of escape.

LUCY   My father, I know, hath been drinking hard with the prisoners, and I fancy he is now taking his nap in his own room. If I can procure the keys, shall I go off with thee, my dear?

MACHEATH   If we are together, 'twill be impossible to lie concealed. As soon as the search begins to be a little cool, I will send to thee. 'Till then my heart is thy prisoner.

LUCY   Come then, my dear husband, owe thy life to me. And though you love me not, be grateful. But that Polly runs in my head strangely.

MACHEATH   A moment of time may make us unhappy forever.

AIR 40.   The lass of Patie's mill

LUCY

> *I like the fox shall grieve,*
> *   Whose mate hath left her side,*
> *Whom hounds, from morn to eve,*
> *   Chase o'er the country wide.*
> *Where can my lover hide?*
> *   Where cheat the weary pack?*
> *If love be not his guide,*
> *   He never will come back!*

Act 3

SCENE 1 *Newgate*

LOCKIT, LUCY

LOCKIT   To be sure, wench, you must have been aiding and abetting to help him to this escape.

LUCY   Sir, here hath been Peachum and his daughter Polly, and to be sure they know the ways of Newgate as well as if they had been born and bred in the place all their lives. Why must all your suspicion light upon me?

LOCKIT Lucy, Lucy, I will have none of these shuffling[9] answers.

LUCY Well then—if I know anything of him I wish I may be burnt!

LOCKIT Keep your temper, Lucy, or I shall pronounce you guilty.

LUCY Keep yours, sir. I do wish I may be burnt. I do. And what can I say more to convince you?

LOCKIT Did he tip handsomely? How much did he come down with? Come hussy, don't cheat your father, and I shall not be angry with you. Perhaps you have made a better bargain with him than I could have done. How much, my good girl?

LUCY You know, sir, I am fond of him, and would have given money to have kept him with me.

LOCKIT Ah Lucy! Thy education might have put thee more upon thy guard, for a girl in the bar of an ale house is always besieged.

LUCY Dear sir, mention not my education, for 'twas to that I owe my ruin.

AIR 41. If love's a sweet passion

When young at the bar you first taught me to score,
And bid me be free of my lips, and no more,
I was kissed by the parson, the squire, and the sot;
When the guest was departed, the kiss was forgot.
But his kiss was so sweet, and so closely he pressed,
That I languished and pined 'till I granted the rest.

If you can forgive me, sir, I will make a fair confession, for to be sure he hath been a most barbarous villain to me.

LOCKIT And so you have let him escape, hussy, have you?

LUCY When a woman loves, a kind look, a tender word can persuade her to anything. And I could ask no other bribe.

LOCKIT Thou wilt always be a vulgar slut, Lucy. If you would not be looked upon as a fool, you should never do anything but upon the foot of interest. Those that act otherwise are their own bubbles.[1]

LUCY But love, sir, is a misfortune that may happen to the most discreet woman, and in love we are all fools alike. Notwithstanding all he swore, I am now fully convinced that Polly Peachum is actually his wife. Did I let him escape (fool that I was!) to go to her? Polly will wheedle herself into his money, and then Peachum will hang him, and cheat us both.

LOCKIT So I am to be ruined because, forsooth, you must be in love! A very pretty excuse!

LUCY I could murder that impudent happy strumpet. I gave him his life, and that creature enjoys the sweets of it. Ungrateful Macheath!

AIR 42. South Sea ballad

My love is all madness and folly,
Alone I lie,
Toss, tumble, and cry,
What a happy creature is Polly!
Was e'er such a wretch as I!
With rage I redden like scarlet,
That my dear inconstant varlet,

9. Evasive.   1. Dupes.

> *Stark blind to my charms,*
> *Is lost in the arms*
> *Of that jilt, that inveigling harlot!*
> *Stark blind to my charms,*
> *Is lost in the arms*
> *Of that jilt, that inveigling harlot!*
> *This, this my resentment alarms.*

LOCKIT   And so, after all this mischief, I must stay here to be entertained with your caterwauling, Mistress Puss! Out of my sight, wanton strumpet! You shall fast and mortify yourself into reason, with now and then a little handsome discipline to bring you to your senses. Go.

SCENE 2

LOCKIT

Peachum then intends to outwit me in this affair; but I'll be even with him. The dog is leaky[2] in his liquor, so I'll ply him that way, get the secret from him, and turn this affair to my own advantage. Lions, wolves, and vultures don't live together in herds, droves, or flocks. Of all animals of prey, man is the only sociable one. Every one of us preys upon his neighbor, and yet we herd together. Peachum is my companion, my friend. According to the custom of the world, indeed, he may quote thousands of precedents for cheating me. And shall not I make use of the privilege of friendship to make him a return?

AIR 43.   Packington's pound

> *Thus gamesters united in friendship are found,*
> *Though they know that their industry all is a cheat;*
> *They flock to their prey at the dice-box's sound,*
> *And join to promote one another's deceit.*
> *But if by mishap*
> *They fail of a chap,[3]*
> *To keep in their hands, they each other entrap.*
> *Like pikes, lank with hunger, who miss of their ends,*
> *They bite their companions, and prey on their friends.*

Now, Peachum, you and I, like honest tradesmen, are to have a fair trial which of us two can overreach the other. Lucy! [*Enter* LUCY] Are there any of Peachum's people now in the house?
LUCY   Filch, sir, is drinking a quartern[4] of strong waters in the next room with Black Moll.
LOCKIT   Bid him come to me.

SCENE 3

LOCKIT, FILCH

LOCKIT   Why, boy, thou lookest as if thou wert half starved, like a shotten herring.[5]

---

2. A blabbermouth.
3. Customer or sucker.
4. Quarter of a pint.
5. A herring exhausted by spawning.

FILCH   One had need have the constitution of a horse to go through the business. Since the favorite child-getter[6] was disabled by a mishap, I have picked up a little money by helping the ladies to a pregnancy against their being called down to sentence. But if a man cannot get an honest livelihood any easier way, I am sure 'tis what I can't undertake for another Session.

LOCKIT   Truly, if that great man should tip off,[7] 'twould be an irreparable loss. The vigor and prowess of a knight-errant never saved half the ladies in distress that he hath done. But, boy, can'st thou tell me where thy master is to be found?

FILCH   At his lock, sir, at the Crooked Billet.

LOCKIT   Very well. I have nothing more with you. [*Exit* FILCH.] I'll go to him there, for I have many important affairs to settle with him; and in the way of those transactions, I'll artfully get into his secret. So that Macheath shall not remain a day longer out of my clutches.

SCENE 4 *A gaming-house*

MACHEATH *in a fine tarnished coat,* BEN BUDGE, MATT OF THE MINT

MACHEATH   I am sorry, gentlemen, the road was so barren of money. When my friends are in difficulties, I am always glad that my fortune can be serviceable to them. [*Gives them money.*] You see, gentlemen, I am not a mere court friend, who professes everything and will do nothing.

AIR 44.   Lillibullero

> The modes of the court so common are grown,
>   That a true friend can hardly be met;
> Friendship for interest is but a loan,
>   Which they let out for what they can get.
>   'Tis true, you find
>   Some friends so kind,
> Who will give you good counsel themselves to defend.
>   In sorrowful ditty,
>   They promise, they pity,
> But shift you for money, from friend to friend.

But we, gentlemen, have still honor enough to break through the corruptions of the world. And while I can serve you, you may command me.

BEN   It grieves my heart that so generous a man should be involved in such difficulties, as oblige him to live with such ill company, and herd with gamesters.

MATT   See the partiality of mankind! One man may steal a horse, better than another look over a hedge.[8] Of all mechanics,[9] of all servile handicraftsmen, a gamester is the vilest. But yet, as many of the quality are of the profession, he is admitted amongst the politest company. I wonder we are not more respected.

6. Stud.
7. Die.
8. I.e., a mere look at a horse can get some people in trouble.
9. Workers who use their hands.

MACHEATH There will be deep play tonight at Marybone, and consequently money may be picked up upon the road. Meet me there, and I'll give you the hint who is worth setting.[1]

MATT The fellow with a brown coat with a narrow gold binding, I am told, is never without money.

MACHEATH What do you mean, Matt? Sure you will not think of meddling with him! He's a good honest kind of a fellow, and one of us.

BEN To be sure, sir, we will put ourselves under your direction.

MACHEATH Have an eye upon the moneylenders. A rouleau,[2] or two, would prove a pretty sort of an expedition. I hate extortion.

MATT Those rouleaus are very pretty things. I hate your bank bills; there is such a hazard in putting them off.[3]

MACHEATH There is a certain man of distinction, who in his time hath nicked me out of a great deal of the ready.[4] He is in my cash,[5] Ben. I'll point him out to you this evening, and you shall draw upon him for the debt. The company are met; I hear the dicebox in the other room. So, gentlemen, your servant. You'll meet me at Marybone.

SCENE 5 *Peachum's Lock*

A table with wine, brandy, pipes, and tobacco

PEACHUM, LOCKIT

LOCKIT The Coronation account,[6] brother Peachum, is of so intricate a nature, that I believe it will never be settled.

PEACHUM It consists indeed of a great variety of articles. It was worth to our people, in fees of different kinds, above ten installments.[7] This is part of the account, brother, that lies open before us.

LOCKIT A lady's tail[8]—of rich brocade—that, I see, is disposed of.

PEACHUM To Mrs. Diana Trapes, the tallywoman, and she will make a good hand on't in shoes and slippers, to trick out young ladies, upon their going into keeping.[9]

LOCKIT But I don't see any article of the jewels.

PEACHUM Those are so well known, that they must be sent abroad. You'll find them entered under the article of exportation. As for the snuffboxes, watches, swords, etc., I thought it best to enter them under their several heads.

LOCKIT Seven and twenty women's pockets[1] complete, with the several things therein contained; all sealed, numbered, and entered.

PEACHUM But, brother, it is impossible for us now to enter upon this affair. We should have the whole day before us. Besides, the account of the last half year's plate[2] is in a book by itself, which lies at the other office.

---

1. Robbing.
2. Roll of gold coins.
3. Converting them into money.
4. Money.
5. He owes me.
6. Register of goods stolen during the coronation of George II (1727).

7. Public installations of the new Lord Mayor of London.
8. Train.
9. Becoming mistresses.
1. Purses worn around the waist.
2. Silver or gold utensils.

LOCKIT Bring us then more liquor. Today shall be for pleasure, tomorrow for business. Ah brother, those daughters of ours are two slippery hussies. Keep a watchful eye upon Polly, and Macheath in a day or two shall be our own again.

AIR 45. Down in the North Country

> *What gudgeons³ are we men!*
>   *Every woman's easy prey.*
> *Though we have felt the hook, again*
>   *We bite and they betray.*
>
> *The bird that hath been trapped,*
>   *When he hears his calling mate,*
> *To her he flies, again he's clapped*
>   *Within the wiry grate.*

PEACHUM But what signifies catching the bird, if your daughter Lucy will set open the door of the cage?

LOCKIT If men were answerable for the follies and frailties of their wives and daughters, no friends could keep a good correspondence together for two days. This is unkind of you, brother; for among good friends, what they say or do goes for nothing.

[*Enter a* SERVANT.]

SERVANT Sir, here's Mrs. Diana Trapes wants to speak with you.

PEACHUM Shall we admit her, brother Lockit?

LOCKIT By all means. She's a good customer, and a fine-spoken woman. And a woman who drinks and talks so freely, will enliven the conversation.

PEACHUM Desire her to walk in.

[Exit SERVANT.]

SCENE 6

PEACHUM, LOCKIT, MRS. TRAPES

PEACHUM Dear Mrs. Dye, your servant. One may know by your kiss that your gin is excellent.

MRS. TRAPES I was always very curious⁴ in my liquors.

LOCKIT There is no perfumed breath like it. I have been long acquainted with the flavor of those lips, han't I, Mrs. Dye?

MRS. TRAPES Fill it up. I take as large draughts of liquor, as I did of love. I hate a flincher in either.

AIR 46. A shepherd kept sheep

> *In the days of my youth I could bill like a dove, fa, la, la, etc.*
> *Like a sparrow at all times was ready for love, fa, la, la, etc.*
> *The life of all mortals in kissing should pass,*
> *Lip to lip while we're young—then the lip to the glass, fa, etc.*

3. Minnows.　　　　4. Choosy.

But now, Mr. Peachum, to our business. If you have blacks of any kind, brought in of late, mantoes[5]—velvet scarfs, petticoats—let it be what it will, I am your chap. For all my ladies are very fond of mourning.

PEACHUM   Why, look ye, Mrs. Dye, you deal so hard with us that we can afford to give the gentlemen who venture their lives for the goods little or nothing.

MRS. TRAPES   The hard times oblige me to go very near[6] in my dealing. To be sure, of late years I have been a great sufferer by the Parliament—three thousand pounds would hardly make me amends. The Act for destroying the Mint[7] was a severe cut upon our business. 'Till then, if a customer stepped out of the way, we knew where to have her. No doubt you know Mrs. Coaxer. There's a wench now (till today) with a good suit of clothes of mine upon her back, and I could never set eyes upon her for three months together. Since the Act too against imprisonment for small sums,[8] my loss there too hath been very considerable, and it must be so, when a lady can borrow a handsome petticoat or a clean gown, and I not have the least hank[9] upon her! And o' my conscience, nowadays most ladies take a delight in cheating, when they can do it with safety.

PEACHUM   Madam, you had a handsome gold watch of us t'other day for seven guineas. Considering we must have our profit, to a gentleman upon the road, a gold watch will be scarce worth the taking.

MRS. TRAPES   Consider, Mr. Peachum, that watch was remarkable, and not of very safe sale. If you have any black velvet scarfs, they are a handsome winter wear, and take with most gentlemen who deal with my customers. 'Tis I that put the ladies upon a good foot. 'Tis not youth or beauty that fixes their price. The gentlemen always pay according to their dress, from half a crown to two guineas; and yet those hussies make nothing of bilking of me. Then too, allowing for accidents—I have eleven fine customers now down under the surgeon's hands. What with fees and other expenses, there are great goings-out, and no comings-in, and not a farthing to pay for at least a month's clothing. We run great risks, great risks indeed.

PEACHUM   As I remember, you said something just now of Mrs. Coaxer.

MRS. TRAPES   Yes, sir. To be sure I stripped her of a suit of my own clothes about two hours ago; and have left her as she should be, in her shift, with a lover of hers at my house. She called him upstairs, as he was going to Marybone in a hackney coach. And I hope, for her own sake and mine, she will persuade the Captain to redeem her, for the Captain is very generous to the ladies.

LOCKIT   What Captain?

MRS. TRAPES   He thought I did not know him. An intimate acquaintance of yours, Mr. Peachum. Only Captain Macheath—as fine as a lord.

PEACHUM   Tomorrow, dear Mrs. Dye, you shall set your own price upon any of the goods you like. We have at least half a dozen velvet scarfs, and all at your service. Will you give me leave to make you a present of this suit of night-clothes for your own wearing? But are you sure it is Captain Macheath?

5. Mantles or cloaks. "Blacks": mourning clothes.
6. Stingy.
7. The status of the Mint district as a sanctuary for outlaws had been undermined by recent statutes.
8. Previous to this act, someone could be arrested for owing any sum, however small.
9. Hold.

MRS. TRAPES   Though he thinks I have forgot him, nobody knows him better. I have taken a great deal of the Captain's money in my time at second hand, for he always loved to have his ladies well dressed.

PEACHUM   Mr. Lockit and I have a little business with the Captain—you understand me—and we will satisfy you for Mrs. Coaxer's debt.

LOCKIT   Depend upon it. We will deal like men of honor.

MRS. TRAPES   I don't inquire after your affairs, so whatever happens, I wash my hands on't. It hath always been my maxim, that one friend should assist another. But if you please, I'll take one of the scarfs home with me. 'Tis always good to have something in hand.

SCENE 7 Newgate

LUCY

Jealousy, rage, love, and fear are at once tearing me to pieces. How I am weather-beaten and shattered with distresses!

AIR 47. One evening, having lost my way

> *I'm like a skiff on the ocean tossed,*
> *Now high, now low, with each billow born,*
> *With her rudder broke, and her anchor lost,*
> *Deserted and all forlorn.*
> *While thus I lie rolling and tossing all night,*
> *That Polly lies sporting on seas of delight!*
> *Revenge, revenge, revenge,*
> *Shall appease my restless sprite.*

I have the ratsbane[1] ready. I run no risk, for I can lay her death upon the gin, and so many die of that naturally that I shall never be called in question. But say I were to be hanged—I never could be hanged for anything that would give me greater comfort than the poisoning that slut.

[*Enter* FILCH.]

FILCH   Madam, here's our Miss Polly come to wait upon you.

LUCY   Show her in.

SCENE 8

LUCY, POLLY

LUCY   Dear madam, your servant. I hope you will pardon my passion when I was so happy to see you last. I was so overrun with the spleen[2] that I was perfectly out of myself. And really when one hath the spleen, everything is to be excused by a friend.

AIR 48.   Now Roger, I'll tell thee, because thou'rt my son

> *When a wife's in her pout,*
> *(As she's sometimes, no doubt!)*
> *The good husband as meek as a lamb,*
> *Her vapors[3] to still,*

---

1. Poison.
2. Fashionable seizure of peevishness or melan-   choly.
3. Ill humor or whims.

> *First grants her her will,*
> *And the quieting draught is a dram.*
> *Poor man! And the quieting draught is a dram.*

I wish all our quarrels might have so comfortable a reconciliation.

POLLY I have no excuse for my own behavior, madam, but my misfortunes. And really, madam, I suffer too upon your account.

LUCY But, Miss Polly, in the way of friendship, will you give me leave to propose a glass of cordial to you?

POLLY Strong waters are apt to give me the headache. I hope, madam, you will excuse me.

LUCY Not the greatest lady in the land could have better in her closet,[4] for her own private drinking. You seem mighty low in spirits, my dear.

POLLY I am sorry, madam, my health will not allow me to accept of your offer. I should not have left you in the rude manner I did when we met last, madam, had not my papa hauled me away so unexpectedly. I was indeed somewhat provoked, and perhaps might use some expressions that were disrespectful. But really, madam, the Captain treated me with so much contempt and cruelty that I deserved your pity rather than your resentment.

LUCY But since his escape, no doubt all matters are made up again. Ah Polly, Polly! 'Tis I am the unhappy wife, and he loves you as if you were only his mistress.

POLLY Sure, madam, you cannot think me so happy as to be the object of your jealousy. A man is always afraid of a woman who loves him too well, so that I must expect to be neglected and avoided.

LUCY Then our cases, my dear Polly, are exactly alike. Both of us indeed have been too fond.

AIR 49.   O Bessy Bell

POLLY	*A curse attends that woman's love,*
	Who always would be pleasing.
LUCY	*The pertness of the billing dove,*
	Like tickling, is but teasing.
POLLY	*What then in love can woman do?*
LUCY	*If we grow fond they shun us.*
POLLY	*And when we fly them, they pursue.*
LUCY	*But leave us when they've won us.*

Love is so very whimsical in both sexes, that it is impossible to be lasting. But my heart is particular, and contradicts my own observation.

POLLY But really, Mistress Lucy, by his last behavior I think I ought to envy you. When I was forced from him, he did not show the least tenderness. But perhaps he hath a heart not capable of it.

AIR 50.   Would Fate to me Belinda give

> *Among the men, coquettes we find,*
> *Who court by turns all womankind;*
> *And we grant all their hearts desired,*
> *When they are flattered, and admired.*

---

4. Small private room.

The coquettes of both sexes are self-lovers, and that is a love no other whatever can dispossess. I fear, my dear Lucy, our husband is one of those.

LUCY Away with these melancholy reflections. Indeed, my dear Polly, we are both of us a cup too low. Let me prevail upon you, to accept of my offer.

AIR 51. Come, sweet lass

Come sweet lass,
Let's banish sorrow
'Till tomorrow;
Come, sweet lass,
Let's take a chirping⁵ glass.
Wine can clear
The vapors of despair,
And make us light as air;
Then drink, and banish care.

I can't bear, child, to see you in such low spirits. And I must persuade you to what I know will do you good. [*Aside.*] I shall now soon be even with the hypocritical strumpet.

SCENE 9

POLLY

All this wheedling of Lucy cannot be for nothing. At this time too, when I know she hates me! The dissembling of a woman is always the forerunner of mischief. By pouring strong waters down my throat, she thinks to pump some secrets out of me. I'll be upon my guard, and won't taste a drop of her liquor, I'm resolved.

SCENE 10

LUCY, *with strong waters.* POLLY

LUCY Come, Miss Polly.

POLLY Indeed, child, you have given yourself trouble to no purpose. You must, my dear, excuse me.

LUCY Really, Miss Polly, you are so squeamishly affected about taking a cup of strong waters as a lady before company. I vow, Polly, I shall take it monstrously ill if you refuse me. Brandy and men (though women love them never so well) are always taken by us with some reluctance—unless 'tis in private.

POLLY I protest, madam, it goes against me.—What do I see! Macheath again in custody! Now every glimmering of happiness is lost. [*Drops the glass of liquor on the ground.*]

LUCY [*Aside.*] Since things are thus, I'm glad the wench hath escaped; for by this event, 'tis plain she was not happy enough to deserve to be poisoned.

5. Cheering.

SCENE 11[6]

LOCKIT, MACHEATH, PEACHUM, LUCY, POLLY

LOCKIT Set your heart to rest, Captain. You have neither the chance of love or money for another escape, for you are ordered to be called down upon your trial immediately.

PEACHUM Away, hussies! This is not a time for a man to be hampered with his wives. You see, the gentleman is in chains already.

LUCY O husband, husband, my heart longed to see thee; but to see thee thus distracts me!

POLLY Will not my dear husband look upon his Polly? Why hadst thou not flown to me for protection? With me thou hadst been safe.

AIR 52. The last time I went o'er the moor

POLLY	*Hither, dear husband, turn your eyes.*
LUCY	*Bestow one glance to cheer me.*
POLLY	*Think with that look, thy Polly dies.*
LUCY	*O shun me not, but hear me.*
POLLY	*'Tis Polly sues.*
LUCY	*—'Tis Lucy speaks.*
POLLY	*Is thus true love requited?*
LUCY	*My heart is bursting*
POLLY	*—Mine too breaks.*
LUCY	*Must I—*
POLLY	*—Must I be slighted?*

MACHEATH What would you have me say, ladies? You see, this affair will soon be at an end, without my disobliging either of you.

PEACHUM But the settling this point, Captain, might prevent a lawsuit between your two widows.

AIR 53. Tom Tinker's my true love

MACHEATH *Which way shall I turn me? How can I decide?*
Wives, the day of our death, are as fond as a bride.
One wife is too much for most husbands to hear,
But two at a time there's no mortal can bear.
This way, and that way, and which way I will,
What would comfort the one, t'other wife would take ill.

POLLY But if his own misfortunes have made him insensible to mine, a father sure will be more compassionate. Dear, dear sir, sink[7] the material evidence, and bring him off at his trial. Polly upon her knees begs it of you.

AIR 54. I am a poor shepherd undone

When my hero in court appears,
And stands arraigned for his life,
Then think of poor Polly's tears;

---

6. For an illustration of this scene by William Hogarth, see the color insert in this volume.   7. Suppress.

> For ah! Poor Polly's his wife.
> Like the sailor he holds up his hand,
> Distressed on the dashing wave.
> To die a dry death at land,
> Is as had as a wat'ry grave.
> And alas, poor Polly!
> Alack, and well-a-day!
> Before I was in love,
> Oh! every month was May.

LUCY If Peachum's heart is hardened, sure you, sir, will have more compassion on a daughter. I know the evidence is in your power: how then can you be a tyrant to me? [*Kneeling.*]

AIR 55. Ianthe the lovely

> When he holds up his hand arraigned for his life,
> Oh think of your daughter, and think I'm his wife!
> What are cannons, or bombs, or clashing of swords?
> For death is more certain by witnesses' words.
> Then nail up their lips, that dread thunder allay;
> And each month of my life will hereafter be May.

LOCKIT Macheath's time is come, Lucy. We know our own affairs, therefore let us have no more whimpering or whining.

AIR 56. A cobbler there was

> Ourselves, like the great, to secure a retreat,
> When matters require it, must give up our gang.
> And good reason why,
> Or, instead of the fry,
> Even Peachum and I,
> Like poor petty rascals, might hang, hang;
> Like poor petty rascals, might hang.

PEACHUM Set your heart at rest, Polly. Your husband is to die today. Therefore, if you are not already provided, 'tis high time to look about for another. There's comfort for you, you slut.

LOCKIT We are ready, sir, to conduct you to the Old Bailey.

AIR 57. Bonny Dundee

MACHEATH
> The charge is prepared; the lawyers are met;
> The judges all ranged (a terrible show!).
> I go, undismayed, for death is a debt,
> A debt on demand. So take what I owe.
> Then farewell my love—dear charmers, adieu.
> Contented I die—'tis the better for you.
> Here ends all dispute the rest of our lives,
> For this way at once I please all my wives.

Now, gentlemen, I am ready to attend you.

SCENE 12

LUCY, POLLY, FILCH

POLLY   Follow them, Filch, to the court. And when the trial is over, bring me a particular account of his behavior, and of everything that happened. You'll find me here with Miss Lucy. [*Exit* FILCH.] But why is all this music?

LUCY   The prisoners whose trials are put off till next Session are diverting themselves.

POLLY   Sure there is nothing so charming as music, I'm fond of it to distraction. But alas! Now all mirth seems an insult upon my affliction. Let us retire, my dear Lucy, and indulge our sorrows. The noisy crew, you see, are coming upon us.   [*Exeunt.*]
      [*A Dance of Prisoners in Chains, etc.*]

SCENE 13 The condemned hold

MACHEATH, in a melancholy posture

AIR 58.   Happy groves

> *O cruel, cruel, cruel case!*
> *Must I suffer this disgrace?*

AIR 59.   Of all the girls that are so smart

> *Of all the friends in time of grief,*
> *When threat'ning death looks grimmer,*
> *Not one so sure can bring relief,*
> *As this best friend, a brimmer.*[8]   [*Drinks.*]

AIR 60.   Britons strike home

> *Since I must swing, I scorn, I scorn to wince or whine.*   [*Rises.*]

AIR 61.   Chevy Chase

> *But now again my spirits sink;*
> *I'll raise them high with wine.*
>   [*Drinks a glass of wine.*]

AIR 62.   To old Sir Simon the King

> *But valor the stronger grows,*
> *The stronger liquor we're drinking.*
> *And how can we feel our woes,*
> *When we've lost the trouble of thinking?*   [*Drinks.*]

AIR 63.   Joy to great Caesar

> *If thus—A man can die*
> *Much bolder with brandy.*
>   [*Pours out a bumper of brandy.*]

8. Brimming goblet.

AIR 64. There was an old woman

So I drink off this bumper. And now I can stand the test.
And my comrades shall see, that I die as brave as the best. [*Drinks.*]

AIR 65. Did you ever hear of a gallant sailor

But can I leave my pretty hussies,
Without one tear, or tender sigh?

AIR 66. Why are mine eyes still flowing

Their eyes, their lips, their busses[9]
Recall my love. Ah must I die?

AIR 67. Green sleeves

Since laws were made for every degree,
To curb vice in others, as well as me,
I wonder we han't better company,
Upon Tyburn Tree!
But gold from law can take out the sting;
And if rich men like us were to swing,
'Twould thin the land, such numbers to string
Upon Tyburn Tree!

JAILER Some friends of yours, Captain, desire to be admitted. I leave you together.

SCENE 14

MACHEATH, BEN BUDGE, MATT OF THE MINT

MACHEATH For my having broke prison, you see, gentlemen, I am ordered immediate execution. The sheriff's officers, I believe, are now at the door. That Jemmy Twitcher should peach me, I own surprised me! 'Tis a plain proof that the world is all alike, and that even our gang can no more trust one another than other people. Therefore, I beg you, gentlemen, look well to yourselves, for in all probability you may live some months longer.

MATT We are heartily sorry, Captain, for your misfortune. But 'tis what we must all come to.

MACHEATH Peachum and Lockit, you know, are infamous scoundrels. Their lives are as much in your power as yours are in theirs. Remember your dying friend! 'Tis my last request. Bring those villains to the gallows before you, and I am satisfied.

MATT We'll do't.

JAILER Miss Polly and Miss Lucy entreat a word with you.

MACHEATH Gentlemen, adieu.

SCENE 15

LUCY, MACHEATH, POLLY

MACHEATH Lucy, my dear Polly, whatsoever hath passed between us is now at an end. If you are fond of marrying again, the best advice I can

---

9. Kisses.

give you, is to ship yourselves off for the West Indies,[1] where you'll have a fair chance of getting a husband apiece; or by good luck, two or three, as you like best.

POLLY   How can I support this sight!

LUCY   There is nothing moves one so much as a great man in distress.

AIR 68.   All you that must take a leap

LUCY	*Would I might be hanged!*
POLLY	*And I would so too!*
LUCY	*To be hanged with you.*
POLLY	*My dear, with you.*
MACHEATH	*O leave me to thought! I fear! I doubt!*
	I tremble! I droop! See, my courage is out.
	[*Turns up the empty bottle.*]
POLLY	*No token of love?*
MACHEATH	*See, my courage is out.*
	[*Turns up the empty pot.*]
LUCY	*No token of love?*
POLLY	*Adieu.*
LUCY	*Farewell.*
MACHEATH	*But hark! I hear the toll of the bell.*[2]
CHORUS	*Tol de rol lol, etc.*

JAILER   Four women more, Captain, with a child apiece! See, here they come. [*Enter women and children.*]

MACHEATH   What—four wives more! This is too much. Here—tell the sheriff's officers I am ready. [*Exit* MACHEATH *guarded.*]

SCENE 16

To them, enter PLAYER *and* BEGGAR

PLAYER   But, honest friend, I hope you don't intend that Macheath shall be really executed.

BEGGAR   Most certainly, sir. To make the piece perfect, I was for doing strict poetical justice. Macheath is to be hanged; and for the other personages of the drama, the audience must have supposed they were all either hanged or transported.

PLAYER   Why then, friend, this is a downright deep tragedy. The catastrophe is manifestly wrong, for an opera must end happily.

BEGGAR   Your objection, sir, is very just, and is easily removed. For you must allow that in this kind of drama 'tis no matter how absurdly things are brought about. So—you rabble there—run and cry a reprieve. Let the prisoner be brought back to his wives in triumph.

PLAYER   All this we must do, to comply with the taste of the town.

BEGGAR   Through the whole piece you may observe such a similitude of manners in high and low life, that it is difficult to determine whether (in the fashionable vices) the fine gentlemen imitate the gentlemen of the road, or the gentlemen of the road the fine gentlemen. Had the play

---

1. In the sequel to *The Beggar's Opera*, Polly does find a husband in the West Indies, where fortunes could be made.

2. Rung five minutes before the condemned were taken to Tyburn.

remained as I at first intended, it would have carried a most excellent moral. 'Twould have shown that the lower sort of people have their vices in a degree as well as the rich, and that they are punished for them.[3]

SCENE 17

To them, MACHEATH *with rabble, etc.*

MACHEATH   So, it seems, I am not left to my choice, but must have a wife at last. Look ye, my dears, we will have no controversy now. Let us give this day to mirth, and I am sure she who thinks herself my wife will testify her joy by a dance.

ALL   Come, a dance, a dance.

MACHEATH   Ladies, I hope you will give me leave to present a partner to each of you. And (if I may without offense) for this time, I take Polly for mine. [*To* POLLY.] And for life, you slut, for we were really married. As for the rest—But at present keep your own secret.

A DANCE

AIR 69.   Lumps of pudding

Thus I stand like the Turk, with his doxies around;
From all sides their glances his passion confound;
For black, brown, and fair, his inconstancy burns,
And the different beauties subdue him by turns;
Each calls forth her charms, to provoke his desires;
Though willing to all, with but one he retires.
But think of this maxim, and put off your sorrow,
The wretch of today may be happy tomorrow.

CHORUS   *But think of this maxim, etc.*

FINIS

1728

3. *Unlike* the rich.

WILLIAM HOGARTH
1697–1764

William Hogarth was a Londoner born and bred; the life of the city, both high and low, fills all his work. His early life was hard. When his father, a writer and teacher, failed in business, the family was confined to the area of the Fleet, the debtor's prison. Hogarth never forgot "the cruel treatment" of his father by booksellers, and he resolved to make his living without relying on dealers; he would always be aggressively independent. Apprenticed as an engraver, he trained himself to sketch scenes quickly or catch them in memory. He also learned to paint, studying with the Serjeant Painter to the King, Sir James Thornhill, whose daughter he married (late in life Hogarth himself would become Serjeant Painter). Gradually he won a reputation for portraits and conversation pieces—group portraits in which members of a family or assembly interact in a social situation. But his popular fame was forged by sets of pictures that told a story: *A Harlot's Progress* (1731–32), *A Rake's Progress* (1734–35), and *Marriage A-la-Mode* (1743–45). First Hogarth painted these Modern Moral Subjects (as he called them), then prints were made and sold in large editions. He also found new ways to market and protect his work; a copyright bill to ban cheap imitations of prints was known as "Hogarth's Act." Despite this success, however, his ambition to redefine British standards of art led to frustration. The high regard and high prices for continental old masters were too well entrenched to be undermined. Hogarth did not get prestigious commissions, and his *Analysis of Beauty* (1753), an effort to fix "the fluctuating ideas of taste" by appealing to practical observations, not academic rules, was poorly received. Political and aesthetic controversies embittered his final years.

Writers have always loved Hogarth's satiric art, and many have claimed him as one of their own. Swift, Fielding, and Sterne associated their work with his; Horace Walpole considered him more "a writer of comedy with a pencil" than a painter; Charles Lamb compared him to Shakespeare; and William Hazlitt included him among the great English comic writers. This emphasis may slight Hogarth's importance in the history of art. His attempts to found a British school that looked at life and nature directly, not through a haze of ideas or reverence for the past, and to give pleasure to common people, not only to critics and connoisseurs, opened the eyes of many artists to come. But Hogarth is also a great storyteller, someone to *read*. Like novels and plays, his pictures have plots and morals; they ask us not only to look but also to think. Yet looking and thinking are always intertwined. The mind delights in riddles, according to Hogarth; and as he revised his work he stuffed in more and more clues, like a mystery writer. A feast of interpretation draws the reader in. So many expressive details crowd the pictures, so many keys to character and meaning, that viewers often become obsessed with figuring them out. Even inanimate objects can speak; playwrights rely on words, as Walpole pointed out, but "it was reserved to Hogarth to write a scene of furniture."

The furniture is particularly eloquent in *Marriage A-la-Mode*; note, for example, the fallen chairs in Plates 2 and 6. Hogarth took special pains with this series. The audience at which he aimed, as well as the subject matter, belonged to high society; and the art too is highly refined. A sinuous line weaves through each picture, leading the reader on, and each piece of bric-a-brac carries a message of lavish excess. Yet the story itself is brutally straightforward. A disastrous forced marriage stands at the center: a rich but miserly merchant buys the worthless son of an aristocrat for his restless daughter, and with nothing in common the couple destroy one another. The crisis of values that Hogarth depicts was bringing about radical changes in English life. In the tension between a fading aristocracy, both morally and financially bankrupt, and an upwardly mobile middle class, greedy for power but culturally insecure, the marriage reflects a society that has lost all sense of right and wrong. The artist plays no favorites. The aristocratic Squanderfields are not only vain, effete, and dissipated but also lacking in taste; the wan mythological paintings on their walls are just the sort of pretentious, overpriced art that Hogarth hates. But the vulgar Dutch art on the merchant's walls (in Plate 6) seems even worse, and his daughter falls for every extravagant, spurious fashion (in Plate 4). Nor do the parasites who live off these easy marks offer any hope. Lawyer and doctor, bawd and servant pave the road to ruin. Hogarth's satire warns against the spreading corruption of modern times, when self-interest eats into marriage and old values die. Look hard, he tells the public. These objects make up the world we live in. We might become these people.

Many commentaries have been written on Hogarth's pictures. The notes printed here were supplied by the editors of this volume.

Marriage A-la-Mode

Plate 1. *The Marriage Contract*.   Lord Squanderfield points to the family tree, going back to William the Conquerer, that his son will bring to the marriage. Coronets are blazed all over the room, from the top of the canopy at the upper left to the lower right on the prostrate dog's side, incised just behind the shoulder. The earl, though hobbled by gout, is proud. But he has run out of money: construction has stopped on the Palladian mansion seen through the window. Sitting across from him, a squinting merchant grasps the marriage settlement. Some of the coins and banknotes he has placed on the table have been taken up by a scrawny usurer, who hands the earl a mortgage in return. At the right the betrothed sit back to back, uncaring as the dogs chained to each other below. The vacuous viscount pinches snuff and gazes at himself in a mirror, which ominously reflects the image of lawyer Silvertongue, who sharpens his pen as he bends unctuously over the bride-to-be. Pouting, she twirls her wedding ring in a handkerchief. Disasters from mythology cover the walls. A bombastic portrait of the earl as Jupiter, astride a cannon, dominates the room; and in a candle sconce on the right Medusa glowers over the scene.

Plate 2. *After the Marriage.* By now the couple are used to ignoring each other. The morning after a spree, the rumpled, exhausted viscount slouches in a chair. His broken sword has dropped on the carpet, and a lapdog sniffs at a woman's cap in his pocket—souvenirs of the night. Lolling and stretching in an unladylike pose, his wife too is half asleep. She has spent the night home but not alone. *Hoyle on Whist* lies before her, cards are scattered on the floor, and the overturned chair, book of music, and violin cases suggest that some player may have departed in haste. A steward carries away a sheaf of bills—only one paid—and the household ledger; a Methodist (*Regeneration* is in his pocket), he petitions heaven to look down on these heathens. Oriental idols decorate the mantel over the fireplace, surmounted by a broken-nosed Roman bust that frowns like the steward and a painting of Cupid playing the bagpipes. On the left, amid the shrubbery of a rococo clock, a cat leers over fish and a Buddha smiles. In the next room, a dozing servant fails to notice that a candle has set fire to a chair. Next to a row of saints, a curtain does not quite cover a bawdy painting from which a naked foot peeps.

Plate 3. *The Scene with the Quack.* The husband has come to this chamber of medical horrors in search of a cure. The pillbox he holds toward the quack has not done its job, and he raises his cane as if with a playful threat. Evidently the little girl who stands between his legs is infected. She dabs a sore on her lip, and her ageless face may hint that she is not as young and pure as she looks. Her cap resembles the cap in Plate 2; she is the husband's mistress. Perhaps the beauty spot on his neck also covers a sore. The bowlegged Monsieur de la Pillule comfortably wipes his glasses; he has seen all this before. Between the two men an angry woman, fortified by a massive hoop skirt, opens a knife. She may be the wife of the quack, defending her man, or else a bawd who resents the charge that her girls are damaged goods. Medical oddities and monstrosities clutter the room, along with portents of death. The viscount's cane points to a cabinet where a wigged head looks at a skeleton that seems to be groping a cadaver; the tripod above evokes a gallows tree. At the far left, in front of a laboratory door, are two of the doctor's inventions: machines for setting bones and uncorking bottles. Their similarity to instruments of torture hints at how useful the doctor's assistance will be.

Plate 4. *The Countess's Levee.*   In her bedchamber at rising (*levée;* French), the countess receives some guests and puts on a show. Her husband is now earl (note the coronets), and they have a child (note the rattle on her chair). While a hairdresser curls her locks, she hangs on the words of Silvertongue, who makes himself at home (note his portrait on the upper right wall). Tonight they will be going to a masquerade ball, like the one on the screen he gestures toward; his left hand holds the tickets. At the far right a puffy, bedizened castrato sings, accompanied by a flute. His audience includes a self-absorbed dandy in curl-papers; a man who appreciatively smirks and opens his hand, from which a fan dangles; a snoring husband, holding his riding-crop like a baton; and his enraptured wife, who leans forward as if about to swoon. Unobserved by the others, a black servant, bearing a cup of chocolate, smiles in amazement at these precious airs. At the lower left another black servant, a boy in a turban, grins at gewgaws purchased at an auction. His finger points both to Actaeon's horns, the sign of a cuckold, and to the couple as they arrange their tryst. Wall paintings illustrate unnatural sex: Lot's seduction by his daughters, Jupiter embracing Io, and the rape of Ganymede.

Plate 5. ***The Death of the Earl.*** The melodramatic tableau at the center, as the earl totters toward death and the countess kneels to beg forgiveness, imitates paintings of Christ descending from the cross while Mary Magdalen mourns. But the surroundings are sordid. At a house of ill repute, the Turk's Head Bagnio, the countess and Silvertongue have been surprised in bed. The earl has broken in (key and socket on the floor) and drawn his sword, and the lawyer has run him through. As the horrified owner and constable enter, under a watchman's lantern, the killer, still in his nightshirt, flees through a window. A fire, outside the picture on the lower right, casts lurid light on the victim; the shadow of the tongs encircles the murder weapon. Costumed as a nun and friar, the lovers have come from a masquerade, and their discarded masks and clothes show they were in haste. Pills (presumably mercury, prescribed for venereal disease) have spilled from an overturned table on the right, beside an advertisement for the bagnio, a corset, and a bundle of firewood. The portrait of a streetwalker, a squirrel perched on her hand, leers over the countess; on the wall behind the earl an uplifted blade is about to sever a child, in the Judgment of Solomon. At the top left St. Luke, the patron of artists, inscribes these transgressions.

Plate 6. *The Death of the Countess.* "Counseller Silvertongues Last Dying Speech," a paper on the floor announces, and a bottle of laudanum has dropped beside it. News of her lover's execution has driven the countess to poison herself. Slumped in a chair, she is already dead; on the far right a doctor steals away. Her father calmly slides the ring from her finger. This is his house; a window with cobwebs and broken panes opens on London Bridge, in the heart of the City. No luxury here. The furnishings are sparse, the floor is bare, and the dining table holds only one egg and a few leftovers, including a pathetic boar's head from which a starving hound is tearing scraps. The art is equally cheap: a pissing boy, a jumbled still life, a pipe set alight by the glowing nose of a drunk. At the center, beneath a coatrack, a stout apothecary (stomach pump and julep in his pocket) points toward the empty bottle in reproof and pokes the servant who brought it—an idiot wearing a coat many sizes too large, the merchant's hand-me-down. The service staff is completed by a withered old woman who holds out the countess's little child for one last hug and kiss. But the mark on the child's cheek and the brace on its leg imply that disease has passed to the next generation. This noble family will have no heir.

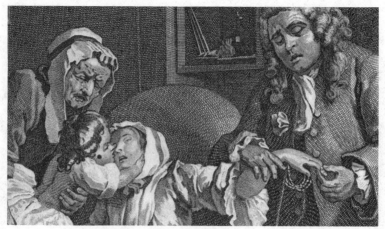

SAMUEL JOHNSON
1709–1784

amuel Johnson was famous as a talker in his own time, and his conversation (preserved by James Boswell and others) has been famous ever since. But his wisdom survives above all in his writings: a few superb poems; the grave *Rambler* essays, which established his reputation as a stylist and a moralist; the lessons about life in *Rasselas* and the *Lives of the Poets*; and literary criticism that ranks among the best in English. The virtues of the talk and the writings are the same. They come hot from a mind well stored with knowledge, searingly honest, humane, and quick to seize the unexpected but appropriate image of truth. Johnson's wit is timeless, for it deals with the great facts of human experience, with hope and happiness and loss and duty and the fear of death. Whatever topic he addresses, whatever the form in which he writes, he holds to one commanding purpose: to see life as it is.

Two examples must suffice here. When Anna Williams wondered why a man should make a beast of himself through drunkenness, Johnson answered that "he who makes a beast of himself gets rid of the pain of being a man." In this reply Williams's tired metaphor is so charged with an awareness of the dark aspects of human life that it comes almost unbearably alive. Such moments characterize Johnson's writings as well. For instance, in reviewing the book of a fatuous would-be philosopher who blandly explained away the pains of poverty by declaring that a kindly providence compensates the poor by making them more hopeful, more healthy, more easily pleased, and less sensitive than the rich, Johnson retorted: "The poor indeed are insensible of many little vexations which sometimes embitter the possessions and pollute the enjoyments of the rich. They are not pained by casual incivility, or mortified by the mutilation of a compliment; but this happiness is like that of a malefactor who ceases to feel the cords that bind him when the pincers are tearing his flesh."

Johnson had himself known the pains of poverty. During his boyhood and youth in Lichfield, his father's bookshop and other businesses plunged into debt, so that he was forced to leave Oxford before he had taken a degree. An early marriage to a well-to-do widow, Elizabeth ("Tetty") Porter, more than twenty years older than he, enabled him to open a school. But the school failed, and he moved to London to make his way as a writer. The years between 1737, when he first arrived there with his pupil David Garrick (who later became the leading actor of his generation), and 1755, when the publication of the *Dictionary* established his reputation, were often difficult. He supported himself at first as best he could by doing hack work for the *Gentleman's Magazine*, but gradually his own original writings began to attract attention.

In 1747 Johnson published the Plan of his *Dictionary*, and he spent the next seven years compiling it—although he had expected to finish it in three. When in 1748 Dr. Adams, a friend from Oxford days, questioned his ability to carry out such a work alone so fast and reminded him that the *Dictionary* of the French Academy had needed forty academicians working for forty years, Johnson replied with humorous jingoism: "Sir, thus it is. This is the proportion. Let me see; forty times forty is sixteen hundred. As three to sixteen hundred, so is the proportion of an Englishman to a Frenchman."

Johnson's achievement in compiling the *Dictionary* seems even greater when we realize that he was writing some of his best essays and poems during the same period. Although the booksellers who published the *Dictionary* paid him what was then the large sum of £1575, it was not enough to enable him to support his household, buy materials, and pay the wages of the six assistants whom he employed year by year until the task was accomplished. He therefore had to earn more money by writing. In 1749, his early tragedy *Irene* (pronounced *I-re-nĕ*) was produced at long last by his old friend Garrick, by then the manager of Drury Lane. The play was not a success, although Johnson made some profit from it. In the same year appeared his finest poem, "The Vanity of Human Wishes." With the *Rambler* (1750–52) and the *Idler* (1758–60), two series of periodical essays, Johnson found a devoted audience, but his pleasure was tempered by the death of his wife in 1752. He never remarried.

Boswell said of the *Rambler* essays that "in no writings whatever can be found more bark and steel [i.e., quinine and iron] for the mind." Moral strength and health; the importance of applying reason to experience; the test of virtue by what we do, not what we say or "feel"; faith in God: these are the centers to which Johnson's moral writings always return. What Johnson uniquely offers us is the quality of his understanding of the human condition, based on wide reading but always ultimately referred to his own passionate and often anguished experience. Such understanding had to be fought for again and again.

Johnson is thought of as the great generalizer, but what gives his generalizations strength is that they are rooted in the particulars of his self-knowledge. He had constantly to fight against what he called "filling the mind" with illusions to avoid the call of duty, his own black melancholy, and the realities of life. The portrait (largely a self-portrait) of Sober in *Idler* 31 is revealing: he occupies his idle hours with crafts and hobbies and has now taken up chemistry—he "sits and counts the drops as they come from his retort, and forgets that, whilst a drop is falling, a moment flies away."

His theme of themes is expressed in the title "The Vanity of Human Wishes": the dangerous but all-pervasive power of wishful thinking, the feverish intrusion of desires and hopes that distort reality and lead to false expectations. Almost all of Johnson's major writings—verse satire, moral essay, or the prose fable *Rasselas* (1759)—express this theme. In *Rasselas* it is called "the hunger of imagination, which preys upon life," picturing things as one would like them to be, not as they are. The travelers who are the fable's protagonists pursue some formula for happiness; they reflect our naive hope, against the lessons of experience, that one choice of life will make us happy forever.

Johnson also developed a style of his own: balanced, extended sentences, phrases, or clauses moving to carefully controlled rhythms, in language that is characteristically general, often Latinate, and frequently polysyllabic. This style is far from Swift's simplicity or Addison's neatness, but it never becomes obscure or turgid, for even a very complex sentence reveals—as it should—the structure of the thought, and the learned words are always precisely used. While reading early scientists to collect words for the *Dictionary*, Johnson developed a new vocabulary: for example, *obtund, exuberate, fugacity,* and *frigorific*. But he used many of these strange words in conversation as well as in his writings, often with a peculiarly Johnsonian felicity, describing the operations of the mind with a scientific precision.

After Johnson received his pension in 1762, he no longer had to write for a living, and because he held that "no man but a blockhead" ever wrote for any other reason, he produced as little as he decently could during the last twenty years of his life. His edition of Shakespeare, long delayed, was published in 1765, with a fine preface and fascinating notes. His last important work is the *Lives of the Poets*, which came out in two parts in 1779 and 1781. These biographical and critical prefaces were commissioned by a group of booksellers who had joined together to publish a large collection of the English poets and who wished to give their venture the prestige that Johnson would lend it. The poets to be included (except for four insisted on by Johnson) were selected by the booksellers according to current fashions. Therefore the collection begins with Abraham Cowley and John Milton and ends with Thomas Gray, and it omits such standard poets as Chaucer, Spenser, Sidney, Donne, and Marvell.

In the *Lives of the Poets* and in the earlier *Life of Richard Savage* (1744), Johnson did much to advance the art of biography in England. Biography had long been associated with panegyrics or scandalous memoirs; and therefore, Johnson's insistence on truth, even about the subject's defects, and on concrete, often minute, details was a new departure. "The biographical part of literature is what I love most," Johnson said, for he found every biography useful in revealing the human nature that all of us share. His insistence on truth in biography (and knowing that Boswell intended to write his life, he insisted that he should write it truthfully) was owing to his conviction that only a truthful work can be trusted to help us with the business of living.

The ideal poet, according to Johnson, has a genius for making the things we see every day seem new. The same might be said of Johnson himself as a critic. Johnson is our great champion, in criticism, of common sense and the common reader. Without denying the right of the poet to flights of imagination, he also insists that poems must make sense, please readers, and help us not only understand the world but cope with it. Johnson holds poems to the truth, as he sees it: the principles of nature, logic, religion, and morality. Not even Shakespeare can be excused when "he sacrifices virtue to convenience" and "seems to write without any moral purpose." Yet Johnson is no worshiper of authority or mere "correctness." As a critic he is always the empiricist, testing theory by practice. His determination to judge literature by its truth to life, not by abstract rules, is perfectly illustrated by his treatment of the doctrine of the three unities in the Preface to Shakespeare. Johnson is never afraid to state the obvious, whether the lack of human interest in *Paradise Lost* or Shakespeare's temptation by puns. But at its best, as in the praise of Milton or Shakespeare, his criticism engages some of the deepest questions about literature: why it endures, and how it helps us endure.

The Vanity of Human Wishes   This poem is an imitation of Juvenal's *Satire 10*. Although it closely follows the order and the ideas of the Latin poem, it remains a very personal work, for Johnson has used the Roman Stoic's satire as a means of expressing his own sense of the tragic and comic in human life. He has tried to reproduce in English verse the qualities he thought especially Juvenalian: stateliness, pointed sentences, and declamatory grandeur. The poem is difficult because of the extreme compactness of the style: every line is forced to convey the greatest possible amount of meaning. Johnson believed that "great thoughts are always general," but he certainly did not intend that the general should fade into the abstract: observe, for example, how he makes personified nouns concrete, active, and dramatic by using them as subjects of active and dramatic verbs: "Hate *dogs* their flight, and Insult *mocks* their end" (line 78). But the difficulty of the poem is also related to its theme, the difficulty of seeing anything clearly on this earth. In a world of blindness and illusion, human beings must struggle to find a point of view that will not deceive them, and a happiness that can last.

The Vanity of Human Wishes

In Imitation of the Tenth Satire of Juvenal

Let Observation, with extensive view,
Survey mankind, from China to Peru;
Remark each anxious toil, each eager strife,
And watch the busy scenes of crowded life;
5   Then say how hope and fear, desire and hate
O'erspread with snares the clouded maze of fate,

Where wavering man, betrayed by venturous Pride
To tread the dreary paths without a guide,
As treacherous phantoms in the mist delude,
10 Shuns fancied ills, or chases airy good.
How rarely Reason guides the stubborn choice,
Rules the bold hand, or prompts the suppliant voice;
How nations sink, by darling schemes oppressed,
When Vengeance listens to the fool's request.
15 Fate wings with every wish the afflictive dart,
Each gift of nature, and each grace of art;
With fatal heat impetuous courage glows,
With fatal sweetness elocution flows,
Impeachment stops the speaker's powerful breath,
20 And restless fire precipitates on death.
   But scarce observed, the knowing and the bold
Fall in the general massacre of gold;
Wide-wasting pest! that rages unconfined,
And crowds with crimes the records of mankind;
25 For gold his sword the hireling ruffian draws,
For gold the hireling judge distorts the laws;
Wealth heaped on wealth, nor truth nor safety buys,
The dangers gather as the treasures rise.
   Let History tell where rival kings command,
30 And dubious title° shakes the madded land,   *claim of right*
When statutes glean the refuse of the sword,
How much more safe the vassal than the lord;
Low skulks the hind° beneath the rage of power,   *peasant*
And leaves the wealthy traitor in the Tower,[1]
35 Untouched his cottage, and his slumbers sound,
Though Confiscation's vultures hover round.
   The needy traveler, serene and gay,
Walks the wild heath, and sings his toil away.
Does envy seize thee? crush the upbraiding joy,
40 Increase his riches and his peace destroy;
New fears in dire vicissitude invade,
The rustling brake° alarms, and quivering shade,   *thicket*
Nor light nor darkness bring his pain relief,
One shows the plunder, and one hides the thief.
45 Yet still one general cry the skies assails,
And gain and grandeur load the tainted gales;
Few know the toiling statesman's fear or care,
The insidious rival and the gaping heir.
   Once more, Democritus,[2] arise on earth,
50 With cheerful wisdom and instructive mirth,
See motley life in modern trappings dressed,
And feed with varied fools the eternal jest:
Thou who couldst laugh where Want enchained Caprice,
Toil crushed Conceit, and man was of a piece;

---

1. I.e., the Tower of London, which served as a prison. Johnson first wrote "bonny traitor," recalling the Jacobite uprising of 1745 and the execution of four of its Scot leaders.

2. A Greek philosopher of the late 5th century B.C.E., remembered as the "laughing philosopher" because men's follies only moved him to mirth.

55 Where Wealth unloved without a mourner died;
And scarce a sycophant was fed by Pride;
Where ne'er was known the form of mock debate,
Or seen a new-made mayor's unwieldy state;[3]
Where change of favorites made no change of laws,
60 And senates heard before they judged a cause;
How wouldst thou shake at Britain's modish tribe,
Dart the quick taunt, and edge the piercing gibe?
Attentive truth and nature to descry,
And pierce each scene with philosophic eye.
65 To thee were solemn toys or empty show
The robes of pleasure and the veils of woe:
All aid the farce, and all thy mirth maintain,
Whose joys are causeless, or whose griefs are vain.
    Such was the scorn that filled the sage's mind,
70 Renewed at every glance on human kind;
How just that scorn ere yet thy voice declare,
Search every state, and canvass every prayer.
    Unnumbered suppliants crowd Preferment's gate,
Athirst for wealth, and burning to be great;
75 Delusive Fortune hears the incessant call,
They mount, they shine, evaporate,[4] and fall.
On every stage the foes of peace attend,
Hate dogs their flight, and Insult mocks their end.
Love ends with hope, the sinking statesman's door
80 Pours in the morning worshiper no more;[5]
For growing names the weekly scribbler lies,
To growing wealth the dedicator flies;
From every room descends the painted face,
That hung the bright palladium[6] of the place;
85 And smoked in kitchens, or in auctions sold,
To better features yields the frame of gold;
For now no more we trace in every line
Heroic worth, benevolence divine:
The form distorted justifies the fall,
90 And Detestation rids the indignant wall.
    But will not Britain hear the last appeal,
Sign her foes' doom, or guard her favorites' zeal?
Through Freedom's sons no more remonstrance rings,
Degrading nobles and controlling kings;
95 Our supple tribes repress their patriot throats,
And ask no questions but the price of votes;
With weekly libels and septennial ale,[7]
Their wish is full to riot and to rail.

---

3. Pomp. Mayors organized costly processions.
4. Disperse in vapors, like fireworks.
5. Statesmen gave interviews and received friends and petitioners at levees, or morning receptions.
6. An image of Pallas Athena, that fell from heaven and was preserved at Troy. Not until it was stolen by Diomedes could the city fall to the Greeks.

7. Ministers and even the king freely bought support by bribing members of Parliament, who in turn won elections by buying votes. "Weekly libels": politically motivated lampoons published in the weekly newspapers. "Septennial ale": the ale given away by candidates at parliamentary elections, held at least every seven years.

In full-blown dignity, see Wolsey[8] stand,
100   Law in his voice, and fortune in his hand:
To him the church, the realm, their powers consign,
Through him the rays of regal bounty shine;
Turned by his nod the stream of honor flows,
His smile alone security bestows:
105   Still to new heights his restless wishes tower,
Claim leads to claim, and power advances power;
Till conquest unresisted ceased to please,
And rights submitted, left him none to seize.
At length his sovereign frowns—the train of state
110   Mark the keen glance, and watch the sign to hate.
Where'er he turns, he meets a stranger's eye,
His suppliants scorn him, and his followers fly;
At once is lost the pride of awful state,
The golden canopy, the glittering plate,
115   The regal palace, the luxurious board,
The liveried army, and the menial lord.
With age, with cares, with maladies oppressed,
He seeks the refuge of monastic rest.
Grief aids disease, remembered folly stings,
120   And his last sighs reproach the faith of kings.
     Speak thou, whose thoughts at humble peace repine,
Shall Wolsey's wealth, with Wolsey's end be thine?
Or liv'st thou now, with safer pride content,
The wisest justice on the banks of Trent?
125   For why did Wolsey, near the steeps of fate,
On weak foundations raise the enormous weight?
Why but to sink beneath misfortune's blow,
With louder ruin to the gulfs below?
     What gave great Villiers[9] to the assassin's knife,
130   And fixed disease on Harley's[1] closing life?
What murdered Wentworth, and what exiled Hyde,[2]
By kings protected, and to kings allied?
What but their wish indulged in courts to shine,
And power too great to keep or to resign?
135   When first the college rolls receive his name,
The young enthusiast quits his ease for fame;
Through all his veins the fever of renown
Burns from the strong contagion of the gown:[3]
O'er Bodley's dome[4] his future labors spread,
140   And Bacon's[5] mansion trembles o'er his head.

8. Thomas Cardinal Wolsey (ca. 1475–1530), lord chancellor and favorite of Henry VIII. Shakespeare dramatized his fall in *Henry VIII*.
9. George Villiers, first duke of Buckingham, favorite of James I and Charles I, was assassinated in 1628.
1. Robert Harley, earl of Oxford, chancellor of the exchequer and later lord treasurer under Queen Anne (1710–14), impeached and imprisoned by the Whigs in 1715.
2. Edward Hyde, earl of Clarendon ("to kings allied" because his daughter married James, duke

of York), lord chancellor under Charles II (impeached in 1667, he fled to the Continent). Thomas Wentworth, earl of Strafford, intimate and adviser of Charles I, impeached by the Long Parliament and executed in 1641.
3. Academic robe; here associated with the poisoned shirt that tormented Hercules.
4. The Bodleian Library, Oxford.
5. Roger Bacon (ca. 1214–1294), scientist and philosopher, taught at Oxford, where his study, according to tradition, would collapse if a man greater than he should appear at Oxford.

Are these thy views? proceed, illustrious youth,
And Virtue guard thee to the throne of Truth!
Yet should thy soul indulge the generous heat,
Till captive Science° yields her last retreat;   *knowledge*
145   Should Reason guide thee with her brightest ray,
And pour on misty Doubt resistless day;
Should no false kindness lure to loose delight,
Nor praise relax, nor difficulty fright;
Should tempting Novelty thy cell refrain,
150   And Sloth effuse her opiate fumes in vain;
Should Beauty blunt on fops her fatal dart,
Nor claim the triumph of a lettered heart;
Should no disease thy torpid veins invade,
Nor Melancholy's phantoms haunt thy shade;
155   Yet hope not life from grief or danger free,
Nor think the doom of man reversed for thee:
Deign on the passing world to turn thine eyes,
And pause a while from letters, to be wise;
There mark what ills the scholar's life assail,
160   Toil, envy, want, the patron,[6] and the jail.
See nations slowly wise, and meanly just,
To buried merit raise the tardy bust.
If dreams yet flatter, once again attend,
Hear Lydiat's life, and Galileo's[7] end.
165   Nor deem, when Learning her last prize bestows,
The glittering eminence exempt from foes;
See when the vulgar 'scapes, despised or awed,
Rebellion's vengeful talons seize on Laud.[8]
From meaner minds, though smaller fines content,
170   The plundered palace or sequestered rent;[9]
Marked out by dangerous parts° he meets   *accomplishments*
       the shock,
And fatal Learning leads him to the block:
Around his tomb let Art and Genius weep,
But hear his death, ye blockheads, hear and sleep.
175   The festal blazes, the triumphal show,
The ravished standard, and the captive foe,
The senate's thanks, the gazette's pompous tale,
With force resistless o'er the brave prevail.
Such bribes the rapid Greek° o'er Asia whirled,   *Alexander the Great*
180   For such the steady Romans shook the world;
For such in distant lands the Britons shine,
And stain with blood the Danube or the Rhine;
This power has praise that virtue scarce can warm,
Till fame supplies the universal charm.
185   Yet Reason frowns on War's unequal game,

6. In the first edition, "garret." For the reason of the change see Boswell's *Life of Johnson* (p. 841).
7. Astronomer (1564–1642) who was imprisoned as a heretic by the Inquisition in 1633; he died blind. Thomas Lydiat (1572–1646), Oxford scholar, died impoverished because of his Royalist sympathies.

8. Appointed archbishop of Canterbury by Charles I, William Laud followed rigorously High Church policies and was executed by order of the Long Parliament in 1645.
9. During the Commonwealth, the estates of many Royalists were pillaged and their incomes confiscated ("sequestered") by the state.

Where wasted nations raise a single name,
And mortgaged states their grandsires' wreaths regret
From age to age in everlasting debt;
Wreaths which at last the dear-bought right convey
190 To rust on medals, or on stones decay.
　　On what foundation stands the warrior's pride?
How just his hopes, let Swedish Charles[1] decide;
A frame of adamant, a soul of fire,
No dangers fright him, and no labors tire;
195 O'er love, o'er fear, extends his wide domain,
Unconquered lord of pleasure and of pain;
No joys to him pacific scepters yield,
War sounds the trump, he rushes to the field;
Behold surrounding kings their powers combine,
200 And one capitulate, and one resign;[2]
Peace courts his hand, but spreads her charms in vain;
"Think nothing gained," he cries, "till naught remain,
On Moscow's walls till Gothic standards fly,
And all be mine beneath the polar sky."
205 The march begins in military state,
And nations on his eye suspended wait;
Stern Famine guards the solitary coast,
And Winter barricades the realms of Frost;
He comes, nor want nor cold his course delay—
210 Hide, blushing Glory, hide Pultowa's day:
The vanquished hero leaves his broken bands,
And shows his miseries in distant lands;
Condemned a needy supplicant to wait,
While ladies interpose, and slaves debate.
215 But did not Chance at length her error mend?
Did no subverted empire mark his end?
Did rival monarchs give the fatal wound?
Or hostile millions press him to the ground?
His fall was destined to a barren strand,
220 A petty fortress, and a dubious hand;[3]
He left the name at which the world grew pale,
To point a moral, or adorn a tale.
　　All times their scenes of pompous woes afford,
From Persia's tyrant to Bavaria's lord.[4]
225 In gay hostility, and barbarous pride,
With half mankind embattled at his side,
Great Xerxes comes to seize the certain prey,
And starves exhausted regions in his way;
Attendant Flattery counts his myriads o'er,

1. Charles XII of Sweden (1682–1718). Defeated by the Russians at Pultowa (1709), he escaped to Turkey and tried to form an alliance against Russia with the sultan. Returning to Sweden, he attacked Norway and was killed in the attack on Fredrikshald.
2. Frederick IV of Denmark capitulated to Charles in 1700. Augustus II of Poland resigned his throne to Charles in 1704.
3. It was disputed whether Charles was shot by the enemy or by his own aide-de-camp.
4. The Elector Charles Albert caused the War of the Austrian Succession (1740–48) when he contested the crown of the empire with Maria Theresa ("Fair Austria" in line 245). "Persia's tyrant": Xerxes invaded Greece and was totally defeated in the sea battle off Salamis, 480 B.C.E.

230 Till counted myriads soothe his pride no more;
Fresh praise is tried till madness fires his mind,
The waves he lashes, and enchains the wind;[5]
New powers are claimed, new powers are still bestowed,
Till rude resistance lops the spreading god;
235 The daring Greeks deride the martial show,
And heap their valleys with the gaudy foe;
The insulted sea with humbler thoughts he gains,
A single skiff to speed his flight remains;
The encumbered oar scarce leaves the dreaded coast
240 Through purple billows and a floating host.
  The bold Bavarian, in a luckless hour,
Tries the dread summits of Caesarean power,
With unexpected legions bursts away,
And sees defenseless realms receive his sway;
245 Short sway! fair Austria spreads her mournful charms,
The queen, the beauty, sets the world in arms;
From hill to hill the beacon's rousing blaze
Spreads wide the hope of plunder and of praise;
The fierce Croatian, and the wild Hussar,[6]
250 With all the sons of ravage crowd the war;
The baffled prince in honor's flattering bloom
Of hasty greatness finds the fatal doom,
His foes' derision, and his subjects' blame,
And steals to death from anguish and from shame.
255   Enlarge my life with multitude of days!
In health, in sickness, thus the suppliant prays;
Hides from himself his state, and shuns to know,
That life protracted is protracted woe.
Time hovers o'er, impatient to destroy,
260 And shuts up all the passages of joy;
In vain their gifts the bounteous seasons pour,
The fruit autumnal, and the vernal flower;
With listless eyes the dotard views the store,
He views, and wonders that they please no more;
265 Now pall the tasteless meats, and joyless wines,
And Luxury with sighs her slave resigns.
Approach, ye minstrels, try the soothing strain,
Diffuse the tuneful lenitives of pain:°   *painkillers*
No sounds, alas! would touch the impervious ear,
270 Though dancing mountains witnessed Orpheus[7] near;
Nor lute nor lyre his feeble powers attend,
Nor sweeter music of a virtuous friend,
But everlasting dictates crowd his tongue,
Perversely grave, or positively wrong.
275 The still returning tale, and lingering jest,
Perplex the fawning niece and pampered guest,
While growing hopes scarce awe the gathering sneer,

5. When storms destroyed Xerxes' boats, he commanded his men to punish the wind and sea.
6. Hungarian light cavalry.
7. A legendary poet who played on the lyre so beautifully that even stones were moved.

And scarce a legacy can bribe to hear;
The watchful guests still hint the last offense,
280   The daughter's petulance, the son's expense,
Improve° his heady rage with treacherous skill,   *increase*
And mold his passions till they make his will.
Unnumbered maladies his joints invade,
Lay siege to life and press the dire blockade;
285   But unextinguished avarice still remains,
And dreaded losses aggravate his pains;
He turns, with anxious heart and crippled hands,
His bonds of debt, and mortgages of lands;
Or views his coffers with suspicious eyes,
290   Unlocks his gold, and counts it till he dies.
But grant, the virtues of a temperate prime
Bless with an age exempt from scorn or crime;
An age that melts with unperceived decay,
And glides in modest innocence away;
295   Whose peaceful day Benevolence endears,
Whose night congratulating Conscience cheers;
The general favorite as the general friend:
Such age there is, and who shall wish its end?
Yet even on this her load Misfortune flings,
300   To press the weary minutes' flagging wings;
New sorrow rises as the day returns,
A sister sickens, or a daughter mourns.
Now kindred Merit fills the sable bier,
Now lacerated Friendship claims a tear;
305   Year chases year, decay pursues decay,
Still drops some joy from withering life away;
New forms arise, and different views engage,
Superfluous lags the veteran[8] on the stage,
Till pitying Nature signs the last release,
310   And bids afflicted Worth retire to peace.
But few there are whom hours like these await,
Who set unclouded in the gulfs of Fate.
From Lydia's monarch[9] should the search descend,
By Solon cautioned to regard his end,
315   In life's last scene what prodigies surprise,
Fears of the brave, and follies of the wise!
From Marlborough's[1] eyes the streams of dotage flow,
And Swift[2] expires a driveler and a show.
The teeming mother, anxious for her race,°   *family*
320   Begs for each birth the fortune of a face:
Yet Vane[3] could tell what ills from beauty spring;
And Sedley[4] cursed the form that pleased a king.
Ye nymphs of rosy lips and radiant eyes,

8. I.e., of life, not of war.
9. Croesus, the wealthy and fortunate king, was warned by Solon not to count himself happy until he ceased to live. He lost his crown to Cyrus the Great of Persia.
1. John Churchill, duke of Marlborough, England's brilliant general during most of the

War of the Spanish Succession (1702–13).
2. Jonathan Swift, who passed the last four years of his life in utter senility.
3. Anne Vane, mistress of Frederick, Prince of Wales (son of George II).
4. Catherine Sedley, mistress of James II.

Whom Pleasure keeps too busy to be wise,
325 Whom Joys with soft varieties invite,
By day the frolic, and the dance by night;
Who frown with vanity, who smile with art,
And ask the latest fashion of the heart;
What care, what rules your heedless charms shall save,
330 Each nymph your rival, and each youth your slave?
Against your fame with Fondness Hate combines,
The rival batters, and the lover mines.[5]
With distant voice neglected Virtue calls,
Less heard and less, the faint remonstrance falls;
335 Tired with contempt, she quits the slippery reign,
And Pride and Prudence take her seat in vain.
In crowd at once, where none the pass defend,
The harmless freedom, and the private friend.
The guardians yield, by force superior plied:
340 To Interest, Prudence; and to Flattery, Pride.
Now Beauty falls betrayed, despised, distressed,
And hissing Infamy proclaims the rest.
   Where then shall Hope and Fear their objects find?
Must dull Suspense° corrupt the stagnant mind?   *uncertainty*
345 Must helpless man, in ignorance sedate,
Roll darkling down the torrent of his fate?
Must no dislike alarm, no wishes rise,
No cries invoke the mercies of the skies?
Inquirer, cease; petitions yet remain,
350 Which Heaven may hear, nor deem religion vain.
Still raise for good the supplicating voice,
But leave to Heaven the measure and the choice.
Safe in his power, whose eyes discern afar
The secret ambush of a specious prayer.
355 Implore his aid, in his decisions rest,
Secure, whate'er he gives, he gives the best.
Yet when the sense of sacred presence fires,
And strong devotion to the skies aspires,
Pour forth thy fervors for a healthful mind,
360 Obedient passions, and a will resigned;
For love, which scarce collective man can fill;[6]
For patience sovereign o'er transmuted ill;
For faith, that panting for a happier seat,
Counts death kind Nature's signal of retreat:
365 These goods for man the laws of Heaven ordain,
These goods he grants, who grants the power to gain;
With these celestial Wisdom calms the mind,
And makes the happiness she does not find.

1749

---

5. Plants mines beneath, as in the siege of a fortress.

6. Which humankind as a whole can hardly over-task.

On the Death of Dr. Robert Levet[1]

Condemned to Hope's delusive mine,
  As on we toil from day to day,
By sudden blasts, or slow decline,
  Our social comforts drop away.

5 Well tried through many a varying year,
  See Levet to the grave descend;
Officious,[2] innocent, sincere,
  Of every friendless name the friend.

Yet still he fills Affection's eye,
10   Obscurely wise, and coarsely kind;
Nor, lettered Arrogance, deny
  Thy praise to merit unrefined.

When fainting Nature called for aid,
  And hovering Death prepared the blow,
15 His vigorous remedy displayed
  The power of art without the show.

In Misery's darkest caverns known,
  His useful care was ever nigh,
Where hopeless Anguish poured his groan,
20   And lonely Want retired to die.

No summons mocked by chill delay,
  No petty gain disdained by pride,
The modest wants of every day
  The toil of every day supplied.

25 His virtues walked their narrow round,
  Nor made a pause, nor left a void;
And sure the Eternal Master found
  The single talent well employed.[3]

The busy day, the peaceful night,
30   Unfelt, uncounted, glided by;
His frame was firm, his powers were bright,
  Though now his eightieth year was nigh.

Then with no throbbing fiery pain,
  No cold gradations of decay,
35 Death broke at once the vital chain,
  And freed his soul the nearest way.

1783

1. An unlicensed physician who lived in Johnson's house for many years and died in 1782. His practice was among the very poor. Boswell wrote: "He was of a strange grostesque appearance, stiff and formal in his manner, and seldom said a word while any company was present."

2. "Kind, doing good offices" (Johnson's *Dictionary*).
3. In the parable of the talents (Matthew 25.14–30), Jesus suggests that salvation will be granted to those who make good use of their abilities, however small.

Rambler No. 4

[ON FICTION]

Saturday, March 31, 1750

Simul et jucunda et idonea dicere vitae.
—HORACE, *Art of Poetry*, 334

And join both profit and delight in one.
—CREECH

The works of fiction with which the present generation seems more particularly delighted are such as exhibit life in its true state, diversified only by accidents that daily happen in the world, and influenced by passions and qualities which are really to be found in conversing with mankind.

This kind of writing may be termed, not improperly, the comedy of romance, and is to be conducted nearly by the rules of comic poetry. Its province is to bring about natural events by easy means, and to keep up curiosity without the help of wonder: it is therefore precluded from the machines[1] and expedients of the heroic romance, and can neither employ giants to snatch away a lady from the nuptial rites, nor knights to bring her back from captivity; it can neither bewilder its personages in deserts, nor lodge them in imaginary castles.

I remember a remark made by Scaliger upon Pontanus,[2] that all his writings are filled with the same images; and that if you take from him his lilies and his roses, his satyrs and his dryads, he will have nothing left that can be called poetry. In like manner, almost all the fictions of the last age will vanish if you deprive them of a hermit and a wood, a battle and a shipwreck.

Why this wild strain of imagination found reception so long in polite and learned ages, it is not easy to conceive; but we cannot wonder that while readers could be procured, the authors were willing to continue it; for when a man had by practice gained some fluency of language, he had no further care than to retire to his closet, let loose his invention, and heat his mind with incredibilities; a book was thus produced without fear of criticism, without the toil of study, without knowledge of nature, or acquaintance with life.

The task of our present writers is very different; it requires, together with that learning which is to be gained from books, that experience which can never be attained by solitary diligence, but must arise from general converse and accurate observation of the living world. Their performances have, as Horace expresses it, *plus oneris quanto veniae minus,*[3] little indulgence, and therefore more difficulty. They are engaged in portraits of which everyone knows the original, and can detect any deviation from exactness of resemblance. Other writings are safe, except from the malice of learning, but these are in danger from every common reader; as the slipper ill executed was censured by a shoemaker who happened to stop in his way at the Venus of Apelles.[4]

---

1. The technical term in neoclassical critical theory for the supernatural agents who intervene in human affairs in epic and tragedy.
2. Julius Caesar Scaliger (1484–1558) criticized the Latin poems of the Italian poet Jovianus Pontanus (1426–1503).
3. *Epistles* 2.1.170.

4. According to Pliny the Younger (*Naturalis Historia* 35.85), the Greek painter Apelles of Kos (4th century B.C.E.) corrected the drawing of a sandal after hearing a shoemaker criticize it as faulty, but when the flattered artisan dared to find fault with the drawing of a leg, the artist bade him "stick to his last."

But the fear of not being approved as just copiers of human manners is not the most important concern that an author of this sort ought to have before him. These books are written chiefly to the young, the ignorant, and the idle, to whom they serve as lectures of conduct, and introductions into life. They are the entertainment of minds unfurnished with ideas, and therefore easily susceptible of impressions; not fixed by principles, and therefore easily following the current of fancy; not informed by experience, and consequently open to every false suggestion and partial account.

That the highest degree of reverence should be paid to youth, and that nothing indecent should be suffered to approach their eyes or ears, are precepts extorted by sense and virtue from an ancient writer by no means eminent for chastity of thought.[5] The same kind, though not the same degree, of caution, is required in everything which is laid before them, to secure them from unjust prejudices, perverse opinions, and incongruous combinations of images.

In the romances formerly written, every transaction and sentiment was so remote from all that passes among men that the reader was in very little danger of making any applications to himself; the virtues and crimes were equally beyond his sphere of activity; and he amused himself with heroes and with traitors, deliverers and persecutors, as with beings of another species, whose actions were regulated upon motives of their own, and who had neither faults nor excellencies in common with himself.

But when an adventurer is leveled with the rest of the world, and acts in such scenes of the universal drama as may be the lot of any other man, young spectators fix their eyes upon him with closer attention, and hope, by observing his behavior and success, to regulate their own practices when they shall be engaged in the like part.

For this reason these familiar histories may perhaps be made of greater use than the solemnities of professed morality, and convey the knowledge of vice and virtue with more efficacy than axioms and definitions. But if the power of example is so great as to take possession of the memory by a kind of violence, and produce effects almost without the intervention of the will, care ought to be taken that when the choice is unrestrained, the best examples only should be exhibited; and that which is likely to operate so strongly should not be mischievous or uncertain in its effects.

The chief advantage which these fictions have over real life is that their authors are at liberty, though not to invent, yet to select objects, and to cull from the mass of mankind those individuals upon which the attention ought most to be employed; as a diamond, though it cannot be made, may be polished by art, and placed in such situation as to display that luster which before was buried among common stones.

It is justly considered as the greatest excellency of art to imitate nature; but it is necessary to distinguish those parts of nature which are most proper for imitation: greater care is still required in representing life, which is so often discolored by passion or deformed by wickedness. If the world be promiscuously[6] described, I cannot see of what use it can be to read the account; or why it may not be as safe to turn the eye immediately upon mankind as upon a mirror which shows all that presents itself without discrimination.

5. Juvenal's *Satires* 14.1–58.
6. Indiscriminately.

It is therefore not a sufficient vindication of a character that it is drawn as it appears, for many characters ought never to be drawn; nor of a narrative that the train of events is agreeable to observation and experience, for that observation which is called knowledge of the world will be found much more frequently to make men cunning than good. The purpose of these writings is surely not only to show mankind, but to provide that they may be seen hereafter with less hazard; to teach the means of avoiding the snares which are laid by Treachery for Innocence, without infusing any wish for that superiority with which the betrayer flatters his vanity; to give the power of counteracting fraud without the temptation to practice it; to initiate youth by mock encounters in the art of necessary defense, and to increase prudence without impairing virtue.

Many writers, for the sake of following nature, so mingle good and bad qualities in their principal personages that they are both equally conspicuous; and as we accompany them through their adventures with delight, and are led by degrees to interest ourselves in their favor, we lose the abhorrence of their faults because they do not hinder our pleasure, or perhaps regard them with some kindness for being united with so much merit.[7]

There have been men indeed splendidly wicked, whose endowments threw a brightness on their crimes, and whom scarce any villainy made perfectly detestable because they never could be wholly divested of their excellencies; but such have been in all ages the great corrupters of the world, and their resemblance ought no more to be preserved than the art of murdering without pain.

Some have advanced, without due attention to the consequences of this notion, that certain virtues have their correspondent faults, and therefore that to exhibit either apart is to deviate from probability. Thus men are observed by Swift to be "grateful in the same degree as they are resentful." This principle, with others of the same kind, supposes man to act from a brute impulse, and pursue a certain degree of inclination without any choice of the object; for, otherwise, though it should be allowed that gratitude and resentment arise from the same constitution of the passions, it follows not that they will be equally indulged when reason is consulted; yet, unless that consequence be admitted, this sagacious maxim becomes an empty sound, without any relation to practice or to life.

Nor is it evident that even the first motions to these effects are always in the same proportion. For pride, which produces quickness of resentment, will obstruct gratitude by unwillingness to admit that inferiority which obligation implies; and it is very unlikely that he who cannot think he receives a favor will acknowledge or repay it.

It is of the utmost importance to mankind that positions of this tendency should be laid open and confuted; for while men consider good and evil as springing from the same root, they will spare the one for the sake of the other, and in judging, if not of others at least of themselves, will be apt to estimate their virtues by their vices. To this fatal error all those will contribute who confound the colors of right and wrong, and, instead of helping to

7. Johnson is probably thinking of such popular novels as Tobias Smollett's *Roderick Random* (1748) and Henry Fielding's *Tom Jones* (1749), as opposed to the model of virtue provided by Samuel Richardson's *Clarissa* (1747–48).

settle their boundaries, mix them with so much art that no common mind is able to disunite them.

In narratives where historical veracity has no place, I cannot discover why there should not be exhibited the most perfect idea of virtue; of virtue not angelical, nor above probability (for what we cannot credit, we shall never imitate), but the highest and purest that humanity can reach, which, exercised in such trials as the various revolutions of things shall bring upon it, may, by conquering some calamities and enduring others, teach us what we may hope, and what we can perform. Vice (for vice is necessary to be shown) should always disgust; nor should the graces of gaiety, nor the dignity of courage, be so united with it as to reconcile it to the mind. Wherever it appears, it should raise hatred by the malignity of its practices, and contempt by the meanness of its stratagems: for while it is supported by either parts[8] or spirit, it will be seldom heartily abhorred. The Roman tyrant was content to be hated if he was but feared;[9] and there are thousands of the readers of romances willing to be thought wicked if they may be allowed to be wits. It is therefore to be steadily inculcated that virtue is the highest proof of understanding, and the only solid basis of greatness; and that vice is the natural consequence of narrow thoughts; that it begins in mistake, and ends in ignominy.

Rambler No. 5[1]

[ON SPRING]

Tuesday, *April* 3, 1750

Et nunc omnis ager, nunc omnis parturit arbos,
Nunc frondent silvae, nunc formosissimus annus.
—VIRGIL, *Eclogues* 3.5.56

Now ev'ry field, now ev'ry tree is green;
Now genial nature's fairest face is seen.
—ELPHINSTON

Every man is sufficiently discontented with some circumstances of his present state, to suffer his imagination to range more or less in quest of future happiness, and to fix upon some point of time, in which, by the removal of the inconvenience which now perplexes him, or acquisition of the advantage which he at present wants, he shall find the condition of his life very much improved.

When this time, which is too often expected with great impatience, at last arrives, it generally comes without the blessing for which it was desired; but we solace ourselves with some new prospect, and press forward again with equal eagerness.

---

8. Abilities.
9. The emperor Tiberius (see Suetonius's *Lives of the Caesars*).
1. The *Rambler*, almost wholly written by Johnson himself, appeared every Tuesday and Saturday from March 20, 1750, to March 14, 1752—years in which Johnson was writing the *Dictionary*. It is a successor of the *Tatler* and the *Spectator*, but it is much more serious in tone than the earlier periodicals. Johnson's reputation as a moralist and a stylist was established by these essays; because of them Boswell first conceived the ambition to seek Johnson's acquaintance.

It is lucky for a man, in whom this temper prevails, when he turns his hopes upon things wholly put of his own power; since he forbears then to precipitate[2] his affairs, for the sake of the great event that is to complete his felicity, and waits for the blissful hour, with less neglect of the measures necessary to be taken in the mean time.

I have long known a person of this temper, who indulged his dream of happiness with less hurt to himself than such chimerical wishes commonly produce, and adjusted his scheme with such address, that his hopes were in full bloom three parts of the year, and in the other part never wholly blasted. Many, perhaps, would be desirous of learning by what means he procured to himself such a cheap and lasting satisfaction. It was gained by a constant practice of referring the removal of all his uneasiness to the coming of the next spring; if his health was impaired, the spring would restore it; if what he wanted was at a high price, it would fall in value in the spring.

The spring, indeed, did often come without any of these effects, but he was always certain that the next would be more propitious; nor was ever convinced that the present spring would fail him before the middle of summer; for he always talked of the spring as coming till it was past, and when it was once past, everyone agreed with him that it was coming.

By long converse with this man, I am, perhaps, brought to feel immoderate pleasure in the contemplation of this delightful season; but I have the satisfaction of finding many, whom it can be no shame to resemble, infected with the same enthusiasm; for there is, I believe, scarce any poet of eminence, who has not left some testimony of his fondness for the flowers, the zephyrs, and the warblers of the spring. Nor has the most luxuriant imagination been able to describe the serenity and happiness of the golden age, otherwise than by giving a perpetual spring, as the highest reward of uncorrupted innocence.

There is, indeed, something inexpressibly pleasing, in the annual renovation of the world, and the new display of the treasures of nature. The cold and darkness of winter, with the naked deformity of every object on which we turn our eyes, make us rejoice at the succeeding season, as well for what we have escaped, as for what we may enjoy; and every budding flower, which a warm situation brings early to our view, is considered by us as a messenger to notify the approach of more joyous days.

The spring affords to a mind, so free from the disturbance of cares or passions as to be vacant[3] to calm amusements, almost every thing that our present state makes us capable of enjoying. The variegated verdure of the fields and woods, the succession of grateful odors, the voice of pleasure pouring out its notes on every side, with the gladness apparently conceived by every animal, from the growth of his food, and the clemency of the weather, throw over the whole earth an air of gaiety, significantly expressed by the smile of nature.

Yet there are men to whom these scenes are able to give no delight, and who hurry away from all the varieties of rural beauty, to lose their hours, and divert their thoughts by cards, or assemblies, a tavern dinner, or the prattle of the day.

---

2. "To hurry blindly or rashly" (Johnson's *Dictionary*).
3. "At leisure" (Johnson's *Dictionary*).

It may be laid down as a position which will seldom deceive, that when a man cannot bear his own company there is something wrong. He must fly from himself, either because he feels a tediousness in life from the equipoise of an empty mind, which, having no tendency to one motion more than another but as it is impelled by some external power, must always have recourse to foreign objects; or he must be afraid of the intrusion of some unpleasing ideas, and, perhaps, is struggling to escape from the remembrance of a loss, the fear of a calamity, or some other thought of greater horror.

Those whom sorrow incapacitates to enjoy the pleasures of contemplation, may properly apply to such diversions, provided they are innocent, as lay strong hold on the attention; and those, whom fear of any future affliction chains down to misery, must endeavor to obviate the danger.

My considerations shall, on this occasion, be turned on such as are burthensome to themselves merely because they want subjects for reflection, and to whom the volume of nature is thrown open, without affording them pleasure or instruction, because they never learned to read the characters.

A French author has advanced this seeming paradox, that *very few men know how to take a walk;* and, indeed, it is true, that few know how to take a walk with a prospect of any other pleasure, than the same company would have afforded them at home.

There are animals that borrow their color from the neighboring body, and, consequently, vary their hue as they happen to change their place. In like manner it ought to be the endeavor of every man to derive his reflections from the objects about him; for it is to no purpose that he alters his position, if his attention continues fixed to the same point. The mind should be kept open to the access of every new idea, and so far disengaged from the predominance of particular thoughts, as easily to accommodate itself to occasional entertainment.

A man that has formed this habit of turning every new object to his entertainment, finds in the productions of nature an inexhaustible stock of materials upon which he can employ himself, without any temptations to envy or malevolence; faults, perhaps, seldom totally avoided by those, whose judgment is much exercised upon the works of art. He has always a certain prospect of discovering new reasons for adoring the sovereign author of the universe, and probable hopes of making some discovery of benefit to others, or of profit to himself. There is no doubt but many vegetables and animals have qualities that might be of great use, to the knowledge of which there is not required much force of penetration, or fatigue of study, but only frequent experiments, and close attention. What is said by the chemists of their darling mercury, is, perhaps, true of everybody through the whole creation, that if a thousand lives should be spent upon it, all its properties would not be found out.

Mankind must necessarily be diversified by various tastes, since life affords and requires such multiplicity of employments, and a nation of naturalists[4] is neither to be hoped, or desired; but it is surely not improper to point out a fresh amusement to those who languish in health, and repine in plenty, for want of some source of diversion that may be less easily exhausted, and to

4. "A student in physicks, or natural philosophy" (Johnson's *Dictionary*).

inform the multitudes of both sexes, who are burthened with every new day, that there are many shows which they have not seen.

He that enlarges his curiosity after the works of nature, demonstrably multiplies the inlets to happiness; and, therefore, the younger part of my readers, to whom I dedicate this vernal speculation, must excuse me for calling upon them, to make use at once of the spring of the year, and the spring of life; to acquire, while their minds may be yet impressed with new images, a love of innocent pleasures, and an ardor for useful knowledge; and to remember, that a blighted spring makes a barren year, and that the vernal flowers, however beautiful and gay, are only intended by nature as preparatives to autumnal fruits.

Rambler No. 60

[BIOGRAPHY]

Saturday, *October* 13, 1750

—Quid sit pulchrum, quid turpe, quid utile, quid non,
Plenius ac melius Chrysippo et Crantore dicit.
—HORACE, *Epistles*, 1.2.3–4

Whose works the beautiful and base contain,
Of vice and virtue more instructive rules,
Than all the sober sages of the schools.
—FRANCIS

All joy or sorrow for the happiness or calamities of others is produced by an act of the imagination, that realizes the event, however fictitious, or approximates it,[1] however remote, by placing us, for a time, in the condition of him whose fortune we contemplate; so that we feel, while the deception lasts, whatever motions would be excited by the same good or evil happening to ourselves.

Our passions are therefore more strongly moved, in proportion as we can more readily adopt the pains or pleasure proposed to our minds, by recognizing them as once our own, or considering them as naturally incident to our state of life. It is not easy for the most artful writer to give us an interest in happiness or misery, which we think ourselves never likely to feel, and with which we have never yet been made acquainted. Histories of the downfall of kingdoms, and revolutions of empires, are read with great tranquility; the imperial tragedy pleases common auditors only by its pomp of ornament, and grandeur of ideas; and the man whose faculties have been engrossed by business, and whose heart never fluttered but at the rise or fall of stocks, wonders how the attention can be seized, or the affections agitated, by a tale of love.

Those parallel circumstances, and kindred images to which we readily conform our minds, are, above all other writings, to be found in narratives

1. Brings it near.

of the lives of particular persons; and therefore no species of writing seems more worthy of cultivation than biography, since none can be more delightful or more useful, none can more certainly enchain the heart by irresistible interest, or more widely diffuse instruction to every diversity of condition.

The general and rapid narratives of history, which involve a thousand fortunes in the business of a day, and complicate[2] innumerable incidents in one great transaction, afford few lessons applicable to private life, which derives its comforts and its wretchedness from the right or wrong management of things, which nothing but their frequency makes considerable, *Parva si non fiunt quotidie*, says Pliny,[3] and which can have no place in those relations which never descend below the consultation of senates, the motions of armies, and the schemes of conspirators.

I have often thought that there has rarely passed a life of which a judicious and faithful narrative would not be useful. For, not only every man has in the mighty mass of the world great numbers in the same condition with himself, to whom his mistakes and miscarriages, escapes and expedients, would be of immediate and apparent use; but there is such an uniformity in the state of man, considered apart from adventitious and separable decorations and disguises, that there is scarce any possibility of good or ill, but is common to humankind. A great part of the time of those who are placed at the greatest distance by fortune, or by temper, must unavoidably pass in the same manner; and though, when the claims of nature are satisfied, caprice, and vanity, and accident, begin to produce discriminations and peculiarities, yet the eye is not very heedful or quick, which cannot discover the same causes still[4] terminating their influence in the same effects, though sometimes accelerated, sometimes retarded, or perplexed by multiplied combinations. We are all prompted by the same motives, all deceived by the same fallacies, all animated by hope, obstructed by danger, entangled by desire, and seduced by pleasure.

It is frequently objected to relations of particular lives, that they are not distinguished by any striking or wonderful vicissitudes. The scholar who passed his life among his books, the merchant who conducted only his own affairs, the priest whose sphere of action was not extended beyond that of his duty, are considered as no proper objects of public regard, however they might have excelled in their several stations, whatever might have been their learning, integrity, and piety. But this notion arises from false measures of excellence and dignity, and must be eradicated by considering, that in the esteem of uncorrupted reason, what is of most use is of most value.

It is, indeed, not improper to take honest advantages of prejudice, and to gain attention by a celebrated name; but the business of the biographer is often to pass slightly over those performances and incidents, which produce vulgar greatness, to lead the thoughts into domestic privacies, and display the minute details of daily life, where exterior appendages are cast aside, and men excel each other only by prudence and by virtue. The account of Thuanus[5] is, with great propriety, said by its author to have been written,

---

2. Join.
3. Pliny the Younger's *Epistles* 3.1. Johnson translates the phrase in the preceding clause.
4. Always.

5. Jacques-Auguste de Thou (1553–1617), an important French historian, of whom Nicholas Rigault wrote a brief biography, a sentence of which Johnson quotes and translates below.

that it might lay open to posterity the private and familiar character of that man, *cujus ingenium et candorem ex ipsius scriptis sunt olim semper miraturi,* whose candor and genius will to the end of time be by his writings preserved in admiration.

There are many invisible circumstances which, whether we read as inquirers after natural or moral knowledge, whether we intend to enlarge our science, or increase our virtue, are more important than public occurrences. Thus Sallust, the great master of nature, has not forgot, in his account of Catiline,[6] to remark that *his walk was now quick, and again slow,* as an indication of a mind revolving something with violent commotion. Thus the story of Melancthon[7] affords a striking lecture on the value of time, by informing us that when he made an appointment, he expected not only the hour, but the minute to be fixed, that the day might not run out in the idleness of suspense; and all the plans and enterprises of De Witt are now of less importance to the world, than that part of his personal character, which represents him as careful of his health, and negligent of his life.[8]

But biography has often been allotted to writers who seem very little acquainted with the nature of their task, or very negligent about the performance. They rarely afford any other account than might be collected from public papers, but imagine themselves writing a life when they exhibit a chronological series of actions or preferments; and so little regard the manners or behavior of their heroes, that more knowledge may be gained of a man's real character, by a short conversation with one of his servants, than from a formal and studied narrative, begun with his pedigree, and ended with his funeral.

If now and then they condescend to inform the world of particular facts, they are not always so happy as to select the most important. I know not well what advantage posterity can receive from the only circumstance by which Tickell has distinguished Addison from the rest of mankind, the irregularity of his pulse:[9] nor can I think myself overpaid for the time spent in reading the life of Malherbe, by being enabled to relate, after the learned biographer,[1] that Malherbe had two predominant opinions; one, that the looseness of a single woman might destroy all her boast of ancient descent; the other, that the French beggars made use very improperly and barbarously of the phrase *noble gentleman,* because either word included the sense of both.

There are, indeed, some natural reasons why these narratives are often written by such as were not likely to give much instruction or delight, and why most accounts of particular persons are barren and useless. If a life be delayed till interest and envy are at an end, we may hope for impartiality, but must expect little intelligence;[2] for the incidents which give excellence to biography are of a volatile and evanescent kind, such as soon escape the memory, and are rarely transmitted by tradition. We know how few can portray a living acquaintance, except by his most prominent and observable particularities, and the grosser features of his mind; and it may be easily

---

6. Sallust, a Roman historian of the 1st century B.C.E., wrote an account of Catiline's conspiracy against the Roman state.
7. Camerarius wrote a life of Melancthon, a German theologian of the 16th century.
8. Sir William Temple, characterizing the Dutch statesman John De Witt.

9. From Thomas Tickell's preface to Addision's *Works* (1721).
1. The life of the French poet François de Malherbe (1555–1628) was written by Honorat de Racan.
2. Information.

imagined how much of this little knowledge may be lost in imparting it, and how soon a succession of copies will lose all resemblance of the original.

If the biographer writes from personal knowledge, and makes haste to gratify the public curiosity, there is danger lest his interest, his fear, his gratitude, or his tenderness, overpower his fidelity, and tempt him to conceal, if not to invent. There are many who think it an act of piety to hide the faults or failings of their friends, even when they can no longer suffer by their detection; we therefore see whole ranks of characters adorned with uniform panegyric, and not to be known from one another, but by extrinsic and casual circumstances. "Let me remember," says Hale, "when I find myself inclined to pity a criminal, that there is likewise a pity due to the country."[3] If we owe regard to the memory of the dead, there is yet more respect to be paid to knowledge, to virtue, and to truth.

Idler No. 31[1]

[ON IDLENESS]

Saturday, *November* 18, 1758

Many moralists have remarked, that Pride has of all human vices the widest dominion, appears in the greatest multiplicity of forms, and lies hid under the greatest variety of disguises; of disguises, which, like the moon's *veil of brightness*, are both *its luster and its shade*,[2] and betray it to others, though they hide it from ourselves.

It is not my intention to degrade Pride from this pre-eminence of mischief, yet I know not whether Idleness may not maintain a very doubtful and obstinate competition.

There are some that profess Idleness in its full dignity, who call themselves the Idle, as Busiris in the play "calls himself the Proud";[3] who boast that they do nothing, and thank their stars that they have nothing to do; who sleep every night till they can sleep no longer, and rise only that exercise may enable them to sleep again; who prolong the reign of darkness by double curtains, and never see the sun but to "tell him how they hate his beams";[4] whose whole labor is to vary the postures of indulgence, and whose day differs from their night but as a couch or chair differs from a bed.

These are the true and open votaries of Idleness, for whom she weaves the garlands of poppies, and into whose cup she pours the waters of oblivion; who exist in a state of unruffled stupidity, forgetting and forgotten; who have long ceased to live, and at whose death the survivors can only say, that they have ceased to breathe.

But Idleness predominates in many lives where it is not suspected; for being a vice which terminates in itself, it may be enjoyed without injury to

3. From Gilbert Burnet's *Life and Death of Sir Matthew Hale* (1682).
1. Johnson wrote and published the *Idler*, a periodical similar to the *Rambler*, from 1758 until 1760.

2. Quoted from Samuel Butler's *Hudibras* 2.1.907–08.
3. Edward Young's *Busiris* (1719) 1.1.13.
4. *Paradise Lost* 4.37.

others; and is therefore not watched like Fraud, which endangers property, or like Pride, which naturally seeks its gratifications in another's inferiority. Idleness is a silent and peaceful quality, that neither raises envy by ostentation, nor hatred by opposition; and therefore nobody is busy to censure or detect it.

As Pride sometimes is hid under humility, Idleness is often covered by turbulence and hurry. He that neglects his known duty and real employment, naturally endeavors to crowd his mind with something that may bar out the remembrance of his own folly, and does any thing but what he ought to do with eager diligence, that he may keep himself in his own favor.

Some are always in a state of preparation, occupied in previous measures, forming plans, accumulating materials, and providing for the main affair. These are certainly under the secret power of Idleness. Nothing is to be expected from the workman whose tools are forever to be sought. I was once told by a great master, that no man ever excelled in painting, who was eminently curious about pencils and colors.

There are others to whom Idleness dictates another expedient, by which life may be passed unprofitably away without the tediousness of many vacant hours. The art is, to fill the day with petty business, to have always something in hand which may raise curiosity, but not solicitude, and keep the mind in a state of action, but not of labor.

This art has for many years been practiced by my old friend Sober, with wonderful success. Sober is a man of strong desires and quick imagination, so exactly balanced by the love of ease, that they can seldom stimulate him to any difficult undertaking; they have, however, so much power, that they will not suffer him to lie quite at rest, and though they do not make him sufficiently useful to others, they make him at least weary of himself.

Mr. Sober's chief pleasure is conversation; there is no end of his talk or his attention; to speak or to hear is equally pleasing; for he still fancies that he is teaching or learning something, and is free for the time from his own reproaches.

But there is one time at night when he must go home, that his friends may sleep; and another time in the morning, when all the world agrees to shut out interruption. These are the moments of which poor Sober trembles at the thought. But the misery of these tiresome intervals, he has many means of alleviating. He has persuaded himself that the manual arts are undeservedly overlooked; he has observed in many trades the effects of close thought, and just ratiocination. From speculation he proceeded to practice, and supplied himself with the tools of a carpenter, with which he mended his coalbox very successfully, and which he still continues to employ, as he finds occasion.

He has attempted at other times the crafts of the shoemaker, tinman, plumber, and potter; in all these arts he has failed, and resolves to qualify himself for them by better information. But his daily amusement is chemistry. He has a small furnace, which he employs in distillation, and which has long been the solace of his life. He draws oils and waters, and essences and spirits, which he knows to be of no use; sits and counts the drops as they come from his retort, and forgets that, whilst a drop is falling, a moment flies away.

Poor Sober![5] I have often teased him with reproof, and he has often promised reformation; for no man is so much open to conviction as the Idler, but there is none on whom it operates so little. What will be the effect of this paper I know not; perhaps he will read it and laugh, and light the fire in his furnace; but my hope is that he will quit his trifles, and betake himself to rational and useful diligence.

Rasselas   Johnson wrote *Rasselas* in January 1759 during the evenings of one week, a remarkable instance of his ability to write rapidly and brilliantly under the pressure of necessity. His mother lay dying in Lichfield. Her son, famous for his *Dictionary*, was nonetheless oppressed by poverty and in great need of ready money with which to make her last days comfortable, pay her funeral expenses, and settle her small debts. He was paid £100 for the first edition of *Rasselas*, but not in time to attend her deathbed or her funeral.

Rasselas is a philosophical fable cast in the popular form of an Oriental tale, a type of fiction that owed its popularity to the vogue of the *Arabian Nights*, first translated into English in the early eighteenth century. Because the work is a fable, we should not approach it as a novel: psychologically credible characters and a series of intricately involved actions that lead to a necessary resolution and conclusion are not to be found in *Rasselas*. Instead we are meant to reflect on the ideas and to savor the melancholy resonance and intelligence of the stately prose that expresses them. Johnson arranges the incidents of the fable to test a variety of possible solutions to a problem: What choice of life will bring us happiness? (*The Choice of Life* was his working title for the book.) Many ways of life are examined in turn, and each is found wanting. Johnson does not pretend to have solved the problem. Rather, he locates the sources of discontent in a basic principle of human nature: the "hunger of imagination which preys incessantly upon life" (chapter 32) and which lures us to "listen with credulity to the whispers of fancy and pursue with eagerness the phantoms of hope" (chapter 1). The tale is a gentle satire on one of the perennial topics of satirists: the folly of all of us who stubbornly cling to our illusions despite the evidence of experience. *Rasselas* is not all darkness and gloom, for Johnson's theme invites comic as well as tragic treatment, and some of the episodes evoke that laughter of the mind that is the effect of high comedy. In its main theme, however—the folly of cherishing the dream of ever attaining unalloyed happiness in a world that can never wholly satisfy our desires—and in many of the sayings of its characters, especially of the sage Imlac, *Rasselas* expresses some of Johnson's own deepest convictions.

The History of Rasselas, Prince of Abyssinia

Chapter 1. Description of a Palace in a Valley

Ye who listen with credulity to the whispers of fancy, and pursue with eagerness the phantoms of hope; who expect that age will perform the promises of youth, and that the deficiencies of the present day will be supplied by the morrow—attend to the history of Rasselas, prince of Abyssinia.

Rasselas was the fourth son of the mighty emperor in whose dominions the Father of Waters[1] begins his course; whose bounty pours down the streams of plenty, and scatters over half the world the harvests of Egypt.

---

5. Sober represents aspects of Johnson's own character. He was much given to indolence, and he performed chemical experiments in a small laboratory in his garret.

1. The Nile.

According to the custom which has descended from age to age among the monarchs of the torrid zone, Rasselas was confined in a private palace, with the other sons and daughters of Abyssinian royalty, till the order of succession should call him to the throne.

The place which the wisdom or policy of antiquity had destined for the residence of the Abyssinian princes was a spacious valley[2] in the kingdom of Amhara, surrounded on every side by mountains, of which the summits overhang the middle part. The only passage by which it could be entered was a cavern that passed under a rock, of which it has long been disputed whether it was the work of nature or of human industry. The outlet of the cavern was concealed by a thick wood, and the mouth which opened into the valley was closed with gates of iron, forged by the artificers of ancient days, so massy that no man could, without the help of engines, open or shut them.

From the mountains on every side rivulets descended that filled all the valley with verdure and fertility, and formed a lake in the middle, inhabited by fish of every species, and frequented by every fowl whom nature has taught to dip the wing in water. This lake discharged its superfluities by a stream, which entered a dark cleft of the mountain on the northern side, and fell with dreadful noise from precipice to precipice till it was heard no more.

The sides of the mountains were covered with trees, the banks of the brooks were diversified with flowers; every blast[3] shook spices from the rocks, and every month dropped fruits upon the ground. All animals that bite the grass, or browse the shrub, whether wild or tame, wandered in this extensive circuit, secured from beasts of prey by the mountains which confined them. On one part were flocks and herds feeding in the pastures, on another all the beasts of chase frisking in the lawns; the sprightly kid was bounding on the rocks, the subtle monkey frolicking in the trees, and the solemn elephant reposing in the shade. All the diversities of the world were brought together, the blessings of nature were collected, and its evils extracted and excluded.

The valley, wide and fruitful, supplied its inhabitants with the necessaries of life, and all delights and superfluities were added at the annual visit which the emperor paid his children, when the iron gate was opened to the sound of music, and during eight days everyone that resided in the valley was required to propose whatever might contribute to make seclusion pleasant, to fill up the vacancies of attention, and lessen the tediousness of time. Every desire was immediately granted. All the artificers of pleasure were called to gladden the festivity; the musicians exerted the power of harmony, and the dancers showed their activity before the princes, in hope that they should pass their lives in this blissful captivity, to which those only were admitted whose performance was thought able to add novelty to luxury. Such was the appearance of security and delight which this retirement afforded, that they to whom it was new always desired that it might be perpetual; and as those on whom the iron gate had once closed were never suffered to return, the effect of longer experience could not be known. Thus every year produced new schemes of delight and new competitors for imprisonment.

2. Johnson had read of the Happy Valley in the Portuguese Jesuit Father Lobo's book on Abyssinia, which he translated in 1735. This description also owes something to the description of the Garden in *Paradise Lost* 4, and Coleridge's "Kubla Khan" may owe something to it.
3. "A gust or puff of wind" (Johnson's *Dictionary*).

The palace stood on an eminence, raised about thirty paces[4] above the surface of the lake. It was divided into many squares or courts, built with greater or less magnificence according to the rank of those for whom they were designed. The roofs were turned into arches of massy stone, joined with a cement that grew harder by time, and the building stood from century to century, deriding the solstitial rains and equinoctial hurricanes, without need of reparation.

This house, which was so large as to be fully known to none but some ancient officers, who successively inherited the secrets of the place, was built as if suspicion herself had dictated the plan. To every room there was an open and secret passage; every square had a communication with the rest, either from the upper stories by private galleries, or by subterranean passages from the lower apartments. Many of the columns had unsuspected cavities, in which a long race of monarchs had reposited their treasures. They then closed up the opening with marble, which was never to be removed but in the utmost exigencies of the kingdom, and recorded their accumulations in a book, which was itself concealed in a tower, not entered but by the emperor, attended by the prince who stood next in succession.

Chapter 2. The Discontent of Rasselas in the Happy Valley

Here the sons and daughters of Abyssinia lived only to know the soft vicissitudes of pleasure and repose, attended by all that were skillful to delight, and gratified with whatever the senses can enjoy. They wandered in gardens of fragrance, and slept in the fortresses of security. Every art was practiced to make them pleased with their own condition. The sages who instructed them told them of nothing but the miseries of public life, and described all beyond the mountains as regions of calamity, where discord was always raging, and where man preyed upon man.

To heighten their opinion of their own felicity, they were daily entertained with songs, the subject of which was the *happy valley*. Their appetites were excited by frequent enumerations of different enjoyments, and revelry and merriment was the business of every hour, from the dawn of morning to the close of even.

These methods were generally successful; few of the princes had ever wished to enlarge their bounds, but passed their lives in full conviction that they had all within their reach that art or nature could bestow, and pitied those whom fate had excluded from this seat of tranquility, as the sport of chance and the slaves of misery.

Thus they rose in the morning and lay down at night, pleased with each other and with themselves; all but Rasselas, who, in the twenty-sixth year of his age, began to withdraw himself from their pastimes and assemblies, and to delight in solitary walks and silent meditation. He often sat before tables covered with luxury, and forgot to taste the dainties that were placed before him; he rose abruptly in the midst of the song, and hastily retired beyond the sound of music. His attendants observed the change, and endeavored to renew his love of pleasure. He neglected their officiousness, repulsed their invitations, and spent day after day on the banks of rivulets sheltered with

4. About 150 feet.

trees, where he sometimes listened to the birds in the branches, sometimes observed the fish playing in the stream, and anon cast his eyes upon the pastures and mountains filled with animals, of which some were biting the herbage, and some sleeping among the bushes.

This singularity of his humor made him much observed. One of the sages, in whose conversation he had formerly delighted, followed him secretly, in hope of discovering the cause of his disquiet. Rasselas, who knew not that anyone was near him, having for some time fixed his eyes upon the goats that were browsing among the rocks, began to compare their condition with his own.

"What," said he, "makes the difference between man and all the rest of the animal creation? Every beast that strays beside me has the same corporal necessities with myself; he is hungry, and crops the grass, he is thirsty, and drinks the stream, his thirst and hunger are appeased, he is satisfied, and sleeps; he rises again, and he is hungry, he is again fed, and is at rest. I am hungry and thirsty like him, but when thirst and hunger cease, I am not at rest; I am, like him, pained with want, but am not, like him, satisfied with fullness. The intermediate hours are tedious and gloomy; I long again to be hungry that I may again quicken my attention. The birds peck the berries or the corn, and fly away to the groves, where they sit in seeming happiness on the branches, and waste their lives in tuning one unvaried series of sounds. I likewise can call the lutanist and the singer, but the sounds that pleased me yesterday weary me today, and will grow yet more wearisome tomorrow. I can discover within me no power of perception which is not glutted with its proper pleasure, yet I do not feel myself delighted. Man has surely some latent sense for which this place affords no gratification, or he has some desires distinct from sense, which must be satisfied before he can be happy."

After this he lifted up his head, and seeing the moon rising, walked towards the palace. As he passed through the fields, and saw the animals around him, "Ye," said he, "are happy, and need not envy me that walk thus among you, burthened with myself; nor do I, ye gentle beings, envy your felicity, for it is not the felicity of man. I have many distresses from which ye are free; I fear pain when I do not feel it; I sometimes shrink at evils recollected, and sometimes start at evils anticipated. Surely the equity of Providence has balanced peculiar sufferings with peculiar enjoyments."

With observations like these the prince amused himself as he returned, uttering them with a plaintive voice, yet with a look that discovered[5] him to feel some complacence in his own perspicacity, and to receive some solace of the miseries of life from consciousness of the delicacy with which he felt, and the eloquence with which he bewailed them. He mingled cheerfully in the diversions of the evening, and all rejoiced to find that his heart was lightened.

Chapter 3. The Wants of Him That Wants Nothing

On the next day his old instructor, imagining that he had now made himself acquainted with his disease of mind, was in the hope of curing it by counsel, and officiously sought an opportunity of conference, which the

5. Showed.

prince, having long considered him as one whose intellects were exhausted, was not very willing to afford. "Why," said he, "does this man thus intrude upon me; shall I be never suffered to forget those lectures which pleased only while they were new, and to become new again must be forgotten?" He then walked into the wood, and composed himself to his usual meditations; when, before his thoughts had taken any settled form, he perceived his pursuer at his side, and was at first prompted by his impatience to go hastily away; but, being unwilling to offend a man whom he had once reverenced and still loved, he invited him to sit down with him on the bank.

The old man, thus encouraged, began to lament the change which had been lately observed in the prince, and to inquire why he so often retired from the pleasures of the palace, to loneliness and silence. "I fly from pleasure," said the prince, "because pleasure has ceased to please; I am lonely because I am miserable, and am unwilling to cloud with my presence the happiness of others." "You, sir," said the sage, "are the first who has complained of misery in the *happy valley*. I hope to convince you that your complaints have no real cause. You are here in full possession of all that the emperor of Abyssinia can bestow; here is neither labor to be endured nor danger to be dreaded, yet here is all that labor or danger can procure or purchase. Look round and tell me which of your wants is without supply; if you want nothing, how are you unhappy?"

"That I want nothing," said the prince, "or that I know not what I want, is the cause of my complaint; if I had any known want, I should have a certain wish; that wish would excite endeavor, and I should not then repine to see the sun move so slowly towards the western mountain, or lament when the day breaks, and sleep will no longer hide me from myself. When I see the kids and the lambs chasing one another, I fancy that I should be happy if I had something to pursue. But, possessing all that I can want, I find one day and one hour exactly like another, except that the latter is still more tedious than the former. Let your experience inform me how the day may now seem as short as in my childhood, while nature was yet fresh and every moment showed me what I never had observed before. I have already enjoyed too much; give me something to desire."

The old man was surprised at this new species of affliction and knew not what to reply, yet was unwilling to be silent. "Sir," said he, "if you had seen the miseries of the world you would know how to value your present state." "Now," said the prince, "you have given me something to desire. I shall long to see the miseries of the world, since the sight of them is necessary to happiness."

Chapter 4. The Prince Continues to Grieve and Muse

At this time the sound of music proclaimed the hour of repast, and the conversation was concluded. The old man went away sufficiently discontented to find that his reasonings had produced the only conclusion which they were intended to prevent. But in the decline of life shame and grief are of short duration; whether it be that we bear easily what we have born long, or that, finding ourselves in age less regarded, we less regard others; or, that we look with slight regard upon afflictions, to which we know that the hand of death is about to put an end.

The prince, whose views were extended to a wider space, could not speedily quiet his emotions. He had been before terrified at the length of life which nature promised him, because he considered that in a long time much must be endured; he now rejoiced in his youth, because in many years much might be done.

This first beam of hope, that had been ever darted into his mind, rekindled youth in his cheeks, and doubled the luster of his eyes. He was fired with the desire of doing something, though he knew not yet with distinctness, either end or means.

He was now no longer gloomy and unsocial; but, considering himself as master of a secret stock of happiness, which he could enjoy only by concealing it, he affected to be busy in all schemes of diversion, and endeavored to make others pleased with the state of which he himself was weary. But pleasures never can be so multiplied or continued, as not to leave much of life unemployed; there were many hours, both of the night and day, which he could spend without suspicion in solitary thought. The load of life was much lightened: he went eagerly into the assemblies, because he supposed the frequency of his presence necessary to the success of his purposes; he retired gladly to privacy, because he had now a subject of thought.

His chief amusement was to picture to himself that world which he had never seen; to place himself in various conditions; to be entangled in imaginary difficulties, and to be engaged in wild adventures: but his benevolence always terminated his projects in the relief of distress, the detection of fraud, the defeat of oppression, and the diffusion of happiness.

Thus passed twenty months of the life of Rasselas. He busied himself so intensely in visionary bustle, that he forgot his real solitude; and, amidst hourly preparations for the various incidents of human affairs, neglected to consider by what means he should mingle with mankind.

One day, as he was sitting on a bank, he feigned to himself an orphan virgin robbed of her little portion[6] by a treacherous lover, and crying after him for restitution and redress. So strongly was the image impressed upon his mind, that he started up in the maid's defense, and ran forward to seize the plunderer, with all the eagerness of real pursuit. Fear naturally quickens the flight of guilt. Rasselas could not catch the fugitive with his utmost efforts; but, resolving to weary, by perseverance, him whom he could not surpass in speed, he pressed on till the foot of the mountain stopped his course.

Here he recollected himself, and smiled at his own useless impetuosity. Then raising his eyes to the mountain, "This," said he, "is the fatal obstacle that hinders at once the enjoyment of pleasure, and the exercise of virtue. How long is it that my hopes and wishes have flown beyond this boundary of my life, which yet I never have attempted to surmount!"

Struck with this reflection, he sat down to muse, and remembered, that since he first resolved to escape from his confinement, the sun had passed twice over him in his annual course. He now felt a degree of regret with which he had never been before acquainted. He considered how much might have been done in the time which had passed, and left nothing real behind it. He compared twenty months with the life of man. "In life," said he, "is not

6. Money or goods.

to be counted the ignorance of infancy, or imbecility[7] of age. We are long before we are able to think, and we soon cease from the power of acting. The true period of human existence may be reasonably estimated as forty years, of which I have mused away the four and twentieth part. What I have lost was certain, for I have certainly possessed it; but of twenty months to come who can assure me?"

The consciousness of his own folly pierced him deeply, and he was long before he could be reconciled to himself. "The rest of my time," said he, "has been lost by the crime or folly of my ancestors, and the absurd institutions of my country; I remember it with disgust, yet without remorse: but the months that have passed since new light darted into my soul, since I formed a scheme of reasonable felicity, have been squandered by my own fault. I have lost that which can never be restored: I have seen the sun rise and set for twenty months, an idle gazer on the light of heaven. In this time the birds have left the nest of their mother, and committed themselves to the woods and to the skies: the kid has forsaken the teat, and learned by degrees to climb the rocks in quest of independent sustenance. I only have made no advances, but am still helpless and ignorant. The moon, by more than twenty changes, admonished me of the flux of life; the stream that rolled before my feet upbraided my inactivity. I sat feasting on intellectual luxury, regardless alike of the examples of the earth, and the instructions of the planets. Twenty months are past, who shall restore them!"

These sorrowful meditations fastened upon his mind; he passed four months in resolving to lose no more time in idle resolves, and was awakened to more vigorous exertion by hearing a maid, who had broken a porcelain cup, remark that what cannot be repaired is not to be regretted.

This was obvious; and Rasselas reproached himself that he had not discovered it, having not known, or not considered, how many useful hints are obtained by chance, and how often the mind, hurried by her own ardor to distant views, neglects the truths that lie open before her. He, for a few hours, regretted his regret, and from that time bent his whole mind upon the means of escaping from the valley of happiness.

Chapter 5. The Prince Meditates His Escape

He now found that it would be very difficult to effect that which it was very easy to suppose effected. When he looked round about him, he saw himself confined by the bars of nature which had never yet been broken, and by the gate, through which none that once had passed it were ever able to return. He was now impatient as an eagle in a grate.[8] He passed week after week in clambering the mountains, to see if there was any aperture which the bushes might conceal, but found all the summits inaccessible by their prominence. The iron gate he despaired to open; for it was not only secured with all the power of art, but was always watched by successive sentinels, and was by its position exposed to the perpetual observation of all the inhabitants.

He then examined the cavern through which the waters of the lake were discharged; and, looking down at a time when the sun shone strongly upon

7. Weakness.
8. Barred cage.

its mouth, he discovered it to be full of broken rocks, which, though they permitted the stream to flow through many narrow passages, would stop anybody of solid bulk. He returned discouraged and dejected; but, having now known the blessing of hope, resolved never to despair.

In these fruitless searches he spent ten months. The time, however, passed cheerfully away: in the morning he rose with new hope, in the evening applauded his own diligence, and in the night slept sound after his fatigue. He met a thousand amusements which beguiled his labor, and diversified his thoughts. He discerned the various instincts of animals, and properties of plants, and found the place replete with wonders, of which he purposed to solace himself with the contemplation, if he should never be able to accomplish his flight; rejoicing that his endeavors, though yet unsuccessful, had supplied him with a source of inexhaustible enquiry.

But his original curiosity was not yet abated; he resolved to obtain some knowledge of the ways of men. His wish still continued, but his hope grew less. He ceased to survey any longer the walls of his prison, and spared to search by new toils for interstices which he knew could not be found, yet determined to keep his design always in view, and lay hold on any expedient that time should offer.

Chapter 6. A Dissertation on the Art of Flying

Among the artists that had been allured into the happy valley, to labor for the accommodation and pleasure of its inhabitants, was a man eminent for his knowledge of the mechanic powers, who had contrived many engines[9] both of use and recreation. By a wheel, which the stream turned, he forced the water into a tower, whence it was distributed to all the apartments of the palace. He erected a pavillion in the garden, around which he kept the air always cool by artificial showers. One of the groves appropriated to the ladies, was ventilated by fans, to which the rivulet that run through it gave a constant motion; and instruments of soft music were placed at proper distances, of which some played by the impulse of the wind, and some by the power of the stream.

This artist was sometimes visited by Rasselas, who was pleased with every kind of knowledge, imagining that the time would come when all his acquisitions should be of use to him in the open world. He came one day to amuse himself in his usual manner, and found the master busy in building a sailing chariot: he saw that the design was practicable upon a level surface, and with expressions of great esteem solicited its completion. The workman was pleased to find himself so much regarded by the prince, and resolved to gain yet higher honors. "Sir," said he, "you have seen but a small part of what the mechanic sciences can perform. I have been long of opinion, that, instead of the tardy conveyance of ships and chariots, man might use the swifter migration of wings; that the fields of air are open to knowledge, and that only ignorance and idleness need crawl upon the ground."

This hint rekindled the prince's desire of passing the mountains; having seen what the mechanist had already performed, he was willing to fancy that he could do more; yet resolved to inquire further before he suffered hope to afflict him by disappointment. "I am afraid," said he to the artist, "that your

9. Machines. "Mechanic powers": the forces that cause things to move.

Unknown engraver, *Rasselas*, 1787. Rasselas pulls the artist to shore. *The History of Rasselas, Prince of Abissinia, a tale, in two volumes.*

imagination prevails over your skill, and that you now tell me rather what you wish than what you know. Every animal has his element assigned him; the birds have the air, and man and beasts the earth." "So," replied the mechanist, "fishes have the water, in which yet beasts can swim by nature, and men by art. He that can swim needs not despair to fly: to swim is to fly in a grosser fluid, and to fly is to swim in a subtler.[1] We are only to proportion our power of resistance to the different density of the matter through which we are to pass. You will be necessarily upborn by the air, if you can renew any impulse upon it, faster than the air can recede from the pressure."

"But the exercise of swimming," said the prince, "is very laborious; the strongest limbs are soon wearied; I am afraid the act of flying will be yet more violent, and wings will be of no great use, unless we can fly further than we can swim."

"The labor of rising from the ground," said the artist, "will be great, as we see it in the heavier domestic fowls; but, as we mount higher, the earth's attraction, and the body's gravity, will be gradually diminished, till we shall arrive at a region where the man will float in the air without any tendency to fall: no care will then be necessary, but to move forwards, which the gentlest impulse will effect. You, Sir, whose curiosity is so extensive, will easily conceive with what pleasure a philosopher, furnished with wings, and hovering in the sky, would see the earth, and all its inhabitants, rolling beneath him, and presenting to him successively, by its diurnal motion, all the countries within the same parallel. How must it amuse the pendent spectator to see the moving scene of land and ocean, cities and deserts! To survey with equal security the marts of trade, and the fields of battle; mountains infested by barbarians, and fruitful regions gladdened by plenty, and lulled by peace! How easily shall we then trace the Nile through all his passage; pass over to distant regions, and examine the face of nature from one extremity of the earth to the other!"

"All this," said the prince, "is much to be desired, but I am afraid that no man will be able to breathe in these regions of speculation and tranquil-

1. Thinner.

ity. I have been told, that respiration is difficult upon lofty mountains, yet from these precipices, though so high as to produce great tenuity of the air, it is very easy to fall: therefore I suspect, that from any height, where life can be supported, there may be danger of too quick descent."

"Nothing," replied the artist, "will ever be attempted, if all possible objections must be first overcome. If you will favor my project I will try the first flight at my own hazard. I have considered the structure of all volant[2] animals, and find the folding continuity of the bat's wings most easily accommodated to the human form. Upon this model I shall begin my task tomorrow, and in a year expect to tower into the air beyond the malice or pursuit of man. But I will work only on this condition, that the art shall not be divulged, and that you shall not require me to make wings for any but ourselves."

"Why," said Rasselas, "should you envy others so great an advantage? All skill ought to be exerted for universal good; every man has owed much to others, and ought to repay the kindness that he has received."

"If men were all virtuous," returned the artist, "I should with great alacrity teach them all to fly. But what would be the security of the good, if the bad could at pleasure invade them from the sky? Against an army sailing through the clouds neither walls, nor mountains, nor seas, could afford any security. A flight of northern savages might hover in the wind, and light at once with irresistible violence upon the capital of a fruitful region that was rolling under them. Even this valley, the retreat of princes, the abode of happiness, might be violated by the sudden descent of some of the naked nations that swarm on the coast of the southern sea."

The prince promised secrecy, and waited for the performance, not wholly hopeless of success. He visited the work from time to time, observed its progress, and remarked many ingenious contrivances to facilitate motion, and unite levity with strength. The artist was every day more certain that he should leave vultures and eagles behind him, and the contagion of his confidence seized upon the prince.

In a year the wings were finished, and, on a morning appointed, the maker appeared furnished for flight on a little promontory: he waved his pinions a while to gather air, then leaped from his stand, and in an instant dropped into the lake. His wings, which were of no use in the air, sustained him in the water, and the prince drew him to land, half dead with terror and vexation.

Chapter 7. The Prince Finds a Man of Learning

The prince was not much afflicted by this disaster, having suffered himself to hope for a happier event, only because he had no other means of escape in view. He still persisted in his design to leave the happy valley by the first opportunity.

His imagination was now at a stand; he had no prospect of entering into the world; and, notwithstanding all his endeavors to support himself, discontent by degrees preyed upon him, and he began again to lose his thoughts in sadness, when the rainy season, which in these countries is periodical, made it inconvenient to wander in the woods.

2. Able to fly.

The rain continued longer and with more violence than had been ever known; the clouds broke on the surrounding mountains, and the torrents streamed into the plain on every side, till the cavern was too narrow to discharge the water. The lake overflowed its banks, and all the level of the valley was covered with the inundation. The eminence, on which the palace was built, and some other spots of rising ground, were all that the eye could now discover. The herds and flocks left the pastures, and both the wild beasts and the tame retreated to the mountains.

This inundation confined all the princes to domestic amusements, and the attention of Rasselas was particularly seized by a poem, which Imlac rehearsed,[3] upon the various conditions of humanity. He commanded the poet to attend him in his apartment, and recite his verses a second time; then entering into familiar talk, he thought himself happy in having found a man who knew the world so well, and could so skillfully paint the scenes of life. He asked a thousand questions about things, to which, though common to all other mortals, his confinement from childhood had kept him a stranger. The poet pitied his ignorance, and loved his curiosity, and entertained him from day to day with novelty and instruction, so that the prince regretted the necessity of sleep, and longed till the morning should renew his pleasure.

As they were sitting together, the prince commanded Imlac to relate his history, and to tell by what accident he was forced, or by what motive induced, to close his life in the happy valley. As he was going to begin his narrative, Rasselas was called to a concert, and obliged to restrain his curiosity till the evening.

Chapter 8. The History of Imlac

The close of the day is, in the regions of the torrid zone, the only season of diversion and entertainment, and it was therefore midnight before the music ceased, and the princesses retired. Rasselas then called for his companion and required him to begin the story of his life.

"Sir," said Imlac, "my history will not be long: the life that is devoted to knowledge passes silently away, and is very little diversified by events. To talk in public, to think in solitude, to read and to hear, to inquire, and answer inquiries, is the business of a scholar. He wanders about the world without pomp or terror, and is neither known nor valued but by men like himself.

"I was born in the kingdom of Goiama,[4] at no great distance from the fountain of the Nile. My father was a wealthy merchant, who traded between the inland countries of Africk and the ports of the Red Sea. He was honest, frugal and diligent, but of mean sentiments, and narrow comprehension: he desired only to be rich, and to conceal his riches, lest he should be spoiled[5] by the governors of the province."

"Surely," said the prince, "my father must be negligent of his charge, if any man in his dominions dares take that which belongs to another. Does he not know that kings are accountable for injustice permitted as well as done? If I were emperor, not the meanest of my subjects should be oppressed with impunity. My blood boils when I am told that a merchant durst not enjoy his

3. Recited.
4. Mentioned by Father Lobo, in the western

part of Abyssinian dominions.
5. Robbed.

honest gains for fear of losing them by the rapacity of power. Name the governor who robbed the people, that I may declare his crimes to the emperor."

"Sir," said Imlac, "your ardor is the natural effect of virtue animated by youth: the time will come when you will acquit your father, and perhaps hear with less impatience of the governor. Oppression is, in the Abyssinian dominions, neither frequent nor tolerated; but no form of government has been yet discovered, by which cruelty can be wholly prevented. Subordination supposes power on one part and subjection on the other; and if power be in the hands of men, it will sometimes be abused. The vigilance of the supreme magistrate may do much, but much will still remain undone. He can never know all the crimes that are committed, and can seldom punish all that he knows."

"This," said the prince, "I do not understand, but I had rather hear thee than dispute. Continue thy narration."

"My father," proceeded Imlac, "originally intended that I should have no other education, than such as might qualify me for commerce; and discovering in me great strength of memory, and quickness of apprehension, often declared his hope that I should be some time the richest man in Abyssinia."

"Why," said the prince, "did thy father desire the increase of his wealth, when it was already greater than he durst discover or enjoy? I am unwilling to doubt thy veracity, yet inconsistencies cannot both be true."

"Inconsistencies," answered Imlac, "cannot both be right, but, imputed to man, they may both be true. Yet diversity is not inconsistency. My father might expect a time of greater security. However, some desire is necessary to keep life in motion, and he, whose real wants are supplied, must admit those of fancy."

"This," said the prince, "I can in some measure conceive. I repent that I interrupted thee."

"With this hope," proceeded Imlac, "he sent me to school; but when I had once found the delight of knowledge, and felt the pleasure of intelligence[6] and the pride of invention, I began silently to despise riches, and determined to disappoint the purpose of my father, whose grossness of conception raised my pity. I was twenty years old before his tenderness would expose me to the fatigue of travel, in which time I had been instructed, by successive masters, in all the literature of my native country. As every hour taught me something new, I lived in a continual course of gratifications; but, as I advanced towards manhood, I lost much of the reverence with which I had been used to look on my instructors; because, when the lesson was ended, I did not find them wiser or better than common men.

"At length my father resolved to initiate me in commerce, and, opening one of his subterranean treasuries, counted out ten thousand pieces of gold. 'This, young man,' said he, 'is the stock with which you must negotiate.[7] I began with less than the fifth part, and you see how diligence and parsimony have increased it. This is your own to waste or to improve. If you squander it by negligence or caprice, you must wait for my death before you will be rich: if, in four years, you double your stock, we will thenceforward let subordination cease, and live together as friends and partners; for he shall always be equal with me, who is equally skilled in the art of growing rich.'

6. Information or knowledge.
7. Do business.

"We laid our money upon camels, concealed in bales of cheap goods, and travelled to the shore of the Red Sea. When I cast my eye on the expanse of waters my heart bounded like that of a prisoner escaped. I felt an unextinguishable curiosity kindle in my mind, and resolved to snatch this opportunity of seeing the manners of other nations, and of learning sciences unknown in Abyssinia.

"I remembered that my father had obliged me to the improvement of my stock, not by a promise which I ought not to violate, but by a penalty which I was at liberty to incur; and therefore determined to gratify my predominant desire, and by drinking at the fountains of knowledge, to quench the thirst of curiosity.

"As I was supposed to trade without connection with my father, it was easy for me to become acquainted with the master of a ship, and procure a passage to some other country. I had no motives of choice to regulate my voyage; it was sufficient for me that, wherever I wandered, I should see a country which I had not seen before. I therefore entered a ship bound for Surat,[8] having left a letter for my father declaring my intention.

Chapter 9. The History of Imlac Continued

"When I first entered upon the world of waters, and lost sight of land, I looked round about me with pleasing terror, and thinking my soul enlarged by the boundless prospect, imagined that I could gaze round for ever without satiety; but, in a short time, I grew weary of looking on barren uniformity, where I could only see again what I had already seen. I then descended into the ship, and doubted for a while whether all my future pleasures would not end like this in disgust and disappointment. Yet, surely, said I, the ocean and the land are very different; the only variety of water is rest and motion, but the earth has mountains and valleys, deserts and cities: it is inhabited by men of different customs and contrary opinions; and I may hope to find variety in life, though I should miss it in nature.

"With this thought I quieted my mind; and amused myself during the voyage, sometimes by learning from the sailors the art of navigation, which I have never practiced, and sometimes by forming schemes for my conduct in different situations, in not one of which I have been ever placed.

"I was almost weary of my naval amusements when we landed safely at Surat. I secured my money, and purchasing some commodities for show, joined myself to a caravan that was passing into the inland country. My companions, for some reason or other, conjecturing that I was rich, and, by my inquiries and admiration, finding that I was ignorant, considered me as a novice whom they had a right to cheat, and who was to learn at the usual expense the art of fraud. They exposed me to the theft of servants, and the exaction of officers,[9] and saw me plundered upon false pretenses, without any advantage to themselves, but that of rejoicing in the superiority of their own knowledge."

"Stop a moment," said the prince. "Is there such depravity in man, as that he should injure another without benefit to himself? I can easily conceive that

8. A port in India.
9. Officials or agents.

all are pleased with superiority; but your ignorance was merely accidental, which, being neither your crime nor your folly, could afford them no reason to applaud themselves; and the knowledge which they had, and which you wanted, they might as effectually have shown by warning, as betraying you."

"Pride," said Imlac, "is seldom delicate, it will please itself with very mean advantages; and envy feels not its own happiness, but when it may be compared with the misery of others. They were my enemies because they grieved to think me rich, and my oppressors because they delighted to find me weak."

"Proceed," said the prince: "I doubt not of the facts which you relate, but imagine that you impute them to mistaken motives."

"In this company," said Imlac, "I arrived at Agra, the capital of Indostan, the city in which the great Mogul commonly resides. I applied myself to the language of the country, and in a few months was able to converse with the learned men; some of whom I found morose and reserved, and others easy and communicative; some were unwilling to teach another what they had with difficulty learned themselves; and some showed that the end[1] of their studies was to gain the dignity of instructing.

"To the tutor of the young princes I recommended myself so much, that I was presented to the emperor as a man of uncommon knowledge. The emperor asked me many questions concerning my country and my travels; and though I cannot now recollect any thing that he uttered above the power of a common man, he dismissed me astonished at his wisdom, and enamored of his goodness.

"My credit was now so high, that the merchants, with whom I had traveled, applied to me for recommendations to the ladies of the court. I was surprised at their confidence of solicitation, and gently reproached them with their practices on the road. They heard me with cold indifference, and showed no tokens of shame or sorrow.

"They then urged their request with the offer of a bribe; but what I would not do for kindness I would not do for money; and refused them, not because they had injured me, but because I would not enable them to injure others; for I knew they would have made use of my credit to cheat those who should buy their wares.

"Having resided at Agra till there was no more to be learned, I traveled into Persia, where I saw many remains of ancient magnificence, and observed many new accommodations[2] of life. The Persians are a nation eminently social, and their assemblies afforded me daily opportunities of remarking characters and manners, and of tracing human nature through all its variations.

"From Persia I passed into Arabia, where I saw a nation at once pastoral and warlike; who live without any settled habitation; whose only wealth is their flocks and herds; and who have yet carried on, through all ages, an hereditary war with all mankind, though they neither covet nor envy their possessions.

Chapter 10. Imlac's History Continued. A Dissertation upon Poetry

"Wherever I went, I found that poetry was considered as the highest learning, and regarded with a veneration somewhat approaching to that which

---

1. Purpose.
2. "Conveniences, things requisite to ease or refreshment" (Johnson's *Dictionary*).

man would pay to the angelic nature. And yet it fills me with wonder that, in almost all countries, the most ancient poets are considered as the best: whether it be that every other kind of knowledge is an acquisition gradually attained, and poetry is a gift conferred at once; or that the first poetry of every nation surprised them as a novelty, and retained the credit by consent which it received by accident at first; or whether, as the province of poetry is to describe nature and passion, which are always the same, the first writers took possession of the most striking objects for description and the most probable occurrences for fiction, and left nothing to those that followed them, but transcription of the same events, and new combinations of the same images—whatever be the reason, it is commonly observed that the early writers are in possession of nature, and their followers of art; that the first excel in strength and invention, and the latter in elegance and refinement.

"I was desirous to add my name to this illustrious fraternity. I read all the poets of Persia and Arabia, and was able to repeat by memory the volumes that are suspended in the mosque of Mecca.[3] But I soon found that no man was ever great by imitation. My desire of excellence impelled me to transfer my attention to nature and to life. Nature was to be my subject, and men to be my auditors: I could never describe what I had not seen; I could not hope to move those with delight or terror, whose interests and opinions I did not understand.

"Being now resolved to be a poet, I saw everything with a new purpose; my sphere of attention was suddenly magnified; no kind of knowledge was to be overlooked. I ranged mountains and deserts for images and resemblances, and pictured upon my mind every tree of the forest and flower of the valley. I observed with equal care the crags of the rock and the pinnacles of the palace. Sometimes I wandered along the mazes of the rivulet, and sometimes watched the changes of the summer clouds. To a poet nothing can be useless. Whatever is beautiful, and whatever is dreadful, must be familiar to his imagination; he must be conversant with all that is awfully[4] vast or elegantly little. The plants of the garden, the animals of the wood, the minerals of the earth, and meteors of the sky, must all concur to store his mind with inexhaustible variety: for every idea[5] is useful for the enforcement or decoration of moral or religious truth; and he who knows most will have most power of diversifying his scenes, and of gratifying his reader with remote allusions and unexpected instruction.

"All the appearances of nature I was therefore careful to study, and every country which I have surveyed has contributed something to my poetical powers."

"In so wide a survey," said the prince, "you must surely have left much unobserved. I have lived till now within the circuit of these mountains, and yet cannot walk abroad without the sight of something which I have never beheld before, or never heeded."

"The business of a poet," said Imlac, "is to examine, not the individual, but the species; to remark general properties and large appearances; he does not number the streaks of the tulip, or describe the different shades in the

---

3. In the 7th century, seven peerless Arabic poems were supposed to have been transcribed in gold and hung up in a mosque.

4. Awe-inspiringly.
5. Mental image.

verdure of the forest. He is to exhibit in his portraits of nature such prominent and striking features as recall the original to every mind, and must neglect the minuter discriminations, which one may have remarked and another have neglected, for those characteristics which are alike obvious to vigilance and carelessness.

"But the knowledge of nature is only half the task of a poet; he must be acquainted likewise with all the modes of life. His character requires that he estimate the happiness and misery of every condition; observe the power of all the passions in all their combinations, and trace the changes of the human mind, as they are modified by various institutions and accidental influences of climate or custom, from the sprightliness of infancy to the despondence of decrepitude. He must divest himself of the prejudices of his age or country; he must consider right and wrong in their abstracted and invariable state; he must disregard present laws and opinions, and rise to general and transcendental[6] truths, which will always be the same. He must, therefore, content himself with the slow progress of his name, contemn the applause of his own time, and commit his claims to the justice of posterity. He must write as the interpreter of nature and the legislator of mankind, and consider himself as presiding over the thoughts and manners of future generations, as a being superior to time and place.

"His labor is not yet at an end; he must know many languages and many sciences; and, that his style may be worthy of his thoughts, must by incessant practice familiarize to himself every delicacy of speech and grace of harmony."

Chapter 11. Imlac's Narrative Continued. A Hint on Pilgrimage

Imlac now felt the enthusiastic fit, and was proceeding to aggrandize his own profession, when the prince cried out: "Enough! thou hast convinced me that no human being can ever be a poet. Proceed with thy narration."

"To be a poet," said Imlac, "is indeed very difficult." "So difficult," returned the prince, "that I will at present hear no more of his labors. Tell me whither you went when you had seen Persia."

"From Persia," said the poet, "I traveled through Syria, and for three years resided in Palestine, where I conversed with great numbers of the northern and western nations of Europe, the nations which are now in possession of all power and all knowledge, whose armies are irresistible, and whose fleets command the remotest parts of the globe. When I compared these men with the natives of our own kingdom, and those that surround us, they appeared almost another order of beings. In their countries it is difficult to wish for anything that may not be obtained; a thousand arts, of which we never heard, are continually laboring for their convenience and pleasure; and whatever their own climate has denied them is supplied by their commerce."

"By what means," said the prince, "are the Europeans thus powerful, or why, since they can so easily visit Asia and Africa for trade or conquest, cannot the Asiatics and Africans invade their coasts, plant colonies in their ports, and give laws to their natural princes? The same wind that carries them back would bring us thither."

6. "General; pervading many particulars" (Johnson's *Dictionary*).

"They are more powerful, sir, than we," answered Imlac, "because they are wiser; knowledge will always predominate over ignorance, as man governs the other animals. But why their knowledge is more than ours, I know not what reason can be given, but the unsearchable will of the Supreme Being."

"When," said the prince with a sigh, "shall I be able to visit Palestine, and mingle with this mighty confluence of nations? Till that happy moment shall arrive, let me fill up the time with such representations as thou canst give me. I am not ignorant of the motive that assembles such numbers in that place, and cannot but consider it as the center of wisdom and piety, to which the best and wisest men of every land must be continually resorting."

"There are some nations," said Imlac, "that send few visitants to Palestine; for many numerous and learned sects in Europe concur to censure pilgrimage as superstitious, or deride it as ridiculous."

"You know," said the prince, "how little my life has made me acquainted with diversity of opinions. It will be too long to hear the arguments on both sides; you, that have considered them, tell me the result."

"Pilgrimage," said Imlac, "like many other acts of piety, may be reasonable or superstitious, according to the principles upon which it is performed. Long journeys in search of truth are not commanded. Truth, such as is necessary to the regulation of life, is always found where it is honestly sought. Change of place is no natural cause of the increase of piety, for it inevitably produces dissipation of mind. Yet, since men go every day to view the fields where great actions have been performed, and return with stronger impressions of the event, curiosity of the same kind may naturally dispose us to view that country whence our religion had its beginning; and I believe no man surveys those awful scenes without some confirmation of holy resolutions. That the Supreme Being may be more easily propitiated in one place than in another is the dream of idle superstition, but that some places may operate upon our own minds in an uncommon manner is an opinion which hourly experience will justify. He who supposes that his vices may be more successfully combated in Palestine, will, perhaps, find himself mistaken, yet he may go thither without folly; he who thinks they will be more freely pardoned, dishonors at once his reason and religion."

"These," said the prince, "are European distinctions. I will consider them another time. What have you found to be the effect of knowledge? Are those nations happier than we?"

"There is so much infelicity," said the poet, "in the world that scarce any man has leisure from his own distresses to estimate the comparative happiness of others. Knowledge is certainly one of the means of pleasure, as is confessed by the natural desire which every mind feels of increasing its ideas. Ignorance is mere privation, by which nothing can be produced; it is a vacuity in which the soul sits motionless and torpid for want of attraction; and, without knowing why, we always rejoice when we learn, and grieve when we forget. I am therefore inclined to conclude that if nothing counteracts the natural consequence of learning, we grow more happy as our minds take a wider range.

"In enumerating the particular comforts of life, we shall find many advantages on the side of the Europeans. They cure wounds and diseases with which we languish and perish. We suffer inclemencies of weather which they can obviate. They have engines for the despatch of many laborious works, which we must perform by manual industry. There is such communication between distant places that one friend can hardly be said to be absent from another. Their policy removes all public inconveniences; they have roads cut through their mountains, and bridges laid upon their rivers. And, if we descend to the privacies of life, their habitations are more commodious, and their possessions are more secure."

"They are surely happy," said the prince, "who have all these conveniencies, of which I envy none so much as the facility with which separated friends interchange their thoughts."

"The Europeans," answered Imlac, "are less unhappy than we, but they are not happy. Human life is everywhere a state in which much is to be endured, and little to be enjoyed."

Chapter 12. The Story of Imlac Continued

"I am not yet willing," said the prince, "to suppose that happiness is so parsimoniously distributed to mortals; nor can believe but that, if I had the choice of life, I should be able to fill every day with pleasure. I would injure no man, and should provoke no resentment: I would relieve every distress, and should enjoy the benedictions of gratitude. I would choose my friends among the wise, and my wife among the virtuous; and therefore should be in no danger from treachery, or unkindness. My children should, by my care, be learned and pious, and would repay to my age what their childhood had received. What would dare to molest him who might call on every side to thousands enriched by his bounty, or assisted by his power? And why should not life glide quietly away in the soft reciprocation of protection and reverence? All this may be done without the help of European refinements, which appear by their effects to be rather specious than useful. Let us leave them and pursue our journey."

"From Palestine," said Imlac, "I passed through many regions of Asia; in the more civilized kingdoms as a trader, and among the barbarians of the mountains as a pilgrim. At last I began to long for my native country, that I might repose after my travels, and fatigues, in the places where I had spent my earliest years, and gladden my old companions with the recital of my adventures. Often did I figure to myself those, with whom I had sported away the gay hours of dawning life, sitting round me in its evening, wondering at my tales, and listening to my counsels.

"When this thought had taken possession of my mind, I considered every moment as wasted which did not bring me nearer to Abyssinia. I hastened into Egypt, and, notwithstanding my impatience, was detained ten months in the contemplation of its ancient magnificence, and in enquiries after the remains of its ancient learning. I found in Cairo a mixture of all nations; some brought thither by the love of knowledge, some by the hope of gain, and many by the desire of living after their own manner without observation, and of lying hid in the obscurity of multitudes: for, in a city, populous as Cairo, it is possible to obtain at the same time the gratifications of society, and the secrecy of solitude.

"From Cairo I traveled to Suez, and embarked on the Red Sea, passing along the coast till I arrived at the port from which I had departed twenty years before. Here I joined myself to a caravan and re-entered my native country.

"I now expected the caresses of my kinsmen, and the congratulations of my friends, and was not without hope that my father, whatever value he had set upon riches, would own with gladness and pride a son who was able to add to the felicity and honor of the nation. But I was soon convinced that my thoughts were vain. My father had been dead fourteen years, having divided his wealth among my brothers, who were removed to some other provinces. Of my companions the greater part was in the grave, of the rest some could with difficulty remember me, and some considered me as one corrupted by foreign manners.

"A man used to vicissitudes is not easily dejected. I forgot, after a time, my disappointment, and endeavored to recommend myself to the nobles of the kingdom: they admitted me to their tables, heard my story, and dismissed me. I opened a school, and was prohibited to teach. I then resolved to sit down in the quiet of domestic life, and addressed a lady that was fond of my conversation, but rejected my suit, because my father was a merchant.

"Wearied at last with solicitation and repulses, I resolved to hide myself for ever from the world, and depend no longer on the opinion or caprice of others. I waited for the time when the gate of the *happy valley* should open, that I might bid farewell to hope and fear: the day came; my performance was distinguished with favor, and I resigned myself with joy to perpetual confinement."

"Hast thou here found happiness at last?" said Rasselas. "Tell me without reserve; art thou content with thy condition? or, dost thou wish to be again wandering and inquiring? All the inhabitants of this valley celebrate their lot, and, at the annual visit of the emperor, invite others to partake of their felicity."

"Great prince," said Imlac, "I shall speak the truth: I know not one of all your attendants who does not lament the hour when he entered this retreat. I am less unhappy than the rest, because I have a mind replete with images, which I can vary and combine at pleasure. I can amuse my solitude by the renovation of the knowledge which begins to fade from my memory, and by recollection of the accidents of my past life. Yet all this ends in the sorrowful consideration, that my acquirements are now useless, and that none of my pleasures can be again enjoyed. The rest, whose minds have no impression but of the present moment, are either corroded by malignant passions, or sit stupid in the gloom of perpetual vacancy."

"What passions can infest those," said the prince, "who have no trials? We are in a place where impotence precludes malice, and where all envy is repressed by community[7] of enjoyments."

"There may be community," said Imlac, "of material possessions, but there can never be community of love or of esteem. It must happen that one will please more than another; he that knows himself despised will always be envious; and still more envious and malevolent, if he is condemned to live in the presence of those who despise him. The invitations, by which they allure others to a state which they feel to be wretched, proceed from the natural malignity of hopeless misery. They are weary of themselves, and of each other, and expect to find relief in new companions. They envy the liberty

7. Joint possession.

which their folly has forfeited, and would gladly see all mankind imprisoned like themselves.

"From this crime, however, I am wholly free. No man can say that he is wretched by my persuasion. I look with pity on the crowds who are annually soliciting admission to captivity, and wish that it were lawful for me to warn them of their danger."

"My dear Imlac," said the prince, "I will open to thee my whole heart. I have long meditated an escape from the happy valley. I have examined the mountains on every side, but find myself insuperably barred: teach me the way to break my prison; thou shalt be the companion of my flight, the guide of my rambles, the partner of my fortune, and my sole director in the *choice of life.*"

"Sir," answered the poet, "your escape will be difficult, and, perhaps, you may soon repent your curiosity. The world, which you figure to yourself smooth and quiet as the lake in the valley, you will find a sea foaming with tempests, and boiling with whirlpools: you will be sometimes overwhelmed by the waves of violence, and sometimes dashed against the rocks of treachery. Amidst wrongs and frauds, competitions and anxieties, you will wish a thousand times for these seats of quiet, and willingly quit hope to be free from fear."

"Do not seek to deter me from my purpose," said the prince: "I am impatient to see what thou hast seen; and, since thou art thyself weary of the valley, it is evident, that thy former state was better than this. Whatever be the consequence of my experiment, I am resolved to judge with my own eyes of the various conditions of men, and then to make deliberately my *choice of life.*"

"I am afraid," said Imlac, "you are hindered by stronger restraints than my persuasions; yet, if your determination is fixed, I do not counsel you to despair. Few things are impossible to diligence and skill."

Chapter 13. Rasselas Discovers the Means of Escape

The prince now dismissed his favorite to rest, but the narrative of wonders and novelties filled his mind with perturbation. He revolved all that he had heard, and prepared innumerable questions for the morning.

Much of his uneasiness was now removed. He had a friend to whom he could impart his thoughts, and whose experience could assist him in his designs. His heart was no longer condemned to swell with silent vexation. He thought that even the *happy valley* might be endured with such a companion, and that, if they could range the world together, he should have nothing further to desire.

In a few days the water was discharged, and the ground dried. The prince and Imlac then walked out together to converse without the notice of the rest. The prince, whose thoughts were always on the wing, as he passed by the gate, said, with a countenance of sorrow, "Why art thou so strong, and why is man so weak?"

"Man is not weak," answered his companion; "knowledge is more than equivalent to force. The master of mechanics laughs at strength. I can burst the gate, but cannot do it secretly. Some other expedient must be tried."

As they were walking on the side of the mountain, they observed that the conies,[8] which the rain had driven from their burrows, had taken shelter among the bushes, and formed holes behind them, tending upwards in an oblique line. "It has been the opinion of antiquity," said Imlac, "that human reason borrowed many arts from the instinct of animals; let us, therefore, not think ourselves degraded by learning from the coney. We may escape by piercing the mountain in the same direction. We will begin where the summit hangs over the middle part, and labor upward till we shall issue out beyond the prominence."

The eyes of the prince, when he heard this proposal, sparkled with joy. The execution was easy, and the success certain.

No time was now lost. They hastened early in the morning to choose a place proper for their mine. They clambered with great fatigue among crags and brambles, and returned without having discovered any part that favored their design. The second and the third day were spent in the same manner, and with the same frustration. But, on the fourth, they found a small cavern, concealed by a thicket, where they resolved to make their experiment.

Imlac procured instruments proper to hew stone and remove earth, and they fell to their work on the next day with more eagerness than vigor. They were presently exhausted by their efforts, and sat down to pant upon the grass. The prince, for a moment, appeared to be discouraged. "Sir," said his companion, "practice will enable us to continue our labor for a longer time; mark, however, how far we have advanced, and you will find that our toil will some time have an end. Great works are performed, not by strength, but perseverance: yonder palace was raised by single stones, yet you see its height and spaciousness. He that shall walk with vigor three hours a day will pass in seven years a space equal to the circumference of the globe."

They returned to their work day after day, and, in a short time, found a fissure in the rock, which enabled them to pass far with very little obstruction. This Rasselas considered as a good omen. "Do not disturb your mind," said Imlac, "with other hopes or fears than reason may suggest: if you are pleased with prognostics of good, you will be terrified likewise with tokens of evil, and your whole life will be a prey to superstition. Whatever facilitates our work is more than an omen, it is a cause of success. This is one of those pleasing surprises which often happen to active resolution. Many things difficult to design prove easy to performance."

Chapter 14. Rasselas and Imlac Receive an Unexpected Visit

They had now wrought their way to the middle, and solaced their toil with the approach of liberty, when the prince, coming down to refresh himself with air, found his sister Nekayah standing before the mouth of the cavity. He started and stood confused, afraid to tell his design, and yet hopeless to conceal it. A few moments determined him to repose on her fidelity, and secure her secrecy by a declaration without reserve.

"Do not imagine," said the princess, "that I came hither as a spy: I had long observed from my window, that you and Imlac directed your walk every day towards the same point, but I did not suppose you had any better reason

8. Rabbits.

for the preference than a cooler shade, or more fragrant bank; nor followed you with any other design than to partake of your conversation. Since then not suspicion but fondness has detected you, let me not lose the advantage of my discovery. I am equally weary of confinement with yourself, and not less desirous of knowing what is done or suffered in the world. Permit me to fly with you from this tasteless tranquility, which will yet grow more loathsome when you have left me. You may deny me to accompany you, but cannot hinder me from following."

The prince, who loved Nekayah above his other sisters, had no inclination to refuse her request, and grieved that he had lost an opportunity of showing his confidence by a voluntary communication. It was therefore agreed that she should leave the valley with them; and that, in the mean time, she should watch, lest any other straggler should, by chance or curiosity, follow them to the mountain.

At length their labor was at an end; they saw light beyond the prominence, and, issuing to the top of the mountain, beheld the Nile, yet a narrow current, wandering beneath them.

The prince looked round with rapture, anticipated all the pleasures of travel, and in thought was already transported beyond his father's dominions. Imlac, though very joyful at his escape, had less expectation of pleasure in the world, which he had before tried, and of which he had been weary.

Rasselas was so much delighted with a wider horizon, that he could not soon be persuaded to return into the valley. He informed his sister that the way was open, and that nothing now remained but to prepare for their departure.

Chapter 15. The Prince and Princess Leave the Valley, and See Many Wonders

The prince and princess had jewels sufficient to make them rich whenever they came into a place of commerce, which, by Imlac's direction, they hid in their clothes, and, on the night of the next full moon, all left the valley. The princess was followed only by a single favorite, who did not know whither she was going.

They clambered through the cavity, and began to go down on the other side. The princess and her maid turned their eyes towards every part, and, seeing nothing to bound their prospect, considered themselves as in danger of being lost in a dreary vacuity. They stopped and trembled. "I am almost afraid," said the princess, "to begin a journey of which I cannot perceive an end, and to venture into this immense plain where I may be approached on every side by men whom I never saw." The prince felt nearly the same emotions, though he thought it more manly to conceal them.

Imlac smiled at their terrors, and encouraged them to proceed; but the princess continued irresolute till she had been imperceptibly drawn forward too far to return.

In the morning they found some shepherds in the field, who set milk and fruits before them. The princess wondered that she did not see a palace ready for her reception, and a table spread with delicacies; but, being faint and hungry, she drank the milk and ate the fruits, and thought them of a higher flavor than the products of the valley.

They traveled forward by easy journeys, being all unaccustomed to toil or difficulty, and knowing, that though they might be missed, they could not be pursued. In a few days they came into a more populous region, where Imlac was diverted with the admiration which his companions expressed at the diversity of manners, stations and employments.

Their dress was such as might not bring upon them the suspicion of having any thing to conceal, yet the prince, wherever he came, expected to be obeyed, and the princess was frighted, because those that came into her presence did not prostrate themselves before her. Imlac was forced to observe them with great vigilance, lest they should betray their rank by their unusual behavior, and detained them several weeks in the first village to accustom them to the sight of common mortals.

By degrees the royal wanderers were taught to understand that they had for a time laid aside their dignity, and were to expect only such regard as liberality and courtesy could procure. And Imlac, having, by many admonitions, prepared them to endure the tumults of a port, and the ruggedness of the commercial race, brought them down to the seacoast.

The prince and his sister, to whom every thing was new, were gratified equally at all places, and therefore remained for some months at the port without any inclination to pass further. Imlac was content with their stay, because he did not think it safe to expose them, unpracticed in the world, to the hazards of a foreign country.

At last he began to fear lest they should be discovered, and proposed to fix a day for their departure. They had no pretensions to judge for themselves, and referred the whole scheme to his direction. He therefore took passage in a ship to Suez; and, when the time came, with great difficulty prevailed on the princess to enter the vessel. They had a quick and prosperous voyage, and from Suez traveled by land to Cairo.

Chapter 16. They Enter Cairo, and Find Every Man Happy

As they approached the city, which filled the strangers with astonishment, "This," said Imlac to the prince, "is the place where travelers and merchants assemble from all the corners of the earth. You will here find men of every character and every occupation. Commerce is here honorable. I will act as a merchant, and you shall live as strangers, who have no other end of travel than curiosity. It will soon be observed that we are rich; our reputation will procure us access to all whom we shall desire to know; you will see all the conditions of humanity, and enable yourself at leisure to make your *choice of life.*"

They now entered the town, stunned by the noise, and offended by the crowds. Instruction had not yet so prevailed over habit, but that they wondered to see themselves pass undistinguished along the street, and met by the lowest of the people without reverence or notice. The princess could not at first bear the thought of being leveled with the vulgar,[9] and for some days continued in her chamber, where she was served by her favorite, Pekuah, as in the palace of the valley.

9. Ordinary people.

Imlac, who understood traffic,[1] sold part of the jewels the next day, and hired a house, which he adorned with such magnificence that he was immediately considered as a merchant of great wealth. His politeness attracted many acquaintance, and his generosity made him courted by many dependents. His table was crowded by men of every nation, who all admired his knowledge, and solicited his favor. His companions, not being able to mix in the conversation, could make no discovery[2] of their ignorance or surprise, and were gradually initiated in the world as they gained knowledge of the language.

The prince had, by frequent lectures, been, taught the use and nature of money; but the ladies could not for a long time comprehend what the merchants did with small pieces of gold and silver, or why things of so little use should be received as equivalent to the necessaries of life.

They studied the language two years, while Imlac was preparing to set before them the various ranks and conditions of mankind. He grew acquainted with all who had anything uncommon in their fortune or conduct. He frequented the voluptuous and the frugal, the idle and the busy, the merchants and the men of learning.

The prince being now able to converse with fluency, and having learned the caution necessary to be observed in his intercourse with strangers, began to accompany Imlac to places of resort, and to enter into all assemblies, that he might make his *choice of life*.

For some time he thought choice needless, because all appeared to him equally happy. Wherever he went he met gaiety and kindness, and heard the song of joy or the laugh of carelessness. He began to believe that the world overflowed with universal plenty, and that nothing was withheld either from want or merit; that every hand showered liberality, and every heart melted with benevolence: "And who then," says he, "will be suffered to be wretched?"

Imlac permitted the pleasing delusion, and was unwilling to crush the hope of inexperience, till one day, having sat awhile silent, "I know not," said the prince, "what can be the reason that I am more unhappy than any of our friends. I see them perpetually and unalterably cheerful, but feel my own mind restless and uneasy. I am unsatisfied with those pleasures which I seem most to court; I live in the crowds of jollity, not so much to enjoy company as to shun myself, and am only loud and merry to conceal my sadness."

"Every man," said Imlac, "may, by examining his own mind, guess what passes in the minds of others; when you feel that your own gaiety is counterfeit, it may justly lead you to suspect that of your companions not to be sincere. Envy is commonly reciprocal. We are long before we are convinced that happiness is never to be found, and each believes it possessed by others, to keep alive the hope of obtaining it for himself. In the assembly where you passed the last night, there appeared such sprightliness of air, and volatility of fancy, as might have suited beings of an higher order, formed to inhabit serener regions, inaccessible to care or sorrow; yet, believe me, prince, there was not one who did not dread the moment when solitude should deliver him to the tyranny of reflection."

1. Commerce.
2. Exposure.

"This," said the prince, "may be true of others, since it is true of me; yet, whatever be the general infelicity of man, one condition is more happy than another, and wisdom surely directs us to take the least evil in the *choice of life.*"

"The causes of good and evil," answered Imlac, "are so various and uncertain, so often entangled with each other, so diversified by various relations, and so much subject to accidents which cannot be foreseen, that he who would fix his condition upon incontestable reasons of preference must live and die inquiring and deliberating."

"But, surely," said Rasselas, "the wise men, to whom we listen with reverence and wonder, chose that mode of life for themselves which they thought most likely to make them happy."

"Very few," said the poet, "live by choice. Every man is placed in his present condition by causes which acted without his foresight, and with which he did not always willingly cooperate; and therefore you will rarely meet one who does not think the lot of his neighbor better than his own."

"I am pleased to think," said the prince, "that my birth has given me at least one advantage over others, by enabling me to determine for myself. I have here the world before me. I will review it at leisure; surely happiness is somewhere to be found."

Chapter 17. The Prince Associates with Young Men of Spirit and Gaiety

Rasselas rose next day, and resolved to begin his experiments upon life. "Youth," cried he, "is the time of gladness: I will join myself to the young men, whose only business is to gratify their desires, and whose time is all spent in a succession of enjoyments."

To such societies he was readily admitted, but a few days brought him back weary and disgusted. Their mirth was without images,[3] their laughter without motive; their pleasures were gross and sensual, in which the mind had no part; their conduct was at once wild and mean; they laughed at order and at law, but the frown of power dejected, and the eye of wisdom abashed them.

The prince soon concluded, that he should never be happy in a course of life of which he was ashamed. He thought it unsuitable to a reasonable being to act without a plan, and to be sad or cheerful only by chance. "Happiness," said he, "must be something solid and permanent, without fear and without uncertainty."

But his young companions had gained so much of his regard by their frankness and courtesy, that he could not leave them without warning and remonstrance. "My friends," said he, "I have seriously considered our manners and our prospects, and find that we have mistaken our own interest. The first years of man must make provision for the last. He that never thinks never can be wise. Perpetual levity must end in ignorance; and intemperance, though it may fire the spirits for an hour, will make life short or miserable. Let us consider that youth is of no long duration, and that in maturer age, when the enchantments of fancy shall cease, and phantoms of delight dance no more about us, we shall have no comforts but the esteem of wise

3. Ideas.

men, and the means of doing good. Let us, therefore, stop, while to stop is in our power: let us live as men who are sometime to grow old, and to whom it will be the most dreadful of all evils not to count their past years but by follies, and to be reminded of their former luxuriance of health only by the maladies which riot has produced."

They stared a while in silence one upon another, and, at last, drove him away by a general chorus of continued laughter.

The consciousness that his sentiments were just, and his intentions kind, was scarcely sufficient to support him against the horror of derision. But he recovered his tranquillity, and pursued his search.

Chapter 18. *The Prince Finds a Wise and Happy Man*

As he was one day walking in the street, he saw a spacious building which all were, by the open doors, invited to enter: he followed the stream of people, and found it a hall or school of declamation, in which professors read lectures to their auditory.[4] He fixed his eye upon a sage raised above the rest, who discoursed with great energy on the government of the passions. His look was venerable, his action graceful, his pronunciation clear, and his diction elegant. He showed with great strength of sentiment and variety of illustration that human nature is degraded and debased, when the lower faculties predominate over the higher; that when fancy, the parent of passion, usurps the dominion of the mind, nothing ensues but the natural effect of unlawful government, perturbation, and confusion; that she betrays the fortresses of the intellect to rebels, and excites her children to sedition against reason, their lawful sovereign. He compared reason to the sun, of which the light is constant, uniform and lasting; and fancy to a meteor, of bright but transitory luster, irregular in its motion, and delusive in its direction.

He then communicated the various precepts given from time to time for the conquest of passion, and displayed the happiness of those who had obtained the important victory, after which man is no longer the slave of fear, nor the fool of hope; is no more emaciated by envy, inflamed by anger, emasculated by tenderness, or depressed by grief; but walks on calmly through the tumults or the privacies of life, as the sun pursues alike his course through the calm or the stormy sky.

He enumerated many examples of heroes immovable by pain or pleasure, who looked with indifference on those modes or accidents to which the vulgar give the names of good and evil. He exhorted his hearers to lay aside their prejudices, and arm themselves against the shafts of malice or misfortune, by invulnerable patience; concluding that this state only was happiness, and that this happiness was in everyone's power.

Rasselas listened to him with the veneration due to the instructions of a superior being, and, waiting for him at the door, humbly implored the liberty of visiting so great a master of true wisdom. The lecturer hesitated a moment, when Rasselas put a purse of gold into his hand, which he received with a mixture of joy and wonder.

"I have found," said the prince at his return to Imlac, "a man who can teach all that is necessary to be known; who, from the unshaken throne of

4. Audience.

rational fortitude, looks down on the scenes of life changing beneath him. He speaks, and attention watches his lips. He reasons, and conviction closes his periods.[5] This man shall be my future guide; I will learn his doctrines, and imitate his life."

"Be not too hasty," said Imlac, "to trust or to admire the teachers of morality: they discourse like angels, but they live like men."

Rasselas, who could not conceive how any man could reason so forcibly without feeling the cogency of his own arguments, paid his visit in a few days, and was denied admission. He had now learned the power of money, and made his way by a piece of gold to the inner apartment, where he found the philosopher in a room half darkened, with his eyes misty and his face pale. "Sir," said he, "you are come at a time when all human friendship is useless; what I suffer cannot be remedied, what I have lost cannot be supplied. My daughter, my only daughter, from whose tenderness I expected all the comforts of my age, died last night of a fever. My views, my purposes, my hopes are at an end; I am now a lonely being, disunited from society."

"Sir," said the prince, "mortality is an event by which a wise man can never be surprised; we know that death is always near, and it should therefore always be expected." "Young man," answered the philosopher, "you speak like one that has never felt the pangs of separation." "Have you then forgot the precepts," said Rasselas, "which you so powerfully enforced? Has wisdom no strength to arm the heart against calamity? Consider that external things are naturally variable, but truth and reason are always the same." "What comfort," said the mourner, "can truth and reason afford me? Of what effect are they now, but to tell me that my daughter will not be restored?"

The prince, whose humanity would not suffer him to insult misery with reproof, went away, convinced of the emptiness of rhetorical sound, and the inefficacy of polished periods and studied sentences.[6]

Chapter 19. A Glimpse of Pastoral Life

He was still eager upon the same inquiry; and having heard of a hermit that lived near the lowest cataract of the Nile, and filled the whole country with the fame of his sanctity, resolved to visit his retreat, and inquire whether that felicity which public life could not afford was to be found in solitude; and whether a man whose age and virtue made him venerable could teach any peculiar art of shunning evils, or enduring them.

Imlac and the princess agreed to accompany him, and, after the necessary preparations, they began their journey. Their way lay through fields, where shepherds tended their flocks and the lambs were playing upon the pasture. "This," said the poet, "is the life which has been often celebrated for its innocence and quiet; let us pass the heat of the day among the shepherds' tents, and know whether all our searches are not to terminate in pastoral simplicity."

The proposal pleased them, and they induced the shepherds, by small presents and familiar questions, to tell their opinion of their own state. They were so rude and ignorant, so little able to compare the good with the evil of

5. Completed sentences.
6. Maxims or moral axioms.

the occupation, and so indistinct in their narratives and descriptions, that very little could be learned from them. But it was evident that their hearts were cankered with discontent; that they considered themselves as condemned to labor for the luxury of the rich, and looked up with stupid malevolence toward those that were placed above them.

The princess pronounced with vehemence that she would never suffer these envious savages to be her companions, and that she should not soon be desirous of seeing any more specimens of rustic happiness; but could not believe that all the accounts of primeval pleasures were fabulous,[7] and was yet in doubt whether life had anything that could be justly preferred to the placid gratifications of fields and woods. She hoped that the time would come, when, with a few virtuous and elegant companions, she could gather flowers planted by her own hand, fondle the lambs of her own ewe, and listen, without care, among brooks and breezes, to one of her maidens reading in the shade.

Chapter 20. The Danger of Prosperity

On the next day they continued their journey, till the heat compelled them to look round for shelter. At a small distance they saw a thick wood, which they no sooner entered than they perceived that they were approaching the habitations of men. The shrubs were diligently cut away to open walks where the shades were darkest; the boughs of opposite trees were artificially interwoven; seats of flowery turf were raised in vacant spaces, and a rivulet, that wantoned along the side of a winding path, had its banks sometimes opened into small basins, and its stream sometimes obstructed by little mounds of stone heaped together to increase its murmurs.

They passed slowly through the wood, delighted with such unexpected accommodations, and entertained each other with conjecturing what, or who, he could be, that, in those rude and unfrequented regions, had leisure and art for such harmless luxury.

As they advanced, they heard the sound of music, and saw youths and virgins dancing in the grove; and, going still further, beheld a stately palace built upon a hill surrounded with woods. The laws of eastern hospitality allowed them to enter, and the master welcomed them like a man liberal and wealthy.

He was skilful enough in appearances soon to discern that they were no common guests, and spread his table with magnificence. The eloquence of Imlac caught his attention, and the lofty courtesy of the princess excited his respect. When they offered to depart he entreated their stay, and was the next day still more unwilling to dismiss them than before. They were easily persuaded to stop, and civility grew up in time to freedom and confidence.

The prince now saw all the domestics cheerful, and all the face of nature smiling round the place, and could not forbear to hope that he should find here what he was seeking; but when he was congratulating the master upon his possessions, he answered with a sigh, "My condition has indeed the appearance of happiness, but appearances are delusive. My prosperity puts my life in danger; the Bassa[8] of Egypt is my enemy, incensed only by my

7. Fictional.
8. Pasha, a Turkish viceroy.

wealth and popularity. I have been hitherto protected against him by the princes of the country; but, as the favor of the great is uncertain, I know not how soon my defenders may be persuaded to share the plunder with the Bassa. I have sent my treasures into a distant country, and, upon the first alarm, am prepared to follow them. Then will my enemies riot in my mansion, and enjoy the gardens which I have planted."

They all joined in lamenting his danger, and deprecating his exile; and the princess was so much disturbed with the tumult of grief and indignation, that she retired to her apartment. They continued with their kind inviter a few days longer, and then went forward to find the hermit.

Chapter 21. The Happiness of Solitude. The Hermit's History

They came on the third day, by the direction of the peasants, to the hermit's cell: it was a cavern in the side of a mountain, over-shadowed with palm-trees; at such a distance from the cataract, that nothing more was heard than a gentle uniform murmur, such as composed the mind to pensive meditation, especially when it was assisted by the wind whistling among the branches. The first rude essay of nature had been so much improved by human labor, that the cave contained several apartments, appropriated to different uses, and often afforded lodging to travelers, whom darkness or tempests happened to overtake.

The hermit sat on a bench at the door, to enjoy the coolness of the evening. On one side lay a book with pens and papers, on the other mechanical instruments of various kinds. As they approached him unregarded, the princess observed that he had not the countenance of a man that had found, or could teach, the way to happiness.

They saluted him with great respect, which he repaid like a man not unaccustomed to the forms of courts. "My children," said he, "if you have lost your way, you shall be willingly supplied with such conveniencies for the night as this cavern will afford. I have all that nature requires, and you will not expect delicacies in a hermit's cell."

They thanked him, and, entering, were pleased with the neatness and regularity of the place. The hermit set flesh and wine before them, though he fed only upon fruits and water. His discourse was cheerful without levity, and pious without enthusiasm.[9] He soon gained the esteem of his guests, and the princess repented of her hasty censure.

At last Imlac began thus: "I do not now wonder that your reputation is so far extended; we have heard at Cairo of your wisdom, and came hither to implore your direction for this young man and maiden in the *choice of life*."

"To him that lives well," answered the hermit, "every form of life is good; nor can I give any other rule for choice, than to remove from all apparent evil."

"He will remove most certainly from evil," said the prince, "who shall devote himself to that solitude which you have recommended by your example."

"I have indeed lived fifteen years in solitude," said the hermit, "but have no desire that my example should gain any imitators. In my youth I professed

---

9. "A vain belief of private revelation; a vain confidence of divine favor or communication" (Johnson's *Dictionary*).

arms, and was raised by degrees to the highest military rank. I have traversed wide countries at the head of my troops, and seen many battles and sieges. At last, being disgusted by the preferment of a younger officer, and feeling that my vigor was beginning to decay, I resolved to close my life in peace, having found the world full of snares, discord, and misery. I had once escaped from the pursuit of the enemy by the shelter of this cavern, and therefore chose it for my final residence. I employed artificers to form it into chambers, and stored it with all that I was likely to want.

"For some time after my retreat, I rejoiced like a tempest-beaten sailor at his entrance into the harbor, being delighted with the sudden change of the noise and hurry of war, to stillness and repose. When the pleasure of novelty went away, I employed my hours in examining the plants which grow in the valley, and the minerals which I collected from the rocks. But that inquiry is now grown tasteless and irksome. I have been for some time unsettled and distracted: my mind is disturbed with a thousand perplexities of doubt, and vanities of imagination, which hourly prevail upon me, because I have no opportunities of relaxation or diversion. I am sometimes ashamed to think that I could not secure myself from vice, but by retiring from the exercise of virtue, and begin to suspect that I was rather impelled by resentment, than led by devotion, into solitude. My fancy riots in scenes of folly, and I lament that I have lost so much, and have gained so little. In solitude, if I escape the example of bad men, I want likewise the counsel and conversation of the good. I have been long comparing the evils with the advantages of society, and resolve to return into the world tomorrow. The life of a solitary man will be certainly miserable, but not certainly devout."

They heard his resolution with surprise, but, after a short pause, offered to conduct him to Cairo. He dug up a considerable treasure which he had hid among the rocks, and accompanied them to the city, on which, as he approached it, he gazed with rapture.

Chapter 22. The Happiness of a Life Led according to Nature

Rasselas went often to an assembly of learned men, who met at stated times to unbend their minds and compare their opinions. Their manners were somewhat coarse, but their conversation was instructive, and their disputations acute, though sometimes too violent, and often continued till neither controvertist remembered upon what question they began. Some faults were almost general among them; everyone was desirous to dictate to the rest, and everyone was pleased to hear the genius or knowledge of another depreciated.

In this assembly Rasselas was relating his interview with the hermit, and the wonder with which he heard him censure a course of life which he had so deliberately chosen, and so laudably followed. The sentiments of the hearers were various. Some were of opinion that the folly of his choice had been justly punished by condemnation to perpetual perseverance. One of the youngest among them, with great vehemence, pronounced him an hypocrite. Some talked of the right of society to the labor of individuals, and considered retirement as a desertion of duty. Others readily allowed that there was a time when the claims of the public were satisfied, and when a man might properly sequester himself, to review his life and purify his heart.

One, who appeared more affected with the narrative than the rest, thought it likely that the hermit would in a few years go back to his retreat, and perhaps, if shame did not restrain, or death intercept him, return once more from his retreat into the world. "For the hope of happiness," said he, "is so strongly impressed that the longest experience is not able to efface it. Of the present state, whatever it be, we feel and are forced to confess the misery; yet when the same state is again at a distance, imagination paints it as desirable. But the time will surely come when desire will be no longer our torment, and no man shall be wretched but by his own fault."

"This," said a philosopher who had heard him with tokens of great impatience, "is the present condition of a wise man. The time is already come when none are wretched but by their own fault. Nothing is more idle than to inquire after happiness, which nature has kindly placed within our reach. The way to be happy is to live according to nature, in obedience to that universal and unalterable law with which every heart is originally impressed; which is not written on it by precept, but engraven by destiny, not instilled by education, but infused at our nativity. He that lives according to nature will suffer nothing from the delusions of hope, or importunities of desire; he will receive and reject with equability of temper, and act or suffer as the reason of things shall alternately prescribe. Other men may amuse themselves with subtle definitions, or intricate ratiocination. Let them learn to be wise by easier means; let them observe the hind of the forest, and the linnet of the grove; let them consider the life of animals, whose motions are regulated by instinct; they obey their guide, and are happy. Let us therefore, at length, cease to dispute, and learn to live; throw away the encumbrance of precepts, which they who utter them with so much pride and pomp do not understand, and carry with us this simple and intelligible maxim, that deviation from nature is deviation from happiness."

When he had spoken, he looked round him with a placid air, and enjoyed the consciousness of his own beneficence. "Sir," said the prince with great modesty, "as I, like all the rest of mankind, am desirous of felicity, my closest attention has been fixed upon your discourse. I doubt not the truth of a position which a man so learned has so confidently advanced. Let me only know what it is to live according to nature."

"When I find young men so humble and so docile," said the philosopher, "I can deny them no information which my studies have enabled me to afford. To live according to nature, is to act always with due regard to the fitness arising from the relations and qualities of causes and effects; to concur with the great and unchangeable scheme of universal felicity; to co-operate with the general disposition and tendency of the present system of things."

The prince soon found that this was one of the sages whom he should understand less as he heard him longer. He therefore bowed and was silent; and the philosopher, supposing him satisfied, and the rest vanquished, rose up and departed with the air of a man that had co-operated with the present system.

Chapter 23. The Prince and His Sister Divide between Them the Work of Observation

Rasselas returned home full of reflections, doubtful how to direct his future steps. Of the way to happiness he found the learned and simple equally ignorant; but, as he was yet young, he flattered himself that he had time remaining for more experiments, and further inquiries. He communicated to Imlac his observations and his doubts, but was answered by him with new doubts, and remarks that gave him no comfort. He therefore discoursed more frequently and freely with his sister, who had yet the same hope with himself, and always assisted him to give some reason why, though he had been hitherto frustrated, he might succeed at last.

"We have hitherto," said she, "known but little of the world: we have never yet been either great or mean. In our own country, though we had royalty, we had no power, and in this we have not yet seen the private recesses of domestic peace. Imlac favors not our search, lest we should in time find him mistaken. We will divide the task between us: you shall try what is to be found in the splendor of courts, and I will range the shades of humbler life. Perhaps command and authority may be the supreme blessings, as they afford most opportunities of doing good: or, perhaps, what this world can give may be found in the modest habitations of middle fortune; too low for great designs, and too high for penury and distress."

Chapter 24. The Prince Examines the Happiness of High Stations

Rasselas applauded the design, and appeared next day with a splendid retinue at the court of the Bassa. He was soon distinguished for his magnificence, and admitted, as a prince whose curiosity had brought him from distant countries, to an intimacy with the great officers, and frequent conversation with the Bassa himself.

He was at first inclined to believe, that the man must be pleased with his own condition, whom all approached with reverence, and heard with obedience, and who had the power to extend his edicts to a whole kingdom. "There can be no pleasure," said he, "equal to that of feeling at once the joy of thousands all made happy by wise administration. Yet, since, by the law of subordination, this sublime delight can be in one nation but the lot of one, it is surely reasonable to think that there is some satisfaction more popular[1] and accessible, and that millions can hardly be subjected to the will of a single man, only to fill his particular breast with incommunicable content."

These thoughts were often in his mind, and he found no solution of the difficulty. But as presents and civilities gained him more familiarity, he found that almost every man who stood high in employment hated all the rest, and was hated by them, and that their lives were a continual succession of plots and detections, stratagems and escapes, faction and treachery. Many of those, who surrounded the Bassa, were sent only to watch and report his conduct; every tongue was muttering censure and every eye was searching for a fault.

At last the letters of revocation arrived, the Bassa was carried in chains to Constantinople, and his name was mentioned no more.

1. Common.

"What are we now to think of the prerogatives of power," said Rasselas to his sister; "is it without any efficacy to good? or, is the subordinate degree only dangerous, and the supreme safe and glorious? Is the Sultan the only happy man in his dominions? or, is the Sultan himself subject to the torments of suspicion, and the dread of enemies?"

In a short time the second Bassa was deposed. The Sultan, that had advanced him, was murdered by the Janisaries,[2] and his successor had other views and different favorites.

Chapter 25. The Princess Pursues Her Inquiry with More Diligence Than Success

The princess, in the mean time, insinuated herself into many families; for there are few doors, through which liberality, joined with good humor, cannot find its way. The daughters of many houses were airy[3] and cheerful, but Nekayah had been too long accustomed to the conversation of Imlac and her brother to be much pleased with childish levity and prattle which had no meaning. She found their thoughts narrow, their wishes low, and their merriment often artificial. Their pleasures, poor as they were, could not be preserved pure, but were embittered by petty competitions and worthless emulation. They were always jealous of the beauty of each other; of a quality to which solicitude can add nothing, and from which detraction can take nothing away. Many were in love with triflers like themselves, and many fancied that they were in love when in truth they were only idle. Their affection was seldom fixed on sense or virtue, and therefore seldom ended but in vexation. Their grief, however, like their joy, was transient; everything floated in their mind unconnected with the past or future, so that one desire easily gave way to another, as a second stone cast into the water effaces and confounds the circles of the first.

With these girls she played as with inoffensive animals, and found them proud of her countenance,[4] and weary of her company.

But her purpose was to examine more deeply, and her affability easily persuaded the hearts that were swelling with sorrow to discharge their secrets in her ear: and those whom hope flattered, or prosperity delighted, often courted her to partake their pleasures.

The princess and her brother commonly met in the evening in a private summer-house on the bank of the Nile, and related to each other the occurrences of the day. As they were sitting together, the princess cast her eyes upon the river that flowed before her. "Answer," said she, "great father of waters, thou that rollest thy floods through eighty nations, to the invocations of the daughter of thy native king. Tell me if thou waterest, through all thy course, a single habitation from which thou dost not hear the murmurs of complaint?"

"You are then," said Rasselas, "not more successful in private houses than I have been in courts." "I have, since the last partition of our provinces,[5] said the princess, "enabled myself to enter familiarly into many families,

2. Guards of the Turkish ruler.
3. "Gay; sprightly; full of mirth" (Johnson's Dictionary).

4. Patronage, favor.
5. Division of our responsibilities.

where there was the fairest show of prosperity and peace, and know not one house that is not haunted by some fury that destroys its quiet.

"I did not seek ease among the poor, because I concluded that there it could not be found. But I saw many poor whom I had supposed to live in affluence. Poverty has, in large cities, very different appearances: it is often concealed in splendor, and often in extravagance. It is the care of a very great part of mankind to conceal their indigence from the rest: they support themselves by temporary expedients, and every day is lost in contriving for the morrow.

"This, however, was an evil, which, though frequent, I saw with less pain, because I could relieve it. Yet some have refused my bounties; more offended with my quickness to detect their wants, than pleased with my readiness to succor them: and others, whose exigencies compelled them to admit my kindness, have never been able to forgive their benefactress. Many, however, have been sincerely grateful without the ostentation of gratitude, or the hope of other favors."

Chapter 26. The Princess Continues Her Remarks upon Private Life

Nekayah, perceiving her brother's attention fixed, proceeded in her narrative.

"In families where there is or is not poverty, there is commonly discord. If a kingdom be, as Imlac tells us, a great family, a family likewise is a little kingdom, torn with factions and exposed to revolutions. An unpracticed observer expects the love of parents and children to be constant and equal; but this kindness seldom continues beyond the years of infancy: in a short time the children become rivals to their parents. Benefits are allayed[6] by reproaches, and gratitude debased by envy.

"Parents and children seldom act in concert; each child endeavors to appropriate the esteem or fondness of the parents, and the parents, with yet less temptation, betray each other to their children. Thus, some place their confidence in the father, and some in the mother, and by degrees the house is filled with artifices and feuds.

"The opinions of children and parents, of the young and the old, are naturally opposite, by the contrary effects of hope and despondence, of expectation and experience, without crime or folly on either side. The colors of life in youth and age appear different, as the face of nature in spring and winter. And how can children credit the assertions of parents, which their own eyes show them to be false?

"Few parents act in such a manner as much to enforce their maxims by the credit of their lives. The old man trusts wholly to slow contrivance and gradual progression; the youth expects to force his way by genius, vigor, and precipitance. The old man pays regard to riches, and the youth reverences virtue. The old man deifies prudence; the youth commits himself to magnanimity and chance. The young man, who intends no ill, believes that none is intended, and therefore acts with openness and candor; but his father, having suffered the injuries of fraud, is impelled to suspect, and too often

6. To allay is "to join anything to another, so as to abate its predominant qualities" (Johnson's *Dictionary*).

allured to practice it. Age looks with anger on the temerity of youth, and youth with contempt on the scrupulosity[7] of age. Thus parents and children, for the greatest part, live on to love less and less; and, if those whom nature has thus closely united are the torments of each other, where shall we look for tenderness and consolation?"

"Surely," said the prince, "you must have been unfortunate in your choice of acquaintance: I am unwilling to believe that the most tender of all relations is thus impeded in its effects by natural necessity."

"Domestic discord," answered she, "is not inevitably and fatally necessary, but yet is not easily avoided. We seldom see that a whole family is virtuous; the good and evil cannot well agree, and the evil can yet less agree with one another. Even the virtuous fall sometimes to variance, when their virtues are of different kinds, and tending to extremes. In general, those parents have most reverence who most deserve it; for he that lives well cannot be despised.

"Many other evils infest private life. Some are the slaves of servants whom they have trusted with their affairs. Some are kept in continual anxiety to the caprice of rich relations, whom they cannot please, and dare not offend. Some husbands are imperious, and some wives perverse; and, as it is always more easy to do evil than good, though the wisdom or virtue of one can very rarely make many happy, the folly or vice of one may often make many miserable."

"If such be the general effect of marriage," said the prince, "I shall for the future think it dangerous to connect my interest with that of another, lest I should be unhappy by my partner's fault."

"I have met," said the princess, "with many who live single for that reason; but I never found that their prudence ought to raise envy. They dream away their time without friendship, without fondness, and are driven to rid themselves of the day, for which they have no use, by childish amusements, or vicious delights. They act as beings under the constant sense of some known inferiority that fills their minds with rancor, and their tongues with censure. They are peevish at home, and malevolent abroad; and, as the outlaws of human nature, make it their business and their pleasure to disturb that society which debars them from its privileges. To live without feeling or exciting sympathy, to be fortunate without adding to the felicity of others, or afflicted without tasting the balm of pity, is a state more gloomy than solitude; it is not retreat but exclusion from mankind. Marriage has many pains, but celibacy has no pleasures."

"What then is to be done?" said Rasselas; "the more we inquire, the less we can resolve. Surely he is most likely to please himself that has no other inclination to regard."

Chapter 27. Disquisition upon Greatness

The conversation had a short pause. The prince, having considered his sister's observations, told her, that she had surveyed life with prejudice, and supposed misery where she did not find it. "Your narrative," says he, "throws yet a darker gloom upon the prospects of futurity: the predictions of Imlac

---

7. "Fear of acting in any manner" (Johnson's *Dictionary*).

were but faint sketches of the evils painted by Nekayah. I have been lately, convinced that quiet is not the daughter of grandeur, or of power: that her presence is not to be bought by wealth, nor enforced by conquest. It is evident, that as any man acts in a wider compass, he must be more exposed to opposition from enmity or miscarriage from chance; whoever has many to please or to govern, must use the ministry of many agents, some of whom will be wicked, and some ignorant; by some he will be misled, and by others betrayed. If he gratifies one he will offend another: those that are not favored will think themselves injured; and, since favors can be conferred but upon few, the greater number will be always discontented."

"The discontent," said the princess, "which is thus unreasonable, I hope that I shall always have spirit to despise, and you, power to repress."

"Discontent," answered Rasselas, "will not always be without reason under the most just or vigilant administration of public affairs. None, however attentive, can always discover that merit which indigence or faction may happen to obscure; and none, however powerful, can always reward it. Yet, he that sees inferior desert[8] advanced above him, will naturally impute that preference to partiality or caprice; and, indeed, it can scarcely be hoped that any man, however magnanimous by nature, or exalted by condition, will be able to persist for ever in fixed and inexorable justice of distribution: he will sometimes indulge his own affections, and sometimes those of his favorites; he will permit some to please him who can never serve him; he will discover in those whom he loves qualities which in reality they do not possess; and to those, from whom he receives pleasure, he will in his turn endeavor to give it. Thus will recommendations sometimes prevail which were purchased by money, or by the more destructive bribery of flattery and servility.

"He that has much to do will do something wrong, and of that wrong must suffer the consequences; and, if it were possible that he should always act rightly, yet when such numbers are to judge of his conduct, the bad will censure and obstruct him by malevolence, and the good sometimes by mistake.

"The highest stations cannot therefore hope to be the abodes of happiness, which I would willingly believe to have fled from thrones and palaces to seats of humble privacy and placid obscurity. For what can hinder the satisfaction, or intercept the expectations, of him whose abilities are adequate to his employments, who sees with his own eyes the whole circuit of his influence, who chooses by his own knowledge all whom he trusts, and whom none are tempted to deceive by hope or fear? Surely he has nothing to do but to love and to be loved, to be virtuous and to be happy."

"Whether perfect happiness would be procured by perfect goodness," said Nekayah, "this world will never afford an opportunity of deciding. But this, at least, may be maintained, that we do not always find visible happiness in proportion to visible virtue. All natural and almost all political evils, are incident alike to the bad and good: they are confounded in the misery of a famine, and not much distinguished in the fury of a faction; they sink together in a tempest, and are driven together from their country by invaders. All that virtue can afford is quietness of conscience, a steady prospect of a happier state; this may enable us to endure calamity with patience; but remember that patience must suppose pain."

8. Merit; one deserving reward.

Chapter 28. *Rasselas and Nekayah Continue Their Conversation*

"Dear princess," said Rasselas, "you fall into the common errors of exaggeratory declamation, by producing, in a familiar disquisition,[9] examples of national calamities, and scenes of extensive misery, which are found in books rather than in the world, and which, as they are horrid, are ordained to be rare. Let us not imagine evils which we do not feel, nor injure life by misrepresentations. I cannot bear that querulous eloquence which threatens every city with a siege like that of Jerusalem,[1] that makes famine attend on every flight of locusts, and suspends pestilence on the wing of every blast that issues from the south.

"On necessary and inevitable evils, which overwhelm kingdoms at once, all disputation is vain: when they happen they must be endured. But it is evident, that these bursts of universal distress are more dreaded than felt: thousands and ten thousands flourish in youth, and wither in age, without the knowledge of any other than domestic evils, and share the same pleasures and vexations whether their kings are mild or cruel, whether the armies of their country pursue their enemies, or retreat before them. While courts are disturbed with intestine[2] competitions, and ambassadors are negotiating in foreign countries, the smith still plies his anvil, and the husbandman drives his plow forward; the necessaries of life are required and obtained, and the successive business of the seasons continues to make its wonted revolutions.

"Let us cease to consider what, perhaps, may never happen, and what, when it shall happen, will laugh at human speculation. We will not endeavor to modify the motions of the elements, or to fix the destiny of kingdoms. It is our business to consider what beings like us may perform; each laboring for his own happiness, by promoting within his circle, however narrow, the happiness of others.

"Marriage is evidently the dictate of nature; men and women were made to be companions of each other, and therefore I cannot be persuaded but that marriage is one of the means of happiness."

"I know not," said the princess, "whether marriage be more than one of the innumerable modes of human misery. When I see and reckon the various forms of connubial infelicity, the unexpected causes of lasting discord, the diversities of temper, the oppositions of opinion, the rude collisons of contrary desire where both are urged by violent impulses, the obstinate contests of disagreeing virtues, where both are supported by consciousness of good intention, I am sometimes disposed to think with the severer casuists of most nations, that marriage is rather permitted than approved, and that none, but by the instigation of a passion too much indulged, entangle themselves with indissoluble compacts."

"You seem to forget," replied Rasselas, "that you have, even now, represented celibacy as less happy than marriage. Both conditions may be bad, but they cannot both be worst. Thus it happens when wrong opinions are entertained, that they mutually destroy each other, and leave the mind open to truth."

"I did not expect," answered the princess, "to hear that imputed to falsehood which is the consequence only of frailty. To the mind, as to the eye, it

9. Family discussion of a question.
1. In 70 C.E. the Romans, under Titus, besieged
and destroyed Jerusalem.
2. Internal, domestic.

is difficult to compare with exactness objects vast in their extent, and various in their parts. Where we see or conceive the whole at once we readily note the discriminations and decide the preference: but of two systems, of which neither can be surveyed by any human being in its full compass of magnitude and multiplicity of complication, where is the wonder, that judging of the whole by parts, I am alternately affected by one and the other as either presses on my memory or fancy? We differ from ourselves just as we differ from each other, when we see only part of the question, as in the multifarious relations of politics and morality: but when we perceive the whole at once, as in numerical computations, all agree in one judgment, and none ever varies his opinion."

"Let us not add," said the prince, "to the other evils of life, the bitterness of controversy, nor endeavor to vie with each other in subtleties of argument. We are employed in a search, of which both are equally to enjoy the success, or suffer by the miscarriage. It is therefore fit that we assist each other. You surely conclude too hastily from the infelicity of marriage against its institution; will not the misery of life prove equally that life cannot be the gift of heaven? The world must be peopled by marriage, or peopled without it."

"How the world is to be peopled," returned Nekayah, "is not my care, and needs not be yours. I see no danger that the present generation should omit to leave successors behind them: we are not now inquiring for the world, but for ourselves."

Chapter 29. *The Debate on Marriage Continued*

"The good of the whole," says Rasselas, "is the same with the good of all its parts. If marriage be best for mankind it must be evidently best for individuals, or a permanent and necessary duty must be the cause of evil, and some must be inevitably sacrificed to the convenience of others. In the estimate which you have made of the two states, it appears that the incommodities of a single life are, in a great measure, necessary and certain, but those of the conjugal state accidental and avoidable.

"I cannot forbear to flatter myself that prudence and benevolence will make marriage happy. The general folly of mankind is the cause of general complaint. What can be expected but disappointment and repentance from a choice made in the immaturity of youth, in the ardor of desire, without judgment, without foresight, without inquiry after conformity of opinions, similarity of manners, rectitude of judgment, or purity of sentiment.

"Such is the common process of marriage. A youth and maiden meeting by chance, or brought together by artifice, exchange glances, reciprocate civilities, go home, and dream of one another. Having little to divert attention, or diversify thought, they find themselves uneasy when they are apart, and therefore conclude that they shall be happy together. They marry, and discover what nothing but voluntary blindness had before concealed; they wear out life in altercations, and charge nature with cruelty.

"From those early marriages proceeds likewise the rivalry of parents and children: the son is eager to enjoy the world before the father is willing to forsake it, and there is hardly room at once for two generations. The daughter begins to bloom before the mother can be content to fade, and neither can forbear to wish for the absence of the other.

"Surely all these evils may be avoided by that deliberation and delay which prudence prescribes to irrevocable choice. In the variety and jollity of youthful pleasures life may be well enough supported without the help of a partner. Longer time will increase experience, and wider views will allow better opportunities of inquiry and selection: one advantage, at least, will be certain; the parents will be visibly older than their children."

"What reason cannot collect," said Nekayah, "and what experiment has not yet taught, can be known only from the report of others. I have been told that late marriages are not eminently happy. This is a question too important to be neglected, and I have often proposed it to those, whose accuracy of remark, and comprehensiveness of knowledge, made their suffrages[3] worthy of regard. They have generally determined that it is dangerous for a man and woman to suspend their fate upon each other, at a time when opinions are fixed, and habits are established; when friendships have been contracted on both sides, when life has been planned into method, and the mind has long enjoyed the contemplation of its own prospects.

"It is scarcely possible that two traveling through the world under the conduct of chance should have been both directed to the same path, and it will not often happen that either will quit the track which custom has made pleasing. When the desultory levity of youth has settled into regularity, it is soon succeeded by pride ashamed to yield, or obstinacy delighting to contend. And even though mutual esteem produces mutual desire to please, time itself, as it modifies unchangeably the external mien, determines likewise the direction of the passions, and gives an inflexible rigidity to the manners. Long customs are not easily broken: he that attempts to change the course of his own life very often labors in vain; and how shall we do that for others which we are seldom able to do for ourselves?"

"But surely," interposed the prince, "you suppose the chief motive of choice forgotten or neglected. Whenever I shall seek a wife, it shall be my first question, whether she be willing to be led by reason?"

"Thus it is," said Nekayah, "that philosophers are deceived. There are a thousand familiar[4] disputes which reason never can decide; questions that elude investigation, and make logic ridiculous; cases where something must be done, and where little can be said. Consider the state of mankind, and inquire how few can be supposed to act upon any occasions, whether small or great, with all the reasons of action present to their minds. Wretched would be the pair above all names of wretchedness, who should be doomed to adjust by reason every morning all the minute detail of a domestic day.

"Those who marry at an advanced age will probably escape the encroachments of their children; but, in diminution of this advantage, they will be likely to leave them, ignorant and helpless, to a guardian's mercy: or, if that should not happen, they must at least go out of the world before they see those whom they love best either wise or great.

"From their children, if they have less to fear, they have less also to hope, and they lose, without equivalent, the joys of early love, and the convenience of uniting with manners pliant and minds susceptible of new impressions, which might wear away their dissimilitudes by long cohabitation, as soft bodies, by continual attrition, conform their surfaces to each other.

3. Opinions.   4. Domestic.

"I believe it will be found that those who marry late are best pleased with their children, and those who marry early with their partners."

"The union of these two affections," said Rasselas, "would produce all that could be wished. Perhaps there is a time when marriage might unite them, a time neither too early for the father, nor too late for the husband."

"Every hour," answered the princess, "confirms my prejudice in favor of the position so often uttered by the mouth of Imlac, 'That nature sets her gifts on the right hand and on the left.' Those conditions, which flatter hope and attract desire, are so constituted that, as we approach one, we recede from another. There are goods so opposed that we cannot seize both, but, by too much prudence, may pass between them at too great a distance to reach either. This is often the fate of long consideration; he does nothing who endeavors to do more than is allowed to humanity. Flatter not yourself with contrarieties of pleasure. Of the blessings set before you make your choice, and be content. No man can taste the fruits of autumn, while he is delighting his scent with the flowers of the spring: no man can, at the same time, fill his cup from the source and from the mouth of the Nile."

Chapter 30. Imlac Enters, and Changes the Conversation

Here Imlac entered, and interrupted them. "Imlac," said Rasselas, "I have been taking from the princess the dismal history of private life, and am almost discouraged from further search."

"It seems to me," said Imlac, "that while you are making the choice of life, you neglect to live. You wander about a single city, which, however large and diversified, can now afford few novelties, and forget that you are in a country, famous among the earliest monarchies for the power and wisdom of its inhabitants; a country where the sciences first dawned that illuminate the world, and beyond which the arts cannot be traced of civil society or domestic life.

"The old Egyptians have left behind them monuments of industry and power before which all European magnificence is confessed to fade away. The ruins of their architecture are the schools of modern builders, and from the wonders which time has spared we may conjecture, though uncertainly, what it has destroyed."

"My curiosity," said Rasselas, "does not very strongly lead me to survey piles of stone, or mounds of earth; my business is with man. I came hither not to measure fragments of temples, or trace choked aqueducts, but to look upon the various scenes of the present world."

"The things that are now before us," said the princess, "require attention, and deserve it. What have I to do with the heroes or the monuments of ancient times? with times which never can return, and heroes, whose form of life was different from all that the present condition of mankind requires or allows."

"To know anything," returned the poet, "we must know its effects; to see men we must see their works, that we may learn what reason has dictated, or passion has incited, and find what are the most powerful motives of action. To judge rightly of the present we must oppose it to the past; for all judgment is comparative, and of the future nothing can be known. The truth is, that no mind is much employed upon the present: recollection and anticipation fill up almost all our moments. Our passions are joy and grief, love and hatred, hope and fear. Of joy and grief the past is the object, and the future of hope and fear; even love and hatred respect the past, for the cause must have been before the effect.

"The present state of things is the consequence of the former, and it is natural to inquire what were the sources of the good that we enjoy, or of the evil that we suffer. If we act only for ourselves, to neglect the study of history is not prudent: if we are entrusted with the care of others, it is not just. Ignorance, when it is voluntary, is criminal; and he may properly be charged with evil who refused to learn how he might prevent it.

"There is no part of history so generally useful as that which relates the progress of the human mind, the gradual improvement of reason, the successive advances of science, the vicissitudes of learning and ignorance, which are the light and darkness of thinking beings, the extinction and resuscitation of arts, and all the revolutions of the intellectual world. If accounts of battles and invasions are peculiarly the business of princes, the useful or elegant arts are not to be neglected; those who have kingdoms to govern, have understandings to cultivate.

"Example is always more efficacious than precept. A soldier is formed in war, and a painter must copy pictures. In this, contemplative life has the advantage: great actions are seldom seen, but the labors of art are always at hand for those who desire to know what art has been able to perform.

"When the eye or the imagination is struck with any uncommon work the next transition of an active mind is to the means by which it was performed. Here begins the true use of such contemplation; we enlarge our comprehension by new ideas, and perhaps recover some art lost to mankind, or learn what is less perfectly known in our own country. At least we compare our own with former times, and either rejoice at our improvements, or, what is the first motion towards good, discover our defects."

"I am willing," said the prince, "to see all that can deserve my search." "And I," said the princess, "shall rejoice to learn something of the manners of antiquity."

"The most pompous monument of Egyptian greatness, and one of the most bulky works of manual industry," said Imlac, "are the pyramids; fabrics[5] raised before the time of history, and of which the earliest narratives afford us only uncertain traditions. Of these the greatest is still standing, very little injured by time."

"Let us visit them tomorrow," said Nekayah. "I have often heard of the pyramids, and shall not rest, till I have seen them within and without with my own eyes."

Chapter 31. They Visit the Pyramids

The resolution being thus taken, they set out the next day. They laid tents upon their camels, being resolved to stay among the pyramids till their curiosity was fully satisfied. They traveled gently, turned aside to everything remarkable, stopped from time to time and conversed with the inhabitants, and observed the various appearances of towns ruined and inhabited, of wild and cultivated nature.

5. Buildings.

When they came to the great pyramid, they were astonished at the extent of the base, and the height of the top. Imlac explained to them the principles upon which the pyramidal form was chosen for a fabric intended to coextend its duration with that of the world; he showed that its gradual diminution gave it such stability as defeated all the common attacks of the elements, and could scarcely be overthrown by earthquakes themselves, the least resistible of natural violence. A concussion that should shatter the pyramid would threaten the dissolution of the continent.

They measured all its dimensions, and pitched their tents at its foot. Next day they prepared to enter its interior apartments, and having hired the common guides, climbed up to the first passage, when the favorite of the princess, looking into the cavity, stepped back and trembled. "Pekuah," said the princess, "of what art thou afraid?" "Of the narrow entrance," answered the lady, "and of the dreadful gloom. I dare not enter a place which must surely be inhabited by unquiet souls. The original possessors of these dreadful vaults will start up before us, and perhaps shut us in forever." She spoke, and threw her arms round the neck of her mistress.

"If all your fear be of apparitions," said the prince, "I will promise you safety. There is no danger from the dead; he that is once buried will be seen no more."

"That the dead are seen no more," said Imlac, "I will not undertake to maintain, against the concurrent and unvaried testimony of all ages, and of all nations. There is no people, rude or learned, among whom apparitions of the dead are not related and believed. This opinion, which perhaps prevails as far as human nature is diffused, could become universal only by its truth; those that never heard of one another would not have agreed in a tale which nothing but experience can make credible. That it is doubted by single cavilers can very little weaken the general evidence; and some who deny it with their tongues confess it by their fears.

"Yet I do not mean to add new terrors to those which have already seized upon Pekuah. There can be no reason why specters should haunt the pyramid more than other places, or why they should have power or will to hurt innocence and purity. Our entrance is no violation of their privileges; we can take nothing from them, how then can we offend them?"

"My dear Pekuah," said the princess, "I will always go before you, and Imlac shall follow you. Remember that you are the companion of the princess of Abyssinia."

"If the princess is pleased that her servant should die," returned the lady, "let her command some death less dreadful than enclosure in this horrid cavern. You know I dare not disobey you; I must go if you command me, but if I once enter, I never shall come back."

The princess saw that her fear was too strong for expostulation or reproof, and, embracing her, told her that she should stay in the tent till their return. Pekuah was yet not satisfied, but entreated the princess not to pursue so dreadful a purpose as that of entering the recesses of the pyramid. "Though I cannot teach courage," said Nekayah, "I must not learn cowardice, nor leave at last undone what I came hither only to do."

Chapter 32. They Enter the Pyramid

Pekuah descended to the tents, and the rest entered the pyramid. They passed through the galleries, surveyed the vaults of marble, and examined the chest in which the body of the founder is supposed to have been reposited. They then sat down in one of the most spacious chambers to rest a while before they attempted to return.

"We have now," said Imlac, "gratified our minds with an exact view of the greatest work of man, except the wall of China.

"Of the wall it is very easy to assign the motive. It secured a wealthy and timorous nation from the incursions of barbarians, whose unskillfulness in arts made it easier for them to supply their wants by rapine than by industry, and who from time to time poured in upon the habitations of peaceful commerce, as vultures descend upon domestic fowl. Their celerity and fierceness made the wall necessary, and their ignorance made it efficacious.

"But for the pyramids, no reason has ever been given adequate to the cost and labor of the work. The narrowness of the chambers proves that it could afford no retreat from enemies, and treasures might have been reposited at far less expense with equal security. It seems to have been erected only in compliance with that hunger of imagination which preys incessantly upon life, and must be always appeased by some employment. Those who have already all that they can enjoy must enlarge their desires. He that has built for use till use is supplied, must begin to build for vanity, and extend his plan to the utmost power of human performance, that he may not be soon reduced to form another wish.

"I consider this mighty structure as a monument of the insufficiency of human enjoyments. A king, whose power is unlimited, and whose treasures surmount all real and imaginary wants, is compelled to solace, by the erection of a pyramid, the satiety of dominion and tastelessness of pleasures, and to amuse the tediousness of declining life by seeing thousands laboring without end, and one stone, for no purpose, laid upon another. Whoever thou art, that, not content with a moderate condition, imaginest happiness in royal magnificence, and dreamest that command or riches can feed the appetite of novelty with perpetual gratifications, survey the pyramids, and confess thy folly!"

Chapter 33. The Princess Meets with an Unexpected Misfortune

They rose up, and returned through the cavity at which they had entered, and the princess prepared for her favorite a long narrative of dark labyrinths, and costly rooms, and of the different impressions which the varieties of the way had made upon her. But when they came to their train, they found every one silent and dejected: the men discovered[6] shame and fear in their countenances, and the women were weeping in the tents.

What had happened they did not try to conjecture, but immediately inquired. "You had scarcely entered into the pyramid," said one of the attendants, "when a troop of Arabs rushed upon us: we were too few to resist them, and too slow to escape. They were about to search the tents, set us on our

6. Revealed, betrayed. "Train": retinue.

camels, and drive us along before them, when the approach of some Turkish horsemen put them to flight; but they seized the lady Pekuah with her two maids, and carried them away: the Turks are now pursuing them by our instigation, but I fear they will not be able to overtake them."

The princess was overpowered with surprise and grief. Rasselas, in the first heat of his resentment, ordered his servants to follow him, and prepared to pursue the robbers with his saber in his hand. "Sir," said Imlac, "what can you hope from violence or valor? the Arabs are mounted on horses trained to battle and retreat; we have only beasts of burden. By leaving our present station we may lose the princess, but cannot hope to regain Pekuah."

In a short time the Turks returned, having not been able to reach the enemy. The princess burst out into new lamentations, and Rasselas could scarcely forbear to reproach them with cowardice; but Imlac was of opinion, that the escape of the Arabs was no addition to their misfortune, for, perhaps, they would have killed their captives rather than have resigned them.

Chapter 34. *They Return to Cairo without Pekuah*

There was nothing to be hoped from longer stay. They returned to Cairo repenting of their curiosity, censuring the negligence of the government, lamenting their own rashness which had neglected to procure a guard, imagining many expedients by which the loss of Pekuah might have been prevented, and resolving to do something for her recovery, though none could find any thing proper to be done.

Nekayah retired to her chamber, where her women attempted to comfort her, by telling her that all had their troubles, and that lady Pekuah had enjoyed much happiness in the world for a long time, and might reasonably expect a change of fortune. They hoped that some good would befall her wheresoever she was, and that their mistress would find another friend who might supply her place.

The princess made them no answer, and they continued the form of condolence, not much grieved in their hearts that the favorite was lost.

Next day the prince presented to the Bassa a memorial[7] of the wrong which he had suffered, and a petition for redress. The Bassa threatened to punish the robbers, but did not attempt to catch them, nor, indeed, could any account or description be given by which he might direct the pursuit.

It soon appeared that nothing would be done by authority. Governors, being accustomed to hear of more crimes than they can punish, and more wrongs than they can redress, set themselves at ease by indiscriminate negligence, and presently[8] forget the request when they lose sight of the petitioner.

Imlac then endeavored to gain some intelligence by private agents. He found many who pretended to an exact knowledge of all the haunts of the Arabs, and to regular correspondence with their chiefs, and who readily undertook the recovery of Pekuah. Of these, some were furnished with money for their journey, and came back no more; some were liberally paid for accounts which a few days discovered to be false. But the princess would not suffer any means, however improbable, to be left untried. While she was

7. Statement of facts.   8. Immediately.

doing something she kept her hope alive. As one expedient failed, another was suggested; when one messenger returned unsuccessful, another was dispatched to a different quarter.

Two months had now passed, and of Pekuah nothing had been heard; the hopes which they had endeavored to raise in each other grew more languid, and the princess, when she saw nothing more to be tried, sunk down inconsolable in hopeless dejection. A thousand times she reproached herself with the easy compliance by which she permitted her favorite to stay behind her. "Had not my fondness," said she, "lessened my authority, Pekuah had not dared to talk of her terrors. She ought to have feared me more than specters. A severe look would have overpowered her; a peremptory command would have compelled obedience. Why did foolish indulgence prevail upon me? Why did I not speak and refuse to hear?"

"Great princess," said Imlac, "do not reproach yourself for your virtue, or consider that as blameable by which evil has accidentally been caused. Your tenderness for the timidity of Pekuah was generous and kind. When we act according to our duty, we commit the event to him by whose laws our actions are governed, and who will suffer none to be finally punished for obedience. When, in prospect of some good, whether natural or moral, we break the rules prescribed us, we withdraw from the direction of superior wisdom, and take all consequences upon ourselves. Man cannot so far know the connection of causes and events, as that he may venture to do wrong in order to do right. When we pursue our end by lawful means, we may always console our miscarriage by the hope of future recompense. When we consult only our own policy, and attempt to find a nearer way to good, by overleaping the settled boundaries of right and wrong, we cannot be happy even by success, because we cannot escape the consciousness of our fault; but, if we miscarry, the disappointment is irremediably embittered. How comfortless is the sorrow of him, who feels at once the pangs of guilt, and the vexation of calamity which guilt has brought upon him?

"Consider, princess, what would have been your condition, if the lady Pekuah had entreated to accompany you, and, being compelled to stay in the tents, had been carried away; or how would you have borne the thought, if you had forced her into the pyramid, and she had died before you in agonies of terror."

"Had either happened," said Nekayah, "I could not have endured life till now: I should have been tortured to madness by the remembrance of such cruelty, or must have pined away in abhorrence of myself."

"This at least," said Imlac, "is the present reward of virtuous conduct, that no unlucky consequence can oblige us to repent it."

Chapter 35. *The Princess Languishes for Want of Pekuah*

Nekayah, being thus reconciled to herself, found that no evil is insupportable but that which is accompanied with consciousness of wrong. She was, from that time, delivered from the violence of tempestuous sorrow, and sunk into silent pensiveness and gloomy tranquillity. She sat from morning to evening recollecting all that had been done or said by her Pekuah, treasured up with might recall to mind any little incident or careless conversation. The sentiments of her, whom she now expected to see no more, were treasured in her memory as rules of life, and she deliberated to no other end than to conjecture on any occasion what would have been the opinion and counsel of Pekuah.

The women, by whom she was attended, knew nothing of her real condition, and therefore she could not talk to them but with caution and reserve. She began to remit[9] her curiosity, having no great care to collect notions which she had no convenience of uttering. Rasselas endeavored first to comfort and afterwards to divert her; he hired musicians, to whom she seemed to listen, but did not hear them, and procured masters to instruct her in various arts, whose lectures, when they visited her again, were again to be repeated. She had lost her taste of pleasure and her ambition of excellence. And her mind, though forced into short excursions, always recurred to the image of her friend.

Imlac was every morning earnestly enjoined to renew his inquiries, and was asked every night whether he had yet heard of Pekuah, till not being able to return the princess the answer that she desired, he was less and less willing to come into her presence. She observed his backwardness, and commanded him to attend her. "You are not," said she, "to confound impatience with resentment, or to suppose that I charge you with negligence, because I repine at your unsuccessfulness. I do not much wonder at your absence; I know that the unhappy are never pleasing, and that all naturally avoid the contagion of misery. To hear complaints is wearisome alike to the wretched and the happy; for who would cloud by adventitious grief the short gleams of gaiety which life allows us? or who, that is struggling under his own evils, will add to them the miseries of another?

"The time is at hand, when none shall be disturbed any longer by the sighs of Nekayah: my search after happiness is now at an end. I am resolved to retire from the world with all its flatteries and deceits, and will hide myself in solitude, without any other care than to compose my thoughts, and regulate my hours by a constant succession of innocent occupations, till, with a mind purified from all earthly desires, I shall enter into that state, to which all are hastening, and in which I hope again to enjoy the friendship of Pekuah."

"Do not entangle your mind," said Imlac, "by irrevocable determinations, nor increase the burden of life by a voluntary accumulation of misery: the weariness of retirement will continue or increase when the loss of Pekuah is forgotten. That you have been deprived of one pleasure is no very good reason for rejection of the rest."

"Since Pekuah was taken from me," said the princess, "I have no pleasure to reject or to retain. She that has no one to love or trust has little to hope. She wants the radical principle of happiness. We may, perhaps, allow that what satisfaction this world can afford, must arise from the conjunction of wealth, knowledge and goodness: wealth is nothing but as it is bestowed, and knowledge nothing but as it is communicated: they must therefore be imparted to others, and to whom could I now delight to impart them? Goodness affords the only comfort which can be enjoyed without a partner, and goodness may be practised in retirement."

"How far solitude may admit goodness, or advance it, I shall not," replied Imlac, "dispute at present. Remember the confession of the pious hermit.

9. Slacken.

You will wish to return into the world, when the image of your companion has left your thoughts." "That time," said Nekayah, "will never come. The generous frankness, the modest obsequiousness,[1] and the faithful secrecy of my dear Pekuah, will always be more missed, as I shall live longer to see vice and folly."

"The state of a mind oppressed with a sudden calamity," said Imlac, "is like that of the fabulous inhabitants of the new created earth, who, when the first night came upon them, supposed that day never would return. When the clouds of sorrow gather over us, we see nothing beyond them, nor can imagine how they will be dispelled: yet a new day succeeded to the night, and sorrow is never long without a dawn of ease. But they who restrain themselves from receiving comfort, do as the savages would have done, had they put out their eyes when it was dark. Our minds, like our bodies, are in continual flux; something is hourly lost, and something acquired. To lose much at once is inconvenient to either, but while the vital powers remain uninjured, nature will find the means of reparation. Distance has the same effect on the mind as on the eye, and while we glide along the stream of time, whatever we leave behind us is always lessening, and that which we approach increasing in magnitude. Do not suffer life to stagnate; it will grow muddy for want of motion: commit yourself again to the current of the world; Pekuah will vanish by degrees; you will meet in your way some other favorite, or learn to diffuse yourself in general conversation."

"At least," said the prince, "do not despair before all remedies have been tried: the inquiry after the unfortunate lady is still continued, and shall be carried on with yet greater diligence, on condition that you will promise to wait a year for the event, without any unalterable resolution."

Nekayah thought this a reasonable demand, and made the promise to her brother, who had been advised by Imlac to require it. Imlac had, indeed, no great hope of regaining Pekuah, but he supposed, that if he could secure the interval of a year, the princess would be then in no danger of a cloister.

Chapter 36. Pekuah Is Still Remembered. The Progress of Sorrow

Nekayah, seeing that nothing was omitted for the recovery of her favorite, and having, by her promise, set her intention of retirement at a distance, began imperceptibly to return to common cares and common pleasures. She rejoiced without her own consent at the suspension of her sorrows, and sometimes caught herself with indignation in the act of turning away her mind from the remembrance of her, whom yet she resolved never to forget.

She then appointed a certain hour of the day for meditation on the merits and fondness of Pekuah, and for some weeks retired constantly at the time fixed, and returned with her eyes swollen and her countenance clouded. By degrees she grew less scrupulous, and suffered any important and pressing avocation to delay the tribute of daily tears. She then yielded to less occasions; sometimes forgot what she was indeed afraid to remember, and, at last, wholly released herself from the duty of periodical affliction.

Her real love of Pekuah was yet not diminished. A thousand occurrences brought her back to memory, and a thousand wants, which nothing but the

1. Obedience.

confidence of friendship can supply, made her frequently regretted. She, therefore, solicited Imlac never to desist from inquiry, and to leave no art of intelligence untried, that, at least, she might have the comfort of knowing that she did not suffer by negligence or sluggishness. "Yet what," said she, "is to be expected from our pursuit of happiness, when we find the state of life to be such, that happiness itself is the cause of misery? Why should we endeavor to attain that, of which the possession cannot be secured? I shall henceforward fear to yield my heart to excellence, however bright, or to fondness, however tender, lest I should lose again what I have lost in Pekuah."

Chapter 37. *The Princess Hears News of Pekuah*

In seven months, one of the messengers, who had been sent away upon the day when the promise was drawn from the princess, returned, after many unsuccessful rambles, from the borders of Nubia, with an account that Pekuah was in the hands of an Arab chief, who possessed a castle or fortress on the extremity of Egypt. The Arab, whose revenue was plunder, was willing to restore her, with her two attendants, for two hundred ounces of gold.

The price was no subject of debate. The princess was in ecstasies when she heard that her favorite was alive, and might so cheaply be ransomed. She could not think of delaying for a moment Pekuah's happiness or her own, but entreated her brother to send back the messenger with the sum required. Imlac, being consulted, was not very confident of the veracity of the relator, and was still more doubtful of the Arab's faith, who might, if he were too liberally trusted, detain at once the money and the captives. He thought it dangerous to put themselves in the power of the Arab, by going into his district, and could not expect that the rover[2] would so much expose himself as to come into the lower country, where he might be seized by the forces of the Bassa.

It is difficult to negotiate where neither will trust. But Imlac, after some deliberation, directed the messenger to propose that Pekuah should be conducted by ten horsemen to the monastery of St. Anthony, which is situated in the deserts of Upper Egypt, where she should be met by the same number, and her ransom should be paid.

That no time might be lost, as they expected that the proposal would not be refused, they immediately began their journey to the monastery; and, when they arrived, Imlac went forward with the former messenger to the Arab's fortress. Rasselas was desirous to go with them, but neither his sister nor Imlac would consent. The Arab, according to the custom of his nation, observed the laws of hospitality with great exactness to those who put themselves into his power, and, in a few days, brought Pekuah with her maids, by easy journeys, to their place appointed, where receiving the stipulated price, he restored her with great respect to liberty and her friends, and undertook to conduct them back toward Cairo beyond all danger of robbery or violence.

The princess and her favorite embraced each other with transport too violent to be expressed, and went out together to pour the tears of tenderness in secret, and exchange professions of kindness and gratitude. After a few hours they returned into the refectory of the convent, where, in the

2. Robber.

presence of the prior and his brethren, the prince required of Pekuah the history of her adventures.

Chapter 38. *The Adventures of the Lady Pekuah*

"At what time, and in what manner, I was forced away," said Pekuah, "your servants have told you. The suddenness of the event struck me with surprise, and I was at first rather stupified than agitated with any passion of either fear or sorrow. My confusion was increased by the speed and tumult of our flight while we were followed by the Turks, who, as it seemed, soon despaired to overtake us, or were afraid of those whom they made a show of menacing.

"When the Arabs saw themselves out of danger they slackened their course, and, as I was less harassed by external violence, I began to feel more uneasiness in my mind. After some time we stopped near a spring shaded with trees in a pleasant meadow, where we were set upon the ground, and offered such refreshments as our masters were partaking. I was suffered to sit with my maids apart from the rest, and none attempted to comfort or insult us. Here I first began to feel the full weight of my misery. The girls sat weeping in silence, and from time to time looked on me for succor. I knew not to what condition we were doomed, nor could conjecture where would be the place of our captivity, or whence to draw any hope of deliverance. I was in the hands of robbers and savages, and had no reason to suppose that their pity was more than their justice, or that they would forbear the gratification of any ardor of desire, or caprice of cruelty. I, however, kissed my maids, and endeavored to pacify them by remarking, that we were yet treated with decency, and that, since we were now carried beyond pursuit, there was no danger of violence to our lives.

"When we were to be set again on horseback, my maids clung round me, and refused to be parted, but I commanded them not to irritate those who had us in their power. We traveled the remaining part of the day through an unfrequented and pathless country, and came by moonlight to the side of a hill, where the rest of the troop was stationed. Their tents were pitched, and their fires kindled, and our chief was welcomed as a man much beloved by his dependents.

"We were received into a large tent, where we found women who had attended their husbands in the expedition. They set before us the supper which they had provided, and I eat it rather to encourage my maids than to comply with any appetite of my own. When the meat was taken away they spread the carpets for repose. I was weary, and hoped to find in sleep that remission of distress which nature seldom denies. Ordering myself therefore to be undressed, I observed that the women looked very earnestly upon me, not expecting, I suppose, to see me so submissively attended. When my upper vest was taken off, they were apparently struck with the splendor of my clothes, and one of them timorously laid her hand upon the embroidery. She then went out, and, in a short time, came back with another woman, who seemed to be of higher rank, and greater authority. She did, at her entrance, the usual act of reverence, and, taking me by the hand, placed me in a smaller tent, spread with finer carpets, where I spent the night quietly with my maids.

"In the morning, as I was sitting on the grass, the chief of the troop came towards me: I rose up to receive him, and he bowed with great respect.

'Illustrious lady,' said he, 'my fortune is better than I had presumed to hope; I am told by my women that I have a princess in my camp.' 'Sir,' answered I, 'your women have deceived themselves and you; I am not a princess, but an unhappy stranger who intended soon to have left this country, in which I am now to be imprisoned for ever.' 'Whoever, or whencesoever, you are,' returned the Arab, 'your dress, and that of your servants, show your rank to be high, and your wealth to be great. Why should you, who can so easily procure your ransom, think yourself in danger of perpetual captivity? The purpose of my incursions is to increase my riches, or more properly to gather tribute. The sons of Ishmael[3] are the natural and hereditary lords of this part of the continent, which is usurped by late invaders, and low-born tyrants, from whom we are compelled to take by the sword what is denied to justice. The violence of war admits no distinction; the lance that is lifted at guilt and power will sometimes fall on innocence and gentleness.'

"'How little,' said I, 'did I expect that yesterday it should have fallen upon me.'

"'Misfortunes,' answered the Arab, 'should always be expected. If the eye of hostility could learn reverence or pity, excellence like yours had been exempt from injury. But the angels of affliction spread their toils alike for the virtuous and the wicked, for the mighty and the mean. Do not be disconsolate; I am not one of the lawless and cruel rovers of the desert; I know the rules of civil life: I will fix your ransom, give a passport to your messenger, and perform my stipulation with nice punctuality.'[4]

"You will easily believe that I was pleased with his courtesy; and finding that his predominant passion was desire of money, I began now to think my danger less, for I knew that no sum would be thought too great for the release of Pekuah. I told him that he should have no reason to charge me with ingratitude, if I was used with kindness, and that any ransom, which could be expected for a maid of common rank, would be paid, but that he must not persist to rate me as a princess. He said, he would consider what he should demand, and then, smiling, bowed and retired.

"Soon after the women came about me, each contending to be more officious[5] than the other, and my maids themselves were served with reverence. We traveled onward by short journeys. On the fourth day the chief told me, that my ransom must be two hundred ounces of gold, which I not only promised him, but told him, that I would add fifty more, if I and my maids were honorably treated.

"I never knew the power of gold before. From that time I was the leader of the troop. The march of every day was longer or shorter as I commanded, and the tents were pitched where I chose to rest. We now had camels and other conveniencies for travel, my own women were always at my side, and I amused myself with observing the manners of the vagrant nations,[6] and with viewing remains of ancient edifices with which these deserted countries appear to have been, in some distant age, lavishly embellished.

"The chief of the band was a man far from illiterate: he was able to travel by the stars or the compass, and had marked in his erratic expeditions such

3. Arabs, who claim descent from Ishmael, a son of Abraham.
4. Scrupulous exactness. "Civil": civilized.

5. Ready to serve.
6. Nomads.

places as are most worthy the notice of a passenger.[7] He observed to me, that buildings are always best preserved in places little frequented, and difficult of access: for, when once a country declines from its primitive splendor, the more inhabitants are left, the quicker ruin will be made. Walls supply stones more easily than quarries, and palaces and temples will be demolished to make stables of granite, and cottages of porphyry.

Chapter 39. *The Adventures of Pekuah Continued*

"We wandered about in this manner for some weeks, whether, as our chief pretended, for my gratification, or, as I rather suspected, for some convenience of his own. I endeavored to appear contented where sullenness and resentment would have been of no use, and that endeavor conduced much to the calmness of my mind; but my heart was always with Nekayah, and the troubles of the night much overbalanced the amusements of the day. My women, who threw all their cares upon their mistress, set their minds at ease from the time when they saw me treated with respect, and gave themselves up to the incidental alleviations of our fatigue without solicitude or sorrow. I was pleased with their pleasure, and animated with their confidence. My condition had lost much of its terror, since I found that the Arab ranged the country merely to get riches. Avarice is an uniform and tractable vice: other intellectual distempers are different in different constitutions of mind; that which soothes the pride of one will offend the pride of another; but to the favor of the covetous there is a ready way, bring money and nothing is denied.

"At last we came to the dwelling of our chief, a strong and spacious house built with stone in an island of the Nile, which lies, as I was told, under the tropic. 'Lady,' said the Arab, 'you shall rest after your journey a few weeks in this place, where you are to consider yourself as sovereign. My occupation is war: I have therefore chosen this obscure residence, from which I can issue unexpected, and to which I can retire unpursued. You may now repose in security: here are few pleasures, but here is no danger.' He then led me into the inner apartments, and seating me on the richest couch, bowed to the ground. His women, who considered me as a rival, looked on me with malignity; but being soon informed that I was a great lady detained only for my ransom, they began to vie with each other in obsequiousness and reverence.

"Being again comforted with new assurances of speedy liberty, I was for some days diverted from impatience by the novelty of the place. The turrets overlooked the country to a great distance, and afforded a view of many windings of the stream. In the day I wandered from one place to another as the course of the sun varied the splendor of the prospect, and saw many things which I had never seen before. The crocodiles and river-horses[8] are common in this unpeopled region, and I often looked upon them with terror, though I knew that they could not hurt me. For some time I expected to see mermaids and tritons, which, as Imlac has told me, the European travelers have stationed in the Nile, but no such beings ever appeared, and the Arab, when I inquired after them, laughed at my credulity.

"At night the Arab always attended me to a tower set apart for celestial observations, where he endeavored to teach me the names and courses of

7. Traveler.   8. Hippopotamuses.

the stars. I had no great inclination to this study, but an appearance of attention was necessary to please my instructor, who valued himself for his skill,
and, in a little while, I found some employment requisite to beguile the
tediousness of time, which was to be passed always amidst the same objects.
I was weary of looking in the morning on things from which I had turned
away weary in the evening: I therefore was at last willing to observe the stars
rather than do nothing, but could not always compose my thoughts, and was
very often thinking on Nekayah when others imagined me contemplating
the sky. Soon after the Arab went upon another expedition, and then my
only pleasure was to talk with my maids about the accident by which we
were carried away, and the happiness that we should all enjoy at the end of
our captivity."

"There were women in your Arab's fortress," said the princess, "why did
you not make them your companions, enjoy their conversation, and partake
their diversions? In a place where they found business or amusement, why
should you alone sit corroded with idle melancholy? or why could not you
bear for a few months that condition to which they were condemned for life?"

"The diversions of the women," answered Pekuah, "were only childish play,
by which the mind accustomed to stronger operations could not be kept busy.
I could do all which they delighted in doing by powers merely sensitive,[9] while
my intellectual faculties were flown to Cairo. They ran from room to room as
a bird hops from wire to wire in his cage. They danced for the sake of motion,
as lambs frisk in a meadow. One sometimes pretended to be hurt that the rest
might be alarmed, or hid herself that another might seek her. Part of their
time passed in watching the progress of light bodies that floated on the river,
and part in marking the various forms into which clouds broke in the sky.

"Their business was only needlework, in which I and my maids sometimes helped them; but you know that the mind will easily straggle from the
fingers, nor will you suspect that captivity and absence from Nekayah could
receive solace from silken flowers.

"Nor was much satisfaction to be hoped from their conversation: for of
what could they be expected to talk? They had seen nothing; for they had
lived from early youth in that narrow spot: of what they had not seen they
could have no knowledge, for they could not read. They had no ideas but of
the few things that were within their view, and had hardly names for anything but their clothes and their food. As I bore a superior character, I was
often called to terminate their quarrels, which I decided as equitably as I
could. If it could have amused me to hear the complaints of each against the
rest, I might have been often detained by long stories, but the motives of their
animosity were so small that I could not listen without intercepting the tale."

"How," said Rasselas, "can the Arab, whom you represented as a man of
more than common accomplishments, take any pleasure in his seraglio, when
it is filled only with women like these. Are they exquisitely beautiful?"

"They do not," said Pekuah, "want that unaffecting and ignoble beauty
which may subsist without spriteliness or sublimity, without energy of
thought or dignity of virtue. But to a man like the Arab such beauty was only
a flower casually plucked and carelessly thrown away. Whatever pleasures he

9. "Having sense or perception, but not reason" (Johnson's *Dictionary*).

might find among them, they were not those of friendship or society. When they were playing about him he looked on them with inattentive superiority: when they vied for his regard he sometimes turned away disgusted. As they had no knowledge, their talk could take nothing from the tediousness of life: as they had no choice, their fondness, or appearance of fondness, excited in him neither pride nor gratitude; he was not exalted in his own esteem by the smiles of a woman who saw no other man, nor was much obliged by that regard, of which he could never know the sincerity, and which he might often perceive to be exerted not so much to delight him as to pain a rival. That which he gave, and they received, as love, was only a careless distribution of superfluous time, such love as man can bestow upon that which he despises, such as has neither hope nor fear, neither joy nor sorrow."

"You have reason, lady, to think yourself happy," said Imlac, "that you have been thus easily dismissed. How could a mind, hungry for knowledge, be willing, in an intellectual famine, to lose such a banquet as Pekuah's conversation?"

"I am inclined to believe," answered Pekuah, "that he was for some time in suspense; for, notwithstanding his promise, whenever I proposed to dispatch a messenger to Cairo, he found some excuse for delay. While I was detained in his house he made many incursions into the neighboring countries, and, perhaps, he would have refused to discharge me, had his plunder been equal to his wishes. He returned always courteous, related his adventures, delighted to hear my observations, and endeavored to advance my acquaintance with the stars. When I importuned him to send away my letters, he soothed me with professions of honor and sincerity; and, when I could be no longer decently denied, put his troop again in motion, and left me to govern in his absence. I was much afflicted by this studied procrastination, and was sometimes afraid that I should be forgotten; that you would leave Cairo, and I must end my days in an island of the Nile.

"I grew at last hopeless and dejected, and cared so little to entertain him, that he for a while more frequently talked with my maids. That he should fall in love with them, or with me, might have been equally fatal, and I was not much pleased with the growing friendship. My anxiety was not long; for, as I recovered some degree of cheerfulness, he returned to me, and I could not forbear to despise my former uneasiness.

"He still delayed to send for my ransom, and would, perhaps, never have determined, had not your agent found his way to him. The gold, which he would not fetch, he could not reject when it was offered. He hastened to prepare for our journey hither, like a man delivered from the pain of an intestine conflict. I took leave of my companions in the house, who dismissed me with cold indifference."

Nekayah, having heard her favorite's relation, rose and embraced her, and Rasselas gave her an hundred ounces of gold, which she presented to the Arab for the fifty that were promised.

Chapter 40. The History of a Man of Learning

They returned to Cairo, and were so well pleased at finding themselves together, that none of them went much abroad. The prince began to love learning, and one day declared to Imlac, that he intended to devote himself to science,[1] and pass the rest of his days in literary solitude.

"Before you make your final choice," answered Imlac, "you ought to examine its hazards, and converse with some of those who are grown old in the company of themselves. I have just left the observatory of one of the most learned astronomers in the world, who has spent forty years in unwearied attention to the motions and appearances of the celestial bodies, and has drawn out his soul in endless calculations. He admits a few friends once a month to hear his deductions and enjoy his discoveries. I was introduced as a man of knowledge worthy of his notice. Men of various ideas and fluent conversation are commonly welcome to those whose thoughts have been long fixed upon a single point, and who find the images of other things stealing away. I delighted him with my remarks, he smiled at the narrative of my travels, and was glad to forget the constellations, and descend for a moment into the lower world.

"On the next day of vacation[2] I renewed my visit, and was so fortunate as to please him again. He relaxed from that time the severity of his rule, and permitted me to enter at my own choice. I found him always busy, and always glad to be relieved. As each knew much which the other was desirous of learning, we exchanged our notions with great delight. I perceived that I had every day more of his confidence, and always found new cause of admiration in the profundity of his mind. His comprehension is vast, his memory capacious and retentive, his discourse is methodical, and his expression clear.

"His integrity and benevolence are equal to his learning. His deepest researches and most favorite studies are willingly interrupted for any opportunity of doing good by his counsel or his riches. To his closest retreat,[3] at his most busy moments, all are admitted that want his assistance: 'For though I exclude idleness and pleasure, I will never,' says he, 'bar my doors against charity. To man is permitted the contemplation of the skies, but the practice of virtue is commanded.'"

"Surely," said the princess, "this man is happy."

"I visited him," said Imlac, "with more and more frequency, and was every time more enamored of his conversation: he was sublime without haughtiness, courteous without formality, and communicative without ostentation. I was at first, great princess, of your opinion, thought him the happiest of mankind, and often congratulated him on the blessing that he enjoyed. He seemed to hear nothing with indifference but the praises of his condition, to which he always returned a general answer, and diverted the conversation to some other topic.

"Amidst this willingness to be pleased, and labor to please, I had quickly reason to imagine that some painful sentiment pressed upon his mind. He often looked up earnestly towards the sun, and let his voice fall in the midst of his discourse. He would sometimes, when we were alone, gaze upon me in silence with the air of a man who longed to speak what he was yet resolved to suppress. He would often send for me with vehement injunctions of haste, though, when I came to him, he had nothing extraordinary to say. And some-

1. Knowledge.
2. Leisure.

3. Most secluded place of privacy.

times, when I was leaving him, he would call me back, pause a few moments and then dismiss me.

Chapter 41. *The Astronomer Discovers the Cause of His Uneasiness*

"At last the time came when the secret burst his reserve. We were sitting together last night in the turret of his house, watching the emersion of a satellite of Jupiter. A sudden tempest clouded the sky, and disappointed our observation. We sat a while silent in the dark, and then he addressed himself to me in these words: 'Imlac, I have long considered thy friendship as the greatest blessing of my life. Integrity without knowledge is weak and useless, and knowledge without integrity is dangerous and dreadful. I have found in thee all the qualities requisite for trust, benevolence, experience, and fortitude. I have long discharged an office which I must soon quit at the call of nature, and shall rejoice in the hour of imbecility[4] and pain to devolve it upon thee.'

"I thought myself honored by this testimony, and protested that whatever could conduce to his happiness would add likewise to mine.

"'Hear, Imlac, what thou wilt not without difficulty credit. I have possessed for five years the regulation of weather, and the distribution of the seasons: the sun has listened to my dictates, and passed from tropic to tropic by my direction; the clouds, at my call, have poured their waters, and the Nile has overflowed at my command; I have restrained the rage of the dog-star, and mitigated the fervors of the crab.[5] The winds alone, of all the elemental powers, have hitherto refused my authority, and multitudes have perished by equinoctial tempests which I found myself unable to prohibit or restrain. I have administered this great office with exact justice, and made to the different nations of the earth an impartial dividend of rain and sunshine. What must have been the misery of half the globe, if I had limited the clouds to particular regions, or confined the sun to either side of the equator?'

Chapter 42. *The Opinion of the Astronomer Is Explained and Justified*

"I suppose he discovered in me, through the obscurity of the room, some tokens of amazement and doubt, for, after a short pause, he proceeded thus:

"'Not to be easily credited will neither surprise nor offend me; for I am, probably, the first of human beings to whom this trust has been imparted. Nor do I know whether to deem this distinction a reward or punishment; since I have possessed it I have been far less happy than before, and nothing but the consciousness of good intention could have enabled me to support the weariness of unremitted vigilance.'

"'How long, Sir,' said I, 'has this great office been in your hands?'

"'About ten years ago,' said he, 'my daily observations of the changes of the sky led me to consider, whether, if I had the power of the seasons, I could confer greater plenty upon the inhabitants of the earth. This contemplation fastened on my mind, and I sat days and nights in imaginary dominion, pouring upon this country and that the showers of fertility, and seconding every

4. Feebleness.
5. The fourth sign of the zodiac (Cancer). "The

dog-star": Sirius was supposed to cause the heat ("dog days") of summer.

fall of rain with a due proportion of sunshine. I had yet only the will to do good, and did not imagine that I should ever have the power.

"'One day as I was looking on the fields withering with heat, I felt in my mind a sudden wish that I could send rain on the southern mountains, and raise the Nile to an inundation. In the hurry of my imagination I commanded rain to fall, and, by comparing the time of my command, with that of the inundation, I found that the clouds had listened to my lips.'

"'Might not some other cause,' said I, 'produce this concurrence? the Nile does not always rise on the same day.'

"'Do not believe,' said he with impatience, 'that such objections could escape me: I reasoned long against my own conviction, and labored against truth with the utmost obstinacy. I sometimes suspected myself of madness, and should not have dared to impart this secret but to a man like you, capable of distinguishing the wonderful from the impossible, and the incredible from the false.'

"'Why, Sir,' said I, 'do you call that incredible, which you know, or think you know, to be true?'

"'Because,' said he, 'I cannot prove it by any external evidence; and I know too well the laws of demonstration to think that my conviction ought to influence another, who cannot, like me, be conscious of its force. I therefore shall not attempt to gain credit by disputation. It is sufficient that I feel this power, that I have long possessed, and every day exerted it. But the life of man is short, the infirmities of age increase upon me, and the time will soon come when the regulator of the year must mingle with the dust. The care of appointing a successor has long disturbed me; the night and the day have been spent in comparisons of all the characters which have come to my knowledge, and I have yet found none so worthy as thyself.'

Chapter 43. *The Astronomer Leaves Imlac His Directions*

"'Hear therefore, what I shall impart, with attention, such as the welfare of a world requires. If the task of a king be considered as difficult, who has the care only of a few millions, to whom he cannot do much good or harm, what must be the anxiety of him, on whom depends the action of the elements, and the great gifts of light and heat!—Hear me therefore with attention.

"'I have diligently considered the position of the earth and sun, and formed innumerable schemes in which I changed their situation. I have sometimes turned aside the axis of the earth, and sometimes varied the ecliptic of the sun: but I have found it impossible to make a disposition by which the world may be advantaged; what one region gains, another loses by any imaginable alteration, even without considering the distant parts of the solar system with which we are unacquainted. Do not, therefore, in thy administration of the year, indulge thy pride by innovation; do not please thyself with thinking that thou canst make thyself renowned to all future ages, by disordering the seasons. The memory of mischief is no desirable fame. Much less will it become thee to let kindness or interest prevail. Never rob other countries of rain to pour it on thine own. For us the Nile is sufficient.'

"I promised that when I possessed the power, I would use it with inflexible integrity, and he dismissed me, pressing my hand. 'My heart,' said he, 'will be now at rest, and my benevolence will no more destroy my quiet: I have found a man of wisdom and virtue, to whom I can cheerfully bequeath the inheritance of the sun.'"

The prince heard this narration with very serious regard, but the princess smiled, and Pekuah convulsed herself with laughter. "Ladies," said Imlac, "to mock the heaviest of human afflictions is neither charitable nor wise. Few can attain this man's knowledge, and few practice his virtues; but all may suffer his calamity. Of the uncertainties of our present state, the most dreadful and alarming is the uncertain continuance of reason."

The princess was recollected, and the favorite was abashed. Rasselas, more deeply affected, inquired of Imlac, whether he thought such maladies of the mind frequent, and how they were contracted.

Chapter 44. The Dangerous Prevalence[6] of Imagination

"Disorders of intellect," answered Imlac, "happen much more often than superficial observers will easily believe. Perhaps, if we speak with rigorous exactness, no human mind is in its right state. There is no man whose imagination does not sometimes predominate over his reason, who can regulate his attention wholly by his will, and whose ideas will come and go at his command. No man will be found in whose mind airy notions do not sometimes tyrannize, and force him to hope or fear beyond the limits of sober probability. All power of fancy over reason is a degree of insanity; but while this power is such as we can control and repress, it is not visible to others, nor considered as any depravation of the mental faculties; it is not pronounced madness but when it comes ungovernable, and apparently influences speech or action.

"To indulge the power of fiction, and send imagination out upon the wing, is often the sport of those who delight too much in silent speculation. When we are alone we are not always busy; the labor of excogitation is too violent to last long; the ardor of inquiry will sometimes give way to idleness or satiety. He who has nothing external that can divert him must find pleasure in his own thoughts, and must conceive himself what he is not; for who is pleased with what he is? He then expatiates in boundless futurity, and culls from all imaginable conditions that which for the present moment he should most desire, amuses his desires with impossible enjoyments, and confers upon his pride unattainable dominion. The mind dances from scene to scene, unites all pleasures in all combinations, and riots in delights which nature and fortune, with all their bounty, cannot bestow.

"In time, some particular train of ideas fixes the attention; all other intellectual gratifications are rejected; the mind, in weariness or leisure, recurs constantly to the favorite conception, and feasts on the luscious falsehood, whenever she is offended with the bitterness of truth. By degrees the reign of fancy is confirmed; she grows first imperious, and in time despotic. Then fictions begin to operate as realities, false opinions fasten upon the mind, and life passes in dreams of rapture or of anguish.

"This, sir, is one of the dangers of solitude, which the hermit has confessed not always to promote goodness, and the astronomer's misery has proved to be not always propitious to wisdom."

6. Predominance.

"I will no more," said the favorite, "imagine myself the queen of Abyssinia. I have often spent the hours which the princess gave to my own disposal, in adjusting ceremonies and regulating the court; I have repressed the pride of the powerful, and granted the petitions of the poor; I have built new palaces in more happy situations, planted groves upon the tops of mountains, and have exulted in the beneficence of royalty, till, when the princess entered, I had almost forgotten to bow down before her."

"And I," said the princess, "will not allow myself any more to play the shepherdess in my waking dreams. I have often soothed my thoughts with the quiet and innocence of pastoral employments, till I have in my chamber heard the winds whistle, and the sheep bleat; sometimes freed the lamb entangled in the thicket, and sometimes with my crook encountered the wolf. I have a dress like that of the village maids, which I put on to help my imagination, and a pipe on which I play softly, and suppose myself followed by my flocks."

"I will confess," said the prince, "an indulgence of fantastic delight more dangerous than yours. I have frequently endeavored to image the possibility of a perfect government, by which all wrong should be restrained, all vice reformed, and all the subjects preserved in tranquility and innocence. This thought produced innumerable schemes of reformation, and dictated many useful regulations and salutary edicts. This has been the sport, and sometimes the labor, of my solitude; and I start, when I think with how little anguish I once supposed the death of my father and my brothers."

"Such," says Imlac, "are the effects of visionary schemes; when we first form them, we know them to be absurd, but familiarize them by degrees, and in time lose sight of their folly."

Chapter 45. They Discourse with an Old Man

The evening was now far past, and they rose to return home. As they walked along the bank of the Nile, delighted with the beams of the moon quivering on the water, they saw at a small distance an old man, whom the prince had often heard in the assembly of the sages. "Yonder," said he, "is one whose years have calmed his passions, but not clouded his reason. Let us close the disquisitions of the night by inquiring what are his sentiments of his own state, that we may know whether youth alone is to struggle with vexation, and whether any better hope remains for the latter part of life."

Here the sage approached and saluted them. They invited him to join their walk, and prattled a while, as acquaintance that had unexpectedly met one another. The old man was cheerful and talkative, and the way seemed short in his company. He was pleased to find himself not disregarded, accompanied them to their house, and, at the prince's request, entered with them. They placed him in the seat of honor, and set wine and conserves before him.

"Sir," said the princess, "an evening walk must give to a man of learning like you pleasures which ignorance and youth can hardly conceive. You know the qualities and the causes of all that you behold, the laws by which the river flows, the periods in which the planets perform their revolutions. Everything must supply you with contemplation, and renew the consciousness of your own dignity."

"Lady," answered he, "let the gay and the vigorous expect pleasure in their excursions; it is enough that age can obtain ease. To me the world has lost its novelty; I look round, and see what I remember to have seen in happier days. I rest against a tree, and consider that in the same shade I once disputed upon the annual overflow of the Nile with a friend who is now silent in the grave. I cast my eyes upward, fix them on the changing moon, and think with pain on the vicissitudes of life. I have ceased to take much delight in physical truth; for what have I to do with those things which I am soon to leave?"

"You may at least recreate[7] yourself," said Imlac, "with the recollection of an honorable and useful life, and enjoy the praise which all agree to give you."

"Praise," said the sage with a sigh, "is to an old man an empty sound. I have neither mother to be delighted with the reputation of her son, nor wife to partake the honors of her husband. I have outlived my friends and my rivals. Nothing is now of much importance; for I cannot extend my interest beyond myself. Youth is delighted with applause, because it is considered as the earnest of some future good, and because the prospect of life is far extended; but to me, who am now declining to decrepitude, there is little to be feared from the malevolence of men, and yet less to be hoped from their affection or esteem. Something they may yet take away, but they can give me nothing. Riches would now be useless, and high employment would be pain. My retrospect of life recalls to my view many opportunities of good neglected, much time squandered upon trifles, and more lost in idleness and vacancy. I leave many great designs unattempted, and many great attempts unfinished. My mind is burthened with no heavy crime, and therefore I compose myself to tranquility; endeavor to abstract my thoughts from hopes and cares which, though reason knows them to be vain, still try to keep their old possession of the heart; expect,[8] with serene humility, that hour which nature cannot long delay; and hope to possess, in a better state, that happiness which here I could not find, and that virtue which here I have not attained."

He arose and went away, leaving his audience not much elated with the hope of long life. The prince consoled himself with remarking that it was not reasonable to be disappointed by this account; for age had never been considered as the season of felicity, and if it was possible to be easy in decline and weakness, it was likely that the days of vigor and alacrity might be happy; that the noon of life might be bright, if the evening could be calm.

The princess suspected that age was querulous and malignant, and delighted to repress the expectations of those who had newly entered the world. She had seen the possessors of estates look with envy on their heirs, and known many who enjoy pleasure no longer than they can confine it to themselves.

Pekuah conjectured that the man was older than he appeared, and was willing to impute his complaints to delirious dejection; or else supposed that he had been unfortunate, and was therefore discontented. "For nothing," said she, "is more common than to call our own condition the condition of life."

Imlac, who had no desire to see them depressed, smiled at the comforts which they could so readily procure to themselves, and remembered that, at the same age, he was equally confident of unmingled prosperity, and equally fertile of consolatory expedients. He forbore to force upon them unwelcome knowledge, which time itself would too soon impress. The princess and her

7. Refresh.   8. Await.

lady retired; the madness of the astronomer hung upon their minds, and they desired Imlac to enter upon his office, and delay next morning the rising of the sun.

Chapter 46. The Princess and Pekuah Visit the Astronomer

The princess and Pekuah, having talked in private of Imlac's astronomer, thought his character at once so amiable and so strange, that they could not be satisfied without a nearer knowledge, and Imlac was requested to find the means of bringing them together.

This was somewhat difficult; the philosopher had never received any visits from women, though he lived in a city that had in it many Europeans who followed the manners of their own countries, and many from other parts of the world that lived there with European liberty. The ladies would not be refused, and several schemes were proposed for the accomplishment of their design. It was proposed to introduce them as strangers in distress, to whom the sage was always accessible; but, after some deliberation, it appeared, that by this artifice, no acquaintance could be formed, for their conversation would be short, and they could not decently importune him often. "This," said Rasselas, "is true; but I have yet a stronger objection against the misrepresentation of your state. I have always considered it as treason against the great republic of human nature, to make any man's virtues the means of deceiving him, whether on great or little occasions. All imposture weakens confidence and chills benevolence. When the sage finds that you are not what you seemed, he will feel the resentment natural to a man who, conscious of great abilities, discovers that he has been tricked by understandings meaner than his own, and, perhaps, the distrust, which he can never afterwards wholly lay aside, may stop the voice of counsel, and close the hand of charity; and where will you find the power of restoring his benefactions to mankind, or his peace to himself?"

To this no reply was attempted, and Imlac began to hope that their curiosity would subside; but next day Pekuah told him, she had now found an honest pretense for a visit to the astronomer, for she would solicit permission to continue under him the studies in which she had been initiated by the Arab, and the princess might go with her either as a fellow-student, or because a woman could not decently come alone. "I am afraid," said Imlac, "that he will be soon weary of your company: men advanced far in knowledge do not love to repeat the elements of their art, and I am not certain, that even of the elements, as he will deliver them connected with inferences, and mingled with reflections, you are a very capable auditress." "That," said Pekuah, "must be my care: I ask of you only to take me thither. My knowledge is, perhaps, more than you imagine it, and by concurring always with his opinions I shall make him think it greater than it is."

The astronomer, in pursuance of this resolution, was told, that a foreign lady, traveling in search of knowledge, had heard of his reputation, and was desirous to become his scholar. The uncommonness of the proposal raised at once his surprise and curiosity, and when, after a short deliberation, he consented to admit her, he could not stay without impatience till the next day.

The ladies dressed themselves magnificently, and were attended by Imlac to the astronomer, who was pleased to see himself approached with respect by persons of so splendid an appearance. In the exchange of the first civilities he was timorous and bashful; but when the talk became regular, he recollected his powers, and justified the character which Imlac had given. Inquiring of Pekuah what could have turned her inclination towards astronomy, he received from her a history of her adventure at the pyramid, and of the time passed in the Arab's island. She told her tale with ease and elegance, and her conversation took possession of his heart. The discourse was then turned to astronomy: Pekuah displayed what she knew: he looked upon her as a prodigy of genius, and entreated her not to desist from a study which she had so happily begun.

They came again and again, and were every time more welcome than before. The sage endeavored to amuse them, that they might prolong their visits, for he found his thoughts grow brighter in their company; the clouds of solicitude vanished by degrees, as he forced himself to entertain them, and he grieved when he was left at their departure to his old employment of regulating the seasons.

The princess and her favorite had now watched his lips for several months, and could not catch a single word from which they could judge whether he continued, or not, in the opinion of his preternatural commission. They often contrived to bring him to an open declaration, but he easily eluded all their attacks, and on which side soever they pressed him escaped from them to some other topic.

As their familiarity increased they invited him often to the house of Imlac, where they distinguished him by extraordinary respect. He began gradually to delight in sublunary pleasures. He came early and departed late; labored to recommend himself by assiduity and compliance; excited their curiosity after new arts, that they might still want his assistance; and when they made any excursion of pleasure or inquiry, entreated to attend them.

By long experience of his integrity and wisdom, the prince and his sister were convinced that he might be trusted without danger; and lest he should draw any false hopes from the civilities which he received, discovered to him their condition, with the motives of their journey, and required his opinion on the choice of life.

"Of the various conditions which the world spreads before you, which you shall prefer," said the sage, "I am not able to instruct you. I can only tell that I have chosen wrong. I have passed my time in study without experience; in the attainment of sciences which can, for the most part, be but remotely useful to mankind. I have purchased knowledge at the expense of all the common comforts of life: I have missed the endearing elegance of female friendship, and the happy commerce of domestic tenderness. If I have obtained any prerogatives above other students, they have been accompanied with fear, disquiet, and scrupulosity; but even of these prerogatives, whatever they were, I have, since my thoughts have been diversified by more intercourse with the world, begun to question the reality. When I have been for a few days lost in pleasing dissipation, I am always tempted to think that my inquiries have ended in error, and that I have suffered much, and suffered it in vain."

Imlac was delighted to find that the sage's understanding was breaking through its mists, and resolved to detain him from the planets till he should forget his task of ruling them, and reason should recover its original influence.

From this time the astronomer was received into familiar friendship, and partook of all their projects and pleasures: his respect kept him attentive, and the activity of Rasselas did not leave much time unengaged. Something was always to be done; the day was spent in making observations which furnished talk for the evening, and the evening was closed with a scheme for the morrow.

The sage confessed to Imlac, that since he had mingled in the gay tumults of life, and divided his hours by a succession of amusements, he found the conviction of his authority over the skies fade gradually from his mind, and began to trust less to an opinion which he never could prove to others, and which he now found subject to variation from causes in which reason had no part. "If I am accidentally left alone for a few hours," said he, "my inveterate persuasion rushes upon my soul, and my thoughts are chained down by some irresistible violence, but they are soon disentangled by the prince's conversation, and instantaneously released at the entrance of Pekuah. I am like a man habitually afraid of specters, who is set at ease by a lamp, and wonders at the dread which harassed him in the dark, yet, if his lamp be extinguished, feels again the terrors which he knows that when it is light he shall feel no more. But I am sometimes afraid lest I indulge my quiet by criminal negligence, and voluntarily forget the great charge with which I am entrusted. If I favor myself in a known error, or am determined by my own ease in a doubtful question of this importance, how dreadful is my crime!"

"No disease of the imagination," answered Imlac, "is so difficult of cure, as that which is complicated with the dread of guilt: fancy and conscience then act interchangeably upon us, and so often shift their places, that the illusions of one are not distinguished from the dictates of the other. If fancy presents images not moral or religious, the mind drives them away when they give it pain, but when melancholic[9] notions take the form of duty, they lay hold on the faculties without opposition, because we are afraid to exclude or banish them. For this reason the superstitious are often melancholy, and the melancholy almost always superstitious.

"But do not let the suggestions of timidity overpower your better reason: the danger of neglect can be but as the probability of the obligation, which, when you consider it with freedom, you find very little, and that little growing every day less. Open your heart to the influence of the light, which, from time to time, breaks in upon you: when scruples importune you, which you in your lucid moments know to be vain, do not stand to parley, but fly to business or to Pekuah, and keep this thought always prevalent, that you are only one atom of the mass of humanity, and have neither such virtue nor vice, as that you should be singled out for supernatural favors or afflictions."

Chapter 47. The Prince Enters, and Brings a New Topic

"All this," said the astronomer, "I have often thought, but my reason has been so long subjugated by an uncontrollable and overwhelming idea, that it durst not confide in its own decisions. I now see how fatally I betrayed my quiet, by suffering chimeras to prey upon me in secret; but melancholy

---

9. Obsessive. According to Johnson's *Dictionary*, one definition of melancholy is "a kind of madness in which the mind is always fixed on one object."

shrinks from communication, and I never found a man before, to whom I could impart my troubles, though I had been certain of relief. I rejoice to find my own sentiments confirmed by yours, who are not easily deceived, and can have no motive or purpose to deceive. I hope that time and variety will dissipate the gloom that has so long surrounded me, and the latter part of my days will be spent in peace."

"Your learning and virtue," said Imlac, "may justly give you hopes."

Rasselas then entered with the princess and Pekuah, and inquired whether they had contrived any new diversion for the next day. "Such," said Nekayah, "is the state of life, that none are happy but by the anticipation of change: the change itself is nothing; when we have made it, the next wish is to change again. The world is not yet exhausted; let me see something tomorrow which I never saw before."

"Variety," said Rasselas, "is so necessary to content, that even the happy valley disgusted me by the recurrence of its luxuries; yet I could not forbear to reproach myself with impatience, when I saw the monks of St. Anthony support without complaint, a life, not of uniform delight, but uniform hardship."

"Those men," answered Imlac, "are less wretched in their silent convent than the Abyssinian princes in their prison of pleasure. Whatever is done by the monks is incited by an adequate and reasonable motive. Their labor supplies them with necessaries; it therefore cannot be omitted, and is certainly rewarded. Their devotion prepares them for another state, and reminds them of its approach, while it fits them for it. Their time is regularly distributed; one duty succeeds another, so that they are not left open to the distraction of unguided choice, nor lost in the shades of listless inactivity. There is a certain task to be performed at an appropriated hour; and their toils are cheerful, because they consider them as acts of piety, by which they are always advancing towards endless felicity."

"Do you think," said Nekayah, "that the monastic rule is a more holy and less imperfect state than any other? May not he equally hope for future happiness who converses openly with mankind, who succors the distressed by his charity, instructs the ignorant by his learning, and contributes by his industry to the general system of life; even though he should omit some of the mortifications which are practiced in the cloister, and allow himself such harmless delights as his condition may place within his reach?"

"This," said Imlac, "is a question which has long divided the wise, and perplexed the good. I am afraid to decide on either part. He that lives well in the world is better than he that lives well in a monastery. But perhaps everyone is not able to stem the temptations of public life; and if he cannot conquer, he may properly retreat. Some have little power to do good, and have likewise little strength to resist evil. Many are weary of their conflicts with adversity, and are willing to eject those passions which have long busied them in vain. And many are dismissed by age and diseases from the more laborious duties of society. In monasteries the weak and timorous may be happily sheltered, the weary may repose, and the penitent may meditate. Those retreats of prayer and contemplation have something so congenial to the mind of man, that, perhaps, there is scarcely one that does not purpose to close his life in pious abstraction with a few associates serious as himself."

"Such," said Pekuah, "has often been my wish, and I have heard the princess declare, that she should not willingly die in a crowd."

"The liberty of using harmless pleasures," proceeded Imlac, "will not be disputed; but it is still to be examined what pleasures are harmless. The evil of any pleasure that Nekayah can image is not in the act itself, but in its consequences. Pleasure, in itself harmless, may become mischievous, by endearing to us a state which we know to be transient and probatory,[1] and withdrawing our thoughts from that, of which every hour brings us nearer to the beginning, and of which no length of time will bring us to the end. Mortification is not virtuous in itself, nor has any other use, but that it disengages us from the allurements of sense. In the state of future perfection, to which we all aspire, there will be pleasure without danger, and security without restraint."

The princess was silent, and Rasselas, turning to the astronomer, asked him, whether he could not delay her retreat, by showing her something which she had not seen before.

"Your curiosity," said the sage, "has been so general, and your pursuit of knowledge so vigorous, that novelties are not now very easily to be found: but what you can no longer procure from the living may be given by the dead. Among the wonders of this country are the catacombs, or the ancient repositories, in which the bodies of the earliest generations were lodged, and where, by the virtue of the gums which embalmed them, they yet remain without corruption."

"I know not," said Rasselas, "what pleasure the sight of the catacombs can afford; but, since nothing else is offered, I am resolved to view them, and shall place this with many other things which I have done, because I would do something."

They hired a guard of horsemen, and the next day visited the catacombs. When they were about to descend into the sepulchral caves, "Pekuah," said the princess, "we are now again invading the habitations of the dead; I know that you will stay behind; let me find you safe when I return." "No, I will not be left," answered Pekuah; "I will go down between you and the prince."

They then all descended, and roved with wonder through the labyrinth of subterraneous passages, where the bodies were laid in rows on either side.

Chapter 48. Imlac Discourses on the Nature of the Soul

"What reason," said the prince, "can be given, why the Egyptians should thus expensively preserve those carcasses which some nations consume with fire, others lay to mingle with the earth, and all agree to remove from their sight, as soon as decent rites can be performed?"

"The original of ancient customs," said Imlac, "is commonly unknown; for the practice often continues when the cause has ceased; and concerning superstitious ceremonies it is vain to conjecture; for what reason did not dictate reason cannot explain. I have long believed that the practice of embalming arose only from tenderness to the remains of relations or friends, and to this opinion I am more inclined, because it seems impossible that this care should have been general: had all the dead been embalmed, their repositories

---

1. Serving as a trial or test.

must in time have been more spacious than the dwellings of the living. I suppose only the rich or honorable were secured from corruption, and the rest left to the course of nature.

"But it is commonly supposed that the Egyptians believed the soul to live as long as the body continued undissolved, and therefore tried this method of eluding death."

"Could the wise Egyptians," said Nekayah, "think so grossly of the soul? If the soul could once survive its separation, what could it afterwards receive or suffer from the body?"

"The Egyptians would doubtless think erroneously," said the astronomer, "in the darkness of heathenism, and the first dawn of philosophy. The nature of the soul is still disputed amidst all our opportunities of clearer knowledge: some yet say, that it may be material, who, nevertheless, believe it to be immortal."

"Some," answered Imlac, "have indeed said that the soul is material, but I can scarcely believe that any man has thought it, who knew how to think; for all the conclusions of reason enforce the immateriality of mind, and all the notices of sense and investigations of science concur to prove the unconsciousness of matter.

"It was never supposed that cogitation is inherent in matter, or that every particle is a thinking being. Yet if any part of matter be devoid of thought, what part can we suppose to think? Matter can differ from matter only in form, density, bulk, motion, and direction of motion: to which of these, however varied or combined, can consciousness be annexed? To be round or square, to be solid or fluid, to be great or little, to be moved slowly or swiftly one way or another, are modes of material existence, all equally alien from the nature of cogitation. If matter be once without thought, it can only be made to think by some new modification, but all the modifications which it can admit are equally unconnected with cogitative powers."

"But the materialists," said the astronomer, "urge that matter may have qualities with which we are unacquainted."

"He who will determine," returned Imlac, "against that which he knows, because there may be something which he knows not; he that can set hypothetical possibility against acknowledged certainty, is not to be admitted among reasonable beings. All that we know of matter is, that matter is inert, senseless and lifeless; and if this conviction cannot be opposed but by referring us to something that we know not, we have all the evidence that human intellect can admit. If that which is known may be overruled by that which is unknown, no being, not omniscient, can arrive at certainty."

"Yet let us not," said the astronomer, "too arrogantly limit the Creator's power."

"It is no limitation of omnipotence," replied the poet, "to suppose that one thing is not consistent with another, that the same proposition cannot be at once true and false, that the same number cannot be even and odd, that cogitation cannot be conferred on that which is created incapable of cogitation."

"I know not," said Nekayah, "any great use of this question. Does that immateriality, which, in my opinion, you have sufficiently proved, necessarily include eternal duration?"

"Of immateriality," said Imlac, "our ideas are negative, and therefore obscure. Immateriality seems to imply a natural power of perpetual duration as a consequence of exemption from all causes of decay: whatever perishes, is destroyed by the solution of its contexture,[2] and separation of its parts; nor can we conceive how that which has no parts, and therefore admits no solution, can be naturally corrupted or impaired."

"I know not," said Rasselas, "how to conceive anything without extension: what is extended must have parts, and you allow, that whatever has parts may be destroyed."

"Consider your own conceptions," replied Imlac, "and the difficulty will be less. You will find substance without extension. An ideal form is no less real than material bulk: yet an ideal form has no extension. It is no less certain, when you think on a pyramid, that your mind possesses the idea of a pyramid, than that the pyramid itself is standing. What space does the idea of a pyramid occupy more than the idea of a grain of corn? or how can either idea suffer laceration? As is the effect such is the cause; as thought is, such is the power that thinks; a power impassive and indiscerptible."[3]

"But the Being," said Nekayah, "whom I fear to name, the Being which made the soul, can destroy it."

"He, surely, can destroy it," answered Imlac, "since, however unperishable, it receives from a superior nature its power of duration. That it will not perish by any inherent cause of decay, or principle of corruption, may be shown by philosophy; but philosophy can tell no more. That it will not be annihilated by him that made it, we must humbly learn from higher authority."

The whole assembly stood a while silent and collected. "Let us return," said Rasselas, "from this scene of mortality. How gloomy would be these mansions of the dead to him who did not know that he shall never die; that what now acts shall continue its agency, and what now thinks shall think on for ever. Those that lie here stretched before us, the wise and the powerful of ancient times, warn us to remember the shortness of our present state: they were, perhaps, snatched away while they were busy, like us, in the choice of life."

"To me," said the princess, "the choice of life is become less important; I hope hereafter to think only on the choice of eternity."

They then hastened out of the caverns, and, under the protection of their guard, returned to Cairo.

Chapter 49. The Conclusion, in Which Nothing Is Concluded

It was now the time of the inundation of the Nile: a few days after their visit to the catacombs, the river began to rise.

They were confined to their house. The whole region being under water gave them no invitation to any excursions, and being well supplied with materials for talk, they diverted themselves with comparisons of the different forms of life which they had observed, and with various schemes of happiness which each of them had formed.

Pekuah was never so much charmed with any place as the convent of St. Anthony, where the Arab restored her to the princess, and wished only to fill it with pious maidens, and to be made prioress of the order; she was

2. Dissolution of its structure.
3. Not to be separated.

weary of expectation and disgust,[4] and would gladly be fixed in some unvariable state.

The princess thought that, of all sublunary things, knowledge was the best: she desired first to learn all sciences, and then purposed to found a college of learned women, in which she would preside, that, by conversing with the old and educating the young, she might divide her time between the acquisition and communication of wisdom, and raise up for the next age models of prudence, and patterns of piety.

The prince desired a little kingdom, in which he might administer justice in his own person, and see all the parts of government with his own eyes; but he could never fix the limits of his dominion, and was always adding to the number of his subjects.

Imlac and the astronomer were contented to be driven along the stream of life, without directing their course to any particular port.

Of these wishes that they had formed, they well knew that none could be obtained. They deliberated a while what was to be done, and resolved, when the inundation should cease, to return to Abyssinia.[5]

1759

A Dictionary of the English Language

Before Johnson, no standard dictionary of the English language existed. The lack had troubled speakers of English for some time, both because Italian and French academies had produced major dictionaries of their own tongues and because, in the absence of any authority, English seemed likely to change utterly from one generation to another. Many eighteenth-century authors feared that their own language would soon become obsolete: as Alexander Pope wrote in *An Essay on Criticism,*

> Our sons their fathers' failing language see,
> And such as Chaucer is, shall Dryden be.

A dictionary could help slow such change, and commercially it would be a book that everyone would need to buy. In 1746 a group of London publishers commissioned Johnson, still an unknown author, to undertake the project. He hoped to finish it in three years; it took him nine. But the quantity and quality of work he accomplished, aided only by six part-time assistants, made him famous as "Dictionary Johnson." The *Dictionary* remained a standard reference book for one hundred years.

Johnson's achievement is notable in three respects: its size (forty thousand words), the wealth of illustrative quotations, and the excellence of the definitions. No earlier English dictionary rivaled the scope of Johnson's two large folio volumes. About 114,000 quotations, gathered from the best English writers from Sidney to the eighteenth century, exemplify the usage of words as well as their meanings. Above all, it was the definitions, however, that established the authority of Johnson's *Dictionary.* A small selection is only too likely to concentrate on a few amusing or notorious definitions, but the great majority are full, clear, and totally free from eccentricity. Indeed, many of them are still repeated in modern dictionaries. Language, Johnson knew, cannot be fixed once and for all; many of the words he defines have radically changed meaning since the eighteenth century. Yet Johnson did more than any other person of his time to preserve the ideal of a standard English.

4. Aversion.
5. Their destination is their home country, but the text does not say whether they will return to the Happy Valley.

From A Dictionary of the English Language

From *Preface*

* * *

A large work is difficult because it is large, even though all its parts might singly be performed with facility; where there are many things to be done, each must be allowed its share of time and labor, in the proportion only which it bears to the whole; nor can it be expected that the stones which form the dome of a temple should be squared and polished like the diamond of a ring.

Of the event of this work, for which, having labored it with so much application, I cannot but have some degree of parental fondness, it is natural to form conjectures. Those who have been persuaded to think well of my design will require that it should fix our language, and put a stop to those alterations which time and chance have hitherto been suffered to make in it without opposition. With this consequence I will confess that I flattered myself for a while;[1] but now begin to fear that I have indulged expectation which neither reason nor experience can justify. When we see men grow old and die at a certain time one after another, from century to century, we laugh at the elixir that promises to prolong life to a thousand years; and with equal justice may the lexicographer be derided, who being able to produce no example of a nation that has preserved their words and phrases from mutability, shall imagine that his dictionary can embalm his language and secure it from corruption and decay, that it is in his power to change sublunary nature, or clear the world at once from folly, vanity, and affectation.

With this hope, however, academies have been instituted, to guard the avenues of their languages, to retain fugitives, and repulse intruders; but their vigilance and activity have hitherto been vain; sounds are too volatile and subtle for legal restraints; to enchain syllables, and to lash the wind, are equally the undertakings of pride, unwilling to measure its desires by its strength. The French language has visibly changed under the inspection of the academy;[2] the style of Amelot's translation of father Paul is observed by Le Courayer to be *un peu passé;*[3] and no Italian will maintain that the diction of any modern writer is not perceptibly different from that of Boccace, Machiavel, or Caro.[4]

Total and sudden transformations of a language seldom happen; conquests and migrations are now very rare: but there are other causes of change, which, though slow in their operation, and invisible in their progress, are perhaps as much superior to human resistance as the revolutions of the sky, or intumescence[5] of the tide. Commerce, however necessary, however lucrative, as it depraves the manners, corrupts the language; they that have frequent intercourse with strangers, to whom they endeavor to accommodate

1. Johnson's Plan (1747) had called for "a dictionary by which the pronunciation of our language may be fixed, and its attainment facilitated; by which its purity may be preserved, its use ascertained, and its duration lengthened."
2. The French academy, founded to purify the French language, had produced a dictionary in 1694; but revisions were necessary within a few years.
3. A bit old-fashioned (French). Le Courayer's translation (1736) of Father Paolo Sarpi's *History of the Council of Trent* superseded Amelot's (1683).
4. Like Boccaccio (1313–1375) and Machiavelli (1469–1527), Annibale Caro (1507–1566) was a classic Italian stylist whose work had preceded the dictionary published in 1612 by the Italian academy.
5. Swelling.

themselves, must in time learn a mingled dialect, like the jargon which serves the traffickers[6] on the Mediterranean and Indian coasts. This will not always be confined to the exchange, the warehouse, or the port, but will be communicated by degrees to other ranks of the people, and be at last incorporated with the current speech.

There are likewise internal causes equally forcible. The language most likely to continue long without alteration would be that of a nation raised a little, and but a little, above barbarity, secluded from strangers, and totally employed in procuring the conveniencies of life; either without books, or, like some of the Mahometan countries, with very few: men thus busied and unlearned, having only such words as common use requires, would perhaps long continue to express the same notions by the same signs. But no such constancy can be expected in a people polished by arts, and classed by subordination, where one part of the community is sustained and accommodated by the labor of the other. Those who have much leisure to think, will always be enlarging the stock of ideas, and every increase of knowledge, whether real or fancied, will produce new words, or combinations of words. When the mind is unchained from necessity, it will range after convenience; when it is left at large in the fields of speculation, it will shift opinions; as any custom is disused, the words that expressed it must perish with it; as any opinion grows popular, it will innovate speech in the same proportion as it alters practice.

As by the cultivation of various sciences, a language is amplified, it will be more furnished with words deflected from their original sense; the geometrician will talk of a courtier's zenith, or the eccentric virtue of a wild hero, and the physician of sanguine expectations and phlegmatic delays.[7] Copiousness of speech will give opportunities to capricious choice, by which some words will be preferred, and others degraded; vicissitudes of fashion will enforce the use of new, or extend the signification of known terms. The tropes[8] of poetry will make hourly encroachments, and the metaphorical will become the current sense: pronunciation will be varied by levity or ignorance, and the pen must at length comply with the tongue; illiterate writers will at one time or other, by public infatuation, rise into renown, who, not knowing the original import of words, will use them with colloquial licentiousness, confound distinction, and forget propriety. As politeness increases, some expressions will be considered as too gross and vulgar for the delicate, others as too formal and ceremonious for the gay and airy; new phrases are therefore adopted, which must, for the same reasons, be in time dismissed. Swift, in his petty treatise on the English language,[9] allows that new words must sometimes be introduced, but proposes that none should be suffered to become obsolete. But what makes a word obsolete, more than general agreement to forbear it? and how shall it be continued, when it conveys an offensive idea, or recalled again into the mouths of mankind, when it has once by disuse become unfamiliar, and by unfamiliarity unpleasing.

6. Traders.
7. "Sanguine" and "phlegmatic" once referred only to the physiological predominance of blood or phlegm. "Zenith" (the point of the sky directly overhead) and "eccentric" (deviating from the center) were originally astronomical and geomet-rical terms.
8. "A change of a word from its original signification" (Johnson's *Dictionary*).
9. "A Proposal for Correcting, Improving, and Ascertaining the English Tongue" (1712). "Petty": little.

There is another cause of alteration more prevalent than any other, which yet in the present state of the world cannot be obviated. A mixture of two languages will produce a third distinct from both, and they will always be mixed, where the chief part of education, and the most conspicuous accomplishment, is skill in ancient or in foreign tongues. He that has long cultivated another language, will find its words and combinations crowd upon his memory; and haste or negligence, refinement or affectation, will obtrude borrowed terms and exotic expressions.

The great pest of speech is frequency of translation. No book was ever turned from one language into another, without imparting something of its native idiom; this is the most mischievous and comprehensive innovation; single words may enter by thousands, and the fabric of the tongue continue the same, but new phraseology changes much at once; it alters not the single stones of the building, but the order[1] of the columns. If an academy should be established for the cultivation of our style, which I, who can never wish to see dependence multiplied, hope the spirit of English liberty will hinder or destroy, let them, instead of compiling grammars and dictionaries, endeavor with all their influence to stop the license of translators, whose idleness and ignorance, if it be suffered to proceed, will reduce us to babble a dialect of France.

If the changes that we fear be thus irresistible, what remains but to acquiesce with silence, as in the other insurmountable distresses of humanity? It remains that we retard what we cannot repel, that we palliate what we cannot cure. Life may be lengthened by care, though death cannot be ultimately defeated: tongues, like governments, have a natural tendency to degeneration; we have long preserved our constitution, let us make some struggles for our language.

In hope of giving longevity to that which its own nature forbids to be immortal, I have devoted this book, the labor of years, to the honor of my country, that we may no longer yield the palm of philology without a contest to the nations of the continent. The chief glory of every people arises from its authors: whether I shall add anything by my own writings to the reputation of English literature, must be left to time. Much of my life has been lost under the pressures of disease; much has been trifled away; and much has always been spent in provision for the day that was passing over me; but I shall not think my employment useless or ignoble, if by my assistance foreign nations, and distant ages, gain access to the propagators of knowledge, and understand the teachers of truth; if my labors afford light to the repositories of science, and add celebrity to Bacon, to Hooker, to Milton, and to Boyle.[2]

When I am animated by this wish, I look with pleasure on my book, however defective; and deliver it to the world with the spirit of a man that has endeavored well. That it will immediately become popular I have not promised to myself: a few wild blunders and risible absurdities, from which no work of such multiplicity was ever free, may for a time furnish folly with laughter, and harden ignorance in contempt; but useful diligence will at last prevail, and

---

1. Architectural mode (Doric, etc.), which determines the style and proportions of columns.
2. Leading physicist and chemist (1627–1691).

"Science": knowledge. Richard Hooker wrote *The Laws of Ecclesiastical Polity* (1594–97), a famous defense of the Church of England.

there never can be wanting some who distinguish desert;[3] who will consider that no dictionary of a living tongue ever can be perfect, since while it is hastening to publication, some words are budding, and some falling away; that a whole life cannot be spent upon syntax and etymology, and that even a whole life would not be sufficient; that he, whose design includes whatever language can express, must often speak of what he does not understand; that a writer will sometimes be hurried by eagerness to the end, and sometimes faint with weariness under a task, which Scaliger compares to the labors of the anvil and the mine;[4] that what is obvious is not always known, and what is known is not always present; that sudden fits of inadvertency will surprise vigilance, slight avocations[5] will reduce attention, and casual eclipses of the mind will darken learning; and that the writer shall often in vain trace his memory at the moment of need, for that which yesterday he knew with intuitive readiness, and which will come uncalled into his thoughts tomorrow.

In this work, when it shall be found that much is omitted, let it not be forgotten that much likewise is performed; and though no book was ever spared out of tenderness to the author, and the world is little solicitous to know whence proceeded the faults of that which it condemns; yet it may gratify curiosity to inform it, that the *English Dictionary* was written with little assistance of the learned, and without any patronage of the great;[6] not in the soft obscurities of retirement, or under the shelter of academic bowers, but amidst inconvenience and distraction, in sickness and in sorrow: and it may repress the triumph of malignant criticism to observe, that if our language is not here fully displayed, I have only failed in an attempt which no human powers have hitherto completed. If the lexicons of ancient tongues, now immutably fixed, and comprised in a few volumes, be yet, after the toil of successive ages, inadequate and delusive; if the aggregated knowledge and cooperating diligence of the Italian academicians did not secure them from the censure of Beni;[7] if the embodied critics of France, when fifty years had been spent upon their work, were obliged to change its economy,[8] and give their second edition another form, I may surely be contented without the praise of perfection, which, if I could obtain, in this gloom of solitude, what would it avail me? I have protracted my work till most of those whom I wished to please have sunk into the grave,[9] and success and miscarriage are empty sounds: I therefore dismiss it with frigid tranquility, having little to fear or hope from censure or from praise.

[SOME DEFINITIONS: A SMALL ANTHOLOGY][1]

ANTHO'LOGY. *n.*
1. A collection of flowers.
To CANT. *v.*
  To talk in the jargon of particular professions, or in any kind of formal affected language, or with a peculiar and studied tone of voice.

3. Merit.
4. Joseph Justus Scaliger (1540–1609), a great scholar and lexicographer, wrote Latin verses suggesting that criminals should be condemned to lexicography.
5. Whatever calls one aside.
6. See Johnson's letter to Lord Chesterfield in Boswell's *Life of Johnson* on p. 839.

7. Paolo Beni's *L'Anticrusca* (1612) violently attacked the first edition of the *Vocabolario* (the Italian dictionary).
8. Organization.
9. Johnson's wife had died three years earlier.
1. Johnson's definitions include etymologies and illustrative quotations, some of which are omitted in this selection.

Men *cant* endlessly about *materia forma;* and hunt chimeras by rules of art, or dress up ignorance in words of bulk or sound, which may stop up the mouth of inquiry.—*Glanville's Scepsis Scientifica.*

ENTHU'SIASM. *n.*

1. A vain belief of private revelation; a vain confidence of divine favor or communication.

> *Enthusiasm* is founded neither on reason nor divine revelation, but rises from the conceits of a warmed or overweening brain.—*Locke.*

GE'NIUS. *n.*

1. The protecting or ruling power of men, places, or things.

> And as I awake, sweet music breathe,
> Sent by some spirit to mortals good,
> Or th' unseen *genius* of the wood.—*Milton.*

2. A man endowed with superior faculties.
3. Mental power or faculties.
4. Disposition of nature by which anyone is qualified for some peculiar employment.
5. Nature; disposition.

IMA'GINATION, *n.*

1. Fancy; the power of forming ideal pictures; the power of representing things absent to one's self or others.
2. Conception; image in the mind; idea.
3. Contrivance; scheme.

LEXICO'GRAPHER. *n.*

A writer of dictionaries; a harmless drudge, that busies himself in tracing the original, and detailing the signification of words.

MELANCHO'LY. *n.*

1. A disease, supposed to proceed from a redundance of black bile.
2. A kind of madness, in which the mind is always fixed on one object.
3. A gloomy, pensive, discontented temper.

NA'TURE. *n.*

1. An imaginary being supposed to preside over the material and animal world.

> Thou, *nature*, art my goddess; to thy law
> My services are bound.—*Shakespeare.*

2. The native state or properties of anything, by which it is discriminated from others.
3. The constitution of an animated body.
4. Disposition of mind; temper.
5. The regular course of things.
6. The compass of natural existence.
7. Natural affection, or reverence; native sensations.
8. The state or operation of the material world.
9. Sort; species.
10. Sentiments or images adapted to nature, or comfortable to truth and reality.
11. Physics; the science which teaches the qualities of things.

> *Nature* and *nature's* laws lay hid in night,
> God said, Let Newton be, and all was light.—*Pope.*

NE'TWORK. *n.*

Anything reticulated or decussated, at equal distances, with interstices between the intersections.

OATS. *n.*

A grain, which in England is generally given to horses, but in Scotland supports the people.

PA'STERN. *n.*

1. The knee of an horse.[2]

PA'TRON. *n.*

1. One who countenances, supports, or protects. Commonly a wretch who supports with insolence, and is paid with flattery.

PE'NSION. *n.*

An allowance made to anyone without an equivalent. In England it is generally understood to mean pay given to a state hireling for treason to his country.[3]

SA'TIRE. *n.*

A poem in which wickedness or folly is censured. Proper *satire* is distinguished, by the generality of the reflections, from a *lampoon*, which is aimed against a particular person; but they are too frequently confounded.

TO'RY. *n.*

One who adheres to the ancient constitution of the state, and the apostolical hierarchy of the church of England, opposed to a whig.

> The knight is more a *tory* in the country than the town, because it more advances his interest.—*Addison.*

WHIG. *n.*

2. The name of a faction.

> Whoever has a true value for church and state, should avoid the extremes of *whig* for the sake of the former, and the extremes of tory on the account of the latter.—*Swift.*

WIT. *n.*

1. The powers of the mind; the mental faculties; the intellects. This is the original signification.

2. Imagination; quickness of fancy.

3. Sentiments produced by quickness of fancy.

4. A man of fancy.

5. A man of genius.

6. Sense; judgment.

7. In the plural. Sound mind; intellect not crazed.

8. Contrivance; stratagem; power of expedients.

1755

---

2. "A lady once asked him how he came to define *Pastern* the *knee* of a horse: instead of making an elaborate defense, as she expected, he at once answered, 'Ignorance, Madam, pure ignorance'"
(Boswell).

3. In 1762 Johnson was awarded a pension, but he did not revise the definition in later editions.

The Preface to Shakespeare   This is the finest piece of Shakespeare criticism in the eighteenth century; it culminates a critical tradition that began with John Dryden's remarks on Shakespeare and continued as the plays were edited by Nicholas Rowe, Alexander Pope, Lewis Theobald, and William Warburton. Johnson addresses the standard topics: Shakespeare is the poet of nature, not learning; the creator of characters who spring to life; and a writer whose works express the full range of human passions. But the Preface also takes a fresh look not only at the plays but at the first principles of criticism. Resisting "bardolatry"—uncritical worship of Shakespeare—Johnson points out his faults as well as his virtues and finds that his truth to life, or "just representations of general nature," surpasses that of all other modern writers. The Preface is most original when it attacks the long-standing critical reverence for the unities of time and place. What seems real on the stage, Johnson argues, does not depend on artificial rules but on what the mind is willing to imagine.

Johnson's edition of Shakespeare also contained footnotes and brief introductions to each of the plays. Reprinted here are his afterwords to *Twelfth Night* and *Othello*.

From The Preface to Shakespeare

[SHAKESPEARE'S EXCELLENCE, GENERAL NATURE]

That praises are without reason lavished on the dead, and that the honors due only to excellence are paid to antiquity, is a complaint likely to be always continued by those who, being able to add nothing to truth, hope for eminence from the heresies of paradox; or those who, being forced by disappointment upon consolatory expedients, are willing to hope from posterity what the present age refuses, and flatter themselves that the regard which is yet denied by envy will be at last bestowed by time.

Antiquity, like every other quality that attracts the notice of mankind, has undoubtedly votaries that reverence it not from reason but from prejudice. Some seem to admire indiscriminately whatever has been long preserved, without considering that time has sometimes cooperated with chance; all perhaps are more willing to honor past than present excellence; and the mind contemplates genius through the shades of age, as the eye surveys the sun through artificial opacity. The great contention of criticism is to find the faults of the moderns and the beauties of the ancients. While an author is yet living we estimate his powers by his worst performance; and when he is dead we rate them by his best.

To works, however, of which the excellence is not absolute and definite, but gradual and comparative; to works not raised upon principles demonstrative and scientific, but appealing wholly to observation and experience, no other test can be applied than length of duration and continuance of esteem. What mankind have long possessed they have often examined and compared; and if they persist to value the possession, it is because frequent comparisons have confirmed opinion in its favor. As among the works of nature no man can properly call a river deep or a mountain high, without the knowledge of many mountains and many rivers; so in the productions of genius, nothing can be styled excellent till it has been compared with other works of the same kind. Demonstration[1] immediately displays its power and has nothing to

---

1. "The highest degree of deducible or argumental evidence" (Johnson's *Dictionary*).

hope or fear from the flux of years; but works tentative and experimental must be estimated by their proportion to the general and collective ability of man, as it is discovered in a long succession of endeavors. Of the first building that was raised, it might be with certainty determined that it was round or square, but whether it was spacious or lofty must have been referred to time. The Pythagorean scale of numbers[2] was at once discovered to be perfect; but the poems of Homer we yet know not to transcend the common limits of human intelligence, but by remarking that nation after nation, and century after century, has been able to do little more than transpose his incidents, new name his characters, and paraphrase his sentiments.

The reverence due to writings that have long subsisted arises, therefore, not from any credulous confidence in the superior wisdom of past ages, or gloomy persuasion of the degeneracy of mankind, but is the consequence of acknowledged and indubitable positions, that what has been longest known has been most considered, and what is most considered is best understood.

The poet of whose works I have undertaken the revision may now begin to assume the dignity of an ancient and claim the privilege of established fame and prescriptive veneration. He has long outlived his century, the term commonly fixed as the test of literary merit.[3] Whatever advantages he might once derive from personal allusions, local customs, or temporary opinions, have for many years been lost; and every topic of merriment or motive of sorrow which the modes of artificial life afforded him now only obscure the scenes which they once illuminated. The effects of favor and competition are at an end; the tradition of his friendships and his enmities has perished; his works support no opinion with arguments nor supply any faction with invectives; they can neither indulge vanity nor gratify malignity; but are read without any other reason than the desire of pleasure, and are therefore praised only as pleasure is obtained; yet, thus unassisted by interest or passion, they have passed through variations of taste and changes of manners, and, as they devolved from one generation to another, have received new honors at every transmission.

But because human judgment, though it be gradually gaining upon certainty, never becomes infallible, and approbation, though long continued, may yet be only the approbation of prejudice or fashion, it is proper to inquire by what peculiarities of excellence Shakespeare has gained and kept the favor of his countrymen.

Nothing can please many, and please long, but just representations of general nature. Particular manners can be known to few, and therefore few only can judge how nearly they are copied. The irregular combinations of fanciful invention may delight awhile by that novelty of which the common satiety of life sends us all in quest; but the pleasures of sudden wonder are soon exhausted, and the mind can only repose on the stability of truth.

Shakespeare is, above all writers, at least above all modern writers, the poet of nature, the poet that holds up to his readers a faithful mirror of manners and of life. His characters are not modified by the customs of particular places, unpracticed by the rest of the world; by the peculiarities of studies or professions, which can operate but upon small numbers; or by

2. Pythagoras discovered the ratios that determine the principal intervals of the musical scale.
3. Horace's *Epistles* 2.1.39.

the accidents of transient fashions or temporary opinions: they are the genuine progeny of common humanity, such as the world will always supply and observation will always find. His persons act and speak by the influence of those general passions and principles by which all minds are agitated and the whole system of life is continued in motion. In the writings of other poets a character is too often an individual: in those of Shakespeare it is commonly a species.

It is from this wide extension of design that so much instruction is derived. It is this which fills the plays of Shakespeare with practical axioms and domestic wisdom. It was said of Euripides[4] that every verse was a precept; and it may be said of Shakespeare that from his works may be collected a system of civil and economical prudence. Yet his real power is not shown in the splendor of particular passages, but by the progress of his fable[5] and the tenor of his dialogue; and he that tries to recommend him by select quotations will succeed like the pedant in Hierocles[6] who, when he offered his house to sale, carried a brick in his pocket as a specimen.

It will not easily be imagined how much Shakespeare excels in accommodating his sentiments to real life but by comparing him with other authors. It was observed of the ancient schools of declamation that the more diligently they were frequented, the more was the student disqualified for the world, because he found nothing there which he should ever meet in any other place. The same remark may be applied to every stage but that of Shakespeare. The theater, when it is under any other direction, is peopled by such characters as were never seen, conversing in a language which was never heard, upon topics which will never arise in the commerce of mankind. But the dialogue of this author is often so evidently determined by the incident which produces it, and is pursued with so much ease and simplicity, that it seems scarcely to claim the merit of fiction, but to have been gleaned by diligent selection out of common conversation and common occurrences.

Upon every other stage the universal agent is love, by whose power all good and evil is distributed and every action quickened or retarded. To bring a lover, a lady, and a rival into the fable; to entangle them in contradictory obligations, perplex them with oppositions of interest, and harass them with violence of desires inconsistent with each other; to make them meet in rapture, and part in agony; to fill their mouths with hyperbolical joy and outrageous sorrow; to distress them as nothing human ever was distressed; to deliver them as nothing human ever was delivered, is the business of a modern dramatist. For this, probability is violated, life is misrepresented, and language is depraved. But love is only one of many passions; and as it has no great influence upon the sum of life, it has little operation in the dramas of a poet who caught his ideas from the living world and exhibited only what he saw before him. He knew that any other passion, as it was regular or exorbitant, was a cause of happiness or calamity.

Characters thus ample and general were not easily discriminated and preserved; yet perhaps no poet ever kept his personages more distinct from each other. I will not say with Pope that every speech may be assigned to

---

4. The Greek tragic poet (ca. 480–406 B.C.E.). The observation is Cicero's.
5. Plot. "The series or contexture of events which constitute a poem epic or dramatic" (Johnson's

Dictionary).
6. Hierocles of Alexandria (5th century C.E.), Greek philosopher.

the proper speaker,[7] because many speeches there are which have nothing characteristical; but perhaps though some may be equally adapted to every person, it will be difficult to find that any can be properly transferred from the present possessor to another claimant. The choice is right when there is reason for choice.

Other dramatists can only gain attention by hyperbolical or aggravated characters, by fabulous and unexampled excellence or depravity, as the writers of barbarous romances invigorated the reader by a giant and a dwarf; and he that should form his expectations of human affairs from the play or from the tale would be equally deceived. Shakespeare has no heroes; his scenes are occupied only by men, who act and speak as the reader thinks that he should himself have spoken or acted on the same occasion; even where the agency is supernatural, the dialogue is level with life. Other writers disguise the most natural passions and most frequent incidents so that he who contemplates them in the book will not know them in the world: Shakespeare approximates[8] the remote, and familiarizes the wonderful; the event which he represents will not happen, but, if it were possible, its effects would probably be such as he has assigned; and it may be said that he has not only shown human nature as it acts in real exigencies, but as it would be found in trials to which it cannot be exposed.

This therefore is the praise of Shakespeare, that his drama is the mirror of life; that he who has mazed his imagination in following the phantoms which other writers raise up before him, may here be cured of his delirious ecstasies by reading human sentiments in human language, by scenes from which a hermit may estimate the transactions of the world, and a confessor predict the progress of the passions.

[SHAKESPEARE'S FAULTS. THE THREE DRAMATIC UNITIES]

Shakespeare with his excellencies has likewise faults, and faults sufficient to obscure and overwhelm any other merit. I shall show them in the proportion in which they appear to me, without envious malignity or superstitious veneration. No question can be more innocently discussed than a dead poet's pretensions to renown; and little regard is due to that bigotry which sets candor[9] higher than truth.

His first defect is that to which may be imputed most of the evil in books or in men. He sacrifices virtue to convenience, and is so much more careful to please than to instruct that he seems to write without any moral purpose. From his writings indeed a system of social duty may be selected, for he that thinks reasonably must think morally, but his precepts and axioms drop casually from him; he makes no just distribution of good or evil, nor is always careful to show in the virtuous a disapprobation of the wicked; he carries his persons indifferently through right and wrong, and at the close dismisses them without further care, and leaves their examples to operate by chance. This fault the barbarity of his age cannot extenuate; for it is always a writer's duty to make the world better, and justice is a virtue independent on time or place.

---

7. In the preface to his edition of Shakespeare's plays (1725).
8. Brings near.
9. Kindness.

The plots are often so loosely formed that a very slight consideration may improve them, and so carelessly pursued that he seems not always fully to comprehend his own design. He omits opportunities of instructing or delighting which the train of his story seems to force upon him, and apparently rejects those exhibitions which would be more affecting for the sake of those which are more easy.

It may be observed that in many of his plays the latter part is evidently neglected. When he found himself near the end of his work, and in view of his reward, he shortened the labor to snatch the profit. He therefore remits his efforts where he should most vigorously exert them, and his catastrophe is improbably produced or imperfectly represented.

He had no regard to distinction of time or place, but gives to one age or nation, without scruple, the customs, institutions, and opinions of another, at the expense not only of likelihood but of possibility. These faults Pope has endeavored, with more zeal than judgment, to transfer to his imagined interpolators. We need not wonder to find Hector quoting Aristotle, when we see the loves of Theseus and Hippolyta combined with the Gothic mythology of fairies.[1] Shakespeare, indeed, was not the only violator of chronology, for in the same age Sidney, who wanted not the advantages of learning, has, in his *Arcadia*, confounded the pastoral with the feudal times, the days of innocence, quiet, and security with those of turbulence, violence, and adventure.

In his comic scenes he is seldom very successful when he engages his characters in reciprocations of smartness and contests of sarcasm; their jests are commonly gross, and their pleasantry licentious; neither his gentlemen nor his ladies have much delicacy, nor are sufficiently distinguished from his clowns[2] by any appearance of refined manners. Whether he represented the real conversation of his time is not easy to determine: the reign of Elizabeth is commonly supposed to have been a time of stateliness, formality, and reserve; yet perhaps the relaxations of that severity were not very elegant. There must, however, have been always some modes of gaiety preferable to others, and a writer ought to choose the best.

In tragedy his performance seems constantly to be worse as his labor is more. The effusions of passion, which exigence forces out, are for the most part striking and energetic; but whenever he solicits his invention, or strains his faculties, the offspring of his throes is tumor,[3] meanness, tediousness, and obscurity.

In narration he affects a disproportionate pomp of diction and a wearisome train of circumlocution, and tells the incident imperfectly in many words which might have been more plainly delivered in few. Narration in dramatic poetry is naturally tedious, as it is unanimated and inactive, and obstructs the progress of the action; it should therefore always be rapid and enlivened by frequent interruption. Shakespeare found it an encumbrance, and instead of lightening it by brevity, endeavored to recommend it by dignity and splendor.

His declamations or set speeches are commonly cold and weak, for his power was the power of nature; when he endeavored, like other tragic writers, to catch opportunities of amplification and, instead of inquiring what the

---

1. In *Troilus and Cressida* 2.2.166 and in *A Midsummer Night's Dream*, respectively.

2. Rustics.

3. Inflated grandeur, false magnificence.

occasion demanded, to show how much his stores of knowledge could supply, he seldom escapes without the pity or resentment of his reader.

It is incident to him to be now and then entangled with an unwieldy sentiment which he cannot well express, and will not reject; he struggles with it awhile, and, if it continues stubborn, comprises it in words such as occur, and leaves it to be disentangled and evolved[4] by those who have more leisure to bestow upon it.

Not that always where the language is intricate the thought is subtle, or the image always great where the line is bulky; the equality of words to things is very often neglected, and trivial sentiments and vulgar[5] ideas disappoint the attention, to which they are recommended by sonorous epithets and swelling figures.

But the admirers of this great poet have most reason to complain when he approaches nearest to his highest excellence, and seems fully resolved to sink them in dejection and mollify them with tender emotions by the fall of greatness, the danger of innocence, or the crosses of love. What he does best, he soon ceases to do. He is not long soft and pathetic without some idle conceit or contemptible equivocation. He no sooner begins to move than he counteracts himself; and terror and pity, as they are rising in the mind, are checked and blasted by sudden frigidity.

A quibble[6] is to Shakespeare what luminous vapors are to the traveler: he follows it at all adventures; it is sure to lead him out of his way, and sure to engulf him in the mire. It has some malignant power over his mind, and its fascinations are irresistible. Whatever be the dignity or profundity of his disquisitions, whether he be enlarging knowledge or exalting affection, whether he be amusing[7] attention with incidents, or enchaining it in suspense, let but a quibble spring up before him, and he leaves his work unfinished. A quibble is the golden apple for which he will always turn aside from his career[8] or stoop from his elevation. A quibble, poor and barren as it is, gave him such delight that he was content to purchase it by the sacrifice of reason, propriety, and truth. A quibble was to him the fatal Cleopatra for which he lost the world, and was content to lose it.

It will be thought strange that in enumerating the defects of this writer, I have not yet mentioned his neglect of the unities; his violation of those laws which have been instituted and established by the joint authority of poets and critics.

For his other deviations from the art of writing, I resign him to critical justice without making any other demand in his favor than that which must be indulged to all human excellence: that his virtues be rated with his failings. But from the censure which this irregularity may bring upon him I shall, with due reverence to that learning which I must oppose, adventure to try how I can defend him.

His histories, being neither tragedies nor comedies, are not subject to any of their laws; nothing more is necessary to all the praise which they expect

---

4. Unfolded.
5. "Mean; low; being of the common rate" (Johnson's *Dictionary*).
6. Pun.
7. "To entertain with tranquility; to fill with thoughts that engage the mind, without distracting it" (Johnson's *Dictionary*).

8. Course of action; the ground on which a race is run. In Greek legend Atalanta refused to marry any man who could not defeat her in a foot race. Hippomenes won her by dropping, as he ran, three of the golden apples of the Hesperides, which she paused to pick up.

than that the changes of action be so prepared as to be understood; that the incidents be various and affecting, and the characters consistent, natural, and distinct. No other unity is intended, and therefore none is to be sought.

In his other works he has well enough preserved the unity of action. He has not, indeed, an intrigue regularly perplexed and regularly unraveled: he does not endeavor to hide his design only to discover it, for this is seldom the order of real events, and Shakespeare is the poet of nature: but his plan has commonly what Aristotle requires,[9] a beginning, a middle, and an end; one event is concatenated with another, and the conclusion follows by easy consequence. There are, perhaps, some incidents that might be spared, as in other poets there is much talk that only fills up time upon the stage; but the general system makes gradual advances, and the end of the play is the end of expectation.

To the unities of time and place he has shown no regard; and perhaps a nearer view of the principles on which they stand will diminish their value and withdraw from them the veneration which, from the time of Corneille,[1] they have very generally received, by discovering that they have given more trouble to the poet than pleasure to the auditor.

The necessity of observing the unities of time and place arises from the supposed necessity of making the drama credible. The critics hold it impossible that an action of months or years can be possibly believed to pass in three hours; or that the spectator can suppose himself to sit in the theater while ambassadors go and return between distant kings, while armies are levied and towns besieged, while an exile wanders and returns, or till he whom they saw courting his mistress shall lament the untimely fall of his son. The mind revolts from evident falsehood, and fiction loses its force when it departs from the resemblance of reality.

From the narrow limitation of time necessarily arises the contraction of place. The spectator who knows that he saw the first act at Alexandria cannot suppose that he sees the next at Rome, at a distance to which not the dragons of Medea[2] could, in so short a time, have transported him; he knows with certainty that he has not changed his place; and he knows that place cannot change itself, that what was a house cannot become a plain, that what was Thebes can never be Persepolis.

Such is the triumphant language with which a critic exults over the misery of an irregular poet, and exults commonly without resistance or reply. It is time, therefore, to tell him by the authority of Shakespeare that he assumes, as an unquestionable principle, a position which, while his breath is forming it into words, his understanding pronounces to be false. It is false that any representation is mistaken for reality; that any dramatic fable in its materiality was ever credible or, for a single moment, was ever credited.

The objection arising from the impossibility of passing the first hour at Alexandria and the next at Rome supposes that when the play opens the spectator really imagines himself at Alexandria, and believes that his walk to the theater has been a voyage to Egypt, and that he lives in the days of Antony and Cleopatra. Surely he that imagines this may imagine more. He

9. *Poetics* 7.
1. Pierre Corneille (1606–1684), the French playwright, discussed the unities in his *Discours*

des trois unités (1660).
2. According to legend, Medea fled the scene of her crimes in a chariot drawn by dragons.

that can take the stage at one time for the palace of the Ptolemies may take it in half an hour for the promontory of Actium. Delusion, if delusion be admitted, has no certain limitation; if the spectator can be once persuaded that his old acquaintances are Alexander and Caesar, that a room illuminated with candles is the plain of Pharsalia or the bank of Granicus, he is in a state of elevation above the reach of reason or of truth, and from the heights of empyrean poetry may despise the circumscriptions of terrestrial nature. There is no reason why a mind thus wandering in ecstasy should count the clock, or why an hour should not be a century in that calenture[3] of the brain that can make the stage a field.

The truth is that the spectators are always in their senses, and know, from the first act to the last, that the stage is only a stage, and that the players are only players. They came to hear a certain number of lines recited with just gesture and elegant modulation. The lines relate to some action, and an action must be in some place; but the different actions that complete a story may be in places very remote from each other; and where is the absurdity of allowing that space to represent first Athens, and then Sicily, which was always known to be neither Sicily nor Athens but a modern theater?

By supposition, as place is introduced, time may be extended; the time required by the fable elapses, for the most part, between the acts; for, of so much of the action as is represented, the real and poetical duration is the same. If, in the first act, preparations for war against Mithridates are represented to be made in Rome, the event of the war may, without absurdity, be represented, in the catastrophe, as happening in Pontus; we know that there is neither war nor preparation for war; we know that we are neither in Rome nor Pontus, that neither Mithridates nor Lucullus are before us. The drama exhibits successive imitations of successive actions; and why may not the second imitation represent an action that happened years after the first, if it be so connected with it that nothing but time can be supposed to intervene? Time is, of all modes of existence, most obsequious[4] to the imagination; a lapse of years is as easily conceived as a passage of hours. In contemplation we easily contract the time of real actions, and therefore willingly permit it to be contracted when we only see their imitation.

It will be asked how the drama moves if it is not credited. It is credited with all the credit due to a drama. It is credited, whenever it moves, as a just picture of a real original; as representing to the auditor what he would himself feel if he were to do or suffer what is there feigned to be suffered or to be done. The reflection that strikes the heart is not that the evils before us are real evils, but that they are evils to which we ourselves may be exposed. If there be any fallacy, it is not that we fancy the players, but that we fancy ourselves, unhappy for a moment; but we rather lament the possibility than suppose the presence of misery, as a mother weeps over her babe when she remembers that death may take it from her. The delight of tragedy proceeds from our consciousness of fiction; if we thought murders and treasons real, they would please no more.

Imitations produce pain or pleasure, not because they are mistaken for realities, but because they bring realities to mind. When the imagination is

---

3. A delirium produced by tropical heat, which causes sailors to leap into the sea under the delusion that it is a green field.
4. "Obedient; compliant" (Johnson's *Dictionary*).

recreated[5] by a painted landscape, the trees are not supposed capable to give us shade or the fountains coolness; but we consider how we should be pleased with such fountains playing beside us and such woods waving over us. We are agitated in reading the history of *Henry the Fifth*; yet no man takes his book for the field of Agincourt. A dramatic exhibition is a book recited with concomitants that increase or diminish its effect. Familiar[6] comedy is often more powerful on the theater than in the page; imperial tragedy is always less. The humor of Petruchio may be heightened by grimace; but what voice or what gesture can hope to add dignity or force to the soliloquy of Cato?[7]

A play read affects the mind like a play acted. It is therefore evident that the action is not supposed to be real; and it follows that between the acts a longer or shorter time may be allowed to pass, and that no more account of space or duration is to be taken by the auditor of a drama than by the reader of a narrative, before whom may pass in an hour the life of a hero or the revolutions of an empire.

Whether Shakespeare knew the unities and rejected them by design or deviated from them by happy ignorance, it is, I think, impossible to decide and useless to inquire. We may reasonably suppose that, when he rose to notice, he did not want[8] the counsels and admonitions of scholars and critics, and that he at last deliberately persisted in a practice which he might have begun by chance. As nothing is essential to the fable but unity of action, and as the unities of time and place arise evidently from false assumptions, and, by circumscribing the extent of the drama, lessen its variety, I cannot think it much to be lamented that they were not known by him, or not observed: nor, if such another poet could arise, should I very vehemently reproach him that his first act passed at Venice and his next in Cyprus.[9] Such violations of rules merely positive[1] become the comprehensive genius of Shakespeare, and such censures are suitable to the minute and slender criticism of Voltaire.

> *Non usque adeo permiscuit imis*
> *Longus summa dies, ut non, si voce Metelli*
> *Serventur leges, malint a Caesare tolli.*[2]

Yet when I speak thus slightly of dramatic rules, I cannot but recollect how much wit and learning may be produced against me; before such authorities I am afraid to stand: not that I think the present question one of those that are to be decided by mere authority, but because it is to be suspected that these precepts have not been so easily received but for better reasons than I have yet been able to find. The result of my inquiries, in which it would be ludicrous to boast of impartiality, is that the unities of time and place are not essential to a just drama, that though they may sometimes conduce to pleasure, they are always to be sacrificed to the nobler beauties of variety and instruction; and that a play written with nice observation of critical rules is to be contemplated as an elaborate curiosity, as the product of superfluous

---

5. Delighted.
6. Domestic.
7. In Addison's tragedy *Cato* (5.1), the hero soliloquizes on immortality shortly before committing suicide. Petruchio is the hero of Shakespeare's comedy *The Taming of the Shrew*.
8. Lack.

9. As is the case in *Othello*.
1. Arbitrary; not natural.
2. Lucan's *Pharsalia* 3.138–40: "The course of time has not wrought such confusion that the laws would not rather be trampled on by Caesar than saved by Metellus."

and ostentatious art, by which is shown rather what is possible than what is necessary.

He that without diminution of any other excellence shall preserve all the unities unbroken deserves the like applause with the architect who shall display all the orders of architecture in a citadel without any deduction for its strength; but the principal beauty of a citadel is to exclude the enemy, and the greatest graces of a play are to copy nature and instruct life. * * *

[TWELFTH NIGHT]

This play is in the graver part elegant and easy, and in some of the lighter scenes exquisitely humorous. Ague-cheek is drawn with great propriety, but his character is, in a great measure, that of natural fatuity, and is therefore not the proper prey of a satirist. The soliloquy of Malvolio is truly comick; he is betrayed to ridicule merely by his pride. The marriage of Olivia, and the succeeding perplexity, though well enough contrived to divert on the stage, wants credibility, and fails to produce the proper instruction required in the drama, as it exhibits no just picture of life.

[OTHELLO]

The beauties of this play impress themselves so strongly upon the attention of the reader that they can draw no aid from critical illustration. The fiery openness of Othello, magnanimous, artless, and credulous, boundless in his confidence, ardent in his affection, inflexible in his resolution, and obdurate in his revenge; the cool malignity of Iago, silent in his resentment, subtle in his designs, and studious at once of his interest and his vengeance; the soft simplicity of Desdemona, confident of merit and conscious of innocence, her artless perseverance in her suit, and her slowness to suspect that she can be suspected are such proofs of Shakespeare's skill in human nature as, I suppose, it is vain to seek in any modern writer. The gradual progress which Iago makes in the Moor's conviction and the circumstances which he employs to inflame him are so artfully natural that, though it will perhaps not be said of him as he says of himself that he is "a man not easily jealous," yet we cannot but pity him when at last we find him "perplexed in the extreme."

There is always danger lest wickedness conjoined with abilities should steal upon[3] esteem, though it misses of approbation; but the character of Iago is so conducted that he is from the first scene to the last hated and despised.

Even the inferior characters of this play would be very conspicuous in any other piece, not only for their justness but their strength. Cassio is brave, benevolent, and honest, ruined only by his want of stubbornness to resist an insidious invitation. Roderigo's suspicious credulity and impatient submission to the cheats which he sees practiced upon him and which by persuasion he suffers to be repeated exhibit a strong picture of a weak mind betrayed by unlawful desires to a false friend; and the virtue of Emilia is such as we often find worn loosely but not cast off, easy to commit small crimes but quickened and alarmed at atrocious villainies.

The scenes from the beginning to the end are busy, varied by happy interchanges,[4] and regularly promoting the progression of the story; and the

3. Imperceptibly gain.
4. Apt successions of actions and events.

narrative in the end,[5] though it tells but what is known already, yet is necessary to produce the death of Othello.

Had the scene opened in Cyprus and the preceding incidents been occasionally related, there had been little wanting to a drama of the most exact and scrupulous regularity.[6]

1765

FROM LIVES OF THE POETS

From Cowley[1]

[METAPHYSICAL WIT]

Wit, like all other things subject by their nature to the choice of man, has its changes and fashions, and at different times takes different forms. About the beginning of the seventeenth century appeared a race of writers that may be termed the metaphysical poets,[2] of whom in a criticism on the works of Cowley it is not improper to give some account.

The metaphysical poets were men of learning, and to show their learning was their whole endeavor; but, unluckily resolving to show it in rhyme, instead of writing poetry they only wrote verses, and very often such verses as stood the trial of the finger better than of the ear; for the modulation was so imperfect that they were only found to be verses by counting the syllables.

If the father of criticism[3] has rightly denominated poetry *tekhnē mimē-tikè, an imitative art*, these writers will without great wrong lose their right to the name of poets, for they cannot be said to have imitated anything: they neither copied nature nor life; neither painted the forms of matter nor represented the operations of intellect.

Those however who deny them to be poets allow them to be wits. Dryden confesses of himself and his contemporaries that they fall below Donne in wit, but maintains that they surpass him in poetry.[4]

If wit be well described by Pope as being "that which has been often thought, but was never before so well expressed,"[5] they certainly never attained nor ever sought it, for they endeavored to be singular in their thoughts, and were careless of their diction. But Pope's account of wit is undoubtedly erroneous; he depresses it below its natural dignity, and reduces it from strength of thought to happiness of language.

If by a more noble and more adequate conception that be considered as wit which is at once natural and new, that which though not obvious is,

5. Concluding explanation to Othello of Iago's plots.
6. Adherence to rules of good drama. "Occasionally": when the chance arose.
1. Abraham Cowley (1618–1667) was much admired during the middle of the 17th century. His reputation began to decline before 1700, but he was remembered as a writer of false wit, especially in his collection of love poems, *The Mistress* (1647).
2. Presumably Johnson took this now common designation from a hint in Dryden's "A Discourse Concerning the Original and Progress of Satire." Dryden condemned Donne because "he affects the metaphysics . . . and perplexes the minds of the fair sex with nice speculations of philosophy, when he should engage their hearts, and entertain them with the softnesses of love."
3. Aristotle in his *Poetics*.
4. "A Discourse . . . of Satire."
5. *An Essay on Criticism*, lines 297–98.

upon its first production, acknowledged to be just; if it be that which he that never found it, wonders how he missed; to wit of this kind the metaphysical poets have seldom risen. Their thoughts are often new, but seldom natural; they are not obvious, but neither are they just;[6] and the reader, far from wondering that he missed them, wonders more frequently by what perverseness of industry they were ever found.

But wit, abstracted from its effects upon the hearer, may be more rigorously and philosophically considered as a kind of *discordia concors*;[7] a combination of dissimilar images, or discovery of occult resemblances in things apparently unlike. Of wit, thus defined, they have more than enough. The most heterogeneous ideas are yoked by violence together; nature and art are ransacked for illustrations, comparisons, and allusions; their learning instructs, and their subtlety surprises; but the reader commonly thinks his improvement dearly bought, and, though he sometimes admires, is seldom pleased.

From this account of their compositions it will be readily inferred that they were not successful in representing or moving the affections. As they were wholly employed on something unexpected and surprising, they had no regard to that uniformity of sentiment which enables us to conceive and to excite the pains and the pleasure of other minds; they never inquired what on any occasion they should have said or done, but wrote rather as beholders than partakers of human nature; as beings looking upon good and evil, impassive and at leisure; as Epicurean deities making remarks on the actions of men and the vicissitudes of life, without interest and without emotion. Their courtship was void of fondness and their lamentation of sorrow. Their wish was only to say what they hoped had been never said before.

Nor was the sublime more within their reach than the pathetic; for they never attempted that comprehension and expanse of thought which at once fills the whole mind, and of which the first effect is sudden astonishment, and the second rational admiration. Sublimity is produced by aggregation, and littleness by dispersion. Great thoughts are always general, and consist in positions not limited by exceptions, and in descriptions not descending to minuteness. It is with great propriety that subtlety, which in its original import means exility[8] of particles, is taken in its metaphorical meaning for nicety of distinction. Those writers who lay on the watch for novelty could have little hope of greatness; for great things cannot have escaped former observation. Their attempts were always analytic: they broke every image into fragments, and could no more represent by their slender conceits and labored particularities the prospects of nature or the scenes of life, than he who dissects a sunbeam with a prism can exhibit the wide effulgence of a summer noon.

What they wanted however of the sublime they endeavored to supply by hyperbole;[9] their amplification had no limits: they left not only reason but fancy behind them, and produced combinations of confused magnificence that not only could not be credited, but could not be imagined.

Yet great labor directed by great abilities is never wholly lost: if they frequently threw away their wit upon false conceits, they likewise sometimes struck out unexpected truth: if their conceits were farfetched, they were

6. Exact, proper.
7. A harmonious discord (Latin). Johnson is himself being witty in using this phrase, a familiar philosophical concept denoting the general har-

mony of God's creation despite its manifold and often contradictory particulars.
8. Thinness, smallness.
9. An image heightened beyond reality.

often worth the carriage.[1] To write on their plan it was at least necessary to read and think. No man could be born a metaphysical poet, nor assume the dignity of a writer by descriptions copied from descriptions, by imitations borrowed from imitations, by traditional imagery and hereditary similes, by readiness of rhyme and volubility of syllables.

1779

From Milton[1]

["LYCIDAS"]

One of the poems on which much praise has been bestowed is *Lycidas*; of which the diction is harsh, the rhymes uncertain, and the numbers[2] unpleasing. What beauty there is, we must therefore seek in the sentiments and images. It is not to be considered as the effusion of real passion; for passion runs not after remote allusions and obscure opinions. Passion plucks no berries from the myrtle and ivy, nor calls upon Arethuse and Mincius, nor tells of "rough satyrs and fauns with cloven heel." Where there is leisure for fiction there is little grief.

In this poem there is no nature, for there is no truth; there is no art, for there is nothing new. Its form is that of a pastoral, easy, vulgar, and therefore disgusting:[3] whatever images it can supply are long ago exhausted; and its inherent improbability always forces dissatisfaction on the mind. When Cowley tells of Hervey that they studied together,[4] it is easy to suppose how much he must miss the companion of his labors and the partner of his discoveries; but what image of tenderness can be excited by these lines!

> We drove afield, and both together heard
> What time the grayfly winds her sultry horn,
> Battening our flocks with the fresh dews of night.

We know that they never drove afield, and that they had no flocks to batten; and though it be allowed that the representation may be allegorical, the true meaning is so uncertain and remote that it is never sought because it cannot be known when it is found.

Among the flocks and copses and flowers appear the heathen deities, Jove and Phoebus, Neptune and Aeolus, with a long train of mythological imagery, such as a college easily supplies. Nothing can less display knowledge or less exercise invention than to tell how a shepherd has lost his companion and must now feed his flocks alone, without any judge of his skill in piping; and how one god asks another god what is become of Lycidas, and

1. In the *Life of Addison*, Johnson wrote: "A simile may be compared to lines converging at a point, and is more excellent as the lines approach from greater distance."
1. Johnson's treatment of Milton as man and poet offended many ardent Miltonians in his own day and damaged his reputation as a critic in the following century. He did not admire Milton's character, and he detested his politics and religion. But no one has praised *Paradise Lost* more hand-somely. Especially offensive in the 19th century was his attack on "Lycidas." Johnson disliked modern pastorals, believing that the tradition had been worn threadbare. His views on the genre may be read in *Rambler* no. 36 and no. 37.
2. Versification.
3. Distasteful, because too facile and common.
4. Cowley's "On the Death of Mr. William Hervey" (1656).

how neither god can tell. He who thus grieves will excite no sympathy; he who thus praises will confer no honor.

This poem has yet a grosser fault. With these trifling fictions are mingled the most awful and sacred truths, such as ought never to be polluted with such irreverent combinations. The shepherd likewise is now a feeder of sheep, and afterwards an ecclesiastical pastor, a superintendent of a Christian flock. Such equivocations are always unskillful; but here they are indecent,[5] and at least approach to impiety, of which, however, I believe the writer not to have been conscious.

Such is the power of reputation justly acquired that its blaze drives away the eye from nice examination. Surely no man could have fancied that he read *Lycidas* with pleasure had he not known its author.

[*PARADISE LOST*]

Those little pieces may be dispatched without much anxiety; a greater work calls for greater care. I am now to examine *Paradise Lost*, a poem which, considered with respect to design, may claim the first place, and with respect to performance the second, among the productions of the human mind.

By the general consent of critics the first praise of genius is due to the writer of an epic poem, as it requires an assemblage of all the powers which are singly sufficient for other compositions. Poetry is the art of uniting pleasure with truth, by calling imagination to the help of reason. Epic poetry undertakes to teach the most important truths by the most pleasing precepts, and therefore relates some great event in the most affecting manner. History must supply the writer with the rudiments of narration, which he must improve and exalt by a nobler art, must animate by dramatic energy, and diversify by retrospection and anticipation; morality must teach him the exact bounds and different shades of vice and virtue; from policy and the practice of life he has to learn the discriminations of character and the tendency of the passions, either single or combined; and physiology[6] must supply him with illustrations and images. To put these materials to poetical use is required an imagination capable of painting nature and realizing fiction. Nor is he yet a poet till he has attained the whole extension of his language, distinguished all the delicacies of phrase, and all the colors of words, and learned to adjust their different sounds to all the varieties of metrical modulation.

Bossu is of opinion that the poet's first work is to find a *moral*, which his fable is afterwards to illustrate and establish.[7] This seems to have been the process only of Milton: the moral of other poems is incidental and consequent; in Milton's only it is essential and intrinsic. His purpose was the most useful and the most arduous: "to vindicate the ways of God to man";[8] to show the reasonableness of religion, and the necessity of obedience to the Divine Law.

To convey this moral there must be a *fable*, a narration artfully constructed, so as to excite curiosity and surprise expectation. In this part of his work Milton must be confessed to have equaled every other poet. He has

5. Unbecoming, lacking in decorum.
6. "The doctrine of the constitution of the works of nature" (Johnson's *Dictionary*).
7. René le Bossu's treatise on the epic poem, *Traité du Poëme Épique*, 1675, was much admired in the late 17th and early 18th centuries.
8. Milton wrote "justify," not "vindicate" (*Paradise Lost* 1.26). It was Pope, in *An Essay on Man* 1.16, who used "vindicate."

involved in his account of the Fall of Man the events which preceded, and those that were to follow it: he has interwoven the whole system of theology with such propriety that every part appears to be necessary, and scarcely any recital is wished shorter for the sake of quickening the progress of the main action.

The subject of an epic poem is naturally an event of great importance. That of Milton is not the destruction of a city, the conduct of a colony, or the foundation of an empire. His subject is the fate of worlds, the revolutions of heaven and of earth; rebellion against the Supreme King raised by the highest order of created beings; the overthrow of their host and the punishment of their crime; the creation of a new race of reasonable creatures; their original happiness and innocence, their forfeiture of immortality, and their restoration to hope and peace.

Great events can be hastened or retarded only by persons of elevated dignity. Before the greatness displayed in Milton's poem all other greatness shrinks away. The weakest of his agents are the highest and noblest of human beings, the original parents of mankind; with whose actions the elements consented; on whose rectitude or deviation of will depended the state of terrestrial nature and the condition of all the future inhabitants of the globe.

Of the other agents in the poem, the chief are such as it is irreverence to name on slight occasions. The rest were lower powers;

> of which the least could wield
> Those elements, and arm him with the force
> Of all their regions;[9]

powers which only the control of Omnipotence restrains from laying creation waste, and filling the vast expanse of space with ruin and confusion. To display the motives and actions of beings thus superior, so far as human reason can examine them or human imagination represent them, is the task which this mighty poet has undertaken and performed.

In the examination of epic poems much speculation is commonly employed upon the *characters*. The characters in the *Paradise Lost* which admit of examination are those of angels and of man; of angels good and evil, of man in his innocent and sinful state.

Among the angels the virtue of Raphael is mild and placid, of easy condescension and free communication; that of Michael is regal and lofty, and, as may seem, attentive to the dignity of his own nature. Abdiel and Gabriel appear occasionally, and act as every incident requires; the solitary fidelity of Abdiel is very amiably painted.[1]

Of the evil angels the characters are more diversified. To Satan, as Addison observes, such sentiments are given as suit "the most exalted and most depraved being."[2] Milton has been censured by Clarke for the impiety which sometimes breaks from Satan's mouth. For there are thoughts, as he justly remarks, which no observation of character can justify, because no good man would willingly permit them to pass, however transiently, through his own mind.[3] To make Satan speak as a rebel, without any such expressions as might taint the reader's imagination, was indeed one of the great

9. *Paradise Lost* 6.221.
1. *Paradise Lost* 5.803ff.
2. *Spectator* 303.
3. John Clarke's *Essay upon Study* (1731).

difficulties in Milton's undertaking, and I cannot but think that he has extricated himself with great happiness. There is in Satan's speeches little that can give pain to a pious ear. The language of rebellion cannot be the same with that of obedience. The malignity of Satan foams in haughtiness and obstinacy; but his expressions are commonly general, and no otherwise offensive than as they are wicked.

The other chiefs of the celestial rebellion are very judiciously discriminated in the first and second books; and the ferocious character of Moloch appears, both in the battle and the council, with exact consistency.

To Adam and Eve are given during their innocence such sentiments as innocence can generate and utter. Their love is pure benevolence and mutual veneration; their repasts are without luxury and their diligence without toil. Their addresses to their Maker have little more than the voice of admiration and gratitude. Fruition left them nothing to ask, and Innocence left them nothing to fear.

But with guilt enter distrust and discord, mutual accusation, and stubborn self-defense; they regard each other with alienated minds, and dread their Creator as the avenger of their transgression. At last they seek shelter in his mercy, soften to repentance, and melt in supplication. Both before and after the Fall the superiority of Adam is diligently sustained.

Of the *probable* and the *marvelous*,[4] two parts of a vulgar epic poem which immerge the critic in deep consideration, the *Paradise Lost* requires little to be said. It contains the history of a miracle, of Creation and Redemption; it displays the power and the mercy of the Supreme Being: the probable therefore is marvelous, and the marvelous is probable. The substance of the narrative is truth; and as truth allows no choice, it is, like necessity, superior to rule. To the accidental or adventitious parts, as to every thing human, some slight exceptions may be made. But the main fabric is immovably supported.

It is justly remarked by Addison[5] that this poem has, by the nature of its subject, the advantage above all others, that it is universally and perpetually interesting. All mankind will, through all ages, bear the same relation to Adam and to Eve, and must partake of that good and evil which extend to themselves.

Of the *machinery*, so called from *theòs apò mēkhanēs*,[6] by which is meant the occasional interposition of supernatural power, another fertile topic of critical remarks, here is no room to speak, because every thing is done under the immediate and visible direction of Heaven; but the rule is so far observed that no part of the action could have been accomplished by any other means.

Of *episodes*[7] I think there are only two, contained in Raphael's relation of the war in heaven and Michael's prophetic account of the changes to happen in this world. Both are closely connected with the great action; one was necessary to Adam as a warning, the other as a consolation.

To the completeness or *integrity* of the design nothing can be objected; it has distinctly and clearly what Aristotle requires, a beginning, a middle, and an end. There is perhaps no poem of the same length from which so little

---

4. Actions in an epic poem that are wonderful because they exceed the probable.
5. *Spectator* 273.
6. Aristotle's *Poetics* 15.10. *Deus ex machina*, the intervention of supernatural powers into the affairs of humans.
7. Incidental but related narratives within an epic poem. Johnson is citing *Paradise Lost* 5.577ff. and 11.334ff.

can be taken without apparent mutilation. Here are no funeral games, nor is there any long description of a shield. The short digressions at the beginning of the third, seventh, and ninth books might doubtless be spared; but superfluities so beautiful who would take away? or who does not wish that the author of the *Iliad* had gratified succeeding ages with a little knowledge of himself? Perhaps no passages are more frequently or more attentively read than those extrinsic paragraphs; and since the end of poetry is pleasure, that cannot be unpoetical with which all are pleased.

The questions, whether the action of the poem be strictly *one*,[8] whether the poem can be properly termed *heroic*, and who is the hero, are raised by such readers as draw their principles of judgment rather from books than from reason. Milton, though he entitled *Paradise Lost* only a "poem," yet calls it himself "heroic song."[9] Dryden, petulantly and indecently, denies the heroism of Adam because he was overcome; but there is no reason why the hero should not be unfortunate except established practice, since success and virtue do not go necessarily together. Cato is the hero of Lucan, but Lucan's authority will not be suffered by Quintilian to decide. However, if success be necessary, Adam's deceiver was at last crushed; Adam was restored to his Maker's favor, and therefore may securely resume his human rank.

After the scheme and fabric of the poem must be considered its component parts, the sentiments, and the diction.

The *sentiments*, as expressive of manners or appropriated to characters, are for the greater part unexceptionably just. Splendid passages containing lessons of morality or precepts of prudence occur seldom. Such is the original formation of this poem that as it admits no human manners till the Fall, it can give little assistance to human conduct. Its end is to raise the thoughts above sublunary cares or pleasures. Yet the praise of that fortitude, with which Abdiel maintained his singularity of virtue against the scorn of multitudes, may be accommodated to all times; and Raphael's reproof of Adam's curiosity after the planetary motions, with the answer returned by Adam, may be confidently opposed to any rule of life which any poet has delivered.[1]

The thoughts which are occasionally called forth in the progress are such as could only be produced by an imagination in the highest degree fervid and active, to which materials were supplied by incessant study and unlimited curiosity. The heat of Milton's mind might be said to sublimate his learning, to throw off into his work the spirit of science,[2] unmingled with its grosser parts.

He had considered creation in its whole extent, and his descriptions are therefore learned. He had accustomed his imagination to unrestrained indulgence, and his conceptions therefore were extensive. The characteristic quality of his poem is sublimity. He sometimes descends to the elegant, but his element is the great. He can occasionally invest himself with grace; but his natural port is gigantic loftiness. He can please when pleasure is required; but it is his peculiar power to astonish.

He seems to have been well acquainted with his own genius, and to know what it was that Nature had bestowed upon him more bountifully than

8. I.e., a single action dealing with a single character.
9. *Paradise Lost* 9.25.

1. *Paradise Lost* 8.65ff.
2. Knowledge.

upon others; the power of displaying the vast, illuminating the splendid, enforcing the awful, darkening the gloomy, and aggravating the dreadful: he therefore chose a subject on which too much could not be said, on which he might tire his fancy without the censure of extravagance.

* * *

The defects and faults of *Paradise Lost*, for faults and defects every work of man must have, it is the business of impartial criticism to discover. As in displaying the excellence of Milton I have not made long quotations, because of selecting beauties there had been no end, I shall in the same general manner mention that which seems to deserve censure; for what Englishman can take delight in transcribing passages, which, if they lessen the reputation of Milton, diminish in some degree the honor of our country?

* * *

The plan of *Paradise Lost* has this inconvenience, that it comprises neither human actions nor human manners. The man and woman who act and suffer are in a state which no other man or woman can ever know. The reader finds no transaction in which he can be engaged, beholds no condition in which he can by any effort of imagination place himself; he has, therefore, little natural curiosity or sympathy.

We all, indeed, feel the effects of Adam's disobedience; we all sin like Adam, and like him must all bewail our offenses; we have restless and insidious enemies in the fallen angels, and in the blessed spirits we have guardians and friends; in the Redemption of mankind we hope to be included: in the description of heaven and hell we are surely interested, as we are all to reside hereafter either in the regions of horror or of bliss.

But these truths are too important to be new: they have been taught to our infancy; they have mingled with our solitary thoughts and familiar conversation, and are habitually interwoven with the whole texture of life. Being therefore not new they raise no unaccustomed emotion in the mind: what we knew before, we cannot learn; what is not unexpected, cannot surprise.

Of the ideas suggested by these awful scenes, from some we recede with reverence, except when stated hours require their association; and from others we shrink with horror, or admit them only as salutary inflictions, as counterpoises to our interests and passions. Such images rather obstruct the career of fancy than incite it.

Pleasure and terror are indeed the genuine sources of poetry; but poetical pleasure must be such as human imagination can at least conceive, and poetical terror such as human strength and fortitude may combat. The good and evil of Eternity are too ponderous for the wings of wit; the mind sinks under them in passive helplessness, content with calm belief and humble adoration.

Known truths however may take a different appearance, and be conveyed to the mind by a new train of intermediate images. This Milton has undertaken, and performed with pregnancy and vigor of mind peculiar to himself. Whoever considers the few radical[3] positions which the Scriptures

3. Original or primary.

afforded him will wonder by what energetic operation he expanded them to such extent and ramified them to so much variety, restrained as he was by religious reverence from licentiousness of fiction.

Here is a full display of the united force of study and genius; of a great accumulation of materials, with judgment to digest and fancy to combine them: Milton was able to select from nature or from story, from ancient fable or from modern science, whatever could illustrate or adorn his thoughts. An accumulation of knowledge impregnated his mind, fermented by study and exalted by imagination.

* * *

But original deficience cannot be supplied. The want of human interest is always felt. *Paradise Lost* is one of the books which the reader admires and lays down, and forgets to take up again. None ever wished it longer than it is. Its perusal is a duty rather than a pleasure. We read Milton for instruction, retire harassed and overburdened, and look elsewhere for recreation; we desert our master, and seek for companions.

* * *

Dryden remarks that Milton has some flats among his elevations.[4] This is only to say that all the parts are not equal. In every work one part must be for the sake of others; a palace must have passages, a poem must have transitions. It is no more to be required that wit should always be blazing than that the sun should always stand at noon. In a great work there is a vicissitude[5] of luminous and opaque parts, as there is in the world a succession of day and night. Milton, when he has expatiated in the sky, may be allowed sometimes to revisit earth; for what other author ever soared so high or sustained his flight so long?

* * *

The highest praise of genius is original invention. Milton cannot be said to have contrived the structure of an epic poem, and therefore owes reverence to that vigor and amplitude of mind to which all generations must be indebted for the art of poetical narration, for the texture of the fable, the variation of incidents, the interposition of dialogue, and all the stratagems that surprise and enchain attention. But of all the borrowers from Homer Milton is perhaps the least indebted. He was naturally a thinker for himself, confident of his own abilities and disdainful of help or hindrance; he did not refuse admission to the thoughts or images of his predecessors, but he did not seek them. From his contemporaries he neither courted nor received support; there is in his writings nothing by which the pride of other authors might be gratified or favor gained, no exchange of praise or solicitation of support. His great works were performed under discountenance and in blindness, but difficulties vanished at his touch; he was born for whatever is arduous; and his work is not the greatest of heroic poems, only because it is not the first.

1779

4. Preface to *Sylvae*.   5. Regular change.

From Pope

Of his intellectual character, the constituent and fundamental principle was good sense, a prompt and intuitive perception of consonance and propriety. He saw immediately, of his own conceptions, what was to be chosen, and what to be rejected; and, in the works of others, what was to be shunned, and what was to be copied.

But good sense alone is a sedate and quiescent quality, which manages its possessions well, but does not increase them; it collects few materials for its own operations, and preserves safety, but never gains supremacy. Pope had likewise genius; a mind active, ambitious, and adventurous, always investigating, always aspiring; in its widest searches still longing to go forward, in its highest flights still wishing to be higher; always imagining something greater than it knows, always endeavoring more than it can do.

To assist these powers, he is said to have had great strength and exactness of memory. That which he had heard or read was not easily lost; and he had before him not only what his own meditation suggested, but what he had found in other writers that might be accommodated to his present purpose.

These benefits of nature he improved by incessant and unwearied diligence; he had recourse to every source of intelligence, and lost no opportunity of information; he consulted the living as well as the dead; he read his compositions to his friends, and was never content with mediocrity when excellence could be attained. He considered poetry as the business of his life, and however he might seem to lament his occupation, he followed it with constancy: to make verses was his first labor, and to mend them was his last.

From his attention to poetry he was never diverted. If conversation offered anything that could be improved, he committed it to paper; if a thought, or perhaps an expression more happy than was common, rose to his mind, he was careful to write it; an independent distich was preserved for an opportunity of insertion, and some little fragments have been found containing lines, or parts of lines, to be wrought upon at some other time.

He was one of those few whose labor is their pleasure; he was never elevated to negligence, nor wearied to impatience; he never passed a fault unamended by indifference, nor quitted it by despair. He labored his works first to gain reputation, and afterwards to keep it.

Of composition there are different methods. Some employ at once memory and invention, and, with little intermediate use of the pen, form and polish large masses by continued meditation, and write their productions only when, in their own opinion, they have completed them. It is related of Virgil[1] that his custom was to pour out a great number of verses in the morning, and pass the day in retrenching exuberances and correcting inaccuracies. The method of Pope, as may be collected from his translation, was to write his first thoughts in his first words, and gradually to amplify, decorate, rectify, and refine them.

With such faculties and such dispositions, he excelled every other writer in *poetical prudence;* he wrote in such a manner as might expose him to

1. By Suetonius, in his brief life of the poet.

few hazards. He used almost always the same fabric of verse; and, indeed, by those few essays which he made of any other, he did not enlarge his reputation. Of this uniformity the certain consequence was readiness and dexterity. By perpetual practice, language had in his mind a systematical arrangement; having always the same use for words, he had words so selected and combined as to be ready at his call. This increase of facility he confessed himself to have perceived in the progress of his translation.

But what was yet of more importance, his effusions were always voluntary, and his subjects chosen by himself. His independence secured him from drudging at a task, and laboring upon a barren topic: he never exchanged praise for money, nor opened a shop of condolence or congratulation. His poems, therefore, were scarce ever temporary.[2] He suffered coronations and royal marriages to pass without a song, and derived no opportunities from recent events, nor any popularity from the accidental disposition of his readers. He was never reduced to the necessity of soliciting the sun to shine upon a birthday, of calling the Graces and Virtues to a wedding, or of saying what multitudes have said before him. When he could produce nothing new, he was at liberty to be silent.

His publications were for the same reason never hasty. He is said to have sent nothing to the press till it had lain two years under his inspection: it is at least certain that he ventured nothing without nice examination. He suffered the tumult of imagination to subside, and the novelties of invention to grow familiar. He knew that the mind is always enamored of its own productions, and did not trust his first fondness. He consulted his friends, and listened with great willingness to criticism; and, what was of more importance, he consulted himself, and let nothing pass against his own judgment.

He professed to have learned his poetry from Dryden, whom, whenever an opportunity was presented, he praised through his whole life with unvaried liberality; and perhaps his character may receive some illustration, if he be compared with his master.

Integrity of understanding and nicety of discernment were not allotted in a less proportion to Dryden than to Pope. The rectitude of Dryden's mind was sufficiently shown by the dismission of his poetical prejudices,[3] and the rejection of unnatural thoughts and rugged numbers. But Dryden never desired to apply all the judgment that he had. He wrote, and professed to write, merely for the people; and when he pleased others, he contented himself. He spent no time in struggles to rouse latent powers; he never attempted to make that better which was already good, nor often to mend what he must have known to be faulty. He wrote, as he tells us, with very little consideration; when occasion or necessity called upon him, he poured out what the present moment happened to supply, and, when once it had passed the press, ejected it from his mind; for when he had no pecuniary interest, he had no further solicitude.

Pope was not content to satisfy; he desired to excel, and therefore always endeavored to do his best: he did not court the candor,[4] but dared the judgment of his reader, and, expecting no indulgence from others, he showed none to himself. He examined lines and words with minute and punctilious

---

2. Topical or transitory.
3. Prepossessions. Dryden's early poems were

influenced by the metaphysical poets.
4. Kindness, sweetness of temper.

observation, and retouched every part with indefatigable diligence, till he had left nothing to be forgiven.

For this reason he kept his pieces very long in his hands, while he considered and reconsidered them. The only poems which can be supposed to have been written with such regard to the times as might hasten their publication were the two satires of *Thirty-Eight*; of which Dodsley[5] told me that they were brought to him by the author, that they might be fairly copied. "Almost every line," he said, "was then written twice over; I gave him a clean transcript, which he sent some time afterwards to me for the press, with almost every line written twice over a second time."

His declaration, that his care for his works ceased at their publication, was not strictly true. His parental attention never abandoned them; what he found amiss in the first edition, he silently corrected in those that followed. He appears to have revised the *Iliad*, and freed it from some of its imperfections; and the *Essay on Criticism* received many improvements after its first appearance. It will seldom be found that he altered without adding clearness, elegance, or vigor. Pope had perhaps the judgment of Dryden; but Dryden certainly wanted the diligence of Pope.

In acquired knowledge, the superiority must be allowed to Dryden, whose education was more scholastic, and who before he became an author had been allowed more time for study, with better means of information. His mind has a larger range, and he collects his images and illustrations from a more extensive circumference of science. Dryden knew more of man in his general nature, and Pope in his local manners. The notions of Dryden were formed by comprehensive speculation, and those of Pope by minute attention. There is more dignity in the knowledge of Dryden, and more certainty in that of Pope.

Poetry was not the sole praise of either; for both excelled likewise in prose; but Pope did not borrow his prose from his predecessor. The style of Dryden is capricious and varied, that of Pope is cautious and uniform; Dryden obeys the motions of his own mind, Pope constrains his mind to his own rules of composition; Dryden is sometimes vehement and rapid; Pope is always smooth, uniform, and gentle. Dryden's page is a natural field, rising into inequalities, and diversified by the varied exuberance of abundant vegetation; Pope's is a velvet lawn, shaven by the scythe, and leveled by the roller.

Of genius, that power which constitutes a poet; that quality without which judgment is cold and knowledge is inert; that energy which collects, combines, amplifies, and animates; the superiority must, with some hesitation, be allowed to Dryden. It is not to be inferred that of this poetical vigor Pope had only a little, because Dryden had more; for every other writer since Milton must give place to Pope; and even of Dryden it must be said that if he has brighter paragraphs, he has not better poems. Dryden's performances were always hasty, either excited by some external occasion, or extorted by domestic necessity; he composed without consideration, and published without correction. What his mind could supply at call, or gather in one excursion, was all that he sought, and all that he gave. The dilatory caution of Pope enabled him to condense his sentiments, to multiply his images, and to accumulate all that study might produce, or chance might supply. If the flights

5. Robert Dodsley, the publisher.

of Dryden therefore are higher, Pope continues longer on the wing. If of Dryden's fire the blaze is brighter, of Pope's the heat is more regular and constant. Dryden often surpasses expectation, and Pope never falls below it. Dryden is read with frequent astonishment, and Pope with perpetual delight.

This parallel will, I hope, when it is well considered, be found just; and if the reader should suspect me, as I suspect myself, of some partial fondness for the memory of Dryden, let him not too hastily condemn me; for meditation and inquiry may, perhaps, show him the reasonableness of my determination.

1781

JAMES BOSWELL
1740–1795

The discovery of a vast number of James Boswell's personal papers (believed until 1925 to have been destroyed by his literary executors) has made it possible to know the author of *The Life of Samuel Johnson* as well as we can know anybody, dead or living. His published letters and journals have made modern readers aware of the serious and absurd, the charming and repellent sides of his character. At twenty-two, when he met Johnson, he had already trained himself to listen, to observe, and to remember until he found time to write it all down. Only rarely did he take notes while a conversation was in progress, since to do so would of course have been a serious breach of social etiquette. His unusual memory and disciplined art enabled him to re-create and vividly preserve the many "scenes" that distinguish his journals as they do the *Life*.

Boswell was the eldest son and heir of Alexander Boswell of Auchinleck (pronounced *Affléck*) in Ayrshire, a judge who bore the courtesy title of Lord Auchinleck. As a member of an ancient family and heir to its large estate, Boswell was in the technical sense of the term a gentleman, with entrée into the best circles of Edinburgh and London. By temperament he was unstable, emotionally and sexually skittish. After attending the universities of Edinburgh and Glasgow and studying law in Holland, he made the grand tour of Europe; in Switzerland he met and succeeded in captivating the two foremost French men of letters, Jean-Jacques Rousseau and Voltaire. He visited the beleaguered hero of Corsica, General Pasquale de Paoli, whose revolt against Genoa seemed to European liberals to embody all the civic and military virtues of Republican Rome. Upon returning to England, Boswell wrote *An Account of Corsica* (1768). It was promptly translated into Dutch, German, French, and Italian, and its young author found himself with a considerable European reputation.

By 1769, Boswell was established in what was to prove a successful law practice in Edinburgh and had married his cousin, Margaret Montgomerie. But he kept his ties to London and Johnson. In 1773, he fullfilled a plan first suggested by Johnson ten years earlier to tour the Scottish Highlands and Hebrides together. Almost every aspect of the adventure should have made it impossible. Johnson, nearing his sixty-fourth birthday and after years of sedentary city living, found himself astride a horse in wild country or in open boats in autumn weather. As a devout Anglican, he was an outspoken enemy of the Presbyterian church. As a lover of London, he was a stranger to the primitive life of the Highlands. Moreover, for many years he had half-jestingly, half-seriously, made Scots the butt of his wit. But such were

Boswell's social tact and Johnson's vigor and curiosity that the tour was a great success. Johnson's *Journey to the Western Islands of Scotland* (1775) is a thoughtful account of the way that people live in the Hebrides (though some Scots were offended). Boswell's *Journal of a Tour to the Hebrides* (1785), a preliminary study for the *Life*, is a lively and entertaining diary that amused Johnson himself.

In 1786, four years after Johnson's death, Boswell abandoned his Scottish practice; moved to London; was admitted to the English bar (but never actually practiced); and, often depressed and drunken, began the *Life*. Fortunately he had the help and encouragement of the distinguished literary scholar Edmond Malone, without whose guidance he might never have finished his task.

Boswell had an overwhelming amount of material to deal with: his own journals, all of Johnson's letters that he could find, Johnson's voluminous writings, and every scrap of information that his friends would furnish—all of which had to be collected, verified, and somehow reduced to unity. The *Life* is a record not of Johnson alone but of literary England during the last half of the century. But Boswell wrote with his eye on the object, and that object was Samuel Johnson, toward whom such eminent persons as Sir Joshua Reynolds, Edmund Burke, Oliver Goldsmith, Lord Chesterfield—even the king himself—always face. Individual episodes are designed to reveal the great protagonist in a variety of aspects, and the world that Boswell created and populated is sustained by the vitality of his hero.

Boswell's gift is not only narrative but also dramatic. A gifted mimic, he often writes like a theatrical improviser, creating scenes with living people and playing simultaneously the roles of contriver of the dialogue, director of the plot, actor in the drama, and applauding audience—for Boswell kept an eye on his own performance. The quintessence of Boswell as both a social genius and a literary artist is to be found in his description of his visit to Voltaire: "I placed myself by him. I touched the keys in unison with his imagination. I wish you had heard the music."

Although the Johnson of popular legend is largely Boswell's creation, there was much in his life about which Boswell had no firsthand knowledge. At their first meeting, Johnson was fifty-four, a widower, already established as "Dictionary" Johnson and the author of the *Rambler*, and pensioned by the crown. Boswell knew nothing at firsthand of the long, hard years during which Johnson made his way painfully up from obscurity to fame. Hence the *Life* is the portrait of a sage. Its chief glory is conversation: the talk of a man who has experienced broadly, read widely, and observed and reflected on his observations; whose ideas are constantly brought to the test of experience; and whose experience is habitually transmuted into ideas. The book is as large as life and as human as its central character.

From Boswell on the Grand Tour

[BOSWELL INTERVIEWS VOLTAIRE][1]

And whence do I now write to you, my friend?[2] From the château of Monsieur de Voltaire. I had a letter for him from a Swiss colonel at The Hague. I came hither Monday and was presented to him. He received me with dignity

1. Voltaire was the name assumed by François-Marie Arouet (1694–1778), the most famous French writer of his generation. Playwright, poet, satirist, philosopher, enemy of the church, and irrepressible ironist, he (after a stormy career) was living in splendor at his chateau at Ferney near the border of Switzerland and France, just outside Geneva. His housekeeper and mistress

was his niece Marie-Louise Denis. He and Jean-Jacques Rousseau, whom Boswell had just visited and flattered, were deadly enemies.
2. This passage is taken from a letter, dated December 28, 1764, written to Boswell's closest friend, a young clergyman named William Temple.

and that air of a man who has been much in the world which a Frenchman acquires in perfection. I saw him for about half an hour before dinner. He was not in spirits. Yet he gave me some brilliant sallies. He did not dine with us, and I was obliged to post away immediately after dinner, because the gates of Geneva shut before five and Ferney is a good hour from town. I was by no means satisfied to have been so little time with the monarch of French literature. A happy scheme sprung up in my adventurous mind. Madame Denis, the niece of Monsieur de Voltaire, had been extremely good to me. She is fond of our language. I wrote her a letter in English begging her interest to obtain for me the privilege of lodging a night under the roof of Monsieur de Voltaire, who, in opposition to our sun, rises in the evening. I was in the finest humor and my letter was full of wit. I told her, "I am a hardy and a vigorous Scot. You may mount me to the highest and coldest garret. I shall not even refuse to sleep upon two chairs in the bedchamber of your maid. I saw her pass through the room where we sat before dinner." I sent my letter on Tuesday by an express. It was shown to Monsieur de Voltaire, who with his own hand wrote this answer in the character of Madame Denis: "You will do us much honor and pleasure. We have few beds. But you will (*shall*) not sleep on two chairs. My uncle, though very sick, hath guessed at your merit. I know it better; for I have seen you longer." * * *

I returned yesterday to this enchanted castle. The magician appeared a very little before dinner. But in the evening he came into the drawing room in great spirits. I placed myself by him. I touched the keys in unison with his imagination. I wish you had heard the music. He was all brilliance. He gave me continued flashes of wit. I got him to speak English, which he does in a degree that made me now and then start up and cry, "Upon my soul this is astonishing!" When he talked our language he was animated with the soul of a Briton. He had bold flights. He had humor. He had an extravagance; he had a forcible oddity of style that the most comical of our *dramatis personae* could not have exceeded. He swore bloodily, as was the fashion when he was in England.[3] He hummed a ballad; he repeated nonsense. Then he talked of our Constitution with a noble enthusiasm. I was proud to hear this from the mouth of an illustrious Frenchman. At last we came upon religion. Then did he rage. The company went to supper. Monsieur de Voltaire and I remained in the drawing room with a great Bible before us; and if ever two mortal men disputed with vehemence, we did. Yes, upon that occasion he was one individual and I another. For a certain portion of time there was a fair opposition between Voltaire and Boswell. The daring bursts of his ridicule confounded my understanding. He stood like an orator of ancient Rome. Tully[4] was never more agitated than he was. He went too far. His aged frame trembled beneath him. He cried, "Oh, I am very sick; my head turns round," and he let himself gently fall upon an easy chair. He recovered. I resumed our conversation, but changed the tone. I talked to him serious and earnest. I demanded of him an honest confession of his real sentiments. He gave it me with candor and with a mild eloquence which touched my heart. I did not believe him capable of

3. In 1726, to avoid imprisonment because of a quarrel with a nobleman, Voltaire had gone into exile in England, where he remained for three years, meeting many distinguished English writers and statesmen and learning to admire the British Constitution and the English principle of religious toleration. His *Lettres philosophiques sur les Anglais* (1734) expressed his admiration of English institutions and indirectly criticized France.

4. Marcus Tullius Cicero.

thinking in the manner that he declared to me was "from the bottom of his heart." He expressed his veneration—his love—of the Supreme Being, and his entire resignation to the will of Him who is all-wise. He expressed his desire to resemble the Author of Goodness by being good himself. His sentiments go no farther. He does not inflame his mind with grand hopes of the immortality of the soul. He says it may be, but he knows nothing of it. And his mind is in perfect tranquility. I was moved; I was sorry. I doubted his sincerity. I called to him with emotion, "Are you sincere? are you really sincere?" He answered "Before God, I am." Then with the fire of him whose tragedies have so often shone on the theater of Paris, he said, "I suffer much. But I suffer with patience and resignation; not as a Christian—but as a man."

Temple, was not this an interesting scene? Would a journey from Scotland to Ferney have been too much to obtain such a remarkable interview? * * *

1764   1928

From The Life of Samuel Johnson, LL.D.

[PLAN OF THE *LIFE*]

* * * Had Dr. Johnson written his own life, in conformity with the opinion which he has given, that every man's life may be best written by himself;[1] had he employed in the preservation of his own history, that clearness of narration and elegance of language in which he has embalmed so many eminent persons, the world would probably have had the most perfect example of biography that was ever exhibited. But although he at different times, in a desultory manner, committed to writing many particulars of the progress of his mind and fortunes, he never had persevering diligence enough to form them into a regular composition. Of these memorials a few have been preserved; but the greater part was consigned by him to the flames, a few days before his death.

As I had the honor and happiness of enjoying his friendship for upwards of twenty years; as I had the scheme of writing his life constantly in view; as he was well apprised of this circumstance, and from time to time obligingly satisfied my inquiries, by communicating to me the incidents of his early years; as I acquired a facility in recollecting, and was very assiduous in recording, his conversation, of which the extraordinary vigor and vivacity constituted one of the first features of his character; and as I have spared no pains in obtaining materials concerning him, from every quarter where I could discover that they were to be found, and have been favored with the most liberal communications by his friends; I flatter myself that few biographers have entered upon such a work as this with more advantages; independent of literary abilities, in which I am not vain enough to compare myself with some great names who have gone before me in this kind of writing. * * *

Instead of melting down my materials into one mass, and constantly speaking in my own person, by which I might have appeared to have more merit in the execution of the work, I have resolved to adopt and enlarge upon the

1. *Idler* 84.

excellent plan of Mr. Mason, in his *Memoirs of Gray*.[2] Wherever narrative is necessary to explain, connect, and supply, I furnish it to the best of my abilities; but in the chronological series of Johnson's life, which I trace as distinctly as I can, year by year, I produce, wherever it is in my power, his own minutes, letters, or conversation, being convinced that this mode is more lively, and will make my readers better acquainted with him than even most of those were who actually knew him, but could know him only partially; whereas there is here an accumulation of intelligence from various points, by which his character is more fully understood and illustrated.

Indeed I cannot conceive a more perfect mode of writing any man's life than not only relating all the most important events of it in their order, but interweaving what he privately wrote, and said, and thought; by which mankind are enabled as it were to see him live, and to "live o'er each scene"[3] with him, as he actually advanced through the several stages of his life. Had his other friends been as diligent and ardent as I was, he might have been almost entirely preserved. As it is, I will venture to say that he will be seen in this work more completely than any man who has ever yet lived.

And he will be seen as he really was; for I profess to write, not his panegyric, which must be all praise, but his Life; which, great and good as he was, must not be supposed to be entirely perfect. To be as he was, is indeed subject of panegyric enough to any man in this state of being; but in every picture there should be shade as well as light, and when I delineate him without reserve, I do what he himself recommended, both by his precept and his example. * * *

I am fully aware of the objections which may be made to the minuteness on some occasions of my detail of Johnson's conversation, and how happily it is adapted for the petty exercise of ridicule, by men of superficial understanding and ludicrous fancy; but I remain firm and confident in my opinion, that minute particulars are frequently characteristic, and always amusing, when they relate to a distinguished man. I am therefore exceedingly unwilling that anything, however slight, which my illustrious friend thought it worth his while to express, with any degree of point, should perish. * * *

Of one thing I am certain, that considering how highly the small portion which we have of the table-talk and other anecdotes of our celebrated writers is valued, and how earnestly it is regretted that we have not more, I am justified in preserving rather too many of Johnson's sayings, than too few; especially as from the diversity of dispositions it cannot be known with certainty beforehand, whether what may seem trifling to some, and perhaps to the collector himself, may not be most agreeable to many; and the greater number that an author can please in any degree, the more pleasure does there arise to a benevolent mind. * * *

[JOHNSON'S EARLY YEARS. MARRIAGE AND LONDON]

[*1709*] Samuel Johnson was born at Lichfield, in Staffordshire, on the 18th of September, N.S.,[4] 1709; and his initiation into the Christian Church was not

2. William Mason, poet and dramatist, published his life of Thomas Gray in 1774:
3. Pope's Prologue to Addison's *Cato*, line 4.
4. New Style. In 1752, Great Britain adopted the Gregorian calendar, introduced in 1582 by Pope Gregory XIII to correct the accumulated inaccuracies of Julius Caesar's calendar, which had been in use since 46 B.C.E. By 1752, the error amounted

delayed; for his baptism is recorded, in the register of St. Mary's parish in that city, to have been performed on the day of his birth. His father is there styled *Gentleman*, a circumstance of which an ignorant panegyrist has praised him for not being proud; when the truth is, that the appellation of Gentleman, though now lost in the indiscriminate assumption of *Esquire*, was commonly taken by those who could not boast of gentility. His father was Michael Johnson, a native of Derbyshire, of obscure extraction, who settled in Lichfield as a bookseller and stationer. His mother was Sarah Ford, descended of an ancient race of substantial yeomanry in Warwickshire. They were well advanced in years when they married, and never had more than two children, both sons; Samuel, their first-born, who lived to be the illustrious character whose various excellence I am to endeavor to record, and Nathanael, who died in his twenty-fifth year.

Mr. Michael Johnson was a man of a large and robust body, and of a strong and active mind; yet, as in the most solid rocks veins of unsound substance are often discovered, there was in him a mixture of that disease, the nature of which eludes the most minute inquiry, though the effects are well known to be a weariness of life, an unconcern about those things which agitate the greater part of mankind, and a general sensation of gloomy wretchedness. From him then his son inherited, with some other qualities, "a vile melancholy," which in his too strong expression of any disturbance of the mind, "made him mad all his life, at least not sober." Michael was, however, forced by the narrowness of his circumstances to be very diligent in business, not only in his shop, but by occasionally resorting to several towns in the neighborhood, some of which were at a considerable distance from Lichfield. At that time booksellers' shops in the provincial towns of England were very rare, so that there was not one even in Birmingham, in which town old Mr. Johnson used to open a shop every market day. He was a pretty good Latin scholar, and a citizen so creditable as to be made one of the magistrates of Lichfield; and, being a man of good sense, and skill in his trade, he acquired a reasonable share of wealth, of which however he afterwards lost the greatest part, by engaging unsuccessfully in a manufacture of parchment. He was a zealous highchurch man and royalist, and retained his attachment to the unfortunate house of Stuart, though he reconciled himself, by casuistical arguments of expediency and necessity, to take the oaths imposed by the prevailing power. * * *

Johnson's mother was a woman of distinguished understanding. I asked his old schoolfellow, Mr. Hector,[5] surgeon of Birmingham, if she was not vain of her son. He said, "She had too much good sense to be vain, but she knew her son's value." Her piety was not inferior to her understanding; and to her must be ascribed those early impressions of religion upon the mind of her son, from which the world afterwards derived so much benefit. He told me that he remembered distinctly having had the first notice of Heaven, "a place to which good people went," and hell, "a place to which bad people went," communicated to him by her, when a little child in bed with her; and that it might be the better fixed in his memory, she sent him to repeat it to Thomas Jack-

---

to eleven days. Dates before September 2, 1752, must be corrected by adding eleven days or by using the Julian date, followed by "O.S." (Old Style).

5. Edmund Hector, a lifelong friend of Johnson.

son, their manservant; he not being in the way, this was not done; but there was no occasion for any artificial aid for its preservation. * * *

[1728] That a man in Mr. Michael Johnson's circumstances should think of sending his son to the expensive University of Oxford, at his own charge, seems very improbable. The subject was too delicate to question Johnson upon. But I have been assured by Dr. Taylor[6] that the scheme never would have taken place had not a gentleman of Shropshire, one of his schoolfellows, spontaneously undertaken to support him at Oxford, in the character of his companion; though, in fact, he never received any assistance whatever from that gentleman.

He, however, went to Oxford, and was entered a Commoner of Pembroke College on the 31st of October, 1728, being then in his nineteenth year.

The Reverend Dr. Adams,[7] who afterwards presided over Pembroke College with universal esteem, told me he was present, and gave me some account of what passed on the night of Johnson's arrival at Oxford. On that evening, his father, who had anxiously accompanied him, found means to have him introduced to Mr. Jorden, who was to be his tutor. * * *

His father seemed very full of the merits of his son, and told the company he was a good scholar, and a poet, and wrote Latin verses. His figure and manner appeared strange to them; but he behaved modestly and sat silent, till upon something which occurred in the course of conversation, he suddenly struck in and quoted Macrobius; and thus he gave the first impression of that more extensive reading in which he had indulged himself.

His tutor, Mr. Jorden, fellow of Pembroke, was not, it seems, a man of such abilities as we should conceive requisite for the instructor of Samuel Johnson, who gave me the following account of him. "He was a very worthy man, but a heavy man, and I did not profit much by his instructions. Indeed, I did not attend him much. The first day after I came to college I waited upon him, and then stayed away four. On the sixth, Mr. Jorden asked me why I had not attended. I answered I had been sliding in Christ Church meadow. And this I said with as much *nonchalance* as I am now talking to you. I had no notion that I was wrong or irreverent to my tutor." BOSWELL: "That, Sir, was great fortitude of mind." JOHNSON: "No, Sir; stark insensibility." * * *

[1729] The "morbid melancholy," which was lurking in his constitution, and to which we may ascribe those particularities and that aversion to regular life, which, at a very early period, marked his character, gathered such strength in his twentieth year as to afflict him in a dreadful manner. While he was at Lichfield, in the college vacation of the year 1729, he felt himself overwhelmed with an horrible hypochondria,[8] with perpetual irritation, fretfulness, and impatience; and with a dejection, gloom, and despair, which made existence misery. From this dismal malady he never afterwards was perfectly relieved; and all his labors, and all his enjoyments, were but temporary interruptions of its baleful influence. He told Mr. Paradise[9] that he was sometimes so languid and inefficient that he could not distinguish the hour upon the town-clock. * * *

6. A well-to-do clergyman who had been Johnson's schoolfellow in Lichfield.
7. The Reverend William Adams, D.D., elected master of Pembroke in 1775.
8. Depression.
9. John Paradise, a member of the Essex Head Club, which Johnson founded in 1783.

To Johnson, whose supreme enjoyment was the exercise of his reason, the disturbance or obscuration of that faculty was the evil most to be dreaded. Insanity, therefore, was the object of his most dismal apprehension; and he fancied himself seized by it, or approaching to it, at the very time when he was giving proofs of a more than ordinary soundness and vigor of judgment. That his own diseased imagination should have so far deceived him, is strange; but it is stranger still that some of his friends should have given credit to his groundless opinion, when they had such undoubted proofs that it was totally fallacious; though it is by no means surprising that those who wish to depreciate him should, since his death, have laid hold of this circumstance, and insisted upon it with very unfair aggravation. * * *

Dr. Adams told me that Johnson, while he was at Pembroke College, "was caressed and loved by all about him, was a gay and frolicsome fellow, and passed there the happiest part of his life." But this is a striking proof of the fallacy of appearances, and how little any of us know of the real internal state even of those whom we see most frequently; for the truth is, that he was then depressed by poverty, and irritated by disease. When I mentioned to him this account as given me by Dr. Adams, he said, "Ah, Sir, I was mad and violent. It was bitterness which they mistook for frolic. I was miserably poor, and I thought to fight my way by my literature and my wit; so I disregarded all power and all authority." * * *

[1734] In a man whom religious education has secured from licentious indulgences, the passion of love, when once it has seized him, is exceedingly strong; being unimpaired by dissipation,[1] and totally concentrated in one object. This was experienced by Johnson, when he became the fervent admirer of Mrs. Porter, after her first husband's death. Miss Porter told me that when he was first introduced to her mother, his appearance was very forbidding: he was then lean and lank, so that his immense structure of bones was hideously striking to the eye, and the scars of the scrofula were deeply visible. He also wore his hair,[2] which was straight and stiff, and separated behind: and he often had, seemingly, convulsive starts and odd gesticulations, which tended to excite at once surprise and ridicule. Mrs. Porter was so much engaged by his conversation that she overlooked all these external disadvantages, and said to her daughter, "This is the most sensible man that I ever saw in my life."

[1735] Though Mrs. Porter was double the age of Johnson, and her person and manner, as described to me by the late Mr. Garrick,[3] were by no means pleasing to others, she must have had a superiority of understanding and talents, as she certainly inspired him with a more than ordinary passion; and she having signified her willingness to accept of his hand, he went to Lichfield to ask his mother's consent to the marriage, which he could not but be conscious was a very imprudent scheme, both on account of their disparity of years and her want of fortune. But Mrs. Johnson knew too well the ardor of her son's temper, and was too tender a parent to oppose his inclinations.

I know not for what reason the marriage ceremony was not performed at Birmingham; but a resolution was taken that it should be at Derby, for which

---

1. Scattered attention.
2. I.e., he wore no wig.
3. David Garrick (1717–1779), the most famous

actor of his day. In 1736 he was one of Johnson's three pupils in an unsuccessful school at Edial.

place the bride and bridegroom set out on horseback, I suppose in very good humor. But though Mr. Topham Beauclerk[4] used archly to mention Johnson's having told him, with much gravity, "Sir, it was a love marriage on both sides," I have had from my illustrious friend the following curious account of their journey to church upon the nuptial morn:

9th July: "Sir, she had read the old romances, and had got into her head the fantastical notion that a woman of spirit should use her lover like a dog. So, Sir, at first she told me that I rode too fast, and she could not keep up with me; and, when I rode a little slower, she passed me, and complained that I lagged behind. I was not to be made the slave of caprice; and I resolved to begin as I meant to end. I therefore pushed on briskly, till I was fairly out of her sight. The road lay between two hedges, so I was sure she could not miss it; and I contrived that she should soon come up with me. When she did, I observed her to be in tears." * * *

[1737] Johnson now thought of trying his fortune in London, the great field of genius and exertion, where talents of every kind have the fullest scope and the highest encouragement. It is a memorable circumstance that his pupil David Garrick went thither at the same time, with intention to complete his education, and follow the profession of the law, from which he was soon diverted by his decided preference for the stage.[5] * * *

[1744] * * * He produced one work this year, fully sufficient to maintain the high reputation which he had acquired. This was *The Life of Richard Savage;*[6] a man of whom it is difficult to speak impartially without wondering that he was for some time the intimate companion of Johnson; for his character was marked by profligacy, insolence, and ingratitude: yet, as he undoubtedly had a warm and vigorous, though unregulated mind, had seen life in all its varieties, and been much in the company of the statesmen and wits of his time, he could communicate to Johnson an abundant supply of such materials as his philosophical curiosity most eagerly desired; and as Savage's misfortunes and misconduct had reduced him to the lowest state of wretchedness as a writer for bread, his visits to St. John's Gate[7] naturally brought Johnson and him together.

It is melancholy to reflect that Johnson and Savage were sometimes in such extreme indigence that they could not pay for a lodging; so that they have wandered together whole nights in the streets. Yet in these almost incredible scenes of distress, we may suppose that Savage mentioned many of the anecdotes with which Johnson afterwards enriched the life of his unhappy companion, and those of other poets.

---

4. Pronounced *bo-clare*. A descendant of Charles II and the actress Nell Gwynn, he was brilliant and dissolute.

5. Johnson had hoped to complete his tragedy *Irene* and to get it produced, but this was not accomplished until Garrick staged it in 1749. Meanwhile Johnson struggled against poverty, at first as a writer and translator for Edward Cave's *Gentleman's Magazine.* He gradually won recognition but was never financially secure until he was pensioned in 1762. Garrick succeeded in the theater much more rapidly than did Johnson in literature.

6. The poet Richard Savage courted and gained notoriety by claiming to be the illegitimate son of Earl Rivers and the Countess of Macclesfield, whose husband had divorced her because of her unfaithfulness with Rivers. Savage publicized his claim and persecuted his alleged mother. Johnson and many others believed Savage's story and resented what they considered the lady's inhumanity. Savage was a gifted man, but he lived in poverty as a hack writer, although he was long assisted by Pope and others. He died in a debtor's prison in Bristol in 1743.

7. Where Cave published the *Gentleman's Magazine.*

He told Sir Joshua Reynolds that one night in particular, when Savage and he walked round St. James's Square for want of a lodging, they were not at all depressed by their situation; but in high spirits and brimful of patriotism, traversed the square for several hours, inveighed against the minister, and "resolved they would *stand by their country.*" * * *

[1752] That there should be a suspension of his literary labors during a part of the year 1752[8] will not seem strange when it is considered that soon after closing his *Rambler,* he suffered a loss which, there can be no doubt, affected him with the deepest distress. For on the 17th of March, O.S., his wife died. * * *

The following very solemn and affecting prayer was found, after Dr. Johnson's decease, by his servant, Mr. Francis Barber, who delivered it to my worthy friend the Reverend Mr. Strahan, Vicar of Islington, who at my earnest request has obligingly favored me with a copy of it, which he and I compared with the original:

"April 26, 1752, being after 12 at night of the 25th.

"O Lord! Governor of heaven and earth, in whose hands are embodied and departed spirits, if thou hast ordained the souls of the dead to minister to the living, and appointed my departed wife to have care of me, grant that I may enjoy the good effects of her attention and ministration, whether exercised by appearance, impulses, dreams or in any other manner agreeable to thy government. Forgive my presumption, enlighten my ignorance, and however meaner agents are employed, grant me the blessed influences of thy holy Spirit, through Jesus Christ our Lord. Amen." * * *

One night when Beauclerk and Langton[9] had supped at a tavern in London, and sat till about three in the morning, if came into their heads to go and knock up Johnson, and see if they could prevail on him to join them in a ramble. They rapped violently at the door of his chambers in the Temple,[1] till at last he appeared in his shirt, with his little black wig on the top of his head, instead of a nightcap, and a poker in his hand, imagining, probably, that some ruffians were coming to attack him. When he discovered who they were, and was told their errand, he smiled, and with great good humor agreed to their proposal: "What, is it you, you dogs! I'll have a frisk with you." He was soon dressed, and they sallied forth together into Covent Garden, where the greengrocers and fruiterers were beginning to arrange their hampers, just come in from the country. Johnson made some attempts to help them; but the honest gardeners stared so at his figure and manner and odd interference, that he soon saw his services were not relished. They then repaired to one of the neighboring taverns, and made a bowl of that liquor called *Bishop,*[2] which Johnson had always liked; while in joyous contempt of sleep, from which he had been roused, he repeated the festive lines,

8. Johnson's important works written before the publication of the *Dictionary* are the poems "London" (1738) and "The Vanity of Human Wishes" (1749), the *Life of Savage* (1744), and the essays that made up his periodical the *Rambler* (1750–52).
9. Bennet Langton. As a boy he so much admired the *Rambler* that he sought Johnson's acquain-

tance. They became lifelong friends.
1. Because Johnson lived in Inner Temple Lane between 1760 and 1765, the "frisk" could not have taken place in the year of his wife's death, where Boswell, for his own convenience, placed it.
2. A drink made of wine, sugar, and either lemon or orange.

Short, O short then be thy reign,
And give us to the world again![3]

They did not stay long, but walked down to the Thames, took a boat, and rowed to Billingsgate. Beauclerk and Johnson were so well pleased with their amusement that they resolved to persevere in dissipation for the rest of the day: but Langton deserted them, being engaged to breakfast with some young ladies. Johnson scolded him for "leaving his social friends, to go and sit with a set of wretched un-idea'd girls." Garrick being told of this ramble, said to him smartly, "I heard of your frolic t' other night. You'll be in the *Chronicle*." Upon which Johnson afterwards observed, "*He* durst not do such a thing. His *wife* would not *let* him!" * * *

[THE LETTER TO CHESTERFIELD]

[1754] Lord Chesterfield,[4] to whom Johnson had paid the high compliment of addressing to his Lordship the *Plan* of his *Dictionary*, had behaved to him in such a manner as to excite his contempt and indignation. The world has been for many years amused with a story confidently told, and as confidently repeated with additional circumstances, that a sudden disgust was taken by Johnson upon occasion of his having been one day kept long in waiting in his Lordship's antechamber, for which the reason assigned was that he had company with him; and that at last, when the door opened, out walked Colley Cibber;[5] and that Johnson was so violently provoked when he found for whom he had been so long excluded, that he went away in a passion, and never would return. I remember having mentioned this story to George Lord Lyttelton, who told me he was very intimate with Lord Chesterfield; and holding it as a well-known truth, defended Lord Chesterfield, by saying, that Cibber, who had been introduced familiarly by the back stairs, had probably not been there above ten minutes. It may seem strange even to entertain a doubt concerning a story so long and so widely current, and thus implicitly adopted, if not sanctioned, by the authority which I have mentioned; but Johnson himself assured me that there was not the least foundation for it. He told me that there never was any particular incident which produced a quarrel between Lord Chesterfield and him; but that his Lordship's continued neglect was the reason why he resolved to have no connection with him. When the *Dictionary* was upon the eve of publication, Lord Chesterfield, who, it is said, had flattered himself with expectations that Johnson would dedicate the work to him, attempted, in a courtly manner, to soothe, and insinuate himself with the sage, conscious, as it should seem, of the cold indifference with which he had treated its learned author; and further attempted to conciliate him, by writing two papers in *The World*, in recommendation of the work; and it must be confessed that they contain some studied compliments, so finely turned, that if there had been no previous offense, it is probable that Johnson would have been highly delighted. Praise, in general,

3. Misquoted from Lansdowne's "Drinking Song to Sleep."
4. Philip Dormer Stanhope, earl of Chesterfield (1694–1773), statesman; wit, man of fashion. His *Letters*, written for the guidance of his natural son, are famous for their worldly good sense and for their expression of the ideal of an 18th-century gentleman.
5. Cibber (1671–1757), playwright, comic actor, and (after 1730) poet laureate. A fine actor but a very bad poet, Cibber was a constant object of ridicule by the wits of the town. Pope made him king of the Dunces in the *Dunciad* of 1743.

was pleasing to him; but by praise from a man of rank and elegant accomplishments, he was peculiarly gratified. * * *

This courtly device failed of its effect. Johnson, who thought that "all was false and hollow,"[6] despised the honeyed words, and was even indignant that Lord Chesterfield should, for a moment, imagine that he could be dupe of such an artifice. His expression to me concerning Lord Chesterfield, upon this occasion, was, "Sir, after making great professions, he had, for many years, taken no notice of me; but when my *Dictionary* was coming out, he fell a-scribbling in *The World* about it. Upon which, I wrote him a letter expressed in civil terms, but such as might show him that I did not mind what he said or wrote, and that I had done with him."

This is that celebrated letter of which so much has been said, and about which curiosity has been so long excited, without being gratified. I for many years solicited Johnson to favor me with a copy of it, that so excellent a composition might not be lost to posterity. He delayed from time to time to give it me; till at last in 1781, when we were on a visit at Mr. Dilly's,[7] at Southill in Bedfordshire, he was pleased to dictate it to me from memory. He afterwards found among his papers a copy of it, which he had dictated to Mr. Baretti,[8] with its title and corrections, in his own handwriting. This he gave to Mr. Langton; adding that if it were to come into print, he wished it to be from that copy. By Mr. Langton's kindness, I am enabled to enrich my work with a perfect transcript of what the world has so eagerly desired to see.

TO THE RIGHT HONORABLE THE EARL OF CHESTERFIELD

February 7, 1755

MY LORD,

I have been lately informed, by the proprietor of *The World*, that two papers, in which my Dictionary is recommended to the public, were written by your Lordship. To be so distinguished, is an honor, which, being very little accustomed to favors from the great, I know not well how to receive, or in what terms to acknowledge.

When, upon some slight encouragement, I first visited your Lordship, I was overpowered, like the rest of mankind, by the enchantment of your address; and could not forbear to wish that I might boast myself *Le vainqueur du vainqueur de la terre*[9]—that I might obtain that regard for which I saw the world contending; but I found my attendance so little encouraged that neither pride nor modesty would suffer me to continue it. When I had once addressed your Lordship in public, I had exhausted all the art of pleasing which a retired and uncourtly scholar can possess. I had done all that I could; and no man is well pleased to have his all neglected, be it ever so little.

Seven years, my Lord, have now passed since I waited in your outward rooms, or was repulsed from your door; during which time I have

6. *Paradise Lost* 2.112.
7. Southill was the country home of Charles and Edward Dilly, publishers. The firm published all of Boswell's serious works and shared in the publication of Johnson's *Lives of the Poets* (1779–81).
8. Giuseppe Baretti, an Italian writer and lexi-cographer whom Johnson introduced into his circle.
9. The conqueror of the conqueror of the earth (French). From the first line of Scudéry's epic *Alaric* (1654).

been pushing on my work through difficulties of which it is useless to complain, and have brought it, at last, to the verge of publication, without one act of assistance, one word of encouragement, or one smile of favor. Such treatment I did not expect, for I never had a patron before.

The shepherd in Virgil grew at last acquainted with Love, and found him a native of the rocks.[1]

Is not a patron, my Lord, one who looks with unconcern on a man struggling for life in the water, and, when he has reached ground, encumbers him with help? The notice which you have been pleased to take of my labors, had it been early, had been kind; but it has been delayed till I am indifferent, and cannot enjoy it; till I am solitary, and cannot impart it; till I am known, and do not want it. I hope it is no very cynical asperity not to confess obligations where no benefit has been received, or to be unwilling that the public should consider me as owing that to a patron which Providence has enabled me to do for myself.

Having carried on my work thus far with so little obligation to any favorer of learning, I shall not be disappointed though I should conclude it, if less be possible, with less; for I have been long wakened from that dream of hope in which I once boasted myself with so much exultation, my Lord, your Lordship's most humble, most obedient servant,

SAM. JOHNSON.

"While this was the talk of the town," says Dr. Adams, in a letter to me, "I happened to visit Dr. Warburton,[2] who finding that I was acquainted with Johnson, desired me earnestly to carry his compliments to him, and to tell him that he honored him for his manly behavior in rejecting these condescensions of Lord Chesterfield, and for resenting the treatment he had received from him, with a proper spirit. Johnson was visibly pleased with this compliment, for he had always a high opinion of Warburton. Indeed, the force of mind which appeared in this letter was congenial with that which Warburton himself amply possessed."

There is a curious minute circumstance which struck me, in comparing the various editions of Johnson's imitations of Juvenal. In the tenth satire, one of the couplets upon the vanity of wishes even for literary distinction stood thus:

> Yet think what ills the scholar's life assail,
> Toil, envy, want, the *garret*, and the jail.

But after experiencing the uneasiness which Lord Chesterfield's fallacious patronage made him feel, he dismissed the word *garret* from the sad group, and in all the subsequent editions the line stands

> Toil, envy, want, the *patron*, and the jail.

[1762] The accession of George the Third to the throne of these kingdoms[3] opened a new and brighter prospect to men of literary merit, who had been honored with no mark of royal favor in the preceding reign. His present Majesty's education in this country, as well as his taste and beneficence, prompted

1. *Eclogues* 8.44.
2. William Warburton, bishop of Gloucester, friend and literary executor of Pope, editor of Pope and Shakespeare, theological controversialist.
3. In 1760.

him to be the patron of science and the arts; and early this year Johnson, having been represented to him as a very learned and good man, without any certain provision, his Majesty was pleased to grant him a pension of three hundred pounds a year. The Earl of Bute,[4] who was then Prime Minister, had the honor to announce this instance of his Sovereign's bounty, concerning which many and various stories, all equally erroneous, have been propagated: maliciously representing it as a political bribe to Johnson, to desert his avowed principles, and become the tool of a government which he held to be founded in usurpation. I have taken care to have it in my power to refute them from the most authentic information. Lord Bute told me that Mr. Wedderburne, now Lord Loughborough, was the person who first mentioned this subject to him. Lord Loughborough told me that the pension was granted to Johnson solely as the reward of his literary merit, without any stipulation whatever, or even tacit understanding that he should write for administration. His Lordship added that he was confident the political tracts which Johnson afterwards did write, as they were entirely consonant with his own opinions, would have been written by him though no pension had been granted to him.[5] * * *

[A MEMORABLE YEAR: BOSWELL MEETS JOHNSON]

[1763] This is to me a memorable year; for in it I had the happiness to obtain the acquaintance of that extraordinary man whose memoirs I am now writing; an acquaintance which I shall ever esteem as one of the most fortunate circumstances in my life. * * *

Mr. Thomas Davies the actor, who then kept a bookseller's shop in Russel Street, Covent Garden, told me that Johnson was very much his friend, and came frequently to his house, where he more than once invited me to meet him; but by some unlucky accident or other he was prevented from coming to us. * * *

At last, on Monday the 16th of May, when I was sitting in Mr. Davies's back parlor, after having drunk tea with him and Mrs. Davies, Johnson unexpectedly came into the shop; and Mr. Davies having perceived him through the glass door in the room in which we were sitting, advancing towards us— he announced his awful approach to me, somewhat in the manner of an actor in the part of Horatio, when he addresses Hamlet on the appearance of his father's ghost, "Look, my Lord, it comes." I found that I had a very perfect idea of Johnson's figure, from the portrait of him painted by Sir Joshua Reynolds soon after he had published his *Dictionary*, in the attitude of sitting in his easy chair in deep meditation, which was the first picture his friend did for him, which Sir Joshua very kindly presented to me, and from which an engraving has been made for this work. Mr. Davies mentioned my name, and respectfully introduced me to him. I was much agitated; and recollecting his prejudice against the Scotch, of which I had heard much, I said to Davies, "Don't tell where I come from."—"From Scotland," cried Davies roguishly.

4. An intimate friend of George III's mother, he early gained an ascendancy over the young prince and was largely responsible for the king's autocratic views. He was hated in England both as a favorite and as a Scot.
5. Johnson's few political pamphlets in the 1770s invariably supported the policies of the crown. The best known is his answer to the American colonies, "Taxation No Tyranny" (1775). His dislike of the Americans was in large part due to the fact they owned slaves.

"Mr. Johnson," said I, "I do indeed come from Scotland, but I cannot help it." I am willing to flatter myself that I meant this as light pleasantry to soothe and conciliate him, and not as an humiliating abasement at the expense of my country. But however that might be, this speech was somewhat unlucky; for with that quickness of wit for which he was so remarkable, he seized the expression "come from Scotland," which I used in the sense of being of that country; and, as if I had said that I had come away from it, or left it, retorted, "That, Sir, I find, is what a very great many of your countrymen cannot help." This stroke stunned me a good deal; and when we had sat down, I felt myself not a little embarrassed, and apprehensive of what might come next. He then addressed himself to Davies: "What do you think of Garrick? He has refused me an order for the play for Miss Williams,[6] because he knows the house will be full, and that an order would be worth three shillings." Eager to take any opening to get into conversation with him, I ventured to say, "O Sir, I cannot think Mr. Garrick would grudge such a trifle to you." "Sir," said he, with a stern look, "I have known David Garrick longer than you have done: and I know no right you have to talk to me on the subject." Perhaps I deserved this check; for it was rather presumptuous in me, an entire stranger, to express any doubt of the justice of his animadversion upon his old acquaintance and pupil. I now felt myself much mortified, and began to think that the hope which I had long indulged of obtaining his acquaintance was blasted. And, in truth, had not my ardor been uncommonly strong, and my resolution uncommonly persevering, so rough a reception might have deterred me forever from making any further attempts. Fortunately, however, I remained upon the field not wholly discomfited. * * *

I was highly pleased with the extraordinary vigor of his conversation, and regretted that I was drawn away from it by an engagement at another place. I had, for a part of the evening, been left alone with him, and had ventured to make an observation now and then, which he received very civilly; so that I was satisfied that though there was a roughness in his manner, there was no ill nature in his disposition. Davies followed me to the door, and when I complained to him a little of the hard blows which the great man had given me, he kindly took upon him to console me by saying, "Don't be uneasy. I can see he likes you very well."

A few days afterwards I called on Davies, and asked him if he thought I might take the liberty of waiting on Mr. Johnson at his chambers in the Temple. He said I certainly might, and that Mr. Johnson would take it as a compliment. So upon Tuesday the 24th of May, after having been enlivened by the witty sallies of Messieurs Thornton, Wilkes, Churchill, and Lloyd,[7] with whom I had passed the morning, I boldly repaired to Johnson. His chambers were on the first floor of No. 1, Inner Temple Lane, and I entered them with an impression given me by the Reverend Dr. Blair,[8] of Edinburgh, who had been introduced to him not long before, and described his having "found the giant in his den"; an expression, which, when I came to be pretty

6. Mrs. Anna Williams (1706–1783), a blind poet and friend of Mrs. Johnson. She continued to live in Johnson's house after his wife's death and habitually sat up to make tea for him whenever he came home.
7. Robert Lloyd, poet and essayist. Bonnell Thornton, journalist. Charles Churchill, satirist.

For Wilkes, see p. 852. The four were bound together by a common love of wit and dissipation. Boswell enjoyed their company in 1763.
8. The Reverend Hugh Blair (1718–1800), Scottish divine and professor of rhetoric and *belles lettres* at the University of Edinburgh.

well acquainted with Johnson, I repeated to him, and he was diverted at this picturesque account of himself. Dr. Blair had been presented to him by Dr. James Fordyce.[9] At this time the controversy concerning the pieces published by Mr. James Macpherson, as translations of *Ossian*, was at its height.[1] Johnson had all along denied their authenticity; and, what was still more provoking to their admirers, maintained that they had no merit. The subject having been introduced by Dr. Fordyce, Dr. Blair, relying on the internal evidence of their antiquity, asked Dr. Johnson whether he thought any man of a modern age could have written such poems? Johnson replied, "Yes, Sir, many men, many women, and many children." Johnson, at this time, did not know that Dr. Blair had just published a dissertation, not only defending their authenticity, but seriously ranking them with the poems of Homer and Virgil; and when he was afterwards informed of this circumstance, he expressed some displeasure at Dr. Fordyce's having suggested the topic, and said, "I am not sorry that they got thus much for their pains. Sir, it was like leading one to talk of a book when the author is concealed behind the door."

He received me very courteously; but, it must be confessed that his apartment, and furniture, and morning dress, were sufficiently uncouth. His brown suit of clothes looked very rusty; he had on a little old shriveled unpowdered wig, which was too small for his head; his shirt neck and knees of his breeches were loose; his black worsted stockings ill drawn up; and he had a pair of unbuckled shoes by way of slippers. But all these slovenly particularities were forgotten the moment that he began to talk. Some gentlemen, whom I do not recollect, were sitting with him; and when they went away, I also rose; but he said to me, "Nay, don't go." "Sir," said I, "I am afraid that I intrude upon you. It is benevolent to allow me to sit and hear you." He seemed pleased with this compliment, which I sincerely paid him, and answered, "Sir, I am obliged to any man who visits me." I have preserved the following short minute of what passed this day:

"Madness frequently discovers itself merely by unnecessary deviation from the usual modes of the world. My poor friend Smart showed the disturbance of his mind by falling upon his knees, and saying his prayers in the street, or in any other unusual place. Now although, rationally speaking, it is greater madness not to pray at all than to pray as Smart did, I am afraid there are so many who do not pray, that their understanding is not called in question."

Concerning this unfortunate poet, Christopher Smart, who was confined in a madhouse, he had, at another time, the following conversation with Dr. Burney:[2] BURNEY. "How does poor Smart do, Sir; is he likely to recover?" JOHNSON. "It seems as if his mind had ceased to struggle with the disease; for he grows fat upon it." BURNEY. "Perhaps, Sir, that may be from want of exercise." JOHNSON. "No, Sir; he has partly as much exercise as he used to have, for he digs in the garden. Indeed, before his confinement, he used for exercise to walk to the ale house; but he was *carried* back again. I did not think he ought to be shut up. His infirmities were not noxious to society. He insisted

9. A Scottish preacher.
1. Macpherson had imposed on most of his contemporaries, Scottish and English, by convincing them of the genuineness of prose poems that he had concocted but that he claimed to have translated from the original Gaelic of Ossian, a blind epic poet of the 3rd century. The vogue of the poems both in Europe and in America was enormous.
2. Dr. Charles Burney (1726–1814), historian of music and father of the novelist and diarist Frances Burney, whom Johnson befriended in his old age.

on people praying with him; and I'd as lief pray with Kit Smart as anyone else. Another charge was that he did not love clean linen; and I have no passion for it."—Johnson continued. "Mankind have a great aversion to intellectual labor; but even supposing knowledge to be easily attainable, more people would be content to be ignorant than would take even a little trouble to acquire it."

Talking of Garrick, he said, "He is the first man in the world for sprightly conversation."

When I rose a second time he again pressed me to stay, which I did. * * *

[GOLDSMITH. SUNDRY OPINIONS. JOHNSON MEETS HIS KING]

As Dr. Oliver Goldsmith will frequently appear in this narrative, I shall endeavor to make my readers in some degree acquainted with his singular character. He was a native of Ireland, and a contemporary with Mr. Burke[3] at Trinity College, Dublin, but did not then give much promise of future celebrity. He, however, observed to Mr. Malone,[4] that "though he made no great figure in mathematics, which was a study in much repute there, he could turn an ode of Horace into English better than any of them." He afterwards studied physic[5] at Edinburgh, and upon the Continent; and I have been informed, was enabled to pursue his travels on foot, partly by demanding at universities to enter the lists as a disputant, by which, according to the custom of many of them, he was entitled to the premium of a crown, when luckily for him his challenge was not accepted; so that, as I once observed to Dr. Johnson, he *disputed* his passage through Europe. He then came to England, and was employed successively in the capacities of an usher[6] to an academy, a corrector of the press, a reviewer, and a writer for a newspaper. He had sagacity enough to cultivate assiduously the acquaintance of Johnson, and his faculties were gradually enlarged by the contemplation of such a model. To me and many others it appeared that he studiously copied the manner of Johnson, though, indeed, upon a smaller scale.

At this time I think he had published nothing with his name, though it was pretty generally known that *one Dr. Goldsmith* was the author of *An Enquiry into the Present State of Polite Learning in Europe*, and of *The Citizen of the World*, a series of letters supposed to be written from London by a Chinese. No man had the art of displaying, with more advantage as a writer, whatever literary acquisitions he made. "*Nihil quod tetigit non ornavit.*"[7] His mind resembled a fertile, but thin soil. There was a quick, but not a strong vegetation, of whatever chanced to be thrown upon it. No deep root could be struck. The oak of the forest did not grow there; but the elegant shrubbery and the fragrant parterre[8] appeared in gay succession. It has been generally circulated and believed that he was a mere fool in conversation; but, in truth, this has been greatly exaggerated. He had, no doubt, a more than common share of that hurry of ideas which we often find in his countrymen, and which sometimes produces a laughable confu-

3. Edmund Burke (1729–1797), statesman, orator, and political philosopher.
4. Edmond Malone (1741–1812), distinguished editor and literary scholar. He helped Boswell in the writing and publication of the *Life*.
5. Medicine.

6. An assistant teacher; then a disagreeable and ill-paid job.
7. He touched nothing that he did not adorn (Latin). From Johnson's epitaph for Goldsmith's monument in Westminster Abbey.
8. A flower garden with beds laid out in patterns.

sion in expressing them. He was very much what the French call *un étourdi*,[9] and from vanity and an eager desire of being conspicuous wherever he was, he frequently talked carelessly without knowledge of the subject, or even without thought. His person was short, his countenance coarse and vulgar, his deportment that of a scholar awkwardly affecting the easy gentleman. Those who were in any way distinguished, excited envy in him to so ridiculous an excess that the instances of it are hardly credible. When accompanying two beautiful young ladies with their mother on a tour in France, he was seriously angry that more attention was paid to them than to him; and once at the exhibition of the *Fantoccini*[1] in London, when those who sat next him observed with what dexterity a puppet was made to toss a pike, he could not bear that it should have such praise, and exclaimed with some warmth, "Pshaw! I can do it better myself." * * *

I had as my guests this evening at the Mitre Tavern, Dr. Johnson, Dr. Goldsmith, Mr. Thomas Davies, Mr. Eccles, an Irish gentleman, for whose agreeable company I was obliged to Mr. Davies, and the Reverend Mr. John Ogilvie,[2] who was desirous of being in company with my illustrious friend, while I, in my turn, was proud to have the honor of showing one of my countrymen upon what easy terms Johnson permitted me to live with him. * * *

Mr. Ogilvie was unlucky enough to choose for the topic of his conversation the praises of his native country. He began with saying that there was very rich land round Edinburgh. Goldsmith, who had studied physic there, contradicted this, very untruly, with a sneering laugh. Disconcerted a little by this, Mr. Ogilvie then took new ground, where, I suppose, he thought himself perfectly safe; for he observed that Scotland had a great many noble wild prospects. JOHNSON. "I believe, Sir, you have a great many. Norway, too, has noble wild prospects; and Lapland is remarkable for prodigious noble wild prospects. But, Sir, let me tell you, the noblest prospect which a Scotchman ever sees, is the highroad that leads him to England!" This unexpected and pointed sally produced a roar of applause. After all, however, those who admire the rude grandeur of nature cannot deny it to Caledonia. * * *

At night Mr. Johnson and I supped in a private room at the Turk's Head Coffeehouse, in the Strand. "I encourage this house," said he, "for the mistress of it is a good civil woman, and has not much business.

"Sir, I love the acquaintance of young people; because, in the first place, I don't like to think myself growing old. In the next place, young acquaintances must last longest, if they do last; and then, Sir, young men have more virtue than old men: they have more generous sentiments in every respect. I love the young dogs of this age: they have more wit and humor and knowledge of life than we had; but then the dogs are not so good scholars. Sir, in my early years I read very hard. It is a sad reflection, but a true one, that I knew almost as much at eighteen as I do now. My judgment, to be sure, was not so good; but I had all the facts. I remember very well, when I was at Oxford, an old gentleman said to me, 'Young man, ply your book diligently now, and acquire a stock of knowledge; for when years come upon you, you will find that poring upon books will be but an irksome task.'" * * *

---

9. One who acts without thought.
1. Puppets (Italian).

2. A Presbyterian minister and poet.

He again insisted on the duty of maintaining subordination of rank. "Sir, I would no more deprive a nobleman of his respect than of his money. I consider myself as acting a part in the great system of society, and I do to others as I would have them to do to me. I would behave to a nobleman as I should expect he would behave to me, were I a nobleman and he Sam. Johnson. Sir, there is one Mrs. Macaulay[3] in this town, a great republican. One day when I was at her house, I put on a very grave countenance, and said to her, 'Madam, I am now become a convert to your way of thinking. I am convinced that all mankind are upon an equal footing; and to give you an unquestionable proof, Madam, that I am in earnest, here is a very sensible, civil, well-behaved fellow citizen, your footman; I desire that he may be allowed to sit down and dine with us.' I thus, Sir, showed her the absurdity of the leveling doctrine.[4] She has never liked me since. Sir, your levelers wish to level *down* as far as themselves; but they cannot bear leveling *up* to themselves. They would all have some people under them; why not then have some people above them?" * * *

At supper this night he talked of good eating with uncommon satisfaction. "Some people," he said, "have a foolish way of not minding, or pretending not to mind, what they eat. For my part, I mind my belly very studiously, and very carefully; for I look upon it that he who does not mind his belly will hardly mind anything else." He now appeared to me *Jean Bull philosophe*,[5] and he was, for the moment, not only serious but vehement. Yet I have heard him, upon other occasions, talk with great contempt of people who were anxious to gratify their palates; and the 206th number of his *Rambler* is a masterly essay against gulosity.[6] His practice, indeed, I must acknowledge, may be considered as casting the balance of his different opinions upon this subject; for I never knew any man who relished good eating more than he did. When at table, he was totally absorbed in the business of the moment; his looks seemed riveted to his plate; nor would he, unless when in very high company, say one word, or even pay the least attention to what was said by others, till he had satisfied his appetite, which was so fierce, and indulged with such intenseness, that while in the act of eating, the veins of his forehead swelled, and generally a strong perspiration was visible. To those whose sensations were delicate, this could not but be disgusting; and it was doubtless not very suitable to the character of a philosopher, who should be distinguished by self-command. But it must be owned that Johnson, though he could be rigidly *abstemious*, was not a *temperate* man either in eating or drinking. He could refrain, but he could not use moderately. He told me that he had fasted two days without inconvenience, and that he had never been hungry but once. They who beheld with wonder how much he eat upon all occasions when his dinner was to his taste, could not easily conceive what he must have meant by hunger; and not only was he remarkable for the extraordinary quantity which he eat, but he was, or affected to be, a man of very nice discernment in the science of cookery. * * *

3. Catharine Macaulay, a distinguished feminist, historian, and propounder of libertarian and egalitarian ideas.
4. Leveler: "One who destroys superiority; one who endeavours to bring all to the same state of equality" (Johnson's *Dictionary*).
5. I.e., John Bull (the typical hardheaded Englishman) in the role of philosopher.
6. Greediness.

[*1767*] In February, 1767, there happened one of the most remarkable incidents of Johnson's life, which gratified his monarchical enthusiasm, and which he loved to relate with all its circumstances, when requested by his friends. This was his being honored by a private conversation with his Majesty, in the library at the Queen's house. He had frequently visited those splendid rooms and noble collection of books, which he used to say was more numerous and curious than he supposed any person could have made in the time which the King had employed. Mr. Barnard, the librarian, took care that he should have every accommodation that could contribute to his ease and convenience, while indulging his literary taste in that place; so that he had here a very agreeable resource at leisure hours.

His Majesty having been informed of his occasional visits, was pleased to signify a desire that he should be told when Dr. Johnson came next to the library. Accordingly, the next time that Johnson did come, as soon as he was fairly engaged with a book, on which, while he sat by the fire, he seemed quite intent, Mr. Barnard stole round to the apartment where the King was, and, in obedience to his Majesty's commands, mentioned that Dr. Johnson was then in the library. His Majesty said he was at leisure, and would go to him; upon which Mr. Barnard took one of the candles that stood on the King's table, and lighted his Majesty through a suite of rooms, till they came to a private door into the library, of which his Majesty had the key. Being entered, Mr. Barnard stepped forward hastily to Dr. Johnson, who was still in a profound study, and whispered him, "Sir, here is the King." Johnson started up, and stood still. His Majesty approached him, and at once was courteously easy.

His Majesty began by observing that he understood he came sometimes to the library; and then mentioning his having heard that the Doctor had been lately at Oxford, asked him if he was not fond of going thither. To which Johnson answered that he was indeed fond of going to Oxford sometimes, but was likewise glad to come back again. The King then asked him what they were doing at Oxford. Johnson answered, he could not much commend their diligence, but that in some respects they were mended, for they had put their press under better regulations, and were at that time printing Polybius. He was then asked whether there were better libraries at Oxford or Cambridge. He answered, he believed the Bodleian was larger than any they had at Cambridge; at the same time adding, "I hope, whether we have more books or not than they have at Cambridge, we shall make as good use of them as they do." Being asked whether All Souls or Christ Church library was the largest, he answered, "All Souls library is the largest we have, except the Bodleian." "Aye," said the King, "that is the public library."

His Majesty inquired if he was then writing anything. He answered, he was not, for he had pretty well told the world what he knew, and must now read to acquire more knowledge. The King, as it should seem with a view to urge him to rely on his own stores as an original writer, and to continue his labors, then said "I do not think you borrow much from anybody." Johnson said he thought he had already done his part as a writer. "I should have thought so too," said the King, "if you had not written so well."—Johnson observed to me, upon this, that "No man could have paid a handsomer compliment; and it was fit for a king to pay. It was decisive." When asked by another friend, at Sir Joshua Reynolds's, whether he made any reply to this high compliment, he answered,

"No, Sir. When the King had said it, it was to be so. It was not for me to bandy civilities with my sovereign." Perhaps no man who had spent his whole life in courts could have shown a more nice and dignified sense of true politeness than Johnson did in this instance. * * *

[FEAR OF DEATH]

[1769] When we were alone, I introduced the subject of death, and endeavored to maintain that the fear of it might be got over. I told him that David Hume said to me, he was no more uneasy to think he should *not be* after this life, than that he *had not been* before he began to exist. JOHNSON. "Sir, if he really thinks so, his perceptions are disturbed; he is mad: if he does not think so, he lies. He may tell you, he holds his finger in the flame of a candle, without feeling pain; would you believe him? When he dies, he at least gives up all he has." BOSWELL. "Foote,[7] Sir, told me, that when he was very ill he was not afraid to die." JOHNSON. "It is not true, Sir. Hold a pistol to Foote's breast, or to Hume's breast, and threaten to kill them, and you'll see how they behave." BOSWELL. "But may we not fortify our minds for the approach of death?" Here I am sensible I was in the wrong, to bring before his view what he ever looked upon with horror; for although when in a celestial frame, in his *Vanity of Human Wishes*, he has supposed death to be "kind Nature's signal for retreat," from this stage of being to "a happier seat," his thoughts upon this awful change were in general full of dismal apprehensions. His mind resembled the vast amphitheater, the Colosseum at Rome. In the center stood his judgment, which, like a mighty gladiator, combated those apprehensions that, like the wild beasts of the arena, were all around in cells, ready to be let out upon him. After a conflict, he drove them back into their dens; but not killing them, they were still assailing him. To my question, whether we might not fortify our minds for the approach of death, he answered, in a passion, "No, Sir, let it alone. It matters not how a man dies, but how he lives. The act of dying is not of importance, it lasts so short a time." He added (with an earnest look), "A man knows it must be so, and submits. It will do him no good to whine."

I attempted to continue the conversation. He was so provoked that he said, "Give us no more of this"; and was thrown into such a state of agitation that he expressed himself in a way that alarmed and distressed me; showed an impatience that I should leave him, and when I was going away, called to me sternly, "Don't let us meet tomorrow." * * *

[OSSIAN. "TALKING FOR VICTORY"]

MR. BOSWELL TO DR. JOHNSON

Edinburgh, Feb. 2, 1775.

* * * As to Macpherson, I am anxious to have from yourself a full and pointed account of what has passed between you and him. It is confidently told here that before your book[8] came out he sent to you, to let you know that he understood you meant to deny the authenticity of

---

7. Samuel Foote, actor and dramatist, famous for his wit and his skill in mimicry.
8. Johnson's *Journey to the Western Islands*

(1775), in which he had publicly expressed his views on the Ossianic poems.

Ossian's poems; that the originals were in his possession; that you might have inspection of them, and might take the evidence of people skilled in the Erse language; and that he hoped, after this fair offer, you would not be so uncandid[9] as to assert that he had refused reasonable proof. That you paid no regard to his message, but published your strong attack upon him; and then he wrote a letter to you, in such terms as he thought suited to one who had not acted as a man of veracity. * * *

What words were used by Mr. Macpherson in his letter to the venerable sage, I have never heard; but they are generally said to have been of a nature very different from the language of literary contest. Dr. Johnson's answer appeared in the newspapers of the day, and has since been frequently republished; but not with perfect accuracy. I give it as dictated to me by himself, written down in his presence, and authenticated by a note in his own handwriting, *"This, I think, is a true copy."*

MR. JAMES MACPHERSON,

   I received your foolish and impudent letter. Any violence offered me I shall do my best to repel; and what I cannot do for myself, the law shall do for me. I hope I shall never be deterred from detecting what I think a cheat, by the menaces of a ruffian.

   What would you have me retract? I thought your book an imposture; I think it an imposture still. For this opinion I have given my reasons to the public, which I here dare you to refute. Your rage I defy. Your abilities, since your Homer, are not so formidable; and what I hear of your morals inclines me to pay regard not to what you shall say, but to what you shall prove. You may print this if you will.

SAM. JOHNSON.

Mr. Macpherson little knew the character of Dr. Johnson if he supposed that he could be easily intimidated; for no man was ever more remarkable for personal courage. He had, indeed, an awful dread of death, or rather, "of something after death";[1] and what rational man, who seriously thinks of quitting all that he has ever known, and going into a new and unknown state of being, can be without that dread? But his fear was from reflection; his courage natural. His fear, in that one instance, was the result of philosophical and religious consideration. He feared death, but he feared nothing else, not even what might occasion death. Many instances of his resolution may be mentioned. One day, at Mr. Beauclerk's house in the country, when two large dogs were fighting, he went up to them, and beat them till they separated; and at another time, when told of the danger there was that a gun might burst if charged with many balls, he put in six or seven, and fired it off against a wall. Mr. Langton told me that when they were swimming together near Oxford, he cautioned Dr. Johnson against a pool which was reckoned particularly dangerous; upon which Johnson directly swam into it. He told me himself that one night he was attacked in the street by four men, to whom he would not yield, but kept them all at bay, till the watch came up, and carried both him and

9. Unfair, malicious.   1. *Hamlet* 3.1.80.

them to the roundhouse.[2] In the playhouse at Lichfield, as Mr. Garrick informed me, Johnson having for a moment quitted a chair which was placed for him between the side-scenes, a gentleman took possession of it, and when Johnson on his return civilly demanded his seat, rudely refused to give it up; upon which Johnson laid hold of it, and tossed him and the chair into the pit. Foote, who so successfully revived the old comedy, by exhibiting living characters, had resolved to imitate Johnson on the stage, expecting great profits from his ridicule of so celebrated a man. Johnson being informed of his intention, and being at dinner at Mr. Thomas Davies's the bookseller, from whom I had the story, he asked Mr. Davies what was the common price of an oak stick; and being answered six-pence, "Why then, Sir," said he, "give me leave to send your servant to purchase me a shilling one. I'll have a double quantity; for I am told Foote means to *take me off,* as he calls it, and I am determined the fellow shall not do it with impunity." Davies took care to acquaint Foote of this, which effectually checked the wantonness of the mimic. Mr. Macpherson's menaces made Johnson provide himself with the same implement of defense; and had he been attacked, I have no doubt that, old as he was, he would have made his corporal prowess be felt as much as his intellectual. * * *

[1776] I mentioned a new gaming club, of which Mr. Beauclerk had given me an account, where the members played to a desperate extent. JOHNSON. "Depend upon it, Sir, this is mere talk. *Who* is ruined by gaming? You will not find six instances in an age. There is a strange rout made about deep play:[3] whereas you have many more people ruined by adventurous trade, and yet we do not hear such an outcry against it." THRALE.[4] "There may be few people absolutely ruined by deep play; but very many are much hurt in their circumstances by it." JOHNSON. "Yes, Sir, and so are very many by other kinds of expense." I had heard him talk once before in the same manner; and at Oxford he said, he wished he had learnt to play at cards. The truth, however, is that he loved to display his ingenuity in argument; and therefore would sometimes in conversation maintain opinions which he was sensible were wrong, but in supporting which, his reasoning and wit would be most conspicuous. He would begin thus: "Why, Sir, as to the good or evil of card playing——" "Now," said Garrick, "he is thinking which side he shall take." He appeared to have a pleasure in contradiction, especially when any opinion whatever was delivered with an air of confidence; so that there was hardly any topic, if not one of the great truths of religion and morality, that he might not have been incited to argue, either for or against. Lord Elibank[5] had the highest admiration of his powers. He once observed to me, "Whatever opinion Johnson maintains, I will not say that he convinces me; but he never fails to show me that he has good reasons for it." I have heard Johnson pay his Lordship this high compliment: "I never was in Lord Elibank's company without learning something." * * *

2. "The constable's prison, in which disorderly persons, found in the street, are confined" (Johnson's *Dictionary*).
3. High-stakes gambling. "Rout": fuss.
4. Johnson met Henry Thrale, the wealthy brewer, and his charming wife, Hester, in 1765. Thereafter he spent much of his time at their house at Streatham near London. There he enjoyed the good things of life, as well as the companionship of Mrs. Thrale and her children. Henry Thrale died in 1781. His widow's marriage to Gabriel Piozzi, an Italian musician, in 1784, caused Johnson to quarrel with her and darkened the last months of his life.
5. Prominent in Scottish literary circles. Johnson, who admired him, had visited him on his tour of Scotland with Boswell in 1773.

[DINNER WITH WILKES]

My worthy booksellers and friends, Messieurs Dilly in the Poultry, at whose hospitable and well-covered table I have seen a greater number of literary men than at any other, except that of Sir Joshua Reynolds, had invited me to meet Mr. Wilkes[6] and some more gentlemen on Wednesday, May 15. "Pray," said I, "let us have Dr. Johnson."—"What, with Mr. Wilkes? not for the world," said Mr. Edward Dilly, "Dr. Johnson would never forgive me."—"Come," said I, "if you'll let me negotiate for you, I will be answerable that all shall go well." DILLY. "Nay, if you will take it upon you, I am sure I shall be very happy to see them both here."

Notwithstanding the high veneration which I entertained for Dr. Johnson, I was sensible that he was sometimes a little actuated by the spirit of contradiction, and by means of that I hoped I should gain my point. I was persuaded that if I had come upon him with a direct proposal, "Sir, will you dine in company with Jack Wilkes?" he would have flown into a passion, and would probably have answered, "Dine with Jack Wilkes, Sir! I'd as soon dine with Jack Ketch."[7] I therefore, while we were sitting quietly by ourselves at his house in an evening, took occasion to open my plan thus: "Mr. Dilly, Sir, sends his respectful compliments to you, and would be happy if you would do him the honor to dine with him on Wednesday next along with me, as I must soon go to Scotland." JOHNSON. "Sir, I am obliged to Mr. Dilly. I will wait upon him—" BOSWELL. "Provided, Sir, I suppose, that the company which he is to have, is agreeable to you." JOHNSON. "What do you mean, Sir? What do you take me for? Do you think I am so ignorant of the world as to imagine that I am to prescribe to a gentleman what company he is to have at his table?" BOSWELL. "I beg your pardon, Sir, for wishing to prevent you from meeting people whom you might not like. Perhaps he may have some of what he calls his patriotic[8] friends with him." JOHNSON. "Well, Sir, and what then? What care *I* for his *patriotic friends?* Poh!" BOSWELL. "I should not be surprised to find Jack Wilkes there." JOHNSON. "And if Jack Wilkes *should* be there, what is that to *me*, Sir? My dear friend, let us have no more of this. I am sorry to be angry with you; but really it is treating me strangely to talk to me as if I could not meet any company whatever, occasionally." BOSWELL. "Pray forgive me, Sir: I meant well. But you shall meet whoever comes, for me." Thus I secured him, and told Dilly that he would find him very well pleased to be one of his guests on the day appointed.

Upon the much-expected Wednesday, I called on him about half an hour before dinner, as I often did when we were to dine out together, to see that he was ready in time, and to accompany him. I found him buffeting his books, as upon a former occasion, covered with dust, and making no prepa-

6. John Wilkes (1727–1797) was disapproved of by the Christian and Tory Johnson in every way. He was profane and dissolute, and his personal life was a public scandal. For more than a decade he had been notorious as a courageous and resourceful opponent of the authoritarian policies of the king and his ministers and had been the envenomed critic of Lord Bute, to whom Johnson owed his pension. When Johnson met him he had totally defeated his enemies, had served as lord mayor, and was again a member of Parliament, a post from which he had been expelled and driven into exile as an outlaw in 1764. Boswell had found Wilkes a gay and congenial companion in Italy in 1764.
7. A famous public hangman.
8. In Tory circles the word had come to be used ironically of those who opposed the government. The "patriots" considered themselves the defenders of the ancient liberties of the English. They included the partisans of both Wilkes and the American colonists.

ration for going abroad. "How is this, Sir?" said I. "Don't you recollect that you are to dine at Mr. Dilly's?" JOHNSON. "Sir, I did not think of going to Dilly's: it went out of my head. I have ordered dinner at home with Mrs. Williams." BOSWELL. "But, my dear Sir, you know you were engaged to Mr. Dilly, and I told him so. He will expect you, and will be much disappointed if you don't come." JOHNSON. "You must talk to Mrs. Williams about this."

Here was a sad dilemma. I feared that what I was so confident I had secured would yet be frustrated. He had accustomed himself to show Mrs. Williams such a degree of humane attention as frequently imposed some restraint upon him; and I knew that if she should be obstinate, he would not stir. I hastened downstairs to the blind lady's room, and told her I was in great uneasiness, for Dr. Johnson had engaged to me to dine this day at Mr. Dilly's, but that he had told me he had forgotten his engagement, and had ordered dinner at home. "Yes, Sir," said she, pretty peevishly, "Dr. Johnson is to dine at home."—"Madam," said I, "his respect for you is such that I know he will not leave you unless you absolutely desire it. But as you have so much of his company, I hope you will be good enough to forgo it for a day; as Mr. Dilly is a very worthy man, has frequently had agreeable parties at his house for Dr. Johnson, and will be vexed if the Doctor neglects him today. And then, Madam, be pleased to consider my situation; I carried the message, and I assured Mr. Dilly that Dr. Johnson was to come, and no doubt he has made a dinner, and invited a company, and boasted of the honor he expected to have. I shall be quite disgraced if the Doctor is not there." She gradually softened to my solicitations, which were certainly as earnest as most entreaties to ladies upon any occasion, and was graciously pleased to empower me to tell Dr. Johnson that all things considered, she thought he should certainly go. I flew back to him, still in dust, and careless of what should be the event, "indifferent in his choice to go or stay";[9] but as soon as I had announced to him Mrs. Williams' consent, he roared, "Frank, a clean shirt," and was very soon dressed. When I had him fairly seated in a hackney coach with me, I exulted as much as a fortune hunter who has got an heiress into a post chaise with him to set out for Gretna Green.[1]

When we entered Mr. Dilly's drawing room, he found himself in the midst of a company he did not know. I kept myself snug and silent, watching how he would conduct himself. I observed him whispering to Mr. Dilly, "Who is that gentleman, Sir?"—"Mr. Arthur Lee."—JOHNSON. "Too, too, too" (under his breath), which was one of his habitual mutterings. Mr. Arthur Lee could not but be very obnoxious to Johnson, for he was not only a *patriot* but an *American*.[2] He was afterwards minister from the United States at the court of Madrid. "And who is the gentleman in lace?"—"Mr. Wilkes, Sir." This information confounded him still more; he had some difficulty to restrain himself, and taking up a book, sat down upon a window seat and read, or at least kept his eye upon it intently for some time, till he composed himself. His feelings, I dare say, were awkward enough. But he

9. Addison's *Cato* 5.1.40. Boswell cleverly adapts to his own purpose Cato's words, "Indifferent in his choice to sleep or die."
1. A village just across the Scottish border where runaway couples were married by the local innkeeper or the blacksmith.
2. Johnson was extremely hostile to the rebel-

ling American colonists. On one occasion he said, "I am willing to love all mankind, except an American." Lee had been educated in England and Scotland, and had recently been admitted to the English bar. He had been a loyal supporter of Wilkes.

no doubt recollected his having rated me for supposing that he could be at all disconcerted by any company, and he, therefore, resolutely set himself to behave quite as an easy man of the world, who could adapt himself at once to the disposition and manners of those whom he might chance to meet.

The cheering sound of "Dinner is upon the table," dissolved his reverie, and we *all* sat down without any symptom of ill humor. There were present, beside Mr. Wilkes, and Mr. Arthur Lee, who was an old companion of mine when he studied physic at Edinburgh, Mr. (now Sir John) Miller, Dr. Lettsom, and Mr. Slater the druggist. Mr. Wilkes placed himself next to Dr. Johnson, and behaved to him with so much attention and politeness that he gained upon him insensibly. No man eat more heartily than Johnson, or loved better what was nice and delicate. Mr. Wilkes was very assiduous in helping him to some fine veal. "Pray give me leave, Sir—It is better here—A little of the brown—Some fat, Sir—A little of the stuffing—Some gravy—Let me have the pleasure of giving you some butter—Allow me to recommend a squeeze of this orange—or the lemon, perhaps, may have more zest."—"Sir, Sir, I am obliged to you, Sir," cried Johnson, bowing, and turning his head to him with a look for some time of "surly virtue," but, in a short while, of complacency.

Foote being mentioned, Johnson said, "He is not a good mimic." One of the company added, "A merry Andrew, a buffoon." JOHNSON. "But he has wit too, and is not deficient in ideas, or in fertility and variety of imagery, and not empty of reading; he has knowledge enough to fill up his part. One species of wit he has in an eminent degree, that of escape. You drive him into a corner with both hands; but he's gone, Sir, when you think you have got him—like an animal that jumps over your head. Then he has a great range for wit; he never lets truth stand between him and a jest, and he is sometimes mighty coarse. Garrick is under many restraints from which Foote is free." WILKES. "Garrick's wit is more like Lord Chesterfield's." JOHNSON. "The first time I was in company with Foote was at Fitzherbert's. Having no good opinion of the fellow, I was resolved not to be pleased; and it is very difficult to please a man against his will. I went on eating my dinner pretty sullenly, affecting not to mind him. But the dog was so very comical, that I was obliged to lay down my knife and fork, throw myself back upon my chair, and fairly laugh it out. No, Sir, he was irresistible. He upon one occasion experienced, in an extraordinary degree, the efficacy of his powers of entertaining. Amongst the many and various modes which he tried of getting money, he became a partner with a small-beer[3] brewer, and he was to have a share of the profits for procuring customers amongst his numerous acquaintance. Fitzherbert was one who took his small beer; but it was so bad that the servants resolved not to drink it. They were at some loss how to notify their resolution, being afraid of offending their master, who they knew liked Foote much as a companion. At last they fixed upon a little black boy, who was rather a favorite, to be their deputy, and deliver their remonstrance; and having invested him with the whole authority of the kitchen, he was to inform Mr. Fitzherbert, in all their names, upon a certain day, that they would drink Foote's small beer no longer. On that day Foote happened to dine at Fitzherbert's, and this boy served at table; he was so delighted with Foote's stories, and merriment, and gri-

3. Weak beer, served in the servants' hall.

mace, that when he went downstairs, he told them, 'This is the finest man I have ever seen. I will not deliver your message. I will drink his small beer.'"

Somebody observed that Garrick could not have done this. WILKES. "Garrick would have made the small beer still smaller. He is now leaving the stage; but he will play Scrub[4] all his life." I knew that Johnson would let nobody attack Garrick but himself, as Garrick once said to me, and I had heard him praise his liberality; so to bring out his commendation of his celebrated pupil, I said, loudly, "I have heard Garrick is liberal." JOHNSON. "Yes, Sir, I know that Garrick has given away more money than any man in England that I am acquainted with, and that not from ostentatious views. Garrick was very poor when he began life; so when he came to have money, he probably was very unskillful in giving away, and saved when he should not. But Garrick began to be liberal as soon as he could; and I am of opinion, the reputation of avarice which he has had, has been very lucky for him, and prevented his having many enemies. You despise a man for avarice, but do not hate him. Garrick might have been much better attacked for living with more splendor than is suitable to a player: if they had had the wit to have assaulted him in that quarter, they might have galled him more. But they have kept clamoring about his avarice, which has rescued him from much obloquy and envy."

Talking of the great difficulty of obtaining authentic information for biography, Johnson told us, "When I was a young fellow I wanted to write the *Life of Dryden*, and in order to get materials, I applied to the only two persons then alive who had seen him; these were old Swinney,[5] and old Cibber. Swinney's information was no more than this, that at Will's Coffeehouse Dryden had a particular chair for himself, which was set by the fire in winter, and was then called his winter chair; and that it was carried out for him to the balcony in summer, and was then called his summer chair. Cibber could tell no more but that he remembered him a decent old man, arbiter of critical disputes at Will's. You are to consider that Cibber was then at a great distance from Dryden, had perhaps one leg only in the room, and durst not draw in the other." BOSWELL. "Yet Cibber was a man of observation?" JOHNSON. "I think not." BOSWELL. "You will allow his *Apology* to be well done." JOHNSON. "Very well done, to be sure, Sir. That book is a striking proof of the justice of Pope's remark:

> Each might his several province well command,
> Would all but stoop to what they understand."[6]

BOSWELL. "And his plays are good." JOHNSON. "Yes; but that was his trade; *l'esprit du corps*: he had been all his life among players and play writers. I wondered that he had so little to say in conversation, for he had kept the best company, and learnt all that can be got by the ear. He abused Pindar to me, and then showed me an ode of his own, with an absurd couplet, making a linnet soar on an eagle's wing. I told him that when the ancients made a simile, they always made it like something real."

Mr. Wilkes remarked that "among all the bold flights of Shakespeare's imagination, the boldest was making Birnam Wood march to Dunsinane;[7]

---

4. The servant of Squire Sullen in Farquhar's *Beaux' Stratagem*, a favorite role of Garrick.
5. Owen Mac Swinney, a playwright.

6. *An Essay on Criticism* 1.66–67.
7. *Macbeth* 5.5.30–52.

creating a wood where there never was a shrub; a wood in Scotland! ha! ha! ha!" And he also observed, that "the clannish slavery of the Highlands of Scotland was the single exception to Milton's remark of 'The mountain nymph, sweet Liberty,'[8] being worshiped in all hilly countries."—"When I was at Inverary," said he, "on a visit to my old friend, Archibald, Duke of Argyle, his dependents congratulated me on being such a favorite of his Grace. I said, 'It is then, gentlemen, truly lucky for me; for if I had displeased the Duke, and he had wished it, there is not a Campbell among you but would have been ready to bring John Wilkes's head to him in a charger.[9] It would have been only

> Off with his head! So much for Aylesbury.'[1]

I was then member for Aylesbury." * * *

Mr. Arthur Lee mentioned some Scotch who had taken possession of a barren part of America, and wondered why they should choose it. JOHNSON. "Why, Sir, all barrenness is comparative. The *Scotch* would not know it to be barren." BOSWELL. "Come, come, he is flattering the English. You have now been in Scotland, Sir, and say if you did not see meat and drink enough there." JOHNSON. "Why yes, Sir; meat and drink enough to give the inhabitants sufficient strength to run away from home." All these quick and lively sallies were said sportively, quite in jest, and with a smile, which showed that he meant only wit. Upon this topic he and Mr. Wilkes could perfectly assimilate; here was a bond of union between them, and I was conscious that as both of them had visited Caledonia, both were fully satisfied of the strange narrow ignorance of those who imagine that it is a land of famine. But they amused themselves with persevering in the old jokes. When I claimed a superiority for Scotland over England in one respect, that no man can be arrested there for a debt merely because another swears it against him; but there must first be the judgment of a court of law ascertaining its justice; and that a seizure of the person, before judgment is obtained, can take place only if his creditor should swear that he is about to fly from the country, or, as it is technically expressed, is *in meditatione fugae*: WILKES. "That, I should think, may be safely sworn of all the Scotch nation." JOHNSON (to Mr. Wilkes). "You must know, Sir, I lately took my friend Boswell and showed him genuine civilized life in an English provincial town. I turned him loose at Lichfield, my native city, that he might see for once real civility: for you know he lives among savages in Scotland, and among rakes in London." WILKES. "Except when he is with grave, sober, decent people like you and me." JOHNSON (smiling). "And we ashamed of him."

They were quite frank and easy. Johnson told the story of his asking Mrs. Macaulay to allow her footman to sit down with them, to prove the ridiculousness of the argument for the equality of mankind; and he said to me afterwards, with a nod of satisfaction, "You saw Mr. Wilkes acquiesced." * * *

This record, though by no means so perfect as I could wish, will serve to give a notion of a very curious interview, which was not only pleasing at the time, but had the agreeable and benignant effect of reconciling any animos-

8. "L'Allegro," line 36.
9. Platter.
1. "Off with his head! So much for Bucking-

ham." A line in Cibber's version of Shakespeare's *Richard III*.

ity and sweetening any acidity, which in the various bustle of political contest, had been produced in the minds of two men, who, though widely
different, had so many things in common—classical learning, modern literature, wit, and humor, and ready repartee—that it would have been much to
be regretted if they had been forever at a distance from each other.

Mr. Burke gave me much credit for this successful "negotiation"; and
pleasantly said that there was nothing to equal it in the whole history of the
Corps Diplomatique. * * *

[DREAD OF SOLITUDE]

[1777] I talked to him of misery being "the doom of man" in this life, as displayed in his *Vanity of Human Wishes.* Yet I observed that things were done
upon the supposition of happiness; grand houses were built, fine gardens
were made, splendid places of public amusement were contrived, and crowded
with company. JOHNSON. "Alas, Sir, these are all only struggles for happiness.
When I first entered Ranelagh,[2] it gave an expansion and gay sensation to my
mind, such as I never experienced anywhere else. But, as Xerxes wept when
he viewed his immense army, and considered that not one of that great multitude would be alive a hundred years afterwards, so it went to my heart to
consider that there was not one in all that brilliant circle that was not afraid
to go home and think; but that the thoughts of each individual there, would
be distressing when alone." * * *

["A BOTTOM OF GOOD SENSE." BET FLINT. "CLEAR YOUR MIND OF CANT"]

[1781] Talking of a very respectable author, he told us a curious circumstance in his life, which was that he had married a printer's devil.[3] REYN-
OLDS. "A printer's devil, Sir! Why, I thought a printer's devil was a creature
with a black face and in rags." JOHNSON. "Yes, Sir. But I suppose, he had
her face washed, and put clean clothes on her." Then looking very serious,
and very earnest: "And she did not disgrace him; the woman had a bottom
of good sense." The word *bottom* thus introduced was so ludicrous when
contrasted with his gravity, that most of us could not forbear tittering and
laughing; though I recollect that the Bishop of Killaloe kept his countenance with perfect steadiness, while Miss Hannah More[4] slyly hid her face
behind a lady's back who sat on the same settee with her. His pride could not
bear that any expression of his should excite ridicule, when he did not intend
it; he therefore resolved to assume and exercise despotic power, glanced
sternly around, and called out in a strong tone, "Where's the merriment?"
Then collecting himself, and looking awful, to make us feel how he could
impose restraint, and as it were searching his mind for a still more ludicrous
word, he slowly pronounced, "I say the *woman* was *fundamentally* sensible";
as if he had said, "hear this now, and laugh if you dare." We all sat composed
as at a funeral. * * *

He gave us an entertaining account of Bet Flint, a woman of the town,
who, with some eccentric talents and much effrontery, forced herself upon

2. Pleasure gardens in Chelsea, where concerts
were held, fireworks displayed, and food and
drink sold.
3. Apprentice in a print shop.

4. Bluestocking and religious writer (1745–1833),
one of the promoters of the Sunday School movement.

his acquaintance. "Bet," said he, "wrote her own Life in verse, which she brought to me, wishing that I would furnish her with a Preface to it" (laughing). "I used to say of her that she was generally slut and drunkard; occasionally, whore and thief. She had, however, genteel lodgings, a spinnet on which she played, and a boy that walked before her chair. Poor Bet was taken up on a charge of stealing a counterpane, and tried at the Old Bailey. Chief Justice ———, who loved a wench, summed up favorably, and she was acquitted. After which Bet said, with a gay and satisfied air, 'Now that the counterpane is *my own*, I shall make a petticoat of it.'" * * *

[1783] I have no minute of any interview with Johnson till Thursday, May 15, when I find what follows: BOSWELL. "I wish much to be in Parliament, Sir." JOHNSON. "Why, Sir, unless you come resolved to support any administration, you would be the worse for being in Parliament, because you would be obliged to live more expensively." BOSWELL. "Perhaps, Sir, I should be the less happy for being in Parliament. I never would sell my vote, and I should be vexed if things went wrong." JOHNSON. "That's cant,[5] Sir. It would not vex you more in the house than in the gallery: public affairs vex no man." BOSWELL. "Have not they vexed yourself a little, Sir? Have not you been vexed by all the turbulence of this reign, and by that absurd vote of the House of Commons, 'That the influence of the Crown has increased, is increasing, and ought to be diminished?'" JOHNSON. "Sir, I have never slept an hour less, nor eat an ounce less meat. I would have knocked the factious dogs on the head, to be sure; but I was not *vexed*." BOSWELL. "I declare, Sir, upon my honor, I did imagine I was vexed, and took a pride in it; but it *was*, perhaps, cant; for I own I neither ate less, nor slept less." JOHNSON. "My dear friend, clear your *mind* of cant. You may *talk* as other people do: you may say to a man, 'Sir, I am your most humble servant.' You are *not* his most humble servant. You may say, 'These are bad times; it is a melancholy thing to be reserved to such times.' You don't mind the times. You tell a man, 'I am sorry you had such bad weather the last day of your journey, and were so much wet.' You don't care sixpence whether he is wet or dry. You may *talk* in this manner; it is a mode of talking in society: but don't *think* foolishly." * * *

[JOHNSON PREPARES FOR DEATH]

My anxious apprehensions at parting with him this year proved to be but too well founded; for not long afterwards he had a dreadful stroke of the palsy, of which there are very full and accurate accounts in letters written by himself, to show with what composure of mind, and resignation to the Divine Will, his steady piety enabled him to behave. * * *

Two days after he wrote thus to Mrs. Thrale:

"On Monday, the 16th, I sat for my picture, and walked a considerable way with little inconvenience. In the afternoon and evening I felt myself light and easy, and began to plan schemes of life. Thus I went to bed, and in a short time waked and sat up, as has been long my custom, when I felt a confusion and indistinctness in my head, which lasted, I suppose, about half a minute. I was alarmed, and prayed God that however he might afflict my body, he would spare my understanding. This prayer,

5. "A whining pretension to goodness in formal and affected terms" (Johnson's *Dictionary*).

that I might try the integrity of my faculties, I made in Latin verse. The lines were not very good, but I knew them not to be very good: I made them easily, and concluded myself to be unimpaired in my faculties.

"Soon after I perceived that I had suffered a paralytic stroke, and that my speech was taken from me. I had no pain, and so little dejection in this dreadful state, that I wondered at my own apathy, and considered that perhaps death itself, when it should come, would excite less horror than seems now to attend it.

"In order to rouse the vocal organs, I took two drams. Wine has been celebrated for the production of eloquence. I put myself into violent motion, and I think repeated it; but all was vain. I then went to bed and strange as it may seem, I think, slept. When I saw light, it was time to contrive what I should do. Though God stopped my speech, he left me my hand; I enjoyed a mercy which was not granted to my dear friend Lawrence,[6] who now perhaps overlooks me as I am writing, and rejoices that I have what he wanted. My first note was necessarily to my servant, who came in talking, and could not immediately comprehend why he should read what I put into his hands.

"I then wrote a card to Mr. Allen,[7] that I might have a discreet friend at hand, to act as occasion should require. In penning this note, I had some difficulty; my hand, I knew not how nor why, made wrong letters. I then wrote to Dr. Taylor to come to me, and bring Dr. Heberden; and I sent to Dr. Brocklesby, who is my neighbor.[8] My physicians are very friendly, and give me great hopes; but you may imagine my situation. I have so far recovered my vocal powers as to repeat the Lord's Prayer with no very imperfect articulation. My memory, I hope, yet remains as it was; but such an attack produces solicitude for the safety of every faculty." * * *

[1784] To Mr. Henry White, a young clergyman, with whom he now formed an intimacy, so as to talk to him with great freedom, he mentioned that he could not in general accuse himself of having been an undutiful son. "Once, indeed," said he, "I was disobedient; I refused to attend my father to Uttoxeter market. Pride was the source of that refusal, and the remembrance of it was painful. A few years ago, I desired to atone for this fault; I went to Uttoxeter in very bad weather, and stood for a considerable time bareheaded in the rain, on the spot where my father's stall used to stand. In contrition I stood, and I hope the penance was expiatory."

"I told him," says Miss Seward,[9] "in one of my latest visits to him, of a wonderful learned pig, which I had seen at Nottingham; and which did all that we have observed exhibited by dogs and horses. The subject amused him. 'Then,' said he, 'the pigs are a race unjustly calumniated. *Pig* has, it seems, not been wanting to *man*, but *man* to *pig*. We do not allow *time* for his education, we kill him at a year old.' Mr. Henry White, who was present, observed that if this instance had happened in or before Pope's time, he would not have been justified in instancing the swine as the lowest degree of groveling

6. Dr. Thomas Lawrence, president of the Royal College of Physicians and Johnson's own doctor, had died paralyzed shortly before this was written.
7. Edmund Allen, a printer, Johnson's landlord and neighbor.
8. These two physicians attended Johnson on his deathbed.
9. Anna Seward, "the Swan of Lichfield," a poet.

instinct.[1] Dr. Johnson seemed pleased with the observation, while the person who made it proceeded to remark that great torture must have been employed, ere the indocility of the animal could have been subdued. 'Certainly,' said the Doctor; 'but,' turning to me, 'how old is your pig?' I told him, three years old. 'Then,' said he, 'the pig has no cause to complain; he would have been killed the first year if he had not been *educated*, and protracted existence is a good recompense for very considerable degrees of torture.'"

[JOHNSON FACES DEATH]

As Johnson had now very faint hopes of recovery, and as Mrs. Thrale was no longer devoted to him, it might have been supposed that he would naturally have chosen to remain in the comfortable house of his beloved wife's daughter,[2] and end his life where he began it. But there was in him an animated and lofty spirit, and however complicated diseases might depress ordinary mortals, all who saw him, beheld and acknowledged the *invictum animum Catonis*.[3] Such was his intellectual ardor even at this time that he said to one friend, "Sir, I look upon every day to be lost, in which I do not make a new acquaintance"; and to another, when talking of his illness, "I will be conquered; I will not capitulate." And such was his love of London, so high a relish had he of its magnificent extent, and variety of intellectual entertainment, that he languished when absent from it, his mind having become quite luxurious from the long habit of enjoying the metropolis; and, therefore, although at Lichfield, surrounded with friends, who loved and revered him, and for whom he had a very sincere affection, he still found that such conversation as London affords, could be found nowhere else. These feelings, joined, probably, to some flattering hopes of aid from the eminent physicians and surgeons in London, who kindly and generously attended him without accepting fees, made him resolve to return to the capital. * * * Death had always been to him an object of terror; so that, though by no means happy, he still clung to life with an eagerness at which many have wondered. At any time when he was ill, he was very much pleased to be told that he looked better. An ingenious member of the Eumelian Club[4] informs me that upon one occasion when he said to him that he saw health returning to his cheek, Johnson seized him by the hand and exclaimed, "Sir, you are one of the kindest friends I ever had." * * *

Dr. Heberden, Dr. Brocklesby, Dr. Warren, and Dr. Butter, physicians, generously attended him, without accepting any fees, as did Mr. Cruikshank, surgeon; and all that could be done from professional skill and ability was tried, to prolong a life so truly valuable. He himself, indeed, having, on account of his very bad constitution, been perpetually applying himself to medical inquiries, united his own efforts with those of the gentlemen who attended him; and imagining that the dropsical collection of water which oppressed him might be drawn off by making incisions in his body, he, with his usual resolute defiance of pain, cut deep, when he thought that his surgeon had done it too tenderly.

---

1. *An Essay on Man* 1.221.
2. Lucy Porter.
3. The unconquered soul of Cato (Latin). An

adaptation of a phrase in Horace's *Odes* 2.1.24.
4. A club to which Boswell and Reynolds belonged.

About eight or ten days before his death, when Dr. Brocklesby paid him his morning visit, he seemed very low and desponding, and said, "I have been as a dying man all night." He then emphatically broke out in the words of Shakespeare:

> "Canst thou not minister to a mind diseased;
> Pluck from the memory a rooted sorrow,
> Raze out the written troubles of the brain,
> And with some sweet oblivious antidote
> Cleanse the stuffed bosom of that perilous stuff
> Which weighs upon the heart?"

To which Dr. Brocklesby readily answered, from the same great poet:

> "—Therein the patient
> Must minister to himself."[5]

Johnson expressed himself much satisfied with the application. * * *

Amidst the melancholy clouds which hung over the dying Johnson, his characteristical manner showed itself on different occasions.

When Dr. Warren, in the usual style, hoped that he was better; his answer was, "No, Sir; you cannot conceive with what acceleration I advance towards death."

A man whom he had never seen before was employed one night to sit up with him. Being asked next morning how he liked his attendant, his answer was, "Not at all, Sir: the fellow's an idiot; he is as awkward as a turnspit[6] when first put into the wheel, and as sleepy as a dormouse."

Mr. Windham[7] having placed a pillow conveniently to support him, he thanked him for his kindness, and said, "That will do—all that a pillow can do." * * *

Johnson, with that native fortitude, which, amidst all his bodily distress and mental sufferings, never forsook him, asked Dr. Brocklesby, as a man in whom he had confidence, to tell him plainly whether he could recover. "Give me," said he, "a direct answer." The Doctor having first asked him if he could bear the whole truth, which way soever it might lead, and being answered that he could, declared that, in his opinion, he could not recover without a miracle. "Then," said Johnson, "I will take no more physic, not even my opiates; for I have prayed that I may render up my soul to God unclouded." In this resolution he persevered, and, at the same time, used only the weakest kinds of sustenance. Being pressed by Mr. Windham to take somewhat more generous nourishment, lest too low a diet should have the very effect which he dreaded, by debilitating his mind, he said, "I will take anything but inebriating sustenance."

The Reverend Mr. Strahan,[8] who was the son of his friend, and had been always one of his great favorites, had, during his last illness, the satisfaction of contributing to soothe and comfort him. That gentleman's house, at Islington, of which he is Vicar, afforded Johnson, occasionally and easily, an agree-

---

5. *Macbeth* 5.3.40–46.
6. "A dog kept to turn the roasting-spit by running within a tread-wheel connected to it" (*OED*).
7. William Windham, one of Johnson's younger

friends, later a member of Parliament.
8. The Reverend George Strahan (pronounced *Strawn*), who later published Johnson's *Prayers and Meditations*.

able change of place and fresh air; and he attended also upon him in town in the discharge of the sacred offices of his profession.

Mr. Strahan has given me the agreeable assurance that, after being in much agitation, Johnson became quite composed, and continued so till his death.

Dr. Brocklesby, who will not be suspected of fanaticism, obliged me with the following account:

> "For some time before his death, all his fears were calmed and absorbed by the prevalence of his faith, and his trust in the merits and *propitiation* of Jesus Christ." * * *

Johnson having thus in his mind the true Christian scheme, at once rational and consolatory, uniting justice and mercy in the Divinity, with the improvement of human nature, previous to his receiving the Holy Sacrament in his apartment, composed and fervently uttered this prayer:

> "Almighty and most merciful Father, I am now as to human eyes, it seems, about to commemorate, for the last time, the death of thy Son Jesus Christ, our Saviour and Redeemer. Grant, O Lord, that my whole hope and confidence may be in his merits, and thy mercy; enforce and accept my imperfect repentance; make this commemoration available to the confirmation of my faith, the establishment of my hope, and the enlargement of my charity; and make the death of thy Son Jesus Christ effectual to my redemption. Have mercy upon me, and pardon the multitude of my offenses. Bless my friends; have mercy upon all men. Support me, by thy Holy Spirit, in the days of weakness, and at the hour of death; and receive me, at my death, to everlasting happiness, for the sake of Jesus Christ. Amen."

Having * * * made his will on the 8th and 9th of December, and settled all his worldly affairs, he languished till Monday, the 13th of that month, when he expired, about seven o'clock in the evening, with so little apparent pain that his attendants hardly perceived when his dissolution took place. * * *

1791

LAURENCE STERNE
1713–1768

No other novelist of the eighteenth century loved to play with conventions—of narrative, of print, of moral thought and feeling—as much as Laurence Sterne, and none has exerted so much influence on experiments in the art of fiction in the centuries that followed. Born in Ireland to an English military family that moved around often, Sterne was sent at ten to grammar school in Yorkshire in the north of England, never living with his parents again. He obtained his bachelor's (1737) and master's (1740) degrees from Cambridge University and settled into a quiet career as a country clergyman near York. In 1741 he married Elizabeth; the union would not be happy. He wrote a little about provincial politics but remained virtually unknown until 1759.

At the end of that year, Sterne published the first two volumes of his masterpiece, *The Life and Opinions of Tristram Shandy, Gentleman*, at York, after failing to interest a London bookseller in it. By the spring of 1760, Sterne was a major celebrity, feted and fashionable throughout the English literary world. Some readers objected to the work's bawdiness, especially after his vocation as a clergyman become widely known with the publication of *The Sermons of Mr. Yorick* in May 1760—his own sermons, attributed to a character in his novel, now recognized as his alter ego (or one of them). But his fame, and *Tristram Shandy* itself, grew through the 1760s: two more volumes appeared in 1761, volumes 5 and 6 in 1762, volumes 7 and 8 in 1765, and the final, 9th volume in 1767, extending the success of his debut.

The work has been difficult to classify. It comically attempts to account for the narrator's life by starting at his conception but can barely get started. Tristram describes the sexual oddities and elaborate theories of naming children, childbirth, and many other notions and habits of his father, Walter Shandy; and introduces Walter's gentle brother, Toby, a wounded veteran who re-creates the scene of his battle injury in miniature in a garden on the Shandy country estate, and other (mostly male) characters, all of whom interact in domestic scenes. The story is interrupted by long, learned digressions and parodies of learning. Sterne subverted the conventions that determined what a book is, putting chapters out of order, marking the death of Yorick in volume 1 with an entirely black page, inviting the reader to provide a description of another character by leaving a page blank, starting a mundane sentence of Uncle Toby's in volume 1 and not concluding it until volume 2. Sterne's experimental style and literary games owe much to Renaissance traditions of learned wit developed by writers such as François Rabelais and Robert Burton, traditions that extend to his own century in the satirical "Scriblerian" writings of Pope and Swift. Some readers question whether *Tristram Shandy* should be called a novel at all. The psychological depth of Sterne's characters and the intimacy of the Shandy household nonetheless immerse readers in a fully realized fictional world in a way we now expect from novels at their most affecting and humanizing.

Sterne published his second and final work of fiction, *A Sentimental Journey through France and Italy*, in two short volumes just three weeks before he died of tuberculosis in 1768. In some ways, Sterne seems to anticipate his own end with Yorick, the novel's narrator, who mentions a cough in the closing pages. Readers also could not forget the black page for him in *Tristram*, nor his literary ancestor, Yorick the dead jester whose skull provokes Hamlet's musings in the graveyard scene of Shakespeare's great tragedy (in act 5; scene 1). Despite these hints, Sterne in Yorick presents one of literature's great portraits of vitality and vibrant feeling. The novel narrates his sensations in near microscopic detail, from the individual beatings of his heart to the sensitive pressure on his fingertips. In so doing Sterne introduces a new "sentimental" focus to literature, in which episodic encounters suffused with affect—sympathy, erotic desire, pathos— are more important than plot. The short, unnumbered chapters of *A Sentimental Journey*, with titles (sometimes repeated) signifying the places and people occasioning Yorick's moving experiences, trace his trip through France from Calais to the passes in the Alps that lead to Italy, where he does not quite arrive. (The novel's title anticipates Italian sections Sterne did not live to complete.) As originally printed, the brief chapters left a lot of blank space, testifying perhaps to how difficult Sterne found it, at the end of his life, to fill up pages. The radical experimentation of *Tristram Shandy* was also somewhat reduced, though his love of literary play leads him to place the work's preface some seven chapters after the beginning, to include verbatim a "Fragment" of another work supposedly found in a butter wrapper, and to use idiosyncratic typography copiously, especially his characteristic long dash.

Sterne's *Sentimental Journey* caused a sensation, perhaps even more so than *Tristram*, in Britain and on the Continent. In the year of its appearance, a successful German translation came out; it was the first of Sterne's works to appear in French, in 1769. The novel spurred a vogue for dramatizing personal feelings, in literature and life, among both women and men. Sterne's immediate literary heirs include the Scottish novelist Henry Mackenzie, whose short, fragmentary *Man of Feeling* appeared in 1771. The term *sentimental* came into wide use; authors appended the phrase "a sentimental novel" as a descriptor to numerous titles from the 1770s onward. In Germany, where Sterne's works were immensely popular, there arose a "cult of Lorenzo," named after the monk whom Yorick meets in Calais: graves of Lorenzo sprouted up in various German locales, and devotees of the book exchanged snuffboxes as Yorick and the monk do. Artists depicted its most famous personages and scenes: Joseph Wright painted "The Captive" after the novel's chapter of that name; Wright, Angelika Kauffmann, and others painted the encounter with Maria; Lady Emma Hamilton, the famous English beauty, rendered herself and her lover, naval hero Horatio Lord Nelson, in needlepoint as Maria and Yorick (see p. 933, below). European critics and philosophers, from Voltaire and Germaine de Staël to Johann Gottfried von Herder, passionately took to *A Sentimental Journey*. German critic Gotthold Lessing said he would gladly have given five years of his own life so that Sterne could have written more.

The feelings described and evoked in *A Sentimental Journey* have implications much more challenging than anything readers now are liable to associate with the idea of sentimentalism. "Sterne is the great master of *ambiguity*," wrote the German philosopher Friedrich Nietzsche: "the reader who demands to know exactly what Sterne really thinks of a thing, whether he is making a serious or a laughing face, must be given up for lost." Often, Nietzsche says, Sterne is making both faces, somehow, at once. Among Yorick's most uncertain and suggestive encounters are those with women, of various social stations—a chambermaid, a shopkeeper, a count's sister at Calais—animated by delicate innuendo and slight but erotic physical contact. Yet he can declare, "I have something within me which cannot bear the shock of the least indecent insinuation"—and mean it. During these intimate exchanges, the reader may pause to pursue the implications of nearly any word or phrase. When Yorick offers his hand to the count's sister, he remarks, "she had a black pair of silk gloves, open only at the thumb and two forefingers, so accepted it without reserve," and that word *so* alone hints at an elaborate ethics and erotics of sentimental touch. Critics have detected elements of undercutting parody even in Sterne's most celebrated scenes of pathos, such as Yorick's meeting with Maria. Sterne's prose further opens up the meanings of such scenes by techniques of delay. Often Yorick introduces an idea or anecdote out of context, without apparent motivation, and the reader must wait for its relevance to the story to arrive. Sterne travels through a narrative terrain in which it seems anything at all may surprise the reader and then come to make sense in the whole that it enhances. Praised by Nietzsche as "the most liberated spirit of all time," Sterne has appealed across the centuries to modernists such as Virginia Woolf and James Joyce, and postmodernists including Italo Calvino, Salman Rushdie, Carlos Fuentes, and David Foster Wallace have all found his experimentation inspiring. His freedom of technique, thought, and feeling continues to open paths for any writing that aspires to be truly new.

Sterne fairly closely oversaw the printing of *A Sentimental Journey*, and the text here follows that of the first edition, preserving its typography and other elements. We also reproduce, without correcting, Sterne's French, which often omits diacritical marks and contains other errors. The language translated in the footnotes is French, unless otherwise noted.

A Sentimental Journey through France and Italy

—They order, said I, this matter better in France[1]—

—You have been in France? said my gentleman,[2] turning quick upon me with the most civil triumph in the world.—Strange! quoth I, debating the matter with myself, that one and twenty miles' sailing, for 'tis absolutely no further from Dover to Calais, should give a man these rights[3]—I'll look into them: so giving up the argument—I went straight to my lodgings, put up half a dozen shirts and a black pair of silk breeches—"the coat I have on," said I, looking at the sleeve, "will do"—took a place in the Dover stage; and the packet[4] sailing at nine the next morning—by three I had got sat down to my dinner upon a fricasseed chicken, so incontestably in France, that had I died that night of an indigestion, the whole world could not have suspended the effects of the *droits d'aubaine*[5]—my shirts, and black pair of silk breeches—portmanteau and all must have gone to the King of France—even the little picture which I have so long worn, and so often have told thee, Eliza,[6] I would carry with me into my grave, would have been torn from my neck.—Ungenerous!—to seize upon the wreck of an unwary passenger, whom your subjects had beckoned to their coast—By heaven! Sire, it is not well done; and much does it grieve me, 'tis the monarch of a people so civilized and courteous, and so renowned for sentiment and fine feelings, that I have to reason with—

But I have scarce set foot in your dominions—

CALAIS.

When I had finished my dinner, and drank the King of France's health, to satisfy my mind that I bore him no spleen,[7] but, on the contrary, high honor for the humanity of his temper—I rose up an inch taller for the accommodation.

—No—said I—the Bourbon is by no means a cruel race:[8] they may be misled like other people; but there is a mildness in their blood. As I acknowledged this, I felt a suffusion of a finer kind upon my cheek—more warm and friendly to man, than what Burgundy (at least of two livres a bottle,[9] which was such as I had been drinking) could have produced.

—Just God! said I, kicking my portmanteau aside, what is there in this world's goods which should sharpen our spirits, and make so many kind-hearted brethren of us fall out so cruelly as we do by the way?

1. The novel begins, typically for Sterne, in mid-conversation, and we never learn what "this matter" is.
2. Valet, male servant.
3. The rights to speak authoritatively about how things are done in France. Calais is the French port city where boats from the English port of Dover disembark.
4. Ship traveling on a regular schedule between two ports.
5. "All the effects of strangers (Swiss and Scotch excepted) dying in France, are seized by virtue of this law, though the heir be on the spot—the profit of these contingencies being farmed, there is no redress" [Sterne's note]. "Farmed" (in Sterne's note): taken as a fee.
6. During the composition of *A Sentimental Journey*, Sterne was also writing a journal, also under the name of Yorick, addressed to a young, married Englishwoman in India named Elizabeth Draper, whom he addressed as Eliza, with whom he carried on a deeply "sentimental" attachment. It was finally published in 1904 as *The Journal to Eliza*; scholars also refer to it as *The Continuation of the Bramine's Journal*.
7. Spite.
8. Family from a common ancestor. "Bourbon": royal house of France, of which King Louis XV (1710–1774) was head when Sterne wrote.
9. A moderately priced wine. A livre, an old French unit of currency, was worth one to one and a half British shillings in the 18th century.

When man is at peace with man, how much lighter than a feather is the heaviest of metals in his hand! he pulls out his purse, and holding it airily and uncompressed, looks round him, as if he sought for an object to share it with—In doing this, I felt every vessel in my frame dilate—the arteries beat all cheerily together, and every power which sustained life, performed it with so little friction, that 'twould have confounded the most *physical precieuse* in France: with all her materialism, she could scarce have called me a machine[1]—

I'm confident, said I to myself, I should have overset her creed.[2]

The accession of that idea carried nature, at that time, as high as she could go—I was at peace with the world before, and this finished the treaty with myself—

—Now, was I a King of France, cried I—what a moment for an orphan to have begged his father's portmanteau of me!

THE MONK.

CALAIS.

I had scarce uttered the words, when a poor monk of the order of St. Francis[3] came into the room to beg something for his convent. No man cares to have his virtues the sport of contingencies—or one man may be generous, as another man is puissant—*sed non, quo ad hanc*[4]—or be it as it may—for there is no regular reasoning upon the ebbs and flows of our humors; they may depend upon the same causes, for aught I know, which influence the tides themselves—'twould oft be no discredit to us, to suppose it was so; I'm sure at least for myself, that in many a case I should be more highly satisfied to have it said by the world, "I had had an affair with the moon, in which there was neither sin nor shame," than have it pass altogether as my own act and deed, wherein there was so much of both.

—But be this as it may. The moment I cast my eyes upon him, I was pre-determined not to give him a single sou;[5] and accordingly I put my purse into my pocket—buttoned it up—set myself a little more upon my center, and advanced up gravely to him: there was something, I fear, forbidding in my look: I have his figure this moment before my eyes, and think there was that in it which deserved better.

The monk, as I judged from the break in his tonsure,[6] a few scattered white hairs upon his temples being all that remained of it, might be about seventy—but from his eyes, and that sort of fire which was in them, which seemed more tempered by courtesy than years, could be no more than sixty—Truth might lie between—He was certainly sixty-five; and the general air of his countenance, notwithstanding something seemed to have been planting wrinkles in it before their time, agreed to the account.

---

1. Fashionable philosophy in France espoused the idea that humans were purely physical beings ("machines") without immaterial souls. "Precieuse": a witty, intellectual Frenchwoman who holds such a view.
2. Changed her beliefs.
3. Religious order whose members travel about to preach and minister to the poor, begging for subsistence.
4. Latin, which Sterne translates, roughly, in the next phrase.
5. Coin of little value worth five centimes, the twentieth part of a franc.
6. The top of a monk's head where it is shaved bare.

It was one of those heads which Guido[7] has often painted—mild, pale—penetrating, free from all commonplace ideas of fat contented ignorance looking downwards upon the earth—it looked forwards; but looked, as if it looked at something beyond this world. How one of his order came by it, heaven above, who let it fall upon a monk's shoulders, best knows; but it would have suited a Brahmin, and had I met it upon the plains of Indostan,[8] I had reverenced it.

The rest of his outline may be given in a few strokes; one might put it into the hands of any one to design, for 'twas neither elegant or otherwise, but as character and expression made it so: it was a thin, spare form, something above the common size, if it lost not the distinction by a bend forwards in the figure—but it was the attitude of Entreaty; and as it now stands presented to my imagination, it gained more than it lost by it.

When he had entered the room three paces, he stood still; and laying his left hand upon his breast (a slender white staff with which he journeyed being in his right)—when I had got close up to him, he introduced himself with the little story of the wants of his convent, and the poverty of his order—and did it with so simple a grace—and such an air of deprecation was there in the whole cast of his look and figure—I was bewitched not to have been struck with it—

—A better reason was, I had predetermined not to give him a single sou.

THE MONK.

CALAIS.

—'Tis very true, said I, replying to a cast upwards with his eyes, with which he had concluded his address—'tis very true—and heaven be their resource who have no other but the charity of the world, the stock of which, I fear, is no way sufficient for the many *great claims* which are hourly made upon it.

As I pronounced the words *great claims,* he gave a slight glance with his eye downwards upon the sleeve of his tunic—I felt the full force of the appeal—I acknowledge it, said I—a coarse habit, and that but once in three years, with meager diet—are no great matters; and the true point of pity is, as they can be earned in the world with so little industry, that your order should wish to procure them by pressing upon a fund which is the property of the lame, the blind, the aged, and the infirm—the captive who lies down counting over and over again the days of his afflictions, languishes also for his share of it; and had you been of the *Order of Mercy,*[9] instead of the order of St. Francis, poor as I am, continued I, pointing at my portmanteau, full cheerfully should it have been opened to you, for the ransom of the unfortunate—The monk made me a bow—But of all others, resumed I, the unfortunate of our own country, surely, have the first rights; and I have left thousands in distress upon our own shore—The monk gave a cordial wave with his head—as much as to say, No doubt, there is misery enough in every corner of the world, as well as within our convent—But we distinguish, said I, laying my hand upon the sleeve of his tunic, in return for his appeal—we distinguish, my good father! betwixt those

7. Guido Reni (1575–1642), Italian baroque painter.
8. Hindustan, name for northern India. "Brah-min": member of the priest caste in India.
9. Or Mercedarians, who ransomed Christian captives taken by Mediterranean pirates.

who wish only to eat the bread of their own labor—and those who eat the bread of other people's, and have no other plan in life but to get through it in sloth and ignorance, *for the love of God.*

The poor Franciscan made no reply: a hectic[1] of a moment passed across his cheek, but could not tarry—Nature seemed to have done with her resentments in him; he showed none—but letting his staff fall within his arm, he pressed both his hands with resignation upon his breast, and retired.

THE MONK.

CALAIS.

My heart smote me the moment he shut the door—Psha! said I with an air of carelessness, three several times—but it would not do: every ungracious syllable I had uttered, crowded back into my imagination: I reflected, I had no right over the poor Franciscan, but to deny him; and that the punishment of that was enough to the disappointed without the addition of unkind language: I considered his gray hairs—his courteous figure seemed to reenter and gently ask me what injury he had done me?—and why I could use him thus—I would have given twenty livres for an advocate—I have behaved very ill, said I within myself; but I have only just set out upon my travels; and shall learn better manners as I get along.

THE DESOBLIGEANT.

CALAIS.

When a man is discontented with himself, it has one advantage however, that it puts him into an excellent frame of mind for making a bargain. Now there being no traveling through France and Italy without a chaise—and nature generally prompting us to the thing we are fittest for, I walked out into the coachyard to buy or hire something of that kind to my purpose: an old desobligeant[2] in the furthest corner of the court hit my fancy at first sight, so I instantly got into it, and, finding it in tolerable harmony with my feelings, I ordered the waiter to call Monsieur Dessein,[3] the master of the hotel—but Monsieur Dessein being gone to vespers, and not caring to face the Franciscan, whom I saw on the opposite side of the court, in conference with a lady just arrived at the inn—I drew the taffeta curtain betwixt us, and being determined to write my journey, I took out my pen and ink, and wrote the preface to it in the *desobligeant.*

PREFACE

IN THE DESOBLIGEANT.

It must have been observed by many a peripatetic philosopher,[4] that nature has set up by her own unquestionable authority certain boundaries and fences

1. Flush.
2. Unfriendly. "A chaise, so called in France, from its holding but one person" [Sterne's note].
3. Sterne met Pierre Quillacq (1726–1793), the hotel keeper known as "Dessein" in his travels

through Calais. *Dessin* means "design."
4. Philosopher who travels. Aristotelians were called peripatetics because of Aristotle's habit of walking in the Lyceum while teaching.

to circumscribe the discontent of man: she has effected her purpose in the quietest and easiest manner, by laying him under almost insuperable obligations to work out his ease, and to sustain his sufferings at home. It is there only that she has provided him with the most suitable objects to partake of his happiness, and bear a part of that burden, which, in all countries and ages, has ever been too heavy for one pair of shoulders. 'Tis true, we are endued with an imperfect power of spreading our happiness sometimes beyond *her* limits, but 'tis so ordered, that, from the want[5] of languages, connections, and dependencies, and from the difference in education, customs, and habits, we lie under so many impediments in communicating our sensations out of our own sphere, as often amount to a total impossibility.

It will always follow from hence, that the balance of sentimental commerce is always against the expatriated adventurer: he must buy what he has little occasion for at their own price—his conversation will seldom be taken in exchange for theirs without a large discount—and this by the by eternally driving him into the hands of more equitable brokers for such conversation as he can find, it requires no great spirit of divination to guess at his party—

This brings me to my point; and naturally leads me (if the see-saw of this *desobligeant* will but let me get on) into the efficient as well as the final causes[6] of traveling—

Your idle people that leave their native country and go abroad for some reason or reasons which may be derived from one of these general causes—

Infirmity of body,

Imbecility of mind, or

Inevitable necessity.

The first two include all those who travel by land or by water, laboring with pride, curiosity, vanity, or spleen, subdivided and combined *in infinitum*.

The third class includes the whole army of peregrine martyrs; more especially those travelers who set out upon their travels with the benefit of the clergy,[7] either as delinquents traveling under the direction of governors recommended by the magistrate—or young gentlemen transported by the cruelty of parents and guardians, and traveling under the direction of governors recommended by Oxford, Aberdeen, and Glasgow.[8]

There is a fourth class, but their number is so small that they would not deserve a distinction, was it not necessary in a work of this nature to observe the greatest precision and nicety, to avoid a confusion of character. And these men I speak of, are such as cross the seas and sojourn in a land of strangers, with a view of saving money for various reasons and upon various pretenses: but as they might also save themselves and others a great deal of unnecessary trouble by saving their money at home—and as their reasons for traveling are the least complex of any other species of emigrants, I shall distinguish these gentlemen by the name of

Simple Travelers.

Thus the whole circle of travelers may be reduced to the following *heads:*

---

5. Lack.
6. Two of Aristotle's four types of cause: "efficient," that which brings something about, and "final," the purpose to which something is directed.
7. A legal practice under which first-time offenders get a lighter sentence. "Peregrine": traveling.

8. Sterne refers to young aristocrats forced to make the grand tour of Europe under the supervision of clergymen or governors from colleges in the three university towns mentioned. "Transported": alludes to the practice of sending offenders abroad as punishment for their crimes.

Idle Travelers,
Inquisitive Travelers,
Lying Travelers,
Proud Travelers,
Vain Travelers,
 Splenetic Travelers.
Then follow the Travelers of Necessity.
 The Delinquent and Felonious Traveler,
 The Unfortunate and Innocent Traveler,
 The Simple Traveler,
 And last of all (if you please)
 The Sentimental Traveler (meaning thereby myself), who have traveled, and of which I am now sitting down to give an account—as much out of *necessity,* and the *besoin de voyager,*[9] as any one in the class.

I am well aware, at the same time, as both my travels and observations will be altogether of a different cast from any of my forerunners; that I might have insisted upon a whole nitch[1] entirely to myself—but I should break in upon the confines of the *Vain* Traveler, in wishing to draw attention towards me, till I have some better grounds for it, than the mere *novelty of my vehicle.*

It is sufficient for my reader, if he has been a traveler himself, that with study and reflection hereupon he may be able to determine his own place and rank in the catalogue—it will be one step towards knowing himself, as it is great odds but[2] he retains some tincture and resemblance of what he imbibed or carried out, to the present hour.

The man who first transplanted the grape of Burgundy to the Cape of Good Hope (observe he was a Dutchman) never dreamt of drinking the same wine at the Cape, that the same grape produced upon the French mountains—he was too phlegmatic for that—but undoubtedly he expected to drink some sort of vinous liquor; but whether good, bad, or indifferent—he knew enough of this world to know, that it did not depend upon his choice, but that what is generally called *chance* was to decide his success: however, he hoped for the best: and in these hopes, by an intemperate confidence in the fortitude of his head, and the depth of his discretion, *mynheer* might possibly overset both in his new vineyard, and by discovering[3] his nakedness, become a laughing-stock to his people.

Even so it fares with the poor traveler, sailing and posting[4] through the politer kingdoms of the globe in pursuit of knowledge and improvements.

Knowledge and improvements are to be got by sailing and posting for that purpose; but whether useful knowledge and real improvements is all a lottery—and even where the adventurer is successful, the acquired stock must be used with caution and sobriety, to turn to any profit—but as the chances run prodigiously the other way both as to the acquisition and application, I am of opinion, that a man would act wisely, if he could prevail upon himself to live contented without foreign knowledge or foreign improvements, especially if he lives in a country that has no absolute want of either—and indeed, much grief of heart has it oft and many a time cost me, when I have

9. Need to travel.
1. Niche.
2. Highly likely that.

3. Revealing. *"Mynheer"*: my master (Dutch). "Overset": overturn.
4. Traveling on horseback, with haste.

observed how many a foul step the Inquisitive Traveler has measured to see sights and look into discoveries, all which, as Sancho Panza said to Don Quixote, they might have seen dry-shod at home.[5] It is an age so full of light, that there is scarce a country or corner of Europe, whose beams are not crossed and interchanged with others—Knowledge in most of its branches, and in most affairs, is like music in an Italian street, whereof those may partake who pay nothing—But there is no nation under heaven—and God is my record (before whose tribunal I must one day come and give an account of this work)—that I do not speak it vauntingly—but there is no nation under heaven abounding with more variety of learning—where the sciences may be more fitly wooed, or more surely won, than here—where art is encouraged, and will so soon rise high—where Nature (take her altogether) has so little to answer for—and, to close all, where there is more wit and variety of character to feed the mind with—Where then, my dear countrymen, are you going—

—We are only looking at this chaise, said they—Your most obedient servant, said I, skipping out of it, and pulling off my hat—We were wondering, said one of them, who, I found, was an *inquisitive traveler*—what could occasion its motion.—'Twas the agitation, said I coolly, of writing a preface—I never heard, said the other, who was a *simple traveler*, of a preface wrote in a *Desobligeant.*—It would have been better, said I, in a *Vis-à-Vis.*[6]

As an Englishman does not travel to see Englishmen, I retired to my room.

CALAIS.

I perceived that something darkened the passage more than myself, as I stepped along it to my room; it was effectually Monsieur Dessein, the master of the hotel, who had just returned from vespers, and, with his hat under his arm, was most complaisantly following me, to put me in mind of my wants. I had wrote myself pretty well out of conceit[7] with the *Desobligeant;* and Monsieur Dessein speaking of it with a shrug, as if it would no way suit me, it immediately struck my fancy that it belonged to some *innocent traveler*, who, on his return home, had left it to Monsieur Dessein's honor to make the most of.[8] Four months had elapsed since it had finished its career of Europe in the corner of Monsieur Dessein's coach-yard; and having sallied out from thence but a vamped-up business at the first, though it had been twice taken to pieces on Mount Sennis,[9] it had not profited much by its adventures—but by none so little as the standing so many months unpitied in the corner of Monsieur Dessein's coach-yard. Much indeed was not to be said for it—but something might—and when a few words will rescue misery out of her distress, I hate the man who can be a churl of[1] them.

—Now was I the master of this hotel, said I, laying the point of my forefinger on Monsieur Dessein's breast, I would inevitably make a point of getting rid of this unfortunate *Desobligeant*—it stands swinging reproaches at you every time you pass by it—

5. In *Don Quixote* by Miguel de Cervantes (1547–1616), Sancho remarks to his wife (not to the Don) on the benefits of staying home (part 2, chapter 5).
6. A light carriage in which two travelers sit face to face.
7. So as not to be pleased.

8. To sell it for as much as possible.
9. At the pass at Mount Cenis in the Alps, travelers had their coaches or chaises taken apart, and the pieces were carried to and reassembled on the other side. "A vamped-up business at the first": originally fabricated out of pieces.
1. Be stingy with.

Mon Dieu![2] said Monsieur Dessein—I have no interest—Except the interest, said I, which men of a certain turn of mind take, Monsieur Dessein, in their own sensations—I'm persuaded, to a man who feels for others as well as for himself, every rainy night, disguise it as you will, must cast a damp upon your spirits—You suffer, Monsieur Dessein, as much as the machine—

I have always observed, when there is as much *sour* as *sweet* in a compliment, that an Englishman is eternally at a loss within himself, whether to take it or let it alone: a Frenchman never is: Monsieur Dessein made me a bow.

C'est bien vrai,[3] said he—But in this case I should only exchange one disquietude for another, and with loss; figure to yourself, my dear sir, that in giving you a chaise which would fall to pieces before you had got half-way to Paris—figure to yourself how much I should suffer, in giving an ill impression of myself to a man of honor, and lying at the mercy, as I must do, *d'un homme d'esprit.*[4]

The dose was made up exactly after my own prescription; so I could not help taking it—and returning Monsieur Dessein his bow, without more casuistry we walked together towards his remise, to take a view of his magazine[5] of chaises.

IN THE STREET.

CALAIS.

It must needs to be a hostile kind of a world, when the buyer (if it be but of a sorry post-chaise) cannot go forth with the seller thereof into the street, to terminate the difference betwixt them, but he instantly falls into the same frame of mind, and views his conventionist with the same sort of eye, as if he was going along with him to Hyde Park Corner[6] to fight a duel. For my own part, being but a poor swordsman, and no way a match for Monsieur *Dessein*, I felt the rotation of all the movements within me to which the situation is incident—I looked at Monsieur *Dessein* through and through—eyed him as he walked along in profile—then, *en face*[7]—thought he looked like a Jew—then a Turk—disliked his wig—cursed him by my gods—wished him at the devil—

—And is all this to be lighted up in the heart for a beggarly account of three or four louis d'ors,[8] which is the most I can be overreached in?—Base passion! said I, turning myself about, as a man naturally does upon a sudden reverse of sentiment—base ungentle passion! thy hand is against every man, and every man's hand against thee[9]—Heaven forbid! said she, raising her hand up to her forehead, for I had turned full in front upon the lady whom I had seen in conference with the monk—she had followed us unperceived.— Heaven forbid, indeed! said I, offering her my own—she had a black pair of silk gloves, open only at the thumb and two forefingers, so accepted it without reserve—and I led her up to the door of the Remise.

Monsieur *Dessein* had *diabled*[1] the key above fifty times, before he found out he had come with a wrong one in his hand: we were as impatient as him-

2. My God!
3. That's quite true.
4. Of a man of spirit.
5. Stock, supply. "Remise": carriage house.
6. In the southeastern corner of Hyde Park, London, where many famous duels in the period were fought. "Conventionist": one of the parties

to a contract.
7. Full in the face.
8. French gold coins worth seventeen shillings each.
9. See Genesis 16.12.
1. Deviled; from *diable!*, a mild French curse.

self to have it opened; and so attentive to the obstacle, that I continued holding her hand almost without knowing it: so that Monsieur *Dessein* left us
together, with her hand in mine, and with our faces turned towards the door
of the Remise, and said he would be back in five minutes.

Now a colloquy of five minutes, in such a situation, is worth one of as many
ages, with your faces turned towards the street. In the latter case, 'tis drawn
from the objects and occurrences without—when your eyes are fixed upon a
dead blank—you draw purely from yourselves. A silence of a single moment
upon Monsieur *Dessein's* leaving us, had been fatal to the situation—she had
infallibly turned about—so I begun the conversation instantly.—

But what were the temptations (as I write not to apologize for the weaknesses of my heart in this tour,—but to give an account of them)—shall be
described with the same simplicity with which I felt them.

THE REMISE DOOR.

CALAIS.

When I told the reader that I did not care to get out of the *Desobligeant,*
because I saw the monk in close conference with a lady just arrived at the
inn—I told him the truth; but I did not tell him the whole truth; for I was full
as much restrained by the appearance and figure of the lady he was talking
to. Suspicion crossed my brain, and said, he was telling her what had passed;
something jarred upon it within me—I wished him at his convent.

When the heart flies out before the understanding, it saves the judgment
a world of pains—I was certain she was of a better order of beings—
however, I thought no more of her, but went on and wrote my preface.

The impression returned upon my encounter with her in the street; a
guarded frankness with which she gave me her hand, showed, I thought,
her good education and her good sense; and as I led her on, I felt a pleasurable ductility about her, which spread a calmness over all my spirits—

—Good God! how a man might lead such a creature as this round the
world with him!—

I had not yet seen her face—'twas not material; for the drawing was
instantly set about, and long before we had got to the door of the Remise,
Fancy had finished the whole head, and pleased herself as much with its
fitting her goddess, as if she had dived into the Tiber[2] for it—But thou art a
seduced, and a seducing slut; and albeit thou cheatest us seven times a day
with thy pictures and images, yet with so many charms dost thou do it, and
thou deckest out thy pictures in the shapes of so many angels of light, 'tis a
shame to break with thee.

When we had got to the door of the Remise, she withdrew her hand from
across her forehead, and let me see the original—it was a face of about six
and twenty—of a clear transparent brown, simply set off without rouge or
powder—it was not critically[3] handsome, but there was that in it, which in
the frame of mind I was in, attached me much more to it—it was interesting;
I fancied it wore the characters of a widowed look, and in that state of its

2. River running through Rome, where many statues and other antiquities were discovered in the 18th
century.
3. Exactly.

declension, which had passed the two first paroxysms of sorrow, and was quietly beginning to reconcile itself to its loss—but a thousand other distresses might have traced the same lines; I wished to know what they had been—and was ready to inquire (had the same *bon ton*[4] of conversation permitted, as in the days of Esdras)—*"What aileth thee? and why art thou disquieted? and why is thy understanding troubled?"*[5]—In a word, I felt benevolence for her; and resolved some way or other to throw in my mite of courtesy—if not of service.

Such were my temptations—and in this disposition to give way to them, was I left alone with the lady with her hand in mine, and with our faces both turned closer to the door of the Remise than what was absolutely necessary.

THE REMISE DOOR.

CALAIS.

This certainly, fair lady! said I, raising her hand up a little lightly as I began, must be one of Fortune's whimsical doings: to take two utter strangers by their hands—of different sexes, and perhaps from different corners of the globe, and in one moment place them together in such a cordial situation as Friendship herself could scarce have achieved for them, had she projected it for a month—

—And your reflection upon it, shows how much, Monsieur, she has embarrassed you by the adventure.—

When the situation is what we would wish, nothing is so ill-timed as to hint at the circumstances which make it so: you thank Fortune, continued she—you had reason—the heart knew it, and was satisfied; and who but an English philosopher would have sent notices of it to the brain to reverse the judgment?

In saying this she disengaged her hand with a look which I thought a sufficient commentary upon the text.

It is a miserable picture which I am going to give of the weakness of my heart, by owning that it suffered a pain, which worthier occasions could not have inflicted.—I was mortified with the loss of her hand, and the manner in which I had lost it carried neither oil nor wine to the wound:[6] I never felt the pain of a sheepish inferiority so miserably in my life.

The triumphs of a true feminine heart are short upon these discomfitures. In a very few seconds she laid her hand upon the cuff of my coat, in order to finish her reply; so some way or other, God knows how, I regained my situation.

—She had nothing to add.

I forthwith began to model a different conversation for the lady, thinking from the spirit as well as moral of this, that I had been mistaken in her character; but upon turning her face towards me, the spirit which had animated the reply was fled—the muscles relaxed, and I beheld the same unprotected look of distress which first won me to her interest—melancholy! to see such sprightliness the prey of sorrow.—I pitied her from my soul; and though it may

---

4. Fashionable style.
5. 2 Esdras 10.31.

6. See Luke 10.33–34.

seem ridiculous enough to a torpid heart,—I could have taken her into my arms, and cherished her, though it was in the open street, without blushing.

The pulsations of the arteries along my fingers pressing across hers, told her what was passing within me: she looked down—a silence of some moments followed.

I fear, in this interval, I must have made some slight efforts towards a closer compression of her hand, from a subtle sensation I felt in the palm of my own—not as if she was going to withdraw hers—but as if she thought about it—and I had infallibly lost it a second time, had not instinct more than reason directed me to the last resource in these dangers—to hold it loosely and in a manner as if I was every moment going to release it of myself; so she let it continue till Monsieur *Dessein* returned with the key; and in the meantime I set myself to consider how I should undo the ill impressions which the poor monk's story, in case he had told it her, must have planted in her breast against me.

THE SNUFF-BOX.

CALAIS.

The good old monk was within six paces of us, as the idea of him crossed my mind; and was advancing towards us a little out of the line, as if uncertain whether he should break in upon us or no.—He stopped, however, as soon as he came up to us, with a world of frankness; and having a horn snuff-box in his hand, he presented it open to me—You shall taste mine— said I, pulling out my box (which was a small tortoise one) and putting it unto his hand—'Tis most excellent, said the monk. Then do me the favor, I replied, to accept of the box and all, and when you take a pinch out of it, sometimes recollect it was the peace offering of a man who once used you unkindly, but not from his heart.

The poor monk blushed as red as scarlet. *Mon Dieu!* said he, pressing his hands together—you never used me unkindly.—I should think, said the lady, he is not likely. I blushed in my turn, but from what movements I leave to the few who feel to analyze—Excuse me, Madame, replied I—I treated him most unkindly and from no provocations—'Tis impossible, said the lady.—My God! cried the monk, with a warmth of asseveration which seemed not to belong to him—the fault was in me, and in the indiscretion of my zeal—The lady opposed it, and I joined with her in maintaining it was impossible, that a spirit so regulated as his, could give offense to any.

I knew not that contention could be rendered so sweet and pleasurable a thing to the nerves as I then felt it.—We remained silent without any sensation of that foolish pain which takes place, when in such a circle you look for ten minutes in one another's faces without saying a word. Whilst this lasted, the monk rubbed his horn box upon the sleeve of his tunic; and as soon as it had acquired a little air of brightness by the friction—he made a low bow, and said, 'twas too late to say whether it was the weakness or goodness of our tempers which had involved us in this contest—But be it as it would—he begged we might exchange boxes[7]—In saying this, he pre-

7. This famous scene gave rise to "Lorenzo cults" in Germany, in which sensitive male friends exchanged their snuffboxes.

sented his to me with one hand, as he took mine from me in the other; and having kissed it—with a stream of good nature in his eyes he put it into his bosom—and took his leave.

I guard this box, as I would the instrumental[8] parts of my religion, to help my mind on to something better: in truth, I seldom go abroad without it: and oft and many a time have I called up by it the courteous spirit of its owner to regulate my own, in the justlings of the world; they had found full employment for his, as I learnt from his story, till about the forty-fifth year of his age, when upon some military services ill requited, and meeting at the same time with a disappointment in the tenderest of passions, he abandoned the sword and the sex[9] together, and took sanctuary, not so much in his convent as in himself.

I feel a damp upon my spirits, as I am going to add, that in my last return through Calais, upon inquiring after Father Lorenzo, I heard he had been dead near three months, and was buried, not in his convent, but, according to his desire, in a little cemetery belonging to it, about two leagues off: I had a strong desire to see where they had laid him—when upon pulling out his little horn box, as I sat by his grave, and plucking up a nettle or two at the head of it, which had no business to grow there, they all struck together so forcibly upon my affections, that I burst into a flood of tears—but I am as weak as a woman; and I beg the world not to smile, but pity me.

THE REMISE DOOR.

CALAIS.

I had never quitted the lady's hand all this time; and had held it so long, that it would have been indecent to have let it go, without first pressing it to my lips: the blood and spirits, which had suffered a revulsion[1] from her, crowded back to her, as I did it.

Now the two travelers, who had spoke to me in the coachyard, happening at that crisis to be passing by, and observing our communications, naturally took it into their heads that we must be *man and wife* at least; so stopping as soon as they came up to the door of the Remise, the one of them, who was the inquisitive traveler, asked us, if we set out for Paris the next morning?—I could only answer for myself, I said; and the lady added, she was for Amiens.[2]—We dined there yesterday, said the simple traveler—You go directly through the town, added the other, in your road to Paris. I was going to return a thousand thanks for the intelligence, *that Amiens was in the road to Paris*; but, upon pulling out my poor monk's little horn box to take a pinch of snuff—I made them a quiet bow, and wishing them a good passage to Dover— they left us alone—

—Now where would be the harm, said I to myself, if I was to beg of this distressed lady to accept of half of my chaise?—and what mighty mischief could ensue?

Every dirty passion, and bad propensity in my nature, took the alarm, as I stated the proposition—It will oblige you to have a third horse, said

8. Useful, effective.
9. Women. A common way (for men, mostly) to refer to women.

1. Withdrawal.
2. Cathedral city about ninety miles north of Paris.

AVARICE, which will put twenty livres out of your pocket.—You know not who she is, said CAUTION—or what scrapes the affair may draw you into, whispered COWARDICE—

Depend upon it, Yorick! said DISCRETION, 'twill be said you went off with a mistress, and came by assignation to Calais for that purpose—

—You can never after, cried HYPOCRISY aloud, show your face in the world—or rise, quoth MEANNESS, in the church—or be anything in it, said PRIDE, but a lousy prebendary.[3]

—But 'tis a civil thing, said I—and as I generally act from the first impulse, and therefore seldom listen to these cabals, which serve no purpose that I know of, but to encompass the heart with adamant[4]—I turned instantly about to the lady—

—But she had glided off unperceived, as the cause was pleading, and had made ten or a dozen paces down the street, by the time I had made the determination; so I set off after her with a long stride, to make her the proposal with the best address I was master of: but observing she walked with her cheek half resting upon the palm of her hand—with the slow, short-measured step of thoughtfulness, and with her eyes, as she went step by step, fixed upon the ground, it struck me, she was trying the same cause herself.—God help her! said I, she has some mother-in-law, or tartufish[5] aunt, or nonsensical old woman, to consult upon the occasion, as well as myself: so not caring to interrupt the process, and deeming it more gallant to take her at discretion than by surprise, I faced about, and took a short turn or two before the door of the Remise, whilst she walked musing on one side.

IN THE STREET.

CALAIS.

Having, on first sight of the lady, settled the affair in my fancy, "that she was of the better order of beings"—and then laid it down as a second axiom, as indisputable as the first, that she was a widow, and wore a character of distress—I went no further; I got ground enough for the situation which pleased me—and had she remained close beside my elbow till midnight, I should have held true to my system, and considered her only under that general idea.

She had scarce got twenty paces distant from me, ere something within me called out for a more particular inquiry—it brought on the idea of a further separation—I might possibly never see her more—the heart is for saving what it can; and I wanted the traces through which my wishes might find their way to her, in case I should never rejoin her myself: in a word, I wished to know her name—her family's—her condition;[6] and as I knew the place to which she was going, I wanted to know from whence she came: but there was no coming at all this intelligence: a hundred little delicacies stood in the way. I formed a score different plans—There was no such thing as a man's asking her directly—the thing was impossible.

3. A clergyman with a small income, usually associated with a cathedral.
4. Impenetrably hard substance. "Cabals": secret, malicious factions.

5. Hypocritically stern in matters of religion or conscience, after the title character in the comedy *Tartuffe* (1664) by Molière (1622–1673).
6. Rank or social standing.

A little French *debonair* captain, who came dancing down the street, showed me, it was the easiest thing in the world; for popping in betwixt us, just as the lady was returning back to the door of the Remise, he introduced himself to my acquaintance, and before he had well got announced, begged I would do him the honor to present him to the lady—I had not been presented myself—so turning about to her, he did it just as well by asking her, if she had come from Paris?—No, she was going that route, she said.—*Vous n'etes pas de Londre?*[7]—She was not, she replied.—Then Madame must have come through Flanders.—*Apparemment vous etez Flammande?*[8] said the French captain.—The lady answered, she was.—*Peutetre, de Lisle?*[9] added he.—She said she was not of Lisle.—Nor Arras?—nor Cambray?—nor Ghent?[1]—nor Brussels? She answered, she was of Brussels.

He had had the honor, he said, to be at the bombardment of it last war— that it was finely situated, *pour cela*[2]—and full of noblesse when the Imperialists were driven out by the French[3] (the lady made a slight curtsy)—so giving her an account of the affair, and of the share he had had in it—he begged the honor to know her name—so made his bow.

—*Et Madame a son Mari?*[4]—said he, looking back when he had made two steps—and without staying for an answer—danced down the street.

Had I served seven years' apprenticeship to good breeding, I could not have done as much.

THE REMISE.

CALAIS.

As the little French captain left us, Monsieur Dessein came up with the key of the Remise in his hand, and forthwith let us into his magazine of chaises.

The first object which caught my eye, as Monsieur Dessein opened the door of the Remise, was another old tattered *Desobligeant,* and notwithstanding it was the exact picture of that which had hit my fancy so much in the coach-yard but an hour before—the very sight of it stirred up a disagreeable sensation within me now; and I thought 'twas a churlish beast into whose heart the idea could first enter, to construct such a machine; nor had I much more charity for the man who could think of using it.

I observed the lady was as little taken with it as myself: so Monsieur Dessein led us on to a couple of chaises which stood abreast, telling us, as he recommended them, that they had been purchased by my Lord A. and B. to go the *grand tour,* but had gone no further than Paris, so were in all respects as good as new—They were too good—so I passed on to a third, which stood behind, and forthwith began to chaffer[5] for the price—But 'twill scarce hold two, said I, opening the door and getting in—Have the goodness, Madam, said Monsieur Dessein, offering his arm, to step in—The lady hesitated half

7. Are you not from London?
8. Apparently you are Flemish.
9. Perhaps you're from Lille?
1. City in the Flemish region of Belgium. Lisle (Lille), Arras, and Cambray (Cambrai) are cities in northern France.
2. For that.

3. During the War of the Austrian Succession, the French took Brussels in 1746 from forces of Empress Maria Theresa of Austria, with whom the British were allied.
4. And is Madam married?
5. Haggle.

a second, and stepped in; and the waiter that moment beckoning to speak to Monsieur Dessein, he shut the door of the chaise upon us, and left us.

THE REMISE.
CALAIS.

C'est bien comique, 'tis very droll, said the lady smiling, from the reflection that this was the second time we had been left together by a parcel of non-sensical contingencies—*c'est bien comique,* said she—

—There wants nothing, said I, to make it so, but the comic use which the gallantry of a Frenchman would put it to—to make love the first moment, and an offer of his person[6] the second.

'Tis their *fort,*[7] replied the lady.

It is supposed so at least—and how it has come to pass, continued I, I know not; but they have certainly got the credit of understanding more of love, and making it better than any other nation upon earth; but for my own part, I think them errant bunglers, and in truth the worst set of marksmen that ever tried Cupid's patience.

—To think of making love by *sentiments!*

I should as soon think of making a genteel suit of clothes out of remnants:— and to do it—pop—at first sight by declaration—is submitting the offer and themselves with it, to be sifted with all their *pours* and *contres,*[8] by an unheated mind.

The lady attended as if she expected I should go on.

Consider then, Madam, continued I, laying my hand upon hers—

That grave people hate love for the name's sake—

That selfish people hate it for their own—

Hypocrites for heaven's—

And that all of us, both old and young, being ten times worse frightened than hurt by the very *report*—What a want of knowledge in this branch of commerce a man betrays, who ever lets the word come out of his lips, till an hour or two at least after the time that his silence upon it becomes torment-ing. A course of small, quiet attentions, not so pointed as to alarm—nor so vague as to be misunderstood—with now and then a look of kindness, and little or nothing said upon it—leaves Nature for your mistress, and she fashions it to her mind.—

Then I solemnly declare, said the lady, blushing—you have been making love to me all this while.

THE REMISE.
CALAIS.

Monsieur *Dessein* came back to let us out of the chaise, and acquaint the lady, the Count de L——, her brother, was just arrived at the hotel. Though I had infinite good will for the lady, I cannot say, that I rejoiced in my heart at the event—and could not help telling her so—for it is fatal to a proposal, Madam, said I, that I was going to make you—

6. Himself.　　　　　　　　　　　　　　8. Pros and cons.
7. Distinguishing strength.

—You need not tell me what the proposal was, said she, laying her hand upon both mine, as she interrupted me.—A man, my good Sir, has seldom an offer of kindness to make to a woman, but she has a presentiment of it some moments before—

Nature arms her with it, said I, for immediate preservation—But I think, said she, looking in my face, I had no evil to apprehend—and to deal frankly with you, had determined to accept it.—If I had—(she stopped a moment)—I believe your good will would have drawn a story from me, which would have made pity the only dangerous thing in the journey.

In saying this, she suffered me to kiss her hand twice, and with a look of sensibility mixed with a concern, she got out of the chaise—and bid adieu.

IN THE STREET.

CALAIS.

I never finished a twelve-guinea bargain[9] so expeditiously in my life: my time seemed heavy upon the loss of the lady, and knowing every moment of it would be as two, till I put myself into motion—I ordered post-horses[1] directly, and walked towards the hotel.

Lord! said I, hearing the town clock strike four, and recollecting that I had been little more than a single hour in Calais—

—What a large volume of adventures may be grasped within this little span of life by him who interests his heart in everything, and who, having eyes to see what time and chance are perpetually holding out to him as he journeyeth on his way, misses nothing he can *fairly* lay his hands on.—

—If this won't turn out something—another will—no matter—'tis an assay upon human nature—I get my labor for my pains—'tis enough—the pleasure of the experiment has kept my senses and the best part of my blood awake, and laid the gross to sleep.

I pity the man who can travel from *Dan to Beersheba*,[2] and cry, 'Tis all barren—and so it is; and so is all the world to him, who will not cultivate the fruits it offers. I declare, said I, clapping my hands cheerily together, that was I in a desert, I would find out wherewith in it to call forth my affections—If I could not do better, I would fasten them upon some sweet myrtle, or seek some melancholy cypress to connect myself to—I would court their shade, and greet them kindly for their protection—I would cut my name upon them, and swear they were the loveliest trees throughout the desert: if their leaves withered, I would teach myself to mourn, and when they rejoiced, I would rejoice along with them.

The learned SMELFUNGUS[3] traveled from Boulogne to Paris—from Paris to Rome—and so on—but he set out with the spleen and jaundice, and every object he passed by was discolored or distorted—He wrote an account of them, but 'twas nothing but the account of his miserable feelings.

---

9. A low price, for a presumably rather cheap chaise.
1. Used by travelers for hire as well as by the post.
2. Biblical phrase indicating the extent of regions settled by the tribes of Israel, from the north to the south.
3. Sterne's disparaging name for novelist Tobias Smollett (1721–1771), author of *Travels through France and Italy* (1766), which took an often critical view of people and places he visited.

I met Smelfungus in the grand portico of the Pantheon[4]—he was just coming out of it—'Tis nothing but a huge cock-pit,[5] said he—I wish you had said nothing worse of the Venus of Medicis,[6] replied I—for in passing through Florence, I had heard he had fallen foul upon the goddess, and used her worse than a common strumpet, without the least provocation in nature.

I popped upon Smelfungus again at Turin, in his return home; and a sad tale of sorrowful adventures had he to tell, "wherein he spoke of moving accidents by flood and field, and of the cannibals which each other eat: the Anthropophagi"[7]—he had been flea'd alive, and bedeviled, and used worse than St. Bartholomew,[8] at every stage he had come at—

—I'll tell it, cried Smelfungus, to the world. You had better tell it, said I, to your physician.[9]

Mundungus,[1] with an immense fortune, made the whole tour; going on from Rome to Naples—from Naples to Venice—from Venice to Vienna—to Dresden, to Berlin, without one generous connection or pleasurable anecdote to tell of; but he had traveled straight on, looking neither to his right hand or his left, lest Love or Pity should seduce him out of his road.

Peace be to them! if it is to be found; but heaven itself, was it possible to get there with such tempers, would want objects to give it—Every gentle spirit would come flying upon the wings of Love to hail their arrival—Nothing would the souls of Smelfungus and Mundungus hear of, but fresh anthems of joy, fresh raptures of love, and fresh congratulations of their common felicity—I heartily pity them: they have brought up no faculties for this work; and was the happiest mansion in heaven to be allotted to Smelfungus and Mundungus, they would be so far from being happy, that the souls of Smelfungus and Mundungus would do penance there to all eternity.

MONTRIUL.[2]

I had once lost my portmanteau from behind my chaise, and twice got out in the rain, and one of the times up to the knees in dirt, to help the postilion[3] to tie it on, without being able to find out what was wanting—Nor was it till I got to Montriul, upon the landlord's asking me if I wanted not a servant, that it occurred to me, that that was the very thing.

A servant! That I do most sadly, quoth I—Because, Monsieur, said the landlord, there is a clever young fellow, who would be very proud of the honor to serve an Englishman—But why an English one, more than any other?— They are so generous, said the landlord—I'll be shot if this is not a livre out of my pocket, quoth I to myself, this very night—But they have wherewithal to be so, Monsieur, added he—Set down one livre more for that, quoth I—It

---

4. Ancient domed temple in Rome.
5. A place where cockfights are held. Sterne provides a note to Smollett's *Travels*.
6. Statue of Venus in the Uffizi Gallery, Florence.
7. See *Othello*, 1.3.134–35.
8. One of the twelve apostles, flayed ("flea'd") alive in 44 C.E. (alluding to fleas in inns).
9. Smollett himself was a physician.

1. Identified as Dr. Samuel Sharp, whose *Letters from Italy* (1766) was critical of the Italians. The name Mundungus suggests refuse and was also a common name for foul-smelling tobacco.
2. Montreuil (here misspelled by Sterne), a town about forty-five miles south of Calais.
3. Rider of the lead coach horse who directs the coach when there is no coachman.

was but last night, said the landlord, *qu'un my Lord Anglois presentoit un ecu a la fille de chambre*[4]—*Tant pis, pour Mademoiselle Janatone,*[5] said I.

Now Janatone being the landlord's daughter, and the landlord supposing I was young in French, took the liberty to inform me, I should not have said *tant pis*— but, *tant mieux. Tant mieux, toujours,*[6] *Monsieur,* said he, when there is anything to be got—*tant pis,* when there is nothing. It comes to the same thing, said I. *Pardonnez moi,* said the landlord.

I cannot take a fitter opportunity to observe, once for all, that *tant pis* and *tant mieux* being two of the great hinges in French conversation, a stranger would do well to set himself right in the use of them, before he gets to Paris.

A prompt French Marquis at our ambassador's table demanded of Mr. H——, if he was H—— the poet? No, said H—— mildly—*Tant pis,* replied the Marquis.

It is H—— the historian,[7] said another.—*Tant mieux,* said the Marquis. And Mr. H——, who is a man of an excellent heart, returned thanks for both.

When the landlord had set me right in this matter, he called in La Fleur, which was the name of the young man he had spoke of—saying only first, That as for his talents, he would presume to say nothing—Monsieur was the best judge what would suit him; but for the fidelity of La Fleur, he would stand responsible in all he was worth.

The landlord delivered this in a manner which instantly set my mind to the business I was upon—and La Fleur, who stood waiting without, in that breathless expectation which every son of nature of us have felt in our turns, came in.

MONTRIUL.

I am apt to be taken with all kinds of people at first sight; but never more so, than when a poor devil comes to offer his service to so poor a devil as myself; and as I know this weakness, I always suffer my judgment to draw back something on that very account—and this more or less, according to the mood I am in, and the case—and I may add the gender too of the person I am to govern.

When La Fleur entered the room, after every discount I could make for my soul, the genuine look and air of the fellow determined the matter at once in his favor; so I hired him first—and then began to inquire what he could do: But I shall find out his talents, quoth I, as I want them—besides, a Frenchman can do everything.

Now poor La Fleur could do nothing in the world but beat a drum, and play a march or two upon the fife. I was determined to make his talents do: and can't say my weakness was ever so insulted by my wisdom, as in the attempt.

La Fleur had set out early in life, as gallantly as most Frenchmen do, with *serving*[8] for a few years: at the end of which, having satisfied the sentiment, and found moreover, that the honor of beating a drum was likely to be its own

---

4. That an English lord presented an écu (about three livres, a suspiciously big tip) to the chambermaid.
5. So much the worse for Miss Janatone.
6. So much the better, so much the better, always.

7. David Hume, Scottish philosopher and historian, instead of John Home, Scottish poet and tragedian (whose last name is pronounced *Hume*).
8. In the army.

reward, as it opened no further track of glory to him—he retired *a ses terres,*[9] and lived *comme il plaisoit a Dieu*[1]—that is to say, upon nothing.

—And so, quoth *Wisdom,* you have hired a drummer to attend you in this tour of yours through France and Italy! Psha! said I, and do not one half of our gentry go with a hum-drum *compagnon du voiage*[2] the same round, and have the piper and the devil and all to pay besides? When man can extricate himself with an *equivoque*[3] in such an unequal match—he is not ill off—But you can do something else, La Fleur? said I—O *qu'oui!*—he could make spatterdashes,[4] and play a little upon the fiddle—Bravo! said Wisdom—Why I play a bass myself, said I—we shall do very well.—You can shave, and dress a wig a little, La Fleur?—He had all the dispositions[5] in the world—It is enough for heaven! said I, interrupting him—and ought to be enough for me—So supper coming in, and having a frisky English spaniel on one side of my chair, and a French valet, with as much hilarity in his countenance as ever nature painted in one, on the other—I was satisfied to my heart's content with my empire; and if monarchs knew what they would be at, they might be as satisfied as I was.

MONTRIUL.

As La Fleur went the whole tour of France and Italy with me, and will be often upon the stage, I must interest the reader a little further in his behalf, by saying, that I had never less reason to repent of the impulses which generally do determine me, than in regard to this fellow—he was a faithful, affectionate, simple soul as ever trudged after the heels of a philosopher; and notwithstanding his talents of drum-beating and spatterdash-making, which, though very good in themselves, happened to be of no great service to me, yet was I hourly recompensed by the festivity of his temper—it supplied all defects—I had a constant resource in his looks, in all difficulties and distresses of my own—I was going to have added, of his too; but La Fleur was out of the reach of everything; for whether it was hunger or thirst, or cold or nakedness, or watchings,[6] or whatever stripes of ill luck La Fleur met with in our journeyings, there was no index in his physiognomy to point them out by—he was eternally the same; so that if I am a piece of a philosopher,[7] which Satan now and then puts into my head I am—it always mortifies the pride of the conceit, by reflecting how much I owe to the complexional philosophy[8] of this poor fellow, for shaming me into one of a better kind. With all this, La Fleur had a small cast of the coxcomb—but he seemed at first sight to be more a coxcomb of nature than of art; and before I had been three days in Paris with him—he seemed to be no coxcomb at all.

MONTRIUL.

The next morning, La Fleur entering upon his employment, I delivered to him the key of my portmanteau with an inventory of my half a dozen shirts

9. To his land (La Fleur had apparently deserted).
1. As it pleased God.
2. Traveling companion.
3. Play on words. Sterne plays on La Fleur's drumming ("hum-drum") and piping (with the expression "pay the piper," to face the consequences of one's actions).

4. Leggings to keep stockings and trousers from getting spattered. "O *qu'oui*": yes indeed.
5. Abilities.
6. Inability to sleep.
7. A philosopher to some degree, one who bears adversity "philosophically."
8. Philosophical temperament.

and silk pair of breeches; and bid him fasten all upon the chaise—get the horses put to—and desire the landlord to come in with his bill.

C'est un garçon de bonne fortune,[9] said the landlord, pointing through the window to half a dozen wenches who had got round about La Fleur, and were most kindly taking their leave of him, as the postilion was leading out the horses. La Fleur kissed all their hands round and round again, and thrice he wiped his eyes, and thrice he promised he would bring them all pardons from Rome.[1]

The young fellow, said the landlord, is beloved by all the town, and there is scarce a corner in Montriul where the want of him will not be felt: he has but one misfortune in the world, continued he, "He is always in love."—I am heartily glad of it, said I—'twill save me the trouble every night of putting my breeches under my head. In saying this, I was making not so much La Fleur's eloge,[2] as my own, having been in love, with one princess or other, almost all my life, and I hope I shall go on so till I die, being firmly persuaded, that if ever I do a mean action, it must be in some interval betwixt one passion and another: whilst this interregnum[3] lasts, I always perceive my heart locked up—I can scarce find in it to give Misery a sixpence; and therefore I always get out of it as fast as I can, and the moment I am rekindled, I am all generosity and good will again; and would do anything in the world, either for or with any one, if they will but satisfy me there is no sin in it.

—But in saying this—surely I am commending the passion—not myself.

A FRAGMENT.

—The town of Abdera, notwithstanding Democritus lived there, trying all the powers of irony and laughter to reclaim it, was the vilest and most profligate town in all Thrace.[4] What for poisons, conspiracies, and assassinations— libels, pasquinades,[5] and tumults, there was no going there by day—'twas worse by night.

Now, when things were at the worst, it came to pass, that the *Andromeda* of Euripides[6] being represented at Abdera, the whole orchestra was delighted with it: but of all the passages which delighted them, nothing operated more upon their imaginations, than the tender strokes of nature, which the poet had wrought up in that pathetic speech of Perseus.[7]

O Cupid, prince of Gods and men, &c.

Every man almost spoke pure iambics the next day, and talked of nothing but Perseus his pathetic[8] address—"O Cupid, prince of Gods and men"—in every street of Abdera, in every house—"O Cupid! Cupid!"—in every mouth, like the natural notes of some sweet melody which drops from it whether it

---

9. He's a fortunate young man (literal trans.); an expression implying that La Fleur is lucky in love.

1. Implying that the young women who know him may well need pardons from the Vatican.
2. Commendation.
3. Period between the reigns of monarchs.
4. This anecdote is adapted from Robert Burton (1577–1640), *The Anatomy of Melancholy* (1621). Abdera is an ancient city in Thrace, a region in the north of Greece. Democritus (ca. 460–ca.

370 B.C.E.) was called the laughing philosopher because he laughed at human follies.
5. Public lampoons.
6. Greek dramatist (ca. 480–406 B.C.E.), whose tragedy *Andromeda* (412 B.C.E.) is lost.
7. Legendary Greek hero who saves Andromeda from the sea monster Cetus.
8. Moving. "Iambics": iambic trimeter, the poetic meter in which the spoken parts of most Greek tragedy are written.

will or no—nothing but "Cupid! Cupid! prince of Gods and men"—The fire caught—and the whole city, like the heart of one man, opened itself to Love.

No pharmacopolist could sell one grain of hellebore[9]—not a single armorer had a heart to forge one instrument of death—Friendship and Virtue met together, and kissed each other in the street—the golden age returned, and hung over the town of Abdera—every Abderite took his oaten pipe, and every Abderitish woman left her purple web, and chastely sat her down and listened to the song—

'Twas only in the power, says the Fragment, of the God whose empire extendeth from heaven to earth, and even to the depths of the sea, to have done this.

MONTRIUL.

When all is ready, and every article is disputed and paid for in the inn, unless you are a little soured by the adventure, there is always a matter to compound[1] at the door, before you can get into your chaise, and that is with the sons and daughters of poverty, who surround you. Let no man say, "let them go to the devil"—'tis a cruel journey to send a few miserables, and they have had sufferings enow without it: I always think it better to take a few sous out in my hand; and I would counsel every gentle traveler to do so likewise; he need not be so exact in setting down his motives for giving them—They will be registered elsewhere.[2]

For my own part, there is no man gives so little as I do; for few that I know have so little to give: but as this was the first public act of my charity in France, I took the more notice of it.

A well-a-way! said I, I have but eight sous in the world showing them in my hand, and there are eight poor men and eight poor women for 'em.

A poor tattered soul, without a shirt on, instantly withdrew his claim, by retiring two steps out of the circle, and making a disqualifying bow on his part. Had the whole parterre cried out, *Place aux dames*,[3] with one voice, it would not have conveyed the sentiment of a deference for the sex with half the effect.

Just Heaven! for what wise reasons hast thou ordered it, that beggary and urbanity, which are at such variance in other countries, should find a way to be at unity in this?

—I insisted upon presenting him with a single sou, merely for his *politesse*.[4]

A poor little dwarfish, brisk fellow, who stood over against me in the circle, putting something first under his arm, which had once been a hat, took his snuff-box out of his pocket, and generously offered a pinch on both sides of him: it was a gift of consequence, and modestly declined—The poor little fellow pressed it upon them with a nod of welcomeness—*Prenez en*[5]—*prenez*, said he, looking another way; so they each took a pinch—Pity thy box should ever want one, said I to myself; so I put a couple of sous into it—taking a small pinch out of his box to enhance their value, as I did it—He felt the

---

9. Herb thought to cure madness. "Pharmacopolist": seller of drugs.
1. To settle (with money).
2. In heaven.

3. Give way to the ladies.
4. Courtesy.
5. Take some.

weight of the second obligation more than that of the first—'twas doing him an honor—the other was only doing him a charity—and he made me a bow down to the ground for it.

—Here! said I to an old soldier with one hand, who had been campaigned and worn out to death in the service—here's a couple of sous for thee. *Vive le Roi!*[6] said the old soldier.

I had then but three sous left: so I gave one, simply *pour l'amour de Dieu*,[7] which was the footing on which it was begged—The poor woman had a dislocated hip; so it could not be well upon any other motive.

Mon cher et tres charitable Monsieur[8]—There's no opposing this, said I.

My Lord Anglois[9]—the very sound was worth the money—so I gave *my last sous for it*. But in the eagerness of giving, I had overlooked a *pauvre honteux*,[1] who had no one to ask a sou for him, and who, I believed, would have perished ere he could have asked one for himself; he stood by the chaise, a little without the circle, and wiped a tear from a face which I thought had seen better days—Good God! said I—and I have not one single sou left to give him—But you have a thousand! cried all the powers of nature, stirring within me—so I gave him—no matter what—I am ashamed to say *how much*, now—and was ashamed to think how little, then: so if the reader can form any conjecture of my disposition, as these two fixed points are given him, he may judge within a livre or two what was the precise sum.

I could afford nothing for the rest, but *Dieu vous benisse—Et le bon Dieu vous benisse encore*[2]—said the old soldier, the dwarf, &c. The *pauvre honteux* could say nothing—he pulled out a little handkerchief, and wiped his face as he turned away—and I thought he thanked me more than them all.

THE BIDET.

Having settled all these little matters, I got into my post-chaise with more ease than ever I got into a post-chaise in my life; and La Fleur having got one large jackboot on the far side of a little *bidet*,[3] and another on this (for I count nothing of his legs)—he cantered away before me as happy and as perpendicular as a prince.—

—But what is happiness! what is grandeur in this painted scene of life! A dead ass, before we had got a league,[4] put a sudden stop to La Fleur's career—his bidet would not pass by it—a contention arose betwixt them, and the poor fellow was kicked out of his jackboots the very first kick.

La Fleur bore his fall like a French Christian, saying neither more or less upon it, than, Diable! so presently got up and came to the charge again astride his bidet, beating him up to it as he would have beat his drum.

The bidet flew from one side of the road to the other, then back again— then this way—then that way, and in short every way but by the dead ass.—La Fleur insisted upon the thing—and the bidet threw him.

What's the matter, La Fleur, said I, with this bidet of thine?—*Monsieur*, said he, *c'est un cheval le plus opiniatré du monde*[5]—Nay, if he is a conceited

---

6. Long live the king!
7. For the love of God.
8. My dear, most charitable gentleman.
9. My English lord.
1. A poor man ashamed to be begging.

2. May God bless you, and good God bless you again.
3. Post-horse [Sterne's note].
4. About three miles.
5. The most stubborn horse in the world.

beast, he must go his own way, replied I—so La Fleur got off him, and giving him a good sound lash, the bidet took me at my word, and away he scampered back to Montriul.—*Peste!*[6] said La Fleur.

It is not *mal a propos*[7] to take notice here, that though La Fleur availed himself but of two different terms of exclamation in this encounter—namely, *Diable!* and *Peste!* that there are nevertheless three in the French language, like the positive, comparative, and superlative, one or the other of which serve for every unexpected throw of the dice in life.

Le Diable! which is the first, and positive degree, is generally used upon ordinary emotions of the mind, where small things only fall out contrary to your expectations—such as—the throwing once doublets[8]—La Fleur's being kicked off his horse, and so forth—cuckoldom, for the same reason, is always—*Le Diable!*

But in cases where the cast has something provoking in it, as in that of the bidet's running away after, and leaving La Fleur aground in jackboots—'tis the second degree.

'Tis then *Peste!*

And for the third[9]—

—But here my heart is wrung with pity and fellow-feeling, when I reflect what miseries must have been their lot, and how bitterly so refined a people must have smarted, to have forced them upon the use of it.—

Grant me, O ye powers which touch the tongue with eloquence in distress!—whatever is my *cast*, grant me but decent words to exclaim in, and I will give my nature way.

—But as these were not to be had in France, I resolved to take every evil just as it befell me, without any exclamation at all.

La Fleur, who had made no such covenant with himself, followed the bidet with his eyes till it was got out of sight—and then, you may imagine, if you please, with what word he closed the whole affair.

As there was no hunting down a frightened horse in jackboots, there remained no alternative but taking La Fleur either behind the chaise, or into it.—

I preferred the latter, and in half an hour we got to the post-house at Nampont.[1]

NAMPONT.

THE DEAD ASS.

—And this, said he, putting the remains of a crust into his wallet—and this should have been thy portion, said he, hadst thou been alive to have shared it with me. I thought by the accent, it had been an apostrophe to his child; but 'twas to his ass, and to the very ass we had seen dead in the road, which had occasioned La Fleur's misadventure. The man seemed to lament it much; and it instantly brought into my mind Sancho's lamentation for his;[2] but he did it with more true touches of nature.

---

6. What a plague!
7. Inappropriate.
8. Throwing a pair of ones in dice; snake eyes.
9. Yorick never says what the third is, though

several grosser obscenities suggest themselves.
1. Town about ten miles south of Montreuil.
2. In *Don Quixote*, Sancho laments when his ass is stolen.

The mourner was sitting upon a stone bench at the door, with the ass's pannel[3] and its bridle on one side, which he took up from time to time— then laid them down—looked at them and shook his head. He then took his crust of bread out of his wallet again, as if to eat it; held it some time in his hand—then laid it upon the bit of his ass's bridle—looked wistfully at the little arrangement he had made—and then gave a sigh.

The simplicity of his grief drew numbers about him, and La Fleur amongst the rest, whilst the horses were getting ready; as I continued sitting in the post-chaise, I could see and hear over their heads.

—He said he had come last from Spain, where he had been from the furthest borders of Franconia;[4] and had got so far on his return home, when his ass died. Every one seemed desirous to know what business could have taken so old and poor a man so far a journey from his own home.

It had pleased heaven, he said, to bless him with three sons, the finest lads in all Germany; but having in one week lost two of the eldest of them by the smallpox, and the youngest falling ill of the same distemper, he was afraid of being bereft of them all; and made a vow, if Heaven would not take him from him also, he would go in gratitude to St. Iago[5] in Spain.

When the mourner got thus far on his story, he stopped to pay nature his tribute—and wept bitterly.

He said, Heaven had accepted the conditions, and that he had set out from his cottage with this poor creature, who had been a patient partner of his journey—that it had eat the same bread with him all the way, and was unto him as a friend.

Everybody who stood about, heard the poor fellow with concern—La Fleur offered him money.—The mourner said, he did not want it—it was not the value of the ass—but the loss of him.—The ass, he said, he was assured loved him—and upon this told them a long story of a mischance upon their passage over the Pyrenean mountains,[6] which had separated them from each other three days; during which time the ass had sought him as much as he had sought the ass, and that they had neither scarce eat or drank till they met.

Thou has one comfort, friend, said I, at least, in the loss of thy poor beast; I'm sure thou hast been a merciful master to him.—Alas! said the mourner, I thought so, when he was alive—but now that he is dead I think otherwise.—I fear the weight of myself and my afflictions together have been too much for him—they have shortened the poor creature's days, and I fear I have them to answer for.—Shame on the world! said I to myself—Did we love each other, as this poor soul but loved his ass—'twould be something.—

NAMPONT.

THE POSTILLION.

The concern which the poor fellow's story threw me into, required some attention: the postillion paid not the least to it, but set off upon the *pavè*[7] in a full gallop.

---

3. A wooden saddle for an ass.
4. Region in southwest Germany.
5. Shrine in northwest Spain, where the body of the apostle St. James supposedly lies.

6. The Pyrenees, mountain range that forms a border between France and Spain.
7. Pavement.

The thirstiest soul in the most sandy desert of Arabia could not have wished more for a cup of cold water, than mine did for grave and quiet movements; and I should have had an high opinion of the postillion, had he but stolen off with me in something like a pensive pace.—On the contrary, as the mourner finished his lamentation, the fellow gave an unfeeling lash to each of his beasts, and set off clattering like a thousand devils.

I called to him as loud as I could, for heaven's sake to go slower—and the louder I called, the more unmercifully he galloped.—The deuce take him and his galloping too—said I—he'll go on tearing my nerves to pieces till he has worked me into a foolish passion, and then he'll go slow, that I may enjoy the sweets of it.

The postillion managed the point to a miracle: by the time he had got to the foot of a steep hill about half a league from Nampont, he had put me out of temper with him—and then with myself, for being so.

My case then required a different treatment; and a good rattling gallop would have been of real service to me.—

—Then, prithee, get on—get on, my good lad, said I.

The postillion pointed to the hill—I then tried to return back to the story of the poor German and his ass—but I had broke the clue[8]—and could no more get into it again, than the postillion could into a trot.—

—The deuce go, said I, with it all! Here am I sitting as candidly disposed to make the best of the worst, as ever wight[9] was, and all runs counter.

There is one sweet lenitive[1] at least for evils, which Nature holds out to us: so I took it kindly at her hands, and fell asleep; and the first word which roused me was *Amiens*.[2]

—Bless me! said I, rubbing my eyes—this is the very town where my poor lady is to come.

AMIENS.

The words were scarce out of my mouth, when the Count de L***'s post-chaise, with his sister in it, drove hastily by: she had just time to make me a bow of recognition—and of that particular kind of it, which told me she had not yet done with me. She was as good as her look; for, before I had quite finished my supper, her brother's servant came into the room with a billet,[3] in which she said she had taken the liberty to charge me with a letter, which I was to present myself to Madame R*** the first morning I had nothing to do at Paris. There was only added, she was sorry, but from what *penchant* she had not considered, that she had been prevented telling me her story—that she still owed it me; and if my route should ever lay through Brussels, and I had not by then forgot the name of Madame de L***—that Madame de L*** would be glad to discharge her obligation.

Then I will meet thee, said I, fair spirit! at Brussels—'tis only returning from Italy through Germany to Holland, by the route of Flanders, home—'twill scarce be ten posts out of my way;[4] but were it ten thousand! with what a moral delight will it crown my journey, in sharing in the sickening incidents

---

8. Lost the thread (of his mood).
9. Fellow (archaic).
1. Soothing medicine.
2. About fifty miles south of Nampont.

3. A note.
4. Because a post is about six miles, Yorick drastically underestimates the distance out of his way.

of a tale of misery told to me by such a sufferer! to see her weep! and though I cannot dry up the fountain of her tears, what an exquisite sensation is there still left, in wiping them away from off the cheeks of the first and fairest of women, as I'm sitting with my handkerchief in my hand in silence the whole night besides her?

There was nothing wrong in the sentiment; and yet I instantly reproached my heart with it in the bitterest and most reprobate of expressions.

It had ever, as I told the reader, been one of the singular blessings of my life, to be almost every hour of it miserably in love with some one; and my last flame happening to be blown out by a whiff of jealousy on the sudden turn of a corner, I had lighted it up afresh at the pure taper of Eliza but about three months before—swearing as I did it, that it should last me through the whole journey—Why should I dissemble the matter? I had sworn to her eternal fidelity—she had a right to my whole heart—to divide my affections was to lessen them—to expose them, was to risk them: where there is risk, there may be loss—and what wilt thou have, Yorick! to answer to a heart so full of trust and confidence—so good, so gentle, and unreproaching!

—I will not go to Brussels, replied I, interrupting myself—but my imagination went on—I recalled her looks at that crisis of our separation, when neither of us had power to say Adieu! I looked at the picture she had tied in a black ribband about my neck—and blushed as I looked at it—I would have given the world to have kissed it—but was ashamed—and shall this tender flower, said I, pressing it between my hands—shall it be smitten to its very root—and smitten, Yorick! by thee, who hast promised to shelter it in thy breast?

Eternal fountain of happiness! said I, kneeling down upon the ground— be thou my witness—and every pure spirit which tastes it, be my witness also, That I would not travel to Brussels, unless Eliza went along with me, did the road lead me towards heaven.

In transports of this kind, the heart, in spite of the understanding, will always say too much.

THE LETTER.

AMIENS.

Fortune had not smiled upon La Fleur; for he had been unsuccessful in his feats of chivalry—and not one thing had offered to signalize his zeal for my service from the time he had entered into it, which was almost four and twenty hours. The poor soul burned with impatience; and the Count de L***'s servant coming with the letter, being the first practicable occasion which offered, La Fleur had laid hold of it; and in order to do honor to his master, had taken him into a back parlor in the Auberge,[5] and treated him with a cup or two of the best wine in Picardy;[6] and the Count de L***'s servant, in return, and not to be behindhand in politeness with La Fleur, had taken him back with him to the Count's hotel. La Fleur's *prevenancy*[7] (for there was a passport in his very looks) soon set every servant in the kitchen at

5. Inn.
6. Region in which Amiens is located.

7. Courteous anticipation of others' desires.

ease with him; and as a Frenchman, whatever be his talents, has no sort of prudery in showing them, La Fleur, in less than five minutes, had pulled out his fife, and leading off the dance himself with the first note, set the *fille de chambre, the maitre d'hotel,* the cook, the scullion, and all the household, dogs and cats, besides an old monkey, a-dancing. I suppose there never was a merrier kitchen since the flood.[8]

Madame de L***, in passing from her brother's apartments to her own, hearing so much jollity below stairs, rung up her *fille de chambre* to ask about it; and hearing it was the English gentleman's servant who had set the whole house merry with his pipe, she ordered him up.

As the poor fellow could not present himself empty, he had loadened himself in going up-stairs with a thousand compliments to Madame de L***, on the part of his master—added a long apocrypha[9] of inquiries after Madame de L***'s health—told her, that Monsieur his master was *au desespoir*[1] for her re-establishment from the fatigues of her journey—and, to close all, that Monsieur had received the letter which Madame had done him the honor—And he has done me the honor, said Madame de L***, interrupting La Fleur, to send a billet in return.

Madame de L*** had said this with such a tone of reliance upon the fact, that La Fleur had not power to disappoint her expectations—he trembled for my honor—and possibly might not altogether be unconcerned for his own, as a man capable of being attached to a master who could be a-wanting *en egards vis a vis d'une femme;*[2] so that when Madame de L*** asked La Fleur if he had brought a letter—*O qu'oui,* said La Fleur; so laying down his hat upon the ground, and taking hold of the flap of his right side pocket with his left hand, he began to search for the letter with his right—then contrariwise—*Diable!*— then sought every pocket—pocket by pocket, round, not forgetting his fob— *Peste!*—then La Fleur emptied them upon the floor—pulled out a dirty cravat—a handkerchief—a comb—a whip lash—a night-cap—then gave a peep into his hat—*Quelle etourderie!*[3] He had left the letter upon the table in the Auberge—he would run for it, and be back with it in three minutes.

I had just finished my supper when La Fleur came in to give me an account of his adventure: he told the whole story simply as it was; and only added, that if Monsieur had forgot (*par hazard*)[4] to answer Madame's letter, the arrangement gave him an opportunity to recover the *faux pas*—and if not, that things were only as they were.

Now I was not altogether sure of my *etiquette* whether I ought to have wrote or no; but if I had—a devil himself could not have been angry: 'twas but the officious zeal of a well-meaning creature for my honor; and however he might have mistook the road—or embarrassed me in so doing—his heart was in no fault—I was under no necessity to write—and what weighed more than all—he did not look as if he had done amiss.

—'Tis all very well, La Fleur, said I.—'Twas sufficient. La Fleur flew out of the room like lightning, and returned with pen, ink, and paper, in his

---

8. Of Noah. *"Fille de chambre"*: chambermaid. *"Maître d'hôtel"*: butler. *"Scullion"*: kitchen maid.
9. Additional material that is not genuine. (La Fleur pretends Yorick inquired after the lady's health, when he did not.)

1. Disconsolate.
2. Lacking in his attentions to a woman.
3. How thoughtless (of me)!
4. By chance.

hand; and coming up to the table, laid them close before me, with such a delight in his countenance, that I could not help taking up the pen.

I begun and begun again; and though I had nothing to say, and that nothing might have been expressed in half a dozen lines, I made half a dozen different beginnings, and could no way please myself.

In short, I was in no mood to write.

La Fleur stepped out and brought a little water in a glass to dilute my ink— then fetched sand and seal-wax—It was all one; I wrote, and blotted, and tore off, and burnt, and wrote again—*Le Diable l'emporte,*[5] said I half to myself—I cannot write this selfsame letter, throwing the pen down despairingly as I said it.

As soon as I had cast down the pen, La Fleur advanced with the most respectful carriage up to the table, and making a thousand apologies for the liberty he was going to take, told me he had a letter in his pocket wrote by a drummer in his regiment to a corporal's wife, which, he durst say, would suit the occasion.

I had a mind to let the poor fellow have his humor—Then prithee, said I, let me see it.

La Fleur instantly pulled out a little dirty pocket-book crammed full of small letters and billet-doux[6] in a sad condition, and laying it upon the table, and then untying the string which held them all together, run them over one by one, till he came to the letter in question—*La voila,* said he, clapping his hands: so unfolding it first, he laid it before me, and retired three steps from the table whilst I read it.

THE LETTER.

Madame,

Je suis penetré de la douleur la plus vive, et reduit en même temps au desespoir par ce retour imprevû du Corporal qui rend notre entrevue de ce soir la chose du monde la plus impossible.

Mais vive la joie! et toute la mienne sera de penser a vous.

L'amour n'est *rien* sans sentiment.

Et le sentiment est encore *moins* sans amour.

On dit qu'on ne doit jamais se desesperer.

On dit aussi que Monsieur le Corporal monte la garde Mercredi; alors ce sera mon tour.

Chacun a son tour.

En attendant—Vive l'amour! et vive la bagatelle!

Je suis, Madame,

Avec toutes les sentiments les plus respecteux et les plus tendres tout a vous,

Jaques Roque[7]

---

5. The Devil take it!
6. Love letters.
7. Madam, I am penetrated with most keen sadness, and at the same time am reduced to despair at this unexpected return of the corporal, which makes our meeting tonight the most impossible thing in the world. Yet long live joy! And all my joy will be to think of you. Love is *nothing* without sentiment. And sentiment is still less without love. They say one should never despair. They also say that Mister Corporal is on guard-duty [literally, will "mount guard"] on Wednesday: then it will be my turn. *Everyone has his turn.* Meanwhile long live love! And trifles! I am, Madam, with all the most respectful and tender sentiments, entirely yours, Jaques Roque.

It was but changing the Corporal into the Count—and saying nothing about mounting guard on Wednesday—and the letter was neither right or wrong—so to gratify the poor fellow, who stood trembling, for my honor, his own, and the honor of his letter—I took the cream gently off it, and whipping it up in my own way—I sealed it up and sent him with it to Madame de L* * * and the next morning we pursued our journey to Paris.

PARIS.

When a man can contest the point by dint of equipage, and carry all on floundering before him with half a dozen lackeys and a couple of cooks—'tis very well in such a place as Paris—he may drive in at which end of a street he will.[8]

A poor prince who is weak in cavalry, and whose whole infantry does not exceed a single man, had best quit the field; and signalize himself in the cabinet,[9] if he can get up into it—I say *up into it*—for there is no descending perpendicular amongst 'em with a *"Me voici! mes enfans"*[1]—here I am—whatever many may think.

I own my first sensations, as soon as I was left solitary and alone in my own chamber in the hotel, were far from being so flattering as I had prefigured them. I walked up gravely to the window in my dusty black coat, and looking through the glass saw all the world in yellow, blue, and green, running at the ring of pleasure.—The old with broken lances, and in helmets which had lost their vizards[2]—the young in armor bright which shone like gold, beplumed with each gay feather of the east—all—all tilting at it like fascinated knights in tournaments of yore for fame and love.—

Alas, poor Yorick![3] cried I, what art thou doing here? On the very first onset of all this glittering clatter thou art reduced to an atom—seek—seek some winding alley, with a tourniquet the end of it, where chariot never rolled or flambeau[4] shot its rays—there thou mayest solace thy soul in converse sweet with some kind *grisset*[5] of a barber's wife, and get into such coteries!—

—May I perish! if I do, said I, pulling out the letter which I had to present to Madame de R***.—I'll wait upon this lady, the very first thing I do. So I called La Fleur to go seek me a barber directly—and come back and brush my coat.

THE WIG.

PARIS.

When the barber came, he absolutely refused to have anything to do with my wig: 'twas either above or below his art: I had nothing to do, but to take one ready made of his own recommendation.

—But I fear, friend! said I, this buckle won't stand.—You may immerge it, replied he, into the ocean, and it will stand—

---

8. Streets in Paris in the 18th century were extremely narrow.
9. The center of power as opposed the field of battle; also a private room.
1. Here I am! my children.
2. Visors. Yorick continues the military metaphor, seeing the streets of modern Paris as filled with chivalric knights and ladies from a romance.
3. See *Hamlet* 5.1.184. Sterne also uses the line in *Tristram Shandy* as he laments his character Yorick's death.
4. Torch. "Tourniquet": turnstile.
5. Shopgirl.

What a great scale is everything upon in this city! thought I—The utmost stretch of an English periwig-maker's ideas could have gone no further than to have "dipped it into a pail of water"—What difference! 'tis like time to eternity.

I confess I do hate all cold conceptions, as I do the puny ideas which engender them; and am generally so struck with the great works of nature, that for my own part, if I could help it, I never would make a comparison less than a mountain at least. All that can be said against the French sublime[6] in this instance of it, is this—that the grandeur is *more* in the *word*, and *less* in the *thing*. No doubt the ocean fills the mind with vast ideas; but Paris being so far inland, it was not likely I should run post a hundred miles out of it, to try the experiment—The Parisian barber meant nothing.—

The pail of water standing besides the great deep, makes certainly but a sorry figure in speech—but 'twill be said—it has one advantage—'tis in the next room, and the truth of the buckle may be tried in it, without more ado, in a single moment.

In honest truth, and upon a more candid revision of the matter, *the French expression professes more than it performs.*

I think I can see the precise and distinguishing marks of national characters more in these nonsensical *minutiæ*, than in the most important matters of state; where great men of all nations talk and stalk so much alike, that I would not give ninepence to choose amongst them.

I was so long in getting from under my barber's hands, that it was too late of thinking of going with my letter to Madame R*** that night: but when a man is once dressed at all points for going out, his reflections turn to little account; so taking down the name of the Hotel de Modene where I lodged, I walked forth without any determination where to go—I shall consider of that, said I, as I walk along.

THE PULSE.

PARIS.

Hail ye small sweet courtesies of life, for smooth do ye make the road of it! like grace and beauty which beget inclinations to love at first sight: 'tis ye who open this door and let the stranger in.

—Pray, Madame, said I, have the goodness to tell me which way I must turn to go to the Opera Comique:[7]—Most willingly, Monsieur, said she, laying aside her work—

I had given a cast with my eye into half a dozen shops as I came along in search of a face not likely to be disordered by such an interruption; till at last, this hitting my fancy, I had walked in.

She was working a pair of ruffles as she sat in a low chair on the far side of the shop facing the door—

—*Tres volentieres;* most willingly, said she, laying her work down upon a chair next her, and rising up from the low chair she was sitting in, with so cheerful a movement and so cheerful a look, that had I been laying out fifty louis d'ors with her, I should have said—"This woman is grateful."

---

6. The awe-inspiring in nature or art.   7. Paris theater presenting comic operas.

You must turn, Monsieur, said she, going with me to the door of the shop, and pointing the way down the street I was to take—you must turn first to your left hand—*mais prenez guarde*[8]—there are two turns; and be so good as to take the second—then go down a little way and you'll see a church, and when you are past it, give yourself the trouble to turn directly to the right, and that will lead you to the foot of the *Pont Neuf*,[9] which you must cross—and there any one will do himself the pleasure to show you—

She repeated her instructions three times over to me, with the same good-natured patience the third time as the first—and if *tones and manners* have a meaning, which certainly they have, unless to hearts which shut them out—she seemed really interested, that I should not lose myself.

I will not suppose it was the woman's beauty, notwithstanding she was the handsomest grisset, I think, I ever saw, which had much to do with the sense I had of her courtesy; only I remember, when I told her how much I was obliged to her, that I looked very full in her eyes,—and that I repeated my thanks as often as she had done her instructions.

I had not got ten paces from the door, before I found I had forgot every tittle of what she had said—so looking back, and seeing her still standing in the door of the shop as if to look whether I went right or not—I returned back, to ask her whether the first turn was to my right or left—for that I had absolutely forgot.—Is it possible? said she, half laughing.—'Tis very possible, replied I, when a man is thinking more of a woman, than of her good advice.

As this was the real truth—she took it, as every woman takes a matter of right, with a slight courtesy.[1]

—*Attendez!*[2] said she, laying her hand upon my arm to detain me, whilst she called a lad out of the back-shop to get ready a parcel of gloves. I am just going to send him, said she, with a packet into that quarter, and if you will have the complaisance to step in, it will be ready in a moment, and he shall attend you to the place.—So I walked in with her to the far side of the shop, and taking up the ruffle in my hand which she laid upon the chair, as if I had a mind to sit, she sat down herself in her low chair, and I instantly sat myself down besides her.

—He will be ready, Monsieur, said she, in a moment—And in that moment, replied I, most willingly would I say something very civil to you for all these courtesies. Any one may do a casual act of good nature, but a continuation of them shows it is a part of the temperature;[3] and certainly, added I, if it is the same blood which comes from the heart, which descends to the extremes (touching her wrist), I am sure you must have one of the best pulses of any woman in the world—Feel it, said she, holding out her arm. So laying down my hat, I took hold of her fingers in one hand, and applied the two forefingers of my other to the artery—

—Would to heaven! my dear Eugenius,[4] thou hadst passed by, and beheld me sitting in my black coat, and in my lack-a-day-sical manner, counting the throbs of it, one by one, with as much true devotion as if I had been watching the critical ebb or flow of her fever—How wouldst thou have laughed and

8. But take care.
9. New Bridge, the oldest standing bridge in Paris.
1. Curtsy.
2. Wait a moment!

3. Character, disposition.
4. Sterne's name in his fiction for his friend John Hall-Stevenson.

moralized upon my new profession—and thou shouldst have laughed and moralized on—Trust me, my dear Eugenius, I should have said, "there are worse occupations in this world *than feeling a woman's pulse.*"—But a Grisset's! thou wouldst have said—and in an open shop! Yorick—

—So much the better: for when my views are direct,[5] Eugenius, I care not if all the world saw me feel it.

THE HUSBAND.

PARIS.

I had counted twenty pulsations, and was going on fast towards the fortieth, when her husband coming unexpected from a back parlor into the shop, put me a little out of my reckoning—'Twas nobody but her husband, she said—so I began a fresh score—Monsieur is so good, quoth she, as he passed by us, as to give himself the trouble of feeling my pulse—The husband took off his hat, and making me a bow, said, I did him too much honor—and having said that, he put on his hat and walked out.

Good God! said I to myself, as he went out—and can this man be the husband of this woman!

Let it not torment the few who know what must have been the grounds of this exclamation, if I explain it to those who do not.

In London a shopkeeper and a shopkeeper's wife seem to be one bone and one flesh:[6] in the several endowments of mind and body, sometimes the one, sometimes the other has it, so as in general to be upon a par, and to tally with each other as nearly as man and wife need to do.

In Paris, there are scarce two orders of beings more different: for the legislative and executive powers of the shop not resting in the husband, he seldom comes there—in some dark and dismal room behind, he sits commerceless in his thrum nightcap,[7] the same rough son of Nature that Nature left him.

The genius of a people where nothing but the monarchy is *salique*,[8] having ceded this department, with sundry others, totally to the women—by a continual higgling[9] with customers of all ranks and sizes from morning to night, like so many rough pebbles shook long together in a bag, by amicable collisions, they have worn down their asperities and sharp angles, and not only become round and smooth, but will receive, some of them, a polish like a brilliant.[1]—Monsieur *le Mari*[2] is little better than the stone under your foot—

—Surely—surely, man! it is not good for thee to sit alone[3]—thou wast made for social intercourse and gentle greetings, and this improvement of our natures from it, I appeal to, as my evidence.

—And how does it beat, Monsieur? said she.—With all the benignity, said I, looking quietly in her eyes, that I expected—She was going to say something civil in return—but the lad came into the shop with the gloves—A *propos*, said I; I want a couple of pair myself.

5. Straightforward, true.
6. See Genesis 2.23–24.
7. Cap made of waste thread and yarn.
8. Referring to a law that excludes women from ascending the throne, as in France (unlike

Britain).
9. Haggling.
1. Finely cut diamond.
2. Mr. Husband.
3. See Genesis 2.18.

THE GLOVES.

PARIS.

The beautiful Grisset rose up when I said this, and going behind the counter, reached down a parcel and untied it: I advanced to the side over-against her: they were all too large. The beautiful Grisset measured them one by one across my hand—It would not alter the dimensions—She begged I would try a single pair, which seemed to be the least—She held it open—my hand slipped into it at once—It will not do, said I, shaking my head a little—No, said she, doing the same thing.

There are certain combined looks of simple subtlety—where whim, and sense, and seriousness, and nonsense, are so blended, that all the languages of Babel set loose together could not express them—they are communicated and caught so instantaneously, that you can scarce say which party is the infecter. I leave it to your men of words to swell pages about it—it is enough in the present to say again, the gloves would not do; so folding our hands within our arms, we both lolled upon the counter—it was narrow, and there was just room for the parcel to lay between us.

The beautiful Grisset looked sometimes at the gloves, then sideways to the window, then at the gloves—and then at me. I was not disposed to break silence—I followed her example: so I looked at the gloves, then to the window, then at the gloves, and then at her—and so on alternately.

I found I lost considerably in every attack—she had a quick black eye, and shot through two such long and silken eye-lashes with such penetration, that she looked into my very heart and reins[4]—It may seem strange, but I could actually feel she did—

—It is no matter, said I, taking up a couple of the pairs next me, and putting them into my pocket.

I was sensible the beautiful Grisset had not asked above a single livre above the price—I wished she had asked a livre more, and was puzzling my brains how to bring the matter about—Do you think, my dear Sir, said she, mistaking my embarrassment, that I could ask a *sous* too much of a stranger—and of a stranger whose politeness, more than his want of gloves, has done me the honor to lay himself at my mercy?—*M'en croyez capable?*[5]—Faith! not I, said I; and if you were, you are welcome—So counting the money into her hand, and with a lower bow than one generally makes to a shopkeeper's wife, I went out, and her lad with his parcel followed me.

THE TRANSLATION.

PARIS.

There was nobody in the box I was let into but a kindly old French officer. I love the character, not only because I honor the man whose manners are softened by a profession which makes bad men worse; but that I once knew one—for he is no more—and why should I not rescue one page from viola-

---

4. Literally kidneys, a biblical term referring to the seat of affections.
5. Do you think me capable of that?

tion by writing his name in it, and telling the world it was Captain Tobias Shandy, the dearest of my flock and friends, whose philanthropy I never think of at this long distance from his death[6]—but my eyes gush out with tears. For his sake, I have a predilection for the whole corps of veterans; and so I strode over the two back rows of benches, and placed myself beside him.

The old officer was reading attentively a small pamphlet, it might be the book of the opera, with a large pair of spectacles. As soon as I sat down, he took his spectacles off, and putting them into a shagreen[7] case, returned them and the book into his pocket together. I half rose up, and made him a bow.

Translate this into any civilized language in the world—the sense is this:

"Here's a poor stranger come into the box—he seems as if he knew nobody; and is never likely, was he to be seven years in Paris, if every man he comes near keeps his spectacles upon his nose—'tis shutting the door of conversation absolutely in his face—and using him worse than a German."

The French officer might as well have said it all aloud: and if he had, I should in course have put the bow I made him into French too, and told him, "I was sensible of his attention, and returned him a thousand thanks for it."

There is not a secret so aiding to the progress of sociality, as to get master of this *shorthand*, and be quick in rendering the several turns of looks and limbs, with all their inflections and delineations, into plain words. For my own part, by long habitude, I do it so mechanically, that when I walk the streets of London, I go translating all the way; and have more than once stood behind in the circle,[8] where not three words have been said, and have brought off twenty different dialogues with me, which I could have fairly wrote down and sworn to.

I was going one evening to Martini's concert[9] at Milan, and was just entering the door of the hall, when the Marquesina di F***[1] was coming out in a sort of a hurry—she was almost upon me before I saw her; so I gave a spring to one side to let her pass—She had done the same, and on the same side too; so we ran our heads together: she instantly got to the other side to get out: I was just as unfortunate as she had been; for I had sprung to that side, and opposed her passage again—We both flew together to the other side, and then back—and so on—it was ridiculous; we both blushed intolerably; so I did at last the thing I should have done at first—I stood stock still, and the Marquesina had no more difficulty. I had no power to go into the room, till I had made her so much reparation as to wait and follow her with my eye to the end of the passage—She looked back twice, and walked along it rather sideways, as if she would make room for any one coming up stairs to pass her—No, said I—that's a vile translation: the Marquesina has a right to the best apology I can make her; and that opening is left for me to do it in—so I ran and begged pardon for the embarrassment I had given her, saying it was my intention to have made her way. She answered, she was guided by the same intention towards me—so we reciprocally thanked each other. She was at the top of the

6. Uncle Toby is a principal character in Sterne's *Tristram Shandy* (he is never called Tobias). It is confusing that Yorick himself is said in *Tristram* to have died around 1748, but the action of *A Sentimental Journey* takes place in 1762. We have no date of Uncle Toby's death.
7. A kind of rough, untanned leather.

8. A group of people conversing.
9. Perhaps a concert by Giovanni Battista Martini (1706–1784), Italian composer, musician, music teacher, and Franciscan friar.
1. Not definitively identified. The Italian title would be *Marchesa* (Marchioness).

stairs; and seeing no *chicheshee*[2] near her, I begged to hand her to her coach— so we went down the stairs, stopping at every third step to talk of the concert and the adventure—Upon my word, Madame, said I, when I had handed her in, I made six different efforts to let you go out—And I made six efforts, replied she, to let you enter—I wish to heaven you would make a seventh, said I—With all my heart, said she, making room—Life is too short to be long about the forms of it—so I instantly stepped in, and she carried me home with her— And what became of the concert, St. Cecilia,[3] who, I suppose, was at it, knows more than I.

I will only add, that the connection which arose out of that translation, gave me more pleasure than any one I had the honor to make in Italy.

THE DWARF.

PARIS.

I had never heard the remark made by any one in my life, except by one; and who that was will probably come out in this chapter;[4] so that being pretty much unprepossessed, there must have been grounds for what struck me the moment I cast my eyes over the *parterre*[5]—and that was the unaccountable sport of nature in forming such numbers of dwarfs—No doubt she sports at certain times in almost every corner of the world; but in Paris, there is no end to her amusements—The goddess seems almost as merry as she is wise.

As I carried my idea out of the *opera comique* with me, I measured everybody I saw walking in the streets by it—Melancholy application! especially where the size was extremely little—the face extremely dark—the eyes quick—the nose long—the teeth white—the jaw prominent—to see so many miserables, by force of accidents driven out of their own proper class into the very verge of another, which it gives me pain to write down—every third man a pygmy!—some by rickety heads and hump backs—others by bandy legs—a third set arrested by the hand of Nature in the sixth and seventh years of their growth—a fourth, in their perfect and natural state like dwarf apple-trees; from the first rudiments and stamina[6] of their existence, never meant to grow higher.

A medical traveler might say, 'tis owing to undue bandages[7]—a splenetic one, to want of air—and an inquisitive traveler, to fortify the system, may measure the height of their houses—the narrowness of their streets, and in how few feet square in the sixth and seventh stories such numbers of the *Bourgeoisie* eat and sleep together; but I remember, Mr. Shandy the elder, who accounted for nothing like anybody else, in speaking one evening of these matters, averred, that children, like other animals, might be increased almost to any size, provided they came right into the world;[8] but the misery was, the citizens of Paris were so cooped up, that they had not actually room

2. I.e., a chichesbeo; in Italian society an escort of a married woman, sometimes also her lover.
3. Patron saint of music and musicians.
4. Smollett remarks on the number of dwarves in France and Italy in his *Travels*.
5. Ground floor of the theater behind the orchestra.
6. Original nature, constitution.

7. Smollett in his *Travels* had identified the swaddling of infants (in "bandages") in France and Italy as the cause of dwarfism.
8. Walter Shandy, Tristram's father, a principal character in *Tristram Shandy*. His theories of the developmental effects of various circumstances at an infant's birth are one of the novel's major themes.

enough to get[9] them—I do not call it getting anything, said he—'tis getting nothing—Nay, continued he, rising in his argument, 'tis getting worse than nothing, when all you have got, after twenty or five and twenty years of the tenderest care and most nutritious aliment[1] bestowed upon it, shall not at last be as high as my leg. Now, Mr. Shandy being very short, there could be nothing more said of it.

As this is not a work of reasoning, I leave the solution as I found it, and content myself with the truth only of the remark which is verified in every lane and by-lane of Paris. I was walking down that which leads from the Carousal to the Palais Royal,[2] and observing a little boy in some distress at the side of the gutter, which ran down the middle of it, I took hold of his hand, and helped him over. Upon turning up his face to look at him after, I perceived he was about forty—Never mind, said I; some good body will do as much for me, when I am ninety.

I feel some little principles within me, which incline me to be merciful towards this poor blighted part of my species, who have neither size or strength to get on in the world—I cannot bear to see one of them trod upon; and had scarce got seated beside my old French officer,[3] ere the disgust was exercised, by seeing the very thing happen under the box we sat in.

At the end of the orchestra and betwixt that and the first side-box there is a small esplanade[4] left, where, when the house is full, numbers of all ranks take sanctuary. Though you stand, as in the parterre, you pay the same price as in the orchestra. A poor defenseless being of this order had got thrust, somehow or other, into this luckless place—the night was hot, and he was surrounded by beings two feet and a half higher than himself. The dwarf suffered inexpressibly on all sides; but the thing which incommoded him most, was a tall corpulent German, near seven feet high, who stood directly betwixt him and all possibility of his seeing either the stage or the actors. The poor dwarf did all he could to get a peep at what was going forwards by seeking for some little opening betwixt the German's arm and his body, trying first one side, then the other; but the German stood square in the most unaccommodating posture that can be imagined—the dwarf might as well have been placed at the bottom of the deepest draw-well in Paris; so he civilly reached up his hand to the German's sleeve, and told him his distress—The German turned his head back, looked down upon him as Goliath did upon David—and unfeelingly resumed his posture.

I was just then taking a pinch of snuff out of my monk's little horn box—And how would thy meek and courteous spirit, my dear monk! so tempered to *bear and forbear!*—how sweetly would it have lent an ear to this poor soul's complaint!

The old French officer, seeing me lift up my eyes with an emotion, as I made the apostrophe, took the liberty to ask me what was the matter—I told him the story in three words, and added, how inhuman it was.

By this time the dwarf was driven to extremes, and in his first transports, which are generally unreasonable, had told the German he would cut off

9. Beget.
1. Sustenance.
2. The royal palace. "Carousal": the inner court of the Tuileries gardens.

3. An awkwardness by Sterne: Yorick had described leaving the theater but picks up the story back inside.
4. Open space.

his long queue[5] with his knife—The German looked back coolly, and told him he was welcome, if he could reach it.

An injury sharpened by an insult, be it to who it will, makes every man of sentiment a party:[6] I could have leaped out of the box to have redressed it.—The old French officer did it with much less confusion; for leaning a little over, and nodding to a centinel,[7] and pointing at the same time with his finger to the distress—the centinel made his way up to it.—There was no occasion to tell the grievance—the thing told itself; so thrusting back the German instantly with his musket—he took the poor dwarf by the hand, and placed him before him.—This is noble! said I, clapping my hands together—And yet you would not permit this, said the old officer, in England.

—In England, dear Sir, said I, *we sit all at our ease*.[8]

The old French officer would have set me at unity with myself, in case I had been at variance,—by saying it was a *bon mot*[9]—and as a *bon mot* is always worth something at Paris, he offered me a pinch of snuff.

THE ROSE.

PARIS.

It was now my turn to ask the old French officer, "what was the matter?" for a cry of *"Haussez les mains, Monsieur l'Abbe,"*[1] re-echoed from a dozen different parts of the parterre, was as unintelligible to me, as my apostrophe to the monk had been to him.

He told me, it was some poor Abbe in one of the upper loges, who he supposed had got planted perdu[2] behind a couple of grissets, in order to see the opera, and that the parterre espying him were insisting upon his holding up both his hands during the representation.—And can it be supposed, said I, that an ecclesiastic would pick the Grisset's pockets? The old French officer smiled, and whispering in my ear, opened a door of knowledge which I had no idea of—

Good God! said I, turning pale with astonishment—is it possible, that a people so smit with sentiment should at the same time be so unclean, and so unlike themselves—*Quelle grossierte!*[3] added I.

The French officer told me it was an illiberal sarcasm at the church, which had begun in the theater about the time the *Tartuffe* was given in it, by Molière[4]—but, like other remains of Gothic[5] manners, was declining—Every nation, continued he, have their refinements and *grossiertes*, in which they take the lead, and lose it of one another by turns—that he had been in most countries, but never in one where he found not some delicacies, which others seemed to want. *Le POUR et le CONTRE se trovent en chaque nation;*[6] there is a balance, said he, of good and bad everywhere; and nothing but the knowing it is so, can emancipate one half of the world from the prepossessions which it holds against the other—that the advantage of travel, as it regarded the

---

5. Pigtail.
6. Take sides (with the person injured).
7. Armed guard stationed to prevent disturbances in theaters.
8. Seats were installed in all parts of London theaters in the 17th century.
9. Witty remark.

1. Put your hands up, Mr. Priest.
2. In a dangerous position.
3. What coarseness!
4. See p. 877, n. 5.
5. Barbaric.
6. Roughly translated by the next sentence.

sçavoir vivre,[7] was by seeing a great deal both of men and manners; it taught us mutual toleration; and mutual toleration, concluded he, making me a bow, taught us mutual love.

The old French officer delivered this with an air of such candor and good sense, as coincided with my first favorable impressions of his character—I thought I loved the man; but I fear I mistook the object—'twas my own way of thinking—the difference was, I could not have expressed it half so well.

It is alike troublesome to both the rider and his beast—if the latter goes pricking up his ears, and starting all the way at every object which he never saw before—I have as little torment of this kind as any creature alive; and yet I honestly confess, that many a thing gave me pain, and that I blushed at many a word the first month—which I found inconsequent and perfectly innocent the second.

Madame de Rambouliet,[8] after an acquaintance of about six weeks with her, had done me the honor to take me in her coach about two leagues out of town—Of all women, Madame de Rambouliet is the most correct; and I never wish to see one of more virtues and purity of heart—In our return back, Madame de Rambouliet desired me to pull the cord—I asked her if she wanted anything—*Rien que pisser*,[9] said Madame de Rambouliet.

Grieve not, gentle traveler, to let Madame de Rambouliet p—ss on—And, ye fair mystic nymphs! go each one *pluck your rose*,[1] and scatter them in your path—for Madame de Rambouliet did no more—I handed Madame de Rambouliet out of the coach; and had I been the priest of the chaste CASTALIA,[2] I could not have served at her fountain with a more respectful decorum.

END OF VOL. I.

THE FILLE DE CHAMBRE.

PARIS.

What the old French officer had delivered upon traveling, bringing Polonius's advice to his son upon the same subject into my head[1]—and that bringing in *Hamlet*; and *Hamlet* the rest of Shakespeare's works, I stopped at the Quai de Conti in my return home, to purchase the whole set.

The bookseller said he had not a set in the world.—*Comment!*[2] said I; taking one up out of a set which lay upon the counter betwixt us.—He said they were sent him only to be got bound, and were to be sent back to Versailles in the morning to the Count de B****.[3]

—And does the Count de B****, said I, read Shakespeare? *C'est un Esprit fort*,[4] replied the bookseller.—He loves English books; and what is more to his honor, Monsieur, he loves the English too. You speak this so civilly, said

---

7. Knowing of how to live.
8. Another probably fictional name, perhaps an anachronistic reference to Catherine de Vivonne, Marquise de Rambouillet (1588–1665), who ran a fashionable salon and was satirized in the comedy *Les Précieuses ridicules* (1659) by Molière.
9. Nothing but to urinate. "Pull the cord": to signal the driver to stop.
1. Go to the toilet.
2. Nymph who escaped pursuit by Apollo by throwing herself into a spring on Mount Parnassus.

1. See *Hamlet* 1.3.55–81, in which Polonius offers his son, Laertes, advice about how to comport himself while traveling.
2. What?
3. Variously identified as Claude de Thiard, Comte de Bissy (1721–1810) and Jacques Célestin du Merdy de Catuélan (1733–ca. 1790), both translators of English works into French. Versailles is the site of the French royal court.
4. He's a man of strong intellect.

I, that it is enough to oblige an Englishman to lay out a Louis d'or or two at your shop—The bookseller made a bow, and was going to say something, when a young decent girl of about twenty, who by her air and dress seemed to be *fille de chambre* to some devout woman of fashion, came into the shop and asked for *Les Egarements du Cœur & de l'Esprit:*[5] the bookseller gave her the book directly; she pulled out a little green satin purse, run round with a ribband of the same color, and putting her finger and thumb into it, she took out the money and paid for it. As I had nothing more to stay me in the shop, we both walked out of the door together.

—And what have you to do, my dear, said I, with *The Wanderings of the Heart,* who scarce know yet you have one; nor, till love has first told you it, or some faithless shepherd has made it ache, canst thou ever be sure it is so.—*Le Dieu m'en guard!*[6] said the girl.—With reason, said I—for if it is a good one, 'tis pity it should be stolen; 'tis a little treasure to thee, and gives a better air to your face, than if it was dressed out with pearls.

The young girl listened with a submissive attention, holding her satin purse by its ribband in her hand all the time—'Tis a very small one, said I, taking hold of the bottom of it—she held it towards me—and there is very little in it, my dear, said I; but be but as good as thou art handsome, and heaven will fill it: I had a parcel of crowns in my hand to pay for Shakespeare; and as she had let go the purse entirely, I put a single one in; and tying up the ribband in a bow-knot, returned it to her.

The young girl made me more a humble courtesy than a low one—'twas one of those quiet, thankful sinkings, where the spirit bows itself down—the body does no more than tell it. I never gave a girl a crown in my life which gave me half the pleasure.

My advice, my dear, would not have been worth a pin to you, said I, if I had not given this along with it: but now, when you see the crown, you'll remember it—so don't, my dear, lay it out in ribbands.

Upon my word, Sir, said the girl, earnestly, I am incapable—in saying which, as is usual in little bargains of honor, she gave me her hand—*En verite, Monsieur, je mettrai cet argent apart,*[7] said she.

When a virtuous convention is made betwixt man and woman, it sanctifies their most private walks; so notwithstanding it was dusky, yet as both our roads lay the same way, we made no scruple of walking along the Quai de Conti together.

She made me a second courtesy in setting off, and before we got twenty yards from the door, as if she had not done enough before, she made a sort of a little stop to tell me again—she thanked me.

It was a small tribute, I told her, which I could not avoid paying to virtue, and would not be mistaken in the person I had been rendering it to for the world—but I see innocence, my dear, in your face—and foul befall the man who ever lays a snare in its way!

The girl seemed affected some way or other with what I said—she gave a low sigh—I found I was not empowered to inquire at all after it—so said nothing more till I got to the corner of the Rue de Nevers, where we were to part.

5. *The Wanderings of the Heart and Spirit* (1736–38), French novel by Claude-Prosper Jolyot de Crébillon (1707–1777), called Crébillon *fils* (i.e., the son; his father was also a writer.)
6. May God protect me!
7. And truly, sir, I will set this coin apart.

—But is this the way, my dear, said I, to the Hotel de Modene? she told me it was—or, that I might go by the Rue de Guineygaude, which was the next turn.— Then I'll go, my dear, by the Rue de Guineygaude, said I, for two reasons; first I shall please myself, and next I shall give you the protection of my company as far on your way as I can. The girl was sensible I was civil—and said, she wished the Hotel de Modene was in the Rue de St. Pierre—You live there? said I.— She told me she was *fille de chambre* to Madame R****—Good God! said I, 'tis the very lady for whom I have brought a letter from Amiens—The girl told me that Madame R****, she believed, expected a stranger with a letter, and was impatient to see him—so I desired the girl to present my compliments to Madame R****, and say I would certainly wait upon her in the morning.

We stood still at the corner of the Rue de Nevers whilst this passed—We then stopped a moment whilst she disposed of her *Egarements du Cœur*, &c. more commodiously than carrying them in her hand—they were two volumes; so I held the second for her whilst she put the first into her pocket; and then she held her pocket, and I put in the other after it.

'Tis sweet to feel by what fine-spun threads our affections are drawn together.

We set off afresh, and as she took her third step, the girl put her hand within my arm—I was just bidding her—but she did it of herself with that undeliberating simplicity, which showed it was out of her head that she had never seen me before. For my own part, I felt the conviction of consanguinity[8] so strongly, that I could not help turning half round to look in her face, and see if I could trace out anything in it of a family likeness—Tut! said I, are we not all relations?

When we arrived at the turning up of the Rue de Guineygaude, I stopped to bid her adieu for good and all: the girl would thank me again for my company and kindness—She bid me adieu twice—I repeated it as often; and so cordial was the parting between us, that had it happened anywhere else, I'm not sure but I should have signed it with a kiss of charity, as warm and holy as an apostle.

But in Paris, as none kiss each other but the men—I did, what amounted to the same thing—

—I bid God bless her.

THE PASSPORT.

PARIS.

When I got home to my hotel, La Fleur told me I had been inquired after by the Lieutenant de Police—The deuce take it! said I—I know the reason. It is time the reader should know it, for in the order of things in which it happened, it was omitted; not that it was out of my head; but that, had I told it then, it might have been forgot now—and now is the time I want it.

I had left London with so much precipitation, that it never entered my mind that we were at war with France;[9] and had reached Dover, and looked through my glass at the hills beyond Boulogne, before the idea presented itself; and with this in its train, that there was no getting there without a

8. Of being related to her by blood.
9. The action of the novel takes place in 1762, during the Seven Years' War (1756–63) between France and Britain.

passport. Go but to the end of a street, I have a mortal aversion for returning back no wiser than I set out; and as this was one of the greatest efforts I had ever made for knowledge, I could less bear the thoughts of it; so hearing the Count de **** had hired the packet, I begged he would take me in his *suite*.[1] The Count had some little knowledge of me, so made little or no difficulty— only said, his inclination to serve me could reach no further than Calais, as he was to return by way of Brussels to Paris; however, when I had once passed there, I might get to Paris without interruption; but that in Paris I must make friends and shift[2] for myself.—Let me get to Paris, Monsieur le Count, said I—and I shall do very well. So I embarked, and never thought more of the matter.

When La Fleur told me the Lieutenant de Police had been inquiring after me—the thing instantly recurred—and by the time La Fleur had well told me, the master of the hotel came into my room to tell me the same thing, with this addition to it, that my passport had been particularly asked after: the master of the hotel concluded with saying, He hoped I had one.—Not I, faith! said I.

The master of the hotel retired three steps from me, as from an infected person, as I declared this—and poor La Fleur advanced three steps towards me, and with that sort of movement which a good soul makes to succor a distressed one—the fellow won my heart by it; and from that single *trait*, I knew his character as perfectly, and could rely upon it as firmly, as if he had served me with fidelity for seven years.

Mon seignior! cried the master of the hotel—but recollecting himself as he made the exclamation, he instantly changed the tone of it—If Monsieur, said he, has not a passport (*apparament*)[3] in all likelihood he has friends in Paris who can procure him one.—Not that I know of, quoth I, with an air of indifference.—Then, *certes*, replied he, you'll be sent to the Bastille or the Chatelet, *au moins*.[4] Poo! said I, the king of France is a good-natured soul—he'll hurt nobody.—*Cela n'empeche pas*,[5] said he—you will certainly be sent to the Bastille tomorrow morning.—But I've taken your lodgings for a month, answered I, and I'll not quit them a day before the time for all the kings of France in the world. La Fleur whispered in my ear, that nobody could oppose the king of France.

Pardi![6] said my host, *ces Messieurs Anglois sont des gens tres extraordinaires*[7]—and having both said and sworn it—he went out.

THE PASSPORT.

THE HOTEL AT PARIS.

I could not find in my heart to torture La Fleur's with a serious look upon the subject of my embarrassment, which was the reason I had treated it so cavalierly; and to show him how light it lay upon my mind, I dropt the subject entirely; and whilst he waited upon me at supper, talked to him

1. Party, retinue.
2. Fend, make do.
3. Apparently.
4. At least. The Bastille was a prison for state criminals in Paris. The Châtelet was a fortified bridge tower, also used as a prison. "Certes":

certainly.
5. But that doesn't matter.
6. Of course, certainly.
7. English gentlemen are very extraordinary people.

with more than usual gaiety about Paris, and of the opera comique.—La Fleur had been there himself, and had followed me through the streets as far as the bookseller's shop; but seeing me come out with the young *fille de chambre*, and that we walked down the Quai de Conti together, La Fleur deemed it unnecessary to follow me a step further—so making his own reflections upon it, he took a shorter cut—and got to the hotel in time to be informed of the affair of the police against my arrival.

As soon as the honest creature had taken away, and gone down to sup himself, I then began to think a little seriously about my situation.—

—And here, I know, Eugenius, thou wilt smile at the remembrance of a short dialogue which passed betwixt us the moment I was going to set out—I must tell it here.

Eugenius, knowing that I was as little subject to be overburdened with money as thought, had drawn me aside to interrogate me how much I had taken care for; upon telling him the exact sum, Eugenius shook his head, and said it would not do; so pulled out his purse in order to empty it into mine.—I've enough in conscience, Eugenius, said I.—Indeed, Yorick, you have not, replied Eugenius—I know France and Italy better than you.—But you don't consider, Eugenius, said I, refusing his offer, that before I have been three days in Paris, I shall take care to say or do something or other for which I shall get clapped up into the Bastille, and that I shall live there a couple of months entirely at the king of France's expense.—I beg pardon, said Eugenius, dryly: really, I had forgot that resource.

Now the event I treated gaily came seriously to my door.

Is it folly, or nonchalance, or philosophy, or pertinacity—or what is it in me, that, after all, when La Fleur had gone down stairs, and I was quite alone, I could not bring down my mind to think of it otherwise than I had then spoken of it to Eugenius?

—And as for the Bastille! the terror is in the word—Make the most of it you can, said I to myself, the Bastille is but another word for a tower—and a tower is but another word for a house you can't get out of—Mercy on the gouty! for they are in it twice a year—but with nine livres a day, and pen and ink and paper and patience, albeit a man can't get out, he may do very well within—at least for a month or six weeks; at the end of which, if he is a harmless fellow, his innocence appears, and he comes out a better and wiser man than he went in.

I had some occasion (I forget what) to step into the courtyard, as I settled this account; and remember I walked downstairs in no small triumph with the conceit of my reasoning—Beshrew[8] the *somber* pencil! said I vauntingly— for I envy not its powers, which paints the evils of life with so hard and deadly a coloring. The mind sits terrified at the objects she has magnified herself, and blackened: reduce them to their proper size and hue, she over-looks them—'Tis true said I, correcting the proposition—the Bastille is not an evil to be despised—but strip it of its towers—fill up the fossè[9]— unbarricade the doors—call it simply a confinement, and suppose 'tis some tyrant of a distemper—and not of a man, which holds you in it—the evil vanishes, and you bear the other half without complaint.

8. Curse.
9. A ditch fronting a fortification for defensive purposes.

I was interrupted in the heyday of this soliloquy, with a voice which I took to be of a child, which complained "it could not get out."—I looked up and down the passage, and seeing neither man, woman, or child, I went out without further attention.

In my return back through the passage, I heard the same words repeated twice over; and looking up, I saw it was a starling hung in a little cage.—"I can't get out—I can't get out," said the starling.[1]

I stood looking at the bird: and to every person who came through the passage it ran fluttering to the side towards which they approached it, with the same lamentation of its captivity—"I can't get out," said the starling— God help thee! said I, but I'll let thee out, cost what it will; so I turned about the cage to get to the door; it was twisted and double twisted so fast with wire, there was no getting it open without pulling the cage to pieces—I took both hands to it.

The bird flew to the place where I was attempting his deliverance, and thrusting his head through the trellis,[2] pressed his breast against it, as if impatient—I fear, poor creature! said I, I cannot set thee at liberty—"No," said the starling—"I can't get out—I can't get out," said the starling.

I vow, I never had my affections more tenderly awakened; or do I remember an incident in my life, where the dissipated spirits, to which my reason had been a bubble, were so suddenly called home.[3] Mechanical as the notes were, yet so true in tune to nature were they chanted, that in one moment they overthrew all my systematic reasonings upon the Bastille; and I heavily walked upstairs, unsaying every word I had said in going down them.

Disguise thyself as thou wilt, still, slavery! said I—still thou art a bitter draught! and though thousands in all ages have been made to drink of thee, thou art no less bitter on that account.—'tis thou, thrice sweet and gracious goddess, addressing myself to LIBERTY, whom all in public or in private worship, whose taste is grateful, and ever wilt be so, till NATURE herself shall change—no *tint* of words can spot thy snowy mantle, or chymic[4] power turn thy scepter into iron—with thee to smile upon him as he eats his crust, the swain is happier than his monarch, from whose court thou art exiled— Gracious heaven! cried I, kneeling down upon the last step but one in my ascent, grant me but health, thou great Bestower of it, and give me but this fair goddess as my companion—and shower down thy miters, if it seems good unto thy divine providence, upon those heads which are aching for them.[5]

THE CAPTIVE.

PARIS.

The bird in his cage pursued me into my room; I sat down close to my table, and leaning my head upon my hand, I began to figure[6] to myself the miseries of confinement. I was in a right frame for it, and so I gave full scope to my imagination.

1. Like parrots, European starlings can imitate a variety of sounds, including human speech.
2. Lattice or grate, part of the cage.
3. Made natural and reasonable again. "A bubble": a dupe.
4. Chemical.

5. A miter, the ceremonial headwear of a bishop, signifies the peak of worldly success in Yorick's profession, the church, which he does not desire or ache for, as long as he has liberty.
6. Imagine.

I was going to begin with the millions of my fellow creatures, born to no inheritance but slavery:[7] but finding, however affecting the picture was, that I could not bring it near me, and that the multitude of sad groups in it did but distract me.—

—I took a single captive, and having first shut him up in his dungeon, I then looked through the twilight of his grated door to take his picture.

I beheld his body half wasted away with long expectation and confinement, and felt what kind of sickness of the heart it was which arises from hope deferred. Upon looking nearer I saw him pale and feverish: in thirty years the western breeze had not once fanned his blood—he had seen no sun, no moon, in all that time—nor had the voice of friend or kinsman breathed through his lattice—his children—

—But here my heart began to bleed—and I was forced to go on with another part of the portrait.

He was sitting upon the ground upon a little straw, in the furthest corner of his dungeon, which was alternately his chair and bed: a little calendar of small sticks were laid at the head, notched all over with the dismal days and nights he had passed there—he had one of these little sticks in his hand, and with a rusty nail he was etching another day of misery to add to the heap. As I darkened the little light he had, he lifted up a hopeless eye towards the door, then cast it down—shook his head, and went on with his work of affliction. I heard his chains upon his legs, as he turned his body to lay his little stick upon the bundle—He gave a deep sigh—I saw the iron enter into his soul[8]—I burst into tears—I could not sustain the picture of confinement which my fancy had drawn—I started up from my chair, and calling La Fleur—I bid him bespeak[9] me a *remise,* and have it ready at the door of the hotel by nine in the morning.

—I'll go directly, said I, myself to Monsieur le Duc de Choiseul.[1]

La Fleur would have put me to bed; but not willing he should see anything upon my cheek which would cost the honest fellow a heartache—I told him I would go to bed by myself—and bid him go do the same.

THE STARLING.

ROAD TO VERSAILLES.

I got into my *remise* the hour I proposed: La Fleur got up behind, and I bid the coachman make the best of his way to Versailles.

As there was nothing in this road, or rather nothing which I look for in traveling, I cannot fill up the blank better than with a short history of this selfsame bird, which became the subject of the last chapter.

Whilst the Honorable Mr.**** was waiting for a wind at Dover, it had been caught upon the cliffs before it could well fly, by an English lad who was his groom; who not caring to destroy it, had taken it in his breast into the packet—and by course of feeding it, and taking it once under his protection, in a day or two grew fond of it, and got it safe along with him to Paris.

7. Sterne corresponded with a former slave, Ignatius Sancho, who urged him to address the evil of slavery in his works. For this correspondence, see the NAEL Archive.
8. The Anglican Book of Common Prayer translates Psalms 105.18, describing Joseph's captivity, as "the iron entered into his soul."
9. Call for, order.
1. French secretary of state, minister of war, and minister of the navy.

At Paris the lad had laid out a livre in a little cage for the starling, and as he had little to do better the five months his master stayed there, he taught it in his mother's tongue the four simple words—(and no more)—to which I owned myself so much its debtor.

Upon his master's going on for Italy—the lad had given it to the master of the hotel—But his little song for liberty being in an *unknown* language at Paris—the bird had little or no store set by him—so La Fleur bought both him and his cage for me for a bottle of Burgundy.

In my return from Italy I brought him with me to the country in whose language he had learned his notes—and telling the story of him to Lord A—Lord A begged the bird of me—in a week Lord A gave him to Lord B—Lord B made a present of him to Lord C—and Lord C's gentleman sold him to Lord D's for a shilling—Lord D gave him to Lord E—and so on—half round the alphabet— From that rank he passed into the lower house,[2] and passed the hands of as many commoners—But as all these wanted to *get in*[3]—and my bird wanted to *get out*—he had almost as little store set by him in London as in Paris.

It is impossible but many of my readers must have heard of him; and if any by mere chance have ever seen him—I beg leave to inform them, that that bird was my bird—or some vile copy set up to represent him.

I have nothing further to add upon him, but that from that time to this, I have borne this poor starling as the crest to my arms.—Thus:

—And let the heralds' officers[4] twist his neck about if they dare.

THE ADDRESS.

VERSAILLES.

I should not like to have my enemy take a view of my mind when I am going to ask protection of any man: for which reason I generally endeavor to protect myself; but this going to Monsieur le Duc de C**** was an act of compulsion—had it been an act of choice, I should have done it, I suppose, like other people.

How many mean plans of dirty address, as I went along, did my servile heart form! I deserved the Bastille for every one of them.

2. The lower house of Parliament, the House of Commons. I.e., he went from being owned by lords to being owned by commoners.

3. Into Parliament, or fashionable society.
4. Officials who determine the legitimacy of families' coats of arms.

Then nothing would serve me, when I got within sight of Versailles, but putting words and sentences together, and conceiving attitudes and tones to wreathe myself into Monsieur le Duc de C****'s good graces—This will do—said I—Just as well, retorted I again, as a coat carried up to him by an adventurous tailor, without taking his measure—Fool! continued I—see Monsieur le Duc's face first—observe what character is written in it—take notice in what posture he stands to hear you—mark the turns and expressions of his body and limbs—and for the tone—the first sound which comes from his lips will give it you; and from all these together you'll compound an address at once upon the spot, which cannot disgust the Duke—the ingredients are his own, and most likely to go down.

Well! said I, I wish it well over—Coward again! as if man to man was not equal throughout the whole surface of the globe; and if in the field—why not face to face in the cabinet[5] too? And trust me, Yorick, whenever it is not so, man is false to himself, and betrays his own succors ten times, where nature does it once. Go to the Duc de C**** with the Bastille in thy looks—My life for it, thou wilt be sent back to Paris[6] in half an hour, with an escort.

I believe so, said I—Then I'll go to the Duke, by heaven! with all the gaiety and debonairness in the world.—

—And there you are wrong again, replied I—A heart at ease, Yorick, flies into no extremes—'tis ever on its center.—Well! well! cried I, as the coachman turned in at the gates—I find I shall do very well: and by the time he had wheeled round the court, and brought me up to the door, I found myself so much the better for my own lecture, that I neither ascended the steps like a victim to justice, who was to part with life upon the topmost,—nor did I mount them with a skip and a couple of strides, as I do when I fly up, Eliza! to thee, to meet it.

As I entered the door of the saloon,[7] I was met by a person who possibly might be the maitre d'hotel, but had more the air of one of the under secretaries, who told me the Duc de C**** was busy—I am utterly ignorant, said I, of the forms of obtaining an audience, being an absolute stranger, and what is worse in the present conjuncture of affairs, being an Englishman too.—He replied, that did not increase the difficulty.—I made him a slight bow, and told him, I had something of importance to say to Monsieur le Duc. The secretary looked towards the stairs, as if he was about to leave me to carry up this account to some one—But I must not mislead you, said I—for what I have to say is of no manner of importance to Monsieur le Duc de C****—but of great importance to myself.—C'est une autre affaire,[8] replied he—Not at all, said I, to a man of gallantry.—But pray, good sir, continued I, when can a stranger hope to have accesse? In not less than two hours, said he, looking at his watch. The number of equipages in the courtyard seemed to justify the calculation, that I could have no nearer a prospect—and as walking backwards and forwards in the saloon, without a soul to commune with, was for the time as bad as being in the Bastille itself, I instantly went back to my remise, and bid the coachman to drive me to the Cordon Bleu, which was the nearest hotel.

I think there is a fatality in it—I seldom go to the place I set out for.

5. Here, room in which affairs of state are conducted.
6. Where the Bastille is located.
7. Lofty room in which guests are received.
8. Well, that's another story.

LE PATISSER.[9]

VERSAILLES.

Before I had got half-way down the street I changed my mind: as I am at Versailles, thought I, I might as well take a view of the town; so I pulled the cord, and ordered the coachman to drive round some of the principal streets—I suppose the town is not very large, said I.—The coachman begged pardon for setting me right, and told me it was very superb, and that numbers of the first dukes and marquises and counts had hotels[1]—The Count de B****, of whom the bookseller at the Quai de Conti had spoke so handsomely the night before, came instantly into my mind.—And why should I not go, thought I, to the Count de B****, who has so high an idea of English books and Englishmen—and tell him my story? So I changed my mind a second time—In truth it was the third; for I had intended that day for Madame de R**** in the Rue St. Pierre, and had devoutly sent her word by her *fille de chambre* that I would assuredly wait upon her—but I am governed by circumstances—I cannot govern them: so seeing a man standing with a basket on the other side of the street, as if he had something to sell, I bid La Fleur go up to him and inquire for the Count's hotel.

La Fleur returned a little pale: and told me it was a Chevalier de St. Louis selling *patès*[2]—It is impossible, La Fleur, said I.—La Fleur could no more account for the phenomenon than myself; but persisted in his story: he had seen the croix set in gold, with its red ribband, he said, tied to his button-hole—and had looked into the basket and seen the *patès* which the Chevalier was selling; so could not be mistaken in that.

Such a reverse in man's life awakens a better principle than curiosity: I could not help looking for some time at him as I sat in the *remise*—the more I looked at him, his croix, and his basket, the stronger they wove themselves into my brain—I got out of the *remise* and went towards him.

He was begirt with a clean linen apron which fell below his knees, and with a sort of a bib that went half way up his breast; upon the top of this, but a little below the hem, hung his croix. His basket of little *patès* was covered over with a white damask napkin: another of the same kind was spread at the bottom; and there was a look of *propreté* and neatness throughout, that one might have bought his *patès* of him, as much from appetite as sentiment.

He made an offer of them to neither; but stood still with them at the corner of a hotel, for those to buy who chose it, without solicitation.

He was about forty-eight—of a sedate look, something approaching to gravity. I did not wonder.—I went up rather to the basket than him, and having lifted up the napkin, and taken one of his *patès* into my hand—I begged he would explain the appearance which affected me.

He told me in a few words, that the best part of his life had passed in the service, in which, after spending a small patrimony,[3] he had obtained a company and the croix with it; but that at the conclusion of the last peace, his regiment being reformed, and the whole corps, with those of some other regiments, left without any provision—he found himself in a wide world without friends, without a livre—and indeed, said he, without anything but this—(pointing, as he said it, to his croix)—The poor chevalier won my pity, and he finished the scene with winning my esteem too.

The king, he said, was the most generous of princes, but his generosity could neither relieve or reward every one, and it was only his misfortune to be amongst the number. He had a little wife, he said, whom he loved, who did the *patisserie;* and added, he felt no dishonor in defending her and himself from want in this way—unless Providence had offered him a better.

It would be wicked to withhold a pleasure from the good, in passing over what happened to this poor Chevalier of St. Louis about nine months after.

It seems he usually took his stand near the iron gates which lead up to the palace, and as his croix had caught the eye of numbers, numbers had made the same inquiry which I had done—He had told the same story, and always with so much modesty and good sense, that it had reached at last the king's ears—who hearing the Chevalier had been a gallant officer, and respected by the whole regiment as a man of honor and integrity—he broke up his little trade by a pension of fifteen hundred livres a year.

As I have told this to please the reader, I beg he will allow me to relate another, out of its order, to please myself—the two stories reflect light upon each other,—and 'tis a pity they should be parted.

THE SWORD.

RENNES.[4]

When states and empires have their periods of declension, and feel in their turns what distress and poverty is—I stop not to tell the causes which gradually brought the house d'E**** in Brittany into decay. The Marquis d'E**** had fought up against his condition with great firmness; wishing to preserve, and still show to the world some little fragments of what his ancestors had been—their indiscretions had put it out of his power. There was enough left for the little exigencies of *obscurity*—but he had two boys who looked up to him for *light*—he thought they deserved it. He had tried his sword—it could not open the way—the *mounting* was too expensive[5]—and simple economy was not a match for it—there was no resource but commerce.

In any other province in France, save Brittany, this was smiting the root forever of the little tree his pride and affection wished to see reblossom—But in Brittany, there being a provision for this,[6] he availed himself of it; and taking an occasion when the states[7] were assembled at Rennes, the Marquis,

4. Town in the west of France, capital of Brittany.
5. He tried to keep his house's reputation via a military career (the sword) but could not afford the associated costs.
6. In other parts of France, it was forbidden for the nobility to engage in activities not in keeping with their station (such as commerce), but in Brittany, nobles could suspend their status, and temporarily become commoners, to do so.
7. Representatives of the body politic, including the nobility.

attended with his two boys, entered the court; and having pleaded the right of an ancient law of the duchy, which, though seldom claimed, he said, was no less in force, he took his sword from his side—Here—said he—take it; and be trusty guardians of it, till better times put me in condition to reclaim it.

The president accepted the Marquis's sword—he stayed a few minutes to see it deposited in the archives of his house—and departed.

The Marquis and his whole family embarked the next day for Martinico,[8] and in about nineteen or twenty years of successful application to business, with some unlooked-for bequests from distant branches of his house— returned home to reclaim his nobility and to support it.

It was an incident of good fortune which will never happen to any traveler, but a sentimental one, that I should be at Rennes at the very time of this solemn requisition: I call it solemn—it was so to me.

The Marquis entered the court with his whole family: he supported his lady—his eldest son supported his sister, and his youngest was at the other extreme of the line next his mother—he put his handkerchief to his face twice—

—There was a dead silence. When the Marquis had approached within six paces of the tribunal, he gave the Marchioness to his youngest son, and advancing three steps before his family—he reclaimed his sword. His sword was given him, and the moment he got it into his hand, he drew it almost out of the scabbard—'twas the shining face of a friend he had once given up—he looked attentively along it, beginning at the hilt, as if to see whether it was the same—when observing a little rust which it had contracted near the point, he brought it near his eye, and bending his head down over it—I think I saw a tear fall upon the place: I could not be deceived by what followed.

"I shall find," said he, "some *other way* to get it off."

When the Marquis had said this, he returned his sword into its scabbard, made a bow to the guardians of it—and with his wife and daughter, and his two sons following him, walked out.

O how I envied him his feelings!

THE PASSPORT.

VERSAILLES.

I found no difficulty in getting admittance to Monsieur le Count de B****. The set of Shakespeares was laid upon the table, and he was tumbling them over. I walked up close to the table, and giving first such a look at the books as to make him conceive I knew what they were—I told him I had come without any one to present me, knowing I should meet with a friend in his apartment, who, I trusted, would do it for me—it is my countryman the great Shakespeare, said I, pointing to his works—*et ayez la bontè, mon cher ami*, apostrophizing his spirit, added I, *de me faire cet honneur-la*.[9]—

The Count smiled at the singularity of the introduction; and seeing I looked a little pale and sickly, insisted upon my taking an arm-chair: so I sat

8. Martinique, French colony in the Caribbean.
9. And have the goodness, my dear friend . . . to do me the honor.

down; and to save him conjectures upon a visit so out of all rule, I told him simply of the incident in the bookseller's shop, and how that had impelled me rather to go to him with the story of a little embarrassment I was under, than to any other man in France—And what is your embarrassment? let me hear it, said the Count. So I told him the story just as I have told it the reader—

—And the master of my hotel, said I, as I concluded it, will needs have it, Monsieur le Count, that I should be sent to the Bastille—but I have no apprehensions, continued I—for in falling into the hands of the most polished people in the world, and being conscious I was a true man, and not come to spy the nakedness of the land,[1] I scarce thought I laid at their mercy.—It does not suit the gallantry of the French, Monsieur le Count, said I, to show it against invalids.

An animated blush came into the Count de B****'s cheeks as I spoke this—*Ne craignez rien*—don't fear, said he—Indeed I don't, replied I again—Besides, continued I a little sportingly—I have come laughing all the way from London to Paris, and I do not think Monsieur le Duc de Choiseul is such an enemy to mirth, as to send me back crying for my pains.

—My application to you, Monsieur le Compte de B**** (making him a low bow) is to desire he will not.

The Count heard me with great good nature, or I had not said half as much—and once or twice said—*C'est bien dit.*[2] So I rested my cause there—and determined to say no more about it.

The Count led the discourse: we talked of indifferent things—of books, and politics, and men—and then of women—God Bless them all! said I, after much discourse about them—there is not a man upon earth who loves them so much as I do: after all the foibles I have seen, and all the satires I have read against them, still I love them; being firmly persuaded that a man, who has not a sort of an affection for the whole sex, is incapable of ever loving a single one as he ought.

Heh bien! Monsieur l'Anglois,[3] said the Count, gaily—you are not come to spy the nakedness of the land—I believe you—*ni encore,*[4] I dare say *that* of our women—But permit me to conjecture—if, *par hazard,* they fell in your way—that the prospect would not affect you.

I have something within me which cannot bear the shock of the least indecent insinuation: in the sportability of chitchat I have often endeavored to conquer it, and with infinite pain have hazarded a thousand things to a dozen of the sex together—the least of which I could not venture to a single one to gain heaven.

Excuse me, Monsieur le Count, said I—as for the nakedness of your land, if I saw it, I should cast my eyes over it with tears in them—and for that of your women (blushing at the idea he had excited in me) I am so evangelical in this, and have such a fellow-feeling for whatever is *weak* about them, that I would cover it with a garment, if I knew how to throw it on—But I could wish, continued I, to spy the *nakedness* of their hearts, and through the different disguises of customs, climates, and religion, find out what is good in them to fashion my own by—and therefore am I come.

---

1. See Genesis 42.9.

2. That's well said.
3. Well, English sir!

It is for this reason, Monsieur le Compte, continued I, that I have not seen the Palais Royal—nor the Luxembourg—nor the Façade of the Louvre[5]—nor have attempted to swell the catalogues we have of pictures, statues, and churches—I conceive every fair being as a temple, and would rather enter in, and see the original drawings, and loose sketches hung up in it, than the transfiguration of Raphael[6] itself.

The thirst of this, continued I, as impatient as that which inflames the breast of the connoisseur, has led me from my own home into France—and from France will lead me through Italy—'tis a quiet journey of the heart in pursuit of NATURE, and those affections which rise out of her, which make us love each other—and the world, better than we do.

The Count said a great many civil things to me upon the occasion; and added, very politely, how much he stood obliged to Shakespeare for making me known to him—But, *a-propos*, said he,—Shakespeare is full of great things—he forgot a small punctilio of announcing your name—it puts you under a necessity of doing it yourself.

THE PASSPORT.

VERSAILLES.

There is not a more perplexing affair in life to me, than to set about telling any one who I am—for there is scarce anybody I cannot give a better account of than of myself; and I have often wished I could do it in a single word—and have an end of it. It was the only time and occasion in my life I could accomplish this to any purpose—for Shakespeare lying upon the table, and recollecting I was in his books, I took up *Hamlet*, and turning immediately to the grave-diggers scene in the fifth act, I laid my finger upon YORICK, and advancing the book to the Count, with my finger all the way over the name—Me, *voici!*[7] said I.

Now whether the idea of poor Yorick's skull was put out of the Count's mind by the reality of my own, or by what magic he could drop a period of seven or eight hundred years, makes nothing in this account—'tis certain the French conceive better than they combine—I wonder at nothing in this world, and the less at this; inasmuch as one of the first of our own church, for whose candor and paternal sentiments I have the highest veneration, fell into the same mistake in the very same case.—"He could not bear," he said, "to look into sermons wrote by the king of Denmark's jester."[8]—Good my lord! said I—but there are two Yoricks. The Yorick your lordship thinks of has been dead and buried eight hundred years ago; he flourished in Horwendillus's court[9]—the other Yorick is myself, who have flourished, my

4. Nor.

5. Palace in Paris where the royal collections were housed. The Palais-Royal is a Paris palace, housing a magnificent art collection. The Luxembourg palace and gardens in Paris were a tourist destination.

6. *The Transfiguration of Christ*, an eminent (though unfinished) painting, by the Italian master Raphael (1483–1520), displayed at the Vatican.

7. Right here! Yorick identifies himself by point-ing to the name of the dead jester whom Hamlet eulogizes in Shakespeare's play.

8. Alluding perhaps to the reaction of William Warburton, bishop of Gloucester, to Sterne's *Sermons* (2 vols., 1760), published under the name "Mr. Yorick."

9. In Shakespeare's historical sources for *Hamlet*, King Horwendillus of Denmark is murdered, whose death Amleth (Hamlet) must avenge. Sterne's *Tristram Shandy* places the ancestor of

lord, in no court—He shook his head—Good God! said I, you might as well confound Alexander the Great with Alexander the Copper-smith, my lord—'Twas all one, he replied—

—If Alexander king of Macedon could have translated your lordship, said I—I'm sure your lordship would not have said so.[1]

The poor Count de B**** fell but into the same *error*—

—*Et, Monsieur, est il Yorick?* cried the Count.—*Je le suis,* said I.—*Vous?*—*Moi—moi qui ai l'honneur de vous parler, Monsieur le Compte—Mon Dieu!* said he, embracing me—*Vous etes Yorick!*[2]

The Count instantly put the Shakespeare into his pocket—and left me alone in his room.

THE PASSPORT.

VERSAILLES.

I could not conceive why the Count de B**** had gone so abruptly out of the room, any more than I could conceive why he had put the Shakespeare into his pocket—*Mysteries which must explain themselves are not worth the loss of time which a conjecture about them takes up:* 'twas better to read Shakespeare; so taking up *Much Ado about Nothing,* I transported myself instantly from the chair I sat in to Messina in Sicily, and got so busy with Don Pedro and Benedick and Beatrice,[3] that I thought not of Versailles, the Count, or the passport.

Sweet pliability of man's spirit, that can at once surrender itself to illusions, which cheat expectation and sorrow of their weary moments!—long—long since had ye numbered out my days, had I not trod so great a part of them upon this enchanted ground; when my way is too rough for my feet, or too steep for my strength, I get off it, to some smooth velvet path which fancy has scattered over with rosebuds of delights; and having taken a few turns in it, come back strengthened and refreshed—When evils press sore upon me, and there is no retreat from them in this world, then I take a new course—I leave it—and as I have a clearer idea of the Elysian fields than I have of heaven, I force myself, like Æneas, into them—I see him meet the pensive shade of his forsaken Dido[4]—and wish to recognize it—I see the injured spirit wave her head, and turn off silent from the author of her miseries and dishonors—I lose the feelings for myself in hers—and in those affections which were wont to make me mourn for her when I was at school.

Surely this is not walking in a vain shadow—nor does man disquiet himself in vain by it[5]—he oftener does so in trusting the issue of his commotions to reason only.—I can safely say for myself, I was never able to conquer any one single bad sensation in my heart so decisively, as by beating up as fast as I could for some kindly and gentle sensation to fight it upon its own ground.

his Yorick in the court of this king.
1. Yorick continues to address the bishop, not the count. "Translated": ordered (a bishop) to be moved from one see to another.
2. And sir, are you Yorick? . . . I am he. . . . You? Me—me who has the honor of addressing you, Count—My God! . . . You are Yorick!
3. In Shakespeare's *Much Ado About Nothing*

(1598–99), set in Messina, Don Pedro seeks to facilitate the match between the combative lovers Beatrice and Benedick.
4. In book VI of Virgil's *Aeneid,* the hero Aeneas meets Dido, the lover he forsook, in Hades, and then visits the Elysian fields, the place where heroes and the virtuous spend the afterlife.
5. See Psalms 39.6.

When I had got to the end of the third act, the Count de B**** entered with my passport in his hand. Monsieur le Duc de C****, said the Count, is as good a prophet, I dare say, as he is a statesman—*Un homme qui rit,* said the duke, *ne sera jamais dangereuz.*[6]—Had it been for any one but the king's jester, added the Count, I could not have got it these two hours.—*Pardonnez moi,*[7] Monsieur le Compte, said I—I am not the king's jester.—But you are Yorick?—Yes.—*Et vous plaisantez?*[8]—I answered, Indeed I did jest—but was not paid for it—'twas entirely at my own expense.

We have no jester at court, Monsieur le Compte, said I; the last we had was in the licentious reign of Charles the Second[9]—since which time our manners have been so gradually refining, that our court at present is so full of patriots, who wish for *nothing* but the honors and wealth of their country—and our ladies are all so chaste, so spotless, so good, so devout— there is nothing for a jester to make a jest of—

Voila un persiflage![1] cried the Count.

THE PASSPORT.

VERSAILLES.

As the passport was directed to all lieutenant-governors, governors, and commandants of cities, generals of armies, justiciaries,[2] and all officers of justice, to let Mr. Yorick the king's jester, and his baggage, travel quietly along—I own the triumph of obtaining the passport was not a little tarnished by the figure I cut in it—But there is nothing unmixt in this world, and some of the gravest of our divines have carried it so far as to affirm, that enjoyment itself was attended even with a sigh—and that the greatest *they knew of* terminated *in a general way,* in little better than a convulsion.

I remember the grave and learned Bevoriskius,[3] in his commentary upon the generations from Adam, very naturally breaks off in the middle of a note to give an account to the world of a couple of sparrows upon the out-edge of his window, which had incommoded him all the time he wrote, and at last had entirely taken him off from his genealogy.

—'Tis strange! writes Bevoriskius, but the facts are certain, for I have had the curiosity to mark them down one by one with my pen—but the cock-sparrow during the little time that I could have finished the other half this note, has actually interrupted me with the reiteration of his caresses three and twenty times and a half.

How merciful, adds Bevoriskius, is heaven to his creatures!

Ill-fated Yorick! that the gravest of thy brethren should be able to write that to the world, which stains thy face with crimson, to copy in even thy study.

But this is nothing to my travels—So I twice—twice beg pardon for it.

6. A man who laughs will never be dangerous.
7. Excuse me.
8. And you're kidding, right?
9. In his diary, Samuel Pepys reports in 1668 that playwright Thomas Killigrew received "the title of king's fool or jester," though this was likely a joke.

1. And there's a joke!
2. Judicial jurisdictions.
3. Johan van Beverwyck (1594–1647), called Beverovicius, Dutch physician and magistrate. The passage that Yorick will "quote" loosely resembles remarks in a work published by van Beverwyck in 1672.

CHARACTER.

VERSAILLES.

And how do you find the French? said the Count de B****, after he had given me the passport.

The reader may suppose, that after so obliging a proof of courtesy, I could not be at a loss to say something handsome to the inquiry.

—*Mais passe, pour cela*[4]—Speak frankly, said he: do you find all the urbanity in the French which the world give us the honor of?—I had found everything, I said, which confirmed it—*Vraiment*, said the Count.—*Les Francois sont polis.*[5]—To an excess, replied I.

The Count took notice of the word *excesse;* and would have it I meant more than I said. I defended myself a long time as well as I could against it—he insisted I had a reserve, and that I would speak my opinion frankly.

I believe, Monsieur le Compte, said I, that man has a certain compass,[6] as well as an instrument; and that the social and other calls have occasion by turns for every key in him; so that if you begin a note too high or too low, there must be a want either in the upper or under part, to fill up the system of harmony.—The Count de B**** did not understand music, so desired me to explain it some other way. A polished nation, my dear Count, said I, makes everyone its debtor; and besides, urbanity itself, like the fair sex, has so many charms; it goes against the heart to say it can do ill: and yet, I believe, there is but a certain line of perfection, that man, take him altogether, is empowered to arrive at—if he gets beyond, he rather exchanges qualities, than gets them. I must not presume to say how far this has affected the French in the subject we are speaking of—but should it ever be the case of the English, in the progress of their refinements, to arrive at the same polish which distinguishes the French, if we did not lose the *politesse du cœur,*[7] which inclines men more to human actions, than courteous ones—we should at least lose that distinct variety and originality of character, which distinguishes them, not only from each other, but from all the world besides.

I had a few of King William's shillings[8] as smooth as glass in my pocket; and foreseeing they would be of use in the illustration of my hypothesis, I had got them into my hand, when I had proceeded so far—

See, Monsieur le Compte, said I, rising up, and laying them before him upon the table—by jingling and rubbing one against another for seventy years together in one body's pocket or another's, they are become so much alike, you can scarce distinguish one shilling from another.

The English, like ancient medals,[9] kept more apart, and passing but few people's hands, preserve the first sharpnesses which the fine hand of nature has given them—they are not so pleasant to feel—but, in return, the legend is so visible, that at the first look you see whose image and superscription they bear.—But the French, Monsieur le Compte, added I, wishing to soften what I had said, have so many excellencies, they can the better spare this—

---

4. But you don't need to answer.
5. Truly . . . the French are polite.
6. The range of notes that a musical instrument or voice can make.
7. Politeness of the heart.
8. Shillings first circulated during the reign of William III (1689–1702).

they are a loyal, a gallant, a generous, an ingenious, and good-tempered people as is under heaven—if they have a fault—they are too *serious*.

Mon Dieu! cried the Count, rising out of his chair.

Mais vous plaisantez,[1] said he, correcting his exclamation.—I laid my hand upon my breast, and with earnest gravity assured him, it was my most settled opinion.

The Count said he was mortified he could not stay to hear my reasons, being engaged to go that moment to dine with the Duc de C****.

But if it is not too far to come to Versailles to eat your soup[2] with me, I beg, before you leave France, I may have the pleasure of knowing you retract your opinion—or, in what manner you support it.—But if you do support it, Monsieur Anglois, said he, you must do it with all your powers, because you have the whole world against you.—I promised the Count I would do myself the honor of dining with him before I set out for Italy—so took my leave.

THE TEMPTATION.

PARIS.

When I alighted at the hotel, the porter told me a young woman with a bandbox[3] had been that moment inquiring for me.—I do not know, said the porter, whether she is gone away or no. I took the key of my chamber of him, and went upstairs; and when I had got within ten steps of the top of the landing before my door, I met her coming easily down.

It was the fair *fille de chambre* I had walked along the Quai de Conti with: Madame de R**** had sent her upon some commissions to a *merchande des modes*[4] within a step or two of the Hotel de Modene; and as I had failed in waiting upon her, had bid her inquire if I had left Paris, and if so, whether I had not left a letter addressed to her.

As the fair *fille de chambre* was so near my door, she turned back, and went into the room with me for a moment or two whilst I wrote a card.

It was a fine still evening in the latter end of the month of May—the crimson window curtains (which were of the same color of those of the bed) were drawn close—the sun was setting and reflected through them so warm a tint into the fair *fille de chambre*'s face—I thought she blushed—the idea of it made me blush myself—we were quite alone; and that super-induced a second blush before the first could get off.

There is a sort of a pleasing half guilty blush, where the blood is more in fault than the man—'tis sent impetuous from the heart, and virtue flies after it—not to call it back, but to make the sensation of it more delicious to the nerves—'tis associated.—

But I'll not describe it.—I felt something at first within me which was not in strict unison with the lesson of virtue I had given her the night before—I sought five minutes for a card—I knew I had not one.—I took up a pen—I laid it down again—my hand trembled—the devil was in me.

I know as well as any one, he is an adversary, whom if we resist, he will fly from us—but I seldom resist him at all; from a terror that though I may

9. Old commemorative coins, prized by collectors.
1. My God! . . . But you're joking.
2. Have a meal. As elsewhere, Sterne turns a

French expression into English.
3. A box that holds items of fabric.
4. A dealer in fabrics.

conquer, I may still get a hurt in the combat—so I give up the triumph, for security; and instead of thinking to make him fly, I generally fly myself.

The fair *fille de chambre* came close up to the bureau where I was looking for a card—took up first the pen I cast down, then offered to hold me the ink; she offered it so sweetly, I was going to accept it—but I durst not—I have nothing, my dear, said I, to write upon.—Write it, said she, simply, upon anything.—

I was just going to cry out, Then I will write it, fair girl! upon thy lips.—

If I do, said I, I shall perish—so I took her by the hand, and led her to the door, and begged she would not forget the lesson I had given her—She said, Indeed she would not—and as she uttered it with some earnestness, she turned about, and gave me both her hands, closed together, into mine—it was impossible not to compress them in that situation—I wished to let them go; and all the time I held them, I kept arguing within myself against it—and still I held them on.—In two minutes I found I had all the battle to fight over again—and I felt my legs and every limb about me tremble at the idea.

The foot of the bed was within a yard and a half of the place where we were standing—I had still hold of her hands—and how it happened I can give no account, but I neither asked her—nor drew her—nor did I think of the bed—but so it did happen, we both sat down.

I'll just show you, said the fair *fille de chambre*, the little purse I have been making today to hold your crown. So she put her hand into her right pocket, which was next me, and felt for it some time—then into the left— "She had lost it."—I never bore expectation more quietly—it was in her right pocket at last—she pulled it out; it was of green taffeta, lined with a little bit of white quilted satin, and just big enough to hold the crown—she put it into my hand—it was pretty; and I held it ten minutes with the back of my hand resting upon her lap—looking sometimes at the purse, sometimes on one side of it.

A stitch or two had broke out in the gathers of my stock—the fair *fille de chambre*, without saying a word, took out her little hussive,[5] threaded a small needle, and sewed it up—I foresaw it would hazard the glory of the day; and as she passed her hand in silence across and across my neck in the manœuver, I felt the laurels[6] shake which fancy had wreathed about my head.

A strap had given way in her walk, and the buckle of her shoe was just falling off—See, said the *fille de chambre*, holding up her foot—I could not for my soul but fasten the buckle in return, and putting in the strap—and lifting up the other foot with it, when I had done, to see both were right—in doing it too suddenly—it unavoidably threw the fair *fille de chambre* off her center—and then—

THE CONQUEST.

Yes——and then—Ye whose clay-cold heads and luke-warm hearts can argue down or mask your passions—tell me, what trespass is it that man should have them? or how his spirit stands answerable, to the Father of spirits but for his conduct under them?

---

5. Sewing case.

If Nature has so wove her web of kindness that some threads of love and desire are entangled with the piece—must the whole web be rent in drawing them out?—Whip me such stoics, great Governor of nature! said I to myself—Wherever thy providence shall place me for the trials of my virtue—whatever is my danger—whatever is my situation—let me feel the movements which rise out of it, and which belong to me as a man—and if I govern them as a good one—I will trust the issues[7] to thy justice, for thou hast made us—and not we ourselves.

As I finished my address, I raised the fair *fille de chambre* up by the hand, and led her out of the room—she stood by me till I locked the door and put the key in my pocket—*and then*—the victory being quite decisive—and not till then, I pressed my lips to her cheek, and taking her by the hand again, led her safe to the gate of the hotel.

THE MYSTERY.

PARIS.

If a man knows the heart, he will know it was impossible to go back instantly to my chamber—it was touching a cold key with a flat third to it, upon the close of a piece of music,[8] which had called forth my affections—therefore when I let go the hand of the *fille de chambre*, I remained at the gate of the hotel for some time, looking at every one who passed by, and forming conjectures upon them, till my attention got fixed upon a single object which confounded all kind of reasoning upon him.

It was a tall figure of a philosophic, serious, adust[9] look, which passed and repassed sedately along the street, making a turn of about sixty paces on each side of the gate of the hotel—the man was about fifty-two—had a small cane under his arm—was dressed in a dark drab-colored coat, waistcoat, and breeches, which seemed to have seen some years' service—they were still clean, and there was a little air of frugal *properté* throughout him. By his pulling off his hat, and his attitude of accosting a good many in his way, I saw he was asking charity; so I got a sous or two out of my pocket ready to give him, as he took me in his turn—he passed by me without asking anything—and yet did not go five steps further before he asked charity of a little woman—I was much more likely to have given of the two—He had scarce done with the woman, when he pulled off his hat to another who was coming the same way.—An ancient gentleman came slowly—and, after him, a young smart one—He let them both pass, and asked nothing: I stood observing him half an hour, in which time he had made a dozen turns backwards and forwards, and found that he invariably pursued the same plan.

There were two things very singular in this, which set my brain to work, and to no purpose—the first was, why the man should *only* tell his story to the sex—and secondly—what kind of story it was, and what species of eloquence it could be, which softened the hearts of the women, which he knew 'twas to no purpose to practice upon the men.

There were two other circumstances which entangled this mystery—the one was, he told every woman what he had to say in her ear, and in a way

---

6. Decoration given to a victor in battle.
7. Results.

8. A dissonant note, unpleasing at the close of a piece.

which had much more the air of a secret than a petition—the other was, it was always successful—he never stopped a woman, but she pulled out her purse, and immediately gave him something.

I could form no system to explain the phenomenon.

I had got a riddle to amuse me for the rest of the evening, so I walked upstairs to my chamber.

THE CASE OF CONSCIENCE.

PARIS.

I was immediately followed up by the master of the hotel, who came into my room to tell me I must provide lodgings elsewhere.—How so, friend? said I.— He answered, I had had a young woman locked up with me two hours that evening in my bedchamber, and 'twas against the rules of his house.—Very well, said I, we'll all part friends then—for the girl is no worse—and I am no worse—and you will be just as I found you.—It was enough, he said, to over-throw the credit[1] of his hotel.—*Voyez vous, Monsieur,*[2] said he, pointing to the foot of the bed we had been sitting upon.—I own it had something of the appearance of an evidence;[3] but my pride not suffering me to enter into any detail of the case, I exhorted him to let his soul sleep in peace, as I resolved to let mine do that night, and that I would discharge what I owed him at breakfast.

I should not have minded, *Monsieur,* said he, if you had had twenty girls— 'Tis a score more, replied I, interrupting him, than I ever reckoned upon— Provided, added he, it had been but in a morning.—And does the difference of the time of the day at Paris make a difference in the sin?—It made a dif-ference, he said, in the scandal.—I like a good distinction in my heart; and cannot say I was intolerably out of temper with the man. I own it is necessary, reassumed the master of the hotel, that a stranger at Paris should have the opportunities presented to him of buying lace and silk stockings, and ruffles, *et tout cela*[4]—and 'tis nothing if a woman comes with a bandbox.—O' my conscience, said I, she had one; but I never looked into it.—Then *Monsieur,* said he, has bought nothing.—Not one earthly thing, replied I.—Because, said he, I could recommend one to you who would use you *en conscience.*[5]— But I must see her this night, said I.—He made me a low bow, and walked down.

Now shall I triumph over this *maitre d'hotel,* cried I—and what then?— Then I shall let him see I know he is a dirty fellow.—And what then?—What then!—I was too near myself to say it was for the sake of others.—I had no good answer left—there was more of spleen than principle in my project, and I was sick of it before the execution.

In a few minutes the Grisset came in with her box of lace—I'll buy noth-ing, however, said I, within myself.

The Grisset would show me everything—I was hard to please: she would not seem to see it; she opened her little magazine,[6] and laid all her laces one after another before me—unfolded and folded them up again one by one

---

9. Gloomy.
1. To ruin the reputation.
2. You see, sir.

3. Of wrongdoing.
4. And all of that.
5. Fairly.

with the most patient sweetness—I might buy—or not—she would let me have everything at my own price—the poor creature seemed anxious to get a penny; and laid herself out to win me, and not so much in a manner which seemed artful, as in one I felt simple and caressing.

If there is not a fund of honest cullibility[7] in man, so much the worse—my heart relented, and I gave up my second resolution as quietly as the first—Why should I chastise one for the trespass of another? If thou art tributary[8] to this tyrant of an host, thought I, looking up in her face, so much harder is thy bread.

If I had not had more than four *Louis d'ors* in my purse, there was no such thing as rising up and showing her the door, till I had first laid three of them out in a pair of ruffles.

—The master of the hotel will share the profit with her—no matter—then I have only paid as many a poor soul has *paid* before me, for an act he *could* not do, or think of.

THE RIDDLE.

PARIS.

When La Fleur came up to wait upon me at supper, he told me how sorry the master of the hotel was for his affront to me in bidding me change my lodgings.

A man who values a good night's rest will not lay down with enmity in his heart, if he can help it—so I bid La Fleur tell the master of the hotel, that I was sorry on my side for the occasion I had given him—and you may tell him, if you will, La Fleur, added I, that if the young woman should call again, I shall not see her.

This was a sacrifice not to him, but myself, having resolved, after so narrow an escape, to run no more risks, but to leave Paris, if it was possible, with all the virtue I entered in.

C'est deroger à noblesse, Monsieur,[9] said La Fleur, making me a bow down to the ground as he said it—*Et encore, Monsieur,*[1] said he, may change his sentiments—and if (*par hazard*) he should like to amuse himself—I find no amusement in it, said I, interrupting him—

Mon Dieu! said La Fleur—and took away.

In an hour's time he came to put me to bed, and was more than commonly officious—something hung upon his lips to say to me, or ask me, which he could not get off: I could not conceive what it was; and indeed gave myself little trouble to find it out, as I had another riddle so much more interesting upon my mind, which was that of the man's asking charity before the door of the hotel—I would have given anything to have got to the bottom of it; and that, not out of curiosity—'tis so low a principle of inquiry, in general, I would not purchase the gratification of it with a two-sous piece—but a secret, I thought, which so soon and so certainly softened the heart of every woman you came near, was a secret at least equal to the philosopher's stone:[2] had I had both the Indies, I would have given up one to have been master of it.

6. Portable case that holds items for sale.
7. Gullibility.
8. Someone who must pay tribute.

9. That would be to relinquish your nobility, sir.
1. And furthermore, sir.
2. In alchemy, a substance capable of turning base

I tossed and turned it almost all night long in my brains to no manner of purpose; and when I awoke in the morning, I found my spirit as much troubled with my *dreams,* as ever the king of Babylon had been with his; and I will not hesitate to affirm, it would have puzzled all the wise men of Paris as much as those of Chaldea,[3] to have given its interpretation.

LE DIMANCHE.[4]

PARIS.

It was Sunday; and when La Fleur came in, in the morning, with my coffee and roll and butter, he had got himself so gallantly arrayed, I scarce knew him.

I had convenanted at Montriul to give him a new hat with a silver button and loop, and four Louis d'ors *pour s'adoniser,*[5] when we got to Paris; and the poor fellow, to do him justice, had done wonders with it.

He had bought a bright, clean, good scarlet coat, and a pair of breeches of the same—They were not a crown worse, he said, for the wearing—I wished him hanged for telling me—they looked so fresh, that tho' I know the thing could not be done, yet I would rather have imposed upon my fancy with thinking I had bought them new for the fellow, than that they had come out of the *Rue de Friperie.*[6]

This is a nicety which makes not the heart sore at Paris.

He had purchased moreover a handsome blue satin waistcoat, fancifully enough embroidered—this was indeed something the worse for the service it had done, but 'twas clean scoured—the gold had been touched up, and upon the whole was rather showy than otherwise—and as the blue was not violent, it suited with the coat and breeches very well: he had squeezed out of the money, moreover, a new bag and a solitaire; and had insisted with the *fripier*[7] upon a gold pair of garters to his breeches' knees—He had purchased muslin ruffles, *bien brodées,*[8] with four livres of his own money—and a pair of white silk stockings for five more—and, to top all, nature had given him a handsome figure, without costing him a sous.

He entered the room thus set off, with his hair dressed in the first style, and with a handsome *bouquet* in his breast—in a word, there was that look of festivity in everything about him, which at once put me in mind it was Sunday[9]— and by combining both together, it instantly struck me, that the favor he wished to ask of me the night before, was to spend the day as everybody in Paris spent it besides. I had scarce made the conjecture, when La Fleur, with infinite humility, but with a look of trust, as if I should not refuse him, begged I would grant him the day, *pour faire le galant vis à vis de sa maitresse.*[1]

Now it was the very thing I intended to do myself *vis à vis* Madame de R****—I had retained the *remise* on purpose for it, and it would not have mortified my vanity to have had a servant so well dressed as La Fleur was, to have got up behind it: I never could have worse spared him.

metals to gold.
3. In Daniel 2.1–11, King Nebuchadnezzar demands that the wise men of Babylon in Chaldea interpret his dreams.
4. Sunday.
5. To deck himself out.

6. Street where secondhand clothes are sold.
7. Used clothing salesman. "Bag and solitaire": a wig bag and black ribbon necktie.
8. Nicely embroidered.
9. The day off for servants.
1. To gallantly attend his mistress.

But we must *feel*, not argue, in these embarrassments—the sons and daughters of service part with liberty, but not with Nature, in their contracts; they are flesh and blood, and have their little vanities and wishes in the midst of the house of bondage, as well as their taskmasters—no doubt they have set their self-denials at a price—and their expectations are so unreasonable, that I would often disappoint them, but that their condition puts it so much in my power to do it.

Behold!—Behold, I am thy servant—disarms me at once of the powers of a master—

—Thou shalt go, La Fleur! said I.

—And what mistress, La Fleur, said I, canst thou have picked up in so little a time at Paris? La Fleur laid his hand upon his breast, and said 'twas a *petite demoiselle*,[2] at Monsieur le Compte de B****'s.—La Fleur had a heart made for society; and, to speak the truth of him, let as few occasions slip him as his master—so that somehow or other—but how—heaven knows—he had connected himself with the *demoiselle* upon the landing of the staircase, during the time I was taken up with my passport; and as there was time enough for me to win the Count to my interest, La Fleur had contrived to make it do to win the maid to his—the family, it seems, was to be at Paris that day, and he had made a party with her, and two or three more of the Count's household, upon the *boulevards*.

Happy people! that once a week at least are sure to lay down all your cares together; and dance and sing, and sport away the weights of grievance, which bow down the spirit of other nations to the earth.

THE FRAGMENT.

PARIS.

La Fleur had left me something to amuse myself with for the day more than I had bargained for, or could have entered either into his head or mine.

He had brought the little print of butter upon a currant leaf; and as the morning was warm, he had begged a sheet of waste paper to put betwixt the currant leaf and his hand—As that was plate sufficient, I bad him lay it upon the table as it was, and as I resolved to stay within all day, I ordered him to call upon the *traiteur*,[3] to bespeak my dinner, and leave me to breakfast by myself.

When I had finished the butter, I threw the currant leaf out of the window, and was going to do the same by the waste paper—but stopping to read a line first, and that drawing me on to a second and third—I thought it better worth; so I shut the window, and drawing a chair up to it, I sat down to read it.

It was in the old French of Rabelais's time,[4] and for aught I know might have been wrote by him—it was moreover in a Gothic letter, and that so faded and gone off by damps and length of time, it cost me infinite trouble to

2. Young woman.
3. Caterer.

4. The first half of the 16th century, the time of French comic author François Rabelais (ca. 1494–1553).

make anything of it—I threw it down; and then wrote a letter to Eugenius—then I took it up again and embroiled my patience with it afresh—and then to cure that, I wrote a letter to Eliza.—Still it kept hold of me; and the difficulty of understanding it increased but the desire.

I got my dinner; and after I had enlightened my mind with a bottle of Burgundy, I at it again—and after two or three hours poring upon it, with almost as deep attention as ever Gruter or Jacob Spon[5] did upon a nonsensical inscription, I thought I made sense of it; but to make sure of it, the best way, I imagined, was to turn it into English, and see how it would look then—so I went on leisurely as a trifling man does, sometimes writing a sentence—then taking a turn or two—and then looking how the world went, out of the window; so that it was nine o'clock at night before I had done it—I then begun and read it as follows.

THE FRAGMENT.

PARIS.

—Now as the notary's wife disputed the point with the notary with too much heat—I wish, said the notary, throwing down the parchment, that there was another notary here only to set down and attest all this—

—And what would you do then, Monsieur? said she, rising hastily up—the notary's wife was a little fume[6] of a woman, and the notary thought it well to avoid a hurricane by a mild reply—I would go, answered he, to bed.—You may go to the devil, answered the notary's wife.

Now there happening to be but one bed in the house, the other two rooms being unfurnished, as is the custom at Paris, and the notary not caring to lie in the same bed with a woman who had but that moment sent him pell-mell to the devil, went forth with his hat and cane and short cloak, the night being very windy, and walked out ill at ease towards the *Pont Neuf*.

Of all the bridges which ever were built, the whole world who have passed over the *Pont Neuf* must own, that it is the noblest—the finest—the grandest—the lightest—the longest—the broadest that ever conjoined land and land together upon the face of the terraqueous[7] globe—

By this it seems as if the author of the fragment had not been a Frenchman.[8]

The worst fault which divines and the doctors of the Sorbonne[9] can allege against it, is, that if there is but a capful of wind in or about Paris, 'tis more blasphemously *sacre Dieu'd*[1] there than in any other aperture of the whole city—and with reason, good and cogent, Messieurs; for it comes against you without crying *garde d'eau*,[2] and with such unpremeditable[3] puffs, that of the few who cross it with their hats on, not one in fifty but hazards two livres and a half, which is its full worth.

The poor notary, just as he was passing by the sentry, instinctively clapped his cane to the side of it, but in raising it up, the point of his cane catching

---

5. French historian and antiquarian (1647–1685). Gruter is Jan Gruytère (1560–1627), Dutch historian.
6. One who tends to fume in anger.
7. Formed of land and water.
8. An irony: the French were known to take great pride in the bridges of Paris.
9. Ancient university in Paris.
1. Cursed. Literally, "Holy God-ed."
2. Watch out for the water! Then-common cry of warning in France when dumping dirty water, emptying chamber pots, etc., out a window.
3. Unpredictable.

hold of the loop of the sentinel's hat, hoisted it over the spikes of the balustrade clear into the Seine—

—'Tis an ill wind, said a boatsman, who catched it, which blows nobody any good. The sentry, being a Gascon, incontinently twirled up his whiskers, and leveled his harquebus.[4]

Harquebuses in those days went off with matches; and an old woman's paper lanthorn at the end of the bridge happening to be blown out, she had borrowed the sentry's match to light it—it gave a moment's time for the Gascon's blood to run cool, and turn the accident better to his advantage—'Tis an ill wind, said he, catching off the notary's castor,[5] and legitimating the capture with the boatman's adage.

The poor notary crossed the bridge, and passing along the Rue de Dauphine into the fauxbourgs of St. Germain,[6] lamented himself as he walked along in this manner:

Luckless man! that I am, said the notary, to be the sport of hurricanes all my days—to be born to have the storm of ill language leveled against me and my profession wherever I go—to be forced into marriage by the thunder of the church to a tempest of a woman—to be driven forth out of my house by domestic winds, and despoiled of my castor by pontific[7] ones—to be here, bareheaded, in a windy night at the mercy of the ebbs and flows of accidents—where am I to lay my head?—miserable man! what wind in the two and thirty points of the whole compass can blow unto thee, as it does to the rest of thy fellow-creatures, good!

As the notary was passing on by a dark passage, complaining in this sort, a voice called out to a girl, to bid her run for the next notary—now the notary being the next, and availing himself of his situation, walked up the passage to the door, and passing through an old sort of a saloon, was ushered into a large chamber, dismantled of everything but a long military pike—a breastplate—a rusty old sword, and bandolier, hung up equidistant in four different places against the wall.

An old personage, who had heretofore been a gentleman, and unless decay of fortune taints the blood along with it, was a gentleman at that time, lay supporting his head upon his hand, in his bed; a little table with a taper burning was set close beside it, and close by the table was placed a chair—the notary sat him down in it; and pulling out his inkhorn and a sheet or two of paper which he had in his pocket, he placed them before him, and dipping his pen in his ink, and leaning his breast over the table, he disposed everything to make the gentleman's last will and testament.

Alas! Monsieur le Notaire,[8] said the gentleman, raising himself up a little, I have nothing to bequeath, which will pay the expense of bequeathing, except the history of myself, which I could not die in peace unless I left it as a legacy to the world; the profits arising out of it I bequeath to you for the pains of taking it from me—it is a story so uncommon, it must be read by all mankind—it will make the fortunes of your house—the notary dipped his pen into his inkhorn—Almighty Director of every event in my life! said the

---

4. An early portable gun, supported by a tripod. "Gascon": native of Gascony, proverbially boastful.
5. Hat made from beaver fur.

6. The Faubourg Saint Germain, now a part of Paris, was then a suburb just west of the city.
7. Pertaining to a bridge, also evoking the church (punning on "pontiff," the pope).

old gentleman, looking up earnestly, and raising his hands towards heaven—
thou whose hand hast led me on through such a labyrinth of strange passages
down into this scene of desolation, assist the decaying memory of an old,
infirm, and broken-hearted man—direct my tongue by the spirit of thy eternal truth, that this stranger may set down naught but what is written in that
Book,[9] from whose records, said he, clasping his hands together, I am to be
condemned or acquitted!—The notary held up the point of his pen betwixt
the taper and his eye—

—It is a story, Monsieur le Notaire, said the gentleman, which will rouse
up every affection in nature—it will kill the humane, and touch the heart
of cruelty herself with pity—

—The notary was inflamed with a desire to begin, and put his pen a third
time into his inkhorn—and the old gentleman turning a little more towards
the notary, began to dictate his story in these words—

—And where is the rest of it, La Fleur? said I, as he just then entered the
room.

THE FRAGMENT AND THE BOUQUET[1].

PARIS.

When La Fleur came up close to the table, and was made to comprehend
what I wanted, he told me there were only two other sheets of it, which he
had wrapt round the stalks of a *bouquet* to keep it together, which he had
presented to the *demoiselle* upon the *boulevards*—Then, prithee, La Fleur,
said I, step back to her to the Count de B****'s hotel, and *see if you canst
get*—There is no doubt of it, said La Fleur—and away he flew.

In a very little time the poor fellow came back quite out of breath, with
deeper marks of disappointment in his looks than could arise from the
simple irreparability of the fragment.—*Juste ciel!*[2] in less than two minutes
that the poor fellow had taken his last tender farewell of her—his faithless
mistress had given his *gage d'amour*[3] to one of the Count's footmen—the
footman to a young seamstress—and the seamstress to a fiddler, with my
fragment at the end of it—Our misfortunes were involved together—I gave
a sigh—and La Fleur echoed it back again to my ear.

—How perfidious! cried La Fleur—How unlucky! said I.—

—I should not have been mortified, Monsieur, quoth La Fleur, if she had
lost it—Nor I, La Fleur, said I, had I found it.

Whether I did or no, will be seen hereafter.

THE ACT OF CHARITY.

PARIS.

The man who either disdains or fears to walk up a dark entry, may be an
excellent good man, and fit for a hundred things; but he will not do to make
a good sentimental traveler. I count little of the many things I see pass at

---

8. Sir Notary.
9. I.e., the book into which a record of each person's actions in life is entered.

1. Nosegay [Sterne's note].
2. Good heavens!
3. Pledge of love.

broad noonday, in large and open streets.—Nature is shy, and hates to act before spectators; but in such an unobserved corner, you sometimes see a single short scene of hers, worth all the sentiments of a dozen French plays compounded together—and yet they are *absolutely* fine;—and whenever I have a more brilliant affair upon my hands than common, as they suit a preacher just as well as a hero, I generally make my sermon out of 'em—and for the text—"Cappadocia, Pontus and Asia, Phrygia and Pamphylia"[4]—is as good as any one in the Bible.

There is a long dark passage issuing out from the Opera Comique into a narrow street; 'tis trod by a few who humbly wait for a *fiacre*[5] or wish to get off quietly o' foot when the opera is done. At the end of it, towards the theater, 'tis lighted by a small candle, the light of which is almost lost before you get half-way down, but near the door—'tis more for ornament than use: you see it as a fixed star of the least magnitude; it burns—but does little good to the world, that we know of.

In returning along this passage, I discerned, as I approached within five or six paces of the door, two ladies standing arm in arm with their backs against the wall, waiting, as I imagined, for a *fiacre*—as they were next the door, I thought they had a prior right; so edged myself up within a yard or little more of them, and quietly took my stand—I was in black, and scarce seen.

The lady next me was a tall lean figure of a woman, of about thirty-six; the other of the same size and make, of about forty; there was no mark of wife or widow in any one part of either of them—they seemed to be two upright vestal[6] sisters, unsapped by caresses, unbroke in upon by tender salutations: I could have wished to have made them happy—their happiness was destined, that night, to come from another quarter.

A low voice, with a good turn of expression, and sweet cadence at the end of it, begged for a twelve-sous piece betwixt them, for the love of heaven. I thought it singular that a beggar should fix the quota of an alms—and that the sum should be twelve times as much as what is usually given in the dark. They both seemed astonished at it as much as myself.—Twelve sous! said one—A twelve-sous piece! said the other—and made no reply.

The poor man said, he knew not how to ask less of ladies of their rank; and bowed down his head to the ground.

Poo! said they—we have no money.

The beggar remained silent for a moment or two, and renewed his supplication.

Do not, my fair young ladies, said he, stop your good ears against me—Upon my word, honest man! said the younger, we have no change—Then God bless you, said the poor man, and multiply those joys which you can give to others without change!—I observed the elder sister put her hand into her pocket—I'll see, said she, if I have a sous—A sous! give twelve, said the supplicant; Nature has been bountiful to you, be bountiful to a poor man.

I would, friend, with all my heart, said the younger, if I had it.

---

4. Acts 2.9–10. At Pentecost, inspired by the Holy Spirit, the apostles address people from these and other places in their own languages. A sermon on such a biblical text, Yorick says, could well employ the style of contemporary French tragedy (which Sterne found excessively sentimental and preachy).
5. Hackney-coach [Sterne's note].
6. Virginal, like the priestesses of the Roman deity Vesta, goddess of the home and hearth.

My fair charitable! said he, addressing himself to the elder—what is it but your goodness and humanity which makes your bright eyes so sweet, that they outshine the morning even in this dark passage? and what was it which made the Marquis de Santerre and his brother[7] say so much of you both as they just passed by?

The two ladies seemed much affected; and impulsively at the same time they both put their hands into their pocket, and each took out a twelve-sous piece.

The contest betwixt them and the poor supplicant was no more—it was continued betwixt themselves, which of the two should give the twelve-sous piece in charity—and to end the dispute, they both gave it together, and the man went away.

THE RIDDLE EXPLAINED.

PARIS.

I stepped hastily after him: it was the very man whose success in asking charity of the women before the door of the hotel had so puzzled me—and I found at once his secret, or at least the basis of it—'twas flattery.

Delicious essence! how refreshing art thou to nature! how strongly are all its powers and all its weaknesses on thy side! how sweetly dost thou mix with the blood, and help it through the most difficult and tortuous passages to the heart!

The poor man, as he was not straitened[8] for time, had given it here in a larger dose: 'tis certain he had a way of bringing it into less form, for the many sudden cases[9] he had to do with in the streets; but how he contrived to correct, sweeten, concenter, and qualify it—I vex not my spirit with the inquiry—it is enough, the beggar gained two twelve-sous pieces—and they can best tell the rest, who have gained much greater matters by it.

PARIS.

We get forwards in the world, not so much by doing services, as receiving them: you take a withering twig, and put it in the ground; and then you water it because you have planted it.

Monsieur le Compte de B****, merely because he had done me one kindness in the affair of my passport, would go on and do me another, the few days he was at Paris, in making me known to a few people of rank; and they were to present me to others, and so on.

I had got master of my *secret*, just in time to turn these honors to some little account; otherwise, as is commonly the case, I should have dined or supped a single time or two round, and then by *translating* French looks and attitudes into plain English, I should presently have seen, that I had got hold of the *couvert*[1] of some more entertaining guest; and in course should have resigned all my places one after another, merely upon the principle that I could not keep them.—As it was, things did not go much amiss.

7. Two passing noblemen, though the name may suggest they are without land (*sans terre*).
8. Pressed.
9. Less perfectly shaped for quicker, less deliber- ate encounters.
1. Plate, napkin, knife, fork, and spoon [Sterne's note].

I had the honor of being introduced to the old Marquis de B****: in days of yore he had signalized himself by some small feats of chivalry in the *Cour d'amour*, and had dressed himself out to the idea of tilts[2] and tournaments ever since—the Marquis de B**** wished to have it thought the affair was somewhere else than in his brain. "He could like to take a trip to England," and asked much of the English ladies. Stay where you are, I beseech you Monsieur le Marquis, said I—Les Messieurs Anglois[3] can scarce get a kind look from them as it is.—The Marquis invited me to supper.

Monsieur P**** the farmer-general[4] was just as inquisitive about our taxes.—They were very considerable, he heard—If we knew but how to collect them, said I, making him a low bow.

I could never have been invited to Monsieur P****'s concerts upon any other terms.

I had been misrepresented to Madame de Q*** as an *esprit*[5]—Madame de Q*** was an *esprit* herself; she burnt with impatience to see me, and hear me talk. I had not taken my seat, before I saw she did not care a sous whether I had any wit or no—I was let in, to be convinced she had.—I call heaven to witness I never once opened the door of my lips.

Madame de Q*** vowed to every creature she met, "she had never had a more improving conversation with a man in her life."

There are three epochas[6] in the empire of a Frenchwoman—She is coquette—then deist—then *devôte*:[7] the empire during these is never lost—she only changes her subjects: when thirty-five years and more have unpeopled her dominions of the slaves of love, she repeoples it with slaves of infidelity—and then with the slaves of the Church.

Madame de V*** was vibrating betwixt the first of these epochas: the color of the rose was shading fast away—she ought to have been a deist five years before the time I had the honor to pay my first visit.

She placed me upon the same sofa with her, for the sake of disputing the point of religion more closely—In short Madame de V*** told me she believed nothing.

I told Madame de V*** it might be her principle; but I was sure it could not be her interest to level the outworks,[8] without which I could not conceive how such a citadel as hers could be defended—that there was not a more dangerous thing in the world than for a beauty to be a deist—that it was a debt I owed my creed, not to conceal it from her—that I had not been five minutes sat upon the sofa besides her, but I had begun to form designs—and what is it but the sentiments of religion, and the persuasion they had existed in her breast, which could have checked them as they rose up.

We are not adamant, said I, taking hold of her hand—and there is need of all restraints, till age in her own time steals in and lays them on us—but, my dear lady, said I, kissing her hand—'tis too—too soon—

2. Jousts. The Marquis is a knight at the court of Love ("*Cour d'amour*").
3. English gentlemen.
4. Tax collector. An allusion to Alexandre-Jean-Joseph Le Riche de la Popelinière (1692–1762).
5. A wit, a person of spirit.

6. Epochs, stages.
7. One devoted to religion. "Deist": one who believes in God but not the doctrines of any Christian church or the supernatural events described in the Bible.
8. Outer fortifications.

I declare I had the credit all over Paris of unperverting Madame de V***.—She affirmed to Monsieur D***[9] and the Abbe M***,[1] that in one half-hour I had said more for revealed religion[2] than all their Encyclopedia had said against it—I was lifted directly into Madame de V***'s *Coterie*— and she put off the epocha of deism for two years.

I remember it was in this *Coterie*, in the middle of a discourse, in which I was showing the necessity of a *first cause*, that the young Count de Faineant[3] took me by the hand to the furthest corner of the room to tell me my *solitaire* was pinned too strait about my neck.—It should be *plus badinant*,[4] said the Count, looking down upon his own—but a word, Monsieur Yorick, *to the wise*— —And *from the wise*, Monsieur le Compte, replied I, making him a bow—*is enough*.

The Count de Faineant embraced me with more ardor than ever I was embraced by mortal man.

For three weeks together, I was of every man's opinion I met.—*Pardi! ce Monsieur Yorick a autant d'esprit que nous autres.—Il raisonne bien*, said another.—*C'est un bon enfant*,[5] said a third.—And at this price I could have eaten and drank and been merry all the days of my life at Paris; but 'twas a dishonest *reckoning*—I grew ashamed of it—It was the gain of a slave—every sentiment of honor revolted against it—the higher I got, the more was I forced upon my *beggarly system*—the better the *Coterie*—the more children of Art—I languished for those of Nature: and one night, after a most vile prostitution of myself to half a dozen different people, I grew sick—went to bed—ordered La Fleur to get me horses in the morning to set out for Italy.

MARIA.

MOULINES.[6]

I never felt what the distress of plenty was in any one shape till now—to travel it through the Bourbonnois, the sweetest part of France—in the hey- day of the vintage,[7] when Nature is pouring her abundance into every one's lap, and every eye is lifted up—a journey through each step of which music beats time to *Labor*, and all her children are rejoicing as they carry in their clusters—to pass through this with my affections flying out, and kindling at every group before me—and every one of 'em was pregnant with adventures.

Just heaven!—it would fill up twenty volumes—and alas! I have but a few small pages left of this to crowd it into—and half of these must be taken up with the poor Maria my friend Mr. Shandy met with near Moulines.[8]

The story he had told of that disordered maid affected me not a little in

---

9. Denis Diderot (1713–1784), author and editor of the massive *Encyclopédie, ou dictionnaire rai- sonné des sciences, des arts et des métiers* (Ency- clopaedia, or a systematic dictionary of the sciences, arts, and crafts, 1751–72), to which he contributed many articles.
1. Identified as Abbé André Morellet (1727–1819), a relatively orthodox divine who wrote many of the articles about theology in the *Encyclopédie*.
2. Religion as revealed by Holy Scripture, not as reasoned out by intellect.
3. Idler. "First cause": the idea that the universe must be caused by a prime mover, God, who him- self has no prior cause.

4. More loose.
5. By Jove! Mr Yorick is as witty as we are. . . . He reasons well. . . . He's a good fellow.
6. Moulins, capital of the old province of Bour- bonnais (corresponding to the modern depart- ment of Allier) in central France, about 160 miles south of Paris.
7. When wine grapes are harvested.
8. In book 9 of *Tristram Shandy*, Tristram describes this encounter with Maria, who went mad after having her marriage prevented by a wicked priest. The present scene in *A Sentimental Journey* made her a preeminent figure of pathos in sentimental literature, paintings, and prints.

the reading; but when I got within the neighborhood where she lived, it returned so strong into my mind, that I could not resist an impulse which prompted me to go half a league out of the road, to the village where her parents dwelt, to inquire after her.

'Tis going, I own, like the Knight of the Woeful Countenance,[9] in quest of melancholy adventures—but I know not how it is, but I am never so perfectly conscious of the existence of a soul within me, as when I am entangled in them.

The old mother came to the door, her looks told me the story before she opened her mouth—She had lost her husband; he had died, she said, of anguish, for the loss of Maria's senses, about a month before.—She had feared at first, she added, that it would have plundered her poor girl of what little understanding was left—but, on the contrary, it had brought her more to herself—still she could not rest—her poor daughter, she said, crying, was wandering somewhere about the road—

—Why does my pulse beat languid as I write this? and what made La Fleur, whose heart seemed only to be tuned to joy, to pass the back of his hand twice across his eyes, as the woman stood and told it? I beckoned to the postilion to turn back into the road.

When we had got within half a league of Moulines, at a little opening in the road leading to a thicket, I discovered poor Maria sitting under a poplar—she was sitting with her elbow in her lap, and her head leaning on one side within her hand—a small brook ran at the foot of the tree.

I bid the postilion go on with the chaise to Moulines—and La Fleur to bespeak my supper—and that I would walk after him.

She was dressed in white, and much as my friend described her, except that her hair hung loose, which before was twisted within a silk net.—She had, superadded likewise to her jacket, a pale-green ribband, which fell across her shoulder to the waist; at the end of which hung her pipe.—Her goat[1] had been as faithless as her lover; and she had got a little dog in lieu of him, which she had kept tied by a string to her girdle: as I looked at her dog, she drew him towards her with the string.—"Thou shalt not leave me, Sylvio," said she. I looked in Maria's eyes, and saw she was think-

A needlepoint thought to be by Emma Hamilton, model and society celebrity, representing herself and her lover, naval hero Horatio Lord Nelson, as Maria and Yorick (late 18th century). National Maritime Museum, London.

9. A title Cervantes gives his protagonist Don Quixote.
1. In *Tristram Shandy*, Maria had tended a goat. Tristram asked if she found a resemblance between it and him.

ing more of her father than of her lover or her little goat; for as she uttered them the tears trickled down her cheeks.

I sat down close by her; and Maria let me wipe them away as they fell, with my handkerchief.—I then steeped it in my own—and then in hers—and then in mine—and then I wiped hers again—and as I did it, I felt such undescribable emotions within me, as I am sure could not be accounted for from any combinations of matter and motion.[2]

I am positive I have a soul; nor can all the books with which materialists have pestered the world ever convince me of the contrary.

MARIA.

When Maria had come a little to herself, I asked her if she remembered a pale thin person of a man, who had sat down betwixt her and her goat about two years before? She said, she was unsettled much at that time, but remembered it upon two accounts—that ill as she was she saw the person pitied her; and next, that her goat had stolen his handkerchief, and she had beat him for the theft—she had washed it, she said, in the brook, and kept it ever since in her pocket to restore it to him in case she should ever see him again, which, she added, he had half promised her. As she told me this, she took the handkerchief out of her pocket to let me see it; she had folded it up neatly in a couple of vine leaves, tied round with a tendril—on opening it, I saw an S marked in one of the corners.

She had since that, she told me, strayed as far as Rome, and walked round St. Peter's once—and returned back—that she found her way alone across the Apennines[3]—had traveled over all Lombardy without money—and through the flinty roads of Savoy without shoes—how she had borne it, and how she had got supported, she could not tell—but *God tempers the wind,* said Maria, to the shorn lamb.[4]

Shorn indeed! and to the quick, said I; and wast thou in my own land, where I have a cottage, I would take thee to it and shelter thee: thou shouldst eat of my own bread and drink of my own cup—I would be kind to thy Sylvio—in all thy weaknesses and wanderings I would seek after thee and bring thee back—when the sun went down I would say my prayers; and when I had done thou shouldst play thy evening song upon thy pipe, nor would the incense of my sacrifice be worse accepted for entering heaven along with that of a broken heart.

Nature melted within me, as I uttered this; and Maria observing, as I took out my handkerchief, that it was steeped too much already to be of use, would needs go wash it in the stream.—And where will you dry it, Maria? said I—I'll dry it in my bosom, said she—'twill do me good.

And is your heart still so warm, Maria? said I.

I touched upon the string on which hung all her sorrows—she looked with wistful disorder for some time in my face; and then, without saying anything, took her pipe, and played her service to the Virgin—The string I had touched ceased to vibrate—in a moment or two Maria returned to herself—let her pipe fall—and rose up.

2. What the universe consists of according to materialist philosophers.
3. The mountain range that runs the length of the Italian peninsula.
4. A French proverb.

And where are you going, Maria? said I.—She said to Moulines.—Let us go, said I, together.—Maria put her arm within mine, and lengthening the string, to let the dog follow—in that order we entered Moulines.

MARIA.

MOULINES.

Though I hate salutations and greetings in the marketplace,[5] yet when we got into the middle of this, I stopped to take my last look and last farewell of Maria. Maria, though not tall, was nevertheless of the first order of fine forms—affliction had touched her looks with something that was scarce earthly—still she was feminine—and so much was there about her of all that the heart wishes, or the eye looks for in woman, that could the traces be ever worn out of her brain, and those of Eliza's out of mine, she should *not only eat of my bread and drink of my own cup*, but Maria should lay in my bosom, and be unto me as a daughter.

Adieu, poor luckless maiden!—Imbibe the oil and wine which the compassion of a stranger, as he journeyeth on his way, now pours into thy wounds[6]— the being who has twice bruised thee can only bind them up forever.

THE BOURBONNOIS.

There was nothing from which I had painted out for myself so joyous a riot of the affections, as in this journey in the vintage, through this part of France; but pressing through this gate of sorrow to it, my sufferings have totally unfitted me: in every scene of festivity I saw Maria in the background of the piece, sitting pensive under her poplar; and I had got almost to Lyons before I was able to cast a shade across her—

—Dear sensibility! source inexhausted of all that's precious in our joys, or costly in our sorrows! thou chainest thy martyr down upon his bed of straw—and 'tis thou who lifts him up to HEAVEN—eternal fountain of our feelings!—'tis here I trace thee—and this is thy divinity which stirs within me—not, that in some sad and sickening moments, *"my soul shrinks back upon herself, and startles at destruction"*[7]—mere pomp of words!—but that I feel some generous joys and generous cares beyond myself—all comes from thee, great—great SENSORIUM[8] of the world! which vibrates, if a hair of our heads but falls upon the ground, in the remotest desert of thy creation.— Touched with thee, Eugenius draws my curtain when I languish—hears my tale of symptoms, and blames the weather for the disorder of his nerves. Thou givest a portion of it sometimes to the roughest peasant who traverses the bleakest mountains—he finds the lacerated lamb of another's flock— This moment I beheld him leaning with his head against his crook, with piteous inclination looking down upon it—Oh! had I come one moment sooner!—it bleeds to death—his gentle heart bleeds with it—

Peace to thee, generous swain!—I see thou walkest off with anguish— but thy joys shall balance it—for happy is thy cottage—and happy is the sharer of it—and happy are the lambs which sport about you.

5. See Mark 12.38.
6. See Luke 10.33–34.
7. Closely following the play *Cato* (1713), 5.1.5–6,

by Joseph Addison (1672–1719).
8. The complete ensemble of the sensory apparatus of feeling beings.

THE SUPPER.

A shoe coming loose from the fore foot of the thill-horse, at the beginning of the ascent of mount Taurira,[9] the postilion dismounted, twisted the shoe off, and put it in his pocket; as the ascent was of five or six miles, and that horse our main dependence, I made a point of having the shoe fastened on again, as well as we could; but the postilion had thrown away the nails, and the hammer in the chaise-box being of no great use without them, I submitted to go on.

He had not mounted half a mile higher, when coming to a flinty piece of road, the poor devil lost a second shoe, and from off his other fore-foot; I then got out of the chaise in good earnest; and seeing a house about a quarter of a mile to the left hand, with a great deal to do,[1] I prevailed upon the postilion to turn up to it. The look of the house, and of everything about it, as we drew nearer, soon reconciled me to the disaster.—It was a little farmhouse, surrounded with about twenty acres of vineyard, about as much corn—and close to the house, on one side, was a *potagerie*[2] of an acre and a half, full of everything which could make plenty in a French peasant's house—and on the other side was a little wood, which furnished wherewithal to dress it. It was about eight in the evening when I got to the house—so I left the postilion to manage his point as he could—and for mine, I walked directly into the house.

The family consisted of an old gray-headed man and his wife, with five or six sons and sons-in-law, and their several wives, and a joyous genealogy out of 'em.

They were all sitting down together to their lentil soup; a large wheaten loaf was in the middle of the table; and a flagon of wine at each end of it, promised joy thro' the stages of the repast—'twas a feast of love.

The old man rose up to meet me, and with a respectful cordiality would have me sit down at the table; my heart was sat down the moment I entered the room; so I sat down at once like a son of the family; and to invest myself in the character as speedily as I could, I instantly borrowed the old man's knife, and taking up the loaf, cut myself a hearty luncheon;[3] and as I did it, I saw a testimony in every eye, not only of an honest welcome, but of a welcome mixed with thanks that I had not seemed to doubt it.

Was it this; or tell me, Nature, what else it was which made this morsel so sweet—and to what magic I owe it, that the draught I took of their flagon was so delicious with it, that they remain upon my palate to this hour?

If the supper was to my taste—the grace which followed it was much more so.

THE GRACE.

When supper was over, the old man gave a knock upon the table with the haft of his knife—to bid them prepare for the dance: the moment the signal was given, the women and girls ran all together into a back apartment to tie up their hair—and the young men to the door to wash their faces, and change

---

9. The climbing road to Tarare, a town twenty-eight miles northwest of Lyon. "Thill-horse": in a team of horses, the one closest to the wheels and carriage.

1. By a big effort.
2. Kitchen garden. "Corn": wheat.
3. "As much food as one's hand can hold" (Johnson's *Dictionary*, 1755).

their sabots;[4] and in three minutes every soul was ready upon a little esplanade before the house to begin—The old man and his wife came out last, and placing me betwixt them, sat down upon a sofa of turf by the door.

The old man had some fifty years ago been no mean performer upon the vielle[5]—and, at the age he was then of, touched it well enough for the purpose. His wife sung now and then a little to the tune—then intermitted—and joined her old man again as their children and grandchildren danced before them.

It was not till the middle of the second dance, from some pauses in the movement wherein they all seemed to look up, I fancied I could distinguish an elevation of spirit different from that which is the cause or the effect of simple jollity.—In a word, I thought I beheld *Religion* mixing in the dance—but as I had never seen her so engaged, I should have looked upon it now, as one of the illusions of an imagination which is eternally misleading me, had not the old man, as soon the dance ended, said that this was their constant way; and that all his life long he had made it a rule, after supper was over, to call out his family to dance and rejoice; believing, he said, that a cheerful and contented mind was the best sort of thanks to heaven that an illiterate peasant could pay—

—Or a learned prelate[6] either, said I.

THE CASE OF DELICACY.

When you have gained the top of mount Taurira, you run presently down to Lyons—adieu then to all rapid movements! 'Tis a journey of caution; and it fares better with sentiments, not to be in a hurry with them; so I contracted with a voiturin[7] to take his time with a couple of mules, and convey me in my own chaise safe to Turin through Savoy.

Poor, patient, quiet, honest people! fear not: your poverty, the treasury of your simple virtues, will not be envied you by the world, nor will your valleys be invaded by it.—Nature! in the midst of thy disorders, thou art still friendly to the scantiness thou hast created—with all thy great works about thee, little hast thou left to give, either to the scythe or to the sickle—but to that little thou grantest safety and protection; and sweet are the dwellings which stand so sheltered.

Let the way-worn traveler vent his complaints upon the sudden turns and dangers of your roads—your rocks—your precipices—the difficulties of getting up—the horrors of getting down—mountains impracticable—and cataracts, which roll down great stones from their summits, and block his up road.—The peasants had been all day at work in removing a fragment of this kind between St. Michael and Madane;[8] and by the time my voiturin got to the place, it wanted full two hours of completing before a passage could any how be gained: there was nothing but to wait with patience—'twas a wet and tempestuous night: so that by the delay, and that together, the voiturin found himself obliged to take up five miles short of his stage[9] at a little decent kind of an inn by the roadside.

---

4. Wooden shoes of French peasants.
5. A four-stringed instrument played with a wheel, a hurdy-gurdy.
6. High church official, such as a bishop.
7. One who furnishes conveyance for travelers crossing the Alps.
8. St. Michel and Modane, two alpine towns about ten miles apart near the French–Italian border.
9. Appointed stopping place on the road.

I forthwith took possession of my bedchamber—got a good fire—ordered supper; and was thanking heaven it was no worse—when a voiture[1] arrived with a lady in it and her servant-maid.

As there was no other bedchamber in the house, the hostess, without much nicety, led them into mine, telling them, as she ushered them in, that there was nobody in it but an English gentleman—that there were two good beds in it, and a closet within the room which held another—the accent in which she spoke of this third bed did not say much for it—however, she said there were three beds, and but three people—and she durst say, the gentleman would do anything to accommodate matters.—I left not the lady a moment to make a conjecture about it—so instantly made a declaration I would do anything in my power.

As this did not amount to an absolute surrender of my bedchamber, I still felt myself so much the proprietor, as to have a right to do the honors of it[2]—so I desired the lady to sit down—pressed her into the warmest seat—called for more wood—desired the hostess to enlarge the plan of the supper, and to favor us with the very best wine.

The lady had scarce warmed herself five minutes at the fire, before she began to turn her head back, and give a look at the beds; and the oftener she cast her eyes that way, the more they returned perplexed—I felt for her—and for myself; for in a few minutes, what by her looks, and the case itself, I found myself as much embarrassed as it was possible the lady could be herself.

That the beds we were to lay in were in one and the same room, was enough simply by itself to have excited all this—but the position of them, for they stood parallel, and so very close to each other, as only to allow space for a small wicker chair betwixt them, rendered the affair still more oppressive to us—they were fixed up moreover near the fire, and the projection of the chimney on one side, and a large beam which crossed the room on the other, formed a kind of recess for them that was no way favorable to the nicety of our sensations—if anything could have added to it, it was that the two beds were both of 'em so very small, as to cut us off from every idea of the lady and the maid lying together; which in either of them, could it have been feasible, my lying besides them, tho' a thing not to be wished, yet there was nothing in it so terrible which the imagination might not have passed over without torment.

As for the little room within, it offered little or no consolation to us; 'twas a damp cold closet, with a half-dismantled window shutter, and with a window which had neither glass or oil paper[3] in it to keep out the tempest of the night. I did not endeavor to stifle my cough[4] when the lady gave a peep into it; so it reduced the case in course to this alternative—that the lady should sacrifice her health to her feelings, and take up with the closet herself, and abandon the bed next mine to her maid—or that the girl should take the closet, &c. &c.

The lady was a Piedmontese[5] of about thirty, with a glow of health in her cheeks.—The maid was a Lyonoise[6] of twenty, and as brisk and lively a French girl as ever moved.—There were difficulties every way—and the obstacle of the stone in the road, which brought us into the distress, great as

1. Carriage.
2. Dispose of it as I saw fit.
3. Paper waterproofed with oil used in lieu of window glass.
4. Sterne perhaps alludes to his own tuberculosis.
5. From Piedmont, in the upper northwest of Italy.
6. Lyonnaise, from Lyon, France.

it appeared whilst the peasants were removing it, was but a pebble to what lay in our ways now—I have only to add, that it did not lessen the weight which hung upon our spirits, that we were both too delicate to communicate what we felt to each other upon the occasion.

We sat down to supper; and had we not had more generous wine to it than a little inn in Savoy could have furnished, our tongues had been tied up, till necessity herself had set them at liberty—but the lady having a few bottles of Burgundy in her voiture, sent down her Fille de Chambre for a couple of them; so that by the time supper was over, and we were left alone, we felt ourselves inspired with a strength of mind sufficient to talk, at least, without reserve upon our situation. We turned it every way, and debated and considered it in all kind of lights in the course of a two hours' negotiation; at the end of which the articles were settled finally betwixt us, and stipulated for in form and manner of a treaty of peace—and I believe with as much religion and good faith on both sides, as in any treaty which has yet had the honor of being handed down to posterity.

They were as follows:

First. As the right of the bedchamber is in Monsieur—and he thinking the bed next to the fire to be the warmest, he insists upon the concession on the lady's side of taking up with it.

Granted, on the part of Madame; with a proviso, that as the curtains of that bed are of a flimsy transparent cotton, and appear likewise too scanty to draw close, that the Fille de Chambre shall fasten up the opening, either by corking pins,[7] or needle and thread, in such manner as shall be deemed a sufficient barrier on the side of Monsieur.

2dly. It is required on the part of Madame, that Monsieur shall lay the whole night through in his robe de chambre.[8]

Rejected: inasmuch as Monsieur is not worth a robe de chambre; he having nothing in his portmanteau but six shirts and a black silk pair of breeches.

The mentioning the silk pair of breeches made an entire change of the article—for the breeches were accepted as an equivalent for the robe de chambre; and so it was stipulated and agreed upon, that I should lay in my black silk breeches all night.

3dly. It was insisted upon, and stipulated for by the lady, that after Monsieur was got to bed, and the candle and fire extinguished, that Monsieur should not speak one single word the whole night.

Granted; provided Monsieur's saying his prayers might not be deemed an infraction of the treaty.

There was but one point forgot in this treaty, and that was the manner in which the lady and myself should be obliged to undress and get to bed—there was but one way of doing it, and that I leave to the reader to devise; protesting as I do, that if it is not the most delicate in nature, 'tis the fault of his own imagination—against which this is not my first complaint.

Now when we were got to bed, whether it was the novelty of the situation, or what it was, I know not; but so it was, I could not shut my eyes; I tried this side and that, and turned and turned again, till a full hour after midnight; when Nature and patience both wearing out—O my God! said I—

7. Pins of the largest size.
8. Nightgown.

—You have broke the treaty, Monsieur, said the lady, who had no more slept than myself.—I begged a thousand pardons—but insisted it was no more than an ejaculation—she maintained 'twas an entire infraction of the treaty—I maintained it was provided for in the clause of the third article.

The lady would by no means give up her point, though she weakened her barrier by it; for in the warmth of the dispute, I could hear two or three corking-pins fall out of the curtain to the ground.

Upon my word and honor, Madame, said I—stretching my arm out of bed by way of asseveration—

—(I was going to have added, that I would not have trespassed against the remotest idea of decorum for the world)—

—But the Fille de Chambre hearing there were words between us, and fearing that hostilities would ensue in course,[9] had crept silently out of her closet, and it being totally dark, had stolen so close to our beds, that she had got herself into the narrow passage which separated them, and had advanced so far up as to be in a line betwixt her mistress and me—

So that when I stretched out my hand, I caught hold of the Fille de Chambre's

END OF VOL. II.

1768

9. As a result.

FRANCES BURNEY
1752–1840

People have often made the mistake of underestimating Frances Burney. In person, as in her writing, she seemed a proper, self-effacing lady. Many readers still call her "Fanny," as if familiarity could make her harmless. But she saw through such poses. Sir Joshua Reynolds said that "if he was conscious to himself of any trick, or any affectation, there is nobody he should so much fear as this little Burney!" And Samuel Johnson teased her by claiming that "your shyness, & slyness, & pretending to know nothing, never took *me* in, whatever you may do with others. *I* always knew you for a *toadling!*" (according to legend, little toads may look submissive but actually carry poison). Although her writing crackles with humor, it can be relentless—and sometimes cruel—in exposing bad manners or a selfish heart.

She learned quite young how to hide in a crowd. A devoted daughter of Charles Burney, a popular teacher and historian of music, Frances grew up in a large family that gave her many opportunities to study character and mix discreetly in society. Her first novel, *Evelina, or, A Young Lady's Entrance into the World* (1778), was written in secret and published anonymously. But delighted readers, including Johnson, Burke, and Hester Thrale, soon found her out and sang her praises; and a second novel, *Cecilia* (1782), confirmed her reputation. Her home life was less happy, however; she and her stepmother disliked each other, and she fell in love with a young clergyman who never got around to proposing. In 1786, to please her father, she accepted a place as a lady-in-waiting at court, where the paralyzing etiquette and lack of independence tormented her for the next five years, until she finally managed to resign. At forty-one she married a French émigré, General Alexandre-Gabriel-Jean-Baptiste d'Arblay. Despite the disapproval of her father—d'Arblay was penniless, Catholic, and politically liberal—the marriage was happy. Madame d'Arblay soon bore a son, and her novel *Camilla* (1796) brought in good money. After she joined her husband in France, in 1802, the Napoleonic wars prevented them from returning to England for ten years; the pain of an outcast dominates her last novel, *The Wanderer, or Female Difficulties* (1814). But she never stopped writing, producing a doctored version of her father's *Memoirs* (1832) and more of the diaries and letters that, edited after her death by a niece, made her famous again.

Burney wrote all her life—not only novels and plays but perpetual letters and journals, recording whatever she saw for friends and family as well as herself. Even the most informal pages display her gifts: a knack for catching character, a wonderful ear for dialogue, wry humor, and a swift pace that carries the reader along from moment to moment. Her special subject is embarrassment—often her own. In scenes like her flight from the king, where she is torn between opposite notions of the right thing to do, shame and comedy mingle. These trepidations can also be incredibly painful, as in her gripping account of a mastectomy. Despite her propriety, Burney looks at the world and its institutions with the clear eyes of an outsider, aware of the gaps between what people say and what they do. She frees herself to write with utter honesty by pretending, at first, that nobody is going to read her. But her private thoughts are reported so fully and faithfully that, in the end, every reader can share them.

From The Journal and Letters

[FIRST JOURNAL ENTRY]

Poland Street, London, March 27, 1768[1]

To have some account of my thoughts, manners, acquaintance and actions, when the hour arrives at which time is more nimble than memory, is the reason which induces me to keep a journal: a journal in which I must confess my *every* thought, must open my whole heart! But a thing of this kind ought to be addressed to somebody—I must imagine myself to be talking— talking to the most intimate of friends—to one in whom I should take delight in confiding, and feel remorse in concealment: but who must this friend be?—to make choice of one to whom I can but *half* rely, would be to frustrate entirely the intention of my plan. The only one I could wholly, totally confide in, lives in the same house with me, and not only never *has*, but never *will*, leave me one secret *to* tell her.[2] To whom, then *must* I dedicate my wonderful, surprising and interesting adventures?—to *whom* dare I reveal my private opinion of my nearest relations? the secret thoughts of my dearest friends? my own hopes, fears, reflections and dislikes—Nobody!

1. This is the first page of Burney's first journal, begun when she was fifteen.
2. Burney's younger sister Susanna. In 1773, when Burney spent the summer away from home, she began a journal for her sister, continuing it off and on until 1800, when Susanna died.

To Nobody, then, will I write my Journal! since To Nobody can I be wholly unreserved—to Nobody can I reveal every thought, every wish of my heart, with the most unlimited confidence, the most unremitting sincerity to the end of my life! For what chance, what accident can end my connections with Nobody? No secret *can* I conceal from No—body, and to No—body can I be *ever* unreserved. Disagreement cannot stop our affection, Time itself has no power to end our friendship. The love, the esteem I entertain for Nobody, No-body's self has not power to destroy. From Nobody I have nothing to fear, the secrets sacred to friendship, Nobody will not reveal, when the affair is doubtful, Nobody will not look towards the side least favourable.—

I will suppose you, then, to be my best friend; tho' God forbid you ever should! my dearest companion—and a romantick girl, for mere oddity may perhaps be more sincere—more *tender*—than if you were a friend in propria personae[3]—in as much as imagination often exceeds reality. In your breast my errors may create pity without exciting contempt; may raise your compassion, without eradicating your love.

From this moment, then, my dear girl—but why, permit me to ask, must a *female* be made Nobody? Ah! my dear, what were this world good for, *were* Nobody a female? And now I have done with *perambulation*.

[MR. BARLOW'S PROPOSAL]

About 2 o'clock, while I was dawdling in the study, and waiting for an opportunity to speak, John came in, and said "A gentleman is below, who asks for Miss Burney,—Mr. Barlow."[4]

I think I was never more distressed in my life—to have taken pains to avoid a private conversation so highly disagreeable to me, and at last to be forced into it at so unfavourable a juncture,—for I had now 2 letters from him, both unanswered and consequently open to his conjectures. I exclaimed "Lord!—how provoking! what shall I do?"

My father looked uneasy and perplexed:—he said something about not being hasty, which I did not desire him to explain. Terrified lest he should hint at the advantage of an early establishment—like Mr. Crisp[5]—quick from the study—but slow enough afterwards—I went down stairs.—I saw my mother pass from the front into the back parlour; which did not add to the *graciousness* of my reception of poor Mr. Barlow, who I found alone in the front parlor. I was not sorry that none of the family were there, as I now began to seriously dread any protraction of this affair.

He came up to me, and with an air of *tenderness* and satisfaction, began some anxious enquiries about my health, but I interrupted him with saying "I fancy, sir, you have not received a letter I—I—"

I stopt, for I could not say which I had *sent*!

"A letter?—no, ma'am!"

"You will have it, then, to-morrow, sir."

3. As a real person.
4. Thomas Barlow had met Burney early in May and immediately wrote to declare that he loved and admired her. She did not reciprocate his feelings: "his language is stiff & uncommon, he has a great desire to please, but no elegance of manners; nei- ther, though he may be very worthy, is he at all agreeable." Her family, however, approved of the match and encouraged her to accept him.
5. Samuel Crisp, an old family friend, had been a mentor to Burney. "Early establishment": marriage when young.

We were both silent for a minute or two, when he said "In consequence, I presume, ma'am, of the one I—"

"Yes, sir!" cried I.

"And pray—ma'am—Miss Burney!—may I—beg to ask the contents? that is—the—the—" he could not go on.

"Sir—I—it was only—it was merely—in short, you will see it tomorrow."

"But if you would favor me with the contents now, I could perhaps answer it at once?"

"Sir, it requires no answer!"

A second silence ensued. I was really distressed myself to see *his* distress, which was very apparent. After some time, he stammered out something of *hoping*—and *beseeching*,—which, gathering more firmness, I announced— "I am much obliged to you, sir, for the too good opinion you are pleased to have of me—but I should be sorry you should lose any more time upon my account—as I have no thoughts at all of changing my situation and abode."

* * *

He remonstrated very earnestly. "This is the severest decision!—Surely you must allow that the *social state* is what we were all meant for?—that we were created for one another?—that to form such a resolution is contrary to the design of our being?—"

"All this may be true,—" said I;—"I have nothing to say in contradiction to it—but you know there are many odd characters in the world—and perhaps I am one of them."

"O no, no, no,—that can never be!—but is it possible you can have so bad an opinion of the married state? It seems to me the *only* state for happiness!—"

"Well, sir, *you* are attached to the married life—I am to the single— therefore, *every man in his humor*[6]—do *you* follow *your* opinion,—and let *me* follow *mine*."

"But surely—is not this—*singular?*—"

"I give you leave, sir," cried I, laughing, "to think me singular—odd— queer—nay, even whimsical, if you please."

"But, my *dear* Miss Burney, only—"

"I entreat you, sir, to take my answer—You really pain me by being so urgent.—"

"That would not I do for the world!—I only beg you to suffer me— perhaps in future—"

"No, indeed; I shall never change—I do assure you you will find me very obstinate!"

He began to lament his own destiny. I grew extremely tired of saying so often the same thing;—but I could not absolutely turn him out of the house, and indeed he seemed so dejected and unhappy, that I made it my study to soften my refusal as much as I could without leaving room for future expectation.

About this time, my mother came in. We both rose.—I was horridly provoked at my situation—

---

6. Title of a play (1598) by Ben Jonson.

"I am only come in for a letter," cried she,—"pray don't let me disturb you.—" And away she went.

This could not but be encouraging to him, for she was no sooner gone, than he began again the same story, and seemed determined not to give up his cause. He hoped, at least, that I would allow him to enquire after my health?—

"I must beg you, sir, to send me no more letters."

He seemed much hurt.

"You had better, sir, think of me no more—if you study your own happiness—"

"I *do* study my own happiness—more than I have ever had any probability of doing before—!"

"You have made an unfortunate choice, sir; but you will find it easier to forget it than you imagine. You have only to suppose I was not at Mr. Burney's on May Day—and it was a mere chance my being there—and then you will be—"

"But if I *could*—could I also forget seeing you at old Mrs. Burney's?—and if I did—can I forget that I see you now?—"

"O yes!—in 3 months time you may forget you ever knew me. You will not find it so difficult as you suppose."

"You have heard, ma'am, of an old man being growed young?—perhaps you believe *that*?—But you will not deny me leave to sometimes see you?—"

"My father, sir, is seldom,—hardly ever, indeed, at home—"

"I have never seen the doctor—but I hope he would not refuse me permission to enquire after your health? I have no wish without his consent."

"Though I acknowledge myself to be *singular* I would not have you think me either *affected* or *trifling*,—and therefore I must assure you that I am *fixed* in the answer I have given you; *unalterably* fixed."

* * *

He then took his leave:—returned back—took leave—and returned again:—I now made a more formal reverence of the head, at the same time expressing my good wishes for his welfare, in a sort of way that implied I expected never to see him again—he would fain have taken a more *tender* leave of me,—but I repulsed him with great surprise and displeasure. I did not, however, as he was so terribly sorrowful, refuse him my hand, which he had made sundry vain attempts to take in the course of our conversation; but when I withdrew it, as I did presently, I rang the bell, to prevent him again returning from the door.

Though I was really sorry for the unfortunate and misplaced attachment which this young man professes for me, yet I could almost have *jumped* for joy when he was gone, to think that the affair was thus finally over.

Indeed I think it hardly possible for a woman to be in a more irksome situation, than when rejecting a worthy man who is all humility, respect and submission, and who throws himself and his fortune at her feet.

* * *

The next day—a day the remembrance of which will be never erased from my memory—my father first spoke to me *in favor* of Mr. Barlow! and desired me not to be *peremptory* in the answer I had still to write, though it was to appear written previously.

I scarce made any answer—I was terrified to death—I felt the utter impossibility of resisting not merely my father's *persuasion*, but even his *advice*.—I felt, too, that I had no *argumentative* objections to make to Mr. Barlow, his character—disposition—situation—I knew nothing against—but O!—I felt he was no companion for my heart!—I wept like an infant when alone—eat nothing—seemed as if already married—and passed the whole day in more misery than, merely on my own account, I ever passed one before in my life,—except when a child, upon the loss of my own beloved mother—and ever revered and most dear grandmother!

After supper, I went into the study, while my dear father was alone, to wish him good night, which I did as cheerfully as I could, though pretty evidently in dreadful uneasiness. When I had got to the door, he called me back, and asked some questions concerning a new court mourning,[7] kindly saying he would assist Susette and me in our fitting-out, which he accordingly did, and affectionately embraced me, saying "I wish I could do more for thee, Fanny!" "O Sir!—" cried I—"*I* wish for nothing!—only let me live with you!—"—"My life!" cried he, kissing me kindly, "Thee shalt live with me for ever, if thee wilt! Thou canst not think I meant to get rid of thee?"

"I could not, sir! I could not!" cried I, "I could not outlive such a thought—" and, as I kissed him—O! how gratefully and thankfully! with what a relief to my heart! I saw his dear eyes full of tears! a mark of his tenderness which I shall never forget!

"God knows"—continued he—"I wish not to part with my girls!—they are my greatest comfort!—only—do not be too hasty!—"

Thus relieved, restored to future hopes, I went to bed as light, happy and thankful as if escaped from destruction.

From that day to this, my father, I thank heaven, has never again mentioned Mr. Barlow.

["DOWN WITH HER, BURNEY!"]

Streatham, September 15, 1778[8]

I was then looking over the "Life of Cowley," which he[9] had himself given me to read, at the same time that he gave to Mrs. Thrale that of Waller. They are now printed, though they will not be published for some time. But he bade me put it away.

"Do," cried he, "put away that now, and prattle with us; I can't make this little Burney prattle, and I am sure she prattles well; but I shall teach her another lesson than to sit thus silent before I have done with her."

"To talk," cried I, "is the only lesson I shall be backward to learn from you, sir."

*   *   *

7. A period of general mourning had been ordered after the death of George III's sister Caroline, queen of Denmark.

8. *Evelina* was published in January 1778 and enthusiastically received. After her authorship became known, Burney was invited to Streatham Park, the country house of Henry and Hester Lynch Thrale. Samuel Johnson spent much of his time there and was then writing his *Lives of the Poets*. He and Hester Thrale became fond of Burney.

9. Johnson.

Mrs. Thrale. "To morrow, Sir, Mrs. Montagu[1] dines here! and then you will have talk enough."

Dr. Johnson began to seesaw, with a countenance strongly expressive of *inward fun,*—and, after enjoying it some time in silence, he suddenly, and with great animation, turned to me, and cried *"Down* with her, Burney!—*down* with her!—spare her not! attack her, fight her, and *down* with her at once!—*You* are a *rising* wit,—*she* is at the *top,*—and when *I* was beginning the world, and was nothing and nobody, the joy of my life was to fire at all the established wits!—and then, every body loved to hallow[2] me on;—but there is no game *now,* and *now,* every body would be glad to see me *conquered:* but *then,* when I was *new,*—to vanquish the great ones was all the delight of my poor little dear soul!—So at her, Burney!—at her, and *down* with her!"

O how we were all amused! By the way, I must tell you that Mrs. Montagu is in very great estimation here, even with Dr. Johnson himself, when others do not praise her *improperly*: Mrs Thrale ranks her as the *first of women,* in the literary way.

*   *   *

I should have told you that Miss Gregory, daughter of the Gregory who wrote the "Letters," or, "Legacy of Advice,"[3] lives with Mrs. Montagu, and was invited to accompany her.

"Mark, now," said Dr. Johnson, "if I contradict her tomorrow. I am determined, let her say what she will, that I will not contradict her."

Mrs. T.—Why, to be sure, sir, you did put her a little out of countenance last time she came. Yet you were neither rough, nor cruel, nor ill-natured; but still, when a lady changes color, we imagine her feelings are not quite composed.

Dr. J.—Why, madam, I won't answer that I shan't contradict her again, if she provokes me as she did then; but a less provocation I will withstand. I believe I am not high in her good graces already; and I begin (added he, laughing heartily) to tremble for my admission into her new house. I doubt I shall never see the inside of it.

(Mrs. Montagu is building a most superb house.)

Mrs. T.—Oh, I warrant you, she fears you, indeed; but that, you know, is nothing uncommon; and dearly I love to hear your disquisitions; for certainly she is the first woman for literary knowledge in England, and if in England, I hope I may say in the world.

Dr. J.—I believe you may, madam. She diffuses more knowledge in her conversation than any woman I know, or, indeed, almost any man.

Mrs. T.—I declare I know no man equal to her, take away yourself and Burke, for that art. And you who love magnificence, won't quarrel with her, as everybody else does, for her love of finery.

Dr. J.—No, I shall not quarrel with her upon that topic. (Then, looking earnestly at me,) "Nay," he added, "it's very handsome!"

"What, sir?" cried I, amazed.

---

1. Elizabeth Montagu, known as "Queen of the Blues" (or bluestockings), a group of intellectual women, was probably the most respected literary woman in England; she had written the famous *Essay on Shakespear* (1769).
2. A cry inciting hunters to the chase.
3. John Gregory, *A Father's Legacy to His Daughters* (1774).

"Why, your cap:—I have looked at it some time, and I like it much. It has not that vile bandeau[4] across it, which I have so often cursed."

Did you ever hear anything so strange? nothing escapes him. My Daddy Crisp is not more minute in his attentions: nay, I think he is even less so.

Mrs. T.—Well, sir, that bandeau you quarreled with was worn by every woman at court the last birthday,[5] and I observed that all the men found fault with it.

Dr. J.—The truth is, women, take them in general, have no idea of grace. Fashion is all they think of. I don't mean Mrs. Thrale and Miss Burney, when I talk of women!—they are goddesses!—and therefore I except them.

Mrs. T.—Lady Ladd never wore the bandeau, and said she never would, because it is unbecoming.

Dr. J.—(*Laughing.*) Did not she? then is Lady Ladd a charming woman, and I have yet hopes of entering into engagements with her!

Mrs. T.—Well, as to that I can't say; but to be sure, the only similitude I have yet discovered in you, is in size: there you agree mighty well.

Dr. J.—Why, if anybody could have worn the bandeau, it must have been Lady Ladd; for there is enough of her to carry it off; but you are too little for anything ridiculous; that which seems nothing upon a Patagonian,[6] will become very conspicuous upon a Lilliputian, and of you there is so little in all, that one single absurdity would swallow up half of you.

Some time after, when we had all been a few minutes wholly silent, he turned to me and said:

"Come, Burney, shall you and I study our parts against[7] Mrs. Montagu comes?"

"Miss Burney," cried Mr. Thrale, "you must get up your courage for this encounter! I think you should begin with Miss Gregory; and down with her first."

Dr. J.—No, no, always fly at the eagle! down with Mrs. Montagu herself! I hope she will come full of "Evelina"!

[A YOUNG AND AGREEABLE INFIDEL]

Bath, June 1780

Miss White[8] is young and pleasing in her appearance, not pretty, but agreeable in her face, and soft, gentle and well bred in her manners. Our conversation, for some time, was upon the common Bath topics,—but when Mrs. Lambart left us,—called to receive more company, we went, insensibly, into graver matters.

As I soon found, by the looks and expressions of this young lady, that she was of a *peculiar cast*, I left all choice of subjects to herself, determined quietly to follow as she led. And very soon, and I am sure I know not how, we had for topics the follies and vices of mankind,—and indeed she spared not for lashing them!—The *women* she rather excused than defended, laying to the

---

4. A narrow headband.
5. June 4, the king's birthday.
6. The Indians of Patagonia, whose average height was more than six feet, were commonly thought to be giants.
7. Before.
8. Lydia Rogers White (ca. 1763–1827) would become a well-known London hostess and wit.

door of the *men* their faults and imperfections;—but the *men*, she said, were *all* bad,—*all*, in one word, and without exception, *sensualists*.

I stared much at a severity of speech for which her softness of manner had so ill prepared me,—and she, perceiving my surprise, said "I am sure I ought to apologise for speaking *my* opinion to *you*,—*you*, who have so just and so uncommon a knowledge of human nature,—I have long wished ardently to have the honour of conversing with you,—but your party has, altogether, been regarded as so formidable, that I have not had courage to approach it."

I made, as what could I do else, disqualifying speeches, and she then led to discoursing of happiness and misery;—the *latter* she held to be the *invariable* lot of us all,—and "*one* word," she added, "we have in our language, and in all other, for which there is never any essential necessity,— and that is *pleasure*." And her eyes filled with tears as she spoke.

"How you amaze me!" cried I: "I have met with *misanthropes* before, but never with so complete a one,—and I can hardly think I hear right when I see how young you are."

She then, in rather indirect terms, gave me to understand that she was miserable *at home*,—and in *very direct* terms that she was wretched *abroad*, and openly said that to affliction she was born, and in affliction she must die, for that the world was so vilely formed as to render happiness *impossible* for its inhabitants.

There was something in this freedom of repining that I could by no means approve, and as I found by all her manner that she had a disposition to even *respect* whatever I said, why I now grew very serious, and frankly told her that I could not think it consistent with either truth or religion to cherish such notions.

"One thing," answered she, "there is which I believe *might* make me happy,—but for that I have no inclination;—it is an amorous disposition. But that I do not possess; I can make myself no happiness by intrigue."

"I hope not, indeed!" cried I, almost confounded by her extraordinary notions and speeches,—"but surely there are worthier subjects of happiness attainable."—

"No, I believe there are not,—and the reason the men are happier than us, is because they are more sensual."

"I would not *think such thoughts*," cried I, clasping my hands with an involuntary vehemence, "for worlds!"—

The Miss Caldwells then interrupted us, and seated themselves next to us,—but Miss White paid them little attention at first, and soon after none at all, but, in a low voice, continued her discourse with me; recurring to the same subject of happiness and misery, upon which, after again asserting the folly of ever hoping for the former, she made this speech—

"There may be, indeed, *one moment* of happiness,—which must be the finding one worthy of exciting a passion which one should dare own to himself! *That* would, indeed, be a moment worth living for! but that can never happen,—I am sure not to *me*,—the men are so low, so vicious,—so worthless!—no, there is not one such to be found."

* * *

"Well,—you are a most extraordinary character indeed! I must confess I have seen *nothing like you!*"

"I hope, however, *I* shall find something like myself,—and, like the magnet rolling in the dust, attract some metal as I go."

"That you may *attract* what you please, is of all things most likely;—but if you wait to be happy for a friend resembling *yourself*, I shall no longer wonder at your despondency."

"O!" cried she, raising her eyes in ecstasy, "*could* I find such a one!—male or female,—for sex would be indifferent to me, with such a one I would go to *live* directly."

I half laughed,—but was perplexed in my own mind whether to be *sad* or *merry* at such a speech.

"But then," she continued, "after *making*—should I *lose* such a friend—I would not survive!"

"Not survive?" repeated I; "what can you mean?"

She looked down, but said nothing.

"Surely you cannot mean," said I, *very* gravely indeed, "to put a violent end to your life?"

"I should not," said she, again looking up, "hesitate a moment."

I was quite thunderstruck,—and for some time could not say a word;—but when I *did* speak, it was in a style of exhortation so serious and earnest I am ashamed to write it to you lest you should think it too much.

She gave me an attention that was even *respectful*, but when I urged her to tell me by what *right* she thought herself entitled to *rush unlicensed on Eternity*,[9] she said—"By the right of believing I shall be *extinct*."

I really felt *horror'd*!

"Where, for heaven's sake," I cried, "where have you picked up such dreadful reasoning?"

"In *Hume*," said she;—"I have read his *Essays*[1] repeatedly."

"I am sorry to find they have power to do so much mischief; you should not have read them, at least, till a man equal to Hume in *abilities* had answered him. Have you read any more infidel writers?"

"Yes,—Bolingbroke,[2]—the divinest of all writers!"

"And do you read nothing upon the *right* side?"

"Yes,—the Bible, till I was sick to death of it, every Sunday evening to my mother."

"Have you read Beattie on the immutability of Truth?"[3]

"No."

"Give me leave, then, to recommend it to you. After Hume's *Essays*, you *ought* to read it. And even, for *lighter* reading, if you were to look at Mason's elegy on Lady Coventry,[4] it might be of no disservice to you."

* * *

9. Burney echoes lines from William Mason's dramatic poem *Elfrida* (1752).
1. The edition of David Hume's *Essays* published in 1777, the year after his death, included two essays previously suppressed: "Of Suicide," which argues that suicide is not a transgression, and "Of the Immortality of the Soul," which argues that immortality is unlikely and cannot be proved.
2. The philosophical *Letters, or Essays, addressed to Alexander Pope* (1754) by Henry St. John, Vis-

count Bolingbroke, advocates a religion and ethics based on nature rather than on the teachings of the established church.
3. James Beattie, *An Essay on the Nature and Immutability of Truth, in Opposition to Sophistry and Scepticism* (1770), attempts to refute Hume and other "infidels."
4. Burney quotes eight lines on immortality from William Mason's elegy "On the Death of a Lady" (1760).

This was the chief of our conversation,—which indeed made an impression upon me I shall not easily get rid of, a young and agreeable *infidel* is even a shocking sight,—and with her romantic, flighty and unguarded turn of mind, what could happen to her that could surprise?

Poor misguided girl![5]

[ENCOUNTERING THE KING]

Kew Palace, Monday February 2, 1789

What an adventure had I this morning! one that has occasioned me the severest personal terror I ever experienced in my life.

Sir Lucas Pepys still persisting that exercise and air were absolutely necessary to save me from illness, I have continued my walks, varying my gardens from Richmond to Kew, according to the accounts I received of the movements of the King. For this I had her majesty's permission, on the representation of Sir Lucas.

This morning, when I received my intelligence of the king, from Dr. John Willis,[6] I begged to know where I might walk in safety? In Kew Garden, he said, as the king would be in Richmond.

"Should any unfortunate circumstance," I cried, "at any time, occasion my being seen by his majesty, do not mention my name, but let me run off, without call or notice."

This he promised. Everybody, indeed, is ordered to keep out of sight.

Taking, therefore, the time I had most at command, I strolled into the garden; I had proceeded, in my quick way, nearly half the round, when I suddenly perceived, through some trees, two or three figures. Relying on the instructions of Dr. John, I concluded them to be workmen, and gardeners;—yet tried to look sharp,—and in so doing, as they were less shaded, I thought I saw the person of his majesty!

Alarmed past all possible expression, I waited not to know more, but turning back, ran off with all my might—But what was my terror to hear myself pursued!—to hear the voice of the king himself, loudly and hoarsely calling after me "Miss Burney! Miss Burney!—"

I protest I was ready to die;—I knew not in what state he might be at the time; I only knew the orders to keep out of his way were universal; that the queen would highly disapprove any unauthorised meeting, and that the very action of my running away might deeply, in his present irritable state, offend him.

Nevertheless, on I ran,—too terrified to stop, and in search of some short passage, for the garden is full of little labyrinths, by which I might escape.

The steps still pursued me, and still the poor hoarse and altered voice rang in my ears:—more and more footsteps resounded frightfully behind me,—the attendants all running, to catch their eager master, and the voices of the two Doctor Willises loudly exhorting him not to heat himself so unmercifully.

5. A fictional version of the "young infidel" plays a major role in Burney's last novel, *The Wanderer* (1814).
6. In 1788, two years after Burney joined the court, George III began to have fits of madness or delirium (today diagnosed as resulting from porphyria, a hereditary disease). He was kept in isolation at Kew, under the control of two physicians, Francis and John Willis.

Heavens how I ran!—I do not think I should have felt the hot lava from Vesuvius,—at least not the hot cinders, had I so ran during its eruption. My feet were not sensible that they even touched the ground.

Soon after, I heard other voices, shriller though less nervous, call out "Stop! Stop!—Stop!—"

I could by no means consent,—I knew not what was purposed,—but I recollected fully my agreement with Dr. John that very morning, that I should decamp if surprised, and not be named.

My own fears and repugnance, also, after a flight and disobedience like this, were doubled in the thought of not escaping; I knew not to what I might be exposed, should the malady be then high, and take the turn of resentment.

Still, therefore, on I flew,—and such was my speed, so almost incredible to relate, or recollect, that I fairly believe no one of the whole party could have overtaken me, if these words, from one of the attendants, had not reached me: "Dr. Willis begs you to stop!—"

"I cannot!—I cannot!—" I answered, still flying on,—when he called out "You *must*, ma'am, it hurts the king to run.—"

Then, indeed, I stopt!—in a state of fear really amounting to agony!—I turned round,—I saw the two doctors had got the king between them, and about 8 attendants of Dr. Willis's were hovering about. They all slacked their pace, as they saw me stand still,—but such was the excess of my alarm, that I was wholly insensible to the effects of a race which, at any other time, would have required an hour's recruit.[7]

As they approached, some little presence of mind happily came to my command; it occurred to me that, to appease the wrath of my flight, I must now show some confidence; I therefore faced them as undauntedly as I was able,—only charging the nearest of the attendants to stand by my side.

When they were within a few yards of me, the king called out "Why did you run away?—"

Shocked at a question impossible to answer, yet a little assured by the mild tone of his voice, I instantly forced myself forward, to meet him—though the internal sensation which satisfied me this was a step the most proper, to appease his suspicions and displeasure, was so violently combated by the tremor of my nerves, that I fairly think I may reckon it the greatest effort of personal courage I have ever made.

The effort answered,—I looked up, and met all his wonted benignity of countenance, though something still of wildness in his eyes. Think, however, of my surprise, to feel him put both his hands round my two shoulders, and then kiss my cheek!—I wonder I did not really sink, so exquisite was my affright when I saw him spread out his arms!—Involuntarily, I concluded he meant to crush me:—but the Willises, who have never seen him till this fatal illness, not knowing how very extraordinary an action this was from him, simply smiled and looked pleased, supposing, perhaps, it was his customary salutation!

I have reason, however, to believe it was but the joy of a heart unbridled, now, by the forms and proprieties of established custom, and sober reason. He looked almost in *rapture* at the meeting, from the moment I advanced; and to see any of his household thus by accident, seemed such a near

7. Renewal of strength.

approach to liberty and recovery, that who can wonder it should serve rather to elate[8] than lessen what yet remains of his disorder?—

He now spoke in such terms of his pleasure in seeing me, that I soon lost the whole of my terror, though it had threatened to almost lose *me*: astonishment to find him so nearly *well*, and gratification to see him so pleased, removed every uneasy feeling, and the joy that succeeded, in my conviction of his recovery, made me ready to throw myself at his feet to express it.

What a conversation followed!—when he saw me fearless, he grew more and more alive, and made me walk close by his side, away from the attendants, and even the Willises themselves, who, to indulge him, retreated. I own myself not completely *composed*, but *alarm* I could entertain no more.—

Everything that came uppermost in his mind he mentioned; he seemed to have just such remains of his flightiness, as heated his imagination, without deranging his reason, and robbed him of all control over his speech, though nearly in his perfect state of mind as to his opinions.

What did he not say!—He opened his whole heart to me,—expounded all his sentiments, and acquainted me with all his intentions.

* * *

He next talked to me a great deal of my dear father, and made a thousand inquiries concerning his history of music. This brought him to his favorite theme, Handel;[9] and he told me innumerable anecdotes of him, and particularly that celebrated tale of Handel's saying of himself, when a boy, "While that boy lives, my music will never want a protector—" And this, he said, I might relate to my father.

Then he ran over most of his oratorios, attempting to sing the subjects of several airs and choruses, but so dreadfully hoarse, that the sound was terrible.

Dr. Willis, quite alarmed at this exertion, feared he would do himself harm, and again proposed a separation. "No! no! no!" he exclaimed, "not yet,—I have something I must just mention first."

Dr. Willis, delighted to comply, even when uneasy at compliance, again gave way.

The good king then greatly affected me,—he began upon my revered old friend, Mrs. Delany![1]—and he spoke of her with such warmth, such kindness:—"She was my *friend*!" he cried, "and I *loved* her as a friend!—I have made a memorandum when I lost her!—I will show it you—"

He pulled out a pocketbook, and rummaged some time, but to no purpose—

The tears stood in his eyes,—he wiped them,—and Dr. Willis again became very anxious,—"Come, sir," he cried, "now do you come in, and let the lady go on her walk,—come, now you have talked a long while,—so will go in,—if your majesty pleases."

"No!—no!—" he cried, "I want to ask her a few questions,—I have lived so long out of the world, I know nothing!—"

This touched me to the heart.

8. Heighten.
9. From childhood, George III had been a devotee of George Frideric Handel (1685–1759), the great German-English composer. George III, who loved German music, took a keen interest in Charles Burney's pioneering work, *A General His-* *tory of Music*; the third and fourth volumes were just about to be published.
1. Mary Delany, a figure at court and accomplished artist of works in cut paper, was regarded by Burney as "the pattern of a perfect fine lady," and had died the previous year.

* * *

What a scene! how variously was I affected by it!—but, upon the whole, how inexpressibly thankful to see him so nearly himself! so little removed from recovery.

[A MASTECTOMY]

Paris, March 22, 1812[2]

Separated as I have now so long—long been from my dearest father—brothers—sisters—nieces, and native friends, I would spare, at least, their kind hearts any grief for me but what they must inevitably feel in reflecting upon the sorrow of such an absence to one so tenderly attached to all her first and forever so dear and regretted ties—nevertheless, if they should hear that I have been dangerously ill from any hand but my own, they might have doubts of my perfect recovery which my own alone can obviate. And how can I hope they will escape hearing what has reached Seville to the south, and Constantinople to the east? from both I have had messages—yet nothing could urge me to this communication till I heard that M. de Boinville[3] had written it to his wife, without any precaution, because in ignorance of my plan of silence. Still I must hope it may never travel to my dearest father—But to you, my beloved Esther, who, living more in the world, will surely hear it ere long, to you I will write the whole history, certain that, from the moment you know any evil has befallen me your kind kind heart will be constantly anxious to learn its extent and its circumstances, as well as its termination.

About August, in the year 1810, I began to be annoyed by a small pain in my breast, which went on augmenting from week to week, yet, being rather heavy than acute, without causing me any uneasiness with respect to consequences: Alas, "what was the ignorance?" The most sympathizing of partners, however, was more disturbed: not a start, not a wry face, not a movement that indicated pain was unobserved, and he early conceived apprehensions to which I was a stranger. He pressed me to see some surgeon; I revolted from the idea, and hoped, by care and warmth, to make all succor unnecessary. Thus passed some months, during which Madame de Maisonneuve, my particularly intimate friend, joined with M. d'Arblay to press me to consent to an examination. I thought their fears groundless, and could not make so great a conquest over my repugnance. I relate this false confidence, now, as a warning to my dear Esther—my sisters and nieces, should any similar sensations excite similar alarm. M. d'Arblay now revealed his uneasiness to another of our kind friends, Mme. de Tracy, who wrote to me a long and eloquent letter upon the subject, that began to awaken very unpleasant surmises; and a conference with her ensued, in which her urgency and representations, aided by her long experience of disease, and most miserable existence by art, subdued me, and, most painfully and reluctantly, I ceased to object, and M. d'Arblay summoned a physician—M. Bourdois? Maria will cry;—No, my dear Maria, I would not give your beau frere[4]

---

2. Burney (now Madame d'Arblay) sent this letter to Esther Burney, her sister; it describes an operation performed the previous September.
3. Because Chastel de Boinville's wife was English, it was likely that news of the illness

would spread to the Burney family in England.
4. Brother-in-law. Maria (or Marianne), Esther Burney's daughter, had married Antoine Bourdois, whose brother was a prominent French physician.

that trouble; not him, but Dr. Jouart, the physician of Miss Potts. Thinking but slightly of my statement, he gave me some directions that produced no fruit—on the contrary, I grew worse, and M. d'Arblay now would take no denial to my consulting M. Dubois, who had already attended and cured me in an abscess of which Maria, my dearest Esther, can give you the history. M. Dubois, the most celebrated surgeon of France, was then appointed accoucheur to the empress, and already lodged in the Tuilleries,[5] and in constant attendance: but nothing could slacken the ardour of M. d'Arblay to obtain the first advice. Fortunately for his kind wishes, M. Dubois had retained a partial regard for me from the time of his former attendance, and, when applied to through a third person, he took the first moment of liberty, granted by a *promenade* taken by the empress, to come to me. It was now I began to perceive my real danger, M. Dubois gave me a prescription to be pursued for a month, during which time he could not undertake to see me again, and pronounced nothing—but uttered so many charges to me to be tranquil, and to suffer no uneasiness, that I could not but suspect there was room for terrible inquietude. My alarm was increased by the nonappearance of M. d'Arblay after his departure. They had remained together some time in the book room, and M. d'Arblay did not return—till, unable to bear the suspense, I begged him to come back. He, also, sought then to tranquilize me—but in words only; his looks were shocking! his features, his whole face displayed the bitterest woe. I had not, therefore, much difficulty in telling myself what he endeavored not to tell me—that a small operation would be necessary to avert evil consequences!—Ah, my dearest Esther, for this I felt no courage—my dread and repugnance, from a thousand reasons *besides* the pain, almost shook all my faculties, and, for some time, I was rather confounded and stupified than affrighted.—Direful, however, was the effect of this interview; the pains became quicker and more violent, and the hardness of the spot affected increased. I took, but vainly, my proscription, and every symptom grew more serious.

* * *

A physician was now called in, Dr. Moreau, to hear if he could suggest any new means: but Dr. Larrey[6] had left him no resources untried. A formal consultation now was held, of Larrey, Ribe, and Moreau—and, in fine, I was formally condemned to an operation by all three. I was as much astonished as disappointed—for the poor breast was no where discoloured, and not much larger than its healthy neighbor. Yet I felt the evil to be deep, so deep, that I often thought if it could not be dissolved, it could only with life be extirpated. I called up, however, all the reason I possessed, or could assume, and told them that—if they saw no other alternative, I would not resist their opinion and experience:—the good Dr. Larrey, who, during his long attendance had conceived for me the warmest friendship, had now tears in his eyes; from my dread he had expected resistance.

* * *

---

5. The royal palace in Paris. "Accoucheur": obstetrician.
6. Dominique-Jean Larrey, "Napoleon's surgeon," is remembered for his courage on the battlefield and his innovative procedures.

All hope of escaping this evil now at an end, I could only console or employ my mind in considering how to render it less dreadful to M. d'Arblay. M. Dubois had pronounced "il faut s'attendre à souffrir, Je ne veux pas vous tromper—Vous souffrirez—vous souffrirez *beaucoup!*—"[7] M. Ribe had *charged* me to cry! to withhold or restrain myself might have seriously bad consequences, he said. M. Moreau, in echoing this injunction, inquired whether I had cried or screamed at the birth of Alexander—Alas, I told him, it had not been possible to do otherwise; Oh then, he answered, there is no fear!—What terrible inferences were here to be drawn! I desired, therefore, that M. d'Arblay might be kept in ignorance of the day till the operation should be over. To this they agreed, except M. Larrey, with high approbation: M. Larrey looked dissentient, but was silent. M. Dubois protested he would not undertake to act, after what he had seen of the agitated spirits of M. d'Arblay if he were present: nor would he suffer me to know the time myself over night; I obtained with difficulty a promise of 4 hours warning, which were essential to me for sundry regulations.

From this time, I assumed the best spirits in my power, *to meet the coming blow*;—and support my too sympathizing partner.

* * *

Sundry necessary works and orders filled up my time entirely till one o'clock, when all was ready—but Dr. Moreau then arrived, with news that M. Dubois could not attend till three. Dr. Aumont went away—and the coast was clear. This, indeed, was a dreadful interval. I had no longer any thing to do—I had only to think—two hours thus spent seemed never-ending. I would fain have written to my dearest father—to you, my Esther—to Charlotte James—Charles—Amelia Lock—but my arm prohibited me: I strolled to the salon—I saw it fitted with preparations, and I recoiled—But I soon returned; to what effect disguise from myself what I must so soon know?—yet the sight of the immense quantity of bandages, compresses, spunges, lint—made me a little sick:—I walked backwards and forwards till I quieted all emotion, and became by degrees, nearly stupid—torpid, without sentiment or consciousness;—and thus I remained till the clock struck three. A sudden spirit of exertion then returned,—I defied my poor arm, no longer worth sparing, and took my long banished pen to write a few words to M. d'Arblay—and a few more for Alex, in case of a fatal result. These short billets I could only deposit safely, when the cabriolets[8]—one—two—three—four—succeeded rapidly to each other in stopping at the door. Dr. Moreau instantly entered my room, to see if I were alive. He gave me a wine cordial, and went to the salon. I rang for my maid and nurses,—but before I could speak to them, my room, without previous message, was entered by 7 men in black, Dr. Larrey, M. Dubois, Dr. Moreau, Dr. Aumont, Dr. Ribe, and a pupil of Dr. Larrey, and another of M. Dubois. I was now awakened from my stupor—and by a sort of indignation—Why so many? and without leave?—But I could not utter a syllable. M. Dubois acted as commander in chief. Dr. Larrey kept out of sight; M. Dubois ordered a bedstead into the middle of the

7. You must expect to suffer. I do not want to deceive you—you will suffer—you will suffer *greatly* (French). Operations were then performed without anesthestics.
8. Carriages.

room. Astonished, I turned to Dr. Larrey, who had promised that an arm chair would suffice; but he hung his head, and would not look at me. Two *old mattresses* M. Dubois then demanded, and an old sheet. I now began to tremble violently, more with distaste and horror of the preparations even than of the pain. These arranged to his liking, he desired me to mount the bedstead. I stood suspended, for a moment, whether I should not abruptly escape—I looked at the door, the windows—I felt desperate—but it was only for a moment, my reason then took the command, and my fears and feelings struggled vainly against it. I called to my maid—she was crying, and the two nurses stood, transfixed, at the door. "Let those women all go!" cried M. Dubois. This order recovered me my voice—"No," I cried, "let them stay! *qu'elles restent!*" This occasioned a little dispute, that re-animated me—The maid, however, and one of the nurses ran off—I charged the other to approach, and she obeyed. M. Dubois now tried to issue his commands *en militaire*,[9] but I resisted all that were resistable—I was compelled, however, to submit to taking off my long robe de chambre,[1] which I had meant to retain—Ah, then, how did I think of my sisters!—not one, at so dreadful an instant, at hand, to protect—adjust—guard me—I regretted that I had refused Mme de Maisonneuve—Mme Chastel—no one upon whom I could rely—my departed angel![2]—how did I think of her!—how did I long—long for my Esther—my Charlotte!—My distress was, I suppose, apparent, though not my wishes, for M. Dubois himself now softened, and spoke soothingly. "Can *you*," I cried, "feel for an operation that, to *you*, must seem so trivial?"— "Trivial?" he repeated—taking up a bit of paper, which he tore, unconsciously, into a million pieces, "*oui—c'est peu de chose—mais—*"[3] he stammered, and could not go on. No one else attempted to speak, but I was softened myself, when I saw even M. Dubois grow agitated, while Dr. Larrey kept always aloof, yet a glance showed me he was pale as ashes. I knew not, positively, then, the immediate danger, but every thing convinced me danger was hovering about me, and that this experiment could alone save me from its jaws. I mounted, therefore, unbidden, the bedstead—and M. Dubois placed me upon the mattress, and spread a cambric handkerchief upon my face. It was transparent, however, and I saw, through it, that the bedstead was instantly surrounded by the 7 men and my nurse. I refused to be held; but when, bright through the cambric, I saw the glitter of polished steel—I closed my eyes. I would not trust to convulsive fear the sight of the terrible incision. A silence the most profound ensued, which lasted for some minutes, during which, I imagine, they took their orders by signs, and made their examination—Oh what a horrible suspension!—I did not breathe—and M. Dubois tried vainly to find any pulse. This pause, at length, was broken by Dr. Larrey, who in a voice of solemn melancholy, said "Qui me tiendra ce sein?[4]—"

No one answered; at least not verbally; but this aroused me from my passively submissive state, for I feared they imagined the whole breast infected— feared it too justly,—for, again through the cambric, I saw the hand of M. Dubois held up, while his forefinger first described a straight line from top to bottom of the breast, secondly a cross, and thirdly a circle; intimating that

9. In military fashion (French). Most of the attending physicians had been army surgeons.
1. Dressing gown.
2. Susanna, Burney's favorite sister, had died in 1800.
3. Yes—it is not much—but— (French).
4. Who will hold this breast for me? (French).

the whole was to be taken off. Excited by this idea, I started up, threw off my veil, and, in answer to the demand "Qui me tiendra ce sein?" cried "C'est moi, Monsieur!"[5] and I held my hand under it, and explained the nature of my sufferings, which all sprang from one point, though they darted into every part. I was heard attentively, but in utter silence, and M. Dubois then, re-placed me as before, and, as before, spread my veil over my face. How vain, alas, my representation! immediately again I saw the fatal finger describe the cross— and the circle—Hopeless, then, desperate, and self-given up, I closed once more my eyes, relinquishing all watching, all resistance, all interference, and sadly resolute to be wholly resigned.

My dearest Esther,—and all my dears to whom she communicates this doleful ditty, will rejoice to hear that this resolution once taken, was firmly adhered to, in defiance of a terror that surpasses all description, and the most torturing pain. Yet—when the dreadful steel was plunged into the breast— cutting through veins—arteries—flesh—nerves—I needed no injunctions not to restrain my cries. I began a scream that lasted unintermittingly during the whole time of the incision—and I almost marvel that it rings not in my ears still! so excruciating was the agony. When the wound was made, and the instrument was withdrawn, the pain seemed undiminished, for the air that suddenly rushed into those delicate parts felt like a mass of minute but sharp and forked poniards,[6] that were tearing the edges of the wound—but when again I felt the instrument—describing a curve—cutting against the grain, if I may so say, while the flesh resisted in a manner so forcible as to oppose and tire the hand of the operator, who was forced to change from the right to the left—then, indeed, I thought I must have expired. I attempted no more to open my eyes,—they felt as if hermetically shut, and so firmly closed, that the eyelids seemed indented into the cheeks. The instrument this second time withdrawn, I concluded the operation over,—Oh no! presently the terrible cutting was renewed—and worse than ever, to separate the bottom, the foundation of this dreadful gland from the parts to which it adhered—Again all description would be baffled—yet again all was not over,—Dr. Larrey rested but his own hand, and—Oh heaven!—I then felt the knife rackling[7] against the breast bone—scraping it!—This performed, while I yet remained in utterly speechless torture, I heard the voice of Mr. Larrey,—(all others guarded a dead silence) in a tone nearly tragic, desire every one present to pronounce if anything more remained to be done; or if he thought the operation complete. The general voice was yes,—but the finger of Mr. Dubois— which I literally *felt* elevated over the wound, though I saw nothing, and though he touched nothing, so indescribably sensitive was the spot—pointed to some further requisition[8]—and again began the scraping!—and, after this, Dr. Moreau thought he discerned a peccant atom—and still, and still, M. Dubois demanded atom after atom—My dearest Esther, not for days, not for weeks, but for months I could not speak of this terrible business without nearly again going through it! I could not *think* of it with impunity! I was sick, I was disordered by a single question—even now, 9 months after it is over, I have a head ache from going on with the account! and this miserable account,

5. *I* will (French).
6. Daggers.
7. Raking (?).

8. Necessity. Surgical practice of the time dictated that "the whole diseased structure" be cut out, no matter how long or painful the operation.

which I began 3 months ago, at least, I dare not revise, nor read, the recollection is still so painful.

To conclude, the evil was so profound, the case so delicate, and the precautions necessary for preventing a return so numerous, that the operation, including the treatment and the dressing, lasted 20 minutes! a time, for sufferings so acute, that was hardly supportable—However, I bore it with all the courage I could exert, and never moved, nor stopped them, nor resisted, nor remonstrated, nor spoke—except once or twice, during the dressings, to say "Ah Messieurs! que je vous plains!—"[9] for indeed I was sensible to the feeling concern with which they all saw what I endured, though my speech was principally—*very* principally meant for Dr. Larrey. Except this, I uttered not a syllable, save, when so often they re-commenced, calling out "Avertissez moi, Messieurs! avertissez moi![1]—" Twice, I believe, I fainted; at least, I have two total chasms in my memory of this transaction, that impede my tying together what passed. When all was done, and they lifted me up that I might be put to bed, my strength was so totally annihilated, that I was obliged to be carried, and could not even sustain my hands and arms, which hung as if I had been lifeless; while my face, as the nurse has told me, was utterly colorless. This removal made me open my eyes—and I then saw my good Dr. Larrey, pale nearly as myself, his face streaked with blood, and its expression depicting grief, apprehension, and almost horror.

When I was in bed,—my poor M. d'Arblay—who ought to write you himself his own history of this morning—was called to me—and afterwards our Alex.—

[M. D'ARBLAY'S POSTSCRIPT]

No! No my dearest and ever more dear friends, I shall not make a *fruitless* attempt. No language could convey what I felt in the deadly course of these seven hours. Nevertheless, every one *of you, my dearest dearest friends*, can guess, must even know it. Alexandre had no less feeling, but showed more fortitude. He, perhaps, will be more able to describe to you, nearly at least, the torturing state of my poor heart and soul. Besides, I must own, to you, that these details which were, till just now, quite unknown to me, have almost killed me, and I am only able to thank God that this more than half angel has had the sublime courage to deny herself the comfort I might have offered her, to spare me, not the sharing of her excruciating pains, that was impossible, but the witnessing so terrific a scene, and perhaps the remorse to have rendered it more tragic. For I don't flatter myself I could have got through it—I must confess it.

Thank heaven! She is now surprisingly well, and in good spirits, and we hope to have many many still happy days. May that of peace soon arrive, and enable me to embrace better than with my pen my beloved and ever ever more dear friends of the town and country. Amen. Amen![2]

---

9. How I pity you! (French).
1. Give me warning! (French).
2. The wound healed without infection. Burney

returned to England later in 1812 and lived for twenty-eight more years.

Liberty

No idea resonated more strongly in the minds of Britons in the eighteenth century than liberty. Writers explained its political significance in many, at times contradictory ways. It was seen by some as the natural right of every human being, and by others as a uniquely British birthright. Its origins were hotly debated: as their model of liberty, some took the ancient Roman Republic, others the ancient, "Gothic" constitution of pre-Norman England. To other minds, it was a distinctly modern product: either of the volatile, bloody period of the English civil wars and Commonwealth (when Milton's defense of liberty, "Areopagitica," appeared), or of the remarkably bloodless Glorious Revolution of 1688, which established the stability some felt was needed for true liberty to be enjoyed. Some thought liberty could prosper only in a society where power lay in the hands of independent landowners, while others felt it thrived best on the fluidity of commerce, markets, and credit. In different contexts throughout the eighteenth century, ideologues across the political spectrum, both Tories and Whigs, appealed to some understanding of British liberty as a fundamental, guiding principle.

But the concept of liberty applied far beyond the spheres of economics and politics. It became the basis for a new social ethos: as the influential philosopher Anthony Ashley Cooper, third earl of Shaftesbury (1671–1713), remarked, "all politeness is owing to liberty." And English literature itself derived its character from the elaboration of the concept. Most practically, the eighteenth century witnessed a growing respect for the freedom of the press and the end of prepublication censorship. As an abstract idea and a piece of political ideology, liberty also absorbed the attention of leading writers: Henry Fielding, William Collins, James Thomson, and Joseph Warton, among many others, wrote idealistic (and in Thomson's case, rather long) poems addressed to it in the 1730s and 1740s. Perhaps most profoundly, a reverence for liberty granted an imaginative, intellectual, and sentimental expansiveness to English literature: frequently contrasted with the French neoclassicists' supposedly slavish regard for the rules of good writing (which was thought to be of a piece with France's royal absolutism), the English love of liberty fostered literary naturalness, truth, and originality. In "The Preface to Shakespeare," Samuel Johnson defends Shakespeare's disregard of the unities of time and place in these terms, declaring that such violations of the rules suit "the comprehensive genius of Shakespeare."

It is, therefore, the most considerable of historical ironies that liberty-loving eighteenth-century Britain engaged as extensively as it did in the slave trade. In the early 1660s, when the events in Behn's *Oroonoko* are supposed to have taken place, this engagement was gathering momentum. Later, in 1713, the Treaty of Utrecht secured Great Britain the contract (*asiento*) to monopolize the export of slaves to Spain's American colonies. Bristol and then Liverpool developed into prosperous slave ports, trading manufactured goods to Africa for human cargo, which crossed the Atlantic on ships that returned to England with sugar and money. By the 1780s, when Britain shipped a third of a million slaves to the New World, the national economy depended on this so-called Triangle Trade. Though slavery was not new to Africa, the Middle Passage—the deadly voyage across the Atlantic—made the suffering and degradation it inflicted newly terrible, brutal, and global. The former slave Olaudah Equiano describes the experience of such a crossing in his autobiography.

The stark contradiction of Britons' love of liberty and their profit from slavery is reflected in English political philosophy and law. John Locke's chapter "Of Slavery" from the *Second Treatise of Civil Government* sets forth the idea that "the natural

William Blake, *Europe Supported by Africa & America*, 1796. Blake follows the allegorical tradition of representing the continents as beautiful women. The armbands on Africa and America signify their enslavement, but their strength supports Europe, and unlike hers, their eyes meet the viewer's. From John Stedman, *Narrative of a Five Years Expedition against the Revolted Negroes of Surinam . . . from the Year 1772, to 1777* (1796).

liberty of man is to be free from any superior power on earth," but Locke also invested in the slave trade and upheld the notion that slavery was necessary in various writings. And though William Blackstone wrote in his commentaries on English law that "a slave or negro, the moment he lands in England, falls under the protection of the laws," and thus becomes a freeman, he later added another clause: "though the master's right to his service may probably still continue" (1769).

Yet the eighteenth-century language of liberty was not merely hypocritical. It provided terms in which a range of injustices, inequalities, and abridgements of rights could be attacked and thus became a language of world-transforming, even revolutionary importance. It helped stimulate the growth of feminism, as Mary Astell ironically explores its applicability to women, Mary Wortley Montagu laments the "eternal chains" of oppressive matrimony in "Epistle from Mrs. Yonge to Her Husband" (1724), and Mary Wollstonecraft later affirms that both genders deserve "to breathe the sharp invigorating air of freedom" in *A Vindication of the Rights of Woman* (1792). It also inspired the British abolitionist movement, which gained particular fervor in the 1780s; a bill abolishing the slave trade finally became law in Britain in 1807. That did not put an end, of course, to illegal trade, let alone to already existing slavery itself. The conflict between boasts of liberty and the enslavement of human beings then passed from Britain to America, where its consequences would be written in blood.

JOHN LOCKE

A t Stowe in Buckinghamshire, the greatest of eighteenth-century English land-scape gardens, a bust of John Locke appears in a temple with busts of Pope, Newton, Milton, Shakespeare, Queen Elizabeth I, and other "British Worthies." The inscription under his name says that he, "best of all philosophers, understood the powers of the human mind, the nature, end, and bounds of civil government; and with equal sagacity refuted the slavish system of usurped authority over the rights, the consciences, or the reason of mankind." Locke's reputation as the philosopher of political liberty in the eighteenth century was not always this easy to read, nor was it as pervasive as his influence as a philosopher of "the powers of the human mind" (see the selection from the *Essay Concerning Human Understanding*, p. 106, for his program for the liberation of mankind's reason). Other Whig writers from Locke's era arguably influenced the developing discourse of liberty as much as or more than his *Two Treatises of Government* did (published 1690). Indeed, it is not clear the radicalism of the *Treatises* was always appreciated. Scholars have found they were mostly composed during the years 1679–81, before the Glorious Revolution (1688), not after it: the works represent not an after-the-fact justification of deposing a tyranni-cal king, James II, but rather a more dangerous meditation on the people's right to depose tyrants during the turbulent years of Charles II's reign. In any case, the inscription at Stowe, executed half a century later in the 1730s to buoy the Whig and Tory opposition to Robert Walpole's putatively corrupt, tyrannical Whig administra-tion, attests to Locke's continuing relevance to defenders of liberty as eighteenth-century politics evolved. A classic articulation of the rights and freedoms of the individual, Locke's second *Treatise* has come to occupy a preeminent place in political theory.

The degree of Locke's own opposition to slavish systems was far from unambiguous, however. Though he maintains that all men are born free, he himself invested in the Royal Africa Company (formed 1672) and a group of "Bahamas Adventurers": both enterprises were predicated on slavery. Scholars have also argued that he helped draft "The Fundamental Constitutions of Carolina" (1669), with his employer Lord Ashley, which granted each freeman "absolute power and authority over his negro slaves." (Ashley would become the first Earl of Shaftesbury, himself the great Whig paragon of liberty.) The selection included here from the second *Treatise* indicates both Locke's detestation of the condition of slavery and his allowance for its justification: if he can somehow consider slaveholders the "lawful conquerors" of their slaves, who themselves may have committed some base act or other, Locke may defend the slave-owning and slave-trading societies he wished to legitimize. Over Britons, however, he believed that civil government should never be tyrannical, because of their natural rights to liberty and property. Locke's first *Treatise* (not printed here) attacked the writings of Sir Robert Filmer, who insisted that kings hold a patriarchal authority over their subjects ultimately derived from God's authority over all mankind. The second *Treatise* describes the origins and ends of legitimate political society, from the state of nature, in which mankind discovers the natural rights to liberty and property, to the institution of civil government, designed solely to protect these rights and allow them best to flourish.

From Two Treatises of Government

An Essay Concerning the True Original, Extent, and End of Civil Government

CHAPTER IV. OF SLAVERY

22. The natural liberty of man is to be free from any superior power on earth, and not to be under the will or legislative authority of man, but to have only the law of nature for his rule. The liberty of man in society is to be under no other legislative power, but that established, by consent, in the commonwealth; nor under the dominion of any will, or restraint of any law, but what that legislative shall enact, according to the trust put in it. Freedom then is not what *Sir R. F.* tells us, *O.A.* 55, "A liberty for every one to do what he lists, to live as he pleases, and not to be tied by any laws":[1] but freedom of men under government is to have a standing rule to live by, common to every one of that society, and made by the legislative power erected in it, a liberty to follow my own will in all things, where the rule prescribes not, [and] not to be subject to the inconstant, uncertain, unknown, arbitrary will of another man; as freedom of nature is to be under no other restraint but the law of nature.

23. This freedom from absolute, arbitrary power is so necessary to and closely joined with a man's preservation that he cannot part with it but by what forfeits his preservation and life together. For a man, not having the power of his own life,[2] cannot by compact or his own consent enslave himself to any one, nor put himself under the absolute, arbitrary power of another, to take away his life, when he pleases. Nobody can give more power than he has himself; and he that cannot take away his own life cannot give another power over it. Indeed having, by his fault, forfeited his own life by some act that deserves death; he to whom he has forfeited it may (when he has him in his power) delay to take it, and make use of him to his own service, and he does him no injury by it. For whenever he finds the hardship of his slavery outweigh the value of his life, 'tis in his power by resisting the will of his master to draw on himself the death he desires.

24. This is the perfect condition of slavery, which is nothing else but the state of war continued between a lawful conqueror and a captive. For if once compact enter between them[3] and make an agreement for a limited power on the one side, and obedience on the other, the state of war and slavery ceases, as long as the compact endures. For as has been said, no man can by agreement pass over to another that which he hath not in himself, a power over his own life.

I confess we find among the Jews as well as other nations that men did sell themselves; but, 'tis plain this was only to drudgery, not to slavery. For it is evident the person sold was not under an absolute, arbitrary, despotical power. For the master could not have power to kill him at any time whom at

---

1. Sir Robert Filmer (1588–1653), a defender of royal prerogative and the divine right of kings, is Locke's chief opponent in the first *Treatise*. Locke here refers to page 55 of the 1679 republication of Filmer's *Observations upon Aristotle's Politics* (originally published 1652).
2. In chapter 2, section 6 of the second *Treatise*,

Locke explained that the law of nature, which is essentially the will of God as our reason reveals it to us, dictates that human beings may not commit suicide.
3. I.e., once their relationship attains the status of a legal agreement or contract.

a certain time he was obliged to let go free out of his service: and the master of such a servant was so far from having an arbitrary power over his life, that he could not, at pleasure, so much as maim him, but the loss of an eye, or tooth, set him free, *Exod.* XXI.

CHAPTER IX. OF THE ENDS OF POLITICAL SOCIETY AND GOVERNMENT

123. If man in the state of nature be so free, as has been said; if he be absolute lord of his own person[4] and possessions, equal to the greatest and subject to nobody, why will he part with his freedom? Why will he give up this empire, and subject himself to the dominion and control of any other power? To which 'tis obvious to answer that though in the state of nature he hath such a right, yet the enjoyment of it is very uncertain and constantly exposed to the invasion of others; for all being kings as much as he, every man his equal, and the greater part no strict observers of equity and justice, the enjoyment of the property he has in this state is very unsafe, very insecure. This makes him willing to quit this condition, which however free is full of fears and continual dangers: and 'tis not without reason that he seeks out and is willing to join in society with others who are already united or have a mind to unite for the mutual preservation of their lives, liberties, and estates, which I call by the general name, property.

124. The great and chief end therefore of men's uniting into commonwealths and putting themselves under government is the preservation of their property. To which in the state of nature there are many things wanting.

First, there wants an established, settled, known law, received and allowed by common consent to be the standard of right and wrong, and the common measure to decide all controversies between them. For though the law of nature be plain and intelligible to all rational creatures; yet men being biased by their interest, as well as ignorant for want of study of it, are not apt to allow of it as a law binding to them in the application of it to their particular cases.

125. Secondly, in the state of nature there wants a known and indifferent[5] judge, with authority to determine all differences according to the established law. For everyone in that state being both judge and executioner of the law of nature, men being partial to themselves, passion and revenge is very apt to carry them too far, and with too much heat in their own cases, as well as negligence and unconcernedness make them too remiss in other men's.

126. Thirdly, in the state of nature there often wants power to back and support the sentence when right, and to give it due execution. They who by any injustice offended will seldom fail where they are able by force to make good their injustice; such resistance many times makes the punishment dangerous and frequently destructive to those who attempt it.

127. Thus mankind, notwithstanding all the privileges of the state of nature, being but in an ill condition while they remain in it, are quickly driven into society. Hence it comes to pass that we seldom find any number

---

4. Body, physical being. Locke earlier defines "the state of nature," the "state all men are naturally in," as "a state of perfect freedom to order their actions and dispose of their possessions and persons as they think fit, within the bounds of the law of nature, without asking leave or depending upon the will of any other man" (chapter 2, section 4).

5. Impartial.

of men live any time together in this state. The inconveniencies that they are therein exposed to by the irregular and uncertain exercise of the power every man has of punishing the transgressions of others make them take sanctuary under the established laws of government, and therein seek the preservation of their property. 'Tis this makes them so willingly give up every one his single power of punishing to be exercised by such alone as shall be appointed to it amongst them; and by such rules as the community, or those authorized by them to that purpose, shall agree on. And in this we have the original right and rise of both the legislative and executive power,[6] as well as of the governments and societies themselves.

128. For in the state of nature, to omit the liberty he has of innocent delights, a man has two powers. The first is to do whatsoever he thinks fit for the preservation of himself and others within the permission of the law of nature; by which law common to them all, he and all the rest of mankind are one community, make up one society distinct from all other creatures, and were it not for the corruption and viciousness of degenerate men, there would be no need of any other, no necessity that men should separate from this great and natural community and associate into lesser combinations. The other power a man has in the state of nature is the power to punish the crimes committed against that law. Both these he gives up when he joins in a private, if I may so call it, or particular political society, and incorporates into any commonwealth[7] separate from the rest of mankind.

129. The first power, *viz.* of doing whatsoever he thought fit for the preservation of himself and the rest of mankind, he gives up to be regulated by laws made by the society, so far forth as the preservation of himself and the rest of that society shall require; which laws of the society in many things confine the liberty he had by the law of nature.

130. Secondly, the power of punishing he wholly gives up, and engages his natural force, which he might before employ in the execution of the law of nature, by his own single authority, as he thought fit, to assist the executive power of the society, as the law thereof shall require. For being now in a new state wherein he is to enjoy many conveniences from the labor, assistance, and society of others in the same community, as well as protection from its whole strength; he is to part also with as much of his natural liberty in providing for himself, as the good, prosperity, and safety of the society shall require; which is not only necessary but just, since the other members of the society do the like.

131. But though men when they enter into society give up the equality, liberty, and executive power they had in the state of nature into the hands of the society, to be so far disposed of by the legislative as the good of the society shall require; yet it being only with an intention in everyone, the better to preserve himself, his liberty, and property, (for no rational creature can be supposed to change his condition with an intention to be worse), the power of the society, or legislative constituted by them, can never be supposed to extend farther than the common good; but is obliged to secure everyone's property by providing against those three defects above-mentioned, that made the state of nature so unsafe and uneasy. And so whoever has the

6. A branch of government charged with executing the laws of a state.

7. A political unit formed for the common good of its members.

legislative or supreme power of any commonwealth is bound to govern by established standing laws, promulgated and known to the people, and not by extemporary decrees; by indifferent and upright judges, who are to decide controversies by those laws; and to employ the force of the community at home, only in the execution of such laws, or abroad to prevent or redress foreign injuries, and secure the community from inroads and invasion. And all this to be directed to no other end, but the peace, safety, and public good of the people.

1690

MARY ASTELL

Mary Astell challenged many orthodoxies, including the ideas that women should not be educated, that they are intellectually inferior to men, and that they ought to marry at practically any cost (see *Some Reflections upon Marriage*, p. 249). Yet she was also a vigorous Tory controversialist who defended the doctrine of the divine right of kings, argued that English subjects owe (at least) "passive obedience" to their monarchs, and denounced toleration of Dissenters. Astell devoted much of her writing to political controversy: she published three substantial political pamphlets in 1704 alone. Her four-hundred-page magnum opus, *The Christian Religion as Profess'd by a Daughter of the Church of England* (1705), explicitly attacks Locke's *Two Treatises of Government*; at various places in her work, she criticizes his theological essay *The Reasonableness of Christianity* (1695); and she even mocks what she sees as the political tendency of his epistemology in his *Essay Concerning Human Understanding* (1689). Her Tory convictions also color her discussions of gender relations. In *Some Reflections upon Marriage*, she consistently draws parallels between a wife's duty of obedience to her husband and the obedience that subjects owe their sovereigns: a woman who marries "elects a monarch for life" and "gives him an authority she cannot recall however he misapply it." She devoutly held her belief in obedience, authority, and hierarchy—it was far more than a mere concession to the status quo—and this stance set her against the Whig theorists who supported the rights of subjects to disobey unjust power.

Yet Astell's involvement in contemporary political debate made certain ironies irresistible to her. Her most famous work, the "Preface, in Answer to Some Objections" added to the third edition of *Reflections upon Marriage* (1706; the word *some* was dropped from the title) is filled with the language of freedom, tyranny, rights, and slavery. In the Preface, she singles out some of Locke's pronouncements in the chapter "Of Slavery" from the *Second Treatise of Government* for ironic commentary. "If all men are born free, how is it that all women are born slaves?" she asks. Such questions expose the hypocrisy of male advocates of liberty who refuse to extend it to domestic relationships. And perhaps Astell's ironies do more. While she would never espouse the right to rebel against unjust authority in a marriage or a monarchy, some readers find in the Preface an awareness of domestic tyranny too keen to be piously constrained, and detect in Astell's deftly ironic repetition of the formulaic praises of liberty the seeds of women's liberation. Much of the Preface catalogs strong, sensible women from both the Old and New Testaments to prove that the Bible does not proclaim women's natural intellectual inferiority. In the paragraphs included here, Astell approaches an outright denunciation of the "arbitrary power" that men exercise in families. Through the very sarcasm with which she accepts the subjection of wives in marriage, she draws close to applying a doctrine of English political liberty to women.

From A Preface, in Answer to Some Objections to *Reflections upon Marriage*

* * *

[T]his design, which is unfortunately accused of being so destructive to the government, of the men I mean, is entirely her own.[1] She neither advised with friends, nor turned over[2] ancient or modern authors, nor prudently submitted to the correction of such as are, or such as *think* they are good judges, but with an *English* spirit and genius set out upon the forlorn hope, meaning no hurt to anybody, nor designing any thing but the public good, and to retrieve, if possible, the native liberty, the rights and privileges of the subject.

Far be it from her to stir up sedition of any sort, none can abhor it more; and she heartily wishes that our masters[3] would pay their civil and ecclesiastical governors the same submission which they themselves exact from their domestic subjects. Nor can she imagine how she any way undermines the masculine empire or blows the trumpet of rebellion to the moiety[4] of mankind. Is it by exhorting women not to expect to have their own will in any thing, but to be entirely submissive when once they have made choice of a lord and master, though he happen not to be so wise, so kind, or even so just a governor as was expected?[5] She did not indeed advise them to think his folly wisdom, nor his brutality that love and worship he promised in his matrimonial oath, for this required a flight of wit and sense much above her poor ability, and proper only to masculine understandings. However she did not in any manner prompt them to resist or to abdicate the perjured spouse, though the laws of God and the land make special provision for it in a case wherein, as is to be feared, few men can truly plead not guilty.[6]

* * *

If mankind had never sinned, reason would always have been obeyed, there would have been no struggle for dominion, and brutal power would not have prevailed. But in the lapsed state of mankind, and now that men will not be guided by their reason but by their appetites, and do not what they *ought* but what they *can*, the reason, or that which stands for it, the will and pleasure of the governor, is to be the reason of those who will not be guided by their own, and must take place for order's sake, although it should not be conformable to right reason. Nor can there be any society great or little,

1. As in earlier editions, Astell does not put her name on the third edition's title page, but she here affirms that she, the author, is a woman (referring to herself in the third person).
2. Ransacked.
3. Men in general, masters of women.
4. Half; here referring to the female half of humankind.

5. Astell advises in the body of *Some Reflections upon Marriage* that women accept their marriages, no matter how tyrannical their husbands are.
6. In Astell's time, both ecclesiastical and civil law allowed wives the right to petition for legal separation (not divorce) from husbands who were egregiously, physically cruel to them.

from empires down to private families, without a last resort to determine the affairs of the society by an irresistible sentence.[7] Now unless this supremacy be fixed somewhere, there will be a perpetual contention about it, such is the love of dominion; and let the reason of things be what it may, those who have least force or cunning to supply it[8] will have the disadvantage. So that since women are acknowledged to have least bodily strength, their being commanded to obey is in pure kindness to them, and for their quiet and security, as well as for the exercise of their virtue.[9] But does it follow that domestic governors have more sense than their subjects, any more than that other governors have? We do not find any man thinks the worse of his own understanding because another has superior power; or concludes himself less capable of a post of honor and authority because he is not preferred[1] to it. How much time would lie on men's hands, how empty would the places of concourse be, and how silent most companies, did men forbear to censure their governors; that is, in effect, to think themselves wiser. Indeed, government would be much more desirable than it is did it invest the possessor with a superior understanding as well as power. And if mere power gives a right to rule, there can be no such thing as usurpation; but a highway-man, so long as he has strength to force, has also a right to require our obedience.

Again, if absolute sovereignty be not necessary in a state, how comes it to be so in a family? or if in a family why not in a state; since no reason can be alleged for the one that will not hold more strongly for the other? If the authority of the husband, so far as it extends, is sacred and inalienable, why not of the prince? The domestic sovereign is without dispute elected,[2] and the stipulations and contracts are mutual. Is it not then partial[3] in men to the last degree to contend for and practice that arbitrary dominion in their families which they abhor and exclaim against in the state? For if arbitrary power is evil in itself, and an improper method of governing rational and free agents, it ought not to be practiced anywhere. Nor is it less but rather more mischievous in families than in kingdoms, by how much 100,000 tyrants are worse than one. What though a husband can't deprive a wife of life without being responsible to the law, he may however do what is much more grievous to a generous mind, render life miserable, for which she has no redress, scarce pity, which is afforded to every other complainant; it being thought a wife's duty to suffer everything without complaint. If *all men are born free*, how is it that all women are born slaves? as they must be if the being subjected to the *inconstant, uncertain, unknown, arbitrary will* of men be the *perfect condition of slavery?* and if the essence of freedom consists, as our masters say it does, in having *a standing rule to live by?*[4] And why is slavery so much condemned and strove against in one case and so highly applauded and held so necessary and so sacred in another?

* * *

7. I.e., no society can subsist without vesting power in some ultimate authority that incontrovertibly decides contentious questions.
8. To occupy the place of supremacy.
9. Here Astell presents the crucial link between her politics and her feminism: women must look favorably on absolute sovereignty because political instability threatens them, the weakest members of society, the most.

1. Promoted.
2. The wife "elects" her husband when she consents to marry him.
3. Unfair, or biased.
4. The last three italicized phrases quote the first and third paragraphs of the chapter "Of Slavery" (sections 22 and 24) from John Locke's *Second Treatise of Government* (p. 962).

Again, men are possessed of all places of power, trust, and profit; they make laws and exercise the magistracy. Not only the sharpest sword, but even all the swords and blunderbusses are theirs, which by the strongest logic in the world gives them the best title to everything they please to claim as their prerogative. Who shall contend with them? Immemorial prescription[5] is on their side in these parts of the world, ancient tradition and modern usage! Our fathers have all along both taught and practiced superiority over the weaker sex, and consequently women are by nature inferior to men, as was to be demonstrated. An argument which must be acknowledged unanswerable; for as well as I love my sex, I will not pretend a reply to *such* demonstration!

Only let me beg to be informed, to whom we poor fatherless maids and widows who have lost their masters owe subjection? It can't be to all men in general, unless all men were agreed to give the same commands. Do we then fall as strays to the first who finds us? By the maxims of some men and the conduct of some women, one would think so. But whoever he be that thus happens to become our master, if he allows us to be reasonable creatures and does not merely compliment us with that title, since no man denies our readiness to use our tongues, it would tend I should think to our master's advantage, and therefore he may please to be advised, to teach us to improve our reason. But if reason is only allowed us by way of raillery, and the secret maxim is that we have none, or little more than brutes, 'tis the best way to confine us with chain and block to the chimney-corner, which probably might save the estates of some families and the honor of others.

I do not propose this to prevent a rebellion, for women are not so well united as to form an insurrection. They are for the most part wise enough to love their chains and to discern how very becomingly they set. They think as humbly of themselves as their masters can wish with respect to the other sex, but in regard to their own they have a spice of masculine ambition: every one would lead, and none would follow—both sexes being too apt to envy and too backward in emulating, and take more delight in detracting from their neighbor's virtue than in improving their own. And therefore as to those women who find themselves born for slavery and are so sensible of their own meanness as to conclude it impossible to attain to anything excellent, since they are or ought to be best acquainted with their own strength and genius, she's a fool who would attempt their deliverance or improvement. No, let them enjoy the great honor and felicity of their tame, submissive, and depending temper! Let the men applaud and let them glory in this wonderful humility! Let them receive the flatteries and grimaces of the other sex, live unenvied by their own, and be as much beloved as one such woman can afford to love another! Let them enjoy the glory of treading in the footsteps of their predecessors, and of having the prudence to avoid that audacious attempt of soaring beyond their sphere! Let them housewife[6] or play, dress, and be pretty entertaining company! Or, which is better, relieve the poor to ease their own compassions, read pious books, say their prayers and go to church, because they have been taught and used to do so, without being able to give a better reason for their faith and practice! Let them not by any means aspire at being women of understanding, because no man can endure a woman of superior

5. Title or claim based on long possession.   6. Perform domestic duties.

sense or would treat a reasonable woman civilly, but that he thinks he stands on higher ground and that she is so wise as to make exceptions in his favor and to take her measures by his directions. They may pretend to sense indeed since mere pretences only render one the more ridiculous! Let them in short be what is called *very* women, for this is most acceptable to all sorts of men; or let them aim at the title of *good devout* women, since some men can bear with this; but let them not judge of the sex by their own scantling.[7] For the great Author of nature and fountain of all perfection never designed that the mean and imperfect, but that the most complete and excellent, of his creatures in every kind should be the standard to the rest.

*　*　*

1706

7. Small ability.

JAMES THOMSON

James Thomson's *Liberty* (1735–36), a poem of some thirty-five hundred lines that portrays British freedom as the culmination of the progress of European civilization, is now no longer much read. But his short ode "Rule, Britannia" remains one of the nation's most popular patriotic songs. Set to music by Thomas Arne, the poem was composed for *Alfred* (1740), a masque in honor of Frederick, Prince of Wales, whom opponents of Robert Walpole's administration such as Thomson, Bolingbroke, and Pope supported. Many writers of the era evoke the image of Alfred the Great (849–899) to locate the origins of British liberty in a Gothic past, free of modern corruption: the ode was originally sung by an actor dressed as an ancient bard, accompanied by a British harp. The poem's depiction of Britons as exceptionally unfit for slavery and willing to fight for their freedom at home and abroad both criticizes the contemporary antiwar policy of Walpole and contributes to a national self-image that will shape Britain's role in the world in the centuries to come.

T. Medland, **The Gothic Temple of Liberty**, engraving, 1796. New buildings like this one (ca. 1748) at Stowe Landscape Garden revived the ancient Gothic architectural style to recall the liberty enjoyed by the forebears of modern Britons, who feared their nation was becoming slavish and corrupt. From *Stowe. A Description of the House and Gardens* (1796).

Ode: Rule, Britannia

1

When *Britain* first, at heaven's command,
  Arose from out the azure main°   *open ocean*
This was the charter of the land,
  And guardian angels sung *this* strain:
5   "Rule, *Britannia*, rule the waves;
    Britons never will be slaves."

2

The nations, not so blest as thee,
  Must, in their turns, to tyrants fall:
While thou shalt flourish great and free,
10   The dread and envy of them all.
    "Rule," etc.

3

Still more majestic shalt thou rise,
  More dreadful, from each foreign stroke:
As the loud blast that tears the skies,
15   Serves but to root thy native oak.
    "Rule," etc.

4

Thee haughty tyrants ne'er shall tame:
  All their attempts to bend thee down
Will but arouse thy generous flame;
20   But work their woe, and thy renown.
    "Rule," etc.

5

To thee belongs the rural reign;
  Thy cities shall with commerce shine:
All thine shall be the subject main,
25   And every shore it circles thine.
    "Rule," etc.

6

The Muses, still° with freedom found,   *always*
  Shall to thy happy coast repair:
Blest isle! with matchless beauty crowned,
30   And manly hearts to guard the fair.
    "Rule, *Britannia*, rule the waves;
    Britons never will be slaves."

1740   1745–46

DAVID HUME

D avid Hume (1711–1776) declared that he "was seized very early with a passion for literature," which, he said, "has been the ruling passion of my life, and the great source of my enjoyments." Now we think of Hume as the most devastatingly brilliant of British philosophers. But epistemology and moral philosophy were only part of his larger literary enterprise, and in his time he was known better as a historian and an essayist on various topics—matters of taste, culture, politics, history, economics—than he was as the great philosophical skeptic who undermined commonsense notions of causation and personal identity. The selection included here comes from Hume's first collection, *Essays, Moral and Political* (1741; rev. ed. 1742), which, though published anonymously, launched the body of writing that would soon establish his reputation after the disappointing indifference that greeted his massive, brilliant *Treatise of Human Nature* (1739–40). Hume went on to produce other collections of essays and the popular and influential *History of England* (1754–62) in six volumes, which surveyed the development of politics, commerce, and the arts and sciences in Great Britain from ancient times to the Revolution of 1688, for the first time, Hume thought, from a nonpartisan perspective. A Scot and a skeptic, Hume was in a position to survey British culture and history from a critical distance that sometimes produced anger or bafflement in his readers, though these reactions augmented more than mitigated his fame. His detractors brought up his reputed atheism when opportunities arose for him to take important public positions—on different occasions he was denied professorships in Scottish universities on these grounds—though his most probing religious writing, including the *Dialogues Concerning Natural Religion* (1779), was suppressed until after his death.

Hume's style as an essayist is familiar, polished, and urbane; he wears his learning lightly and gracefully. But even these performances reveal a subtle mind unwilling to accept any easy answer or comforting ideological piety. The selection included here celebrates the freedom of the press in Britain, on which many of Hume's fellow subjects congratulated themselves, in contrast to the heavier legal restrictions imposed on writers on the Continent. But typically for Hume this liberty results less from a high-minded British embrace of rationalized principle than from passion, specifically the intense "jealousy" energizing Britain's mix of monarchy and republic. Later, indeed, he came to have second thoughts: the final version of the essay excises the last three paragraphs praising liberty and dourly concludes that "unbounded liberty of the press . . . is one of those evils, attending those mixed forms of government." The earlier version, reproduced here, offers a more positive view, but still a complex one, noting that the freedom to publish can help contain political rebelliousness even while allowing its expression. The essay is true to Hume's abiding belief that liberty produces a stronger, richer (if not more rational) social fabric.

Of the Liberty of the Press

There is nothing more apt to surprise a foreigner than the extreme liberty we enjoy in this country of communicating whatever we please to the public, and of openly censuring every measure which is entered into by the king or his ministers. If the administration resolve upon war, 'tis affirmed that either willfully or ignorantly they mistake the interest of the nation, and that peace in the present situation of affairs is infinitely preferable. If the passion of the ministers be for peace, our political writers breathe nothing but war and devastation, and represent the pacific conduct of the government as mean and pusillanimous. As this liberty is not indulged in any other government, either republican or monarchical, in Holland and Venice, no more than in France or Spain,[1] it may very naturally give occasion to these two questions: how it happens that Great Britain alone enjoys such a peculiar privilege? and, whether the unlimited exercise of this liberty be advantageous or prejudicial to the public?

As to the first question, why the laws indulge us in such an extraordinary liberty? I believe the reason may be derived from our mixed form of government, which is neither wholly monarchical, nor wholly republican. 'Twill be found, if I mistake not, a true observation in politics that the two extremes in government, of liberty and slavery, approach nearest to each other; and, that as you depart from the extremes, and mix a little of monarchy with liberty, the government becomes always the more free; and, on the other hand, when you mix a little of liberty with monarchy, the yoke becomes always the more grievous and intolerable.[2] In a government such as that of France, which is entirely absolute, and where laws, custom, and religion all concur to make the people fully satisfied with their condition, the monarch cannot entertain the least jealousy[3] against his subjects, and is therefore apt to indulge them in great liberties both of speech and action. In a government altogether republican such as that of Holland, where there is no magistrate[4] so eminent as to give jealousy to the state, there is also no danger in intrusting the magistrates with very large discretionary powers, and though many advantages result from such powers in the preservation of peace and order; yet they lay a considerable restraint on men's actions, and make every private subject pay a great respect to the government. Thus it is evident that the two extremes of absolute monarchy and of a republic approach very near to each other in the most material circumstances. In the first, the magistrate has no jealousy of the people: in the second, the people have no jealousy of the magistrate: which want of jealousy begets a mutual confidence and trust in both cases, and produces a species of liberty in monarchies and of arbitrary power in republics.

To justify the other part of the foregoing observation, that in every government the means are most wide of each other, and that the mixtures of monarchy and liberty render the yoke either more easy or more grievous; I must take notice of a remark of Tacitus with regard to the Romans under the emperors, that they neither could bear total slavery nor total liberty: Nec totam servitutem, nec totam libertatem pati possunt.[5] This remark a famous

---

1. The former pair typify republics; the latter, absolutist monarchies.
2. In the following examples, Hume argues that Holland and France exemplify the "extremes" of liberty and slavery, respectively, which in the final analysis resemble one another, while imperial Rome and modern Britain are described as political mixtures that prove to differ profoundly.
3. Suspicion as toward a competitor or rival; here for power in the state.
4. Governmental official.
5. Hume translates the Latin in the preceding phrase. The quotation is from the *Histories* (1.16.28) of Roman historian Tacitus (55?–117?).

poet has translated and applied to the English in his admirable description of Queen Elizabeth's policy and happy government.

> Et fit aimer son joug a l'Anglois indompté,
> Qui ne peut ni servir, ni vivre en liberté . . .
> HENRIADE, *liv*. I.[6]

According to these remarks, therefore, we are to consider the Roman government as a mixture of despotism and liberty, where the despotism prevailed; and the English government as a mixture of the same kind, but where the liberty predominates. The consequences are exactly conformable to the foregoing observation; and such as may be expected from those mixed forms of government, which beget a mutual watchfulness and jealousy. The Roman emperors were, many of them, the most frightful tyrants that ever disgraced humanity; and 'tis evident their cruelty was chiefly excited by their jealousy, and by their observing that all the great men of Rome bore with impatience the dominion of a family which, but a little before, was noways superior to their own. On the other hand, as the republican part of the government prevails in England, though with a great mixture of monarchy, 'tis obliged for its own preservation to maintain a watchful jealousy over the magistrates, to remove all discretionary powers, and to secure every one's life and fortune by general and inflexible laws. No action must be deemed a crime but what the law has plainly determined to be such: no crime must be imputed to a man but from a legal proof before his judges; and even these judges must be his fellow-subjects, who are obliged by their own interest to have a watchful eye over the encroachments and violence of the ministers. From these causes it proceeds that there is as much liberty, and even, perhaps, licentiousness in Britain, as there were formerly slavery and tyranny in Rome.

These principles account for the great liberty of the press in these kingdoms, beyond what is indulged in any other government. 'Tis sufficiently known that despotic power would soon steal in upon us were we not extreme watchful to prevent its progress, and were there not an easy method of conveying the alarum from one end of the kingdom to the other. The spirit of the people must frequently be roused to curb the ambition of the court; and the dread of rousing this spirit must be employed to prevent that ambition. Nothing is so effectual to this purpose as the liberty of the press, by which all the learning, wit, and genius of the nation may be employed on the side of liberty, and every one be animated to its defense. As long, therefore, as the republican part of our government can maintain itself against the monarchical, it must be extreme jealous[7] of the liberty of the press, as of the utmost importance to its preservation.

Since therefore the liberty of the press is so essential to the support of our mixed government, this sufficiently decides the second question, "Whether this liberty be advantageous or prejudicial?"; there being nothing

---

6. The famous poet is François-Marie Arouet, known as Voltaire (1694–1778). The lines on Elizabeth are from his epic poem *La Henriade* (1728): She made her yoke agreeable to the unconquered English, who could neither serve nor live in freedom (French).

7. Here vigilant in guarding as a possession.

of greater importance in every state than the preservation of the ancient government, especially if it be a free one. But I would fain go a step farther and assert that such a liberty is attended with so few inconveniencies that it may be claimed as the common right of mankind, and ought to be indulged them almost in every government: except the ecclesiastical, to which indeed it would be fatal. We need not dread from this liberty any such ill consequences as followed from the harangues of the popular demagogues of Athens and tribunes of Rome. A man reads a book or pamphlet alone and coolly. There is none present from whom he can catch the passion by contagion. He is not hurried away by the force and energy of action. And should he be wrought up to never so seditious a humor,[8] there is no violent resolution presented to him by which he can immediately vent his passion. The liberty of the press, therefore, however abused, can scarce ever excite popular tumults or rebellion. And as to those murmurs or secret discontents it may occasion, 'tis better they should get vent in words, that they may come to the knowledge of the magistrate before it be too late, in order to his providing a remedy against them. Mankind, 'tis true, have always a greater propension to believe what is said to the disadvantage of their governors than the contrary; but this inclination is inseparable from them whether they have liberty or not. A whisper may fly as quick and be as pernicious as a pamphlet. Nay, it will be more pernicious, where men are not accustomed to think freely, or distinguish betwixt truth and falsehood.

It has also been found as the experience of mankind increases that the people are no such dangerous monster as they have been represented, and that 'tis in every respect better to guide them like rational creatures than to lead or drive them like brute beasts. Before the United Provinces[9] set the example, toleration was deemed incompatible with good government; and 'twas thought impossible that a number of religious sects could live together in harmony and peace, and have all of them an equal affection to their common country, and to each other. England has set a like example of civil liberty; and though this liberty seems to occasion some small ferment at present, it has not as yet produced any pernicious effects; and it is to be hoped that men, being every day more accustomed to the free discussion of public affairs, will improve in their judgment of them and be with greater difficulty seduced by every idle rumor and popular clamor.

'Tis a very comfortable reflection to the lovers of liberty that this peculiar privilege of Britain is of a kind that cannot easily be wrested from us, but must last as long as our government remains in any degree free and independent. 'Tis seldom that liberty of any kind is lost all at once. Slavery has so frightful an aspect to men accustomed to freedom that it must steal in upon them by degrees, and must disguise itself in a thousand shapes in order to be received. But if the liberty of the press ever be lost, it must be lost all at once. The general laws against sedition and libeling are at present as strong as they possibly can be made. Nothing can impose a farther restraint, but

---

8. Mood.   9. Holland, noted for its religious toleration.

either the clapping an IMPRIMATUR[1] upon the press, or the giving very large discretionary powers to the court to punish whatever displeases them. But these concessions would be such a bare-faced violation of liberty that they will probably be the last efforts of a despotic government. We may conclude that the liberty of Britain is gone for ever when these attempts shall succeed.

1741, 1742

1. Let it be printed (Latin). This word was applied by the Vatican to indicate that a book may be published and is often employed, as here, to refer to the general practice of prepublication licensing of texts.

EDMUND BURKE

Edmund Burke (1729–1797) commanded both an acute capacity for political analysis and a confident, passionate, often poetic gift for dramatizing what he took to be the stakes of the great historical events of his time. Born and educated in Dublin, the son of an Anglican father and Catholic mother, he came to London in 1750 to study law. But he made his first mark in the world as a philosopher, publishing *A Philosophical Enquiry into the Origin of Our Ideas of the Sublime and the Beautiful* in 1757, a work that has exercised considerable influence on the study of aesthetics to the present day. Its main claim is that we respond with instinctive feeling to certain objects— beautiful ones with pleasure, sublime ones with a type of pain—before the intervention of reason. His insight into human passion deeply informed his later career in politics, both as an analyst of events and their causes and as the most moving orator of his day. Many of his twenty-nine years in Parliament were spent in opposition: he was a voice of conscience and protest not only against Tory governments in power but often against his fellow Whigs. Most of the time he fought for the losing side. He sought to reconcile Britain with its American colonies and avoid war; argued against the persecution of Irish Catholics; and presided over the trial of Warren Hastings, governor-general of India, whose administration Burke found rapacious and corrupt. To different degrees, such campaigns ended in failure. Some of Burke's most famous and lasting political thinking appears in his works opposing the French Revolution, including *Reflections on the Revolution in France* (1790). In it he denounces what he saw as the destructively "metaphysical," rationalistic spirit of the revolutionaries, which led them to neglect the ways in which history and human emotions knit the fabric of society together—a neglect that resulted in recklessness and cruelty.

Burke's speech recommending Britain's conciliation with its American colonies (1775), delivered on the eve of the American War for Independence, has powerfully resonated long past its historical moment. Burke both unfolds the complex origins of liberty in British history and shows how the idea helps establish the very political identity of the people soon to become the citizens of the United States. The speech has long been popular with Americans: in the early nineteenth century, for instance, anti-abolitionists were fond of citing Burke's depiction of the fierce commitment to liberty of the white South (though he had not meant that as praise). Most characteristic of Burke's political thinking is the speech's description of liberty as a complex, concrete reality, not as "abstract liberty," which, "like other mere abstractions, is not to be found." More than an ideal, the meaning of liberty emerges from a richly detailed weave of particular historical processes.

From Speech on the Conciliation with the American Colonies

* * *

In [the] character of the Americans a love of freedom is the predominating feature which marks and distinguishes the whole: and as an ardent is always a jealous affection, your colonies become suspicious, restive, and untractable, whenever they see the least attempt to wrest from them by force, or shuffle from them by chicane, what they think the only advantage worth living for. This fierce spirit of liberty is stronger in the English colonies, probably, than in any other people of the earth, and this from a great variety of powerful causes; which, to understand the true temper of their minds, and the direction which this spirit takes, it will not be amiss to lay open somewhat more largely.

First, the people of the colonies are descendants of Englishmen. England, Sir, is a nation which still, I hope, respects, and formerly adored, her freedom. The colonists emigrated from you when this part of your character was most predominant; and they took this bias and direction the moment they parted from your hands. They are therefore not only devoted to liberty, but to liberty according to English ideas and on English principles. Abstract liberty, like other mere abstractions, is not to be found. Liberty inheres in some sensible object;[1] and every nation has formed to itself some favorite point, which by way of eminence becomes the criterion of their happiness. It happened, you know, Sir, that the great contests for freedom in this country were from the earliest times chiefly upon the question of taxing. Most of the contests in the ancient commonwealths turned primarily on the right of election of magistrates, or on the balance among the several orders of the state. The question of money was not with them so immediate. But in England it was otherwise. On this point of taxes the ablest pens and most eloquent tongues have been exercised, the greatest spirits have acted and suffered. In order to give the fullest satisfaction concerning the importance of this point, it was not only necessary for those who in argument defended the excellence of the English Constitution to insist on this privilege of granting money as a dry point of fact, and to prove that the right had been acknowledged in ancient parchments and blind usages to reside in a certain body called a House of Commons: they went much further: they attempted to prove, and they succeeded, that in theory it ought to be so, from the particular nature of a House of Commons, as an immediate representative of the people, whether the old records had delivered this oracle or not. They took infinite pains to inculcate, as a fundamental principle, that in all monarchies the people must in effect themselves, mediately or immediately, possess the power of granting their own money, or no shadow of liberty could subsist. The colonies draw from you, as with their life-blood, these ideas and principles. Their love of liberty, as with you, fixed and attached on this specific point of taxing. Liberty might be safe or might be endangered in twenty other particulars without their being much pleased or alarmed. Here they felt its pulse; and as they found that beat, they thought themselves sick or sound. I do not say whether they were right or wrong in applying your general

1. I.e., an object perceived by the senses.

arguments to their own case. It is not easy, indeed, to make a monopoly of theorems and corollaries. The fact is, that they did thus apply those general arguments; and your mode of governing them, whether through lenity or indolence, through wisdom or mistake, confirmed them in the imagination, that they, as well as you, had an interest in these common principles.

They were further confirmed in this pleasing error by the form of their provincial legislative assemblies. Their governments are popular in an high degree: some are merely popular;[2] in all, the popular representative is the most weighty; and this share of the people in their ordinary government never fails to inspire them with lofty sentiments, and with a strong aversion from whatever tends to deprive them of their chief importance.

If anything were wanting to this necessary operation of the form of government, religion would have given it a complete effect. Religion, always a principle of energy, in this new people is no way worn out or impaired; and their mode of professing it is also one main cause of this free spirit. The people are Protestants, and of that kind which is the most adverse to all implicit submission of mind and opinion. This is a persuasion not only favorable to liberty, but built upon it. I do not think, Sir, that the reason of this averseness in the dissenting churches from all that looks like absolute government is so much to be sought in their religious tenets as in their history. Every one knows that the Roman Catholic religion is at least coeval with most of the governments where it prevails, that it has generally gone hand in hand with them, and received a great favor and every kind of support from authority. The Church of England, too, was formed from her cradle under the nursing care of regular government. But the dissenting interests have sprung up in direct opposition to all the ordinary powers of the world, and could justify that opposition only on a strong claim to natural liberty. Their very existence depended on the powerful and unremitted assertion of that claim. All Protestantism, even the most cold and passive, is a sort of dissent. But the religion most prevalent in our northern colonies is a refinement on the principle of resistance: it is the dissidence of dissent, and the protestantism of the Protestant religion. This religion, under a variety of denominations agreeing in nothing but in the communion of the spirit of liberty, is predominant in most of the northern provinces, where the Church of England, notwithstanding its legal rights, is in reality no more than a sort of private sect, not composing, most probably, the tenth of the people. The colonists left England when this spirit was high, and in the emigrants was the highest of all; and even that stream of foreigners which has been constantly flowing into these colonies has, for the greatest part, been composed of dissenters from the establishments of their several countries, and have brought with them a temper and character far from alien to that of the people with whom they mixed.

Sir, I can perceive, by their manner, that some gentlemen object to the latitude of this description, because in the southern colonies the Church of England forms a large body, and has a regular establishment. It is certainly true. There is, however, a circumstance attending these colonies, which, in my opinion, fully counterbalances this difference, and makes the spirit of liberty still more high and haughty than in those to the northward. It is, that

2. Entirely elected by the people. In 18th-century England the masses could not vote.

in Virginia and the Carolinas they have a vast multitude of slaves. Where this is the case in any part of the world, those who are free are by far the most proud and jealous of their freedom. Freedom is to them not only an enjoyment, but a kind of rank and privilege. Not seeing there, that freedom, as in countries where it is a common blessing, and as broad and general as the air, may be united with much abject toil, with great misery, with all the exterior of servitude, liberty looks, amongst them, like something that is more noble and liberal. I do not mean, Sir, to commend the superior morality of this sentiment, which has at least as much pride as virtue in it,[3] but I cannot alter the nature of man. The fact is so; and these people of the southern colonies are much more strongly, and with an higher and more stubborn spirit, attached to liberty, than those to the northward. Such were all the ancient commonwealths; such were our Gothic ancestors; such in our days were the Poles;[4] and such will be all masters of slaves, who are not slaves themselves. In such a people, the haughtiness of domination combines with the spirit of freedom, fortifies it, and renders it invincible.

Permit me, Sir, to add another circumstance in our colonies, which contributes no mean part towards the growth and effect of this untractable spirit: I mean their education. In no country, perhaps, in the world is the law so general a study. * * * This study renders men acute, inquisitive, dexterous, prompt in attack, ready in defense, full of resources. In other countries, the people, more simple, and of a less mercurial cast, judge of an ill principle in government only by an actual grievance; here they anticipate the evil, and judge the pressure of the grievance by the badness of the principle. They augur misgovernment at a distance, and snuff the approach of tyranny in every tainted breeze.

The last cause of this disobedient spirit in the colonies is hardly less powerful than the rest, as it is not merely moral, but laid deep in the natural constitution of things. Three thousand miles of ocean lie between you and them. No contrivance can prevent the effect of this distance in weakening government. Seas roll, and months pass, between the order and the execution; and the want of a speedy explanation of a single point is enough to defeat an whole system. You have, indeed, winged ministers of vengeance, who carry your bolts in their pounces[5] to the remotest verge of the sea: but there a power steps in, that limits the arrogance of raging passions and furious elements, and says, "So far shalt thou go, and no farther."[6] Who are you, that should fret and rage, and bite the chains of Nature? Nothing worse happens to you than does to all nations who have extensive empire; and it happens in all the forms into which empire can be thrown. In large bodies, the circulation of power must be less vigorous at the extremities. Nature has said it. The Turk cannot govern Egypt, and Arabia, and Kurdistan, as he governs Thrace; nor has he the same dominion in Crimea and Algiers which he has at Brusa and Smyrna. Despotism itself is obliged to truck and huckster. The Sultan gets such obedience as he can. He governs with a loose rein, that he may govern at all; and the whole of the force and vigor of his

3. Burke himself passionately opposed slavery. In 1765 he had argued against American representation in Parliament on the ground that slaveowners had no right to make laws for free men.
4. Slavery was abolished in Poland in 1772.

5. Talons; gunpowder. Burke compares the ships of the British navy to Milton's avenging angels.
6. A reference to King Canute, who could not command the sea.

authority in his center is derived from a prudent relaxation in all his borders. Spain, in her provinces, is perhaps not so well obeyed as you are in yours. She complies, too; she submits; she watches times. This is the immutable condition, the eternal law, of extensive and detached empire.

Then, Sir, from these six capital sources, of descent, of form of government, of religion in the northern provinces, of manners in the southern, of education, of the remoteness of situation from the first mover of government—from all these causes a fierce spirit of liberty has grown up. It has grown with the growth of the people in your colonies, and increased with the increase of their wealth: a spirit, that, unhappily meeting with an exercise of power in England, which, however lawful, is not reconcilable to any ideas of liberty, much less with theirs, has kindled this flame that is ready to consume us.

*   *   *

1775

SAMUEL JOHNSON

Samuel Johnson detested slavery and the owners of slaves. Once, "in company with some very grave men at Oxford, his toast was, 'Here's to the next insurrection of the Negroes in the West Indies,'" and in his pamphlet *Taxation No Tyranny* (1775), he put the American rebels down with a devastating question: "How is it that we hear the loudest yelps for liberty among the drivers of Negroes?" Although slavery had been abolished in England in 1772, serfdom still existed in Scotland, and the British remained heavily involved in the slave trade. In 1777 a black slave, Joseph Knight, sued for freedom from the Scottish master he had escaped. On his behalf Johnson dictated this argument to Boswell.

[A Brief to Free a Slave]

It must be agreed that in most ages many countries have had part of their inhabitants in a state of slavery; yet it may be doubted whether slavery can ever be supposed the natural condition of man. It is impossible not to conceive that men in their original state were equal; and very difficult to imagine how one would be subjected to another but by violent compulsion. An individual may, indeed, forfeit his liberty by a crime; but he cannot by that crime forfeit the liberty of his children. What is true of a criminal seems true likewise of a captive. A man may accept life from a conquering enemy on condition of perpetual servitude; but it is very doubtful whether he can entail[1] that servitude on his descendants; for no man can stipulate without commission for another. The condition which he himself accepts, his son or grandson perhaps would have rejected. If we should admit, what perhaps

1. Settle unalterably.

may with more reason be denied, that there are certain relations between man and man which may make slavery necessary and just,[2] yet it can never be proved that he who is now suing for his freedom ever stood in any of those relations. He is certainly subject by no law, but that of violence, to his present master,[3] who pretends no claim to his obedience, but that he bought him from a merchant of slaves, whose right to sell him never was examined. It is said that, according to the constitutions of Jamaica, he was legally enslaved; these constitutions are merely positive;[4] and apparently injurious to the rights of mankind, because whoever is exposed to sale is condemned to slavery without appeal; by whatever fraud or violence he might have been originally brought into the merchant's power. In our own time princes have been sold, by wretches to whose care they were entrusted, that they might have an European education; but when once they were brought to a market in the plantations, little would avail either their dignity or their wrongs. The laws of Jamaica afford a Negro no redress. His color is considered as a sufficient testimony against him. It is to be lamented that moral right should ever give way to political convenience. But if temptations of interest are sometimes too strong for human virtue, let us at least retain a virtue where there is no temptation to quit it. In the present case there is apparent right on one side, and no convenience on the other. Inhabitants of this island can neither gain riches nor power by taking away the liberty of any part of the human species. The sum of the argument is this:—No man is by nature the property of another: The defendant is, therefore, by nature free: The rights of nature must be some way forfeited before they can be justly taken away: That the defendant has by any act forfeited the rights of nature we require to be proved; and if no proof of such forfeiture can be given, we doubt not but the justice of the court will declare him free.[5]

1777   1792

2. Boswell, who strongly disagreed with Johnson's "prejudice" against slavery, argued that "to abolish a *status*, which in all ages GOD has sanctioned, and man has continued, would not only be *robbery* to an innumerable class of our fellow subjects; but it would be extreme cruelty to the African savages."
3. Knight had been kidnapped as a child.
4. Arbitrarily instituted (opposed to *natural* laws).
5. Knight was set free by the Scottish court.

OLAUDAH EQUIANO

The Interesting Narrative of the Life of Olaudah Equiano, or Gustavus Vassa, the African, Written by Himself, published in 1789, is the classic story of an eighteenth-century African's descent into slavery and rise to freedom. It describes how its author (ca. 1745–1797) was raised in an Ibo village (in modern Nigeria), kidnapped by African raiders, and sold into slavery. Particularly powerful is its account of the horrors of the Middle Passage to the New World. There, an English naval officer bought him to serve as a cabin boy and renamed him Gustavus Vassa, after a sixteenth-century Swedish hero who freed his people from the Danes (such names concealed the status of a slave, because slavery was frowned on by the British Navy).

During years at sea, as well as a period at a London school, Equiano acquired a basic education. He also underwent baptism, a ritual that many slaves expected to make them free. But his hopes were cruelly disappointed when, after six years' service, he was suddenly sold and shipped to the West Indies. There a Quaker merchant, Robert King, purchased him, employed him as a clerk and a seaman, and eventually allowed him, in 1766, to buy his freedom. Equiano went back to England, working first as a hairdresser and later voyaging all over the world, even taking part in an effort to find a passage to India by way of the North Pole. Scholars have raised doubts about the account that the *Interesting Narrative* gives of the early parts of Equiano's life: parish and British naval records indicate he was born not in Africa but in South Carolina and hence did not himself undergo the Middle Passage. Whether fact or fiction— scholars may never determine conclusively—the description of his days in Africa, abduction, and suffering in the slave ship gives a voice to countless Africans who faced such experiences and dramatizes the undeniable realities of the slave trade to a white readership. Equiano's publication of his story is a culmination of his involvement in the abolitionist movement through the 1780s and was an important contribution to that movement, not only for its explicit arguments against the slave trade but also for its demonstration that someone of African descent could be humane, intelligent, a good Christian, and a free and eloquent British subject. The book went through many editions and made Equiano famous. He married an Englishwoman, fathered two daughters, and died in London in 1797.

The *Life of Equiano* combines several literary genres. It is a captivity narrative, a spiritual autobiography, a travel memoir, an adventure story, and an abolitionist tract. The early chapters describe the healthy, cheerful, and virtuous life of Africans, contrasted with European inhumanity, and the later chapters show how much a black man can achieve, when given a chance. Equiano does not disguise the strains of his position as he is pulled between different identities and different worlds. His main purpose, however, is clearly to force his readers to face the ordeals a slave must endure—to live in his skin. If *Oroonoko* taught Europeans to sympathize with Africans, Equiano taught them that a black man could speak for himself.

William Blake, *A Coromantyn Free Negro, or Ranger, Armed,* 1796. Blake depicts the strength and independence of one of the African soldiers in Surinam promised their freedom for fighting with whites to suppress a slave rebellion. His scarlet cap signifies liberty. From John Stedman, *Narrative of a Five Years Expedition against the Revolted Negroes of Surinam . . . from the Year 1772, to 1777* (1796).

From The Interesting Narrative of the Life of Olaudah Equiano, or Gustavus Vassa, the African, Written by Himself

[THE MIDDLE PASSAGE][1]

The first object which saluted my eyes when I arrived on the coast was the sea, and a slave ship, which was then riding at anchor, and waiting for its cargo. These filled me with astonishment, which was soon converted into terror when I was carried on board. I was immediately handled and tossed up to see if I were sound by some of the crew; and I was now persuaded that I had gotten into a world of bad spirits, and that they were going to kill me. Their complexions too differing so much from ours, their long hair, and the language they spoke, (which was very different from any I had ever heard) united to confirm me in this belief. Indeed such were the horrors of my views and fears at the moment, that, if ten thousand worlds had been my own, I would have freely parted with them all to have exchanged my condition with that of the meanest slave in my own country. When I looked round the ship too and saw a large furnace of copper boiling, and a multitude of black people of every description chained together, every one of their countenances expressing dejection and sorrow, I no longer doubted of my fate; and, quite overpowered with horror and anguish, I fell motionless on the deck and fainted. When I recovered a little I found some black people about me, who I believe were some of those who brought me on board, and had been receiving their pay; they talked to me in order to cheer me, but all in vain. I asked them if we were not to be eaten by those white men with horrible looks, red faces, and loose hair. They told me I was not; and one of the crew brought me a small portion of spirituous liquor in a wine glass; but, being afraid of him, I would not take it out of his hand. One of the blacks therefore took it from him and gave it to me, and I took a little down my palate, which, instead of reviving me, as they thought it would, threw me into the greatest consternation at the strange feeling it produced, having never tasted any such liquor before. Soon after this the blacks who brought me on board went off, and left me abandoned to despair. I now saw myself deprived of all chance of returning to my native country, or even the least glimpse of hope of gaining the shore, which I now considered as friendly; and I even wished for my former slavery in preference to my present situation, which was filled with horrors of every kind, still heightened by my ignorance of what I was to undergo. I was not long suffered to indulge my grief; I was soon put down under the decks, and there I received such a salutation in my nostrils as I had never experienced in my life; so that, with the loathsomeness of the stench, and crying together, I became so sick and low that I was not able to eat, nor had I the least desire to taste any thing. I now wished for the last friend, death, to relieve me; but soon, to my grief, two of the white men offered me eatables; and, on my refusing to eat, one of them held me fast by the hands, and laid me across I think the windlass, and tied my feet, while the other flogged me severely. I had never experienced any thing of

---

1. After his kidnapping, young Equiano passes from one African master to another. The last of these, a merchant, treats him like a member of the family, until one morning the boy is suddenly wakened and hurried away to the seacoast.

this kind before; and although, not being used to the water, I naturally feared that element the first time I saw it, yet nevertheless, could I have got over the nettings,[2] I would have jumped over the side, but I could not; and, besides, the crew used to watch us very closely who were not chained down to the decks, lest we should leap into the water; and I have seen some of these poor African prisoners most severely cut for attempting to do so, and hourly whipped for not eating. This indeed was often the case with myself. In a little time after, amongst the poor chained men, I found some of my own nation, which in a small degree gave ease to my mind. I inquired of these what was to be done with us; they gave me to understand we were to be carried to these white people's country to work for them. I then was a little revived, and thought, if it were no worse than working, my situation was not so desperate: but still I feared I should be put to death, the white people looked and acted, as I thought, in so savage a manner; for I had never seen among any people such instances of brutal cruelty; and this not only shewn towards us blacks, but also to some of the whites themselves. One white man in particular I saw, when we were permitted to be on deck, flogged so unmercifully with a large rope near the foremast, that he died in consequence of it; and they tossed him over the side as they would have done a brute. This made me fear these people the more; and I expected nothing less than to be treated in the same manner. I could not help expressing my fears and apprehensions to some of my countrymen: I asked them if these people had no country, but lived in this hollow place (the ship): they told me they did not, but came from a distant one. "Then," said I, "how comes it in all our country we never heard of them?" They told me because they lived so very far off. I then asked where were their women? had they any like themselves? I was told they had: "and why," said I, "do we not see them?" they answered, because they were left behind. I asked how the vessel could go? they told me they could not tell; but that there were cloths put upon the masts by the help of the ropes I saw, and then the vessel went on; and the white men had some spell or magic they put in the water when they liked in order to stop the vessel. I was exceedingly amazed at this account, and really thought they were spirits. I therefore wished much to be from amongst them, for I expected they would sacrifice me: but my wishes were vain; for we were so quartered that it was impossible for any of us to make our escape. While we stayed on the coast I was mostly on deck; and one day, to my great astonishment, I saw one of these vessels coming in with the sails up. As soon as the whites saw it, they gave a great shout, at which we were amazed; and the more so as the vessel appeared larger by approaching nearer. At last she came to an anchor in my sight, and when the anchor was let go I and my countrymen who saw it were lost in astonishment to observe the vessel stop; and were now convinced it was done by magic. Soon after this the other ship got her boats out, and they came on board of us, and the people of both ships seemed very glad to see each other. Several of the strangers also shook hands with us black people, and made motions with their hands, signifying I suppose we were to go to their country; but we did not understand them. At last, when the ship we were in had got in all her cargo, they made ready with many fearful noises, and we were all put under deck, so that we could not

2. A network of small ropes around the ship kept slaves from jumping overboard.

see how they managed the vessel. But this disappointment was the least of my sorrow. The stench of the hold while we were on the coast was so intolerably loathsome, that it was dangerous to remain there for any time, and some of us had been permitted to stay on the deck for the fresh air; but now that the whole ship's cargo were confined together, it became absolutely pestilential. The closeness of the place, and the heat of the climate, added to the number in the ship, which was so crowded that each had scarcely room to turn himself, almost suffocated us. This produced copious perspirations, so that the air soon became unfit for respiration, from a variety of loathsome smells, and brought on a sickness among the slaves, of which many died, thus falling victims to the improvident avarice, as I may call it, of their purchasers. This wretched situation was again aggravated by the galling of the chains, now become insupportable; and the filth of the necessary tubs,[3] into which the children often fell, and were almost suffocated. The shrieks of the women, and the groans of the dying, rendered the whole a scene of horror almost inconceivable. Happily perhaps for myself I was soon reduced so low here that it was thought necessary to keep me almost always on deck; and from[4] my extreme youth I was not put in fetters. In this situation I expected every hour to share the fate of my companions, some of whom were almost daily brought upon deck at the point of death, which I began to hope would soon put an end to my miseries. Often did I think many of the inhabitants of the deep much more happy than myself. I envied them the freedom they enjoyed, and as often wished I could change my condition for theirs. Every circumstance I met with served only to render my state more painful, and heighten my apprehensions, and my opinion of the cruelty of the whites. One day they had taken a number of fishes; and when they had killed and satisfied themselves with as many as they thought fit, to our astonishment who were on the deck, rather than give any of them to us to eat as we expected, they tossed the remaining fish into the sea again, although we begged and prayed for some as well as we could, but in vain; and some of my countrymen, being pressed by hunger, took an opportunity, when they thought no one saw them, of trying to get a little privately; but they were discovered, and the attempt procured them some very severe floggings.

One day, when we had a smooth sea and moderate wind, two of my wearied countrymen who were chained together (I was near them at the time), preferring death to such a life of misery, somehow made through the nettings and jumped into the sea; immediately another quite dejected fellow, who, on account of his illness, was suffered to be out of irons, also followed their example; and I believe many more would very soon have done the same if they had not been prevented by the ship's crew, who were instantly alarmed. Those of us that were the most active were in a moment put down under the deck, and there was such a noise and confusion amongst the people of the ship as I never heard before, to stop her, and get the boat out to go after the slaves. However two of the wretches were drowned, but they got the other, and afterwards flogged him unmercifully for thus attempting to prefer death to slavery. In this manner we continued to undergo more hardships than I can now relate, hardships which are inseparable from this

---

3. Latrines.   4. Because of.

accursed trade. Many a time we were near suffocation from the want of fresh air, which we were often without for whole days together. This, and the stench of the necessary tubs, carried off many. During our passage I first saw flying fishes, which surprised me very much: they used frequently to fly across the ship, and many of them fell on the deck. I also now first saw the use of the quadrant; I had often with astonishment seen the mariners make observations with it, and I could not think what it meant. They at last took notice of my surprise; and one of them, willing to increase it, as well as to gratify my curiosity, made me one day look through it. The clouds appeared to me to be land, which disappeared as they passed along. This heightened my wonder; and I was now more persuaded than ever that I was in another world, and that every thing about me was magic. At last we came in sight of the island of Barbados,[5] at which the whites on board gave a great shout, and made many signs of joy to us. We did not know what to think of this; but as the vessel drew nearer we plainly saw the harbor, and other ships of different kinds and sizes; and we soon anchored amongst them off Bridge Town. Many merchants and planters now came on board, though it was in the evening. They put us in separate parcels,[6] and examined us attentively. They also made us jump, and pointed to the land, signifying we were to go there. We thought by this we should be eaten by these ugly men, as they appeared to us; and, when soon after we were all put down under the deck again, there was much dread and trembling among us, and nothing but bitter cries to be heard all the night from these apprehensions, insomuch that at last the white people got some old slaves from the land to pacify us. They told us we were not to be eaten, but to work, and were soon to go on land, where we should see many of our country people. This report eased us much; and sure enough, soon after we were landed, there came to us Africans of all languages. We were conducted immediately to the merchant's yard, where we were pent up altogether like so many sheep in a fold, without regard to sex or age. As every object was new to me, every thing I saw filled me with surprise. What struck me first was that the houses were built with stories, and in every other respect different from those in Africa; but I was still more astonished on seeing people on horseback. I did not know what this could mean; and indeed I thought these people were full of nothing but magical arts. While I was in this astonishment one of my fellow prisoners spoke to a countryman of his about the horses, who said they were the same kind they had in their country. I understood them, though they were from a distant part of Africa, and I thought it odd I had not seen any horses there; but afterwards, when I came to converse with different Africans, I found they had many horses amongst them, and much larger than those I then saw. We were not many days in the merchant's custody before we were sold after their usual manner, which is this:—On a signal given (as the beat of a drum) the buyers rush at once into the yard where the slaves are confined, and make a choice of that parcel they like best. The noise and clamor with which this is attended, and the eagerness visible in the countenances of the buyers, serve not a little to increase the apprehensions of the terrified Africans, who may well be supposed to consider them as the ministers of that destruction to

5. The easternmost Caribbean island, then an important center for the trade of sugar and slaves.

6. Groups sorted to be sold as one lot.

which they think themselves devoted.[7] In this manner, without scruple, are relations and friends separated, most of them never to see each other again. I remember in the vessel in which I was brought over, in the men's apartment, there were several brothers, who, in the sale, were sold in different lots; and it was very moving on this occasion to see and hear their cries at parting. O, ye nominal Christians! might not an African ask you, learned you this from your God, who says unto you, Do unto all men as you would men should do unto you? Is it not enough that we are torn from our country and friends to toil for your luxury and lust of gain? Must every tender feeling be likewise sacrificed to your avarice? Are the dearest friends and relations, now rendered more dear by their separation from their kindred, still to be parted from each other, and thus prevented from cheering the gloom of slavery with the small comfort of being together and mingling their sufferings and sorrows? Why are parents to lose their children, brothers their sisters, or husbands their wives? Surely this is a new refinement in cruelty, which, while it has no advantage to atone for it, thus aggravates distress, and adds fresh horrors even to the wretchedness of slavery.

* * *

[A FREE MAN][8]

Every day now brought me nearer my freedom, and I was impatient till we proceeded again to sea, that I might have an opportunity of getting a sum large enough to purchase it. I was not long ungratified; for, in the beginning of the year 1766, my master bought another sloop, named the *Nancy*, the largest I had ever seen. She was partly laden, and was to proceed to Philadelphia; our Captain had his choice of three, and I was well pleased he chose this, which was the largest; for, from his having a large vessel, I had more room, and could carry a larger quantity of goods with me. Accordingly, when we had delivered our old vessel, the *Prudence*, and completed the lading of the *Nancy*, having made near three hundred per cent, by four barrels of pork I brought from Charlestown, I laid in as large a cargo as I could, trusting to God's providence to prosper my undertaking. With these views I sailed for Philadelphia. On our passage, when we drew near the land, I was for the first time surprised at the sight of some whales, having never seen any such large sea monsters before; and as we sailed by the land one morning I saw a puppy whale close by the vessel; it was about the length of a wherry boat, and it followed us all the day till we got within the Capes. We arrived safe and in good time at Philadelphia, and I sold my goods there chiefly to the Quakers. They always appeared to be a very honest discreet sort of people, and never attempted to impose on me; I therefore liked them, and ever after chose to deal with them in preference to any others.

One Sunday morning while I was here, as I was going to church, I chanced to pass a meeting house. The doors being open, and the house full of people,

<hr/>

7. Doomed.
8. Frustrated in his hope to be set free in England, Equiano is shipped to Montserrat, a British colony in the Leeward Islands of the West Indies. Robert King, a prosperous Quaker merchant from Philadelphia, buys him, treats him

kindly, and values him as a reliable worker. By being useful to a friendly sea captain, Thomas Farmer, Equiano has opportunities to travel and trade goods for money. Eventually King promises to let him purchase his freedom for his original cost: £40.

it excited my curiosity to go in. When I entered the house, to my great surprise, I saw a very tall woman standing in the midst of them, speaking in an audible voice something which I could not understand. Having never seen anything of this kind before, I stood and stared about me for some time, wondering at this odd scene. As soon as it was over I took an opportunity to make inquiry about the place and people, when I was informed they were called Quakers.[9] I particularly asked what that woman I saw in the midst of them had said, but none of them were pleased to satisfy me; so I quitted them, and soon after, as I was returning, I came to a church crowded with people; the church-yard was full likewise, and a number of people were even mounted on ladders, looking in at the windows. I thought this a strange sight, as I had never seen churches, either in England or the West Indies, crowded in this manner before. I therefore made bold to ask some people the meaning of all this, and they told me the Rev. Mr. George Whitfield[1] was preaching. I had often heard of this gentleman, and had wished to see and hear him; but I had never before had an opportunity. I now therefore resolved to gratify myself with the sight, and I pressed in amidst the multitude. When I got into the church I saw this pious man exhorting the people with the greatest fervor and earnestness, and sweating as much as I ever did while in slavery on Montserrat beach. I was very much struck and impressed with this; I thought it strange I had never seen divines exert themselves in this manner before, and I was no longer at a loss to account for the thin congregations they preached to.

When we had discharged our cargo here, and were loaded again, we left this fruitful land once more, and set sail for Montserrat. My traffic had hitherto succeeded so well with me, that I thought, by selling my goods when we arrived at Montserrat, I should have enough to purchase my freedom. But, as soon as our vessel arrived there, my master came on board, and gave orders for us to go to St. Eustatia,[2] and discharge our cargo there, and from thence proceed for Georgia. I was much disappointed at this; but thinking, as usual, it was of no use to murmur at the decrees of fate, I submitted without repining, and we went to St. Eustatia. After we had discharged our cargo there we took in a live cargo, as we call a cargo of slaves. Here I sold my goods tolerably well; but, not being able to lay out all my money in this small island to as much advantage as in many other places, I laid out only part, and the remainder I brought away with me neat.[3] We sailed from hence for Georgia, and I was glad when we got there, though I had not much reason to like the place from my last adventure in Savannah;[4] but I longed to get back to Montserrat and procure my freedom, which I expected to be able to purchase when I returned. As soon as we arrived here I waited on my careful doctor, Mr. Brady, to whom I made the most grateful acknowledgments in my power for his former kindness and attention during my illness.

---

9. Quaker meetings are not led by clergy; any worshiper who feels inspired by God can rise to speak.
1. Whitefield (1714–1770), a famous evangelist who helped found Methodism, was in Britain, not Philadelphia, in 1766. It is possible that Equiano had heard him preach the previous year, in Savannah, Georgia. Equiano's later conversion to Methodism will become a dominant theme of his life story.
2. An island in the Netherlands Antilles (West Indies).
3. Intact.
4. The year before, a drunken slave owner and his servant had beaten Equiano so brutally that he nearly died.

While we were here an odd circumstance happened to the Captain and me, which disappointed us both a good deal. A silversmith, whom we had brought to this place some voyages before, agreed with the Captain to return with us to the West Indies, and promised at the same time to give the Captain a great deal of money, having pretended to take a liking to him, and being, as we thought, very rich. But while we stayed to load our vessel this man was taken ill in a house where he worked, and in a week's time became very bad. The worse he grew the more he used to speak of giving the Captain what he had promised him, so that he expected something considerable from the death of this man, who had no wife or child, and he attended him day and night. I used also to go with the Captain, at his own desire, to attend him; especially when we saw there was no appearance of his recovery; and, in order to recompense me for my trouble, the Captain promised me ten pounds, when he should get the man's property. I thought this would be of great service to me, although I had nearly money enough to purchase my freedom, if I should get safe this voyage to Montserrat. In this expectation I laid out above eight pounds of my money for a suit of superfine clothes to dance with at my freedom, which I hoped was then at hand. We still continued to attend this man, and were with him even on the last day he lived, till very late at night, when we went on board. After we were got to bed, about one or two o'clock in the morning, the Captain was sent for, and informed the man was dead. On this he came to my bed, and, waking me, informed me of it, and desired me to get up and procure a light, and immediately go to him. I told him I was very sleepy, and wished he would take somebody else with him, or else, as the man was dead, and could want no farther attendance, to let all things remain as they were till next morning. "No, no," said he, "we will have the money tonight, I cannot wait till tomorrow; so let us go." Accordingly I got up and struck a light, and away we both went and saw the man as dead as we could wish. The Captain said he would give him a grand burial, in gratitude for the promised treasure; and desired that all the things belonging to the deceased might be brought forth. Among others, there was a nest of trunks of which he had kept the keys whilst the man was ill, and when they were produced we opened them with no small eagerness and expectation; and as there were a great number within one another, with much impatience we took them one out of the other. At last, when we came to the smallest, and had opened it, we saw it was full of papers, which we supposed to be notes; at the sight of which our hearts leapt for joy; and that instant the Captain, clapping his hands, cried out, "Thank God, here it is." But when we took up the trunk, and began to examine the supposed treasure and long-looked-for bounty, (alas! alas! how uncertain and deceitful are all human affairs!) what had we found! While we were embracing a substance we grasped an empty nothing. The whole amount that was in the nest of trunks was only one dollar and a half; and all that the man possessed would not pay for his coffin. Our sudden and exquisite joy was now succeeded by as sudden and exquisite pain; and my Captain and I exhibited, for some time, most ridiculous figures—pictures of chagrin and disappointment! We went away greatly mortified, and left the deceased to do as well as he could for himself, as we had taken so good care of him when alive for nothing. We set sail once more for Montserrat, and arrived there safe; but much out of humor with our friend the silversmith. When we had unladen the vessel, and I had sold my venture, finding myself master of about forty-seven pounds, I consulted my true friend, the Captain, how I should proceed in offering my master the money for my freedom. He told me to come on a certain morning, when he and my master would be at breakfast together. Accordingly, on that morning I went, and met the Captain there, as he had appointed. When I went in I made my obeisance to my master, and with my money in my hand, and many fears in my heart, I prayed him to be as good as his offer to me, when he was pleased to promise me my freedom as soon as I could purchase it. This speech seemed to confound him; he began to recoil; and my heart that instant sank within me. "What," said he, "give you your freedom? Why, where did you get the money? Have you got forty pounds sterling?" "Yes, sir," I answered. "How did you get it?" replied he. I told him, very honestly. The Captain then said he knew I got the money very honestly and with much industry, and that I was particularly careful. On which my master replied, I got money much faster than he did; and said he would not have made me the promise he did if he had thought I should have got money so soon. "Come, come," said my worthy Captain, clapping my master on the back, "Come, Robert" (which was his name), "I think you must let him have his freedom; you have laid your money out very well; you have received good interest for it all this time, and here is now the principal at last. I know Gustavus has earned you more than an hundred a-year, and he will still save you money, as he will not leave you:—Come, Robert, take the money." My master then said, he would not be worse than his promise; and, taking the money, told me to go to the Secretary at the Register Office, and get my manumission[5] drawn up. These words of my master were like a voice from heaven to me: in an instant all my trepidation was turned into unutterable bliss; and I most reverently bowed myself with gratitude, unable to express my feelings, but by the overflowing of my eyes, while my true and worthy friend, the Captain, congratulated us both with a peculiar degree of heartfelt pleasure. As soon as the first transports of my joy were over, and that I had expressed my thanks to these my worthy friends in the best manner I was able, I rose with a heart full of affection and reverence, and left the room, in order to obey my master's joyful mandate of going to the Register Office. As I was leaving the house I called to mind the words of the Psalmist, in the 126th Psalm, and like him, "I glorified God in my heart, in whom I trusted." These words had been impressed on my mind from the very day I was forced from Deptford[6] to the present hour, and I now saw them, as I thought, fulfilled and verified. My imagination was all rapture as I flew to the Register Office, and in this respect, like the apostle Peter[7] (whose deliverance from prison was so sudden and extraordinary, that he thought he was in a vision), I could scarcely believe I was awake. Heavens! who could do justice to my feelings at this moment! Not conquering heroes themselves, in the midst of a triumph—Not the tender mother who had just regained her long-lost infant, and presses it to her heart—Not the weary hungry mariner, at the sight of the desired friendly port—Not the lover, when he once more embraces his beloved mistress, after she had been ravished from his arms!—All within my breast was tumult, wildness, and delirium! My feet scarcely touched the ground, for they were

5. Release from slavery.
6. The port near London from which Equiano

was sold by his English master.
7. Acts, chap. xii, ver. 9 [Equiano's note].

winged with joy, and, like Elijah, as he rose to Heaven,[8] they "were with lightning sped as I went on." Every one I met I told of my happiness, and blazed about the virtue of my amiable master and captain.

When I got to the office and acquainted the Register with my errand he congratulated me on the occasion, and told me he would draw up my manumission for half price, which was a guinea. I thanked him for his kindness; and having received it and paid him, I hastened to my master to get him to sign it, that I might be fully released. Accordingly he signed the manumission that day, so that, before night, I who had been a slave in the morning, trembling at the will of another, was become my own master, and completely free. I thought this was the happiest day I had ever experienced; and my joy was still heightened by the blessings and prayers of the sable race, particularly the aged, to whom my heart had ever been attached with reverence.

As the form of my manumission has something peculiar in it, and expresses the absolute power and dominion one man claims over his fellow, I shall beg leave to present it before my readers at full length:

Montserrat.—To all men unto whom these presents shall come: I Robert King, of the parish of St. Anthony in the said island, merchant, send greeting: Know ye, that I the aforesaid Robert King, for and in consideration of the sum of seventy pounds current money of the said island,[9] to me in hand paid, and to the intent that a negro man-slave, named Gustavus Vassa, shall and may become free, have manumitted, emancipated, enfranchised, and set free, and by these presents do manumit, emancipate, enfranchise, and set free, the aforesaid negro man-slave, named Gustavus Vassa, for ever, hereby giving, granting, and releasing unto him, the said Gustavus Vassa, all right, title, dominion, sovereignty, and property, which, as lord and master over the aforesaid Gustavus Vassa, I had, or now I have, or by any means whatsoever I may or can hereafter possibly have over him the aforesaid negro, for ever. In witness whereof I the above-said Robert King have unto these presents set my hand and seal, this tenth day of July, in the year of our Lord one thousand seven hundred and sixty-six.

ROBERT KING

Signed, sealed, and delivered in the presence of Terrylegay, Montserrat.

Registered the within manumission at full length, this eleventh day of July, 1766, in liber D.[1]

TERRYLEGAY, REGISTER.

In short, the fair as well as black people immediately styled me by a new appellation, to me the most desirable in the world, which was Freeman, and at the dances I gave my Georgia superfine blue clothes made no indifferent appearance, as I thought.

* * *

1789

---

8. 2 Kings 2.11.
9. The equivalent of £40 in British money.

1. Book or register D.

JAMES THOMSON
1700–1748

James Thomson, the first and most popular nature poet of the century, did not see London until he was twenty-five years old. He grew up in the picturesque border country of Roxboroughshire in Scotland and, after studying divinity in Edinburgh, went to London in 1725, bringing with him, in addition to a memory well stored with images of the external world, the earliest version of his descriptive poem "Winter" in 405 lines of blank verse. Published in 1726, it soon became popular. Thomson went on to publish "Summer" (1727), "Spring" (1728), and "Autumn" in the first collected edition of *The Seasons* (1730), to which he added the "Hymn to the Seasons." During the next sixteen years, because of constant revisions and additions, the poem grew in length to 5,541 lines. *The Seasons* continued to be popular well into the Romantic period; between 1730 and 1800 it was printed fifty times. Thomson's last poem, *The Castle of Indolence* (1748), is a witty imitation of Spenser; it moves from a playful portrait of the idleness of the poet and his friends to a celebration of industry and progress.

The Seasons set the fashion for the poetry of natural description. Generations of readers learned to look at the external world through Thomson's eyes and with the emotions that he had taught them to feel. The *eye* dominates the literature of external nature during the eighteenth century as the *imagination* was to do in the poetry of William Wordsworth. And Thomson amazed his readers by his capacity to see: the general effects of light and cloud and foliage or the particular image of a leaf tossed in the gale or the slender feet of a robin or the delicate film of ice at the edge of a brook. He tries to view each season from every perspective, as it might be perceived by a bird in the sky or by the tiniest insect, by God or a painter or Milton or Sir Isaac Newton (whom Thomson commemorated in a popular ode). As the poem grew, it became an *omnium gatherum* of contemporary ideas and interests: natural history; ideas about the nature of man and society, primitive and civilized; the conception of created nature as a source of religious experience, as an object of religious veneration, and as a continuing revelation of a Creator whose presence fills the world.

From The Seasons

From *Autumn*

[EVENING AND NIGHT][1]

The western sun withdraws the shortened day;
And humid evening, gliding o'er the sky,
In her chill progress, to the ground condensed
1085   The vapors throws. Where creeping waters ooze,

---

1. This passage, like many in *The Seasons*, went through extensive revisions. The opening lines on the harvest moon shining through fog (1082–1102) originally belonged to "Winter"; the descriptions of the aurora borealis (1108–37) and wildfire (1150–64) first appeared in "Summer." Scientific and visionary, divine and human perspectives are contrasted and join together in an intricate harmony.

Where marshes stagnate, and where rivers wind,
Cluster the rolling fogs, and swim along
The dusky-mantled lawn. Meanwhile the moon,
Full-orbed and breaking through the scattered clouds,
1090 Shows her broad visage in the crimsoned east.
Turned to the sun direct, her spotted disk
(Where mountains rise, umbrageous dales descend,[2]
And caverns deep, as optic tube° descries)   telescope
A smaller earth, gives all his blaze again,
1095 Void of its flame, and sheds a softer day.
Now through the passing cloud she seems to stoop,
Now up the pure cerulean rides sublime.
Wide the pale deluge° floats, and streaming mild   moonlight
O'er the skied[3] mountain to the shadowy vale,
1100 While rocks and floods reflect the quivering gleam,
The whole air whitens with a boundless tide
Of silver radiance trembling round the world.
    But when, half blotted from the sky, her light
Fainting, permits the starry fires to burn
1105 With keener luster through the depth of heaven;
Or quite extinct her deadened orb appears,
And scarce appears, of sickly beamless white;
Oft in this season, silent from the north
A blaze of meteors[4] shoots—ensweeping first
1110 The lower skies, they all at once converge
High to the crown[5] of heaven, and, all at once
Relapsing quick, as quickly reascend,
And mix and thwart,° extinguish and renew,   cross
All ether coursing[6] in a maze of light.
1115   From look to look, contagious through the crowd,
The panic runs, and into wondrous shapes
The appearance throws—armies in meet° array,   fitting
Thronged with aerial spears and steeds of fire;
Till, the long lines of full-extended war
1120 In bleeding fight commixed, the sanguine flood
Rolls a broad slaughter o'er the plains of heaven.
As thus they scan the visionary scene,
On all sides swells the superstitious din,
Incontinent; and busy frenzy talks
1125 Of blood and battle; cities overturned,
And late at night in swallowing earthquake sunk,
Or hideous wrapped in fierce ascending flame;
Of sallow famine, inundation, storm;
Of pestilence, and every great distress;
1130 Empires subversed,° when ruling fate has struck   overthrown
The unalterable hour; even nature's self

2. Observation of the moon had revealed shadows ("umbrageous dales"), hence an irregular surface.
3. I.e., seeming to touch the sky.
4. Not meteors as we think of them, but the aurora borealis, or northern lights (multicolored, streaming pulses of light in the upper atmo- sphere). The aurora had often been associated with cosmic battles, in both literature and popular superstition.
5. The corona or central ring of the aurora.
6. Running through all the upper sky.

Is deemed to totter on the brink of time.
Not so the man of philosophic eye
And inspect sage:° the waving brightness he   *wise examination*
1135 Curious surveys, inquisitive to know
The causes and materials, yet unfixed,[7]
Of this appearance beautiful and new.
    Now black and deep the night begins to fall,
A shade immense! Sunk in the quenching gloom,
1140 Magnificent and vast, are heaven and earth.
Order confounded lies, all beauty void,
Distinction lost, and gay variety
One universal blot—such the fair power
Of light to kindle and create the whole.
1145 Drear is the state of the benighted wretch
Who then bewildered wanders through the dark
Full of pale fancies and chimeras° huge;   *imaginary monsters*
Nor visited by one directive ray
From cottage streaming or from airy hall.
1150 Perhaps, impatient as he stumbles on,
Struck from the root of slimy rushes, blue
The wildfire[8] scatters round, or, gathered, trails
A length of flame deceitful o'er the moss;
Whither decoyed by the fantastic blaze,
1155 Now lost and now renewed, he sinks absorbed,
Rider and horse, amid the miry gulf—
While still, from day to day, his pining wife
And plaintive children his return await,
In wild conjecture lost. At other times,
1160 Sent by the better genius of the night,
Innoxious,° gleaming on the horse's mane,   *harmless*
The meteor[9] sits, and shows the narrow path
That winding leads through pits of death, or else
Instructs him how to take the dangerous ford.
1165   The lengthened night elapsed, the morning shines
Serene, in all her dewy beauty bright,
Unfolding fair the last autumnal day.
And now the mounting sun dispels the fog;
The rigid hoarfrost melts before his beam;
1170 And, hung on every spray, on every blade
Of grass, the myriad dewdrops twinkle round.

1730

---

7. Unexplained by science.
8. Will-o'-the-wisp or ignis fatuus, a flitting phosphorescent light thought to kindle from the gas of decaying swamp grasses ("slimy rushes").

9. The ignis lambens, or St. Elmo's fire, a halo of light that shines on the tips of certain objects during electrical storms.

THOMAS GRAY
1716–1771

The man who wrote the English poem most loved by those whom Samuel Johnson called "the common reader" was a scholarly recluse who lived the quiet life of a university professor in the stagnant atmosphere of mid-eighteenth-century Cambridge. Born in London, Thomas Gray was the only one of twelve children to survive, and his family life was desperately unhappy. At eight he left home for Eton, where he made intimate friends: Richard West, a fellow poet; Thomas Ashton; and Horace Walpole, the son of the prime minister. After four years at Cambridge, Gray left without a degree to take the grand tour of France and Italy as Walpole's guest. The death of West in 1742 desolated Gray, and memories of West haunt much of his verse. He spent the rest of his life in Cambridge, pursuing his studies and writing wonderful letters as well as a handful of poems. Two high-flown Pindaric odes, "The Progress of Poesy" (1754) and "The Bard" (1757), display his learning and his love of nature and the sublime.

Most of Gray's poems take part in a contemporary reaction against the wit and satiric elegance of Pope's couplets; poets sought a new style, at once intimate and prophetic. Gray was not easily satisfied; he constantly revised his poems and published very little. Because he held that "the language of the age is never the language of poetry," he often uses archaic words and a word order borrowed from Latin, where a verb can precede its subject (as in line 35 of the "Elegy Written in a Country Churchyard": "Awaits alike the inevitable hour"). But the "Elegy" stands alone in his work. It balances Latinate phrases with living English speech, and the learning of a scholar with a common humanity that everyone can share. Johnson, who did not usually like Gray's poetry, acknowledged that the "Elegy" would live on:

> The Churchyard abounds with images that find a mirror in every mind, and with sentiments to which every bosom returns an echo. The four stanzas beginning "Yet even these bones" are to me original: I have never seen the notions in any other place; yet he that reads them here, persuades himself that he has always felt them. Had Gray written often thus, it had been vain to blame, and useless to praise him.

Ode on a Distant Prospect of Eton College

Anthrōpos ikanē prophasis eis tò dustukheīn.[1]
MENANDER

Ye distant spires, ye antique towers,
  That crown the watery glade,
Where grateful Science° still adores   *Learning*
  Her Henry's holy shade;[2]
5 And ye, that from the stately brow

---

1. I am a man: sufficient reason for being miserable (Greek).
2. Henry VI founded Eton in 1440.

Of Windsor's heights[3] the expanse below
Of grove, of lawn, of mead survey,
Whose turf, whose shade, whose flowers among
Wanders the hoary Thames along
His silver-winding way.

Ah happy hills, ah pleasing shade,
Ah fields beloved in vain,
Where once my careless childhood strayed,
A stranger yet to pain!
I feel the gales, that from ye blow,
A momentary bliss bestow,
As waving fresh their gladsome wing,
My weary soul they seem to soothe,
And, redolent of joy and youth,
To breathe a second spring.

Say, Father Thames, for thou hast seen
Full many a sprightly race
Disporting on thy margent° green   *bank*
The paths of pleasure trace,
Who foremost now delight to cleave
With pliant arm thy glassy wave?
The captive linnet which enthrall?°   *imprison*
What idle progeny succeed[4]
To chase the rolling circle's° speed,   *hoop's*
Or urge the flying ball?

While some on earnest business bent
Their murmuring labors[5] ply
'Gainst graver hours, that bring constraint
To sweeten liberty:
Some bold adventurers disdain
The limits of their little reign,
And unknown regions dare descry:
Still as they run they look behind,
They hear a voice in every wind,
And snatch a fearful joy.

Gay hope is theirs by fancy fed,
Less pleasing when possessed;
The tear forgot as soon as shed,
The sunshine of the breast:
Theirs buxom° health of rosy hue,   *zestful, jolly*
Wild wit, invention ever new,
And lively cheer of vigor born;
The thoughtless day, the easy night,
The spirits pure, the slumbers light,
That fly the approach of morn.

---

3. Windsor Castle, across the Thames valley
from Eton.

4. I.e., follow in succession Gray's generation.
5. Recited lessons for school.

Alas, regardless of their doom,
   The little victims play!
No sense have they of ills to come,
   Nor care beyond today.
55 Yet see how all around 'em wait
The ministers of human fate,
   And black Misfortune's baleful train!
Ah, show them where in ambush stand
To seize their prey the murderous band!
60   Ah, tell them they are men!

These shall the fury Passions tear,
   The vultures of the mind,
Disdainful Anger, pallid Fear,
   And Shame that skulks behind;
65 Or pining Love shall waste their youth,
Or Jealousy with rankling tooth,
   That inly gnaws the secret heart,
And Envy wan, and faded Care,
Grim-visaged comfortless Despair,
70   And Sorrow's piercing dart.

Ambition this shall tempt to rise,
   Then whirl the wretch from high,
To bitter Scorn a sacrifice,
   And grinning Infamy.
75 The stings of Falsehood those shall try,
And hard Unkindness' altered eye,
   That mocks the tear it forced to flow;
And keen Remorse with blood defiled,
And moody Madness laughing wild
80   Amid severest woe.

Lo, in the vale of years beneath
   A grisly troop are seen,
The painful family of Death,
   More hideous than their queen:
85 This racks the joints, this fires the veins,
That every laboring sinew strains,
   Those in the deeper vitals rage:
Lo, Poverty, to fill the band,
That numbs the soul with icy hand,
90   And slow-consuming Age.

To each his sufferings: all are men,
   Condemned alike to groan;
The tender for another's pain,
   The unfeeling for his own.
95 Yet ah! why should they know their fate?
Since sorrow never comes too late,
   And happiness too swiftly flies.
Thought would destroy their paradise.

No more; where ignorance is bliss,
100   'Tis folly to be wise.

1742   1747

Ode on the Death of a Favorite Cat[1]

Drowned in a Tub of Goldfishes

'Twas on a lofty vase's side,
Where China's gayest art had dyed
    The azure flowers that blow;°   *bloom*
Demurest of the tabby kind,
5   The pensive Selima reclined,
    Gazed on the lake below.

Her conscious tail her joy declared;
The fair round face, the snowy beard,
    The velvet of her paws,
10   Her coat, that with the tortoise vies,
Her ears of jet, and emerald eyes,
    She saw; and purred applause.

Still had she gazed; but 'midst the tide
Two angel forms were seen to glide,
15   The genii of the stream:
Their scaly armor's Tyrian° hue   *purple*
Through richest purple to the view
    Betrayed a golden gleam.

The hapless nymph with wonder saw:
20   A whisker first and then a claw,
    With many an ardent wish,
She stretched in vain to reach the prize.
What female heart can gold despise?
    What cat's averse to fish?

25   Presumptuous maid! with looks intent
Again she stretched, again she bent,
    Nor knew the gulf between.
(Malignant Fate sat by and smiled)
The slippery verge her feet beguiled,
30   She tumbled headlong in.

Eight times emerging from the flood
She mewed to every watery god,
    Some speedy aid to send.

1. Selima, one of Horace Walpole's cats, had recently drowned in a china cistern. Gray wrote this memorial at Walpole's request. For an illus- tration of this poem by William Blake, see the color insert in this volume.

No dolphin came, no nereid° stirred: *sea nymph*
35   Nor cruel Tom, nor Susan² heard.
      A favorite has no friend!

From hence, ye beauties, undeceived,
Know, one false step is ne'er retrieved,
      And be with caution bold.
40   Not all that tempts your wandering eyes
And heedless hearts is lawful prize;
      Nor all that glisters gold.

1747   1748

Elegy Written in a Country Churchyard

The curfew¹ tolls the knell of parting day,
   The lowing herd wind slowly o'er the lea,
The plowman homeward plods his weary way,
   And leaves the world to darkness and to me.

5   Now fades the glimmering landscape on the sight,
   And all the air a solemn stillness holds,
Save where the beetle wheels his droning flight,
   And drowsy tinklings lull the distant folds;

Save that from yonder ivy-mantled tower
10   The moping owl does to the moon complain
Of such, as wandering near her secret bower,
   Molest her ancient solitary reign.

Beneath those rugged elms, that yew tree's shade,
   Where heaves the turf in many a moldering heap,
15   Each in his narrow cell forever laid,
   The rude° forefathers of the hamlet sleep.   *uneducated*

The breezy call of incense-breathing Morn,
   The swallow twittering from the straw-built shed,
The cock's shrill clarion, or the echoing horn,°   *hunter's horn*
20   No more shall rouse them from their lowly bed.

For them no more the blazing hearth shall burn,
   Or busy housewife ply her evening care;
No children run to lisp their sire's return,
   Or climb his knees the envied kiss to share.

25   Oft did the harvest to their sickle yield,
   Their furrow oft the stubborn glebe° has broke;   *soil*
How jocund did they drive their team afield!
   How bowed the woods beneath their sturdy stroke!

2. Servants' names.   1. A bell rung in the evening.

Let not Ambition mock their useful toil,
30   Their homely joys, and destiny obscure;
Nor Grandeur hear with a disdainful smile
The short and simple annals of the poor.

The boast of heraldry,° the pomp of power,   *noble birth*
And all that beauty, all that wealth e'er gave,
35 Awaits alike the inevitable hour.
The paths of glory lead but to the grave.

Nor you, ye proud, impute to these the fault,
If Memory o'er their tomb no trophies[2] raise,
Where through the long-drawn aisle and fretted[3] vault
40   The pealing anthem swells the note of praise.

Can storied urn[4] or animated° bust   *lifelike*
Back to its mansion call the fleeting breath?
Can Honor's voice provoke° the silent dust,   *call forth*
Or Flattery soothe the dull cold ear of Death?

45 Perhaps in this neglected spot is laid
Some heart once pregnant with celestial fire;
Hands that the rod of empire might have swayed,°   *wielded*
Or waked to ecstasy the living lyre.

But Knowledge to their eyes her ample page
50   Rich with the spoils of time did ne'er unroll;
Chill Penury repressed their noble rage,°   *inspiration*
And froze the genial° current of the soul.   *creative*

Full many a gem of purest ray serene,
The dark unfathomed caves of ocean bear:
55 Full many a flower is born to blush unseen,
And waste its sweetness on the desert air.

Some village Hampden,[5] that with dauntless breast
The little tyrant of his fields withstood;
Some mute inglorious Milton here may rest,
60   Some Cromwell guiltless of his country's blood.

The applause of listening senates to command,
The threats of pain and ruin to despise,
To scatter plenty o'er a smiling land,
And read their history in a nation's eyes,

65 Their lot forbade: nor circumscribed alone
Their growing virtues, but their crimes confined;

2. An ornamental or symbolic group of figures depicting the achievements of the deceased.
3. Decorated with intersecting lines in relief.
4. A funeral urn with an epitaph or pictured story inscribed on it.

5. John Hampden (1594–1643), who, both as a private citizen and as a member of Parliament, zealously defended the rights of the people against the autocratic policies of Charles I.

Forbade to wade through slaughter to a throne,
And shut the gates of mercy on mankind,

The struggling pangs of conscious truth to hide,
70   To quench the blushes of ingenuous shame,
Or heap the shrine of Luxury and Pride
With incense kindled at the Muse's flame.

Far from the madding crowd's ignoble strife,
Their sober wishes never learned to stray;
75   Along the cool sequestered vale of life
They kept the noiseless tenor of their way.

Yet even these bones from insult to protect
Some frail memorial still erected nigh,
With uncouth rhymes and shapeless sculpture decked,[6]
80   Implores the passing tribute of a sigh.

Their name, their years, spelt by the unlettered Muse,
The place of fame and elegy supply:
And many a holy text around she strews,
That teach the rustic moralist to die.

85   For who to dumb Forgetfulness a prey,
This pleasing anxious being e'er resigned,
Left the warm precincts of the cheerful day,
Nor cast one longing lingering look behind?

On some fond breast the parting soul relies,
90   Some pious drops the closing eye requires;
Even from the tomb the voice of Nature cries,
Even in our ashes live their wonted fires.

For thee, who mindful of the unhonored dead
Dost in these lines their artless tale relate;
95   If chance,° by lonely contemplation led,   *perchance*
Some kindred spirit shall inquire thy fate,

Haply some hoary-headed swain may say,
"Oft have we seen him at the peep of dawn
Brushing with hasty steps the dews away
100   To meet the sun upon the upland lawn.

"There at the foot of yonder nodding beech
That wreathes its old fantastic roots so high,
His listless length at noontide would he stretch,
And pore upon the brook that babbles by.

105   "Hard by yon wood, now smiling as in scorn,
Muttering his wayward fancies he would rove,

---

6. Cf. "storied urn or animated bust" dedicated inside the church to "the proud" (line 41).

Now drooping, woeful wan, like one forlorn,
　　Or crazed with care, or crossed in hopeless love.

"One morn I missed him on the customed hill,
110　　Along the heath and near his favorite tree;
Another came; nor yet beside the rill,
　　Nor up the lawn, nor at the wood was he;

"The next with dirges due in sad array
　　Slow through the churchway path we saw him borne.
115　Approach and read (for thou canst read) the lay,
　　Graved on the stone beneath yon aged thorn."

The Epitaph

Here rests his head upon the lap of Earth
　　A youth to Fortune and to Fame unknown.
Fair Science° frowned not on his humble birth,　　　　　　Learning
120　　*And Melancholy marked him for her own.*

Large was his bounty, and his soul sincere,
　　Heaven did a recompense as largely send:
He gave to Misery all he had, a tear,
　　He gained from Heaven ('twas all he wished) a friend.

125　*No farther seek his merits to disclose,*
　　Or draw his frailties from their dread abode
(There they alike in trembling hope repose),
　　The bosom of his Father and his God.

ca. 1742–50　　　　　　　　　　　　　　　　　　　　　1751

WILLIAM COLLINS
1721–1759

William Collins was born in Chichester and was educated at Winchester and Oxford. Coming up to London from the university, he tried to establish himself as an author, but he was given rather to planning than to writing books. He came to know Samuel Johnson, who later remembered him affectionately as a man of learning who "loved fairies, genii, giants, and monsters" and who "delighted to rove through the meanders of enchantment." In 1746 Collins published his *Odes on Several Descriptive and Allegorical Subjects*, his part in an undertaking, with his friend Joseph Warton, to create a new poetry, more lyrical and fanciful than that of Alexander Pope's generation. Collins's *Odes* address personified abstractions (Fear, Pity, the Passions), which are imagined as vivid presences that overwhelm the poet as he calls them to life. In form, these poems represent a new version of the classical Great Ode, derived from Greek poet Pindar (ca. 522–ca. 443 B.C.E.), which treats lofty themes in an elevated style; Collins returned to Pindar's regularity of structure, after the relative freedom of most English odes written in preceding decades. But the originality of the *Odes* lies in their intensity of vision, which risks obscurity in quest of the sublime.

To his disappointment, contemporaries preferred his early *Persian Eclogues* to the more difficult *Odes*. Inheriting some money, the poet traveled for a while, but fits of depression gradually deepened into total debility. He spent his last years in Chichester, forgotten by all but a small circle of loyal friends. As the century progressed he gained in reputation. The Romantics admired his poems and felt akin to him. Coleridge said that "Ode on the Poetical Character" "has inspired and whirled me along with greater agitations of enthusiasm than any the most *impassioned* scene in Schiller or Shakespeare."

Ode on the Poetical Character   Critics have acclaimed this ode as an early, dramatic engagement with one of the central concerns of the Romantic age— the origin and role of the creative imagination and, indeed, of the poet himself.

In the strophe an analogy is drawn between the magic girdle of Venus, which only the chaste can wear, and the cest, or girdle, of Fancy, or the creative imagination. In the epode the creation of the world is presented as an act of the divine imagination. Inspired by God, Fancy gives birth to another sublime creation, the spirit of poetry.

In the antistrophe, John Milton is regarded as the type of poet divinely able to wear the girdle of Fancy. Collins pictures himself pursuing the "guiding steps" (line 71) of Milton, as of Edmund Spenser (in the strophe)—both poet-prophets. His movement away from the elegant school of Edmund Waller (and, by implication, that of Alexander Pope) is "In vain" (line 72), however, for he lives in an uninspired age.

Ode on the Poetical Character

Strophe

> As once, if not with light regard,
> I read aright that gifted bard
> (Him[1] whose school above the rest
> His loveliest Elfin Queen has blest),
> 5 One, only one, unrivaled fair
> Might hope the magic girdle wear,
> At solemn tourney hung on high,
> The wish of each love-darting eye;[2]
> Lo! to each other nymph in turn applied,
> 10   As if, in air unseen, some hovering hand,
> Some chaste and angel-friend to virgin-fame,
>   With whispered spell had burst the starting band,
> It left unblest her loathed dishonored side;
>   Happier, hopeless fair, if never
> 15   Her baffled hand with vain endeavor
> Had touched that fatal zone° to her denied!   girdle
> Young Fancy thus, to me divinest name,

1. Edmund Spenser.
2. *The Faerie Queene* 4.5 tells of the contest of many beautiful ladies for the girdle of Venus.

To whom, prepared and bathed in Heaven
The cest° of amplest power is given: *girdle*
20   To few the godlike gift assigns,
To gird their blest, prophetic loins,[3]
And gaze her visions wild, and feel unmixed her flame!

Epode

The band, as fairy legends say,
Was wove on that creating day,
25   When He,[4] who called with thought to birth
Yon tented sky, this laughing earth,
And dressed with springs, and forests tall,
And poured the main engirting all,
Long by the loved Enthusiast[5] wooed,
30   Himself in some diviner mood,
Retiring, sate with her alone,
And placed her on his sapphire throne;
The whiles, the vaulted shrine around,
Seraphic wires were heard to sound,
35   Now sublimest triumph swelling,
Now on love and mercy dwelling;
And she, from out the veiling cloud,
Breathed her magic notes aloud:
And thou, thou rich-haired Youth of Morn,[6]
40   And all thy subject life was born!
The dangerous Passions kept aloof,
Far from the sainted growing woof:
But near it sate ecstatic Wonder,
Listening the deep applauding thunder:
45   And Truth, in sunny vest arrayed,
By whose the tarsel's° eyes were made;   *falcon's*
All the shadowy tribes of Mind,
In braided dance their murmurs joined,
And all the bright uncounted Powers
50   Who feed on Heaven's ambrosial flowers.
Where is the bard, whose soul can now
Its high presuming hopes avow?
Where he who thinks, with rapture blind,
This hallow'd work[7] for him designed?

Antistrophe

55   High on some cliff, to Heaven up-piled,
Of rude access, of prospect wild,
Where, tangled round the jealous° steep,   *vigilant*
Strange shades o'erbrow the valleys deep,

3. Pronounced *lines*.
4. God, on the day of creation.
5. I.e., Fancy; literally, *enthusiast* means "one possessed by a god."

6. Apollo, god of the sun and of poetry, associated with the archetypal poet.
7. The girdle of Fancy.

And holy Genii guard the rock,
60 Its glooms embrown, its springs unlock,
While on its rich ambitious head,
An Eden, like his° own, lies spread: *Milton's*
I view that oak, the fancied glades among,
By which as Milton lay, his evening ear,
65 From many a cloud that dropped ethereal dew,
Nigh sphered in Heaven its native strains could hear:
On which that ancient trump he reached was hung;
        Thither oft, his glory greeting,
        From Waller's myrtle[8] shades retreating,
70 With many a vow from Hope's aspiring tongue,
My trembling feet his guiding steps pursue;
        In vain—such bliss to one alone,°   *Milton*
        Of all the sons of soul was known,
        And Heaven, and Fancy, kindred powers,
75   Have now o'erturned the inspiring bowers,
Or curtained close such scene from every future view.

                                                        1746

Ode to Evening[1]

If aught of oaten stop,[2] or pastoral song,
May hope, chaste Eve, to soothe thy modest ear,
        Like thy own solemn springs,
        Thy springs and dying gales,
5 O nymph reserved, while now the bright-haired sun
Sits in yon western tent, whose cloudy skirts,
        With brede° ethereal wove,   *embroidery*
        O'erhang his wavy bed:
Now air is hushed, save where the weak-eyed bat,
10 With short shrill shriek flits by on leathern wing,
        Or where the beetle winds
        His small but sullen horn,
As oft he rises 'midst the twilight path,
Against the pilgrim borne in heedless hum:
15   Now teach me, maid composed,
        To breathe some softened strain,
Whose numbers,° stealing through thy darkening vale,   *measures*
May not unseemly with its stillness suit,
        As, musing slow, I hail
20   Thy genial° loved return!   *life-giving*
For when thy folding-star[3] arising shows
His paly circlet, at his warning lamp

---

8. The symbol of love poetry. Edmund Waller (1606–1687), whose poetry is thought of as trivial compared with Milton's grandeur.
1. Collins borrowed the metrical structure and the rhymeless lines of this ode from Milton's translation of Horace, *Odes* 1.5 (1673). The text printed here is based on the revised version, published in Dodsley's *Miscellany* (1748).
2. Finger hole in a shepherd's flute.
3. The evening star, which signals the hour for herding the sheep into the sheepfold.

The fragrant Hours, and elves
Who slept in flowers the day,
25 And many a nymph who wreaths her brows with sedge,
And sheds the freshening dew, and, lovelier still,
The pensive Pleasures sweet,
Prepare thy shadowy car.
Then lead, calm vot'ress, where some sheety lake
30 Cheers the lone heath, or some time-hallowed pile
Or upland fallows gray
Reflect its last cool gleam.
But when chill blustering winds, or driving rain,
Forbid my willing feet, be mine the hut
35 That from the mountain's side
Views wilds, and swelling floods,
And hamlets brown, and dim-discovered spires,
And hears their simple bell, and marks o'er all
Thy dewy fingers draw
40 The gradual dusky veil.
While Spring shall pour his showers, as oft he wont,
And bathe thy breathing tresses, meekest Eve;
While Summer loves to sport
Beneath thy lingering light;
45 While sallow Autumn fills thy lap with leaves;
Or Winter, yelling through the troublous air,
Affrights thy shrinking train,
And rudely rends thy robes;
So long, sure-found beneath the sylvan shed,
50 Shall Fancy, Friendship, Science, rose-lipped Health,
Thy gentlest influence own,
And hymn thy favorite name!

1746, 1748

CHRISTOPHER SMART
1722–1771

In 1756 Christopher Smart, who had won prizes at Pembroke College, Cambridge, as a scholar and poet and was known in London as a wit and bon vivant, was seized by religious mania: "a preternatural excitement to prayer," according to Hester Thrale, "which he held it as a duty not to control or repress." If Smart had been content to pray in private, his life might have ended as happily as it began, but he insisted on kneeling down in the streets, in parks, and in assembly rooms. He became a public nuisance, and the public took its revenge. For most of the next seven years Smart was confined, first in St. Luke's hospital, then in a private madhouse. There, severed from his wife, his children, and his friends, he began to write a bold new sort of poetry:

vivid, concise, abrupt, syntactically daring. Few of his contemporaries noticed it. After Smart's release from the madhouse (1763) he fell into debt—he had always been profligate—and his masterpiece, *A Song to David* (1763), was almost completely ignored (for the complete text of *A Song to David*, go to the NAEL Archive). He died, forgotten, in a debtor's prison. But in the nineteenth century his reputation revived, and with the publication of *Jubilate Agno* in 1939 his poems became newly famous.

Jubilate Agno (Rejoice in the Lamb), written a few lines at a time during Smart's confinement, is (1) a record of his daily life and thoughts; (2) the notebook of a scholar, crammed with puns and obscure learning, which sets out elaborate correspondences between the world of the Bible and modern England; and (3) a personal testament or book of worship, antiphonally arranged in lines beginning alternately with *Let* and *For*, which seeks to join the material and spiritual universes in one unending prayer. It has also come to be recognized, since first published in 1939 by W. F. Stead, as a poem—a poem unique in English for its ecstatic sense of the presence of the divine spirit. The most famous passage describes Smart's cat, Jeoffry, his only companion during the years of confinement: "For I am possessed of a cat, surpassing in beauty, from whom I take occasion to bless Almighty God." At once a real cat, lovingly observed in all its frisks, and visible evidence of the providential plan, Jeoffry celebrates the Maker, as all things do, in his very being.

From Jubilate Agno

[MY CAT JEOFFRY]

For I will consider my Cat Jeoffry.
For he is the servant of the Living God duly and daily serving him.
For at the first glance of the glory of God in the East° he   *sunrise*
    worships in his way.
For is this done by wreathing his body seven times round with elegant
    quickness.
5   For then he leaps up to catch the musk, wch is the blessing of God
    upon his prayer.
For he rolls upon prank° to work it in.   *prankishly*
For having done duty and received blessing he begins to consider
    himself.
For this he performs in ten degrees.
For first he looks upon his fore-paws to see if they are clean.
10 For secondly he kicks up behind to clear away there.
For thirdly he works it upon stretch with the fore-paws extended.
For fourthly he sharpens his paws by wood.
For fifthly he washes himself.
For Sixthly he rolls upon wash.
15 For Seventhly he fleas himself, that he may not be interrupted upon
    the beat.
For Eighthly he rubs himself against a post.
For Ninthly he looks up for his instructions.
For Tenthly he goes in quest of food.
For having consider'd God and himself he will consider his neighbor.
20 For if he meets another cat he will kiss her in kindness.
For when he takes his prey he plays with it to give it a chance.

For one mouse in seven escapes by his dallying.

For when his day's work is done his business more properly begins.

For he keeps the Lord's watch in the night against the adversary.

25 For he counteracts the powers of darkness by his electrical skin & glaring eyes.

For he counteracts the Devil, who is death, by brisking about the life.

For in his morning orisons he loves the sun and the sun loves him.

For he is of the tribe of Tiger.

For the Cherub Cat is a term of the Angel Tiger.[1]

30 For he has the subtlety and hissing of a serpent, which in goodness he suppresses.

For he will not do destruction if he is well-fed, neither will he spit without provocation.

For he purrs in thankfulness, when God tells him he's a good Cat.

For he is an instrument for the children to learn benevolence upon.

For every house is incomplete without him & a blessing is lacking in the spirit.

35 For the Lord commanded Moses concerning the cats at the departure of the Children of Israel from Egypt.[2]

For every family had one cat at least in the bag.

For the English Cats are the best in Europe.

For he is the cleanest in the use of his fore-paws of any quadrupede.

For the dexterity of his defence is an instance of the love of God to him exceedingly.

40 For he is the quickest to his mark of any creature.

For he is tenacious of his point.

For he is a mixture of gravity and waggery.

For he knows that God is his Saviour.

For there is nothing sweeter than his peace when at rest.

45 For there is nothing brisker than his life when in motion.

For he is of the Lord's poor and so indeed is he called by benevolence perpetually—Poor Jeoffry! poor Jeoffry! the rat has bit thy throat.

For I bless the name of the Lord Jesus that Jeoffry is better.

For the divine spirit comes about his body to sustain it in compleat cat.

For his tongue is exceeding pure so that it has in purity what it wants in music.

50 For he is docile and can learn certain things.

For he can set up with gravity which is patience upon approbation.

For he can fetch and carry, which is patience in employment.

For he can jump over a stick which is patience upon proof positive.

For he can spraggle upon waggle[3] at the word of command.

55 For he can jump from an eminence into his master's bosom.

For he can catch the cork and toss it again.

For he is hated by the hypocrite and miser.

For the former is afraid of detection.

For the latter refuses the charge.

60 For he camels his back to bear the first notion of business.

For he is good to think on, if a man would express himself neatly.

1. As a cherub is a small angel, so a cat is a small tiger.
2. No cats are mentioned in the Bible.
3. He can sprawl when his master waggles a finger or stick.

For he made a great figure in Egypt for his signal services.
For he killed the Icneumon-rat very pernicious by land.[4]
For his ears are so acute that they sting again.
65 For from this proceeds the passing° quickness of his   surpassing
    attention.
For by stroking of him I have found out electricity.
For I perceived God's light about him both wax and fire.
For the Electrical fire is the spiritual substance, which God sends
    from heaven to sustain the bodies both of man and beast.
For God has blessed him in the variety of his movements.
70 For, though he cannot fly, he is an excellent clamberer.
For his motions upon the face of the earth are more than any other
    quadrupede.
For he can tread to all the measures upon the music.
For he can swim for life.
For he can creep.

1759–63   1939

4. The ichneumon, which resembles a weasel, was venerated and domesticated by the ancient Egyptians.

OLIVER GOLDSMITH
ca. 1730–1774

Oliver Goldsmith was born in Ireland, the son of an Anglican clergyman whose geniality he inherited and whose improvidence he imitated. Disfigured by smallpox, he grew up homely, ungainly, apparently stupid, and certainly idle. Nonetheless, he was sent to Trinity College, Dublin, as a sizar—that is, a student who did menial jobs for well-to-do undergraduates—and took his A.B. in 1749. After studying medicine at the University of Edinburgh he wandered for a while on the Continent, visiting Holland, France, Italy, and Switzerland. He returned to England in 1756 with a mysteriously acquired M.D. and tried in vain to support himself as a physician among the poor in the borough of Southwark. Eventually he drifted into the profession of hack writer for Ralph Griffiths, the proprietor of the *Monthly Review*, and later worked for and with the benevolent publisher John Newbery. His first success, *An Inquiry into the Present State of Polite Learning in Europe* (1759), attributes the decline of the fine arts in mid-eighteenth-century Europe to the lack of enlightened patronage and to the malign influence of criticism and scholarship. Soon he became a famous author and an intimate of the brilliant circle around Samuel Johnson. Although his writings brought in a great deal of money, extravagance and generosity kept him always in debt. He died owing the prodigious sum (for a man whose only source of income was writing) of £2000.

The variety and excellence of Goldsmith's work are astonishing. His easy and pleasant prose style and shrewd observations of character and scene enliven his essays, especially those in the series *The Citizen of the World* (1762), and his popular novel *The Vicar of Wakefield* (1766). Two plays, *The Good-Natured Man* (1768) and *She Stoops to Conquer* (1773), achieve a sort of hearty and mirthful comedy— unspoiled by the fashionable sentimentality of the moment—that is unique in the century. His two major poems, *The Traveler, or A Prospect of Society* (1764) and *The Deserted Village*, are distinguished for the unforced grace of their couplets and for an air of simplicity that is far from simple to achieve.

The Deserted Village[1]

Sweet Auburn! loveliest village of the plain,
Where health and plenty cheered the laboring swain,
Where smiling spring its earliest visit paid,
And parting summer's lingering blooms delayed:
5   Dear lovely bowers of innocence and ease,
Seats of my youth, when every sport could please,
How often have I loitered o'er thy green,
Where humble happiness endeared each scene;
How often have I paused on every charm,
10   The sheltered cot,° the cultivated farm,   cottage
The never-failing brook, the busy mill,
The decent church that topped the neighboring hill,
The hawthorn bush, with seats beneath the shade,
For talking age and whispering lovers made;
15   How often have I blessed the coming day,°   Sunday
When toil remitting lent its turn to play,
And all the village train, from labor free,
Led up their sports beneath the spreading tree,
While many a pastime circled in the shade,
20   The young contending as the old surveyed;
And many a gambol frolicked o'er the ground,
And sleights of art and feats of strength went round;
And still as each repeated pleasure tired,
Succeeding sports the mirthful band inspired;
25   The dancing pair that simply sought renown,
By holding out to tire each other down;
The swain mistrustless of his smutted face,
While secret laughter tittered round the place;
The bashful virgin's sidelong looks of love,
30   The matron's glance that would those looks reprove:
These were thy charms, sweet village! sports like these,
With sweet succession, taught even toil to please;
These round thy bowers their cheerful influence shed,
These were thy charms—But all these charms are fled.
35   Sweet smiling village, loveliest of the lawn,
Thy sports are fled, and all thy charms withdrawn;
Amidst thy bowers the tyrant's hand is seen,

1. *The Deserted Village* is an idealization of English rural life mingled with poignant memories of the poet's own youth in Lissoy, Ireland. Goldsmith was seriously concerned about the effects of the agricultural revolution then in progress, which was being hastened by Enclosure Acts. Either for the sake of more profitable farming or to create vast private parks and landscape

Thomas Gainsborough, *The Cottage Door,* ca. 1778. Gainsborough painted several versions of this idealized, cozy view of home, motherhood, and childhood as experienced by peasants in rural Britain.

> And desolation saddens all thy green:
> One only master grasps the whole domain,
> 40 And half a tillage stints thy smiling plain;
> No more thy glassy brook reflects the day,
> But choked with sedges, works its weedy way;
> Along thy glades, a solitary guest,
> The hollow-sounding bittern guards its nest;
> 45 Amidst thy desert walks the lapwing flies,
> And tires their echoes with unvaried cries.
> Sunk are thy bowers, in shapeless ruin all,

gardens, arable land was being "enclosed"—i.e., taken out the hands of small proprietors—thus displacing yeoman farmers who, like their ancestors, had lived for generations in small villages, grazing their cattle on common land and raising food on small holdings. The only alternative available to many such people was to seek employment in the city or to migrate to America. In the poem, Goldsmith opposes "luxury" (the increase of wealth, the growth of cities, and the costly country estates of great noblemen and wealthy merchants) to "rural virtue" (the old agrarian economy that supported a sturdy population of independent peasants). His poem is thus at once a nostalgic lament for a doomed way of life and a denunciation of what he regarded as the corrupting, destructive force of new wealth.

And the long grass o'ertops the moldering wall;
And trembling, shrinking from the spoiler's hand,
50 Far, far away thy children leave the land.
     Ill fares the land, to hastening ills a prey,
Where wealth accumulates, and men decay;
Princes and lords may flourish, or may fade;
A breath can make them, as a breath has made;
55 But a bold peasantry, their country's pride.
When once destroyed, can never be supplied.
     A time there was, ere England's griefs began,
When every rood° of ground maintained its man;   *quarter acre*
For him light labor spread her wholesome store,
60 Just gave what life required, but gave no more:
His best companions, innocence and health;
And his best riches, ignorance of wealth.
     But times are altered; Trade's unfeeling train
Usurp the land and dispossess the swain;
65 Along the lawn, where scattered hamlets rose,
Unwieldy wealth, and cumbrous° pomp repose;   *oppressive*
And every want to opulence allied,
And every pang that folly pays to pride.
These gentle hours that plenty bade to bloom,
70 Those calm desires that asked but little room,
Those healthful sports that graced the peaceful scene,
Lived in each look, and brightened all the green;
These far departing seek a kinder shore,
And rural mirth and manners are no more.
75   Sweet Auburn! parent of the blissful hour,
Thy glades forlorn confess the tyrant's power.
Here, as I take my solitary rounds,
Amidst thy tangling walks, and ruined grounds,
And, many a year elapsed, return to view
80 Where once the cottage stood, the hawthorn grew,
Remembrance wakes with all her busy train,
Swells at my breast, and turns the past to pain.
     In all my wanderings round this world of care,
In all my griefs—and God has given my share—
85 I still had hopes my latest hours to crown,
Amidst these humble bowers to lay me down;
To husband out life's taper at the close,
And keep the flame from wasting by repose.
I still had hopes, for pride attends us still,
90 Amidst the swains to show my book-learned skill,
Around my fire an evening group to draw,
And tell of all I felt, and all I saw;
And, as an hare whom hounds and horns pursue,
Pants to the place from whence at first she flew,
95 I still had hopes, my long vexations past,
Here to return—and die at home at last.
     O blest retirement, friend to life's decline,
Retreats from care that never must be mine,
How happy he who crowns in shades like these,

100 A youth of labor with an age of ease;
Who quits a world where strong temptations try,
And, since 'tis hard to combat, learns to fly!
For him no wretches, born to work and weep,
Explore the mine, or tempt the dangerous deep;
105 No surly porter stands in guilty state
To spurn imploring famine from the gate;
But on he moves to meet his latter end,
Angels around befriending virtue's friend;
Bends to the grave with unperceived decay,
110 While Resignation gently slopes the way;
And, all his prospects brightening to the last,
His Heaven commences ere the world be passed!
     Sweet was the sound when oft at evening's close,
Up yonder hill the village murmur rose;
115 There, as I passed with careless steps and slow,
The mingling notes came softened from below;
The swain responsive as the milkmaid sung,
The sober herd that lowed to meet their young,
The noisy geese that gabbled o'er the pool,
120 The playful children just let loose from school;
The watchdog's voice that bayed the whispering wind,
And the loud laugh that spoke the vacant° mind;   *idle, carefree*
These all in sweet confusion sought the shade,
And filled each pause the nightingale had made.
125 But now the sounds of population fail,
No cheerful murmurs fluctuate in the gale,
No busy steps the grass-grown footway tread,
For all the bloomy flush of life is fled.
All but yon widowed, solitary thing
130 That feebly bends beside the plashy° spring;   *boggy*
She, wretched matron, forced, in age, for bread,
To strip the brook with mantling cresses spread,
To pick her wintry faggot from the thorn,
To seek her nightly shed, and weep till morn;
135 She only left of all the harmless train,
The sad historian of the pensive° plain.   *gloomy*
     Near yonder copse, where once the garden smiled,
And still where many a garden flower grows wild,
There, where a few torn shrubs the place disclose,
140 The village preacher's modest mansion rose.
A man he was, to all the country dear,
And passing rich with forty pounds a year;
Remote from towns he ran his godly race,
Nor e'er had changed, nor wished to change his place;
145 Unpracticed he to fawn, or seek for power,
By doctrines fashioned to the varying hour;
Far other aims his heart had learned to prize,
More skilled to raise the wretched than to rise.
His house was known to all the vagrant train,
150 He chid their wanderings, but relieved their pain;
The long-remembered beggar was his guest,

Whose beard descending swept his aged breast;
The ruined spendthrift, now no longer proud,
Claimed kindred there, and had his claims allowed;
155 The broken soldier, kindly bade to stay,
Sate by his fire, and talked the night away;
Wept o'er his wounds, or tales of sorrow done,
Shouldered his crutch, and showed how fields were won.
Pleased with his guests, the good man learned to glow,
160 And quite forgot their vices in their woe;
Careless their merits, or their faults to scan,
His pity gave ere charity began.
    Thus to relieve the wretched was his pride,
And even his failings leaned to Virtue's side;
165 But in his duty prompt at every call,
He watched and wept, he prayed and felt, for all.
And, as a bird each fond endearment tries,
To tempt its new-fledged offspring to the skies,
He tried each art, reproved each dull delay,
170 Allured to brighter worlds, and led the way.
    Beside the bed where parting life was laid,
And sorrow, guilt, and pain, by turns dismayed,
The reverend champion stood. At his control,
Despair and anguish fled the struggling soul;
175 Comfort came down the trembling wretch to raise,
And his last faltering accents whispered praise.
    At church, with meek and unaffected grace,
His looks adorned the venerable place;
Truth from his lips prevailed with double sway,
180 And fools, who came to scoff, remained to pray.
The service past, around the pious man,
With steady zeal each honest rustic ran;
Even children followed with endearing wile,
And plucked his gown, to share the good man's smile.
185 His ready smile a parent's warmth expressed,
Their welfare pleased him, and their cares distressed;
To them his heart, his love, his griefs were given,
But all his serious thoughts had rest in Heaven.
As some tall cliff that lifts its awful form,
190 Swells from the vale, and midway leaves the storm,
Though round its breast the rolling clouds are spread,
Eternal sunshine settles on its head.
    Beside yon straggling fence that skirts the way,
With blossomed furze unprofitably gay,
195 There, in his noisy mansion, skilled to rule,
The village master taught his little school;
A man severe he was, and stern to view,
I knew him well, and every truant knew;
Well had the boding tremblers learned to trace
200 The day's disasters in his morning face;
Full well they laughed with counterfeited glee,
At all his jokes, for many a joke had he;
Full well the busy whisper circling round,

Conveyed the dismal tidings when he frowned;
205 Yet he was kind, or if severe in aught,
The love he bore to learning was in fault;[2]
The village all declared how much he knew;
'Twas certain he could write, and cipher too;
Lands he could measure, terms and tides[3] presage,
210 And even the story ran that he could gauge.[4]
In arguing too, the parson owned his skill,
For even though vanquished, he could argue still;
While words of learned length, and thundering sound,
Amazed the gazing rustics ranged around;
215 And still they gazed, and still the wonder grew,
That one small head could carry all he knew.
    But past is all his fame. The very spot
Where many a time he triumphed, is forgot.
Near yonder thorn, that lifts its head on high,
220 Where once the signpost caught the passing eye,
Low lies that house where nut-brown draughts inspired,
Where graybeard Mirth and smiling Toil retired,
Where village statesmen talked with looks profound,
And news much older than their ale went round.
225 Imagination fondly stoops to trace
The parlor splendors of that festive place:
The whitewashed wall, the nicely sanded floor,
The varnished clock that clicked behind the door;
The chest contrived a double debt to pay,
230 A bed by night, a chest of drawers by day;
The pictures placed for ornament and use,
The twelve good rules, the royal game of goose;[5]
The hearth, except when winter chilled the day,
With aspen boughs, and flowers, and fennel gay,
235 While broken teacups, wisely kept for show,
Ranged o'er the chimney, glistened in a row.
    Vain transitory splendors! Could not all
Reprieve the tottering mansion from its fall!
Obscure it sinks, nor shall it more impart
240 An hour's importance to the poor man's heart;
Thither no more the peasant shall repair
To sweet oblivion of his daily care;
No more the farmer's news, the barber's tale,
No more the woodman's ballad shall prevail;
245 No more the smith his dusky brow shall clear,
Relax his ponderous strength, and lean to hear;
The host himself no longer shall be found
Careful to see the mantling bliss[6] go round;
Nor the coy maid, half willing to be pressed,

---

2. Because the *l* was silent, *fault* and *aught* rhymed perfectly.
3. Feasts and seasons in the church year. "Terms": dates on which rent, wages, etc. were due and tenancy began or ended.
4. Measure the content of casks and other vessels.

5. A game in which counters were moved on a board, according to the throw of the dice. "The twelve good rules" of conduct, attributed to Charles I, were printed in a broadside that was often seen on the walls of taverns.
6. Foaming bliss, i.e., foaming ale.

250   Shall kiss the cup to pass it to the rest.
       Yes! let the rich deride, the proud disdain,
    These simple blessings of the lowly train,
    To me more dear, congenial to my heart,
    One native charm, than all the gloss of art;
255   Spontaneous joys, where nature has its play,
    The soul adopts, and owns their first-born sway;
    Lightly they frolic o'er the vacant mind,
    Unenvied, unmolested, unconfined.
    But the long pomp, the midnight masquerade,
260   With all the freaks of wanton wealth arrayed,
    In these, ere triflers half their wish obtain,
    The toiling pleasure sickens into pain;
    And, even while fashion's brightest arts decoy,
    The heart distrusting asks, if this be joy.
265   Ye friends to truth, ye statesmen, who survey
    The rich man's joys increase, the poor's decay,
    'Tis yours to judge how wide the limits stand
    Between a splendid and an happy land.
    Proud swells the tide with loads of freighted ore,
270   And shouting Folly hails them from her shore;
    Hoards, even beyond the miser's wish abound,
    And rich men flock from all the world around.
    Yet count our gains. This wealth is but a name
    That leaves our useful products still the same.
275   Not so the loss. The man of wealth and pride
    Takes up a space that many poor supplied;
    Space for his lake, his park's extended bounds,
    Space for his horses, equipage, and hounds;
    The robe that wraps his limbs in silken sloth
280   Has robbed the neighboring fields of half their growth;
    His seat, where solitary sports are seen,
    Indignant spurns the cottage from the green;
    Around the world each needful product flies,
    For all the luxuries the world supplies.
285   While thus the land adorned for pleasure all
    In barren splendor feebly waits the fall.
       As some fair female unadorned and plain,
    Secure to please while youth confirms her reign,
    Slights every borrowed charm that dress supplies,
290   Nor shares with art the triumph of her eyes:
    But when those charms are past, for charms are frail,
    When time advances, and when lovers fail,
    She then shines forth, solicitous to bless,
    In all the glaring impotence of dress:
295   Thus fares the land, by luxury betrayed;
    In nature's simplest charms at first arrayed;
    But verging to decline, its splendors rise,
    Its vistas strike, its palaces surprise;
    While scourged by famine from the smiling land,
300   The mournful peasant leads his humble band;
    And while he sinks without one arm to save,

The country blooms—a garden, and a grave.
   Where then, ah where, shall Poverty reside,
To 'scape the pressure of contiguous Pride?
305 If to some common's fenceless limits strayed,
He drives his flock to pick the scanty blade,
Those fenceless fields the sons of wealth divide,
And even the bare-worn common is denied.
   If to the city sped—What waits him there?
310 To see profusion that he must not share;
To see ten thousand baneful arts combined
To pamper luxury, and thin mankind;
To see those joys the sons of pleasure know,
Extorted from his fellow creature's woe.
315 Here, while the courtier glitters in brocade,
There the pale artist° plies the sickly trade;   *artisan*
Here, while the proud their long-drawn pomps display,
There the black gibbet glooms beside the way.
The dome where Pleasure holds her midnight reign,
320 Here, richly decked, admits the gorgeous train;
Tumultuous grandeur crowds the blazing square,
The rattling chariots clash, the torches glare.
Sure scenes like these no troubles e'er annoy!
Sure these denote one universal joy!
325 Are these thy serious thoughts?—Ah, turn thine eyes
Where the poor houseless shivering female lies.
She once, perhaps, in village plenty blest,
Has wept at tales of innocence distressed;
Her modest looks the cottage might adorn,
330 Sweet as the primrose peeps beneath the thorn;
Now lost to all; her friends, her virtue fled,
Near her betrayer's door she lays her head,
And pinched with cold, and shrinking from the shower,
With heavy heart deplores that luckless hour,
335 When idly first, ambitious of the town,
She left her wheel° and robes of country brown.   *spinning wheel*
   Do thine, sweet Auburn, thine, the loveliest train,
Do thy fair tribes participate her pain?
Even now, perhaps, by cold and hunger led,
340 At proud men's doors they ask a little bread!
   Ah, no. To distant climes, a dreary scene,
Where half the convex world intrudes between,
Through torrid tracts with fainting steps they go,
Where wild Altama[7] murmurs to their woe.
345 Far different there from all that charmed before,
The various terrors of that horrid shore;
Those blazing suns that dart a downward ray,
And fiercely shed intolerable day;
Those matted woods where birds forget to sing,
350 But silent bats in drowsy clusters cling;
Those poisonous fields with rank luxuriance crowned,

7. The Altamaha River in Georgia.

Where the dark scorpion gathers death around;
Where at each step the stranger fears to wake
The rattling terrors of the vengeful snake;
355 Where crouching tigers[8] wait their hapless prey,
And savage men, more murderous still than they;
While oft in whirls the mad tornado flies,
Mingling the ravaged landscape with the skies.
Far different these from every former scene,
360 The cooling brook, the grassy-vested green,
The breezy covert of the warbling grove,
That only sheltered thefts of harmless love.
       Good Heaven! what sorrows gloomed that parting day,
That called them from their native walks away;
365 When the poor exiles, every pleasure past,
Hung round their bowers, and fondly looked their last,
And took a long farewell, and wished in vain
For seats like these beyond the western main;
And shuddering still to face the distant deep,
370 Returned and wept, and still returned to weep.
The good old sire, the first prepared to go
To new-found worlds, and wept for other's woe.
But for himself, in conscious virtue brave,
He only wished for worlds beyond the grave.
375 His lovely daughter, lovelier in her tears,
The fond companion of his helpless years,
Silent went next, neglectful of her charms,
And left a lover's for a father's arms.
With louder plaints the mother spoke her woes,
380 And blessed the cot where every pleasure rose;
And kissed her thoughtless babes with many a tear,
And clasped them close in sorrow doubly dear;
Whilst her fond husband strove to lend relief
In all the silent manliness of grief.
385   O luxury! Thou cursed by Heaven's decree,
How ill exchanged are things like these for thee!
How do thy portions, with insidious joy,
Diffuse their pleasures only to destroy!
Kingdoms, by thee, to sickly greatness grown,
390 Boast of a florid vigor not their own.
At every draught more large and large they grow,
A bloated mass of rank unwieldy woe;
Till sapped their strength, and every part unsound,
Down, down they sink, and spread a ruin round.
395   Even now the devastation is begun,
And half the business of destruction done;
Even now, methinks, as pondering here I stand,
I see the rural Virtues leave the land.
Down where yon anchoring vessel spreads the sail,
400 That idly waiting flaps with every gale,
Downward they move, a melancholy band,

8. Not the Asian tiger but the puma.

Pass from the shore, and darken all the strand.
Contented Toil, and hospitable Care,
And kind connubial Tenderness are there;
405 And Piety, with wishes placed above,
And steady Loyalty, and faithful Love:
And thou, sweet Poetry, thou loveliest maid,
Still° first to fly where sensual joys invade;   *always*
Unfit in these degenerate times of shame,
410 To catch the heart, or strike for honest fame;
Dear charming Nymph, neglected and decried,
My shame in crowds, my solitary pride;
Thou source of all my bliss, and all my woe,
That found'st me poor at first, and keep'st me so;
415 Thou guide by which the nobler arts excel,
Thou nurse of every virtue, fare thee well.
Farewell, and O! where'er thy voice be tried
On Torno's cliffs, or Pambamarca's side,[9]
Whether where equinoctial fervors glow,
420 Or winter wraps the polar world in snow,
Still let thy voice, prevailing over time,
Redress the rigors of the inclement clime;
Aid slighted truth, with thy persuasive strain
Teach erring man to spurn the rage of gain;
425 Teach him that states of native strength possessed,
Though very poor, may still be very blest;
That Trade's proud empire hastes to swift decay,
As ocean sweeps the labored mole[1] away;
While self-dependent power can time defy,
430 As rocks resist the billows and the sky.[2]

1770

9. The river Torne in Sweden falls into the Gulf of Bothnia. Pambamarca is a mountain in Ecuador.
1. The laboriously built breakwater.

2. Johnson composed the last four lines of the poem.

GEORGE CRABBE
1754–1832

George Crabbe (1754–1832) survived through the Romantic period, but his first successful poem is very much a part of eighteenth-century literature. Born to poverty in a small, decayed Suffolk seaport, Aldeburgh, he was apprenticed to a surgeon but could not manage to earn a living by practicing in his native village. In 1780 Crabbe went to London where, finding neither a patron nor a position and reduced to desperate straits, he sent an appeal to Edmund Burke, who recognized his merit and gave him timely help. Through Burke's influence *The Library* was published, Samuel

Johnson agreed to correct *The Village* (1783), and Crabbe was ordained a minister in the Anglican Church. His appointment as chaplain to the duke of Rutland enabled him to marry the woman to whom he had long been engaged.

After 1785 Crabbe published nothing until 1807, when *The Parish Register* appeared. It was followed by *The Borough* (1810), *Tales* (1812), and *Tales of the Hall* (1819). In these poems, which won the admiration of William Wordsworth, Sir Walter Scott, and Lord Byron, Crabbe developed his powers of narrative and characterization. *The Village* was widely read, although its unrelieved realism and gloom set it sharply apart from conventional poems on rural life. Indeed, it is an angry, scornful reply to the sentimental cult of rural simplicity, innocence, and happiness. It mocks the naïveté of pastoral conventions and systematically answers Oliver Goldsmith's idealization of villagers, and their life, in *The Deserted Village*. Crabbe had experienced the degrading effect of hopeless poverty, had observed rural vice, and knew the gulf that sometimes separated the landed gentry from their laboring tenants. Out of recollections of Aldeburgh and the neighboring seacoast, he fashioned for his poem a setting whose withered nature seems the only proper background for the rugged people who inhabit it. The accuracy of the details created a poetry of the ugly and the barren that has always appealed to readers who prefer plain truth to pretty illusions.

From The Village

From *Book 1*

The village life, and every care that reigns
O'er youthful peasants and declining swains;
What labor yields, and what, that labor past,
Age, in its hour of languor, finds at last;
5   What forms the real picture of the poor,
Demand a song—the Muse can give no more.
    Fled are those times when, in harmonious strains,
The rustic poet praised his native plains.
No shepherds now, in smooth altérnate° verse,   *metrically regular*
10   Their country's beauty or their nymphs' rehearse;
Yet still for these we frame the tender strain,
Still in our lays fond Corydons[1] complain,
And shepherds' boys their amorous pains reveal,
The only pains, alas! they never feel.
15   On Mincio's banks, in Caesar's bounteous reign,
If Tityrus[2] found the Golden Age again,
Must sleepy bards the flattering dream prolong,
Mechanic echoes of the Mantuan song?[3]
From Truth and Nature shall we widely stray,
20   Where Virgil, not where Fancy, leads the way?
    Yes, thus the Muses sing of happy swains,
Because the Muses never knew their pains.
They boast their peasants' pipes; but peasants now
Resign their pipes and plod behind the plow;
25   And few, amid the rural tribe, have time

---

1. Corydon is a stock name for a shepherd in pastorals, used by both Theocritus and Virgil.
2. One of the speakers in Virgil's *Eclogues* 1.

3. Virgil was born near Mantua, in Italy, not far from the river Mincius.

To number syllables, and play with rhyme;
Save honest Duck,[4] what son of verse could share
The poet's rapture, and the peasant's care?
Or the great labors of the field degrade,
30   With the new peril of a poorer trade?
     From this chief cause these idle praises spring,
That themes so easy few forbear to sing;
For no deep thought the trifling subjects ask:
To sing of shepherds is an easy task.
35   The happy youth assumes the common strain,
A nymph his mistress, and himself a swain;
With no sad scenes he clouds his tuneful prayer,
But all, to look like her, is painted fair.
     I grant indeed that fields and flocks have charms
40   For him that grazes or for him that farms;
But when amid such pleasing scenes I trace
The poor laborious natives of the place,
And see the midday sun, with fervid ray,
On their bare heads and dewy temples play;
45   While some, with feebler heads and fainter hearts,
Deplore their fortune, yet sustain their parts:
Then shall I dare these real ills to hide
In tinsel trappings of poetic pride?
     No; cast by Fortune on a frowning coast,
50   Which neither groves nor happy valleys boast;
Where other cares than those the Muse relates,
And other shepherds dwell with other mates;
By such examples taught, I paint the cot,°   cottage
As Truth will paint it, and as bards will not:
55   Nor you, ye poor, of lettered scorn complain,
To you the smoothest song is smooth in vain;
O'ercome by labor, and bowed down by time,
Feel you the barren flattery of a rhyme?
Can poets soothe you, when you pine for bread,
60   By winding myrtles round your ruined shed?
Can their light tales your weighty griefs o'erpower,
Or glad with airy mirth the toilsome hour?
     Lo! where the heath, with withering brake grown o'er,
Lends the light turf that warms the neighboring poor;
65   From thence a length of burning sand appears,
Where the thin harvest waves its withered ears;
Rank weeds, that every art and care defy,
Reign o'er the land, and rob the blighted rye:
There thistles stretch their prickly arms afar,
70   And to the ragged infant threaten war;
There poppies, nodding, mock the hope of toil;
There the blue bugloss paints the sterile soil;
Hardy and high, above the slender sheaf,
The slimy mallow waves her silky leaf;

4. Stephen Duck (1705–1756), the "Thresher Poet," was a self-educated agricultural laborer whose verses attracted attention and finally won him the patronage of Queen Caroline.

75 O'er the young shoot the charlock throws a shade,
  And clasping tares cling round the sickly blade;
  With mingled tints the rocky coasts abound,
  And a sad splendor vainly shines around.
  So looks the nymph whom wretched arts adorn,
80 Betrayed by man, then left for man to scorn;
  Whose cheek in vain assumes the mimic rose,
  While her sad eyes the troubled breast disclose;
  Whose outward splendor is but folly's dress,
  Exposing most, when most it gilds distress.
85 Here joyless roam a wild amphibious race,
  With sullen woe displayed in every face;
  Who far from civil arts and social fly,
  And scowl at strangers with suspicious eye.
  Here too the lawless merchant of the main
90 Draws from his plow the intoxicated swain;
  Want only claimed the labor of the day,
  But vice now steals his nightly rest away.
  Where are the swains, who, daily labor done,
  With rural games played down the setting sun;
95 Who struck with matchless force the bounding ball,
  Or made the ponderous quoit obliquely fall;
  While some huge Ajax, terrible and strong,
  Engaged some artful stripling of the throng,
  And fell beneath him, foiled, while far around
100 Hoarse triumph rose, and rocks returned the sound?
  Where now are these?—Beneath yon cliff they stand,
  To show the freighted pinnace where to land;[5]
  To load the ready steed with guilty haste;
  To fly in terror o'er the pathless waste;
105 Or, when detected in their straggling course,
  To foil their foes by cunning or by force;
  Or yielding part (which equal knaves demand)
  To gain a lawless passport[6] through the land.
  Here, wandering long amid these frowning fields,
110 I sought the simple life that Nature yields;
  Rapine and Wrong and Fear usurped her place,
  And a bold, artful, surly, savage race;
  Who, only skilled to take the finny tribe,
  The yearly dinner, or septennial bribe,[7]
115 Wait on the shore, and, as the waves run high,
  On the tossed vessel bend their eager eye,
  Which to their coast directs its venturous way;
  Theirs, or the ocean's, miserable prey.
  As on their neighboring beach yon swallows stand,
120 And wait for favoring winds to leave the land,
  While still for flight the ready wing is spread:
  So waited I the favoring hour, and fled;

---

5. Smuggling was common on the East Anglian coast.
6. License to import or travel.

7. Paid to electors by candidates for election to Parliament. Because Parliament is elected at least every seven years, the bribes are "septennial."

Fled from these shores where guilt and famine reign,
And cried, "Ah! hapless they who still remain;
125 Who still remain to hear the ocean roar,
Whose greedy waves devour the lessening shore;
Till some fierce tide, with more imperious sway,
Sweeps the low hut and all it holds away;
When the sad tenant weeps from door to door,
130 And begs a poor protection from the poor!"
       But these are scenes where Nature's niggard hand
Gave a spare portion to the famished land;
Hers is the fault, if here mankind complain
Of fruitless toil and labor spent in vain.
135 But yet in other scenes, more fair in view,
Where Plenty smiles—alas! she smiles for few—
And those who taste not, yet behold her store,   ⎤
Are as the slaves that dig the golden ore,   ⎬
The wealth around them makes them doubly poor.   ⎦
140   Or will you deem them amply paid in health,
Labor's fair child, that languishes with wealth?
Go, then! and see them rising with the sun,
Through a long course of daily toil to run;
See them beneath the dog star's raging heat,
145 When the knees tremble and the temples beat;
Behold them, leaning on their scythes, look o'er
The labor past, and toils to come explore;
See them alternate suns and showers engage,
And hoard up aches and anguish for their age;
150 Through fens and marshy moors their steps pursue,
When their warm pores imbibe the evening dew;
Then own that labor may as fatal be
To these thy slaves, as thine excess to thee.
       Amid this tribe too oft a manly pride
155 Strives in strong toil the fainting heart to hide;
There may you see the youth of slender frame
Contend, with weakness, weariness, and shame;
Yet, urged along, and proudly loath to yield,
He strives to join his fellows of the field;
160 Till long-contending nature droops at last,
Declining health rejects his poor repast,
His cheerless spouse the coming danger sees,
And mutual murmurs urge the slow disease.
       Yet grant them health, 'tis not for us to tell,
165 Though the head droops not, that the heart is well;
Or will you praise that homely, healthy fare,
Plenteous and plain, that happy peasants share?
Oh! trifle not with wants you cannot feel,
Nor mock the misery of a stinted meal,
170 Homely, not wholesome; plain, not plenteous; such
As you who praise would never deign to touch.
       Ye gentle souls, who dream of rural ease,
Whom the smooth stream and smoother sonnet please;
Go! if the peaceful cot your praises share,

175 Go, look within, and ask if peace be there:
If peace be his—that drooping weary sire,
Or theirs, that offspring round their feeble fire;
Or hers, that matron pale, whose trembling hand
Turns on the wretched hearth the expiring brand!

* * *

1780–83   1783

WILLIAM COWPER
1731–1800

There are no saner poems in the language than William Cowper's, yet they were written by a man who was periodically insane and who for forty years lived day to day with the possibility of madness. After attempting suicide in 1763, he believed that he was damned for having committed the unforgivable sin, the "sin against the Holy Ghost." From then on, a refugee from life, he looked for hope in Evangelicalism and found shelter first, in 1765, in the pious family of the clergyman Morley Unwin, and after Unwin's death, with his widow, Mary Unwin, who cared for Cowper until her death in 1796. Their move to rural Olney (pronounced *Own-y*) in 1768 brought them under the influence of the strenuous and fervent Evangelical minister John Newton, author of "Amazing Grace." With him Cowper wrote the famous *Olney Hymns*, still familiar to Methodists and other Nonconformists. But a second attack of madness, in 1773, not only frustrated his planned marriage to Mary Unwin but left him for the rest of his life with the assurance that he had been cast out by God. He never again attended services, and the main purpose of his life thereafter was to divert his mind from numb despair by every possible innocent device. He gardened, he kept pets, he walked, he wrote letters (some of the best of the century), he conversed, he read—and he wrote poetry. When it was published, it brought him a measure of fame that his modest nature could never have hoped for.

Cowper's major work is *The Task* (1785), undertaken at the bidding of Lady Austen, a friend who, when he complained that he had no subject, directed him to write about the sofa in his parlor. It began with a mock-heroic account of the development of the sofa from a simple stool, but it grew into a long meditative poem of more than five thousand lines. The poet describes his small world of country, village, garden, and parlor, and from time to time he glances toward the great world to condemn cities and worldliness, war and slavery, luxury and corruption. The tone is muted, the sensibility delicate, the language on the whole precise and clear. Cowper does not strive to be great, yet his contemporaries recognized their own concerns in his pious and humorous musings. Blake, Wordsworth, and Coleridge felt close to him, and so did many literary women. No eighteenth-century poet was more beloved.

From The Task

From *Book 1*

[A LANDSCAPE DESCRIBED. RURAL SOUNDS]

150   Thou[1] knowest my praise of nature most sincere,
    And that my raptures are not conjured up
    To serve occasions of poetic pomp,
    But genuine, and art partner of them all.
    How oft upon yon eminence our pace
155   Has slackened to a pause, and we have borne
    The ruffling wind, scarce conscious that it blew,
    While admiration, feeding at the eye,
    And still unsated, dwelt upon the scene.
    Thence with what pleasure have we just discerned
160   The distant plow slow moving, and beside
    His laboring team, that swerved not from the track,
    The sturdy swain diminished to a boy!
    Here Ouse,[2] slow winding through a level plain
    Of spacious meads with cattle sprinkled o'er,
165   Conducts the eye along its sinuous course
    Delighted. There, fast rooted in their bank,
    Stand, never overlooked, our favorite elms,
    That screen the herdsman's solitary hut;
    While far beyond, and overthwart the stream
170   That, as with molten glass, inlays the vale,
    The sloping land recedes into the clouds;
    Displaying on its varied side the grace
    Of hedgerow beauties numberless, square tower,
    Tall spire, from which the sound of cheerful bells
175   Just undulates upon the listening ear,
    Groves, heaths, and smoking villages, remote.
    Scenes must be beautiful, which, daily viewed,
    Please daily, and whose novelty survives
    Long knowledge and the scrutiny of years—
180   Praise justly due to those that I describe.
      Nor rural sights alone, but rural sounds,
    Exhilarate the spirit, and restore
    The tone of languid Nature. Mighty winds,
    That sweep the skirt of some far-spreading wood
185   Of ancient growth, make music not unlike
    The dash of ocean on his winding shore,
    And lull the spirit while they fill the mind;
    Unnumbered branches waving in the blast,
    And all their leaves fast fluttering, all at once.
190   Nor less composure waits upon the roar
    Of distant floods, or on the softer voice
    Of neighboring fountain, or of rills that slip
    Through the cleft rock, and, chiming as they fall

---

1. Mary Unwin.
2. The village of Olney, where Cowper and Mary Unwin were living, is situated on the river Ouse.

Upon loose pebbles, lose themselves at length
195 In matted grass, that with a livelier green
Betrays the secret of their silent course.
Nature inanimate employs sweet sounds,
But animated nature sweeter still,
To soothe and satisfy the human ear.
200 Ten thousand warblers cheer the day, and one
The livelong night: nor these alone, whose notes
Nice-fingered art[3] must emulate in vain,
But cawing rooks, and kites that swim sublime
In still repeated circles, screaming loud,
205 The jay, the pie,° and even the boding owl   magpie
That hails the rising moon, have charms for me.
Sounds inharmonious in themselves and harsh,
Yet heard in scenes where peace forever reigns,
And only there, please highly for their sake.

[CRAZY KATE]

There often wanders one, whom better days
535 Saw better clad, in cloak of satin trimmed
With lace, and hat with splendid ribband bound.
A servingmaid was she, and fell in love
With one who left her, went to sea, and died.
Her fancy followed him through foaming waves
540 To distant shores; and she would sit and weep
At what a sailor suffers; fancy, too,
Delusive most where warmest wishes are,
Would oft anticipate his glad return,
And dream of transports she was not to know.
545 She heard the doleful tidings of his death—
And never smiled again! And now she roams
The dreary waste; there spends the livelong day,
And there, unless when charity forbids,
The livelong night. A tattered apron hides,
550 Worn as a cloak, and hardly hides, a gown
More tattered still; and both but ill conceal
A bosom heaved with never-ceasing sighs.
She begs an idle pin of all she meets,
And hoards them in her sleeve; but needful food,
555 Though pressed with hunger oft, or comelier clothes,
Though pinched with cold, asks never.—Kate is crazed!

---

3. Refined skill, such as that of a flutist imitating the nightingale's song.

From *Book 3*

[THE STRICKEN DEER]

I was a stricken deer, that left the herd
Long since; with many an arrow deep infixed
110   My panting side was charged, when I withdrew
To seek a tranquil death in distant shades.
There was I found by one who had himself
Been hurt by the archers. In his side he bore,
And in his hands and feet, the cruel scars.
115   With gentle force soliciting[4] the darts,
He drew them forth, and healed, and bade me live.
Since then, with few associates, in remote
And silent woods I wander, far from those
My former partners of the peopled scene;
120   With few associates, and not wishing more.
Here much I ruminate, as much I may,
With other views of men and manners now
Than once, and others of a life to come.
I see that all are wanderers, gone astray
125   Each in his own delusions; they are lost
In chase of fancied happiness, still wooed
And never won. Dream after dream ensues;
And still they dream that they shall still succeed,
And still are disappointed. Rings the world
130   With the vain stir. I sum up half mankind
And add two-thirds of the remaining half,
And find the total of their hopes and fears
Dreams, empty dreams.

From *Book 4*

[THE WINTER EVENING: A BROWN STUDY]

Come evening once again, season of peace,
Return sweet evening, and continue long!
245   Methinks I see thee in the streaky west,
With matron-step slow-moving, while the night
Treads on thy sweeping train; one hand employed
In letting fall the curtain of repose
On bird and beast, the other charged for man
250   With sweet oblivion of the cares of day;
Not sumptuously adorned, nor needing aid
Like homely featured night, of clustering gems;
A star or two just twinkling on thy brow
Suffices thee; save that the moon is thine
255   No less than hers, not worn indeed on high
With ostentatious pageantry, but set
With modest grandeur in thy purple zone,[5]

4. "To endeavor to draw out by the use of gentle force" (*OED*).
5. Encircling band. Evening is seen both as a per- sonified goddess, whose "zone" is her royal belt, and as a natural phenomenon, where the "zone" is a stripe of color in the sky.

Resplendent less, but of an ampler round.[6]
Come then and thou shalt find thy votary calm,
260 Or make me so. Composure is thy gift.
And whether I devote thy gentle hours
To books, to music, or the poet's toil,
To weaving nets for bird-alluring fruit;
Or twining silken threads round ivory reels
265 When they command whom man was born to please;[7]
I slight thee not, but make thee welcome still.
    Just when our drawing rooms begin to blaze
With lights by clear reflection multiplied
From many a mirror, in which he of Gath,
270 Goliah,[8] might have seen his giant bulk
Whole without stooping, towering crest and all,
My pleasures too begin. But me perhaps
The glowing hearth may satisfy awhile
With faint illumination that uplifts
275 The shadow to the ceiling, there by fits
Dancing uncouthly to the quivering flame.
Not undelightful is an hour to me
So spent in parlor twilight; such a gloom
Suits well the thoughtful or unthinking mind,
280 The mind contemplative, with some new theme
Pregnant, or indisposed alike to all.
Laugh ye, who boast your more mercurial powers
That never feel a stupor, know no pause,
Nor need one. I am conscious,° and confess,   *conscious of*
285 Fearless, a soul that does not always think.
Me oft has fancy ludicrous and wild
Soothed with a waking dream of houses, towers,
Trees, churches, and strange visages expressed
In the red cinders, while with poring eye
290 I gazed, myself creating what I saw.
Nor less amused have I quiescent watched
The sooty films that play upon the bars,[9]
Pendulous and foreboding, in the view
Of superstition prophesying still,
295 Though still deceived, some stranger's near approach.[1]
'Tis thus the understanding takes repose
In indolent vacuity of thought,
And sleeps and is refreshed. Meanwhile the face
Conceals the mood lethargic with a mask
300 Of deep deliberation, as° the man   *as if*
Were tasked to his full strength, absorbed and lost.
Thus oft reclined at ease, I lose an hour
At evening, till at length the freezing blast

6. The moon looks larger at evening, when just over the horizon, than at night, when it is higher and brighter.
7. I.e., women.
8. Goliah, the giant of Gath slain by David (1 Samuel 17.19–51).
9. The grate of a fireplace.
1. The piece of soot that often flaps on the bars of a grate was called a "stranger" and was supposed to portend an unexpected visitor. Cf. lines 272–310 with Coleridge's "Frost at Midnight."

That sweeps the bolted shutter, summons home
305 The recollected powers, and snapping short
The glassy threads with which the fancy weaves
Her brittle toys, restores me to myself.
How calm is my recess, and how the frost,
Raging abroad, and the rough wind, endear
310 The silence and the warmth enjoyed within.
I saw the woods and fields at close of day,
A variegated show; the meadows green,
Though faded; and the lands where lately waved
The golden harvest, of a mellow brown,
315 Upturned so lately by the forceful share.°   plowshare
I saw far off the weedy fallows[2] smile
With verdure not unprofitable, grazed
By flocks fast feeding and selecting each
His favorite herb; while all the leafless groves
320 That skirt the horizon wore a sable hue,
Scarce noticed in the kindred dusk of eve.
Tomorrow brings a change, a total change!
Which even now, though silently performed
And slowly, and by most unfelt, the face
325 Of universal nature undergoes.
Fast falls a fleecy shower. The downy flakes,
Descending and with never-ceasing lapse,[3]
Softly alighting upon all below,
Assimilate all objects. Earth receives
330 Gladly the thickening mantle, and the green
And tender blade that feared the chilling blast,
Escapes unhurt beneath so warm a veil.

1785

The Castaway

Obscurest night involved the sky,
    The Atlantic billows roared,
When such a destined wretch as I,
    Washed headlong from on board,
5 Of friends, of hope, of all bereft,
His floating home forever left.

No braver chief[1] could Albion boast
    Than he with whom he went,
Nor ever ship left Albion's coast,

---

2. Plowed but unseeded land.
3. Gentle downward glide.
1. George, Lord Anson (1697–1762), in whose

Voyage (1748) Cowper, years before writing this poem, had read the story of the sailor washed overboard in a storm.

10   With warmer wishes sent.
      He loved them both, but both in vain,
      Nor him beheld, nor her again.

      Not long beneath the whelming brine,
          Expert to swim, he lay;
15   Nor soon he felt his strength decline,
          Or courage die away;
      But waged with death a lasting strife,
      Supported by despair of life.

      He shouted; nor his friends had failed
20   To check the vessel's course,
      But so the furious blast prevailed,
          That, pitiless perforce,
      They left their outcast mate behind,
      And scudded still before the wind.

25   Some succor yet they could afford;
          And, such as storms allow,
      The cask, the coop, the floated cord,
          Delayed not to bestow.
      But he (they knew) nor ship, nor shore,
30   Whate'er they gave, should visit more.

      Nor, cruel as it seemed, could he
          Their haste himself condemn,
      Aware that flight, in such a sea,
          Alone could rescue them;
35   Yet bitter felt it still to die
      Deserted, and his friends so nigh.

      He long survives, who lives an hour
          In ocean, self-upheld;
      And so long he, with unspent power,
40   His destiny repelled;
      And ever, as the minutes flew,
      Entreated help, or cried, "Adieu!"

      At length, his transient respite past,
          His comrades, who before
45   Had heard his voice in every blast,
          Could catch the sound no more.
      For then, by toil subdued, he drank
      The stifling wave, and then he sank.

      No poet wept him; but the page
50   Of narrative sincere,
      That tells his name, his worth, his age,
          Is wet with Anson's tear.
      And tears by bards or heroes shed
      Alike immortalize the dead.

55 I therefore purpose not, or dream,
  Descanting on his fate,
 To give the melancholy theme
  A more enduring date:
 But misery still delights to trace
60 Its semblance in another's case.

 No voice divine the storm allayed,
  No light propitious shone,
 When, snatched from all effectual aid,
  We perished, each alone;
65 But I beneath a rougher sea,
 And whelmed in deeper gulfs than he.

1799   1803

APPENDIXES

General Bibliography

This bibliography consists of a list of suggested general readings on English literature. Bibliographies for the authors in *The Norton Anthology of English Literature* are available online in the NAEL Archive (digital.wwnorton.com/englishlit10abc and digital.wwnorton.com/englishlit10def).

Suggested General Readings

Histories of England and of English Literature

Even the most distinguished of the comprehensive general histories written in past generations have come to seem outmoded. Innovative research in social, cultural, and political history has made it difficult to write a single coherent account of England from the Middle Ages to the present, let alone to accommodate in a unified narrative the complex histories of Scotland, Ireland, Wales, and the other nations where writing in English has flourished. Readers who wish to explore the historical matrix out of which the works of literature collected in this anthology emerged are advised to consult the studies of particular periods listed in the appropriate sections of this bibliography. The multivolume *Oxford History of England* and *New Oxford History of England* are useful, as are the three-volume *Peoples of the British Isles: A New History*, ed. Stanford Lehmberg, 1992; the nine-volume *Cambridge Cultural History of Britain*, ed. Boris Ford, 1992; the three-volume *Cambridge Social History of Britain, 1750–1950*, ed. F. M. L. Thompson, 1992; and the multivolume *Penguin History of Britain*, gen. ed. David Cannadine, 1996–. For Britain's imperial history, readers can consult the five-volume *Oxford History of the British Empire*, ed. Roger Louis, 1998–99, as well as *Gender and Empire*, ed. Philippa Levine, 2004. Given the cultural centrality of London, readers may find particular interest in *The London Encyclopaedia*, ed. Ben Weinreb et al., 3rd ed., 2008; Roy Porter, *London: A Social History*, 1994; and Jerry White, *London in the Nineteenth Century: "A Human Awful Wonder of God,"* 2007, and *London in the Twentieth Century: A City and Its People*, 2001.

Similar observations may be made about literary history. In the light of such initiatives as women's studies, new historicism, and postcolonialism, the range of authors deemed significant has expanded, along with the geographical and conceptual boundaries of literature in English. Attempts to capture in a unified account the great sweep of literature from *Beowulf* to the early twenty-first century have largely given way to studies of individual genres, carefully delimited time periods, and specific authors. For these more focused accounts, see the listings by period. Among the large-scale literary surveys, *The Cambridge Guide to Literature in English*, 3rd ed., 2006, is useful, as is the nine-volume *Penguin History of Literature*, 1993–94. *The Feminist Companion to Literature in English*, ed. Virginia Blain, Isobel Grundy, and Patricia Clements, 1990, is an important resource, and the editorial materials in *The Norton Anthology of Literature by Women*, 3rd ed., 2007, eds. Sandra M. Gilbert and Susan Gubar, constitute a concise history and set of biographies of women authors since the Middle Ages. *Annals of English Literature, 1475–1950*, rev. 1961, lists important publications year by year, together with the significant literary events for each year. Six volumes have been published in the *Oxford English Literary History*, gen. ed. Jonathan Bate, 2002–: Laura Ashe, *1000–1350: Conquest and Transformation*;

James Simpson, *1350–1547: Reform and Cultural Revolution*; Philip Davis, *1830–1880: The Victorians*; Chris Baldick, *1830–1880: The Modern Movement*; Randall Stevenson, *1960–2000: The Last of England?*; and Bruce King, *1948–2000: The Internationalization of English Literature*. See also *The Cambridge History of Medieval English Literature*, ed. David Wallace, 1999; *The Cambridge History of Early Medieval English Literature*, ed. Clare E. Lees, 2012; *The Cambridge History of Early Modern English Literature*, ed. David Loewenstein and Janel Mueller, 2003; *The Cambridge History of English Literature, 1660–1780*, ed. John Richetti, 2005; *The Cambridge History of English Romantic Literature*, ed. James Chandler, 2009; *The Cambridge History of Victorian Literature*, ed. Kate Flint, 2012; and *The Cambridge History of Twentieth-Century English Literature*, ed. Laura Marcus and Peter Nicholls, 2005.

Helpful treatments and surveys of English meter, rhyme, and stanza forms are Paul Fussell Jr., *Poetic Meter and Poetic Form*, rev. 1979; Donald Wesling, *The Chances of Rhyme: Device and Modernity*, 1980; Charles O. Hartman, *Free Verse: An Essay in Prosody*, 1983; John Hollander, *Rhyme's Reason: A Guide to English Verse*, rev. 1989; Derek Attridge, *Poetic Rhythm: An Introduction*, 1995; Robert Pinsky, *The Sounds of Poetry: A Brief Guide*, 1998; Mark Strand and Eavan Boland, eds., *The Making of a Poem: A Norton Anthology of Poetic Forms*, 2000; Helen Vendler, *Poems, Poets, Poetry*, 3rd ed., 2010; Virginia Jackson and Yopie Prins, eds., *The Lyric Theory Reader*, 2013; and Jonathan Culler, *Theory of the Lyric*, 2015.

On the development and functioning of the novel as a form, see Ian Watt, *The Rise of the Novel*, 1957; Gérard Genette, *Narrative Discourse: An Essay in Method*, 1980; *Theory of the Novel: A Historical Approach*, ed. Michael McKeon, 2000; McKeon, *The Origins of the English Novel, 1600–1740*, 15th anniversary ed., 2002; and *The Novel*, ed. Franco Moretti, 2 vols., 2006–07. *The Cambridge History of the English Novel*, eds. Robert L. Caserio and Clement Hawes, 2012; *A Companion to the English Novel*, eds. Stephen Arata et al., 2015; eight volumes have been published from *The Oxford History of the Novel in English*, 2011–16. On women novelists and readers, see Nancy Armstrong, *Desire and Domestic Fiction: A Political History of the Novel*, 1987; and Catherine Gallagher, *Nobody's Story: The Vanishing Acts of Women Writers in the Marketplace, 1670–1820*, 1994.

On the history of playhouse design, see Richard Leacroft, *The Development of the English Playhouse: An Illustrated Survey of Theatre Building in England from Medieval to Modern Times*, 1988. For a survey of the plays that have appeared on these and other stages, see Allardyce Nicoll, *British Drama*, rev. 1962; the eight-volume *Revels History of Drama in English*, gen. eds. Clifford Leech and T. W. Craik, 1975–83; and Alfred Harbage, *Annals of English Drama, 975–1700*, 3rd ed., 1989, rev. S. Schoenbaum and Sylvia Wagonheim; and the three volumes of *The Cambridge History of British Theatre*, eds. Jane Milling, Peter Thomson, and Joseph Donohue, 2004.

On some of the key intellectual currents that are at once reflected in and shaped by literature and contemporary literary criticism, Arthur O. Lovejoy's classic studies *The Great Chain of Being*, 1936, and *Essays in the History of Ideas*, 1948, remain valuable, along with such works as Georg Simmel, *The Philosophy of Money*, 1907; Lovejoy and George Boas, *Primitivism and Related Ideas in Antiquity*, 1935; Norbert Elias, *The Civilizing Process*, orig. pub. 1939, English trans. 1969; Simone de Beauvoir, *The Second Sex*, 1949; Frantz Fanon, *Black Skin, White Masks*, 1952, new trans. 2008; Ernst Cassirer, *The Philosophy of Symbolic Forms*, 4 vols., 1953–96; Ernst Kantorowicz, *The King's Two Bodies: A Study in Medieval Political Theology*, 1957, new ed. 1997; Hannah Arendt, *The Human Condition*, 1958; Richard Popkin, *The History of Skepticism from Erasmus to Descartes*, 1960; M. H. Abrams, *Natural Supernaturalism: Tradition and Revolution in Romantic Literature*, 1971; Michel Foucault, *Madness and Civilization: A History of Insanity in the Age of Reason*, Eng.

trans. 1965, and *The Order of Things: An Archaeology of the Human Sciences*, Eng. trans. 1970; Gaston Bachelard, *The Poetics of Space*, Eng. trans. 1969; Martin Jay, *The Dialectical Imagination: A History of the Frankfurt School and the Institute of Social Research, 1923–1950*, 1973, new ed. 1996; Hayden White, *Metahistory*, 1973; Roland Barthes, *The Pleasure of the Text*, Eng. trans. 1975; Jacques Derrida, *Of Grammatology*, Eng. trans. 1976, and *Dissemination*, Eng. trans. 1981; Richard Rorty, *Philosophy and the Mirror of Nature*, 1979; Gilles Deleuze and Félix Guattari, *A Thousand Plateaus*, 1980; Raymond Williams, *Keywords: A Vocabulary of Culture and Society*, rev. 1983; Pierre Bourdieu, *Distinction: A Social Critique of the Judgment of Taste*, Eng. trans. 1984; Michel de Certeau, *The Practice of Everyday Life*, Eng. trans. 1984; Hans Blumenberg, *The Legitimacy of the Modern Age*, Eng. trans. 1985; Jürgen Habermas, *The Philosophical Discourse of Modernity*, Eng. trans, 1987; Slavoj Žižek, *The Sublime Object of Ideology*, 1989; Homi Bhabha, *The Location of Culture*, 1994; Judith Butler, *The Psychic Life of Power: Theories in Subjection*, 1997; and Sigmund Freud, *Writings on Art and Literature*, ed. Neil Hertz, 1997.

Reference Works

The single most important tool for the study of literature in English is the *Oxford English Dictionary*, 2nd ed. 1989, 3rd ed. in process. The most current edition is available online to subscribers. The *OED* is written on historical principles: that is, it attempts not only to describe current word use but also to record the history and development of the language from its origins before the Norman conquest to the present. It thus provides, for familiar as well as archaic and obscure words, the widest possible range of meanings and uses, organized chronologically and illustrated with quotations. The *OED* can be searched as a conventional dictionary arranged a–z and also by subject, usage, region, origin, and timeline (the first appearance of a word). Beyond the *OED* there are many other valuable dictionaries, such as *The American Heritage Dictionary* (5th ed., 2016), *The Oxford Dictionary of Abbreviations*, *The Concise Oxford Dictionary of English Etymology*, *The Oxford Dictionary of English Grammar*, *A New Dictionary of Eponyms*, *The Oxford Essential Dictionary of Foreign Terms in English*, *The Oxford Dictionary of Idioms*, *The Concise Oxford Dictionary of Linguistics*, *The Oxford Guide to World English*, and *The Concise Oxford Dictionary of Proverbs*. Other valuable reference works include *The Cambridge Encyclopedia of the English Language*, 2nd ed., ed. David Crystal, 2003; *The Concise Oxford Companion to the English Language*; *Pocket Fowler's Modern English Usage*; and the numerous guides to specialized vocabularies, slang, regional dialects, and the like.

There is a steady flow of new editions of most major and many minor writers in English, along with a ceaseless outpouring of critical appraisals and scholarship. James L. Harner's *Literary Research Guide: An Annotated List of Reference Sources in English Literary Studies* (6th ed., 2009; online ed. available to subscribers at www.mlalrg.org/public) offers thorough, evaluative annotations of a wide range of sources. For the historical record of scholarship and critical discussion, *The New Cambridge Bibliography of English Literature*, ed. George Watson, 5 vols. (1969–77) and *The Cambridge Bibliography of English Literature*, 3rd ed., 5 vols. (1941–2000) are useful. The *MLA International Bibliography* (also online) is a key resource for following critical discussion of literatures in English. Ranging from 1926 to the present; it includes journal articles, essays, chapters from collections, books, and dissertations, and covers folklore, linguistics, and film. The *Annual Bibliography of English Language and Literature* (*ABELL*), compiled by the Modern Humanities Research Association, lists monographs, periodical articles, critical editions of literary works, book reviews, and collections of essays published anywhere in the world; unpublished doctoral dissertations are covered for the period 1920–99

(available online to subscribers and as part of Literature Online, http://literature.
proquest.com/marketing/index.jsp).

For compact biographies of English authors, see the multivolume *Oxford Dictionary of National Biography* (*DNB*), ed. H. C. G. Matthew and Brian Harrison, 2004; since 2004 the *DNB* has been extended online with three annual updates. Handy reference books of authors, works, and various literary terms and allusions include many volumes in the *Cambridge Companion* and *Oxford Companion* series (e.g., *The Cambridge Companion to Narrative*, ed David Herman, 2007; *The Oxford Companion to English Literature*, ed. Dinah Birch, rev. 2016; *The Cambridge Companion to Allegory*, ed. Rita Copeland and Peter Struck, 2010; etc.). Likewise, *The Princeton Encyclopedia of Poetry and Poetics*, ed. Roland Greene and others, 4th ed., is available online to subscribers in ProQuest Ebook Central. Handbooks that define and illustrate literary concepts and terms are *The Penguin Dictionary of Literary Terms and Literary Theory*, ed. J. A. Cuddon and M. A. R. Habib, 5th ed., 2015; William Harmon, *A Handbook to Literature*, 12th ed., 2011; *Critical Terms for Literary Study*, ed. Frank Lentricchia and Thomas McLaughlin, rev. 1995; and M. H. Abrams and Geoffrey Harpham, *A Glossary of Literary Terms*, 11th ed., 2014. Also useful are Richard Lanham, *A Handlist of Rhetorical Terms*, 2nd ed., 2012; Arthur Quinn, *Figures of Speech: 60 Ways to Turn a Phrase*, 1995; and the *Barnhart Concise Dictionary of Etymology*, ed. Robert K. Barnhart, 1995; and George Kennedy, *A New History of Classical Rhetoric*, 2009.

On the Greek and Roman backgrounds, see *The Cambridge History of Classical Literature* (vol. 1: *Greek Literature*, 1982; vol. 2: *Latin Literature*, 1989), both available online; *The Oxford Companion to Classical Literature*, ed. M. C. Howatson, 3rd ed., 2011; Gian Biagio Conte, *Latin Literature: A History*, 1994; *The Oxford Classical Dictionary*, 4th ed., 2012; Richard Rutherford, *Classical Literature: A Concise History*, 2005; and Mark P. O. Morford, Robert J. Lenardon, and Michael Sham, *Classical Mythology*, 10th ed., 2013. The Loeb Classical Library of Greek and Roman texts is now available online to subscribers at www.loebclassics.com.

Digital resources in the humanities have vastly proliferated since the previous edition of *The Norton Anthology of English Literature* and are continuing to grow rapidly. The NAEL Archive (accessed at digital.wwnorton.com/englishlit10abc and digital.wwnorton.com/englishlit10def) is the gateway to an extensive array of annotated texts, images, and other materials especially gathered for the readers of this anthology. Among other useful electronic resources for the study of English literature are enormous digital archives, available to subscribers: Early English Books Online (EEBO), http://eebo.chadwyck.com/home; Literature Online, http://literature.proquest.com/marketing/index.jsp; and Eighteenth Century Collections Online (ECCO), www.gale.com/primary-sources/eighteenth-century-collections-online. There are also numerous free sites of variable quality. Many of the best of these are period or author specific and hence are listed in the period/author bibiliographies in the NAEL Archive. Among the general sites, one of the most useful and wide-ranging is Voice of the Shuttle (http://vos.ucsb.edu), which includes in its aggregation links to Bartleby.com and Project Gutenberg.

Literary Criticism and Theory

Nine volumes of the *Cambridge History of Literary Criticism* have been published, 1989– : *Classical Criticism*, ed. George A. Kennedy; *The Middle Ages*, ed. Alastair Minnis and Ian Johnson; *The Renaissance*, ed. Glyn P. Norton; *The Eighteenth Century*, ed. H. B. Nisbet and Claude Rawson; *Romanticism*, ed. Marshall Brown; *The Nineteenth Century ca. 1830–1914*, ed. M. A. R. Habib; *Modernism and the New Criticism*, ed. A. Walton Litz, Louis Menand, and Lawrence Rainey; *From Formalism to Poststructuralism*, ed. Raman Selden; and *Twentieth-Century Historical, Philosoph-*

ical, and Psychological Perspectives, ed. Christa Knellwolf and Christopher Norris. See also M. H. Abrams, *The Mirror and the Lamp: Romantic Theory and the Critical Tradition*, 1953; William K. Wimsatt and Cleanth Brooks, *Literary Criticism: A Short History*, 1957; René Wellek, *A History of Modern Criticism: 1750–1950*, 9 vols., 1955–93; Frank Lentricchia, *After the New Criticism*, 1980; and J. Hillis Miller, *On Literature*, 2002. Raman Selden, Peter Widdowson, and Peter Brooker have written *A Reader's Guide to Contemporary Literary Theory*, 5th ed., 2015. Other useful resources include *The Johns Hopkins Guide to Literary Theory and Criticism*, 2nd ed., 2004; *Literary Theory, an Anthology*, eds. Julie Rivkin and Michael Ryan, 1998; and *The Norton Anthology of Theory and Criticism*, 3rd ed., gen. ed. Vincent Leitch, 2018.

Modern approaches to English literature and literary theory were shaped by certain landmark works: William Empson, *Seven Types of Ambiguity*, 1930, 3rd ed. 1953, *Some Versions of Pastoral*, 1935, and *The Structure of Complex Words*, 1951; F. R. Leavis, *Revaluation*, 1936, and *The Great Tradition*, 1948; Lionel Trilling, *The Liberal Imagination*, 1950; T. S. Eliot, *Selected Essays*, 3rd ed. 1951, and *On Poetry and Poets*, 1957; Erich Auerbach, *Mimesis: The Representation of Reality in Western Literature*, 1953; William K. Wimsatt, *The Verbal Icon*, 1954; Northrop Frye, *Anatomy of Criticism*, 1957; Wayne C. Booth, *The Rhetoric of Fiction*, 1961, rev. ed. 1983; and W. J. Bate, *The Burden of the Past and the English Poet*, 1970. René Wellek and Austin Warren, *Theory of Literature*, rev. 1970, is a useful introduction to the variety of scholarly and critical approaches to literature up to the time of its publication. Jonathan Culler's *Literary Theory: A Very Short Introduction*, 1997, discusses recurrent issues and debates.

Beginning in the late 1960s, there was a significant intensification of interest in literary theory as a specific field. Certain forms of literary study had already been influenced by the work of the Russian linguist Roman Jakobson and the Russian formalist Viktor Shklovsky and, still more, by conceptions that derived or claimed to derive from Marx and Engels, but the full impact of these theories was not felt until what became known as the "theory revolution" of the 1970s and '80s. For Marxist literary criticism, see Georg Lukács, *Theory of the Novel*, 1920, trans. 1971; *The Historical Novel*, 1937, trans. 1983; and *Studies in European Realism*, trans. 1964; Walter Benjamin's essays from the 1920s and '30s represented in *Illuminations*, trans. 1986, and *Reflections*, trans. 1986; Mikhail Bakhtin's essays from the 1930s represented in *The Dialogic Imagination*, trans. 1981, and *Rabelais and His World*, 1941, trans. 1968; *Selections from the Prison Notebooks of Antonio Gramsci*, ed. and trans. Quintin Hoare and Geoffrey Smith, 1971; Raymond Williams, *Marxism and Literature*, 1977; Tony Bennett, *Formalism and Marxism*, 1979; Fredric Jameson, *The Political Unconscious: Narrative as a Socially Symbolic Act*, 1981; and Terry Eagleton, *Literary Theory: An Introduction*, 3rd ed., 2008, and *The Ideology of the Aesthetic*, 1990.

Structural linguistics and anthropology gave rise to a flowering of structuralist literary criticism; convenient introductions include Robert Scholes, *Structuralism in Literature: An Introduction*, 1974, and Jonathan Culler, *Structuralist Poetics*, 1975. Poststructuralist challenges to this approach are epitomized in such influential works as Jacques Derrida, *Writing and Difference*, 1967, trans. 1978, and Paul de Man, *Blindness and Insight: Essays in the Rhetoric of Contemporary Criticism*, 1971, 2nd ed., 1983. Poststructuralism is discussed in Jonathan Culler, *On Deconstruction*, 1982; Slavoj Žižek, *The Sublime Object of Ideology*, 1989; Fredric Jameson, *Postmodernism; or the Cultural Logic of Late Capitalism*, 1991; John McGowan, *Postmodernism and Its Critics*, 1991; and *Beyond Structuralism*, ed. Wendell Harris, 1996. A figure who greatly influenced both structuralism and poststructuralism is Roland Barthes, in *Mythologies*, trans. 1972, and *S/Z*, trans. 1974. Among other influential contributions to literary theory are the psychoanalytic approach in Harold Bloom, *The Anxiety of*

Influence, 1973; and the reader-response approach in Stanley Fish, *Is There a Text in This Class?: The Authority of Interpretive Communities*, 1980. For a retrospect on the theory decades, see Terry Eagleton, *After Theory*, 2003.

Influenced by these theoretical currents but not restricted to them, modern feminist literary criticism was fashioned by such works as Patricia Meyer Spacks, *The Female Imagination*, 1975; Ellen Moers, *Literary Women*, 1976; Elaine Showalter, *A Literature of Their Own*, 1977; and Sandra Gilbert and Susan Gubar, *The Madwoman in the Attic*, 1979. Subsequent studies include Jane Gallop, *The Daughter's Seduction: Feminism and Psychoanalysis*, 1982; Luce Irigaray, *This Sex Which Is Not One*, trans. 1985; Gayatri Chakravorty Spivak, *In Other Worlds: Essays in Cultural Politics*, 1987; Sandra Gilbert and Susan Gubar, *No Man's Land: The Place of the Woman Writer in the Twentieth Century*, 3 vols., 1988–94; Barbara Johnson, *A World of Difference*, 1989; Judith Butler, *Gender Trouble*, 1990; and the critical views sampled in Elaine Showalter, *The New Feminist Criticism*, 1985; *The Hélène Cixous Reader*, ed. Susan Sellers, 1994; *Feminist Literary Theory: A Reader*, ed. Mary Eagleton, 3rd ed., 2010; and *Feminisms: An Anthology of Literary Theory and Criticism*, eds. Robyn R. Warhol and Diane Price Herndl, 2nd ed., 1997; *The Cambridge Companion to Feminist Literary Theory*, ed. Ellen Rooney, 2006; *Feminist Literary Theory and Criticism*, ed. Sandra Gilbert and Susan Gubar, 2007; and *Feminist Literary Theory: A Reader*, ed. Mary Eagleton, 3rd ed., 2011.

Just as feminist critics used poststructuralist and psychoanalytic methods to place literature in conversation with gender theory, a new school emerged placing literature in conversation with critical race theory. Comprehensive introductions include *Critical Race Theory: The Key Writings That Formed the Movement*, eds. Kimberlé Crenshaw et al.; *The Routledge Companion to Race and Ethnicity*, ed. Stephen Caliendo and Charlton McIlwain, 2010; and *Critical Race Theory: An Introduction*, ed. Richard Delgado and Jean Stefancic, 3rd ed., 2017. For an important precursor in cultural studies, see Stuart Hall et al., *Policing the Crisis*, 1978. Seminal works include Henry Louis Gates, Jr., *The Signifying Monkey: A Theory of African-American Literature*, 1988; Patricia Williams, *The Alchemy of Race and Rights*, 1991; Toni Morrison, *Playing the Dark: Whiteness and the Literary Imagination*, 1992; Cornel West, *Race Matters*, 2001; and Gene Andrew Jarrett, *Representing the Race: A New Political History of African American Literature*, 2011. Helpful anthologies and collections of essays have emerged in recent decades, such as *The Oxford Companion to African American Literature*, eds., William L. Andrews, Frances Smith Foster, and Trudier Harris, 1997; also their *Concise Companion*, 2001; *The Cambridge Companion to Jewish American Literature*, eds. Hana Wirth-Nesher and Michael P. Kramer, 2003; *The Routledge Companion to Anglophone Caribbean Literature*, eds. Michael A. Bucknor and Alison Donnell, 2011; *The Routledge Companion to Latino/a Literature*, eds. Suzanne Bost and Frances R. Aparicio, 2013; *A Companion to African American Literature*, ed. Gene Andrew Jarrett, 2013; *The Routledge Companion to Asian American and Pacific Islander Literature*, ed. Rachel Lee, 2014; *The Cambridge Companion to Asian American Literature*, eds. Crystal Parikh and Daniel Y. Kim, 2015; and *The Cambridge Companion to British Black and Asian Literature (1945–2010)*, ed. Deirdre Osborne, 2016.

Gay literature and queer studies are represented in *Inside/Out: Lesbian Theories, Gay Theories*, ed. Diana Fuss, 1991; *The Lesbian and Gay Studies Reader*, eds. Henry Abelove, Michele Barale, and David Halperin, 1993; *The Columbia Anthology of Gay Literature: Readings from Western Antiquity to the Present Day*, ed. Byrne R. S. Fone, 1998; and by such books as Eve Sedgwick, *Between Men: English Literature and Male Homosocial Desire*, 1985, and *Epistemology of the Closet*, 1990; Diana Fuss, *Essentially Speaking: Feminism, Nature, and Difference*, 1989; Terry Castle, *The Apparitional Lesbian: Female Homosexuality and Modern Culture*, 1993; Leo Bersani, *Homos*, 1995; Gregory Woods, *A History of Gay Literature: The Male Tradition*,

1998; David Halperin, *How to Do the History of Homosexuality*, 2002; Judith Halberstam, *In a Queer Time and Place: Transgender Bodies, Subcultural Lives*, 2005; Heather Love, *Feeling Backward: Loss and the Politics of Queer History*, 2009; *The Cambridge History of Gay and Lesbian Literature*, eds. E. L. McCallum and Mikko Tuhkanen, 2014; and *The Cambridge Companion to Lesbian Literature*, ed. Jodie Medd, 2015.

New historicism is represented in Stephen Greenblatt, *Learning to Curse*, 1990; in the essays collected in *The New Historicism Reader*, ed. Harold Veeser, 1993; in *New Historical Literary Study: Essays on Reproducing Texts, Representing History*, eds. Jeffrey N. Cox and Larry J. Reynolds, 1993; and in Catherine Gallagher and Stephen Greenblatt, *Practicing New Historicism*, 2000. The related social and historical dimension of texts is discussed in Jerome McGann, *Critique of Modern Textual Criticism*, 1983; and *Scholarly Editing: A Guide to Research*, ed. D. C. Greetham, 1995. Characteristic of new historicism is an expansion of the field of literary interpretation still further in cultural studies; for a broad sampling of the range of interests, see Lawrence Grossberg, Cary Nelson, and Paula Treichler, eds., *Cultural Studies*, 1992; *The Cultural Studies Reader*, ed. Simon During, 3rd ed., 2007; and *A Cultural Studies Reader: History, Theory, Practice*, eds. Jessica Munns and Gita Rajan, 1996.

This expansion of the field is similarly reflected in postcolonial studies: see Frantz Fanon, *Black Skin, White Masks*, 1952, new trans. 2008, and *The Wretched of the Earth*, 1961, new trans. 2004; Edward Said, *Orientalism*, 1978, and *Culture and Imperialism*, 1993; *The Post-Colonial Studies Reader*, 2nd ed., 2006; and such influential books as Homi Bhabha, ed., *Nation and Narration*, 1990, and *The Location of Culture*, 1994; Robert J. C. Young, *Postcolonialism: An Historical Introduction*, 2001; Bill Ashcroft, Gareth Griffiths, and Helen Tiffin, *The Empire Writes Back: Theory and Practice in Post-Colonial Literatures*, 2nd ed. 2002; Elleke Boehmer, *Colonial and Postcolonial Literature*, 2nd ed. 2005; and *The Cambridge History of Postcolonial Literature*, ed. Ato Quayson, 2011; *The Cambridge Companion to the Postcolonial Novel*, ed. Ato Quayson, 2015; and *The Cambridge Companion to Postcolonial Poetry*, ed. Jahan Ramazani, 2017.

In the wake of the theory revolution, critics have focused on a wide array of topics, which can only be briefly surveyed here. One current of work, focusing on the history of emotion, is represented in Brian Massumi, *Parables for the Virtual*, 2002; Sianne Ngai, *Ugly Feelings*, 2005; *The Affect Theory Reader*, eds. Melissa Gregg and Gregory J. Seigworth, 2010; and Judith Butler, *Senses of the Subject*, 2015. A somewhat related current, examining the special role of traumatic memory in literature, is exemplified in Cathy Caruth, *Trauma: Explorations in Memory*, 1995; and Dominic LaCapra, *Writing History, Writing Trauma*, 2000. Work on the literary implications of cognitive science may be glimpsed in *Introduction to Cognitive Cultural Studies*, ed. Lisa Zunshine, 2010. Interest in quantitative approaches to literature was sparked by Franco Moretti, *Graphs, Maps, Trees: Abstract Models for Literary History*, 2005. For the growing field of digital humanities, see also Moretti, *Distant Reading*, 2013; *Defining Digital Humanities: A Reader*, eds. Melissa Terras, Julianne Nyhan, and Edward Vanhoutte, 2014; and *A New Companion to Digital Humanities*, eds. Susan Schreibman, Ray Siemens, and John Unsworth, 2nd ed., 2016. There has also been a flourishing of ecocriticism, or studies of literature and the environment, including *The Ecocriticism Reader: Landmarks in Literary Ecology*, eds. Cheryll Glotfelty and Harold Fromm, 1996; *Writing the Environment*, eds. Richard Kerridge and Neil Sammells, 1998; Jonathan Bate, *The Song of the Earth*, 2002; Lawrence Buell, *The Future of Environmental Criticism: Environmental Crisis and Literary Imagination*, 2005; Timothy Morton, *Ecology Without Nature*, 2009; and *The Oxford Handbook of Ecocriticism*, ed. Greg Garrard, 2014. Related are the emerging fields of animal studies and posthumanism, where key works include

Bruno Latour, *We Have Never Been Modern,* 1993; Steve Baker, *Postmodern Animal,* 2000; Jacques Derrida, *The Animal That Therefore I Am,* trans. 2008; Cary Wolfe, *Animal Rites: American Culture, the Discourse of Species, and Posthumanist Theory,* 2003, and *What is Posthumanism?* 2009; Kari Weil, *Thinking Animals: Why Animal Studies Now?* 2012; and Aaron Gross and Anne Vallely, eds. *Animals and the Human Imagination: A Companion to Animal Studies,* 2012; and *Critical Animal Studies: Thinking the Unthinkable,* ed. John Sorenson, 2014. The relationship between literature and law is central to such works as *Interpreting Law and Literature: A Hermeneutic Reader,* eds. Sanford Levinson and Steven Mailloux, 1988; *Law's Stories: Narrative and Rhetoric in the Law,* eds. Peter Brooks and Paul Gerwertz, 1998; and *Literature and Legal Problem Solving: Law and Literature as Ethical Discourse,* Paul J. Heald, 1998. Ethical questions in literature have been usefully explored by, among others, Geoffrey Galt Harpham in *Getting It Right: Language, Literature, and Ethics,* 1997, and Derek Attridge in *The Singularity of Literature,* 2004. Finally, approaches to literature, such as formalism and literary biography, that seemed superseded in the theoretical ferment of the late twentieth century, have had a powerful resurgence. A renewed interest in form is evident in Susan Stewart, *Poetry and the Fate of the Senses,* 2002; *Reading for Form,* eds. Susan J. Wolfson and Marshall Brown, 2007; and Caroline Levine, *Forms: Whole, Rhythm, Hierarchy, Network,* 2015. Interest in the history of the book was spearheaded by D. F. McKenzie's *Bibliography and the Sociology of Texts,* 1986; Jerome McGann's *The Textual Condition,* 1991; and Roger Chartier's *The Order of Books: Readers, Authors, and Libraries in Europe Between the Fourteenth and Eighteenth Centuries,* 1994. See also *The Cambridge History of the Book in Britain,* 7 vols., 1998–2017; and *The Practice and Representation of Reading in England,* eds. James Raven, Helen Small, and Naomi Tadmor, 2007; *The Book History Reader,* eds. David Finkelstein and Alistair McCleery, 2nd ed., 2006; and *The Cambridge Companion to the History of the Book,* ed. Leslie Howsam, 2014.

Anthologies representing a range of recent approaches include *Modern Criticism and Theory,* ed. David Lodge, 1988; *Contemporary Literary Criticism,* ed. Robert Con Davis and Ronald Schlieffer, 4th ed., 1998; and *The Norton Anthology of Theory and Criticism,* gen. ed. Vincent Leitch, 3rd ed., 2018.

Literary Terminology*

Using simple technical terms can sharpen our understanding and streamline our discussion of literary works. Some terms, such as the ones in section A, help us address the internal style, structure, form, and kind of works. Other terms, such as those in section B, provide insight into the material forms in which literary works have been produced.

In analyzing what they called "rhetoric," ancient Greek and Roman writers determined the elements of what we call "style" and "structure." Our literary terms are derived, via medieval and Renaissance intermediaries, from the Greek and Latin sources. In the definitions that follow, the etymology, or root, of the word is given when it helps illuminate the word's current usage.

Most of the examples are drawn from texts in this anthology.

Words **boldfaced** within definitions are themselves defined in this appendix. Some terms are defined within definitions; such words are *italicized*.

A. Terms of Style, Structure, Form, and Kind

accent (synonym "stress"): a term of **rhythm.** The special force devoted to the voicing of one syllable in a word over others. In the noun "accent," for example, the accent, or stress, is on the first syllable.

act: the major subdivision of a play, usually divided into **scenes.**

aesthetics (from Greek, "to feel, apprehend by the senses"): the philosophy of artistic meaning as a distinct mode of apprehending untranslatable truth, defined as an alternative to rational enquiry, which is purely abstract. Developed in the late eighteenth century by the German philosopher Immanuel Kant especially.

Alexandrine: a term of **meter.** In French verse a line of twelve syllables, and, by analogy, in English verse a line of six stresses. See **hexameter.**

allegory (Greek "saying otherwise"): saying one thing (the "vehicle" of the allegory) and meaning another (the allegory's "tenor"). Allegories may be momentary aspects of a work, as in **metaphor** ("John is a lion"), or, through extended metaphor, may constitute the basis of narrative, as in Bunyan's *Pilgrim's Progress*: this second meaning is the dominant one. See also **symbol** and **type.** Allegory is one of the most significant **figures of thought.**

alliteration (from Latin "litera," alphabetic letter): a **figure of speech.** The repetition of an initial consonant sound or consonant cluster in consecutive or closely positioned words. This pattern is often an inseparable part of the meter in Germanic languages, where the tonic, or accented **syllable,** is usually the first syllable. Thus all Old English poetry and some varieties of Middle English poetry use alliteration as part of their basic metrical practice. *Sir Gawain and the Green Knight*, line 1: "Sithen the sege and the assaut was sesed at Troye" (see vol. A, p. 204). Otherwise used for local effects; Stevie Smith, "Pretty," lines 4–5: "And in the pretty pool the pike stalks / He stalks his prey . . ." (see vol. F, p. 733).

*This appendix was devised and compiled by James Simpson with the collaboration of all the editors. We especially thank Professor Lara Bovilsky of the University of Oregon at Eugene, for her help.

allusion: Literary allusion is a passing but illuminating reference within a literary text to another, well-known text (often biblical or **classical**). Topical allusions are also, of course, common in certain modes, especially **satire.**

anagnorisis (Greek "recognition"): the moment of **protagonist's** recognition in a narrative, which is also often the moment of moral understanding.

anapest: a term of **rhythm.** A three-syllable foot following the rhythmic pattern, in English verse, of two unstressed (uu) syllables followed by one stressed (/). Thus, for example, "Illinois."

anaphora (Greek "carrying back"): a **figure of speech.** The repetition of words or groups of words at the beginning of consecutive sentences, clauses, or phrases. Blake, "London," lines 5–8: "In every cry of every Man, / In every Infant's cry of fear, / In every voice, in every ban . . ." (see vol. D, p. 141); Louise Bennett, "Jamaica Oman," lines 17–20: "Some backa man a push, some side-a / Man a hole him han, / Some a lick sense eena him head, / Some a guide him pon him plan!" (see vol. F, p. 860).

animal fable: a **genre.** A short narrative of speaking animals, followed by moralizing comment, written in a low style and gathered into a collection. Robert Henryson, "The Preaching of the Swallow" (see vol. A, p. 523).

antithesis (Greek "placing against"): a **figure of thought.** The juxtaposition of opposed terms in clauses or sentences that are next to or near each other. Milton, *Paradise Lost* 1.777–80: "They but now who seemed / In bigness to surpass Earth's giant sons / Now less than smallest dwarfs, in narrow room / Throng numberless" (see vol. B, p. 1514).

apostrophe (from Greek "turning away"): a **figure of thought.** An address, often to an absent person, a force, or a quality. For example, a poet makes an apostrophe to a Muse when invoking her for inspiration.

apposition: a term of **syntax.** The repetition of elements serving an identical grammatical function in one sentence. The effect of this repetition is to arrest the flow of the sentence, but in doing so to add extra semantic nuance to repeated elements. This is an especially important feature of Old English poetic style. See, for example, Caedmon's *Hymn* (vol. A, p. 31), where the phrases "heaven-kingdom's Guardian," "the Measurer's might," "his mind-plans," and "the work of the Glory-Father" each serve an identical syntactic function as the direct objects of "praise."

assonance (Latin "sounding to"): a **figure of speech.** The repetition of identical or near identical stressed vowel sounds in words whose final consonants differ, producing half-rhyme. Tennyson, "The Lady of Shalott," line 100: "His broad clear brow in sunlight glowed" (see vol. E, p. 149).

aubade (originally from Spanish "alba," dawn): a **genre.** A lover's dawn song or lyric bewailing the arrival of the day and the necessary separation of the lovers; Donne, "The Sun Rising" (see vol. B, p. 926). Larkin recasts the genre in "Aubade" (see vol. F, p. 930).

autobiography (Greek "self-life writing"): a **genre.** A narrative of a life written by the subject; Wordsworth, *The Prelude* (see vol. D, p. 362). There are subgenres, such as the spiritual autobiography, narrating the author's path to conversion and subsequent spiritual trials, as in Bunyan's *Grace Abounding.*

ballad stanza: a **verse form.** Usually a **quatrain** in alternating **iambic tetrameter** and **iambic trimeter** lines, rhyming abcb. See "Sir Patrick Spens" (vol. D, p. 36); Louise Bennett's poems (vol. F, pp. 857–61); Eliot, "Sweeney among the Nightingales" (vol. F, p. 657); Larkin, "This Be The Verse" (vol. F, p. 930).

ballade: a **verse form**. A form consisting usually of three stanzas followed by a four-line envoi (French, "send off"). The last line of the first stanza establishes a **refrain**, which is repeated, or subtly varied, as the last line of each stanza. The form was derived from French medieval poetry; English poets, from the fourteenth to the sixteenth centuries especially, used it with varying stanza forms. Chaucer, "Complaint to His Purse" (see vol. A, p. 363).

bathos (Greek "depth"): a **figure of thought**. A sudden and sometimes ridiculous descent of tone; Pope, *The Rape of the Lock* 3.157–58: "Not louder shrieks to pitying heaven are cast, / When husbands, or when lapdogs breathe their last" (see vol. C, p. 518).

beast epic: a **genre**. A continuous, unmoralized narrative, in prose or verse, relating the victories of the wholly unscrupulous but brilliant strategist Reynard the Fox over all adversaries. Chaucer arouses, only to deflate, expectations of the genre in *The Nun's Priest's Tale* (see vol. A, p. 344).

biography (Greek "life-writing"): a **genre**. A life as the subject of an extended narrative. Thus Izaak Walton, *The Life of Dr. Donne* (see vol. B, p. 976).

blank verse: a **verse form**. Unrhymed **iambic pentameter** lines. Blank verse has no stanzas, but is broken up into uneven units (verse paragraphs) determined by sense rather than form. First devised in English by Henry Howard, earl of Surrey, in his translation of two books of Virgil's *Aeneid* (see vol. B, p. 141), this very flexible verse type became the standard form for dramatic poetry in the seventeenth century, as in most of Shakespeare's plays. Milton and Wordsworth, among many others, also used it to create an English equivalent to **classical epic**.

blazon: strictly, a heraldic shield; in rhetorical usage, a **topos** whereby the individual elements of a beloved's face and body are singled out for **hyperbolic** admiration. Spenser, *Epithalamion*, lines 167–84 (see vol. B, p. 495). For an inversion of the **topos**, see Shakespeare, Sonnet 130 (vol. B, p. 736).

burlesque (French and Italian "mocking"): a work that adopts the **conventions** of a genre with the aim less of comically mocking the genre than of satirically mocking the society so represented (see **satire**). Thus Pope's *Rape of the Lock* (see vol. C, p. 507) does not mock **classical epic** so much as contemporary mores.

caesura (Latin "cut") (plural "caesurae"): a term of **meter**. A pause or breathing space within a line of verse, generally occurring between syntactic units; Louise Bennett, "Colonization in Reverse," lines 5–8: "By de hundred, by de tousan, / From country an from town, / By de ship-load, by de plane-load, / Jamaica is Englan boun" (see vol. F, p. 858), where the caesurae occur in lines 5 and 7.

canon (Greek "rule"): the group of texts regarded as worthy of special respect or attention by a given institution. Also, the group of texts regarded as definitely having been written by a certain author.

catastrophe (Greek "overturning"): the decisive turn in **tragedy** by which the plot is resolved and, usually, the **protagonist** dies.

catharsis (Greek "cleansing"): According to Aristotle, the effect of **tragedy** on its audience, through their experience of pity and terror, was a kind of spiritual cleansing, or catharsis.

character (Greek "stamp, impression"): a person, personified animal, or other figure represented in a literary work, especially in narrative and drama. The more a character seems to generate the action of a narrative, and the less he or she seems merely to serve a preordained narrative pattern, the "fuller," or more "rounded," a character is said to be. A "stock" character, common particularly in many comic genres, will perform a predictable function in different works of a given genre.

chiasmus (Greek "crosswise"): a **figure of speech**. The inversion of an already established sequence. This can involve verbal echoes: Pope, "Eloisa to Abelard," line 104, "The crime was common, common be the pain" (see vol. C, p. 529); or it can be purely a matter of syntactic inversion: Pope, *Epistle to Dr. Arbuthnot*, line 8: "They pierce my thickets, through my grot they glide" (see vol. C, p. 544).

classical, classicism, classic: Each term can be widely applied, but in English literary discourse, "classical" primarily describes the works of either Greek or Roman antiquity. "Classicism" denotes the practice of art forms inspired by classical antiquity, in particular the observance of rhetorical norms of **decorum** and balance, as opposed to following the dictates of untutored inspiration, as in Romanticism. "Classic" denotes an especially famous work within a given **canon.**

climax (Greek "ladder"): a moment of great intensity and structural change, especially in drama. Also a **figure of speech** whereby a sequence of verbally linked clauses is made, in which each successive clause is of greater consequence than its predecessor. Bacon, *Of Studies*: "Studies serve for pastimes, for ornaments, and for abilities. Their chief use for pastimes is in privateness and retiring; for ornament, is in discourse; and for ability, is in judgement" (see vol. B, p. 1223–24).

comedy: a **genre**. A term primarily applied to drama, and derived from ancient drama, in opposition to **tragedy.** Comedy deals with humorously confusing, sometimes ridiculous situations in which the ending is, nevertheless, happy. A comedy often ends in one or more marriages. Shakespeare, *Twelfth Night* (see vol. B, p. 741).

comic mode: Many genres (e.g., **romance, fabliau, comedy**) involve a happy ending in which justice is done, the ravages of time are arrested, and that which is lost is found. Such genres participate in a comic mode.

connotation: To understand connotation, we need to understand **denotation.** While many words can denote the same concept—that is, have the same basic meaning—those words can evoke different associations, or connotations. Contrast, for example, the clinical-sounding term "depression" and the more colorful, musical, even poetic phrase "the blues."

consonance (Latin "sounding with"): a **figure of speech**. The repetition of final consonants in words or stressed syllables whose vowel sounds are different. Herbert, "Easter," line 13: "Consort, both heart and lute . . ." (see vol. B, p. 1258).

convention: a repeatedly recurring feature (in either form or content) of works, occurring in combination with other recurring formal features, which constitutes a convention of a particular genre.

couplet: a **verse form**. In English verse two consecutive, rhyming lines usually containing the same number of stresses. Chaucer first introduced the **iambic pentameter** couplet into English (*Canterbury Tales*); the form was later used in many types of writing, including drama; imitations and translations of **classical epic** (thus *heroic couplet*); essays; and **satire** (see Dryden and Pope). The *distich* (Greek "two lines") is a couplet usually making complete sense; Aemilia Lanyer, *Salve Deus Rex Judaeorum*, lines 5–6: "Read it fair queen, though it defective be, / Your excellence can grace both it and me" (see vol. B, p. 981).

dactyl (Greek "finger," because of the finger's three joints): a term of **rhythm.** A three-syllable foot following the rhythmic pattern, in English verse, of one stressed followed by two unstressed syllables. Thus, for example, "Oregon."

decorum (Latin "that which is fitting"): a rhetorical principle whereby each formal aspect of a work should be in keeping with its subject matter and/or audience.

deixis (Greek "pointing"): relevant to **point of view.** Every work has, implicitly or explicitly, a "here" and a "now" from which it is narrated. Words that refer to or imply this point from which the voice of the work is projected (such as "here," "there," "this," "that," "now," "then") are examples of deixis, or "deictics." This technique is especially important in drama, where it is used to create a sense of the events happening as the spectator witnesses them.

denotation: A word has a basic, "prosaic" (factual) meaning prior to the associations it connotes (see **connotation**). The word "steed," for example, might call to mind a horse fitted with battle gear, to be ridden by a warrior, but its denotation is simply "horse."

denouement (French "unknotting"): the point at which a narrative can be resolved and so ended.

dialogue (Greek "conversation"): a **genre.** Dialogue is a feature of many genres, especially in both the **novel** and drama. As a genre itself, dialogue is used in philosophical traditions especially (most famously in Plato's *Dialogues*), as the representation of a conversation in which a philosophical question is pursued among various speakers.

diction, or **"lexis"** (from, respectively, Latin *dictio* and Greek *lexis*, each meaning "word"): the actual words used in any utterance—speech, writing, and, for our purposes here, literary works. The choice of words contributes significantly to the style of a given work.

didactic mode (Greek "teaching mode"): **Genres** in a didactic mode are designed to instruct or teach, sometimes explicitly (e.g., sermons, philosophical **discourses, georgic**), and sometimes through the medium of fiction (e.g., **animal fable, parable**).

diegesis (Greek for "narration"): a term that simply means "narration," but is used in literary criticism to distinguish one kind of story from another. In a *mimetic* story, the events are played out before us (see **mimesis**), whereas in diegesis someone recounts the story to us. Drama is for the most part *mimetic*, whereas the novel is for the most part diegetic. In novels the narrator is not, usually, part of the action of the narrative; s/he is therefore extradiegetic.

dimeter (Greek "two measure"): a term of **meter.** A two-stress line, rarely used as the meter of whole poems, though used with great frequency in single poems by Skelton, e.g., "The Tunning of Elinour Rumming" (see vol. B, p. 39). Otherwise used for single lines, as in Herbert, "Discipline," line 3: "O my God" (see vol. B, p. 1274).

discourse (Latin "running to and fro"): broadly, any nonfictional speech or writing; as a more specific genre, a philosophical meditation on a set theme. Thus Newman, *The Idea of a University* (see vol. E, p. 64).

dramatic irony: a feature of narrative and drama, whereby the audience knows that the outcome of an action will be the opposite of that intended by a **character.**

dramatic monologue (Greek "single speaking"): a **genre.** A poem in which the voice of a historical or fictional **character** speaks, unmediated by any narrator, to an implied though silent audience. See Tennyson, "Ulysses" (vol. E, p. 156); Browning, "The Bishop Orders His Tomb" (vol. E, p. 332); Eliot, "The Love Song of J. Alfred Prufrock" (vol. F, p. 654); Carol Ann Duffy, "Medusa" and "Mrs Lazarus" (vol. F, pp. 1211–13).

ecphrasis (Greek "speaking out"): a **topos** whereby a work of visual art is represented in a literary work. Auden, "Musée des Beaux Arts" (see vol. F, p. 815).

elegy: a **genre**. In **classical** literature elegy was a form written in elegiac **couplets** (a **hexameter** followed by a **pentameter**) devoted to many possible topics. In Ovidian elegy a lover meditates on the trials of erotic desire (e.g., Ovid's *Amores*). The **sonnet** sequences of both Sidney and Shakespeare exploit this genre, and, while it was still practiced in classical tradition by Donne ("On His Mistress" [see vol. B, p. 942]), by the later seventeenth century the term came to denote the poetry of loss, especially through the death of a loved person. See Tennyson, *In Memoriam* (vol. E, p. 173); Yeats, "In Memory of Major Robert Gregory" (vol. F, p. 223); Auden, "In Memory of W. B. Yeats" (see vol. F, p. 815); Heaney, "Clearances" (vol. F, p. 1104).

emblem (Greek "an insertion"): a **figure of thought**. A picture allegorically expressing a moral, or a verbal picture open to such interpretation. Donne, "A Hymn to Christ," lines 1–2: "In what torn ship soever I embark, / That ship shall be my emblem of thy ark" (see vol. B, p. 966).

end-stopping: the placement of a complete syntactic unit within a complete poetic line, fulfilling the metrical pattern; Auden, "In Memory of W. B. Yeats," line 42: "Earth, receive an honoured guest" (see vol. F, p. 817). Compare **enjambment**.

enjambment (French "striding," encroaching): The opposite of **end-stopping**, enjambment occurs when the syntactic unit does not end with the end of the poetic line and the fulfillment of the metrical pattern. When the sense of the line overflows its meter and, therefore, the line break, we have enjambment; Auden, "In Memory of W. B. Yeats," lines 44–45: "Let the Irish vessel lie / Emptied of its poetry" (see vol. F, p. 817).

epic (synonym, *heroic poetry*): a **genre**. An extended narrative poem celebrating martial heroes, invoking divine inspiration, beginning in medias res (see **order**), written in a high style (including the deployment of **epic similes**; on high style, see **register**), and divided into long narrative sequences. Homer's *Iliad* and Virgil's *Aeneid* were the prime models for English writers of epic verse. Thus Milton, *Paradise Lost* (see vol. B, p. 1495); Wordsworth, *The Prelude* (see vol. D, p. 362); and Walcott, *Omeros* (see vol. F, p. 947). With its precise repertoire of stylistic resources, epic lent itself easily to **parodic** and **burlesque** forms, known as **mock epic**; thus Pope, *The Rape of the Lock* (see vol. C, p. 507).

epigram: a **genre**. A short, pithy poem wittily expressed, often with wounding intent. See Jonson, *Epigrams* (see vol. B, p. 1089).

epigraph (Greek "inscription"): a **genre**. Any formal statement inscribed on stone; also the brief formulation on a book's title page, or a quotation at the beginning of a poem, introducing the work's themes in the most compressed form possible.

epistle (Latin "letter"): a **genre**. The letter can be shaped as a literary form, involving an intimate address often between equals. The *Epistles* of Horace provided a model for English writers from the sixteenth century. Thus Wyatt, "Mine own John Poins" (see vol. B, p. 131), or Pope, "An Epistle to a Lady" (vol. C, p. 655). Letters can be shaped to form the matter of an extended fiction, as the eighteenth-century epistolary **novel** (e.g., Samuel Richardson's *Pamela*).

epitaph: a **genre**. A pithy formulation to be inscribed on a funeral monument. Thus Ralegh, "The Author's Epitaph, Made by Himself" (see vol. B, p. 532).

epithalamion (Greek "concerning the bridal chamber"): a **genre**. A wedding poem, celebrating the marriage and wishing the couple good fortune. Thus Spenser, *Epithalamion* (see vol. B, p. 491).

epyllion (plural "epyllia") (Greek: "little epic"): a **genre**. A relatively short poem in the meter of epic poetry. See, for example, Marlowe, *Hero and Leander* (vol. B, p 660).

essay (French "trial, attempt"): a **genre**. An informal philosophical meditation, usually in prose and sometimes in verse. The journalistic periodical essay was developed in the early eighteenth century. Thus Addison and Steele, periodical essays (see vol. C, p. 462); Pope, *An Essay on Criticism* (see vol. C, p. 490).

euphemism (Greek "sweet saying"): a **figure of thought**. The figure by which something distasteful is described in alternative, less repugnant terms (e.g., "he passed away").

exegesis (Greek "leading out"): interpretation, traditionally of the biblical text, but, by transference, of any text.

exemplum (Latin "example"): an example inserted into a usually nonfictional writing (e.g., sermon or **essay**) to give extra force to an abstract thesis. Thus Johnson's example of "Sober" in his essay "On Idleness" (see vol. C, p. 732).

fabliau (French "little story," plural *fabliaux*): a **genre**. A short, funny, often bawdy narrative in low style (see **register**) imitated and developed from French models, most subtly by Chaucer; see *The Miller's Prologue and Tale* (vol. A, p. 282).

farce (French "stuffing"): a **genre**. A play designed to provoke laughter through the often humiliating antics of stock **characters**. Congreve's *The Way of the World* (see vol. C, p. 188) draws on this tradition.

figures of speech: Literary language often employs patterns perceptible to the eye and/or to the ear. Such patterns are called "figures of speech"; in classical rhetoric they were called "schemes" (from Greek *schema*, meaning "form, figure").

figures of thought: Language can also be patterned conceptually, even outside the rules that normally govern it. Literary language in particular exploits this licensed linguistic irregularity. Synonyms for figures of thought are "trope" (Greek "twisting," referring to the irregularity of use) and "conceit" (Latin "concept," referring to the fact that these figures are perceptible only to the mind). Be careful not to confuse **trope** with **topos** (a common error).

first-person narration: relevant to **point of view**, a narrative in which the voice narrating refers to itself with forms of the first-person pronoun ("I," "me," "my," etc., or possibly "we," "us," "our"), and in which the narrative is determined by the limitations of that voice. Thus Mary Wollstonecraft Shelley, *Frankenstein*.

frame narrative: Some narratives, particularly collections of narratives, involve a frame narrative that explains the genesis of, and/or gives a perspective on, the main narrative or narratives to follow. Thus Chaucer, *Canterbury Tales*; Mary Wollstonecraft Shelley, *Frankenstein*; or Conrad, *Heart of Darkness*.

free indirect style: relevant to **point of view**, a narratorial voice that manages, without explicit reference, to imply, and often implicitly to comment on, the voice of a **character** in the narrative itself. Virginia Woolf, "A Sketch of the Past," where the voice, although strictly that of the adult narrator, manages to convey the child's manner of perception: "—I begin: the first memory. This was of red and purple flowers on a black background—my mother's dress."

genre and mode: The **style**, structure, and, often, length of a work, when coupled with a certain subject matter, raise expectations that a literary work conforms to a certain **genre** (French "kind"). Good writers might upset these expectations, but they remain aware of the expectations and thwart them purposefully. Works in different genres may nevertheless participate in the same **mode**, a broader category designating the fundamental perspectives governing various genres of writing. For mode, see **tragic, comic, satiric,** and **didactic modes**. Genres are fluid, sometimes very fluid (e.g., the **novel**); the word "usually" should be added to almost every account of the characteristics of a given genre!

georgic (Greek "farming"): a **genre**. Virgil's *Georgics* treat agricultural and occasionally scientific subjects, giving instructions on the proper management of farms. Unlike **pastoral**, which treats the countryside as a place of recreational idleness among shepherds, the georgic treats it as a place of productive labor. For an English poem that critiques both genres, see Crabbe, "The Village" (vol. C, p. 1019).

hermeneutics (from the Greek god Hermes, messenger between the gods and humankind): the science of interpretation, first formulated as such by the German philosophical theologian Friedrich Schleiermacher in the early nineteenth century.

heroic poetry: see **epic**.

hexameter (Greek "six measure"): a term of **meter**. The hexameter line (a six-stress line) is the meter of **classical** Latin **epic**; while not imitated in that form for epic verse in English, some instances of the hexameter exist. See, for example, the last line of a Spenserian stanza, *Faerie Queene* 1.1.2: "O help thou my weake wit, and sharpen my dull tong" (vol. B, p. 253), or Yeats, "The Lake Isle of Innisfree," line 1: "I will arise and go now, and go to Innisfree" (vol. F, p. 215).

homily (Greek "discourse"): a **genre**. A sermon, to be preached in church; *Book of Homilies* (see vol. B, p. 165). Writers of literary fiction sometimes exploit the homily, or sermon, as in Chaucer, *The Pardoner's Tale* (see vol. A, p. 329).

homophone (Greek "same sound"): a **figure of speech**. A word that sounds identical to another word but has a different meaning ("bear" / "bare").

hyperbaton (Greek "overstepping"): a term of **syntax**. The rearrangement, or inversion, of the expected word order in a sentence or clause. Gray, "Elegy Written in a Country Churchyard," line 38: "If Memory o'er their tomb no trophies raise" (vol. C, p. 999). Poets can suspend the expected syntax over many lines, as in the first sentences of the *Canterbury Tales* (vol. A, p. 261) and of *Paradise Lost* (vol. B, p. 1495).

hyperbole (Greek "throwing over"): a **figure of thought**. Overstatement, exaggeration; Marvell, "To His Coy Mistress," lines 11–12: "My vegetable love should grow / Vaster than empires, and more slow" (see vol. B, p. 1347); Auden, "As I Walked Out One Evening," lines 9–12: " 'I'll love you, dear, I'll love you / Till China and Africa meet / And the river jumps over the mountain / And the salmon sing in the street" (see vol. F, p. 813).

hypermetrical (adj.; Greek "over measured"): a term of **meter**; the word describes a breaking of the expected metrical pattern by at least one extra syllable.

hypotaxis, or **subordination** (respectively Greek and Latin "ordering under"): a term of **syntax**. The subordination, by the use of subordinate clauses, of different elements of a sentence to a single main verb. Milton, *Paradise Lost* 9.513–15: "As when a ship by skillful steersman wrought / Nigh river's mouth or foreland, where the wind / Veers oft, as oft so steers, and shifts her sail; So varied he" (vol. B, p. 1654). The contrary principle to **parataxis**.

iamb: a term of **rhythm**. The basic foot of English verse; two syllables following the rhythmic pattern of unstressed followed by stressed and producing a rising effect. Thus, for example, "Vermont."

imitation: the practice whereby writers strive ideally to reproduce and yet renew the **conventions** of an older form, often derived from **classical** civilization. Such a practice will be praised in periods of classicism (e.g., the eighteenth century) and repudiated in periods dominated by a model of inspiration (e.g., Romanticism).

irony (Greek "dissimulation"): a **figure of thought**. In broad usage, irony designates the result of inconsistency between a statement and a context that undermines the statement. "It's a beautiful day" is unironic if it's a beautiful day; if, however, the weather is terrible, then the inconsistency between statement and context is ironic. The effect is often amusing; the need to be ironic is sometimes produced by censorship of one kind or another. Strictly, irony is a subset of allegory: whereas allegory says one thing and means another, irony says one thing and means its opposite. For an extended example of irony, see Swift's "Modest Proposal." See also **dramatic irony**.

journal (French "daily"): a **genre**. A diary, or daily record of ephemeral experience, whose perspectives are concentrated on, and limited by, the experiences of single days. Thus Pepys, *Diary* (see vol. C, p. 86).

lai: a **genre**. A short narrative, often characterized by images of great intensity; a French term, and a form practiced by Marie de France (see vol. A, p. 160).

legend (Latin "requiring to be read"): a **genre**. A narrative of a celebrated, possibly historical, but mortal **protagonist**. To be distinguished from **myth**. Thus the "Arthurian legend" but the "myth of Proserpine."

lexical set: Words that habitually recur together (e.g., January, February, March, etc.; or red, white, and blue) form a lexical set.

litotes (from Greek "smooth"): a **figure of thought**. Strictly, understatement by denying the contrary; More, *Utopia*: "differences of no slight import" (see vol. B, p. 47). More loosely, understatement; Swift, "A Tale of a Tub": "Last week I saw a woman flayed, and you will hardly believe how much it altered her person for the worse" (see vol. C, p. 274). Stevie Smith, "Sunt Leones," lines 11–12: "And if the Christians felt a little blue— / Well people being eaten often do" (see vol. F, p. 729).

lullaby: a **genre**. A bedtime, sleep-inducing song for children, in simple and regular meter. Adapted by Auden, "Lullaby" (see vol. F, p. 809).

lyric (from Greek "lyre"): Initially meaning a song, "lyric" refers to a short poetic form, without restriction of meter, in which the expression of personal emotion, often by a voice in the first person, is given primacy over narrative sequence. Thus "The Wife's Lament" (see vol. A, p. 123); Yeats, "The Wild Swans at Coole" (see vol. F, p. 223).

masque: a **genre**. Costly entertainments of the Stuart court, involving dance, song, speech, and elaborate stage effects, in which courtiers themselves participated.

metaphor (Greek "carrying across," etymologically parallel to Latin "translation"): One of the most significant **figures of thought**, metaphor designates identification or implicit identification of one thing with another with which it is not literally identifiable. Blake, "London," lines 11–12: "And the hapless Soldier's sigh / Runs in blood down Palace walls" (see vol. D, p. 141).

meter: Verse (from Latin *versus*, turned) is distinguished from prose (from Latin *prorsus*, "straightforward") as a more compressed form of expression, shaped by metrical norms. **Meter** (Greek "measure") refers to the regularly recurring sound pattern of verse lines. The means of producing sound patterns across lines differ in different poetic traditions. Verse may be **quantitative**, or determined by the quantities of syllables (set patterns of long and short syllables), as in Latin and Greek poetry. It may be **syllabic**, determined by fixed numbers of syllables in the line, as in the verse of Romance languages (e.g., French and Italian). It may be **accentual**, determined by the number of accents, or stresses in the line, with variable numbers of syllables, as in Old English and some varieties of Middle English alliterative verse. Or it may be **accentual-syllabic**, determined by the numbers of accents, but possessing a regular pattern of stressed and unstressed syllables, so as to produce regular numbers of syllables per line. Since Chaucer, English verse has worked primarily within the many possibilities of accentual-syllabic meter. The unit of meter is the **foot**. In English verse the number of feet per line corresponds to the number of accents in a line. For the types and examples of different meters, see **monometer, dimeter, trimester, tetrameter, pentameter,** and **hexameter.** In the definitions below, "u" designates one unstressed syllable, and "/" one stressed syllable.

metonymy (Greek "change of name"): one of the most significant **figures of thought.** Using a word to **denote** another concept or other concepts, by virtue of habitual association. Thus "The Press," designating printed news media. Fictional names often work by associations of this kind. Closely related to **synecdoche.**

mimesis (Greek for "imitation"): A central function of literature and drama has been to provide a plausible imitation of the reality of the world beyond the literary work; mimesis is the representation and imitation of what is taken to be reality.

mise-en-abyme (French for "cast into the abyss"): Some works of art represent themselves in themselves; if they do so effectively, the represented artifact also represents itself, and so ad infinitum. The effect achieved is called "*mise-en-abyme.*" Hoccleve's *Complaint,* for example, represents a depressed man reading about a depressed man. This sequence threatens to become a *mise-en-abyme.*

monometer (Greek "one measure"): a term of **meter.** An entire line with just one stress; *Sir Gawain and the Green Knight,* line 15, "most (u) grand (/)" (see vol. A, p. 204).

myth: a **genre.** The narrative of **protagonists** with, or subject to, superhuman powers. A myth expresses some profound foundational truth, often by accounting for the origin of natural phenomena. To be distinguished from **legend.** Thus the "Arthurian legend" but the "myth of Proserpine."

novel: an extremely flexible **genre** in both form and subject matter. Usually in prose, giving high priority to narration of events, with a certain expectation of length, novels are preponderantly rooted in a specific, and often complex, social world; sensitive to the realities of material life; and often focused on one **character** or a small circle of central characters. By contrast with chivalric **romance** (the main European narrative genre prior to the novel), novels tend to eschew the marvelous in favor of a recognizable social world and credible action. The novel's openness allows it to participate in all modes, and to be co-opted for a huge variety of subgenres. In English literature the novel dates from the late seventeenth century and has been astonishingly successful in appealing to a huge readership, particularly in the nineteenth and twentieth centuries. The English and Irish tradition of the novel includes, for example, Fielding, Austen, the Brontë sisters, Dickens, George Eliot, Conrad, Woolf, Lawrence, and Joyce, to name but a few very great exponents of the genre.

novella: a **genre.** A short **novel,** often characterized by imagistic intensity. Conrad, *Heart of Darkness* (see vol. F, p. 73).

occupatio (Latin "taking possession"): a **figure of thought.** Denying that one will discuss a subject while actually discussing it; also known as "praeteritio" (Latin "passing by"). See Chaucer, *Nun's Priest's Tale,* lines 414–32 (see vol. A, p. 353).

ode (Greek "song"): a **genre.** A **lyric** poem in elevated, or high style (see **register**), often addressed to a natural force, a person, or an abstract quality. The Pindaric ode in English is made up of **stanzas** of unequal length, while the Horatian ode has stanzas of equal length. For examples of both types, see, respectively, Wordsworth, "Ode: Intimations of Immortality" (vol. D, p. 348); and Marvell, "An Horatian Ode" (vol. B, p. 1356), or Keats, "Ode on Melancholy" (vol. D, p. 981). For a fuller discussion, see the headnote to Jonson's "Ode on Cary and Morison" (vol. B, p. 1102).

omniscient narrator (Latin "all-knowing narrator"): relevant to **point of view.** A narrator who, in the fiction of the narrative, has complete access to both the deeds and the thoughts of all **characters** in the narrative. Thus Thomas Hardy, "On the Western Circuit" (see vol. F, p. 36).

onomatopoeia (Greek "name making"): a **figure of speech.** Verbal sounds that imitate and evoke the sounds they denotate. Hopkins, "Binsey Poplars," lines 10–12 (about some felled trees): "O if we but knew what we do / When we delve [dig] or hew— / Hack and rack the growing green!" (see vol. E, p. 598).

order: A story may be told in different narrative orders. A narrator might use the sequence of events as they happened, and thereby follow what **classical** rhetoricians called the *natural order*; alternatively, the narrator might reorder the sequence of events, beginning the narration either in the middle or at the end of the sequence of events, thereby following an *artificial order*. If a narrator begins in the middle of events, he or she is said to begin *in medias res* (Latin "in the middle of the matter"). For a brief discussion of these concepts, see Spenser, *Faerie Queene*, "A Letter of the Authors" (vol. B, p. 249). Modern narratology makes a related distinction, between *histoire* (French "story") for the natural order that readers mentally reconstruct, and *discours* (French, here "narration") for the narrative as presented. See also **plot** and **story.**

ottava rima: a **verse form.** An eight-line stanza form, rhyming abababcc, using **iambic pentameter;** Yeats, "Sailing to Byzantium" (see vol. F, p. 230). Derived from the Italian poet Boccaccio, an eight-line stanza was used by fifteenth-century English poets for inset passages (e.g., Christ's speech from the Cross in Lydgate's *Testament*, lines 754–897). The form in this rhyme scheme was used in English poetry for long narrative by, for example, Byron (*Don Juan*; see vol. D, p. 669).

oxymoron (Greek "sharp blunt"): a **figure of thought.** The conjunction of normally incompatible terms; Milton, *Paradise Lost* 1.63: "darkness visible" (see vol. B, p. 1497).

panegyric: a **genre.** Demonstrative, or epideictic (Greek "showing"), rhetoric was a branch of **classical** rhetoric. Its own two main branches were the rhetoric of praise on the one hand and of vituperation on the other. Panegyric, or eulogy (Greek "sweet speaking"), or encomium (plural *encomia*), is the term used to describe the speeches or writings of praise.

parable: a **genre.** A simple story designed to provoke, and often accompanied by, **allegorical** interpretation, most famously by Christ as reported in the Gospels.

paradox (Greek "contrary to received opinion"): a **figure of thought.** An apparent contradiction that requires thought to reveal an inner consistency. Chaucer, "Troilus's Song," line 12: "O sweete harm so quainte" (see vol. A, p. 362).

parataxis, or **coordination** (respectively Greek and Latin "ordering beside"): a term of **syntax.** The coordination, by the use of coordinating conjunctions, of different main clauses in a single sentence. Malory, *Morte Darthur:* "So Sir Lancelot departed and took his sword under his arm, and so he walked in his mantle, that noble knight, and put himself in great jeopardy" (see vol. A, p. 539). The opposite principle to **hypotaxis.**

parody: a work that uses the **conventions** of a particular genre with the aim of comically mocking a **topos,** a genre, or a particular exponent of a genre. Shakespeare parodies the topos of **blazon** in Sonnet 130 (see vol. B, p. 736).

pastoral (from Latin *pastor*, "shepherd"): a **genre.** Pastoral is set among shepherds, making often refined **allusion** to other apparently unconnected subjects (sometimes politics) from the potentially idyllic world of highly literary if illiterate shepherds. Pastoral is distinguished from **georgic** by representing recreational rural idleness, whereas the georgic offers instruction on how to manage rural labor. English writers had classical models in the *Idylls* of Theocritus in Greek and Virgil's *Eclogues* in Latin. Pastoral is also called bucolic (from the Greek word for "herdsman"). Thus Spenser, *Shepheardes Calender* (see vol. B, p. 241).

pathetic fallacy: the attribution of sentiment to natural phenomena, as if they were in sympathy with human feelings. Thus Milton, *Lycidas,* lines 146–47: "With cowslips wan that hang the pensive head, / And every flower that sad embroidery wears" (see vol. B, p. 1472). For critique of the practice, see Ruskin (who coined the term), "Of the Pathetic Fallacy" (vol. E, p. 386).

pentameter (Greek "five measure"): a term of **meter.** In English verse, a five-stress line. Between the late fourteenth and the nineteenth centuries, this meter, frequently employing an iambic rhythm, was the basic line of English verse. Chaucer, Shakespeare, Milton, and Wordsworth each, for example, deployed this very flexible line as their primary resource; Milton, *Paradise Lost* 1.128: "O Prince, O Chief of many thronèd Powers" (see vol. B, p. 1499).

performative: Verbal expressions have many different functions. They can, for example, be descriptive, or constative (if they make an argument), or performative, for example. A performative utterance is one that makes something happen in the world by virtue of its utterance. "I hereby sentence you to ten years in prison," if uttered in the appropriate circumstances, itself performs an action; it makes something happen in the world. By virtue of its performing an action, it is called a "performative." See also **speech act.**

peripeteia (Greek "turning about"): the sudden reversal of fortune (in both directions) in a dramatic work.

periphrasis (Greek "declaring around"): a **figure of thought.** Circumlocution; the use of many words to express what could be expressed in few or one; Sidney, *Astrophil and Stella* 39.1–4 (vol. B, p. 593).

persona (Latin "sound through"): originally the mask worn in the Roman theater to magnify an actor's voice; in literary discourse persona (plural *personae*) refers to the narrator or speaker of a text, whose voice is coherent and whose person need have no relation to the person of the actual author of a text. Eliot, "The Love Song of J. Alfred Prufrock" (see vol. F, p. 654).

personification, or **prosopopoeia** (Greek "person making"): a **figure of thought.** The attribution of human qualities to nonhuman forces or objects; Keats, "Ode on a Grecian Urn," lines 1–2: "Thou still unvanish'd bride of quietness, / Thou foster-child of silence and slow time" (see vol. D, p. 979).

plot: the sequence of events in a story as narrated, as distinct from **story,** which refers to the sequence of events as we reconstruct them from the plot. See also **order.**

point of view: All of the many kinds of writing involve a point of view from which a text is, or seems to be, generated. The presence of such a point of view may be powerful and explicit, as in many novels, or deliberately invisible, as in much drama. In some genres, such as the **novel,** the narrator does not necessarily tell the story from a position we can predict; that is, the needs of a particular story, not the **conventions** of the genre, determine the narrator's position. In other genres, the narrator's position is fixed by convention; in certain kinds of love poetry, for example, the narrating voice is always that of a suffering lover. Not only does the point of view significantly inform the style of a work, but it also informs the structure of that work.

protagonist (Greek "first actor"): the hero or heroine of a drama or narrative.

pun: a figure of thought. A sometimes irresolvable doubleness of meaning in a single word or expression; Shakespeare, Sonnet 135, line 1: "Whoever hath her wish, thou hast thy *Will*" (see vol. B, p. 736).

quatrain: a verse form. A stanza of four lines, usually rhyming abcb, abab, or abba. Of many possible examples, see Crashaw, "On the Wounds of Our Crucified Lord" (see vol. B, p. 1296).

refrain: usually a single line repeated as the last line of consecutive stanzas, sometimes with subtly different wording and ideally with subtly different meaning as the poem progresses. See, for example, Wyatt, "Blame not my lute" (see vol. B, p. 128).

register: The register of a word is its stylistic level, which can be distinguished by degree of technicality but also by degree of formality. We choose our words from different registers according to context, that is, audience and/or environment. Thus a chemist in a laboratory will say "sodium chloride," a cook in a kitchen "salt." A formal register designates the kind of language used in polite society (e.g., "Mr. President"), while an informal or colloquial register is used in less formal or more relaxed social situations (e.g., "the boss"). In **classical** and medieval rhetoric, these registers of formality were called *high style* and *low style*. A *middle style* was defined as the style fit for narrative, not drawing attention to itself.

rhetoric: the art of verbal persuasion. **Classical** rhetoricians distinguished three areas of rhetoric: the forensic, to be used in law courts; the deliberative, to be used in political or philosophical deliberations; and the demonstrative, or epideictic, to be used for the purposes of public praise or blame. Rhetorical manuals covered all the skills required of a speaker, from the management of style and structure to delivery. These manuals powerfully influenced the theory of poetics as a separate branch of verbal practice, particularly in the matter of style.

rhyme: a figure of speech. The repetition of identical vowel sounds in stressed syllables whose initial consonants differ ("dead" / "head"). In poetry, rhyme often links the end of one line with another. *Masculine rhyme*: full rhyme on the final syllable of the line ("decays" / "days"). *Feminine rhyme*: full rhyme on syllables that are followed by unaccented syllables ("fountains" / "mountains"). *Internal rhyme*: full rhyme within a single line; Coleridge, *The Rime of the Ancient Mariner*, line 7: "The guests are met, the feast is set" (see vol. D, p. 448). *Rhyme riche*: rhyming on **homophones**; Chaucer, *General Prologue*, lines 17–18: "seeke" / "seke." *Off rhyme* (also known as *half rhyme*, *near rhyme*, or *slant rhyme*): differs from perfect rhyme in changing the vowel sound and/or the concluding consonants expected of perfect rhyme; Byron, "They say that Hope is Happiness," lines 5–7: "most" / "lost." *Pararhyme*: stressed vowel sounds differ but are flanked by identical or similar consonants; Owen, "Miners," lines 9–11: "simmer" / "summer" (see vol. F, p. 163).

rhyme royal: a verse form. A **stanza** of seven **iambic pentameter** lines, rhyming ababbcc; first introduced by Chaucer and called "royal" because the form was used by James I of Scotland for his *Kingis Quair* in the early fifteenth century. Chaucer, "Troilus's Song" (see vol. A, p. 362).

rhythm: Rhythm is not absolutely distinguishable from **meter.** One way of making a clear distinction between these terms is to say that rhythm (from the Greek "to flow") denotes the patterns of sound within the feet of verse lines and the combination of those feet. Very often a particular meter will raise expectations that a given rhythm will be used regularly through a whole line or a whole poem. Thus in English verse the pentameter regularly uses an iambic rhythm. Rhythm, however, is much more fluid than meter, and many lines within the same poem using a single meter will frequently exploit different rhythmic possibilities. For examples of different rhythms, see **iamb, trochee, anapest, spondee,** and **dactyl.**

romance: a **genre.** From the twelfth to the sixteenth century, the main form of European narrative, in either verse or prose, was that of chivalric romance. Romance, like the later **novel,** is a very fluid genre, but romances are often characterized by (i) a tripartite structure of social integration, followed by disintegration, involving moral tests and often marvelous events, itself the prelude to reintegration in a happy ending, frequently of marriage; and (ii) aristocratic social milieux. Thus *Sir Gawain and the Green Knight* (see vol. A, p. 204); Spenser's (unfinished) *Faerie Queene* (vol. B, p. 249). The immensely popular, fertile genre was absorbed, in both domesticated and undomesticated form, by the novel. For an adaptation of romance, see Chaucer, *Wife of Bath's Tale* (vol. A, p. 300).

sarcasm (Greek "flesh tearing"): a **figure of thought.** A wounding expression, often expressed ironically; Boswell, *Life of Johnson*: Johnson [asked if any man of the modern age could have written the **epic** poem *Fingal*] replied, "Yes, Sir, many men, many women, and many children" (see vol. C, p. 844).

satire (Latin for "a bowl of mixed fruits"): a **genre.** In Roman literature (e.g., Juvenal), the communication, in the form of a letter between equals, complaining of the ills of contemporary society. The genre in this form is characterized by a first-person narrator exasperated by social ills; the letter form; a high frequency of contemporary reference; and the use of invective in **low-style** language. Pope practices the genre thus in the *Epistle to Dr. Arbuthnot* (see vol. C, p. 543). Wyatt's "Mine own John Poins" (see vol. B, p. 131) draws ultimately on a gentler, Horatian model of the genre.

satiric mode: Works in a very large variety of genres are devoted to the more or less savage attack on social ills. Thus Swift's travel narrative *Gulliver's Travels* (see vol. C, p. 279), his **essay** "A Modest Proposal" (vol. C, p. 454), Pope's mock-**epic** *The Dunciad* (vol. C, p. 555), and Gay's *Beggar's Opera* (vol. C, p. 659), to look no further than the eighteenth century, are all within a satiric mode.

scene: a subdivision of an **act,** itself a subdivision of a dramatic performance and/or text. The action of a scene usually occurs in one place.

sensibility (from Latin, "capable of being perceived by the senses"): as a literary term, an eighteenth-century concept derived from moral philosophy that stressed the social importance of fellow feeling and particularly of sympathy in social relations. The concept generated a literature of "sensibility," such as the sentimental **novel** (the most famous of which was Goethe's *Sorrows of the Young Werther* [1774]), or sentimental poetry, such as Cowper's passage on the stricken deer in *The Task* (see vol. C, p. 1024).

short story: a **genre.** Generically similar to, though shorter and more concentrated than, the **novel;** often published as part of a collection. Thus Mansfield, "The Daughters of the Late Colonel" (see vol. F, p. 698).

simile (Latin "like"): a **figure of thought.** Comparison, usually using the word "like" or "as," of one thing with another so as to produce sometimes surprising analogies. Donne, "The Storm," lines 29–30: "Sooner than you read this line did the gale, / Like shot, not feared till felt, our sails assail." Frequently used, in extended form, in **epic** poetry; Milton, *Paradise Lost* 1.338–46 (see vol. B, p. 1504).

soliloquy (Latin "single speaking"): a **topos** of drama, in which a **character,** alone or thinking to be alone on stage, speaks so as to give the audience access to his or her private thoughts. Thus Viola's soliloquy in Shakespeare, *Twelfth Night* 2.2.17– 41 (vol. B, p. 758).

sonnet: a verse form. A form combining a variable number of units of rhymed lines to produce a fourteen-line poem, usually in rhyming **iambic pentameter** lines. In English there are two principal varieties: the Petrarchan sonnet, formed by an octave (an eight-line stanza, often broken into two **quatrains** having the same rhyme scheme, typically abba abba) and a sestet (a six-line stanza, typically cdecde or cdcdcd); and the Shakespearean sonnet, formed by three quatrains (abab cdcd efef) and a **couplet** (gg). The declaration of a sonnet can take a sharp turn, or "volta," often at the decisive formal shift from octave to sestet in the Petrarchan sonnet, or in the final couplet of a Shakespearean sonnet, introducing a trenchant counterstatement. Derived from Italian poetry, and especially from the poetry of Petrarch, the sonnet was first introduced to English poetry by Wyatt, and initially used principally for the expression of unrequited erotic love, though later poets used the form for many other purposes. See Wyatt, "Whoso list to hunt" (vol. B, p. 121); Sidney, *Astrophil and Stella* (vol. B, p. 586); Shakespeare, *Sonnets* (vol. B, p. 723); Wordsworth, "London, 1802" (vol. D, p. 357); McKay, "If We Must Die" (vol. F, p. 854); Heaney, "Clearances" (vol. F, p. 1104).

speech act: Words and deeds are often distinguished, but words are often (perhaps always) themselves deeds. Utterances can perform different speech acts, such as promising, declaring, casting a spell, encouraging, persuading, denying, lying, and so on. See also **performative.**

Spenserian stanza: a verse form. The stanza developed by Spenser for *The Faerie Queene*; nine **iambic** lines, the first eight of which are **pentameters,** followed by one **hexameter,** rhyming ababbcbcc. See also, for example, Shelley, *Adonais* (vol. D, p. 856), and Keats, *The Eve of St. Agnes* (vol. D, p. 961).

spondee: a term of **meter.** A two-syllable foot following the rhythmic pattern, in English verse, of two stressed syllables. Thus, for example, "Utah."

stanza (Italian "room"): groupings of two or more lines, though "stanza" is usually reserved for groupings of at least four lines. Stanzas are often joined by rhyme, often in sequence, where each group shares the same metrical pattern and, when rhymed, rhyme scheme. Stanzas can themselves be arranged into larger groupings. Poets often invent new **verse forms,** or they may work within established forms.

story: a narrative's sequence of events, which we reconstruct from those events as they have been recounted by the narrator (i.e., the **plot**). See also **order.**

stream of consciousness: usually a **first-person** narrative that seems to give the reader access to the narrator's mind as it perceives or reflects on events, prior to organizing those perceptions into a coherent narrative. Thus (though generated from a **third-person** narrative) Joyce, *Ulysses,* "Penelope" (see vol. F, p. 604).

style (from Latin for "writing instrument"): In literary works the manner in which something is expressed contributes substantially to its meaning. The expressions "sun," "mass of helium at the center of the solar system," "heaven's golden orb" all designate "sun," but do so in different manners, or styles, which produce different meanings. The manner of a literary work is its "style," the effect of which is its "tone." We often can intuit the tone of a text; from that intuition of tone we can analyze the stylistic resources by which it was produced. We can analyze the style of literary works through consideration of different elements of style; for example, **diction, figures of thought, figures of speech, meter and rhythm, verse form, syntax, point of view.**

sublime: As a concept generating a literary movement, the sublime refers to the realm of experience beyond the measurable, and so beyond the rational, produced especially by the terrors and grandeur of natural phenomena. Derived especially from the first-century Greek treatise *On the Sublime*, sometimes attributed to Longinus, the notion of the sublime was in the later eighteenth century a spur to Romanticism.

syllable: the smallest unit of sound in a pronounced word. The syllable that receives the greatest stress is called the *tonic* syllable.

symbol (Greek "token"): a **figure of thought.** Something that stands for something else, and yet seems necessarily to evoke that other thing. In Neoplatonic, and therefore Romantic, theory, to be distinguished from **allegory** thus: whereas allegory involves connections between vehicle and tenor agreed by convention or made explicit, the meanings of a symbol are supposedly inherent to it. For discussion, see Coleridge, "On Symbol and Allegory" (vol. D, p. 507).

synecdoche (Greek "to take with something else"): a **figure of thought.** Using a part to express the whole, or vice versa; e.g., "all hands on deck." Closely related to **metonymy.**

syntax (Greek "ordering with"): Syntax designates the rules by which sentences are constructed in a given language. Discussion of meter is impossible without some reference to syntax, since the overall effect of a poem is, in part, always the product of a subtle balance of meter and sentence construction. Syntax is also essential to the understanding of prose style, since prose writers, deprived of the full shaping possibilities of meter, rely all the more heavily on syntactic resources. A working command of syntactical practice requires an understanding of the parts of speech (nouns, verbs, adjectives, adverbs, conjunctions, pronouns, prepositions, and interjections), since writers exploit syntactic possibilities by using particular combinations and concentrations of the parts of speech.

taste (from Italian "touch"): Although medieval monastic traditions used eating and tasting as a metaphor for reading, the concept of taste as a personal ideal to be cultivated by, and applied to, the appreciation and judgment of works of art in general was developed in the eighteenth century.

tercet: a **verse form.** A stanza or group of three lines, used in larger forms such as **terza rima,** the **Petrarchan sonnet,** and the **villanelle.**

terza rima: a **verse form.** A sequence of rhymed **tercets** linked by rhyme thus: aba bcb cdc, etc. first used extensively by Dante in *The Divine Comedy,* the form was adapted in English **iambic pentameters** by Wyatt and revived in the nineteenth century. See Wyatt, "Mine own John Poins" (vol. B, p. 131); Shelley, "Ode to the West Wind" (vol. D, p. 806); and Morris, "The Defence of Guinevere" (vol. E, p. 560). For modern adaptations see Eliot, lines 78–149 (though unrhymed) of "Little Gidding" (vol. F, pp. 679–81); Heaney, "Station Island" (vol. F, p. 1102); Walcott, *Omeros* (vol. F, p. 947).

tetrameter (Greek "four measure"): a term of **meter.** A line with four stresses. Coleridge, *Christabel,* line 31: "She stole along, she nothing spoke" (see vol. D, p. 468).

theme (Greek "proposition"): In literary criticism the term designates what the work is about; the theme is the concept that unifies a given work of literature.

third-person narration: relevant to **point of view.** A narration in which the narrator recounts a narrative of **characters** referred to explicitly or implicitly by third-person pronouns ("he," she," etc.), without the limitation of a **first-person narration.** Thus Johnson, *The History of Rasselas.*

topographical poem (Greek "place writing"): a **genre.** A poem devoted to the meditative description of particular places. Thus Gray, "Ode on a Distant Prospect of Eton College" (see vol. C, p. 994).

topos (Greek "place," plural *topoi*): a commonplace in the content of a given kind of literature. Originally, in **classical** rhetoric, the topoi were tried-and-tested stimuli to literary invention: lists of standard headings under which a subject might be investigated. In medieval narrative poems, for example, it was commonplace to begin with a description of spring. Writers did, of course, render the commonplace uncommon, as in Chaucer's spring scene at the opening of *The Canterbury Tales* (see vol. A, p. 261).

tradition (from Latin "passing on"): A literary tradition is whatever is passed on or revived from the past in a single literary culture, or drawn from others to enrich a writer's culture. "Tradition" is fluid in reference, ranging from small to large referents: thus it may refer to a relatively small aspect of texts (e.g., the tradition of **iambic pentameter**), or it may, at the other extreme, refer to the body of texts that constitute a **canon.**

tragedy: a **genre.** A dramatic representation of the fall of kings or nobles, beginning in happiness and ending in catastrophe. Later transferred to other social milieux. The opposite of **comedy;** thus Shakespeare, *Othello* (see vol. B, p. 806).

tragic mode: Many genres (**epic** poetry, **legend**ary chronicles, **tragedy,** the **novel**) either do or can participate in a tragic mode, by representing the fall of noble **protagonists** and the irreparable ravages of human society and history.

tragicomedy: a **genre.** A play in which potentially tragic events turn out to have a happy, or **comic,** ending. Thus Shakespeare, *Measure for Measure.*

translation (Latin "carrying across"): the rendering of a text written in one language into another.

trimeter (Greek "three measure"): a term of **meter.** A line with three stresses. Herbert, "Discipline," line 1: "Throw away thy rod" (see vol. B, p. 1274).

triplet: a **verse form.** A **tercet** rhyming on the same sound. Pope inserts triplets among heroic **couplets** to emphasize a particular thought; see *Essay on Criticism,* 315–17 (vol. C, p. 497).

trochee: a term of **rhythm.** A two-syllable foot following the pattern, in English verse, of stressed followed by unstressed syllable, producing a falling effect. Thus, for example, "Texas."

type (Greek "impression, figure"): a **figure of thought.** In Christian allegorical interpretation of the Old Testament, pre-Christian figures were regarded as "types," or foreshadowings, of Christ or the Christian dispensation. *Typology* has been the source of much visual and literary art in which the parallelisms between old and new are extended to nonbiblical figures; thus the virtuous plowman in *Piers Plowman* becomes a type of Christ.

unities: According to a theory supposedly derived from Aristotle's *Poetics,* the events represented in a play should have unity of time, place, and action: that the play take up no more time than the time of the play, or at most a day; that the space of action should be within a single city; and that there should be no subplot. See Johnson, *The Preface to Shakespeare* (vol. C, p. 807).

vernacular (from Latin *verna*, "servant"): the language of the people, as distinguished from learned and arcane languages. From the later Middle Ages especially, the "vernacular" languages and literatures of Europe distinguished themselves from the learned languages and literatures of Latin, Greek, and Hebrew.

verse form: The terms related to **meter** and **rhythm** describe the shape of individual lines. Lines of verse are combined to produce larger groupings, called verse forms. These larger groupings are in the first instance **stanzas**. The combination of a certain meter and stanza shape constitutes the verse form, of which there are many standard kinds.

villanelle: a **verse form**. A fixed form of usually five **tercets** and a **quatrain** employing only two rhyme sounds altogether, rhyming aba for the tercets and abaa for the quatrain, with a complex pattern of two **refrains**. Derived from a French fixed form. Thomas, "Do Not Go Gentle into That Good Night" (see vol. F, p. 833).

wit: Originally a synonym for "reason" in Old and Middle English, "wit" became a literary ideal in the Renaissance as brilliant play of the full range of mental resources. For eighteenth-century writers, the notion necessarily involved pleasing expression, as in Pope's definition of true wit as "Nature to advantage dressed, / What oft was thought, but ne'er so well expressed" (*Essay on Criticism*, lines 297–98; see vol. C, p. 496–97). See also Johnson, *Lives of the Poets*, "Cowley," on "metaphysical wit" (see vol. C, p. 817). Romantic theory of the imagination deprived wit of its full range of apprehension, whence the word came to be restricted to its modern sense, as the clever play of mind that produces laughter.

zeugma (Greek "a yoking"): a **figure of thought**. A figure whereby one word applies to two or more words in a sentence, and in which the applications are surprising, either because one is unusual, or because the applications are made in very different ways; Pope, *Rape of the Lock* 3.7–8, in which the word "take" is used in two senses: "Here thou, great Anna! whom three realms obey, / Dost sometimes counsel take— and sometimes tea" (see vol. C, p. 515).

B: Publishing History, Censorship

By the time we read texts in published books, they have already been treated—that is, changed by authors, editors, and printers—in many ways. Although there are differences across history, in each period literary works are subject to pressures of many kinds, which apply before, while, and after an author writes. The pressures might be financial, as in the relations of author and patron; commercial, as in the marketing of books; and legal, as in, during some periods, the negotiation through official and unofficial censorship. In addition, texts in all periods undergo technological processes, as they move from the material forms in which an author produced them to the forms in which they are presented to readers. Some of the terms below designate important material forms in which books were produced, disseminated, and surveyed across the historical span of this anthology. Others designate the skills developed to understand these processes. The anthology's introductions to individual periods discuss the particular forms these phenomena took in different eras.

bookseller: In England, and particularly in London, commercial bookmaking and -selling enterprises came into being in the early fourteenth century. These were loose organizations of artisans who usually lived in the same neighborhoods (around St. Paul's Cathedral in London). A bookseller or dealer would coordinate the production of hand-copied books for wealthy patrons (see **patronage**), who would order books to be custom-made. After the introduction of **printing** in the late fifteenth century, authors generally sold the rights to their work to booksellers, without any further **royalties**. Booksellers, who often had their own shops, belonged to the **Stationers' Company**. This system lasted into the eighteenth century. In 1710, however, authors were for the first time granted **copyright**, which tipped the commercial balance in their favor, against booksellers.

censorship: The term applies to any mechanism for restricting what can be published. Historically, the reasons for imposing censorship are heresy, sedition, blasphemy, libel, or obscenity. External censorship is imposed by institutions having legislative sanctions at their disposal. Thus the pre-Reformation Church imposed the Constitutions of Archbishop Arundel of 1409, aimed at repressing the Lollard "heresy." After the Reformation, some key events in the history of censorship are as follows: 1547, when anti-Lollard legislation and legislation made by Henry VIII concerning treason by writing (1534) were abolished; the Licensing Order of 1643, which legislated that works be licensed, through the Stationers' Company, prior to publication; and 1695, when the last such Act stipulating prepublication licensing lapsed. Postpublication censorship continued in different periods for different reasons. Thus, for example, British publication of D. H. Lawrence's *Lady Chatterley's Lover* (1928) was obstructed (though unsuccessfully) in 1960, under the Obscene Publications Act of 1959. Censorship can also be international: although not published in Iran, Salman Rushdie's *Satanic Verses* (1988) was censored in that country, where the leader, Ayatollah Ruhollah Khomeini, proclaimed a fatwa (religious decree) promising the author's execution. Very often censorship is not imposed externally, however: authors or publishers can censor work in anticipation of what will incur the wrath of readers or the penalties of the law. Victorian and Edwardian publishers of **novels**, for example, urged authors to remove potentially offensive material, especially for serial publication in popular magazines.

codex: the physical format of most modern books and medieval manuscripts, consisting of a series of separate leaves gathered into quires and bound together, often with a cover. In late antiquity, the codex largely replaced the scroll, the standard form of written documents in Roman culture.

copy text: the particular text of a work used by a textual editor as the basis of an edition of that work.

copyright: the legal protection afforded to authors for control of their work's publication, in an attempt to ensure due financial reward. Some key dates in the history of copyright in the United Kingdom are as follows: 1710, when a statute gave authors the exclusive right to publish their work for fourteen years, and fourteen years more if the author were still alive when the first term had expired; 1842, when the period of authorial control was extended to forty-two years; and 1911, when the term was extended yet further, to fifty years after the author's death. In 1995 the period of protection was harmonized with the laws in other European countries to be the life of the author plus seventy years. In the United States no works first published before 1923 are in copyright. Works published since 1978 are, as in the United Kingdom, protected for the life of the author plus seventy years.

folio: the leaf formed by both sides of a single page. Each folio has two sides: a *recto* (the front side of the leaf, on the right side of a double-page spread in an open codex), and a *verso* (the back side of the leaf, on the left side of a double-page spread). Modern book pagination follows the pattern 1, 2, 3, 4, while medieval manuscript pagination follows the pattern 1r, 1v, 2r, 2v. "Folio" can also designate the size of a printed book. Books come in different shapes, depending originally on the number of times a standard sheet of paper is folded. One fold produces a large volume, a *folio* book; two folds produce a *quarto*, four an *octavo*, and six a very small *duodecimo*. Generally speaking, the larger the book, the grander and more expensive. Shakespeare's plays were, for example, first printed in quartos, but were gathered into a folio edition in 1623.

foul papers: versions of a work before an author has produced, if she or he has, a final copy (a "fair copy") with all corrections removed.

incunabulum (plural "incunabula"): any printed book produced in Europe before 1501. Famous incunabula include the Gutenberg Bible, printed in 1455.

manuscript (Latin, "written by hand"): Any text written physically by hand is a manuscript. Before the introduction of **printing** with moveable type in 1476, all texts in England were produced and reproduced by hand, in manuscript. This is an extremely labor-intensive task, using expensive materials (e.g., **vellum**, or **parchment**); the cost of books produced thereby was, accordingly, very high. Even after the introduction of printing, many texts continued to be produced in manuscript. This is obviously true of letters, for example, but until the eighteenth century, poetry written within aristocratic circles was often transmitted in manuscript copies.

paleography (Greek "ancient writing"): the art of deciphering, describing, and dating forms of handwriting.

parchment: animal skin, used as the material for handwritten books before the introduction of paper. See also **vellum**.

patronage, patron (Latin "protector"): Many technological, legal, and commercial supports were necessary before professional authorship became possible. Although some playwrights (e.g., Shakespeare) made a living by writing for the theater, other authors needed, principally, the large-scale reproductive capacities of **printing** and the security of **copyright** to make a living from writing. Before these conditions obtained, many authors had another main occupation, and most authors had to rely on patronage. In different periods, institutions or individuals offered material support, or patronage, to authors. Thus in Anglo-Saxon England, monasteries afforded the conditions of writing to monastic authors. Between the twelfth and the seventeenth centuries, the main source of patronage was the royal court. Authors offered patrons prestige and ideological support in return for financial support. Even as the conditions of professional authorship came into being at the beginning of the eighteenth century, older forms of direct patronage were not altogether displaced until the middle of the century.

periodical: Whereas journalism, strictly, applies to daily writing (from French *jour*, "day"), periodical writing appears at larger, but still frequent, intervals, characteristically in the form of the **essay**. Periodicals were developed especially in the eighteenth century.

printing: Printing, or the mechanical reproduction of books using moveable type, was invented in Germany in the mid-fifteenth century by Johannes Gutenberg; it quickly spread throughout Europe. William Caxton brought printing into England from the Low Countries in 1476. Much greater powers of reproduction at much lower prices transformed every aspect of literary culture.

publisher: the person or company responsible for the commissioning and publicizing of printed matter. In the early period of **printing**, publisher, printer, and bookseller were often the same person. This trend continued in the ascendancy of the **Stationers' Company**, between the middle of the sixteenth and the end of the seventeenth centuries. Toward the end of the seventeenth century, these three functions began to separate, leading to their modern distinctions.

quire: When medieval manuscripts were assembled, a few loose sheets of parchment or paper would first be folded together and sewn along the fold. This formed a quire (also known as a "gathering" or "signature"). Folded in this way, four large sheets of parchment would produce eight smaller manuscript leaves. Multiple quires could then be bound together to form a codex.

royalties: an agreed-upon proportion of the price of each copy of a work sold, paid by the publisher to the author, or an agreed-upon fee paid to the playwright for each performance of a play.

scribe: In **manuscript** culture, the scribe is the copyist who reproduces a text by hand.

scriptorium (plural "scriptoria"): a place for producing written documents and manuscripts.

serial publication: generally referring to the practice, especially common in the nineteenth century, of publishing novels a few chapters at a time, in periodicals.

Stationers' Company: The Stationers' Company was an English guild incorporating various tradesmen, including printers, publishers, and booksellers, skilled in the production and selling of books. It was formed in 1403, received its royal charter in 1557, and served as a means both of producing and of regulating books. Authors would sell the manuscripts of their books to individual stationers, who incurred the risks and took the profits of producing and selling the books. The stationers entered their rights over given books in the Stationers' Register. They also regulated the book trade and held their monopoly by licensing books and by being empowered to seize unauthorized books and imprison resisters. This system of licensing broke down in the social unrest of the Civil War and Interregnum (1640–60), and it ended in 1695. Even after the end of licensing, the Stationers' Company continued to be an intrinsic part of the **copyright** process, since the 1710 copyright statute directed that copyright had to be registered at Stationers' Hall.

subscription: An eighteenth-century system of bookselling somewhere between direct **patronage** and impersonal sales. A subscriber paid half the cost of a book before publication and half on delivery. The author received these payments directly. The subscriber's name appeared in the prefatory pages.

textual criticism: Works in all periods often exist in many subtly or not so subtly different forms. This is especially true with regard to manuscript textual reproduction, but it also applies to printed texts. Textual criticism is the art, developed from the fifteenth century in Italy but raised to new levels of sophistication from the eighteenth century, of deciphering different historical states of texts. This art involves the analysis of textual **variants,** often with the aim of distinguishing authorial from scribal forms.

variants: differences that appear among different manuscripts or printed editions of the same text.

vellum: animal skin, used as the material for handwritten books before the introduction of paper. See also **parchment.**

watermark: the trademark of a paper manufacturer, impressed into the paper but largely invisible unless held up to light.

Geographic Nomenclature

The British Isles refers to the prominent group of islands off the northwest coast of Europe, especially to the two largest, **Great Britain** and **Ireland**. At present these comprise two sovereign states: **the Republic of Ireland**, and **the United Kingdom of Great Britain and Northern Ireland**—known for short as the **United Kingdom** or the **U.K.** Most of the smaller islands are part of the **U.K.** but a few, like the **Isle of Man** and the tiny **Channel Islands**, are largely independent. The **U.K.** is often loosely referred to as "Britain" or "Great Britain" and is sometimes called simply, if inaccurately, "England." For obvious reasons, the latter usage is rarely heard among the inhabitants of the other countries of the U.K.—**Scotland, Wales,** and **Northern Ireland** (sometimes called **Ulster**). England is by far the most populous part of the kingdom, as well as the seat of its capital, London.

From the first to the fifth century C.E. most of what is now **England** and **Wales** was a province of the Roman Empire called **Britain** (in Latin, **Britannia**). After the fall of Rome, much of the island was invaded and settled by peoples from northern Germany and Denmark speaking what we now call Old English. These peoples are collectively known as the Anglo-Saxons, and the word **England** is related to the first element of their name. By the time of the Norman Conquest (1066) most of the kingdoms founded by the Anglo-Saxons and subsequent Viking invaders had coalesced into the kingdom of **England**, which, in the latter Middle Ages, conquered and largely absorbed the neighboring Celtic kingdom of **Wales**. In 1603 James VI of **Scotland** inherited the island's other throne as James I of **England**, and for the next hundred years—except for the two decades of Puritan rule—**Scotland** (both its English-speaking **Lowlands** and its Gaelic-speaking **Highlands**) and **England** (with **Wales**) were two kingdoms under a single king. In 1707 the Act of Union welded them together as **the United Kingdom of Great Britain. Ireland,** where English rule had begun in the twelfth century and been tightened in the sixteenth, was incorporated by the 1800–1801 Act of Union into **the United Kingdom of Great Britain and Ireland**. With the division of Ireland and the establishment of **the Irish Free State** after World War I, this name was modified to its present form, and in 1949 **the Irish Free State** became **the Republic of Ireland,** or **Éire.** In 1999 **Scotland** elected a separate parliament it had relinquished in 1707, and **Wales** elected an assembly it lost in 1409; neither Scotland nor Wales ceased to be part of the **United Kingdom.**

The **British Isles** are further divided into counties, which in **Great Britain** are also known as shires. This word, with its vowel shortened in pronunciation, forms the suffix in the names of many counties, such as **Yorkshire, Wiltshire, Somersetshire.**

The Latin names **Britannia** (Britain), **Caledonia** (Scotland), and **Hibernia** (Ireland) are sometimes used in poetic diction; so too is **Britain's** ancient Celtic name, **Albion.** Because of its accidental resemblance to *albus* (Latin for "white"), **Albion** is especially associated with the chalk cliffs that seem to gird much of the English coast like defensive walls.

The **British Empire** took its name from **the British Isles** because it was created not only by the **English** but also by the **Irish, Scots,** and **Welsh,** as well as by civilians and servicemen from other constituent countries of the empire. Some of the empire's **overseas colonies,** or **crown colonies,** were populated largely by settlers of European origin and their descendants. These predominantly white **settler colonies,** such as **Canada, Australia,** and **New Zealand,** were allowed significant self-government in the nineteenth century and recognized as **dominions** in the early twentieth century. The white dominions became members of the Commonwealth of Nations, also called the Commonwealth, the British Commonwealth, and "the Old Commonwealth" at different times, an association of sovereign states under the symbolic leadership of the British monarch.

Other overseas colonies of the empire had mostly indigenous populations (or, in the Caribbean, the descendants of imported slaves, indentured servants, and others). These colonies were granted political independence after World War II, later than the dominions, and have often been referred to since as postcolonial nations. In South and Southeast Asia, India and Pakistan gained independence in 1947, followed by other countries including Sri Lanka (formerly Ceylon), Burma (now Myanmar), Malaya (now Malaysia), and Singapore. In West and East Africa, the Gold Coast was decolonized as Ghana in 1957, Nigeria in 1960, Sierra Leone in 1961, Uganda in 1962, Kenya in 1963, and so forth, while in southern Africa, the white minority government of South Africa was already independent in 1931, though majority rule did not come until 1994. In the Caribbean, Jamaica and Trinidad and Tobago won independence in 1962, followed by Barbados in 1966, and other islands of the British West Indies in the 1970s and '80s. Other regions with nations emerging out of British colonial rule included Central America (British Honduras, now Belize), South America (British Guiana, now Guyana), the Pacific islands (Fiji), and Europe (Cyprus, Malta). After decolonization, many of these nations chose to remain within a newly conceived Commonwealth and are sometimes referred to as "New Commonwealth" countries. Some nations, such as Ireland, Pakistan, and South Africa, withdrew from the Commonwealth, though South Africa and Pakistan eventually rejoined, and others, such as Burma (now Myanmar), gained independence outside the Commonwealth. Britain's last major overseas colony, Hong Kong, was returned to Chinese sovereignty in 1997, but while Britain retains only a handful of dependent territories, such as Bermuda and Montserrat, the scope of the Commonwealth remains vast, with 30 percent of the world's population.

British Money

One of the most dramatic changes to the system of British money came in 1971. In the system previously in place, the pound consisted of 20 shillings, each containing 12 pence, making 240 pence to the pound. Since 1971, British money has been calculated on the decimal system, with 100 pence to the pound. Britons' experience of paper money did not change very drastically: as before, 5- and 10-pound notes constitute the majority of bills passing through their hands (in addition, 20- and 50- pound notes have been added). But the shift necessitated a whole new way of thinking about and exchanging coins and marked the demise of the shilling, one of the fundamental units of British monetary history. Many other coins, still frequently encountered in literature, had already passed. These include the groat, worth 4 pence (the word "groat" is often used to signify a trifling sum); the angel (which depicted the archangel Michael triumphing over a dragon), valued at 10 shillings; the mark, worth in its day two-thirds of a pound or 13 shillings 4 pence; and the sovereign, a gold coin initially worth 22 shillings 6 pence, later valued at 1 pound, last circulated in 1932. One prominent older coin, the guinea, was worth a pound and a shilling; though it has not been minted since 1813, a very few quality items or prestige awards (like the purse in a horse race) may still be quoted in guineas. (The table below includes some other well-known, obsolete coins.) Colloquially, a pound was (and is) called a quid; a shilling a bob; sixpence, a tanner; a copper could refer to a penny, a half-penny, or a farthing (¼ penny).

Old Currency	New Currency
1 pound note	1 pound coin (or note in Scotland)
10 shilling (half-pound note)	50 pence
5 shilling (crown)	
2½ shilling (half crown)	20 pence
2 shilling (florin)	10 pence
1 shilling	5 pence
6 pence	
2½ pence	1 penny
2 pence	
1 penny	
½ penny	
¼ penny (farthing)	

Throughout its tenure as a member of the European Union, Britain contemplated but did not make the change to the EU's common currency, the Euro. Many Britons strongly identify their country with its rich commercial history and tend to view their currency patriotically as a national symbol. Now, with the planned withdrawal of the United Kingdom from the EU, the pound seems here to stay.

Even more challenging than sorting out the values of obsolete coins is calculating for any given period the purchasing power of money, which fluctuates over time by its very nature. At the beginning of the twentieth century, 1 pound was worth about 5 American dollars, though those bought three to four times what they now do. Now, the pound buys anywhere from $1.20 to $1.50. As difficult as it is to generalize, it is clear that money used to be worth much more than it is currently. In Anglo-Saxon times, the most valuable circulating coin was the silver penny: four would buy a sheep. Beyond long-term inflationary trends, prices varied from times of plenty to those marked by poor harvests; from peacetime to wartime; from the country to the metropolis (life in London has always been very expensive); and wages varied according to the availability of labor (wages would sharply rise, for instance, during the devastating Black Death in the fourteenth century). The following chart provides a glimpse of some actual prices of given periods and their changes across time, though all the variables mentioned above prevent them from being definitive. Even from one year to the next, an added tax on gin or tea could drastically raise prices, and a lottery ticket could cost much more the night before the drawing than just a month earlier. Still, the prices quoted below do indicate important trends, such as the disparity of incomes in British society and the costs of basic commodities. In the chart on the following page, the symbol £ is used for pound, s. for shilling, d. for a penny (from Latin *denarius*); a sum would normally be written £2.19.3, i.e., 2 pounds, 19 shillings, 3 pence. (This is Leopold Bloom's budget for the day depicted in Joyce's novel *Ulysses* [1922]; in the new currency, it would be about £2.96.)

circa	1390	1590	1650	1750	1815	1875	1950
food and drink	gallon (8 pints) of ale, 1.5d.	tankard of beer, .5d.	coffee, 1d. a dish	"drunk for a penny, dead drunk for two-pence" (gin shop sign in Hogarth print)	ounce of laudanum, 3d.	pint of beer, 3d.	pint of Guinness stout, 11d.
	gallon (8 pints) of wine, 3 to 4d.	pound of beef, 2s. 5d.	chicken, 1s. 4d.	dinner at a steakhouse, 1s.	ham and potato dinner for two, 7s.	dinner in a good hotel, 5s.	pound of beef, 2s. 2d.
	pound of cinnamon, 1 to 3s.	pound of cinnamon, 10s. 6d.	pound of tea, £3 10s.	pound of tea, 16s.	bottle of French claret, 12s.	pound of tea, 2s.	dinner on railway car, 7s. 6d.
entertainment	no cost to watch a cycle play	admission to public theater, 1 to 3d.	falcon, £11 5s.	theater tickets, 1 to 5s.	admission to Covent Garden theater, 1 to 7s.	theater tickets, 6d. to 7s.	admission to Old Vic theater, 1s. 6d. to 10s. 6d.
	contributory admission to professional troupe theater	cheap seat in private theater, 6d.	billiard table, £25	admission to Vauxhall Gardens, 1s.	annual subscription to Almack's (exclusive club), 10 guineas	admission to Madam Tussaud's waxworks, 1s.	admission to Odeon cinema, Manchester, 1s 3d.
	maintenance for royal hounds at Windsor, .75d. a day	"to see a dead Indian" (quoted in *The Tempest*), 1.25d. (ten "doits")	three-quarter length portrait painting, £31	lottery ticket, £20 (shares were sold)	Jane Austen's piano, 30 guineas	annual fees at a gentleman's club, 7 to 10 guineas	tropical fish tank, £4 4s.

circa	1390	1590	1650	1750	1815	1875	1950
reading	cheap romance, 1s.	play quarto, 6d.	pamphlet, 1 to 6d.	issue of The Gentleman's Magazine, 6d.	issue of Edinburgh Review, 6s.	copy of the Times, 3d.	copy of the Times, 3d.
	a Latin Bible, 2 to £4	Shakespeare's First Folio (1623), £1	student Bible, 6s.	cheap edition of Milton, 2s.	membership in circulating library (3rd class), £1 4s. a year	illustrated edition of Through the Looking-glass, 6s.	issue of Eagle comics, 4.5d.
	payment for illuminating a liturgical book, £22 9s.	Foxe's Acts and Monuments, 24s.	Hobbes's Leviathan, 8s.	Johnson's Dictionary, folio, 2 vols., £4 10s.	1st edition of Austen's Pride and Prejudice, 18s.	1st edition of Trollope's The Way We Live Now, 2 vols., £1 1s.	Orwell's Nineteen Eighty Four, paperback, 3s. 6d.
transportation	night's supply of hay for horse, 2d.	wherry (whole boat) across Thames, 1d.	day's journey, coach, 10s.	boat across Thames, 4d.	coach ride, outside, 2 to 3d. a mile; inside, 4 to 5d. a mile	15-minute journey in a London cab, 1s. 6d.	London tube fare, about 2d. a mile
	coach, £8	hiring a horse for a day, 12d.	coach horse, £30	coach fare, London to Edinburgh, 10s.	palanquin transport in Madras, 5s. a day	railway, 3rd class, London to Plymouth, 18s. 8d. (about 1d. a mile)	petrol, 3s. a gallon
	quality horse, £10	hiring a coach for a day, 10s.	fancy carriage, £170	transport to America, £5	passage, Liverpool to New York, £10	passage to India, 1st class, £50	midsize Austin sedan, £449 plus £188 4s. 2d. tax
clothes	clothing allowance for peasant, 3s. a year	shoes with buckles, 8d.	footman's frieze coat, 15s.	working woman's gown, 6s. 6d.	checked muslin, 7s. per yard	flannel for a cheap petticoat, 1s. 3d. a yard	woman's sun frock, £3 13s. 10d.

shoes for gentry wearer, 4d.	woman's gloves, £1 5s.	falconer's hat, 10s.	gentleman's suit, £8	hiring a dressmaker for a pelisse, 8s.	overcoat for an Eton schoolboy, £1 1s.	tweed sports jacket, £3 16s. 6d.
hat for gentry wearer, 10d.	fine cloak, £16	black cloth for mourning household of an earl, £100	very fine wig, £30	ladies silk stockings, 12s.	set of false teeth, £2 10s.	"Teddy boy" drape suit, £20
hiring a skilled building worker, 4d. a day	actor's daily wage during playing season, 1s.	agricultural laborer, 6s. 5d. a week	price of boy slave, £32	lowest-paid sailor on Royal Navy ship, 10s. 9d. a month	seasonal agricultural laborer, 14s. a week	minimum wage, agricultural laborer, £4 14s. per 47-hour week
wage for professional scribe, £2 3s. 4d. a year + cloak	household servant 2 to £5 a year + food, clothing	tutor to nobleman's children, £30 a year	housemaid's wage, £6 to £8 a year	contributor to Quarterly Review, 10 guineas per sheet	housemaid's wage, £10 to £25 a year	shorthand typist, £367 a year
minimum income to be called gentleman, £10 a year; for knighthood, 40 to £400	minimum income for eligibility for knighthood, £30 a year	Milton's salary as Secretary of Foreign Tongues, £288 a year	Boswell's allowance, £200 a year	minimum income for a "genteel" family, £100 a year	income of the "comfortable" classes, £800 and up a year	middle manager's salary, £1,480 a year
income from land of richest magnates, £3,500 a year	income from land of average earl, £4,000 a year	Earl of Bedford's income, £8,000 a year	Duke of Newcastle's income, £40,000 a year	Mr. Darcy's income, *Pride and Prejudice*, £10,000	Trollope's income, £4,000 a year	barrister's salary, £2,032 a year

labor/incomes

The British Baronage

The English monarchy is in principle hereditary, though at times during the Middle Ages the rules were subject to dispute. In general, authority passes from father to eldest surviving son, to daughters in order of seniority if there is no son, to a brother if there are no children, and in default of direct descendants to collateral lines (cousins, nephews, nieces) in order of closeness. There have been breaks in the order of succession (1066, 1399, 1688), but so far as possible the usurpers have always sought to paper over the break with a legitimate, i.e., hereditary, claim. When a queen succeeds to the throne and takes a husband, he does not become king unless he is in the line of blood succession; rather, he is named prince consort, as Albert was to Victoria. He may father kings, but is not one himself.

The original Saxon nobles were the king's thanes, ealdormen, or earls, who provided the king with military service and counsel in return for booty, gifts, or landed estates. William the Conqueror, arriving from France, where feudalism was fully developed, considerably expanded this group. In addition, as the king distributed the lands of his new kingdom, he also distributed dignities to men who became known collectively as "the baronage." "Baron" in its root meaning signifies simply "man," and barons were the king's men. As the title was common, a distinction was early made between greater and lesser barons, the former gradually assuming loftier and more impressive titles. The first English "duke" was created in 1337; the title of "marquess," or "marquis" (pronounced "markwis"), followed in 1385, and "viscount" ("vyekount") in 1440. Though "earl" is the oldest title of all, an earl now comes between a marquess and a viscount in order of dignity and precedence, and the old term "baron" now designates a rank just below viscount. "Baronets" were created in 1611 as a means of raising revenue for the crown (the title could be purchased for about £1,000); they are marginal nobility and have never sat in the House of Lords.

Kings and queens are addressed as "Your Majesty," princes and princesses as "Your Highness," the other hereditary nobility as "My Lord" or "Your Lordship." Peers receive their titles either by inheritance (like Lord Byron, the sixth baron of that line) or from the monarch (like Alfred, Lord Tennyson, created 1st Baron Tennyson by Victoria). The children, even of a duke, are commoners unless they are specifically granted some other title or inherit their father's title from him. A peerage can be forfeited by act of attainder, as for example when a lord is convicted of treason; and, when forfeited, or lapsed for lack of a successor, can be bestowed on another family. Thus in 1605 Robert Cecil was made first earl of Salisbury in the third creation, the first creation dating from 1149, the second from 1337, the title having been in abeyance since 1539. Titles descend by right of succession and do not depend on tenure of land; thus, a title does not always indicate where a lord dwells or holds power. Indeed, noble titles do not always refer to a real place at all. At Prince Edward's marriage in 1999, the queen created him earl of Wessex, although the old kingdom of Wessex has had no political existence since the Anglo-Saxon period, and the name was all but forgotten until it was resurrected by Thomas Hardy as the setting of his novels. (This is perhaps but one of many ways in which the world of the aristocracy increasingly resembles the realm of literature.)

The king and queen	(These are all of the royal line.)
Prince and princess	
Duke and duchess	(These may or may not be of the royal
Marquess and marchioness	line, but are ordinarily remote from the
Earl and countess	succession.)
Viscount and viscountess	
Baron and baroness	
Baronet and lady	

Scottish peers sat in the parliament of Scotland, as English peers did in the parliament of England, till at the Act of Union (1707) Scottish peers were granted sixteen seats in the English House of Lords, to be filled by election. (In 1963, all Scottish lords were allowed to sit.) Similarly, Irish peers, when the Irish parliament was abolished in 1801, were granted the right to elect twenty-eight of their number to the House of Lords in Westminster. (Now that the Republic of Ireland is a separate nation, this no longer applies.) Women members (peeresses) were first allowed to sit in the House as nonhereditary Life Peers in 1958 (when that status was created for members of both genders); women first sat by their own hereditary right in 1963. Today the House of Lords still retains some power to influence or delay legislation, but its future is uncertain. In 1999, the hereditary peers (then amounting to 750) were reduced to 92 temporary members elected by their fellow peers. Holders of Life Peerages remain, as do senior bishops of the Church of England and high-court judges (the "Law Lords").

Below the peerage the chief title of honor is "knight." Knighthood, which is not hereditary, is generally a reward for services rendered. A knight (Sir John Black) is addressed, using his first name, as "Sir John"; his wife, using the last name, is "Lady Black"—unless she is the daughter of an earl or nobleman of higher rank, in which case she will be "Lady Arabella." The female equivalent of a knight bears the title of "Dame." Though the word *knight* itself comes from the Anglo-Saxon *cniht*, there is some doubt as to whether knighthood amounted to much before the arrival of the Normans. The feudal system required military service as a condition of land tenure, and a man who came to serve his king at the head of an army of tenants required a title of authority and badges of identity—hence the title of knighthood and the coat of arms. During the Crusades, when men were far removed from their land (or even sold it in order to go on crusade), more elaborate forms of fealty sprang up that soon expanded into orders of knighthood. The Templars, Hospitallers, Knights of the Teutonic Order, Knights of Malta, and Knights of the Golden Fleece were but a few of these companionships; not all of them were available at all times in England.

Gradually, with the rise of centralized government and the decline of feudal tenures, military knighthood became obsolete, and the rank largely honorific; sometimes, as under James I, it degenerated into a scheme of the royal government for making money. For hundreds of years after its establishment in the fourteenth century, the Order of the Garter was the only English order of knighthood, an exclusive courtly companionship. Then, during the late seventeenth, the eighteenth, and the nineteenth centuries, a number of additional orders were created, with names such as the Thistle, Saint Patrick, the Bath, Saint Michael, and Saint George, plus a number of special Victorian and Indian orders. They retain the terminology, ceremony, and dignity of knighthood, but the military implications are vestigial.

Although the British Empire now belongs to history, appointments to the Order of the British Empire continue to be conferred for services to that empire at home or abroad. Such honors (commonly referred to as "gongs") are granted by the monarch in her New Year's and Birthday lists, but the decisions are now made by the government in power. In recent years there have been efforts to popularize and democratize the dispensation of honors, with recipients including rock stars and actors. But this does not prevent large sectors of British society from regarding both knighthood and the peerage as largely irrelevant to modern life.

The Royal Lines of England and Great Britain

England

SAXONS AND DANES

Egbert, king of Wessex	802–839
Ethelwulf, son of Egbert	839–858
Ethelbald, second son of Ethelwulf	858–860
Ethelbert, third son of Ethelwulf	860–866
Ethelred I, fourth son of Ethelwulf	866–871
Alfred the Great, fifth son of Ethelwulf	871–899
Edward the Elder, son of Alfred	899–924
Athelstan the Glorious, son of Edward	924–940
Edmund I, third son of Edward	940–946
Edred, fourth son of Edward	946–955
Edwy the Fair, son of Edmund	955–959
Edgar the Peaceful, second son of Edmund	959–975
Edward the Martyr, son of Edgar	975–978 (murdered)
Ethelred II, the Unready, second son of Edgar	978–1016
Edmund II, Ironside, son of Ethelred II	1016–1016
Canute the Dane	1016–1035
Harold I, Harefoot, natural son of Canute	1035–1040
Hardecanute, son of Canute	1040–1042
Edward the Confessor, son of Ethelred II	1042–1066
Harold II, brother-in-law of Edward	1066–1066 (died in battle)

HOUSE OF NORMANDY

William I, the Conqueror	1066–1087
William II, Rufus, third son of William I	1087–1100 (shot from ambush)
Henry I, Beauclerc, youngest son of William I	1100–1135

HOUSE OF BLOIS

Stephen, son of Adela, daughter of William I	1135–1154

HOUSE OF PLANTAGENET

Henry II, son of Geoffrey Plantagenet by Matilda, daughter of Henry I	1154–1189
Richard I, Coeur de Lion, son of Henry II	1189–1199
John Lackland, son of Henry II	1199–1216
Henry III, son of John	1216–1272
Edward I, Longshanks, son of Henry III	1272–1307
Edward II, son of Edward I	1307–1327 (deposed)
Edward III of Windsor, son of Edward II	1327–1377
Richard II, grandson of Edward III	1377–1399 (deposed)

HOUSE OF LANCASTER

Henry IV, son of John of Gaunt, son of Edward III	1399–1413
Henry V, Prince Hal, son of Henry IV	1413–1422
Henry VI, son of Henry V	1422–1461 (deposed), 1470–1471 (deposed)

HOUSE OF YORK

Edward IV, great-great-grandson of Edward III	1461–1470 (deposed), 1471–1483
Edward V, son of Edward IV	1483–1483 (murdered)
Richard III, Crookback	1483–1485 (died in battle)

HOUSE OF TUDOR

Henry VII, married daughter of Edward IV	1485–1509
Henry VIII, son of Henry VII	1509–1547
Edward VI, son of Henry VIII	1547–1553
Mary I, "Bloody," daughter of Henry VIII	1553–1558
Elizabeth I, daughter of Henry VIII	1558–1603

HOUSE OF STUART

James I (James VI of Scotland)	1603–1625
Charles I, son of James I	1625–1649 (executed)

COMMONWEALTH & PROTECTORATE

Council of State	1649–1653
Oliver Cromwell, Lord Protector	1653–1658
Richard Cromwell, son of Oliver	1658–1660 (resigned)

HOUSE OF STUART (RESTORED)

Charles II, son of Charles I   1660–1685

James II, second son of Charles I   1685–1688

(INTERREGNUM, 11 DECEMBER 1688 TO 13 FEBRUARY 1689)

HOUSE OF ORANGE-NASSAU

William III of Orange, by
    Mary, daughter of Charles I   1689–1701
    and Mary II, daughter of James II   –1694

Anne, second daughter of James II   1702–1714

Great Britain

HOUSE OF HANOVER

George I, son of Elector of Hanover and
    Sophia, granddaughter of James I   1714–1727

George II, son of George I   1727–1760

George III, grandson of George II   1760–1820

George IV, son of George III   1820–1830

William IV, third son of George III   1830–1837

Victoria, daughter of Edward, fourth son
    of George III   1837–1901

HOUSE OF SAXE-COBURG AND GOTHA

Edward VII, son of Victoria   1901–1910

HOUSE OF WINDSOR (NAME ADOPTED 17 JULY 1917)

George V, second son of Edward VII   1910–1936

Edward VIII, eldest son of George V   1936–1936 (abdicated)

George VI, second son of George V   1936–1952

Elizabeth II, daughter of George VI   1952–

Religions in Great Britain

In the late sixth century C.E., missionaries from Rome introduced Christianity to the Anglo-Saxons—actually, reintroduced it, since it had briefly flourished in the southern parts of the British Isles during the Roman occupation, and even after the Roman withdrawal had persisted in the Celtic regions of Scotland and Wales. By the time the earliest poems included in *The Norton Anthology of English Literature* were composed (i.e., the seventh century), therefore, there had been a Christian presence in the British Isles for hundreds of years. The conversion of the Germanic occupiers of England can, however, be dated only from 597. Our knowledge of the religion of pre-Christian Britain is sketchy, but it is likely that vestiges of Germanic polytheism assimilated into, or coexisted with, the practice of Christianity: fertility rites were incorporated into the celebration of Easter resurrection, rituals commemorating the dead into All-Hallows Eve and All Saints Day, and elements of winter solstice festivals into the celebration of Christmas. The most durable polytheistic remains are our days of the week, each of which except "Saturday" derives from the name of a Germanic pagan god, and the word "Easter," deriving, according to the Anglo-Saxon scholar Bede (d. 735), from the name of a Germanic pagan goddess, Eostre. In English literature such "folkloric" elements sometimes elicit romantic nostalgia. Geoffrey Chaucer's "Wife of Bath" looks back to a magical time before the arrival of Christianity in which the land was "fulfilled of fairye." Hundreds of years later, the seventeenth-century writer Robert Herrick honors the amalgamation of Christian and pagan elements in agrarian British culture in such poems as "Corinna's Gone A-Maying" and "The Hock Cart."

Medieval Christianity was fairly uniform, if complex, across Western Europe—hence called "catholic," or universally shared. The Church was composed of the so-called "regular" and "secular" orders, the regular orders being those who followed a rule in a community under an abbot or an abbess (i.e., monks, nuns, friars and canons), while the secular clergy of priests served parish communities under the governance of a bishop. In the unstable period from the sixth until the twelfth century, monasteries were the intellectual powerhouse of the Church. From the beginning of the thirteenth century, with the development of an urban Christian spirituality in Europe, friars dominated the recently invented institution of universities, as well as devoting themselves, in theory at least, to the urban poor.

The Catholic Church was also an international power structure. With its hierarchy of pope, cardinals, archbishops, and bishops, it offered a model of the centralized, bureaucratic state from the late eleventh century. That ecclesiastical power structure coexisted alongside a separate, often less centralized and feudal structure of lay authorities, with theoretically different and often competing spheres of social responsibilities. The sharing of lay and ecclesiastical authority in medieval England was sometimes a source of conflict. Chaucer's pilgrims are on their way to visit the memorial shrine to one victim of such exemplary struggle: Thomas à Becket, Archbishop of Canterbury, who opposed the policies of King Henry II, was assassinated by indirect suggestion of the king in 1170, and later made a saint. The Church, in turn, produced its own victims: Jews were subject to persecution in the late twelfth century in England, before being expelled in 1290. From the beginning of the fifteenth century, the English Church targeted Lollard heretics (see below) with capital punishment, for the first time.

As an international organization, the Church conducted its business in the universal language of Latin. Thus although in the period the largest segment of literate persons was made up of clerics, the clerical contribution to great literary writing in vernacular languages (e.g., French and English) was, so far as we know, relatively modest, with some great exceptions in the later Middle Ages (e.g., William Langland). Lay, vernacular writers of the period certainly reflect the importance of the Church as an institution and the pervasiveness of religion in the rituals that marked everyday life, as well as contesting institutional authority. From the late fourteenth century, indeed, England witnessed an active and articulate, proto-Protestant movement known as Lollardy, which attacked clerical hierarchy and promoted vernacular scriptures.

Beginning in 1517 the German monk Martin Luther, in Wittenberg, Germany, openly challenged many aspects of Catholic practice and by 1520 had completely repudiated the authority of the pope, setting in train the Protestant Reformation. Luther argued that the Roman Catholic Church had strayed far from the pattern of Christianity laid out in scripture. He rejected Catholic doctrines for which no biblical authority was to be found, such as the belief in Purgatory, and translated the Bible into German, on the grounds that the importance of scripture for all Christians made its translation into the vernacular tongue essential. Luther was not the first to advance such views— Lollard followers of the Englishman John Wycliffe had translated the Bible in the late fourteenth century. But Luther, protected by powerful German rulers, was able to speak out with impunity and convert others to his views, rather than suffer the persecution usually meted out to heretics. Soon other reformers were following in Luther's footsteps: of these, the Swiss Ulrich Zwingli and the French Jean Calvin would be especially influential for English religious thought.

At first England remained staunchly Catholic. Its king, Henry VIII, was so severe to heretics that the pope awarded him the title "Defender of the Faith," which British monarchs have retained to this day. In 1534, however, Henry rejected the authority of the pope to prevent his divorce from his queen, Catherine of Aragon, and his marriage to his mistress, Ann Boleyn. In doing so, Henry appropriated to himself ecclesiastical as well as secular authority. Thomas More, author of *Utopia*, was executed in 1535 for refusing to endorse Henry's right to govern the English church. Over the following six years, Henry consolidated his grip on the ecclesiastical establishment by dissolving the powerful, populous Catholic monasteries and redistributing their massive landholdings to his own lay followers. Yet Henry's church largely retained Catholic doctrine and liturgy. When Henry died and his young son, Edward, came to the throne in 1547, the English church embarked on a more Protestant path, a direction abruptly reversed when Edward died and his older sister Mary, the daughter of Catherine of Aragon, took the throne in 1553 and attempted to reintroduce Roman Catholicism. Mary's reign was also short, however, and her successor, Elizabeth I, the daughter of Ann Boleyn, was a Protestant. Elizabeth attempted to establish a "middle way" Christianity, compromising between Roman Catholic practices and beliefs and reformed ones.

The Church of England, though it laid claim to a national rather than pan-European authority, aspired like its predecessor to be the universal church of all English subjects. It retained the Catholic structure of parishes and dioceses and the Catholic hierarchy of bishops, though the ecclesiastical authority was now the Archbishop of Canterbury and the Church's "Supreme Governor" was the monarch. Yet disagreement and controversy persisted. Some members of the Church of England wanted to retain many of the ritual and liturgical elements of Catholicism. Others, the Puritans, advocated a more thoroughgoing reformation. Most Puritans remained within the Church of England, but a minority, the "Separatists" or "Congregationalists," split from the established church altogether. These dissenters no longer thought of the ideal church as an organization to which everybody belonged; instead, they conceived it as a more exclusive group of likeminded people, one not necessarily attached to a larger body of believers.

In the seventeenth century, the succession of the Scottish king James to the English throne produced another problem. England and Scotland were separate nations, and in the sixteenth century Scotland had developed its own national Presbyterian church, or "kirk," under the leadership of the reformer John Knox. The kirk retained fewer Catholic liturgical elements than did the Church of England, and its authorities, or "presbyters," were elected by assemblies of their fellow clerics, rather than appointed by the king. James I and his son Charles I, especially the latter, wanted to bring the Scottish kirk into conformity with Church of England practices. The Scots violently resisted these efforts, with the collaboration of many English Puritans, in a conflict that eventually developed into the English Civil War in the mid-seventeenth century. The effect of these disputes is visible in the poetry of such writers as John Milton, Robert Herrick, Henry Vaughan, and Thomas Traherne, and in the prose of Thomas Browne, Lucy Hutchinson, and Dorothy Waugh. Just as in the mid-sixteenth century, when a succession of monarchs with different religious commitments destabilized the church, so the seventeenth century endured spiritual whiplash. King Charles I's highly ritualistic Church of England was violently overturned by the Puritan victors in the Civil War—until 1660, after the death of the Puritan leader, Oliver Cromwell, when the Church of England was restored along with the monarchy.

The religious and political upheavals of the seventeenth century produced Christian sects that de-emphasized the ceremony of the established church and rejected as well its top-down authority structure. Some of these groups were ephemeral, but the Baptists (founded in 1608 in Amsterdam by the English expatriate John Smyth) and Quakers, or Society of Friends (founded by George Fox in the 1640s), flourished outside the established church, sometimes despite cruel persecution. John Bunyan, a Baptist, wrote the Christian allegory *Pilgrim's Progress* while in prison. Some dissenters, like the Baptists, shared the reformed reverence for the absolute authority of scripture but interpreted the scriptural texts differently from their fellow Protestants. Others, like the Quakers, favored, even over the authority of the Bible, the "inner light" or voice of individual conscience, which they took to be the working of the Holy Spirit in the lives of individuals.

The Protestant dissenters were not England's only religious minorities. Despite crushing fines and the threat of imprisonment, a minority of Catholics under Elizabeth and James openly refused to give their allegiance to the new church, and others remained secret adherents to the old ways. John Donne was brought up in an ardently Catholic family, and several other writers converted to Catholicism as adults—Ben Jonson for a considerable part of his career, Elizabeth Carey and Richard Crashaw permanently, and at profound personal cost. In the eighteenth century, Catholics remained objects of suspicion as possible agents of sedition, especially after the "Glorious Revolution" in 1688 deposed the Catholic James II in favor of the Protestant William and Mary. Anti-Catholic prejudice affected John Dryden, a Catholic convert, as well as the lifelong Catholic Alexander Pope. By contrast, the English colony of Ireland remained overwhelmingly Roman Catholic, the fervor of its religious commitment at least partly inspired by resistance to English occupation. Starting in the reign of Elizabeth, England shored up its own authority in Ireland by encouraging Protestant immigrants from Scotland to settle in the north of Ireland, producing a virulent religious divide the effects of which are still playing out today.

A small community of Jews had moved from France to London after 1066, when the Norman William the Conqueror came to the English throne. Although despised and persecuted by many Christians, they were allowed to remain as moneylenders to the Crown, until the thirteenth century, when the king developed alternative sources of credit. At this point, in 1290, the Jews were expelled from England. In 1655 Oliver Cromwell permitted a few to return, and in the late seventeenth and early eighteenth centuries the Jewish population slowly increased, mainly by immigration from Germany. In the mid-eighteenth century some prominent Jews had their children brought up as Christians so as to facilitate their full integration into English society: thus the nineteenth-century writer and politician Benjamin Disraeli, although he and his father were members of the Church of England, was widely considered a Jew insofar as his ancestry was Jewish.

In the late seventeenth century, as the Church of England reasserted itself, Catholics, Jews, and dissenting Protestants found themselves subject to significant legal restrictions. The Corporation Act, passed in 1661, and the Test Act, passed in 1673, excluded all who refused to take communion in the Church of England from voting, attending university, or working in government or in the professions. Members of religious minorities, as well as Church of England communicants, paid mandatory taxes in support of Church of England ministers and buildings. In 1689 the dissenters gained the right to worship in public, but Jews and Catholics were not permitted to do so.

During the eighteenth century, political, intellectual, and religious history remained closely intertwined. The Church of England came to accommodate a good deal of variety. "Low church" services resembled those of the dissenting Protestant churches, minimizing ritual and emphasizing the sermon; the "high church" retained more elaborate ritual elements, yet its prestige was under attack on several fronts. Many Enlightenment thinkers subjected the Bible to rational critique and found it wanting: the philosopher David Hume, for instance, argued that the "miracles" described therein were more probably lies or errors than real breaches of the laws of nature. Within the Church of England, the "broad church" Latitudinarians welcomed this rationalism, advocating theological openness and an emphasis on ethics rather than dogma. More radically, the Unitarian movement rejected the divinity of Christ while professing to accept his ethical teachings. Taking a different tack, the preacher John Wesley, founder of Methodism, responded to the rationalists' challenge with a newly fervent call to evangelism and personal discipline; his movement was particularly successful in Wales. Revolutions in America and France at the end of the century generated considerable millenarian excitement and fostered more new religious ideas, often in conjunction with a radical social agenda. Many important writers of the Romantic period were indebted to traditions of protestant dissent: Unitarian and rationalist protestant ideas influenced William Hazlitt, Anna Barbauld, Mary Wollstonecraft, and the young Samuel Taylor Coleridge. William Blake created a highly idiosyncratic poetic mythology loosely indebted to radical strains of Christian mysticism. Others were even more heterodox: Lord Byron and Robert Burns, brought up as Scots Presbyterians, rebelled fiercely, and Percy Shelley's writing of an atheistic pamphlet resulted in his expulsion from Oxford.

Great Britain never erected an American-style "wall of separation" between church and state, but in practice religion and secular affairs grew more and more distinct during the nineteenth century. In consequence, members of religious minorities no longer seemed to pose a threat to the commonweal. A movement to repeal the Test Act failed in the 1790s, but a renewed effort resulted in the extension of the franchise to dissenting Protestants in 1828 and to Catholics in 1829. The numbers of Roman Catholics in England were swelled by immigration from Ireland, but there were also some prominent English adherents. Among writers, the converts John Newman and Gerard Manley Hopkins are especially important. The political participation and social integration of Jews presented a thornier challenge. Lionel de Rothschild, repeatedly elected to represent London in Parliament during the 1840s and 1850s, was not permitted to take his seat there because he refused to take his oath of office "on the true faith of a Christian"; finally, in 1858, the Jewish Disabilities Act allowed him to omit these words. Only in 1871, however, were Oxford and Cambridge opened to non-Anglicans.

Meanwhile geological discoveries and Charles Darwin's evolutionary theories increasingly cast doubt on the literal truth of the Creation story, and close philological analysis of the biblical text suggested that its origins were human rather than divine. By the end of the nineteenth century, many writers were bearing witness to a world in which Christianity no longer seemed fundamentally plausible. In his poetry and prose, Thomas Hardy depicts a world devoid of benevolent providence. Matthew Arnold's poem "Dover Beach" is in part an elegy to lost spiritual assurance, as the "Sea of Faith" goes out like the tide: "But now I only hear / Its melancholy, long, withdrawing roar / Retreating." For Arnold, literature must replace religion as a source of spiritual truth, and intimacy between individuals substitute for the lost communal solidarity of the universal church.

The work of many twentieth-century writers shows the influence of a religious upbringing or a religious conversion in adulthood. T. S. Eliot and W. H. Auden embrace Anglicanism, William Butler Yeats spiritualism. James Joyce repudiates Irish Catholicism but remains obsessed with it. Yet religion, or lack of it, is a matter of individual choice and conscience, not social or legal mandate. In the past fifty years, church attendance has plummeted in Great Britain. Although 71 percent of the population still identified itself as "Christian" on the 2000 census, only about 7 percent of these regularly attend religious services of any denomination. Meanwhile, immigration from former British colonies has swelled the ranks of religions once uncommon in the British Isles—Muslim, Sikh, Hindu, Buddhist—though the numbers of adherents remain small relative to the total population.

The Universe According to Ptolemy

Ptolemy was a Roman astronomer of Greek descent, born in Egypt during the second century C.E.; for nearly fifteen hundred years after his death his account of the design of the universe was accepted as standard. During that time, the basic pattern underwent many detailed modifications and was fitted out with many astrological and pseudoscientific trappings. But in essence Ptolemy's followers portrayed the earth as the center of the universe, with the sun, planets, and fixed stars set in transparent spheres orbiting around it. In this scheme of things, as modified for Christian usage, Hell was usually placed under the earth's surface at the center of the cosmic globe, while Heaven, the abode of the blessed spirits, was in the outermost, uppermost circle, the empyrean. But in 1543 the Polish astronomer Copernicus proposed an alternative hypothesis—that the earth rotates around the sun, not vice versa; and despite theological opposition, observations with the new telescope and careful mathematical calculations insured ultimate acceptance of the new view.

The map of the Ptolemaic universe below is a simplified version of a diagram in Peter Apian's *Cosmography* (1584). In such a diagram, the Firmament is the sphere that contained the fixed stars; the Crystalline Sphere, which contained no heavenly bodies, is a late innovation, included to explain certain anomalies in the observed movement of the heavenly bodies; and the Prime Mover is the sphere that, itself put into motion by God, imparts rotation around the earth to all the other spheres.

Milton, writing in the mid-seventeenth century, used two universes. The Copernican universe, though he alludes to it, was too large, formless, and unfamiliar to be the setting for the war between Heaven and Hell in *Paradise Lost*. He therefore used the Ptolemaic cosmos, but placed Heaven well outside this smaller earth-centered universe, Hell far beneath it, and assigned the vast middle space to Chaos.

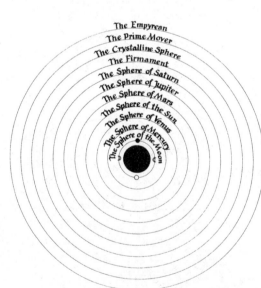

PERMISSIONS ACKNOWLEDGMENTS

TEXT CREDITS

Aphra Behn: *The Complete Text of OROONOKO*, edited by Joanna Lipking. Copyright © 1993 by Joanna Lipking and W. W. Norton & Company, Inc. Reprinted by permission of W. W. Norton & Company, Inc.
James Boswell: *Boswell Interviews Voltaire* from BOSWELL ON THE GRAND TOUR: GERMANY AND SWITZERLAND, 1764, edited by F. A. Pottle. Reprinted with the permission of Yale Boswell Editions.
Thomas Gray: From the manuscript of *Elegy Written in a Country Churchyard*. Transcribed by kind permission of the Provost and Fellows of Eton College.
Samuel Johnson: Excerpt from the manuscript of *The Vanity of Human Wishes*. Reprinted with permission.
Lady Mary Wortley Montagu: Poems from LADY MARY WORTLEY MONTAGU, ESSAYS AND POEMS, 1977, Revised 1993, edited by R. Halsband and I. Grundy. Reprinted with permission.
Samuel Pepys: Excerpts from THE DIARY OF SAMUEL PEPYS, 11 volumes, edited by Robert Latham and William Matthews. Copyright © 1972, 1986 by The Master, Fellows and Scholars of Magdalen College, Cambridge, Robert Latham, and the Executors of William Matthews. Copyright © 2000 by the Regents of the University of California. Reprinted by permission of the publisher, the University of California Press and HarperCollins Publishers Ltd.
Alexander Pope: From the manuscript of AN ESSAY ON MAN, MS Eng 233.21 transcribed by permission of the Houghton Library, Harvard University.
Christopher Smart: *My Cat Jeoffry* from JUBILATE AGNO, edited by W. H. Bond. Copyright © 1954 by W. H. Bond. Reprinted by permission of HarperCollins Publishers Ltd.

IMAGE CREDITS

Pp. 2–3: Bridgeman-Giraudon / Art Resource, NY; p. 9: The Granger Collection, NYC: p. 13: © Look and Learn / Peter Jackson Collection / Bridgeman Images; p. 18: National Portrait Gallery (London); p. 23: Private Collection / The Stapleton Collection / Bridgeman Images; p. 29: Lewis Walpole Library; p. 116: Museum of London/Heritage Images / Getty Images; p. 129: Warwick Castle, Warwickshire / Bridgeman Images; p. 183: © Hulton-Deutsch Collection / Getty Images; p. 283: Map of Lilliput (engraving), English School, (19th century) / Private Collection / © Look and Learn / Bridgeman Images; p. 323: Map showing location of Brobdingnag from first edition of 'Travels into Several Remote Nations of the World' 'Gulliver's Travels': AF Fotografie / Alamy Stock Photo; p. 366: Map from 'Gulliver's Travels' by Jonathan Swift (1667–1745) (engraving) (b/w photo), English School / Private Collection / Bridgeman Images; p. 379: AF Fotografie / Alamy Stock Photo; p. 408: AF Fotografie / Alamy Stock Photo; p. 472: Private Collection / The Bridgeman Art Library;. 563: Universal History Archive/Getty Images; p. 568: ullstein bild/ullstein bild via Getty Images; p. 630: Art Resource; p. 705: Reproduced by the permission of the Print Collection, Miriam and Ira D. Wallach Division of Art, Prints and Photographs, The New York Public Library, Astor, Lenox and Tilden Foundations; p. 706: Reproduced by the permission of the Print Collection, Miriam and Ira D. Wallach Division of Art, Prints and Photographs, The New York Public Library, Astor, Lenox and Tilden Foundations; p. 707: Reproduced by the permission of the Print Collection, Miriam and Ira D. Wallach Division of Art, Prints and Photographs, The New York Public Library, Astor, Lenox and Tilden Foundations; p. 708: Reproduced by the permission of the Print Collection, Miriam and Ira D. Wallach Division of Art, Prints and Photographs, The New York Public Library, Astor, Lenox and Tilden Foundations; p. 709: Reproduced by the permission of the Print Collection, Miriam and Ira D. Wallach Division of Art, Prints and Photographs, The New York Public Library, Astor, Lenox and Tilden Foundations; p. 710: Reproduced by the permission of the Print Collection, Miriam and Ira D. Wallach Division of Art, Prints and Photographs, The New York Public Library, Astor, Lenox and Tilden Foundations; p. 742: Public Domain; p. 909: Reproduced by kind permission of Cambridge University Library; p. 933: © National Maritime Museum, Greenwich, London/The Image Works; p. 960: William Blake / John Gabriel Stedman / Private Collection / Archives Charmet / The Bridgeman Art Library International; p. 970: From Stowe, *A Description of House and Gardens* / PD; p. 981: William Blake / John Gabriel Stedman / Private Collection / Archives Charmet / The Bridgeman Art Library International; p. 1010: © The Huntington Library, Art Collection & Botanical Gardens / The Bridgeman Art Library International.

COLOR INSERT CREDITS

C1: National Gallery of Scotland, Edinburgh, Scotland / Bridgeman Art Library; C2: Museum of London, UK / Bridgeman Art Library; C3: Réunion des Musées Nationaux / Art Resource, NY; C4 (top): Bristol City Museum and Art Gallery, UK / Bridgeman Art Library; C4 (bottom): Private Collection / Bridgeman Art Library; C5: Tate Gallery, London / Art Resource, NY; C6 (top): Somerset Maugham Theatre Collection, London, UK / Bridgeman Art Library; C6 (bottom): Giraudon / Art Resource, NY; C7 (top): Private Collection / Phillips, Fine Art Auctioneers, NY / Bridgeman Art Library; C7 (bottom): © 2003 State Hermitage Museum, St. Petersburg, Russia; C8 (top): The Huntington Library, Art Collections & Botanical Gardens / The Bridgeman Art Library; C8 (bottom): © Yale Center for British Art, Paul Mellon Collection, USA / Bridgeman Art Library.

Index